GAME DESIGNERS
Logan Bonner, Jason Bulmahn,
Stephen Radney-MacFarland, and Mark Seifter

ADDITIONAL WRITING
James Jacobs

DEVELOPERS
Adam Daigle, Lyz Liddell, and Erik Mona

EDITORS
Amirali Attar Olyaee, Judy Bauer,
Christopher Paul Carey, James Case, Jaym Gates,
Leo Glass, Jason Keeley, Avi Kool, Lyz Liddell,
Luis Loza, Erik Mona, Adrian Ng, Lacy Pellazar,
Elsa Sjunneson-Henry, and Jason Tondro

COVER ARTIST
Wayne Reynolds

INTERIOR ARTISTS
Giorgio Baroni, Rogier van de Beek,
Yanis Cardin, Sergio Cosmai, Biagio D'Alessandro,
Michele Esposito, Giorgio Falconi, Taylor Fischer,
Mariusz Gandzel, Igor Grechanyi, Hai Hoang,
Roman Roland Kuteynikov, Setiawan Lie,
Valeria Lutfullina, Damien Mammoliti, Rob McCaleb,
Andrea Tentori Montalto, Stefano Moroni,
Federico Musetti, Alexander Nanitchkov,
Mirco Paganessi, Mary Jane Pajaron,
Jose Parodi, Angelo Peluso, Roberto Pitturru,
Konstantin Porubov, Wayne Reynolds,
Kiki Moch Rizky, Riccardo Rullo, Bryan Sola,
Matteo Spirito, Matias Tapia, Ben Wootten, and
Sam Yang

ART DIRECTION AND GRAPHIC DESIGN
Sarah E. Robinson and Sonja Morris

CREATIVE DIRECTOR
James Jacobs

PUBLISHER
Erik Mona

SPECIAL THANKS
Dave Arneson, Monte Cook, Ron Edwards,
Gary Gygax, Daniel Solis, John Stavropoulos,
Jonathan Tweet, Skip Williams, and all the
participants in the Pathfinder Playtest

Paizo Inc.
7120 185th Ave NE, Ste 120
Redmond, WA 98052-0577

paizo® paizo.com

TABLE OF CONTENTS

5

7

11

With a haunting moan, shambling bodies rose up from the forgotten battlefield. Given foul unlife by the necromancy of the Whispering Tyrant, the corpses still wore the tattered raiment of their former lives. These crusaders had been the first to stand against the lich when he returned, and they were the first to fall in his rebirth.

"Aroden is dead!" Valeros spat out the dead god's name like a curse as he drew his sword and readied his battered shield. "He's not coming back to save us this time." Kyra and Merisiel shared his sentiment. The Whispering Tyrant was back, and it was up to them to return the lich to his grave.

As Kyra strode up beside Valeros, blade in hand, she called out a prayer to her goddess. Sarenrae's light would guide and fortify her against the coming darkness, but there would be no direct divine intervention in this war. Victory would be bought with the sweat and blood of mortals, and both the brave and the innocent would give their lives.

Merisiel nodded to the others, a look of determination upon her face. Quickly scanning the horde, she found her first target and let fly a small blade. It sank to the hilt in the rotting eye socket of one of the dead crusaders, but while the foul creature staggered back, it did not fall. Unfazed, she drew another dagger and prepared to throw again.

Provoked by the attack, the undead advanced as one, a wave of rotting flesh and clattering bone that descended on the heroes…

CHAPTER 1: INTRODUCTION

Pathfinder is a fantasy tabletop roleplaying game (RPG) where you and a group of friends gather to tell a tale of brave heroes and cunning villains in a world filled with terrifying monsters and amazing treasures. More importantly, Pathfinder is a game where your character's choices determine how the story unfolds.

Pathfinder adventures take place in the Age of Lost Omens, a perilous fantasy world rife with ancient empires; sprawling city-states; and countless tombs, dungeons, and monster lairs packed with plunder. A Pathfinder character's adventures might take them to forsaken underwater ruins, haunted gothic crypts, or magical universities in jungle cities. A world of endless adventure awaits!

WHAT IS A ROLEPLAYING GAME?

A roleplaying game is an interactive story where one player, the Game Master (GM), sets the scene and presents challenges, while other players take the roles of player characters (PCs) and attempt to overcome those challenges. Danger comes in the form of monsters, devious traps, and the machinations of adversarial agents, but Pathfinder also provides political schemes, puzzles, interpersonal drama, and much, much more.

The game is typically played in a group of four to seven players, with one of those players serving as the group's Game Master. The GM prepares, presents, and presides over the game's world and story, posing challenges and playing adversaries, allies, and bystanders alike. As each scene leads into the next, each player contributes to the story, responding to situations according to the personality and abilities of their character. Dice rolls, combined with preassigned statistics, add an element of chance and determine whether characters succeed or fail at actions they attempt.

THE FLOW OF THE GAME

Pathfinder is played in sessions, during which players gather in person or online for a few hours to play the game. A complete Pathfinder story can be as short as a single session, commonly referred to as a "one-shot," or it can stretch on for multiple sessions, forming a campaign that might last for months or even years. If the Game Master enjoys telling the story and the players are entertained, the game can go as long as you like.

A session can be mostly action, with battles with vile beasts, escapes from fiendish traps, and the completion of heroic quests. Alternatively, it could include negotiating with a baron for rights to a fort, infiltrating an army of lumbering frost giants, or bargaining with an angel for a strand of hair required for an elixir to revive a slain friend. Ultimately it's up to you and your group to determine what kind of game you are playing, from dungeon exploration to a nuanced political drama, or anything in between.

THE PLAYERS

Everyone involved in a Pathfinder game is a player, including the Game Master, but for the sake of simplicity, "player" usually refers to participants other than the GM. Before the game begins, players invent a history and personality for their characters, using the rules to determine their characters' statistics, abilities, strengths, and weaknesses. The GM might limit the options available during character creation, but the limits are discussed ahead of time so everyone can create interesting heroes. In general, the only limits to character concepts are the players' imaginations and the GM's guidelines.

During the game, players describe the actions their characters take and roll dice, using their characters' abilities. The GM resolves the outcome of these actions. Some players enjoy acting out (or roleplaying) what they do as if they were their characters, while others describe their characters' actions as if narrating a story. Do whatever feels best!

If this is your first experience with a roleplaying game, it is recommended that you take on the role of a player to familiarize yourself with the rules and the world.

THE FIRST RULE

The first rule of Pathfinder is that this game is *yours*. Use it to tell the stories you want to tell, be the character you want to be, and share exciting adventures with friends. If any other rule gets in the way of your fun, as long as your group agrees, you can alter or ignore it to fit your story. The true goal of Pathfinder is for everyone to enjoy themselves.

DICE

Pathfinder requires a set of polyhedral dice. Each die has a different number of sides—four, six, eight, or more. When these dice are mentioned in the text, they're indicated by a "d" followed by the number of sides on the die. Pathfinder uses 4-sided dice (or d4), 6-sided dice (d6), 8-sided dice (d8), 10-sided dice (d10), 12-sided dice (d12), and 20-sided dice (d20). If you need to roll multiple dice, a number before the "d" tells you how many. For example, "4d6" means you should roll four dice, all 6-sided. If a rule asks for d%, you generate a number from 1 to 100 by rolling two 10-sided dice, treating one as the tens place and the other as the ones place.

THE GAME MASTER

While the other players create and control their characters, the Game Master (or GM) is in charge of the story and world. The GM describes all the situations player characters experience in an adventure, considers how the actions of player characters affect the story, and interprets the rules along the way.

The GM can create a new adventure—crafting a narrative, selecting monsters, and assigning treasure on their own—or they can instead rely on a published adventure, using it as a basis for the session and modifying it as needed to accommodate their individual players and the group's style of play. Some even run games that combine original and published content, mixed together to form a new narrative.

Being the GM is a challenge, requiring you to adjudicate the rules, narrate the story, and juggle other responsibilities. But it can also be very rewarding and worth all the work required to run a good game. If it is your first time running a game, remember that the only thing that matters is that everyone has a good time, and that includes you. Everything else will come naturally with practice and patience.

GAMING IS FOR ALL

Whether you are the GM or a player, participating in a tabletop roleplaying game includes a social contract: everyone has gathered together to have fun telling a story. For many, roleplaying is a way to escape the troubles of everyday life. Be mindful of everyone at the table and what they want out of the game, so that everyone can have fun. When a group gathers for the first time, they should talk about what they hope to experience at the table, as well as any topics they want to avoid. Everyone should understand that elements might come up that make some players feel uncomfortable or even unwelcome, and everyone should agree to respect those boundaries during play. That way, everyone can enjoy the game together.

Pathfinder is a game for everyone, regardless of their age, gender, race or ethnicity, religion, sexual orientation, or any other identities and life experiences. It is the responsibility of all of the players, not just the GM, to make sure the table is fun and welcoming to all.

TOOLS OF PLAY

In addition to this book, there are a few things you will need to play Pathfinder. These supplies can be found at your local hobby shop or online at **paizo.com**.

Character Sheet: Each player will need a character sheet to create their character and to record what happens to that character during play. You can find a character sheet in the back of this book and online as a free pdf.

Dice: The players and GM will need at least one set of polyhedral dice, although most participants bring their own. Six-sided dice are quite common, but all the dice in the set can be found at hobby game stores or online. See the Dice sidebar on page 7 for more on the different kinds of dice and how they are discussed in the text.

Adventure: Every table needs an adventure to play, whether it's designed by the GM or found in a published resource. You can find a variety of exciting adventures and even entire Adventure Path campaigns at **paizo.com**.

Bestiary: From terrifying dragons to mischievous gremlins, monsters are a common threat that the PCs might face, and each type has its own statistics and abilities. These can be found in the *Pathfinder Bestiary*, an absolutely invaluable book for GMs. Monster statistics can also be found online for free at **paizo.com/prd**.

Maps and Miniatures: The chaos of combat can be difficult to imagine, so many groups use maps to represent the battlefield. These maps are marked with a 1-inch grid, and each square represents 5 feet in the game. Miniatures and illustrated tokens called pawns are used to represent the characters and the adversaries they face.

Additional Accessories: There are a number of additional accessories you can add to your game to enhance the experience, including tools that help you track turns in combat, decks of cards for referencing common rules, digital character-creation tools, and even background music and sound-effect sets.

BASICS OF PLAY

Before creating your first character or adventure, you should understand a number of basic concepts used in the game. New concepts are presented in bold to make them easy to find, but this chapter is only an introduction to the basics of play. The complete game rules are defined in later chapters, and the Glossary and Index in the back of this book will help you find specific rules you need.

DEFINING CHARACTERS

In Pathfinder, the players take on the role of **player characters (PCs)**, while the Game Master portrays **nonplayer characters (NPCs)** and **monsters**. While PCs and NPCs are both important to the story, they serve very different purposes in the game. PCs are the protagonists—the narrative is about them—while NPCs and monsters are allies, contacts, adversaries, and villains. That said, PCs, NPCs, and monsters share several characteristics.

Level is one of the most important statistics of the game, as it conveys the approximate power and capabilities of every individual creature. PCs range in level from 1st, at the start of the character's adventuring career, to 20th, the very height of power. As the characters overcome challenges, defeat foes, and complete adventures, they accumulate **Experience Points (XP)**. Every time a character amasses 1,000 XP, they go up a level, gaining new abilities so they can take on even greater challenges. A 1st-level PC might face off against a giant rat or a group of bandits, but at 20th level, that same character might be able to bring ruin to an entire city with a single spell.

In addition to level, characters are defined by **ability scores**, which measure a character's raw potential and are

INTRODUCTION 1

INTRODUCTION

ANCESTRIES &
BACKGROUNDS

CLASSES

SKILLS

FEATS

EQUIPMENT

SPELLS

THE AGE OF
LOST OMENS

PLAYING THE
GAME

GAME
MASTERING

CRAFTING
& TREASURE

APPENDIX

used to calculate most of their other statistics. There are six ability scores in the game. **Strength** represents a character's physical might, while **Dexterity** represents agility and the ability to avoid danger. **Constitution** indicates a character's overall health and well-being. **Intelligence** represents raw knowledge and problem-solving ability, while **Wisdom** measures a character's insight and the ability to evaluate a situation. Finally, **Charisma** indicates charm, persuasiveness, and force of personality. Ability scores for ordinary folk range from as low as 3 to as high as 18, with 10 representing average human capabilities. High-level characters can have ability scores that range much higher than 18.

An ability score that's above the average increases your chance of success at tasks related to the ability score, while those below the average decrease your chance. This adjustment is called an **ability modifier**.

Your player character is also defined by some key choices you make. The first choice is a PC's **ancestry**, representing the character's parents and heritage, such as human, elf, or goblin. Next up is the PC's **background**, which describes their upbringing, from lowly street urchin to wealthy noble. Finally, and most importantly, a PC's **class** defines the majority of their aptitudes and abilities, like a wizard's command of powerful arcane spells or a druid's power to transform into a fearsome beast!

In addition to these key choices, player characters also have a number of **feats**—individual abilities selected during character creation and as the character increases in level. Every feat has a type to denote where its explanation can be found (for example, elf feats can be found in the elf ancestry) and its theme (wizard feats, for example, grant abilities that deal with spells). Finally, characters have **skills** that measure their ability to hide, swim, bargain, and perform other common tasks.

CREATING A NARRATIVE

Characters and their choices create the story of Pathfinder, but how they interact with each other and the world around them is governed by rules. So, while you might decide that your character undertakes an epic journey to overcome terrifying foes and make the world a safer place, your character's chance of success is determined by their abilities, the choices you make, and the roll of the dice.

The GM determines the premise and background of most adventures, although character histories and personalities certainly play a part. Once a game session begins, the players take turns describing what their characters attempt to do, while the GM determines the outcome, with the table working together toward a specific goal. The GM also describes the environment, other characters' actions, and events. For example, the GM might announce that the characters' hometown is under attack by marauding trolls. The characters might track the trolls to a nearby swamp—only to discover that the trolls were driven from their swamp by a fearsome dragon! The PCs then have the choice of taking on an entire tribe of trolls, the dragon, or both. Whatever they decide, their success depends on their choices and the die rolls they make during play.

A single narrative—including the setup, plot, and conclusion—is called an **adventure**. A series of adventures creates an even larger narrative, called a **campaign**. An adventure might take several sessions to complete, whereas a campaign might take months or even years!

THE WORLD AS A PARTICIPANT

Aside from characters and monsters, the world of Pathfinder itself can be a force at the table and in the narrative. While the presence of the larger world can sometimes be an obvious hazard, such as when a powerful storm lashes the countryside, the world can also act in subtle, small ways. Traps and treasures are just as important in many tales as cunning beasts. To help you understand these game elements, many of them use the same characteristics as characters and monsters. For example, most environmental hazards have a level, which indicates how dangerous they are, and the level of a magic item gives you a sense of its overall power and impact on a story.

PLAYING THE GAME

In a Pathfinder game, three modes of play determine the pacing of each scene in the story. Most of your character's time is spent in **exploration**, uncovering mysteries, solving problems, and interacting with other characters. The Age of Lost Omens abounds with danger, however, and characters often find themselves in an **encounter**, fighting savage beasts and terrifying monsters. Finally, time moves quickly when the characters enjoy **downtime**, a respite from the world's troubles and a chance to rest and train for future expeditions. Throughout an adventure, game play moves between these three modes many times, as needed for the story. The more you play the game, the more you'll see that each mode has its own play style, but moving from mode to mode has few hard boundaries.

During the game, your character will face situations where the outcome is uncertain. A character might need to climb a sheer cliff, track down a wounded chimera, or sneak past a sleeping dragon, all of which are dangerous tasks with a price for failure. In such cases, the acting character (or characters) will be asked to attempt a **check** to determine whether or not they succeed. A check is usually made by rolling a single 20-sided die (a d20) and adding a number based on the relevant ability. In such cases, rolling high is always good.

Once a check is rolled, the GM compares the result to a target number called the **difficulty class (DC)** to determine the outcome. If the result of the check is equal to or greater than the DC, the check is successful. If it is less, the check is a failure. Beating the DC by 10 or more is referred to as a **critical success**, which usually grants an especially positive outcome. Similarly, failing the check by 10 or more is a **critical failure** (sometimes called a fumble). This sometimes results in additional negative effects. You also often score a critical success by rolling a 20 on the die when attempting a check (before adding anything). Likewise, rolling a 1 on the die when attempting a check often results in a critical failure. Note that not all checks have a special effect on a critical success or critical failure and such results should be treated just like an ordinary success or failure instead.

For example, in pursuit of the wounded chimera, your character might find the path blocked by a fast-moving river. You decide to swim across, but the GM declares this a dangerous task and asks you to roll an Athletics skill check (since swimming is covered by the Athletics skill). On your character sheet, you see that your character has a +8 modifier for such checks. Rolling the d20, you get an 18, for a total of 26. The GM compares this to the DC (which was 16) and finds that you got a critical success (since the result exceeded the DC by 10). Your character swims quickly across the river and continues the pursuit, drenched but unharmed. Had you gotten a result less than 26 but equal to or greater than 16, your character would have made it halfway across the river. Had your result been less than 16, your character might have been swept downriver or, worse, been pulled under the current and begun to drown!

Checks like this are the heart of the game and are rolled all the time, in every mode of play, to determine the outcome of tasks. While the roll of the die is critical, the statistic you add to the roll (called a **modifier**) often makes the difference between success and failure. Every character is made up of many such statistics governing what the character is good at, each consisting of a relevant ability modifier plus a **proficiency** bonus, and sometimes modified further by other factors, such as bonuses or penalties from gear, spells, feats, magic items, and other special circumstances.

Proficiency is a simple way of assessing your character's general level of training and aptitude for a given task. It is broken into five different ranks: **untrained**, **trained**, **expert**, **master**, and **legendary**. Each rank grants a different proficiency bonus. If you're untrained at a statistic, your proficiency bonus is +0—you must rely solely on the raw potential of your ability modifier. If your proficiency rank for a statistic is trained, expert, master, and legendary, your bonus equals your character's level plus another number based on the rank (2, 4, 6, and 8, respectively). Proficiency ranks are part of almost every statistic in the game.

EXPLORATION

Most of the time, your character will explore the world, interact with characters, travel from place to place, and overcome challenges. This is called exploration. Game play is relatively free-form during exploration, with players responding to the narrative whenever they have an idea of what to do next. Leaving town via horseback, following the trail of a marauding orc tribe, avoiding the tribe's scouts, and convincing a local hunter to help in an upcoming fight are all examples of things that might occur during exploration.

Throughout this mode of play, the GM asks the players what their characters are doing as they explore. This is important in case a conflict arises. If combat breaks out, the tasks the PCs undertook while exploring might give them an edge or otherwise inform how the combat begins.

ENCOUNTERS

In the course of your adventures, there will be times when a simple skill check is not enough to resolve a challenge—when fearsome monsters stand in your character's way and the only choice is to do battle. In Pathfinder, this is called an encounter. Encounters usually involve combat, but they can also be used in situations where timing is critical, such as during a chase or when dodging hazards.

While exploration is handled in a free-form manner, encounters are more structured. The players and GM roll **initiative** to determine who acts in what order. The encounter occurs over a number of **rounds**, each of which is equal to about 6 seconds of time in the world of the game. During a round, each participant takes a **turn**. When it's your turn to act, you can use up to three **actions**. Most simple things, such as drawing a weapon, moving a short distance, opening a door, or swinging a sword, use a single action to perform. There are also **activities** that use more than a single

INTRODUCTION

1

INTRODUCTION

ANCESTRIES &
BACKGROUNDS

CLASSES

SKILLS

FEATS

EQUIPMENT

SPELLS

THE AGE OF
LOST OMENS

PLAYING THE
GAME

GAME
MASTERING

CRAFTING
& TREASURE

APPENDIX

action to perform; these are often special abilities from your character's class and feats. One common activity in the game is casting a spell, which usually uses two actions.

Free actions, such as dropping an object, don't count toward the three actions you can take on your turn. Finally, each character can use up to one **reaction** during a round. This special type of action can be used even when it's not your turn, but only in response to certain events, and only if you have an ability that allows it. Rogues, for example, can select a feat that lets them use their reaction to dodge an incoming attack.

Attacking another creature is one of the most common actions in combat, and is done by using the **Strike** action. This requires an attack roll—a kind of check made against the **Armor Class (AC)** of the creature you're attacking. Strikes can be made using weapons, spells, or even parts of a creature's body, like a fist, claw, or tail. You add a modifier to this roll based on your proficiency rank with the type of attack you're using, your ability scores, and any other bonuses or penalties based on the situation. The target's AC is calculated using their proficiency rank in the armor they're wearing and their Dexterity modifier. An attack deals damage if it hits, and rolling a critical success results in the attack dealing double damage!

You can use more than one Strike action on your turn, but each additional attack after the first becomes less accurate. This is reflected by a **multiple attack penalty** that starts at –5 on the second attack, but increases to –10

on the third. There are many ways to reduce this penalty, and it resets at the end of your turn.

If your character finds themself the target of a magical *lightning bolt* or the freezing breath of a fearsome white dragon, you will be called on to attempt a **saving throw**, representing your character's ability to avoid danger or otherwise withstand an assault to their mind or body. A saving throw is a check attempted against the DC of the spell or special ability targeting your character. There are three types of saving throws, and a character's proficiency in each says a great deal about what they can endure. A **Fortitude** saving throw is used when your character's health or vitality is under attack, such as from poison or disease. A **Reflex** saving throw is called for when your character must dodge away from danger, usually something that affects a large area, such as the scorching blast of a *fireball* spell. Finally, a **Will** saving throw is often your defense against spells and effects that target your character's mind, such as a *charm* or *confusion* spell. For all saving throws, a success lessens the harmful effect, and scoring a critical success usually means your character escapes unscathed.

Attacks, spells, hazards, and special abilities frequently either deal **damage** to a character or impose one or more **conditions**—and sometimes both. Damage is subtracted from a creature's **Hit Points (HP)**—a measure of health—and when a creature is reduced to 0 HP, it falls unconscious and may die! A combat encounter typically lasts until one side has been defeated, and while this can mean retreat or surrender, it most often happens because one side is dead or dying. Conditions can hinder a creature for a time, limiting the actions they can use and applying penalties to future checks. Some conditions are even permanent, requiring a character to seek out powerful magic to undo their effects.

DOWNTIME

Characters don't spend every waking moment adventuring. Instead, they recover from wounds, plan future conquests, or pursue a trade. In Pathfinder, this is called downtime, and it allows time to pass quickly while characters work toward long-term tasks or objectives. Most characters can practice a trade in downtime, earning a few coins, but those with the right skills can instead spend time crafting, creating new gear or even magic items. Characters can also use downtime to retrain, replacing one character choice with another to reflect their evolving priorities. They might also research a problem, learn new spells, or even run a business or kingdom!

KEY TERMS

There are a number of important terms that you'll need to know as you create your first character or adventure. Some of the most important terms mentioned on previous pages are also included here for reference.

ABILITY SCORE

Each creature has six ability scores: Strength, Dexterity, Constitution, Intelligence, Wisdom, and Charisma. These scores represent a creature's raw potential and basic attributes. The higher the score, the greater the creature's potential in that ability. Ability scores are described in full later in this chapter.

ALIGNMENT

Alignment represents a creature's fundamental moral and ethical attitude.

ANCESTRY

An ancestry is the broad family of people that a character belongs to. Ancestry determines a character's starting Hit Points, languages, senses, and Speed, and it grants access to ancestry feats. Ancestries can be found in Chapter 2.

ARMOR CLASS (AC)

All creatures in the game have an Armor Class. This score represents how hard it is to hit and damage a creature. It serves as the Difficulty Class for hitting a creature with an attack.

ATTACK

When a creature tries to harm another creature, it makes a Strike or uses some other attack action. Most attacks are Strikes made with a weapon, but a character might Strike with their fist, grapple or shove with their hands, or attack with a spell.

BACKGROUND

A background represents what a character experienced before they took up the life of an adventurer. Each background grants a feat and training in one or more skills. You can read more about backgrounds in Chapter 2.

BONUSES AND PENALTIES

Bonuses and penalties apply to checks and certain statistics. There are several types of bonuses and penalties. If you have more than one bonus of the same type, you use only the highest bonus. Likewise, you use only the worst penalty of each type.

CLASS

A class represents the adventuring profession chosen by a character. A character's class determines most of their proficiencies, grants the character Hit Points each time they gain a new level, and gives access to a set of class feats. Classes appear in Chapter 3.

CONDITION

An ongoing effect that changes how a character can act, or that alters some of their statistics, is called a condition. The rules for the basic conditions used in the game can be found in the Conditions Appendix at the back of this book.

CURRENCY

The most common currencies in the game are gold pieces (gp) and silver pieces (sp). One gp is worth 10 sp. In addition, 1 sp is worth 10 copper pieces (cp), and 10 gp are worth 1 platinum piece (pp). Characters begin play with 15 gp (or 150 sp) to spend on equipment.

FEAT

A feat is an ability you can select for your character due to their ancestry, background, class, general training, or skill training. Some feats grant the ability to use special actions.

GAME MASTER (GM)

The Game Master is the player who adjudicates the rules and narrates the various elements of the Pathfinder story and world that the other players explore.

GOLARION

Pathfinder is set on the planet Golarion during the Age of Lost Omens. It is an ancient world with a rich diversity of people and cultures, exciting locations to explore, and deadly villains. More information on the Age of Lost Omens, the world of Golarion, and its deities can be found in Chapter 8.

HIT POINTS (HP)

Hit Points represent the amount of punishment a creature can take before it falls unconscious and begins dying. Damage decreases Hit Points on a 1-to-1 basis, while healing restores Hit Points at the same rate.

Initiative

At the start of an encounter, all creatures involved roll for initiative to determine the order in which they act. The higher the result of its roll, the earlier a creature gets to act. Initiative and combat are described in Chapter 9.

Level

A level is a number that measures something's overall power. Player characters have a level, ranging from 1st to 20th, representing their level of experience. Monsters, NPCs, hazards, diseases, and poisons have levels ranging from –1 to 30 that measure the danger they pose. An item's level, usually within the range of 0 to 20 but sometimes higher, indicates its power and suitability as treasure.

Spells have levels ranging from 1st to 10th, which measure their power; characters and monsters can usually cast only a certain number of spells of any given level.

Nonplayer Character (NPC)

A nonplayer character, controlled by the GM, interacts with players and helps advance the story.

Perception

Perception measures your character's ability to notice hidden objects or unusual situations, and it usually determines how quickly the character springs into action in combat. It is described in full in Chapter 9.

Player Character (PC)

This is a character created and controlled by a player.

Proficiency

Proficiency is a system that measures a character's aptitude at a specific task or quality, and it has five ranks: untrained, trained, expert, master, and legendary. Proficiency gives you a bonus that's added when determining the following modifiers and statistics: AC, attack rolls, Perception, saving throws, skills, and the effectiveness of spells. If you're untrained, your proficiency bonus is +0. If you're trained, expert, master, or legendary, your proficiency bonus equals your level plus 2, 4, 6, or 8, respectively.

Rarity

Some elements of the game have a rarity to denote how often they're encountered in the game world. Rarity primarily applies to equipment and magic items, but spells, feats, and other rules elements also have a rarity. If no rarity appears in the traits of an item, spell, or other game element, it is of common rarity. Uncommon items are available only to those who have special training, grew up in a certain culture, or come from a particular part of the world. Rare items are almost impossible to find and are usually given out only by the GM, while unique ones are literally one-of-a-kind in the game. The GM might alter the way rarity works or change the rarity of individual items to suit the story they want to tell.

Roleplaying

Describing a character's actions, often while acting from the perspective of the character, is called roleplaying. When a player speaks or describes action from the perspective of a character, they are "in character."

Round

A round is a period of time during an encounter in which all participants get a chance to act. A round represents approximately 6 seconds in game time.

Saving Throw (Save)

When a creature is subject to a dangerous effect that must be avoided, it attempts a saving throw to mitigate the effect. You attempt a saving throw automatically—you don't have to use an action or a reaction. Unlike for most checks, the character who isn't acting rolls the d20 for a saving throw, and the creature who is acting provides the DC.

There are three types of saving throws: Fortitude (to resist diseases, poisons, and physical effects), Reflex (to evade effects a character could quickly dodge), and Will (to resist effects that target the mind and personality).

Skill

A skill represents a creature's ability to perform certain tasks that require instruction or practice. Skills are fully described in Chapter 4. Each skill includes ways anyone can use that skill even if untrained, as well as uses that require a character to be trained in the skill.

Speed

Speed is the distance a character can move using a single action, measured in feet.

Spell

Spells are magical effects created by performing mystical incantations and gestures known only to those with special training or inborn abilities. Casting a spell is an activity that usually uses two actions. Each spell specifies what it targets, the actions needed to cast it, its effects, and how it can be resisted. If a class grants spells, the basics of that ability are provided in the class description in Chapter 3, while the spells themselves are detailed in Chapter 7.

Trait

A trait is a keyword that conveys additional information about a rules element, such as a school of magic or rarity. Often, a trait indicates how other rules interact with an ability, creature, item, or another rules element that has that trait. All the traits used in this book appear in the Glossary and Index beginning on page 628.

Turn

During the course of a round, each creature takes a single turn according to initiative. A creature can typically use up to three actions during its turn.

EXAMPLE OF PLAY

The following example is presented to give you a better idea of how the game of Pathfinder is played. In this adventure, Erik is the GM. Lyz is playing Valeros, a daring human fighter, James is playing Merisiel, a deadly elven rogue, and Judy is taking on the role of Kyra, a fiery human cleric of Sarenrae. The group has just defeated a horde of undead and is making its way into an ancient mausoleum.

Erik:	The entrance to the crypt stands before you, a set of crumbling stairs leading down into darkness. A terrible smell issues forth from the doorway—the stench of old, rotted flesh.
Lyz:	I'm not afraid of a foul stink! I draw my sword and ready my shield.
Judy:	The light of Sarenrae will guide us. I cast my *light* spell on my religious symbol.
Erik:	All right, a glowing radiance spills forth, illuminating the stairs. They appear to go down only about 10 feet before opening up into a chamber. Puddles of stagnant water fill the cracks between uneven stone tiles.
James:	I should go first to make sure it's safe. I'm going to draw my rapier and carefully go down the stairs, looking for traps as I go.
Erik:	Sure, but looking for traps is a secret check, so I'll roll for you. What's your Perception modifier?
James:	I have a +5.

Erik rolls a d20 behind his GM screen, hidden from the players' view, and gets a 17 on the die for a total of 22, more than enough to find the trip wire on the third step.

Erik:	Your caution pays off! You spot a thin wire located at ankle height just above the third stair.
James:	I point it out to the others and head down.
Lyz:	I follow right behind Merisiel, avoiding the wire but otherwise keeping an eye out for danger.
Judy:	Me too.
Erik:	Okay! You make it down the stairs to find yourselves in a crypt. Ancient wood coffins are arranged around the room, covered in cobwebs and dust. Directly ahead, on a raised dais, is a stone casket adorned with wicked-looking symbols. You can tell that it was once wrapped in iron chains, but now twisted links are scattered around the room, along with chunks of what must have been the casket's lid. From the damage, it looks like it was shattered from within!
Judy:	Sarenrae protect us. I draw my blade and advance—I want a better look at those symbols.
Lyz:	I'll keep pace with her. I don't like the look of this.
James:	I think I'll stay back here and hide behind one of the coffins.
Erik:	Merisiel takes cover while the two of you advance. As you draw near, the stench of rot

grows stronger until it's almost overpowering. Suddenly you see the source of the horrid odor. Rising up out of the casket is a nightmarish dead thing. It might have once been a human, but it's hard to tell from its withered body. Its flesh is the color of a new bruise, pulled so tight across its bones that it has split in places. It's hairless, with pointed ears, but worst of all, its mouth is lined with tiny, sharp teeth and its tongue is entirely too long.

| Lyz: | So, not a friend? |
| Erik: | Most certainly not. It looks poised to leap at you and attack. Roll for initiative! Valeros and Kyra need to roll Perception, while Merisiel should roll Stealth. |

Everyone rolls for their initiative. Lyz rolls a 2 for Valeros, getting a total of 8. Judy rolls better for Kyra, getting a total of 14. James uses Stealth for Initiative, because Merisiel was hiding at the start of the fight, and rolls a 17 for a total of 25! Erik rolls for the undead creature, getting a 12. Erik records all these totals, putting the characters in order from highest to lowest.

Erik:	Looks like Merisiel gets to act first. Whatever that thing is, you're pretty sure it doesn't know you are there.
James:	Awesome! For my first action, I want to draw a dagger. For my second, I want to move closer.
Erik:	You can get to within 15 feet of it with one Stride action.
James:	Perfect. For my final action, I'm going to throw my dagger at it!

James rolls a 13 and adds 8, due to Merisiel's skill at thrown daggers, for a total of 21, but the range means he takes a −2 penalty for a result of 19. Erik consults his notes to learn that the monster has an AC of 18.

| Erik: | That's a hit! Go ahead and roll damage. |
| James: | Okay, and I get to add extra damage due to sneak attack. |

Rogues have the ability to deal extra damage to foes that haven't acted yet in an encounter. This extra damage also applies to attacks against enemies that are distracted. James rolls 1d4 for the dagger and 1d6 for the sneak attack, and he adds 4 for Merisiel's Dexterity, getting a total of 9.

Erik:	It hisses as the blade sinks into its shoulder. That looks like it hurt, but the undead thing doesn't appear to be slowing down. James, that was all three of your actions. Next up is Kyra!
Judy:	I think this is undead. What do I know about it?
Erik:	You use an action to recall your training about the living dead. Give me a Religion skill check.

INTRODUCTION

1

INTRODUCTION

ANCESTRIES &
BACKGROUNDS

CLASSES

SKILLS

FEATS

EQUIPMENT

SPELLS

THE AGE OF
LOST OMENS

PLAYING THE
GAME

GAME
MASTERING

CRAFTING
& TREASURE

APPENDIX

Judy rolls a 16, adding Kyra's +8 with Religion to get a total of 24.

| Erik: | At first, you thought this thing might be a ghoul, which is a type of undead that feasts on the flesh of the dead, but the terrible smell reveals the truth. This thing is a ghast, a more powerful type of ghoul. You are pretty sure that its stench can make you sick and that its claws can paralyze you with a touch. |
| Judy: | This is bad. I am going to spend my last two actions to cast *bless*. It gives anyone next to me a +1 bonus to attack rolls. |

Casting this spell is an activity that requires two actions to complete, and it has two components. The complex gestures needed to invoke the spell are the somatic component, and Kyra's prayers to her deity are the verbal component.

| Erik: | Okay! The ghast leaps from the casket straight toward Merisiel. The stench of its rotting body is absolutely horrific up close. Attempt a Fortitude save! |

James rolls an 8, for a total of 14.

| Erik: | Not quite enough—you gain the sickened 1 condition, which is going to give you a –1 penalty to most of your d20 rolls. Next, it lunges at you, trying to bite you! |
| James: | Oh no! I use my reaction to nimbly dodge out of the way. |

Erik rolls an attack roll for the ghast, getting an 9 on the die. Looking at the monster's statistics, he adds 11 for a total of 20. Merisiel's AC is normally 19, but the Nimble Dodge feat lets her use her reaction to increase her AC by 2 against a single attack. In this case, it turns the ghast's attack into a miss.

Erik:	Does a 20 hit you?
James:	Nope, just missed!
Erik:	You twist away from the ghast as its tongue leaves a slimy film on your armor. With its final action, the undead menace lashes out at you with its claw.

Erik rolls a second attack with the ghast, this time with its claw. Normally this attack would take a –5 multiple attack penalty, but since the claw has the agile trait, the penalty is only –4. He rolls a 19 on the die, adds 11 for the ghoul's attack modifier and subtracts 4, for a total of 26.

| Erik: | You may have dodged the ghast's bite, but the thing's bony claw rakes across your face! |

Erik knows this is a hit and rolls the ghast's claw damage, getting a total of 8.

| Erik: | Take 8 points of damage, and I need you to attempt a Fortitude saving throw as a numbing sensation spreads from the wound. |

James rolls a Fortitude saving throw. He gets a 4 on the die, and after adding his bonus and the penalty from the sickened condition, it comes out to only a 9.

| James: | This isn't my day. I don't suppose a 9 is good enough? |
| Erik: | I am afraid not. You are paralyzed! |

Erik notes that Merisiel is paralyzed, making her unable to act, but she will get a new saving throw at the end of each of her turns to shake off the effect.

| Erik: | A dry, creaking laugh escapes the ghast's curled lips, but that's the end of its turn. Valeros, you are the last one to act this round. |
| Lyz: | About time, too! I raise my shield and use my final two actions to make a Sudden Charge! |

Sudden Charge is a fighter feat that lets Valeros move up to twice his Speed and attack at the end of his movement, all for only two actions.

| Erik: | As you draw near, the smell is horrific. Attempt a Fortitude save. |

After rolling, Lyz gets a 19 on the Fortitude save.

| Erik: | You fight off the nausea from this thing's stench. Make your attack roll. |

Lyz rolls the die and it comes up a 20.

| Lyz: | I got a 20! That must be a critical success! |
| Erik: | Your blade hits the vile creature right in the neck, dealing double damage! |

Lyz rolls a 5 on her d8, then adds 4 because of Valeros's Strength modifier. Because it is a critical success, she then doubles the total.

Lyz:	A mighty 18 damage! That surely had to kill it!
Erik:	I'm afraid not. Black ichor runs from the deep wound on its neck, but it only turns to look at you. You can see burning hatred in its eyes!
Lyz:	Uh-oh.

That is the end of the first round of combat. The second round begins immediately after this, using the same initiative order as before. The fight is far from over…

USING THIS BOOK

While this chapter is here to teach you the basics of Pathfinder, the rest of this rulebook serves as a reference manual during play, and it is organized to make finding the rule you need as easy as possible. Rules are grouped together in chapters, with the early chapters focusing on character creation. The last two chapters contain rules for GMs, with advice on how to run a game of Pathfinder and a rich array of treasure. The following is a summary of what you can expect to find in each chapter.

CHAPTER 1: INTRODUCTION

This introduction is designed to help you understand the basics of Pathfinder. This chapter also includes the rules for building and leveling up a character. The chapter ends with an example of building a 1st-level character.

CHAPTER 2: ANCESTRIES & BACKGROUNDS

The rules for the most common ancestries in the Age of Lost Omens are in this chapter, including their ancestry feat options. Backgrounds are at the end of this chapter, along with a section about languages, as these are most often influenced by your choice of ancestry.

CHAPTER 3: CLASSES

This chapter contains the rules for all 12 classes. Each class entry includes guidelines on playing the class, rules for building and advancing a character of that class, sample builds, and all of the class feats available to members of that class. This chapter also includes rules for animal companions and familiars, which can be acquired by members of several different classes. At the end of this chapter are the rules for archetypes—special options available to characters as they increase in level. These rules allow a character to dabble in the abilities of another class or concept.

CHAPTER 4: SKILLS

The rules for using skills are presented in this chapter, and they detail what a character can do with a given skill, based on that character's proficiency rank. Ancestry, background, and class can define some of a character's skill proficiencies, and each character can also select a few additional skills to reflect their personality and training.

CHAPTER 5: FEATS

As a character advances in level, they gain additional feats to represent their growing abilities. General feats and skill feats (which are a subset of general feats) are presented in this chapter.

CHAPTER 6: EQUIPMENT

Armor, weapons, and other gear can all be found in this chapter, along with the price for services, cost of living, and animals (such as horses, dogs, and pack animals).

CHAPTER 7: SPELLS

This chapter starts with rules for casting spells, determining their effects, and getting rid of foes' spells (called counteracting). After that, the spell lists for each spellcasting tradition are included, making it easy to quickly find spells by their level. Next are rules for every spell, presented in alphabetical order. Following the spell descriptions are all of the focus spells—special spells granted by specific class abilities and feats. While most spells appear on multiple spell lists, focus spells are granted only to members of a specific class and are grouped together by class for ease of reference. Finally, at the end of the chapter are rules for rituals, complicated and risky spells that any character can cast.

CHAPTER 8: THE AGE OF LOST OMENS

The setting of Golarion is described in this chapter, including a brief overview of the world and its people, followed by a timeline of events. Most importantly, characters who venerate a deity should look to this chapter to find the rules associated with their faith.

CHAPTER 9: PLAYING THE GAME

This important chapter contains the universal rules needed to play Pathfinder, including rules for the various modes of play, the basic actions that every character can perform, the rules for combat, and the rules for death and dying. Every player should be familiar with this chapter, especially the GM.

CHAPTER 10: GAME MASTERING

Packed full of guidelines and advice, this chapter helps Game Masters tell an interesting and compelling story. It also includes advice on creating a fun and encouraging game space and guides for empowering players to create characters they want to play. This chapter also includes rules that are particularly important for the GM to know, such as rules dealing with traps, environmental dangers, and afflictions (such as curses, diseases, and poisons), as well as guidance on setting DCs and handing out rewards to player characters.

CHAPTER 11: CRAFTING & TREASURE

The treasures characters find during their adventures take many forms, from gold and gemstones to powerful magical weapons. This chapter details guidelines for distributing treasure to characters, as well as descriptions of hundreds of magic items. This chapter also contains the rules for alchemical items.

APPENDICES

The back of this book has an appendix with the rules for all of the conditions that you will find in the game. This section also includes a blank character sheet, and an index with a comprehensive glossary of common terms and traits that you'll encounter in the game.

FORMAT OF RULES ELEMENTS

Throughout this rulebook, you will see formatting standards that might look a bit unusual at first. Specifically, the game's rules are set apart in this text using specialized capitalization and italicization. These standards are in place to make this book rules elements easier to recognize.

The names of specific statistics, skills, feats, actions, and some other mechanical elements in Pathfinder are capitalized. This way, when you see the statement "a Strike targets Armor Class," you know that both Strike and Armor Class are referring to rules.

If a word or a phrase is italicized, it is describing a spell or a magic item. This way, when you see the statement "the door is sealed by *lock*," you know that in this case the word denotes the *lock* spell, rather than a physical item.

Pathfinder also uses many terms that are typically expressed as abbreviations, like AC for Armor Class, DC for Difficulty Class, and HP for Hit Points. If you're ever confused about a game term or an abbreviation, you can always turn to the Glossary and Index, beginning on page 628, and look it up.

UNDERSTANDING ACTIONS

Characters and their adversaries affect the world of Pathfinder by using actions and producing effects. This is especially the case during encounters, when every action counts. When you use an action, you generate an effect. This effect might be automatic, but sometimes actions necessitate that you roll a die, and the effect is based on what you rolled.

Throughout this book, you will see special icons to denote actions.

◆ SINGLE ACTIONS

Single actions use this symbol: ◆. They're the simplest, most common type of action. You can use three single actions on your turn in an encounter, in any order you see fit.

⤴ REACTIONS

Reactions use this symbol: ⤴. These actions can be used even when it's not your turn. You get only one reaction per encounter round, and you can use it only when its specific trigger is fulfilled. Often, the trigger is another creature's action.

◈ FREE ACTIONS

Free actions use this symbol: ◈. Free actions don't require you to spend any of your three single actions or your reaction. A free action might have a trigger like a reaction does. If so, you can use it just like a reaction—even if it's not your turn. However, you can use only one free action per trigger, so if you have multiple free actions with the same trigger, you have to decide which to use. If a free action doesn't have a trigger, you use it like a single action, just without spending any of your actions for the turn.

ACTIVITIES

Activities are special tasks that you complete by spending one or more of your actions together. Usually, an activity uses two or more actions and lets you do more than a single action would allow. You have to spend all the actions an activity requires for its effects to happen. Spellcasting is one of the most common activities, as most spells take more than a single action to cast.

Activities that use two actions use this symbol: ◆◆. Activities that use three actions use this symbol: ◆◆◆. A few special activities, such as spells you can cast in an instant, can be performed by spending a free action or a reaction.

All tasks that take longer than a turn are activities. If an activity is meant to be done during exploration, it has the exploration trait. An activity that takes a day or more of commitment and that can be done only during downtime has the downtime trait.

Single Action

Two-Action Activity

Three-Action Activity

Reaction

Free Action

READING RULES

This book contains hundreds of rules elements that give characters new and interesting ways to respond to situations in the game. All characters can use the basic actions found in Chapter 9, but an individual character often has special rules that allow them to do things most other characters can't. Most of these options are feats, which are gained by making certain choices at character creation or when a character advances in level.

Regardless of the game mechanic they convey, rules elements are always presented in the form of a stat block, a summary of the rules necessary to bring the monster, character, item, or other rules element to life during play. Where appropriate, stat blocks are introduced with an explanation of their format. For example, the Ancestry section of Chapter 2 contains rules for each of the game's six core ancestries, and an explanation of these rules appears at the beginning of that chapter.

The general format for stat blocks is shown below. Entries are omitted from a stat block when they don't apply, so not all rule elements have all of the entries given below. Actions, reactions, and free actions each have the corresponding icon next to their name to indicate their type. An activity that can be completed in a single turn has a symbol indicating how many actions are needed to complete it; activities that take longer to perform omit these icons. If a character must attain a certain level before accessing an ability, that level is indicated to the right of the stat block's name. Rules also

often have traits associated with them (traits appear in the Glossary and Index).

Spells, alchemical items, and magic items use a similar format, but their stat blocks contain a number of unique elements (see Chapter 7 for more on reading spells, and Chapter 11 for more on alchemical and magic items).

ACTION OR FEAT NAME ❖   LEVEL

TRAITS

Prerequisites Any minimum ability scores, feats, proficiency ranks, or other prerequisites you must have before you can access this rule element are listed here. Feats also have a level prerequisite, which appears above.

Frequency This is the limit on how many times you can use the ability within a given time.

Trigger Reactions and some free actions have triggers that must be met before they can be used.

Requirements Sometimes you must have a certain item or be in a certain circumstance to use an ability. If so, it's listed in this section.

This section describes the effects or benefits of a rule element. If the rule is an action, it explains what the effect is or what you must roll to determine the effect. If it's a feat that modifies an existing action or grants a constant effect, the benefit is explained here.

Special Any special qualities of the rule are explained in this section. Usually this section appears in feats you can select more than once, explaining what happens when you do.

CHARACTER CREATION

Unless you're the GM, the first thing you need to do when playing Pathfinder is create your character. It's up to you to imagine your character's past experiences, personality, and worldview, and this will set the stage for your roleplaying during the game. You'll use the game's mechanics to determine your character's ability to perform various tasks and use special abilities during the game.

This section provides a step-by-step guide for creating a character using the Pathfinder rules, preceded by a guide to help you understand ability scores. These scores are a critical part of your character, and you will be asked to make choices about them during many of the following steps. The steps of character creation are presented in a suggested order, but you can complete them in whatever order you prefer.

Many of the steps on pages 21–28 instruct you to fill out fields on your character sheet. The character sheet is shown on pages 24–25; you can find a copy in the back of this book or online as a free pdf. The character sheet is designed to be easy to use when you're actually playing the game—but creating a character happens in a different order, so you'll move back and forth through the character sheet as you go through the character creation process. Additionally, the character sheet includes every field you might need, even though not all characters will have something to put in each field. If a field on your character sheet is not applicable to your character, just leave that field blank.

All the steps of character creation are detailed on the following pages; each is marked with a number that corresponds to the sample character sheet on pages 24–25, showing you where the information goes. If the field you need to fill out is on the third or fourth page of the character sheet, which aren't shown, the text will tell you.

If you're creating a higher-level character, it's a good idea to begin with the instructions here, then turn to page 29 for instructions on leveling up characters.

THE SIX ABILITY SCORES

One of the most important aspects of your character is their ability scores. These scores represent your character's raw potential and influence nearly every other statistic on your character sheet. Determining your ability scores is not done all at once, but instead happens over several steps during character creation.

Ability scores are split into two main groups: physical and mental. Strength, Dexterity, and Constitution are physical ability scores, measuring your character's physical power, agility, and stamina. In contrast, Intelligence, Wisdom, and Charisma are mental ability scores and measure your character's learned prowess, awareness, and force of personality.

Excellence in an ability score improves the checks and statistics related to that ability, as described below. When imagining your character, you should also decide what ability scores you want to focus on to give you the best chance at success.

STRENGTH

Strength measures your character's physical power. Strength is important if your character plans to engage in hand-to-hand combat. Your Strength modifier gets added to melee damage rolls and determines how much your character can carry.

DEXTERITY

Dexterity measures your character's agility, balance, and reflexes. Dexterity is important if your character plans to make attacks with ranged weapons or use stealth to surprise foes. Your Dexterity modifier is also added to your character's AC and Reflex saving throws.

CONSTITUTION

Constitution measures your character's overall health and stamina. Constitution is an important statistic for all characters, especially those who fight in close combat. Your Constitution modifier is added to your Hit Points and Fortitude saving throws.

INTELLIGENCE

Intelligence measures how well your character can learn and reason. A high Intelligence allows your character to analyze situations and understand patterns, and it means they can become trained in additional skills and might be able to master additional languages.

WISDOM

Wisdom measures your character's common sense, awareness, and intuition. Your Wisdom modifier is added to your Perception and Will saving throws.

CHARISMA

Charisma measures your character's personal magnetism and strength of personality. A high Charisma score helps you influence the thoughts and moods of others.

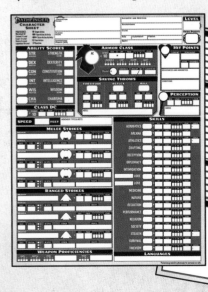

ABILITY SCORE OVERVIEW

Each ability score starts at 10, representing human average, but as you make character choices, you'll adjust these scores by applying ability boosts, which increase a score, and ability flaws, which decrease a score. As you build your character, remember to apply ability score adjustments when making the following decisions.

Ancestry: Each ancestry provides ability boosts, and sometimes an ability flaw. If you are taking any voluntary flaws, apply them in this step (see the sidebar on page 24).

Background: Your character's background provides two ability boosts.

Class: Your character's class provides an ability boost to the ability score most important to your class, called your key ability score.

Determine Scores: After the other steps, you apply four more ability boosts of your choice. Then, determine your ability modifiers based on those scores.

ABILITY BOOSTS

An ability boost normally increases an ability score's value by 2. However, if the ability score to which you're applying an ability boost is already 18 or higher, its value increases by only 1. At 1st level, a character can never have any ability score that's higher than 18.

When your character receives an ability boost, the rules indicate whether it must be applied to a specific ability score or to one of two specific ability scores, or whether it

is a "free" ability boost that can be applied to any ability score of your choice. However, when you gain multiple ability boosts at the same time, you must apply each one to a different score. Dwarves, for example, receive an ability boost to their Constitution score and their Wisdom score, as well as one free ability boost, which can be applied to any score other than Constitution or Wisdom.

ABILITY FLAWS

Ability flaws are not nearly as common in Pathfinder as ability boosts. If your character has an ability flaw—likely from their ancestry—you decrease that ability score by 2.

ABILITY MODIFIERS

Once you've finalized your ability scores, you can use them to determine your ability modifiers, which are used in most other statistics in the game. Find the score in Table 1–1: Ability Modifiers to determine its ability modifier.

TABLE 1–1: ABILITY MODIFIERS

Ability Score	Modifier	Ability Score	Modifier
1	–5	14–15	+2
2–3	–4	16–17	+3
4–5	–3	18–19	+4
6–7	–2	20–21	+5
8–9	–1	22–23	+6
10–11	+0	24–25	+7
12–13	+1	etc...	

ALTERNATIVE METHOD: ROLLING ABILITY SCORES

The standard method of generating ability scores that's described above works great if you want to create a perfectly customized, balanced character. But your GM may decide to add a little randomness to character creation and let the dice decide what kind of character the players are going to play. In that case, you can use this alternative method to generate your ability scores. Be warned—the same randomness that makes this system fun also allows it to sometimes create characters that are significantly more (or less) powerful than the standard ability score system and other Pathfinder rules assume.

If your GM opts for rolling ability scores, follow these alternative steps, ignoring all other instructions and guidelines about applying ability boosts and ability flaws throughout the character generation process.

STEP 1: ROLL AND ASSIGN SCORES

Roll four 6-sided dice (4d6) and discard the lowest die result. Add the three remaining results together and record the sum. (For example, if you rolled a 2, 4, 5, and 6, you would discard the 2 and your total would be 15.) Repeat this process until you've generated six such values. Decide which value you want for each of your ability scores.

STEP 2: ASSIGN ABILITY BOOSTS AND ABILITY FLAWS

Apply the ability boosts your character gains from their ancestry, but your character gets one fewer free ability boost than normal. If your character's ancestry has any ability flaws, apply those next. Finally, apply one ability boost to one of the ability scores specified in the character's background (you do not get the other free ability boost).

These ability boosts cannot raise a score above 18. If this would happen, you can put the ability boost into another ability score instead, as if it were a free ability boost, or you can put it into an ability score of 17 to reach 18 and lose the excess increase.

STEP 3: RECORD SCORES AND MODIFIERS

Record the final scores and assign the ability modifiers according to Table 1-1. When your character receives additional ability boosts at higher levels, you assign them as any character would.

STEP 1
CREATE A CONCEPT

What sort of hero do you want to play? The answer to this question might be as simple as "a brave warrior," or as complicated as "the child of elven wanderers, but raised in a city dominated by humans and devoted to Sarenrae, goddess of the sun." Consider your character's personality, sketch out a few details about their past, and think about how and why they adventure. You'll want to peruse Pathfinder's available ancestries, backgrounds, and classes. The summaries on pages 22–23 might help you match your concept with some of these basic rule elements. Before a game begins, it's also a good idea for the players to discuss how their characters might know each other and how they'll work together throughout the course of their adventures.

There are many ways to approach your character concept. Once you have a good idea of the character you'd like to play, move on to Step 2 to start building your character.

ANCESTRY, BACKGROUND, CLASS, OR DETAILS

If one of Pathfinder's character ancestries, backgrounds, or classes particularly intrigues you, it's easy to build a character concept around these options. The summaries of ancestries and classes on pages 22–23 give a brief overview of these options (full details appear in Chapters 2 and 3, respectively). Each ancestry also has several heritages that might refine your concept further, such as a human with an elf or orc parent, or an arctic or woodland elf. Additionally, the game has many backgrounds to choose from, representing your character's upbringing, their family's livelihood, or their earliest profession. Backgrounds are detailed later in Chapter 2, beginning on page 60.

Building a character around a specific ancestry, background, or class can be a fun way to interact with the world's lore. Would you like to build a typical member of your character's ancestry or class, as described in the relevant entry, or would you prefer to play a character who defies commonly held notions about their people? For example, you could play a dwarf with a wide-eyed sense of wonder and a zest for change, or a performing rogue capable of amazing acrobatic feats but with little interest in sneaking about.

You can draw your concept from any aspect of a character's details. You can use roleplaying to challenge not only the norms of Pathfinder's fictional world, but even real-life societal norms. Your character might challenge gender notions, explore cultural identity, have a disability, or any combination of these suggestions. Your character can live any life you see fit.

FAITH

Perhaps you'd like to play a character who is a devout follower of a specific deity. Pathfinder is a rich world with myriad faiths and philosophies spanning a wide range, from Cayden Cailean, the Drunken Hero of good-hearted

ANCESTRIES AND CLASSES

Each player takes a different approach to creating a character. Some want a character who will fit well into the story, while others look for a combination of abilities that complement each other mechanically. You might combine these two approaches. There is no wrong way!

When you turn the page, you'll see a graphical representation of ancestries and classes that provide at-a-glance information for players looking to make the most of their starting ability scores. In the ancestries overview on page 22, each entry lists which ability scores it boosts, and also indicates any ability flaws the ancestry might have. You can find more about ability boosts and ability flaws in Ability Scores on page 20.

The summaries of the classes on pages 22–23 list each class's key ability score—the ability score used to calculate the potency of many of their class abilities. Characters receive an ability boost in that ability score when you choose their class. This summary also lists one or more secondary ability scores important to members of that class.

Keep in mind a character's background also affects their ability scores, though there's more flexibility in the ability boosts from backgrounds than in those from classes. For descriptions of the available backgrounds, see pages 60–64.

adventuring; to Desna, the Song of Spheres and goddess of dreaming and the stars; to Iomedae, the Inheritor, goddess of honor, justice, and rulership. Pathfinder's major deities appear on pages 437–440. Your character might be so drawn to a particular faith that you decide they should be a champion or cleric of that deity; they might instead be a lay worshipper who applies their faith's teachings to daily life, or simply the child of devout parents.

YOUR ALLIES

You might want to coordinate with other players when forming your character concept. Your characters could have something in common already; perhaps they are relatives, or travelers from the same village. You might discuss mechanical aspects with the other players, creating characters whose combat abilities complement each other. In the latter case, it can be helpful for a party to include characters who deal damage, characters who can absorb damage, and characters who can provide healing. However, Pathfinder's classes include a lot of choices, and there are many options for building each type of character, so don't let these broad categories restrict your decisions.

CHARACTER SHEET

Once you've developed your character's concept, jot down a few sentences summarizing your ideas under the Notes section on the third page of your character sheet. Record any of the details you've already decided, such as your character's name, on the appropriate lines on the first page.

ANCESTRIES

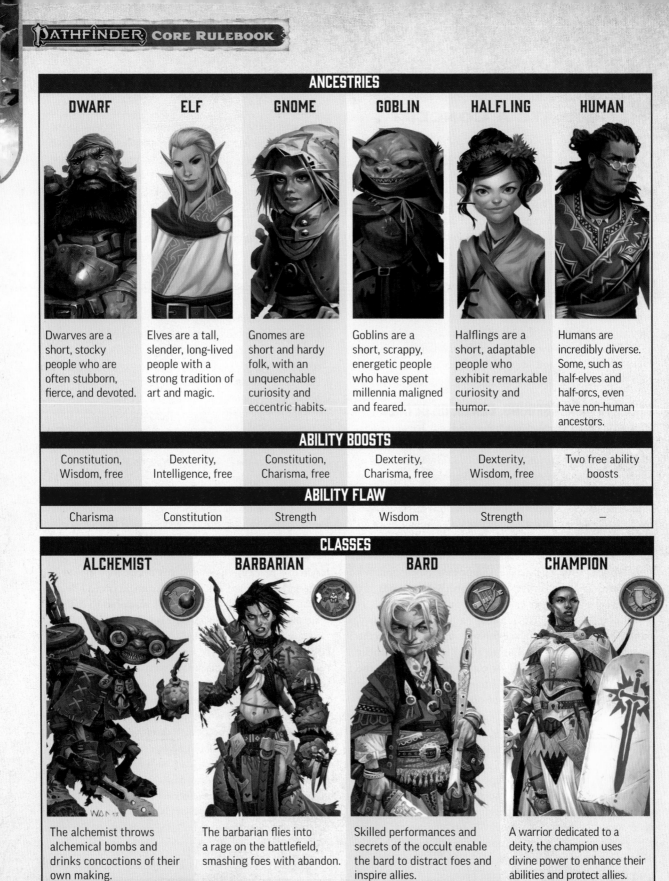

	DWARF	ELF	GNOME	GOBLIN	HALFLING	HUMAN
	Dwarves are a short, stocky people who are often stubborn, fierce, and devoted.	Elves are a tall, slender, long-lived people with a strong tradition of art and magic.	Gnomes are short and hardy folk, with an unquenchable curiosity and eccentric habits.	Goblins are a short, scrappy, energetic people who have spent millennia maligned and feared.	Halflings are a short, adaptable people who exhibit remarkable curiosity and humor.	Humans are incredibly diverse. Some, such as half-elves and half-orcs, even have non-human ancestors.

ABILITY BOOSTS

Constitution, Wisdom, free	Dexterity, Intelligence, free	Constitution, Charisma, free	Dexterity, Charisma, free	Dexterity, Wisdom, free	Two free ability boosts

ABILITY FLAW

Charisma	Constitution	Strength	Wisdom	Strength	–

CLASSES

ALCHEMIST	BARBARIAN	BARD	CHAMPION
The alchemist throws alchemical bombs and drinks concoctions of their own making.	The barbarian flies into a rage on the battlefield, smashing foes with abandon.	Skilled performances and secrets of the occult enable the bard to distract foes and inspire allies.	A warrior dedicated to a deity, the champion uses divine power to enhance their abilities and protect allies.

KEY ABILITY SCORE*

Intelligence	Strength	Charisma	Strength

SECONDARY ABILITY SCORES

Constitution, Dexterity	Constitution, Dexterity	Constitution, Dexterity	Charisma, Constitution

CLASSES

CLERIC 	DRUID	FIGHTER	MONK
The cleric calls on the power of a deity to cast spells that can heal allies or harm foes.	The druid uses the magic of the natural world to bolster allies and strike down enemies.	The fighter is a master of weapons, martial techniques, and powerful attack combinations.	The monk wields the secrets of martial arts in dazzling displays of battlefield prowess.

KEY ABILITY SCORE*

Wisdom	Wisdom	Dexterity or Strength	Dexterity or Strength

SECONDARY ABILITY SCORES

Charisma, Constitution	Constitution, Dexterity	Constitution	Constitution, Wisdom

CLASSES

RANGER	ROGUE	SORCERER	WIZARD
The ranger is a master of using their surroundings, traps, and animal allies to harry enemies.	The rogue is a multitalented master of skulduggery who strikes when enemies least expect it.	The sorcerer's magical might flows from their blood and manifests as fantastic spells and abilities.	The wizard is a scholar whose reservoirs of arcane knowledge powers their wondrous spells and abilities.

KEY ABILITY SCORE*

Dexterity or Strength	Dexterity or other	Charisma	Intelligence

SECONDARY ABILITY SCORES

Constitution, Wisdom	Charisma, Constitution	Dexterity, Constitution	Dexterity, Constitution

* A character receives an ability boost to their class's key ability score.

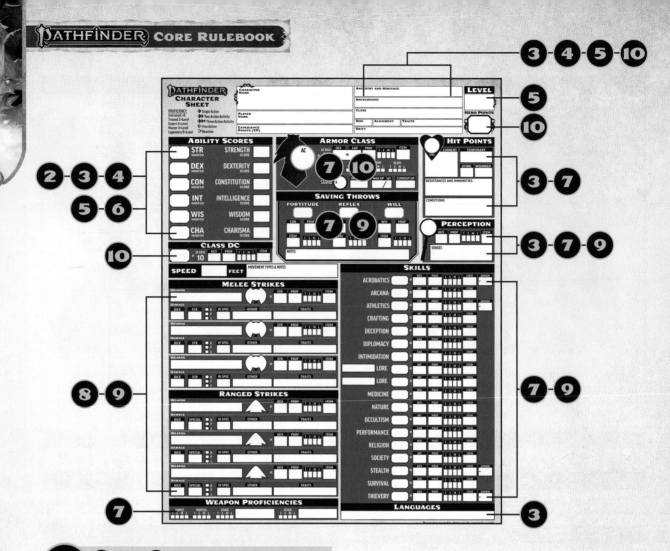

STEP 2
START BUILDING ABILITY SCORES

At this point, you need to start building your character's ability scores. See the overview of ability scores on pages 19–20 for more information about these important aspects of your character and an overview of the process.

Your character's ability scores each start at 10, and as you select your ancestry, background, and class, you'll apply ability boosts, which increase a score by 2, and ability flaws, which decrease a score by 2. At this point, just note a 10 in each ability score and familiarize yourself with the rules for ability boosts and flaws on page 20. This is also a good time to identify which ability scores will be most important to your character. See The Six Ability Scores on page 19 and the class summaries on pages 22–23 for more information.

STEP 3
SELECT AN ANCESTRY

Select an ancestry for your character. The ancestry summaries on page 22 provide an overview of Pathfinder's core ancestry options, and each is fully detailed in Chapter 2. Ancestry determines your character's size, Speed, and languages, and contributes to their Hit Points. Each also grants ability boosts and ability flaws to represent the ancestry's basic capabilities.

You'll make four decisions when you select your character's ancestry:

- Pick the ancestry itself.
- Assign any free ability boosts and decide if you are taking any voluntary flaws.
- Select a heritage from those available within that ancestry, further defining the traits your character was born with.
- Choose an ancestry feat, representing an ability your hero learned at an early age.

CHARACTER SHEET
Write your character's ancestry and heritage in the appropriate space at the top of your character sheet's first page. Adjust your ability scores, adding 2 to an ability score if you gained an ability boost from your ancestry, and subtracting 2 from an ability score if you gained an ability flaw from your ancestry. Note the number of Hit Points your character gains from their ancestry–you'll add more to this number later. Finally, in the appropriate spaces, record your character's size, Speed, and languages. If your character's ancestry provides them with special abilities, write them in the appropriate spaces, such as darkvision in the Senses

INTRODUCTION

1

INTRODUCTION

ANCESTRIES &
BACKGROUNDS

CLASSES

SKILLS

FEATS

EQUIPMENT

SPELLS

THE AGE OF
LOST OMENS

PLAYING THE
GAME

GAME
MASTERING

CRAFTING
& TREASURE

APPENDIX

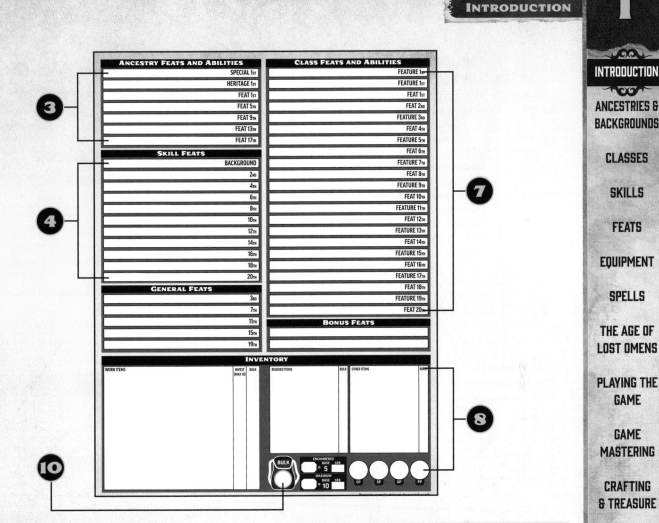

section on the first page and innate spells on the fourth page. Write the ancestry feat you selected in the Ancestry Feat section on your character sheet's second page.

character is trained, then write the name of the Lore skill granted by your background.

STEP 4
PICK A BACKGROUND

Your character's background might represent their upbringing, an aptitude they've been honing since their youth, or another aspect of their life before they became an adventurer. Character backgrounds appear in Chapter 2, starting on page 60. They typically provide two ability boosts (one that can be applied to either of two specific ability scores, and one that is free), training in a specific skill, training in a Lore skill, and a specific skill feat.

CHARACTER SHEET

Record your character's background in the space at the top of the first page of your character sheet. Adjust your ability scores, adding 2 to an ability score if you gained an ability boost from your background. Record the skill feat the background provides in the Skill Feat section of your character sheet's second page. On the first page, check the "T" box next to the name of the specific skill and for one Lore skill to indicate your

STEP 5
CHOOSE A CLASS

At this point, you need to decide your character's class. A class gives your character access to a suite of heroic abilities, determines how effectively they fight, and governs how easily they can shake off or avoid certain harmful effects. Each class is fully detailed in Chapter 3, but the summaries on pages 22–23 provide an overview of each and tells you which ability scores are important when playing that class.

You don't need to write down all of your character's class features yet. You simply need to know which class you want to play, which determines the ability scores that will be most important for your character.

CHARACTER SHEET

Write your character's class in the space at the top of the first page of your character sheet, then write "1" in the Level box to indicate that your character is 1st level. Next to the ability scores, note the class's key ability score, and add 2 to that ability score from the ability boost the

OPTIONAL: VOLUNTARY FLAWS

Sometimes, it's fun to play a character with a major flaw even if you're not playing an ancestry that imposes one. You can elect to take two additional ability flaws when applying the ability boosts and ability flaws from your ancestry. If you do, you can also apply one additional free ability boost. These ability flaws can be assigned to any ability score you like, but you can't apply more than one ability flaw to the same ability score during this step unless you apply both of the additional ability flaws to a score that is already receiving an ability boost during this step. In this case, the first ability flaw cancels the ability boost, and the second ability flaw decreases the score by 2. Likewise, as an exception to the normal rules for ability boosts, you can apply two free ability boosts to an ability score receiving an ability flaw during this step; the first ability boost cancels the ability flaw, and the second ability boost increases the score by 2. For example, a dwarf normally gets an ability boost to Constitution and Wisdom, along with an ability flaw to Charisma. You could apply one ability flaw each to Intelligence and Strength, or you could apply both ability flaws to Wisdom. You could not apply either additional ability flaw to Charisma, though, because it is already receiving dwarves' ability flaw during this step.

class provides. Don't worry about recording the rest of your character's class features and abilities yet—you'll handle that in Step 7.

6 STEP 6
DETERMINE ABILITY SCORES

Now that you've made the main mechanical choices about your character, it's time to finalize their ability scores. Do these three things:

- First, make sure you've applied all the ability boosts and ability flaws you've noted in previous steps (from your ancestry, background, and class).
- Then, apply four more ability boosts to your character's ability scores, choosing a different ability score for each and increasing that ability score by 2.
- Finally, record your starting ability scores and ability modifiers, as determined using Table 1–1: Ability Modifiers.

Remember that each ability boost adds 2 to the base score of 10, and each ability flaw subtracts 2. You should have no ability score lower than 8 or higher than 18.

CHARACTER SHEET

Write your character's starting ability scores in the box provided for each. Record the ability modifier for each ability score in the box to the left of the ability's name.

7 STEP 7
RECORD CLASS DETAILS

Now, record all the benefits and class features that your character receives from the class you've chosen. While you've already noted your key ability score, you'll want to be sure to record the following class features.

- To determine your character's total starting Hit Points, add together the number of Hit Points your character gains from their ancestry (chosen in Step 2) and the number of Hit Points they gain from their class.
- The Initial Proficiencies section of your class entry indicates your character's starting proficiency ranks in a number of areas. Choose which skills your character is trained in and record those, along with the ones set by your class. If your class would make you trained in a skill you're already trained in (typically due to your background), you can select another skill to become trained in.
- See the class advancement table in your class entry to learn the class features your character gains at 1st level—but remember, you already chose an ancestry and background. Some class features require you to make additional choices, such as selecting spells.

CHARACTER SHEET

Write your character's total Hit Points on the first page of your character sheet. Use the proficiency fields (the boxes marked "T," "E," "M," and "L") on your character sheet to record your character's initial proficiencies in Perception, saving throws, and the skills granted by their class; mark "T" if your character is trained, or "E" if your character is expert. Indicate which additional skills you chose for your character to be trained in by marking the "T" proficiency box for each skill you selected. Likewise, record your character's their armor proficiencies in the Armor Class section at the top of the first page and their weapon proficiencies at the bottom of the first page. Record all other class feats and abilities on the second page. Don't worry yet about finalizing any values for your character's statistics—you'll handle that in Step 9.

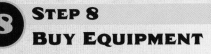

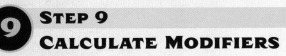

STEP 8
BUY EQUIPMENT

At 1st level, your character has 15 gold pieces (150 silver pieces) to spend on armor, weapons, and other basic equipment. Your character's class lists the types of weapons and armor with which they are trained (or better!). Their weapons determine how much damage they deal in combat, and their armor influences their Armor Class; these calculations are covered in more detail in Step 10. Don't forget essentials such as food and traveling gear! For more on the available equipment and how much it costs, see Chapter 6.

CHARACTER SHEET

Once you've spent your character's starting wealth, calculate any remaining gp, sp, and cp they might still have and write those amounts in Inventory on the second page. Record your character's weapons in the Melee Strikes and Ranged Strikes sections of the first page, depending on the weapon, and the rest of their equipment in the Inventory section on your character sheet's second page. You'll calculate specific numbers for melee Strikes and ranged Strikes with the weapons in Step 9 and for AC when wearing that armor in Step 10.

STEP 9
CALCULATE MODIFIERS

With most of the big decisions for your character made, it's time to calculate the modifiers for each of the following statistics. If your proficiency rank for a statistic is trained, expert, master, and legendary, your bonus equals your character's level plus another number based on the rank (2, 4, 6, and 8, respectively). If your character is untrained, your proficiency bonus is +0.

PERCEPTION

Your character's Perception modifier measures how alert they are. This modifier is equal to their proficiency bonus in Perception plus their Wisdom modifier. For more about Perception, see page 448.

SAVING THROWS

For each kind of saving throw, add your character's Fortitude, Reflex, or Will proficiency bonus (as appropriate) plus the ability modifier associated with that kind of saving throw. For Fortitude saving throws, use your character's Constitution modifier. For Reflex saving throws, use your character's Dexterity modifier. For Will saving throws, use your character's Wisdom modifier. Then add in any bonuses or penalties from abilities, feats, or items that always apply (but not modifiers, bonuses, or penalties that apply only in certain situations). Record this number on the line for that saving throw.

MELEE STRIKES AND RANGED STRIKES

Next to where you've written your character's melee and ranged weapons, calculate the modifier to Strike with each weapon and how much damage that Strike deals. The modifier for a Strike is equal to your character's proficiency bonus with the weapon plus an ability modifier (usually Strength for melee Strikes and Dexterity for ranged Strikes). You also add any item bonus from the weapon and any other permanent bonuses or penalties. You also need to calculate how much damage each weapon's Strike deals. Melee weapons usually add your character's Strength modifier to damage rolls, while ranged weapons might add some or all of your character's Strength modifier, depending on the weapon's traits. See the weapon entries in Chapter 6 for more information.

SPELLS AND SPELLCASTING

Most classes can learn to cast a few focus spells, but the bard, cleric, druid, sorcerer, and wizard all gain spellcasting—the ability to cast a wide variety of spells. If your character's class grants spells, you should take time during Step 7 to learn about the spells they know and how to cast them. The fourth page of the character sheet provides space to note your character's magic tradition and their proficiency rank for spell attack rolls and spell DCs. It also gives ample space to record the spells in your character's repertoire or spellbook, or that you prepare frequently. Each class determines which spells a character can cast, how they are cast, and how many they can cast in a day, but the spells themselves and detailed rules for spellcasting are located in Chapter 7.

SKILLS

In the second box to the right of each skill name on your character sheet, there's an abbreviation that reminds you of the ability score tied to that skill. For each skill in which your character is trained, add your proficiency bonus for that skill (typically +3 for a 1st-level character) to the indicated ability's modifier, as well as any other applicable bonuses and penalties, to determine the total modifier for that skill. For skills your character is untrained in, use the same method, but your proficiency bonus is +0.

CHARACTER SHEET

For Perception and saving throws, write your proficiency bonus and the appropriate ability modifier in the boxes provided, then record the total modifier in the large space. Record the proficiency bonuses, ability modifiers, and total modifiers for your melee Strikes and ranged Strikes in the box after the name of each weapon, and put the damage for each in the space below, along with the traits for that attack. For skills, record the relevant ability modifier and proficiency bonus in the appropriate box for each skill, and then write the total skill modifiers in the spaces to the left.

If your character has any modifiers, bonuses, or penalties from feats or abilities that always apply, add them into the total modifiers. For ones that apply only in certain situations, note them next to the total modifiers.

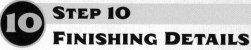

STEP 10
FINISHING DETAILS

Now add the following details to your character sheet in the appropriate spaces.

ALIGNMENT

Your character's alignment is an indicator of their morality and personality. There are nine possible alignments in Pathfinder, as shown on Table 1–2: The Nine Alignments. If your alignment has any components other than neutral, your character gains the traits of those alignment components. This might affect the way various spells, items, and creatures interact with your character.

Your character's alignment is measured by two pairs of opposed values: the axis of good and evil and the axis of law and chaos. A character who isn't committed strongly to either side is neutral on that axis. Keep in mind that alignment is a complicated subject, and even acts that might be considered good can be used for nefarious purposes, and vice versa. The GM is the arbiter of questions about how specific actions might affect your character's alignment.

If you play a champion, your character's alignment must be one allowed for their deity and cause (pages 437–440 and 106–107), and if you play a cleric, your character's alignment must be one allowed for their deity (pages 437–440).

Good and Evil

Your character has a good alignment if they consider the happiness of others above their own and work selflessly to assist others, even those who aren't friends and family. They are also good if they value protecting others from harm, even if doing so puts the character in danger. Your character has an evil alignment if they're willing to victimize others for their own selfish gain, and even more so if they enjoy inflicting harm. If your character falls somewhere in the middle, they're likely neutral on this axis.

Law and Chaos

Your character has a lawful alignment if they value consistency, stability, and predictability over flexibility. Lawful characters have a set system in life, whether it's meticulously planning day-to-day activities, carefully following a set of official or unofficial laws, or strictly adhering to a code of honor. On the other hand, if your character values flexibility, creativity, and spontaneity over consistency, they have a chaotic alignment—though this doesn't mean they make decisions by choosing randomly. Chaotic characters believe that lawful characters are too inflexible to judge each situation by its own merits or take advantage of opportunities, while lawful characters believe that chaotic characters are irresponsible and flighty.

Many characters are in the middle, obeying the law or following a code of conduct in many situations, but bending the rules when the situation requires it. If your character is in the middle, they are neutral on this axis.

Changing Alignment

Alignment can change during play as a character's beliefs change, or as you realize that your character's actions reflect a different alignment than the one on your character sheet. In most cases, you can just change their alignment and continue playing. However, if you play a cleric or champion and your character's alignment changes to one not allowed for their deity (or cause, for champions), your character loses some of their class abilities until they atone (as described in the class).

DEITY

Write down the deity your character worships, if any. Champions and clerics must worship a deity. See pages 437–440 for more about Pathfinder's deities.

AGE

Decide your character's age and note it on the third page of the character sheet. The description for your character's ancestry in Chapter 2 gives some guidance on the age ranges of members of that ancestry. Beyond that, you can play a character of whatever age you like. There aren't any mechanical adjustments to your character for being particularly old, but you might want to take it into account when considering your starting ability scores and future advancement. Particularly young characters can change

TABLE 1-2: THE NINE ALIGNMENTS

	Good	Neutral	Evil
Lawful	Lawful Good (LG)	Lawful Neutral (LN)	Lawful Evil (LE)
Neutral	Neutral Good (NG)	True Neutral (N)	Neutral Evil (NE)
Chaotic	Chaotic Good (CG)	Chaotic Neutral (CN)	Chaotic Evil (CE)

the tone of some of the game's threats, so it's recommended that characters are at least young adults.

GENDER AND PRONOUNS

Characters of all genders are equally likely to become adventurers. Record your character's gender, if applicable, and their pronouns on the third page of the character sheet.

CLASS DC

A class DC sets the difficulty for certain abilities granted by your character's class. This DC equals 10 plus their proficiency bonus for their class DC (+3 for most 1st-level characters) plus the modifier for the class's key ability score.

HERO POINTS

Your character usually begins each game session with 1 Hero Point, and you can gain additional Hero Points during sessions by performing heroic deeds or devising clever strategies. Your character can use Hero Points to gain certain benefits, such as staving off death or rerolling a d20. See page 467 for more about Hero Points.

ARMOR CLASS (AC)

Your character's Armor Class represents how difficult they are to hit in combat. To calculate your AC, add 10 plus your character's Dexterity modifier (up to their armor's Dexterity modifier cap; page 274), plus their proficiency bonus with their armor, plus their armor's item bonus to AC and any other permanent bonuses and penalties.

BULK

Your character's maximum Bulk determines how much weight they can comfortably carry. If they're carrying a total amount of Bulk that exceeds 5 plus their Strength modifier, they are encumbered. A character can't carry a total amount of Bulk that exceeds 10 plus their Strength modifier. The Bulk your character is carrying equals the sum of all of their items; keep in mind that 10 light items make up 1 Bulk. You can find out more about Bulk in Chapter 6: Equipment.

INTRODUCTION

ANCESTRIES & BACKGROUNDS

CLASSES

SKILLS

FEATS

EQUIPMENT

SPELLS

THE AGE OF LOST OMENS

PLAYING THE GAME

GAME MASTERING

CRAFTING & TREASURE

APPENDIX

SAMPLE CHARACTER

This step-by-step example illustrates the process of creating a Pathfinder character.

STEPS 1 AND 2

Adam is making his first Pathfinder character. After talking about it with the rest of the group, he's decided to make a dwarven druid. After jotting down a few ideas, he begins by writing down a 10 for each ability score.

STEP 3

Adam looks up the dwarf entry in Chapter 2. He records the ability boosts to his Constitution and Wisdom scores (bringing both up to 12). He also applies the ability flaw to his Charisma, dropping it to 8. For his free ability boost, he chooses Dexterity to boost his defenses, raising it to 12 as well. He also records the 10 Hit Points the ancestry gives him. Next, he returns to his character sheet to record the size, Speed, language, and darkvision ability he gets from being a dwarf. Finally, he decides on a heritage, writing "rock dwarf" next to dwarf, and he picks an ancestry feat, deciding on Rock Runner, to show his character's strong connection to stone.

STEP 4

Looking through the backgrounds, Adam likes the idea of a solitary dwarven druid, and the nomad background makes for a good choice. For the first ability boost granted by the background, Adam chooses Wisdom, and for the free ability boost, he choses Constitution, taking both up to 14. On the second page, he writes "Assurance (Survival)" in the Skill Feats area, on the Background line. Finally, returning to the first page, he writes "cave" next to the first Lore skill entry and checks the box under the "T" for that skill and Survival.

STEP 5

Adam writes "druid" on the class line of his character sheet and fills in the number 1 in the level box. The druid class grants an ability boost to its key ability score, which is Wisdom, so Adam's character has his Wisdom raised to 16.

STEP 6

Adam applies four more ability boosts to his ability scores to determine his starting scores. After giving it some thought, he applies them to Wisdom (raising it to 18), since that's the most important ability score for his class, and to Strength, Dexterity, and Constitution (raising them to 12, 14, and 16, respectively) to make him better in combat. He then looks at Table 1–1 to determine the ability modifiers for each score and writes all of his ability scores and modifiers down on his character sheet.

STEP 7

As Adam applies his class, he has a number of things to figure out. First, he starts by recording all of his initial proficiencies, marking the appropriate boxes in the Armor Class, Saving Throws, Weapon Proficiencies, Spell Attack Roll, and Spell DCs areas of his sheet. Turning to skills, he marks Nature as trained and notes that once he picks his druid order, he'll become trained in another skill determined by that order. He then gets to choose three more skills (if he had a higher Intelligence, he would have gotten more). He decides on Athletics, Diplomacy, and Medicine, marking all of them as trained. Next, he adds the 8 Hit Points from the druid class and his Constitution modifier of +3 to the 10 Hit Points from his dwarf ancestry for an impressive 21 total Hit Points.

Moving on to class features, Adam marks down wild empathy in the class feats and abilities area, as well as the Shield Block feat in the bonus feats area. He makes note of the anathema for being a druid and records Druidic in his language section. Next, he looks through the druid orders and decides upon the wild order, which gives him his final trained skill (Intimidation), the ability to cast *wild morph*, as well as the Wild Shape feat, which lets him cast a spell to turn into an animal. He writes these spells in the focus spell area of his character sheet and also notes that he has 1 Focus Point to use to cast these spells.

Finally, a druid can cast a limited number of primal spells. Although he can change them every morning, Adam is curious, and he turns to Chapter 7: Spells to decide what spells he might cast. He jots down five cantrips and two 1st-level spells and marks them as prepared.

STEP 8

Next up, Adam turns to Chapter 6: Equipment. He's trained in medium armor, but since wearing metal armor is anathema to druids, he chooses hide armor. For weapons, he decides on a spear, but he buys two just in case he wants to throw the first one. He writes all of these on the front of his character sheet. Adam lists the spear under both melee Strikes and ranged Strikes, and he also writes the claws he gains from *wild morph* under his melee Strikes, because he's sure that he'll be casting that spell a lot. He records the rest of his gear in the Inventory section on the second page, along with coin left over after buying his starting gear.

STEP 9

Adam records all of the ability modifiers for Perception, saving throws, Strikes, and skills. He then puts a "+3" in the box marked Prof to indicate his proficiency bonus for each statistic he's trained in (1 for his level, plus 2 for being trained) and "+5" in any that he is an expert. Then, he adds up his modifiers for each statistic.

STEP 10

Finally, Adam fills out the final details of his character, noting his neutral alignment and calculating his AC and Bulk limits. Last but not least, he fills in some last-minute information about his character and decides on a name. Gar the dwarf druid is ready for his first adventure!

INTRODUCTION

1

INTRODUCTION

ANCESTRIES & BACKGROUNDS

CLASSES

SKILLS

FEATS

EQUIPMENT

SPELLS

THE AGE OF LOST OMENS

PLAYING THE GAME

GAME MASTERING

CRAFTING & TREASURE

APPENDIX

LEVELING UP

The world of Pathfinder is a dangerous place, and your character will face terrifying beasts and deadly traps on their journey into legend. With each challenge resolved, a character earns Experience Points (XP) that allow them to increase in level. Each level grants greater skill, increased resiliency, and new capabilities, allowing your character to face even greater challenges and go on to earn even more impressive rewards.

Each time your character reaches 1,000 Experience Points, their level increases by 1. On your character sheet, indicate your character's new level beside the name of their class, and deduct 1,000 XP from their XP total. If you have any Experience Points left after this, record them—they count toward your next level, so your character is already on their way to advancing yet again!

Next, return to your character's class entry. Increase your character's total Hit Points by the number indicated for your class. Then, take a look at the class advancement table and find the row for your character's new level. Your character gains all the abilities listed for that level, including new abilities specific to your class and additional benefits all characters gain as they level up. For example, all characters gain four ability boosts at 5th level and every 5 levels thereafter.

You can find all the new abilities specific to your class, including class feats, right in your class entry, though you can also use class feats to take an archetype (page 219). Your character's class entry also explains how to apply any ability boosts and skill increases your character gains. If they gain an ancestry feat, head back to the entry for your character's ancestry in Chapter 2 and select another ancestry feat from the list of options. If they gain a skill increase, refer to Chapter 4 when deciding which skill to apply it to. If they gain a general feat or a skill feat, you can choose from the feats listed in Chapter 5. If they can cast spells, see the class entry for details on adding spell slots and spells. It's also a good idea to review your character's spells in Chapter 7 and see if there are heightened versions they can now cast.

Once you've made all your choices for your character's new level, be sure to go over your character sheet and adjust any values that have changed. At a bare minimum, your proficiency bonuses all increase by 1 because you've gained a level, so your AC, attack rolls, Perception, saving throws, skill modifiers, spell attack rolls, and class DC all increase by at least 1. You might need to change other values because of skill increases, ability boosts, or class features that either increase your proficiency rank or increase other statistics at certain levels. If an ability boost increases your character's Constitution modifier, recalculate their maximum Hit Points using their new Constitution modifier (typically this adds 1 Hit Point per level). If an ability boost increases your character's Intelligence modifier, they become trained in an additional skill and language.

Some feats grant a benefit based on your level, such as Toughness, and these benefits are adjusted whenever you gain a level as well.

You can perform the steps in the leveling-up process in whichever order you want. For example, if you wanted to take the skill feat Intimidating Prowess as your skill feat at 10th level, but your character's Strength score was only 14, you could first increase their Strength score to 16 using the ability boosts gained at 10th level, and then take Intimidating Prowess as a skill feat at the same level.

LEVELING-UP CHECKLIST

Every time you gain a level, make sure you do each of the following:

- Increase your level by 1 and subtract 1,000 XP from your XP total.
- Increase your maximum Hit Points by the amount listed in your class entry in Chapter 3.
- Add class features from your class advancement table, including ability boosts and skill increases.
- Select feats as indicated on your class advancement table. For ancestry feats, see Chapter 2. For class feats, see your class entry in Chapter 3. For general feats and skill feats, see Chapter 5.
- Add spells and spell slots if your class grants spellcasting. See Chapter 7 for spells.
- Increase all of your proficiency bonuses by 1 from your new level, and make other increases to your proficiency bonuses as necessary from skill increases or other class features. Increase any other statistics that changed as a result of ability boosts or other abilities.
- Adjust bonuses from feats and other abilities that are based on your level.

CHAPTER 2: ANCESTRIES & BACKGROUNDS

Your character's ancestry determines which people they call their own, whether it's diverse and ambitious humans, insular but vivacious elves, traditionalist and family-focused dwarves, or any of the other folk who call Golarion home. A character's ancestry and their experiences prior to their life as an adventurer—represented by a background—might be key parts of their identity, shape how they see the world, and help them find their place in it.

2

INTRODUCTION

ANCESTRIES &
BACKGROUNDS

CLASSES

SKILLS

FEATS

EQUIPMENT

SPELLS

THE AGE OF
LOST OMENS

PLAYING THE
GAME

GAME
MASTERING

CRAFTING
& TREASURE

APPENDIX

A character has one ancestry and one background, both of which you select during character creation. You'll also select a number of languages for your character. Once chosen, your ancestry and background can't be changed.

This chapter is divided into three parts:

- **Ancestries** express the culture your character hails from. Within many ancestries are heritages—subgroups that each have their own characteristics. An ancestry provides ability boosts (and perhaps ability flaws), Hit Points, ancestry feats, and sometimes additional abilities.
- **Backgrounds**, starting on page 60, describe training or environments your character experienced before becoming an adventurer. Your character's background provides ability boosts, skill training, and a skill feat.
- **Languages**, starting on page 65, let your character communicate with the wonderful and weird people and creatures of the world.

ANCESTRY ENTRIES

Each entry includes details about the ancestry and presents the rules elements described below (all of these but heritages and ancestry feats are listed in a sidebar).

HIT POINTS

This tells you how many Hit Points your character gains from their ancestry at 1st level. You'll add the Hit Points from your character's class (including their Constitution modifier) to this number. For more on calculating Hit Points, see Step 7: Record Class Details, on page 25.

SIZE

This tells you the physical size of members of the ancestry. Medium corresponds roughly to the height and weight range of a human adult, and Small is roughly half that.

SPEED

This entry lists how far a member of the ancestry can move each time they spend an action (such as Stride) to do so.

ABILITY BOOSTS

This lists the ability scores you apply ability boosts to when creating a character of this ancestry. Most ancestries provide ability boosts to two specified ability scores, plus a free ability boost that you can apply to any other score of your choice. For more about ability boosts, see page 20.

ABILITY FLAW

This lists the ability score to which you apply an ability flaw when creating a character of this ancestry. Most ancestries, with the exception of humans, include an ability flaw. For more about applying ability flaws, see page 20.

LANGUAGES

This tells you the languages that members of the ancestry speak at 1st level. If your Intelligence modifier is +1 or higher, you can select more languages from a list given here. More about languages can be found on page 65.

TRAITS

These descriptors have no mechanical benefit, but they're important for determining how certain spells, effects, and other aspects of the game interact with your character.

SPECIAL ABILITIES

Any other entries in the sidebar represent abilities, senses, and other qualities all members of the ancestry manifest. These are omitted for ancestries with no special rules.

HERITAGES

You select a heritage at 1st level to reflect abilities passed down to you from your ancestors or common among those of your ancestry in the environment where you were born or grew up. You have only one heritage and can't change it later. A heritage is not the same as a culture or ethnicity, though some cultures or ethnicities might have more or fewer members from a particular heritage.

ANCESTRY FEATS

This section presents ancestry feats, which allow you to customize your character. You gain your first ancestry feat at 1st level, and you gain another at 5th level, 9th level, 13th level, and 17th level, as indicated in the class advancement table in the descriptions of each class.

Ancestry feats are organized by level. As a starting character, you can choose from only 1st-level ancestry feats, but later choices can be made from any feat of your level or lower. These feats also sometimes list prerequisites—requirements that your character must fulfill to select that feat.

DWARF

Dwarves have a well-earned reputation as a stoic and stern people, ensconced within citadels and cities carved from solid rock. While some see them as dour and humorless crafters of stone and metal, dwarves and those who have spent time among them understand their unbridled zeal for their work, caring far more about quality than quantity. To a stranger, they can seem untrusting and clannish, but to their friends and family, they are warm and caring, their halls filled with the sounds of laughter and hammers hitting anvils.

Dwarves are slow to trust those outside their kin, but this wariness is not without reason. Dwarves have a long history of forced exile from ancestral holds and struggles against the depredations of savage foes, especially giants, goblinoids, orcs, and the horrors that dwell deep below the surface. While trust from a dwarf is hard-won, once gained it is as strong as iron.

If you want to play a character who is as hard as nails, a stubborn and unrelenting adventurer, with a mix of rugged toughness and deep wisdom—or at least dogged conviction—you should play a dwarf.

YOU MIGHT...

- Strive to uphold your personal honor, no matter the situation.
- Appreciate quality craftsmanship in all forms and insist upon it for all your gear.
- Don't waver or back down once you've set your mind to something.

OTHERS PROBABLY...

- See you as stubborn, though whether they see this as an asset or a detriment changes from one person to the next.
- Assume you are an expert in matters related to stonework, mining, precious metals, and gems.
- Recognize the deep connection you have with your family, heritage, and friends.

PHYSICAL DESCRIPTION

Dwarves are short and stocky, standing about a foot shorter than most humans. They have wide, compact bodies and burly frames. Dwarves of all genders pride themselves on the length of their hair, which they often braid into intricate patterns, some of which represent specific clans. A long beard is a sign of masculinity and honor among the dwarves, and thus a clean-shaven male dwarf is considered weak, untrustworthy, or worse.

Dwarves typically reach physical adulthood around the age of 25, though their traditionalist culture places more value on completing coming of age ceremonies unique to each clan than reaching a certain age. A typical dwarf can live to around 350 years old.

SOCIETY

The ancient surface empire the dwarves once ruled fell long ago, overwhelmed by orc and goblinoid enemies. Today's dwarves today retain many of the qualities that propelled their people to greatness in ancient times: fierceness, gumption, and stubbornness in endeavors ranging from battle and craftsmanship to forging ties with family and friends.

While the distance between their mountain Sky Citadels can create vast cultural divides between various dwarf clans, most dwarven societies share a number of similarities. Nearly all dwarven peoples share a passion for stonework, metalwork, and gem-cutting. Most are highly skilled at architecture and mining, and many share a hatred of giants, orcs, and goblinoids.

Few dwarves are seen without their clan dagger strapped to their belt. This dagger is forged just before a dwarf's birth and bears the gemstone of their clan. A parent uses this dagger to cut the infant's umbilical cord, making it the first weapon to taste their blood.

ALIGNMENT AND RELIGION

Dwarves tend to value honor and closely follow the traditions of their clans and kingdoms. They have a strong sense of friendship and justice, though they are often very particular about who they consider a friend. They work hard and play harder—especially when strong ale is involved.

The typical dwarf is lawful good or lawful neutral and prefers to worship deities of those alignments. Torag, god of dwarvenkind, is the dwarves' primary deity, though worship of Torag's family members is also common.

NAMES

Dwarves honor their children with names taken from ancestors or dwarven heroes, and it's quite rare to invent a new name or to borrow a name from another culture for a child. When introducing themselves, dwarves tend to list their family and clan, plus any number of other familial connections and honorifics. Dwarven names usually contain hard consonants and are rarely more or fewer than two syllables.

SAMPLE NAMES

Agna, Bodill, Dolgrin, Edrukk, Grunyar, Ingra, Kazmuk, Kotri, Lupp, Morgrym, Rogar, Rusilka, Torra, Yangrit

DWARF HERITAGES

With their long family lines and hardy physiologies, dwarves take great pride in the resilience their bloodlines provide. Choose one of the following dwarven heritages at 1st level.

ANCIENT-BLOODED DWARF

Dwarven heroes of old could shrug off their enemies' magic, and some of that resistance manifests in you. You gain the Call on Ancient Blood reaction.

CALL ON ANCIENT BLOOD ⟳

Trigger You attempt a saving throw against a magical effect, but you haven't rolled yet.

Your ancestors' innate resistance to magic surges, before slowly ebbing down. You gain a +1 circumstance bonus to the triggering saving throw and until the end of this turn.

DEATH WARDEN DWARF

Your ancestors have been tomb guardians for generations, and the power they cultivated to ward off necromancy has passed on to you. If you roll a success on a saving throw against a necromancy effect, you get a critical success instead.

FORGE DWARF

You have a remarkable adaptation to hot environments from ancestors who inhabited blazing deserts or volcanic chambers beneath the earth. This grants you fire resistance equal to half your level (minimum 1), and you treat environmental heat effects as if they were one step less extreme (incredible heat becomes extreme, extreme heat becomes severe, and so on).

Hit Points
10

Size
Medium

Speed
20 feet

Ability Boosts
Constitution
Wisdom
Free

Ability Flaw
Charisma

Languages
Common
Dwarven
Additional languages equal to your Intelligence modifier (if it's positive). Choose from Gnomish, Goblin, Jotun, Orcish, Terran, Undercommon, and any other languages to which you have access (such as the languages prevalent in your region).

Traits
Dwarf
Humanoid

Darkvision
You can see in darkness and dim light just as well as you can see in bright light, though your vision in darkness is in black and white.

ROCK DWARF

Your ancestors lived and worked among the great ancient stones of the mountains or the depths of the earth. This makes you solid as a rock when you plant your feet. You gain a +2 circumstance bonus to your Fortitude or Reflex DC against attempts to Shove or Trip you. This bonus also applies to saving throws against spells or effects that attempt to knock you prone.

In addition, if any effect would force you to move 10 feet or more, you are moved only half the distance.

STRONG-BLOODED DWARF

Your blood runs hearty and strong, and you can shake off toxins. You gain poison resistance equal to half your level (minimum 1), and each of your successful saving throws against a poison affliction reduces its stage by 2, or by 1 for a virulent poison. Each critical success against an ongoing poison reduces its stage by 3, or by 2 for a virulent poison.

ANCESTRY FEATS

At 1st level, you gain one ancestry feat, and you gain an additional ancestry feat every 4 levels thereafter (at 5th, 9th, 13th, and 17th levels). As a dwarf, you select from among the following ancestry feats.

1ST LEVEL

DWARVEN LORE   FEAT 1
DWARF

You eagerly absorbed the old stories and traditions of your ancestors, your gods, and your people, studying in subjects and techniques passed down for generation upon generation. You gain the trained proficiency rank in Crafting and Religion. If you would automatically become trained in one of those skills (from your background or class, for example), you instead become trained in a skill of your choice. You also become trained in Dwarven Lore.

DWARVEN WEAPON FAMILIARITY   FEAT 1
DWARF

Your kin have instilled in you an affinity for hard-hitting weapons, and you prefer these to more elegant arms. You are trained with the battle axe, pick, and warhammer.

You also gain access to all uncommon dwarf weapons. For the purpose of determining your proficiency, martial dwarf weapons are simple weapons and advanced dwarf weapons are martial weapons.

ROCK RUNNER   FEAT 1
DWARF

Your innate connection to stone makes you adept at moving across uneven surfaces. You can ignore difficult terrain caused by rubble and uneven ground made of stone and earth.

In addition, when you use the Acrobatics skill to Balance on narrow surfaces or uneven ground made of stone or earth, you aren't flat-footed, and when you roll a success at one of these Acrobatics checks, you get a critical success instead.

STONECUNNING   FEAT 1
DWARF

You have a knack for noticing even small inconsistencies and craftsmanship techniques in the stonework around you. You gain a +2 circumstance bonus to Perception checks to notice unusual stonework. This bonus applies to checks to discover mechanical traps made of stone or hidden within stone.

If you aren't using the Seek action or searching, the GM automatically rolls a secret check for you to notice unusual stonework anyway. This check doesn't gain the circumstance bonus, and it takes a –2 circumstance penalty.

UNBURDENED IRON   FEAT 1
DWARF

You've learned techniques first devised by your ancestors during their ancient wars, allowing you to comfortably wear massive suits of armor. Ignore the reduction to your Speed from any armor you wear.

In addition, any time you're taking a penalty to your Speed from some other reason (such as from the encumbered condition or from a spell), deduct 5 feet from the penalty. For example, the encumbered condition normally gives a –10-foot penalty to Speed, but it gives you only a –5-foot penalty. If your Speed is taking multiple penalties, pick only one penalty to reduce.

VENGEFUL HATRED   FEAT 1
DWARF

You heart aches for vengeance against those who have wronged your people. Choose one of the following dwarven ancestral foes when you gain Vengeful Hatred: drow, duergar, giant, or orc. You gain a +1 circumstance bonus to damage with weapons and unarmed attacks against creatures with that trait. If your attack would deal more than one weapon die of damage (as is common at higher levels than 1st), the bonus is equal to the number of weapon dice or unarmed attack dice.

In addition, if a creature critically succeeds at an attack against you and deals damage to you, you gain your bonus to damage against that creature for 1 minute regardless of whether it has the chosen trait.

Special Your GM can add appropriate creature traits to the ancestral foes list if your character is from a community that commonly fights other types of enemies.

5TH LEVEL

BOULDER ROLL ◆◆   FEAT 5
DWARF

Prerequisites Rock Runner

Your dwarven build allows you to push foes around, just like

ANCESTRIES & BACKGROUNDS

2

INTRODUCTION

ANCESTRIES &
BACKGROUNDS

CLASSES

SKILLS

FEATS

EQUIPMENT

SPELLS

THE AGE OF
LOST OMENS

PLAYING THE
GAME

GAME
MASTERING

CRAFTING
& TREASURE

a mighty boulder tumbles through a subterranean cavern. Take a Step into the square of a foe that is your size or smaller, and the foe must move into the empty space directly behind it. The foe must move even if doing so places it in harm's way. The foe can attempt a Fortitude saving throw against your Athletics DC to block your Step. If the foe attempts this saving throw, unless it critically succeeds, it takes bludgeoning damage equal to your level plus your Strength modifier.

If the foe can't move into an empty space (if it is surrounded by solid objects or other creatures, for example), your Boulder Roll has no effect.

DWARVEN WEAPON CUNNING   FEAT 5

DWARF

Prerequisites Dwarven Weapon Familiarity

You've learned cunning techniques to get the best effects out of your dwarven weapons. Whenever you critically hit using a battle axe, pick, warhammer, or a dwarf weapon, you apply the weapon's critical specialization effect.

9TH LEVEL

MOUNTAIN'S STOUTNESS   FEAT 9

DWARF

Your hardiness lets you withstand more punishment than most before going down. Increase your maximum Hit Points by your level. You also decrease the DC of recovery checks when you have the dying condition by 1.

If you also have the Toughness feat, the Hit Points gained from it and this feat are cumulative, and you decrease the DC of recovery checks by 4.

STONEWALKER   FEAT 9

DWARF

You have a deep reverence for and connection to stone. You gain *meld into stone* as a 3rd-level divine innate spell that you can cast once per day.

If you have the Stonecunning dwarf ancestry feat, you can attempt to find unusual stonework and stonework traps that require legendary proficiency in Perception. If you have both Stonecunning and legendary proficiency in Perception, when you're not Seeking and the GM rolls a secret check for you to notice unusual stonework, you keep the bonus from Stonecunning and don't take the –2 circumstance penalty.

13TH LEVEL

DWARVEN WEAPON EXPERTISE   FEAT 13

DWARF

Prerequisites Dwarven Weapon Familiarity

Your dwarven affinity blends with your training, granting you great skill with dwarven weapons. Whenever you gain a class feature that grants you expert or greater proficiency in certain weapons, you also gain that proficiency for battle axes, picks, warhammers, and all dwarven weapons in which you are trained.

DWARVEN ADVENTURERS

Dwarven adventurers tend to work as treasure hunters or sellswords. They often leave their citadels and subterranean cities in search of wealth to enrich their homeland or to reclaim long-lost dwarven treasures or lands taken by the enemies of their kin.

Typical dwarven backgrounds include acolyte, artisan, merchant, miner, and warrior. Dwarves excel at many of the martial classes, such as barbarian, fighter, monk, and ranger, but they also make excellent clerics and druids.

ELF

As an ancient people, elves have seen great change and have the perspective that can come only from watching the arc of history. After leaving the world in ancient times, they returned to a changed land, and they still struggle to reclaim their ancestral homes, most notably from terrible demons that have invaded parts of their lands. To some, the elves are objects of awe—graceful and beautiful, with immense talent and knowledge. Among themselves, however, the elves place far more importance on personal freedom than on living up to these ideals.

Elves combine otherworldly grace, sharp intellect, and mysterious charm in a way that is practically magnetic to members of other ancestries. They are often voraciously intellectual, though their studies delve into a level of detail that most shorter-lived peoples find excessive or inefficient. Valuing kindness and beauty, elves ever strive to improve their manners, appearance, and culture.

Elves are often rather private people, steeped in the secrets of their groves and kinship groups. They're slow to build friendships outside their kinsfolk, but for a specific reason: they subtly and deeply attune to their environment and their companions. There's a physical element to this attunement, but it isn't only superficial. Elves who spend their lives among shorter-lived peoples often develop a skewed perception of their own mortality and tend to become morose after watching generation after generation of companions age and die. These elves are called the Forlorn.

If you want a character who is magical, mystical, and mysterious, you should play an elf.

YOU MIGHT...

- Carefully curate your relationships with people with shorter lifespans, either keeping a careful emotional distance or resigning yourself to outliving them.
- Adopt specialized or obscure interests simply for the sake of mastering them.
- Have features such as eye color, skin tone, hair, or mannerisms that reflect the environment in which you live.

OTHERS PROBABLY...

- Focus on your appearance, either admiring your grace or treating you as if you're physically fragile.
- Assume you practice archery, cast spells, fight demons, and have perfected one or more fine arts.
- Worry that you privately look down on them, or feel like you're condescending and aloof.

PHYSICAL DESCRIPTION

While generally taller than humans, elves possess a fragile grace, accentuated by long features and sharply pointed ears. Their eyes are wide and almond-shaped, featuring large and vibrant-colored pupils that make up the entire visible portion of the eye. These pupils give them an alien look and allow them to see sharply even in very little light.

Elves gradually adapt to their environment and their companions, and they often take on physical traits reflecting their surroundings. An elf who has dwelled in primeval forests for centuries, for example, might exhibit verdant hair and gnarled fingers, while one who's lived in a desert might have golden pupils and skin. Elven fashion, like the elves themselves, tends

ANCESTRIES & BACKGROUNDS

2

INTRODUCTION

ANCESTRIES &
BACKGROUNDS

CLASSES

SKILLS

FEATS

EQUIPMENT

SPELLS

THE AGE OF
LOST OMENS

PLAYING THE
GAME

GAME
MASTERING

CRAFTING
& TREASURE

APPENDIX

to reflect their surroundings. Elves living in the forests and other wilderness locales wear clothing that plays off the terrain and flora of their homes, while those who live in cities tend to wear the latest fashions.

Elves reach physical adulthood around the age of 20, though they aren't considered to be fully emotionally mature by other elves until closer to the passing of their first century, once they've experienced more, held several occupations, and outlived a generation of shorter-lived people. A typical elf can live to around 600 years old.

SOCIETY

Elven culture is deep, rich, and on the decline. Their society peaked millennia ago, long before they fled the world to escape a great calamity. They've since returned, but rebuilding is no easy task. Their inborn patience and intellectual curiosity make elves excellent sages, philosophers, and wizards, and their societies are built upon their inherent sense of wonder and knowledge. Elven architecture displays their deep appreciation of beauty, and elven cities are wondrous works of art.

Elves hold deeply seated ideals of individualism, allowing each elf to explore multiple occupations before alighting on a particular pursuit or passion that suits her best. Elves bear notorious grudges against rivals, which the elves call *ilduliel*, but these antagonistic relationships can sometimes blossom into friendships over time.

ALIGNMENT AND RELIGION

Elves are often emotional and capricious, yet they hold high ideals close to their hearts. As such, many are chaotic good. They prefer deities who share their love of all things mystic and artistic. Desna and Shelyn are particular favorites, the former for her sense of wonder and the latter for her appreciation of artistry. Calistria is the most notorious of elven deities, as she represents many of the elven ideals taken to the extreme.

NAMES

An elf keeps their personal name secret among their family, while giving a nickname when meeting other people. This nickname can change over time, due to events in the elf's life or even on a whim. A single elf might be known by many names by associates of different ages and regions. Elven names consist of multiple syllables and are meant to flow lyrically—at least in the Elven tongue. They so commonly end in "-el" or "-ara" that other cultures sometimes avoid names ending in these syllables to avoid sounding too elven.

SAMPLE NAMES

Aerel, Amrunelara, Caladrel, Dardlara, Faunra, Heldalel, Jathal, Lanliss, Oparal, Seldlon, Soumral, Talathel, Tessara, Variel, Yalandlara, Zordlon

ELF HERITAGES

Elves live long lives and adapt to their environment after dwelling there for a long time. Choose one of the following elven heritages at 1st level.

ARCTIC ELF

You dwell deep in the frozen north and have gained incredible resilience against cold environments, granting you cold resistance equal to half your level (minimum 1). You treat environmental cold effects as if they were one step less extreme (incredible cold becomes extreme, extreme cold becomes severe, and so on).

CAVERN ELF

You were born or spent many years in underground tunnels or caverns where light is scarce. You gain darkvision.

Hit Points
6

Size
Medium

Speed
30 feet

Ability Boosts
Dexterity
Intelligence
Free

Ability Flaw
Constitution

Languages
Common
Elven
Additional languages equal to your Intelligence modifier (if it's positive). Choose from Celestial, Draconic, Gnoll, Gnomish, Goblin, Orcish, Sylvan, and any other languages to which you have access (such as the languages prevalent in your region).

Traits
Elf
Humanoid

Low-Light Vision
You can see in dim light as though it were bright light, so you ignore the concealed condition due to dim light.

SEER ELF

You have an inborn ability to detect and understand magical phenomena. You can cast the *detect magic* cantrip as an arcane innate spell at will. A cantrip is heightened to a spell level equal to half your level rounded up.

In addition, you gain a +1 circumstance bonus to checks to Identify Magic and to Decipher Writing of a magical nature. These skill actions typically use the Arcana, Nature, Occultism, or Religion skill.

WHISPER ELF

Your ears are finely tuned, able to detect even the slightest whispers of sound. As long as you can hear normally, you can use the Seek action to sense undetected creatures in a 60-foot cone instead of a 30-foot cone. You also gain a +2 circumstance bonus to locate undetected creatures that you could hear within 30 feet with a Seek action.

WOODLAND ELF

You're adapted to life in the forest or the deep jungle, and you know how to climb trees and use foliage to your advantage. When Climbing trees, vines, and other foliage, you move at half your Speed on a success and at full Speed on a critical success (and you move at full Speed on a success if you have Quick Climb). This doesn't affect you if you're using a climb Speed.

You can always use the Take Cover action when you are within forest terrain to gain cover, even if you're not next to an obstacle you can Take Cover behind.

ANCESTRY FEATS

At 1st level, you gain one ancestry feat, and you gain an additional ancestry feat every 4 levels thereafter (at 5th, 9th, 13th, and 17th levels). As an elf, you select from among the following ancestry feats.

1ST LEVEL

ANCESTRAL LONGEVITY   FEAT 1
ELF

Prerequisites at least 100 years old

You have accumulated a vast array of lived knowledge over the years. During your daily preparations, you can reflect upon your life experiences to gain the trained proficiency rank in one skill of your choice. This proficiency lasts until you prepare again. Since this proficiency is temporary, you can't use it as a prerequisite for a skill increase or a permanent character option like a feat.

ELVEN LORE   FEAT 1
ELF

You've studied in traditional elven arts, learning about arcane magic and the world around you. You gain the trained proficiency rank in Arcana and Nature. If you would

automatically become trained in one of those skills (from your background or class, for example), you instead become trained in a skill of your choice. You also become trained in Elven Lore.

ELVEN WEAPON FAMILIARITY   FEAT 1
ELF

You favor bows and other elegant weapons. You are trained with longbows, composite longbows, longswords, rapiers, shortbows, and composite shortbows.

In addition, you gain access to all uncommon elf weapons. For the purpose of determining your proficiency, martial elf weapons are simple weapons and advanced elf weapons are martial weapons.

FORLORN   FEAT 1
ELF

Watching your friends age and die fills you with moroseness that protects you against harmful emotions. You gain a +1 circumstance bonus to saving throws against emotion effects. If you roll a success on a saving throw against an emotion effect, you get a critical success instead.

NIMBLE ELF   FEAT 1
ELF

Your muscles are tightly honed. Your Speed increases by 5 feet.

OTHERWORLDLY MAGIC   FEAT 1
ELF

Your elven magic manifests as a simple arcane spell, even if you aren't formally trained in magic. Choose one cantrip from the arcane spell list (page 307). You can cast this cantrip as an arcane innate spell at will. A cantrip is heightened to a spell level equal to half your level rounded up.

UNWAVERING MIEN   FEAT 1
ELF

Your mystic control and meditations allow you to resist external influences upon your consciousness. Whenever you are affected by a mental effect that lasts at least 2 rounds, you can reduce the duration by 1 round.

You still require natural sleep, but you treat your saving throws against effects that would cause you to fall asleep as one degree of success better. This protects only against sleep effects, not against other forms of falling unconscious.

5TH LEVEL

AGELESS PATIENCE   FEAT 5
ELF

You work at a pace born from longevity that enhances your thoroughness. You can voluntarily spend twice as much time as normal on a Perception check or skill check to gain a +2 circumstance bonus to that check. You also don't treat a natural 1 as worse than usual on these checks; you get a

critical failure only if your result is 10 lower than the DC. For example, you could get these benefits if you spent 2 actions to Seek, which normally takes 1 action. You can get these benefits during exploration by taking twice as long exploring as normal, or in downtime by spending twice as much downtime.

The GM might determine a situation doesn't grant you a benefit if a delay would be directly counterproductive to your success, such as a tense negotiation with an impatient creature.

ELVEN WEAPON ELEGANCE   FEAT 5

ELF

Prerequisites Elven Weapon Familiarity

You are attuned to the weapons of your elven ancestors and are particularly deadly when using them. Whenever you critically hit using an elf weapon or one of the weapons listed in Elven Weapon Familiarity, you apply the weapon's critical specialization effect.

9TH LEVEL

ELF STEP ❖   FEAT 9

ELF

You move in a graceful dance, and even your steps are broad. You Step 5 feet twice.

EXPERT LONGEVITY   FEAT 9

ELF

Prerequisites Ancestral Longevity

You've continued to refine the knowledge and skills you've gained through your life. When you choose a skill in which to become trained with Ancestral Longevity, you can also choose a skill in which you are already trained and become an expert in that skill. This lasts until your Ancestral Longevity expires.

When the effects of Ancestral Longevity and Expert Longevity expire, you can retrain one of your skill increases. The skill increase you gain from this retraining must either make you trained in the skill you chose with Ancestral Longevity or make you an expert in the skill you chose with Expert Longevity.

13TH LEVEL

UNIVERSAL LONGEVITY ❖   FEAT 13

ELF

Prerequisites Expert Longevity
Frequency once per day

You've perfected your ability to keep up with all the skills you've learned over your long life, so you're almost never truly untrained at a skill. You reflect on your life experiences, changing the skills you selected with Elven Longevity and Expert Longevity.

ELVEN WEAPON EXPERTISE   FEAT 13

ELF

Prerequisites Elven Weapon Familiarity

Your elven affinity blends with your class training, granting you great skill with elven weapons. Whenever you gain a class feature that grants you expert or greater proficiency in certain weapons, you also gain that proficiency in longbows, composite longbows, longswords, rapiers, shortbows, composite shortbows, and all elf weapons in which you are trained.

ELVEN ADVENTURERS
Many elves adventure to find beauty and discover new things. Typical backgrounds for an elf include emissary, hunter, noble, scholar, or scout. Elves often become rangers or rogues, taking advantage of their dexterity, or alchemists or wizards, exploring their intellectual curiosity.

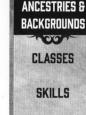

GNOME

Long ago, early gnome ancestors emigrated from the First World, realm of the fey. While it's unclear why the first gnomes wandered to Golarion, this lineage manifests in modern gnomes as bizarre reasoning, eccentricity, obsessive tendencies, and what some see as naivete. These qualities are further reflected in their physical characteristics, such as spindly limbs, brightly colored hair, and childlike and extremely expressive facial features that further reflect their otherworldly origins.

Always hungry for new experiences, gnomes constantly wander both mentally and physically, attempting to stave off a terrible ailment that threatens all of their people. This affliction—the Bleaching—strikes gnomes who fail to dream, innovate, and take in new experiences, in the gnomes' absence of crucial magical essence from the First World. Gnomes latch onto a source of localized magic where they live, typically primal magic, as befits their fey lineage, but this isn't enough to avoid the Bleaching unless they supplement this magic with new experiences. The Bleaching slowly drains the color—literally—from gnomes, and it plunges those affected into states of deep depression that eventually claim their lives. Very few gnomes survive this scourge, becoming deeply morose and wise survivors known as bleachlings.

If you want a character with boundless enthusiasm and an alien, fey outlook on morality and life, you should play a gnome.

YOU MIGHT...

- Embrace learning and hop from one area of study to another without warning.
- Rush into action before fully taking stock of the entire situation.
- Speak, think, and move quickly, and lose patience with those who can't keep up.

OTHERS PROBABLY...

- Appreciate your enthusiasm and the energy with which you approach new situations.
- Struggle to understand your motivations or adapt to your rapid changes of direction.
- See you as unpredictable, flighty, unreliable, or even reckless.

PHYSICAL DESCRIPTION

Most gnomes stand just over 3 feet in height and weigh little more than a human child. They exhibit a wide range of natural skin, hair, and eye colors. For gnomes that haven't begun the Bleaching, nearly any hair and eye color other than white is possible, with vibrant colors most frequent, while skin tones span a slightly narrower spectrum and tend toward earthy tones and pinkish hues, though occasionally green, black, or pale blue. Gnomes' large eyes and dense facial muscles allow them to be particularly expressive in their emotions.

Gnomes typically reach physical maturity at the age of 18, though many gnomes maintain a childlike curiosity about the world even into adulthood. A gnome can theoretically live to any age if she can stave off the Bleaching indefinitely, but in practice gnomes rarely live longer than around 400 years.

SOCIETY

While most gnomes adopt some of the cultural practices of the region in which they live, they tend to pick and choose, adjusting their communities to fit their own fey logic. This often leads to majority gnome communities eventually consisting almost entirely of gnomes, as other people, bewildered by gnomish political decisions, choose to move elsewhere. Gnomes have little culture that they would consider entirely their own. No gnome kingdoms or nations exist on the surface of Golarion, and gnomes wouldn't know what to do with such a state if they had one.

By necessity, few gnomes marry for life, instead allowing relationships to run their course before amicably moving on, the better to stave off the Bleaching with new experiences. Though gnome families tend to be small, many gnome communities raise children communally, with fluid family boundaries. As adults depart the settlement, unrelated adolescents sometimes tag along, creating adopted families to journey together.

ALIGNMENT AND RELIGION

Though gnomes are impulsive tricksters with inscrutable motives and confusing methods, many at least attempt to make the world a better place. They are prone to fits of powerful emotion, and they are often good but rarely lawful. Gnomes most commonly worship deities that value individuality and nature, such as Cayden Cailean, Desna, Gozreh, and Shelyn.

NAMES

Gnome names can get quite complex and polysyllabic. They have little interest in familial names, and most children receive their names purely on a parent's whim. Gnomes rarely concern themselves with how easy their names are to pronounce, and they often go by shorter nicknames. Some even collect and chronicle these nicknames. Among gnomes, the shorter the name, the more feminine it's considered to be.

SAMPLE NAMES

Abroshtor, Bastargre, Besh, Fijit, Halungalom, Krolmnite, Neji, Majet, Pai, Poshment, Queck, Trig, Zarzuket, Zatqualmie

GNOME HERITAGES

A diverse collection of oddballs, gnomes have all sorts of peculiar strains among their bloodlines. Choose one of the following gnome heritages at 1st level.

CHAMELEON GNOME

The color of your hair and skin is mutable, possibly due to latent magic. You can slowly change the vibrancy and the exact color, and the coloration can be different across your body, allowing you to create patterns or other colorful designs. It takes a single action for minor localized shifts and up to an hour for dramatic shifts throughout your body. While you're asleep, the colors shift on their own in tune with your dreams, giving you an unusual coloration each morning. When you're in an area where your coloration is roughly similar to the environment (for instance, forest green in a forest), you can use the single action to make minor localized shifts designed to help you blend into your surroundings. This grants you a +2 circumstance bonus to Stealth checks until your surroundings shift in coloration or pattern.

FEY-TOUCHED GNOME

The blood of the fey is so strong within you that you're truly one of them. You gain the fey trait, in addition to the gnome and humanoid traits. Choose one cantrip from the primal spell list (page 314). You can cast this spell as a primal innate spell at will. A cantrip is heightened to a spell level equal to half your level rounded up. You can change this cantrip to a different one from the same list once per day by meditating to realign yourself with the First World; this is a 10-minute activity that has the concentrate trait.

Hit Points
8

Size
Small

Speed
25 feet

Ability Boosts
Constitution
Charisma
Free

Ability Flaw
Strength

Languages
Common
Gnomish
Sylvan
Additional languages equal to your Intelligence modifier (if it's positive). Choose from Draconic, Dwarven, Elven, Goblin, Jotun, Orcish, and any other languages to which you have access (such as the languages prevalent in your region).

Traits
Gnome
Humanoid

Low-Light Vision
You can see in dim light as though it were bright light, and you ignore the concealed condition due to dim light.

SENSATE GNOME

You see all colors as brighter, hear all sounds as richer, and especially smell all scents with incredible detail. You gain a special sense: imprecise scent with a range of 30 feet. This means you can use your sense of smell to determine the exact location of a creature (as explained on page 465). The GM will usually double the range if you're downwind from the creature or halve the range if you're upwind.

In addition, you gain a +2 circumstance bonus to Perception checks whenever you're trying to locate an undetected creature that is within the range of your scent.

UMBRAL GNOME

Whether from a connection to dark or shadowy fey, from the underground deep gnomes also known as svirfneblin, or another source, you can see in complete darkness. You gain darkvision.

WELLSPRING GNOME

Some other source of magic has a greater hold on you than the primal magic of your fey lineage does. This connection might come from an occult plane or an ancient occult song; a deity, celestial, or fiend; magical effluent left behind by a mage war; or ancient rune magic.

Choose arcane, divine, or occult. You gain one cantrip from that magical tradition's spell list (pages 307–315). You can cast this spell as an innate spell at will, as a spell of your chosen tradition. A cantrip is heightened to a spell level equal to half your level rounded up. Whenever you gain a primal innate spell from a gnome ancestry feat, change its tradition from primal to your chosen tradition.

ANCESTRY FEATS

At 1st level, you gain one ancestry feat, and you gain an additional ancestry feat every 4 levels thereafter (at 5th, 9th, 13th, and 17th level). As a gnome, you select from among the following ancestry feats.

1ST LEVEL

ANIMAL ACCOMPLICE   FEAT 1
GNOME

You build a rapport with an animal, which becomes magically bonded to you. You gain a familiar using the rules on page 217. The type of animal is up to you, but most gnomes choose animals with a burrow Speed.

BURROW ELOCUTIONIST   FEAT 1
GNOME

You recognize the chittering of ground creatures as its own peculiar language. You can ask questions of, receive answers

from, and use the Diplomacy skill with animals that have a burrow Speed, such as badgers, ground squirrels, moles, and prairie dogs. The GM determines which animals count for this ability.

FEY FELLOWSHIP   FEAT 1
GNOME

Your enhanced fey connection affords you a warmer reception from creatures of the First World as well as tools to foil their tricks. You gain a +2 circumstance bonus to both Perception checks and saving throws against fey.

In addition, whenever you meet a fey creature in a social situation, you can immediately attempt a Diplomacy check to Make an Impression on that creature rather than needing to converse for 1 minute. You take a –5 penalty to the check. If you fail, you can engage in 1 minute of conversation and attempt a new check at the end of that time rather than accepting the failure or critical failure result.

Special If you have the Glad-Hand skill feat, you don't take the penalty on your immediate Diplomacy check if the target is a fey.

FIRST WORLD MAGIC   FEAT 1
GNOME

Your connection to the First World grants you a primal innate spell, much like those of the fey. Choose one cantrip from the primal spell list (page 314). You can cast this spell as a primal innate spell at will. A cantrip is heightened to a spell level equal to half your level rounded up.

GNOME OBSESSION   FEAT 1
GNOME

You might have a flighty nature, but when a topic captures your attention, you dive into it headfirst. Pick a Lore skill. You gain the trained proficiency rank in that skill. At 2nd level, you gain expert proficiency in the chosen Lore as well as the Lore granted by your background, if any. At 7th level you gain master proficiency in these Lore skills, and at 15th level you gain legendary proficiency in them.

GNOME WEAPON FAMILIARITY   FEAT 1
GNOME

You favor unusual weapons tied to your people, such as blades with curved and peculiar shapes. You are trained with the glaive and kukri.

In addition, you gain access to all uncommon gnome weapons. For the purpose of determining your proficiency, martial gnome weapons are simple weapons and advanced gnome weapons are martial weapons.

ILLUSION SENSE   FEAT 1
GNOME

Your ancestors spent their days cloaked and cradled in illusions, and as a result, sensing illusion magic is second nature to you. You gain a +1 circumstance bonus to both Perception checks and Will saves against illusions.

When you come within 10 feet of an illusion that can be disbelieved, the GM rolls a secret check for you to disbelieve it, even if you didn't spend an action to Interact with the illusion.

5TH LEVEL

ANIMAL ELOCUTIONIST   FEAT 5

GNOME

Prerequisites Burrow Elocutionist

You hear animal sounds as conversations instead of unintelligent noise, and can respond in turn. You can speak to all animals, not just animals with a burrow Speed. You gain a +1 circumstance bonus to Make an Impression on animals (which usually uses the Diplomacy skill).

ENERGIZED FONT ❖   FEAT 5

GNOME

Prerequisites focus pool, at least one innate spell from a gnome heritage or ancestry feat that shares a tradition with at least one of your focus spells

Frequency once per day

The magic within you provides increased energy you can use to focus. You regain 1 Focus Point, up to your usual maximum.

GNOME WEAPON INNOVATOR   FEAT 5

GNOME

Prerequisites Gnome Weapon Familiarity

You produce outstanding results when wielding unusual weapons. Whenever you critically hit using a glaive, kukri, or gnome weapon, you apply the weapon's critical specialization effect.

9TH LEVEL

FIRST WORLD ADEPT   FEAT 9

GNOME

Prerequisites at least one primal innate spell

Over time your fey magic has grown stronger. You gain *faerie fire* and *invisibility* as 2nd-level primal innate spells. You can cast each of these primal innate spells once per day.

VIVACIOUS CONDUIT   FEAT 9

GNOME

Your connection to the First World has grown, and its positive energy flows into you rapidly. If you rest for 10 minutes, you gain Hit Points equal to your Constitution modifier × half your level. This is cumulative with any healing you receive from Treat Wounds.

13TH LEVEL

GNOME WEAPON EXPERTISE   FEAT 13

GNOME

Prerequisites Gnome Weapon Familiarity

Your gnome affinity blends with your class training, granting you great skill with gnome weapons. Whenever you gain a class feature that grants you expert or greater proficiency in a given weapon or weapons, you also gain that proficiency in the glaive, kukri, and all gnome weapons in which you are trained.

GNOME ADVENTURERS

Adventure is not so much a choice as a necessity for most gnomes. Adventuring gnomes often claim mementos, allowing them to remember and relive their most exciting stories.

Gnomes often consider the entertainer, merchant, or nomad backgrounds. In addition, the animal whisperer, barkeep, gambler, and tinker backgrounds are particularly appropriate.

Gnomes' connection to magic makes spellcasting classes particularly thematic for you, especially classes that match the tradition of your primal innate spells, such as druid or primal sorcerer, though wellspring gnomes might choose others.

GOBLIN

The convoluted histories other people cling to don't interest goblins. These small folk live in the moment, and they prefer tall tales over factual records. The wars of a few decades ago might as well be from the ancient past. Misunderstood by other people, goblins are happy how they are. Goblin virtues are about being present, creative, and honest. They strive to lead fulfilled lives, rather than worrying about how their journeys will end. To tell stories, not nitpick the facts. To be small, but dream big.

Goblins have a reputation as simple creatures who love songs, fire, and eating disgusting things and who hate reading, dogs, and horses—and there are a great many for whom this description fits perfectly. However, great changes have come to goblinkind, and more and more goblins resist conformity to these stereotypes. Even among goblins that are more worldly, many still exemplify their old ways in some small manner, just to a more sensible degree. Some goblins remain deeply fascinated with fire or fearlessly devour a meal that might turn others' stomachs.

Others are endless tinkerers and view their companions' trash as the components of gadgets yet to be made.

Though goblins' culture has splintered radically, their reputation has changed little. As such, goblins who travel to larger cities are frequently subjected to derision, and many work twice as hard at proving their worth.

If you want a character who is eccentric, enthusiastic, and fun-loving, you should play a goblin.

YOU MIGHT...

- Strive to prove that you have a place among other civilized peoples, perhaps even to yourself.
- Fight tooth and nail—sometimes literally—to protect yourself and your friends from danger.
- Lighten the heavy emotional burdens others carry (and amuse yourself) with antics and pranks.

OTHERS PROBABLY...

- Work to ensure you don't accidentally (or intentionally) set too many things on fire.
- Assume you can't—or won't—read.
- Wonder how you survive given your ancestry's typical gastronomic choices, reckless behavior, and love of fire.

PHYSICAL DESCRIPTION

Goblins are stumpy humanoids with large bodies, scrawny limbs, and massively oversized heads with large ears and beady red eyes. Their skin ranges from green to gray to blue, and they often bear scars, boils, and rashes. Goblins average 3 feet tall. Most are bald, with little or no body hair. Their jagged teeth fall out and regrow constantly, and their fast metabolism means they eat constantly and nap frequently. Mutations are also more common among goblins than other peoples, and goblins usually view particularly salient mutations as a sign of power or fortune.

Goblins reach adolescence by the age of 3 and adulthood 4 or 5 years later. Goblins can live 50 years or more, but without anyone to protect them from each other or themselves, few live past 20 years of age.

SOCIETY

Goblins tend to flock to strong leaders, forming small tribes. These tribes rarely number more than a hundred, though the larger a tribe is, the more diligent the leader must be to keep order—a notoriously difficult task. As new threats rise across the Inner Sea region, many tribal elders have put aside their reckless ways in the hope of forging alliances that offer their people a greater chance at survival. Play and creativity matter more to goblins than productivity or study, and their encampments erupt with songs and laughter.

Goblins bond closely with their allies, fiercely protecting those companions who have protected them or offered a sympathetic ear. Goblins tend to assume for their own protection that members of taller ancestries, which goblins often refer to colloquially as "longshanks," won't treat them kindly. Learning to trust longshanks is difficult for a goblin, and it's been only in recent years that such a partnership has even been an option. However, their attitude as a people is changing rapidly, and their short lifespans and poor memories help them adapt quickly.

ALIGNMENT AND RELIGION

Even well-intentioned goblins have trouble following the rules, meaning they're rarely lawful. Most goblin adventurers are chaotic neutral or chaotic good. Organized worship confounds goblins, and most of them would rather pick their own deities, choosing powerful monsters, natural wonders, or anything else they find fascinating. Longshanks might have books upon books about the structures of divinity, but to a goblin, anything can be a god if you want it to. Goblins who spend time around people of other ancestries might adopt some of their beliefs, though, and many goblin adventurers adopt the worship of Cayden Cailean.

NAMES

Goblins keep their names simple. A good name should be easy to pronounce, short enough to shout without getting winded, and taste good to say. The namer often picks a word that rhymes with something they like so that writing songs is easier. Since there aren't any real traditions regarding naming in goblin culture, children often name themselves once they're old enough to do something resembling talking.

Sample Names

Ak, Bokker, Frum, Guzmuk, Krobby, Loohi, Mazmord, Neeka, Omgot, Ranzak, Rickle, Tup, Wakla, Yonk, Zibini

GOBLIN HERITAGES

Goblins, especially those of different tribes, have all sorts of physiological differences, which they often discover only through hazardous "experiments." Choose one of the following goblin heritages at 1st level.

CHARHIDE GOBLIN

Your ancestors have always had a connection to fire and a thicker skin, which allows you to resist burning. You gain fire resistance equal to half your level (minimum 1). You can also recover from being on fire more easily. Your flat check to remove persistent fire damage is DC 10 instead of DC 15, which is reduced to DC 5 if another creature uses a particularly appropriate action to help.

IRONGUT GOBLIN

You can subsist on food that most folks would consider spoiled. You can keep yourself fed with poor meals in a settlement as long as garbage is readily available, without using the Subsist downtime activity. You can eat and drink things when you are sickened.

You gain a +2 circumstance bonus to saving throws against afflictions, against gaining the sickened condition, and to remove the sickened condition. When you roll a success on a Fortitude save affected by this bonus, you get a critical success instead. All these benefits apply only when the affliction or condition resulted from something you ingested.

Hit Points
6

Size
Small

Speed
25 feet

Ability Boosts
Dexterity
Charisma
Free

Ability Flaw
Wisdom

Languages
Common
Goblin
Additional languages equal to your Intelligence modifier (if it's positive). Choose from Draconic, Dwarven, Gnoll, Gnomish, Halfling, Orcish, and any other languages to which you have access (such as the languages prevalent in your region).

Traits
Goblin
Humanoid

Darkvision
You can see in darkness and dim light just as well as you can see in bright light, though your vision in darkness is in black and white.

RAZORTOOTH GOBLIN

Your family's teeth are formidable weapons. You gain a jaws unarmed attack that deals 1d6 piercing damage. Your jaws are in the brawling group and have the finesse and unarmed traits.

SNOW GOBLIN

You are acclimated to living in frigid lands and have skin ranging from sky blue to navy in color, as well as blue fur. You gain cold resistance equal to half your level (minimum 1). You treat environmental cold effects as if they were one step less extreme (incredible cold becomes extreme, extreme cold becomes severe, and so on).

UNBREAKABLE GOBLIN

You're able to bounce back from injuries easily due to an exceptionally thick skull, cartilaginous bones, or some other mixed blessing. You gain 10 Hit Points from your ancestry instead of 6. When you fall, reduce the falling damage you take as though you had fallen half the distance.

ANCESTRY FEATS

At 1st level, you gain one ancestry feat, and you gain an additional ancestry feat every 4 levels thereafter (at 5th, 9th, 13th, and 17th level). As a goblin, you can select from the following ancestry feats.

1ST LEVEL

BURN IT! FEAT 1

`GOBLIN`

Fire fascinates you. Your spells and alchemical items that deal fire damage gain a status bonus to damage equal to half the spell's level or one-quarter the item's level (minimum 1). You also gain a +1 status bonus to any persistent fire damage you deal.

CITY SCAVENGER FEAT 1

`GOBLIN`

You know that the greatest treasures often look like refuse, and you scoff at those who throw away perfectly good scraps. You gain a +1 circumstance bonus to checks to Subsist, and you can use Society or Survival when you Subsist in a settlement.

When you Subsist in a city, you also gather valuable junk that silly longshanks threw away. You can Earn Income using Society or Survival in the same time as you Subsist, without spending any additional days of downtime. You also gain a +1 circumstance bonus to this check.

Special If you have the irongut goblin heritage, increase the bonuses to +2.

GOBLIN LORE FEAT 1

`GOBLIN`

You've picked up skills and tales from your goblin community. You gain the trained proficiency rank in Nature and Stealth.

If you would automatically become trained in one of those skills (from your background or class, for example), you instead become trained in a skill of your choice. You also become trained in Goblin Lore.

GOBLIN SCUTTLE ↻ FEAT 1

`GOBLIN`

Trigger An ally ends a move action adjacent to you.

You take advantage of your ally's movement to adjust your position. You Step.

GOBLIN SONG ◆ FEAT 1

`GOBLIN`

You sing annoying goblin songs, distracting your foes with silly and repetitive lyrics. Attempt a Performance check against the Will DC of a single enemy within 30 feet. This has all the usual traits and restrictions of a Performance check.

You can affect up to two targets within range if you have expert proficiency in Performance, four if you have master proficiency, and eight if you have legendary proficiency.

Critical Success The target takes a –1 status penalty to Perception checks and Will saves for 1 minute.

Success The target takes a –1 status penalty to Perception checks and Will saves for 1 round.

Critical Failure The target is temporarily immune to attempts to use Goblin Song for 1 hour.

GOBLIN WEAPON FAMILIARITY FEAT 1

`GOBLIN`

Others might look upon them with disdain, but you know that the weapons of your people are as effective as they are sharp. You are trained with the dogslicer and horsechopper.

In addition, you gain access to all uncommon goblin weapons. For the purpose of determining your proficiency, martial goblin weapons are simple weapons and advanced goblin weapons are martial weapons.

JUNK TINKER FEAT 1

`GOBLIN`

You can make useful tools out of even twisted or rusted scraps. When using the Crafting skill to Craft, you can make level 0 items, including weapons but not armor, out of junk. This reduces the Price to one-quarter the usual amount but always results in a shoddy item. Shoddy items normally give a penalty, but you don't take this penalty when using shoddy items you made.

You can also incorporate junk to save money while you Craft any item. This grants you a discount on the item as if you had spent 1 additional day working to reduce the cost, but the item is obviously made of junk. At the GM's discretion, this might affect the item's resale value depending on the buyer's tastes.

ROUGH RIDER FEAT 1

`GOBLIN`

You are especially good at riding traditional goblin mounts. You gain the Ride feat, even if you don't meet the prerequisites. You gain a +1 circumstance bonus to Nature checks to use

Command an Animal on a goblin dog or wolf mount. You can always select a wolf as your animal companion, even if you would usually select an animal companion with the mount special ability, such as for a champion's steed ally.

VERY SNEAKY   FEAT 1

GOBLIN

Taller folk rarely pay attention to the shadows at their feet, and you take full advantage of this. You can move 5 feet farther when you take the Sneak action, up to your Speed.

In addition, as long as you continue to use Sneak actions and succeed at your Stealth check, you don't become observed if you don't have cover or greater cover and aren't concealed at the end of the Sneak action, as long as you have cover or greater cover or are concealed at the end of your turn.

5TH LEVEL

GOBLIN WEAPON FRENZY   FEAT 5

GOBLIN

Prerequisites Goblin Weapon Familiarity

You know how to wield your people's vicious weapons. Whenever you score a critical hit using a goblin weapon, you apply the weapon's critical specialization effect.

9TH LEVEL

CAVE CLIMBER   FEAT 9

GOBLIN

After years of crawling and climbing through caverns, you can climb easily anywhere you go. You gain a climb Speed of 10 feet.

SKITTERING SCUTTLE   FEAT 9

GOBLIN

Prerequisites Goblin Scuttle

You can scuttle farther and faster when maneuvering alongside allies. When you use Goblin Scuttle, you can Stride up to half your Speed instead of Stepping.

13TH LEVEL

GOBLIN WEAPON EXPERTISE   FEAT 13

GOBLIN

Prerequisites Goblin Weapon Familiarity

Your goblin affinity blends with your class training, granting you great skill with goblin weapons. Whenever you gain a class feature that grants you expert or greater proficiency in a given weapon or weapons, you also gain that proficiency in the dogslicer, horsechopper, and all goblin weapons in which you are trained.

VERY, VERY SNEAKY   FEAT 13

GOBLIN

Prerequisites Very Sneaky

You can move up to your Speed when you use the Sneak action, and you no longer need to have cover or greater cover or be concealed to Hide or Sneak.

GOBLIN ADVENTURERS

To some degree, almost every goblin is an adventurer, surviving life on the edge using skill and wits. Goblins explore and hunt for treasures by nature, though some become true adventurers in their own rights, often after being separated from their group or tribe.

Goblins often have the acrobat, criminal, entertainer, gladiator, hunter, and street urchin backgrounds. Consider playing an alchemist, since many goblins love fire, or a bard, since many goblins love songs. As scrappy survivors, goblins are often rogues who dart about the shadows, though their inherently charismatic nature also draws them to the pursuit of magical classes such as sorcerer.

HALFLING

Claiming no place as their own, halflings control few settlements larger than villages. Instead, they frequently live among humans within the walls of larger cities, carving out small communities alongside taller folk. Many halflings lead perfectly fulfilling lives in the shadows of their larger neighbors, while others prefer a nomadic existence, traveling the world and taking advantage of opportunities and adventures as they come.

Optimistic and cheerful, blessed with uncanny luck, and driven by powerful wanderlust, halflings make up for their short stature with an abundance of bravado and curiosity. At once excitable and easygoing, they are the best kind of opportunists, and their passions favor joy over violence. Even in the jaws of danger, halflings rarely lose their sense of humor.

Many taller people dismiss halflings due to their size or, worse, treat them like children. Halflings use these prejudices and misconceptions to their advantage, gaining access to opportunities and performing deeds of daring mischief or heroism. A halfling's curiosity is tempered by wisdom and caution, leading to calculated risks and narrow escapes.

While their wanderlust and curiosity sometimes drive them toward adventure, halflings also carry strong ties to house and home, often spending above their means to achieve comfort in their homelife.

If you want to play a character who must contend with these opposing drives toward adventure and comfort, you should play a halfling.

YOU MIGHT...

- Get along well with a wide variety of people and enjoy meeting new friends.
- Find it difficult to resist indulging your curiosity, even when you know it's going to lead to trouble.
- Hold a deep and personal hatred of the practice of slavery and devote yourself to freeing those who still labor against their will.

OTHERS PROBABLY...

- Appreciate your ability to always find a silver lining or something to laugh about, no matter how dire the situation.
- Think you bring good luck with you.
- Underestimate your strength, endurance, and fighting prowess.

PHYSICAL DESCRIPTION

Halflings are short humanoids who look vaguely like smaller humans. They rarely grow to be more than 3 feet in height. Halfling proportions vary, with some looking like shorter adult humans with slightly larger heads and others having proportions closer to those of a human child.

Most halflings prefer to walk barefoot rather than wearing shoes, and those who do so develop roughly calloused soles on their feet over time. Tufts of thick, often-curly hair warm the tops of their broad, tanned feet. Halfling skin tones tend toward rich, tawny shades like amber or oak, and their hair color ranges from a light golden blond to raven black.

Halflings reach physical adulthood around the age of 20. A typical halfling can live to be around 150 years old.

SOCIETY

Despite their jovial and friendly nature, halflings don't usually tend to congregate. They have no cultural homeland in the Inner Sea region, and they instead weave themselves throughout the societies of the world. Halflings eke out whatever living they can manage, many performing menial labor or holding simple service jobs. Some halflings reject city life, instead turning to the open road and traveling from place to place in search of fortune and fame. These nomadic halflings often travel in small groups, sharing hardships and simple pleasures among close friends and family.

Wherever halflings go, they seamlessly blend into the society they find themselves in, adapting to the culture of the predominant ancestry around them and adding their uniquely halfling twists, creating a blend of cultural diffusion that enriches both cultures.

ALIGNMENT AND RELIGION

Halflings are loyal to their friends and their family, but they aren't afraid to do what needs to be done in order to survive. Halfling alignments vary, typically closely in keeping with the alignment of the other ancestries that live around them. Halflings favor gods that either grant luck, like Desna, or encourage guile, like Norgorber, and many appreciate Cayden Cailean's role as a liberator, as well as any religions common among other ancestries around them.

NAMES

Halfling names are usually two to three syllables, with a gentle sound that avoids hard consonants. Preferring their names to sound humble, halflings see overly long or complex names as a sign of arrogance. This goes only for their own people, however—halflings have names that suit them, and they understand that elves and humans might have longer names to suit their own aesthetics. Humans in particular have a tendency to refer to halflings by nicknames, with "Lucky" being common to the point of absurdity.

SAMPLE NAMES

Anafa, Antal, Bellis, Boram, Etune, Filiu, Jamir, Kaleb, Linna, Marra, Miro, Rillka, Sistra, Sumak, Yamyra

HALFLING HERITAGES

Living across the land, halflings of different heritages might appear in regions far from are their ancestors lived. Choose one of the following halfling heritages at 1st level.

GUTSY HALFLING

Your family line is known for keeping a level head and staving off fear when the chips were down, making them wise leaders and sometimes even heroes. When you roll a success on a saving throw against an emotion effect, you get a critical success instead.

HILLOCK HALFLING

Accustomed to a calm life in the hills, your people find rest and relaxation especially replenishing, particularly when indulging in creature comforts. When you regain Hit Points overnight, add your level to the Hit Points regained. When anyone uses the Medicine skill to Treat your Wounds, you can eat a snack to add your level to the Hit Points you regain from their treatment.

Hit Points
6

Size
Small

Speed
25 feet

Ability Boosts
Dexterity
Wisdom
Free

Ability Flaw
Strength

Languages
Common
Halfling
Additional languages equal to your Intelligence modifier (if it's positive). Choose from Dwarven, Elven, Gnomish, Goblin, and any other languages to which you have access (such as the languages prevalent in your region).

Traits
Halfling
Humanoid

Keen Eyes
Your eyes are sharp, allowing you to make out small details about concealed or even invisible creatures that others might miss. You gain a +2 circumstance bonus when using the Seek action to find hidden or undetected creatures within 30 feet of you. When you target an opponent that is concealed from you or hidden from you, reduce the DC of the flat check to 3 for a concealed target or 9 for a hidden one.

NOMADIC HALFLING

Your ancestors have traveled from place to place for generations, never content to settle down. You gain two additional languages of your choice, chosen from among the common and uncommon languages available to you, and every time you take the Multilingual feat, you gain another new language.

TWILIGHT HALFLING

Your ancestors performed many secret acts under the concealing cover of dusk, whether for good or ill, and over time they developed the ability to see in twilight beyond even the usual keen sight of halflings. You gain low-light vision.

WILDWOOD HALFLING

You hail from deep in a jungle or forest, and you've learned how to use your small size to wriggle through undergrowth, vines, and other obstacles. You ignore difficult terrain from trees, foliage, and undergrowth.

ANCESTRY FEATS

At 1st level, you gain one ancestry feat, and you gain an additional ancestry feat every 4 levels thereafter (at 5th, 9th, 13th, and 17th levels). As a halfling, you select from among the following ancestry feats.

1ST LEVEL

DISTRACTING SHADOWS   FEAT 1

HALFLING

You have learned to remain hidden by using larger folk as a distraction to avoid drawing attention to yourself. You can use creatures that are at least one size larger than you (usually Medium or larger) as cover for the Hide and Sneak actions, though you still can't use such creatures as cover for other uses, such as the Take Cover action.

HALFLING LORE   FEAT 1

HALFLING

You've dutifully learned how to keep your balance and how to stick to the shadows where it's safe, important skills passed down through generations of halfling tradition. You gain the trained proficiency rank in Acrobatics and Stealth. If you would automatically become trained in one of those skills (from your background or class, for example), you instead become trained in a skill of your choice. You also become trained in Halfling Lore.

HALFLING LUCK ◈   FEAT 1

FORTUNE HALFLING

Frequency once per day
Trigger You fail a skill check or saving throw.
Your happy-go-lucky nature makes it seem like misfortune

avoids you, and to an extent, that might even be true. You can reroll the triggering check, but you must use the new result, even if it's worse than your first roll.

HALFLING WEAPON FAMILIARITY   FEAT 1

HALFLING

You favor traditional halfling weapons, so you've learned how to use them more effectively. You have the trained proficiency with the sling, halfling sling staff, and shortsword.

In addition, you gain access to all uncommon halfling weapons. For you, martial halfling weapons are simple weapons, and advanced halfling weapons are martial weapons.

SURE FEET   FEAT 1

HALFLING

Whether keeping your balance or scrambling up a tricky climb, your hairy, calloused feet easily find purchase. If you roll a success on an Acrobatics check to Balance or an Athletics check to Climb, you get a critical success instead. You're not flat-footed when you attempt to Balance or Climb.

TITAN SLINGER   FEAT 1

HALFLING

You have learned how to use your sling to fell enormous creatures. When you hit on an attack with a sling against a Large or larger creature, increase the size of the weapon damage die by one step (details on increasing weapon damage die sizes can be found on page 279).

UNFETTERED HALFLING   FEAT 1

HALFLING

You were forced into service as a laborer, either pressed into indentured servitude or shackled by the evils of slavery, but you've since escaped and have trained to ensure you'll never be caught again. Whenever you roll a success on a check to Escape or a saving throw against an effect that would impose the grabbed or restrained condition on you, you get a critical success instead. Whenever a creature rolls a failure on a check to Grapple you, they get a critical failure instead. If a creature uses the Grab ability on you, it must succeed at an Athletics check to grab you instead of automatically grabbing you.

WATCHFUL HALFLING   FEAT 1

HALFLING

Your communal lifestyle causes you to pay close attention to the people around you, allowing you to more easily notice when they act out of character. You gain a +2 circumstance bonus to Perception checks when using the Sense Motive basic action to notice enchanted or possessed characters. If you aren't actively using Sense Motive on an enchanted or possessed character, the GM rolls a secret check, without the usual circumstance and with a –2 circumstance penalty, for you to potentially notice the enchantment or possession anyway.

In addition to using it for skill checks, you can use the Aid basic action to grant a bonus to another creature's saving throw or other check to overcome enchantment or possession.

ANCESTRIES & BACKGROUNDS

2

INTRODUCTION

ANCESTRIES &
BACKGROUNDS

CLASSES

SKILLS

FEATS

EQUIPMENT

SPELLS

THE AGE OF
LOST OMENS

PLAYING THE
GAME

As usual for Aid, you need to prepare by using an action on your turn to encourage the creature to fight against the effect.

5TH LEVEL

CULTURAL ADAPTABILITY   FEAT 5

`HALFLING`

During your adventures, you've honed your ability to adapt to the culture of the predominant ancestry around you. You gain the Adopted Ancestry general feat, and you also gain one 1st-level ancestry feat from the ancestry you chose for the Adopted Ancestry feat.

HALFLING WEAPON TRICKSTER   FEAT 5

`HALFLING`

Prerequisites Halfling Weapon Familiarity

You are particularly adept at fighting with your people's favored weapons. Whenever you critically succeed at an attack roll using a shortsword, a sling, or a halfling weapon, you apply the weapon's critical specialization effect.

9TH LEVEL

GUIDING LUCK   FEAT 9

`HALFLING`

Prerequisites Halfling Luck

Your luck guides you to look the right way and aim your blows unerringly. You can use Halfling Luck twice per day: once in response to its normal trigger, and once when you fail a Perception check or attack roll instead of the normal trigger.

IRREPRESSIBLE   FEAT 9

`HALFLING`

You are easily able to ward off attempts to play on your fears and emotions. When you roll a success on a saving throw against an emotion effect, you get a critical success instead. If your heritage is gutsy halfling, when you roll a critical failure on a saving throw against an emotion effect, you get a failure instead.

13TH LEVEL

CEASELESS SHADOWS   FEAT 13

`HALFLING`

Prerequisites Distracting Shadows

You excel at going unnoticed, especially among a crowd. You no longer need to have cover or be concealed to Hide or Sneak. If you would have lesser cover from creatures, you gain cover and can Take Cover, and if you would have cover from creatures, you gain greater cover.

HALFLING WEAPON EXPERTISE   FEAT 13

`HALFLING`

Prerequisites Halfling, Weapon Familiarity

Your halfling affinity blends with your class training, granting you great skill with halfling weapons. Whenever you gain a class feature that grants you expert or greater proficiency in a given weapon or weapons, you also gain that proficiency in the sling, halfling sling staff, shortsword, and all halfling weapons in which you are trained.

HALFLING ADVENTURERS

Halflings' natural wanderlust and opportunistic nature make them ideal adventurers. Many people put up with their vivacious attitudes in return for the natural talents they provide and the popular superstition that traveling with a halfling is good luck.

Typical backgrounds for halflings include acrobat, criminal, emissary, entertainer, laborer, and street urchin. Halflings make great clerics and rogues, but many also become monks or rangers.

HUMAN

As unpredictable and varied as any of Golarion's peoples, humans have exceptional drive and the capacity to endure and expand. Though many civilizations thrived before humanity rose to prominence, humans have built some of the greatest and the most terrible societies throughout the course of history, and today they are the most populous people in the realms around the Inner Sea.

Humans' ambition, versatility, and exceptional potential have led to their status as the world's predominant ancestry. Their empires and nations are vast, sprawling things, and their citizens carve names for themselves with the strength of their sword arms and the power of their spells. Humanity is diverse and tumultuous, running the gamut from nomadic to imperial, sinister to saintly. Many of them venture forth to explore, to map the expanse of the multiverse, to search for long-lost treasure, or to lead mighty armies to conquer their neighbors—for no better reason than because they can.

If you want a character who can be just about anything, you should play a human.

YOU MIGHT...

- Strive to achieve greatness, either in your own right or on behalf of a cause.
- Seek to understand your purpose in the world.
- Cherish your relationships with family and friends.

OTHERS PROBABLY...

- Respect your flexibility, your adaptability, and—in most cases—your open-mindedness.
- Distrust your intentions, fearing you seek only power or wealth.
- Aren't sure what to expect from you and are hesitant to assume your intentions.

PHYSICAL DESCRIPTION

Humans' physical characteristics are as varied as the world's climes. Humans have a wide variety of skin and hair colors, body types, and facial features. Generally speaking, their skin has a darker hue the closer to the equator they or their ancestors lived.

Humans reach physical adulthood around the age of 15, though mental maturity occurs a few years later. A typical human can live to be around 90 years old. Humans often intermarry with people of other ancestries, giving rise to children who bear the traits of both parents. The most notable half-humans are half-elves and half-orcs.

SOCIETY

Human variety also manifests in terms of their governments, attitudes, and social norms. Though the oldest of human cultures can trace their shared histories thousands of years into the past, when compared to the societies of the elves or dwarves, human civilizations seem in a state of constant flux as empires fragment and new kingdoms subsume the old.

ALIGNMENT AND RELIGION

Humanity is perhaps the most heterogeneous of all the ancestries, with a capacity for great evil and boundless good. Some humans assemble into vast raging hordes, while others build sprawling cities. Considered as a whole, most humans are neutral, yet they tend to congregate into nations or communities of a shared alignment, or at least a shared tendency toward an alignment. Humans also worship a wide range of gods and practice many different religions, tending to seek favor from any divine being they encounter.

NAMES

Unlike many ancestral cultures, which generally cleave to specific traditions and shared histories, humanity's diversity has resulted in a near-infinite set of names. The humans of northern tribes have different names than those dwelling in southern nation-states. Humans throughout much of the world speak Common (though some continents on Golarion have

ANCESTRIES & BACKGROUNDS

2

INTRODUCTION

ANCESTRIES & BACKGROUNDS

CLASSES

SKILLS

FEATS

EQUIPMENT

SPELLS

THE AGE OF LOST OMENS

PLAYING THE GAME

GAME MASTERING

CRAFTING & TREASURE

APPENDIX

their own regional common languages), yet their names are as varied as their beliefs and appearances.

ETHNICITIES

A variety of human ethnic groups—many of which have origins on distant lands—populates the continents bordering Golarion's Inner Sea. Human characters can be any of these ethnicities, regardless of what lands they call home. Information about Golarion's human ethnicities appears on page 430 in Chapter 8.

Characters of human ethnicities in the Inner Sea region speak Common (also known as Taldane), and some ethnicities grant access to an uncommon language.

HALF-ELVES

A half-elf is born to an elf and a human, or to two half-elves. The life of a half-elf can be difficult, often marked by a struggle to fit in. Half-elves don't have their own homeland on Golarion, nor are populations of half-elves particularly tied to one another, since they often have very disparate human and elven traditions. Instead, most half-elves attempt to find acceptance in either human or elven settlements.

Half-elves often appear primarily human, with subtly pointed ears and a taller stature than most full-blooded humans. Half-elves lack the almost alien eyes of their elf parents, though they do have a natural presence—and often a striking beauty—that leads many to become artists or entertainers. Despite this innate appeal, many half-elves have difficulty forming lasting bonds with either humans or elves due to the distance they feel from both peoples as a whole.

Half-elves live longer than other humans, often reaching an age around 150 years. This causes some of them to fear friendship and romance with humans, knowing that they'll likely outlive their companions.

PLAYING A HALF-ELF

You can create a half-elf character by selecting the half-elf heritage at 1st level. This gives you access to elf and half-elf ancestry feats in addition to human ancestry feats.

YOU MIGHT...

- Keep to yourself and find it difficult to form close bonds with others.
- Strongly embrace or reject one side or the other of your parentage.
- Identify strongly with and relate to other people with mixed ancestries.

OTHERS PROBABLY...

- Find you more attractive than humans and more approachable than elves.
- Dismiss your human ethnicity and culture in light of your elven heritage.
- Downplay the challenges of being caught between two cultures.

HALF-ORCS

A half-orc is the offspring of a human and an orc, or of two half-orcs. Because some intolerant people see orcs as more akin to monsters than people, they sometimes hate and fear half-orcs simply due to their lineage. This commonly pushes half-orcs to the margins of society, where some find work in manual labor or as mercenaries, and others fall into crime or cruelty. Many who can't stand the indignities heaped on them in human society find a home among their orc kin or trek into the wilderness to live in peace, apart from society's judgment.

Humans often assume half-orcs are unintelligent or uncivilized, and half-orcs rarely find acceptance among societies with many such folk. To an orc tribe, a half-orc is considered smart enough to make a good war leader but weaker physically than other orcs. Many half-orcs thus end up having low status among orc tribes unless they can prove their strength.

Hit Points
8

Size
Medium

Speed
25 feet

Ability Boosts
Two free ability boosts

Languages
Common
Additional languages equal to your Intelligence modifier (if it's positive). Choose from the list of common languages and any other languages to which you have access (such as the languages prevalent in your region).

Traits
Human
Humanoid

OTHER HALVES

By default, half-elves and half-orcs descend from humans, but your GM might allow you to be the offspring of an elf, orc, or different ancestry. In these cases, the GM will let you select the half-elf or half-orc heritage as the heritage for this other ancestry. The most likely other parent of a half-elf are gnomes and halflings, and the most likely parents of a half-orc are goblins, halflings, and dwarves.

A half-orc has a shorter lifespan than other humans, living to be roughly 70 years old.

PLAYING A HALF-ORC
You can create a half-orc character by selecting the half-orc heritage at 1st level. This gives you access to orc and half-orc ancestry feats in addition to human ancestry feats.

YOU MIGHT...
• Ignore, embrace, or actively counter the common stereotypes about half-orcs.

• Make the most of your size and strength, either physically or socially.
• Keep your distance from people of most other ancestries, in case they unfairly reject you due to your orc ancestors.

OTHERS PROBABLY...
• Assume you enjoy and excel at fighting but aren't inclined toward magical or intellectual pursuits.
• Pity you for the tragic circumstances they assume were involved in your birth.
• Get out of your way and back down rather than face your anger.

HUMAN HERITAGES
Unlike other ancestries, humans don't have significant physiological differences defined by their lineage. Instead, their heritages either reveal their potential as a people or reflect lineages from multiple ancestries. Choose one of the following human heritages at 1st level.

HALF-ELF
Either one of your parents was an elf, or one or both were half-elves. You have pointed ears and other telltale signs of elf heritage. You gain the elf trait and low-light vision. In addition, you can select elf, half-elf, and human feats whenever you gain an ancestry feat.

HALF-ORC
One of your parents was an orc, or one or both were half-orcs. You have a green tinge to your skin and other indicators of orc heritage. You gain the orc trait and low-light vision. In addition, you can select orc, half-orc, and human feats whenever you gain an ancestry feat.

SKILLED HERITAGE
Your ingenuity allows you to train in a wide variety of skills. You become trained in one skill of your choice. At 5th level, you become an expert in the chosen skill.

VERSATILE HERITAGE
Humanity's versatility and ambition have fueled its ascendance to be the most common ancestry in most nations throughout the world. Select a general feat of your choice for which you meet the prerequisites (as with your ancestry feat, you can select this general feat at any point during character creation).

HUMAN ANCESTRY FEATS
At 1st level, you gain one ancestry feat, and you gain an additional ancestry feat every 4 levels thereafter (at 5th, 9th, 13th, and 17th levels). As a human, you choose from among the following ancestry feats.

ANCESTRIES & BACKGROUNDS

2

INTRODUCTION

ANCESTRIES & BACKGROUNDS

CLASSES

SKILLS

FEATS

EQUIPMENT

SPELLS

THE AGE OF LOST OMENS

PLAYING THE GAME

GAME MASTERING

CRAFTING & TREASURE

APPENDIX

1ST LEVEL

ADAPTED CANTRIP   FEAT 1

HUMAN

Prerequisites spellcasting class feature

Through study of multiple magical traditions, you've altered a spell to suit your spellcasting style. Choose one cantrip from a magical tradition other than your own. If you have a spell repertoire or a spellbook, replace one of the cantrips you know or have in your spellbook with the chosen spell. If you prepare spells without a spellbook (if you're a cleric or druid, for example), one of your cantrips must always be the chosen spell, and you prepare the rest normally. You can cast this cantrip as a spell of your class's tradition.

If you swap or retrain this cantrip later, you can choose its replacement from the same alternate tradition or a different one.

COOPERATIVE NATURE   FEAT 1

HUMAN

The short human life span lends perspective and has taught you from a young age to set aside differences and work with others to achieve greatness. You gain a +4 circumstance bonus on checks to Aid.

GENERAL TRAINING   FEAT 1

HUMAN

Your adaptability manifests in your mastery of a range of useful abilities. You gain a 1st-level general feat. You must meet the feat's prerequisites, but if you select this feat during character creation, you can select the feat later in the process in order to determine which prerequisites you meet.

Special You can select this feat multiple times, choosing a different feat each time.

HAUGHTY OBSTINACY   FEAT 1

HUMAN

Your powerful ego makes it harder for others to order you around. If you roll a success on a saving throw against a mental effect that attempts to directly control your actions, you critically succeed instead. If a creature rolls a failure on a check to Coerce you using Intimidation, it gets a critical failure instead (so it can't try to Coerce you again for 1 week).

NATURAL AMBITION   FEAT 1

HUMAN

You were raised to be ambitious and always reach for the stars, leading you to progress quickly in your chosen field. You gain a 1st-level class feat for your class. You must meet the prerequisites, but you can select the feat later in the character creation process in order to determine which prerequisites you meet.

NATURAL SKILL   FEAT 1

HUMAN

Your ingenuity allows you to learn a wide variety of skills. You gain the trained proficiency rank in two skills of your choice.

UNCONVENTIONAL WEAPONRY   FEAT 1

HUMAN

You've familiarized yourself with a particular weapon, potentially from another ancestry or culture. Choose an uncommon simple or martial weapon with a trait corresponding to an ancestry (such as dwarf, goblin, or orc) or that is common in another culture. You gain access to that weapon, and for the purpose of determining your proficiency, that weapon is a simple weapon.

If you are trained in all martial weapons, you can choose an uncommon advanced weapon with such a trait. You gain access to that weapon, and for the purpose of determining your proficiency, that weapon is a martial weapon.

5TH LEVEL

ADAPTIVE ADEPT   FEAT 5

HUMAN

Prerequisites Adapted Cantrip, can cast 3rd-level spells

You've continued adapting your magic to blend your class's tradition with your adapted tradition. Choose a cantrip or 1st-level spell from the same magical tradition as your cantrip from Adapted Cantrip. You gain that spell, adding it to your spell repertoire, spellbook, or prepared spells just like the cantrip from Adapted Spell. You can cast this spell as a spell of your class's magical tradition. If you choose a 1st-level spell, you don't gain access to the heightened versions of that spell, meaning you can't prepare them if you prepare spells and you can't learn them or select the spell as a signature spell if you have a spell repertoire.

CLEVER IMPROVISER   FEAT 5

HUMAN

You've learned how to handle situations when you're out of your depth. You gain the Untrained Improvisation general feat. In addition, you can attempt skill actions that normally require you to be trained, even if you are untrained.

9TH LEVEL

COOPERATIVE SOUL   FEAT 9

HUMAN

Prerequisites Cooperative Nature

You have developed a soul-deep bond with your comrades and maintain an even greater degree of cooperation with them. If you are at least an expert in the skill you are Aiding, you get a success on any outcome rolled to Aid other than a critical success.

INCREDIBLE IMPROVISATION ◆   FEAT 9

HUMAN

Prerequisites Clever Improviser

Frequency once per day

Trigger You attempt a check using a skill you're untrained in.

A stroke of brilliance gives you a major advantage with a skill despite your inexperience. Gain a +4 circumstance bonus to the triggering skill check.

MULTITALENTED
FEAT 9

HUMAN

You've learned to split your focus between multiple classes with ease. You gain a 2nd-level multiclass dedication feat (for more about multiclass archetypes, see page 219), even if you normally couldn't take another dedication feat until you take more feats from your current archetype.

If you're a half-elf, you don't need to meet the feat's ability score prerequisites.

13TH LEVEL

UNCONVENTIONAL EXPERTISE
FEAT 13

HUMAN

Prerequisites Unconventional Weaponry, trained in the weapon you chose for Unconventional Weaponry

You've continued to advance your powers using your unconventional weapon. Whenever you gain a class feature that grants you expert or greater proficiency in certain weapons, you also gain that proficiency in the weapon you chose for Unconventional Weaponry.

HALF-ELF AND HALF-ORC ANCESTRY FEATS

A human with elf or orc blood is called a half-elf or half-orc, respectively, which is represented by the corresponding heritage. If you have the half-elf or half-orc heritage, you can select from additional ancestry feats not available to other humans.

HALF-ELF ANCESTRY FEATS

The following feats are available to half-elves.

1ST LEVEL

ELF ATAVISM
FEAT 1

HALF-ELF

Your elven blood runs particularly strong, granting you features far more elven than those of a typical half-elf. You may also have been raised among elves, steeped in your elven ancestors' heritage. You gain the benefits of the elf heritage of your elven parent or ancestors. You typically can't select a heritage that depends on or improves an elven feature you don't have. For example, you couldn't gain the cavern elf's darkvision ability if you didn't have low-light vision. In these cases, at the GM's discretion, you might gain a different benefit.

Special You can take this feat only at 1st level, and you can't retrain out of this feat or into this feat.

5TH LEVEL

INSPIRE IMITATION
FEAT 5

HALF-ELF

Your own actions inspire your allies to great achievements. Whenever you critically succeed at a skill check, you automatically qualify to use the Aid reaction when attempting to help an ally using the same skill, even without spending an action to prepare to do so.

SUPERNATURAL CHARM
FEAT 5

HALF-ELF

The elven magic in your blood manifests as a force you can use

INTRODUCTION

ANCESTRIES &
BACKGROUNDS

CLASSES

SKILLS

FEATS

EQUIPMENT

SPELLS

THE AGE OF
LOST OMENS

PLAYING THE
GAME

GAME
MASTERING

CRAFTING
& TREASURE

APPENDIX

to become more appealing or alluring. You can cast 1st-level *charm* as an arcane innate spell once per day.

HALF-ORC ANCESTRY FEATS

The following feats are available to half-orcs. Some of these feats are common to people with orc blood, and have the orc trait, while others are specific to half-orcs and have the half-orc trait.

1ST LEVEL

MONSTROUS PEACEMAKER   FEAT 1

HALF-ORC

Your dual human and orc nature has given you a unique perspective, allowing you to bridge the gap between humans and the many intelligent creatures in the world that humans consider monsters. You gain a +1 circumstance bonus to Diplomacy checks against non-humanoid intelligent creatures and against humanoids that are marginalized in human society (at the GM's discretion, but typically at least including giants, goblins, kobolds, and orcs). You also gain this bonus on Perception checks to Sense the Motives of such creatures.

ORC FEROCITY ↺   FEAT 1

ORC

Frequency once per day
Trigger You would be reduced to 0 Hit Points but not immediately killed.

Fierceness in battle runs through your blood, and you refuse to fall from your injuries. You avoid being knocked out and remain at 1 Hit Point, and your wounded condition increases by 1.

ORC SIGHT   FEAT 1

HALF-ORC

Prerequisites low-light vision

Your orc blood is strong enough to grant you the keen vision of your orc forebears. You gain darkvision, allowing you to see in darkness and dim light just as well as you can in bright light. However, in darkness, you see in black and white only.

Special You can take this feat only at 1st level, and you can't retrain out of this feat or into this feat.

ORC SUPERSTITION ↺   FEAT 1

CONCENTRATE   ORC

Trigger You attempt a saving throw against a spell or magical effect, before rolling.

You defend yourself against magic by relying on techniques derived from orc cultural superstitions. You gain a +1 circumstance bonus to your saving throw against the triggering spell or magical effect.

ORC WEAPON FAMILIARITY   FEAT 1

ORC

In combat, you favor the brutal weapons that are traditional

for your orc ancestors. You are trained with the falchion and greataxe. In addition, you gain access to all uncommon orc weapons.

For you, martial orc weapons are simple weapons, and advanced orc weapons are martial weapons.

5TH LEVEL

ORC WEAPON CARNAGE   FEAT 5

ORC

Prerequisites Orc Weapon Familiarity

You are brutally efficient with the weapons of your orc ancestors. Whenever you critically hit using a falchion, a greataxe, or an orc weapon, you apply the weapon's critical specialization effect.

VICTORIOUS VIGOR ↺   FEAT 5

ORC

Trigger You bring a foe to 0 Hit Points.

Your victories in battle fill you with pride and imbue you with the energy to fight a bit longer despite your wounds. You gain temporary Hit Points equal to your Constitution modifier until the end of your next turn.

9TH LEVEL

PERVASIVE SUPERSTITION   FEAT 9

ORC

Prerequisites Orc Superstition

You steep yourself in superstition and practice ancient orc mental exercises for shrugging off the effects of magic. You gain a +1 circumstance bonus to saving throws against spells and magical effects at all times.

13TH LEVEL

INCREDIBLE FEROCITY   FEAT 13

ORC

Prerequisites Orc Ferocity

Given time to collect yourself after a near-death scrape, you can rebuild your ferocity and withstand additional finishing blows. You can use Orc Ferocity with a frequency of once per hour, rather than once per day.

ORC WEAPON EXPERTISE   FEAT 13

ORC

Prerequisites Orc Weapon Familiarity

Your orc affinity blends with your class training, granting you great skill with orc weapons. Whenever you gain a class feature that grants you expert or greater proficiency in a given weapon or weapons, you also gain that proficiency in the falchion, the greataxe, and all orc weapons in which you are trained.

BACKGROUNDS

Backgrounds allow you to customize your character based on their life before adventuring. This is the next step in their life story after their ancestry, which reflects the circumstances of their birth. Your character's background can help you learn or portray more about their personality while also suggesting what sorts of things they're likely to know. Consider what events set your character on their path to the life of an adventurer and how those circumstances relate to their background.

At 1st level when you create your character, you gain a background of your choice. This decision is permanent; you can't change it at later levels. Each background listed here grants two ability boosts, a skill feat, and the trained proficiency rank in two skills, one of which is a Lore skill. If you gain the trained proficiency rank in a skill from your background and would then gain the trained proficiency rank in the same skill from your class at 1st level, you instead become trained in another skill of your choice.

Lore skills represent deep knowledge of a specific subject and are described on page 247. If a Lore skill involves a choice (for instance, a choice of terrain), explain your preference to the GM, who has final say on whether it's acceptable or not. If you'd like some suggestions, the Common Lore Subcategories sidebar on page 248 lists a number of Lore skills that are suitable for most campaigns.

Skill feats expand the functions of your skills and appear in Chapter 5: Feats.

ACOLYTE   BACKGROUND

You spent your early days in a religious monastery or cloister. You may have traveled out into the world to spread the message of your religion or because you cast away the teachings of your faith, but deep down you'll always carry within you the lessons you learned.

Choose two ability boosts. One must be to Intelligence or Wisdom, and one is a free ability boost.

You're trained in the Religion skill and the Scribing Lore skill. You gain the Student of the Canon skill feat.

ACROBAT   BACKGROUND

In a circus or on the streets, you earned your pay by performing as an acrobat. You might have turned to adventuring when the money dried up, or simply decided to put your skills to better use.

Choose two ability boosts. One must be to Strength or Dexterity, and one is a free ability boost.

You're trained in the Acrobatics skill and the Circus Lore skill. You gain the Steady Balance skill feat.

ANIMAL WHISPERER   BACKGROUND

You have always felt a connection to animals, and it was only a small leap to learn to train them. As you travel, you continuously encounter different creatures, befriending them along the way.

Choose two ability boosts. One must be to Wisdom or Charisma, and one is a free ability boost.

You're trained in the Nature skill and a Lore skill related to one terrain inhabited by animals you like (such as Plains Lore or Swamp Lore). You gain the Train Animal skill feat.

ARTISAN   BACKGROUND

As an apprentice, you practiced a particular form of building or crafting, developing specialized skill. You might have been a blacksmith's apprentice toiling over the forge for countless hours, a young tailor sewing garments of all kinds, or a shipwright shaping the hulls of ships.

Choose two ability boosts. One must be to Strength or Intelligence, and one is a free ability boost.

You're trained in the Crafting skill and the Guild Lore skill. You gain the Specialty Crafting skill feat.

ARTIST   BACKGROUND

Your art is your greatest passion, whatever form it takes. Adventuring might help you find inspiration, or simply be a way to survive until you become a world-famous artist.

Choose two ability boosts. One must be to Dexterity or Charisma, and one is a free ability boost.

You're trained in the Crafting skill and the Art Lore skill. You gain the Specialty Crafting skill feat.

BARKEEP   BACKGROUND

You have five specialties: hefting barrels, drinking, polishing steins, drinking, and drinking. You worked in a bar, where you learned how to hold your liquor and rowdily socialize.

Choose two ability boosts. One must be to Constitution or Charisma, and one is a free ability boost.

You're trained in the Diplomacy skill and the Alcohol Lore skill. You gain the Hobnobber skill feat.

BARRISTER   BACKGROUND

Piles of legal manuals, stern teachers, and experience in the courtroom have instructed you in legal matters. You're capable of mounting a prosecution or defense in court, and you tend to keep abreast of local laws, as you never can tell when you might need to know them on short notice.

Choose two ability boosts. One must be to Intelligence or Charisma, and one is a free ability boost.

You're trained in the Diplomacy skill and the Legal Lore skill. You gain the Group Impression skill feat.

INTRODUCTION

ANCESTRIES & BACKGROUNDS

CLASSES

SKILLS

FEATS

EQUIPMENT

SPELLS

THE AGE OF LOST OMENS

PLAYING THE GAME

GAME MASTERING

CRAFTING & TREASURE

APPENDIX

BOUNTY HUNTER — BACKGROUND

Bringing in lawbreakers lined your pockets. Maybe you had an altruistic motive and sought to bring in criminals to make the streets safer, or maybe the coin was motivation enough. Your techniques for hunting down criminals transfer easily to the life of an adventurer.

Choose two ability boosts. One must be to Strength or Wisdom, and one is a free ability boost.

You're trained in the Survival skill and the Legal Lore skill. You gain the Experienced Tracker skill feat.

CHARLATAN — BACKGROUND

You traveled from place to place, peddling false fortunes and snake oil in one town, pretending to be royalty in exile to seduce a wealthy heir in the next. Becoming an adventurer might be your next big scam or an attempt to put your talents to use for a greater cause. Perhaps it's a bit of both, as you realize that after pretending to be a hero, you've become the mask.

Choose two ability boosts. One must be to Intelligence or Charisma, and one is a free ability boost.

You're trained in the Deception skill and the Underworld Lore skill. You gain the Charming Liar skill feat.

CRIMINAL — BACKGROUND

As an unscrupulous independent or as a member of an underworld organization, you lived a life of crime. You might have become an adventurer to seek redemption, to escape the law, or simply to get access to bigger and better loot.

Choose two ability boosts. One must be to Dexterity or Intelligence, and one is a free ability boost.

You're trained in the Stealth skill and the Underworld Lore skill. You gain the Experienced Smuggler skill feat.

DETECTIVE — BACKGROUND

You solved crimes as a police inspector or took jobs for wealthy clients as a private investigator. You might have become an adventurer as part of your next big mystery, but likely it was due to the consequences or aftermath of a prior case.

Choose two ability boosts. One must be to Intelligence or Wisdom, and one is a free ability boost.

You're trained in the Society skill and the Underworld Lore skill. You gain the Streetwise skill feat.

EMISSARY — BACKGROUND

As a diplomat or messenger, you traveled to lands far and wide. Communicating with new people and forming alliances were your stock and trade.

Choose two ability boosts. One must be to Intelligence or Charisma, and one is a free ability boost.

You're trained in the Society skill and a Lore skill related to one city you've visited often. You gain the Multilingual skill feat.

ENTERTAINER — BACKGROUND

Through an education in the arts or sheer dogged practice,

you learned to entertain crowds. You might have been an actor, a dancer, a musician, a street magician, or any other sort of performer.

Choose two ability boosts. One must be to Dexterity or Charisma, and one is a free ability boost.

You're trained in the Performance skill and the Theater Lore skill. You gain the Fascinating Performance skill feat.

FARMHAND   BACKGROUND

With a strong back and an understanding of seasonal cycles, you tilled the land and tended crops. Your farm could have been razed by invaders, you could have lost the family tying you to the land, or you might have simply tired of the drudgery, but at some point you became an adventurer.

Choose two ability boosts. One must be to Constitution or Wisdom, and one is a free ability boost.

You're trained in the Athletics skill and the Farming Lore skill. You gain the Assurance skill feat with Athletics.

FIELD MEDIC   BACKGROUND

In the chaotic rush of battle, you learned to adapt to rapidly changing conditions as you administered to battle casualties. You patched up soldiers, guards, or other combatants, and learned a fair amount about the logistics of war.

Choose two ability boosts. One must be to Constitution or Wisdom, and one is a free ability boost.

You're trained in the Medicine skill and the Warfare Lore skill. You gain the Battle Medic skill feat.

FORTUNE TELLER   BACKGROUND

The strands of fate are clear to you, as you have learned many traditional forms by which laypeople can divine the future. You might have used these skills to guide your community, or simply to make money. But even the slightest peek into these practices connects you to the occult mysteries of the universe.

Choose two ability boosts. One must be to Intelligence or Charisma, and one is a free ability boost.

You're trained in the Occultism skill and the Fortune-Telling Lore skill. You gain the Oddity Identification skill feat.

GAMBLER   BACKGROUND

The thrill of the win drew you into games of chance. This might have been a lucrative sideline that paled in comparison to the real risks of adventuring, or you might have fallen on hard times due to your gambling and pursued adventuring as a way out of a spiral.

Choose two ability boosts. One must be to Dexterity or Charisma, and one is a free ability boost.

You're trained in the Deception skill and the Games Lore skill. You gain the Lie to Me skill feat.

GLADIATOR   BACKGROUND

The bloody games of the arena taught you the art of combat. Before you attained true fame, you departed—or escaped—the arena to explore the world. Your skill at drawing both blood and a crowd's attention pay off in a new adventuring life.

Choose two ability boosts. One must be to Strength or Charisma, and one is a free ability boost.

You're trained in the Performance skill and the Gladiatorial Lore skill. You gain the Impressive Performance skill feat.

GUARD   BACKGROUND

You served in the guard, out of either patriotism or the need for coin. Either way, you know how to get a difficult suspect to talk. However you left the guard, you might think of adventuring as a way to use your skills on a wider stage.

Choose two ability boosts. One must be to Strength or Charisma, and one is a free ability boost.

You're trained in the Intimidation skill and the Legal Lore or Warfare Lore skill. You gain the Quick Coercion skill feat.

HERBALIST   BACKGROUND

As a formally trained apothecary or a rural practitioner of folk medicine, you learned the healing properties of various herbs. You're adept at collecting the right natural cures in all sorts of environments and preparing them properly.

Choose two ability boosts. One must be to Constitution or Wisdom, and one is a free ability boost.

You're trained in the Nature skill and the Herbalism Lore skill. You gain the Natural Medicine skill feat.

HERMIT   BACKGROUND

In an isolated place—like a cave, remote oasis, or secluded mansion—you lived a life of solitude. Adventuring might represent your first foray out among other people in some time. This might be a welcome reprieve from solitude or an unwanted change, but in either case, you're likely still rough around the edges.

Choose two ability boosts. One must be to Constitution or Intelligence, and one is a free ability boost.

You're trained in the Nature or Occultism skill, plus a Lore skill related to the terrain you lived in as a hermit (such as Cave Lore or Desert Lore). You gain the Dubious Knowledge skill feat.

HUNTER   BACKGROUND

You stalked and took down animals and other creatures of the wild. Skinning animals, harvesting their flesh, and cooking them were also part of your training, all of which can give you useful resources while you adventure.

Choose two ability boosts. One must be to Dexterity or Wisdom, and one is a free ability boost.

You're trained in the Survival skill and the Tanning Lore skill. You gain the Survey Wildlife skill feat.

LABORER   BACKGROUND

You've spent years performing arduous physical labor. It was a difficult life, but you somehow survived. You may have embraced adventuring as an easier method to make your way in the world, or you might adventure under someone else's command.

Choose two ability boosts. One must be to Strength or Constitution, and one is a free ability boost.

You're trained in the Athletics skill and the Labor Lore skill. You gain the Hefty Hauler skill feat in Athletics.

MARTIAL DISCIPLE — BACKGROUND

You dedicated yourself to intense training and rigorous study to become a great warrior. The school you attended might have been a traditionalist monastery, an elite military academy, or the local branch of a prestigious mercenary organization.

Choose two ability boosts. One must be to Strength or Dexterity, and one is a free ability boost.

You're trained in your choice of the Acrobatics or Athletics skill. You gain a skill feat: Cat Fall if you chose Acrobatics or Quick Jump if you chose Athletics. You're also trained in the Warfare Lore skill.

MERCHANT — BACKGROUND

In a dusty shop, market stall, or merchant caravan, you bartered wares for coin and trade goods. The skills you picked up still apply in the adventuring life, in which a good deal on a suit of armor could prevent your death.

Choose two ability boosts. One must be to Intelligence or Charisma, and one is a free ability boost.

You're trained in the Diplomacy skill and the Mercantile Lore skill. You gain the Bargain Hunter skill feat.

MINER — BACKGROUND

You earned a living wrenching precious minerals from the lightless depths of the earth. Adventuring might have seemed lucrative or glamorous compared to this backbreaking labor—and if you have to head back underground, this time you plan to do so armed with a real weapon instead of a miner's pick.

Choose two ability boosts. One must be to Strength or Wisdom, and one is a free ability boost.

You're trained in the Survival skill and the Mining Lore skill. You gain the Terrain Expertise skill feat with underground terrain.

NOBLE — BACKGROUND

To the common folk, the life of a noble seems one of idyllic luxury, but growing up as a noble or member of the aspiring gentry, you know the reality: a noble's lot is obligation and intrigue. Whether you seek to escape your duties by adventuring or to better your station, you have traded silks and pageantry for an adventurer's life.

Choose two ability boosts. One must be to Intelligence or Charisma, and one is a free ability boost.

You're trained in the Society skill and your choice of the Genealogy Lore or Heraldry Lore skill. You gain the Courtly Graces skill feat.

NOMAD — BACKGROUND

Traveling far and wide, you picked up basic tactics for surviving on the road and in unknown lands, getting by with few supplies and even fewer comforts. As an adventurer, you travel still, often into even more dangerous places.

Choose two ability boosts. One must be to Constitution or Wisdom, and one is a free ability boost.

You're trained in the Survival skill and a Lore skill related to one terrain you traveled in (such as Desert Lore or Swamp Lore). You gain the Assurance skill feat with Survival.

PRISONER — BACKGROUND

You might have been imprisoned for crimes (whether you were guilty or not), or enslaved for some part of your upbringing. In your adventuring life, you take full advantage of your newfound freedom.

Choose two ability boosts. One must be to Strength or Constitution, and one is a free ability boost.

You're trained in the Stealth skill and the Underworld Lore skill. You gain the Experienced Smuggler skill feat.

SAILOR — BACKGROUND

You heard the call of the sea from a young age. Perhaps you signed onto a merchant's vessel, joined the navy, or even fell in with a crew of pirates and scalawags.

Choose two ability boosts. One must be to Strength or Dexterity, and one is a free ability boost.

You're trained in the Athletics skill and the Sailing Lore skill. You gain the Underwater Marauder skill feat.

SCHOLAR — BACKGROUND

You have a knack for learning, and sequestered yourself from the outside world to learn all you could. You read

about so many wondrous places and things in your books, and always dreamed about one day seeing the real things. Eventually, that curiosity led you to leave your studies and become an adventurer.

Choose two ability boosts. One must be to Intelligence or Wisdom, and one is a free ability boost.

You're trained in your choice of the Arcana, Nature, Occultism, or Religion skill, and gain the Assurance skill feat in your chosen skill. You're also trained in the Academia Lore skill.

SCOUT BACKGROUND

You called the wilderness home as you found trails and guided travelers. Your wanderlust could have called you to the adventuring life, or perhaps you served as a scout for soldiers and found you liked battle.

Choose two ability boosts. One must be to Dexterity or Wisdom, and one is a free ability boost.

You're trained in the Survival skill and a Lore skill related to one terrain you scouted in (such as Forest Lore or Cavern Lore). You gain the Forager skill feat.

STREET URCHIN BACKGROUND

You eked out a living by picking pockets on the streets of a major city, never knowing where you'd find your next meal. While some folk adventure for the glory, you do so to survive.

Choose two ability boosts. One must be to Dexterity or Constitution, and one is a free ability boost.

You're trained in Thievery and a Lore skill for the city you lived in as a street urchin (such as Absalom Lore or Magnimar Lore). You gain the Pickpocket skill feat.

TINKER BACKGROUND

Creating all sorts of minor inventions scratches your itch for problem-solving. Your engineering skills take a particularly creative bent, and no one know what you'll come up with next. It might be a genius device with tremendous potential... or it might explode.

Choose two ability boosts. One must be to Dexterity or Intelligence, and one is a free ability boost.

You're trained in the Crafting skill and the Engineering Lore skill. You gain the Specialty Crafting skill feat.

WARRIOR BACKGROUND

In your younger days, you waded into battle as a mercenary, a warrior defending a nomadic people, or a member of a militia or army. You might have wanted to break out from the regimented structure of these forces, or you could have always been as independent a warrior as you are now.

Choose two ability boosts. One must be to Strength or Constitution, and one is a free ability boost.

You're trained in the Intimidation skill and the Warfare Lore skill. You gain the Intimidating Glare skill feat.

ANCESTRIES & BACKGROUNDS

2

INTRODUCTION

ANCESTRIES &
BACKGROUNDS

CLASSES

SKILLS

FEATS

EQUIPMENT

SPELLS

THE AGE OF
LOST OMENS

PLAYING THE
GAME

GAME
MASTERING

CRAFTING
& TREASURE

APPENDIX

LANGUAGES

The people of the Inner Sea region speak dozens of different languages, along with hundreds of dialects and regional variations. While a character can generally get by with Taldane, also known as Common, knowing another language is vital in some regions. Being able to speak these tongues can help you with negotiation, spying on enemies, or just conducting simple commerce. Languages also afford you the chance to contextualize your character in the world and give meaning to your other character choices.

Your ancestry entry states which languages you know at 1st level. Typically, this means you can both speak and read these languages. Having a positive Intelligence modifier grants a number of additional languages equal to your Intelligence modifier. You can choose these languages from the list presented in your character's ancestry entry and from those available from your region or ethnicity. Ask your GM if there's a language you want to select that isn't on these lists. If your Intelligence changes later on, you adjust your number of languages accordingly.

The languages presented here are grouped according to how common they are throughout the Inner Sea region. Languages that are common are regularly encountered in most places, even among those who aren't native speakers. Languages that are uncommon (see Table 2–2 and Regional Languages) are most frequently spoken by native speakers, but they are also spoken by certain scholars and others interested in the associated cultures.

Druidic is a secret language, and is available only to characters who are druids. In fact, druids are prohibited from teaching the language to non-druids (described further in Anathema on page 130).

It is possible for your character to learn languages later in their adventuring career. Selecting the Multilingual feat, for example, grants a character two new languages chosen from those listed in Table 2–1: Common Languages and Table 2–2: Uncommon Languages. Other abilities and effects might grant access to common or uncommon languages, as detailed in their descriptions.

TABLE 2–1: COMMON LANGUAGES

Language	Speakers
Common	Humans, dwarves, elves, halflings, and other common ancestries
Draconic	Dragons, reptilian humanoids
Dwarven	Dwarves
Elven	Elves, half-elves
Gnomish	Gnomes
Goblin	Goblins, hobgoblins, bugbears
Halfling	Halflings
Jotun	Giants, ogres, trolls, ettins, cyclopes
Orcish	Orcs, half-orcs
Sylvan	Fey, centaurs, plant creatures
Undercommon	Drow, duergars, xulgaths

TABLE 2–2: UNCOMMON LANGUAGES

Language	Speakers
Abyssal	Demons
Aklo	Deros, evil fey, otherworldly monsters
Aquan	Aquatic creatures, water elemental creatures
Auran	Air elemental creatures, flying creatures
Celestial	Angels
Gnoll	Gnolls
Ignan	Fire elemental creatures
Infernal	Devils
Necril	Ghouls, intelligent undead
Shadowtongue	Nidalese, Shadow Plane creatures
Terran	Earth elemental creatures

TABLE 2–3: SECRET LANGUAGE

Language	Speakers
Druidic	Druids

REGIONAL LANGUAGES

Regional languages depend on the game world you're playing in. Chapter 8: The Age of Lost Omens lists the regional languages of the Pathfinder world and where they're spoken (page 432). These languages are uncommon.

Most characters learn the Common language. This is the most widely used language in the region where the campaign takes place. In the Inner Sea region of Golarion, the Common tongue is Taldane, for example. Characters with Common might face a language barrier if they travel somewhere with a different Common language.

SIGN LANGUAGE AND READING LIPS

The language entry for most characters lists languages they use to communicate in spoken words. However, you might know the signed version of a language or know how to read lips. You can learn these by taking the Sign Language and Read Lips skill feats. If you are creating a character who is deaf, hard of hearing, or unable to speak, discuss with your GM whether it makes sense for your character to know sign languages or lip reading. If so, your GM might allow you to select one of these feats for free (even if you don't meet the prerequisites) to represent your character concept.

CHAPTER 3: CLASSES

Just as your character's ancestry plays a key role in expressing their identity and worldview, their class indicates the training they have and will improve upon as an adventurer. Choosing your character's class is perhaps the most important decision you will make for them. Groups of players often create characters whose skills and abilities complement each other mechanically—for example, ensuring your party includes a healer, a combat-oriented character, a stealthy character, and someone with command over magic—so you may wish to discuss options with your group before deciding.

3

INTRODUCTION

ANCESTRIES & BACKGROUNDS

CLASSES

SKILLS

FEATS

EQUIPMENT

SPELLS

THE AGE OF LOST OMENS

PLAYING THE GAME

GAME MASTERING

CRAFTING & TREASURE

APPENDIX

The rules within each class allow you to bring a wealth of character concepts to life. Perhaps you want to create a brilliant but scatterbrained alchemist who can rattle off complex formulas for alchemical items but has trouble remembering his best friend's birthday. Or perhaps you want your character to be a muscle-bound swordswoman who becomes as immovable as a mountain when she hoists a shield. Maybe they'll be a hot-tempered sorcerer whose gesticulating fingers pulse with light from an angelic ancestor. The choices you make for your character within their class—such as a cleric's choice of deity, a fighter's choice of weapon, or a sorcerer's bloodline—bring these visions to life within the context of the rules and the world.

The entries on the pages that follow describe the 12 core classes in Pathfinder. Each entry contains the information you need to play a character of that class, as well as to advance them from their humble beginnings at 1st level to the dizzying heights of power at 20th level. In addition to the class entries, you might need to reference the following sections, which detail additional character options and how to advance your character in level.

- **Leveling Up** on page 31 tells you how to make your character stronger when you get enough Experience Points to reach a new level.
- **Animal Companions and Familiars** on page 214 provides rules to create an animal companion or a familiar to share your adventures with. You must have a class feature or feat that grants you a companion or familiar to use these rules.
- **Archetypes** on page 219 gives you thematic options that allow you to further customize your character's abilities. Though these rules are not recommended for beginners, the archetypes in this book allow you to gain abilities from other classes starting at 2nd level.

READING CLASS ENTRIES

Every class entry includes information about typical members of the class, plus suggestions for roleplaying characters of that class and playing these characters in the game's various modes. Each class provides your character with an ability boost to a key ability score; a number of Hit Points they receive at each level; proficiency ranks for various abilities, equipment, and skills; special abilities from their class features; and more. Your character's class entry also provides the information needed when they gain levels, so it will be a vital reference throughout the course of your campaign.

PLAYING THE CLASS

The first section of each class describes the interests and tendencies typical of that class, as well as information on how others view them. This can help inspire you as you determine your character's actions and define their personality, but you aren't obligated to play your character as this section describes.

KEY ABILITY

This is the ability score that a member of your class cares about the most. Many of your most useful and powerful abilities are tied to this ability in some way.

For instance, this is the ability score you'll use to determine the Difficulty Class (DC) associated with your character's class features and feats. This is called your class DC. If your character is a member of a spellcasting class, this key ability is used to calculate spell DCs and similar values.

Most classes are associated with one key ability score, but some allow you to choose from two options. For instance, if you're a fighter, you can choose either Strength or Dexterity as your key ability. A fighter who chooses Strength will excel in hand-to-hand combat, while those who choose Dexterity prefer ranged or finesse weapons.

Additionally, when you choose your character's class, they gain an ability boost to their key ability score, increasing that ability score by 2. For more about ability boosts, see page 20.

HIT POINTS

This section tells you how many Hit Points your character gains from their class at each level. To determine your character's starting Hit Points, add together the Hit Points they got when you chose their ancestry and the amount listed in this entry, which equals your Constitution modifier plus a fixed number. Classes that intend for characters to rush into battle with weapons bared gain a higher number of Hit Points each level, while those for characters who cast spells or engage in trickery gain fewer.

Each time your character gains a level, they increase their maximum Hit Points by the amount listed in this entry. For more about calculating your character's Constitution modifier and determining their Hit Points, see page 26.

INITIAL PROFICIENCIES

When you choose your character's class, they gain a set of initial proficiencies. Proficiencies measure your character's ability to perform tasks, use abilities, and succeed at checks. Proficiency ranks range from trained to legendary. For instance, a character who is trained with a longbow can use it effectively, while a person who is legendary with the weapon might be able to split an arrow from 100 paces away!

Each class entry specifies your character's initial proficiency rank in Perception, saving throws, attacks, defenses, and either spells or class DC. You gain the trained proficiency rank in at least one skill that is important to your class, and you can choose other skills to gain trained proficiency in—the exact number depends on your class. If your class would make you trained in a skill you're already trained in (typically due to your background), you can select another skill to become trained in.

A proficiency rank can unlock various feats and class features, and it also helps determine the modifier for any check you roll or DC you calculate related to that statistic. If your character is trained in Perception, a saving throw, or another statistic, they gain a proficiency bonus equal to their level + 2, while if they have expert proficiency, they gain a proficiency bonus equal to their level + 4. For more about proficiency ranks, see page 13.

Spellcasting classes grant a proficiency rank for spell attacks and DCs, which are further detailed in each class's entry.

If something isn't listed in your character's class entry, their proficiency rank in that statistic is untrained unless they gain training from another source. If your character is untrained in something, you add a proficiency bonus of +0 when attempting a check or calculating a DC related to that statistic.

ADVANCEMENT TABLE

This table summarizes the feats, skill increases, ability boosts, and other benefits your character gains as they advance in level. The first column of the class table indicates a level, and the second column lists each feature your character receives when they reach that level. The 1st-level entry includes a reminder to select your ancestry and background.

CLASS FEATURES

This section presents all the abilities the class grants your character. An ability gained at a higher level lists the required level next to the ability's name. All classes include the class features detailed below, and each class also gets special class features specific to it. Many class

features require you to choose between options. Unless the specific ability states otherwise, such decisions can't be changed without retraining (as explained on page 481).

CLASS FEATS

This section specifies the levels at which your character gains class feats—special feats that only members of that class can access. Class feats are granted beginning at 1st or 2nd level, depending on the class. Specific class feats are detailed at the end of each class entry.

SKILL FEATS

This section specifies the levels at which your character gains feats with the skill trait, called skill feats. Skill feats can be found in Chapter 5: Feats, beginning on page 254. At 2nd level and every 2 levels thereafter, most classes gain a skill feat, though rogues gain them earlier and more often. Your character must be trained in the corresponding skill to take a skill feat.

GENERAL FEATS

This section specifies the levels at which your character gains general feats. Most classes grant a general feat at 3rd level and every 4 levels thereafter. At each of these levels, you can select any general feat (including skill feats) as long as your character qualifies for it. More information can be found in Chapter 5: Feats (page 254).

SKILL INCREASES

This section specifies the levels at which your character can increase their proficiency rank in a skill. At 3rd level and every 2 levels thereafter, most classes grant a skill increase, though rogues gain them earlier and more often. Your character can use a skill increase to either become trained in one skill in which they're untrained or become an expert in one skill in which they're already trained.

If your character is at least 7th level, they can use a skill increase to become a master of a skill in which they're already an expert. If they're at least 15th level, they can use an increase to become legendary in a skill of which they're already a master.

ABILITY BOOSTS

At 5th level and every 5 levels thereafter, your character boosts four different ability scores. Your character can use these ability boosts to increase their ability scores above 18. Boosting an ability score increases it by 1 if it's already 18 or above, or by 2 if it starts out below 18. For more about ability boosts and applying them during character creation, see page 20.

ANCESTRY FEATS

This section serves as a reminder of the ancestry feats your character gains at 5th, 9th, 13th, and 17th levels. Ancestry feats are detailed in each ancestry entry in Chapter 2, which begins on page 32.

ALCHEMIST — PAGE 70

The alchemist uses their skill at crafting to create alchemical items—such as bombs, elixirs, and poisons—that they use to defeat foes and aid allies. Smart and resourceful, an alchemist often has just the right tool for the job and esoteric knowledge to help their friends get out of a jam.

BARBARIAN — PAGE 82

The barbarian is a fearsome embodiment of rage, focusing the deadly power of their anger against anyone who stands in their way. A barbarian is quick to enter battle and, once their fury has been unleashed, is immensely strong, often unpredictable, and nearly unstoppable.

BARD — PAGE 94

An artist and a scholar, the bard uses performance and esoteric learning to bolster their companions and foil their enemies. Sometimes sneaky and quite often charming, the bard adventures with pizzazz and talent backed up by an impressive repertoire of occult magic.

CHAMPION — PAGE 104

A defender of good who straps on armor and wields a righteous weapon, the champion protects the innocent and vanquishes evil. Steadfast in their beliefs, and devoted to both a deity and an aspect of good, they follow a strict code as they fight to make the world a better place.

CLERIC — PAGE 116

The cleric is dedicated to the worship of a single deity and draws divine magic from this devotion. Clerics can be vastly different depending on who they worship, and whether they're cloistered clerics who pursue one of their deity's domains or war priests who serve as the sword arm of their god.

DRUID — PAGE 128

The druid walks the wild, primordial places of the world without fear, harnessing the primal magic of nature and controlling it with calm purpose. A devotee of the wilderness, the druid finds nourishment in its power, allies among its creatures, and strength in its fury.

FIGHTER — PAGE 140

With calculated daring and fearless determination, the fighter tracks down and confronts their enemies while defending allies from harm. A master of the battlefield, the fighter is quick to exploit opportunities and strike any who stumble within reach of their sword or bow.

MONK — PAGE 154

The monk seeks perfection in all things, and that includes transforming their body into the perfect weapon. They can be walking with calm purpose and contemplating the subtleties of existence in one minute and then transform into a blur of deadly blows in the next.

RANGER — PAGE 166

Resourceful and cunning, the ranger is a hunter, tracker, and warrior who preserves the natural world and protects civilization from its ravages. Whether they use a bow, crossbow, a pair of weapons, or snares, the ranger is a fearsome enemy and great ally in the wild.

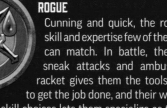

ROGUE — PAGE 178

Cunning and quick, the rogue brings skill and expertise few of their comrades can match. In battle, they excel at sneak attacks and ambushes. Their racket gives them the tools they need to get the job done, and their wide array of skill choices lets them specialize as they see fit.

SORCERER — PAGE 190

The intense magic the sorcerer commands comes from neither study nor worship—it comes from their blood. Their magical abilities depend on whether they have the blood of dragons, angels, fey, aberrant creatures, or some other being flowing through their veins and powering their spells.

WIZARD — PAGE 202

The wizard is the arcane master of spellcasting, plucking incredible power from reality through complicated spell formulas. They stride with confidence, without a need for armor or weapons, enacting their will upon the world and bringing woe upon their enemies.

ALCHEMIST

There's no sight more beautiful to you than a strange brew bubbling in a beaker, and you consume your ingenious elixirs with abandon. You're fascinated by uncovering the secrets of science and the natural world, and you're constantly experimenting in your lab or on the go with inventive concoctions for every eventuality. You are fearless in the face of risk, hurling explosive or toxic creations at your foes. Your unique path toward greatness is lined with alchemical brews that push your mind and body to their limits.

3

INTRODUCTION

ANCESTRIES & BACKGROUNDS

CLASSES

SKILLS

FEATS

EQUIPMENT

SPELLS

THE AGE OF LOST OMENS

PLAYING THE GAME

GAME MASTERING

CRAFTING & TREASURE

APPENDIX

KEY ABILITY

INTELLIGENCE

At 1st level, your class gives you an ability boost to Intelligence.

HIT POINTS

8 plus your Constitution Modifier

You increase your maximum number of HP by this number at 1st level and every level thereafter.

DURING COMBAT ENCOUNTERS...

You lob bombs at your foes, harry your enemies, and support the rest of your party with potent elixirs. At higher levels, your mutagens warp your body into a resilient and powerful weapon.

DURING SOCIAL ENCOUNTERS...

You provide knowledge and experience about alchemical items and related secrets, such as poisons and diseases.

WHILE EXPLORING...

You keep an eye out for trouble with your bombs at the ready, while giving advice on all things alchemical and mysterious.

IN DOWNTIME...

You experiment in an alchemical lab, brewing elixirs, making bombs, and furthering your alchemical knowledge.

YOU MIGHT...

- Enjoy tinkering with strange formulas and alchemical reagents, often with a single-minded dedication and recklessness that gives others pause.
- Get a kick out of wreaking havoc with the alchemical concoctions you've made, and enjoy watching things burn, dissolve, freeze, and jolt.
- Endlessly experiment to discover new, more potent alchemical tools.

OTHERS PROBABLY...

- Think you're some kind of sorcerer or an eccentric wizard and don't understand that you don't cast spells; spellcasters who clumsily dabble in alchemy only heighten this misconception.
- Don't understand your zeal for alchemy, creativity, and invention.
- Assume that if you haven't caused a catastrophe with your experimentations, you inevitably will.

INITIAL PROFICIENCIES

At 1st level, you gain the listed proficiency ranks in the following statistics. You are untrained in anything not listed unless you gain a better proficiency rank in some other way.

PERCEPTION

Trained in Perception

SAVING THROWS

Expert in Fortitude
Expert in Reflex
Trained in Will

SKILLS

Trained in Crafting
Trained in a number of additional skills equal to 3 plus your Intelligence modifier

ATTACKS

Trained in simple weapons
Trained in alchemical bombs
Trained in unarmed attacks

DEFENSES

Trained in light armor
Trained in unarmored defense

CLASS DC

Trained in alchemist class DC

TABLE 3-1: ALCHEMIST ADVANCEMENT

Your Level	Class Features
1	Ancestry and background, initial proficiencies, alchemy, formula book, research field, alchemist feat
2	Alchemist feat, skill feat
3	General feat, skill increase
4	Alchemist feat, skill feat
5	Ability boosts, ancestry feat, field discovery, skill increase
6	Alchemist feat, skill feat
7	Alchemical weapon expertise, general feat, iron will, perpetual infusions, skill increase
8	Alchemist feat, skill feat
9	Alchemical expertise, alertness, ancestry feat, double brew, skill increase
10	Ability boosts, alchemist feat, skill feat
11	General feat, juggernaut, perpetual potency, skill increase
12	Alchemist feat, skill feat
13	Ancestry feat, greater field discovery, light armor expertise, skill increase, weapon specialization
14	Alchemist feat, skill feat
15	Ability boosts, alchemical alacrity, evasion, general feat, skill increase
16	Alchemist feat, skill feat
17	Alchemical mastery, ancestry feat, perpetual perfection, skill increase
18	Alchemist feat, skill feat
19	General feat, light armor mastery, skill increase
20	Ability boosts, alchemist feat, skill feat

CLASS FEATURES

You gain these abilities as an alchemist. Abilities gained at higher levels list the levels at which you gain them next to the features' names.

ANCESTRY AND BACKGROUND

In addition to the abilities provided by your class at 1st level, you have the benefits of your selected ancestry and background, as described in Chapter 2.

INITIAL PROFICIENCIES

At 1st level, you gain a number of proficiencies that represent your basic training. These proficiencies are noted at the start of this class.

ALCHEMY

You understand the complex interactions of natural and unnatural substances and can concoct alchemical items to meet your needs. You can do this using normal reagents and the Craft activity, or you can use special infused reagents that allow you to craft temporary items quickly and at no cost. Over time, you can create more and more alchemical items for free, and since each of

them becomes more and more powerful, you advance in power dramatically, leaving behind those who don't understand your strange science.

You gain the Alchemical Crafting feat (page 258), even if you don't meet that feat's prerequisites, and you gain the four common 1st-level alchemical formulas granted by that feat. The catalog of alchemical items begins on page 543. You can use this feat to create alchemical items as long as you have the items' formulas in your formula book.

INFUSED REAGENTS

You infuse reagents with your own alchemical essence, allowing you to create alchemical items at no cost. Each day during your daily preparations, you gain a number of batches of infused reagents equal to your level + your Intelligence modifier. You can use these reagents for either advanced alchemy or Quick Alchemy, described below. Together, these infused reagents have light Bulk.

As soon as you make your next daily preparations, your infused reagents from the previous day's preparations are instantly destroyed, and nonpermanent effects of your previous day's infused items immediately end. While infused reagents are physical objects, they can't be duplicated, preserved, or created in any way other than your daily preparations. Any such artificial reagents lack the infusion and are useless for advanced alchemy or Quick Alchemy.

ADVANCED ALCHEMY

During your daily preparations, after producing new infused reagents, you can spend batches of those infused reagents to create infused alchemical items. You don't need to attempt a Crafting check to do this, and you ignore both the number of days typically required to create the items and any alchemical reagent requirements. Your advanced alchemy level is equal to your level. For each batch of infused reagents you spend, choose an alchemical item of your advanced alchemy level or lower that's in your formula book, and make a batch of two of that item. These items have the infused trait and remain potent for 24 hours or until your next daily preparations, whichever comes first.

QUICK ALCHEMY

If you need a specific alchemical item on the fly, you can use your infused reagents to quickly create it with the Quick Alchemy action.

QUICK ALCHEMY ❖

ALCHEMIST MANIPULATE

Cost 1 batch of infused reagents
Requirements You have alchemist's tools (page 287), the formula for the alchemical item you're creating, and a free hand.

You swiftly mix up a short-lived alchemical item to use at a moment's notice. You create a single alchemical item of your advanced alchemy level or lower that's in your formula book without having to spend the normal monetary cost in alchemical reagents or needing to attempt a Crafting check. This item has the infused trait, but it remains potent only until the start of your next turn.

FORMULA BOOK

An alchemist keeps meticulous records of the formulas for every item they can create. You start with a standard formula book worth 10 sp or less (as detailed on page 290) for free. The formula book contains the formulas for two common 1st-level alchemical items of your choice, in addition to those you gained from Alchemical Crafting and your research field. The catalog of alchemical items begins on page 543.

Each time you gain a level, you can add the formulas for two common alchemical items to your formula book. These new formulas can be for any level of item you can create. You learn these formulas automatically, but it's also possible to find or buy additional formulas in settlements or from other alchemists, or to invent them with the Inventor feat (page 262).

RESEARCH FIELD

Your inquiries into the alchemical nature of the universe have led you to focus on a particular field of research. You might have a degree from an scientific institute, correspond with other researchers in your field, or work as a genius loner. Choose a field of research. The research fields presented in this book are as follows.

BOMBER

You specialize in explosions and other violent alchemical reactions. You start with the formulas for two 1st-level alchemical bombs in your formula book, in addition to your other formulas.

When throwing an alchemical bomb with the splash trait, you can deal splash damage to only your primary target instead of the usual splash area.

CHIRURGEON

You concentrate on healing others with alchemy. You start with the formulas for two of the following in your formula book, in addition to your other formulas: lesser antidote, lesser antiplague, or lesser elixir of life.

As long as your proficiency rank in Medicine is trained or better, you can attempt a Crafting check instead of a Medicine check for any of Medicine's untrained and trained uses.

MUTAGENIST

You focus on bizarre mutagenic transformations that sacrifice one aspect of a creature's physical or psychological being in order to strengthen another. You start with the formulas for two 1st-level mutagens in your formula book, in addition to your other formulas.

You can gain the benefit of any mutagen, even if it wasn't specifically brewed for you. Whenever your proficiency rank for simple weapons increases, your proficiency rank for unarmed attacks increases to the same rank unless it's already better.

ALCHEMIST FEATS

At 1st level and every even-numbered level thereafter, you gain an alchemist class feat. Alchemist class feats are described beginning on page 76.

SKILL FEATS   2ND

At 2nd level and every 2 levels thereafter, you gain a skill feat. Skill feats can be found in Chapter 5 and have the skill trait. You must be trained or better in the corresponding skill to select a skill feat.

GENERAL FEATS   3RD

At 3rd level and every 4 levels thereafter, you gain a general feat. General feats are listed in Chapter 5.

SAMPLE ALCHEMIST

CHIRURGEON

You use alchemy for medicinal purposes, healing and protecting others across the lands.

ABILITY SCORES
Prioritize Intelligence and Wisdom. Constitution increases your survivability, and Dexterity helps you hit with ranged attacks when violence is necessary.

SKILLS
Crafting, Diplomacy, Medicine, Nature, Occultism, Religion, Society, Survival

RESEARCH FIELD
Chirurgeon

STARTING FEAT
Alchemical Savant

HIGHER-LEVEL FEATS
Poison Resistance (2nd), Efficient Alchemy (4th), Combine Elixirs (6th), Merciful Elixir (10th), Greater Merciful Elixir (14th), Miracle Worker (18th), Craft Philosopher's Stone (20th)

SKILL INCREASES — 3RD
At 3rd level and every 2 levels thereafter, you gain a skill increase. You can use this increase either to increase your proficiency rank to trained in one skill you're untrained in, or to increase your proficiency rank in one skill in which you're already trained to expert.

At 7th level, you can use skill increases to increase your proficiency rank to master in a skill in which you're already an expert, and at 15th level, you can use them to increase your proficiency rank to legendary in a skill in which you're already a master.

ABILITY BOOSTS — 5TH
At 5th level and every 5 levels thereafter, you boost four different ability scores. You can use these ability boosts to increase your ability scores above 18. Boosting an ability score increases it by 1 if it's already 18 or above, or by 2 if it starts out below 18.

ANCESTRY FEATS — 5TH
In addition to the ancestry feat you started with, you gain an ancestry feat at 5th level and every 4 levels thereafter. The list of ancestry feats available to you can be found in your ancestry's entry in Chapter 2.

FIELD DISCOVERY — 5TH
You learn a special discovery depending on your field.

Bomber: When using advanced alchemy to make bombs during your daily preparations, you can use a batch of reagents to create any three bombs instead of just two of the same bomb.

Chirurgeon: When using advanced alchemy to make elixirs of life during your daily preparations, you can create three elixirs with each batch of reagents instead of two.

Mutagenist: When using advanced alchemy to make mutagens during your daily preparations, you can use a batch of reagents to create any three mutagens instead of just two of the same mutagen.

ALCHEMICAL WEAPON EXPERTISE — 7TH
You've trained to more effectively wield the weapons you find in your lab. Your proficiency ranks for simple weapons and alchemical bombs increase to expert.

IRON WILL — 7TH
Your mental defenses are an iron fortress. Your proficiency rank for Will saves increases to expert.

PERPETUAL INFUSIONS — 7TH
You have learned how to create perpetual alchemical infusions that can provide a near-infinite supply of certain simple items. You gain the ability to create two 1st-level alchemical items using Quick Alchemy without spending a batch of infused reagents. The items you can select depend on your research field and must be in your formula book.

Bomber: Choose two of the following formulas: lesser acid flask, lesser alchemist's fire, lesser bottled lightning, lesser liquid ice, lesser tanglefoot bag, lesser thunderstone.

Chirurgeon: Lesser antidote and lesser antiplague.

Mutagenist: Choose two of the following formulas: lesser bestial mutagen, lesser bullheaded mutagen, lesser cognitive mutagen, lesser juggernaut mutagen, lesser quicksilver mutagen, lesser silvertongue mutagen.

ALCHEMICAL EXPERTISE   9TH

Constant practice has increased the effectiveness of your concoctions. Your proficiency rank for your alchemist class DC increases to expert.

ALERTNESS   9TH

You remain alert to threats around you. Your proficiency rank for Perception increases to expert.

DOUBLE BREW   9TH

You know your formulas so well that you can concoct two items at once. When using the Quick Alchemy action, instead of spending one batch of infused reagents to create a single item, you can spend up to two batches of infused reagents to make up to two alchemical items as described in that action. These items do not have to be the same.

JUGGERNAUT   11TH

Your body has become accustomed to physical hazards and resistant to pathogens and ailments. Your proficiency rank for Fortitude saves increases to master. When you roll a success on a Fortitude save, you get a critical success instead.

PERPETUAL POTENCY   11TH

Your perpetual infusions improve, allowing you to use Quick Alchemy to create more powerful items with no cost. The items you can select depend on your research field and must be in your formula book.

Bomber: The moderate versions of the bombs you chose for perpetual infusions.

Chirurgeon: Moderate antidote and antiplague.

Mutagenist: The moderate versions of the mutagens you chose for perpetual infusions.

GREATER FIELD DISCOVERY   13TH

You learn an incredible discovery that advances your understanding of your field.

Bomber: You can increase the splash on your bombs to damage creatures within 10 feet, or 15 feet if you have Expanded Splash.

Chirurgeon: When you use Quick Alchemy to create any type of elixir of life, the creature drinking the elixir gains the maximum Hit Points possible for that elixir, instead of rolling to determine the number of Hit Points regained.

KEY TERMS

You'll see the following key terms in many alchemist abilities.

Additive: Feats with the additive trait allow you to spend actions to add special substances to bombs or elixirs. You can add only one additive to a single alchemical item, and attempting to add another spoils the item. You can typically use actions with the additive trait only when you're creating an infused alchemical item, and some can be used only with the Quick Alchemy action. The additive trait is always followed by a level, such as additive 2. An additive adds its level to the level of the alchemical item you're modifying; the result is the new level of the mixture. The mixture's item level must be no higher than your advanced alchemy level.

Infused: You created an alchemical item with the infused trait using your infused reagents, and it has a limited time before it becomes inert. Any nonpermanent effects from your infused alchemical items, with the exception of afflictions such as slow-acting poisons, end when you make your daily preparations again.

Mutagenist: If you imbibe another mutagen while you are under the effects of a mutagen that you created, you can gain the benefits and the drawbacks of both mutagens at once, despite the fact that they both have the polymorph trait and would not normally function together. If you come under the effects of any further mutagens while benefiting from two mutagens, you lose the benefit of one of the former mutagens of your choice, while retaining the drawbacks of all the mutagens. If you are under the effects of two mutagens and you come under the effect of a non-mutagen polymorph effect, you lose the benefits of the mutagens while retaining the drawbacks of both.

LIGHT ARMOR EXPERTISE   13TH

You've learned how to dodge while wearing light or no armor. Your proficiency ranks for light armor and unarmored defense increase to expert.

WEAPON SPECIALIZATION   13TH

You've learned how to inflict greater injuries with the weapons you know best. You deal 2 additional damage with weapons and unarmed attacks in which you are an expert. This damage increases to 3 if you're a master, and to 4 if you're legendary.

ALCHEMICAL ALACRITY   15TH

Your comfort in concocting items is such that you can create three at a time. When using the Quick Alchemy action, you can spend up to three batches of infused reagents to make up to three alchemical items as described in that action. These items do not have to be the same.

ALCHEMIST FEATS

If you need to look up an alchemist feat by name instead of by level, use this table.

EVASION   15TH

You've learned to move quickly to avoid explosions, dragon's breath, and worse. Your proficiency rank for Reflex saves increases to master. When you roll a success on a Reflex save, you get a critical success instead.

ALCHEMICAL MASTERY   17TH

Your alchemical concoctions are incredibly effective. Your proficiency rank for your alchemist class DC increases to master.

PERPETUAL PERFECTION   17TH

You have perfected your perpetual infusions, allowing you to use Quick Alchemy to create even more powerful items at no cost. The items you can select depend on your research field and must be in your formula book.

Bomber: The greater versions of the bombs you chose for perpetual infusions.

Chirurgeon: Greater antidote and antiplague.

Mutagenist: The greater versions of the mutagens you chose for perpetual infusions.

LIGHT ARMOR MASTERY   19TH

Your skill with light armor improves, increasing your ability to dodge blows. Your proficiency ranks for light armor and unarmored defense increase to master.

ALCHEMIST FEATS

At every level that you gain an alchemist feat, you can select one of the following feats. You must satisfy any prerequisites before taking the feat.

1ST LEVEL

ALCHEMICAL FAMILIAR   FEAT 1

`ALCHEMIST`

You have used alchemy to create life, a simple creature formed from alchemical materials, reagents, and a bit of your own blood. This alchemical familiar appears to be a small creature of flesh and blood, though it might have some unusual or distinguishing aspects depending on your creative process. Like other familiars, your alchemical familiar assists you in your laboratory and on adventures. The familiar uses your Intelligence modifier to determine its Perception, Acrobatics, and Stealth modifiers (see Familiars on page 217 for more information).

ALCHEMICAL SAVANT   FEAT 1

`ALCHEMIST`

Prerequisites trained in Crafting

You can identify alchemical items quickly. When using the Crafting skill to Identify Alchemy on an alchemical item you hold, you can do so as a single action, which has the concentrate and manipulate traits, instead of spending 10 minutes. If you have the formula for the item you are attempting to identify, you gain a +2 circumstance bonus to your check, and if you roll a critical failure, you get a failure instead.

FAR LOBBER   FEAT 1

`ALCHEMIST`

You've learned how to throw a longer distance. When you throw an alchemical bomb, it has a range increment of 30 feet instead of the usual 20 feet.

QUICK BOMBER ◆   FEAT 1

`ALCHEMIST`

You keep your bombs in easy-to-reach pouches from which you draw without thinking. You Interact to draw a bomb, then Strike with it.

INTRODUCTION

ANCESTRIES & BACKGROUNDS

CLASSES

SKILLS

FEATS

EQUIPMENT

SPELLS

THE AGE OF LOST OMENS

PLAYING THE GAME

GAME MASTERING

CRAFTING & TREASURE

APPENDIX

2ND LEVEL

POISON RESISTANCE   FEAT 2

ALCHEMIST

Repeated exposure to toxic reagents has fortified your body against poisons of all kinds. You gain poison resistance equal to half your level, and you gain a +1 status bonus to saving throws against poisons.

REVIVIFYING MUTAGEN   FEAT 2

ALCHEMIST

While under the effect of a mutagen, you can metabolize that mutagen's power to heal yourself. This uses a single action, which has the concentrate and manipulate traits. Once the action is complete, you regain 1d6 Hit Points for every 2 item levels of the mutagen (minimum 1d6), but the mutagen's duration immediately ends, even if you are under the effect of Persistent Mutagen.

SMOKE BOMB ◈   FEAT 2

ADDITIVE 1 | **ALCHEMIST**

Frequency once per round

Trigger You use Quick Alchemy to craft an alchemical bomb with a level at least 1 lower than your advanced alchemy level.

You cause the bomb to create a cloud of thick smoke, in addition to its normal effects. When thrown, the bomb creates a cloud of smoke in a 10-foot-radius burst. You choose which corner of the target's space (or the space in which the bomb lands) the cloud is centered on. Creatures within that area have the concealed condition, and all other creatures are concealed to them. The smoke lasts for 1 minute or until dissipated by a strong wind.

4TH LEVEL

CALCULATED SPLASH   FEAT 4

ALCHEMIST

You have calculated all the angles to maximize a bomb's splash. When you throw an alchemical bomb with the splash trait, you can cause the bomb to deal splash damage equal to your Intelligence modifier (minimum 0) instead of the normal amount.

EFFICIENT ALCHEMY   FEAT 4

ALCHEMIST

Thanks to the time you've spent studying and experimenting, you know how to scale your formulas into larger batches that don't require any additional attention. When spending downtime to Craft alchemical items, you can produce twice as many alchemical items in a single batch without spending additional preparatory time. For instance, if you are creating elixirs of life, you can craft up to eight elixirs in a single batch using downtime, rather than four. This does not reduce the amount of alchemical reagents required or other ingredients needed to craft each item, nor does it increase your rate of progress for days past the base downtime spent. This also does not change the number of items you can create in a batch using advanced alchemy.

SAMPLE ALCHEMIST

BOMBER

You can mix an explosive out of just about anything!

ABILITY SCORES

Prioritize Intelligence and Dexterity. Constitution helps you survive explosions gone wrong, and Wisdom prevents you from bombing the wrong target.

SKILLS

Acrobatics, Arcana, Crafting, Deception, Intimidation, Society, Stealth, Thievery

RESEARCH FIELD

Bomber

STARTING FEAT

Quick Bomber

HIGHER-LEVEL FEATS

Smoke Bomb (2nd), Calculated Splash (4th), Directional Bombs (6th), Sticky Bomb (8th), Expanded Splash (10th), Mega Bomb (20th)

ENDURING ALCHEMY   FEAT 4

ALCHEMIST

You've learned how to make your personal energy last just a little bit longer when quickly brewing ad hoc concoctions. When using Quick Alchemy to create an alchemical tool or elixir, that tool or elixir remains potent until the end of your next turn, instead of losing its potency at the start of your next turn.

6TH LEVEL

COMBINE ELIXIRS ◈   FEAT 6

ADDITIVE 2 | **ALCHEMIST**

Frequency once per round

Trigger You use Quick Alchemy to craft an alchemical item that has the elixir trait and is at least 2 levels lower than your advanced alchemy level.

You've discovered how to mix two elixirs into a single hybrid concoction. You can spend 2 additional batches of infused reagents to add a second elixir to the one you're crafting. The second elixir must also be at least 2 levels lower than your advanced alchemy level, and the combination elixir is an alchemical item two levels higher than the higher of the two elixirs' levels. When this combination elixir is consumed, both the constituent elixirs take effect. For example, you can combine two elixirs of life to create a combined elixir that heals twice the normal amount, or you can combine a lesser darkvision elixir with a lesser eagle-eye elixir to both gain darkvision and find secret doors.

DEBILITATING BOMB ◈   FEAT 6

ADDITIVE 2 | **ALCHEMIST**

Frequency once per round

Trigger You use Quick Alchemy to craft an alchemical bomb that is at least 2 levels lower than your advanced alchemy level.

Your bombs impose additional effects on your enemies. You mix a substance into the bomb that causes one of the following: dazzled, deafened, flat-footed, or a –5-foot status penalty to Speeds. If the attack with that bomb hits, the target must succeed at a Fortitude saving throw or suffer that effect until the start of your next turn. Use your class DC for this saving throw (even if someone else throws the bomb).

DIRECTIONAL BOMBS   FEAT 6

ALCHEMIST

You can lob bombs with great force and a precise trajectory to angle the splash in a cone spraying in a single direction. When throwing an alchemical bomb with the splash trait, instead of splashing all squares adjacent to the target, you can treat the target's space as the first affected square of a 15-foot cone directed away from you, potentially allowing you to avoid allies and splash deeper into enemy lines. If the target takes up more than a single square, the target's square closest to you is the first affected square of the cone.

8TH LEVEL

FERAL MUTAGEN — FEAT 8

ALCHEMIST

Your bestial mutagen brings out the beast lurking within you, granting you especially sharp claws and teeth as well as a ferocious appearance. Whenever you're affected by a bestial mutagen you created, you gain the mutagen's item bonus to your Intimidation checks. In addition, your claws and jaws are increasingly vicious, and they gain the deadly d10 trait. Finally, you can increase the mutagen's penalty to AC from –1 to –2 and, in exchange, increase the damage die size of your claws and jaws by one step.

POWERFUL ALCHEMY — FEAT 8

ALCHEMIST

Alchemical items you create on the fly are particularly potent. When you use Quick Alchemy to create an infused alchemical item that allows a saving throw, you can change its DC to your class DC.

STICKY BOMB ◈ — FEAT 8

ADDITIVE 2 **ALCHEMIST**

Frequency once per round

Trigger You use Quick Alchemy to craft an alchemical bomb, and that bomb's level is at least 2 levels lower than your advanced alchemy level.

You mix in an additive to make your bomb's contents adhere to the target and continue to deal damage. A creature that takes a direct hit from one of your sticky bombs also takes persistent damage equal to and of the same type as the bomb's splash damage. If the bomb already deals persistent damage, combine the two amounts.

10TH LEVEL

ELASTIC MUTAGEN — FEAT 10

ALCHEMIST

You can cause your body to twist and flow like the quicksilver within your mutagens. Whenever you are under the effects of a quicksilver mutagen you created, you can stretch your legs and Step up to 10 feet, and you can squish and compress your body, allowing you to make it through tight spaces as if you were one size smaller, in addition to any effect from Squeezing.

EXPANDED SPLASH — FEAT 10

ALCHEMIST

Prerequisites Calculated Splash

The particularly volatile compounds that you brew into your bombs result in them creating especially large and powerful explosions. When you throw an alchemical bomb you created and that bomb has the splash trait, you can add your Intelligence modifier to the bomb's usual splash damage, and it deals splash damage to every creature within 10 feet of the target.

GREATER DEBILITATING BOMB — FEAT 10

ALCHEMIST

Prerequisites Debilitating Bomb

You have learned enhanced techniques and alchemical secrets that allow you to expand the range of effects you can impose with your bombs. When you use Debilitating Bomb, add the following to the list you can choose from: clumsy 1, enfeebled 1, stupefied 1, or –10-foot status penalty to Speeds.

MERCIFUL ELIXIR ◈ — FEAT 10

ADDITIVE 2 **ALCHEMIST**

Frequency once per round

Trigger You craft an elixir of life using Quick Alchemy, and that elixir is at least 2 levels lower than your advanced alchemy level.

You mix a special additive into your elixir that calms the drinker's body and mind. The elixir of life attempts to counteract one fear effect or one effect imposing the paralyzed condition on the drinker.

POTENT POISONER — FEAT 10

ALCHEMIST

Prerequisites Powerful Alchemy

By concentrating your poisons' toxic components, you make them harder for victims to resist. When you craft an alchemical item with the poison trait by any means, the DC is increased by up to 4, to a maximum of your class DC.

12TH LEVEL

EXTEND ELIXIR — FEAT 12

ALCHEMIST

Integrating your own personal energy into the elixirs you create causes them to affect you for longer. When you consume one of your alchemical items that has the elixir and infused traits and a duration of 1 minute or longer, that elixir's duration is doubled.

INVINCIBLE MUTAGEN — FEAT 12

ALCHEMIST

The fortifying additives you brew into your mutagens make your juggernaut form impervious. Whenever you're affected by a juggernaut mutagen you created, you gain resistance to all physical damage equal to your Intelligence modifier (minimum 0).

UNCANNY BOMBS — FEAT 12

ALCHEMIST

Prerequisites Far Lobber

You lob bombs unerringly, despite obstructions or distance. When you throw an alchemical item with the bomb trait, its range increment increases to 60 feet, you reduce any circumstance bonus to the target's AC from cover by 1, and you automatically succeed at the flat check when targeting a concealed creature.

INTRODUCTION

ANCESTRIES & BACKGROUNDS

CLASSES

SKILLS

FEATS

EQUIPMENT

SPELLS

THE AGE OF LOST OMENS

PLAYING THE GAME

GAME MASTERING

CRAFTING & TREASURE

APPENDIX

SAMPLE ALCHEMIST

MUTAGENIST

You transform yourself and others with mutagens.

ABILITY SCORES
Prioritize Intelligence and Strength. Constitution helps you survive transformations and combat, and Wisdom helps keep your mind intact despite the warping.

SKILLS
Athletics, Arcana, Crafting, Intimidation, Occultism, Society, Stealth, Survival

RESEARCH FIELD
Mutagenist

STARTING FEAT
Alchemical Familiar

HIGHER-LEVEL FEATS
Revivifying Mutagen (2nd), Feral Mutagen (8th), Invincible Mutagen (12th), Persistent Mutagen (16th), Perfect Mutagen (20th)

14TH LEVEL

GLIB MUTAGEN   FEAT 14
ALCHEMIST

Your silvertongue mutagen transcends languages and plausibility. When affected by a silvertongue mutagen you have created, you ignore circumstance penalties to Deception, Diplomacy, Intimidation, and Performance checks. In addition, your words transcend linguistic barriers; everyone listening to you speak hears your words as if you were speaking in their own language (though you do not actually speak that language, nor does this ability allow you to understand any additional languages).

GREATER MERCIFUL ELIXIR   FEAT 14
ALCHEMIST

Prerequisites Merciful Elixir

Your additives contain panaceas that can remedy a plethora of maladies. When you use Merciful Elixir, your elixir can instead attempt to counteract the blinded, deafened, sickened, or slowed condition.

TRUE DEBILITATING BOMB   FEAT 14
ALCHEMIST

Prerequisites Greater Debilitating Bomb

Ever inventive, you have discovered increasingly devastating ways for your bombs to impede and hamper your foes. When you use Debilitating Bomb, add the following to the list of effects you can choose from: enfeebled 2, stupefied 2, or a –15-foot status penalty to Speeds. If you instead apply one of the effects listed in Debilitating Bomb, the target avoids the effect only if the result of its saving throw is a critical success.

16TH LEVEL

ETERNAL ELIXIR   FEAT 16
ALCHEMIST

Prerequisites Extend Elixir

Your body readily accepts and retains minor changes. When you drink one of your alchemical items that has the elixir and infused traits and a duration of 1 minute or more, you can make the elixir's duration indefinite. You can do so only if the elixir's level is half your level or lower. If you later consume a different elixir and make it indefinite, the effect of the previous indefinite elixir ends.

EXPLOITIVE BOMB ◆   FEAT 16
ADDITIVE 2   ALCHEMIST

Frequency once per round

Trigger You craft an alchemical bomb using Quick Alchemy that's at least 2 levels lower than your advanced alchemy level.

You mix a substance into the bomb to foil resistances. The bomb reduces any resistance the enemy has to its damage type by an amount equal to your level, but only for that attack.

GENIUS MUTAGEN FEAT 16

ALCHEMIST

Specialized tweaks to your formula that supplements your genius considerably broaden the benefits you gain from cognitive mutagens. When you're affected by a cognitive mutagen you created, you also gain the mutagen's item bonus to Deception, Diplomacy, Intimidation, Medicine, Nature, Performance, Religion, and Survival checks. In addition, you can communicate telepathically with creatures within 60 feet with whom you share a language. The communication is two-way once you establish it, so a creature you contact can also communicate with you.

PERSISTENT MUTAGEN FEAT 16

ALCHEMIST

Prerequisites Extend Elixir

You've trained your physical form to remain stable within the a given altered state. Once per day, when you consume an alchemical item with the infused and mutagen traits that you have crafted, you can retain its effects until the next time you make your daily preparations instead of its normal duration.

18TH LEVEL

IMPROBABLE ELIXIRS FEAT 18

ALCHEMIST

Your mastery of alchemical secrets enables you to replicate effects most believe can be achieved only via magic. Select a number of potions equal to your Intelligence modifier (minimum 1) of 9th level or lower. You gain formulas to Craft these potions as alchemical items with the elixir trait. When Crafting these alchemical elixirs, you can substitute alchemical reagents for an equal value of magical components, and you can use alchemist's tools instead of any other required tool kits. Other than that, the formula does not change. Once you've chosen the potion formulas, they can't be changed.

MINDBLANK MUTAGEN FEAT 18

ALCHEMIST

With a minor adjustment of ratios in the formula for your serene mutagen, you gain mental protections. When you're affected by a serene mutagen you created, detection, revelation, and scrying effects of 9th level or lower detect nothing from you or your possessions and auras. For instance, *detect magic* would still detect other magic in the area, but not any magic on you.

MIRACLE WORKER FEAT 18

ALCHEMIST

Frequency once every 10 minutes

Your alchemical mastery can resuscitate the recently slain. You can administer a true elixir of life to a creature who has been dead for no more than 2 rounds. When you do, that creature is immediately returned to life with 1 Hit Point and becomes wounded 1.

SAMPLE FORMULA BOOK

You can choose any 1st-level common alchemical items for your formula book, but the list below contains a good selection of starter formulas. A beginner's book with these formulas called *The Fundamentals of Alchemy* has become popular among mainstream alchemists by staying away from controversial topics like mutagens, though it has drawn criticism from fringe alchemists for guiding fledgling alchemists away from more innovative experiments.

Alchemical Item Formulas: Lesser acid flask, lesser alchemist's fire, lesser antidote, lesser antiplague, lesser cheetah's elixir, lesser elixir of life, lesser tanglefoot bag, lesser smokestick.

PERFECT DEBILITATION FEAT 18

ALCHEMIST

You have perfected the formulas for bombs that impede your enemies. When you use Debilitating Bomb, your target avoids the condition the bomb imposes only if it critically succeeds at its saving throw.

20TH LEVEL

CRAFT PHILOSOPHER'S STONE FEAT 20

ALCHEMIST

Your research has paid off, culminating in the legendary philosopher's stone. You learn the formula for the philosopher's stone (page 554) and can add it to your formula book.

MEGA BOMB ❖ FEAT 20

ADDITIVE 3 ALCHEMIST

Prerequisites Expanded Splash

Requirements You are holding an infused alchemical bomb you crafted, with a level at least 3 lower than your advanced alchemy level.

You add an incredibly powerful additive to a held bomb to create a mega bomb, greatly increasing its area and power. You use an Interact action to throw the mega bomb, rather than Strike, and you don't make an attack roll. The mega bomb affects creatures in a 30-foot-radius burst, centered within 60 feet of you. The bomb deals damage as if each creature were the primary target, with a basic Reflex save. On a failed save, a creature also takes any extra effects that affect a primary target (such as flat-footed from bottled lightning). While all targets in the area take splash damage as primary targets, there is no further splash beyond that area. If your next action after creating a mega bomb isn't an Interact action to throw it, the mega bomb denatures and loses all effects.

PERFECT MUTAGEN FEAT 20

ALCHEMIST

You have enhanced the formulas for your mutagens, aligning them perfectly to your physiology. When under the effect of a mutagen you crafted, you do not suffer its drawback.

INTRODUCTION

ANCESTRIES &
BACKGROUNDS

CLASSES

SKILLS

FEATS

EQUIPMENT

SPELLS

THE AGE OF
LOST OMENS

PLAYING THE
GAME

GAME
MASTERING

CRAFTING
& TREASURE

APPENDIX

BARBARIAN

Rage consumes you in battle. You delight in wreaking havoc and using powerful weapons to carve through your enemies, relying on astonishing durability without needing complicated techniques or rigid training. Your rages draw upon a vicious instinct, which you might associate with an animal, a spirit, or some part of yourself. To many barbarians, brute force is a hammer and every problem looks like a nail, whereas others try to hold back the storm of emotions inside them and release their rage only when it matters most.

KEY ABILITY

STRENGTH
At 1st level, your class gives you an ability boost to Strength.

HIT POINTS

12 plus your Constitution Modifier
You increase your maximum number of HP by this number at 1st level and every level thereafter.

INITIAL PROFICIENCIES
At 1st level, you gain the listed proficiency ranks in the following statistics. You are untrained in anything not listed unless you gain a better proficiency rank in some other way.

PERCEPTION
Expert in Perception

SAVING THROWS
Expert in Fortitude
Trained in Reflex
Expert in Will

SKILLS
Trained in Athletics
Trained in a number of
    additional skills equal to 3 plus
    your Intelligence modifier

ATTACKS
Trained in simple weapons
Trained in martial weapons
Trained in unarmed attacks

DEFENSES
Trained in light armor
Trained in medium armor
Trained in unarmored defense

CLASS DC
Trained in barbarian class DC

DURING COMBAT ENCOUNTERS...

You summon your rage and rush to the front lines to smash your way through. Offense is your best defense—you'll need to drop foes before they can exploit your relatively low defenses.

DURING SOCIAL ENCOUNTERS...

You use intimidation to get what you need, especially when gentler persuasion can't get the job done.

WHILE EXPLORING...

You look out for danger, ready to rush headfirst into battle in an instant. You climb the challenging rock wall and drop a rope for others to follow, and you wade into the risky currents to reach the hidden switch beneath the water's surface. If something needs breaking, you're up to the task!

IN DOWNTIME...

You might head to a tavern to carouse, build up the fearsome legend of your mighty deeds, or recruit followers to become a warlord in your own right.

YOU MIGHT...

- Have a deep-seated well of anger, hatred, or frustration.
- Prefer a straightforward approach to one requiring patience and tedium.
- Engage in a regimen of intense physical fitness—and punch anyone who says this conflicts with your distaste for patience and tedium.

OTHERS PROBABLY...

- Rely on your courage and your strength, and trust that you can hold your own in a fight.
- See you as uncivilized or a boorish lout unfit for high society.
- Believe that you are loyal to your friends and allies and will never relent until the fight is done.

TABLE 3-2: BARBARIAN ADVANCEMENT

Your Level	Class Features
1	Ancestry and background, initial proficiencies, rage, instinct, barbarian feat
2	Barbarian feat, skill feat
3	Deny advantage, general feat, skill increase
4	Barbarian feat, skill feat
5	Ability boosts, ancestry feat, brutality, skill increase
6	Barbarian feat, skill feat
7	General feat, juggernaut, skill increase, weapon specialization
8	Barbarian feat, skill feat
9	Ancestry feat, lightning reflexes, raging resistance, skill increase
10	Ability boosts, barbarian feat, skill feat
11	General feat, mighty rage, skill increase
12	Barbarian feat, skill feat
13	Ancestry feat, greater juggernaut, medium armor expertise, skill increase, weapon fury
14	Barbarian feat, skill feat
15	Ability boosts, general feat, greater weapon specialization, indomitable will, skill increase
16	Barbarian feat, skill feat
17	Ancestry feat, heightened senses, skill increase, quick rage
18	Barbarian feat, skill feat
19	Armor of fury, devastator, general feat, skill increase
20	Ability boosts, barbarian feat, skill feat

CLASS FEATURES

You gain these abilities as a barbarian. Abilities gained at higher levels list the requisite levels next to their names.

ANCESTRY AND BACKGROUND

In addition to the abilities provided by your class at 1st level, you have the benefits of your selected ancestry and background, as described in Chapter 2.

INITIAL PROFICIENCIES

At 1st level you gain a number of proficiencies that represent your basic training. These proficiencies are noted in at the start of this class.

RAGE

You gain the Rage action, which lets you fly into a frenzy.

RAGE ◆

BARBARIAN	CONCENTRATE	EMOTION	MENTAL

Requirements You aren't fatigued or raging.

You tap into your inner fury and begin raging. You gain a number of temporary Hit Points equal to your level plus your Constitution modifier. This frenzy lasts for 1 minute, until there are no enemies you can perceive, or until you fall unconscious, whichever comes first. You can't voluntarily stop raging. While you are raging:

- You deal 2 additional damage with melee weapons and unarmed attacks. This additional damage is halved if your weapon or unarmed attack is agile.
- You take a –1 penalty to AC.
- You can't use actions with the concentrate trait unless they also have the rage trait. You can Seek while raging.

After you stop raging, you lose any remaining temporary Hit Points from Rage, and you can't Rage again for 1 minute.

INSTINCT

Your rage wells up from a dominant instinct—one you learned from a tradition or that comes naturally to you. Your instinct gives you an ability, requires you to avoid certain behaviors, grants you increased damage and resistances at higher levels, and allows you to select feats tied to your instinct. For more information, see Instincts on page 86.

BARBARIAN FEATS

At 1st level and every even-numbered level thereafter, you gain a barbarian class feat. Barbarian class feats are described beginning on page 88.

SKILL FEATS   2ND

At 2nd level and every 2 levels thereafter, you gain a skill feat. Skill feats appear in Chapter 5 and have the skill trait. You must be trained or better in the corresponding skill to select a skill feat.

DENY ADVANTAGE   3RD

Your foes struggle to pass your defenses. You aren't flat-footed to hidden, undetected, or flanking creatures of your level or lower, or creatures of your level or lower using surprise attack. However, they can still help their allies flank.

GENERAL FEATS   3RD

At 3rd level and every 4 levels thereafter, you gain a general feat. General feats are listed in Chapter 5.

SKILL INCREASES   3RD

At 3rd level and every 2 levels thereafter, you gain a skill increase. You can use this increase either to increase your proficiency rank to trained in one skill you're untrained in, or to increase your proficiency rank in one skill in which you're already trained to expert.

At 7th level, you can use skill increases to increase your proficiency rank to master in a skill in which you're already an expert, and at 15th level, you can use them to increase your proficiency rank to legendary in a skill in which you're already a master.

ABILITY BOOSTS   5TH

At 5th level and every 5 levels thereafter, you boost four different ability scores. You can use these ability boosts to increase your ability scores above 18. Boosting an ability score increases it by 1 if it's already 18 or above, or by 2 if it starts below 18.

ANCESTRY FEATS   5TH

In addition to the ancestry feat you started with, you gain an ancestry feat at 5th level and every 4 levels thereafter. The list of ancestry feats available to you can be found in your ancestry's entry in Chapter 2.

BRUTALITY   5TH

Your fury makes your weapons lethal. Your proficiency ranks for simple weapons, martial weapons, and unarmed attacks increase to expert. While raging, you gain access to the critical specialization effects for melee weapons and unarmed attacks.

JUGGERNAUT   7TH

Your body is accustomed to physical hardship and resistant to ailments. Your proficiency rank for Fortitude saves increases to master. When you roll a success on a Fortitude save, you get a critical success instead.

WEAPON SPECIALIZATION   7TH

Your rage helps you hit harder. You deal an additional 2 damage with weapons and unarmed attacks in which you have expert proficiency. This damage increases to 3 if you're a master, and 4 if you're legendary. You gain your instinct's specialization ability.

LIGHTNING REFLEXES   9TH

Your reflexes are lightning fast. Your proficiency rank for Reflex saves increases to expert.

RAGING RESISTANCE   9TH

Repeated exposure and toughened skin allow you to fend off harm. While raging, you gain resistance equal to 3 + your Constitution modifier to damage types based on your instinct.

MIGHTY RAGE   11TH

Your rage intensifies and lets you burst into action. Your proficiency rank for your barbarian class DC increases to expert. You gain the Mighty Rage free action.

MIGHTY RAGE ◈

BARBARIAN

Trigger You use the Rage action on your turn.

Use an action that has the rage trait. Alternatively, you can increase the actions of the triggering Rage to 2 to instead use a 2-action activity with the rage trait.

GREATER JUGGERNAUT   13TH

You have a stalwart physiology. Your proficiency rank for Fortitude saves increases to legendary. When you roll a critical failure on a Fortitude save, you get a failure instead. When you fail a Fortitude save against an effect that deals damage, you halve the damage you take.

MEDIUM ARMOR EXPERTISE   13TH

You've learned to defend yourself better against attacks. Your proficiency ranks for light armor, medium armor, and unarmored defense increase to expert.

WEAPON FURY   13TH

Your rage makes you even more effective with the weapons you wield. Your proficiency ranks for simple weapons, martial weapons, and unarmed attacks increase to master.

GREATER WEAPON SPECIALIZATION 15TH

The weapons you've mastered become truly fearsome in your hands. Your damage from weapon specialization increases to 4 with weapons and unarmed attacks in which you're an expert, 6 if you're a master, and 8 if you're legendary. You gain a greater benefit from your instinct's specialization ability.

INDOMITABLE WILL 15TH

Your rage makes it difficult to control you. Your proficiency rank for Will saves increases to master. When you roll a success on a Will save, you get a critical success instead.

HEIGHTENED SENSES 17TH

Your instinct heightens each of your senses further. Your proficiency rank for Perception increases to master.

QUICK RAGE 17TH

You recover from your Rage quickly, and are soon ready to begin anew. After you spend a full turn without raging, you can Rage again without needing to wait 1 minute.

ARMOR OF FURY 19TH

Your training and rage deepen your connection to your armor. Your proficiency ranks for light armor, medium armor, and unarmored defense increase to master.

DEVASTATOR 19TH

Your Strikes are so devastating that you hardly care about resistance, and your barbarian abilities are unparalleled. Your proficiency rank for your barbarian class DC increases to master. Your melee Strikes ignore 10 points of a creature's resistance to their physical damage.

INSTINCTS

You channel your rage through an instinct. You decide what your instinct means to you. It could be a creature or symbol beloved by your clan, or a purely internal source or filter of your rage, such as a belief, curse, heritage, or state of mind. Each instinct grants an instinct ability, plus more abilities you can gain via instinct feats. It also determines what damage you resist with raging resistance and, at higher levels, increases the additional damage you deal when you Rage.

Each instinct lists acts that are anathema to it. Whenever you perform such acts, you lose the instinct's abilities and any instinct feats until you spend 1 day of downtime re-centering yourself, though you keep all of your other barbarian abilities.

ANIMAL INSTINCT

The fury of a wild predator fills you when you Rage, granting you ferocious unarmed attacks. Cultures that revere vicious animals (such as apes or bears) give rise to barbarians with this instinct. You might also be at war with an uncontrollable, animalistic side of your personality, or you might be a descendant of a werewolf or another werecreature. Select an animal from Table 3–3: Animal Instincts that best matches your chosen animal.

TABLE 3-3: ANIMAL INSTINCTS

Animal	Attack	Damage	Traits
Ape	Fist	1d10 B	Grapple, unarmed
Bear	Jaws	1d10 P	Unarmed
	Claw	1d6 S	Agile, unarmed
Bull	Horn	1d10 P	Shove, unarmed
Cat	Jaws	1d10 P	Unarmed
	Claw	1d6 S	Agile, unarmed
Deer	Antler	1d8 P	Charge, unarmed
Frog	Jaws	1d10 B	Unarmed
	Tongue	1d4 B	Agile, unarmed
Shark	Jaws	1d10 P	Grapple, unarmed
Snake	Fangs	1d10 P	Grapple, unarmed
Wolf	Jaws	1d10 P	Trip, unarmed

ANATHEMA

Flagrantly disrespecting an animal of your chosen kind is anathema to your instinct, as is using weapons while raging.

BESTIAL RAGE [INSTINCT ABILITY]

When you Rage, you gain your chosen animal's unarmed attack (or attacks). The specific attack gained, the damage it deals, and its traits are listed on Table 3–3: Animal Instincts. These attacks are in the brawling group. Your Rage action gains the morph, primal, and transmutation traits.

SPECIALIZATION ABILITY

Increase the damage die size for the unarmed attacks granted by your chosen animal by one step, and increase the additional damage from Rage from 2 to 5 for your chosen animal's unarmed attacks. The frog's tongue attack and deer's antler attack gain reach 10 feet. If you have greater weapon specialization, increase the damage from Rage from 5 to 12 for your chosen animal's unarmed attacks.

RAGING RESISTANCE

You resist piercing and slashing damage.

DRAGON INSTINCT

You summon the fury of a mighty dragon and manifest incredible abilities. Perhaps your culture reveres draconic majesty, or you gained your connection by drinking or bathing in dragon's blood or after watching a marauding wyrm burn your village. Select a type of dragon from Table 3–4: Dragon Instincts to be your instinct's dragon type. Chromatic dragons tend to be evil, and metallic dragons tend to be good.

TABLE 3-4: DRAGON INSTINCTS

Dragon	Type	Breath Weapon
Black	Chromatic	Line of acid

INTRODUCTION

ANCESTRIES &
BACKGROUNDS

CLASSES

SKILLS

FEATS

EQUIPMENT

SPELLS

THE AGE OF
LOST OMENS

PLAYING THE
GAME

GAME
MASTERING

CRAFTING
& TREASURE

APPENDIX

Blue	Chromatic	Line of electricity
Green	Chromatic	Cone of poison
Red	Chromatic	Cone of fire
White	Chromatic	Cone of cold
Brass	Metallic	Line of fire
Bronze	Metallic	Line of electricity
Copper	Metallic	Line of acid
Gold	Metallic	Cone of fire
Silver	Metallic	Cone of cold

ANATHEMA

Letting a personal insult against you slide is anathema to your instinct. Choose whether your character respects or abhors your dragon type. If you respect it, defying such a dragon is anathema, and if you abhor it, failing to defeat such a dragon you come across is anathema.

DRACONIC RAGE [INSTINCT ABILITY]

While raging, you can increase the additional damage from Rage from 2 to 4 and change its damage type to match that of your dragon's breath weapon instead of the damage type for your weapon or unarmed attack. If you do this, your Rage action gains the arcane and evocation traits, as well as the trait matching the damage type.

SPECIALIZATION ABILITY

When you use draconic rage, you increase the additional damage from Rage from 4 to 8. If you have greater weapon specialization, instead increase the damage from Rage when using draconic rage from 8 to 16.

RAGING RESISTANCE

You resist piercing damage and the damage type of your dragon's breath weapon.

FURY INSTINCT

Your rage comes from a deep and purely personal well within you. You use your rage as you choose.

ANATHEMA AND INSTINCT ABILITY

You don't have an anathema or an instinct ability. Instead, you gain an additional 1st-level barbarian feat.

SPECIALIZATION ABILITY

Increase the additional damage from Rage from 2 to 6. If you have greater weapon specialization, instead increase the additional damage from Rage to 12.

RAGING RESISTANCE

You resist physical weapon damage, but not physical damage from other sources (such as unarmed attacks).

GIANT INSTINCT

Your rage gives you the raw power and size of a giant. This doesn't necessarily mean you revere giants—you might scoff at them or even aspire to slay them! You could instead

---

seem like a giant to other people due to your exceptional strength or larger-than-life emotions and ego.

ANATHEMA

Failing to face a personal challenge of strength is anathema.

TITAN MAULER [INSTINCT ABILITY]

You can use a weapon built for a Large creature if you are Small or Medium (both normally and when raging). If you're not Small or Medium, you can use a weapon built for a creature one size larger than you. You gain access to one weapon one size larger than you, of any weapon type otherwise available at character creation. It has the normal Price and Bulk for a weapon of its size (page 295). When wielding such a weapon in combat, increase your additional damage from Rage from 2 to 6, but you have the clumsy 1 condition (page 618) because of the weapon's unwieldy size. You can't remove this clumsy condition or ignore its penalties by any means while wielding the weapon.

SPECIALIZATION ABILITY

Increase the damage from Rage when using a larger weapon from 6 to 10; if you have greater weapon specialization, increase it from 10 to 18.

RAGING RESISTANCE

You resist bludgeoning damage and your choice of cold, electricity, or fire, chosen when you gain raging resistance.

SPIRIT INSTINCT

Whether you are emotionally sensitive to the spirits around you; worship ancestors or apparitions; or are haunted by the specter of an ancestor, relative, friend, or foe, your rage takes the form of a spiritual possession.

ANATHEMA

Disrespecting corpses or spirits is anathema to your instinct; defending yourself against undead creatures is not.

SPIRIT RAGE [INSTINCT ABILITY]

When you are raging, you can increase your damage from Rage from 2 to 3 and deal negative or positive damage,

BARBARIAN FEATS

If you need to look up a barbarian feat by name instead of by level, use this table.

Feat	Level
Acute Scent	2
Acute Vision	1
Animal Rage	8
Animal Skin	6
Attack of Opportunity	6
Awesome Blow	14
Brutal Bully	6
Brutal Critical	18
Cleave	6
Collateral Thrash	16
Come and Get Me	10
Contagious Rage	20
Dragon's Rage Breath	6
Dragon's Rage Wings	12
Dragon Transformation	16
Fast Movement	4
Furious Bully	8
Furious Finish	2
Furious Grab	12
Furious Sprint	10
Giant's Lunge	14
Giant's Stature	6
Great Cleave	10
Knockback	10
Moment of Clarity	1
No Escape	2
Perfect Clarity	18
Predator's Pounce	12
Quaking Stomp	20
Raging Athlete	4
Raging Intimidation	1
Raging Thrower	1
Reckless Abandon	16
Renewed Vigor	8
Second Wind	2
Shake It Off	2
Share Rage	8
Spirits' Interference	6
Spirit's Wrath	12
Sudden Charge	1
Sudden Leap	8
Swipe	4
Terrifying Howl	10
Thrash	8
Titan's Stature	12
Vengeful Strike	14
Vicious Evisceration	18
Whirlwind Strike	14
Wounded Rage	4

instead of the normal damage type for your weapon or unarmed attack (choose each time you Rage). If you choose to deal negative or positive damage, your weapon or unarmed attack gains the effects of the *ghost touch* property rune, which makes it more effective against incorporeal creatures, and your Rage action gains the divine and necromancy traits, plus negative or positive, as appropriate.

SPECIALIZATION ABILITY

When using spirit rage, increase the damage from Rage from 3 to 7. If you have greater weapon specialization, instead increase the damage when using spirit rage to 13.

RAGING RESISTANCE

You resist negative damage, as well as damage dealt by the attacks and abilities of undead creatures, regardless of the damage type.

BARBARIAN FEATS

At every level that you gain a barbarian feat, you can select one of the following feats. You must satisfy any prerequisites before selecting the feat.

1ST LEVEL

ACUTE VISION   FEAT 1
`BARBARIAN`
When you are raging, your visual senses improve, granting you darkvision.

MOMENT OF CLARITY ❖   FEAT 1
`BARBARIAN` `CONCENTRATE` `RAGE`
You push back your rage for a moment in order to think clearly. Until the end of this turn, you can use actions with the concentrate trait even if those actions don't have the rage trait.

RAGING INTIMIDATION   FEAT 1
`BARBARIAN`
Your fury fills your foes with fear. While you are raging, your Demoralize and Scare to Death actions (from the Intimidation skill and an Intimidation skill feat, respectively) gain the rage trait, allowing you to use them while raging. As soon as you meet the prerequisites for the skill feats Intimidating Glare and Scare to Death, you gain these feats.

RAGING THROWER   FEAT 1
`BARBARIAN`
Thrown weapons become especially deadly in your fury. You apply the additional damage from Rage to your thrown weapon attacks. If you have the Brutal Critical feat or the devastator class feature, apply their benefits to thrown weapon attacks.

SUDDEN CHARGE ❖❖   FEAT 1
`BARBARIAN` `FLOURISH` `OPEN`
With a quick sprint, you dash up to your foe and swing. Stride twice. If you end your movement within melee reach of at least one enemy, you can make a melee Strike against that enemy. You can use Sudden Charge while Burrowing, Climbing, Flying, or Swimming instead of Striding if you have the corresponding movement type.

2ND LEVEL

ACUTE SCENT   FEAT 2
`BARBARIAN`
Prerequisites Acute Vision or darkvision
When you Rage, your sense of smell improves. You gain imprecise scent with a range of 30 feet.

CLASSES

3

INTRODUCTION

ANCESTRIES &
BACKGROUNDS

CLASSES

SKILLS

FEATS

EQUIPMENT

SPELLS

THE AGE OF
LOST OMENS

PLAYING THE
GAME

GAME
MASTERING

CRAFTING
& TREASURE

APPENDIX

FURIOUS FINISH ❖   FEAT 2

BARBARIAN   RAGE

Desperate to finish the fight, you pour all your rage into one final blow. Make a Strike. If it hits, you gain a circumstance bonus to damage equal to the number of rounds remaining in your Rage (maximum 10). After this Strike, your Rage immediately ends, and you are fatigued until you rest for at least 10 minutes.

NO ESCAPE ⟳   FEAT 2

BARBARIAN   RAGE

Trigger A foe within reach attempts to move away from you.

You keep pace with a retreating foe. Stride up to your Speed, following the foe and keeping it in reach throughout its movement until it stops moving or you've moved your full Speed. You can use No Escape to Burrow, Climb, Fly, or Swim instead of Stride if you have the corresponding movement type.

SECOND WIND   FEAT 2

BARBARIAN

You can enter a second rage, but afterward you need to catch your breath. You can Rage without waiting for 1 minute after the previous Rage (or 1 round, with quick rage), but when you end this second Rage, you're fatigued until you rest for 10 minutes.

SHAKE IT OFF ❖   FEAT 2

BARBARIAN   CONCENTRATE   RAGE

You concentrate on your rage, overcoming fear and fighting back sickness. Reduce your frightened condition value by 1, and attempt a Fortitude save to recover from the sickened condition as if you had spent an action retching; you reduce your sickened condition value by 1 on a failure (but not on a critical failure), by 2 on a success, or by 3 on a critical success.

4TH LEVEL

FAST MOVEMENT   FEAT 4

BARBARIAN

Your rage is a frenzy of rapid movements. While you are raging, you gain a +10-foot status bonus to your Speed.

RAGING ATHLETE   FEAT 4

BARBARIAN

Prerequisites expert in Athletics

Physical obstacles can't hold back your fury. While you are raging, you gain a climb Speed and swim Speed equal to your land Speed, the DC of High Jumps and Long Jumps decreases by 10, and your Leap distance increases by 5 feet when you jump horizontally and by 2 feet when you jump vertically.

SWIPE ❖❖   FEAT 4

BARBARIAN   FLOURISH

You make a wide, arcing swing. Make a single melee Strike and compare the attack roll result to the ACs of up to two foes, each of whom must be within your melee reach and adjacent to the other.

ANIMAL RAGER

The animal within you breaks free, turning you into a feral creature of nature when you rage. You follow your instincts rather than reason, and you find yourself at home in the wilderness.

ABILITY SCORES
Increase your Strength as high as you can, followed by your Constitution and Dexterity. A high Wisdom can improve your senses.

SKILLS
Athletics, Intimidation, Nature, Survival

INSTINCT
Animal instinct

STARTING FEAT
Raging Intimidation

HIGHER-LEVEL FEATS
No Escape (2nd), Animal Skin (6th), Animal Rage (8th), Terrifying Howl (10th), Predator's Pounce (12th)

Roll damage only once and apply it to each creature you hit. A Swipe counts as two attacks for your multiple attack penalty.

If you're using a weapon with the sweep trait, its modifier applies to all your Swipe attacks.

WOUNDED RAGE ⤺   FEAT 4
`BARBARIAN` `RAGE`

Trigger You take damage and are capable of entering a rage.

You roar in pain, awakening the rage within you. You Rage.

6TH LEVEL

ANIMAL SKIN   FEAT 6
`BARBARIAN` `INSTINCT` `MORPH` `PRIMAL` `TRANSMUTATION`

Prerequisites animal instinct

Your proficiency in unarmored defense increases to expert. While you are raging and unarmored, your skin transforms into a thick hide resembling your animal's skin. You gain a +1 status bonus to AC instead of taking a –1 penalty to AC; if you have the greater juggernaut class feature, this status bonus increases to +2. The thickness of your hide gives you a Dexterity modifier cap to your AC of +3.

ATTACK OF OPPORTUNITY ⤺   FEAT 6
`BARBARIAN`

Trigger A creature within your reach uses a manipulate action or a move action, makes a ranged attack, or leaves a square during a move action it's using.

You swat a foe that leaves an opening. Make a melee Strike against the triggering creature. If your attack is a critical hit and the trigger was a manipulate action, you disrupt that action. This Strike doesn't count toward your multiple attack penalty, and your multiple attack penalty doesn't apply to this Strike.

BRUTAL BULLY   FEAT 6
`BARBARIAN`

Prerequisites expert in Athletics

You push your foes around and leave bruises. While raging, when you successfully Disarm, Grapple, Shove, or Trip a foe, you deal that foe bludgeoning damage equal to your Strength modifier; add this to the damage from a critical success to Trip.

CLEAVE ⤺   FEAT 6
`BARBARIAN` `RAGE`

Trigger Your melee Strike kills a creature or knocks it unconscious, and another foe is adjacent to that creature.

You swing clear through one foe and into another. Make a melee Strike against the second foe.

DRAGON'S RAGE BREATH ⬥⬥   FEAT 6
`ARCANE` `BARBARIAN` `CONCENTRATE` `EVOCATION` `INSTINCT` `RAGE`

Prerequisites dragon instinct

Requirements You haven't used this ability since you last Raged.

You breathe deeply and exhale powerful energy in a 30-foot cone or 60-foot line, dealing 1d6 damage per level. The area and damage type match those of your dragon (see Table 3–4 on page 86). If you used this ability in the last hour, the area and the damage are halved (15-foot cone or 30-foot line; 1d6 damage for every 2 levels). Each creature in the area must attempt a basic Reflex save.

GIANT'S STATURE ◆ FEAT 6

`BARBARIAN` `INSTINCT` `POLYMORPH` `PRIMAL` `RAGE` `TRANSMUTATION`

Prerequisites giant instinct

Requirements You are Medium or smaller.

You grow to incredible size. You become Large, increasing your reach by 5 feet and gaining the clumsy 1 condition (page 618) until you stop raging. Your equipment grows with you.

SPIRITS' INTERFERENCE ◆ FEAT 6

`BARBARIAN` `DIVINE` `INSTINCT` `NECROMANCY` `RAGE`

Prerequisites spirit instinct

You call forth protective spirits to ward off ranged attacks. Until your rage ends, anyone making a ranged attack against you must succeed at a DC 5 flat check or the attack misses with no effect.

8TH LEVEL

ANIMAL RAGE ◆ FEAT 8

`BARBARIAN` `CONCENTRATE` `INSTINCT` `POLYMORPH` `PRIMAL` `RAGE` `TRANSMUTATION`

Prerequisites animal instinct

You transform into your animal. You gain the effects of the 3rd-level *animal form* spell except you use your own statistics, temporary Hit Points, and unarmed attacks instead of those granted by *animal form*. You also retain the constant abilities of your gear. If your animal is a frog, your tongue's reach increases to 15 feet. Dismissing the transformation gains the rage trait.

FURIOUS BULLY FEAT 8

`BARBARIAN`

Prerequisites master in Athletics

You bully foes across the battlefield. While raging, you gain a +2 circumstance bonus to Athletics checks for attack actions.

RENEWED VIGOR ◆ FEAT 8

`BARBARIAN` `CONCENTRATE` `RAGE`

You pause to recover your raging vigor. You gain temporary Hit Points equal to half your level plus your Constitution modifier.

SHARE RAGE ◆ FEAT 8

`AUDITORY` `BARBARIAN` `RAGE` `VISUAL`

Requirements You haven't used this ability since you last Raged.

You stoke an ally's fury. While you are raging, one willing creature within 30 feet gains the effects of the Rage action, except it can still use concentrate actions.

SUDDEN LEAP FEAT 8

`BARBARIAN`

You swing at a foe while mid-leap. Make a Leap, High Jump, or Long Jump and attempt one melee Strike at any point during your jump. Immediately after the Strike, you fall to the ground if you're in the air, even if you haven't reached the maximum distance of

your jump. If the distance you fall is no more than the height of your jump, you take no damage and land upright.

When attempting a High Jump or Long Jump during a Sudden Leap, determine the DC using the Long Jump DCs, and increase your maximum distance to double your Speed.

THRASH ◆ FEAT 8

`BARBARIAN` `RAGE`

Requirements You have a foe grabbed.

You thrash the grabbed foe around. It takes bludgeoning damage equal to your Strength modifier plus your ferocious specialization damage plus your Rage damage. The foe must attempt a basic Fortitude save against your class DC.

10TH LEVEL

COME AND GET ME ◆ FEAT 10

`BARBARIAN` `CONCENTRATE` `RAGE`

You open yourself to attacks so you can respond in turn. Until your rage ends, you are flat-footed, and damage rolls against you gain a +2 circumstance bonus. If a creature hits you, that creature is flat-footed to you until the end of your next turn. If you hit it before the end of your next turn, you gain temporary Hit Points equal to your Constitution modifier, or double that on a critical hit. These temporary Hit Points last until the end of your rage.

FURIOUS SPRINT ◆◆ FEAT 10

`BARBARIAN` `RAGE`

You rush forward. Stride up to five times your Speed in a straight line. You can increase the number of actions this activity takes to 3 to Stride up to eight times your Speed in a straight line instead.

GREAT CLEAVE FEAT 10

`BARBARIAN` `RAGE`

Prerequisites Cleave

Your fury carries your weapon through multiple foes. When you Cleave, if your Strike also kills or knocks the target unconscious, you can continue to make melee Strikes until you make a Strike that doesn't kill or knock a creature unconscious, or until there are no creatures adjacent to the most recent creature you attacked while Cleaving, whichever comes first.

KNOCKBACK ◆ FEAT 10

`BARBARIAN` `RAGE`

Requirements Your last action was a successful Strike.

The weight of your swing drives your enemy back. You push the foe back 5 feet, with the effects of a successful Shove. You can follow the foe as normal for a successful Shove.

TERRIFYING HOWL ◆ FEAT 10

`AUDITORY` `BARBARIAN` `RAGE`

Prerequisites Intimidating Glare

You unleash a terrifying howl. Attempt Intimidate checks to Demoralize each creature within 30 feet. Regardless of the results of your checks, each creature is then temporarily immune to Terrifying Howl for 1 minute.

INTRODUCTION

ANCESTRIES & BACKGROUNDS

CLASSES

SKILLS

FEATS

EQUIPMENT

SPELLS

THE AGE OF LOST OMENS

PLAYING THE GAME

GAME MASTERING

CRAFTING & TREASURE

APPENDIX

SAMPLE BARBARIAN

FURY

You keep things simple, because you need only one thing to drive you: your own inner rage.

ABILITY SCORES

Prioritize your Strength, then your Constitution and Dexterity. Wisdom can make you more perceptive.

SKILLS

Acrobatics, Athletics, Intimidation, Stealth

INSTINCT

Fury instinct

STARTING FEAT

Sudden Charge

HIGHER-LEVEL FEATS

Furious Finish (2nd), Fast Movement (4th), Attack of Opportunity (6th), Whirlwind Strike (14th)

12TH LEVEL

DRAGON'S RAGE WINGS ❖   FEAT 12

BARBARIAN | INSTINCT | MORPH | PRIMAL | RAGE | TRANSMUTATION

Prerequisites dragon instinct

You sprout dragon wings from your back of the same color as your chosen dragon. While you are raging, you gain a fly Speed equal to your land Speed. If you are flying when your rage ends, you start to fall but the transformation only completes at the last moment, so you take no damage from the fall and land standing up.

FURIOUS GRAB ❖   FEAT 12

BARBARIAN | RAGE

Requirements Your last action was a successful Strike, and either you have a hand free or your Strike used a grapple weapon.

You grab your foe while it's distracted by your attack. The foe you hit becomes grabbed, as if you had succeeded at an Athletics check to Grapple the foe.

PREDATOR'S POUNCE ❖   FEAT 12

BARBARIAN | FLOURISH | INSTINCT | OPEN | RAGE

Prerequisites animal instinct

Requirements You are unarmored or wearing light armor.

You close the distance to your prey in a blur, pouncing on the creature before it can react. You Stride up to your Speed and make a Strike at the end of your movement.

SPIRIT'S WRATH ❖   FEAT 12

ATTACK | BARBARIAN | CONCENTRATE | INSTINCT | RAGE

Prerequisites spirit instinct

You call forth an ephemeral apparition, typically the ghost of an ancestor or a nature spirit, which takes the form of a wisp. The spirit wisp makes a melee wisp rush unarmed attack against an enemy within 120 feet of you. The wisp's attack modifier is equal to your proficiency bonus for martial weapons plus your Strength modifier plus a +2 item bonus, and it applies the same circumstance and status bonuses and penalties that you have. On a hit, the wisp deals damage equal to 4d8 plus your Constitution modifier. The damage is your choice of negative or positive damage; don't apply your Rage damage or your weapon specialization damage, but circumstance and status bonuses and penalties that would also affect the wisp's damage apply. If your wisp's Strike is a critical hit, the target becomes frightened 1. This attack uses and counts toward your multiple attack penalty as if you were the one attacking.

TITAN'S STATURE   FEAT 12

BARBARIAN | INSTINCT | POLYMORPH | TRANSMUTATION

Prerequisites giant instinct, Giant's Stature

You grow to even greater size. When using Giant's Stature, you can instead become Huge (increasing your reach by 10 feet if you were Medium or smaller) while you are raging. You have the clumsy 1 condition (page 618) as long as you are Huge.

CLASSES

3

INTRODUCTION

ANCESTRIES &
BACKGROUNDS

CLASSES

SKILLS

FEATS

EQUIPMENT

SPELLS

THE AGE OF
LOST OMENS

PLAYING THE
GAME

GAME
MASTERING

CRAFTING
& TREASURE

APPENDIX

14TH LEVEL

AWESOME BLOW   FEAT 14

BARBARIAN | **CONCENTRATE** | **RAGE**

Prerequisites Knockback

Your attacks are so powerful, they can flatten your opponents. When you use Knockback, you can attempt an Athletics check against your target's Fortitude DC.

Critical Success You gain the critical success effect of a Shove, then the critical success effect of a Trip against the target.

Success You gain the success effect of a Shove, then the success effect of a Trip against the target.

Failure You gain the normal effect of Knockback.

GIANT'S LUNGE ◆   FEAT 14

BARBARIAN | **CONCENTRATE** | **INSTINCT** | **RAGE**

Prerequisites giant instinct

You extend your body and prepare to attack foes outside your normal reach. Until your rage ends, all your melee weapons and unarmed attacks gain reach 10. This doesn't increase the reach of any weapon or unarmed attack that already has the reach trait, but it does combine with abilities that increase your reach due to increased size, such as Giant's Stature.

VENGEFUL STRIKE ↺   FEAT 14

BARBARIAN | **RAGE**

Prerequisites Come and Get Me

Trigger A creature within your reach succeeds or critically succeeds at an attack against you.

Requirements You're under the effect of Come and Get Me.

When struck by an enemy, you respond in turn. Make a melee Strike against the triggering creature. This Strike doesn't count toward your multiple attack penalty, and your multiple attack penalty doesn't apply to this Strike.

WHIRLWIND STRIKE ◆◆◆   FEAT 14

BARBARIAN | **FLOURISH** | **OPEN**

You attack all nearby adversaries. Make a melee Strike against each enemy within your melee reach. Each attack counts toward your multiple attack penalty, but do not increase your penalty until you have made all your attacks.

16TH LEVEL

COLLATERAL THRASH   FEAT 16

BARBARIAN | **RAGE**

Prerequisites Thrash

When you Thrash a grabbed foe, you smack that foe into another nearby. Another foe adjacent to the grabbed foe also takes your Thrash damage, with a basic Reflex save against your class DC.

DRAGON TRANSFORMATION ◆   FEAT 16

BARBARIAN | **CONCENTRATE** | **INSTINCT** | **POLYMORPH** | **PRIMAL** | **RAGE** | **TRANSMUTATION**

Prerequisites dragon instinct, Dragon's Rage Wings

You transform into a ferocious Large dragon, gaining the effects of 6th-level *dragon form* except that you use your own AC and

attack modifier; you also apply your extra damage from Rage. The action to Dismiss the transformation gains the rage trait.

At 18th level, you gain a +20-foot status bonus to your fly Speed, your damage bonus with dragon Strikes increases to +12, your breath weapon DC increases to 30, and you gain a +14 status bonus to your breath weapon damage.

RECKLESS ABANDON ◇   FEAT 16

BARBARIAN | **RAGE**

Trigger Your turn begins, and you are at half or fewer Hit Points.

Your blood boils when you take a beating, and you throw caution to the wind to finish the fight. You gain a +2 circumstance bonus to attack rolls, a –2 penalty to AC, and a –1 penalty to saves. These bonuses and penalties last until your Rage ends or until you are above half Hit Points, whichever comes first.

18TH LEVEL

BRUTAL CRITICAL   FEAT 18

BARBARIAN

Your critical hits are particularly devastating. On a critical hit, add one extra damage die. This is in addition to any extra dice you gain if the weapon is deadly or fatal. The target also takes persistent bleed damage equal to two damage dice.

PERFECT CLARITY ↺   FEAT 18

BARBARIAN | **CONCENTRATE** | **FORTUNE** | **RAGE**

Trigger You fail or critically fail an attack roll or Will save.

You burn out all of your rage to ensure that your attack lands and your mind remains free. Reroll the triggering attack roll or Will save with a +2 circumstance bonus, use the better result, and resolve the effect. You then immediately stop raging.

VICIOUS EVISCERATION ◆◆   FEAT 18

BARBARIAN | **RAGE**

You make a vicious attack that maims your enemy. Make a melee Strike. If the Strike hits and deals damage, the target is drained 1, or drained 2 on a critical success.

20TH LEVEL

CONTAGIOUS RAGE   FEAT 20

AUDITORY | **BARBARIAN** | **RAGE** | **VISUAL**

Prerequisites Share Rage

You can drive your allies into a frenzy, granting them incredible benefits. You can ignore the requirements on Share Rage, using it multiple times in a Rage. Allies affected by Share Rage who accept your anathema for the duration of the Rage gain your instinct ability and the specialization ability it gains from weapon specialization, but not greater weapon specialization.

QUAKING STOMP ◆   FEAT 20

BARBARIAN | **MANIPULATE** | **RAGE**

Frequency once per 10 minutes

You stomp the ground with such force that it creates a minor earthquake, with the effects of the *earthquake* spell.

INTRODUCTION

ANCESTRIES &
BACKGROUNDS

CLASSES

SKILLS

FEATS

EQUIPMENT

SPELLS

THE AGE OF
LOST OMENS

PLAYING THE
GAME

GAME
MASTERING

CRAFTING
& TREASURE

APPENDIX

BARD

You are a master of artistry, a scholar of hidden secrets, and a captivating persuader. Using powerful performances, you influence minds and elevate souls to new levels of heroics. You might use your powers to become a charismatic leader, or perhaps you might instead be a counselor, manipulator, scholar, scoundrel, or virtuoso. While your versatility leads some to consider you a beguiling ne'er-do-well and a jack-of-all-trades, it's dangerous to dismiss you as a master of none.

KEY ABILITY

CHARISMA
At 1st level, your class gives you an ability boost to Charisma.

HIT POINTS

8 plus your Constitution modifier
You increase your maximum number of HP by this number at 1st level and every level thereafter.

DURING COMBAT ENCOUNTERS...
You use magical performances to alter the odds in favor of your allies. You confidently alternate between attacks, healing, and helpful spells as needed.

DURING SOCIAL ENCOUNTERS...
You persuade, prevaricate, and threaten with ease.

WHILE EXPLORING...
You're a font of knowledge, folktales, legends, and lore that provide a deeper context and helpful reconnaissance for the group's adventure. Your spells and performances inspire your allies to greater discovery and success.

IN DOWNTIME...
You can earn money and prestige with your performances, gaining a name for yourself and acquiring patrons. Eventually, tales of your talents and triumphs might attract other bards to study your techniques in a bardic college.

YOU MIGHT...
- Have a passion for your art so strong that you forge a spiritual connection with it.
- Take point when tact and nonviolent solutions are required.
- Follow your muse, whether it's a mysterious fey creature, a philosophical concept, a psychic force, or a deity of art or music, and with its aid learn secret lore that few others have.

OTHERS PROBABLY...
- Relish the opportunity to invite you to social events, either as a performer or a guest, but consider you to be something of a curiosity in their social circles.
- Underestimate you compared to other spellcasters, believing you are little more than a foppish minstrel and overlooking the subtle power of your magic.
- Respond favorably to your social charm and abilities, but remain suspicious of your beguiling magic.

INITIAL PROFICIENCIES
At 1st level, you gain the listed proficiency ranks in the following statistics. You are untrained in anything not listed unless you gain a better proficiency rank in some other way.

PERCEPTION
Expert in Perception

SAVING THROWS
Trained in Fortitude
Trained in Reflex
Expert in Will

SKILLS
Trained in Occultism
Trained in Performance
Trained in a number of additional skills equal to 4 plus your Intelligence modifier

ATTACKS
Trained in simple weapons
Trained in the longsword, rapier, sap, shortbow, shortsword, and whip
Trained in unarmed attacks

DEFENSES
Trained in light armor
Trained in unarmored defense

SPELLS
Trained in occult spell attacks
Trained in occult spell DCs

TABLE 3-5: BARD ADVANCEMENT

Your Level	Class Features
1	Ancestry and background, initial proficiencies, occult spellcasting, spell repertoire, composition spells, muse
2	Bard feat, skill feat
3	2nd-level spells, general feat, lightning reflexes, signature spells, skill increase
4	Bard feat, skill feat
5	3rd-level spells, ability boosts, ancestry feat, skill increase
6	Bard feat, skill feat
7	4th-level spells, expert spellcaster, general feat, skill increase
8	Bard feat, skill feat
9	5th-level spells, ancestry feat, great fortitude, resolve, skill increase
10	Ability boots, bard feat, skill feat
11	6th-level spells, bard weapon expertise, general feat, skill increase, vigilant senses
12	Bard feat, skill feat
13	7th-level spells, ancestry feat, light armor expertise, skill increase, weapon specialization
14	Bard feat, skill feat
15	8th-level spells, ability boosts, general feat, master spellcaster, skill increase
16	Bard feat, skill feat
17	9th-level spells, ancestry feat, greater resolve, skill increase
18	Bard feat, skill feat
19	General feat, legendary spellcaster, magnum opus, skill increase
20	Ability boosts, bard feat, skill feat

CLASS FEATURES

You gain these abilities as a bard. Abilities gained at higher levels list the requisite levels next to the features' names.

ANCESTRY AND BACKGROUND

In addition to the abilities provided by your class at 1st level, you have the benefits of your selected ancestry and background, as described in Chapter 2.

INITIAL PROFICIENCIES

At 1st level you gain a number of proficiencies, representing your basic training. These are noted at the start of this class.

OCCULT SPELLCASTING

You draw upon magic from esoteric knowledge. You can cast occult spells using the Cast a Spell activity, and you can supply material, somatic, and verbal components when casting spells (see Casting Spells on page 302). Because you're a bard, you can usually play an instrument for spells requiring somatic or material components, as long

as it takes at least one of your hands to do so. If you use an instrument, you don't need a spell component pouch or another hand free. You can usually also play an instrument for spells requiring verbal components, instead of speaking.

Each day, you can cast up to two 1st-level spells. You must know spells to cast them, and you learn them via the spell repertoire class feature. The number of spells you can cast each day is called your spell slots.

As you increase in level as a bard, your number of spells per day increases, as does the highest level of spells you can cast, as shown on Table 3–6: Bard Spells per Day on page 98.

Some of your spells require you to attempt a spell attack roll to see how effective they are, or have your enemies roll against your spell DC (typically by attempting a saving throw). Since your key ability is Charisma, your spell attack rolls and spell DCs use your Charisma modifier. Details on calculating these statistics appear on page 447.

HEIGHTENING SPELLS

When you get spell slots of 2nd level and higher, you can fill those slots with stronger versions of lower-level spells. This increases the spell's level to match the spell slot. You must have a spell in your spell repertoire at the level you want to cast in order to heighten it to that level. Many spells have specific improvements when they are heightened to certain levels (page 299). The signature spells class feature lets you heighten certain spells freely.

CANTRIPS

Some of your spells are cantrips. A cantrip is a special type of spell that doesn't use spell slots. You can cast a cantrip at will, any number of times per day. A cantrip is automatically heightened to half your level rounded up, which equals the highest level of spell you can cast as a bard. For example, as a 1st-level bard, your cantrips are 1st-level spells, and as a 5th-level bard, your cantrips are 3rd-level spells.

SPELL REPERTOIRE

The collection of spells you can cast is called your spell repertoire. At 1st level, you learn two 1st-level occult spells of your choice and five occult cantrips of your choice. You choose these from the common spells from the occult list (page 311) or from other occult spells to which you have access. You can cast any spell in your spell repertoire by using a spell slot of an appropriate spell level.

You add to this spell repertoire as you increase in level. Each time you get a spell slot (see Table 3–6), you add a spell to your spell repertoire of the same level. At 2nd level, you select another 1st-level spell; at 3rd level, you select two 2nd-level spells, and so on. When you add spells, you might add a higher-level version of a spell you already have, so you can cast a heightened version of that spell.

Though you gain them at the same rate, your spell slots and the spells in your spell repertoire are separate. If a feat or other ability adds a spell to your spell repertoire, it wouldn't give you another spell slot, and vice versa.

Swapping Spells in Your Repertoire

As you gain new spells in your repertoire, you might want to replace some of the spells you previously learned. Each time you gain a level and learn new spells, you can swap out one of your old spells for a different spell of the same level. This spell can be a cantrip. You can also swap out spells by retraining during downtime (page 481).

COMPOSITION SPELLS

You can infuse your performances with magic to create unique effects called compositions. Compositions are a special type of spell that often require you to use the Performance skill when casting them. Composition spells are a type of focus spell. It costs 1 Focus Point to cast a focus spell, and you start with a focus pool of 1 Focus Point. You refill your focus pool during your daily preparations, and you can regain 1 Focus Point by spending 10 minutes using the Refocus activity to perform, write a new composition, or otherwise engage your muse.

Focus spells are automatically heightened to half your level rounded up, much like cantrips. Focus spells don't require spell slots, and you can't cast them using spell slots. Taking feats can give you more focus spells and increase the size of your focus pool, though your focus pool can never hold more than 3 Focus Points. The full rules for focus spells appear on page 300.

You learn the *counter performance* composition spell (page 386), protecting against auditory and visual effects.

Composition Cantrips

Composition cantrips are special composition spells that don't cost Focus Points, so you can use them as often as you like. Composition cantrips are in addition to the cantrips you choose from the occult list. Generally, only feats can give you more composition cantrips. Unlike other cantrips, you can't swap out composition cantrips gained from bard feats at a later level, unless you swap out the specific feat via retraining (page 481).

You learn the *inspire courage* composition cantrip (page 386), which boosts your allies' attacks, damage, and defense against fear.

MUSES

As a bard, you select one muse at 1st level. This muse leads you to great things, and might be a physical creature, a deity, a philosophy, or a captivating mystery.

Enigma

Your muse is a mystery, driving you to uncover the hidden secrets of the multiverse. If your muse is a creature, it might be a dragon or otherworldly being; if a deity, it might be Irori or Nethys. You gain the Bardic Lore feat and add *true strike* to your spell repertoire.

Maestro

Your muse is a virtuoso, inspiring you to greater heights.

If it's a creature, it might be a performance-loving creature such as a choral angel or lillend azata; if a deity, it might be Shelyn. As a bard with a maestro muse, you are an inspiration to your allies and confident of your musical and oratorical abilities. You gain the Lingering Composition feat and add *soothe* to your spell repertoire.

Polymath

Your muse is a jack of all trades, flitting between skills and pursuits. If it's is a creature, it might be an eclectic creature like a fey; if a deity, it might be Desna or Calistria. As a bard with a polymath muse, you are interested in a wide array of topics but rarely dedicated to any one, and you rarely make up your mind—you want to try everything. You gain the Versatile Performance feat and add *unseen servant* to your spell repertoire.

INTRODUCTION

ANCESTRIES & BACKGROUNDS

CLASSES

SKILLS

FEATS

EQUIPMENT

SPELLS

THE AGE OF LOST OMENS

PLAYING THE GAME

GAME MASTERING

CRAFTING & TREASURE

APPENDIX

TABLE 3-6: BARD SPELLS PER DAY

Your Level	Cantrips	Spell Level										
		1st	2nd	3rd	4th	5th	6th	7th	8th	9th	10th
1	5	2	—	—	—	—	—	—	—	—	—
2	5	3	—	—	—	—	—	—	—	—	—
3	5	3	2	—	—	—	—	—	—	—	—
4	5	3	3	—	—	—	—	—	—	—	—
5	5	3	3	2	—	—	—	—	—	—	—
6	5	3	3	3	—	—	—	—	—	—	—
7	5	3	3	3	2	—	—	—	—	—	—
8	5	3	3	3	3	—	—	—	—	—	—
9	5	3	3	3	3	2	—	—	—	—	—
10	5	3	3	3	3	3	—	—	—	—	—
11	5	3	3	3	3	3	2	—	—	—	—
12	5	3	3	3	3	3	3	—	—	—	—
13	5	3	3	3	3	3	3	2	—	—	—
14	5	3	3	3	3	3	3	3	—	—	—
15	5	3	3	3	3	3	3	3	2	—	—
16	5	3	3	3	3	3	3	3	3	—	—
17	5	3	3	3	3	3	3	3	3	2	—
18	5	3	3	3	3	3	3	3	3	3	—
19	5	3	3	3	3	3	3	3	3	3	1*
20	5	3	3	3	3	3	3	3	3	3	1*

* The magnum opus class feature gives you a 10th-level spell slot that works a bit differently from other spell slots.

BARD FEATS 2ND

At 2nd level and every 2 levels thereafter, you gain a bard class feat (page 99).

SKILL FEATS 2ND

At 2nd level and every 2 levels thereafter, you gain a skill feat. Skill feats can be found in Chapter 5 and have the skill trait. You must be trained or better in the corresponding skill to select a skill feat.

GENERAL FEATS 3RD

At 3rd level and every 4 levels thereafter, you gain a general feat. General feats are listed in Chapter 5.

LIGHTNING REFLEXES 3RD

Your reflexes are lightning fast. Your proficiency rank in Reflex saves increases to expert.

SIGNATURE SPELLS 3RD

Experience allows you to cast some spells more flexibly. For each spell level you have access to, choose one spell of that level to be a signature spell. You don't need to learn heightened versions of signature spells separately; instead, you can heighten these spells freely. If you've learned a signature spell at a higher level than its minimum, you can also cast all its lower-level versions without learning those separately. If you swap out a signature spell, you can choose a replacement signature spell of the same spell level at which you learned the previous spell. You can also retrain specifically to change a signature spell to a

different spell of that level without swapping any spells; this takes as much time as retraining a spell normally does.

SKILL INCREASES 3RD

At 3rd level and every 2 levels thereafter, you gain a skill increase. You can use this increase either to increase your proficiency rank to trained in one skill you're untrained in, or to increase your proficiency rank in one skill in which you're already trained to expert.

At 7th level, you can use skill increases to increase your proficiency rank to master in a skill in which you're already an expert, and at 15th level, you can use them to increase your proficiency rank to legendary in a skill in which you're already a master.

ABILITY BOOSTS 5TH

At 5th level and every 5 levels thereafter, you boost four different ability scores. You can use these ability boosts to increase your ability scores above 18. Boosting an ability score increases it by 1 if it's already 18 or above, or by 2 if it starts out below 18.

ANCESTRY FEATS 5TH

In addition to the ancestry feat you started with, you gain an ancestry feat at 5th level and every 4 levels thereafter. The list of feats is in your ancestry's entry in Chapter 2.

EXPERT SPELLCASTER 7TH

Your proficiency ranks for occult spell attack rolls and spell DCs increase to expert.

GREAT FORTITUDE   9TH

Your physique is incredibly hardy. Your proficiency rank for Fortitude saves increases to expert.

RESOLVE   9TH

You've steeled your mind with resolve. Your proficiency rank for Will saves increases to master. When you roll a success at a Will save, you get a critical success instead.

BARD WEAPON EXPERTISE   11TH

You have become thoroughly adept with bardic weapons. You gain expert proficiency in simple weapons, plus the longsword, rapier, sap, shortbow, shortsword, and whip. When you critically succeed at an attack roll using one of these weapons while one of your compositions is active, you apply the critical specialization effect for that weapon.

VIGILANT SENSES   11TH

Through your adventures, you've developed keen awareness and attention to detail. Your proficiency rank for Perception increases to master.

LIGHT ARMOR EXPERTISE   13TH

You've learned how to dodge while wearing light or no armor. Your proficiency ranks for light armor and unarmored defense increase to expert.

WEAPON SPECIALIZATION   13TH

You've learned how to inflict greater injuries with the weapons you know best. You deal 2 additional damage with weapons and unarmed attacks in which you are an expert. This damage increases to 3 damage if you're a master, and 4 damage if you're legendary.

MASTER SPELLCASTER   15TH

You've mastered the occult. Your proficiency ranks for occult spell attack rolls and spell DCs increase to master.

GREATER RESOLVE   17TH

Your unbelievable training grants you mental resiliency. Your proficiency rank for Will saves increases to legendary. When you roll a success at a Will save, you get a critical success. When you roll a critical failure at a Will save, you get a failure instead. When you fail a Will save against a damaging effect, you take half damage.

MAGNUM OPUS   19TH

You have tuned your spellcasting to the highest caliber. Add two common 10th-level occult spells to your repertoire. You gain a single 10th-level spell slot you can use to cast one of those two spells using bard spellcasting. You don't gain more 10th-level spells as you level up, unlike other spell slots, and you can't use 10th-level slots with abilities that give you more spell slots or that let you cast spells without expending spell slots.

KEY TERMS

You'll see the following key terms in many bard class features.

Composition: To cast a composition cantrip or focus spell, you use a type of Performance (page 250). If the spell includes a verbal component, you must use an auditory performance, and if it includes a somatic component, you must use a visual one. The spell gains all the traits of the performance you used. You can cast only one composition spell each turn, and you can have only one active at a time. If you cast a new composition spell, any ongoing effects from your previous composition spell end immediately.

Metamagic: Actions with the metamagic trait tweak the properties of your spells. These actions usually come from metamagic feats. You must use a metamagic action directly before Casting the Spell you want to alter. If you use any action (including free actions and reactions) other than Cast a Spell directly after, you waste the benefits of the metamagic action. Any additional effects added by a metamagic action are part of the spell's effect, not of the metamagic action itself.

LEGENDARY SPELLCASTER   19TH

Your command of occult magic is the stuff of legends. Your proficiency ranks for occult spell attack rolls and spell DCs increase to legendary.

BARD FEATS

At every level that you gain a bard feat, you can select one of the following feats. You must satisfy any prerequisites before selecting the feat.

1ST LEVEL

BARDIC LORE   FEAT 1

`BARD`

Prerequisites enigma muse

Your studies make you informed on every subject. You are trained in Bardic Lore, a special Lore skill that can be used only to Recall Knowledge, but on any topic. If you have legendary proficiency in Occultism, you gain expert proficiency in Bardic Lore, but you can't increase your proficiency rank in Bardic Lore by any other means.

LINGERING COMPOSITION   FEAT 1

`BARD`

Prerequisites maestro muse, focus pool

By adding a flourish, you make your compositions last longer. You learn the *lingering composition* focus spell (page 387). Increase the number of Focus Points in your focus pool by 1.

REACH SPELL ❖   FEAT 1

`BARD` `CONCENTRATE` `METAMAGIC`

You can extend your spells' range. If the next action you use is to Cast a Spell that has a range, increase that spell's range by

BARD FEATS

If you need to look up a bard feat by name instead of by level, use this table.

30 feet. As is standard for increasing spell ranges, if the spell normally has a range of touch, you extend its range to 30 feet.

VERSATILE PERFORMANCE   FEAT 1

BARD

Prerequisites polymath muse

You can rely on the grandeur of your performances rather than ordinary social skills. You can use Performance instead of Diplomacy to Make an Impression and instead of Intimidation to Demoralize. You can also use an acting Performance instead of Deception to Impersonate. You can use your proficiency rank in Performance to meet the requirements of skill feats that require a particular rank in Deception, Diplomacy, or Intimidation.

2ND LEVEL

CANTRIP EXPANSION   FEAT 2

BARD

Study broadens your range of simple spells. Add two additional cantrips from your spell list to your repertoire.

ESOTERIC POLYMATH   FEAT 2

BARD

Prerequisites polymath muse

You keep a book of occult spells, similar to a wizard's spellbook, and can use its spells to supplement your spell repertoire. Add all the spells in your repertoire to this book for free. You can use the Occultism skill to Learn Spells (page 238) and add them to your spellbook by paying the appropriate cost, similar to a wizard.

During your daily preparations, choose any one spell from your book of occult spells. If that spell is already in your spell repertoire, you can treat it as an additional signature spell that day. If it isn't in your repertoire, treat it as though it were until your next daily preparations.

INSPIRE COMPETENCE   FEAT 2

BARD

Prerequisites maestro muse

You learn the *inspire competence* composition cantrip (page 386), which aids your allies' skills.

LOREMASTER'S ETUDE   FEAT 2

BARD FORTUNE

Prerequisites enigma muse, focus pool

You magically unlock memories, making them easier to recall. You learn the *loremaster's etude* composition spell (page 387). Increase the number of Focus Points in your focus pool by 1.

MULTIFARIOUS MUSE   FEAT 2

BARD

Your muse doesn't fall into a single label. Choose a type of muse other than that of your own. You gain a 1st-level feat that requires that muse, and your muse is now also a muse of that type, allowing you to take feats with the other muse as a prerequisite. You don't gain any of the other effects of the muse you chose.

Special You can take this feat multiple times. Each time you do, you must choose a different type of muse other than that of your own.

4TH LEVEL

INSPIRE DEFENSE   FEAT 4

BARD

Prerequisites maestro muse

You learn the *inspire defense* composition cantrip (page 386), which protects you and allies.

MELODIOUS SPELL ❖ FEAT 4

> BARD | CONCENTRATE | MANIPULATE | METAMAGIC

You subtly weave your spellcasting into your performance. If the next action you take is to Cast a Spell, attempt a Performance check against all observers' Perception DCs. If your Performance check is successful against an observer's Perception DC, that observer doesn't notice that you are Casting a Spell, even though normally spells have sensory manifestations that would make spellcasting obvious to those around you, and verbal, somatic, and material components are extremely overt. You hide all of these as part of an ordinary performance.

This hides only the spell's spellcasting actions and manifestations, not its effects, so an observer might still see a ray streak out from you or see you vanish.

TRIPLE TIME FEAT 4

> BARD

You learn the *triple time* composition cantrip (page 387), which speeds up you and your allies for a round.

VERSATILE SIGNATURE FEAT 4

> BARD

Prerequisites polymath muse

While most bards are known for certain signature performances and spells, you're always tweaking your available repertoire. When you make your daily preparations, you can change one of your signature spells to a different spell of that level from your repertoire.

6TH LEVEL

DIRGE OF DOOM FEAT 6

> BARD

You learn the *dirge of doom* composition cantrip (page 386), which frightens your enemies.

HARMONIZE ❖ FEAT 6

> BARD | CONCENTRATE | MANIPULATE | METAMAGIC

Prerequisites maestro muse

You can perform multiple compositions simultaneously. If your next action is to cast a composition, it becomes a harmonized composition. Unlike a normal composition, a harmonized composition doesn't end if you cast another composition, and you can cast another composition on the same turn as a harmonized one. Casting another harmonized composition ends any harmonized composition you have in effect.

STEADY SPELLCASTING FEAT 6

> BARD

You don't lose spells easily. If a reaction would disrupt your spellcasting action, attempt a DC 15 flat check. If you succeed, your action isn't disrupted.

8TH LEVEL

ECLECTIC SKILL FEAT 8

> BARD

Prerequisites polymath muse, master in Occultism

SAMPLE BARD

DANCER

Through myriad styles of dance, you inspire your allies and channel otherworldly magic.

ABILITY SCORES
Make Charisma highest, followed by Dexterity. Add to Constitution for more health and to Intelligence for skills.

SKILLS
Acrobatics, Athletics, Diplomacy, Medicine, Occultism, Performance

MUSE
Maestro

HIGHER-LEVEL FEATS
Inspire Competence (2nd), Triple Time (4th), Allegro (14th)

SPELL REPERTOIRE
1st *color spray, illusory disguise, soothe;* **Cantrips** *detect magic, ghost sound, light, mage hand, read aura*

Your broad experiences translate to a range of skills. You add your level to all skill checks in which you are untrained. You can attempt any skill check that normally requires you to be trained, even if you are untrained. If you have legendary proficiency in Occultism, you can attempt any skill check that normally requires you to have expert proficiency, even if untrained or trained.

INSPIRE HEROICS   FEAT 8
BARD
Prerequisites maestro muse, focus pool
Your performances inspire even greater deeds in your allies. You learn the *inspire heroics* metamagic focus spell (page 387). Increase the number of Focus Points in your focus pool by 1.

KNOW-IT-ALL   FEAT 8
BARD
Prerequisites enigma muse
When you succeed at a Knowledge check, you gain additional information or context. When you critically succeed at a Knowledge check, at the GM's discretion you might gain even more additional information or context than normal.

10TH LEVEL

HOUSE OF IMAGINARY WALLS   FEAT 10
BARD
You erect an imaginary barrier others believe to be real. You learn the *house of imaginary walls* composition cantrip (page 386).

QUICKENED CASTING ◈   FEAT 10
BARD **CONCENTRATE** **METAMAGIC**
Frequency once per day
If your next action is to cast a bard cantrip or a bard spell that is at least 2 levels lower than the highest level bard spell you can cast, reduce the number of actions to cast it by 1 (minimum 1 action).

UNUSUAL COMPOSITION ◈   FEAT 10
BARD **CONCENTRATE** **MANIPULATE** **METAMAGIC**
Prerequisites polymath muse
You can translate the emotion and power of a composition to other mediums. If your next action is to cast a composition spell, you can use a different kind of performance than usual for the composition to change any of its somatic components to verbal components or vice versa. As usual for composition spells, this changes whether the composition is auditory or visual.

12TH LEVEL

ECLECTIC POLYMATH   FEAT 12
BARD
Prerequisites Esoteric Polymath
Your flexible mind can quickly shift spells. If you add a spell to your repertoire during your daily preparations using Esoteric Polymath, when you prepare again, you can choose to keep the

new spell from Esoteric Polymath in your repertoire and instead lose access to another spell of the same level in your repertoire.

INSPIRATIONAL FOCUS — FEAT 12

BARD

Your connection to your muse has granted you unusual focus. If you have spent at least 2 Focus Points since the last time you Refocused, you recover 2 Focus Points when you Refocus instead of 1.

14TH LEVEL

ALLEGRO — FEAT 14

BARD

You can quicken your allies with a fast-paced performance. You learn the *allegro* composition cantrip (page 386).

SOOTHING BALLAD — FEAT 14

BARD

Prerequisites focus pool

You soothe your allies' wounds with the power of your performance. You learn the *soothing ballad* composition spell (page 387). Increase the number of Focus Points in your focus pool by 1.

TRUE HYPERCOGNITION ◆ — FEAT 14

BARD

Prerequisites enigma muse

Your mind works at an incredible pace. You instantly use up to five Recall Knowledge actions. If you have any special abilities or free actions that would normally be triggered when you Recall Knowledge, you can't use them for these actions.

16TH LEVEL

EFFORTLESS CONCENTRATION ◆ — FEAT 16

BARD

Requirement You haven't acted yet on your turn.

You can maintain a spell with hardly a thought. You immediately gain the effects of a Sustain a Spell action, allowing you to extend the duration of one of your active bard spells.

STUDIOUS CAPACITY — FEAT 16

BARD

Prerequisites enigma muse, legendary in Occultism

Your continued study of occult magic has increased your magical capacity, allowing you to cast spells even when it seems impossible. You can cast one spell each day even after you've run out of spell slots of the appropriate spell level, but you can't use this ability to cast a spell of your highest spell level.

18TH LEVEL

DEEP LORE — FEAT 18

BARD

Prerequisites enigma muse, legendary in Occultism

Your repertoire is vast, containing far more spells than usual. Add one spell to your repertoire of each level you can cast.

ETERNAL COMPOSITION — FEAT 18

BARD

Prerequisites maestro muse

The world is a stage upon which you are always playing. You are permanently quickened; you can use your extra action only to cast a composition cantrip that requires 1 action to cast. While in exploration mode, you can declare that you are performing an eligible composition cantrip while using any exploration tactic. Even before your first turn in a combat encounter, that cantrip is active as if you had cast it on your previous turn.

IMPOSSIBLE POLYMATH — FEAT 18

BARD

Prerequisites trained in Arcana, Nature, or Religion, Esoteric Polymath

Your esoteric formulas are so unusual that they allow you to dabble in magic from diverse traditions that other bards don't understand. As long as you're trained in Arcana, you can add arcane spells to your book from Esoteric Polymath; as long as you're trained in Nature, you can add primal spells to your book; and as long as you are trained in Religion, you can add divine spells to your book.

Like your other spells in your book, you can add one of these spells from another tradition to your repertoire as an occult spell each day using Esoteric Polymath, but you can't retain any spells from another tradition when you prepare again, even if you have Eclectic Polymath.

20TH LEVEL

FATAL ARIA — FEAT 20

BARD

Prerequisites focus pool

Your songs overwhelm the target with unbearable emotion, potentially striking them dead on the spot. You learn the *fatal aria* composition spell (page 386). Increase the number of Focus Points in your focus pool by 1.

PERFECT ENCORE — FEAT 20

BARD

Prerequisites magnum opus

You develop another incredible creation. You gain an additional 10th-level spell slot.

SYMPHONY OF THE MUSE — FEAT 20

BARD

Prerequisites Harmonize

You are able to weave countless performances together into a solo symphony. You are no longer limited to a single composition each turn or a single composition at a time; when you use a new composition, all previous compositions' effects continue for their remaining duration.

INTRODUCTION

ANCESTRIES & BACKGROUNDS

CLASSES

SKILLS

FEATS

EQUIPMENT

SPELLS

THE AGE OF LOST OMENS

PLAYING THE GAME

GAME MASTERING

CRAFTING & TREASURE

APPENDIX

CHAMPION

You are an emissary of a deity, a devoted servant who has taken up a weighty mantle, and you adhere to a code that holds you apart from those around you. While champions exist for every alignment, as a champion of good, you provide certainty and hope to the innocent. You have powerful defenses that you share freely with your allies and innocent bystanders, as well as holy power you use to end the threat of evil. Your devotion even attracts the attention of holy spirits who aid you on your journey.

KEY ABILITY

STRENGTH OR DEXTERITY
At 1st level, your class gives you an ability boost to your choice of Strength or Dexterity.

HIT POINTS

10 plus your Constitution modifier
You increase your maximum number of HP by this number at 1st level and every level thereafter.

DURING COMBAT ENCOUNTERS...

You confront enemies in hand-to-hand combat while carefully positioning yourself to protect your allies.

DURING SOCIAL ENCOUNTERS...

You are a voice of hope, striving to reach a peaceful solution that strengthens bonds and yields good results for all.

WHILE EXPLORING...

You overcome barriers both physical and spiritual, providing inspiration to your allies through your actions and—when your fellow adventurers ask for it—providing moral and ethical guidance.

IN DOWNTIME...

You spend much of your time in solemn prayer and contemplation, rigorous training, charity work, and fulfilling the tenets of your code, but that doesn't mean there isn't time to take up a craft or hobby.

YOU MIGHT...

- Believe there is always hope that good will triumph over evil, no matter how grim the odds.
- Know the ends don't justify the means, since evil acts increase the power of evil.
- Have a strong sense of right and wrong, and grow frustrated when greed or shortsightedness breeds evil.

OTHERS PROBABLY...

- See you as a symbol of hope, especially in a time of great need.
- Worry you secretly despise them for not living up to your impossible standard, or that you are unwilling to compromise when necessary.
- Know that you've sworn divine oaths of service they can trust you to keep.

INITIAL PROFICIENCIES

At 1st level, you gain the listed proficiency ranks in the following statistics. You are untrained in anything not listed unless you gain a better proficiency rank in some other way.

PERCEPTION

Trained in Perception

SAVING THROWS

Expert in Fortitude
Trained in Reflex
Expert in Will

SKILLS

Trained in Religion
Trained in one skill determined by your choice of deity
Trained in a number of additional skills equal to 2 plus your Intelligence modifier

ATTACKS

Trained in simple weapons
Trained in martial weapons
Trained in unarmed attacks

DEFENSES

Trained in all armor
Trained in unarmored defense

CLASS DC

Trained in champion class DC

SPELLS

Trained in divine spell attacks
Trained in divine spell DCs

TABLE 3-7: CHAMPION ADVANCEMENT

Your Level	Class Features
1	Ancestry and background, initial proficiencies, champion's code, deity and cause, deific weapon, champion's reaction, devotion spells, champion feat, shield block
2	Champion feat, skill feat
3	Divine ally, general feat, skill increase
4	Champion feat, skill feat
5	Ability boosts, ancestry feat, skill increase, weapon expertise
6	Champion feat, skill feat
7	Armor expertise, general feat, skill increase, weapon specialization
8	Champion feat, skill feat
9	Ancestry feat, champion expertise, divine smite, juggernaut, lightning reflexes, skill increase
10	Ability boosts, champion feat, skill feat
11	Alertness, divine will, exalt, general feat, skill increase
12	Champion feat, skill feat
13	Ancestry feat, armor mastery, skill increase, weapon mastery
14	Champion feat, skill feat
15	Ability boosts, general feat, greater weapon specialization, skill increase
16	Champion feat, skill feat
17	Ancestry feat, champion mastery, legendary armor, skill increase
18	Champion feat, skill feat
19	General feat, hero's defiance, skill increase
20	Ability boosts, champion feat, skill feat

CLASS FEATURES

You gain these abilities as a champion. Abilities gained at higher levels list the requisite levels next to their names.

ANCESTRY AND BACKGROUND

In addition to the abilities provided by your class at 1st level, you have the benefits of your selected ancestry and background, as described in Chapter 2.

INITIAL PROFICIENCIES

At 1st level, you gain a number of proficiencies that represent your basic training, noted at the start of this class.

CHAMPION'S CODE

You follow a code of conduct, beginning with tenets shared by all champions of an alignment (such as good), and continuing with tenets of your cause. Deities often add additional strictures (for instance, Torag's champions can't show mercy to enemies of their people, making it almost impossible for them to follow the redeemer cause). Only rules for good champions appear in this book. Tenets are listed in order of importance, starting with the most important. If a situation places two tenets in conflict, you aren't in a no-win situation; instead, follow the more important tenet. For instance, as a paladin, if an evil king asked you if you're hiding refugees so he could execute them, you could lie to him, since the tenet against lying is less important than preventing harm to innocents. Trying to subvert your code by creating a situation that forces a higher tenet to override a lower tenet (for example, promising not to respect authorities and then, to keep your word, disrespecting authorities) is a violation of the champion code.

If you stray from your alignment or violate your code of conduct, you lose your focus pool and divine ally until you demonstrate your repentance by conducting an *atone* ritual (page 409), but you keep any other champion abilities that don't require those class features. If your alignment shifts but is still one allowed by your deity, your GM might let you retrain your cause while still following the same deity.

THE TENETS OF GOOD

All champions of good alignment follow these tenets.

- You must never perform acts anathema to your deity or willingly commit an evil act, such as murder, torture, or the casting of an evil spell.
- You must never knowingly harm an innocent, or allow immediate harm to one through inaction when you know you could reasonably prevent it. This tenet doesn't force you to take action against possible harm to innocents at an indefinite time in the future, or to sacrifice your life to protect them.

DEITY AND CAUSE

Champions are divine servants of a deity. Choose a deity to follow (pages 437–440); your alignment must be one allowed for followers of your deity. Actions fundamentally opposed to your deity's ideals or alignment are anathema to your faith. A few examples of acts that would be considered anathema appear in each deity's entry. You and your GM determine whether other acts are anathema.

You have one of the following causes. Your cause must match your alignment exactly. Your cause determines your champion's reaction, grants you a devotion spell (page 107), and defines part of your champion's code.

PALADIN (LAWFUL GOOD)

You're honorable, forthright, and committed to pushing back the forces of cruelty. You gain the Retributive Strike champion's reaction and the *lay on hands* devotion spell. After the tenets of good, add these tenets:

- You must act with honor, never taking advantage of others, lying, or cheating.
- You must respect the lawful authority of legitimate leadership wherever you go, and follow its laws.

REDEEMER (NEUTRAL GOOD)

You're full of kindness and forgiveness. You gain the Glimpse of Redemption champion's reaction and the *lay on hands* devotion spell. After the tenets of good, add these:

- You must first try to redeem those who commit evil acts, rather than killing them or meting out punishment. If they then continue on a wicked path, you might need to take more extreme measures.
- You must show compassion for others, regardless of their authority or station.

Liberator [Chaotic Good]

You're committed to defending the freedom of others. You gain the Liberating Step champion's reaction and the *lay on hands* devotion spell. After the tenets of good, add these tenets:

- You must respect the choices others make over their own lives, and you can't force someone to act in a particular way or threaten them if they don't.
- You must demand and fight for others' freedom to make their own decisions. You may never engage in or countenance slavery or tyranny.

DEIFIC WEAPON

You zealously bear your deity's favored weapon. If it's uncommon, you gain access to it. If it's a simple weapon, increase the damage die by one step (d4 to d6, d6 to d8, d8 to d10, d10 to d12).

CHAMPION'S REACTION

Your cause gives you a special reaction: Retributive Strike for paladin, Glimpse of Redemption for redeemer, or Liberating Step for liberator.

RETRIBUTIVE STRIKE ⤾

CHAMPION

Trigger An enemy damages your ally, and both are within 15 feet of you.

You protect your ally and strike your foe. The ally gains resistance to all damage against the triggering damage equal to 2 + your level. If the foe is within reach, make a melee Strike against it.

GLIMPSE OF REDEMPTION ⤾

CHAMPION

Trigger An enemy damages your ally, and both are within 15 feet of you.

Your foe hesitates under the weight of sin as visions of redemption play in their mind's eye. The foe must choose one of the following options:

- The ally is unharmed by the triggering damage.
- The ally gains resistance to all damage against the triggering damage equal to 2 + your level. After the damaging effect is applied, the enemy becomes enfeebled 2 until the end of its next turn.

LIBERATING STEP ⤾

CHAMPION

Trigger An enemy damages, Grabs, or Grapples your ally, and both are within 15 feet of you.

You free an ally from restraint. If the trigger was an ally taking damage, the ally gains resistance to all damage against the triggering damage equal to 2 + your level. The ally can attempt to break free of effects grabbing, restraining, immobilizing, or paralyzing them. They either attempt a new save against one such effect that allows a save, or attempt to Escape from one effect as a free action. If they can move, the ally can Step as a free action, even if they didn't need to escape.

DEVOTION SPELLS

Your deity's power grants you special divine spells called devotion spells, which are a type of focus spell. It costs 1 Focus Point to cast a focus spell, and you start with a focus pool of 1 Focus Point. You refill your focus pool during your daily preparations, and you regain 1 Focus Point by spending 10 minutes using the Refocus activity to pray to your deity or do service toward their causes.

Focus spells are automatically heightened to half your level rounded up. Certain feats can give you more focus spells and increase the size of your focus pool, though your focus pool can never hold more than 3 Focus Points. The full rules are on page 300. You gain a devotion spell depending on your cause, and you are trained in divine spell attack rolls and spell DCs. Your spellcasting ability is Charisma.

CHAMPION FEATS

At 1st level and every even-numbered level thereafter, you gain a champion class feat. Champion class feats are presented beginning on page 109.

SHIELD BLOCK

You gain the Shield Block general feat (page 266), a reaction that lets you reduce damage with your shield.

SKILL FEATS   2ND

At 2nd level and every 2 levels thereafter, you gain a skill feat. Skill feats can be found in Chapter 5 and have the skill trait. You must be trained or better in the corresponding skill to select a skill feat.

DIVINE ALLY   3RD

Your devotion attracts a spirit of your deity's alignment. Once you choose an ally, your choice can't be changed.

The following are divine allies:

Blade Ally: A spirit of battle dwells within your weapon. Select one weapon when you make your daily preparations. In your hands, the weapon gains the effect of a property rune. For a champion following the tenets of good, choose *disrupting*, *ghost touch*, *returning*, or *shifting*. You also gain the weapon's critical specialization effect.

Shield Ally: A spirit of protection dwells within your shield. In your hands, the shield's Hardness increases by 2 and its HP and BT increase by half.

Steed Ally: You gain a young animal companion as a mount (page 214). Ordinarily, your animal companion is one that has the mount special ability, such as a horse. You can select a different animal companion (GM's discretion), but this ability doesn't grant it the mount special ability.

GENERAL FEATS   3RD

At 3rd level and every 4 levels thereafter, you gain a general feat. General feats are listed in Chapter 5.

SKILL INCREASES   3RD

At 3rd level and every 2 levels thereafter, you gain a skill increase. You can use this increase either to increase your proficiency rank to trained in one skill you're untrained in, or to increase your proficiency rank in one skill in which you're already trained to expert.

At 7th level, you can use skill increases to increase your proficiency rank to master in a skill in which you're already an expert, and at 15th level, you can use them to increase your proficiency rank to legendary in a skill in which you're already a master.

ABILITY BOOSTS   5TH

At 5th level and every 5 levels thereafter, boost four different ability scores. You can use these boosts to increase ability scores above 18. Boosting an ability score increases it by 1 if it's already 18 or above, or by 2 if it starts out below 18.

ANCESTRY FEATS   5TH

In addition to the ancestry feat you started with, you gain an ancestry feat at 5th level and every 4 levels thereafter. The list of ancestry feats available to you can be found in your ancestry's entry in Chapter 2.

WEAPON EXPERTISE   5TH

You've dedicated yourself to learning the intricacies of your weapons. Your proficiency ranks for simple weapons and martial weapons increase to expert.

ARMOR EXPERTISE   7TH

You have spent so much time in armor that you know how to make the most of its protection. Your proficiency ranks for light, medium, and heavy armor, as well as for unarmored defense, increase to expert. You gain the armor specialization effects of medium and heavy armor.

WEAPON SPECIALIZATION   7TH

You've learned how to inflict greater injuries with the weapons you know best. You deal 2 additional damage with weapons and unarmed attacks in which you are an expert. This damage increases to 3 if you're a master, and to 4 if you're legendary.

CHAMPION EXPERTISE   9TH

Prayers strengthen your divine power. Your proficiency ranks for your champion class DC and divine spell attack rolls and DCs increase to expert.

DIVINE SMITE   9TH

Your champion's reaction improves.

Paladin: You surround evil targets in a punishing halo. If you hit with your Retributive Strike, the target takes persistent good damage equal to your Charisma modifier.

Redeemer: A guilty conscience assails foes who spurn your Glimpse of Redemption. A foe that responds to your Glimpse of Redemption by dealing damage takes persistent good damage equal to your Charisma modifier.

Liberator: You punish those who ensnare your allies in bondage. If the triggering enemy was using any effects to make your ally grabbed, restrained, immobilized, or paralyzed when you used Liberating Step, that enemy takes persistent good damage equal to your Charisma modifier.

JUGGERNAUT   9TH

Your body is accustomed to physical hardship and resistant to ailments. Your proficiency rank for Fortitude saves increases to master. When you roll a success on a Fortitude save, you get a critical success instead.

LIGHTNING REFLEXES   9TH

Your reflexes are lightning fast. Your proficiency rank for Reflex saves increases to expert.

ALERTNESS   11TH

You remain alert to threats around you. Your proficiency rank for Perception increases to expert.

DIVINE WILL   11TH

Your faith grants mastery of your will. Your proficiency rank for Will saves increases to master. When you roll a success on a Will save, you get a critical success instead.

EXALT   11TH

Your champion's reaction exalts nearby allies, allowing them to benefit as well.

Paladin: When you use Retributive Strike, each ally within 15 feet of you with the target in their melee reach can spend a reaction to Strike the target with a −5 penalty.

Redeemer: You protect multiple allies. You can apply the resistance granted by Glimpse of Redemption to yourself and all allies within 15 feet of you, including the triggering ally, except the resistance is reduced by 2 for all.

Liberator: You can help your whole group get into position. When you use Liberating Step, if your ally doesn't attempt to break free of an effect, you and all allies within 15 feet can Step, in addition to the triggering ally.

ARMOR MASTERY   13TH

Your skill with armor improves, helping you avoid more blows. Your proficiency ranks for light, medium, and heavy armor, as well as for unarmored defense, increase to master.

WEAPON MASTERY   13TH

You fully understand your weapons. Your proficiency ranks for simple and martial weapons increase to master.

GREATER WEAPON SPECIALIZATION   15TH

Your damage from weapon specialization increases to 4 with weapons and unarmed attacks in which you're an expert, 6 if you're a master, and 8 if you're legendary.

CHAMPION MASTERY   17TH

You've mastered your arsenal of champion techniques

and divine spells. Your proficiency ranks for your champion class DC and for divine spell attack rolls and spell DCs increase to master.

LEGENDARY ARMOR   17TH

You shield yourself with steel as easily as with faith. Your proficiency ranks for light, medium, and heavy armor, as well as for unarmored defense, increase to legendary.

HERO'S DEFIANCE   19TH

You can defy fate and continue fighting as long as you have divine energy. You gain the *hero's defiance* devotion spell.

CHAMPION FEATS

At each level that you gain a champion feat, you can select one of the following feats. You must satisfy any prerequisites before selecting the feat.

1ST LEVEL

DEITY'S DOMAIN   FEAT 1
CHAMPION

You embody an aspect of your deity. Choose one of your deity's domains from those listed on page 441. You gain the domain's initial domain spell as a devotion spell.

RANGED REPRISAL   FEAT 1
CHAMPION
Prerequisites paladin cause

You can use Retributive Strike with a ranged weapon. In addition, if the foe that triggered your reaction is within 5 feet of your reach but not in your reach, as part of your reaction you can Step to put the foe in your reach before making a melee Retributive Strike.

UNIMPEDED STEP   FEAT 1
CHAMPION
Prerequisites liberator cause

CHAMPION FEATS

If you need to look up a champion feat by name instead of by level, use this table.

With a burst of divine liberation, your ally's movement from your Liberating Step is unaffected by difficult terrain, greater difficult terrain, narrow surfaces, and uneven ground.

WEIGHT OF GUILT   FEAT 1

CHAMPION

Prerequisites redeemer cause

Guilt clouds the minds of those who ignore your Glimpse of Redemption. Instead of making the triggering creature enfeebled 2, you can make it stupefied 2 for the same duration.

2ND LEVEL

DIVINE GRACE ⤵   FEAT 2

CHAMPION

Trigger You attempt a save against a spell, before you roll.

You call upon your deity's grace, gaining a +2 circumstance bonus to the save.

DRAGONSLAYER OATH   FEAT 2

CHAMPION OATH

Prerequisites tenets of good

You've sworn to slay evil dragons. Add the following tenet to your code after the others: "You must slay evil dragons you encounter as long as you have a reasonable chance of success."

Your Retributive Strike gains a +4 circumstance bonus to damage against an evil dragon, or +6 if you have master proficiency with the weapon you used. Your Glimpse of Redemption's resistance against damage from an evil dragon is 7 + your level. If you use Liberating Step triggered by an evil dragon, your ally gains a +4 circumstance bonus to checks granted by your Liberating Step, and the ally can Step twice afterward.

You don't consider evil dragons to be legitimate authorities, even in nations they rule.

FIENDSBANE OATH   FEAT 2

CHAMPION OATH

Prerequisites tenets of good

You've sworn an oath to banish the corruption of fiends to the dark planes they call home. Add the following tenet to your champion's code after the other tenets: "You must banish or slay fiends you come across as long as you have a reasonable chance of success; in the incredibly unlikely event you find a good fiend, you don't have to banish or kill it."

Your Retributive Strike gains a +4 circumstance bonus to damage against a fiend, or a +6 circumstance bonus if you have master proficiency with the weapon you used. Your Glimpse of Redemption's resistance against damage from a fiend is 7 + your level. If you use Liberating Step triggered by a fiend, your ally gains a +4 circumstance bonus to checks granted by your Liberating Step, and the ally can Step twice afterward.

You don't consider fiends to be legitimate authorities, even in nations ruled by fiends.

SHINING OATH   FEAT 2

CHAMPION OATH

Prerequisites tenets of good

You've sworn an oath to put the undead to rest. Add the following tenet to your champion's code after the other tenets: "You must end the existence of undead you encounter as long as you have a reasonable chance of success; in the unlikely event you find a good undead, you can try to work out a more peaceful way to help it recover from its undead state rather than destroying it in combat, such as helping it complete its unfinished business and find peace."

Your Retributive Strike gains a +4 circumstance bonus to damage against an undead, or +6 if you have master proficiency with the weapon you used. Your Glimpse of Redemption's resistance against damage from an undead is 7 + your level. If you use Liberating Step triggered by an undead, your ally gains a +4 circumstance bonus to checks granted by your Liberating Step, and the ally can Step twice afterward.

You don't consider undead to be legitimate authorities, even in nations ruled by undead.

CLASSES

3

INTRODUCTION

ANCESTRIES &
BACKGROUNDS

CLASSES

SKILLS

FEATS

EQUIPMENT

SPELLS

THE AGE OF
LOST OMENS

PLAYING THE
GAME

GAME
MASTERING

CRAFTING
& TREASURE

APPENDIX

VENGEFUL OATH — FEAT 2

CHAMPION **OATH**

Prerequisites paladin cause

You've sworn an oath to hunt down wicked evildoers and bring them to judgment. Add the following tenet to your code after the others: "You must hunt down and exterminate evil creatures that have committed heinous atrocities as long as you have a reasonable chance of success and aren't engaged in a mission that would prevent your doing so."

You can use *lay on hands* to damage a creature you witness harming an innocent or a good ally as if it were undead; in this case, *lay on hands* deals good damage instead of positive damage and gains the good trait. This good damage can affect non-evil creatures. This doesn't prevent you from healing such a creature with *lay on hands*; you choose whether to heal or harm.

4TH LEVEL

AURA OF COURAGE — FEAT 4

CHAMPION

Prerequisites tenets of good

You stand strong in the face of danger and inspire your allies to do the same. Whenever you become frightened, reduce the condition value by 1 (to a minimum of 0). At the end of your turn when you would reduce your frightened condition value by 1, you also reduce the value by 1 for all allies within 15 feet.

DIVINE HEALTH — FEAT 4

CHAMPION

Prerequisites tenets of good

Your faith makes you resistant to disease, protecting you as you offer succor to the ill. You gain a +1 status bonus to saves against diseases. In addition, if you roll a success on a save against a disease, you get a critical success instead.

MERCY ✦ — FEAT 4

CHAMPION **CONCENTRATE** **METAMAGIC**

Prerequisites devotion spell (*lay on hands*)

Your touch relieves fear and restores movement. If the next action you use is to cast *lay on hands*, you can attempt to counteract a fear effect or an effect imposing the paralyzed condition on the target, in addition to the other benefits of *lay on hands*.

6TH LEVEL

ATTACK OF OPPORTUNITY ↻ — FEAT 6

CHAMPION

Trigger A creature within your reach uses a manipulate action or a move action, makes a ranged attack, or leaves a square during a move action it's using.

You lash out at a foe that leaves an opening. Make a melee Strike against the triggering creature. If your attack is a critical hit and the trigger was a manipulate action, you disrupt

SAMPLE CHAMPION

REDEEMER

Your truth and compassion glow strong as the sun, bringing the evil into the light of your goddess, the Dawnflower.

ABILITY SCORES
Take a high Strength for your combat abilities, and a good Charisma for your devotion spells.

SKILLS
Athletics, Diplomacy, Religion, Medicine

DEITY AND CAUSE
Sarenrae, redeemer

STARTING FEAT
Deity's Domain (truth)

HIGHER-LEVEL FEATS
Shining Oath (2nd), Mercy (4th), Litany Against Wrath (6th), Sense Evil (8th), Devoted Focus (10th), Lasting Doubt (12th), Ultimate Mercy (18th)

---

that action. This Strike doesn't count toward your multiple attack penalty, and your multiple attack penalty doesn't apply to this Strike.

LITANY AGAINST WRATH   FEAT 6
CHAMPION
Prerequisites devotion spells, tenets of good
You excoriate a foe for its wrath against goodly creatures. You can cast the *litany against wrath* devotion spell. Increase the number of Focus Points in your focus pool by 1.

LOYAL WARHORSE   FEAT 6
CHAMPION
Prerequisites divine ally (steed)
You and your mount have grown closer, and your loyalty to each other is unbreakable. The mount you gained through the divine ally class feature is now a mature animal companion (page 214). In addition, your mount never attacks you, even if it is magically compelled to do so.

SHIELD WARDEN   FEAT 6
CHAMPION
Prerequisites divine ally (shield), tenets of good
You use your shield to protect your allies as well as yourself. When you have a shield raised, you can use your Shield Block reaction when an attack is made against an ally adjacent to you. If you do, the shield prevents that ally from taking damage instead of preventing you from taking damage, following the normal rules for Shield Block.

SMITE EVIL ❖   FEAT 6
CHAMPION
Prerequisites divine ally (blade)
Your blade ally becomes an even more powerful tool against evildoers. Select one foe you can see. Until the start of your next turn, your Strikes with the weapon your blade ally inhabits against that foe deal an extra 4 good damage, increasing to 6 if you have master proficiency with this weapon.

If the foe attacks one of your allies, the duration extends to the end of that foe's next turn. If the foe continues to attack your allies each turn, the duration continues to extend.

8TH LEVEL

ADVANCED DEITY'S DOMAIN   FEAT 8
CHAMPION
Prerequisites Deity's Domain
Through your conviction, you have glimpsed the deeper secrets of your deity's domain. You gain an advanced domain spell from the domain you chose with Deity's Domain. You can cast that spell as a devotion spell. Increase the number of Focus Points in your focus pool by 1.

GREATER MERCY   FEAT 8
CHAMPION
Prerequisites Mercy

Your faith enhances your ability to remove conditions. When you use Mercy, you can instead attempt to counteract the blinded, deafened, sickened, or slowed conditions.

HEAL MOUNT   FEAT 8

CHAMPION

Prerequisites divine ally (steed)

Your devotion to your mount manifests as a surge of positive energy. When you cast *lay on hands* on your mount, you can restore 10 Hit Points, plus 10 for each heightened level.

QUICK BLOCK   FEAT 8

CHAMPION

You can block with your shield instinctively. At the start of each of your turns, you gain an additional reaction that you can use only to perform a Shield Block.

SECOND ALLY   FEAT 8

CHAMPION

Prerequisites divine ally

Your inner grace attracts the attention of a second protective spirit. Choose a second type of divine ally and gain its benefits.

SENSE EVIL   FEAT 8

CHAMPION

Prerequisites tenets of good

You sense evil as a queasy or foreboding feeling. When in the presence of an aura of evil that is powerful or overwhelming (page 328), you eventually detect the aura, though you might not do so instantly, and you can't pinpoint the location. This acts as a vague sense, similar to humans' sense of smell. An evil creature using a disguise or otherwise trying to hide its presence attempts a Deception check against your Perception DC to hide its aura from you. If the creature succeeds at its Deception check, it is then temporarily immune to your Sense Evil for 1 day.

10TH LEVEL

DEVOTED FOCUS   FEAT 10

CHAMPION

Prerequisites devotion spells

Your devotion is strong enough to increase your focus to incredible heights. If you have spent at least 2 Focus Points since the last time you Refocused, you recover 2 Focus Points when you Refocus instead of 1.

IMPOSING DESTRIER   FEAT 10

CHAMPION

Prerequisites divine ally (steed), Loyal Warhorse

Under your care, your mount has realized its innate potential. The mount you gained through the divine ally class feature is now a nimble or savage animal companion (page 214). During an encounter, even if you don't use the Command an Animal action, your mount can still use 1 action on your turn to Stride or Strike.

LITANY AGAINST SLOTH   FEAT 10

CHAMPION

Prerequisites devotion spells, tenets of good

You rail against the sin of sloth, turning a foe's laziness against it. You can cast the *litany against sloth* devotion spell. Increase the number of Focus Points in your focus pool by 1.

RADIANT BLADE SPIRIT   FEAT 10

CHAMPION

Prerequisites divine ally (blade)

Your divine ally radiates power, enhancing your chosen weapon. When you choose the weapon for your blade ally during your daily preparations, add the following property runes to the list of effects you can choose from: *flaming* and any aligned properties (*anarchic, axiomatic, holy, or unholy*) that match your cause's alignment.

SHIELD OF RECKONING ↻   FEAT 10

CHAMPION **FLOURISH**

Prerequisites champion's reaction, divine ally (shield), tenets of good, Shield Warden

Trigger A foe's attack against an ally matches the trigger for both your Shield Block reaction and your champion's reaction.

When you shield your ally against an attack, you call upon your power to protect your ally further. You use the Shield Block reaction to prevent damage to an ally and also use your champion's reaction against the foe that attacked your ally.

12TH LEVEL

AFFLICTION MERCY   FEAT 12

CHAMPION

Prerequisites Mercy

The divine grace that flows through you grants reprieve from an affliction. When you use Mercy, you can instead attempt to counteract a curse, disease, or poison.

AURA OF FAITH   FEAT 12

CHAMPION

Prerequisites tenets of good

You radiate an aura of pure belief that imbues your attacks and those of nearby allies with holy power. Your Strikes deal an extra 1 good damage against evil creatures. Also, each good-aligned ally within 15 feet gains this benefit on their first Strike that hits an evil creature each round.

BLADE OF JUSTICE ◆◆   FEAT 12

CHAMPION

Prerequisites paladin cause

You call upon divine power and make a weapon or unarmed Strike against a foe you have witnessed harming an ally or innocent. The Strike deals two extra weapon damage dice if the target of your Strike is evil. Whether or not the target is evil, the Strike applies all effects that normally apply on a Retributive Strike (such as divine smite), and you can convert all the physical damage from the attack into good damage.

INTRODUCTION

ANCESTRIES & BACKGROUNDS

CLASSES

SKILLS

FEATS

EQUIPMENT

SPELLS

THE AGE OF LOST OMENS

PLAYING THE GAME

GAME MASTERING

CRAFTING & TREASURE

APPENDIX

SAMPLE CHAMPION

LIBERATOR

With the name of the Savored Sting on your lips, you free those held against their will and exact revenge upon their captors.

ABILITY SCORES
Focus on Dexterity. Charisma helps your devotion spells and Deception, and good Wisdom and Constitution improve your defenses.

SKILLS
Deception, Religion, Society, Stealth

DEITY AND CAUSE
Calistria, liberator

STARTING FEAT
Unimpeded Step

HIGHER-LEVEL FEATS
Divine Grace (2nd), Aura of Courage (4th), Attack of Opportunity (6th), Liberating Stride (12th)

CHAMPION'S SACRIFICE — FEAT 12

CHAMPION

Prerequisites tenets of good

You can suffer so that others might live. You can cast the *champion's sacrifice* devotion spell. Increase the number of Focus Points in your focus pool by 1.

DIVINE WALL — FEAT 12

CHAMPION

Requirements You are wielding a shield.

You use your shield to harry your enemies, preventing them from stepping away from or around you. All spaces adjacent to you are difficult terrain for your enemies.

LASTING DOUBT — FEAT 12

CHAMPION

Prerequisites redeemer cause

When you cast doubt upon your foes, the effect lasts longer than usual. After being enfeebled 2 by your Glimpse of Redemption, the foe is enfeebled 1 for 1 minute. If you have Weight of Guilt, after being stupefied 2 by your Glimpse of Redemption, the foe is stupefied 1 for 1 minute or until the flat check from stupefied causes it to lose a spell, whichever comes first.

LIBERATING STRIDE — FEAT 12

CHAMPION

Prerequisites liberator cause

Instead of you taking a Step at the end of your Liberating Step, the triggering ally can Stride up to half their Speed. Even if you have exalt, only the triggering ally gains this benefit.

14TH LEVEL

ANCHORING AURA — FEAT 14

CHAMPION

Requirements Fiendsbane Oath

Your aura hampers fiends' teleportation. Your aura attempts to counteract teleportation spells cast by fiends within 15 feet, using the spell level and DC of your devotion spells.

AURA OF LIFE — FEAT 14

CHAMPION

Requirements Shining Oath

Your aura protects against necromantic effects. You and all allies within 15 feet gain resistance 5 to negative energy and a +1 status bonus to saves against necromancy effects.

AURA OF RIGHTEOUSNESS — FEAT 14

CHAMPION

Prerequisites tenets of good

Your righteous aura dampens evil's might. You and all allies within 15 feet gain evil resistance 5.

AURA OF VENGEANCE — FEAT 14

CHAMPION

Requirements exalt, Vengeful Oath

When you call upon others to take retribution, you also guide their aim. When you use Retributive Strike, your allies who make Strikes take only a –2 penalty, instead of a –5 penalty.

DIVINE REFLEXES   FEAT 14

CHAMPION

At the start of each of your turns, you gain an additional reaction that you can use only for your champion's reaction.

LITANY OF RIGHTEOUSNESS   FEAT 14

CHAMPION

Prerequisites tenets of good

You call upon righteousness to expose an evil foe's weakness. You can cast the *litany of righteousness* devotion spell. Increase the number of Focus Points in your focus pool by 1.

WYRMBANE AURA   FEAT 14

CHAMPION

Requirements Dragonslayer Oath

Your aura protects against destructive energies and dragons' breath. You and all allies within 15 feet gain resistance equal to your Charisma modifier to acid, cold, electricity, fire, and poison. If the source of one of these types of damage is a dragon's breath, increase the resistance to half your level.

16TH LEVEL

AUSPICIOUS MOUNT   FEAT 16

CHAMPION

Prerequisites divine ally (steed), Imposing Destrier

Guided by your ongoing care, your steed has developed incredible intelligence and skill. The mount you gained through the divine ally class feature is now a specialized animal companion (page 217). You can select one of the usual specializations or the auspice specialization.

Auspice mounts gain the following benefits: Your companion is marked by your deity's religious symbol as a sacred creature of your deity. Its proficiency rank in Religion increases to expert, it can speak the language associated with your deity's servitors (Celestial for champions who follow the tenets of good), and its Intelligence modifier increases by 2 and its Wisdom modifier by 1.

INSTRUMENT OF ZEAL   FEAT 16

CHAMPION

Prerequisites divine ally (blade), tenets of good

Divine energy fills your weapon. Whenever you critically hit a foe with Smite Evil or a Retributive Strike, your attack adds an extra damage die, and the target is slowed 1 on its next turn.

SHIELD OF GRACE   FEAT 16

CHAMPION

Prerequisites Shield Warden

You protect an ally with both your shield and your body. Whenever you use the Shield Block reaction to prevent damage to an ally, you can evenly split the remaining damage after the Shield Block between the ally and yourself.

18TH LEVEL

CELESTIAL FORM   FEAT 18

CHAMPION

Prerequisites tenets of good

You take on a celestial countenance, appearing like a type of celestial who serves your deity; for example, as an angel, you would gain a halo and feathery wings. You gain a fly Speed equal to your Speed. You gain darkvision if you don't already have it, and you gain the celestial trait and the trait appropriate to the type of servitor you've become (archon, angel, or azata, for example).

ULTIMATE MERCY   FEAT 18

CHAMPION

Prerequisites Mercy

Your mercy transcends the bounds of life and death. When you use Mercy, you can cast *lay on hands* on a creature that died since your last turn to return it to life. The target returns to life with 1 hit point and becomes wounded 1. You can't use Ultimate Mercy if the triggering effect was *disintegrate* or a death effect.

20TH LEVEL

CELESTIAL MOUNT   FEAT 20

CHAMPION

Prerequisites divine ally (steed), tenets of good

Your steed gains incredible celestial powers granted by your deity. It gains darkvision, its maximum Hit Points increase by 40, and it gains weakness 10 to evil damage.

Additionally, it grows wings appropriate to a servitor of your deity (such as metallic wings for an archon), granting it a fly Speed equal to its Speed. It gains the celestial trait and the trait appropriate to the type of servitor it has become (archon, angel, or azata, for example).

RADIANT BLADE MASTER   FEAT 20

CHAMPION

Prerequisites divine ally (blade), Radiant Blade Spirit

Your divine ally turns your chosen weapon into a paragon of its type. When you choose the weapon for your blade divine ally during your preparations, add the following property runes to the list of effects you can choose from: *dancing*, *greater disrupting*, and *keen*.

SHIELD PARAGON   FEAT 20

CHAMPION

Prerequisites divine ally (shield)

Your shield is a vessel of divine protection. When you're wielding your chosen shield, it is always raised, even without you using the Raise a Shield action. Your chosen shield doubles its HP and BT, rather than increasing them by half. If it would be destroyed, it vanishes to your deity's realm instead, where your divine ally repairs it. During your next daily preparations, the shield returns to you fully repaired.

INTRODUCTION

ANCESTRIES &
BACKGROUNDS

CLASSES

SKILLS

FEATS

EQUIPMENT

SPELLS

THE AGE OF
LOST OMENS

PLAYING THE
GAME

GAME
MASTERING

CRAFTING
& TREASURE

APPENDIX

CLERIC

Deities work their will upon the world in infinite ways, and you serve as one of their most stalwart mortal servants. Blessed with divine magic, you live the ideals of your faith, adorn yourself with the symbols of your church, and train diligently to wield your deity's favored weapon. Your spells might protect and heal your allies, or they might punish foes and enemies of your faith, as your deity wills. Yours is a life of devotion, spreading the teachings of your faith through both word and deed.

KEY ABILITY

WISDOM
At 1st level, your class gives you an ability boost to Wisdom.

HIT POINTS

8 plus your Constitution modifier
You increase your maximum number of HP by this number at 1st level and every level thereafter.

DURING COMBAT ENCOUNTERS...

If you're a warpriest, you balance between casting spells and attacking with weapons—typically the favored weapon of your deity. If you're a cloistered cleric, you primarily cast spells. Most of your spells can boost, protect, or heal your allies. Depending on your deity, you get extra spells to heal your allies or harm your enemies.

DURING SOCIAL ENCOUNTERS...

You might make diplomatic overtures or deliver impressive speeches. Because you're wise, you also pick up on falsehoods others tell.

WHILE EXPLORING...

You detect nearby magic and interpret any religious writing you come across. You might also concentrate on a protective spell for your allies in case of attack. After a battle or hazard, you might heal anyone who was hurt.

IN DOWNTIME...

You might perform services at a temple, travel to spread the word of your deity, research scripture, celebrate holy days, or even found a new temple.

YOU MIGHT...

- Visit the temples and holy places sacred to your faith, and have an immediate affinity with other worshippers of your deity.
- Know the teachings of your religion's holy texts and how they apply to a dilemma.
- Cooperate with your allies, provided they don't ask you to go against divine will.

OTHERS PROBABLY...

- Find your devotion impressive, even if they don't understand it.
- Expect you to heal their wounds.
- Rely on you to interact with other religious figures.

INITIAL PROFICIENCIES

At 1st level, you gain the listed proficiency ranks in the following statistics. You are untrained in anything not listed unless you gain a better proficiency rank in some other way.

PERCEPTION
Trained in Perception

SAVING THROWS
Trained in Fortitude
Trained in Reflex
Expert in Will

SKILLS
Trained in Religion
Trained in one skill determined by your choice of deity
Trained in a number of additional skills equal to 2 plus your Intelligence modifier

ATTACKS
Trained in simple weapons
Trained in the favored weapon of your deity. If your deity's favored weapon is uncommon, you also gain access to that weapon.
Trained in unarmed attacks

DEFENSES
Untrained in all armor, though your doctrine might alter this
Trained in unarmored defense

SPELLS
Trained in divine spell attacks
Trained in divine spell DCs

TABLE 3-8: CLERIC ADVANCEMENT

Your Level	Class Features
1	Ancestry and background, initial proficiencies, deity, divine spellcasting, divine font, doctrine
2	Cleric feat, skill feat
3	2nd-level spells, general feat, second doctrine, skill increase
4	Cleric feat, skill feat
5	3rd-level spells, ability boosts, alertness, ancestry feat, skill increase
6	Cleric feat, skill feat
7	4th-level spells, general feat, skill increase, third doctrine
8	Cleric feat, skill feat
9	5th-level spells, ancestry feat, resolve, skill increase
10	Ability boosts, cleric feat, skill feat
11	6th-level spells, fourth doctrine, general feat, lightning reflexes, skill increase
12	Cleric feat, skill feat
13	7th-level spells, ancestry feat, divine defense, skill increase, weapon specialization
14	Cleric feat, skill feat
15	8th-level spells, ability boosts, fifth doctrine, general feat, skill increase
16	Cleric feat, skill feat
17	9th-level spells, ancestry feat, skill increase
18	Cleric feat, skill feat
19	Final doctrine, general feat, miraculous spell, skill increase
20	Ability boosts, cleric feat, skill feat

CLASS FEATURES

You gain these abilities as a cleric. Abilities gained at higher levels list requisite levels next to their names.

ANCESTRY AND BACKGROUND

In addition to the abilities provided by your class at 1st level, you have the benefits of your selected ancestry and background, as described in Chapter 2.

INITIAL PROFICIENCIES

At 1st level, you gain a number of proficiencies that represent your basic training, noted at the start of this class.

DEITY

As a cleric, you are a mortal servitor of a deity you revere above all others. The most common deities in Pathfinder appear on pages 437–440, along with their alignments, areas of concern, and the benefits you get for being a cleric of that deity. Your alignment must be one allowed by your deity, as listed in their entry. Your deity grants you the trained proficiency rank in one skill and with the deity's favored weapon. If the favored weapon is uncommon, you also get access to that weapon.

Your deity also adds spells to your spell list. You can prepare these just like you can any spell on the divine spell list, once you can prepare spells of their level as a cleric.

Some of these spells aren't normally on the divine list, but they're divine spells if you prepare them this way.

ANATHEMA

Acts fundamentally opposed to your deity's alignment or ideals are anathema to your faith. Learning or casting spells, committing acts, and using items that are anathema to your deity remove you from your deity's good graces.

Casting spells with the evil trait is almost always anathema to good deities, and casting good spells is likewise anathema to evil deities; similarly, casting chaotic spells is anathema to lawful deities, and casting lawful spells is anathema to chaotic deities. A neutral cleric who worships a neutral deity isn't limited this way, but their alignment might change over time if they frequently cast spells or use abilities with a certain alignment. Similarly, casting spells that are anathema to the tenets or goals of your faith could interfere with your connection to your deity. For example, casting a spell to create undead would be anathema to Pharasma, the goddess of death. For borderline cases, you and your GM determine which acts are anathema.

If you perform enough acts that are anathema to your deity, or if your alignment changes to one not allowed by your deity, you lose the magical abilities that come from your connection to your deity. The class features that you lose are determined by the GM, but they likely include your divine font and all divine spellcasting. These abilities can be regained only if you demonstrate your repentance by conducting an *atone* ritual (found on page 409).

DIVINE SPELLCASTING

Your deity bestows on you the power to cast divine spells. You can cast divine spells using the Cast a Spell activity, and you can supply material, somatic, and verbal components when casting spells (see Casting Spells on page 302). Because you're a cleric, you can usually hold a divine focus (such as a religious symbol) for spells requiring material components instead of needing to use a spell component pouch.

At 1st level, you can prepare two 1st-level spells and five cantrips each morning from the common spells on the divine spell list in this book (page 309) or from other divine spells to which you gain access. Prepared spells remain available to you until you cast them or until you prepare your spells again. The number of spells you can prepare is called your spell slots.

As you increase in level as a cleric, the number of spells you can prepare each day increases, as does the highest level of spell you can cast, as shown in Table 3–9: Cleric Spells per Day on page 120.

Some of your spells require you to attempt a spell attack roll to see how effective they are, or your enemies to roll against your spell DC (typically by attempting a saving throw). Since your key ability is Wisdom, your spell attack rolls and spell DCs use your Wisdom modifier. Details on calculating these statistics appear on page 447.

Heightening Spells

When you get spell slots of 2nd level and higher, you can fill those slots with stronger versions of lower-level spells. This increases the spell's level, heightening it to match the spell slot. Many spells have specific improvements when they are heightened to certain levels.

Cantrips

A cantrip is a special type of spell that doesn't use spell slots. You can cast a cantrip at will, any number of times per day. A cantrip is always automatically heightened to half your level rounded up—this is usually equal to the highest level of spell you can cast as a cleric. For example, as a 1st-level cleric, your cantrips are 1st-level spells, and as a 5th-level cleric, your cantrips are 3rd-level spells.

DIVINE FONT

Through your deity's blessing, you gain additional spells that channel either the life force called positive energy or its counterforce, negative energy. When you prepare your spells each day, you can prepare additional *heal* or *harm* spells, depending on your deity. The divine font spell your deity provides is listed in the Divine Font entry for your deity on pages 437–440; if both are listed, you can choose between *heal* or *harm*. Once you choose, you can't change your choice short of an ethical shift or divine intervention.

Healing Font: You gain additional spell slots each day at your highest level of cleric spell slots. You can prepare only *heal* spells (page 343) in these slots, and the number of slots is equal to 1 plus your Charisma modifier.

Harmful Font: You gain additional spell slots each day at your highest level of cleric spell slots. You can prepare only *harm* spells (page 343) in these slots, and the number of slots is equal to 1 plus your Charisma modifier.

DOCTRINE

Even among followers of the same deity, there are numerous doctrines and beliefs, which sometimes vary wildly between clerics. At 1st level, you select a doctrine and gain the benefits of its first doctrine. The doctrines presented in this book are cloistered cleric and warpriest. Each doctrine grants you initial benefits at 1st level. At 3rd, 7th, 11th, 15th, and 19th levels, you gain the benefits granted by your doctrine's second, third, fourth, fifth, and final doctrines respectively.

Cloistered Cleric

You are a cleric of the cloth, focusing on divine magic and your connection to your deity's domains.

First Doctrine (1st): You gain the Domain Initiate cleric feat (page 121).

Second Doctrine (3rd): Your proficiency rank for Fortitude saves increases to expert.

Third Doctrine (7th): Your proficiency ranks for divine spell attack rolls and spell DCs increase to expert.

Fourth Doctrine (11th): You gain expert proficiency with your deity's favored weapon. When you critically succeed at an attack roll using that weapon, you apply the weapon's critical specialization effect; use your divine spell DC if necessary.

TABLE 3-9: CLERIC SPELLS PER DAY

Your Level	Cantrips	Spell Level										
		1st	2nd	3rd	4th	5th	6th	7th	8th	9th	10th
1	5	2*	–	–	–	–	–	–	–	–	–
2	5	3*	–	–	–	–	–	–	–	–	–
3	5	3	2*	–	–	–	–	–	–	–	–
4	5	3	3*	–	–	–	–	–	–	–	–
5	5	3	3	2*	–	–	–	–	–	–	–
6	5	3	3	3*	–	–	–	–	–	–	–
7	5	3	3	3	2*	–	–	–	–	–	–
8	5	3	3	3	3*	–	–	–	–	–	–
9	5	3	3	3	3	2*	–	–	–	–	–
10	5	3	3	3	3	3*	–	–	–	–	–
11	5	3	3	3	3	3	2*	–	–	–	–
12	5	3	3	3	3	3	3*	–	–	–	–
13	5	3	3	3	3	3	3	2*	–	–	–
14	5	3	3	3	3	3	3	3*	–	–	–
15	5	3	3	3	3	3	3	3	2*	–	–
16	5	3	3	3	3	3	3	3	3*	–	–
17	5	3	3	3	3	3	3	3	3	2*	–
18	5	3	3	3	3	3	3	3	3	3*	–
19	5	3	3	3	3	3	3	3	3	3	1*†
20	5	3	3	3	3	3	3	3	3	3	1*†

* Your divine font gives you additional *heal* or *harm* spells of this level. The number is equal to 1 + your Charisma modifier.
† The miraculous spell class feature gives you a 10th-level spell slot that works a bit differently from other spell slots.

Fifth Doctrine (15th): Your proficiency ranks for divine spell attack rolls and spell DCs increase to master.

Final Doctrine (19th): Your proficiency ranks for divine spell attack rolls and spell DCs increase to legendary.

WARPRIEST

You have trained in the more militant doctrine of your church, focusing on both spells and battle.

First Doctrine (1st): You're trained in light and medium armor, and you have expert proficiency in Fortitude saves. You gain the Shield Block general feat (page 266), a reaction to reduce damage with a shield. If your deity's weapon is simple, you gain the Deadly Simplicity cleric feat (page 121). At 13th level, if you gain the divine defense class feature, you also gain expert proficiency in light and medium armor.

Second Doctrine (3rd): You're trained in martial weapons.

Third Doctrine (7th): You gain expert proficiency with your deity's favored weapon. When you critically succeed at an attack roll using that weapon, you apply the weapon's critical specialization effect; use your divine spell DC if necessary.

Fourth Doctrine (11th Level): Your proficiency ranks for divine spell attack rolls and spell DCs increase to expert.

Fifth Doctrine (15th Level): Your proficiency rank for Fortitude saves increases to master. When you roll a success at a Fortitude save, you get a critical success instead.

Final Doctrine (19th Level): Your proficiency ranks for divine spell attack rolls and spell DCs increase to master.

CLERIC FEATS   2ND

At 2nd level and every 2 levels thereafter, you gain a cleric class feat. These begin on page 121.

SKILL FEATS   2ND

At 2nd level and every 2 levels thereafter, you gain a skill feat. Skill feats can be found in Chapter 5 and have the skill trait. You must be trained or better in the corresponding skill to select a skill feat.

GENERAL FEATS   3RD

At 3rd level and every 4 levels thereafter, you gain a general feat. General feats are listed in Chapter 5.

SKILL INCREASES   3RD

At 3rd level and every 2 levels thereafter, you gain a skill increase. You can use this increase to either become trained in one skill you're untrained in, or become an expert in one skill in which you're already trained.

You can use any of these skill increases you gain at 7th level or higher to become a master in a skill in which you're already an expert, and any of these skill increases you gain at 15th level or higher to become legendary in a skill in which you're already a master.

ABILITY BOOSTS   5TH

At 5th level and every 5 levels thereafter, you boost four different ability scores. You can use these ability boosts to increase your ability scores above 18. Boosting an ability score increases it by 1 if it's already 18 or above, or by 2 if it starts out below 18.

ALERTNESS   5TH

You remain alert to threats around you. Your proficiency rank for Perception increases to expert.

ANCESTRY FEATS   5TH

In addition to the ancestry feat you started with, you gain an ancestry feat at 5th level and every 4 levels thereafter. The list of ancestry feats available to you can be found in your ancestry's entry in Chapter 2.

RESOLVE   9TH

You've steeled your mind with resolve. Your proficiency rank for Will saves increases to master. When you roll a success at a Will save, you get a critical success instead.

LIGHTNING REFLEXES   11TH

Your reflexes are lightning fast. Your proficiency rank for Reflex saves increases to expert.

DIVINE DEFENSE   13TH

Your training and your deity protect you from harm. Your proficiency rank in unarmored defense increases to expert.

WEAPON SPECIALIZATION   13TH

You've learned how to inflict greater injuries with the weapons you know best. You deal 2 additional damage with weapons and unarmed attacks in which you are an expert. This damage increases to 3 if you're a master, and to 4 if you're legendary.

MIRACULOUS SPELL   19TH

You're exalted by your deity and gain truly incredible spells. You gain a single 10th-level spell slot and can prepare a spell in that slot using divine spellcasting. You don't gain more 10th-level spells as you level up, though you can take the Maker of Miracles feat to gain a second slot.

CLERIC FEATS

At each level that you gain a cleric feat, you can select one of the following feats. You must satisfy any prerequisites before selecting the feat.

1ST LEVEL

DEADLY SIMPLICITY   FEAT 1

CLERIC

Prerequisites deity with a simple favored weapon, trained with your deity's favored weapon

Your deity's weapon is especially powerful in your hands. When you are wielding your deity's favored weapon, increase the damage die size of that weapon by one step.

KEY TERMS

You'll see the following term in many cleric class features.

Metamagic: These actions tweak your spells. You must use a metamagic action directly before Casting the Spell you want to alter. If you use any action (including free actions and reactions) other than Cast a Spell directly after, you waste the benefits of the metamagic action. Effects added by a metamagic action are part of the spell's effect, not of the metamagic action.

If your deity's favored weapon is an unarmed attack (such as a fist, if you worship Irori) and its damage die is smaller than d6, instead increase its damage die size to d6.

DOMAIN INITIATE   FEAT 1

CLERIC

Your deity bestows a special spell related to their powers. Select one domain—a subject of particular interest to you within your religion—from your deity's list. You gain an initial domain spell for that domain, a spell unique to the domain and not available to other clerics. Each domain's theme and domain spells appear in Table 8–2: Domains on page 441.

Domain spells are a type of focus spell. It costs 1 Focus Point to cast a focus spell, and you start with a focus pool of 1 Focus Point. You refill your focus pool during your daily preparations, and you can regain 1 Focus Point by spending 10 minutes using the Refocus activity to pray to your deity or do service toward their causes.

Focus spells are automatically heightened to half your level rounded up. Focus spells don't require spell slots, nor can you cast them using spell slots. Certain feats can give you more focus spells and increase the size of your focus pool, though your focus pool can never hold more than 3 Focus Points. The full rules for focus spells appear on page 300.

Special You can select this feat multiple times, selecting a different domain each time and gaining its domain spell.

HARMING HANDS   FEAT 1

CLERIC

Prerequisites harmful font

The mordant power of your negative energy grows. When you cast *harm*, you roll d10s instead of d8s.

HEALING HANDS   FEAT 1

CLERIC

Prerequisites healing font

Your positive energy is even more vibrant and restorative. When you cast *heal*, you roll d10s instead of d8s.

HOLY CASTIGATION   FEAT 1

CLERIC

Prerequisites good alignment

You combine holy energy with positive energy to damage demons, devils, and their evil ilk. *Heal* spells you cast damage fiends as though they were undead.

INTRODUCTION

ANCESTRIES & BACKGROUNDS

CLASSES

SKILLS

FEATS

EQUIPMENT

SPELLS

THE AGE OF LOST OMENS

PLAYING THE GAME

GAME MASTERING

CRAFTING & TREASURE

APPENDIX

CLERIC FEATS

If you need to look up a cleric feat by name instead of by level, use this table.

REACH SPELL ❖   FEAT 1

`CLERIC` `CONCENTRATE` `METAMAGIC`

You can extend the range of your spells. If the next action you use is to Cast a Spell that has a range, increase that spell's range by 30 feet. As is standard for increasing spell ranges, if the spell normally has a range of touch, you extend its range to 30 feet.

2ND LEVEL

CANTRIP EXPANSION   FEAT 2

`CLERIC`

You study a wider range of simple spells. You can prepare two additional cantrips each day.

COMMUNAL HEALING   FEAT 2

`CLERIC` `HEALING` `POSITIVE`

You're a conduit for positive energy, and as you channel it through you, it heals some of your minor injuries. When you cast the *heal* spell to heal a single creature other than yourself, you regain Hit Points equal to the spell level of the *heal* spell.

EMBLAZON ARMAMENT   FEAT 2

`CLERIC` `EXPLORATION`

Carefully etching a sacred image into a physical object, you steel yourself for battle. You can spend 10 minutes emblazoning a symbol of your deity upon a weapon or shield. The symbol doesn't fade until 1 year has passed, but if you Emblazon an Armament, any symbol you previously emblazoned and any symbol already emblazoned on that item instantly disappears. The item becomes a religious symbol of your deity and can be used as a divine focus while emblazoned, and it gains another benefit determined by the type of item. This benefit applies only to followers of the deity the symbol represents.

- **Shield** The shield gains a +1 status bonus to its Hardness. (This causes it to reduce more damage with the Shield Block reaction.)
- **Weapon** The wielder gains a +1 status bonus to damage rolls.

SAP LIFE   FEAT 2

`CLERIC` `HEALING`

You draw the life force out of your enemies to heal your own wounds. When you cast a *harm* spell and damage at least one living creature, you regain Hit Points equal to the spell level of your *harm* spell. If you aren't a living creature, you gain no benefit from this feat.

TURN UNDEAD   FEAT 2

`CLERIC`

Undead harmed by your positive energy might flee, compelled by an innate aversion to the force opposite undeath. When you use a *heal* spell to damage undead, each undead of your level or lower that critically fails its save gains the fleeing condition for 1 round.

VERSATILE FONT   FEAT 2

`CLERIC`

Prerequisites harmful font or healing font, deity that allows clerics to have both fonts

As you explore your deity's aspects, you move beyond restrictions on healing or harming. You can prepare either *harm* or *heal* in the spell slots gained from the harmful font or healing font.

4TH LEVEL

CHANNEL SMITE ❖❖   FEAT 4

`CLERIC` `DIVINE` `NECROMANCY`

Prerequisites harmful font or healing font

Cost Expend a *harm* or *heal* spell.

You siphon the destructive energies of positive or negative energy through a melee attack and into your foe. Make a melee Strike and add the spell's damage to the Strike's damage. This is negative damage if you expended a *harm* spell or positive damage if you expended a *heal* spell.

The spell is expended with no effect if your Strike fails or hits a creature that isn't damaged by that energy type (such as if you hit a non-undead creature with a *heal* spell).

COMMAND UNDEAD ❖   FEAT 4
CLERIC **CONCENTRATE** **METAMAGIC**

Prerequisites harmful font, evil alignment

You grasp the animating force within an undead creature and bend it to your will. If the next action you use is to cast *harm* targeting one undead creature, you transform the effects of that *harm* spell. Instead of *harm*'s normal effects, the target becomes controlled by you if its level is equal to or lower than your level – 3. It can attempt a Will saving throw to resist being controlled by you. If the target is already under someone else's command, the controlling creature also rolls a saving throw, and the undead uses the better result.

Critical Success The target is unaffected and is temporarily immune for 24 hours.

Success The target is unaffected.

Failure The undead creature becomes a minion under your control. The spell gains a duration of 1 minute, but it is dismissed if you or an ally attacks the minion undead.

Critical Failure As failure, but the duration is 1 hour.

DIRECTED CHANNEL   FEAT 4
CLERIC

You can shape the energy you channel in a single direction, reaching farther and in a more directed fashion. When you cast a version of *harm* or *heal* that has an area, you can make its area a 60-foot cone instead of a 30-foot emanation.

IMPROVED COMMUNAL HEALING   FEAT 4
CLERIC

Prerequisites Communal Healing

You can direct excess channeled energy outward to benefit an ally. You can grant the Hit Points you would regain from Communal Healing to any one creature within the range of your *heal* spell instead of yourself. You can also use Communal Healing when you target only yourself with a *heal* spell, though if you do, you must grant the additional healing to someone other than yourself.

NECROTIC INFUSION ❖   FEAT 4
CLERIC **CONCENTRATE** **METAMAGIC**

Prerequisites harmful font, evil alignment

You pour negative energy into your undead subject to empower its attacks. If the next action you use is to cast *harm* to restore Hit Points to a single undead creature, the target then deals an additional 1d6 negative damage with its melee weapons and unarmed attacks until the end of its next turn.

If the *harm* spell is at least 5th level, this damage increases to 2d6, and if the *harm* spell is at least 8th level, the damage increases to 3d6.

CONTROLLING UNDEAD

Controlled undead gain the minion trait. Minions can use 2 actions per turn and can't use reactions. A minion acts on your turn in combat when you spend an action to issue it verbal commands (this action has the auditory and concentrate traits). If given no commands, undead minions use no actions except to defend themselves or to escape obvious harm. If left unattended for at least 1 minute, mindless undead minions don't act, and intelligent ones act as they please. You can't have more than four undead minions at a time.

6TH LEVEL

CAST DOWN ❖   FEAT 6
CLERIC **CONCENTRATE** **METAMAGIC**

Prerequisites harmful font or healing font

The sheer force of your faith can bring a foe crashing down. If the next action you use is to cast *harm* or *heal* to damage one creature, the target is knocked prone if it takes any damage from the spell. If the target critically fails its save against the spell, it also takes a –10-foot status penalty to its Speed for 1 minute.

DIVINE WEAPON ❖   FEAT 6
CLERIC

Frequency once per turn

Trigger You finish Casting a Spell using one of your divine spell slots on your turn.

You siphon residual spell energy into a weapon you're wielding. Until the end of your turn, the weapon deals an additional 1d4 force damage. You can instead deal an additional 1d6 damage of an alignment type that matches one of your deity's alignment components. As usual for aligned damage, this can damage only creatures of the opposite alignment.

SELECTIVE ENERGY   FEAT 6
CLERIC

As you call down divine power, you can prevent some enemies from benefiting or some allies from being hurt. When you cast a version of *harm* or *heal* that has an area, you can designate a number of creatures equal to your Charisma modifier (minimum 1) that are not targeted by the spell.

STEADY SPELLCASTING   FEAT 6
CLERIC

Confident in your technique, you don't lose spells easily. If a reaction would disrupt your spellcasting action, attempt a DC 15 flat check. If you succeed, your action isn't disrupted.

8TH LEVEL

ADVANCED DOMAIN   FEAT 8
CLERIC

Prerequisites Domain Initiate

Your studies or prayers have unlocked deeper secrets of your deity's domain. You gain an advanced domain spell from one

INTRODUCTION

ANCESTRIES & BACKGROUNDS

CLASSES

SKILLS

FEATS

EQUIPMENT

SPELLS

THE AGE OF LOST OMENS

PLAYING THE GAME

GAME MASTERING

CRAFTING & TREASURE

APPENDIX

SAMPLE CLERIC

GOZREN

Following the Wind and the Waves, you protect the beauty of nature in all its forms.

ABILITY SCORES
Prioritize Wisdom and Strength. Charisma increases your divine font *heal* spells.

SKILLS
Athletics, Nature, Religion, Survival

DEITY
Gozreh (alignment: LN; divine font: *heal*)

DOCTRINE
Warpriest

HIGHER-LEVEL FEATS
Domain Initiate (water, 1st), Divine Weapon (6th)

PREPARED SPELLS
1st *gust of wind, sanctuary, heal* spells from divine font;
Cantrips *detect magic, know direction, light, message, shield*

---

of your domains (as listed in Table 8–2: Domains on page 441). Increase the number of Focus Points in your focus pool by 1.

Special You can select this feat multiple times. Each time, you must select a different advanced domain spell from a domain for which you have an initial domain spell.

ALIGN ARMAMENT ❖ — FEAT 8
CLERIC | DIVINE | EVOCATION

Prerequisites chaotic, evil, good, or lawful deity
Frequency once per round

You bring a weapon into metaphysical concordance with your deity's beliefs. When you select this feat, choose chaotic, evil, good, or lawful. Your choice must match one of your deity's alignment components. This action has the trait corresponding to the chosen alignment component.

When you use this action, you touch a weapon. For 1 round, that weapon deals an additional 1d6 damage of the chosen type to creatures of the opposed alignment. For example, if you chose good, the weapon would deal an extra 1d6 good damage to evil creatures. If you Align an Armament again, any previously aligned armament loses its additional damage.

Special You can select this feat a second time, choosing your deity's other alignment component. When you Align an Armament, you can choose either alignment component.

CHANNELED SUCCOR — FEAT 8
CLERIC

Prerequisites healing font

You can remove conditions with divine grace. You can sacrifice one *heal* spell you've prepared in your extra slots from healing font to cast one of the following spells instead: *remove curse, remove disease, remove paralysis,* or *restoration*. The spell is heightened to the same level as the *heal* spell you sacrificed.

CREMATE UNDEAD — FEAT 8
CLERIC

Your positive energy sets undead alight. When you use a *heal* spell to damage undead, each undead that takes damage also takes persistent fire damage equal to the spell's level.

EMBLAZON ENERGY — FEAT 8
CLERIC

Prerequisites Emblazon Armament

With elemental forces, you make your emblazoned symbols more potent. When you Emblazon an Armament, you can choose from the following effects instead of the effects listed in that feat. These effects have the same restrictions as the base options.

- **Shield** Choose acid, cold, electricity, fire, or sonic. The wielder gain the shield's circumstance bonus to saving throws against that damage type and can use Shield Block against damage of that type. The shield also gains resistance to that damage type equal to half your level if you have a domain spell with a trait matching that type (such as fire).

INTRODUCTION

ANCESTRIES &
BACKGROUNDS

CLASSES

SKILLS

FEATS

EQUIPMENT

SPELLS

THE AGE OF
LOST OMENS

PLAYING THE
GAME

GAME
MASTERING

CRAFTING
& TREASURE

APPENDIX

- **Weapon** Choose acid, cold, electricity, fire, or sonic. The weapon deals an extra 1d4 damage of that type. Increase this extra damage to 1d6 if you have a domain spell with a trait matching that type (such as fire).

10TH LEVEL

CASTIGATING WEAPON FEAT 10

CLERIC

Prerequisites Holy Castigation

The force of your deity's castigation strengthens your body so you can strike down the wicked. After you damage a fiend using a *heal* spell, your weapon or unarmed Strikes deal extra good damage to fiends equal to half the level of the *heal* spell until the end of your next turn. This is cumulative with any good damage the weapon already deals (such as from a *holy* rune).

HEROIC RECOVERY ❖ FEAT 10

CLERIC | CONCENTRATE | METAMAGIC

Prerequisites healing font, good alignment

The restorative power of your healing invigorates the recipient. If the next action you use is to cast *heal* targeting a single living creature and the target regains Hit Points from the spell, it also gains three bonuses until the end of its next turn: a +5-foot status bonus to its Speed, a +1 status bonus to attack rolls, and a +1 status bonus to damage rolls.

IMPROVED COMMAND UNDEAD FEAT 10

CLERIC

Prerequisites harmful font, Command Undead, evil alignment

Undead creatures find it all but impossible to resist your commands. When you use Command Undead, if the undead succeeds at its save but doesn't critically succeed, it is your minion for 1 round. If the undead fails its save, it is your minion for 10 minutes. If it critically fails, it is your minion for 24 hours.

REPLENISHMENT OF WAR FEAT 10

CLERIC

Prerequisites expert in your deity's favored weapon

Striking out against your enemies draws praise and protection from your deity. When you damage a creature with a Strike using your deity's favored weapon, you gain a number of temporary Hit Points equal to half your level, or equal to your level if the Strike was a critical hit. These temporary Hit Points last until the start of your next turn.

12TH LEVEL

DEFENSIVE RECOVERY ❖ FEAT 12

CLERIC | CONCENTRATE | METAMAGIC

Prerequisites harmful font or healing font

Your faith provides temporary protection in addition to healing. If the next action you use is to cast *harm* or *heal* on a single target and the target regains Hit Points from the spell, it also gains a +2 status bonus to AC and saving throws for 1 round.

DOMAIN FOCUS FEAT 12

CLERIC

Prerequisites one or more domain spells

Your devotion to your deity's domains grows greater, and so does the power granted to you. If you have spent at least 2 Focus Points since the last time you Refocused, you recover 2 Focus Points when you Refocus instead of 1.

EMBLAZON ANTIMAGIC FEAT 12

CLERIC

Prerequisites Emblazon Armament

Your deity's symbol protects against offensive magic. When you Emblazon an Armament, you can choose from the following effects instead of the effects listed in that feat. These effects have the same restrictions as the base options.

- **Shield** When the wielder has the shield raised, they gain the shield's circumstance bonus to saving throws against magic, and they can use Shield Block against damage from their enemies' spells.
- **Weapon** When the weapon's wielder critically hits with the weapon, they can attempt to counteract a spell on their target, using their level as the counteract level. If they attempt to do so, the emblazoned symbol immediately disappears.

SHARED REPLENISHMENT FEAT 12

CLERIC

Prerequisites Replenishment of War

When your deity blesses your warlike acts, you can extend that favor to your allies. You can grant the temporary Hit Points from Replenishment of War to an ally within 10 feet instead of gaining them yourself. You can grant these temporary Hit Points to a different ally each time, meaning you might be able to grant them to multiple creatures in a single turn.

14TH LEVEL

DEITY'S PROTECTION FEAT 14

CLERIC

Prerequisites Advanced Domain

When you call upon your deity's power to fulfill the promise of their domain, you gain divine protection. After you cast a domain spell, you gain resistance to all damage until the start of your next turn. The amount of resistance is equal to the level of the domain spell you cast.

EXTEND ARMAMENT ALIGNMENT FEAT 14

CLERIC

Prerequisites Align Armament

The alignment you impose on a weapon lasts much longer. The duration of Align Armament increases to 1 minute.

FAST CHANNEL FEAT 14

CLERIC

Prerequisites harmful font or healing font

Divine power is always at your fingertips, swiftly responding

SAMPLE CLERIC

PHARASMIN

A follower of the Lady of Graves, you respect the sanctity of both life and death.

ABILITY SCORES
Prioritize Wisdom, with Charisma second to maximize your healing and help you spread the word of your faith.

SKILLS
Diplomacy, Medicine, Occultism, Religion

DEITY
Pharasma (alignment: N; divine font: *heal*)

DOCTRINE
Cloistered cleric (death domain)

HIGHER-LEVEL FEATS
Turn Undead (2nd), Selective Energy (6th)

PREPARED SPELLS
1st *fear, mindlink, heal* spells from divine font; **Cantrips** *detect magic,disrupt undead, daze, light, stabilize*

to your call. When you cast *harm* or *heal* by spending 2 actions, you can get the effects of the 3-action version instead of the 2-action version.

You can do this with *harm* if you have harmful font or *heal* if you have healing font (or both if you have Versatile Font).

SWIFT BANISHMENT ↻ FEAT 14
CLERIC

Trigger You critically hit a creature that is not on its home plane.
Requirements You have a *banishment* spell prepared.
The force of your blow sends your victim back to its home plane. You expend a *banishment* spell you have prepared, affecting the creature you critically hit without needing to cast the spell. The creature can attempt to resist the spell as normal.

16TH LEVEL

ETERNAL BANE FEAT 16
CLERIC

Prerequisites evil alignment
A life of evil has made you a nexus for your deity's vile power. You're continuously surrounded by a *bane* spell with a spell level equal to half your level (rounded up). The radius is 15 feet, and you can't increase it. You can Dismiss the spell; if you do, it returns automatically after 1 minute.

ETERNAL BLESSING FEAT 16
CLERIC

Prerequisites good alignment
Your good deeds have brought your deity's grace to you for all of eternity. You're continuously surrounded by a *bless* spell with a spell level equal to half your level (rounded up). The radius is 15 feet, and you can't increase it. You can Dismiss the spell; if you do, it returns automatically after 1 minute.

RESURRECTIONIST FEAT 16
CLERIC

You can cause a creature you bring back from the brink of death to thrive and continue healing. When you restore Hit Points to a dying creature or bring a dead creature back to life and restore Hit Points to it, you grant that creature fast healing 5 for 1 minute. This fast healing ends if the creature is knocked unconscious.

18TH LEVEL

DOMAIN WELLSPRING FEAT 18
CLERIC

Prerequisites Domain Focus
The intensity of your focus grows from the investment you've placed in your domains. If you have spent at least 3 Focus Points since the last time you Refocused, you recover 3 Focus Points when you Refocus instead of 1.

ECHOING CHANNEL ❖   FEAT 18

| CLERIC | CONCENTRATE | METAMAGIC |

When you pull forth positive or negative energy, you also create a smaller pocket of that energy. If the next action you use is to cast a 2-action *harm* or *heal* to heal or damage a single creature, choose one additional creature adjacent to either you or the target. Target that creature with a 1-action version of the same spell. This spell is the same level as the 2-action *harm* or *heal* you cast and doesn't cost another spell slot.

IMPROVED SWIFT BANISHMENT   FEAT 18

| CLERIC |

Prerequisites Swift Banishment

You easily banish creatures with your weapon. You can use Swift Banishment as long as you have a spell slot of 5th level or higher remaining, even if you don't have *banishment* prepared. You must sacrifice a prepared spell of 5th level or higher, and the *banishment* effect you create is heightened to the level of that spell. Your weapon serves as the special material component of *banishment*, causing the target to take the –2 penalty to its save against any *banishment* you cast using Swift Banishment.

20TH LEVEL

AVATAR'S AUDIENCE   FEAT 20

| CLERIC |

Your extensive service has made you a lesser herald of your deity, which affords you certain privileges. First, any creature you encounter knows instinctively that you speak for your deity. Second, if you conduct the *commune* ritual to contact your deity, you don't have to pay any cost and you automatically get a critical success. Third, once per day, you can cast *plane shift* as a divine innate spell, but only to travel to the realm of your deity. When you cast it this way, its casting time is 1 minute, your religious symbol is a sufficient tuning fork for this spell, and you appear exactly where you want to be. If you're in your deity's realm due to this spell, you can return to the point you left when you cast it by spending a single action, which has the concentrate and divine traits.

MAKER OF MIRACLES   FEAT 20

| CLERIC |

Prerequisites miraculous spell

You are a conduit for truly deific power. You gain an additional 10th-level spell slot.

METAMAGIC CHANNEL ❖   FEAT 20

| CLERIC | CONCENTRATE |

Deep understanding of divine revelations into the nature of vital essence allows you to freely manipulate the effects of your positive or negative energy. Use 1 metamagic action that you perform that normally takes 1 action and can be applied to the *harm* or *heal* spell. If you use it in this way, its effects apply only to a *harm* or *heal* spell.

 # DRUID

The power of nature is impossible to resist. It can bring ruin to the stoutest fortress in minutes, reducing even the mightiest works to rubble, burning them to ash, burying them beneath an avalanche of snow, or drowning them beneath the waves. It can provide endless bounty and breathtaking splendor to those who respect it— and an agonizing death to those who take it too lightly. You are one of those who hear nature's call. You stand in awe of the majesty of its power and give yourself over to its service.

KEY ABILITY

WISDOM
At 1st level, your class gives you an ability boost to Wisdom.

HIT POINTS

8 plus your Constitution modifier
You increase your maximum number of HP by this number at 1st level and every level thereafter.

DURING COMBAT ENCOUNTERS...

You call upon the forces of nature to defeat your enemies and protect your allies. You cast spells that draw upon primal magic to protect yourself and your friends, heal their wounds, or summon deadly animals to fight at your side. Depending on your bond to nature, you might call upon powerful elemental magic or change shape into a terrifying beast.

DURING SOCIAL ENCOUNTERS...

You represent balance and a reasoned approach to problems, looking for solutions that not only are best for the natural world, but also allow the creatures within it to live in harmony and peace. You often propose compromises that allow both sides to gain what they truly need, even if they can't have all that they desire.

WHILE EXPLORING...

Your nature skills are invaluable. You track down enemies, navigate the wilderness, and use spells to detect magical auras around you. You might even ask wild animals to lend their extraordinary senses and scouting abilities to your group.

IN DOWNTIME...

You might craft magic items or potions. Alternatively, your tie to nature might lead you to tend a wilderness area, befriending beasts and healing the wounds caused by civilization. You might even teach sustainable farming and animal husbandry techniques that allow others to subsist off the land without harming the natural balance.

YOU MIGHT...

- Have a deep and meaningful respect for the power of nature.
- Be in constant awe of the natural world, eager to share it with others but wary of their influence upon it.
- Treat plants and animals as allies, working with them to reach your goals.

OTHERS PROBABLY...

- View you as a representative of nature, and are sure you can control it.
- Assume you're a recluse who avoids society and cities and prefers to live in the wild.
- Consider you a mystic, similar to a priest, but answering only to the forces of nature.

INITIAL PROFICIENCIES

At 1st level, you gain the listed proficiency ranks in the following statistics. You are untrained in anything not listed unless you gain a better proficiency rank in some other way.

PERCEPTION

Trained in Perception

SAVING THROWS

Trained in Fortitude
Trained in Reflex
Expert in Will

SKILLS

Trained in Nature
Trained in one skill determined by your druidic order
Trained in a number of additional skills equal to 2 plus your Intelligence modifier

ATTACKS

Trained in simple weapons
Trained in unarmed attacks

DEFENSES

Trained in light armor
Trained in medium armor
Trained in unarmored defense

CLASS DC

Trained in druid class DC

SPELLS

Trained in primal spell attacks
Trained in primal spell DCs

TABLE 3-10: DRUID ADVANCEMENT

Your Level	Class Features
1	Ancestry and background, initial proficiencies, primal spellcasting, anathema, Druidic language, druidic order, Shield Block, wild empathy
2	Druid feat, skill feat
3	2nd-level spells, alertness, general feat, great fortitude, skill increase
4	Druid feat, skill feat
5	3rd-level spells, ability boosts, ancestry feat, lightning reflexes, skill increase
6	Druid feat, skill feat
7	4th-level spells, expert spellcaster, general feat, skill increase
8	Druid feat, skill feat
9	5th-level spells, ancestry feat, skill increase
10	Ability boosts, druid feat, skill feat
11	6th-level spells, druid weapon expertise, general feat, resolve, skill increase
12	Druid feat, skill feat
13	7th-level spells, ancestry feat, medium armor expertise, skill increase, weapon specialization
14	Druid feat, skill feat
15	8th-level spells, ability boosts, general feat, master spellcaster, skill increase
16	Druid feat, skill feat
17	9th-level spells, ancestry feat, skill increase
18	Druid feat, skill feat
19	General feat, legendary spellcaster, skill increase
20	Ability boosts, druid feat, skill feat

CLASS FEATURES

You gain these abilities as a druid. Abilities gained at higher levels list the level at which you gain them next to the features' names.

ANCESTRY AND BACKGROUND

In addition to the abilities provided by your class at 1st level, you have the benefits of your selected ancestry and background, as described in Chapter 2.

INITIAL PROFICIENCIES

At 1st level you gain a number of proficiencies, representing your basic training. These proficiencies are noted at the start of this class.

PRIMAL SPELLCASTING

The power of the wild world flows through you. You can cast primal spells using the Cast a Spell activity, and you can supply material, somatic, and verbal components when casting spells (see Casting Spells on page 302). Because you're a druid, you can usually hold a primal focus (such as holly and mistletoe) for spells requiring material components instead of needing to use a spell component pouch.

At 1st level, you can prepare two 1st-level spells and five cantrips each morning from the common spells on the primal spell list in this book (page 314), or from other primal spells to which you gain access. Prepared spells remain available to you until you cast them or until you prepare your spells again. The number of spells you can prepare is called your spell slots.

As you increase in level as a druid, the number of spells you can prepare each day increases, as does the highest level of spell you can cast, as shown in Table 3–11: Druid Spells per Day on page 132.

Some of your spells require you to attempt a spell attack roll to see how effective they are, or have your enemies roll against your spell DC (typically by attempting a saving throw). Since your key ability is Wisdom, your spell attack rolls and spell DCs use your Wisdom modifier. Details on calculating these statistics appear on page 447.

HEIGHTENING SPELLS

When you gain spell slots of 2nd level and higher, you can fill those slots with stronger versions of lower-level spells. This increases the spell's level, heightening it to match the spell slot. Many spells have specific improvements when they are heightened to certain levels.

CANTRIPS

A cantrip is a special type of spell that doesn't use spell slots. You can cast a cantrip at will, any number of times per day. A cantrip is always automatically heightened to half your level rounded up—this is usually equal to the highest level of spell you can cast as a druid. For example, as a 1st-level druid, your cantrips are 1st-level spells, and as a 5th-level druid, your cantrips are 3rd-level spells.

ANATHEMA

As stewards of the natural order, druids find affronts to nature anathema. If you perform enough acts that are anathema to nature, you lose your magical abilities that come from the druid class, including your primal spellcasting and the benefits of your order. These abilities can be regained only if you demonstrate your repentance by conducting an *atone* ritual (page 409).

The following acts are anathema to all druids:

- Using metal armor or shields.
- Despoiling natural places.
- Teaching the Druidic language to non-druids.

Each druidic order also has additional anathema acts, detailed in the order's entry.

DRUIDIC LANGUAGE

You know Druidic, a secret language known to only druids, in addition to any languages you know through your ancestry. Druidic has its own alphabet. Teaching the Druidic language to non-druids is anathema.

DRUIDIC ORDER

Upon becoming a druid, you align yourself with a druidic order, which grants you a class feat, an order spell (see below), and an additional trained skill tied to your order. While you'll always be a member of your initial order, it's not unheard of for a druid to request to study with other orders in search of greater understanding of the natural world, and PC druids are among the most likely to blend the powers of different orders.

Order spells are a type of focus spell. It costs 1 Focus Point to cast a focus spell, and you start with a focus pool of 1 Focus Point. You refill your focus pool during your daily preparations, and you can regain 1 Focus Point by spending 10 minutes using the Refocus activity to commune with local nature spirits or otherwise tend to the wilderness in a way befitting your order.

Focus spells are automatically heightened to half your level rounded up, much like cantrips. Focus spells don't require spell slots to cast, and you can't cast them using spell slots. Selecting druid feats can give you more focus spells and increase the size of your focus pool, though your focus pool can never hold more than 3 points. The full rules for focus spells appear in Chapter 7 on page 300.

ANIMAL

You have a strong connection to beasts, and you are allied with a beast companion. You are trained in Athletics. You also gain the Animal Companion druid feat. You gain the *heal animal* order spell. Committing wanton cruelty to animals or killing animals unnecessarily is anathema to your order. (This doesn't prevent you from defending yourself against animals or killing them cleanly for food.)

LEAF

You revere plants and the bounty of nature, acting as both a gardener and warden for the wilderness, teaching sustainable techniques to communities, and helping areas regrow after disasters or negligent humanoid expansion. You are trained in Diplomacy. You also gain the Leshy Familiar druid feat. You gain the *goodberry* order spell, and you increase the number of Focus Points in your focus pool by 1. Committing wanton cruelty to plants or killing plants unnecessarily is anathema to your order. (This doesn't prevent you from defending yourself against plants or harvesting them when necessary for survival.)

INTRODUCTION

ANCESTRIES & BACKGROUNDS

CLASSES

SKILLS

FEATS

EQUIPMENT

SPELLS

THE AGE OF LOST OMENS

PLAYING THE GAME

GAME MASTERING

CRAFTING & TREASURE

APPENDIX

TABLE 3-11: DRUID SPELLS PER DAY

Your Level	Cantrips	Spell Level										
		1st	2nd	3rd	4th	5th	6th	7th	8th	9th	10th
1	4	2	–	–	–	–	–	–	–	–	–
2	4	3	–	–	–	–	–	–	–	–	–
3	4	3	2	–	–	–	–	–	–	–	–
4	4	3	3	–	–	–	–	–	–	–	–
5	4	3	3	2	–	–	–	–	–	–	–
6	4	3	3	3	–	–	–	–	–	–	–
7	4	3	3	3	2	–	–	–	–	–	–
8	4	3	3	3	3	–	–	–	–	–	–
9	4	3	3	3	3	2	–	–	–	–	–
10	4	3	3	3	3	3	–	–	–	–	–
11	4	3	3	3	3	3	2	–	–	–	–
12	4	3	3	3	3	3	3	–	–	–	–
13	4	3	3	3	3	3	3	2	–	–	–
14	4	3	3	3	3	3	3	3	–	–	–
15	4	3	3	3	3	3	3	3	2	–	–
16	4	3	3	3	3	3	3	3	3	–	–
17	4	3	3	3	3	3	3	3	3	2	–
18	4	3	3	3	3	3	3	3	3	3	–
19	4	3	3	3	3	3	3	3	3	3	1*
20	4	3	3	3	3	3	3	3	3	3	1*

* The primal hierophant class feature gives you a 10th-level spell slot that works a bit differently from other spell slots.

STORM

You carry the fury of the storm within you, channeling it to terrifying effect and riding the winds through the sky. You are trained in Acrobatics. You also gain the Storm Born druid feat. You gain the *tempest surge* order spell, and you increase the number of Focus Points in your focus pool by 1. Polluting the air or allowing those who cause major air pollution or climate shifts to go unpunished is anathema to your order. (This doesn't force you to take action against merely potential harm to the environment or to sacrifice yourself against an obviously superior foe.)

WILD

The savage, uncontrollable call of the natural world infuses you, granting you the ability to change your shape and take on the ferocious form of a wild creature. You are trained in Intimidation. You also gain the Wild Shape druid feat. You gain the *wild morph* order spell. Becoming fully domesticated by the temptations of civilization is anathema to your order. (This doesn't prevent you from buying and using processed goods or staying in a city for an adventure, but you can never come to rely on these conveniences or truly call such a place your permanent home.)

SHIELD BLOCK

You gain the Shield Block general feat (found on page 266), a reaction that lets you reduce damage with your shield.

WILD EMPATHY

You have a connection to the creatures of the natural world that allows you to communicate with them on a rudimentary level. You can use Diplomacy to Make an Impression on animals and to make very simple Requests of them. In most cases, wild animals will give you time to make your case.

DRUID FEATS   2ND

At 2nd level and every even-numbered level, you gain a druid class feat.

SKILL FEATS   2ND

At 2nd level and every 2 levels thereafter, you gain a skill feat. Skill feats appear in Chapter 5 and have the skill trait. You must be trained or better in the corresponding skill to select a skill feat.

ALERTNESS   3RD

Experience has made you increasingly aware of threats around you, and you react more quickly to danger. Your proficiency rank for Perception increases to expert.

GENERAL FEATS   3RD

At 3rd level and every 4 levels thereafter, you gain a general feat. General feats are listed in Chapter 5.

GREAT FORTITUDE   3RD

Your physique is incredibly hardy. Your proficiency rank for Fortitude saves increases to expert.

SKILL INCREASES 3RD

At 3rd level and every 2 levels thereafter, you gain a skill increase. You can use this increase either to increase your proficiency rank to trained in one skill you're untrained in, or to increase your proficiency rank in one skill in which you're already trained to expert.

At 7th level, you can use skill increases to increase your proficiency rank to master in a skill in which you're already an expert, and at 15th level, you can use them to increase your proficiency rank to legendary in a skill in which you're already a master.

ABILITY BOOSTS 5TH

At 5th level and every 5 levels thereafter, you boost four different ability scores. You can use these ability boosts to increase your ability scores above 18. Boosting an ability score increases it by 1 if it's already 18 or above, or by 2 if it starts out below 18.

ANCESTRY FEATS 5TH

In addition to the ancestry feat you started with, you gain an ancestry feat at 5th level and every 4 levels thereafter. The list of ancestry feats available to you can be found in your ancestry's entry in Chapter 2.

LIGHTNING REFLEXES 5TH

Your reflexes are lightning fast. Your proficiency rank for Reflex saves increases to expert.

EXPERT SPELLCASTER 7TH

Your command of primal forces has deepened, empowering your spells. Your proficiency ranks for primal spell attack rolls and spell DCs increase to expert.

DRUID WEAPON EXPERTISE 11TH

You have become thoroughly familiar with the weapons of your trade. Your proficiency ranks for all simple weapons and unarmed attacks increase to expert.

RESOLVE 11TH

You've steeled your mind with incredible resolve. Your proficiency rank for Will saves increases to master. When you roll a success at a Will save, you get a critical success instead.

MEDIUM ARMOR EXPERTISE 13TH

You've learned to defend yourself better against attacks. Your proficiency ranks for light armor, medium armor, and unarmored defense increase to expert.

WEAPON SPECIALIZATION 13TH

You've learned how to inflict greater injuries with the weapons you know best. You deal 2 additional damage with weapons and unarmed attacks in which you are an expert. This damage increases to 3 if you're a master, and to 4 if you're legendary.

KEY TERMS

You'll see the following key term in many druid class features.

Metamagic: Actions with the metamagic trait tweak the properties of your spells. These actions usually come from metamagic feats. You must use the metamagic action directly before Casting the Spell you want to alter. If you use any action (including free actions and reactions) other than Cast a Spell directly after, you waste the benefits of the metamagic action. Any additional effects added by a metamagic action are part of the spell's effect, not of the metamagic action itself.

MASTER SPELLCASTER 15TH

Primal magic answers your command. Your proficiency ranks for primal spell attack rolls and spell DCs increase to master.

LEGENDARY SPELLCASTER 19TH

You have developed an unparalleled rapport with the magic of nature. Your proficiency ranks for primal spell attack rolls and spell DCs increase to legendary.

PRIMAL HIEROPHANT 19TH

You command the most potent forces of primal magic and can cast a spell of truly incredible power. You gain a single 10th-level spell slot and can prepare a spell in that slot using primal spellcasting. Unlike with other spell slots, you don't gain more 10th-level spells as you level up, though you can take the Hierophant's Power feat to gain a second slot.

DRUID FEATS

At every level that you gain a druid feat, you can select one of the following feats. You must satisfy any prerequisites before selecting the feat.

1ST LEVEL

ANIMAL COMPANION FEAT 1

DRUID

Prerequisites animal order

You gain the service of a young animal companion that travels with you on your adventures and obeys any simple commands you give it to the best of its abilities. See Animal Companions on page 214 for more information.

LESHY FAMILIAR FEAT 1

DRUID

Prerequisites leaf order

You gain a leshy familiar, a Tiny plant that embodies one of the many spirits of nature. Other than taking the form of a plant instead of an animal, this familiar uses all the same rules as other familiars, which are detailed on page 217.

INTRODUCTION

ANCESTRIES & BACKGROUNDS

CLASSES

SKILLS

FEATS

EQUIPMENT

SPELLS

THE AGE OF LOST OMENS

PLAYING THE GAME

GAME MASTERING

CRAFTING & TREASURE

APPENDIX

SAMPLE DRUID

WILD DRUID

Taking on the forms of dangerous creatures, you fight with feral intensity. Though you trust your instincts, you might mistrust the ways of polite society.

ABILITY SCORES

Prioritize Wisdom and Strength so you can cast spells and enter melee combat. You'll also want Dexterity and Constitution to improve your defenses and survivability.

SKILLS

Acrobatics, Athletics, Intimidation, Nature

ORDER

Wild

HIGHER-LEVEL FEATS

Form Control (4th), Insect Shape (6th), Soaring Shape (8th), Plant Shape (10th), Monstrosity Shape (16th)

PREPARED SPELLS

1st *heal, magic fang;* **Cantrips** *dancing lights, detect magic, know direction, produce flame, tanglefoot*

REACH SPELL ❖   FEAT 1

> CONCENTRATE | DRUID | METAMAGIC

You can extend the range of your spells. If the next action you use is to Cast a Spell that has a range, increase that spell's range by 30 feet. As is standard for increasing spell ranges, if the spell normally has a range of touch, you extend its range to 30 feet.

STORM BORN   FEAT 1

> DRUID

Prerequisites storm order

You are at home out in the elements, reveling in the power of nature unleashed. You do not take circumstance penalties to ranged spell attacks or Perception checks caused by weather, and your targeted spells don't require a flat check to succeed against a target concealed by weather (such as fog).

WIDEN SPELL ❖   FEAT 1

> DRUID | MANIPULATE | METAMAGIC

You manipulate the energy of your spell, causing it to spread out and affect a wider area. If the next action you use is to Cast a Spell that has an area of a burst, cone, or line and does not have a duration, increase the area of that spell. Add 5 feet to the radius of a burst that normally has a radius of at least 10 feet (a burst with a smaller radius is not affected). Add 5 feet to the length of a cone or line that is normally 15 feet long or smaller, and add 10 feet to the length of a larger cone or line.

WILD SHAPE   FEAT 1

> DRUID

Prerequisites wild order

You are one with the wild, always changing and adapting to meet any challenge. You gain the *wild shape* order spell, which lets you transform into a variety of forms that you can expand with druid feats.

2ND LEVEL

CALL OF THE WILD   FEAT 2

> DRUID

You call upon the creatures of nature to come to your aid. You can spend 10 minutes in concert with nature to replace one of the spells you've prepared in one of your druid spell slots with a *summon animal* or *summon plants and fungi* spell of the same level.

ENHANCED FAMILIAR   FEAT 2

> DRUID

Prerequisites a familiar

You infuse your familiar with additional primal energy, increasing its abilities. You can select four familiar or master abilities each day, instead of two.

ORDER EXPLORER   FEAT 2

> DRUID

You have learned the secrets of another druidic order,

passing whatever rites of initiation that order requires and gaining access to its secrets. Choose an order other than your own. You gain a 1st-level feat that lists that order as a prerequisite, and you are now a member of that order for the purpose of meeting feat prerequisites. If you commit acts anathema to your new order, you lose all feats and abilities requiring that order but retain your other druid feats and abilities. You don't gain any of the other benefits of the order you chose.

Special You can take this feat multiple times. Each time you do, you must choose a different order other than your own.

POISON RESISTANCE ❖ FEAT 2

DRUID

Your affinity for the natural world grants you protection against some of its dangers. You gain poison resistance equal to half your level, and you gain a +1 status bonus to saving throws against poisons.

4TH LEVEL

FORM CONTROL ❖ FEAT 4

DRUID MANIPULATE METAMAGIC

Prerequisites Strength 14, Wild Shape

With additional care and effort, you can take on an alternate form for a longer period of time. If your next action is to cast *wild shape*, *wild shape*'s spell level is 2 lower than normal (minimum 1st level), but you can remain transformed for up to 1 hour or the listed duration (whichever is longer). You can still Dismiss the form at any time, as permitted by the spell.

MATURE ANIMAL COMPANION FEAT 4

DRUID

Prerequisites Animal Companion

Your animal companion grows up, becoming a mature animal companion, which grants it additional capabilities. See the animal companion rules on page 214 for more information. Your animal companion is better trained than most. During an encounter, even if you don't use the Command an Animal action, your animal companion can still use 1 action on your turn that round to Stride or Strike.

ORDER MAGIC FEAT 4

DRUID

Prerequisites Order Explorer

You have delved deeper into the teaching of a new order, gaining access to a coveted order spell. Choose an order you have selected with Order Explorer. You gain the initial order spell from that order.

Special You can take this feat multiple times. Each time you do, you must choose a different order you have selected with Order Explorer.

THOUSAND FACES FEAT 4

DRUID

Prerequisites Wild Shape

Your form is as mutable as the weather, changing to meet your whim. You add the forms listed in *humanoid form* to your *wild shape* list.

WOODLAND STRIDE FEAT 4

DRUID

Prerequisites leaf order

You can always find a path, almost as if foliage parted before you. You ignore any difficult terrain caused by plants, such as bushes, vines, and undergrowth. Even plants manipulated by magic don't impede your progress.

DRUID FEATS

If you need to look up a druid feat by name instead of by level, use this table.

Feat	Level
Animal Companion	1
Call of the Wild	2
Dragon Shape	12
Effortless Concentration	16
Elemental Shape	10
Enhanced Familiar	2
Ferocious Shape	8
Fey Caller	8
Form Control	4
Green Empathy	6
Green Tongue	12
Healing Transformation	10
Hierophant's Power	20
Impaling Briars	16
Incredible Companion	8
Insect Shape	6
Invoke Disaster	18
Leshy Familiar	1
Leyline Conduit	20
Mature Animal Companion	4
Monstrosity Shape	16
Order Explorer	2
Order Magic	4
Overwhelming Energy	10
Perfect Form Control	18
Plant Shape	10
Poison Resistance	2
Primal Focus	12
Primal Summons	12
Primal Wellspring	18
Reach Spell	1
Side by Side	10
Soaring Shape	8
Specialized Companion	14
Steady Spellcasting	6
Storm Born	1
Storm Retribution	6
Thousand Faces	4
Timeless Nature	14
True Shapeshifter	20
Verdant Metamorphosis	14
Widen Spell	1
Wild Shape	1
Wind Caller	8
Woodland Stride	4

SAMPLE DRUID

STORM DRUID

You call upon the power of nature to let loose bolts of lightning, intense weather, and elemental spells.

ABILITY SCORES
Prioritize Wisdom. You typically stay at range, so take a high Dexterity. You can choose whether to focus more on your health with Constitution or be more knowledgeable and skilled with Intelligence.

SKILLS
Acrobatics, Medicine, Nature, Survival

ORDER
Storm

FEATS
Widen Spell (1st), Storm Retribution (6th), Wind Caller (8th), Primal Focus (12th), Invoke Disaster (18th)

PREPARED SPELLS
1st *burning hands, gust of wind;* **Cantrips** *detect magic, electric arc, know direction, light, ray of frost*

6TH LEVEL

GREEN EMPATHY   FEAT 6
DRUID

Prerequisites leaf order

You can communicate with plants on a basic level and use Diplomacy to Make an Impression on them and to make very simple Requests of them. Non-creature plants typically can't fulfill most requests you might ask of them unless you have access to other magic such as *speak with plants*. Because of your affiliation with the leaf order, plants have a sense that you support them, so you gain a +2 circumstance bonus on your check to Make a Request of a plant using Green Empathy.

INSECT SHAPE   FEAT 6
DRUID

Prerequisites Wild Shape

Your understanding of life expands, allowing you to mimic a wider range of creatures. Add the forms in *insect form* to your *wild shape* list. Whenever you use *wild shape* to polymorph into the non-flying insect form listed in *pest form*, the duration is 24 hours instead of 10 minutes.

STEADY SPELLCASTING   FEAT 6
DRUID

Confident in your technique, you don't lose spells easily. If a reaction would disrupt your spellcasting action, attempt a DC 15 flat check. If you succeed, your action isn't disrupted.

STORM RETRIBUTION ⟳   FEAT 6
DRUID

Prerequisites storm order, *tempest surge* order spell
Trigger An opponent adjacent to you critically hits you with a melee weapon or melee unarmed attack.
Requirements You have at least 1 available Focus Point.

You lash out, directing a burst of storming fury toward a creature that has harmed you. You cast *tempest surge* on the triggering opponent and push that creature, moving it 5 feet away from you if it fails its Reflex save, or 10 feet if it critically fails. This movement is forced movement.

8TH LEVEL

FEROCIOUS SHAPE   FEAT 8
DRUID

Prerequisites Wild Shape

You have mastered the shape of ferocious dinosaurs. Add the forms listed in *dinosaur form* to your *wild shape* list. Whenever you use *wild shape* to take a form that grants you a specific Athletics modifier, you gain a +1 status bonus to your Athletics checks.

FEY CALLER   FEAT 8
DRUID

You have learned some of the tricks the fey use to bend primal magic toward illusions and trickery. Add *illusory disguise,*

CLASSES

3

INTRODUCTION

ANCESTRIES &
BACKGROUNDS

CLASSES

SKILLS

FEATS

EQUIPMENT

SPELLS

THE AGE OF
LOST OMENS

PLAYING THE
GAME

GAME
MASTERING

CRAFTING
& TREASURE

APPENDIX

illusory object, *illusory scene*, and *veil* to your spell list as primal spells.

INCREDIBLE COMPANION   FEAT 8
DRUID

Prerequisites Mature Animal Companion

Your animal companion continues to grow and develop. It becomes a nimble or savage animal companion (your choice), gaining additional capabilities determined by the type of companion (page 214).

SOARING SHAPE   FEAT 8
DRUID

Prerequisites Wild Shape

Wings free you from the shackles of the ground below. Add the bat and bird forms in *aerial form* to your *wild shape* list. If you have Insect Shape, you also add the wasp form to your *wild shape* list. If you have Ferocious Shape, you also add the pterosaur form to your *wild shape* list. Whenever you use *wild shape* to gain a form that grants you a specific Acrobatics modifier, you gain a +1 status bonus to Acrobatics checks.

WIND CALLER   FEAT 8
DRUID

Prerequisites storm order

You bid the winds to lift and carry you through the air. You gain the *stormwind flight* order spell. Increase the number of Focus Points in your focus pool by 1.

10TH LEVEL

ELEMENTAL SHAPE   FEAT 10
DRUID

Prerequisites Wild Shape

You understand the fundamental elements of nature such that you can imbue them into your body and manifest as a living embodiment of those elements. Add the forms in *elemental form* to your *wild shape* list. Whenever you're polymorphed into another form using *wild shape*, you gain resistance 5 to fire.

HEALING TRANSFORMATION ◆   FEAT 10
DRUID METAMAGIC

You can take advantage of shapechanging magic to close wounds and patch injuries. If your next action is to cast a non-cantrip polymorph spell that targets only one creature, your polymorph spell also restores 1d6 Hit Points per spell level to that creature. This is a healing effect.

OVERWHELMING ENERGY ◆   FEAT 10
DRUID MANIPULATE METAMAGIC

With a complex gesture, you call upon the primal power of your spell to overcome enemies' resistances. If the next action you use is to Cast a Spell, the spell ignores an amount of the target's resistance to acid, cold, electricity, fire, or sonic damage equal to your level. This applies to all damage the spell deals, including persistent damage and damage caused

SAMPLE DRUID

LEAF DRUID

You're a nurturing caretaker in tune with the natural world and the magic of life. A little plant creature called a leshy accompanies you.

ABILITY SCORES

Prioritize Wisdom. Take Dexterity and Constitution for your defenses, and Charisma to be more diplomatic or Strength if you want to deal more damage in melee.

SKILLS

Diplomacy, Medicine, Nature, Survival

ORDER

Leaf

FEATS

Call of the Wild (2nd), Woodland Stride (4th), Green Empathy (6th), Plant Shape (10th), Green Tongue (12th)

PREPARED SPELLS

1st *heal, summon plants and fungi;* **Cantrips** *detect magic, know direction, light, stabilize, tanglefoot*

---

by an ongoing effect of the spell, such as the wall created by *wall of fire*. A creature's immunities are unaffected.

PLANT SHAPE   FEAT 10

DRUID

Prerequisites leaf order or Wild Shape

You can take the form of a plant creature. Add the forms listed in *plant form* to your *wild shape* list; if you don't have *wild shape*, you can instead cast *plant form* once per day, heightened to the highest spell level you can cast. Whenever you're polymorphed into another form using *wild shape*, you gain resistance 5 to poison.

SIDE BY SIDE   FEAT 10

DRUID

Prerequisites Animal Companion

You and your animal companion fight in tandem, distracting your foes and keeping them off balance. Whenever you and your animal companion are adjacent to the same foe, you are both flanking that foe with each other, regardless of your actual positions.

12TH LEVEL

DRAGON SHAPE   FEAT 12

DRUID

Prerequisites Soaring Shape

You can take on the form of some of the world's most fearsome creatures. Add the forms listed in *dragon form* to your *wild shape* list. Whenever you're polymorphed into another form using *wild shape*, you gain resistance 5 to your choice of acid, cold, electricity, fire, or poison.

GREEN TONGUE   FEAT 12

DRUID

Prerequisites Green Empathy

You share a special kinship with all things green and living. You (and your leshy familiar, if you have one) are constantly under the effects of *speak with plants*. Most non-creature plants recognize you as a druid of the leaf order and are friendly to you.

PRIMAL FOCUS   FEAT 12

DRUID

Your connection to nature is particularly strong, and the spirits of nature flock around you, helping you replenish your focus. If you have spent at least 2 Focus Points since the last time you Refocused, you recover 2 Focus Points when you Refocus instead of 1.

PRIMAL SUMMONS   FEAT 12

DRUID

Prerequisites Call of the Wild

Whenever you summon an ally, you can empower it with the elemental power of air, earth, fire, or water. You gain the *primal summons* order spell.

INTRODUCTION

ANCESTRIES & BACKGROUNDS

CLASSES

SKILLS

FEATS

EQUIPMENT

SPELLS

THE AGE OF LOST OMENS

PLAYING THE GAME

GAME MASTERING

CRAFTING & TREASURE

APPENDIX

14TH LEVEL

SPECIALIZED COMPANION   FEAT 14

DRUID

Prerequisites Incredible Companion

Your animal companion continues to grow in power and ability, and it is now cunning enough to become specialized. Your animal companion gains one specialization of your choice. (See the Animal Companion section on page 214.)

Special You can select this feat up to three times. Each time, add a different specialization to your companion.

TIMELESS NATURE   FEAT 14

DRUID

With primal magic sustaining you, you cease aging. The overflowing primal energy gives you a +2 status bonus to saves against diseases and primal magic.

VERDANT METAMORPHOSIS   FEAT 14

DRUID

Prerequisites leaf order

You transform into a plant version of yourself. You gain the plant trait and lose any trait that's inappropriate for your new form (typically humanoid for a PC, but also possibly animal or fungus). You can change from a form that looks mostly like your old self into a tree or any other non-creature plant as a single action, which has the concentrate trait. This has the same effect as *tree shape*, except you can turn into any kind of non-creature plant and your AC is 30.

If you rest for 10 minutes while transformed into a non-creature plant during daylight hours under direct sunlight, you recover half your maximum Hit Points. If you take your daily rest in this way, the rest restores you to maximum Hit Points and removes all non-permanent drained, enfeebled, clumsy, and stupefied conditions, as well as all poisons and diseases of 19th level or lower.

16TH LEVEL

EFFORTLESS CONCENTRATION ◈   FEAT 16

DRUID

Trigger Your turn begins.

You maintain a spell with hardly a thought. You immediately gain the effects of the Sustain a Spell action, allowing you to extend the duration of one of your active druid spells.

IMPALING BRIARS   FEAT 16

DRUID

Prerequisites leaf order

You can fill an area with devastating briars that impale and impede your foes. You gain the *impaling briars* order spell. Increase the number of Focus Points in your focus pool by 1.

MONSTROSITY SHAPE   FEAT 16

DRUID

Prerequisites Wild Shape

You can transform into a powerful magical creature. Add the purple worm and sea serpent forms listed in *monstrosity form* to your wild shape list. If you have Soaring Shape, add the phoenix form listed in *aerial form* to your *wild shape* list.

18TH LEVEL

INVOKE DISASTER   FEAT 18

DRUID

Prerequisites Wind Caller

You can invoke nature's fury upon your foes. You gain the *storm lord* order spell. Increase the number of Focus Points in your focus pool by 1.

PERFECT FORM CONTROL   FEAT 18

DRUID

Prerequisites Form Control, Strength 18

Thanks to magic and muscle memory, you can stay in your alternate forms indefinitely; you may have even forgotten your original form. When you use Form Control, instead of lasting 1 hour, *wild shape* is permanent until you Dismiss it.

PRIMAL WELLSPRING   FEAT 18

DRUID

Prerequisites Wild Focus

Your reservoir of Focus Points is a deep wellspring. If you have spent at least 3 Focus Points since the last time you Refocused, you recover 3 Focus Points when you Refocus instead of 1.

20TH LEVEL

HIEROPHANT'S POWER   FEAT 20

DRUID

Prerequisites legendary in Nature

You have entwined yourself with the natural world, and its full power flows through you. You gain an additional 10th-level spell slot.

LEYLINE CONDUIT ◈   FEAT 20

CONCENTRATE **DRUID** **MANIPULATE** **METAMAGIC**

Frequency once per minute

You can cast your spells effortlessly by tapping into the leylines of the world. If your next action is to Cast a Spell of 5th level or lower that has no duration, you don't expend the prepared spell as you cast it.

TRUE SHAPESHIFTER ◈◈   FEAT 20

CONCENTRATE **DRUID**

Prerequisites Dragon Shape, Wild Shape

You transcend the limitations of form. While under the effects of *wild shape*, you can change into any other form on your *wild shape* list; if the durations of the forms would vary, use the shorter of the two durations.

Once per day, you can transform into a kaiju, with the effects of *nature incarnate*; if you have Plant Shape, you can instead transform into a green man.

FIGHTER

Fighting for honor, greed, loyalty, or simply the thrill of battle, you are an undisputed master of weaponry and combat techniques. You combine your actions through clever combinations of opening moves, finishing strikes, and counterattacks whenever your foes are unwise enough to drop their guard. Whether you are a knight, mercenary, sharpshooter, or blade master, you have honed your martial skills into an art form and perform devastating critical attacks on your enemies.

KEY ABILITY	HIT POINTS
STRENGTH OR DEXTERITY	**10 plus your Constitution modifier**
At 1st level, your class gives you an ability boost to your choice of Strength or Dexterity.	You increase your maximum number of HP by this number at 1st level and every level thereafter.

DURING COMBAT ENCOUNTERS...

You strike with unmatched accuracy and use specialized combat techniques. A melee fighter stands between allies and enemies, attacking foes who try to get past. A ranged fighter delivers precise shots from a distance.

DURING SOCIAL ENCOUNTERS...

You can be an intimidating presence. This can be useful when negotiating with enemies, but is sometimes a liability in more genteel interactions.

WHILE EXPLORING...

You keep up your defenses in preparation for combat, and keep an eye out for hidden threats. You also overcome physical challenges in your way, breaking down doors, lifting obstacles, climbing adeptly, and leaping across pits.

IN DOWNTIME...

You might perform manual labor or craft and repair armaments. If you know techniques you no longer favor, you might train yourself in new ones. If you've established your reputation, you might build an organization or a stronghold of your own.

YOU MIGHT...

- Know the purpose and quality of every weapon and piece of armor you own.
- Recognize that the danger of an adventurer's life must be balanced out with great revelry or ambitious works.
- Have little patience for puzzles or problems that require detailed logic or study.

OTHERS PROBABLY...

- Find you intimidating until they get to know you—and maybe even after they get to know you.
- Expect you're all brawn and no brains.
- Respect your expertise in the art of warfare and value your opinion on the quality of armaments.

INITIAL PROFICIENCIES

At 1st level, you gain the listed proficiency ranks in the following statistics. You are untrained in anything not listed unless you gain a better proficiency rank in some other way.

PERCEPTION

Expert in Perception

SAVING THROWS

Expert in Fortitude
Expert in Reflex
Trained in Will

SKILLS

Trained in your choice of Acrobatics or Athletics
Trained in a number of additional skills equal to 3 plus your Intelligence modifier

ATTACKS

Expert in simple weapons
Expert in martial weapons
Trained in advanced weapons
Expert in unarmed attacks

DEFENSES

Trained in all armor
Trained in unarmored defense

CLASS DC

Trained in fighter class DC

TABLE 3-12: FIGHTER ADVANCEMENT

Your Level	Class Features
1	Ancestry and background, initial proficiencies, attack of opportunity, fighter feat, shield block
2	Fighter feat, skill feat
3	Bravery, general feat, skill increase
4	Fighter feat, skill feat
5	Ability boosts, ancestry feat, fighter weapon mastery, skill increase
6	Fighter feat, skill feat
7	Battlefield surveyor, general feat, skill increase, weapon specialization
8	Fighter feat, skill feat
9	Ancestry feat, combat flexibility, juggernaut, skill increase
10	Ability boosts, fighter feat, skill feat
11	Armor expertise, fighter expertise, general feat, skill increase
12	Fighter feat, skill feat
13	Ancestry feat, skill increase, weapon legend
14	Fighter feat, skill feat
15	Ability boosts, evasion, general feat, greater weapon specialization, improved flexibility, skill increase
16	Fighter feat, skill feat
17	Ancestry feat, armor mastery, skill increase
18	Fighter feat, skill feat
19	General feat, skill increase, versatile legend
20	Ability boosts, fighter feat, skill feat

CLASS FEATURES

You gain these abilities as a fighter. Abilities gained at higher levels list the level at which you gain them next to the features' names.

ANCESTRY AND BACKGROUND

In addition to the abilities provided by your class at 1st level, you have the benefits of your selected ancestry and background, as described in Chapter 2.

INITIAL PROFICIENCIES

At 1st level you gain a number of proficiencies that represent your basic training. These proficiencies are noted at the start of this class.

ATTACK OF OPPORTUNITY

Ever watchful for weaknesses, you can quickly attack foes that leave an opening in their defenses. You gain the Attack of Opportunity reaction.

ATTACK OF OPPORTUNITY ⤵

Trigger A creature within your reach uses a manipulate action or a move action, makes a ranged attack, or leaves a square during a move action it's using.

You lash out at a foe that leaves an opening. Make a melee Strike

against the triggering creature. If your attack is a critical hit and the trigger was a manipulate action, you disrupt that action. This Strike doesn't count toward your multiple attack penalty, and your multiple attack penalty doesn't apply to this Strike.

FIGHTER FEATS

At 1st level and every even-numbered level thereafter, you gain a fighter class feat. Fighter class feats are described beginning on page 144.

SHIELD BLOCK

You gain the Shield Block general feat (found on page 266), a reaction that lets you reduce damage with your shield.

SKILL FEATS   2ND

At 2nd level and every 2 levels thereafter, you gain a skill feat. Skill feats can be found in Chapter 5 and have the skill trait. You must be trained or better in the corresponding skill to select a skill feat.

BRAVERY   3RD

Having faced countless foes and the chaos of battle, you have learned how to stand strong in the face of fear and keep on fighting. Your proficiency rank for Will saves increases to expert. When you roll a success at a Will save against a fear effect, you get a critical success instead. In addition, anytime you gain the frightened condition, reduce its value by 1.

GENERAL FEATS   3RD

At 3rd level and every 4 levels thereafter, you gain a general feat. General feats are listed in Chapter 5.

SKILL INCREASES   3RD

At 3rd level and every 2 levels thereafter, you gain a skill increase. You can use this increase either to increase your proficiency rank to trained in one skill you're untrained in, or to increase your proficiency rank in one skill in which you're already trained to expert.

At 7th level, you can use skill increases to increase your proficiency rank to master in a skill in which you're already an expert, and at 15th level, you can use them to increase your proficiency rank to legendary in a skill in which you're already a master.

ABILITY BOOSTS   5TH

At 5th level and every 5 levels thereafter, you boost four different ability scores. You can use these ability boosts to increase your ability scores above 18. Boosting an ability score increases it by 1 if it's already 18 or above, or by 2 if it starts out below 18.

ANCESTRY FEATS   5TH

In addition to the ancestry feat you started with, you gain an ancestry feat at 5th level and every 4 levels thereafter.

INTRODUCTION

ANCESTRIES &
BACKGROUNDS

CLASSES

SKILLS

FEATS

EQUIPMENT

SPELLS

THE AGE OF
LOST OMENS

PLAYING THE
GAME

GAME
MASTERING

CRAFTING
& TREASURE

APPENDIX

The list of ancestry feats available to you can be found in your ancestry's entry in Chapter 2.

FIGHTER WEAPON MASTERY · 5TH

Hours spent training with your preferred weapons, learning and developing new combat techniques, have made you particularly effective with your weapons of choice. Choose one weapon group. Your proficiency rank increases to master with the simple and martial weapons in that group, and to expert with the advanced weapons in that group. You gain access to the critical specialization effects (page 283) of all weapons for which you have master proficiency.

BATTLEFIELD SURVEYOR · 7TH

Whether taking stock of an enemy army or simply standing guard, you excel at observing your foes. Your proficiency rank for Perception increases to master. In addition, you gain a +2 circumstance bonus to Perception checks for initiative, making you faster to react during combat.

WEAPON SPECIALIZATION · 7TH

You've learned how to inflict greater injuries with the weapons you know best. You deal 2 additional damage with weapons and unarmed attacks in which you are an expert. This damage increases to 3 if you're a master, and to 4 if you're legendary.

COMBAT FLEXIBILITY · 9TH

Through your experience in battle, you can prepare your tactics to suit different situations. When you make your daily preparations, you gain one fighter feat of 8th level or lower that you don't already have. You can use that feat until your next daily preparations. You must meet all of the feat's other prerequisites.

JUGGERNAUT · 9TH

Your body is accustomed to physical hardship and resistant to ailments. Your proficiency rank for Fortitude saves increases to master. When you roll a success on a Fortitude save, you get a critical success instead.

ARMOR EXPERTISE · 11TH

You have spent so much time wearing armor that you know how to make the most of its protection. Your proficiency rank for light, medium, and heavy armor, as well as for unarmored defense, increase to expert. You gain the armor specialization effects of medium and heavy armor.

FIGHTER EXPERTISE · 11TH

You've practiced your techniques to make them harder to resist. Your proficiency rank for your fighter class DC increases to expert.

WEAPON LEGEND · 13TH

You've learned fighting techniques that apply to all

KEY TERMS

You'll see the following key terms in many fighter class features.

Flourish: Actions with this trait are special techniques that require too much exertion for you to perform frequently. You can use only 1 action with the flourish trait per turn.

Open: These maneuvers work only as the first salvo in the attacks you make on your turn. You can use an action with the open trait only if you haven't used an action with the attack or open trait yet this turn.

Press: Actions with this trait allow you to follow up earlier attacks. An action with the press trait can be used only if you are currently affected by a multiple attack penalty.

Some actions with the press trait also grant an effect on a failure. The effects that are added on a failure don't apply on a critical failure. If your press action succeeds, you can choose to apply the failure effect instead. (For example, you may wish to do this when an attack deals no damage due to resistance.) Because a press action requires a multiple attack penalty, you can't use one when it's not your turn, even if you use the Ready activity.

Stance: A stance is a general combat strategy that you enter by using an action with the stance trait, and you remain in for some time. A stance lasts until you get knocked out, until its requirements (if any) are violated, until the encounter ends, or until you enter a new stance, whichever comes first. After you take an action with the stance trait, you can't take another one for 1 round. You can enter or be in a stance only in encounter mode.

armaments, and you've developed unparalleled skill with your favorite weapons. Your proficiency ranks for simple and martial weapons increase to master. Your proficiency rank for advanced weapons increases to expert.

You can select one weapon group and increase your proficiency ranks to legendary for all simple and martial weapons in that weapon group, and to master for all advanced weapons in that weapon group.

EVASION · 15TH

You've learned to move quickly to avoid explosions, a dragon's breath, and worse. Your proficiency rank for Reflex saves increases to master. When you roll a success on a Reflex save, you get a critical success instead.

GREATER WEAPON SPECIALIZATION · 15TH

Your damage from weapon specialization increases to 4 with weapons and unarmed attacks in which you're an expert, 6 if you're a master, and 8 if you're legendary.

IMPROVED FLEXIBILITY · 15TH

Your extensive experience gives you even greater ability to adapt to each day's challenges. When you use combat

FIGHTER FEATS

If you need to look up a fighter feat by name instead of by level, use this table.

flexibility, you can gain two fighter feats instead of one. While the first feat must still be 8th level or lower, the second feat can be up to 14th level, and you can use the first feat to meet the prerequisites of the second feat. You must meet all of the feats' prerequisites.

ARMOR MASTERY 17TH

Your skill with armor improves, increasing your ability to prevent blows. Your proficiency ranks for light, medium, and heavy armor, as well as for unarmored defense, increase to master.

VERSATILE LEGEND 19TH

You are nigh-unmatched with any weapon. Your proficiency ranks for simple weapons, martial weapons, and unarmed attacks increase to legendary, and your proficiency rank for advanced weapons increases to master. Your proficiency rank for your fighter class DC increases to master.

FIGHTER FEATS

At each level that you gain a fighter feat, you can select one of the following feats. You must satisfy any prerequisites before taking the feat.

1ST LEVEL

DOUBLE SLICE ◆◆ FEAT 1

FIGHTER

Requirements You are wielding two melee weapons, each in a different hand.

You lash out at your foe with both weapons. Make two Strikes, one with each of your two melee weapons, each using your current multiple attack penalty. Both Strikes must have the same target. If the second Strike is made with a weapon that doesn't have the agile trait, it takes a –2 penalty.

If both attacks hit, combine their damage, and then add any other applicable effects from both weapons. You add any precision damage only once, to the attack of your choice. Combine the damage from both Strikes and apply resistances and weaknesses only once. This counts as two attacks when calculating your multiple attack penalty.

EXACTING STRIKE ◆ FEAT 1

FIGHTER **PRESS**

You make a controlled attack, fully accounting for your momentum. Make a Strike. The Strike gains the following failure effect.

Failure This attack does not count toward your multiple attack penalty.

POINT-BLANK SHOT ◆ FEAT 1

FIGHTER **OPEN** **STANCE**

Requirements You are wielding a ranged weapon.

You take aim to pick off nearby enemies quickly. When using a ranged volley weapon while you are in this stance, you don't take the penalty to your attack rolls from the volley trait. When using a ranged weapon that doesn't have the volley trait, you gain a +2 circumstance bonus to damage rolls on attacks against targets within the weapon's first range increment.

POWER ATTACK ◆◆ FEAT 1

FIGHTER **FLOURISH**

You unleash a particularly powerful attack that clobbers your foe but leaves you a bit unsteady. Make a melee Strike. This counts as two attacks when calculating your multiple attack penalty. If this Strike hits, you deal an extra die of weapon damage. If you're at least 10th level, increase this to two extra dice, and if you're at least 18th level, increase it to three extra dice.

REACTIVE SHIELD ↻

FEAT 1

FIGHTER

Trigger An enemy hits you with a melee Strike.
Requirements You are wielding a shield.

You can snap your shield into place just as you would take a blow, avoiding the hit at the last second. You immediately use the Raise a Shield action and gain your shield's bonus to AC. The circumstance bonus from the shield applies to your AC when you're determining the outcome of the triggering attack.

SNAGGING STRIKE ◆

FEAT 1

FIGHTER

Requirements You have one hand free, and your target is within reach of that hand.

You combine an attack with quick grappling moves to throw an enemy off balance as long as it stays in your reach. Make a Strike while keeping one hand free. If this Strike hits, the target is flat-footed until the start of your next turn or until it's no longer within the reach of your hand, whichever comes first.

SUDDEN CHARGE ◆◆

FEAT 1

FIGHTER · FLOURISH · OPEN

With a quick sprint, you dash up to your foe and swing. Stride twice. If you end your movement within melee reach of at least one enemy, you can make a melee Strike against that enemy. You can use Sudden Charge while Burrowing, Climbing, Flying, or Swimming instead of Striding if you have the corresponding movement type.

2ND LEVEL

AGGRESSIVE BLOCK ◆

FEAT 2

FIGHTER

Trigger You use the Shield Block reaction, and the opponent that triggered Shield Block is adjacent to you and is your size or smaller.

You push back as you block the attack, knocking your foe away or off balance. You use your shield to push the triggering creature, either automatically Shoving it 5 feet or causing it to become flat-footed until the start of your next turn. The triggering creature chooses whether to be moved or become flat-footed. If it chooses to be moved, you choose the direction. If the Shove would cause it to hit a solid object, enter a square of difficult terrain, or enter another creature's space, it must become flat-footed instead of being moved.

ASSISTING SHOT ◆

FEAT 2

FIGHTER

With a quick shot, you interfere with a foe in combat. You can use the Aid action with a ranged weapon you wield. Instead of being within reach of the target, you must be within maximum range of the target. An Assisting Shot uses ammunition and incurs penalties just like any other attack.

BRUTISH SHOVE ◆

FEAT 2

FIGHTER · PRESS

Requirements You are wielding a two-handed melee weapon.

Throwing your weight behind your attack, you hit your

opponent hard enough to make it stumble back. Make a Strike with a two-handed melee weapon. If you hit a target that is your size or smaller, that creature is flat-footed until the end of your current turn, and you can automatically Shove it, with the same benefits as the Shove action (including the critical success effect, if your Strike was a critical hit). If you move to follow the target, your movement doesn't trigger reactions.

This Strike has the following failure effect.

Failure The target becomes flat-footed until the end of your current turn.

COMBAT GRAB ◆❖   FEAT 2

FIGHTER | PRESS

Requirements You have one hand free, and your target is within reach of that hand.

You swipe at your opponent and grab at them. Make a melee Strike while keeping one hand free. If the Strike hits, you grab the target using your free hand. The creature remains grabbed until the end of your next turn or until it Escapes, whichever comes first.

DUELING PARRY ❖   FEAT 2

FIGHTER

Requirements You are wielding only a single one-handed melee weapon and have your other hand or hands free.

You can parry attacks against you with your one-handed weapon. You gain a +2 circumstance bonus to AC until the start of your next turn as long as you continue to meet the requirements.

INTIMIDATING STRIKE ❖❖   FEAT 2

EMOTION | FEAR | FIGHTER | MENTAL

Your blow not only wounds creatures but also shatters their confidence. Make a melee Strike. If you hit and deal damage, the target is frightened 1, or frightened 2 on a critical hit.

LUNGE ❖   FEAT 2

FIGHTER

Requirement You are wielding a melee weapon.

Extending your body to its limits, you attack an enemy that would normally be beyond your reach. Make a Strike with a melee weapon, increasing your reach by 5 feet for that Strike. If the weapon has the disarm, shove, or trip trait, you can use the corresponding action instead of a Strike.

4TH LEVEL

DOUBLE SHOT ◆❖   FEAT 4

FIGHTER | FLOURISH

Requirements You are wielding a ranged weapon with reload 0.

You shoot twice in blindingly fast succession. Make two Strikes, each against a separate target and with a –2 penalty. Both attacks count toward your multiple attack penalty, but the penalty doesn't increase until after you've made both of them.

DUAL-HANDED ASSAULT ◆❖   FEAT 4

FIGHTER | FLOURISH

Requirements You are wielding a one-handed melee weapon and have a free hand.

You snap your free hand over to grip your weapon just long enough to add momentum and deliver a more powerful blow to your opponent. Make a Strike with the required weapon. You quickly switch your grip during the Strike in order to make the attack with two hands. If the weapon doesn't normally have the two-hand trait, increase its weapon damage die by one step for this attack. (Rules on increasing die size appear on page 279.) If the weapon has the two-hand trait, you gain the benefit of that trait and a circumstance bonus to damage equal to the weapon's number of damage dice. When the Strike is complete, you resume gripping the weapon with only one hand. This action doesn't end any stance or fighter feat effect that requires you to have one hand free.

KNOCKDOWN ◆❖❖   FEAT 4

FIGHTER | FLOURISH

Prerequisites trained in Athletics

You make an attack to knock a foe off balance, then follow up immediately with a sweep to topple them. Make a melee Strike. If it hits and deals damage, you can attempt an Athletics check to Trip the creature you hit. If you're wielding a two-handed melee weapon, you can ignore Trip's requirement that you have a hand free. Both attacks count toward your multiple attack penalty, but the penalty doesn't increase until after you've made both of them.

POWERFUL SHOVE ❖   FEAT 4

FIGHTER

Prerequisites Aggressive Block or Brutish Shove

You can push larger foes around with your attack. You can use Aggressive Block or Brutish Shove against a creature up to two sizes larger than you.

When a creature you Shove has to stop moving because it would hit an object, it takes damage equal to your Strength modifier (minimum 1). This happens regardless of how you Shoved the creature.

QUICK REVERSAL ◆❖   FEAT 4

FIGHTER | FLOURISH | PRESS

Requirements You are flanked by at least two enemies.

You turn your foes' flanking against them with a quick reverse. Make a melee Strike against one of the flanking enemies and make a second Strike with the same weapon or unarmed attack against a different enemy that is flanking you. This second Strike has the same multiple attack penalty of the initial attack and doesn't count toward your multiple attack penalty.

SHIELDED STRIDE   FEAT 4

FIGHTER

When your shield is up, your enemies' blows can't touch you.

CLASSES

3

INTRODUCTION

ANCESTRIES &
BACKGROUNDS

CLASSES

SKILLS

FEATS

EQUIPMENT

SPELLS

THE AGE OF
LOST OMENS

PLAYING THE
GAME

GAME
MASTERING

CRAFTING
& TREASURE

APPENDIX

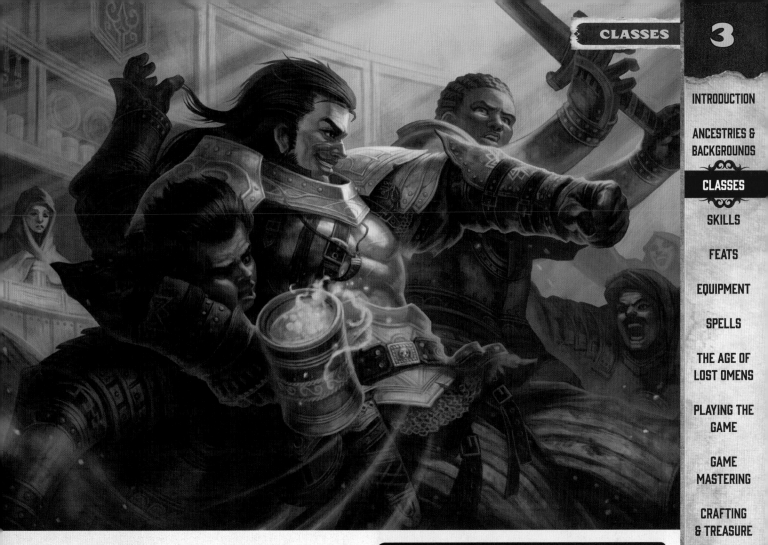

When you have your shield raised, you can Stride to move half your Speed without triggering reactions that are triggered by your movement (such as Attacks of Opportunity). You can use Shielded Stride while Flying or Swimming instead of Striding if you have the corresponding movement type.

SWIPE ◆◆   FEAT 4

FIGHTER **FLOURISH**

You make a wide, arcing swing. Make a melee Strike and compare the attack roll result to the AC of up to two foes, each of whom must be within your melee reach and adjacent to each other. Roll damage only once and apply it to each creature you hit. A Swipe counts as two attacks for your multiple attack penalty.

If you're using a weapon with the sweep trait, its modifier applies to all your Swipe attacks.

TWIN PARRY ◆   FEAT 4

FIGHTER

Requirements You are wielding two melee weapons, one in each hand.

You use your two weapons to parry attacks. You gain a +1 circumstance bonus to AC until the start of your next turn, or a +2 circumstance bonus if either weapon has the parry trait. You lose this circumstance bonus if you no longer meet this feat's requirement.

6TH LEVEL

ADVANCED WEAPON TRAINING   FEAT 6

FIGHTER

You've studied the art of wielding an advanced weapon. Choose a weapon group. You gain proficiency with all advanced weapons in that group as if they were martial weapons of their weapon group.

ADVANTAGEOUS ASSAULT ◆   FEAT 6

FIGHTER **PRESS**

When an enemy's movement is compromised, you deliver a more deadly blow. Make a Strike against a creature that is grabbed, prone, or restrained. You gain a circumstance bonus to damage on this Strike equal to the number of weapon damage dice, or that number + 2 if you're wielding the weapon in two hands. The Strike gains the following failure effect.

Failure You deal damage to the target equal to the number of weapon damage dice, or that number + 2 if you're wielding the weapon in two hands. This damage has the same damage type as the weapon.

DISARMING STANCE ◆   FEAT 6

FIGHTER **STANCE**

Prerequisites trained in Athletics

Requirements You are wielding only a single one-handed melee weapon and have your other hand or hands free.

SAMPLE FIGHTER

BULLY

Using a two-handed weapon, you push your foes about the battlefield and deal grievous wounds. You excel at taking down the biggest enemy standing in your way.

ABILITY SCORES
Prioritizing Strength, Constitution, and Wisdom helps with survivability and increases your damage, and Dexterity allows extra maneuverability.

SKILLS
Athletics, Crafting, Intimidation, Medicine

STARTING FEAT
Power Attack

HIGHER-LEVEL FEATS
Knockdown (4th), Furious Focus (6th), Positioning Assault (8th), Brutal Finish (12th), Savage Critical (18th)

You adopt a fencing stance that improves your control over your weapon. While you are in this stance, you gain a +1 circumstance bonus to Athletics checks to Disarm and a +2 circumstance bonus to your Reflex DC when defending against checks to Disarm you. In addition, you can attempt to Disarm creatures up to two sizes larger than you.

FURIOUS FOCUS   FEAT 6

FIGHTER

Prerequisites Power Attack

You've learned to maintain your balance even when swinging furiously. When you make a Power Attack with a melee weapon you're wielding in two hands, it counts as one attack toward your multiple attack penalty instead of two.

GUARDIAN'S DEFLECTION ↻   FEAT 6

FIGHTER

Trigger An ally within your melee reach is hit by an attack, you can see the attacker, and the ally gaining a +2 circumstance bonus to AC would turn the critical hit into a hit or the hit into a miss.

    Requirements You are wielding a single one-handed melee weapon and have your other hand or hands free.

You use your weapon to deflect the attack against your ally, granting a +2 circumstance bonus to their Armor Class against the triggering attack. This turns the triggering critical hit into a hit, or the triggering hit into a miss.

REFLEXIVE SHIELD   FEAT 6

FIGHTER

You can use your shield to fend off the worst of area effects and other damage. When you Raise your Shield, you gain your shield's circumstance bonus to Reflex saves. If you have the Shield Block reaction, damage you take as a result of a Reflex save can trigger that reaction, even if the damage isn't physical damage.

REVEALING STAB ◆◆   FEAT 6

FIGHTER

Requirements You are wielding a melee weapon that deals piercing damage.

You drive your piercing weapon into an imperceptible foe, revealing its location to your allies. Make a Strike with the required melee weapon. You don't have to attempt a flat check to hit a concealed creature, and you have to succeed at only a DC 5 flat check to target a hidden creature. If you hit and deal damage, you can drive the required weapon into a corporeal target, revealing its current position. You Release the weapon, and it becomes lodged in the target. If the target is concealed, other creatures don't need to succeed at a flat check to hit it. If the target is hidden, other creatures have to succeed at only a DC 5 flat check to target it. The creatures need to be able to see your weapon to gain any of these benefits, and the target can't become undetected to anyone who sees your weapon. If the target is invisible, the weapon remains visible while lodged in it.

This benefit lasts until the weapon is removed from the creature. An adjacent creature or the target can remove the weapon with 2 Interact actions.

SHATTER DEFENSES ◆   FEAT 6

FIGHTER   **PRESS**

Requirements A frightened creature is in your melee reach.
Your offense exploits your enemy's fear. Make a melee Strike against a frightened creature. If you hit and deal damage, the target becomes flat-footed until its frightened condition ends. If the target was already flat-footed to you when you damaged it with this Strike, it can't reduce its frightened value below 1 until the start of your next turn.

SHIELD WARDEN   FEAT 6

FIGHTER

Prerequisites shield block
You use your shield to protect your allies. When you have a shield raised, you can use your Shield Block reaction when an attack is made against an ally adjacent to you. If you do, the shield prevents that ally from taking damage instead of preventing you from taking damage, following the normal rules for Shield Block.

TRIPLE SHOT   FEAT 6

FIGHTER

Prerequisites Double Shot
You can quickly fire multiple shots with greater control. When you use Double Shot, you can make the attacks against the same target. You can add an additional action to Double Shot to make three ranged Strikes instead of two. If you do, the penalty is –4. All attacks count toward your multiple attack penalty, but the penalty doesn't increase until after you've made all of them.

8TH LEVEL

BLIND-FIGHT   FEAT 8

FIGHTER

Prerequisites master in Perception
Your battle instincts make you more aware of concealed and invisible opponents. You don't need to succeed at a flat check to target concealed creatures. You're not flat-footed to creatures that are hidden from you (unless you're flat-footed to them for reasons other than the hidden condition), and you need only a successful DC 5 flat check to target a hidden creature.

While you're adjacent to an undetected creature of your level or lower, it is instead only hidden from you.

DUELING RIPOSTE ↻   FEAT 8

FIGHTER

Prerequisites Dueling Parry
Trigger A creature within your reach critically fails a Strike against you.
Requirements You are benefiting from Dueling Parry.

You riposte against your flailing enemy. Make a melee Strike against or attempt to Disarm the triggering creature.

FELLING STRIKE ◆◆   FEAT 8

FIGHTER

Your attack can ground an airborne foe. Make a Strike. If it hits and deals damage to a flying target, the target falls up to 120 feet. The fall is gradual enough that if it causes the target to hit the ground, the target takes no damage from the fall. If the attack is a critical hit, the target can't Fly, Leap, levitate, or otherwise leave the ground until the end of your next turn.

INCREDIBLE AIM ◆◆   FEAT 8

CONCENTRATE   **FIGHTER**

By spending a moment to focus, you can ensure your attack strikes true. Make a ranged weapon Strike. On this Strike, you gain a +2 circumstance bonus to the attack roll and ignore the target's concealed condition.

MOBILE SHOT STANCE ◆   FEAT 8

FIGHTER   **STANCE**

Your shots become nimble and deadly. While you're in this stance, your ranged Strikes don't trigger Attacks of Opportunity or other reactions that are triggered by a ranged attack.

If you have Attack of Opportunity, you can use it with a loaded ranged weapon you're wielding. The triggering creature must be within 5 feet of you for you to do so.

POSITIONING ASSAULT ◆◆   FEAT 8

FIGHTER   **FLOURISH**

Requirements You are wielding a two-handed melee weapon and your target is within your reach.

With punishing blows, you force your opponent into position. Make a Strike with the required weapon. If you hit, you move the target 5 feet into a space in your reach. This follows the forced movement rules found on page 475.

QUICK SHIELD BLOCK   FEAT 8

FIGHTER

Prerequisites shield block, Reactive Shield
You can bring your shield into place with hardly a thought. At the start of each of your turns, you gain an additional reaction that you can use only to Shield Block.

SUDDEN LEAP ◆◆   FEAT 8

FIGHTER

You make an impressive leap and swing while you soar. Make a Leap, High Jump, or Long Jump and attempt one melee Strike at any point during your jump. Immediately after the Strike, you fall to the ground if you're in the air, even if you haven't reached the maximum distance of your jump. If the distance you fall is no more than the height of your jump, you take no damage and land upright.

When attempting a High Jump or Long Jump during a Sudden Leap, determine the DC using the Long Jump DCs, and increase your maximum distance to double your Speed.

SAMPLE FIGHTER

DUELIST

With one hand free and a blade in the others, you are adept at foiling your opponents by way of misdirection, disarming strikes, and by always being ready for their clumsy attacks.

ABILITY SCORES
Prioritize Strength. Dexterity and Wisdom help with survivability and versatility, and Constitution grants some extra toughness.

SKILLS
Acrobatics, Athletics, Deception, Medicine

STARTING FEAT
Snagging Strike

HIGHER-LEVEL FEATS
Dueling Parry (2nd), Guardian's Deflection (6th), Dueling Riposte (8th), Dueling Dance (12th), Stance Savant (14th)

Special If you have Felling Strike, you can spend 3 actions to make a Sudden Leap and use Felling Strike instead of a normal Strike.

10TH LEVEL

AGILE GRACE   FEAT 10
FIGHTER
Your graceful moves with agile weapons are beyond compare. Your multiple attack penalty with agile weapons and agile unarmed attacks becomes –3 for your second attack and –6 for subsequent attacks (rather than –4 and –8).

CERTAIN STRIKE ❖   FEAT 10
FIGHTER **PRESS**
Even when you don't hit squarely, you can still score a glancing blow. Make a melee Strike. It gains the following failure effect.
Failure Your attack deals any damage it would have dealt on a hit, excluding all damage dice. (This removes damage dice from weapon runes, spells, and special abilities, in addition to weapon damage dice.)

COMBAT REFLEXES   FEAT 10
FIGHTER
You are particularly swift at punishing foes who leave you openings. At the start of each of your turns when you regain your actions, you gain an additional reaction that can be used only to make an Attack of Opportunity.

DEBILITATING SHOT ❖❖   FEAT 10
FIGHTER **FLOURISH**
Aiming for a weak point, you impede your foe with a precise shot. Make a ranged weapon Strike. If it hits and deals damage, the target is slowed 1 until the end of its next turn.

DISARMING TWIST ❖   FEAT 10
FIGHTER **PRESS**
Prerequisites trained in Athletics
Requirements You are wielding only a single one-handed melee weapon and have your other hand or hands free.
After your initial attack redirects your foe's defenses, your follow-up wrests their weapon from their grasp. Make a melee Strike with the required weapon. In addition to its other effects, this Strike gains the success and critical success effects of the Disarm action. The Strike also has the following failure effect.
Failure The target is flat-footed until the end of your current turn.

DISRUPTIVE STANCE ❖   FEAT 10
FIGHTER **STANCE**
The slightest distraction can provoke your wrath, and you're prepared to foil enemies' actions. As long as you are in this stance, you can use Attack of Opportunity when a creature within your reach uses a concentrate action, in addition to manipulate and move actions. Furthermore, you disrupt a

CLASSES

3

INTRODUCTION

ANCESTRIES &
BACKGROUNDS

CLASSES

SKILLS

FEATS

EQUIPMENT

SPELLS

THE AGE OF
LOST OMENS

PLAYING THE
GAME

GAME
MASTERING

CRAFTING
& TREASURE

APPENDIX

triggering concentrate or manipulate action if your Strike hits (not only if it's a critical hit).

FEARSOME BRUTE — FEAT 10

FIGHTER

Fear makes your foes weak and more vulnerable to your attacks. You gain a circumstance bonus to damage rolls for Strikes against frightened creatures. The bonus is equal to double the target's frightened value.

If you have master proficiency in Intimidation, increase the bonus to triple the target's frightened value.

IMPROVED KNOCKDOWN — FEAT 10

FIGHTER

Prerequisites Knockdown

You can dash your foe to the ground with a single blow. When you use Knockdown, instead of making a Strike followed by a Trip, you can attempt a single Strike. If you do and your Strike hits, you also apply the critical success effect of a Trip. If you used a two-handed melee weapon for the Strike, you can use the weapon's damage die size instead of the regular die size for the damage from a critical Trip.

MIRROR SHIELD ↻ — FEAT 10

FIGHTER

Trigger An opponent casting a spell that targets you critically fails a spell attack roll against your AC.

Requirements You have a shield raised.

You reflect the spell back against the triggering opponent. Make a ranged attack against the triggering creature using your highest proficiency with a ranged weapon. If you can cast spells, you can make a spell attack roll instead. If you succeed, your opponent takes the effects of a successful spell attack roll for their own spell (or the effects of a critical success if your attack roll was a critical success).

TWIN RIPOSTE ↻ — FEAT 10

FIGHTER

Trigger A creature within your reach critically fails a Strike against you.

Requirements You are benefiting from Twin Parry.

A clever parry with one weapon leaves your opponent open to an attack with the other weapon. Make a melee Strike or use a Disarm action against the triggering opponent.

12TH LEVEL

BRUTAL FINISH ✦ — FEAT 12

FIGHTER **PRESS**

Requirements You are wielding a melee weapon in two hands. Your final blow can make an impact even if it rebounds off a foe's defenses. Make a Strike with the required weapon. After the Strike, your turn ends. The Strike deals one extra weapon damage die, or two extra weapon damage dice if you're at least 18th level. The Strike also gains the following failure effect.

Failure You deal damage equal to one weapon damage die of

the required weapon. Increase this to two dice if you're at least 18th level.

DUELING DANCE ✦ — FEAT 12

FIGHTER **STANCE**

Prerequisites Dueling Parry

Requirements You are wielding only a single one-handed melee weapon and have your other hand or hands free.

Using your free hand as pivot and balance, you both attack and defend with your weapon. While you are in this stance, you constantly have the benefits of Dueling Parry.

FLINGING SHOVE — FEAT 12

FIGHTER

Prerequisites Aggressive Block or Brutish Shove

Increase the distance you Shove your opponent with Aggressive Block or Brutish Shove to 10 feet on a success or 20 feet on a critical success. When you use Aggressive Block, you can choose whether the target is flat-footed or Shoved. When you make a Brutish Shove, you also Shove the target 5 feet on a failure.

IMPROVED DUELING RIPOSTE — FEAT 12

FIGHTER

Prerequisites Dueling Riposte

Your weapon whirls and darts, striking foes whenever the opportunity presents itself. At the start of each of your turns, you gain an additional reaction that you can use only to make a Dueling Riposte. You can use this extra reaction even if you are not benefiting from Dueling Parry.

INCREDIBLE RICOCHET ✦ — FEAT 12

CONCENTRATE **FIGHTER** **PRESS**

Prerequisites Incredible Aim

After your first shot singles out your opponent's position, you direct another that ricochets around obstacles and strikes unerringly. Make a ranged weapon Strike. You ignore the target's concealed condition and all cover.

LUNGING STANCE ✦ — FEAT 12

FIGHTER **STANCE**

Prerequisites attack of opportunity, Lunge

Requirement You are wielding a melee weapon.

Your body coiled to strike, you can lash out at distant enemies. While you are in this stance, you can use Attack of Opportunity against a creature that is outside your reach but within the reach you would have with a Lunge. If you do, you increase your range with the Strike by 5 feet.

PARAGON'S GUARD ✦ — FEAT 12

FIGHTER **STANCE**

Requirements You are wielding a shield.

Once you've had a moment to set your stance, you always have your shield ready without a thought. While you are in this stance, you constantly have your shield raised as if you'd used the Raise a Shield action, as long as you meet that action's requirements.

SAMPLE FIGHTER

ARCHER

You take out your opponents from a distance with ranged weapons, and you excel at dispatching flying or other hard-to-reach enemies.

ABILITY SCORES
Prioritize Dexterity. Constitution and Wisdom helps with survivability, and Strength adds damage with propulsive weapons.

SKILLS
Acrobatics, Medicine, Stealth, Thievery

STARTING FEAT
Point-Blank Shot

HIGHER-LEVEL FEATS
Double Shot (4th), Triple Shot (6th), Debilitating Shot (10th), Multishot Stance (16th), Impossible Volley (18th)

SPRING ATTACK ◆   FEAT 12

> FIGHTER   PRESS

Requirements You are adjacent to an enemy.

Springing away from one foe, you Strike at another. Stride up to your Speed, but you must end that movement within melee reach of a different enemy. At the end of your movement, make a melee Strike against an enemy now within reach. You can use Spring Attack while Burrowing, Climbing, Flying, or Swimming instead of Striding if you have the corresponding movement type.

14TH LEVEL

DESPERATE FINISHER ↻   FEAT 14

> FIGHTER

Trigger You complete the last action on your turn, and your turn has not ended yet.

Requirements You meet the requirements to use an action with the press trait.

You throw everything into one last press. Use a single action that you know with the press trait as part of Desperate Finisher. You forgo the ability to use reactions until the start of your next turn.

DETERMINATION ◆   FEAT 14

> CONCENTRATE   FIGHTER

Frequency once per day

Your training allows you to shrug off your foes' spells and conditions when the need is dire. Choose a single nonpermanent spell or condition that is affecting you. If you chose a condition, its effect on you ends. If you chose a spell, attempt to counteract the spell (your level is your counteract level, and you attempt a Will save as your counteract check).

This doesn't remove any Hit Point damage normally dealt by the spell or condition, and it doesn't prevent the spell or debilitating effect from affecting other allies or the environment around you. It can't remove an ongoing affliction or prevent such an affliction from inflicting conditions on you later. It can't remove conditions from the situation (such as prone or flanked). If the effect comes from a creature, hazard, or item of 20th level or higher, Determination can't remove its effect on you.

GUIDING FINISH ◆   FEAT 14

> FIGHTER   PRESS

Requirements You are wielding only a single one-handed melee weapon and have your other hand or hands free.

Using your weapon as a lever, you force your opponent to end up right where you want them. Make a Strike with the required weapon. If the Strike hits, you can move the target up to 10 feet into a space in your reach. You can move the target through your space during this movement. This follows the forced movement rules found on page 475. Your Strike gains the following failure effect.

Failure You can force the creature to move as you would on a success, but you can move the target only 5 feet.

GUIDING RIPOSTE — FEAT 14

FIGHTER

Prerequisites Dueling Riposte

By shifting your weight and angling your weapon, you guide your opponent to a more favorable position. When you use Dueling Riposte to Strike and you hit, you can move the target up to 10 feet into a space in your reach. This follows the forced movement rules found on page 475.

IMPROVED TWIN RIPOSTE — FEAT 14

FIGHTER

Prerequisites Twin Riposte

Your weapons are a blur, blocking and biting at your foes. At the start of each of your turns, you gain an additional reaction that you can use only to perform a Twin Riposte. You can use this extra reaction even if you are not benefiting from Twin Parry.

STANCE SAVANT ◈ — FEAT 14

FIGHTER

Trigger You roll initiative.

When there's imminent danger, you drop into a stance with a mere thought. Use an action that has the stance trait.

TWO-WEAPON FLURRY ◆ — FEAT 14

FIGHTER FLOURISH PRESS

Requirements You are wielding two weapons, each in a different hand.

You lash out with both your weapons in a sudden frenzy. Strike twice, once with each weapon.

WHIRLWIND STRIKE ◆▸▸ — FEAT 14

FIGHTER FLOURISH OPEN

You attack all nearby adversaries. Make a melee Strike against each enemy within your melee reach. Each attack counts toward your multiple attack penalty, but do not increase your penalty until you have made all your attacks.

16TH LEVEL

GRACEFUL POISE ◆ — FEAT 16

FIGHTER STANCE

Prerequisites Double Slice

With the right positioning, your off-hand weapon can strike like a scorpion's stinger. While you are in this stance, if you make your second Strike from Double Slice with an agile weapon, Double Slice counts as one attack when calculating your multiple attack penalty.

IMPROVED REFLEXIVE SHIELD — FEAT 16

FIGHTER

Prerequisites Reflexive Shield

Your shield can help save nearby allies. When you use Shield Block against damage resulting from a Reflex save, adjacent allies who would take damage due to Reflex saves against the same effect also benefit from the damage reduction.

MULTISHOT STANCE ◆ — FEAT 16

FIGHTER STANCE

Prerequisites Triple Shot

Requirements You are wielding a ranged weapon with reload 0.

You lock yourself in a stable position so you can fire swiftly and accurately. While you are in this stance, your penalty for Double Shot is reduced to –1, or –2 if you add the extra action to make three Strikes. If you move from your position, this stance ends.

TWINNED DEFENSE ◆ — FEAT 16

FIGHTER STANCE

Prerequisites Twin Parry

Requirements You are wielding two melee weapons, one in each hand.

You're always ready to use your off-hand weapon to interfere with attacks against you. While you are in this stance, you constantly gain the benefits of the Twin Parry action.

18TH LEVEL

IMPOSSIBLE VOLLEY ◆▸▸ — FEAT 18

FIGHTER FLOURISH OPEN

Requirements You are wielding a ranged weapon with the volley trait and reload 0.

You fire a volley at all foes in an area. Make one Strike with a –2 penalty against each enemy within a 10-foot-radius burst centered at or beyond your weapon's volley range. Roll the damage only once for all targets.

Each attack counts toward your multiple attack penalty, but do not increase your penalty until you have made all your attacks.

SAVAGE CRITICAL — FEAT 18

FIGHTER

The wounds you inflict are grievous. When you Strike with a weapon or unarmed attack for which you have legendary proficiency, you critically succeed if you roll a 19 on the die as long as that result is a success. This has no effect on a 19 if the result would be a failure.

20TH LEVEL

BOUNDLESS REPRISALS — FEAT 20

FIGHTER

With a sixth sense for the flow of combat, you can quickly react to any situation as required. At the start of each enemy's turn, you gain a reaction you can use only during that turn.

WEAPON SUPREMACY — FEAT 20

FIGHTER

Your skill with weapons lets you attack swiftly at all times. You're permanently quickened. You can use your extra action only to Strike.

MONK

The strength of your fist flows from your mind and spirit. You seek perfection—honing your body into a flawless instrument and your mind into an orderly bastion of wisdom. You're a fierce combatant renowned for martial arts skills and combat stances that grant you unique fighting moves. While the challenge of mastering many fighting styles drives you to great heights, you also enjoy meditating on philosophical questions and discovering new ways to obtain peace and enlightenment.

KEY ABILITY

STRENGTH OR DEXTERITY
At 1st level, your class gives you an ability boost to your choice of Strength or Dexterity.

HIT POINTS

10 plus your Constitution modifier
You increase your maximum number of HP by this number at 1st level and every level thereafter.

DURING COMBAT ENCOUNTERS...

You speed into the fray, dodging or leaping past obstacles with acrobatic maneuvers. You strike opponents in a rapid flurry of attacks, using your bare fists or wielding specialized weapons that you mastered during your monastic training. Stances let you change up your combat style for different situations, and ki abilities allow you to perform mystic feats like healing yourself and soaring through the air.

DURING SOCIAL ENCOUNTERS...

Your perceptiveness lets you see through falsehoods, and your philosophical training provides insight into any situation.

WHILE EXPLORING...

You climb up walls, dodge traps, overcome obstacles, and leap over pits. You usually stay toward the outside of the group to protect more vulnerable members, and you're well suited to looking for danger or moving stealthily.

IN DOWNTIME...

You diligently exercise, eat healthy foods, meditate, and study various philosophies. You might also take up a craft that you strive to perfect.

YOU MIGHT...

- Maintain a regimen of physical training and meditation.
- Face adversity with a calm and measured approach, never panicking or succumbing to despair.
- Look to the future for ways you can improve, while remaining at peace with your present self.

OTHERS PROBABLY...

- Marvel at your feats of physical prowess.
- Think you're more than a bit uptight, given your vows and tenets.
- Come to you for philosophical advice.

INITIAL PROFICIENCIES

At 1st level, you gain the listed proficiency ranks in the following statistics. You are untrained in anything not listed unless you gain a better proficiency rank in some other way.

PERCEPTION

Trained in Perception

SAVING THROWS

Expert in Fortitude
Expert in Reflex
Expert in Will

SKILLS

Trained in a number of skills equal to 4 plus your Intelligence modifier

ATTACKS

Trained in simple weapons
Trained in unarmed attacks

DEFENSES

Untrained in all armor
Expert in unarmored defense

CLASS DC

Trained in monk class DC

TABLE 3-13: MONK ADVANCEMENT

Your Level	Class Features
1	Ancestry and background, initial proficiencies, flurry of blows, monk feat, powerful fist
2	Monk feat, skill feat
3	General feat, incredible movement +10 feet, mystic strikes, skill increase
4	Monk feat, skill feat
5	Ability boosts, alertness, ancestry feat, expert strikes, skill increase
6	Monk feat, skill feat
7	General feat, incredible movement +15 feet, path to perfection, skill increase, weapon specialization
8	Monk feat, skill feat
9	Ancestry feat, metal strikes, monk expertise, skill increase
10	Ability boosts, monk feat, skill feat
11	General feat, incredible movement +20 feet, second path to perfection, skill increase
12	Monk feat, skill feat
13	Ancestry feat, graceful mastery, master strikes, skill increase
14	Monk feat, skill feat
15	Ability boosts, general feat, greater weapon specialization, incredible movement +25 feet, skill increase, third path to perfection
16	Monk feat, skill feat
17	Adamantine strikes, ancestry feat, graceful legend, skill increase
18	Monk feat, skill feat
19	General feat, incredible movement +30 feet, perfected form, skill increase
20	Ability boosts, monk feat, skill feat

CLASS FEATURES

You gain these abilities as a monk. Abilities gained at higher levels list the requisite levels next to the features' names.

ANCESTRY AND BACKGROUND

In addition to the abilities provided by your class at 1st level, you have the benefits of your selected ancestry and background, as described in Chapter 2.

INITIAL PROFICIENCIES

At 1st level, you gain a number of proficiencies representing your basic training, which are noted at the start of this class.

FLURRY OF BLOWS

You can attack rapidly with fists, feet, elbows, knees, and other unarmed attacks. You gain the Flurry of Blows action.

FLURRY OF BLOWS ◆

FLOURISH MONK

Make two unarmed Strikes. If both hit the same creature, combine their damage for the purpose of resistances and weaknesses. Apply your multiple attack penalty to the Strikes normally. As it has the flourish trait, you can use Flurry of Blows only once per turn.

MONK FEATS

At 1st level and every even-numbered level thereafter, you gain a monk class feat.

POWERFUL FIST

You know how to wield your fists as deadly weapons. The damage die for your fist changes to 1d6 instead of 1d4. Most people take a −2 circumstance penalty when making a lethal attack with nonlethal unarmed attacks, because they find it hard to use their fists with deadly force. You don't take this penalty when making a lethal attack with your fist or any other unarmed attacks.

SKILL FEATS   2ND

At 2nd level and every 2 levels thereafter, you gain a skill feat. Skill feats are listed in Chapter 5 and have the skill trait. You must be trained or better in the corresponding skill to select a skill feat.

GENERAL FEATS   3RD

At 3rd level and every 4 levels thereafter, you gain a general feat. General feats are listed in Chapter 5.

INCREDIBLE MOVEMENT   3RD

You move like the wind. You gain a +10-foot status bonus to your Speed whenever you're not wearing armor. The bonus increases by 5 feet for every 4 levels you have beyond 3rd.

MYSTIC STRIKES   3RD

Focusing your will into your physical attacks imbues them with mystical energy. Your unarmed attacks become magical, allowing them to get past resistances to non-magical attacks. However, you still need an item such as *handwraps of mighty fists* to gain an item bonus to attack rolls or increase your attacks' weapon damage dice.

SKILL INCREASES   3RD

At 3rd level and every 2 levels thereafter, you gain a skill increase. You can use this increase to either become trained in one skill you're untrained in, or become an expert in one skill in which you're already trained.

At 7th level, you can use skill increases to become a master in a skill in which you're already an expert, and at 15th level, you can use them to become legendary in a skill in which you're already a master.

ABILITY BOOSTS   5TH

At 5th level and every 5 levels thereafter, you boost four different ability scores. You can use these ability boosts to increase your ability scores above 18. Boosting an ability score increases it by 1 if it's already 18 or above, or by 2 if it starts out below 18.

ALERTNESS   5TH

You remain alert to threats around you. Your proficiency rank for Perception increases to expert.

ANCESTRY FEATS   5TH

In addition to the ancestry feat you started with, you gain an ancestry feat at 5th level and every 4 levels thereafter. The list of ancestry feats available to you can be found in your ancestry's entry in Chapter 2.

EXPERT STRIKES   5TH

You've practiced martial arts and have now surpassed your former skill. Your proficiency ranks for unarmed attacks and simple weapons increase to expert.

PATH TO PERFECTION   7TH

You have progressed along your own path to enlightenment. Choose your Fortitude, Reflex, or Will saving throw. Your proficiency rank for the chosen saving throw increases to master. When you roll a success on the chosen saving throw, you get a critical success instead.

WEAPON SPECIALIZATION   7TH

You've learned how to inflict greater injuries with the weapons you know best. You deal 2 additional damage with weapons and unarmed attacks in which you are an expert. This damage increases to 3 if you're a master, and 4 if you're legendary.

METAL STRIKES   9TH

You can adjust your body to make unarmed attacks infused with the mystic energy of rare metals. Your unarmed attacks are treated as cold iron and silver. This allows you to deal more damage to a variety of supernatural creatures, such as demons, devils, and fey.

MONK EXPERTISE   9TH

Your proficiency rank for your monk class DC increases to expert. If you have ki spells, your proficiency rank for spell attacks and spell DCs with the tradition of magic you use for your ki spells increases to expert.

SECOND PATH TO PERFECTION   11TH

You've learned to find perfection in every success. Choose a different saving throw than the one you chose for your path to perfection. Your proficiency rank for the chosen saving throw increases to master. If you roll a success with the chosen saving throw, you instead critically succeed.

GRACEFUL MASTERY   13TH

You move with perpetual grace in battle, eluding and turning aside blows. Your proficiency rank for unarmored defense increases to master.

KEY TERMS

You'll see the following key terms in many monk abilities.

Flourish: Actions with this trait are special techniques that require too much exertion for you to perform frequently. You can use only 1 action with the flourish trait per turn.

Incapacitation: An ability with this trait can take a character out of the fight. But when you use an incapacitation effect against a creature of higher level than you, you reduce the degree of success of your attack roll by one step, and that creature improves the degree of success of its saving throws for that effect by one step.

Ki Spells: By tapping into a supernatural inner reserve called ki, you can create magical effects. Certain feats grant you special spells called ki spells, which are a type of focus spell. It costs 1 Focus Point to cast a focus spell. When you gain your first ki spell, you also gain a focus pool of 1 Focus Point. You refill your focus pool during your daily preparations, and you regain 1 Focus Point by spending 10 minutes using the Refocus activity to meditate in order to reach inner peace.

When you first gain a ki spell, decide whether your ki spells are divine spells or occult spells. You become trained in spell attacks and spell DCs of that tradition.

Focus spells are automatically heightened to half your level rounded up. Taking feats can give you more focus spells and increase the size of your focus pool, though your focus pool can never hold more than 3 points. The full rules for focus spells appear on page 300.

Stance: A stance is a general combat strategy that you enter by using an action with the stance trait, and that you remain in for some time. A stance lasts until you get knocked out, until its requirements (if any) are violated, until the encounter ends, or until you enter a new stance, whichever comes first. After you take an action that has the stance trait, you can't take another one for 1 round. You can enter or be in a stance only in encounter mode.

MASTER STRIKES   13TH

You have honed your skill in using your body as a weapon. Your proficiency ranks for unarmed attacks and simple weapons increase to master.

GREATER WEAPON SPECIALIZATION   15TH

Your damage from weapon specialization increases to 4 with weapons and unarmed attacks in which you're an expert, 6 if you're a master, and 8 if you're legendary.

THIRD PATH TO PERFECTION   15TH

You have made great progress in your personal studies of enlightenment. Choose one of the saving throws you selected for path to perfection or second path to perfection. Your proficiency rank for the chosen type of save increases to legendary. When you roll a critical failure on the chosen type of save, you get a failure instead. When you fail at the chosen type of save against an effect that deals damage, you take half damage.

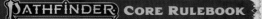

MONK FEATS

If you need to look up a monk feat by name instead of by level, use this table.

ADAMANTINE STRIKES   17TH

When you focus your will into your limbs, your blows are as unyielding as the hardest of metals. Your unarmed attacks are treated as adamantine.

GRACEFUL LEGEND   17TH

Your sublime movement grants you unparalleled protection and offense. Your proficiency rank for unarmored defense increases to legendary, and your proficiency rank for your monk class DC increases to master. If you have ki spells, your proficiency rank for spell attack rolls and spell DCs with the tradition of magic you use for your ki spells increases to master.

PERFECTED FORM   19TH

You have purged incompetence from your techniques. On your first Strike of your turn, if you roll lower than 10, you can treat the attack roll as a 10. This is a fortune effect.

MONK FEATS

Every level at which you gain a monk feat, select one of the following feats. You must satisfy any prerequisites before taking the feat.

1ST LEVEL

CRANE STANCE ❖   FEAT 1

MONK **STANCE**

Requirements You are unarmored.

You enter the stance of a crane, holding your arms in an imitation of a crane's wings and using flowing, defensive motions. You gain a +1 circumstance bonus to AC, but the only Strikes you can make are crane wing attacks. These deal 1d6 bludgeoning damage; are in the brawling group; and have the agile, finesse, nonlethal, and unarmed traits.

While in Crane Stance, reduce the DC for High Jump and Long Jump by 5, and when you Leap, you can move an additional 5 feet horizontally or 2 feet vertically.

DRAGON STANCE ❖   FEAT 1

MONK **STANCE**

Requirements You are unarmored.

You enter the stance of a dragon and make powerful leg strikes like a lashing dragon's tail. You can make dragon tail attacks that deal 1d10 bludgeoning damage. They are in the brawling group and have the backswing, nonlethal, and unarmed traits.

While in Dragon Stance, you can ignore the first square of difficult terrain while Striding.

KI RUSH   FEAT 1

MONK

You can use ki to move with extraordinary speed and make yourself harder to hit. You gain the *ki rush* ki spell and a focus pool of 1 Focus Point. The rules for ki spells are summarized in the sidebar on page 157, and the full rules for focus spells appear on page 300.

KI STRIKE   FEAT 1

MONK

Your study of the flow of mystical energy allows you to harness it into your physical strikes. You gain the *ki strike* ki spell and a focus pool of 1 Focus Point. The rules for ki spells are summarized in the sidebar on page 157, and the full rules for focus spells appear on page 300.

MONASTIC WEAPONRY   FEAT 1

MONK

You have trained with the traditional weaponry of your monastery or school. You gain access to uncommon weapons that have the monk trait and become trained in simple

CLASSES 3

INTRODUCTION

ANCESTRIES &
BACKGROUNDS

CLASSES

SKILLS

FEATS

EQUIPMENT

SPELLS

THE AGE OF
LOST OMENS

PLAYING THE
GAME

GAME
MASTERING

CRAFTING
& TREASURE

APPENDIX

MONK UNARMED ATTACKS

Some monk stances allow you to make special unarmed attacks while in those stances. These attacks are summarized here.

Attack	Damage	Group	Traits
Crane wing	1d6 B	Brawling	Agile, finesse, nonlethal, unarmed
Dragon tail	1d10 B	Brawling	Backswing, nonlethal, unarmed
Falling stone	1d8 B	Brawling	Forceful, nonlethal, unarmed
Iron sweep	1d8 B	Brawling	Nonlethal, parry, sweep, unarmed
Lashing branch	1d8 S	Brawling	Agile, finesse, nonlethal, unarmed
Tiger claw	1d8 S	Brawling	Agile, finesse, nonlethal, unarmed
Wind crash*	1d6 S	Brawling	Agile, nonlethal, propulsive, unarmed
Wolf jaw	1d8 P	Brawling	Agile, backstabber, finesse, nonlethal, unarmed

* *Wild winds stance* is a ki spell, so you can find out more about wind crash on page 402.

and martial monk weapons. When your proficiency rank for unarmed attacks increases to expert or master, your proficiency rank for these weapons increases to expert or master as well.

You can use melee monk weapons with any of your monk feats or monk abilities that normally require unarmed attacks, though not if the feat or ability requires you to use a single specific type of attack, such as Crane Stance.

MOUNTAIN STANCE ❖ FEAT 1

MONK **STANCE**

Trigger You are unarmored and touching the ground.

You enter the stance of an implacable mountain—a technique first discovered by dwarven monks—allowing you to strike with the weight of an avalanche. The only Strikes you can make are falling stone unarmed attacks. These deal 1d8 bludgeoning damage; are in the brawling group; and have the forceful, nonlethal, and unarmed traits.

While in Mountain Stance, you gain a +4 status bonus to AC and a +2 circumstance bonus to any defenses against being Shoved or Tripped. However, you have a Dexterity modifier cap to your AC of +0, meaning you don't add your Dexterity to your AC, and your Speeds are all reduced by 5 feet.

TIGER STANCE ❖ FEAT 1

MONK **STANCE**

Requirements You are unarmored.

You enter the stance of a tiger and can make tiger claw attacks. These deal 1d8 slashing damage; are in the brawling group; and have the agile, finesse, nonlethal, and unarmed traits. On a critical success with your tiger claws, if you deal damage, the target takes 1d4 persistent bleed damage.

As long as your Speed is at least 20 feet while in Tiger Stance, you can Step 10 feet.

WOLF STANCE ❖ FEAT 1

MONK **STANCE**

Requirements You are unarmored.

You enter the stance of a wolf, low to the ground with your hands held like fanged teeth. You can make wolf jaw unarmed attacks. These deal 1d8 piercing damage; are in the brawling group; and have the agile, backstabber, finesse, nonlethal, and unarmed traits.

If you're flanking a target while in Wolf Stance, your wolf jaw unarmed attacks also gain the trip trait.

2ND LEVEL

BRAWLING FOCUS   FEAT 2

MONK

You know how to make the most of your attacks when fighting hand-to-hand. You gain access to the critical specialization effects of unarmed strikes in the brawling group and weapons in the brawling group. If you have Monastic Weaponry, you also gain the critical specialization effects of all monk weapons in which you are trained.

CRUSHING GRAB   FEAT 2

MONK

Like a powerful constrictor, you crush targets in your unyielding grasp. When you successfully Grapple a creature, you can deal bludgeoning damage to that creature equal to your Strength modifier. You can make this attack nonlethal with no penalty.

DANCING LEAF   FEAT 2

MONK

You are as light as a leaf whirling in the breeze. When you Leap or succeed at a High Jump or Long Jump, increase the distance you jump by 5 feet. When calculating the damage you take from falling, don't count any distance fallen while you are adjacent to a wall.

ELEMENTAL FIST   FEAT 2

MONK

Prerequisites Ki Strike

You call upon the power of the elements, infusing your ki with elemental energy and allowing your attacks to deal energy damage. When you cast *ki strike*, in addition to the damage types normally available, you can deliver the extra damage in the form of a gust of storm-tossed wind (dealing electricity damage and gaining the air trait), a chunk of stone (dealing bludgeoning damage and gaining the earth trait), a flickering flame (dealing fire damage), or a crashing wave of frigid water (dealing cold damage and gaining the water trait).

STUNNING FIST   FEAT 2

MONK

Prerequisites Flurry of Blows

The focused power of your flurry threatens to overwhelm your opponent. When you target the same creature with two Strikes from your Flurry of Blows, you can try to stun the creature. If either Strike hits and deals damage, the target must succeed at a Fortitude save against your class DC or be stunned 1 (or stunned 3 on a critical failure). This is an incapacitation effect.

4TH LEVEL

DEFLECT ARROW ⟳   FEAT 4

MONK

Trigger You are the target of a physical ranged attack.

Requirements You're aware of the attack, are not flat-footed against it, and have a hand free.

You gain a +4 circumstance bonus to AC against the triggering attack. If the attack misses, you have deflected it. You cannot use this feat to deflect unusually massive ranged projectiles (such as boulders or ballista bolts).

FLURRY OF MANEUVERS   FEAT 4

MONK

Prerequisites expert in Athletics

You flurry is a combination of maneuvers. You can replace one or both of your attacks during a Flurry of Blows with Grapples, Shoves, or Trips.

FLYING KICK ◆◆   FEAT 4

MONK

You launch yourself at a foe. Make a Leap or attempt a High Jump or Long Jump. At the end of the jump, if you're adjacent to a foe, you can immediately Strike that foe with an unarmed attack, even if the foe is in mid-air. You fall to the ground after the Strike. If the distance you fall is no more than the height of your jump, you land upright and take no damage.

GUARDED MOVEMENT   FEAT 4

MONK

Your guard is up, even while moving. You gain a +4 circumstance bonus to AC against reactions triggered by your movement.

STAND STILL ⟳   FEAT 4

MONK

Trigger A creature within your reach uses a move action or leaves a square during a move action it's using.

You strike out when your foe tries to flee. Make a melee Strike against the triggering creature. If the attack is a critical hit and the trigger was a move action, you disrupt that action.

WHOLENESS OF BODY   FEAT 4

MONK

Prerequisites ki spells

You can restore your health by tapping into your ki. You gain the *wholeness of body* ki spell (page 402). Increase the number of Focus Points in your focus pool by 1.

6TH LEVEL

ABUNDANT STEP   FEAT 6

MONK

Prerequisites incredible movement, ki spells

You can teleport yourself a short distance. You gain the *abundant step* ki spell (page 401). Increase the number of Focus Points in your focus pool by 1.

CLASSES

3

INTRODUCTION

ANCESTRIES &
BACKGROUNDS

CLASSES

SKILLS

FEATS

EQUIPMENT

SPELLS

THE AGE OF
LOST OMENS

PLAYING THE
GAME

GAME
MASTERING

CRAFTING
& TREASURE

APPENDIX

CRANE FLUTTER ⟳   FEAT 6

MONK

Prerequisites Crane Stance

Trigger You are targeted with a melee attack by an attacker you can see.

Requirements You are in Crane Stance.

You interpose your arm between yourself and your opponent. Your circumstance bonus to AC from Crane Stance increases to +3 against the triggering attack. If the attack misses you, you can immediately make a crane wing Strike against the attacker at a –2 penalty, even if the attacker isn't within your reach.

DRAGON ROAR ◆   FEAT 6

AUDITORY   **EMOTION**   **FEAR**   **MENTAL**   **MONK**

Prerequisites Dragon Stance

Requirements You are in Dragon Stance.

You bellow, instilling fear in your enemies. Enemies within a 15-foot emanation must succeed at a Will save against your Intimidation DC or be frightened 1 (frightened 2 on a critical failure). When a creature frightened by the roar begins its turn adjacent to you, it can't reduce its frightened value below 1 on that turn. Your first attack that hits a frightened creature after you roar and before the end of your next turn gains a +4 circumstance bonus to damage.

After you use Dragon Roar, you can't use it again for 1d4 rounds. Its effects end immediately if you leave Dragon Stance. Creatures in the area of your roar are then temporarily immune for 1 minute.

KI BLAST   FEAT 6

MONK

Prerequisites ki spells

You can unleash an impactful cone of force by channeling your ki. You gain the *ki blast* ki spell (page 401). Increase the number of Focus Points in your focus pool by 1.

MOUNTAIN STRONGHOLD ◆   FEAT 6

MONK

Prerequisites Mountain Stance

Requirements You are in Mountain Stance.

You focus on your connection to the earth and call upon the mountain to block attacks against you. You gain a +2 circumstance bonus to AC until the beginning of your next turn.

   Special If you have this feat, the Dexterity modifier cap to your AC while you're in Mountain Stance increases from +0 to +1.

TIGER SLASH ◆◆   FEAT 6

MONK

Prerequisites Tiger Stance

SAMSARAN MONK

KI MONK

Centering yourself, you call forth the internal magical energy that dwells within all living things. This ki can empower your body or flash out as pure energy.

ABILITY SCORES
Prioritize Strength. Wisdom empowers your ki spells, Perception, and Will saves. Constitution and Dexterity help your physical defenses.

SKILLS
Acrobatics, Athletics, Occultism, Stealth

STARTING FEAT
Ki Strike (occult)

HIGHER-LEVEL FEATS
Mountain Stance (1st), Elemental Fist (2nd), Wholeness of Body (4th), Ki Blast (6th), Meditative Focus (12th), Quivering Palm (16th), Empty Body (20th)

Requirements You are in Tiger Stance.

You make a fierce swipe with both hands. Make a tiger claw Strike. It deals two extra weapon damage dice (three extra dice if you're 14th level or higher), and you can push the target 5 feet away as if you had successfully Shoved them. If the attack is a critical success and deals damage, add your Strength modifier to the persistent bleed damage from your tiger claw.

WATER STEP   FEAT 6
MONK

You can Stride across liquid and surfaces that don't support your weight. This benefit lasts only during your movement. If you end your movement on a surface that can't support you, you fall in or it collapses as normal.

WHIRLING THROW ◆   FEAT 6
MONK

Requirements You have a creature grabbed or restrained.

You propel your grabbed or restrained foe a great distance. You can throw the creature any distance up to 10 feet, plus 5 feet × your Strength modifier. If you successfully throw the creature, it takes bludgeoning damage equal to your Strength modifier plus 1d6 per 10 feet you threw it.

Attempt an Athletics check against the foe's Fortitude DC. You take a –2 circumstance penalty to your check if the target is one size larger than you and a –4 circumstance penalty if it's larger than that. You gain a +2 circumstance bonus to your check if the target is one size smaller than you and a +4 circumstance bonus if it's smaller than that.

Critical Success You throw the creature the desired distance and it lands prone.

Success You throw the creature the desired distance.

Failure You don't throw the creature.

Critical Failure You don't throw the creature, and it's no longer grabbed or restrained by you.

WOLF DRAG ◆◆   FEAT 6
MONK

Prerequisites Wolf Stance

Requirements You are in Wolf Stance.

You rip your enemy off their feet. Make a wolf jaw Strike. Your wolf jaw gains the fatal d12 trait for this Strike, and if the attack succeeds, you knock the target prone.

8TH LEVEL

ARROW SNATCHING   FEAT 8
MONK

Prerequisite Deflect Arrow

You pluck missiles from the air and hurl them back at their source. When you successfully deflect an attack with Deflect Arrow, as part of that reaction, you can immediately make a ranged Strike against the attacker using the projectile you deflected. This is a thrown weapon with the same range increment and effect on a hit as the triggering attack.

IRONBLOOD STANCE ✦ FEAT 8

`MONK` `STANCE`

Requirements You are unarmored.

You enter the stance of impenetrable iron, refusing to yield to any blow. You can make iron sweep unarmed attacks. These deal 1d8 bludgeoning damage; are in the brawling group; and have the nonlethal, parry, sweep, and unarmed traits.

While in Ironblood Stance, you gain resistance 2 to all damage. The resistance increases to 3 at 12th level, to 4 at 16th level, and to 5 at 20th level.

MIXED MANEUVER ✦✦ FEAT 8

`MONK`

Prerequisite master in Athletics

You combine two different maneuvers together into a single flowing whole. Choose any two of Grapple, Shove, and Trip. Attempt both of the attacks you chose against the same or different creatures, but don't apply the multiple attack penalty until after resolving both attacks.

TANGLED FOREST STANCE ✦ FEAT 8

`MONK` `STANCE`

Trigger You are unarmored.

You extend your arms like gnarled branches to interfere with your foes' movements. You can make lashing branch unarmed attacks. These deal 1d8 slashing damage; are in the brawling group; and have the agile, finesse, nonlethal, and unarmed traits.

While you're in Tangled Forest Stance and can act, every enemy in your reach that tries to move away from you must succeed at a Reflex save, Acrobatics check, or Athletics check against your class DC or be immobilized for that action. If you prefer, you can allow the enemy to move.

WALL RUN ✦ FEAT 8

`MONK`

You defy gravity, traversing vertical planes as easily as the ground. Stride up to your Speed. You must start your movement on a horizontal surface. During this movement, you can run up vertical surfaces, like walls, at your full Speed. If you end the Stride off the ground, you fall after taking your next action or when your turn ends, whichever comes first (though you can Grab an Edge, if applicable). If you have Water Step or a similar ability, Wall Run lets you run along flimsy vertical surfaces, as well as vertical liquids, such as a waterfall.

WILD WINDS INITIATE FEAT 8

`MONK`

Prerequisites ki spells

You learn a mystical stance that lets you attack from a distance. You gain the *wild winds stance* ki spell (page 402). Increase the number of Focus Points in your focus pool by 1. While entering the stance is a ki spell, the wind crash Strikes the stance grants are not, so you can use them as often as you like while in the stance.

10TH LEVEL

KNOCKBACK STRIKE ✦✦ FEAT 10

`CONCENTRATE` `MONK`

You focus your strength into a blow powerful enough to push an enemy away from you. Make an unarmed Strike. If you hit, attempt an Athletics check to Shove the target. This attack uses the same multiple attack penalty as your Strike, and doesn't count toward your multiple attack penalty.

SLEEPER HOLD ✦ FEAT 10

`ATTACK` `INCAPACITATION` `MONK`

Requirements You have a creature grabbed or restrained.

You pinch crucial points of your target's nervous system, impeding its ability to function. Attempt an Athletics check to Grapple the creature, with the following success and critical success effects instead of the usual effects.

Critical Success The target falls unconscious for 1 minute, though it remains standing and doesn't drop what it holds.

Success The target is clumsy 1 until the end of its next turn.

WIND JUMP FEAT 10

`MONK`

Prerequisites ki spells

You gather the wind beneath you, allowing you to soar as you jump. You gain the *wind jump* ki spell (page 402). Increase the number of Focus Points in your focus pool by 1.

WINDING FLOW ✦ FEAT 10

`MONK`

Frequency once per round

Any journey consists of more than simply reaching your destination. You use two of the following actions in any order: Stand, Step, and Stride. You can't use the same action twice.

12TH LEVEL

DIAMOND SOUL FEAT 12

`MONK`

You have fortified your body and mind against eldritch effects. You gain a +1 status bonus to saving throws against magic.

DISRUPT KI ✦✦ FEAT 12

`MONK` `NEGATIVE`

Make an unarmed Strike. If it deals damage to a living creature, you block that creature's inner life force. The creature takes 2d6 persistent negative damage and is enfeebled 1 until the persistent damage ends. If you're 18th level or higher, this deals 3d6 persistent negative damage instead.

IMPROVED KNOCKBACK FEAT 12

`MONK`

Prerequisites master in Athletics

When you successfully Shove a creature, increase both the distance you can push the creature and the distance you can move to follow along with the target by 5 feet on a success

INTRODUCTION

ANCESTRIES & BACKGROUNDS

CLASSES

SKILLS

FEATS

EQUIPMENT

SPELLS

THE AGE OF LOST OMENS

PLAYING THE GAME

GAME MASTERING

CRAFTING & TREASURE

APPENDIX

SAMPLE MONK

CRANE MONK

Striving for grace in all things, you mimic the fluid movements of the crane. Your strikes are quick as the wind and your mind clear as a placid pool.

ABILITY SCORES
Prioritize Dexterity for finesse attacks and high defenses. A good Wisdom lets you perceive dangers and act quickly, and Constitution improves your hardiness.

SKILLS
Acrobatics, Nature, Religion, Stealth

STARTING FEAT
Crane Stance

HIGHER-LEVEL FEATS
Dancing Leaf (2nd), Flying Kick (4th), Crane Flutter (6th), Winding Flow (10th), Stance Savant (12th), Enduring Quickness (20th)

---

or 10 feet on a critical success. If you push the target into an obstacle, it takes bludgeoning damage equal to 6 plus your Strength modifier, or 8 plus your Strength modifier if you have legendary proficiency in Athletics.

MEDITATIVE FOCUS — FEAT 12

MONK

Prerequisites ki spells

Your meditation is so effective that you can achieve a deep focus. If you have spent at least 2 Focus Points since the last time you Refocused, you recover 2 Focus Points when you Refocus instead of 1.

STANCE SAVANT ⤾ — FEAT 12

MONK

Trigger You roll initiative.

You enter a stance without a thought. Use an action that has the stance trait.

14TH LEVEL

IRONBLOOD SURGE ❖ — FEAT 14

MONK

Prerequisites Ironblood Stance
Requirements You are in Ironblood Stance.

You steel yourself, preparing to resist oncoming attacks and using your muscles to absorb the impact. You gain the benefits of your iron sweep's parry trait (a +1 circumstance bonus to AC until the start of your next turn) and your resistance from Ironblood Stance increases to your Strength modifier (if it's higher) for the same duration.

MOUNTAIN QUAKE ❖ — FEAT 14

MONK

Prerequisites Mountain Stronghold
Requirements You are in Mountain Stance.

You stomp, shaking the earth beneath you. Creatures on the ground within a 20-foot emanation take damage equal to your Strength modifier (minimum 0), which they can resist with a basic Fortitude save. On a failure, they also fall prone. After you use this action, you can't use it again for 1d4 rounds.

Special If you have this feat, the Dexterity modifier cap to your AC while using Mountain Stance increases from +1 to +2.

TANGLED FOREST RAKE ❖ — FEAT 14

MONK

Prerequisites Tangled Forest Stance
Requirements You are in Tangled Forest Stance.

You reposition foes with raking attacks. Make a lashing branch Strike. If you hit and deal damage, you force the target to move 5 feet into a space within your reach. This follows the forced movement rules found on page 475.

TIMELESS BODY — FEAT 14

MONK

You cease aging. In addition, you gain a +2 status bonus to

saving throws against poisons and diseases, and you gain resistance to poison damage equal to half your level.

TONGUE OF SUN AND MOON — FEAT 14

MONK

You have transcended the barriers between words and meaning. You can speak and understand all spoken languages.

WILD WINDS GUST ❖❖ — FEAT 14

AIR | CONCENTRATE | EVOCATION | MANIPULATE | MONK

Prerequisites Wild Winds Initiate
Requirements You are in wild winds stance.

You store up energy and release it in an enormous gust of rushing wind. Make a wind crash Strike against each creature in your choice of a 30-foot cone or a 60 foot line. These attacks all count toward your multiple attack penalty, but the penalty doesn't increase until after you make all the attacks.

16TH LEVEL

ENLIGHTENED PRESENCE — FEAT 16

EMOTION | MENTAL | MONK

You exude an aura of resolve. You and allies within 15 feet of you gain a +2 status bonus to Will saving throws against mental effects.

MASTER OF MANY STYLES ❖ — FEAT 16

MONK

Prerequisites Stance Savant
Requirements This is the first action of your turn.

You move between stances in an unceasing dance. You use an action with the stance trait.

QUIVERING PALM — FEAT 16

MONK

Prerequisites ki spells

Your strikes can kill foes. You gain the *quivering palm* ki spell (page 401). Increase the number of Focus Points in your focus pool by 1.

SHATTERING STRIKE ❖❖ — FEAT 16

MONK

The force of your considered blow shatters objects and defenses alike. Make an unarmed Strike. It bypasses the target's resistances. If the target has Hardness, the Strike treats the Hardness as if it were half its value.

18TH LEVEL

DIAMOND FISTS — FEAT 18

MONK

Your body hardens as you combine your attacks, making your finishing blows more damaging. Your unarmed attacks gain the forceful trait. Any that already had this trait instead increase their weapon damage dice by one step.

EMPTY BODY — FEAT 18

MONK

Prerequisites ki spells

You transmute your body into an ethereal form. You gain the *empty body* ki spell (page 401). Increase the number of Focus Points in your focus pool by 1.

MEDITATIVE WELLSPRING — FEAT 18

MONK

Prerequisites Meditative Focus

When you clear your mind, your focus comes flowing back in a powerful rush. If you have spent at least 3 Focus Points since the last time you Refocused, you recover 3 Focus Points when you Refocus instead of 1.

SWIFT RIVER ❖ — FEAT 18

MONK

Trigger Your turn ends and you have a status penalty to your Speed or are immobilized or slowed.

You flow like water, avoiding all restraints. End one status penalty to your speed, or end one immobilized or slowed condition affecting you.

20TH LEVEL

ENDURING QUICKNESS — FEAT 20

MONK

You move as fast and as high as the wind itself. You're permanently quickened. You can use your extra action to Stride or Leap, or to provide one of the actions needed for a High Jump or Long Jump.

FUSE STANCE — FEAT 20

MONK

Prerequisites at least two stances

You have combined two stances into a single stance all your own. When you take this feat, choose two stances you know and combine them into a single fused stance. Give your new fused stance a unique name. When you enter your fused stance, you gain all the effects of both stances, including the requirements and restrictions.

You can't fuse stances with fundamentally incompatible requirements or restrictions (such as Ironblood Stance and Crane Stance, which both require using only one type of Strike).

IMPOSSIBLE TECHNIQUE ↻ — FEAT 20

FORTUNE | MONK

Trigger An enemy's attack hits you or you fail a saving throw against an enemy's ability.
Requirements You are not armored or fatigued.

You execute a maneuver that defies possibility. If the triggering effect was an enemy's attack hitting you, the enemy rerolls the attack roll and uses the lower result. If the triggering effect was you failing a saving throw, you reroll the saving throw and use the higher result.

INTRODUCTION

ANCESTRIES & BACKGROUNDS

CLASSES

SKILLS

FEATS

EQUIPMENT

SPELLS

THE AGE OF LOST OMENS

PLAYING THE GAME

GAME MASTERING

CRAFTING & TREASURE

APPENDIX

INTRODUCTION

ANCESTRIES &
BACKGROUNDS

CLASSES

SKILLS

FEATS

EQUIPMENT

SPELLS

THE AGE OF
LOST OMENS

PLAYING THE
GAME

GAME
MASTERING

CRAFTING
& TREASURE

APPENDIX

RANGER

Some rangers believe civilization wears down the soul, but still needs to be protected from wild creatures. Others say nature needs to be protected from the greedy, who wish to tame its beauty and plunder its treasures. You could champion either goal, or both. You might be a scout, tracker, or hunter of fugitives or beasts, haunting the edge of civilization or exploring the wilds. You know how to live off the land and are skilled at spotting and taking down both opportune prey and hated enemies.

KEY ABILITY

STRENGTH OR DEXTERITY
At 1st level, your class gives you an ability boost to your choice of Strength or Dexterity.

HIT POINTS

10 + your Constitution modifier
You increase your maximum number of HP by this number at 1st level and every level thereafter.

DURING COMBAT ENCOUNTERS...

You can single out particular foes to hunt, making you better at defeating them. You target and brutalize your chosen foe with either a bow or melee weapons, while supporting your allies with your skills.

DURING SOCIAL ENCOUNTERS...

When you speak, it's with the voice of practical experience, especially involving wilderness exploration.

WHILE EXPLORING...

You guide your allies through the wilderness or follow tracks. You keep an eye out for trouble, constantly alert for danger even when it's not overt.

IN DOWNTIME...

You craft weapons and snares in preparation for your next venture. If you prefer to get outside, you might go on hunts or scout nearby areas to better understand your environment.

YOU MIGHT...

- Respect the raw power of nature and understand how to make the best of its bounty.
- Enjoy the thrill of the hunt.
- Scout out ahead of the party, reconnoitering dangers before combat begins.

OTHERS PROBABLY...

- Call upon you to protect them from the wilds or the encroachment of civilization.
- Expect you to be a quiet or taciturn loner.
- Think there is something dangerous and wild about you.

INITIAL PROFICIENCIES

At 1st level, you gain the listed proficiency ranks in the following statistics. You are untrained in anything not listed unless you gain a better proficiency rank in some other way.

PERCEPTION

Expert in Perception

SAVING THROWS

Expert in Fortitude
Expert in Reflex
Trained in Will

SKILLS

Trained in Nature
Trained in Survival
Trained in a number of additional skills equal to 4 plus your Intelligence modifier

ATTACKS

Trained in simple weapons
Trained in martial weapons
Trained in unarmed attacks

DEFENSES

Trained in light armor
Trained in medium armor
Trained in unarmored defense

CLASS DC

Trained in ranger class DC

TABLE 3-14: RANGER ADVANCEMENT

Your Level	Class Features
1	Ancestry and background, initial proficiencies, hunt prey, hunter's edge, ranger feat
2	Ranger feat, skill feat
3	General feat, iron will, skill increase
4	Ranger feat, skill feat
5	Ability boosts, ancestry feat, skill increase, trackless step, weapon expertise
6	Ranger feat, skill feat
7	Evasion, general feat, skill increase, vigilant senses, weapon specialization
8	Ranger feat, skill feat
9	Ancestry feat, nature's edge, ranger expertise, skill increase
10	Ability boosts, ranger feat, skill feat
11	General feat, juggernaut, medium armor expertise, skill increase, wild stride
12	Ranger feat, skill feat
13	Ancestry feat, skill increase, weapon mastery
14	Ranger feat, skill feat
15	Ability boosts, general feat, greater weapon specialization, improved evasion, incredible senses, skill increase
16	Ranger feat, skill feat
17	Ancestry feat, masterful hunter, skill increase
18	Ranger feat, skill feat
19	General feat, second skin, skill increase, swift prey
20	Ability boosts, ranger feat, skill feat

CLASS FEATURES

You gain these abilities as a ranger. Abilities gained at higher levels list the level at which you gain them next to the features' names.

ANCESTRY AND BACKGROUND

In addition to what you get from your class at 1st level, you have the benefits of your selected ancestry and background, as described in Chapter 2.

INITIAL PROFICIENCIES

At 1st level, you gain a number of proficiencies that represent your basic training. These proficiencies are noted at the start of this class.

HUNT PREY

When you focus your attention on a single foe, you become unstoppable in your pursuit. You gain the Hunt Prey action.

HUNT PREY ❖

CONCENTRATE RANGER

You designate a single creature as your prey and focus your attacks against that creature. You must be able to see or hear the prey, or you must be tracking the prey during exploration.

You gain a +2 circumstance bonus to Perception checks when you Seek your prey and a +2 circumstance bonus to Survival checks when you Track your prey. You also ignore the penalty for making ranged attacks within your second range increment against the prey you're hunting.

You can have only one creature designated as your prey at a time. If you use Hunt Prey against a creature when you already have a creature designated, the prior creature loses the designation and the new prey gains the designation. Your designation lasts until your next daily preparations.

HUNTER'S EDGE

You have trained for countless hours to become a more skilled hunter and tracker, gaining an additional benefit when you Hunt Prey depending on the focus of your training. Choose a hunter's edge.

Flurry: You have trained to unleash a devastating flurry of attacks upon your prey. Your multiple attack penalty for attacks against your hunted prey is –3 (–2 with an agile weapon) on your second attack of the turn instead of –5, and –6 (–4 with an agile weapon) on your third or subsequent attack of the turn, instead of –10.

Precision: You have trained to aim for your prey's weak points. The first time you hit your hunted prey in a round, you also deal 1d8 additional precision damage. (Precision damage increases the damage you already deal, using the same type, but is ineffective against creatures that lack vital organs or weak points.) At 11th level, the extra damage increases to 2d8 precision damage, and at 19th level, the extra damage increases to 3d8 precision damage.

Outwit: You are talented at outwitting and evading your prey. You gain a +2 circumstance bonus to Deception checks, Intimidation checks, Stealth checks, and any checks to Recall Knowledge about the prey, and a +1 circumstance bonus to AC against your prey's attacks.

RANGER FEATS

At 1st level and every even-numbered level, you gain a ranger class feat. Ranger feats are listed beginning on page 170.

SKILL FEATS   2ND

At 2nd level and every 2 levels thereafter, you gain a skill feat. Skill feats appear in Chapter 5 and have the skill trait. You must be trained or better in the corresponding skill to select a skill feat.

GENERAL FEATS   3RD

At 3rd level and every 4 levels thereafter, you gain a general feat. General feats are listed in Chapter 5.

IRON WILL   3RD

Your training has hardened your resolve. Your proficiency rank for Will saves increases to expert.

SKILL INCREASES   3RD

At 3rd level and every 2 levels thereafter, you gain a

skill increase. You can use this increase to either become trained in one skill, or become an expert in one skill in which you're already trained.

At 7th level, you can use skill increases to become a master in a skill in which you're already an expert, and at 15th level, you can use them to become legendary in a skill in which you're already a master.

ABILITY BOOSTS   5TH

At 5th level and every 5 levels thereafter, you boost four different ability scores. You can use these ability boosts to increase your ability scores above 18. Boosting an ability score increases it by 1 if it's already 18 or above, or by 2 if it starts out below 18.

ANCESTRY FEATS   5TH

In addition to the ancestry feat you started with, you gain an ancestry feat at 5th level and every 4 levels thereafter. The list of ancestry feats available to you can be found in your ancestry's entry in Chapter 2.

TRACKLESS STEP   5TH

When you move through natural terrains, you are difficult to track. You always gain the benefits of the Cover Tracks action in such terrains, without moving at half your Speed.

WEAPON EXPERTISE   5TH

You've dedicated yourself to learning the intricacies of your weapons. Your proficiency ranks for simple and martial weapons increases to expert. You gain access to the critical specialization effects of all simple and martial weapons when attacking your hunted prey.

EVASION   7TH

You've learned to move quickly to avoid explosions, dragons' breath, and worse. Your proficiency rank for Reflex saves increases to master. When you roll a success on a Reflex save, you get a critical success instead.

VIGILANT SENSES   7TH

Through your adventuring, you've developed keen awareness and attention to detail. Your proficiency rank for Perception increases to master.

WEAPON SPECIALIZATION   7TH

You've learned how to inflict greater injuries with the weapons you know best. You deal 2 additional damage with weapons and unarmed attacks in which you are an expert. This damage increases to 3 if you're a master, and to 4 if you're legendary.

NATURE'S EDGE   9TH

You always find the weak points in your foes' defenses when they're on unfavorable terrain. Enemies are flat-footed to you if they're in natural difficult terrain, on natural uneven ground, or in difficult terrain resulting from a snare.

KEY TERMS

You'll see these key terms in many ranger class features.

Flourish: Actions with this trait are special techniques that require too much exertion for you to perform frequently. You can use only 1 action with the flourish trait per turn.

Open: These maneuvers work only as the first salvo in the attacks you make on your turn. You can use an action with the open trait only if you haven't used an action with the attack or open trait yet this turn.

Press: Actions with this trait allow you to follow up earlier attacks. An action with the press trait can be used only if you are currently affected by a multiple attack penalty.

Some actions with the press trait also grant an effect on a failure. The effects that are added on a failure don't apply on a critical failure. If your press action succeeds, you can choose to apply the failure effect instead. (For example, you may wish to do this when an attack deals no damage due to resistance.) Because a press action requires a multiple attack penalty, you can't use one when it's not your turn, even if you use the Ready activity.

RANGER EXPERTISE   9TH

You've practiced your techniques to make them harder to resist. Your proficiency rank for your ranger class DC increases to expert.

JUGGERNAUT   11TH

Your body is accustomed to physical hardship and resistant to ailments. Your proficiency rank for Fortitude saves increases to master. When you roll a success on a Fortitude save, you get a critical success instead.

MEDIUM ARMOR EXPERTISE   11TH

You've learned to defend yourself better against attacks. Your proficiency ranks for light armor, medium armor, and unarmored defense increase to expert.

WILD STRIDE   11TH

You move quickly through obstacles, whether they're tumbled stone, tangled undergrowth, or sucking mud. You can ignore the effects of non-magical difficult terrain. As normal for ignoring difficult terrain, this also lets you treat the hindrances of greater difficult terrain as those of difficult terrain.

WEAPON MASTERY   13TH

You fully understand the intricacies of your weapons. Your proficiency ranks for simple and martial weapons increase to master.

GREATER WEAPON SPECIALIZATION   15TH

Your damage from weapon specialization increases to 4 with weapons and unarmed attacks in which you're an expert, 6 if you're a master, and 8 if you're legendary.

RANGER FEATS

If you need to look up a ranger feat by name instead of by level, use this table.

IMPROVED EVASION   15TH

Your ability to elude danger is matchless. Your proficiency rank for Reflex saves increases to legendary. When you roll a critical failure on a Reflex save, you get a failure instead. When you fail a Reflex save against a damaging effect, you take half damage.

INCREDIBLE SENSES   15TH

You notice things almost impossible for an ordinary person to detect. Your proficiency rank for Perception increases to legendary.

MASTERFUL HUNTER   17TH

You have honed your abilities as a hunter to incredible levels. Your proficiency rank for your ranger class DC increases to master. When using a ranged weapon that you have master proficiency in, you can ignore the penalty if attacking your hunted prey within the weapon's second and third range increments.

If you have master proficiency in Perception, you gain a +4 circumstance bonus to Perception checks when you Seek your prey, and if you have master proficiency in Survival, you gain a +4 circumstance bonus to Survival checks when you Track your prey.

You also gain an additional benefit depending on your hunter's edge.

Flurry: You can blend your weapon mastery with skillful targeting to make a series of precise attacks. If you have master proficiency with your weapon, your multiple attack penalty for attacks against your hunted prey is –2 (–1 with an agile weapon) on your second attack of the turn, and –4 (–2 with an agile weapon) on your third and subsequent attacks of the turn.

Precision: Your weapon mastery allows you to hit your prey's vital areas multiple times. The second time in a round you hit your hunted prey, you also deal 1d8 precision damage. At 19th level, your second hit in a round against your hunted prey deals 2d8 precision damage, and your third hit in a round against your hunted prey deals 1d8 precision damage.

Outwit: Your mastery of skills allows you to overwhelm your prey. If you have master proficiency in Deception, Intimidation, Stealth, or the skill you use to Recall Knowledge about your prey, increase the circumstance bonus against the prey with that skill from +2 to +4. If you have master proficiency with your armor, increase the circumstance bonus to AC against the prey from +1 to +2.

SECOND SKIN   19TH

Your armor has become akin to a second skin for you. Your proficiency ranks for light armor, medium armor, and unarmored defense increase to master. When wearing light or medium armor, you can rest normally, rather than receiving poor rest that leaves you fatigued.

SWIFT PREY   19TH

You size up your prey with only a glance. You can use Hunt Prey as a free action if it's your first action of your turn.

RANGER FEATS

At every level that you gain a ranger feat, you can select one of the following. You must satisfy any prerequisites before taking the feat.

1ST LEVEL

ANIMAL COMPANION   FEAT 1

RANGER

You gain the service of a young animal companion that travels with you and obeys simple commands as best as it can. See Animal Companions on page 214. When you Hunt Prey, your animal companion gains the action's benefits and your hunter's edge benefit if you have one.

CROSSBOW ACE   FEAT 1

RANGER

You have a deep understanding of the crossbow. When you're wielding a crossbow and use Hunt Prey or use Interact to reload your crossbow, you gain a +2 circumstance bonus to the damage roll on your next Strike with that crossbow. If the crossbow is a simple crossbow, also increase the damage die size for that attack by one step (page 279). You must make the attack before the end of your next turn or these benefits are lost.

HUNTED SHOT   FEAT 1

FLOURISH **RANGER**

Frequency once per round
Requirement You are wielding a ranged weapon with reload 0.
You take two quick shots against the one you hunt. Make two Strikes against your prey with the required weapon. If both hit the same creature, combine their damage for the purpose of resistances and weaknesses. Apply your multiple attack penalty to each Strike normally.

MONSTER HUNTER   FEAT 1

RANGER

You swiftly assess your prey and apply what you know. As part of the action used to Hunt your Prey, you can attempt a check to Recall Knowledge about your prey. When you critically succeed at identifying your hunted prey with Recall Knowledge, you note a weakness in the creature's defenses. You and allies you tell gain a +1 circumstance bonus to your next attack roll against that prey. You can give bonuses from Monster Hunter only once per day against a particular creature.

TWIN TAKEDOWN   FEAT 1

FLOURISH **RANGER**

Frequency once per round
Requirement You are wielding two melee weapons, each in a different hand.
You swiftly attack your hunted prey with both weapons. Make two Strikes against your hunted prey, one with each of the required weapons. If both hit the same hunted prey, combine their damage for the purpose of its resistances and weaknesses. Apply your multiple attack penalty to each Strike normally.

2ND LEVEL

FAVORED TERRAIN   FEAT 2

RANGER

You have studied a specific terrain to overcome its challenges. Choose aquatic, arctic, desert, forest, mountain, plains, sky, swamp, or underground as your favored terrain. When in that terrain, you can ignore the effects of non-magical difficult terrain.

If you have the wild stride class feature, you gain a second benefit while in your favored terrain, depending on your choice.

- **Aquatic** You gain a swim Speed equal to your Speed. If you already had a swim Speed, you gain a +10-foot status bonus to your swim Speed.
- **Arctic** You need to eat and drink only one-tenth as much as usual, you aren't affected by severe or extreme cold, and you can walk across ice and snow at full Speed without needing to Balance.
- **Desert** You need to eat and drink only one-tenth as much as usual, you aren't affected by severe or extreme heat, and you can walk along sand at full Speed without needing to Balance.
- **Forest, Mountain, or Underground** You gain a climb Speed equal to your Speed. If you already had a climb Speed, you gain a +10-foot status bonus to your climb Speed.
- **Plains** You gain a +10-foot status bonus to your land Speed.
- **Sky** You gain a +10-foot status bonus to your fly Speed, if you have one.

INTRODUCTION

ANCESTRIES & BACKGROUNDS

CLASSES

SKILLS

FEATS

EQUIPMENT

SPELLS

THE AGE OF LOST OMENS

PLAYING THE GAME

GAME MASTERING

CRAFTING & TREASURE

APPENDIX

171

Swamp You can move across bogs at full Speed, even if they are deep enough to be greater difficult terrain or to normally require you to Swim.

HUNTER'S AIM ❖❖   FEAT 2

CONCENTRATE   RANGER

When you focus on aiming, your attack becomes particularly accurate. Make a ranged weapon Strike against your hunted prey. On this Strike, you gain a +2 circumstance bonus to the attack roll and ignore your prey's concealed condition.

MONSTER WARDEN   FEAT 2

RANGER

Prerequisites Monster Hunter

You understand how to defend yourself and others against your prey. When you grant bonuses from Monster Hunter, you and your allies also each gain a +1 circumstance bonus to your next saving throw against that particular creature and to your AC against that creature's next attack against you.

QUICK DRAW ❖   FEAT 2

RANGER

You draw your weapon and attack with the same motion. You Interact to draw a weapon, then Strike with that weapon.

WILD EMPATHY   FEAT 2

RANGER

You have a connection to the creatures of the natural world that allows you to communicate with them on a rudimentary level. You can use Diplomacy to Make an Impression on animals and to make very simple Requests of them. In most cases, wild animals will give you time to make your case.

4TH LEVEL

COMPANION'S CRY   FEAT 4

RANGER

Prerequisites an animal companion

You can urge your companion to do its utmost. You can spend 2 actions to Command an Animal instead of 1 when commanding your animal companion. If you do, your animal companion uses an additional action.

DISRUPT PREY ❖   FEAT 4

RANGER

Trigger Your hunted prey is within your reach, and it uses a manipulate action, uses a move action, or leaves a square during a move action it's using.

Make a melee Strike against your prey. If the attack is a critical hit, you disrupt the triggering action.

FAR SHOT   FEAT 4

RANGER

Your experience in the field has taught you how to focus your aim at a distance, increasing your accuracy. Double your weapons' range increments.

FAVORED ENEMY   FEAT 4

RANGER

You have studied a specific type of wild creature and can hunt it more easily. When you gain this feat, choose animals, beasts, dragons, or both fungi and plants as your favored enemy. When you roll initiative and can see an enemy that belongs to the chosen category, you can Hunt Prey as a free action, designating that enemy.

You can use this free action even if you haven't identified the creature yet with Recall Knowledge. The benefit doesn't apply against favored enemies disguised as other creatures, and the GM determines whether it applies against a creature disguised as a favored enemy.

RUNNING RELOAD ❖   FEAT 4

RANGER

You can reload your weapon on the move. You Stride, Step, or Sneak, then Interact to reload.

SCOUT'S WARNING ❖   FEAT 4

RANGER

Trigger You are about to roll a Perception or Survival check for initiative.

You visually or audibly warn your allies of danger, granting them each a +1 circumstance bonus to their initiative rolls. Depending on whether you use gestures or call out, this action gains either the visual or the auditory trait, respectively.

SNARE SPECIALIST   FEAT 4

RANGER

Prerequisites expert in Crafting, Snare Crafting

You specialize in creating quick traps to obstruct your enemies on the battlefield. If your proficiency rank in Crafting is expert, you gain the formulas for three common or uncommon snares (page 589). If your rank is master, you gain 6. If your rank is legendary, you gain 9.

Each day during your daily preparations, you can prepare four snares from your formula book for quick deployment; if they normally take 1 minute to Craft, you can Craft them with 3 Interact actions. The number of snares increases to six if you have master proficiency in Crafting and eight if you have legendary proficiency in Crafting. Snares prepared in this way don't cost you any resources to Craft.

TWIN PARRY ❖   FEAT 4

RANGER

Requirements You are wielding two melee weapons, one in each hand.

You can use two weapons to deflect attacks. You gain a +1 circumstance bonus to AC until the start of your next turn, or a +2 circumstance bonus if either weapon has the parry trait. You lose this circumstance bonus if you no longer meet this feat's requirement.

CLASSES

3

INTRODUCTION

ANCESTRIES &
BACKGROUNDS

CLASSES

SKILLS

FEATS

EQUIPMENT

SPELLS

THE AGE OF
LOST OMENS

PLAYING THE
GAME

GAME
MASTERING

CRAFTING
& TREASURE

APPENDIX

6TH LEVEL

MATURE ANIMAL COMPANION   FEAT 6

RANGER

Prerequisites Animal Companion

Your animal companion grows up, becoming a mature animal companion and gaining additional capabilities (page 214).

If you have the Hunt Prey action, your animal companion assaults the prey even without your orders. During an encounter, even if you don't use the Command an Animal action, your animal companion can still use 1 action that round on your turn to Stride toward or Strike your prey.

QUICK SNARES   FEAT 6

RANGER

Prerequisites expert in Crafting, Snare Specialist

You can rig a snare in only moments. You can Craft snares that normally take 1 minute to Craft with 3 Interact actions, even if you haven't prepared them.

SKIRMISH STRIKE ❖   FEAT 6

FLOURISH   **RANGER**

Your feet and weapon move in tandem. Either Step and then Strike, or Strike and then Step.

SNAP SHOT   FEAT 6

RANGER

You've learned to react with ranged weapons when a creature is in close quarters. You can use a reaction that normally allows you to make a melee weapon Strike to instead make a ranged weapon Strike. You must be Striking an adjacent target. If necessary for the reaction's trigger, you treat your ranged weapon as if it had a reach of 5 feet. If the reaction has other requirements, such as wielding a specific kind of weapon, Snap Shot doesn't allow you to ignore them; it allows you only to replace a melee weapon Strike with a ranged weapon Strike.

SWIFT TRACKER   FEAT 6

RANGER

Prerequisites expert in Survival, Experienced Tracker

Your keen eyes catch signs of passage even when you're moving. You can move at your full Speed while you Track. If you have master proficiency in Survival, you don't need to attempt a new Survival check every hour while Tracking. If you have legendary proficiency in Survival, you can use another exploration activity while Tracking.

If you roll Survival for initiative while tracking your hunted prey, when you start your first turn of the encounter, you can Stride toward your hunted prey as a free action.

8TH LEVEL

BLIND-FIGHT   FEAT 8

RANGER

Prerequisites master in Perception

Your battle instincts make you more aware of concealed and invisible opponents. You don't need to succeed at a flat check to target concealed creatures. You're not flat-footed to creatures that are hidden from you (unless you're flat-footed to them for reasons other than the hidden condition), and you need only a successful DC 5 flat check to target a hidden creature.

While you're adjacent to an undetected creature of your level or lower, it is instead only hidden from you.

DEADLY AIM ◆ FEAT 8

`OPEN` `RANGER`

Prerequisites weapon specialization

You aim for your prey's weak spots, making your shot more challenging but dealing more damage if you hit. Make a ranged Strike against your hunted prey at a –2 penalty. You gain a +4 circumstance bonus to damage on that Strike. This bonus increases to +6 at 11th level and +8 at 15th level.

HAZARD FINDER FEAT 8

`RANGER`

You have an intuitive ability to sense hazards. You gain a +1 circumstance bonus to Perception checks to find traps and hazards, to AC against their attacks, and to saves against their effects. You can find hazards that would normally require you to Search even if you aren't Searching.

POWERFUL SNARES FEAT 8

`RANGER`

Prerequisites master in Crafting, Snare Specialist

Your snares are particularly difficult for enemies to avoid. When you set a snare, the saving throw DC for that snare is equal to its normal DC or your class DC, whichever is higher.

TERRAIN MASTER FEAT 8

`RANGER`

Prerequisites wild stride, master in Survival, Favored Terrain

You adapt to your surroundings in any natural terrain. You can spend 1 hour practicing in your current terrain in order to make it your favored terrain, replacing your current favored terrain temporarily. If you spend a full day out of the new favored terrain, your favored terrain reverts back to your original choice when you took the Favored Terrain feat.

WARDEN'S BOON ◆ FEAT 8

`RANGER`

By pointing out vulnerabilities, you grant the benefits listed in Hunt Prey and your hunter's edge benefit to an ally until the end of their next turn. Depending on whether you call out or use gestures, this action gains either the auditory or visual trait.

10TH LEVEL

CAMOUFLAGE FEAT 10

`RANGER`

Prerequisites master in Stealth

You alter your appearance to blend in to the wilderness. In natural terrain, you can Sneak even if you're observed.

ANIMAL RANGER

Sharing a powerful bond, you and your beloved animal explore the wilds and fight in tandem.

ABILITY SCORES

Prioritize Dexterity, followed by Constitution and Wisdom. Take Strength if you want to deal more damage.

SKILLS

Acrobatics, Athletics, Medicine, Nature, Stealth, Survival

HUNTER'S EDGE

Outwit

STARTING FEAT

Animal Companion

HIGHER-LEVEL FEATS

Companion's Cry (4th), Mature Animal Companion (6th), Incredible Companion (10th), Side by Side (12th), Specialized Companion (16th), Masterful Companion (18th)

INCREDIBLE COMPANION — FEAT 10

RANGER

Prerequisites Mature Animal Companion

Your animal companion continues to grow and develop. It becomes a nimble or savage animal companion (your choice), gaining additional capabilities determined by the type of companion (page 214).

MASTER MONSTER HUNTER — FEAT 10

RANGER

Prerequisites master in Nature, Monster Hunter

You have a nearly encyclopedic knowledge of all creatures of the world. You can use Nature to Recall Knowledge to identify any creature. In addition, you gain the benefits of Monster Hunter (and Monster Warden, if you have it) on a success as well as a critical success.

PENETRATING SHOT ◆◆ — FEAT 10

OPEN RANGER

Requirements You are wielding a ranged weapon.

You shoot clear through an intervening creature to hit your prey. Choose a target that is giving lesser cover to your hunted prey. Make a single ranged Strike with the required weapon against the chosen target and your hunted prey. This attack ignores any lesser cover the chosen target provides your hunted prey. Roll damage only once, and apply it to each creature you hit. A Penetrating Shot counts as two attacks for your multiple attack penalty.

TWIN RIPOSTE ↻ — FEAT 10

RANGER

Trigger A creature within your reach critically fails a Strike against you.

Requirements You are benefiting from Twin Parry

A clever parry with one weapon leaves your opponent open to an attack with the other weapon. Make a melee Strike or use a Disarm action against the triggering opponent.

WARDEN'S STEP — FEAT 10

RANGER

Prerequisites master in Stealth

You can guide your allies to move quietly through the wilderness. When you Sneak during exploration in natural terrain, you can designate any number of your allies to gain the benefits as if they were using that activity during that exploration. This requires no action on their part.

12TH LEVEL

DISTRACTING SHOT — FEAT 12

RANGER

The sheer power of your attacks, or the overwhelming number of them, leaves an enemy flustered. If you critically hit your hunted prey with a ranged weapon, or hit it at least twice on the same turn with a ranged weapon, it's flat-footed until the start of your next turn.

DOUBLE PREY — FEAT 12

RANGER

You can focus on two foes at once, hunting both of them down. When you use the Hunt Prey action, you can pick two creatures as your prey.

LIGHTNING SNARES — FEAT 12

RANGER

Prerequisites master in Crafting, Snare Specialist

You can rig a trap with incredible speed. When you create a snare that normally takes 1 minute to Craft, you can Craft it using a single Interact action instead.

SECOND STING ◆ — FEAT 12

PRESS RANGER

Requirements You are wielding two melee weapons, each in a different hand.

You read your prey's movements and transform them into openings, so failures with one weapon set up glancing blows with the other. Make a melee Strike with one of the required weapons against your hunted prey. The Strike gains the following failure effect.

Failure You deal the damage the other required weapon would have dealt on a hit, excluding all damage dice. (This removes dice from weapon runes, spells, and special abilities, not just weapon damage dice.)

SIDE BY SIDE — FEAT 12

RANGER

Prerequisites an animal companion

You and your animal companion fight in tandem, distracting your foes and keeping them off balance. Whenever you and your animal companion are adjacent to the same foe, you are both flanking that foe with each other, regardless of your actual positions.

14TH LEVEL

SENSE THE UNSEEN ↻ — FEAT 14

RANGER

Trigger You fail a check to Seek.

When you look for foes, you can catch even the slightest cues, such as their minute movements or the shifting of air currents on your skin. Even though you failed at the triggering check, you automatically sense any undetected creatures in the area where you're Seeking, making them merely hidden to you.

SHARED PREY — FEAT 14

RANGER

Prerequisites Double Prey, Warden's Boon

Hunting as a duo, you and your ally both single out your prey. When you use Hunt Prey and select only one prey, you can grant your Hunt Prey benefits and hunter's edge to an ally in addition to gaining them yourself. The ally retains these benefits until you use Hunt Prey again.

SAMPLE RANGER

ARCHER

You keep your distance from your prey, shooting arrows with incredible precision to hinder or kill those you hunt.

ABILITY SCORES

Prioritize Dexterity, then Wisdom. Choose Strength if you want to use a composite bow or thrown weapon, or Intelligence to be more skilled.

SKILLS

Acrobatics, Athletics, Nature, Stealth, Survival, Thievery

HUNTER'S EDGE

Flurry

STARTING FEAT

Hunted Shot

HIGHER-LEVEL FEATS

Quick Draw (2nd), Far Shot (4th), Skirmish Strike (6th), Deadly Aim (8th), Penetrating Shot (10th), Distracting Shot (12th), Impossible Volley (18th)

STEALTHY COMPANION   FEAT 14

RANGER

Prerequisites Camouflage

You've trained your animal companion to blend in to its surroundings. Your animal companion gains the benefit of the Camouflage feat. If your companion is a specialized ambusher, its proficiency rank for Stealth increases to master (or legendary if it was already master).

TARGETING SHOT ❖   FEAT 14

CONCENTRATE   PRESS   RANGER

Prerequisites Hunter's Aim

You carefully track your prey's position and defenses, allowing you to follow up around obstacles that block your shot. Make a ranged weapon Strike against your hunted prey. You ignore the target's concealed condition and all cover.

WARDEN'S GUIDANCE   FEAT 14

RANGER

You can convey your prey's location to your allies, no matter how well hidden it is. As long as your hunted prey is observed by you, all your allies who roll failures and critical failures when Seeking it get a success instead. Your allies need to be able to see or hear you to gain this benefit. You have to be able to call out or use gestures for your allies to get this benefit.

16TH LEVEL

GREATER DISTRACTING SHOT   FEAT 16

RANGER

Prerequisites Distracting Shot

Even a single missile can throw off your enemy's balance, and more powerful attacks leave it flustered for longer. If you hit your hunted prey with a ranged weapon, it's flat-footed until the start of your next turn. If you critically hit your prey or hit it twice on the same turn with a ranged weapon, it's flat-footed until the end of your next turn instead.

IMPROVED TWIN RIPOSTE   FEAT 16

RANGER

At the start of each of your turns, you gain an additional reaction that you can use only to perform a Twin Riposte against your hunted prey. You can use this extra reaction even if you are not benefiting from Twin Parry.

LEGENDARY MONSTER HUNTER   FEAT 16

RANGER

Prerequisites legendary in Nature, Master Monster Hunter

Your knowledge of monsters is so incredible that it reveals glaring flaws in your prey. Your bonus from Monster Hunter (and the bonus from Monster Warden if you have it) increases from +1 to +2 for you and any allies who benefit.

SPECIALIZED COMPANION   FEAT 16

RANGER

Prerequisites Incredible Companion

Your animal companion has become cunning enough to become specialized. Your animal companion gains one specialization of your choice. (See the Animal Companion section on page 214.)

UBIQUITOUS SNARES   FEAT 16

RANGER

Prerequisites Snare Specialist

You can prepare a seemingly impossible number of snares in advance, and you're ready to spring them on unsuspecting foes. Double the number of prepared snares from Snare Specialist.

18TH LEVEL

IMPOSSIBLE FLURRY ◆◆◆   FEAT 18

FLOURISH **OPEN** **RANGER**

Requirements You are wielding two melee weapons, each in a different hand.

You forgo precision to attack at an impossible speed. Make three melee Strikes with each of the required weapons. All of these Strikes take the maximum multiple attack penalty, as if you had already made two or more attacks this turn.

IMPOSSIBLE VOLLEY ◆◆◆   FEAT 18

RANGER

Requirements You are wielding a ranged weapon with the volley trait and reload 0.

You fire a volley at all foes in an area. Make one Strike with a –2 penalty against each enemy within a 10-foot-radius burst centered at or beyond your weapon's volley range. Roll the damage only once for all targets.

Each attack counts toward your multiple attack penalty, but do not increase your penalty until you have made all your attacks.

MANIFOLD EDGE   FEAT 18

RANGER

Prerequisites hunter's edge, masterful hunter

You've learned every possible edge to use against your foes. When you use Hunt Prey, you can gain a hunter's edge benefit other than the one you selected at 1st level. If you do, you don't gain the additional benefit from masterful hunter.

MASTERFUL COMPANION   FEAT 18

RANGER

Prerequisites masterful hunter, Animal Companion

Your animal companion shares your incredible hunting skills, allowing it to take down your shared prey with ease. When you Hunt Prey, your animal companion gains the masterful hunter benefit associated with your hunter's edge, rather than just your original hunter's edge benefit.

PERFECT SHOT ◆◆◆   FEAT 18

FLOURISH **RANGER**

Requirements You are wielding a loaded ranged weapon with reload 1 or more, and you have not reloaded your weapon since your last turn.

After watching the motions of combat with incredible intensity and precision, you fire at your prey at the perfect moment to deliver maximum pain. Make a ranged Strike with the required weapon against your hunted prey. If you hit, the Strike deals maximum damage. After the Strike, your turn ends.

SHADOW HUNTER   FEAT 18

RANGER

Prerequisites Camouflage

You blend in to your surroundings so well that others have trouble telling you apart from the terrain. While in natural terrain, you're always concealed from all foes if you choose to be, except for your hunted prey.

20TH LEVEL

LEGENDARY SHOT   FEAT 20

RANGER

Prerequisites masterful hunter, legendary in Perception, Far Shot

You focus on your hunted prey, perceiving angles, air resistance, and every variable that would affect your ranged attack. If you have master proficiency with your ranged weapon, you can ignore the penalty for attacking up to five range increments away when attacking your hunted prey.

TO THE ENDS OF THE EARTH   FEAT 20

RANGER

Prerequisites legendary in Survival

Your ability to track your prey has surpassed explanation, allowing you to trace your prey's movements and predict its location with ease. When you use Hunt Prey on a creature within 100 feet, you can follow that creature's movements, allowing you to know the creature's exact location no matter how far away it becomes, as long as it remains your prey. You must be legendary in Nature to track your prey's location across teleportation or planar travel. This feat gains the detection, divination, and primal traits if you're legendary in Nature.

TRIPLE THREAT   FEAT 20

RANGER

Prerequisites Shared Prey

You can divide your attention three ways when hunting. When you use Hunt Prey, you can designate three creatures as prey, designate two creatures as prey and share the effect with one ally (as Shared Prey), or designate one creature as prey and share the effect with two allies.

ULTIMATE SKIRMISHER   FEAT 20

RANGER

Prerequisites wild stride

You are so skilled at navigating the wild, your movement is completely unaffected by terrain. You ignore the effects of all difficult terrain, greater difficult terrain, and hazardous terrain, and you don't trigger traps and hazards that are triggered by moving into an area (such as trip wires and pressure plates), unless you want to.

INTRODUCTION

ANCESTRIES & BACKGROUNDS

CLASSES

SKILLS

FEATS

EQUIPMENT

SPELLS

THE AGE OF LOST OMENS

PLAYING THE GAME

GAME MASTERING

CRAFTING & TREASURE

APPENDIX

ROGUE

You are skilled and opportunistic. Using your sharp wits and quick reactions, you take advantage of your opponents' missteps and strike where it hurts most. You play a dangerous game, seeking thrills and testing your skills, and likely don't care much for any laws that happen to get in your way. While the path of every rogue is unique and riddled with danger, the one thing you all share in common is the breadth and depth of your skills.

KEY ABILITY

DEXTERITY OR OTHER
At 1st level, your class gives you an ability boost to Dexterity or an option from rogue's racket.

HIT POINTS

8 plus your Constitution modifier
You increase your maximum number of HP by this number at 1st level and every level thereafter.

DURING COMBAT ENCOUNTERS...
You move about stealthily so you can catch foes unawares. You're a precision instrument, more useful against a tough boss or distant spellcaster than against rank-and-file soldiers.

DURING SOCIAL ENCOUNTERS...
Your skills give you multiple tools to influence your opposition. Pulling cons and ferreting out information are second nature to you.

WHILE EXPLORING...
You sneak to get the drop on foes and scout for danger or traps. You're a great asset, since you can disable traps, solve puzzles, and anticipate dangers.

IN DOWNTIME...
You might pick pockets or trade in illegal goods. You can also become part of a thieves' guild, or even found one of your own.

YOU MIGHT...
• Hone your skills through intense practice, both on your own and out in the world.
• Know where to attain illicit goods.
• Skirt or break the law because you think it's meaningless or have your own code.

OTHERS PROBABLY...
• Find you charming or fascinating, even if they think they know better than to trust you.
• Come to you when they need someone who is willing to take risks or use questionable methods.
• Suspect you're motivated primarily by greed.

INITIAL PROFICIENCIES
At 1st level, you gain the listed proficiency ranks in the following statistics. You are untrained in anything not listed unless you gain a better proficiency rank in some other way.

PERCEPTION
Expert in Perception

SAVING THROWS
Trained in Fortitude
Expert in Reflex
Expert in Will

SKILLS
Trained in Stealth
Trained in one or more skills determined by your rogue's racket.
Trained in a number of additional skills equal to 7 plus your Intelligence modifier

ATTACKS
Trained in simple weapons
Trained in the rapier, sap, shortbow, and shortsword
Trained in unarmed attacks

DEFENSES
Trained in light armor
Trained in unarmored defense

CLASS DC
Trained in rogue class DC

TABLE 3-15: ROGUE ADVANCEMENT

Your Level	Class Features
1	Ancestry and background, initial proficiencies, rogue's racket, sneak attack 1d6, surprise attack, rogue feat, skill feat
2	Rogue feat, skill feat, skill increase
3	Deny advantage, general feat, skill feat, skill increase
4	Rogue feat, skill feat, skill increase
5	Ability boosts, ancestry feat, skill feat, skill increase, sneak attack 2d6, weapon tricks
6	Rogue feat, skill feat, skill increase
7	Evasion, general feat, skill feat, skill increase, vigilant senses, weapon specialization
8	Rogue feat, skill feat, skill increase
9	Ancestry feat, debilitating strike, great fortitude, skill feat, skill increase
10	Ability boosts, rogue feat, skill feat, skill increase
11	General feat, rogue expertise, skill feat, skill increase, sneak attack 3d6
12	Rogue feat, skill feat, skill increase
13	Ancestry feat, improved evasion, incredible senses, light armor expertise, master tricks, skill feat, skill increase
14	Rogue feat, skill feat, skill increase
15	Ability boosts, double debilitation, general feat, greater weapon specialization, skill feat, skill increase
16	Rogue feat, skill feat, skill increase
17	Ancestry feat, skill feat, skill increase, slippery mind, sneak attack 4d6
18	Rogue feat, skill feat, skill increase
19	General feat, light armor mastery, master strike, skill feat, skill increase
20	Ability boosts, rogue feat, skill feat, skill increase

CLASS FEATURES

You gain these abilities as a rogue. Abilities gained at higher levels list the level at which you gain them next to the features' names.

ANCESTRY AND BACKGROUND

In addition to what you get from your class at 1st level, you have the benefits of your selected ancestry and background, as described in Chapter 2.

INITIAL PROFICIENCIES

At 1st level, you gain a number of proficiencies that represent your basic training. These proficiencies are noted at the start of this class.

ROGUE'S RACKET

As you started on the path of the rogue, you began to develop your own style to pursue your illicit activities. Your racket shapes your rogue techniques and the way you approach a job, while building your reputation in the criminal underworld for a certain type of work. A client with deep pockets might even hire a team of rogues for a particular heist, each specializing in a different racket, in order to cover all the bases. Choose a rogue's racket. The rackets presented in this book are as follows.

RUFFIAN

You prefer to strong-arm or intimidate others rather than rely on finesse or fancy tricks. You might be an enforcer for organized crime, a highway bandit, or a noble who bullies others with threats of your family's power. Or, you might use your skills on the up and up, in a private security detail or as a guard in a city with the right temperament.

You use whatever tools you have at hand to get the job done. You can deal sneak attack damage with any simple weapon, in addition to the weapons listed in the sneak attack class feature. When you critically succeed at an attack roll using a simple weapon and the target has the flat-footed condition (unable to focus on defending itself), you also apply the critical specialization effect for the weapon you're wielding (page 283). You don't gain these benefits if the weapon has a damage die larger than d8 (after applying any abilities that alter its damage die size).

You're trained in Intimidation and medium armor. You can choose Strength as your key ability score. When you gain light armor expertise, you also gain expert proficiency in medium armor, and when you gain light armor mastery, you also gain master proficiency in medium armor.

SCOUNDREL

You use fast-talking, flattery, and a silver tongue to avoid danger and escape tricky situations. You might be a grifter or con artist, traveling from place to place with a new story or scheme. Your racket is also ideal for certain reputable professions, like barrister, diplomat, or politician.

When you successfully Feint (page 246), the target is flat-footed against melee attacks you attempt against it until the end of your next turn. On a critical success, the target is flat-footed against all melee attacks until the end of your next turn, not just yours.

You're trained in Deception and Diplomacy. You can choose Charisma as your key ability score.

THIEF

Nothing beats the thrill of taking something that belongs to someone else, especially if you can do so completely unnoticed. You might be a pickpocket working the streets, a cat burglar sneaking through windows and escaping via rooftops, or a safecracker breaking into carefully guarded vaults. You might even work as a consultant, testing clients' defenses by trying to steal something precious.

When a fight breaks out, you prefer swift, lightweight weapons, and you strike where it hurts. When you attack with a finesse melee weapon, you can add your Dexterity modifier to damage rolls instead of your Strength modifier.

You are trained in Thievery.

SNEAK ATTACK

When your enemy can't properly defend itself, you take advantage to deal extra damage. If you Strike a creature that has the flat-footed condition (page 620) with an agile or finesse melee weapon, an agile or finesse unarmed attack, or a ranged weapon attack, you deal an extra 1d6 precision damage. For a ranged attack with a thrown melee weapon, that weapon must also be agile or finesse.

As your rogue level increases, so does the number of damage dice for your sneak attack. Increase the number of dice by one at 5th, 11th, and 17th levels.

SURPRISE ATTACK

You spring into combat faster than foes can react. On the first round of combat, if you roll Deception or Stealth for initiative, creatures that haven't acted are flat-footed to you.

ROGUE FEATS

At 1st level and every even-numbered level, you gain a rogue class feat.

SKILL FEATS

You gain skill feats more often than others. At 1st level and every level thereafter, you gain a skill feat. Skill feats can be found in Chapter 5 and have the skill trait.

SKILL INCREASES   2ND

You gain more skill increases than members of other classes. At 2nd level and every level thereafter, you gain a skill increase. You can use this increase to either become trained in one skill you're untrained in, or to become an expert in one skill in which you're already trained.

At 7th level, you can use skill increases to become a master in a skill in which you're already an expert, and at 15th level, you can use them to become legendary in a skill in which you're already a master.

DENY ADVANTAGE   3RD

As someone who takes advantage of others' defenses, you are careful not to leave such openings yourself. You aren't flat-footed to hidden, undetected, or flanking creatures of your level or lower, or creatures of your level or lower using surprise attack. However, they can still help their allies flank.

GENERAL FEATS   3RD

At 3rd level and every 4 levels thereafter, you gain a general feat. General feats are listed in Chapter 5.

ABILITY BOOSTS   5TH

At 5th level and every 5 levels thereafter, you boost four different ability scores. You can use these ability boosts to increase your ability scores above 18. Boosting an ability score increases it by 1 if it's already 18 or above, or by 2 if it starts out below 18.

KEY TERMS

You'll see the following key terms in many rogue class features.

Debilitation: Debilitations apply conditions and other negative effects to a creature. When the creature is affected by a new debilitation, any previous one it was affected by ends.

Flourish: Actions with this trait are special techniques that require too much exertion for you to perform frequently. You can use only 1 action with the flourish trait per turn.

INTRODUCTION
ANCESTRIES & BACKGROUNDS
CLASSES
SKILLS
FEATS
EQUIPMENT
SPELLS
THE AGE OF LOST OMENS
PLAYING THE GAME
GAME MASTERING
CRAFTING & TREASURE
APPENDIX

ANCESTRY FEATS   5TH

In addition to the initial ancestry feat you started with, you gain an ancestry feat at 5th level and every 4 levels thereafter. The list of ancestry feats available to you can be found in your ancestry's entry in Chapter 2.

WEAPON TRICKS   5TH

You have become thoroughly familiar with the tools of your trade. You gain expert proficiency in simple weapons, as well as the rapier, sap, shortbow, and shortsword. When you critically succeed at an attack roll against a flat-footed creature while using an agile or finesse simple weapon or any of the listed weapons, you apply the critical specialization effect for the weapon you're wielding.

EVASION   7TH

You've learned to move quickly to avoid explosions, dragons' breath, and worse. Your proficiency rank for Reflex saves increases to master. When you roll a success on a Reflex save, you get a critical success instead.

VIGILANT SENSES   7TH

Through your adventures, you've developed keen awareness and attention to detail. Your proficiency rank for Perception increases to master.

WEAPON SPECIALIZATION   7TH

You've learned how to inflict greater injuries with the weapons you know best. You deal 2 additional damage with weapons and unarmed attacks in which you are an expert. This damage increases to 3 damage if you're a master, and 4 damage if you're legendary.

DEBILITATING STRIKE   9TH

When taking advantage of an opening, you both hinder and harm your foe. You gain the Debilitating Strike free action.

DEBILITATING STRIKE ◈

> ROGUE

Trigger Your Strike hits a flat-footed creature and deals damage.

You apply one of the following debilitations, which lasts until the end of your next turn.

Debilitation The target takes a –10-foot status penalty to its Speeds.

Debilitation The target becomes enfeebled 1.

GREAT FORTITUDE   9TH

Your physique is incredibly hardy. Your proficiency rank for Fortitude saves increases to expert.

ROGUE EXPERTISE   11TH

Your techniques are now harder to resist. Your proficiency rank for your rogue class DC increases to expert.

IMPROVED EVASION   13TH

You elude danger to a degree that few can match.

Your proficiency rank for Reflex saves increases to legendary. When you roll a critical failure on a Reflex save, you get a failure instead. When you fail a Reflex save against a damaging effect, you take half damage.

INCREDIBLE SENSES   13TH

You notice things almost impossible for an ordinary person to detect. Your proficiency rank for Perception increases to legendary.

LIGHT ARMOR EXPERTISE   13TH

You've learned how to dodge while wearing light or no armor. Your proficiency ranks for light armor and unarmored defense increase to expert.

MASTER TRICKS   13TH

You've mastered a rogue's fighting moves. Your proficiency ranks increase to master for all simple weapons plus the rapier, sap, shortbow, and shortsword.

DOUBLE DEBILITATION   15TH

Your opportunistic attacks are particularly detrimental. When you use Debilitating Strike, you can apply two debilitations simultaneously; removing one removes both.

GREATER WEAPON SPECIALIZATION   15TH

Your damage from weapon specialization increases to 4 with weapons and unarmed attacks in which you're an expert, 6 if you're a master, and 8 if you're legendary.

SLIPPERY MIND   17TH

You play mental games and employ cognitive tricks to throw off mind-altering effects. Your proficiency rank for Will saves increases to master. When you roll a success at a Will save, you get a critical success instead.

LIGHT ARMOR MASTERY   19TH

Your skill with light armor improves, increasing your ability to dodge blows. Your proficiency ranks for light armor and unarmored defense increase to master.

MASTER STRIKE   19TH

You can incapacitate an unwary foe with a single strike. Your proficiency rank for your rogue class DC increases to master. You gain the Master Strike free action.

MASTER STRIKE ◈

> INCAPACITATION   ROGUE

Trigger Your Strike hits a flat-footed creature and deals damage.

The target attempts a Fortitude save at your class DC. It then becomes temporarily immune to your Master Strike for 1 day.

Critical Success The target is unaffected.

Success The target is enfeebled 2 until the end of your next turn.

Failure The target is paralyzed for 4 rounds.

Critical Failure The target is paralyzed for 4 rounds, knocked unconscious for 2 hours, or killed (your choice).

ROGUE FEATS

At every level that you gain a rogue feat, you can select one of the following feats. You must satisfy any prerequisites before selecting the feat.

1ST LEVEL

NIMBLE DODGE ⤺   FEAT 1

> ROGUE

Trigger A creature targets you with an attack and you can see the attacker.
Requirements You are not encumbered.

You deftly dodge out of the way, gaining a +2 circumstance bonus to AC against the triggering attack.

TRAP FINDER   FEAT 1

> ROGUE

You have an intuitive sense that alerts you to the dangers and presence of traps. You gain a +1 circumstance bonus to Perception checks to find traps, to AC against attacks made by traps, and to saves against traps. Even if you aren't Searching, you get a check to find traps that normally require you to be Searching. You still need to meet any other requirements to find the trap.

You can disable traps that require a proficiency rank of master in Thievery. If you have master proficiency in Thievery, you can disable traps that require a proficiency rank of legendary instead, and your circumstance bonuses against traps increase to +2.

TWIN FEINT ◆◆   FEAT 1

> ROGUE

Requirements You are wielding two melee weapons, each in a different hand.

You make a dazzling series of attacks with both weapons, using the first attack to throw your foe off guard against a second attack at a different angle. Make one Strike with each of your two melee weapons, both against the same target. The target is automatically flat-footed against the second attack. Apply your multiple attack penalty to the Strikes normally.

YOU'RE NEXT ⤺   FEAT 1

> EMOTION   FEAR   MENTAL   ROGUE

Prerequisites trained in Intimidation
Trigger You reduce an enemy to 0 hit points.

After downing a foe, you menacingly remind another foe that you're coming after them next. Attempt an Intimidation check with a +2 circumstance bonus to Demoralize a single creature that you can see and that can see you. If you have legendary proficiency in Intimidation, you can use this as a free action with the same trigger.

2ND LEVEL

BRUTAL BEATING   FEAT 2

> ROGUE

Prerequisites ruffian racket

The brutality of your critical hits shakes your foes' confidence. Whenever your Strike is a critical hit and deals damage, the target is frightened 1.

DISTRACTING FEINT   FEAT 2

> ROGUE

Prerequisites scoundrel racket

Your Feints are far more distracting than normal, drawing your foes' attention and allowing you and your allies to take greater advantage. While a creature is flat-footed by your Feint, it also takes a –2 circumstance penalty to Perception checks and Reflex saves.

ROGUE FEATS

Use this table to look up rogue feats by name.

SAMPLE ROGUE

SCOUNDREL

Your attacks are made deadly through distraction.

ABILITY SCORES
Prioritize Dexterity, plus Charisma to improve your feints.

SKILLS
Acrobatics, Athletics, Crafting, Deception, Diplomacy, Intimidation, Occultism, Society, Stealth, Thievery

ROGUE'S RACKET
Scoundrel

STARTING FEAT
Trap Finder

HIGHER-LEVEL FEATS
Distracting Feint (2nd), Twist the Knife (6th), Tactical Debilitations (10th), Perfect Distraction (16th)

MINOR MAGIC   FEAT 2
ROGUE

You've dabbled in a variety of tricks, gaining minor magical abilities from a particular tradition. Choose arcane, divine, occult, or primal magic, and gain two cantrips from the common cantrips available to that tradition.

MOBILITY   FEAT 2
ROGUE

You move in a way that denies your enemies the opportunity to retaliate. When you take a Stride action to move half your Speed or less, that movement does not trigger reactions. You can use Mobility when Climbing, Flying, or Swimming instead of Striding if you have the corresponding movement type.

QUICK DRAW ❖   FEAT 2
ROGUE

You draw your weapon and attack with the same motion. You Interact to draw a weapon, then Strike with that weapon.

UNBALANCING BLOW   FEAT 2
ROGUE

Prerequisites thief racket

Interweaving your most powerful attacks in a graceful flow, you temporarily unbalance your foes. Whenever your Strike is a critical hit and deals damage, the target is flat-footed against your attacks until the end of your next turn.

4TH LEVEL

BATTLE ASSESSMENT ❖   FEAT 4
ROGUE | SECRET

With careful observation during battle, you identify an enemy's strengths and weaknesses. The GM rolls a secret Perception check for you against the Deception or Stealth DC (whichever is higher) of an enemy of your choice who is not concealed from you, hidden from you, or undetected by you, and who is engaged in combat. The GM might apply a penalty for the distance between you and the enemy. The enemy is then temporarily immune to your Battle Assessment for 1 day.

Critical Success The GM chooses two of the following pieces of information about the enemy to tell you: which of the enemy's weaknesses is highest, which of the enemy's saving throws has the lowest modifier, one immunity the enemy has, or which of the enemy's resistances is highest. If the event of a tie, the GM should pick one at random.

Success The GM chooses one piece of information from the above list to tell you about the enemy.

Critical Failure The GM gives you false information (the GM makes up the information).

DREAD STRIKER   FEAT 4
ROGUE

You capitalize on your enemies' fear to slip past their defenses. Any creature that has the frightened condition is also flat-footed against your attacks.

CLASSES

3

INTRODUCTION

ANCESTRIES &
BACKGROUNDS

CLASSES

SKILLS

FEATS

EQUIPMENT

SPELLS

THE AGE OF
LOST OMENS

PLAYING THE
GAME

GAME
MASTERING

CRAFTING
& TREASURE

APPENDIX

MAGICAL TRICKSTER — FEAT 4

`ROGUE`

Whether you're using magic items, wielding innate magic, or dabbling in spellcasting, you can sneak spells past your foes' defenses as easily as any blade. When you succeed at a spell attack roll against a flat-footed foe's AC and the spell deals damage, you can add your sneak attack damage to the damage roll. If your single spell leads to multiple separate damage rolls, apply your sneak attack damage only once per target.

POISON WEAPON ❖ — FEAT 4

`MANIPULATE` `ROGUE`

Requirements You are wielding a piercing or slashing weapon and have a free hand.

You apply a poison to the required weapon. If your next attack with that weapon before the end of your next turn hits and deals damage, it applies the effects of the poison, provided that poison can be delivered by contact or injury. If you critically fail the attack roll, the poison is wasted as normal.

Special During your daily preparations, you can prepare a number of simple injury poisons equal to your rogue level. These poisons deal 1d4 poison damage. Only you can apply these poisons properly, and they expire the next time you prepare.

REACTIVE PURSUIT ⟳ — FEAT 4

`ROGUE`

Trigger An adjacent foe moves away from you, and you can reach at least one space adjacent to the foe with a Stride action.

You keep pace with a retreating foe. You Stride, but you must end your movement adjacent to the triggering enemy. Your move does not trigger reactions from the triggering enemy. You can use Reactive Pursuit to Burrow, Climb, Fly, or Swim instead of Stride if you have the corresponding movement type.

SABOTAGE ❖ — FEAT 4

`INCAPACITATION` `ROGUE`

Requirements You have a free hand.

You subtly damage others' equipment. Choose one item that a creature within your reach wields or carries. The item must have moving parts that you could possibly sabotage (a shortbow could be sabotaged, but a longsword could not). Attempt a Thievery check against the Reflex DC of the creature. Damage dealt by Sabotage can't take the item below its Break Threshold.

Critical Success You deal damage equal to four times your Thievery proficiency bonus.

Success You deal damage equal to double your Thievery proficiency bonus.

Critical Failure Temporarily immune to your Sabotage for 1 day.

SAMPLE ROGUE

THIEF

Furtive and swift, you pick locks, find secret doors and traps, and collect all the best loot.

ABILITY SCORES
Prioritize Dexterity. Constitution improves your health and Wisdom helps you notice traps.

SKILLS
Acrobatics, Arcana, Athletics, Crafting, Deception, Diplomacy, Society, Stealth, Thievery

ROGUE'S RACKET
Thief

STARTING FEAT
Nimble Dodge

HIGHER-LEVEL FEATS
Quick Draw (2nd), Skirmish Strike (6th), Sneak Savant (10th), Spring from the Shadows (12th), Implausible Infiltration (18th)

SCOUT'S WARNING ◈   FEAT 4
ROGUE

Trigger You are about to roll a Perception or Survival check for initiative.

You visually or audibly warn your allies of danger, granting them each a +1 circumstance bonus to their initiative rolls. Depending on whether you use gestures or call out, this action gains either the visual or auditory trait, respectively.

6TH LEVEL

GANG UP   FEAT 6
ROGUE

You and your allies harry an opponent in concert. Any enemy is flat-footed against your melee attacks due to flanking as long as the enemy is within both your reach and your ally's. Your allies must still flank an enemy for it to be flat-footed to them.

LIGHT STEP   FEAT 6
ROGUE

You aren't bothered by tricky footing. When you Stride or Step, you can ignore difficult terrain.

SKIRMISH STRIKE ◆   FEAT 6
FLOURISH   **ROGUE**

Your feet and weapon move in tandem. Either Step and then Strike, or Strike and then Step.

TWIST THE KNIFE ◆   FEAT 6
ROGUE

Requirements Your last action was a melee Strike that dealt sneak attack damage to a flat-footed target.

After stabbing your opponent in a weak spot, you tear the wound open. You deal persistent bleed damage to the target equal to your number of sneak attack damage dice.

8TH LEVEL

BLIND-FIGHT   FEAT 8
ROGUE

Prerequisites master in Perception

Your battle instincts make you more aware of concealed and invisible opponents. You don't need to succeed at a flat check to target concealed creatures. You're not flat-footed to creatures that are hidden from you (unless you're flat-footed to them for reasons other than the hidden condition), and you need only a successful DC 5 flat check to target a hidden creature.

While you're adjacent to an undetected creature of your level or lower, it is instead only hidden from you.

DELAY TRAP ↻   FEAT 8
ROGUE

Trigger A trap within your reach is triggered.

You can jam the workings of a trap to delay its effects. Attempt a Thievery check to Disable a Device on the trap; the DC to do so is increased by 5, and the effects are as follows.

Critical Success You prevent the trap from being triggered, or you delay the activation until the start or end of your next turn (your choice).

Success You prevent the trap from being triggered, or you delay the activation until the end of your next turn (whichever is worse for you; GM's choice).

Failure No effect.

Critical Failure You're flat-footed until the start of your next turn.

IMPROVED POISON WEAPON   FEAT 8

ROGUE

Prerequisites Poison Weapon

You deliver poisons in ways that maximize their harmful effects. When you apply a simple poison with Poison Weapon, the poison deals 2d4 poison damage instead of 1d4 poison damage. You don't waste a poison you apply with Poison Weapon on a critically failed attack roll.

NIMBLE ROLL   FEAT 8

ROGUE

Prerequisites Nimble Dodge

You throw yourself into a roll to escape imminent danger. You can use Nimble Dodge before attempting a Reflex save in addition to its original trigger. If you do, the circumstance bonus applies to your Reflex save against the triggering effect.

When you use Nimble Dodge and the triggering attack fails or critically fails, or when you succeed or critically succeed at the saving throw, you can also Stride up to 10 feet as part of the reaction. If you do, the reaction gains the move trait. You can use Nimble Roll while Flying or Swimming instead of Striding if you have the corresponding movement type.

OPPORTUNE BACKSTAB ↻   FEAT 8

ROGUE

Trigger A creature within your melee reach is hit by a melee attack from one of your allies.

When your enemy is hit by your ally, you capitalize upon the distraction. Make a Strike against the triggering creature.

SIDESTEP ↻   FEAT 8

ROGUE

Trigger The attack roll for a Strike targeting you fails or critically fails.

You deftly step out of the way of an attack, letting the blow continue to the creature next to you. You redirect the attack to a creature of your choice that is adjacent to you and within the reach of the triggering attack. The attacker rerolls the Strike's attack roll against the new target.

SLY STRIKER   FEAT 8

ROGUE

Prerequisites sneak attack

Your attacks deal more damage, even against creatures that aren't flat-footed. When you succeed or critically succeed at a Strike against a creature that isn't flat-footed, you also deal 1d6 precision damage. This applies only if you're using a weapon or

unarmed attack you could deal sneak attack damage with. At 14th level, if you would normally deal 3d6 or more sneak attack damage to flat-footed creatures, you deal 2d6 precision damage to creatures that aren't flat-footed.

10TH LEVEL

PRECISE DEBILITATIONS   FEAT 10

ROGUE

Prerequisites thief racket, Debilitating Strike

You carefully aim and gracefully deliver your debilitations. Add the following debilitations to the list you can choose from when you use Debilitating Strike.

- **Debilitation** The target takes an additional 2d6 precision damage from your attacks.
- **Debilitation** The target becomes flat-footed.

SNEAK SAVANT   FEAT 10

ROGUE

Prerequisite master in Stealth

It is almost impossible to spot you without taking effort to look. When you roll a failure on a Sneak action, you get a success instead. You can still critically fail.

TACTICAL DEBILITATIONS   FEAT 10

ROGUE

Prerequisites scoundrel racket, Debilitating Strike

You learn new debilitations that grant you tactical advantages against your foes. Add the following debilitations to the list you can choose from when you use Debilitating Strike.

- **Debilitation** The target can't use reactions.
- **Debilitation** The target can't flank or contribute to allies' flanking.

VICIOUS DEBILITATIONS   FEAT 10

ROGUE

Prerequisites ruffian racket, Debilitating Strike

The debilitations you dish out seriously impair your foes. Add the following debilitations to the list you can choose from when you use Debilitating Strike.

- **Debilitation** The target gains weakness 5 to your choice of bludgeoning, piercing, or slashing damage.
- **Debilitation** The target becomes clumsy 1.

12TH LEVEL

CRITICAL DEBILITATION   FEAT 12

INCAPACITATION   ROGUE

Prerequisites Debilitating Strike

Your debilitations are especially effective on your most powerful attacks. Whenever you critically succeed at an attack roll against an enemy and use Debilitating Strike, add the following debilitation to the list you can choose from.

- **Debilitation** The target attempts a Fortitude save against your class DC with the following effects.

Critical Success The target is unaffected.

Success The target is slowed 1 until the end of your next turn.

Failure The target is slowed 2 until the end of your next turn.

Critical Failure The target is paralyzed until the end of your next turn.

FANTASTIC LEAP ✦✦ FEAT 12

ROGUE

You launch yourself through the air at a foe. Attempt a High Jump or Long Jump. If you attempt a High Jump, determine the distance you can travel using the scale of a Long Jump. At the end of your jump, you can make a melee Strike.

After your Strike, you fall to the ground if you're in the air. If the distance of your fall is no more than the height of your jump, you take no damage and land upright.

FELLING SHOT ✦✦ FEAT 12

ROGUE

Your ranged attacks can shoot an unprepared foe right out of the air. Make a Strike with a ranged weapon or a thrown weapon against a flat-footed creature. If the Strike is a success and deals damage, the target must attempt a Reflex save against your class DC with the following effects.

Success The target is unaffected.

Failure The target falls up to 120 feet. If it hits the ground, it takes no damage from the fall.

Critical Failure As failure, and the target can't fly, jump, levitate, or otherwise leave the ground until the end of your next turn.

REACTIVE INTERFERENCE ⟳ FEAT 12

ROGUE

Trigger An adjacent enemy begins to use a reaction.

Grabbing a sleeve, swiping with your weapon, or creating another obstruction, you reflexively foil an enemy's response. If the triggering creature's level is equal to or lower than yours, you disrupt the triggering reaction. If the triggering creature's level is higher than yours, you must make an attack roll against its AC. On a success, you disrupt the reaction.

SPRING FROM THE SHADOWS ✦ FEAT 12

FLOURISH ROGUE

Leaping out from hiding, you assail your target when they least expect it. You Stride up to your Speed, but you must end your movement next to an enemy you're hidden from or undetected by. You then Strike that enemy; you remain hidden from or undetected by that creature until after you Strike. You can use Spring from the Shadows while Burrowing, Climbing, Flying, or Swimming instead of Striding if you have the corresponding movement type.

14TH LEVEL

DEFENSIVE ROLL ✦ FEAT 14

ROGUE

Frequency once per 10 minutes

Trigger A physical attack would reduce you to 0 Hit Points.

Dropping into a roll to disperse the force of the blow, you can partially evade a lethal attack and stay conscious. You take half damage from the triggering attack.

INSTANT OPENING ✦ FEAT 14

CONCENTRATE ROGUE

You distract your opponent with a few choice words or a rude gesture. Choose a target within 30 feet. It's flat-footed against your attacks until the end of your next turn. Depending on the way you describe your distraction, this action gains either the auditory or visual trait.

LEAVE AN OPENING FEAT 14

ROGUE

When you hit hard enough, you leave an opening so your ally can jump in on the action. Whenever you critically hit a flat-footed opponent with a melee attack and deal damage, the target triggers an Attack of Opportunity reaction from one ally of your choice who has that reaction, as if the enemy had used a manipulate action.

SENSE THE UNSEEN ⟳ FEAT 14

ROGUE

Trigger You fail a check to Seek.

When you look for foes, you catch the slightest of cues. Even though you failed at the triggering check, you automatically sense any undetected creatures in the area where you're Seeking, making them merely hidden to you.

16TH LEVEL

BLANK SLATE FEAT 16

ROGUE

Prerequisites legendary in Deception

Your deceptions confound even the most powerful mortal divinations. Detection, revelation, and scrying effects pass right over you, your possessions, and your auras, detecting nothing unless the detecting effect has a counteract level of 20 or higher. For example, *detect magic* would still detect other magic in the area but not any magic on you, *true seeing* wouldn't reveal you, *locate* or *scrying* wouldn't find you, and so on.

CLOUD STEP FEAT 16

ROGUE

Prerequisites legendary in Acrobatics

Using fantastic acrobatic skill, you can walk for brief stretches across insubstantial surfaces. When you Stride, you can move across water, air, and solid surfaces that can hold only limited weight as if they were normal ground. If you Stride over a trap with a weight-sensitive pressure plate, you don't trigger it. At the end of your turn, you sink, fall, break fragile surfaces, or trigger traps as normal for your current location.

COGNITIVE LOOPHOLE ⟳ FEAT 16

ROGUE

Trigger Your turn ends.

Requirements You are currently affected by a mental effect that you gained by failing, but not critically failing, a saving throw. You can find a loophole in a mental effect to temporarily overcome it. Until the end of your next turn, you ignore a single mental effect that meets the requirement. You can suppress a particular effect using Cognitive Loophole only once.

Special You can use this reaction even if the mental effect is preventing you from using reactions.

DISPELLING SLICE ◆◆ FEAT 16

> ROGUE

Your sneak attack slices through the threads binding magic to a target. Make a Strike against a flat-footed creature (your choice). If your Strike deals sneak attack damage, you attempt to counteract a single spell active on the target. Your counteract level is equal to your rogue level, and your counteract check modifier is equal to your class DC – 10.

PERFECT DISTRACTION ◆ FEAT 16

> ROGUE

Prerequisites legendary in Deception

You use clever tactics to mislead your foes as you sneak away. You Sneak while leaving a decoy behind. The decoy acts as the spell *mislead*, though you aren't invisible, just undetected. You can continue to concentrate to move your decoy, as with the spell, whether or not you remain hidden throughout the duration. Once you use Perfect Distraction, you need to spend 10 minutes to set up another decoy before you can use it again.

18TH LEVEL

IMPLAUSIBLE INFILTRATION ◆◆ FEAT 18

> MAGICAL MOVE ROGUE

Prerequisites legendary in Acrobatics, Quick Squeeze
Requirements You are adjacent to a floor or vertical wall.

You find tiny holes or imperfections that no one else could see and try to somehow fit yourself through them, possibly moving directly through the wall or floor from one side to the other. Your movement attempt fails if the wall or floor is made of something other than wood, plaster, or stone; is thicker than 10 feet; or contains even a thin layer of metal. If you have a climb Speed, you can use this ability to attempt to move through a ceiling.

POWERFUL SNEAK FEAT 18

> ROGUE

You have learned to exploit your enemies' lowered defenses. When you succeed or critically succeed at a Strike using your Strength modifier on the attack roll and you would deal sneak attack damage, you can change the additional damage from sneak attack into ordinary damage of the same type as your Strike, rather than precision damage.

TRICKSTER'S ACE ⟳ FEAT 18

> CONCENTRATE ROGUE

Trigger You specify the trigger when you make your daily preparations (see Requirements below).

Requirements When you make your daily preparations, you must specify a trigger for this reaction using the same restrictions as the triggers for the Ready action. You also choose a single spell from the arcane, divine, occult, or primal list of 4th level or lower. The spell can't have a cost, nor can its casting time be more than 10 minutes. The spell must be able to target a single creature, and you must be a valid target for it.

Whether from jury-rigged magic items, stolen magical essence, or other means, you have a contingency in your back pocket for desperate situations. When the trigger occurs, you cause the spell to come into effect. The spell targets only you, no matter how many creatures it would affect normally. If you define particularly complicated conditions, as determined by the GM, the trigger might fail. Once the contingency is triggered, the spell is expended until your next daily preparations.

20TH LEVEL

HIDDEN PARAGON ⟳ FEAT 20

> ROGUE

Prerequisites legendary in Stealth
Frequency once per hour
Trigger You successfully use Stealth to Hide and become hidden from all of your current foes, or use Stealth to Sneak and become undetected to all your current foes.

When you put your mind to slipping out of sight, you disappear completely. You become invisible for 1 minute, even if you use a hostile action. Not even *glitterdust*, *see invisibility*, or similar effects can reveal you, though creatures can still use the Seek action to locate you as normal.

IMPOSSIBLE STRIKER FEAT 20

> ROGUE

Prerequisites Sly Striker

Your attacks are swift and deadly beyond explanation. Nothing can prevent you from making a sneak attack, even if your opponent can see every blow coming. Instead of dealing the damage from Sly Striker, you can deal your full sneak attack damage to a target even if the target isn't flat-footed.

REACTIVE DISTRACTION ⟳ FEAT 20

> CONCENTRATE MANIPULATE ROGUE

Prerequisites legendary in Deception, Perfect Distraction
Trigger You would be hit by an attack or targeted by an effect, or you are within an effect's area.
Requirements You have Perfect Distraction ready to use.

You reactively switch with your decoy to foil your foe. You use Perfection Distraction, even if you were observed, as long as you end the movement of your Sneak while concealed or in a location with cover or greater cover. Your decoy is targeted by the attack or effect instead of you. In the case of an area effect, if your Sneak doesn't move you out of the area, both you and the decoy are targeted by the effect.

SORCERER

You didn't choose to become a spellcaster—you were born one. There's magic in your blood, whether a divinity touched one of your ancestors, a forebear communed with a primal creature, or a powerful occult ritual influenced your line. Self-reflection and study allow you to refine your inherent magical skills and unlock new, more powerful abilities. The power in your blood carries a risk, however, and you constantly face the choice of whether you'll rise to become a master spellcaster or fall into destruction.

KEY ABILITY

CHARISMA
At 1st level, your class gives you an ability boost to Charisma.

HIT POINTS

6 + your Constitution modifier
You increase your maximum number of HP by this number at 1st level and every level thereafter.

DURING COMBAT ENCOUNTERS...

You use spells to injure your enemies, influence their minds, and hamper their movements. You might be too vulnerable to get into melee combat, or your bloodline might give you abilities that help you hold your own in a brawl. While your magic is powerful, to conserve your best spells—or when you've used them all up—you also rely on cantrips.

DURING SOCIAL ENCOUNTERS...

Your natural charisma makes you good at interacting with people.

WHILE EXPLORING...

You detect the magic around you, finding treasures and warning your adventuring group of magical traps. When the group encounters mysteries or problems related to your bloodline, you try to solve them.

IN DOWNTIME...

You craft magic items or scribe scrolls. Your bloodline might drive you to research your ancestry or associate with affiliated people or creatures.

YOU MIGHT...

- Have a strong independent streak, and whether you embrace or reject your magical heritage, you long to distinguish yourself both as a spellcaster and as an individual.
- View your lineage with fascination, fear, or something in between—anything from wholehearted acceptance to vehement rejection.
- Rely on magic items, such as scrolls and wands, to supplement your limited selection of spells.

OTHERS PROBABLY...

- Marvel at your ability to create magic from thin air and view your abilities with equal parts admiration and mistrust.
- Consider you less dedicated than studious wizards, devoted clerics, and other practitioners of magic, since power comes to you naturally.
- Assume you're as unpredictable as the magic you bring forth, even if your personality proves otherwise.

INITIAL PROFICIENCIES

At 1st level, you gain the listed proficiency ranks in the following statistics. You are untrained in anything not listed unless you gain a better proficiency rank in some other way.

PERCEPTION

Trained in Perception

SAVING THROWS

Trained in Fortitude
Trained in Reflex
Expert in Will

SKILLS

Trained in one or more skills determined by your bloodline
Trained in a number of additional skills equal to 2 plus your Intelligence modifier

ATTACKS

Trained in simple weapons
Trained in unarmed attacks

DEFENSES

Untrained in all armor
Trained in unarmored defense

SPELLS

Trained in spell attack rolls of your spellcasting tradition, as indicated by your bloodline
Trained in spell DCs of your spellcasting tradition, as indicated by your bloodline

TABLE 3-16: SORCERER ADVANCEMENT

Your Level	Class Features
1	Ancestry and background, initial proficiencies, bloodline, sorcerer spellcasting, spell repertoire
2	Skill feat, sorcerer feat
3	2nd-level spells, general feat, signature spells, skill increase
4	Skill feat, sorcerer feat
5	3rd-level spells, ability boosts, ancestry feat, magical fortitude, skill increase
6	Skill feat, sorcerer feat
7	4th-level spells, expert spellcaster, general feat, skill increase
8	Skill feat, sorcerer feat
9	5th-level spells, ancestry feat, lightning reflexes, skill increase
10	Ability boosts, skill feat, sorcerer feat
11	6th-level spells, alertness, general feat, simple weapon expertise, skill increase
12	Skill feat, sorcerer feat
13	7th-level spells, ancestry feat, defensive robes, skill increase, weapon specialization
14	Skill feat, sorcerer feat
15	8th-level spells, ability boosts, general feat, master spellcaster, skill increase
16	Skill feat, sorcerer feat
17	9th-level spells, ancestry feat, skill increase
18	Skill feat, sorcerer feat
19	Bloodline paragon, general feat, legendary spellcaster, skill increase
20	Ability boosts, skill feat, sorcerer feat

CLASS FEATURES

You gain these abilities as a sorcerer. Abilities gained at higher levels list the requisite levels next to their names.

ANCESTRY AND BACKGROUND

In addition to the abilities provided by your class at 1st level, you have the benefits of your selected ancestry and background, as described in Chapter 2.

INITIAL PROFICIENCIES

At 1st level, you gain a number of proficiencies that represent your basic training. These proficiencies are noted at the start of this class.

BLOODLINE

Choose a bloodline that gives you your spellcasting talent. This choice determines the type of spells you cast and the spell list you choose them from, additional spells you learn, and additional trained skills. You also gain Focus Points and special focus spells based on your bloodline. The bloodlines presented in this book are as follows.

Aberrant: A strange and unknowable influence gives you occult spells.

Angelic: Holy grace bestows divine spells upon you.

Demonic: A sinful corruption gives you divine spells.

Diabolic: A bond with devils gives you divine spells.

Draconic: The blood of dragons grants you arcane spells.

Elemental: The power of the elements manifests in you as primal spells.

Fey: Influence from the fey gives you primal spells.

Hag: The blight of a hag has given you occult spells.

Imperial: An ancient power grants you arcane spells.

Undead: The touch of death gives you divine spells.

See Bloodlines on page 194 for more information.

SORCERER SPELLCASTING

Your bloodline provides you with incredible magical power. You can cast spells using the Cast a Spell activity, and you can supply material, somatic, and verbal components when casting spells (see Casting Spells on page 302). Because you're a sorcerer, you can usually replace material components with somatic components, so you don't need to use a spell component pouch.

Each day, you can cast up to three 1st-level spells. You must know spells to cast them, and you learn them via the spell repertoire class feature. The number of spells you can cast each day is called your spell slots.

As you increase in level as a sorcerer, your number of spells per day increases, as does the highest level of spells you can cast, as shown on Table 3–17: Sorcerer Spells per Day on page 193.

Some of your spells require you to attempt a spell attack roll to see how effective they are, or have your enemies roll against your spell DC (typically by attempting a saving throw). Since your key ability is Charisma, your spell attack rolls and spell DCs use your Charisma modifier. Details on calculating these statistics appear on page 447.

HEIGHTENING SPELLS

When you get spell slots of 2nd level and higher, you can fill those slots with stronger versions of lower-level spells. This increases the spell's level to match the spell slot. You must have a spell in your spell repertoire at the level you want to cast in order to heighten it to that level. Many spells have specific improvements when they are heightened to certain levels (page 299). The signature spells class feature lets you heighten certain spells freely.

CANTRIPS

A cantrip is a special type of spell that doesn't use spell slots. You can cast a cantrip at will, any number of times per day. A cantrip is always automatically heightened to half your level rounded up—this is usually equal to the highest level of spell you can cast as a sorcerer. For example, as a 1st-level sorcerer, your cantrips are 1st-level spells, and as a 5th-level sorcerer, your cantrips are 3rd-level spells.

TABLE 3-17: SORCERER SPELLS PER DAY

Your Level	Cantrips	Spell Level 1st	2nd	3rd	4th	5th	6th	7th	8th	9th	10th
1	5	3	–	–	–	–	–	–	–	–	–
2	5	4	–	–	–	–	–	–	–	–	–
3	5	4	3	–	–	–	–	–	–	–	–
4	5	4	4	–	–	–	–	–	–	–	–
5	5	4	4	3	–	–	–	–	–	–	–
6	5	4	4	4	–	–	–	–	–	–	–
7	5	4	4	4	3	–	–	–	–	–	–
8	5	4	4	4	4	–	–	–	–	–	–
9	5	4	4	4	4	3	–	–	–	–	–
10	5	4	4	4	4	4	–	–	–	–	–
11	5	4	4	4	4	4	3	–	–	–	–
12	5	4	4	4	4	4	4	–	–	–	–
13	5	4	4	4	4	4	4	3	–	–	–
14	5	4	4	4	4	4	4	4	–	–	–
15	5	4	4	4	4	4	4	4	3	–	–
16	5	4	4	4	4	4	4	4	4	–	–
17	5	4	4	4	4	4	4	4	4	3	–
18	5	4	4	4	4	4	4	4	4	4	–
19	5	4	4	4	4	4	4	4	4	4	1*
20	5	4	4	4	4	4	4	4	4	4	1*

* The bloodline paragon class feature gives you a 10th-level spell slot that works a bit differently from other spell slots.

SPELL REPERTOIRE

The collection of spells you can cast is called your spell repertoire. At 1st level, you learn two 1st-level spells of your choice and four cantrips of your choice, as well as an additional spell and cantrip from your bloodline (page 194). You choose these from the common spells from the tradition corresponding to your bloodline, or from other spells from that tradition to which you have access. You can cast any spell in your spell repertoire by using a spell slot of an appropriate spell level.

You add to this spell repertoire as you increase in level. Each time you get a spell slot (see Table 3–17), you add a spell of the same level to your spell repertoire. When you gain access to a new level of spells, your first new spell is always your bloodline spell, but you can choose the other spells you gain. At 2nd level, you select another 1st-level spell; at 3rd level, you gain a new bloodline spell and two other 2nd-level spells, and so on. When you add spells, you might choose a higher-level version of a spell you already have so that you can cast a heightened version of that spell.

Though you gain them at the same rate, your spell slots and the spells in your spell repertoire are separate. If a feat or other ability adds a spell to your spell repertoire, it wouldn't give you another spell slot, and vice versa.

SWAPPING SPELLS IN YOUR REPERTOIRE

As you gain new spells in your spell repertoire, you might want to replace some of the spells you previously learned. Each time you gain a level and learn new spells, you can swap out one of your old spells for a different spell of the same level. This spell can be a cantrip, but you can't swap out bloodline spells. You can also swap out spells by retraining during downtime (page 481).

SKILL FEATS   2ND

At 2nd level and every 2 levels thereafter, you gain a skill feat. Skill feats appear in Chapter 5 and have the skill trait. You must be trained or better in the corresponding skill to select a skill feat.

SORCERER FEATS   2ND

At 2nd level and every even-numbered level, you gain a sorcerer class feat. These begin on page 198.

GENERAL FEATS   3RD

At 3rd level and every 4 levels thereafter, you gain a general feat. General feats are listed in Chapter 5.

SIGNATURE SPELLS   3RD

You've learned to cast some of your spells more flexibly. For each spell level you have access to, choose one spell of that level to be a signature spell. You don't need to learn heightened versions of signature spells separately; instead, you can heighten these spells freely. If you've learned a signature spell at a higher level than its minimum, you can also cast all its lower-level versions without learning those separately. If you swap out a signature spell, you can choose a replacement signature spell of the same spell level at which you learned the previous spell. You can also retrain specifically to change a signature spell to a different

INTRODUCTION

ANCESTRIES & BACKGROUNDS

CLASSES

SKILLS

FEATS

EQUIPMENT

SPELLS

THE AGE OF LOST OMENS

PLAYING THE GAME

GAME MASTERING

CRAFTING & TREASURE

APPENDIX

THE BLESSED AND THE DAMNED

Many bloodlines are tied to certain types of creatures, and the reputations of those creatures might color how people see you. If you have the blood of demons, people might fear you; conversely, people of good faiths might assume your angelic blood puts you on their side. These preconceptions aren't necessarily true, and you can certainly use demonic or infernal powers to do good. Having a bloodline tied to creatures of a certain alignment doesn't have any effect on your own alignment unless you want it to; your magic is disconnected from its source. That said, many sorcerers seek out creatures or organizations associated with their bloodlines, which can expose them to these forces' influences.

spell of that level without swapping any spells; this takes as much time as retraining a spell normally does.

SKILL INCREASES   3RD

At 3rd level and every 2 levels thereafter, you gain a skill increase. You can use an increase to either become trained in one skill you're untrained in, or to increase your proficiency rank in one skill in which you're already trained to expert.

At 7th level, you can use skill increases to become a master in a skill in which you're already an expert, and at 15th level, you can use them to become legendary in a skill in which you're already a master.

ABILITY BOOSTS   5TH

At 5th level and every 5 levels thereafter, you boost four different ability scores. You can use these ability boosts to increase your ability scores above 18. Boosting an ability score increases it by 1 if it's already 18 or above, or by 2 if it starts out below 18.

ANCESTRY FEATS   5TH

In addition to the ancestry feat you started with, you gain an ancestry feat at 5th level and every 4 levels thereafter. The list of ancestry feats available to you can be found in your ancestry's entry in Chapter 2.

MAGICAL FORTITUDE   5TH

Magical power has improved your body's resiliency. Your proficiency rank for Fortitude saves increases to expert.

EXPERT SPELLCASTER   7TH

Your inherent magic responds easily and powerfully to your command. Your proficiency ranks for spell attack rolls and spell DCs for spells of your bloodline's tradition increase to expert.

LIGHTNING REFLEXES   9TH

Your reflexes are lightning fast. Your proficiency rank for Reflex saves increases to expert.

ALERTNESS   11TH

You remain alert to threats around you. Your proficiency rank for Perception increases to expert.

SIMPLE WEAPON EXPERTISE   11TH

Training and magic improved your weapon technique. Your proficiency rank for simple weapons increases to expert.

DEFENSIVE ROBES   13TH

The flow of magic and your defensive training combine to help you get out of the way before an attack. Your proficiency rank in unarmored defense increases to expert.

WEAPON SPECIALIZATION   13TH

You've learned to inflict grave wounds with your practiced weapons. You deal 2 additional damage with weapons and unarmed attacks in which you are an expert. This damage increases to 3 if you're a master, and 4 if you're legendary.

MASTER SPELLCASTER   15TH

You have achieved mastery over the magic in your blood. Your proficiency ranks for spell attack rolls and spell DCs for spells of your bloodline's tradition increase to master.

BLOODLINE PARAGON   19TH

You have perfected the magic in your bloodline. Add two common 10th-level spells of your tradition to your repertoire. You gain a single 10th-level spell slot you can use to cast these spells, using sorcerer spellcasting. Unlike other spell slots, you don't gain more 10th-level spells as you level up, and they can't be used for abilities that let you cast spells without expending spell slots or abilities that give you more spell slots. You can take the Bloodline Perfection sorcerer feat to gain a second slot.

LEGENDARY SPELLCASTER   19TH

You demonstrate prodigious talent for spellcasting. Your proficiency ranks for spell attack rolls and spell DCs for spells of your bloodline's tradition increase to legendary.

BLOODLINES

Choose your bloodline, the source of your power. It has a major influence on your abilities, determining your spell list, the tradition of spells you cast, and two trained skills.

BLOODLINE SPELLS

Your bloodline grants you bloodline spells, special spells unique to your lineage. Bloodline spells are a type of focus spell. It costs 1 Focus Point to cast a focus spell, and you start with a focus pool of 1 Focus Point. You refill your focus pool during your daily preparations, and you can regain 1 Focus Point by spending 10 minutes using the Refocus activity. Unlike other characters, you don't need to do anything specific to Refocus, as the power of the blood flowing through your veins naturally replenishes your focus pool.

Focus spells are automatically heightened to half your level rounded up. Focus spells don't require spell slots, nor can you cast them using spell slots. Taking feats can give you more focus spells and increase the size of your focus pool, though your focus pool can never hold more than 3 points. The full rules are on page 300.

READING A BLOODLINE ENTRY

A bloodline entry contains the following information.

Spell List You use this magical tradition and spell list.

Bloodline Skills You become trained in the listed skills.

Granted Spells You automatically add the spells listed here to your spell repertoire, in addition to those you gain through sorcerer spellcasting. At 1st level, you gain a cantrip and a 1st-level spell. You learn the other spells on the list as soon as you gain the ability to cast sorcerer spells of that level.

Bloodline Spells You automatically gain the initial bloodline spell at 1st level and can gain more by selecting the Advanced Bloodline and Greater Bloodline feats.

Blood Magic Whenever you cast a bloodline spell using Focus Points or a granted spell from your bloodline using a spell slot, you gain a blood magic effect. If the blood magic offers a choice, make it before resolving the spell. The blood magic effect occurs after resolving any checks for the spell's initial effects and, against a foe, applies only if the spell is a successful attack or the foe fails its saving throw. If the spell has an area, you must designate yourself or one target in the area when you cast the spell to be the target of the blood magic effect. All references to spell level refer to the level of the spell you cast.

ABERRANT

Something speaks to you from beyond the stars or below the earth. Ancient and unknowable, this alien influence presses against your mind.

Spell List occult (page 311)

Bloodline Skills Intimidation, Occultism

Granted Spells cantrip: *daze*; 1st: *spider sting*; 2nd: *touch of idiocy*; 3rd: *vampiric touch*; 4th: *confusion*; 5th: *black tentacles*; 6th: *feeblemind*; 7th: *warp mind*; 8th: *uncontrollable dance*; 9th: *unfathomable song*

Bloodline Spells initial: *tentacular limbs*; advanced: *aberrant whispers*; greater: *unusual anatomy*

Blood Magic Aberrant whispers shield one target's mind or your own, granting a +2 status bonus to Will saving throws for 1 round.

ANGELIC

One of your forebears hailed from a celestial realm, or your ancestors' devotion led to their lineage being blessed.

Spell List divine (page 309)

Bloodline Skills Diplomacy, Religion

Granted Spells cantrip: *light*; 1st: *heal*; 2nd: *spiritual weapon*; 3rd: *searing light*; 4th: *divine wrath*; 5th: *flame strike*; 6th: *blade barrier*; 7th: *divine decree*; 8th: *divine aura*; 9th: *foresight*

Bloodline Spells initial: *angelic halo*; advanced: *angelic wings*; greater: *celestial brand*

Blood Magic An angelic aura protects you or one target, granting a +1 status bonus to saving throws for 1 round.

DEMONIC

Demons debase all they touch. One of your ancestors fell victim to their corruption, and you are burdened by that sin.

Spell List divine (page 309)

Bloodline Skills Intimidation, Religion

Granted Spells cantrip: *acid splash*; 1st: *fear*; 2nd: *enlarge*; 3rd: *slow*; 4th: *divine wrath*; 5th: *Abyssal plague*; 6th: *disintegrate*; 7th: *divine decree*; 8th: *divine aura*; 9th: *implosion*

INTRODUCTION

ANCESTRIES & BACKGROUNDS

CLASSES

SKILLS

FEATS

EQUIPMENT

SPELLS

THE AGE OF LOST OMENS

PLAYING THE GAME

GAME MASTERING

CRAFTING & TREASURE

APPENDIX

SAMPLE SORCERER

FEY-TOUCHED

Your blood ties you to the magic of the First World and the otherworldly fey. Like them, you're capricious, charming, and hard to pin down.

ABILITY SCORES
Improve your Charisma first. Good Dexterity, Constitution, and Wisdom provide solid defenses.

SKILLS
Deception, Diplomacy, Nature, Stealth

BLOODLINE
Fey

HIGHER-LEVEL FEATS
Reach Spell (1st), Primal Evolution (4th), Advanced Bloodline (6th), Greater Bloodline (10th), Bloodline Focus (12th)

SPELL REPERTOIRE
1st *charm, fleet step, summon fey;* **Cantrips** *dancing lights, daze, detect magic, ghost sound, tanglefoot*

Bloodline Spells initial: *glutton's jaws*; advanced: *swamp of sloth*; greater: *Abyssal wrath*
Blood Magic The corruption of sin weakens a target's defenses or makes you more imposing. Either a target takes a –1 status penalty to AC for 1 round, or you gain a +1 status bonus to Intimidation checks for 1 round.

DIABOLIC
Devils are evil with a silver tongue, and one of your ancestors dallied in darkness or made an infernal pact.
Spell List divine (page 309)
Bloodline Skills Deception, Religion
Granted Spells cantrip: *produce flame*; 1st: *charm*; 2nd: *flaming sphere*; 3rd: *enthrall*; 4th: *suggestion*; 5th: *crushing despair*; 6th: *true seeing*; 7th: *divine decree*; 8th: *divine aura*; 9th: *meteor swarm*
Bloodline Spells initial: *diabolic edict*; advanced: *embrace the pit*; greater: *hellfire plume*
Blood Magic Hellfire scorches a target or fills your tongue with lies. Either a target takes 1 fire damage per spell level (if the spell already deals initial fire damage, combine this with the spell's initial damage before determining weaknesses and resistances), or you gain a +1 status bonus to Deception checks for 1 round.

DRACONIC
The blood of dragons flows through your veins. These beasts are both fearsome in combat and skilled at magic.
Spell List arcane (page 307)
Bloodline Skills Arcana, Intimidation
Granted Spells cantrip: *shield*; 1st: *true strike*; 2nd: *resist energy*; 3rd: *haste*; 4th: *spell immunity*; 5th: *chromatic wall*; 6th: *dragon form*; 7th: *mask of terror*; 8th: *prismatic wall*; 9th: *overwhelming presence*
Bloodline Spells initial: *dragon claws*; advanced: *dragon breath*; greater: *dragon wings*
Blood Magic Draconic scales grow briefly on you or one target, granting a +1 status bonus to AC for 1 round.

Dragon Type
At 1st level, choose the type of dragon that influenced your bloodline. You can't change your dragon type later. This affects how some of your bloodline spells function. The good metallic dragons and their damage types are brass (fire), bronze (electricity), copper (acid), gold (fire), and silver (cold). The evil chromatic dragons and their damage types are black (acid), blue (electricity), green (poison), red (fire), and white (cold).

ELEMENTAL
A genie ancestor or some other elemental influence has imbued your blood with primal fury, affecting how the bloodline spells and granted spells marked with an asterisk (*), as well as your blood magic, function.
Spell List primal (page 314)
Bloodline Skills Intimidation, Nature
Granted Spells cantrip: *produce flame**; 1st: *burning hands**; 2nd: *resist energy*; 3rd: *fireball**; 4th: *freedom of movement*;

CLASSES

3

INTRODUCTION

ANCESTRIES &
BACKGROUNDS

CLASSES

SKILLS

FEATS

EQUIPMENT

SPELLS

THE AGE OF
LOST OMENS

PLAYING THE
GAME

GAME
MASTERING

CRAFTING
& TREASURE

APPENDIX

5th: *elemental form*; 6th: *repulsion*; 7th: *energy aegis*; 8th: *prismatic wall*; 9th: *storm of vengeance*

Bloodline Spells initial: *elemental toss**; advanced: *elemental motion*; greater: *elemental blast**

Blood Magic Elemental energy surrounds you or a target. Either you gain a +1 status bonus to Intimidation checks for 1 round, or a target takes 1 damage per spell level. The damage is bludgeoning or fire, according to your elemental type (see below). If the spell already deals that type of damage, combine it with the spell's initial damage before determining weaknesses and resistances.

ELEMENTAL TYPE

At 1st level, choose the type of elemental that influenced your bloodline: air, earth, fire, or water. If your element is air, you buffet your foes with powerful winds; if it's earth, you toss huge chunks of rock; if it's fire, you incinerate your foes with flame; and if it's water, you inundate your foes with torrents of water. For fire, all marked spells deal fire damage. For other elements, they deal bludgeoning damage. You also add the trait of the element you chose.

FEY

Fey whimsy or a tryst in a moonlit grove put the bewitching magic of the First World into your family's bloodline.

Spell List primal (page 314)

Bloodline Skills Deception, Nature

Granted Spells cantrip: *ghost sound*; 1st: *charm*; 2nd: *hideous laughter*; 3rd: *enthrall*; 4th: *suggestion*; 5th: *cloak of colors*; 6th: *mislead*; 7th: *visions of danger*; 8th: *uncontrollable dance*; 9th: *resplendent mansion*

Bloodline Spells initial: *faerie dust*; advanced: *fey disappearance*; greater: *fey glamour*

Blood Magic Colorful fey glamours dance around you or one target, causing them to be concealed for 1 round. Such obvious concealment can't be used to Hide.

HAG

A hag long ago cursed your family, or you are a descendant of a hag or changeling, and their accursed corruption infests your blood and soul.

Spell List occult (page 311)

Bloodline Skills Deception, Occultism

Granted Spells cantrip: *daze*; 1st: *illusory disguise*; 2nd: *touch of idiocy*; 3rd: *blindness*; 4th: *outcast's curse*; 5th: *mariner's curse*; 6th: *baleful polymorph*; 7th: *warp mind*; 8th: *spiritual epidemic*; 9th: *nature's enmity*

Bloodline Spells initial: *jealous hex*; advanced: *horrific visage*; greater: *you're mine*

KEY TERMS

You'll see the following key terms in many sorcerer abilities.

Metamagic: Actions with the metamagic trait tweak the properties of your spells. These actions usually come from metamagic feats. You must use a metamagic action directly before Casting the Spell you want to alter. If you use any action (including free actions and reactions) other than Cast a Spell directly after, you waste the benefits of the metamagic action. Any additional effects added by a metamagic action are part of the spell's effect, not of the metamagic action itself.

Blood Magic Spiteful curses punish your foes. The first creature that deals damage to you before the end of your next turn takes 2 mental damage per spell level and must attempt a basic Will save.

IMPERIAL

One of your ancestors was a mortal who mastered magic. Such magical blood can remain latent for generations, but in you it manifested in full.

Spell List arcane (page 307)

Bloodline Skills Arcana, Society

Granted Spells cantrip: *detect magic*; 1st: *magic missile*; 2nd: *dispel magic*; 3rd: *haste*; 4th: *dimension door*; 5th: *prying eye*; 6th: *disintegrate*; 7th: *prismatic spray*; 8th: *maze*; 9th: *prismatic sphere*

Bloodline Spells initial: *ancestral memories*; advanced: *extend spell*; greater: *arcane countermeasure*

Blood Magic A surge of ancestral memories grants you or one target a +1 status bonus to skill checks for 1 round.

UNDEAD

The touch of undeath runs through your blood. Your family tree might contain powerful undead, like a vampire, or perhaps you died and returned a bit different.

Spell List divine (page 309)

Bloodline Skills Intimidation, Religion

Granted Spells cantrip: *chill touch*; 1st: *harm*; 2nd: *false life*; 3rd: *bind undead*; 4th: *talking corpse*; 5th: *cloudkill*; 6th: *vampiric exsanguination*; 7th: *finger of death*; 8th: *horrid wilting*; 9th: *wail of the banshee*

Bloodline Spells initial: *touch of undeath*; advanced: *drain life*; greater: *grasping grave*

Blood Magic Necromantic energy flows through you or one target. Either you gain temporary Hit Points equal to the spell's level for 1 round, or a target takes 1 negative damage per spell level (if the spell already deals initial negative damage, combine this with the spell's initial damage before determining weaknesses and resistances).

SORCERER FEATS

At every level at which you gain a sorcerer feat, you can select one of the following feats. You must satisfy any prerequisites before taking the feat.

1ST LEVEL

COUNTERSPELL ↻   FEAT 1

ABJURATION **SORCERER**

Trigger A creature casts a spell that you have in your repertoire.

Requirements You have an unexpended spell slot you could use to cast the triggering spell.

When a foe Casts a Spell you know and you can see its manifestations, you can use your own magic to disrupt it. You expend one of your spell slots to counter the triggering creature's casting of a spell that you have in your repertoire. You lose your spell slot as if you had cast the triggering spell. You then attempt to counteract the triggering spell (page 458).

Special This feat has the trait corresponding to the tradition of spells you cast (arcane, divine, natural, or occult).

DANGEROUS SORCERY   FEAT 1

SORCERER

Your legacy grants you great destructive power. When you Cast a Spell from your spell slots, if the spell deals damage and doesn't have a duration, you gain a status bonus to that spell's damage equal to the spell's level.

FAMILIAR   FEAT 1

SORCERER

An animal serves you and assists your spellcasting. You gain a familiar (rules for familiars are found on page 217).

REACH SPELL ◆   FEAT 1

CONCENTRATE **METAMAGIC** **SORCERER**

You can extend the range of your spells. If the next action you use is to Cast a Spell that has a range, increase that spell's range by 30 feet. As is standard for increasing spell ranges, if the spell normally has a range of touch, you extend its range to 30 feet.

WIDEN SPELL ◆   FEAT 1

MANIPULATE **METAMAGIC** **SORCERER**

You manipulate the energy of your spell, causing it to affect a wider area. If the next action you use is to Cast a Spell that has an area of a burst, cone, or line and does not have a duration, increase the area of that spell. Add 5 feet to the radius of a burst that normally has a radius of at least 10 feet (a burst with a smaller radius is not affected). Add 5 feet to the length of a cone or line that is normally 15 feet long or smaller, and add 10 feet to the length of a larger cone or line.

2ND LEVEL

CANTRIP EXPANSION   FEAT 2

SORCERER

You better understand the basic power of your bloodline. Add two additional cantrips from your spell list to your repertoire.

ENHANCED FAMILIAR   FEAT 2

SORCERER

Prerequisites a familiar

You infuse your familiar with additional magical energy. You can select four familiar or master abilities each day, instead of two.

4TH LEVEL

ARCANE EVOLUTION   FEAT 4

`ARCANE` `SORCERER`

Prerequisites bloodline that grants arcane spells

Your arcane legacy grants you an exceptional aptitude for intellectual and academic pursuits. You become trained in one skill of your choice. Additionally, you keep a book of arcane spells similar to a wizard's spellbook. You add all the spells in your spell repertoire to this book for free, and you can add additional arcane spells to the book by paying the appropriate cost and using your Arcana skill, similarly to how a wizard can Learn Spells to add those spells to his spellbook.

During your daily preparations, choose any one spell from your book of arcane spells. If it isn't in your spell repertoire, add it to your spell repertoire until the next time you prepare. If it's already in your spell repertoire, add it as an additional signature spell for that day.

BESPELL WEAPON ◈   FEAT 4

`SORCERER`

Frequency once per turn

Requirements Your most recent action was to cast a non-cantrip spell.

You siphon the residual energy from the last spell you cast into one weapon you're wielding. Until the end of your turn, the weapon deals an extra 1d6 damage of a type depending on the school of the spell you just cast.

- **Abjuration** force damage
- **Conjuration or Transmutation** the same type as the weapon
- **Divination, Enchantment, or Illusion** mental damage
- **Evocation** a type the spell dealt, or force damage if the spell didn't deal damage
- **Necromancy** negative damage

DIVINE EVOLUTION   FEAT 4

`DIVINE` `SORCERER`

Prerequisites bloodline that grants divine spells

The divine might provided by your bloodline flows through you. You gain an additional spell slot of your highest level, which you can use only to cast your choice of *heal* or *harm*. You can cast either of these spells using that spell slot, even if they aren't in your spell repertoire.

OCCULT EVOLUTION   FEAT 4

`OCCULT` `SORCERER`

Prerequisites bloodline that grants occult spells

Glimpses of the obscure secrets of the universe loan you power. You become trained in one skill of your choice. Additionally, once per day, you can spend 1 minute to choose one mental occult spell you don't know and add it to your spell repertoire. You lose this temporary spell the next time you make your daily preparations (though you can use this ability to add it again later).

PRIMAL EVOLUTION   FEAT 4

`PRIMAL` `SORCERER`

Prerequisites bloodline that grants primal spells

You can call upon the creatures of the wild for aid. You gain an additional spell slot of your highest level, which you can use only to cast *summon animal* or *summon plants and fungi*. You can cast either of these spells using that spell slot, even if it they aren't in your spell repertoire.

SORCERER FEATS

If you need to look up a sorcerer feat by name instead of by level, use this table.

Feat	Level
Advanced Bloodline	6
Arcane Evolution	4
Bespell Weapon	6
Bloodline Conduit	20
Bloodline Focus	12
Bloodline Perfection	20
Bloodline Resistance	8
Bloodline Wellspring	18
Cantrip Expansion	2
Counterspell	1
Crossblooded Evolution	8
Dangerous Sorcery	1
Divine Evolution	4
Effortless Concentration	16
Enhanced Familiar	2
Familiar	1
Greater Bloodline	10
Greater Crossblooded Evolution	18
Greater Mental Evolution	16
Greater Vital Evolution	16
Interweave Dispel	14
Magic Sense	12
Metamagic Mastery	20
Occult Evolution	4
Overwhelming Energy	10
Primal Evolution	4
Quickened Casting	10
Reach Spell	1
Reflect Spell	14
Steady Spellcasting	6
Widen Spell	1

SAMPLE SORCERER

DEMONBLOOD

The grotesque and chaotic creatures of the Abyss left their mark on your family's bloodline. You have a vicious streak and find wanton destruction thrilling.

ABILITY SCORES
Your Charisma is most important, and boosting Strength, Dexterity, and Constitution make you a better combatant.

SKILLS
Athletics, Deception, Intimidation, Religion

BLOODLINE
Demonic

HIGHER-LEVEL FEATS
Dangerous Sorcery (1st), Divine Evolution (4th), Advanced Bloodline (6th), Bloodline Resistance (8th), Greater Bloodline (10th), Bloodline Focus (12th)

SPELL REPERTOIRE
1st *bane, fear, harm;* **Cantrips** *acid splash, chill touch, detect magic, light, shield*

6TH LEVEL

ADVANCED BLOODLINE   FEAT 6
`SORCERER`

Prerequisites bloodline spell

You have studied your bloodline to learn the secrets of its magic. You gain the advanced bloodline spell associated with your bloodline. Increase the number of Focus Points in your focus pool by 1.

STEADY SPELLCASTING   FEAT 6
`SORCERER`

You are confident in your spellcasting technique, and you are more easily able to retain your concentration when you Cast a Spell. If a reaction would disrupt your spellcasting action, attempt a DC 15 flat check. If you succeed, your action isn't disrupted.

8TH LEVEL

BLOODLINE RESISTANCE   FEAT 8
`SORCERER`

Your magical blood makes you more resistant to magic. You gain a +1 status bonus to saving throws against spells and magical effects.

CROSSBLOODED EVOLUTION   FEAT 8
`SORCERER`

Odd interactions in your bloodline provide you with unexpected spells. You can have one spell in your spell repertoire from a tradition other than the one that matches your bloodline. You cast that spell as a spell from your bloodline's tradition. You can swap which spell you add and from which tradition as you could any other sorcerer spell, but you can't have more than one spell from another tradition in your spell repertoire at the same time using this feat.

10TH LEVEL

GREATER BLOODLINE   FEAT 10
`SORCERER`

Prerequisites bloodline spell

Further communion with the legacy of your bloodline has uncovered greater secrets. You gain the greater bloodline spell associated with your bloodline. Increase the number of Focus Points in your focus pool by 1.

OVERWHELMING ENERGY ◆   FEAT 10
`MANIPULATE` `METAMAGIC` `SORCERER`

You alter your spells to overcome resistances. If the next action you use is to Cast a Spell, the spell ignores an amount of the target's resistance to acid, cold, electricity, fire, or sonic damage equal to your level. This applies to all damage the spell deals, including persistent damage and damage caused by an ongoing effect of the spell, such as the wall created by *wall of fire.* A creature's immunities are unaffected.

QUICKENED CASTING ◈ — FEAT 10

CONCENTRATE **METAMAGIC** **SORCERER**

Frequency once per day

In a mentally strenuous process, you modify your casting of a spell to take less time. If your next action is to cast a sorcerer cantrip or a sorcerer spell that is at least 2 levels lower than the highest level sorcerer spell you can cast, reduce the number of actions to cast it by 1 (minimum 1 action).

12TH LEVEL

BLOODLINE FOCUS — FEAT 12

SORCERER

Prerequisites bloodline spell

Your focus recovers faster. If you have spent at least 2 Focus Points since the last time you Refocused, you recover 2 Focus Points when you Refocus instead of 1.

MAGIC SENSE — FEAT 12

DETECTION **DIVINATION** **SORCERER**

You have a literal sixth sense for magic. You can sense the presence of magic auras as though you were always using a 1st-level *detect magic* spell. This detects magic in your field of vision only. When you Seek, you gain the benefits of a 3rd-level *detect magic* spell on things you see (in addition to the normal benefits of Seeking). You can turn this sense off and on with a free action at the start or the end of your turn.

14TH LEVEL

INTERWEAVE DISPEL ◈ — FEAT 14

METAMAGIC **SORCERER**

Prerequisites *dispel magic* in your spell repertoire

You weave dispelling energy into a spell, sending both effects at a foe. If your next action is to cast a single-target spell against a creature, and you either hit the foe with the spell attack roll or the foe fails its saving throw, you can cast *dispel magic* on the foe as a free action, expending a spell slot as normal and targeting one spell effect affecting the foe.

REFLECT SPELL — FEAT 14

SORCERER

Prerequisites Counterspell

When you successfully use Counterspell to counteract a spell that affects targeted creatures or an area, you can turn that spell's effect back on its caster. When reflected, the spell affects only the original caster, even if it's an area spell or it would normally affect more than one creature. The original caster can attempt a save and use other defenses against the reflected spell as normal.

16TH LEVEL

EFFORTLESS CONCENTRATION ◈ — FEAT 16

SORCERER

Trigger Your turn begins.

You maintain a spell with hardly a thought. You immediately gain the effects of the Sustain a Spell action, allowing you to extend the duration of one of your active sorcerer spells.

GREATER MENTAL EVOLUTION — FEAT 16

ARCANE **SORCERER**

Prerequisites Arcane Evolution or Occult Evolution

Your bloodline's deep connection to mental essence greatly enhances your spell repertoire. Add one spell to your spell repertoire for each spell level you can cast.

GREATER VITAL EVOLUTION — FEAT 16

DIVINE **SORCERER**

Prerequisites Divine Evolution or Primal Evolution

Vital power surges through you like a font of energy. Twice per day, you can cast a spell after you've run out of spell slots of the appropriate spell level; the two spells you cast with this feat must be of different spell levels.

18TH LEVEL

BLOODLINE WELLSPRING — FEAT 18

SORCERER

Prerequisites Bloodline Focus

Your blood's power replenishes your focus. If you have spent at least 3 Focus Points since the last time you Refocused, you recover 3 Focus Points when you Refocus instead of 1.

GREATER CROSSBLOODED EVOLUTION — FEAT 18

SORCERER

Prerequisites Crossblooded Evolution

Your bloodline is extraordinarily complex. You can have up to three spells from other traditions in your spell repertoire, rather than just one. These spells must each be of a different spell level, but they don't need to be from the same tradition.

20TH LEVEL

BLOODLINE CONDUIT ◈ — FEAT 20

METAMAGIC **SORCERER**

Frequency once per minute

Your inborn magical nature lets you redirect ambient energies to fuel your spells. If your next action is to Cast a Spell of 5th level or lower that has no duration, you don't expend the spell's slot when you cast it.

BLOODLINE PERFECTION — FEAT 20

SORCERER

Prerequisites bloodline paragon

You command the ultimate powers of your bloodline and tradition. You gain an additional 10th-level spell slot.

METAMAGIC MASTERY — FEAT 20

SORCERER

Altering your spells doesn't take any longer than casting them normally. You can use metamagic single actions as free actions..

INTRODUCTION

ANCESTRIES &
BACKGROUNDS

CLASSES

SKILLS

FEATS

EQUIPMENT

SPELLS

THE AGE OF
LOST OMENS

PLAYING THE
GAME

GAME
MASTERING

CRAFTING
& TREASURE

APPENDIX

WIZARD

You are an eternal student of the arcane secrets of the universe, using your mastery of magic to cast powerful and devastating spells. You treat magic like a science, cross-referencing the latest texts on practical spellcraft with ancient esoteric tomes to discover and understand how magic works. Yet magical theory is vast, and there's no way you can study it all. You either specialize in one of the eight schools of magic, gaining deeper understanding of the nuances of those spells above all others, or favor a broader approach that emphasizes the way all magic comes together at the expense of depth.

KEY ABILITY

INTELLIGENCE
At 1st level, your class gives you an ability boost to Intelligence.

HIT POINTS

6 plus your Constitution modifier
You increase your maximum number of HP by this number at 1st level and every level thereafter.

DURING COMBAT ENCOUNTERS...

You likely try to stay out of the fray, carefully judging when to use your spells. You save your most powerful magic to incapacitate threatening foes and use your cantrips when only weaker foes remain. When enemies pull out tricks like invisibility or flight, you answer with spells like *glitterdust* or *earth bind*, leveling the field for your allies.

DURING SOCIAL ENCOUNTERS...

You provide a well of knowledge about arcane matters and solve arguments with logic.

WHILE EXPLORING...

You locate magical auras and determine the arcane significance of magical writing or phenomena you uncover. When you run across an unusual obstacle to further exploration, you probably have a scroll that will make it easier to overcome.

IN DOWNTIME...

You learn new spells, craft magic items, or scribe scrolls for your party, and seek out new and exciting formulas in addition to spells. You might even forge scholarly connections and establish a school or guild of your own.

YOU MIGHT...

- Have an unquenchable intellectual curiosity about how everything in the world around you works—magic in particular.
- Believe fervently that your school of magic is superior (if you're a specialist) or that true mastery of magic requires knowledge of all schools (if you're a universalist).
- Use esoteric jargon and technical terms to precisely describe the minutiae of magical effects, even though the difference is probably lost on other people.

OTHERS PROBABLY...

- Consider you to be incredibly powerful and potentially dangerous.
- Fear what your magic can do to their minds, bodies, and souls, and ask that you avoid casting spells in polite company, as few can identify whether one of your spells is harmless or malevolent until it's too late.
- Assume you can easily solve all their problems, from dangerous weather to poor crop yields, and ask you for spells that can help them get whatever they desire.

INITIAL PROFICIENCIES

At 1st level, you gain the listed proficiency ranks in the following statistics. You are untrained in anything not listed unless you gain a better proficiency rank in some other way.

PERCEPTION

Trained in Perception

SAVING THROWS

Trained in Fortitude
Trained in Reflex
Expert in Will

SKILLS

Trained in Arcana
Trained in a number of additional skills equal to 2 plus your Intelligence modifier

ATTACKS

Trained in the club, crossbow, dagger, heavy crossbow, and staff
Trained in unarmed attacks

DEFENSES

Untrained in all armor
Trained in unarmored defense

SPELLS

Trained in arcane spell attacks
Trained in arcane spell DCs

TABLE 3-18: WIZARD ADVANCEMENT

Your Level	Class Features
1	Ancestry and background, initial proficiencies, arcane spellcasting, arcane school, arcane bond, arcane thesis, wizard feat
2	Skill feat, wizard feat
3	2nd-level spells, general feat, skill increase
4	Skill feat, wizard feat
5	3rd-level spells, ability boosts, ancestry feat, lightning reflexes, skill increase
6	Skill feat, wizard feat
7	4th-level spells, expert spellcaster, general feat, skill increase
8	Skill feat, wizard feat
9	5th-level spells, ancestry feat, magical fortitude, skill increase
10	Ability boosts, skill feat, wizard feat
11	6th-level spells, alertness, general feat, skill increase, wizard weapon expertise
12	Skill feat, wizard feat
13	7th-level spells, ancestry feat, defensive robes, skill increase, weapon specialization
14	Skill feat, wizard feat
15	8th-level spells, ability boosts, general feat, master spellcaster, skill increase
16	Skill feat, wizard feat
17	9th-level spells, ancestry feat, resolve, skill increase
18	Skill feat, wizard feat
19	Archwizard's spellcraft, legendary archwizard, general feat, skill increase
20	Ability boosts, skill feat, wizard feat

CLASS FEATURES

You gain these abilities as a wizard. Abilities gained at higher levels list the levels next to their names.

ANCESTRY AND BACKGROUND

In addition to the abilities provided by your class at 1st level, you have the benefits of your selected ancestry and background, as described in Chapter 2.

INITIAL PROFICIENCIES

At 1st level, you gain a number of proficiencies that represent your basic training. These proficiencies are noted at the start of this class.

ARCANE SPELLCASTING

Through dedicated study and practice, you can harness arcane power to cast spells. You can cast arcane spells using the Cast a Spell activity, and you can supply material, somatic, and verbal components when casting spells (see Casting Spells on page 302).

At 1st level, you can prepare up to two 1st-level spells and five cantrips each morning from the spells in your spellbook (see below), plus one extra cantrip and spell of your chosen school of each level you can cast if you are a specialist wizard. Prepared spells remain available to you until you cast them or until you prepare your spells again. The number of spells you can prepare is called your spell slots.

As you increase in level as a wizard, your number of spell slots and the highest level of spells you can cast from spell slots increase, shown in Table 3-19: Wizard Spells per Day on page 205.

Some of your spells require you to attempt a spell attack roll to see how effective they are, or have your enemies roll against your spell DC (typically by attempting a saving throw). Since your key ability is Intelligence, your spell attack rolls and spell DCs use your Intelligence modifier. Details on calculating these statistics appear on page 447.

HEIGHTENING SPELLS

When you get spell slots of 2nd level and higher, you can fill those slots with stronger versions of lower-level spells. This increases the spell's level, heightening it to match the spell slot. Many spells have specific improvements when they are heightened to certain levels.

CANTRIPS

A cantrip is a special type of spell that doesn't use spell slots. You can cast a cantrip at will, any number of times per day. A cantrip is always automatically heightened to half your level rounded up—this is usually equal to the highest level of spell you can cast as a wizard. For example, as a 1st-level wizard, your cantrips are 1st-level spells, and as a 5th-level wizard, your cantrips are 3rd-level spells.

SPELLBOOK

Every arcane spell has a written version, usually recorded in a spellbook. You start with a spellbook worth 10 sp or less (as detailed on page 291), which you receive for free and must study to prepare your spells each day. The spellbook contains your choice of 10 arcane cantrips and five 1st-level arcane spells. You choose these from the common spells on the arcane spell list from this book (page 307) or from other arcane spells you gain access to. Your spellbook's form and name are up to you. It might be a musty, leather-bound tome or an assortment of thin metal disks connected to a brass ring; its name might be esoteric, like *The Crimson Libram*, or something more academic, like *A Field Study in Practical Transmutation*.

Each time you gain a level, you add two more arcane spells to your spellbook, of any level of spell you can cast. You can also use the Arcana skill to add other spells that you find in your adventures, as described on page 241.

ARCANE SCHOOL

Many arcane spellcasters delve deeply into a single school of magic in an attempt to master its secrets. If you want to be a specialist wizard, choose a school in which to specialize.

TABLE 3-19: WIZARD SPELLS PER DAY

Your Level	Cantrips	Spell Level									
		1st	2nd	3rd	4th	5th	6th	7th	8th	9th	10th
1	5	2	–	–	–	–	–	–	–	–	–
2	5	3	–	–	–	–	–	–	–	–	–
3	5	3	2	–	–	–	–	–	–	–	–
4	5	3	3	–	–	–	–	–	–	–	–
5	5	3	3	2	–	–	–	–	–	–	–
6	5	3	3	3	–	–	–	–	–	–	–
7	5	3	3	3	2	–	–	–	–	–	–
8	5	3	3	3	3	–	–	–	–	–	–
9	5	3	3	3	3	2	–	–	–	–	–
10	5	3	3	3	3	3	–	–	–	–	–
11	5	3	3	3	3	3	2	–	–	–	–
12	5	3	3	3	3	3	3	–	–	–	–
13	5	3	3	3	3	3	3	2	–	–	–
14	5	3	3	3	3	3	3	3	–	–	–
15	5	3	3	3	3	3	3	3	2	–	–
16	5	3	3	3	3	3	3	3	3	–	–
17	5	3	3	3	3	3	3	3	3	2	–
18	5	3	3	3	3	3	3	3	3	3	–
19	5	3	3	3	3	3	3	3	3	3	1*
20	5	3	3	3	3	3	3	3	3	3	1*

* The archwizard's spellcraft class feature gives you a 10th-level spell slot that works a bit differently from other spell slots.

You gain additional spells and spell slots for spells of your school. Arcane schools are described in detail on page 207.

If you don't choose a school, you're a universalist, a wizard who believes that the path to true knowledge of magic requires a multidisciplinary understanding of all eight schools working together. Though a universalist lacks the focus of a specialist wizard, they have greater flexibility. Universalist wizards are described on page 209.

ARCANE BOND

You place some of your magical power in a bonded item. Each day when you prepare your spells, you can designate a single item you own as your bonded item. This is typically an item associated with spellcasting, such as a wand, ring, or staff, but you are free to designate a weapon or other item. You gain the Drain Bonded Item free action.

DRAIN BONDED ITEM ◆

ARCANE WIZARD

Frequency once per day
Requirements You haven't acted yet on your turn.

You expend the power stored in your bonded item. During your turn, you gain the ability to cast one spell you prepared today and already cast, without spending a spell slot. You must still Cast the Spell and meet the spell's other requirements.

ARCANE THESIS

During your studies to become a full-fledged wizard, you produced a thesis of unique magical research on one of a variety of topics. You gain a special benefit depending on the topic of your thesis research. The arcane thesis topics presented in this book are below; your specific thesis probably has a much longer and more technical title like "On the Methods of Spell Interpolation and the Genesis of a New Understanding of the Building Blocks of Magic."

IMPROVED FAMILIAR ATTUNEMENT

You've long held that fine-tuning the magic that bonds wizard and familiar can improve the mystic connection, compared to the safe yet generic bond most wizards currently use. You've formed such a pact with your familiar, gaining more advantages from it than most wizards. You gain the Familiar wizard feat as a bonus feat. Your familiar gains an extra ability, and it gains an additional extra ability when you reach 6th, 12th, and 18th levels.

Your connection with your familiar alters your arcane bond class feature so that you store your magical energy in your familiar, rather than an item you own; you also gain the Drain Familiar free action instead of Drain Bonded Item. Drain Familiar can be used any time an ability would allow you to use Drain Bonded Item and functions identically, except that you draw magic from your familiar instead of an item.

METAMAGICAL EXPERIMENTATION

You've realized that the practice known as metamagic is a holdover from a time long ago, when wizards had to work out their own spells and variations rather than rely on spells recorded by others and passed down over the years. This allows you efficient access to various metamagic effects.

INTRODUCTION

ANCESTRIES & BACKGROUNDS

CLASSES

SKILLS

FEATS

EQUIPMENT

SPELLS

THE AGE OF LOST OMENS

PLAYING THE GAME

GAME MASTERING

CRAFTING & TREASURE

APPENDIX

SAMPLE SPELLBOOK

You can fill your spellbook with whichever spells you like, but the list below covers a good selection of starter spells for a 1st-level wizard. These are the exact spells found in *Structure and Interpretation of Arcane Magic*, a basic spellbook used by arcane academies and master wizards to teach apprentices good habits in arcane research.

Cantrips: *Acid splash, detect magic, electric arc, light, mage hand, message, prestidigitation, ray of frost, shield,* and *study aura.*

1st Level: *Burning hands, color spray, grease, mage armor,* and *magic missile,* plus one spell of your school if you're a specialist wizard.

You gain a 1st-level metamagic wizard feat as a bonus feat. Starting at 4th level, during your daily preparations, you can gain a metamagic wizard feat of your choice that has a level requirement of no more than half your level, which you can use until your next daily preparations.

Spell Blending

You theorize that spell slots are a shorthand for an underlying energy that powers all spellcasting, and you've found a way to tinker with the hierarchy of spell slots, combining them to fuel more powerful spells.

When you make your daily preparations, you can trade two spell slots of the same level for a bonus spell slot of up to 2 levels higher than the traded spell slots. You can exchange as many spell slots as you have available. Bonus spell slots must be of a level you can normally cast, and each bonus spell slot must be of a different spell level. You can also trade any spell slot for two additional cantrips, though you cannot trade more than one spell slot at a time for additional cantrips in this way.

Spell Substitution

You don't accept the fact that once spells are prepared, they can't be changed until your next daily preparation, and you have uncovered a shortcut allowing you to substitute new spells for those you originally prepared.

You can spend 10 minutes to empty one of your prepared spell slots and prepare a different spell from your spellbook in its place. If you are interrupted during such a swap, the original spell remains prepared and can still be cast. You can try again to swap out the spell later, but you must start the process over again.

WIZARD FEATS

At 1st level and every even-numbered level thereafter, you gain a wizard class feat. These feats begin on page 209.

SKILL FEATS   2ND

At 2nd level and every 2 levels thereafter, you gain a skill feat. Skill feats can be found in Chapter 5 and have the skill trait. You must be trained or better in the corresponding skill to select a skill feat.

GENERAL FEATS   3RD

At 3rd level and every 4 levels thereafter, you gain a general feat. General feats are listed in Chapter 5.

SKILL INCREASES   3RD

At 3rd level and every 2 levels thereafter, you gain a skill increase. You can use this increase either to increase your proficiency rank to trained in one skill you're untrained in, or to increase your proficiency rank in one skill in which you're already trained to expert.

At 7th level, you can use skill increases to increase your proficiency rank to master in a skill in which you're already an expert, and at 15th level, you can use them to increase your proficiency rank to legendary in a skill in which you're already a master.

ABILITY BOOSTS   5TH

At 5th level and every 5 levels thereafter, you boost four different ability scores. You can use these ability boosts to increase your ability scores above 18. Boosting an ability score increases it by 1 if it's already 18 or above, or by 2 if it starts out below 18.

ANCESTRY FEATS   5TH

In addition to the ancestry feat you started with, you gain an ancestry feat at 5th level and every 4 levels thereafter. The list of ancestry feats available to you can be found in your ancestry's entry in Chapter 2.

LIGHTNING REFLEXES   5TH

Your reflexes are lightning fast. Your proficiency rank for Reflex saves increases to expert.

EXPERT SPELLCASTER   7TH

Extended practice of the arcane has improved your capabilities. Your proficiency ranks for arcane spell attack rolls and spell DCs increase to expert.

MAGICAL FORTITUDE   9TH

Magical power has improved your body's resiliency. Your proficiency rank for Fortitude saves increases to expert.

ALERTNESS   11TH

You remain alert to threats around you. Your proficiency rank for Perception increases to expert.

WIZARD WEAPON EXPERTISE   11TH

Through a combination of magic and training, you've learned how to wield wizard weapons more effectively. You gain expert proficiency in the club, crossbow, dagger, heavy crossbow, and staff.

DEFENSIVE ROBES   13TH

The flow of magic and your training combine to help you avoid attacks. Your proficiency rank in unarmored defense increases to expert.

WEAPON SPECIALIZATION   13TH

You've learned how to inflict greater injuries with the weapons you know best. You deal an additional 2 damage with weapons and unarmed attacks in which you are an expert. This damage increases to 3 if you're a master, and 4 if you're legendary.

MASTER SPELLCASTER   15TH

You command superlative spellcasting ability. Your proficiency ranks for arcane spell attack rolls and spell DCs increase to master.

RESOLVE   17TH

You've steeled your mind with resolve. Your proficiency rank for Will saves increases to master. When you roll a success at a Will save, you get a critical success instead.

ARCHWIZARD'S SPELLCRAFT   19TH

You command the most potent arcane magic and can cast a spell of truly incredible power. You gain a single 10th-level spell slot and can prepare a spell in that slot using arcane spellcasting. Unlike with other spell slots, you don't gain more 10th-level spells as you level up, though you can take the Archwizard's Might feat to gain a second slot.

LEGENDARY SPELLCASTER   19TH

You are a consummate spellcaster, with a comprehensive understanding of both arcane theory and practical spellcraft. Your proficiency ranks for arcane spell attack rolls and spell DCs increase to legendary.

ARCANE SCHOOLS

If you specialize in an arcane school, rather than studying each school equally (as universalists do), you gain an extra spell slot for each level of spell you can cast. You can prepare only spells of your chosen arcane school in these extra slots. In addition, you can prepare an extra cantrip of your chosen school. You also add another arcane spell of your chosen school to your spellbook.

You learn a school spell, a special type of spell taught to students of your arcane school. School spells are a type of focus spell. It costs 1 Focus Point to cast a focus spell, and you start with a focus pool of 1 Focus Point. You refill your focus pool during your daily preparations, and you can regain 1 Focus Point by spending 10 minutes using the Refocus activity to study your spellbook or perform arcane research.

Focus spells are automatically heightened to half your level rounded up. Focus spells don't require spell slots, nor can you cast them using spell slots. Certain feats can give you more focus spells and increase the size of your focus pool, though your focus pool can never hold more than 3 Focus Points. The full rules for focus spells appear on page 300.

ABJURATION

As an abjurer, you master the art of protection, strengthening defenses, preventing attacks, and even turning magic against itself. You understand that an ounce of prevention is worth a pound of cure. You add one 1st-level abjuration spell (such as *feather fall*) to your spellbook. You learn the *protective ward* school spell (page 407).

CONJURATION

As a conjurer, you summon creatures and objects from places beyond, and use magic to transport to distant locales.

CONJURER

Your magic summons creatures, transports you, and creates useful items. You know about odd creatures and distant realms.

ABILITY SCORES
Prioritize Intelligence. Dexterity, Constitution, and Wisdom round out your defenses.

SKILLS
Arcana, Crafting, Diplomacy, Nature, Occultism, Religion, Society

SPECIALIZATION
Conjuration

THESIS
Improved Familiar Attunement

HIGHER-LEVEL FEATS
Enhanced Familiar (2nd), Advanced School Spell (8th), Effortless Concentration (16th)

You understand that the true key to victory is strength in numbers. You add one 1st-level conjuration spell (such as *summon animal*) to your spellbook. You learn the *augment summoning* school spell (page 406).

DIVINATION
As a diviner, you master remote viewing and prescience, learning information that can transform investigations, research, and battle strategies. You understand that knowledge is power. You add one 1st-level divination spell (such as *true strike*) to your spellbook. You learn the *diviner's sight* school spell (page 406).

ENCHANTMENT
As an enchanter, you use magic to manipulate others' minds. You might use your abilities to subtly influence others or seize control over them. You understand that the mind surpasses matter. You add one 1st-level enchantment spell (such as *charm*) to your spellbook. You learn the *charming words* school spell (page 406).

EVOCATION
As an evoker, you revel in the raw power of magic, using it to create and destroy with ease. You can call forth elements, forces, and energy to devastate your foes or to assist you in other ways. You understand that the most direct approach is the most elegant. You add one 1st-level evocation spell (such as *shocking grasp*) to your spellbook. You learn the *force bolt* school spell (page 407).

ILLUSION
As an illusionist, you use magic to create images, figments, and phantasms to baffle your enemies. You understand that perception is reality. You add one 1st-level illusion spell (such as *illusory object*) to your spellbook. You learn the *warped terrain* school spell (page 407).

NECROMANCY
As a necromancer, you call upon the powers of life and death. While your school is often vilified for its association with raising the undead, you understand that control over life also means control over healing. You add one 1st-level necromancy spell (such as *grim tendrils*) to your spellbook. You learn the *call of the grave* school spell (page 406).

TRANSMUTATION
As a transmuter, you alter the physical properties of things, transforming creatures, objects, the natural world, and even yourself at your whim. You understand that change is inevitable. You add one 1st-level transmutation spell (such as *magic weapon*) to your spellbook. You learn the *physical boost* school spell (page 407).

INTRODUCTION

ANCESTRIES &
BACKGROUNDS

CLASSES

SKILLS

FEATS

EQUIPMENT

SPELLS

THE AGE OF
LOST OMENS

PLAYING THE
GAME

GAME
MASTERING

CRAFTING
& TREASURE

APPENDIX

UNIVERSALIST WIZARDS

Instead of specializing narrowly in an arcane school, you can become a universalist wizard—by studying all the schools equally, you devote yourself to understanding the full breadth of the arcane arts. For each level of spell you can cast, you can use Drain Bonded item once per day to recall a spell of that level (instead of using it only once per day in total). You gain an extra wizard class feat, and you add one 1st-level spell of your choice to your spellbook.

WIZARD FEATS

At each level that you gain a wizard feat, you can select one of the following feats. You must satisfy any prerequisites before taking the feat.

1ST LEVEL

COUNTERSPELL ↻   FEAT 1

ABJURATION   **ARCANE**   **WIZARD**

Trigger A creature Casts a Spell that you have prepared.

When a foe Casts a Spell and you can see its manifestations, you can use your own magic to disrupt it. You expend a prepared spell to counter the triggering creature's casting of that same spell. You lose your spell slot as if you had cast the

triggering spell. You then attempt to counteract the triggering spell (page 458).

ESCHEW MATERIALS   FEAT 1

WIZARD

You can use clever workarounds to replicate the arcane essence of certain materials. When Casting a Spell that requires material components, you can provide these material components without a spell component pouch by drawing intricate replacement sigils in the air. Unlike when providing somatic components, you still must have a hand completely free. This doesn't remove the need for any materials listed in the spell's cost entry.

FAMILIAR   FEAT 1

WIZARD

You make a pact with creature that serves you and assists your spellcasting. You gain a familiar (page 217).

HAND OF THE APPRENTICE   FEAT 1

WIZARD

Prerequisites universalist wizard

You can magically hurl your weapon at your foe. You gain the *hand of the apprentice* universalist spell. Universalist spells are a type of focus spell, much like school spells. You start with a focus pool of 1 Focus Point. See Arcane Schools on page 207 for more information about focus spells.

KEY TERM

You'll see the following key term in many wizard abilities.

Metamagic: Actions with the metamagic trait tweak the properties of your spells. These actions usually come from metamagic feats. You must use a metamagic action directly before Casting the Spell you want to alter. If you use any action (including free actions and reactions) other than Cast a Spell directly after, you waste the benefits of the metamagic action. Any additional effects added by a metamagic action are part of the spell's effect, not of the metamagic action itself.

REACH SPELL ◆   FEAT 1

CONCENTRATE   METAMAGIC   WIZARD

You can extend the range of your spells. If the next action you use is to Cast a Spell that has a range, increase that spell's range by 30 feet. As is standard for increasing spell ranges, if the spell normally has a range of touch, you extend its range to 30 feet.

WIDEN SPELL ◆   FEAT 1

MANIPULATE   METAMAGIC   WIZARD

You manipulate the energy of your spell, causing it to affect a wider area. If the next action you use is to Cast a Spell that has an area of a burst, cone, or line and does not have a duration, increase the area of that spell. Add 5 feet to the radius of a burst that normally has a radius of at least 10 feet (a burst with a smaller radius is not affected). Add 5 feet to the length of a cone or line that is normally 15 feet long or smaller, and add 10 feet to the length of a larger cone or line.

2ND LEVEL

CANTRIP EXPANSION   FEAT 2

WIZARD

Dedicated study allows you to prepare a wider range of simple spells. You can prepare two additional cantrips each day.

CONCEAL SPELL ◆   FEAT 2

CONCENTRATE   MANIPULATE   METAMAGIC   WIZARD

Hiding your gestures and incantations within other speech and movement, you attempt to conceal the fact that you are Casting a Spell. If the next action you use is to Cast a Spell, attempt a Stealth check against one or more observers' Perception DCs; if the spell has verbal components, you must also attempt a Deception check against the observers' Perception DC. If you succeed at your check (or checks) against an observer's DC, that observer doesn't notice you're casting a spell, even though material, somatic, and verbal components are usually noticeable and spells normally have sensory manifestations that would make spellcasting obvious to those nearby.

This ability hides only the spell's spellcasting actions and manifestations, not its effects, so an observer might still see a ray streak out from you or see you vanish into thin air.

ENHANCED FAMILIAR   FEAT 2

WIZARD

Prerequisites a familiar

You infuse your familiar with additional magical energy. You can select four familiar or master abilities each day, instead of two.

Special If your arcane thesis is improved familiar attunement, your familiar's base number of familiar abilities, before adding any extra abilities from the arcane thesis, is four.

4TH LEVEL

BESPELL WEAPON ◈   FEAT 4

WIZARD

Frequency once per turn

Requirements Your most recent action was to cast a non-cantrip spell.

You siphon spell energy into one weapon you're wielding. Until the end of your turn, the weapon deals an extra 1d6 damage of a type depending on the school of the spell you just cast.

- **Abjuration** force damage
- **Conjuration or Transmutation** the same type as the weapon
- **Divination, Enchantment, or Illusion** mental damage
- **Evocation** a type the spell dealt, or force damage if the spell didn't deal damage
- **Necromancy** negative damage

LINKED FOCUS   FEAT 4

WIZARD

Prerequisites arcane bond, arcane school

Frequency once per day

You have linked your bonded item to the well of energy that powers your school spells. When you Drain your Bonded Item to cast a spell of your arcane school, you also regain 1 Focus Point.

SILENT SPELL ◆   FEAT 4

CONCENTRATE   METAMAGIC   WIZARD

Prerequisites Conceal Spell

You've learned how to cast many of your spells without speaking the words of power you would normally need to provide. If the next action you use is Casting a Spell that has a verbal component and at least one other component, you can remove the verbal component. This makes the spell quieter and allows you to cast it in areas where sound can't carry. However, the spell still has visual manifestations, so this doesn't make the spell any less obvious to someone who sees you casting it. When you use Silent Spell, you can choose to gain the benefits of Conceal Spell, and you don't need to attempt a Deception check because the spell has no verbal components.

6TH LEVEL

SPELL PENETRATION   FEAT 6

WIZARD

You've studied ways of overcoming the innate magical resistance that dragons, otherworldly beings, and certain

other powerful creatures have. Any creature that has a status bonus to saving throws against magic reduces that bonus by 1 against your spells.

STEADY SPELLCASTING — FEAT 6

WIZARD

Confident in your technique, you don't easily lose your concentration when you Cast a Spell. If a reaction would disrupt your spellcasting action, attempt a DC 15 flat check. If you succeed, your action isn't disrupted.

8TH LEVEL

ADVANCED SCHOOL SPELL — FEAT 8

WIZARD

Prerequisites arcane school

You gain access to a powerful new school spell depending on your arcane school. If you're an abjurer, you gain *energy absorption*; if you're a conjurer, you gain *dimensional steps*; if you're a diviner, you gain *vigilant eye*; if you're an enchanter, you gain *dread aura*; if you're an evoker, you gain *elemental tempest*; if you're an illusionist, you gain *invisibility cloak*; if you're a necromancer, you gain *life siphon*; and if you're a transmuter, you gain *shifting form*. The descriptions of these spells are on pages 406–407. Increase the number of Focus Points in your focus pool by 1.

BOND CONSERVATION ◆❖ — FEAT 8

MANIPULATE **METAMAGIC** **WIZARD**

Prerequisites arcane bond
Requirements The last action you used was Drain Bonded Item.

By carefully manipulating the arcane energies stored in your bonded item as you drain it, you can conserve just enough power to cast another, slightly weaker spell. If the next action you use is to Cast a Spell using the energy from Drain Bonded Item, you gain an extra use of Drain Bonded Item. You must use this extra use of Drain Bonded Item before the end of your next turn or you lose it, and you can use this additional use only to cast a spell 2 or more levels lower than the first spell cast with Drain Bonded Item.

UNIVERSAL VERSATILITY — FEAT 8

WIZARD

Prerequisites universalist wizard, Hand of the Apprentice

You can access the fundamental abilities of any school of magic. During your daily preparations, choose one of the eight school spells gained by 1st-level specialist wizards. You can use that school spell until your next daily preparations. When you Refocus, you can choose a different school spell from among those eight school spells, replacing the previous one. Increase the number of Focus Points in your focus pool by 1.

10TH LEVEL

OVERWHELMING ENERGY ◆❖ — FEAT 10

MANIPULATE **METAMAGIC** **WIZARD**

With a complex gesture, you alter the energy of your spell to overcome resistances. If the next action you use is to Cast a Spell, the spell ignores an amount of the target's resistance to acid, cold, electricity, fire, or sonic damage equal to your level. This applies to all damage the spell deals, including persistent damage and damage caused by an ongoing effect of the spell, such as the wall created by *wall of fire*. A creature's immunities are unaffected.

QUICKENED CASTING ◆❖ — FEAT 10

CONCENTRATE **METAMAGIC** **WIZARD**

Frequency once per day

In a mentally strenuous process, you modify your casting of a spell to take less time. If your next action is to cast a wizard cantrip or a wizard spell that is at least 2 levels lower

CLASSES

3

INTRODUCTION

ANCESTRIES & BACKGROUNDS

CLASSES

SKILLS

FEATS

EQUIPMENT

SPELLS

THE AGE OF LOST OMENS

PLAYING THE GAME

GAME MASTERING

CRAFTING & TREASURE

APPENDIX

WIZARD FEATS

If you need to look up a wizard feat by name instead of by level, use this table.

Feat	Level
Advanced School Spell	8
Archwizard's Might	20
Bespell Weapon	4
Bond Conservation	8
Bonded Focus	14
Cantrip Expansion	2
Clever Counterspell	12
Conceal Spell	2
Counterspell	1
Effortless Concentration	16
Enhanced Familiar	2
Eschew Materials	1
Familiar	1
Hand of the Apprentice	1
Infinite Possibilities	18
Linked Focus	4
Magic Sense	12
Metamagic Mastery	20
Overwhelming Energy	10
Quickened Casting	10
Reach Spell	1
Reflect Spell	14
Reprepare Spell	18
Scroll Savant	10
Silent Spell	4
Spell Combination	20
Spell Penetration	6
Spell Tinker	16
Steady Spellcasting	6
Superior Bond	14
Universal Versatility	8
Widen Spell	1

SAMPLE WIZARD

ILLUSIONIST

You cast illusory spells that fool the senses, and you excel at bypassing threats without violence.

ABILITY SCORES
Prioritize Intelligence. Increase Dexterity and Charisma so you can sneak and deceive people with skills as well as spells.

SKILLS
Arcana, Deception, Diplomacy, Occultism, Society, Stealth, Thievery

SPECIALIZATION
Illusion

THESIS
Spell blending

HIGHER-LEVEL FEATS
Conceal Spell (2nd), Silent Spell (4th), Advanced School Spell (8th), Magic Sense (12th)

---

than the highest-level wizard spell you can cast, reduce the number of actions to cast it by 1 (minimum 1 action).

SCROLL SAVANT   FEAT 10

WIZARD

Prerequisites expert in Crafting

During your daily preparations, you can create two temporary scrolls containing arcane spells from your spellbook. These scrolls follow the normal rules for scrolls (page 564), with some additional restrictions. Each scroll must be of a different spell level, and both spell levels must be 2 or more levels lower than your highest-level spell. Any scrolls you create this way become non-magical the next time you make your daily preparations. A temporary scroll has no value.

   If you have master proficiency in arcane spell DCs, you can create three temporary scrolls during your daily preparations, and if you have legendary proficiency, you can create four temporary scrolls.

12TH LEVEL

CLEVER COUNTERSPELL   FEAT 12

WIZARD

Prerequisites Counterspell, Quick Recognize

You creatively apply your prepared spells to Counterspell a much wider variety of your opponents' magic. Instead of being able to counter a foe's spell with Counterspell only if you have that same spell prepared, you can use Counterspell as long as you have the spell the foe is casting in your spellbook. When you use Counterspell in this way, the prepared spell you expend must share a trait other than its tradition with the triggering spell. At the GM's discretion, you can instead use a spell that has an opposing trait or that otherwise logically would counter the triggering spell (such as using a cold or water spell to counter *fireball* or using *remove fear* to counter a fear spell). Regardless of what spell you expend, you take a –2 penalty to your counteract check, though the GM can waive this penalty if the expended spell is especially appropriate.

MAGIC SENSE   FEAT 12

ARCANE   DETECTION   DIVINATION   WIZARD

You have a literal sixth sense for ambient magic in your vicinity. You can sense the presence of magic auras as though you were always using a 1st-level *detect magic* spell. This detects magic in your field of vision only. When you Seek, you gain the benefits of a 3rd-level *detect magic* spell on things you see (in addition to the normal benefits of Seeking). You can turn this sense off and on with a free action at the start or the end of your turn.

14TH LEVEL

BONDED FOCUS   FEAT 14

WIZARD

Prerequisites arcane bond

Your connection to your bonded item increases your focus pool. If you have spent at least 2 Focus Points since the last time you Refocused and your bonded item is in your possession, you recover 2 Focus Points when you Refocus instead of 1.

REFLECT SPELL   FEAT 14

WIZARD

Prerequisites Counterspell

When you successfully use Counterspell to counteract a spell that affects targeted creatures or an area, you can turn that spell's effect back on its caster. When reflected, the spell affects only the original caster, even if it's an area spell or it would normally affect more than one creature. The original caster can attempt a save and use other defenses against the reflected spell as normal.

SUPERIOR BOND   FEAT 14

WIZARD

Prerequisites arcane bond

When you draw upon your bonded item, you can leave a bit of energy within it for later use. You can use Drain Bonded Item one additional time per day, but only to cast a spell 2 or more levels lower than your highest-level spell.

16TH LEVEL

EFFORTLESS CONCENTRATION ◆   FEAT 16

WIZARD

Trigger Your turn begins.

You maintain a spell with hardly a thought. You immediately gain the effects of the Sustain a Spell action, allowing you to extend the duration of one of your active wizard spells.

SPELL TINKER ◆◆   FEAT 16

CONCENTRATE   WIZARD

You've learned to alter choices you make when casting spells on yourself. After casting a spell on only yourself that offers several choices of effect (such as *resist energy*, *spell immunity*, or a polymorph spell that offers several potential forms), you can alter the choice you made when Casting the Spell (for instance, choosing a different type of damage for *resist energy*). However, your tinkering weakens the spell's integrity, reducing its remaining duration by half.

You can't use this feat if the benefits of the spell have already been used up or if the effects of the first choice would persist in any way after switching (for instance, if one of the choices was to create a consumable item you already used, or to heal you), or if the feat would create an effect more powerful than that offered by the base spell. The GM is the final arbiter of what Spell Tinker can be applied to.

18TH LEVEL

INFINITE POSSIBILITIES   FEAT 18

WIZARD

You've found a way to prepare a spell slot that exists in your mind as many different possibilities at once. Once during your daily preparations, you can use a spell slot to hold that infinite potential, rather than using it to prepare a spell. You can use this

spell slot to cast any spell from your spellbook that's at least 2 levels lower than the slot you designate; the spell acts in all ways as a spell of 2 levels lower. You don't have any particular spell prepared in that slot until you cast it.

REPREPARE SPELL   FEAT 18

WIZARD

You've discovered how to reuse some of your spell slots over and over. You can spend 10 minutes to prepare a spell that you already cast today, regaining access to that spell slot. The spell must be of 4th level or lower and one that does not have a duration. You can reprepare a spell in this way even if you've already reprepared that spell previously in the same day.

If you have the spell substitution arcane thesis, you can instead prepare a different spell in an expended slot, as long as the new spell doesn't have a duration. Once you've reprepared a spell in that slot even once, you can use your arcane thesis to substitute only spells without durations into that spell slot.

20TH LEVEL

ARCHWIZARD'S MIGHT   FEAT 20

WIZARD

Prerequisites archwizard's spellcraft

You have mastered the greatest secrets of arcane magic. You gain an additional 10th-level spell slot.

METAMAGIC MASTERY   FEAT 20

WIZARD

Altering your spells doesn't take any longer than casting them normally. You can use metamagic single actions as free actions.

SPELL COMBINATION   FEAT 20

WIZARD

You can merge spells, producing multiple effects with a single casting. One slot of each level of spell you can cast, except 2nd level and 1st level, becomes a spell combination slot (this doesn't apply to cantrips). When you prepare your spells, you can fill a combination slot with a combination of two spells. Each spell in the combination must be 2 or more spell levels below the slot's level, and both must target only one creature or object or have the option to target only one creature or object. Each spell in the combination must also have the same means of determining whether it has an effect—both spells must require a ranged spell attack roll, require the same type of saving throw, or automatically affect the target.

When you cast a combined spell, it affects only one target, even if the component spells normally affect more than one. If any spell in the combination has further restrictions (such as targeting only living creatures), you must abide by all restrictions. The combined spell uses the shorter of the component spells' ranges. Resolve a combined spell as if were a single spell, but apply the effects of both component spells. For example, if the spell's target succeeded at the save against a combined spell, it would apply the success effect of each spell, and if it critically failed, it would apply the critical failure effect of both spells.

INTRODUCTION

ANCESTRIES &
BACKGROUNDS

CLASSES

SKILLS

FEATS

EQUIPMENT

SPELLS

THE AGE OF
LOST OMENS

PLAYING THE
GAME

GAME
MASTERING

CRAFTING
& TREASURE

APPENDIX

ANIMAL COMPANIONS AND FAMILIARS

Some adventurers travel with loyal allies known as animal companions and familiars. The former begin as young animals but acquire impressive physical abilities as you level up, while the latter share a magical bond with you.

ANIMAL COMPANIONS

An animal companion is a loyal comrade who follows your orders without you needing to use Handle an Animal on it. Your animal companion has the minion trait, and it gains 2 actions during your turn if you use the Command an Animal action to command it; this is in place of the usual effects of Command an Animal. If your companion dies, you can spend a week of downtime to replace it at no cost. You can have only one animal companion at a time.

RIDING ANIMAL COMPANIONS

You or an ally can ride your animal companion as long as it is at least one size larger than the rider. If it is carrying a rider, the animal companion can use only its land Speed, and it can't move and Support you on the same turn. However, if your companion has the mount special ability, it's especially suited for riding and ignores both of these restrictions.

YOUNG ANIMAL COMPANIONS

The following are the base statistics for a young animal companion, the first animal companion most characters get. You make adjustments to these statistics depending on the type of animal you choose. As you gain levels, you might make further adjustments as your companion becomes more powerful. Animal companions calculate their modifiers and DCs just as you do with one difference: the only item bonuses they can benefit from are to speed and AC (their maximum item bonus to AC is +2).

PROFICIENCIES

Your animal companion uses your level to determine its proficiency bonuses. It's trained in its unarmed attacks, unarmored defense, barding, all saving throws, Perception, Acrobatics, and Athletics. Animal companions can't use abilities that require greater Intelligence, such as Coerce or Decipher Writing, even if trained in the appropriate skill, unless they have a specialization that allows it.

ABILITY MODIFIERS

An animal companion begins with base ability modifiers of **Str** +2, **Dex** +2, **Con** +1, **Int** –4, **Wis** +1, **Cha** +0. Each type has its own strengths and increases two of these modifiers by 1 each. These increases are already calculated into the stat blocks in Companion Types below.

HIT POINTS

Your animal companion has ancestry Hit Points from its type, plus a number of Hit Points equal to 6 plus its Constitution modifier for each level you have.

MATURE ANIMAL COMPANIONS

To advance a young animal companion to a mature animal companion (usually a result of one of your class feat choices), increase its Strength, Dexterity, Constitution, and Wisdom modifiers by 1. Increase its unarmed attack damage from one die to two dice (for instance 1d8 to 2d8), and its proficiency rank for Perception and all saving throws to expert. Increase its proficiency ranks in Intimidation, Stealth, and Survival to trained, and if it was already trained in one of those skills from its type, increase its proficiency rank in that skill to expert. If your companion is Medium or smaller, it grows by one size.

NIMBLE ANIMAL COMPANIONS

To advance a mature animal companion to a nimble animal companion, increase its Dexterity modifier by 2 and its Strength, Constitution, and Wisdom modifiers by 1. It deals 2 additional damage with its unarmed attacks. Increase its proficiency ranks in Acrobatics and unarmored defense to expert. It also learns the advanced maneuver for its type. Its attacks become magical for the purpose of ignoring resistances.

SAVAGE ANIMAL COMPANIONS

To advance a mature animal companion to a savage animal companion, increase its Strength modifier by 2 and its Dexterity, Constitution, and Wisdom modifiers by 1. It deals 3 additional damage with its unarmed attacks. Increase its proficiency rank in Athletics to expert. It also learns the advanced maneuver for its type. If your companion is Medium or smaller, it grows by one size. Its attacks become magical for the purpose of ignoring resistances.

COMPANION TYPES

The species of animal you choose is called your companion's type. Each companion type has its own statistics. The Size entry indicates your companion's starting size as a young animal companion. Following the size entry are the companion's unarmed attacks, and then its ability modifiers. The Hit Points entry indicates the companion's ancestry Hit Points. The Skill entry indicates an additional trained skill your companion has. The Senses entry lists your companion's special senses. The Speed entry gives your companion's Speeds. The Special entry, if present, lists any other special abilities your companion has, for example whether it often serves as a mount and is particularly appropriate for mounted classes, such as the champion. The Support Benefit entry indicates a special benefit you gain by Commanding the Animal to use the Support action (see below). The Advanced Maneuver entry indicates a powerful new action your companion learns how to use if it becomes a nimble or savage animal companion.

SUPPORT ❖

Requirements The creature is an animal companion.

Your animal companion supports you. You gain the benefits listed in the companion type's Support Benefit entry. If the animal uses the Support action, the only other actions it can use on this turn are basic move actions to get into position to take advantage of the Support benefits; if it has already used any other action this turn, it can't Support you.

BADGER

Your companion is a badger, wolverine, or other big mustelid.
Size Small
Melee ❖ jaws, **Damage** 1d8 piercing
Melee ❖ claw (agile), **Damage** 1d6 slashing
Str +2, **Dex** +2, **Con** +2, **Int** −4, **Wis** +2, **Cha** +0
Hit Points 8
Skill Survival
Senses low-light vision, scent (imprecise, 30 feet)
Speed 25 feet, burrow 10 feet, climb 10 feet
Support Benefit Your badger digs around your foe's position, interfering with its footing. Until the start of your next turn, if you hit and deal damage to a creature your badger threatens, the target can't use a Step action (unless it can Step through difficult terrain) until it moves from its current position.
Advanced Maneuver Badger Rage

BADGER RAGE ❖

> CONCENTRATE EMOTION MENTAL

Requirements The badger isn't fatigued or raging.

The badger enters a state of pure rage that lasts for 1 minute, until there are no enemies it can perceive, or until it falls unconscious, whichever comes first. It can't voluntarily stop raging. While raging, the badger is affected in the following ways.

- It deals 4 additional damage with its bite attacks and 2 additional damage with its claw attacks.
- It takes a −1 penalty to AC.
- It can't use actions that have the concentrate trait unless they also have the rage trait. The animal companion can Seek even while raging.

After it has stopped raging, it can't use Badger Rage again for 1 minute.

BEAR

Your companion is a black, grizzly, polar, or other type of bear.
Size Small
Melee ❖ jaws, **Damage** 1d8 piercing
Melee ❖ claw (agile), **Damage** 1d6 slashing
Str +3, **Dex** +2, **Con** +2, **Int** −4, **Wis** +1, **Cha** +0
Hit Points 8
Skill Intimidation
Senses low-light vision, scent (imprecise, 30 feet)
Speed 35 feet

Support Benefit Your bear mauls your enemies when you create an opening. Until the start of your next turn, each time you hit a creature in the bear's reach with a Strike, the creature takes 1d8 slashing damage from the bear. If your bear is nimble or savage, the slashing damage increases to 2d8.
Advanced Maneuver Bear Hug

BEAR HUG ❖

Requirements The bear's last action was a successful claw Strike.

The bear makes another claw Strike against the same target. If this Strike hits, the target is also grabbed, as if the bear had successfully Grappled the target.

BIRD

Your companion is a bird of prey, such as an eagle, hawk, or owl.
Size Small
Melee ❖ jaws (finesse), **Damage** 1d6 piercing
Melee ❖ talon (agile, finesse), **Damage** 1d4 slashing
Str +2, **Dex** +3, **Con** +1, **Int** −4, **Wis** +2, **Cha** +0
Hit Points 4
Skill Stealth
Senses low-light vision
Speed 10 feet, fly 60 feet
Support Benefit The bird pecks at your foes' eyes when you create an opening. Until the start of your next turn, your Strikes that damage a creature that your bird threatens also deal 1d4 persistent bleed damage, and the target is dazzled until it removes the bleed damage. If your bird is nimble or savage, the persistent bleed damage increases to 2d4.
Advanced Maneuver Flyby Attack

FLYBY ATTACK ❖❖

The bird Flies and makes a talon Strike at any point along the way.

CAT

Your companion is a big cat, such as a leopard or tiger.
Size Small
Melee ❖ jaws (finesse), **Damage** 1d6 piercing
Melee ❖ claw (agile, finesse), **Damage** 1d4 slashing
Str +2, **Dex** +3, **Con** +1, **Int** −4, **Wis** +2, **Cha** +0
Hit Points 4
Skill Stealth
Senses low-light vision, scent (imprecise, 30 feet)
Speed 35 feet
Special Your cat deals 1d4 extra precision damage against flat-footed targets.
Support Benefit Your cat throws your enemies off-balance when you create an opening. Until the start of your next turn, your Strikes that deal damage to a creature that your cat threatens make the target flat-footed until the end of your next turn.
Advanced Maneuver Cat Pounce

CAT POUNCE ❖

> FLOURISH

The cat Strides and then Strikes. If it was undetected at the start of its Cat Pounce, it remains undetected until after the attack.

DROMAEOSAUR

Your companion is a dromaeosaur (also called a raptor), such as a velociraptor or deinonychus.

Size Small

Melee ❖ jaws (finesse); **Damage** 1d8 piercing

Melee ❖ talon (agile, finesse); **Damage** 1d6 slashing

Str +2, **Dex** +3, **Con** +2, **Int** −4, **Wis** +1, **Cha** +0

Hit Points 6

Skill Stealth

Senses low-light vision, scent (imprecise, 30 feet)

Speed 50 feet

Support Benefit Your raptor constantly darts into flanking position. Until the start of your next turn, it counts as being in its space or an empty space of your choice within 10 feet when determining whether you and your companion are flanking; you can choose a different space for each of your attacks).

Advanced Maneuver Darting Attack

DARTING ATTACK ❖

FLOURISH

The raptor Steps up to 10 feet and then Strikes, or Strikes and then Steps up to 10 feet.

HORSE

Your companion is a horse, pony, or similar equine.

Size Medium or Large

Melee ❖ hoof (agile), **Damage** 1d6 bludgeoning

Str +3, **Dex** +2, **Con** +2, **Int** −4, **Wis** +1, **Cha** +0

Hit Points 8

Skill Survival

Senses low-light vision, scent (imprecise, 30 feet)

Speed 40 feet

Special mount

Support Benefit Your horse adds momentum to your charge. Until the start of your next turn, if you moved at least 10 feet on the action before your attack, add a circumstance bonus to damage to that attack equal to twice the number of damage dice. If your weapon already has the jousting weapon trait, increase the trait's damage bonus by 2 per die instead.

Advanced Maneuver Gallop

GALLOP ❖❖

MOVE

The horse Strides twice at a +10-foot circumstance bonus to Speed.

SNAKE

Your companion is a constrictor snake, such as a boa or python.

Size Small

Melee ❖ jaws (finesse); **Damage** 1d8 piercing

Str +3, **Dex** +3, **Con** +1, **Int** −4, **Wis** +1, **Cha** +0

Hit Points 6

Skill Stealth

Senses low-light vision, scent (imprecise, 30 feet)

Speed 20 feet, climb 20 feet, swim 20 feet

Support Benefit Your snake holds your enemies with its coils, interfering with reactions. Until the start of your next turn, any creature your snake threatens can't use reactions triggered by your actions unless its level is higher than yours.

Advanced Maneuver Constrict

CONSTRICT ❖

Requirements The snake has a smaller creature grabbed.

The snake deals 12 bludgeoning damage to the grabbed creature; the creature must attempt a basic Fortitude save. If the snake is a specialized animal companion, increase this damage to 20.

WOLF

Your companion is a wolf or other canine creature, such as a dog.

Size Small

❖ **Melee** jaws (finesse); **Damage** 1d8 piercing

Str +2, **Dex** +3, **Con** +2, **Int** −4, **Wis** +1, **Cha** +0

Hit Points 6

Skill Survival

Senses low-light vision, scent (imprecise, 30 feet)

Speed 40 feet

Support Benefit Your wolf tears tendons with each opening. Until the start of your next turn, your Strikes that damage creatures your wolf threatens give the target a −5-foot status penalty to its Speeds for 1 minute (−10 on a critical success).

CLASSES

3

INTRODUCTION

ANCESTRIES &
BACKGROUNDS

CLASSES

SKILLS

FEATS

EQUIPMENT

SPELLS

THE AGE OF
LOST OMENS

PLAYING THE
GAME

GAME
MASTERING

CRAFTING
& TREASURE

APPENDIX

Advanced Maneuver Knockdown

KNOCKDOWN ❖

Requirements The animal companion's last action was a successful jaws Strike.

The wolf automatically knocks the target of its jaws Strike prone.

SPECIALIZED ANIMAL COMPANIONS

Specialized animal companions are more intelligent and engage in more complex behaviors. The first time an animal gains a specialization, it gains the following: Its proficiency rank for unarmed attacks increases to expert. Its proficiency ranks for saving throws and Perception increase to master. Increase its Dexterity modifier by 1 and its Intelligence modifier by 2. Its unarmed attack damage increases from two dice to three dice, and it increases its additional damage with unarmed attacks from 2 to 4 or from 3 to 6.

Each specialization grants additional benefits. Most animal companions can have only one specialization.

AMBUSHER

In your companion's natural environment, it can use a Sneak action even if it's currently observed. It gains a +2 circumstance bonus to initiative rolls using Stealth, its proficiency rank in Stealth increases to expert (or master if it was already an expert from its type), and its Dexterity modifier increases by 1. Its proficiency rank for unarmored defense increases to expert, or master if it's nimble.

BULLY

Your companion terrorizes foes with dominance displays and pushes them around the battlefield. Its proficiency ranks for Athletics and Intimidation increase to expert (or master if it was already expert from its type), its Strength modifier increases by 1, and its Charisma modifier increases by 3.

DAREDEVIL

Your companion joins the fray with graceful leaps and dives. It gains the deny advantage ability, so it isn't flat-footed to hidden, undetected, or flanking creatures unless such a creature's level is greater than yours. Its proficiency rank in Acrobatics increases to master, and its Dexterity modifier increases by 1. Its proficiency rank in unarmored defense increases to expert, or master if it's nimble.

RACER

Your companion races. It gains a +10-foot status bonus to its Speed, swim Speed, or fly Speed (your choice). Its proficiency in Fortitude saves increases to legendary, and its Constitution modifier increases by 1.

TRACKER

Your companion is an incredible tracker. It can move at full Speed while following tracks. Its proficiency rank in Survival increases to expert (or master if it was already an expert from its type), and its Wisdom modifier increases by 1.

WRECKER

Your companion smashes things. Its unarmed attacks ignore half an object's Hardness. Its Athletics proficiency increases to master, and its Strength modifier increases by 1.

FAMILIARS

Familiars are mystically bonded creatures tied to your magic. Most familiars were originally animals, though the ritual of becoming a familiar makes them something more. You can choose a Tiny animal you want as your familiar, such as a bat, cat, raven, or snake. Some familiars are different, usually described in the ability that granted you a familiar; for example, a druid's leshy familiar is a Tiny plant instead of an animal, formed from a minor nature spirit.

Familiars have the minion trait (page 634), so during an encounter, they gain 2 actions in a round if you spend an action to command them. If your familiar dies, you can spend a week of downtime to replace it at no cost. You can have only one familiar at a time.

MODIFIERS AND AC

Your familiar's save modifiers and AC are equal to yours before applying circumstance or status bonuses or penalties. Its Perception, Acrobatics, and Stealth modifiers are equal to your level plus your spellcasting ability modifier (Charisma if you don't have one, unless otherwise specified). If it attempts an attack roll or other skill check, it uses your level as its modifier. It doesn't have or use its own ability modifiers and can never benefit from item bonuses.

HIT POINTS

Your familiar has 5 Hit Points for each of your levels.

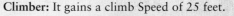

SIZE

Your familiar is Tiny.

SENSES

Your familiar has low-light vision and can gain additional senses from familiar abilities. It can communicate empathically with you as long as it's within 1 mile of you, sharing emotions. It doesn't understand or speak languages normally, but it can gain speech from a familiar ability.

MOVEMENT

Your familiar has either a Speed of 25 feet or a swim Speed of 25 feet (choose one upon gaining the familiar). It can gain other movement types from familiar abilities.

FAMILIAR AND MASTER ABILITIES

Each day, you channel your magic into two abilities, which can be either familiar or master abilities. If your familiar is an animal that naturally has one of these abilities (for instance, an owl has a fly Speed), you must select that ability. Your familiar can't be an animal that naturally has more familiar abilities than your daily maximum familiar abilities.

FAMILIAR ABILITIES

Amphibious: It gains a swim Speed of 25 feet (or Speed of 25 feet if it already has a swim Speed).

Burrower: It gains a burrow Speed of 5 feet, allowing it to dig Tiny holes.

Climber: It gains a climb Speed of 25 feet.

Damage Avoidance: Choose one type of save. It takes no damage when it succeeds at that type of save; this doesn't prevent effects other than damage.

Darkvision: It gains darkvision.

Fast Movement: Increase one of the familiar's Speeds from 25 feet to 40 feet.

Flier: It gains a fly Speed of 25 feet.

Kinspeech: It can understand and speak with animals of the same species. To select this, your familiar must be an animal, it must have the speech ability, and you must be at least 6th level.

Lab Assistant: It can use your Quick Alchemy action. You must have Quick Alchemy, and your familiar must be in your space. This has the same cost and requirement as if you used it. It must have the manual dexterity ability to select this.

Manual Dexterity: It can use up to two of its limbs as if they were hands to use manipulate actions.

Scent: It gains scent (imprecise, 30 feet).

Speech: It understands and speaks a language you know.

MASTER ABILITIES

Cantrip Connection: You can prepare an additional cantrip, or if you have a repertoire, instead designate a cantrip to add to your repertoire every time you select this ability; you can retrain it but can't otherwise change it. You must be able to prepare cantrips or add them to your repertoire to select this.

Extra Reagents: Your familiar grows extra infused reagents on or in its body. You gain an additional batch of infused reagents. You must have the infused reagents ability to select this ability.

Familiar Focus: Once per day, your familiar can use 2 actions with the concentrate trait to regain 1 Focus Point, up to your usual maximum You must have a focus pool to select this.

Lifelink: If your familiar would be reduced to 0 HP by damage, as a reaction with the concentrate trait, you can take the damage. If you do, you take all the damage and your familiar takes none. However, if special effects when a hit damages your familiar (such as snake venom) still apply to your familiar.

Spell Battery: You gain one additional spell slot at least 3 levels lower than your highest-level spell slot; you must be able to cast 4th-level spells using spell slots to select this master ability.

Spell Delivery: If your familiar is in your space, you can cast a spell with a range of touch, transfer its power to your familiar, and command the familiar to deliver the spell. If you do, the familiar uses its 2 actions for the round to move to a target of your choice and touch that target. If it doesn't reach the target to touch it this turn, the spell has no effect.

ARCHETYPES

There are infinite possible character concepts, but you might find that the feats and skill choices from a single class aren't sufficient to fully realize your character. Archetypes allow you to expand the scope of your character's class.

INTRODUCTION

ANCESTRIES & BACKGROUNDS

CLASSES

SKILLS

FEATS

EQUIPMENT

SPELLS

THE AGE OF LOST OMENS

PLAYING THE GAME

GAME MASTERING

CRAFTING & TREASURE

APPENDIX

Applying an archetype requires you to select archetype feats instead of class feats. Start by finding the archetype that best fits your character concept, and select the archetype's dedication feat using one of your class feat choices. Once you have the dedication feat, you can select any feat from that archetype in place of a class feat as long as you meet its prerequisites. The archetype feat you select is still subject to any selection restrictions on the class feat it replaces. For example, if you gained an ability at 6th level that granted you a 4th-level class feat with the dwarf trait, you could swap out that class feat only for an archetype feat of 4th level or lower with the dwarf trait. Archetype feats you gain in place of a class feat are called archetype class feats.

Occasionally, an archetype feat works like a skill feat instead of a class feat. These archetype feats have the skill trait, and you select them in place of a skill feat, otherwise following the same rules above. These are not archetype class feats (for instance, to determine the number of Hit Points you gain from the Fighter Resiliency archetype feat).

Each archetype's dedication feat represents a certain portion of your character's time and focus, so once you select a dedication feat for an archetype, you must satisfy its requirements before you can gain another dedication feat. Typically, you satisfy an archetype dedication feat by gaining a certain number of feats from the archetype's list. You cannot retrain a dedication feat as long as you have any other feats from that archetype.

Sometimes an archetype feat lets you gain another feat, such as the alchemist's basic concoction. You must always meet the prerequisites of the feat you gain in this way.

Two special kinds of archetypes are designated by the class and multiclass traits. The archetypes in this book are all multiclass archetypes.

MULTICLASS ARCHETYPES

Archetypes with the multiclass trait represent diversifying your training into another class's specialties. You can't select a multiclass archetype's dedication feat if you are a member of the class of the same name (for instance, a fighter can't select the Fighter Dedication feat).

CLASS ARCHETYPES

Archetypes with the class trait represent a fundamental divergence from your class's specialties, but one that exists within the context of your class. You can select a class archetype only if you are a member of the class of the same name. Class archetypes always alter or replace some of a class's static class features, in addition to any new feats they offer. It may be possible to take a class archetype at 1st level if it alters or replaces some of the class's initial class features. In that case, you must take that archetype's dedication feat at 2nd level, and after that you proceed normally. You can never have more than one class archetype.

SPELLCASTING ARCHETYPES

Some archetypes grant you a substantial degree of spellcasting, albeit delayed compared to a character from a spellcasting class. In this book, the spellcasting archetypes are bard, cleric, druid, sorcerer, and wizard, the multiclass archetypes for the five main spellcasting classes, but future books might introduce spellcasting archetypes that aren't multiclass archetypes. A spellcasting archetype allows you to use scrolls, staves, and wands in the same way that a member of a spellcasting class can.

Spellcasting archetypes always grant the ability to cast cantrips in their dedication, and then they have a basic spellcasting feat, an expert spellcasting feat, and a master spellcasting feat. These feats share their name with the archetype; for instance, the wizard's master spellcasting feat is called Master Wizard Spellcasting. All spell slots you gain from spellcasting archetypes have restrictions depending on the archetype; for instance, the bard archetype grants you spell slots you can use only to cast occult spells from your bard repertoire, even if you are a sorcerer with occult spells in your sorcerer repertoire.

Basic Spellcasting Feat: Available at 4th level, these feats grant a 1st-level spell slot. At 6th level, they grant you a 2nd-level spell slot. At 8th level, they grant you a 3rd-level spell slot. Archetypes refer to these benefits as the "basic spellcasting benefits."

Expert Spellcasting Feat: Taken at 12th level, these feats make you an expert in spell attack rolls and DCs of the appropriate magical tradition and grant you a 4th-level spell slot. At 14th level, they grant you a 5th-level spell slot, and at 16th level, they grant you a 6th-level spell slot. Archetypes refer to these benefits as the "expert spellcasting benefits."

Master Spellcasting Feat: Upon reaching 18th level, these feats make you a master in spell attack rolls and DCs of the appropriate magical tradition and grant you a 7th-level spell slot. At 20th level, they grant you an 8th-level spell slot. Archetypes refer to these benefits as the "master spellcasting benefits."

ALCHEMIST

You enjoy tinkering with alchemical formulas and substances in your spare time, and your studies have progressed beyond mere experimentation.

MULTICLASS ALCHEMIST CHARACTERS

The free alchemical items from the alchemist archetype are extremely useful to characters of any class. The following are just some of the possible combinations.

- Barbarian alchemists can mix mutagens with their rage to ferocious effect.
- Champion alchemists can focus on alchemical items that boost defenses and heal others, allowing their champion's reaction and *lay on hands* to go further.
- Fighter alchemists can use their alchemy to gain additional options in situations where their usual tactics don't work.
- Ranger alchemists focus on alchemy and snares, getting extra use out of their Crafting skill and supplying bombs for the bomb snare.

- Rogue alchemists can combine a rogue's poison feats with free daily poisons, and bombs present an interesting way to sneak attack with various types of energy damage.
- Spellcaster alchemists often use their alchemical items to take pressure off their repertoire or prepared spells. For instance, a wizard alchemist who can brew up darksight elixirs to grant darkvision can prepare another spell instead of *darkvision*.

ALCHEMIST DEDICATION   FEAT 2

> ARCHETYPE   DEDICATION   MULTICLASS

Prerequisites Intelligence 14

You put your alchemical interest into practice. You become trained in alchemical bombs and Crafting; if you were already trained in Crafting, you instead become trained in a skill of your choice. You become trained in alchemist class DC.

You gain the alchemist's infused reagents class feature, gaining a number of reagents each day equal to your level. You also gain the Alchemical Crafting feat and four additional formulas for 1st-level alchemical items, as well as the ability to create free items during your daily preparations. Your advanced alchemy level is 1 and doesn't increase on its own.

Special You cannot select another dedication feat until you have gained two other feats from the alchemist archetype.

BASIC CONCOCTION   FEAT 4

> ARCHETYPE

Prerequisites Alchemist Dedication

You gain a 1st- or 2nd-level alchemist feat.

QUICK ALCHEMY   FEAT 4

> ARCHETYPE

Prerequisites Alchemist Dedication

You gain the Quick Alchemy action (page 72).

ADVANCED CONCOCTION   FEAT 6

> ARCHETYPE

Prerequisites Basic Concoction

You gain one alchemist feat. For the purpose of meeting its prerequisites, your alchemist level is equal to half your character level.

Special You can select this feat more than once. Each time you select it, you gain another alchemist feat.

EXPERT ALCHEMY   FEAT 6

> ARCHETYPE

Prerequisites Alchemist Dedication, expert in Crafting

Your advanced alchemy level increases to 3. At 10th level, it increases to 5.

MASTER ALCHEMY   FEAT 12

> ARCHETYPE

Prerequisites Expert Alchemy, master in Crafting

Your advanced alchemy level increases to 7. For every level you gain beyond 12th, your advanced alchemy level increases by 1.

BARBARIAN

There's a rage deep inside you that sometimes breaks loose, granting you some of the might of a barbarian in addition to your other abilities.

MULTICLASS BARBARIAN CHARACTERS

The barbarian archetype is a great choice for characters that emphasize Strength and melee attacks more than usual for their class, as long as they can handle Rage's spellcasting restriction. It's especially good for characters looking to add more damage.

BARBARIAN DEDICATION — FEAT 2

ARCHETYPE   DEDICATION   MULTICLASS

Prerequisites Strength 14, Constitution 14

You become trained in Athletics; if you were already trained in Athletics, you instead become trained in a skill of your choice. You become trained in barbarian class DC.

You can use the Rage action (page 84).

Choose an instinct as you would if you were a barbarian. You have that instinct for all purposes and become bound by its anathema, but you don't gain any of the other abilities it grants.

Special You cannot select another dedication feat until you have gained two other feats from the barbarian archetype.

BARBARIAN RESILIENCY — FEAT 4

ARCHETYPE

Prerequisites Barbarian Dedication, class granting no more Hit Points per level than 10 + your Constitution modifier

You gain 3 additional Hit Points for each barbarian archetype class feat you have. As you continue selecting barbarian archetype class feats, you continue to gain additional Hit Points in this way.

BASIC FURY — FEAT 4

ARCHETYPE

Prerequisites Barbarian Dedication

You gain a 1st- or 2nd-level barbarian feat.

ADVANCED FURY — FEAT 6

ARCHETYPE

Prerequisites Basic Fury

You gain one barbarian feat. For the purpose of meeting its prerequisites, your barbarian level is equal to half your character level.

Special You can select this feat more than once. Each time you select it, you gain another barbarian feat.

INSTINCT ABILITY — FEAT 6

ARCHETYPE

Prerequisites Barbarian Dedication

You gain the instinct ability for the instinct you chose for Barbarian Dedication.

JUGGERNAUT'S FORTITUDE — FEAT 12

ARCHETYPE

Prerequisites Barbarian Dedication, expert in Fortitude saves

Your proficiency rank in Fortitude saves increases to master.

BARD

A muse has called you to dabble in occult lore, allowing you to cast a few spells. The deeper you delve, the more powerful your performances become.

MULTICLASS BARD CHARACTERS

The bard archetype grants powerful effects that tend to use actions; it's a great choice if you have actions to spare.

BARD DEDICATION FEAT 2

ARCHETYPE DEDICATION MULTICLASS

Prerequisites Charisma 14

You cast spells like a bard and gain the Cast a Spell activity. You gain a spell repertoire with two common cantrips from the occult spell list, or any other cantrips you learn or discover. You're trained in spell attack rolls and spell DCs for occult spells. Your key spellcasting ability for bard archetype spells is Charisma, and they are occult bard spells. You become trained in Occultism and Performance; for each of these skills in which you were already trained, you instead become trained in a skill of your choice.

Choose a muse as you would if you were a bard. You have that muse for all purposes, allowing you to take that muse's feats, but you don't gain any of the other abilities it grants.

Special You cannot select another dedication feat until you have gained two other feats from the bard archetype.

BASIC BARD SPELLCASTING FEAT 4

ARCHETYPE

Prerequisites Bard Dedication

You gain the basic spellcasting benefits (page 219). Each time you gain a spell slot of a new level from the bard archetype, add a common occult spell or another spell you learned or discovered to your repertoire, of the appropriate spell level.

BASIC MUSE'S WHISPERS FEAT 4

ARCHETYPE

Prerequisites Bard Dedication

You gain a 1st- or 2nd-level bard feat.

ADVANCED MUSE'S WHISPERS FEAT 6

ARCHETYPE

Prerequisites Basic Muse's Whispers

You gain one bard feat. For the purpose of meeting its prerequisites, your bard level is equal to half your character level.

Special You can select this feat more than once. Each time you select it, you gain another bard feat.

COUNTER PERFORM FEAT 6

ARCHETYPE

Prerequisites Bard Dedication

You gain the *counter performance* composition spell. If you don't already have one, you gain a focus pool of 1 Focus Point, which you can Refocus by engaging your muse. (For more on composition spells, see page 97.)

INSPIRATIONAL PERFORMANCE FEAT 8

ARCHETYPE

Prerequisites Bard Dedication

You gain the *inspire courage* composition cantrip.

OCCULT BREADTH FEAT 8

ARCHETYPE

Prerequisites Basic Bard Spellcasting

Your repertoire expands, and you can cast more occult spells each day. Increase the number of spells in your repertoire and the number of spell slots you gain from bard archetype feats by 1 for each spell level other than your two highest spell levels.

EXPERT BARD SPELLCASTING FEAT 12

ARCHETYPE

Prerequisites Basic Bard Spellcasting, master in Occultism

You gain the expert spellcasting benefits (page 219).

MASTER BARD SPELLCASTING FEAT 18

ARCHETYPE

Prerequisites Expert Bard Spellcasting, legendary in Occultism

You gain the master spellcasting benefits (page 219).

CHAMPION

You have sworn a solemn oath to your deity, who has granted you champion powers to aid you in your cause.

MULTICLASS CHAMPION CHARACTERS

The champion archetype greatly improves defenses, particularly armor. It's a great way for a character to gain armor proficiency or a powerful defensive reaction.

CHAMPION DEDICATION   FEAT 2

> ARCHETYPE DEDICATION MULTICLASS

Prerequisites Strength 14, Charisma 14

Choose a deity and cause as you would if you were a champion. You become trained in light, medium, and heavy armor. You become trained in Religion and your deity's associated skill; for each of these skills in which you were already trained, you instead become trained in a skill of your choice. You become trained in champion class DC.

You are bound by your deity's anathema and must follow the champion's code and alignment requirements for your cause. You don't gain any other abilities from your choice of deity or cause.

Special You cannot select another dedication feat until you have gained two other feats from the champion archetype.

BASIC DEVOTION   FEAT 4

> ARCHETYPE

Prerequisites Champion Dedication

You gain a 1st- or 2nd-level champion feat.

CHAMPION RESILIENCY   FEAT 4

> ARCHETYPE

Prerequisites Champion Dedication, class granting no more Hit Points per level than 8 + your Constitution modifier

You gain 3 additional Hit Points for each champion archetype class feat you have. As you continue selecting champion archetype class feats, you continue to gain additional Hit Points in this way.

HEALING TOUCH   FEAT 4

> ARCHETYPE

Prerequisites Champion Dedication

You gain the appropriate devotion spell for your cause (*lay on hands* for the paladin, redeemer, and liberator). If you don't already have one, you gain a focus pool of 1 Focus Point, which you can Refocus by praying or serving your deity. (For more on devotion spells, see page 107.)

ADVANCED DEVOTION   FEAT 6

> ARCHETYPE

Prerequisites Basic Devotion

You gain one champion feat. For the purpose of meeting its prerequisites, your champion level is equal to half your character level.

Special You can select this feat more than once. Each time you select it, you gain another champion feat.

CHAMPION'S REACTION   FEAT 6

> ARCHETYPE

Prerequisites Champion Dedication

You can use the champion's reaction associated with your cause.

DIVINE ALLY   FEAT 6

> ARCHETYPE

Prerequisites Champion Dedication

You gain a divine ally of your choice (page 108).

DIVERSE ARMOR EXPERT   FEAT 14

> ARCHETYPE

Prerequisites Champion Dedication, expert in unarmored defense or one or more types of armor

Your proficiency ranks for light armor, medium armor, heavy armor, and unarmored defense increase to expert.

CLERIC

You are an ordained priest of your deity and have even learned how to cast a few divine spells. Though your main training lies elsewhere, your religious calling provides you divine gifts.

MULTICLASS CLERIC CHARACTERS

The cleric archetype is a great way to create a character of another class who's a devotee of a particular deity. The many domains available to clerics of different deities present a variety of options for focus spells.

- Alchemist clerics work well with the chirurgeon field, healing various ailments with either alchemy or spells.
- Martial clerics are typically looking for a potent domain spell or some healing to use in a pinch.
- Divine sorcerer clerics double down as the ultimate divine spellcasters.
- Other spellcaster clerics diversify their options, becoming theurgic characters who combine two magical traditions.

CLERIC DEDICATION   FEAT 2

ARCHETYPE   DEDICATION   MULTICLASS

Prerequisites Wisdom 14

You cast spells like a cleric. You gain access to the Cast a Spell activity. You can prepare two common cantrips each day from the divine spell list in this book or any other cantrips you learn or discover. You're trained in spell attack rolls and spell DCs for divine spells. Your key spellcasting ability for cleric archetype spells is Wisdom, and they are divine cleric spells. Choose a deity as you would if you were a cleric. You become bound by that deity's anathema. You become trained in Religion and your deity's associated skill; for each of these skills in which you were already trained, you instead become trained in a skill of your choice. You don't gain any other abilities from your choice of deity.

Special You cannot select another dedication feat until you have gained two other feats from the cleric archetype.

BASIC CLERIC SPELLCASTING   FEAT 4

ARCHETYPE

Prerequisites Cleric Dedication

You gain the basic spellcasting benefits (page 219). You can prepare your deity's spells in your spell slots of the appropriate level from the cleric archetype.

BASIC DOGMA   FEAT 4

ARCHETYPE

Prerequisites Cleric Dedication

You gain a 1st- or 2nd-level cleric feat.

ADVANCED DOGMA   FEAT 6

ARCHETYPE

Prerequisites Basic Dogma

You gain one cleric feat. For the purpose of meeting its prerequisites, your cleric level is equal to half your character level.

Special You can select this feat more than once. Each time you select it, you gain another cleric feat.

DIVINE BREADTH   FEAT 8

ARCHETYPE

Prerequisites Basic Cleric Spellcasting

You can cast more divine spells each day. Increase the spell slots you gain from cleric archetype feats by 1 for each spell level other than your two highest spell levels.

EXPERT CLERIC SPELLCASTING   FEAT 12

ARCHETYPE

Prerequisites Basic Cleric Spellcasting, master in Religion

You gain the expert spellcasting benefits (page 219).

MASTER CLERIC SPELLCASTING   FEAT 18

ARCHETYPE

Prerequisites Expert Cleric Spellcasting, legendary in Religion

You gain the master spellcasting benefits (page 219).

DRUID

You have entered a druidic circle and learned a few of the order's secrets, granting you primal power.

MULTICLASS DRUID CHARACTERS

The druid archetype can provide a bit of healing or elemental damage and can increase your utility in a natural environment with spells like *speak with animals* and *meld into stone*.

DRUID DEDICATION   FEAT 2

> ARCHETYPE   DEDICATION   MULTICLASS

Prerequisites Wisdom 14

You cast spells like a druid. You gain access to the Cast a Spell activity. You can prepare two common cantrips each day from the primal spell list in this book or any other cantrips you learn or discover. You're trained in spell attack rolls and spell DCs for primal spells. Your key spellcasting ability for druid archetype spells is Wisdom, and they are primal druid spells.

You learn the Druidic language.

Choose an order as you would if you were a druid. You become a member of that order and are bound by its anathema, allowing you to take the order's feats. You become trained in Nature and your order's associated skill; for each of these skills in which you were already trained, you become trained in a skill of your choice. You don't gain any other abilities from your choice of order.

Special You cannot select another dedication feat until you have gained two other feats from the druid archetype.

BASIC DRUID SPELLCASTING   FEAT 4

> ARCHETYPE

Prerequisites Druid Dedication

You gain the basic spellcasting benefits (page 219).

BASIC WILDING   FEAT 4

> ARCHETYPE

Prerequisites Druid Dedication

You gain a 1st- or 2nd-level druid feat.

ORDER SPELL   FEAT 4

> ARCHETYPE

Prerequisites Druid Dedication

You gain the initial order spell from your order. If you don't already have one, you gain a focus pool of 1 Focus Point, which you can Refocus by being one with nature. (For more on order spells, see page 131.)

ADVANCED WILDING   FEAT 6

> ARCHETYPE

Prerequisites Basic Wilding

You gain one druid feat. For the purpose of meeting its prerequisites, your druid level is equal to half your character level.

Special You can select this feat more than once. Each time you select it, you gain another druid feat.

PRIMAL BREADTH   FEAT 8

> ARCHETYPE

Prerequisites Basic Druid Spellcasting

Increase the spell slots you gain from druid archetype feats by 1 for each spell level other than your two highest spell levels.

EXPERT DRUID SPELLCASTING   FEAT 12

> ARCHETYPE

Prerequisites Basic Druid Spellcasting, master in Nature

You gain the expert spellcasting benefits (page 219).

MASTER DRUID SPELLCASTING   FEAT 18

> ARCHETYPE

Prerequisites Expert Druid Spellcasting, legendary in Nature

You gain the master spellcasting benefits (page 219).

FIGHTER

You have spent time learning the art of warfare, increasing your skill with martial arms and at wearing armor. With further training, you can become a true combat specialist.

MULTICLASS FIGHTER CHARACTERS

The fighter archetype grants access to great feats for characters focusing on any combat style, and it's particularly helpful for characters looking to diversify their offensive abilities or focus on more powerful weapons.

- Barbarian fighters can combine their talents with two-handed weapons with some of the fighter's two-handed feats to devastating effect.
- Champion fighters focus on a style of combat exemplified by their deity. A shield-using champion benefits from the best of both worlds in shield feats.
- Monk fighters are great at combining unusual weapon styles. For instance, a monks isn't hindered by a restriction to keep one hand free, because they want to punch you with that hand anyway.

- Ranger fighters can either specialize in archery or use their fighter feats to pick up an unusual combat style combination.
- Rogue fighters can make good use of fighter's free hand, two-weapon fighting, or archery feats.
- Spellcaster fighters benefit greatly from the additional weapon proficiencies, and fighter is a solid choice for any spellcaster of a particularly martial bent.

FIGHTER DEDICATION   FEAT 2

> ARCHETYPE   DEDICATION   MULTICLASS

Prerequisites Strength 14, Dexterity 14

You become trained in simple weapons and martial weapons. You become trained in your choice of Acrobatics or Athletics; if you are already trained in both of these skills, you instead become trained in a skill of your choice. You become trained in fighter class DC.

Special You cannot select another dedication feat until you have gained two other feats from the fighter archetype.

BASIC MANEUVER   FEAT 4

> ARCHETYPE

Prerequisites Fighter Dedication

You gain a 1st- or 2nd-level fighter feat.

FIGHTER RESILIENCY   FEAT 4

> ARCHETYPE

Prerequisites Fighter Dedication, class granting no more Hit Points per level than 8 + your Constitution modifier

You gain 3 additional Hit Points for each fighter archetype class feat you have. As you continue selecting fighter archetype class feats, you continue to gain additional Hit Points in this way.

OPPORTUNIST   FEAT 4

> ARCHETYPE

Prerequisites Fighter Dedication

You gain the Attack of Opportunity reaction, found on page 142.

ADVANCED MANEUVER   FEAT 6

> ARCHETYPE

Prerequisites Basic Maneuver

You gain a fighter feat. For the purpose of meeting its prerequisites, your fighter level is equal to half your character level.

Special You can select this feat more than once. Each time you select it, you gain another fighter feat.

DIVERSE WEAPON EXPERT   FEAT 12

> ARCHETYPE

Prerequisites Fighter Dedication, expert in any kind of weapon or unarmed attack

Your proficiency ranks for simple weapons and martial weapons increase to expert, and your proficiency rank for advanced weapons increases to trained.

MONK

Monastic training has taught you martial arts and allowed you to hone your mind, body, and spirit to new heights.

MULTICLASS MONK CHARACTERS

The monk archetype is a strong choice for any character that fights unarmored or with unarmed attacks.

- Barbarian monks with the animal instinct can combine the barbarian's excellent unarmed damage with the monk's diverse unarmed special abilities.
- Champion monks are perfect for champions of Irori or other deities who favor unarmed attacks.
- Fighter monks can supplement free-hand fighting and add mobility to the fighter's toolkit.
- Rogue monks are incredibly effective because stances grant some of the best agile finesse attacks and flurry gives more sneak attacks.
- Spellcaster monks can fight with a free hand and still use material components to cast spells.

MONK DEDICATION   FEAT 2

`ARCHETYPE` `DEDICATION` `MULTICLASS`

Prerequisites Strength 14, Dexterity 14

You become trained in unarmed attacks and gain the powerful fist class feature (page 156). You become trained in your choice of Acrobatics or Athletics; if you are already trained in both of these skills, you become trained in a skill of your choice. You become trained in monk class DC.

Special You can't select another dedication feat until you have gained two other feats from the monk archetype.

BASIC KATA   FEAT 4

`ARCHETYPE`

Prerequisites Monk Dedication

You gain a 1st- or 2nd-level monk feat.

MONK RESILIENCY   FEAT 4

`ARCHETYPE`

Prerequisites Monk Dedication, class granting no more Hit Points per level than 8 + your Constitution modifier

You gain 3 additional Hit Points for each monk archetype class feat you have. As you continue selecting monk archetype class feats, you continue to gain additional Hit Points in this way.

ADVANCED KATA   FEAT 6

`ARCHETYPE`

Prerequisites Basic Kata

You gain one monk feat. For the purpose of meeting its prerequisites, your monk level is equal to half your character level.

Special You can select this feat more than once. Each time you select it, you gain another monk feat.

MONK MOVES   FEAT 8

`ARCHETYPE`

Prerequisites Monk Dedication

You gain a +10-foot status bonus to your Speed when you're not wearing armor.

MONK'S FLURRY   FEAT 10

`ARCHETYPE`

Prerequisites Monk Dedication

You gain the Flurry of Blows action (page 156).

PERFECTION'S PATH   FEAT 12

`ARCHETYPE`

Prerequisites Monk Dedication, expert in at least one saving throw

Choose one saving throw (Fortitude, Reflex, or Will) in which you are an expert. Your proficiency rank in the chosen saving throw increases to master.

RANGER

You have studied hunting, tracking, and wilderness survival, adding a ranger's tools to your skill set.

MULTICLASS RANGER CHARACTERS

The ranger archetype has access to excellent options to improve a character's monster knowledge and survival skills, but ranger is of particular interest to any character wanting to become a dedicated archer.

- Alchemist rangers can add snares to their daily free items, benefiting from a strong Crafting modifier, and their Intelligence makes them exceptional with monster knowledge feats. The ranger archetype is also useful to bombers who want to alternate with in bow attacks.

- Champion rangers are particularly fitting for deities who connect thematically to nature or have a bow as their favored weapon. (Or, in the case of Erastil, both!)
- Fighter rangers are among the most fearsome archers, combining the best archery feats from both classes to create a fighting style unique to each fighter ranger.
- Rogue rangers make excellent snipers or ranged skirmishers, and snares let them be on the other side of traps for a change.
- Spellcaster rangers benefit greatly from ranger's feat support, backing up their spells with ranged weapon attacks. Druids have the most thematic overlap with rangers among the spellcasters, allowing you to create a true master of the wilderness.

RANGER DEDICATION   FEAT 2

ARCHETYPE **DEDICATION** **MULTICLASS**

Prerequisites Dexterity 14

You become trained in Survival; if you were already trained in Survival, you instead become trained in another skill of your choice. You become trained in ranger class DC.

You can use the Hunt Prey action (page 168).

Special You cannot select another dedication feat until you have gained two other feats from the ranger archetype.

BASIC HUNTER'S TRICK   FEAT 4

ARCHETYPE

Prerequisites Ranger Dedication

You gain a 1st- or 2nd-level ranger feat.

RANGER RESILIENCY   FEAT 4

ARCHETYPE

Prerequisites Ranger Dedication, class granting no more Hit Points per level than 8 + your Constitution modifier

You gain 3 additional Hit Points for each ranger archetype class feat you have. As you continue selecting ranger archetype class feats, you continue to gain additional Hit Points in this way.

ADVANCED HUNTER'S TRICK   FEAT 6

ARCHETYPE

Prerequisites Basic Hunter's Trick

You gain one ranger feat. For the purpose of meeting its prerequisites, your ranger level is equal to half your character level.

Special You can select this feat more than once. Each time you select it, you gain another ranger feat.

MASTER SPOTTER   FEAT 12

ARCHETYPE

Prerequisites Ranger Dedication, expert in Perception

Your proficiency rank in Perception increases to master.

ROGUE

You've learned to sneak, steal, and disable traps. With time and luck, you'll become capable of moving through the shadows, striking unseen, and escaping without notice.

MULTICLASS ROGUE CHARACTERS

Nearly any character can benefit from the many skills and tricks the rogue archetype grants.

- Alchemist rogues can use the rogue's Poison Weapon to great effect with their daily poisons, and sneak attack is a nice boost to bomb damage.
- Barbarian rogues can become masters in every save and diversify their skills.
- Champion rogues add damage from sneak attack while protecting their flanking partners from harm.
- Fighter rogues combine the fighter's accuracy with extra damage, a deadly combination for archers or finesse fighters.
- Monk rogues have great synergy, since many stances grant powerful Strikes that work with sneak attack.
- Ranger rogues benefit from the shared focus on trailing foes and catching them flat-footed. The flurry edge can get you many sneak attacks, and the precision edge doubles down on precision damage.
- Spellcaster rogues use the rogue multiclass to shore up skills or to pick up tricky rogue feats like Mobility to help keep them safe.

ROGUE DEDICATION   FEAT 2

> **ARCHETYPE** **DEDICATION** **MULTICLASS**

Prerequisites Dexterity 14

You gain a skill feat and the rogue's surprise attack class feature (page 181). You become trained in light armor. In addition, you become trained in Stealth or Thievery plus one skill of your choice; if you are already trained in both Stealth and Thievery, you become trained in an additional skill of your choice. You become trained in rogue class DC.

Special You cannot gain another dedication feat until you have gained two other feats from the rogue archetype.

BASIC TRICKERY   FEAT 4

> **ARCHETYPE**

Prerequisites Rogue Dedication

You gain a 1st- or 2nd-level rogue feat.

SNEAK ATTACKER   FEAT 4

> **ARCHETYPE**

Prerequisites Rogue Dedication

You gain the sneak attack class feature (page 181), except it deals 1d4 damage, increasing to 1d6 at 6th level. You don't increase the number of dice as you gain levels.

ADVANCED TRICKERY   FEAT 6

> **ARCHETYPE**

Prerequisites Basic Trickery

You gain one rogue feat. For the purpose of meeting its prerequisites, your rogue level is equal to half your character level.

Special You can select this feat more than once. Each time you select it, you gain another rogue feat.

SKILL MASTERY   FEAT 8

> **ARCHETYPE**

Prerequisites Rogue Dedication, trained in at least one skill and expert in at least one skill

Increase your proficiency rank in one of your skills from expert to master and in another of your skills from trained to expert. You gain a skill feat associated with one of the skills you chose.

Special You can select this feat up to five times.

UNCANNY DODGE   FEAT 10

> **ARCHETYPE**

Prerequisites Rogue Dedication

You gain the deny advantage class feature (page 181).

EVASIVENESS   FEAT 12

> **ARCHETYPE**

Prerequisites Rogue Dedication, expert in Reflex saves

Your proficiency rank for Reflex saves increases to master.

SORCERER

You coax the magic power in your blood to manifest, accessing magic others don't expect you to have.

MULTICLASS SORCERER CHARACTERS

The sorcerer archetype is a method for anyone to pick up commonly useful spells, such as *invisibility* and *haste*.

SORCERER DEDICATION   FEAT 2

ARCHETYPE **DEDICATION** **MULTICLASS**

Prerequisites Charisma 14

Choose a bloodline. You become trained in the bloodline's two skills; for each of these skills in which you were already trained, you become trained in a skill of your choice.

You cast spells like a sorcerer. You gain access to the Cast a Spell activity. You gain a spell repertoire with two common cantrips from the spell list associated with your bloodline, or any other cantrips you learn or discover. You're trained in spell attack rolls and spell DCs for your tradition's spells. Your key spellcasting ability for sorcerer archetype spells is Charisma, and they are sorcerer spells of your bloodline's

tradition. You don't gain any other abilities from your choice of bloodline.

Special You cannot select another dedication feat until you have gained two other feats from the sorcerer archetype.

BASIC SORCERER SPELLCASTING   FEAT 4

ARCHETYPE

Prerequisites Sorcerer Dedication

You gain the basic spellcasting benefits (page 219). Each time you gain a spell slot of a new level from the sorcerer archetype, add a spell of the appropriate spell level to your repertoire: a common spell of your bloodline's tradition, one of your bloodline's granted spells, or another spell you have learned or discovered.

BASIC BLOOD POTENCY   FEAT 4

ARCHETYPE

Prerequisites Sorcerer Dedication

You gain a 1st- or 2nd-level sorcerer feat.

BASIC BLOODLINE SPELL   FEAT 4

ARCHETYPE

Prerequisites Sorcerer Dedication

You gain your bloodline's initial bloodline spell. If you don't already have one, you also gain a focus pool of 1 Focus Point, which you can Refocus without any special effort. (For more on bloodline spells, see page 194.)

ADVANCED BLOOD POTENCY   FEAT 6

ARCHETYPE

Prerequisites Basic Blood Potency

You gain one sorcerer feat. For the purpose of prerequisites, your sorcerer level is half your character level.

Special You can select this feat more than once. Each time you do, you gain another sorcerer feat.

BLOODLINE BREADTH   FEAT 8

ARCHETYPE

Prerequisites Basic Sorcerer Spellcasting

Your repertoire expands, and you can cast more spells of your bloodline's tradition each day. Increase the number of spells in your repertoire and number of spell slots you gain from sorcerer archetype feats by 1 for each spell level other than your two highest spell levels.

EXPERT SORCERER SPELLCASTING   FEAT 12

ARCHETYPE

Prerequisites Basic Sorcerer Spellcasting; master in Arcana, Nature, Occultism, or Religion, depending on bloodline

You gain the expert spellcasting benefits (page 219).

MASTER SORCERER SPELLCASTING   FEAT 18

ARCHETYPE

Prerequisites Expert Sorcerer Spellcasting; legendary in Arcana, Nature, Occultism, or Religion, depending on bloodline

You gain the master spellcasting benefits (page 219).

Wizard

You have dabbled in the arcane arts and, through discipline and academic study, learned how to cast a few spells.

MULTICLASS WIZARD CHARACTERS

The wizard archetype grants versatile prepared spells, perfect for characters looking to add some extra utility.

WIZARD DEDICATION   FEAT 2

`ARCHETYPE` `DEDICATION` `MULTICLASS`

Prerequisites Intelligence 14

You cast spells like a wizard, gaining a spellbook with four common arcane cantrips of your choice. You gain the Cast a Spell activity. You can prepare two cantrips each day from your spellbook. You're trained in arcane spell attack rolls and spell DCs. Your key spellcasting ability for wizard archetype spells is Int, and they are arcane wizard spells. You become trained in Arcana; if you were already trained in Arcana, you instead become trained in a skill of your choice.

Special You can't select another dedication feat until you have gained two other feats from the wizard archetype.

ARCANE SCHOOL SPELL   FEAT 4

`ARCHETYPE`

Prerequisite Wizard Dedication

Select one arcane school of magic. You gain the school's initial school spell. If you don't already have one, you gain a focus pool of 1 Focus Point, which you can Refocus by studying. (For more on arcane schools, see page 204.)

BASIC ARCANA   FEAT 4

`ARCHETYPE`

Prerequisites Wizard Dedication

You gain a 1st- or 2nd-level wizard feat of your choice.

BASIC WIZARD SPELLCASTING   FEAT 4

`ARCHETYPE`

Prerequisites Wizard Dedication

You gain the basic spellcasting benefits (page 219). Each time you gain a spell slot of a new level from the wizard archetype, add two common spells of that level to your spellbook.

ADVANCED ARCANA   FEAT 6

`ARCHETYPE`

Prerequisites Basic Arcana

You gain one wizard feat. For the purpose of meeting its prerequisites, your wizard level is equal to half your character level.

Special You can select this feat more than once. Each time you select it, you gain another wizard feat.

ARCANE BREADTH   FEAT 8

`ARCHETYPE`

Prerequisites Basic Wizard Spellcasting

You can cast more arcane spells each day. Increase the spell slots you gain from wizard archetype feats by 1 for each spell level other than your two highest spell levels.

EXPERT WIZARD SPELLCASTING   FEAT 12

`ARCHETYPE`

Prerequisites Basic Wizard Spellcasting, master in Arcana

You gain the expert spellcasting benefits (page 219).

MASTER WIZARD SPELLCASTING   FEAT 18

`ARCHETYPE`

Prerequisites Expert Wizard Spellcasting, legendary in Arcana

You gain the master spellcasting benefits (page 219).

INTRODUCTION

ANCESTRIES & BACKGROUNDS

CLASSES

SKILLS

FEATS

EQUIPMENT

SPELLS

THE AGE OF

CHAPTER 4: SKILLS

While your character's ability scores represent their raw talent and potential, skills represent their training and experience at performing certain tasks. Each skill is keyed to one of your character's ability scores and used for an array of related actions. Your character's expertise in a skill comes from several sources, including their background and class. In this chapter, you'll learn about skills, their scope, and the actions they can be used for.

4

INTRODUCTION

ANCESTRIES & BACKGROUNDS

CLASSES

SKILLS

FEATS

EQUIPMENT

SPELLS

THE AGE OF LOST OMENS

PLAYING THE GAME

GAME MASTERING

CRAFTING & TREASURE

APPENDIX

A character's acumen in skills can come from all sorts of training, from practicing acrobatic tricks to studying academic topics to rehearsing a performing art. When you create your character and as they advance in level, you have flexibility as to which skills they become better at and when. Some classes depend heavily on certain skills—such as the alchemist's reliance on Crafting—but for most classes, you can choose whichever skills make the most sense for your character's theme and backstory at 1st level, then use their adventure and downtime experiences to inform how their skills should improve as your character levels up.

A character gains training in certain skills at 1st level: typically two skills from their background, a small number of predetermined skills from their class, and several skills of your choice granted by your class. This training increases your proficiency ranks for those skills to trained instead of untrained and lets you use more of the skills' actions. Sometimes you might gain training in a specific skill from multiple sources, such as if your background granted training in Crafting and you took the alchemist class, which also grants training in Crafting. Each time after the first that you would gain the trained proficiency rank in a given skill, you instead allocate the trained proficiency to any other skill of your choice.

KEY ABILITY

Each skill is tied to a key ability. You add your modifier for this ability to checks and DCs when using that skill. For example, skulking about the shadows of a city at night with Stealth uses your Dexterity modifier, navigating the myriad personalities and power plays of court politics with Society uses your Intelligence modifier, and so on. The key ability for each skill is listed on Table 4–1: Skills, Key Abilities, and Actions on page 235 and also appears in parentheses following the skill's name in the descriptions on the following pages. If the GM deems it appropriate for a certain situation, however, they might have you use a different ability modifier for a skill check or when determining your skill DC.

SKILL ACTIONS

The actions you can perform with a given skill are sorted into those you can use untrained and those that require you to be trained in the skill, as shown on Table 4–1: Skills, Key Abilities, and Actions (page 235). The untrained and trained actions of each skill appear in separate sections within the skill's description.

Anyone can use a skill's untrained actions, but you can use trained actions only if you have a proficiency rank of trained or better in that skill. A circumstance, condition, or effect might bar you from a skill action regardless of your proficiency rank, and sometimes using a skill in a specific situation might require you to have a higher proficiency rank than what is listed on the table. For instance, even though a barbarian untrained in Arcana could identify a construct with a lucky roll using Arcana to Recall Knowledge, the GM might decide that Recalling Knowledge to determine the spells used to create such a construct is beyond the scope of the barbarian's anecdotal knowledge. The GM decides whether a task requires a particular proficiency rank.

IMPROVING SKILLS

As your character advances in level, there are two main ways their skills improve: skill increases and skill feats. Your class lists the levels at which you gain each of these improvements.

SKILL INCREASES

Skill increases improve your proficiency in skills of your choice. You can use these increases to become trained in new skills or increase your proficiency rank in skills you're trained in (from trained to expert at any level, expert to master at 7th level or higher, and master to legendary at 15th level or higher). Unlike when you first become trained at a skill, if two different abilities would make you an expert, master, or legendary in a skill, you don't get to choose a second skill to become expert in—the redundant benefit simply has no effect.

SKILL FEATS

Skill feats are a type of general feat that often grant you a new way to use a skill or make you better at using a skill in a particular way. Skill feats always have the skill trait. These feats appear in Chapter 5.

SKILL CHECKS AND SKILL DCs

When you're actively using a skill, often by performing one of its actions, you might attempt a skill check: rolling a d20 and adding your skill modifier. To determine this modifier, add your ability modifier for the skill's key ability, your proficiency bonus for the skill, and any other bonuses and penalties.

Skill modifier = modifier of the skill's key ability score + proficiency bonus + other bonuses + penalties

---

When writing down the modifier on your character sheet, you should write down only the numbers that always apply—typically just your ability modifier and proficiency bonus at 1st level. At higher levels, you may wear or use items to improve your skills with item bonuses pretty much all the time; you should write those down, too.

The GM sets the DC of a skill check, using the guidelines in Chapter 10: Game Mastering. The most important DCs to remember are the five simple skill DCs below.

Task Difficulty	Simple DC
Untrained	10
Trained	15
Expert	20
Master	30
Legendary	40

When someone or something tests your skill, they attempt a check against your skill DC, which is equal to 10 plus your skill modifier. A skill DC works like any other DC to determine the effect of an opposing creature's skill action.

See page 444 in Chapter 9: Playing the Game for more information about modifiers, bonuses, and penalties.

ARMOR AND SKILLS

Some armor imposes a penalty on specific skill checks and DCs. If a creature is wearing armor that imparts a skill penalty, that penalty is applied to the creature's Strength- and Dexterity-based skill checks and skill DCs, unless the action has the attack trait. Check penalties from armor are detailed on page 274 in Chapter 6: Equipment.

SECRET CHECKS

Sometimes you won't know whether you succeed at a skill check. If an action has the secret trait, the GM rolls the check for you and informs you of the effect without revealing the result of the roll or the degree of success. The GM rolls secret checks when your knowledge about the outcome is imperfect, like when you're searching for a hidden creature or object, attempting to deceive someone, translating a tricky bit of ancient text, or remembering some piece of lore. This way, you as the player don't know things that your character wouldn't. This rule is the default for actions with the secret trait, but the GM can choose not to use secret checks if they would rather some or all rolls be public.

EXPLORATION AND DOWNTIME ACTIVITIES

Some skill activities have the exploration or downtime trait. Exploration activities usually take a minute or more, while downtime activities may take a day or more. They usually can't be used during an encounter, though the GM might bend this restriction. If you're not sure whether you have the time to use one of these activities, ask your GM.

GENERAL SKILL ACTIONS

General skill actions are skill actions that can be used with multiple different skills. When you use a general skill action, you might use your modifier from any skill that lists it as one of the skill's actions, depending on the situation.

General Skill Action	Proficiency	Page
Decipher Writing	Trained	234
Earn Income	Trained	236
Identify Magic	Trained	238
Learn a Spell	Trained	238
Recall Knowledge ❖	Untrained	238
Subsist	Untrained	240

DECIPHER WRITING [TRAINED]

When you encounter particularly archaic or esoteric texts, the GM might require you to Decipher the Writing before you can understand it. You must be trained in the relevant skill to Decipher Writing. Arcana is typically used for writing about magic or science, Occultism for esoteric texts about mysteries and philosophy, Religion for scripture, and Society for coded messages or archaic documents.

DECIPHER WRITING

CONCENTRATE   EXPLORATION   SECRET

You attempt to decipher complicated writing or literature on an obscure topic. This usually takes 1 minute per page of text, but might take longer (typically an hour per page for decrypting ciphers or the like). The text must be in a language you can read, though the GM might allow you to attempt to decipher text written in an unfamiliar language using Society instead.

The DC is determined by the GM based on the state or complexity of the document. The GM might have you roll one check for a short text or a check for each section of a larger text.

Critical Success You understand the true meaning of the text.

Success You understand the true meaning of the text. If it was a coded document, you know the general meaning but might not have a word-for-word translation.

Failure You can't understand the text and take a –2 circumstance penalty to further checks to decipher it.

Critical Failure You believe you understand the text on that page, but you have in fact misconstrued its message.

Sample Decipher Tasks

Trained entry-level philosophy treatise

Expert complex code, such as a cipher

TABLE 4–1: SKILLS, KEY ABILITIES, AND ACTIONS

Skill	Key Ability	Untrained Actions	Trained Actions
Acrobatics	Dexterity	Balance ◆ Tumble Through ◆	Maneuver in Flight ◆ Squeeze [E]
Arcana	Intelligence	Recall Knowledge [G] ◆	Borrow an Arcane Spell [E] Decipher Writing [E, G] Identify Magic [E, G] Learn a Spell [E, G]
Athletics	Strength	Climb ◆ Force Open ◆ Grapple ◆ High Jump ◆◆ Long Jump ◆◆ Shove ◆ Swim ◆ Trip ◆	Disarm ◆
Crafting	Intelligence	Recall Knowledge [G] ◆ Repair [E]	Craft [D] Earn Income [D, G] Identify Alchemy [E]
Deception	Charisma	Create a Diversion ◆ Impersonate [E] Lie	Feint ◆
Diplomacy	Charisma	Gather Information [E] Make an Impression [E] Request ◆	
Intimidation	Charisma	Coerce [E] Demoralize ◆	
Lore	Intelligence	Recall Knowledge [G] ◆	Earn Income [D, G]
Medicine	Wisdom	Administer First Aid ◆◆ Recall Knowledge [G] ◆	Treat Disease [D] Treat Poison ◆ Treat Wounds [E]
Nature	Wisdom	Command an Animal ◆ Recall Knowledge [G] ◆	Identify Magic [E, G] Learn a Spell [E, G]
Occultism	Intelligence	Recall Knowledge [G] ◆	Decipher Writing [E, G] Identify Magic [E, G] Learn a Spell [E, G]
Performance	Charisma	Perform ◆	Earn Income [D, G]
Religion	Wisdom	Recall Knowledge [G] ◆	Decipher Writing [E, G] Identify Magic [E, G] Learn a Spell [E, G]
Society	Intelligence	Recall Knowledge [G] ◆ Subsist [D, G]	Create Forgery [D] Decipher Writing [E, G]
Stealth	Dexterity	Conceal an Object ◆ Hide ◆ Sneak ◆	
Survival	Wisdom	Sense Direction [E] Subsist [D, G]	Cover Tracks [E] Track [E]
Thievery	Dexterity	Palm an Object ◆ Steal ◆	Disable a Device ◆◆ Pick a Lock ◆◆

[D] This skill action can be used only during downtime.

[E] This skill action is used during exploration.

[G] This is a general skill action, with a description appearing on pages 234–240 instead of under the entries for the various skills it's used for.

INTRODUCTION

ANCESTRIES &
BACKGROUNDS

CLASSES

SKILLS

FEATS

EQUIPMENT

SPELLS

THE AGE OF
LOST OMENS

PLAYING THE
GAME

GAME
MASTERING

CRAFTING
& TREASURE

APPENDIX

Master spymaster's code or advanced research notes
Legendary esoteric planar text written in metaphor by an ancient celestial

EXTRA PREPARATION

When Earning Income, you might be able to spend days of downtime to prepare for your task, which adjusts the DC of the skill check. This might involve rehearsing a play, studying a topic, and so on. The GM determines how long preparation takes and how much the DC changes. This is most useful when you're trying a task that's higher level than you; otherwise such tasks have an increased DC!

ENDING OR INTERRUPTING TASKS

When a task you're doing is complete, or if you stop in the middle of one, you normally have to find a new task if you want to keep Earning Income. For instance, if you quit your job working at the docks, you'll need to find another place of employment instead of picking up where you left off. This usually takes 1 day or more of downtime looking for leads on new jobs.

However, you might pause a task due to an adventure or event that wouldn't prevent you from returning to the old job later. The GM might decide that you can pick up where you left off, assuming the task hasn't been completed by others in your absence. Whether you roll a new skill check when you resume is also up to the GM. Generally speaking, if you had a good initial roll and want to keep it, you can, but if you had a bad initial roll, you can't try for a better one by pausing to do something else. If your statistics changed during the break–usually because you leveled up while adventuring–you can attempt a new check.

EARN INCOME (TRAINED)

You can use a skill—typically Crafting, Lore, or Performance—to earn money during downtime. You must be trained in the skill to do so. This takes time to set up, and your income depends on your proficiency rank and how lucrative a task you can find. Because this process requires a significant amount of time and involves tracking things outside the progress of adventures, it won't come up in every campaign.

In some cases, the GM might let you use a different skill to Earn Income through specialized work. Usually, this is scholarly work, such as using Religion in a monastery to study old texts—but giving sermons at a church would still fall under Performance instead of Religion. You also might be able to use physical skills to make money, such as using Acrobatics to perform feats in a circus or Thievery to pick pockets. If you're using a skill other than Crafting, Lore, or Performance, the DC tends to be significantly higher.

EARN INCOME

DOWNTIME

You use one of your skills to make money during downtime. The GM assigns a task level representing the most lucrative job available. You can search for lower-level tasks, with the GM determining whether you find any. Sometimes you can attempt to find better work than the initial offerings, though

TABLE 4-2: INCOME EARNED

Task Level	Failure	Trained	Expert	Master	Legendary
0	1 cp	5 cp	5 cp	5 cp	5 cp
1	2 cp	2 sp	2 sp	2 sp	2 sp
2	4 cp	3 sp	3 sp	3 sp	3 sp
3	8 cp	5 sp	5 sp	5 sp	5 sp
4	1 sp	7 sp	8 sp	8 sp	8 sp
5	2 sp	9 sp	1 gp	1 gp	1 gp
6	3 sp	1 gp, 5 sp	2 gp	2 gp	2 gp
7	4 sp	2 gp	2 gp, 5 sp	2 gp, 5 sp	2 gp, 5 sp
8	5 sp	2 gp, 5 sp	3 gp	3 gp	3 gp
9	6 sp	3 gp	4 gp	4 gp	4 gp
10	7 sp	4 gp	5 gp	6 gp	6 gp
11	8 sp	5 gp	6 gp	8 gp	8 gp
12	9 sp	6 gp	8 gp	10 gp	10 gp
13	1 gp	7 gp	10 gp	15 gp	15 gp
14	1 gp, 5 sp	8 gp	15 gp	20 gp	20 gp
15	2 gp	10 gp	20 gp	28 gp	28 gp
16	2 gp, 5 sp	13 gp	25 gp	36 gp	40 gp
17	3 gp	15 gp	30 gp	45 gp	55 gp
18	4 gp	20 gp	45 gp	70 gp	90 gp
19	6 gp	30 gp	60 gp	100 gp	130 gp
20	8 gp	40 gp	75 gp	150 gp	200 gp
20 (critical success)	–	50 gp	90 gp	175 gp	300 gp

this takes time and requires using the Diplomacy skill to Gather Information, doing some research, or socializing.

When you take on a job, the GM secretly sets the DC of your skill check. After your first day of work, you roll to determine your earnings. You gain an amount of income based on your result, the task's level, and your proficiency rank (as listed on Table 4–2: Income Earned).

You can continue working at the task on subsequent days without needing to roll again. For each day you spend after the first, you earn the same amount as the first day, up until the task's completion. The GM determines how long you can work at the task. Most tasks last a week or two, though some can take months or even years.

Critical Success You do outstanding work. Gain the amount of currency listed for the task level + 1 and your proficiency rank.

Success You do competent work. Gain the amount of currency listed for the task level and your proficiency rank.

Failure You do shoddy work and get paid the bare minimum for your time. Gain the amount of currency listed in the failure column for the task level. The GM will likely reduce how long you can continue at the task.

Critical Failure You earn nothing for your work and are fired immediately. You can't continue at the task. Your reputation suffers, potentially making it difficult for you to find rewarding jobs in that community in the future.

Sample Earn Income Tasks

These examples use Alcohol Lore to work in a bar or Legal Lore to perform legal work.

Trained bartend, do legal research

Expert curate drink selection, present minor court cases

Master run a large brewery, present important court cases

Legendary run an international brewing franchise, present a case in Hell's courts

Crafting Goods for the Market [Crafting]

Using Crafting, you can work at producing common items for the market. It's usually easy to find work making basic items whose level is 1 or 2 below your settlement's level (see Earn Income on page 504). Higher-level tasks represent special commissions, which might require you to Craft a specific item using the Craft downtime activity and sell it to a buyer at full price. These opportunities don't occur as often and might have special requirements—or serious consequences if you disappoint a prominent client.

Practicing a Trade [Lore]

You apply the practical benefits of one of your Lore specialties during downtime by practicing your trade. This is most effective for Lore specialties such as business, law, or sailing, where there's high demand for workers. The GM might increase the DC or determine only low-level tasks are available if you're attempting to use an obscure Lore skill to Earn Income. You might also need specialized tools to accept a job, like mining tools to work in a mine or a merchant's scale to buy and sell valuables in a market.

INCOME EXAMPLES

The following examples show the kinds of tasks your character might take on to Earn Income during low-level and high-level play.

HARSK MAKES TEA

Harsk is a 3rd-level ranger and an expert at harvesting and brewing tea. He has a Tea Lore modifier of +7. He has 30 days of downtime at his disposal and decides to work at a prestigious local tea house. The GM decides this is a 5th-level task if Harsk wants to assist the tea master, or a 2nd-level task if he wants to serve tea. Harsk chooses the tougher task, and the GM secretly sets the DC at 20.

Harsk rolls a 4 on his Tea Lore check for a result of 11. Poor Harsk has failed! He earns only 2 sp for his efforts and continues working for 3 more days, for a total of 8 sp.

At that point, the GM offers Harsk a choice: either he can finish out the week with the tea master and look for a new job, or he can lower his ambitions and serve in the tea house. Harsk, now more aware of his own capabilities, accepts the less prestigious job for now. He moves to his new job and attempts a new Tea Lore check against DC 16. Rolling a 19, he gets a result of 26—a critical success! He earns 5 sp per day (like a success at a 3rd-level task). The GM rules that demand will be high enough that Harsk can work there for the remainder of his downtime if he so chooses, a total of 26 days. Harsk accepts and earns a total of 138 sp (13 gp, 8 sp) that month.

LEM PERFORMS

Lem is a 16th-level bard and legendary with his flute. He has a Performance modifier of +31 with his enchanted flute. With 30 days of downtime ahead of him, Lem wonders if he can find something that might excite him more than performing in front of a bunch of stuffy nobles. He finds a momentous offer indeed—a performance in a celestial realm, and Lem's patron goddess Shelyn might even be in attendance! This is a 20th-level task, and the GM secretly sets the DC at 40.

Lem rolls an 11 on his Performance check for a result of 42. Success! The engagement lasts for a week, and at the end, the grateful celestials present Lem with a beautiful living diamond rose in constant bloom worth 1,400 gold pieces (200 gp per day for 7 days).

With 23 days of downtime left, Lem accepts a 14th-level task performing at a prestigious bardic college for members of a royal court. The GM secretly sets the DC at 32, and Lem critically succeeds, earning 28 gp per day for a total of 644 gp. Between the two performances, Lem has earned just over 2,000 gold pieces during his downtime—though he's not sure he'll ever sell that rose.

STAGING A PERFORMANCE (PERFORMANCE)

You perform for an audience to make money. The available audiences determine the level of your task, since more discerning audiences are harder to impress but provide a bigger payout. The GM determines the task level based on the audiences available. Performing for a typical audience of commoners on the street is a level 0 task, but a performance for a group of artisans with more refined tastes might be a 2nd- or 3rd-level task, and ones for merchants, nobility, and royalty are increasingly higher level. Your degree of success determines whether you moved your audience and whether you were rewarded with applause or rotten fruit.

IDENTIFY MAGIC (TRAINED)

Using the skill related to the appropriate tradition, as explained in Magical Traditions and Skills on page 238, you can attempt to identify a magical item, location, or ongoing effect. In many cases, you can use a skill to attempt to Identify Magic of a tradition other than your own at a higher DC. The GM determines whether you can do this and what the DC is.

IDENTIFY MAGIC

CONCENTRATE | **EXPLORATION** | **SECRET**

Once you discover that an item, location, or ongoing effect is magical, you can spend 10 minutes to try to identify the particulars of its magic. If your attempt is interrupted, you must start over. The GM sets the DC for your check. Cursed or esoteric subjects usually have higher DCs or might even be impossible to identify using this activity alone. Heightening a spell doesn't increase the DC to identify it.

Critical Success You learn all the attributes of the magic, including its name (for an effect), what it does, any means of activating it (for an item or location), and whether it is cursed.

Success For an item or location, you get a sense of what it does and learn any means of activating it. For an ongoing effect (such as a spell with a duration), you learn the effect's name and what it does. You can't try again in hopes of getting a critical success.

Failure You fail to identify the magic and can't try again for 1 day.

Critical Failure You misidentify the magic as something else of the GM's choice.

Magical Traditions and Skills

Each magical tradition has a corresponding skill, as shown on the table below. You must have the trained proficiency rank in a skill to use it to Identify Magic or Learn a Spell. Something without a specific tradition, such as an item with the magical trait, can be identified using any of these skills.

Magical Tradition	Corresponding Skill
Arcane	Arcana
Divine	Religion
Occult	Occultism
Primal	Nature

LEARN A SPELL (TRAINED)

If you're a spellcaster, you can use the skill corresponding to your magical tradition to learn a new spell of that tradition. Table 4–3: Learning a Spell lists the Price of the materials needed to Learn a Spell of each level.

LEARN A SPELL

CONCENTRATE | **EXPLORATION**

Requirements You have a spellcasting class feature, and the spell you want to learn is on your magical tradition's spell list.

You can gain access to a new spell of your tradition from someone who knows that spell or from magical writing like a spellbook or scroll. If you can cast spells of multiple traditions, you can Learn a Spell of any of those traditions, but you must use the corresponding skill to do so. For example, if you were a cleric with the bard multiclass archetype, you couldn't use Religion to add an occult spell to your bardic spell repertoire.

To learn the spell, you must do the following:

- Spend 1 hour per level of the spell, during which you must remain in conversation with a person who knows the spell or have the magical writing in your possession.
- Have materials with the Price indicated in Table 4-3.
- Attempt a skill check for the skill corresponding to your tradition (DC determined by the GM, often close to the DC on Table 4-3). Uncommon or rare spells have higher DCs; full guidelines for the GM appear on page 503.

If you have a spellbook, Learning a Spell lets you add the spell to your spellbook; if you prepare spells from a list, it's added to your list; if you have a spell repertoire, you can select it when you add or swap spells.

Critical Success You expend half the materials and learn the spell.

Success You expend the materials and learn the spell.

Failure You fail to learn the spell but can try again after you gain a level. The materials aren't expended.

Critical Failure As failure, plus you expend half the materials.

TABLE 4-3: LEARNING A SPELL

Spell Level	Price	Typical DC
1st or cantrip	2 gp	15
2nd	6 gp	18
3rd	16 gp	20
4th	36 gp	23
5th	70 gp	26
6th	140 gp	28
7th	300 gp	31
8th	650 gp	34
9th	1,500 gp	36
10th	7,000 gp	41

RECALL KNOWLEDGE (UNTRAINED)

To remember useful information on a topic, you can attempt to Recall Knowledge. You might know basic information about something without needing to attempt a check, but Recall Knowledge requires you to stop and think for a moment so you can recollect more specific

INTRODUCTION

ANCESTRIES &
BACKGROUNDS

CLASSES

SKILLS

FEATS

EQUIPMENT

SPELLS

THE AGE OF
LOST OMENS

PLAYING THE
GAME

GAME
MASTERING

CRAFTING
& TREASURE

APPENDIX

facts and apply them. You might even need to spend time investigating first. For instance, to use Medicine to learn the cause of death, you might need to conduct a forensic examination before attempting to Recall Knowledge.

RECALL KNOWLEDGE ◆❖

CONCENTRATE **SECRET**

You attempt a skill check to try to remember a bit of knowledge regarding a topic related to that skill. The GM determines the DCs for such checks and which skills apply.

Critical Success You recall the knowledge accurately and gain additional information or context.

Success You recall the knowledge accurately or gain a useful clue about your current situation.

Critical Failure You recall incorrect information or gain an erroneous or misleading clue.

The following skills can be used to Recall Knowledge, getting information about the listed topics. In some cases, you can get the GM's permission to use a different but related skill, usually against a higher DC than normal. Some topics might appear on multiple lists, but the skills could give different information. For example, Arcana might tell you about the magical defenses of a golem, whereas Crafting could tell you about its sturdy resistance to physical attacks.

- **Arcana:** Arcane theories, magical traditions, creatures of arcane significance, and arcane planes.
- **Crafting:** Alchemical reactions and creatures, item value, engineering, unusual materials, and constructs.

- **Lore:** The subject of the Lore skill's subcategory.
- **Medicine:** Diseases, poisons, wounds, and forensics.
- **Nature:** The environment, flora, geography, weather, creatures of natural origin, and natural planes.
- **Occultism:** Ancient mysteries, obscure philosophy, creatures of occult significance, and esoteric planes.
- **Religion:** Divine agents, divine planes, theology, obscure myths, and creatures of religious significance.
- **Society:** Local history, key personalities, legal institutions, societal structure, and humanoid culture.

The GM might allow checks to Recall Knowledge using other skills. For example, you might assess the skill of an acrobat using Acrobatics. If you're using a physical skill (like in this example), the GM will most likely have you use a mental ability score—typically Intelligence—instead of the skill's normal physical ability score.

Recall Knowledge Tasks

These examples use Society or Religion.

Untrained name of a ruler, key noble, or major deity

Trained line of succession for a major noble family, core doctrines of a major deity

Expert genealogy of a minor noble, teachings of an ancient priest

Master hierarchy of a genie noble court, major extraplanar temples of a deity

Legendary existence of a long-lost noble heir, secret doctrines of a religion

SUBSIST (UNTRAINED)

If you need to provide food and shelter, you can use the Subsist downtime activity. This typically uses Society if you're in a settlement or Survival if you're in the wild.

SUBSIST

DOWNTIME

You try to provide food and shelter for yourself, and possibly others as well, with a standard of living described on page 294. The GM determines the DC based on the nature of the place where you're trying to Subsist. You might need a minimum proficiency rank to Subsist in particularly strange environments. Unlike most downtime activities, you can Subsist after 8 hours or less of exploration, but if you do, you take a –5 penalty.

Critical Success You either provide a subsistence living for yourself and one additional creature, or you improve your own food and shelter, granting yourself a comfortable living.

Success You find enough food and shelter with basic protection from the elements to provide you a subsistence living.

Failure You're exposed to the elements and don't get enough food, becoming fatigued until you attain sufficient food and shelter.

Critical Failure You attract trouble, eat something you shouldn't, or otherwise worsen your situation. You take a –2 circumstance penalty to checks to Subsist for 1 week. You don't find any food at all; if you don't have any stored up, you're in danger of starving or dying of thirst if you continue failing.

Sample Subsist Tasks

Untrained lush forest with calm weather or large city with plentiful resources
Trained typical hillside or village
Expert typical mountains or insular hamlet
Master typical desert or city under siege
Legendary barren wasteland or city of undead

SKILL DESCRIPTIONS

The following entries describe the skills in the game. The heading for each entry provides the skill's name, with that skill's key ability in parentheses. A brief description of the skill is followed by a list of actions you can use if you're untrained in that skill, and then the actions you can perform if you are trained in that skill. Some actions list sample tasks for each rank to give you a better sense of what you can accomplish as your proficiency increases. As the actions of a skill aren't comprehensive, there may be times when the GM asks you to attempt a skill check without using any of the listed actions, or times when the GM asks you to roll using a different key ability modifier.

Most skills include entries for success and failure, as well as descriptions of what occurs on a critical success or a critical failure. If either of the critical entries is absent, treat those results as a success or failure, as normal.

ACROBATICS (DEX)

Acrobatics measures your ability to perform tasks requiring coordination and grace. When you use the Escape basic action (page 470), you can use your Acrobatics modifier instead of your unarmed attack modifier.

BALANCE ❖

MOVE

Requirements You are in a square that contains a narrow surface, uneven ground, or another similar feature.

You move across a narrow surface or uneven ground, attempting an Acrobatics check against its Balance DC. You are flat-footed while on a narrow surface or uneven ground.

Critical Success You move up to your Speed.

Success You move up to your Speed, treating it as difficult terrain (every 5 feet costs 10 feet of movement).

Failure You must remain stationary to keep your balance (wasting the action) or you fall. If you fall, your turn ends.

Critical Failure You fall and your turn ends.

Sample Balance Tasks

Untrained tangled roots, uneven cobblestones
Trained wooden beam
Expert deep, loose gravel
Master tightrope, smooth sheet of ice
Legendary razor's edge, chunks of floor falling in midair

TUMBLE THROUGH ❖

MOVE

You Stride up to your Speed. During this movement, you can try to move through the space of one enemy. Attempt an Acrobatics check against the enemy's Reflex DC as soon as you try to enter its space. You can Tumble Through using Climb, Fly, Swim, or another action instead of Stride in the appropriate environment.

Success You move through the enemy's space, treating the squares in its space as difficult terrain (every 5 feet costs 10 feet of movement). If you don't have enough Speed to move all the way through its space, you get the same effect as a failure.

Failure Your movement ends, and you trigger reactions as if you had moved out of the square you started in.

ACROBATICS TRAINED ACTIONS

MANEUVER IN FLIGHT ❖

MOVE

Requirements You have a fly Speed.

You try a difficult maneuver while flying. Attempt an Acrobatics check. The GM determines what maneuvers are possible, but they rarely allow you to move farther than your fly Speed.

Success You succeed at the maneuver.

Failure Your maneuver fails. The GM chooses if you simply can't move or if some other detrimental effect happens. The outcome should be appropriate for the maneuver you attempted (for instance, being blown off course if you were trying to fly against a strong wind).

Critical Failure As failure, but the consequence is more dire.

INTRODUCTION

ANCESTRIES & BACKGROUNDS

CLASSES

SKILLS

FEATS

EQUIPMENT

SPELLS

THE AGE OF LOST OMENS

PLAYING THE GAME

GAME MASTERING

CRAFTING & TREASURE

APPENDIX

Sample Maneuver in Flight Tasks

Trained steep ascent or descent

Expert fly against the wind, hover midair

Master reverse direction

Legendary fly through gale force winds

SQUEEZE

`EXPLORATION` `MOVE`

You contort yourself to squeeze through a space so small you can barely fit through. This action is for exceptionally small spaces; many tight spaces are difficult terrain (page 475) that you can move through more quickly and without a check.

Critical Success You squeeze through the tight space in 1 minute per 10 feet of squeezing.

Success You squeeze through in 1 minute per 5 feet.

Critical Failure You become stuck in the tight space. While you're stuck, you can spend 1 minute attempting another Acrobatics check at the same DC. Any result on that check other than a critical failure causes you to become unstuck.

Sample Squeeze Tasks

Trained space barely fitting your shoulders

Master space barely fitting your head

ARCANA (INT)

Arcana measures how much you know about arcane magic and creatures. Even if you're untrained, you can Recall Knowledge (page 238).

- **Recall Knowledge** about arcane theories; magic traditions; creatures of arcane significance (like dragons and beasts); and the Elemental, Astral, and Shadow Planes.

ARCANA TRAINED ACTIONS

You must be trained in Arcana to use it for the following general skill actions (page 234).

- **Decipher Writing** about arcane theory.
- **Identify Magic**, particularly arcane magic.
- **Learn a Spell** from the arcane tradition.

BORROW AN ARCANE SPELL

`CONCENTRATE` `EXPLORATION`

If you're an arcane spellcaster who prepares from a spellbook, you can attempt to prepare a spell from someone else's spellbook. The GM sets the DC for the check based on the spell's level and rarity; it's typically a bit easier than Learning the Spell.

Success You prepare the borrowed spell as part of your normal spell preparation.

Failure You fail to prepare the spell, but the spell slot remains available for you to prepare a different spell. You can't try to prepare this spell until the next time you prepare spells.

ATHLETICS (STR)

Athletics allows you to perform deeds of physical prowess. When you use the Escape basic action (page 470), you can use your Athletics modifier instead of your unarmed attack modifier.

CLIMB ◆

`MOVE`

Requirements You have both hands free.

You move up, down, or across an incline. Unless it's particularly easy, you must attempt an Athletics check. The GM determines the DC based on the nature of the incline and environmental circumstances. You're flat-footed unless you have a climb Speed.

Critical Success You move up, across, or safely down the incline for 5 feet plus 5 feet per 20 feet of your land Speed (a total of 10 feet for most PCs).

Success You move up, across, or safely down the incline for 5 feet per 20 feet of your land Speed (a total of 5 feet for most PCs, minimum 5 feet if your Speed is below 20 feet).

Critical Failure You fall. If you began the climb on stable ground, you fall and land prone.

Sample Climb Tasks

Untrained ladder, steep slope, low-branched tree
Trained rigging, rope, typical tree
Expert wall with small handholds and footholds
Master ceiling with handholds and footholds, rock wall
Legendary smooth surface

TABLE 4–4: CLIMB AND SWIM DISTANCE

This table provides a quick reference for how far you can move with a Climb or Swim action.

	Climb Distance		Swim Distance	
Speed	**Success**	**Critical**	**Success**	**Critical**
5–15 feet	5	5	5	10
20–35 feet	5	10	10	15
40–55 feet	10	15	15	20
60–65 feet	15	20	20	25

FORCE OPEN ❖

ATTACK

Using your body, a lever, or some other tool, you attempt to forcefully open a door, window, container or heavy gate. With a high enough result, you can even smash through walls. Without a crowbar, prying something open takes a –2 item penalty to the Athletics check to Force Open.

Critical Success You open the door, window, container, or gate and can avoid damaging it in the process.

Success You break the door, window, container, or gate open, and the door, window, container, or gate gains the broken condition. If it's especially sturdy, the GM might have it take damage but not be broken.

Critical Failure Your attempt jams the door, window, container, or gate shut, imposing a –2 circumstance penalty on future attempts to Force it Open.

Sample Force Open Tasks

Untrained fabric, flimsy glass
Trained ice, sturdy glass
Expert flimsy wooden door, wooden portcullis
Master sturdy wooden door, iron portcullis, metal bar
Legendary stone or iron door

GRAPPLE ❖

ATTACK

Requirements You have at least one free hand. Your target cannot be more than one size larger than you.

You attempt to grab an opponent with your free hand. Attempt an Athletics check against their Fortitude DC. You can also Grapple to keep your hold on a creature you already grabbed.

Critical Success Your opponent is restrained until the end of your next turn unless you move or your opponent Escapes (page 470).

Success Your opponent is grabbed until the end of your next turn unless you move or your opponent Escapes.

Failure You fail to grab your opponent. If you already had the opponent grabbed or restrained using a Grapple, those conditions on that creature end.

Critical Failure If you already had the opponent grabbed or restrained, it breaks free. Your target can either grab you, as if it succeeded at using the Grapple action against you, or force you to fall and land prone.

HIGH JUMP ❖❖

You Stride, then make a vertical Leap and attempt a DC 30 Athletics check to increase the height of your jump. If you didn't Stride at least 10 feet, you automatically fail your check. This DC might be increased or decreased due to the situation, as determined by the GM.

Critical Success Increase the maximum vertical distance to 8 feet, or increase the maximum vertical distance to 5 feet and maximum horizontal distance to 10 feet.

Success Increase the maximum vertical distance to 5 feet.

Failure You Leap normally.

Critical Failure You don't Leap at all, and instead you fall prone in your space.

Leap

The Leap basic action is used for High Jump and Long Jump. Leap lets you take a careful, short jump. You can Leap up to 10 feet horizontally if your Speed is at least 15 feet, or up to 15 feet horizontally if your Speed is at least 30 feet. You land in the space where your Leap ends (meaning you can typically clear a 5-foot gap if your Speed is between 15 feet and 30 feet, or a 10-foot gap if your Speed is 30 feet or more). If you make a vertical Leap, you can move up to 3 feet vertically and 5 feet horizontally onto an elevated surface.

LONG JUMP ❖❖

You Stride, then make a horizontal Leap and attempt an Athletics check to increase the length of your jump. The DC of the Athletics check is equal to the total distance in feet you're attempting to move during your Leap (so you'd need to succeed at a DC 20 check to Leap 20 feet). You can't Leap farther than your Speed.

If you didn't Stride at least 10 feet, or if you attempt to jump in a different direction than your Stride, you automatically fail your check. This DC might be increased or decreased due to the situation, as determined by the GM.

Success Increase the maximum horizontal distance you Leap to the desired distance.

Failure You Leap normally.

Critical Failure You Leap normally, but then fall and land prone.

SHOVE ◆

ATTACK

Requirements You have at least one hand free. The target can't be more than one size larger than you.

You push an opponent away from you. Attempt an Athletics check against your opponent's Fortitude DC.

Critical Success You push your opponent up to 10 feet away from you. You can Stride after it, but you must move the same distance and in the same direction.

Success You push your opponent back 5 feet. You can Stride after it, but you must move the same distance and in the same direction.

Critical Failure You lose your balance, fall, and land prone.

Forced Movement

The Shove action can force a creature to move. When an effect forces you to move, or if you start falling, the distance you move is defined by the effect that moved you, not by your Speed. Because you're not acting to move, this doesn't trigger reactions triggered by movement.

SWIM ◆

MOVE

You propel yourself through water. In most calm water, you succeed at the action without needing to attempt a check. If you must breathe air and you're submerged in water, you must hold your breath each round. If you fail to hold your breath, you begin to drown (as described on page 478). If the water you are swimming in is turbulent or otherwise dangerous, you might have to attempt an Athletics check to Swim.

If you end your turn in water and haven't succeeded at a Swim action that turn, you sink 10 feet or get moved by the current, as determined by the GM. However, if your last action on your turn was to enter the water, you don't sink or move with the current that turn.

Critical Success You move through the water 10 feet, plus 5 feet per 20 feet of your land Speed (a total of 15 feet for most PCs).

Success You move through the water 5 feet, plus 5 feet per 20 feet of your land Speed (a total of 10 feet for most PCs).

Critical Failure You make no progress, and if you're holding your breath, you lose 1 round of air.

Sample Swim Tasks

Untrained lake or other still water
Trained flowing water, like a river
Expert swiftly flowing river
Master stormy sea
Legendary maelstrom, waterfall

TRIP ◆

ATTACK

Requirements You have at least one hand free. Your target can't be more than one size larger than you.

FALLING

When you fall more than 5 feet, you take falling damage when you land, which is bludgeoning damage equal to half the distance you fell. If you take any damage from a fall, you're knocked prone when you land.

If you fall into water, snow, or another soft substance, calculate the damage from the fall as though your fall were 20 feet shorter. The reduction can't be greater than the depth of the water (so when falling into water that is only 10 feet deep, you treat the fall as 10 feet shorter). You can Grab an Edge as a reaction (page 472) to reduce or eliminate the damage from some falls. More detailed rules for falling damage appear on page 463.

You try to knock an opponent to the ground. Attempt an Athletics check against the target's Reflex DC.

Critical Success The target falls and lands prone and takes 1d6 bludgeoning damage.

Success The target falls and lands prone.

Critical Failure You lose your balance and fall and land prone.

ATHLETICS TRAINED ACTION

DISARM ◆

ATTACK

Requirements You have at least one hand free. The target can't be more than one size larger than you.

You try to knock something out of an opponent's grasp. Attempt an Athletics check against the opponent's Reflex DC.

Critical Success You knock the item out of the opponent's grasp. It falls to the ground in the opponent's space.

Success You weaken your opponent's grasp on the item. Until the start of that creature's turn, attempts to Disarm the opponent of that item gain a +2 circumstance bonus, and the target takes a −2 circumstance penalty to attacks with the item or other checks requiring a firm grasp on the item.

Critical Failure You lose your balance and become flat-footed until the start of your next turn.

CRAFTING (INT)

You can use this skill to create, understand, and repair items. Even if you're untrained, you can Recall Knowledge (page 238).

- **Recall Knowledge** about alchemical reactions, the value of items, engineering, unusual materials, and alchemical or mechanical creatures. The GM determines which creatures this applies to, but it usually includes constructs.

REPAIR

EXPLORATION MANIPULATE

Requirements You have a repair kit (page 291).

You spend 10 minutes attempting to fix a damaged item, placing the item on a stable surface and using the repair kit with

INTRODUCTION

ANCESTRIES & BACKGROUNDS

CLASSES

SKILLS

FEATS

EQUIPMENT

SPELLS

THE AGE OF LOST OMENS

PLAYING THE GAME

GAME MASTERING

CRAFTING & TREASURE

APPENDIX

both hands. The GM sets the DC, but it's usually about the same DC to Repair a given item as it is to Craft it in the first place. You can't Repair a destroyed item.

Critical Success You restore 10 Hit Points to the item, plus an additional 10 Hit Points per proficiency rank you have in Crafting (a total of 20 HP if you're trained, 30 HP if you're an expert, 40 HP if you're a master, or 50 HP if you're legendary).

Success You restore 5 Hit Points to the item, plus an additional 5 per proficiency rank you have in Crafting (for a total of 10 HP if you are trained, 15 HP if you're an expert, 20 HP if you're a master, or 25 HP if you're legendary).

Critical Failure You deal 2d6 damage to the item. Apply the item's Hardness to this damage.

CRAFTING TRAINED ACTIONS

You must be trained in Crafting to use it to Earn Income (page 236).

- **Earn Income** by crafting goods for the market.

CRAFT

DOWNTIME | MANIPULATE

You can make an item from raw materials. You need the Alchemical Crafting skill feat to create alchemical items, the Magical Crafting skill feat to create magic items, and the Snare Crafting feat to create snares.

To Craft an item, you must meet the following requirements:

- The item is your level or lower. An item that doesn't list a level is level 0. If the item is 9th level or higher, you

must be a master in Crafting, and if it's 16th or higher, you must be legendary.

- You have the formula for the item; see Getting Formulas below for more information.
- You have an appropriate set of tools and, in many cases, a workshop. For example, you need access to a smithy to forge a metal shield.
- You must supply raw materials worth at least half the item's Price. You always expend at least that amount of raw materials when you Craft successfully. If you're in a settlement, you can usually spend currency to get the amount of raw materials you need, except in the case of rarer precious materials.

You must spend 4 days at work, at which point you attempt a Crafting check. The GM determines the DC to Craft the item based on its level, rarity, and other circumstances.

If your attempt to create the item is successful, you expend the raw materials you supplied. You can pay the remaining portion of the item's Price in materials to complete the item immediately, or you can spend additional downtime days working on it. For each additional day you spend, reduce the value of the materials you need to expend to complete the item. This amount is determined using Table 4–2: Income Earned (page 236), based on your proficiency rank in Crafting and using your own level instead of a task level. After any of these downtime days, you can complete the item by spending the remaining portion of its Price in materials. If the downtime days you spend are interrupted, you can return to finish the item later, continuing where you left off. An example of Crafting appears in the sidebar.

Critical Success Your attempt is successful. Each additional day spent Crafting reduces the materials needed to complete the item by an amount based on your level + 1 and your proficiency rank in Crafting.

Success Your attempt is successful. Each additional day spent Crafting reduces the materials needed to complete the item by an amount based on your level and your proficiency rank.

Failure You fail to complete the item. You can salvage the raw materials you supplied for their full value. If you want to try again, you must start over.

Critical Failure You fail to complete the item. You ruin 10% of the raw materials you supplied, but you can salvage the rest. If you want to try again, you must start over.

Consumables and Ammunition

You can Craft items with the consumable trait in batches, making up to four of the same item at once with a single check. This requires you to include the raw materials for all the items in the batch at the start, and you must complete the batch all at once. You also Craft non-magical ammunition in batches, using the quantity listed in Table 6–8: Ranged Weapons (typically 10).

Getting Formulas

You can gain access to the formulas for all common items in Chapter 6: Equipment by purchasing a basic crafter's book (page 287). See the rules on page 293 for information on how to acquire other formulas.

IDENTIFY ALCHEMY

CONCENTRATE **EXPLORATION** **SECRET**

Requirements You have alchemist's tools (page 287).

You can identify the nature of an alchemical item with 10 minutes of testing using alchemist's tools. If your attempt is interrupted in any way, you must start over.

Success You identify the item and the means of activating it.

Failure You fail to identify the item but can try again.

Critical Failure You misidentify the item as another item of the GM's choice.

DECEPTION (CHA)

You can trick and mislead others using disguises, lies, and other forms of subterfuge.

CREATE A DIVERSION ◆

MENTAL

With a gesture, a trick, or some distracting words, you can create a diversion that draws creatures' attention elsewhere. If you use a gesture or trick, this action gains the manipulate trait. If you use distracting words, it gains the auditory and linguistic traits.

Attempt a single Deception check and compare it to the

CRAFTING EXAMPLE

Ezren is a 5th-level wizard and an expert in Crafting. He has a Crafting modifier of +13 and the Magical Crafting feat. With 2 weeks of downtime ahead of him, he decides to craft a *striking rune*, a 4th-level item. The GM secretly chooses a DC of 19.

The item has a Price of 65 gp, so Ezren prepares 32 gp, 5 sp worth of raw materials. He has another 32 gp, 5 sp worth of raw materials on hand. After spending 4 days building and incanting spells, he rolls a 12 on his Crafting check, for a result of 25. That's a success! At this point, Ezren can spend the additional 32 gp, 5 sp worth of materials to complete the item immediately for 65 gp.

However, Ezren has 10 more days on his hands, so he decides to spend additional time to complete the item. Because he's a 5th-level character and an expert at Crafting, he reduces the amount he has to pay by 1 gp for each day spent. After spending 10 days working, he reduces the cost to complete the item from 65 gp to 55 gp. He spends the remaining portion of its Price in materials, completes the *striking rune*, and goes out on his next adventure. (He could have stayed home to keep working on the *striking rune*, eventually reducing the item's total Price to just the half he paid up front, but adventuring is far more lucrative!)

If Ezren's Crafting check result were a 29 or higher, he'd have gotten a critical success. In that case, he'd reduce the remaining amount by 2 gp per day, lowering the amount needed to complete the item after 10 additional days of work to 45 gp.

Perception DCs of the creatures whose attention you're trying to divert. Whether or not you succeed, creatures you attempt to divert gain a +4 circumstance bonus to their Perception DCs against your attempts to Create a Diversion for 1 minute.

Success You become hidden to each creature whose Perception DC is less than or equal to your result. (The hidden condition allows you to Sneak away, as described on page 252.) This lasts until the end of your turn or until you do anything except Step or use the Hide or the Sneak action of the Stealth skill (pages 251 and 252). If you Strike a creature, the creature remains flat-footed against that attack, and you then become observed. If you do anything else, you become observed just before you act unless the GM determines otherwise.

Failure You don't divert the attention of any creatures whose Perception DC exceeds your result, and those creatures are aware you were trying to trick them.

IMPERSONATE

CONCENTRATE **EXPLORATION** **MANIPULATE** **SECRET**

You create a disguise to pass yourself off as someone or something you are not. Assembling a convincing disguise takes 10 minutes and requires a disguise kit (found on page 290), but a simpler, quicker disguise might do the job if you're not trying to imitate a specific individual, at the GM's discretion.

INTRODUCTION

ANCESTRIES & BACKGROUNDS

CLASSES

SKILLS

FEATS

EQUIPMENT

SPELLS

THE AGE OF LOST OMENS

PLAYING THE GAME

GAME MASTERING

CRAFTING & TREASURE

APPENDIX

In most cases, creatures have a chance to detect your deception only if they use the Seek action to attempt Perception checks against your Deception DC. If you attempt to directly interact with someone while disguised, the GM rolls a secret Deception check for you against that creature's Perception DC instead. If you're disguised as a specific individual, the GM might give creatures you interact with a circumstance bonus based on how well they know the person you're imitating, or the GM might roll a secret Deception check even if you aren't directly interacting with others.

Success You trick the creature into thinking you're the person you're disguised as. You might have to attempt a new check if your behavior changes.

Failure The creature can tell you're not who you claim to be.

Critical Failure The creature can tell you're not who you claim to be, and it recognizes you if it would know you without a disguise.

LIE

> AUDITORY | CONCENTRATE | LINGUISTIC | MENTAL | SECRET

You try to fool someone with an untruth. Doing so takes at least 1 round, or longer if the lie is elaborate. You roll a single Deception check and compare it against the Perception DC of every creature you are trying to fool. The GM might give them a circumstance bonus based on the situation and the nature of the lie you are trying to tell. Elaborate or highly unbelievable lies are much harder to get a creature to believe than simpler and more believable lies, and some lies are so big that it's impossible to get anyone to believe them.

At the GM's discretion, if a creature initially believes your lie, it might attempt a Perception check later to Sense Motive against your Deception DC to realize it's a lie. This usually happens if the creature discovers enough evidence to counter your statements.

Success The target believes your lie.

Failure The target doesn't believe your lie and gains a +4 circumstance bonus against your attempts to Lie for the duration of your conversation. The target is also more likely to be suspicious of you in the future.

DECEPTION TRAINED ACTION

FEINT ✦

> MENTAL

Requirements You are within melee reach of the opponent you attempt to Feint.

With a misleading flourish, you leave an opponent unprepared for your real attack. Attempt a Deception check against that opponent's Perception DC.

Critical Success You throw your enemy's defenses against you entirely off. The target is flat-footed against melee attacks that you attempt against it until the end of your next turn.

Success Your foe is fooled, but only momentarily. The target is flat-footed against the next melee attack that you attempt against it before the end of your current turn.

Critical Failure Your feint backfires. You are flat-footed against melee attacks the target attempts against you until the end of your next turn.

DIPLOMACY (CHA)

You influence others through negotiation and flattery.

GATHER INFORMATION

> EXPLORATION | SECRET

You canvass local markets, taverns, and gathering places in an attempt to learn about a specific individual or topic. The GM determines the DC of the check and the amount of time it takes (typically 2 hours, but sometimes more), along with any benefit you might be able to gain by spending coin on bribes, drinks, or gifts.

Success You collect information about the individual or topic. The GM determines the specifics.

Critical Failure You collect incorrect information about the individual or topic.

Sample Gather Information Tasks

Untrained talk of the town

Trained common rumor

Expert obscure rumor, poorly guarded secret

Master well-guarded or esoteric information

Legendary information known only to an incredibly select few, or only to extraordinary beings

MAKE AN IMPRESSION

> AUDITORY | CONCENTRATE | EXPLORATION | LINGUISTIC | MENTAL

With at least 1 minute of conversation, during which you engage in charismatic overtures, flattery, and other acts of goodwill, you seek to make a good impression on someone to make them temporarily agreeable. At the end of the conversation, attempt a Diplomacy check against the Will DC of one target, modified by any circumstances the GM sees fit. Good impressions (or bad impressions, on a critical failure) last for only the current social interaction unless the GM decides otherwise.

Critical Success The target's attitude toward you improves by two steps.

Success The target's attitude toward you improves by one step.

Critical Failure The target's attitude toward you decreases by one step.

Changing Attitudes

Your influence on NPCs is measured with a set of attitudes that reflect how they view your character. These are only a brief summary of a creature's disposition. The GM will supply additional nuance based on the history and beliefs of the characters you're interacting with, and their attitudes can change in accordance with the story. The attitudes are detailed in the Conditions Appendix and are summarized here.

- **Helpful:** Willing to help you and responds favorably to your requests.

- **Friendly:** Has a good attitude toward you, but won't necessarily stick their neck out to help you.
- **Indifferent:** Doesn't care about you either way. (Most NPCs start out indifferent.)
- **Unfriendly:** Dislikes you and doesn't want to help you.
- **Hostile:** Actively works against you—and might attack you just because of their dislike.

No one can ever change the attitude of a player character with these skills. You can roleplay interactions with player characters, and even use Diplomacy results if the player wants a mechanical sense of how convincing or charming a character is, but players make the ultimate decisions about how their characters respond.

REQUEST ✦

| AUDITORY | CONCENTRATE | LINGUISTIC | MENTAL |

You can make a request of a creature that's friendly or helpful to you. You must couch the request in terms that the target would accept given their current attitude toward you. The GM sets the DC based on the difficulty of the request. Some requests are unsavory or impossible, and even a helpful NPC would never agree to them.

Critical Success The target agrees to your request without qualifications.

Success The target agrees to your request, but they might demand added provisions or alterations to the request.

Failure The target refuses the request, though they might propose an alternative that is less extreme.

Critical Failure Not only does the target refuse the request, but their attitude toward you decreases by one step due to the temerity of the request.

INTIMIDATION (CHA)

You bend others to your will using threats.

COERCE

| AUDITORY | CONCENTRATE | EMOTION | EXPLORATION | LINGUISTIC | MENTAL |

With threats either veiled or overt, you attempt to bully a creature into doing what you want. You must spend at least 1 minute of conversation with a creature you can see and that can either see or sense you. At the end of the conversation, attempt an Intimidation check against the target's Will DC, modified by any circumstances the GM determines. The attitudes referenced in the effects below are summarized in the Changing Attitudes sidebar on page 246 and described in full in the Conditions Appendix, starting on page 618.

Critical Success The target gives you the information you seek or agrees to follow your directives so long as they aren't likely to harm the target in any way. The target continues to comply for an amount of time determined by the GM but not exceeding 1 day, at which point the target becomes unfriendly (if they weren't already unfriendly or hostile). However, the target is too scared of you to retaliate—at least in the short term.

Success As critical success, but once the target becomes unfriendly, they might decide to act against you—for example, by reporting you to the authorities or assisting your enemies.

Failure The target doesn't do what you say, and if they were not already unfriendly or hostile, they become unfriendly.

Critical Failure The target refuses to comply, becomes hostile if they weren't already, and can't be Coerced by you for at least 1 week.

DEMORALIZE ✦

| AUDITORY | CONCENTRATE | EMOTION | MENTAL |

With a sudden shout, a well-timed taunt, or a cutting put-down, you can shake an enemy's resolve. Choose a creature within 30 feet of you who you're aware of. Attempt an Intimidation check against that target's Will DC. If the target does not understand the language you are speaking, you're not speaking a language, or they can't hear you, you take a -4 circumstance penalty to the check. Regardless of your result, the target is temporarily immune to your attempts to Demoralize it for 10 minutes.

Critical Success The target becomes frightened 2.

Success The target becomes frightened 1.

LORE (INT)

You have specialized information on a narrow topic. Lore features many subcategories. You might have Military Lore, Sailing Lore, Vampire Lore, or any similar subcategory of the skill. Each subcategory counts as its own skill, so applying a skill increase to Planar Lore wouldn't increase your proficiency with Sailing Lore, for example.

You gain a specific subcategory of the Lore skill from your background. The GM determines what other subcategories they'll allow as Lore skills, though these categories are always less broad than any of the other skills that allow you to Recall Knowledge, and they should never be able to fully or mainly take the place of another skill's Recall Knowledge action. For instance, Magic Lore wouldn't enable you to recall the same breadth of knowledge covered by Arcana, Adventuring Lore wouldn't simply give you all the information an adventurer needs, and Planar Lore would not be sufficient to gain all the information spread across various skills and subcategories such as Heaven Lore.

If you have multiple subcategories of Lore that could apply to a check or that would overlap with another skill in the circumstances, you can use the skill with the better skill modifier or the one you would prefer to use. If there's any doubt whether a Lore skill applies to a specific topic or action, the GM decides whether it can be used or not.

Even if you're untrained in Lore, you can use it to Recall Knowledge (page 238).

- **Recall Knowledge** about the subject of your Lore skill's subcategory.

INTRODUCTION

ANCESTRIES & BACKGROUNDS

CLASSES

SKILLS

FEATS

EQUIPMENT

SPELLS

THE AGE OF LOST OMENS

PLAYING THE GAME

GAME MASTERING

CRAFTING & TREASURE

APPENDIX

COMMON LORE SUBCATEGORIES

You can learn any Lore skill your GM gives you permission to take. The following list covers a wide variety of common Lore topics appropriate for most campaigns. Backgrounds often grant you a Lore from this list.

- Academia Lore
- Accounting Lore
- Architecture Lore
- Art Lore
- Circus Lore
- Engineering Lore
- Farming Lore
- Fishing Lore
- Fortune-Telling Lore
- Games Lore
- Genealogy Lore
- Gladiatorial Lore
- Guild Lore
- Heraldry Lore
- Herbalism Lore
- Hunting Lore
- Labor Lore
- Legal Lore
- Library Lore
- Lore about a specific deity (Abadar Lore, Iomedae Lore, etc.)
- Lore about a specific creature or narrow category of creatures (Demon Lore, Owlbear Lore, Vampire Lore, etc.)
- Lore of a specific plane other than the Material Plane, or the plane in which the game is set if not the Material Plane (Abyss Lore, Astral Plane Lore, Heaven Lore, etc.)
- Lore about a specific settlement (Absalom Lore, Magnimar Lore, etc.)
- Lore about a specific terrain (Mountain Lore, River Lore, etc.)
- Lore of a type of food or drink (Alcohol Lore, Baking Lore, Butchering Lore, Cooking Lore, Tea Lore, etc.)
- Mercantile Lore
- Midwifery Lore
- Milling Lore
- Mining Lore
- Sailing Lore
- Scouting Lore
- Scribing Lore
- Stabling Lore
- Tanning Lore
- Theater Lore
- Underworld Lore
- Warfare Lore

LORE TRAINED ACTION

You must be trained in Lore to use it to Earn Income (page 236).

- **Earn Income** by using your knowledge to practice a trade.

MEDICINE (WIS)

You can patch up wounds and help people recover from diseases and poisons. Even if you're untrained in Medicine, you can use it to Recall Knowledge (page 238).

- **Recall Knowledge** about diseases, injuries, poisons, and other ailments. You can use this to perform forensic examinations if you spend 10 minutes (or more, as determined by the GM) checking for evidence such as wound patterns. This is most useful when determining how a body was injured or killed.

ADMINISTER FIRST AID ◆◆

MANIPULATE

Requirements You have healer's tools (page 290).

You perform first aid on an adjacent creature that is dying or bleeding. If a creature is both dying and bleeding, choose which ailment you're trying to treat before you roll. You can Administer First Aid again to attempt to remedy the other effect.

- **Stabilize** Attempt a Medicine check on a creature that has 0 Hit Points and the dying condition. The DC is equal to 5 + that creature's recovery roll DC (typically 15 + its dying value).
- **Stop Bleeding** Attempt a Medicine check on a creature that is taking persistent bleed damage (page 452), giving them a chance to make another flat check to remove the persistent damage. The DC is usually the DC of the effect that caused the bleed.

Success If you're trying to stabilize, the creature loses the dying condition (but remains unconscious). If you're trying to stop bleeding, the creature attempts a flat check to end the bleeding.

Critical Failure If you were trying to stabilize, the creature's dying value increases by 1. If you were trying to stop bleeding, it immediately takes an amount of damage equal to its persistent bleed damage.

MEDICINE TRAINED ACTIONS

TREAT DISEASE

DOWNTIME MANIPULATE

Requirements You have healer's tools (page 290).

You spend at least 8 hours caring for a diseased creature. Attempt a Medicine check against the disease's DC. After you attempt to Treat a Disease for a creature, you can't try again until after that creature's next save against the disease.

Critical Success You grant the creature a +4 circumstance bonus to its next saving throw against the disease.

Success You grant the creature a +2 circumstance bonus to its next saving throw against the disease.

Critical Failure Your efforts cause the creature to take a –2 circumstance penalty to its next save against the disease.

TREAT POISON ◆

MANIPULATE

Requirements You have healer's tools (page 290).

You treat a patient to prevent the spread of poison. Attempt a Medicine check against the poison's DC. After you attempt to

Treat a Poison for a creature, you can't try again until after the next time that creature attempts a save against the poison.

Critical Success You grant the creature a +4 circumstance bonus to its next saving throw against the poison.

Success You grant the creature a +2 circumstance bonus to its next saving throw against the poison.

Critical Failure Your efforts cause the creature to take a –2 circumstance penalty to its next save against the poison.

TREAT WOUNDS

EXPLORATION | HEALING | MANIPULATE

Requirements You have healer's tools (page 290).

You spend 10 minutes treating one injured living creature (targeting yourself, if you so choose). The target is then temporarily immune to Treat Wounds actions for 1 hour, but this interval overlaps with the time you spent treating (so a patient can be treated once per hour, not once per 70 minutes).

The Medicine check DC is usually 15, though the GM might adjust it based on the circumstances, such as treating a patient outside in a storm, or treating magically cursed wounds. If you're an expert in Medicine, you can instead attempt a DC 20 check to increase the Hit Points regained by 10; if you're a master of Medicine, you can instead attempt a DC 30 check to increase the Hit Points regained by 30; and if you're legendary, you can instead attempt a DC 40 check to increase the Hit Points regained by 50. The damage dealt on a critical failure remains the same.

If you succeed at your check, you can continue treating the target to grant additional healing. If you treat them for a total of 1 hour, double the Hit Points they regain from Treat Wounds.

The result of your Medicine check determines how many Hit Points the target regains.

Critical Success The target regains 4d8 Hit Points, and its wounded condition is removed.

Success The target regains 2d8 Hit Points, and its wounded condition is removed.

Critical Failure The target takes 1d8 damage.

NATURE (WIS)

You know a great deal about the natural world, and you command and train animals and magical beasts. Even if you're untrained in Nature, you can use it to Recall Knowledge (page 238).

- **Recall Knowledge** about fauna, flora, geography, weather, the environment, creatures of natural origin (like animals, beasts, fey, and plants), the First World, the Material Plane, and the Elemental Planes.

COMMAND AN ANIMAL ❖

AUDITORY | CONCENTRATE

You issue an order to an animal. Attempt a Nature check against the animal's Will DC. The GM might adjust the DC if the animal has a good attitude toward you, you suggest a course of action it was predisposed toward, or you offer it a treat.

You automatically fail if the animal is hostile or unfriendly to you. If the animal is helpful to you, increase your degree of

---

COMMANDED ANIMALS

Issuing commands to an animal doesn't always go smoothly. An animal is an independent creature with limited intelligence. Most animals understand only the simplest instructions, so you might be able to instruct your animal to move to a certain square but not dictate a specific path to get there, or command it to attack a certain creature but not to make its attack nonlethal. The GM decides the specifics of the action your animal uses.

The animal does what you commanded as soon as it can, usually as its first action on its next turn. If you successfully commanded it multiple times, it does what you said in order. It forgets all commands beyond what it can accomplish on its turn. If multiple people command the same animal, the GM determines how the animal reacts. The GM might also make the DC higher if someone has already tried to Command the Animal that round.

---

success by one step. You might be able to Command an Animal more easily with a feat like Ride (page 266).

Most animals know the Leap, Seek, Stand, Stride, and Strike basic actions. If an animal knows an activity, such as a horse's Gallop, you can Command the Animal to perform the activity, but you must spend as many actions on Command an Animal as the activity's number of actions. You can also spend multiple actions to Command the Animal to perform that number of basic actions on its next turn; for instance, you could spend 3 actions to Command an Animal to Stride three times or to Stride twice and then Strike.

Success The animal does as you command on its next turn.

Failure The animal is hesitant or resistant, and it does nothing.

Critical Failure The animal misbehaves or misunderstands, and it takes some other action determined by the GM.

NATURE TRAINED ACTIONS

You must be trained in Nature to use it for the following general skill actions (page 234).

- **Identify Magic**, particularly primal magic.
- **Learn a Spell** from the primal tradition.

OCCULTISM (INT)

You know a great deal about ancient philosophies, esoteric lore, obscure mysticism, and supernatural creatures. Even if you're untrained in Occultism, you can use it to Recall Knowledge (page 238).

- **Recall Knowledge** about ancient mysteries; obscure philosophies; creatures of occult significance (like aberrations, spirits, and oozes); and the Positive Energy, Negative Energy, Shadow, Astral, and Ethereal Planes.

OCCULTISM TRAINED ACTIONS

You must be trained in Occultism to use it for the following general skill actions (page 234).

INTRODUCTION

ANCESTRIES &
BACKGROUNDS

CLASSES

SKILLS

FEATS

EQUIPMENT

SPELLS

THE AGE OF
LOST OMENS

PLAYING THE
GAME

GAME
MASTERING

CRAFTING
& TREASURE

APPENDIX

- **Decipher Writing** on occult topics, including complex metaphysical systems, syncretic principles, weird philosophies, and incoherent ramblings.
- **Identify Magic**, particularly occult magic.
- **Learn a Spell** from the occult tradition.

PERFORMANCE (CHA)

You are skilled at a form of performance, using your talents to impress a crowd or make a living.

BASIC COMPETENCE

Some performances require you to be more than just charismatic, and if you don't meet the demands of the art form or the audience, the GM might apply a penalty based on the relevant ability score. For example, if you're dancing and have a negative Dexterity modifier, you might take a penalty to your attempt at dancing. Likewise, if you are orating and have a negative Intelligence modifier, you might have to hope your raw Charisma can overcome the penalties from your intellectual shortcomings—or ask someone to help write your speeches!

PERFORMANCE TRAITS

When you use an action that utilizes the Performance skill, it gains one or more traits relevant to the type of performance. The GM might change these depending on the circumstances, but the most common performance-based traits are listed below.

Performance	Additional Traits
Act or perform comedy	Auditory, linguistic, and visual
Dance	Move and visual
Play an instrument	Auditory and manipulate
Orate or sing	Auditory and linguistic

PERFORM ❖

> CONCENTRATE

When making a brief performance—one song, a quick dance, or a few jokes—you use the Perform action. This action is most useful when you want to prove your capability or impress someone quickly. Performing rarely has an impact on its own, but it might influence the DCs of subsequent Diplomacy checks against the observers—or even change their attitudes—if the GM sees fit.

Critical Success Your performance impresses the observers, and they're likely to share stories of your ability.

Success You prove yourself, and observers appreciate the quality of your performance.

Failure Your performance falls flat.

Critical Failure You demonstrate only incompetence.

Sample Perform Tasks

Untrained audience of commoners
Trained audience of artisans
Expert audience of merchants or minor nobles
Master audience of high nobility or minor royalty
Legendary audience of major royalty or otherworldly beings

PERFORMANCE TRAINED ACTION

You must be trained in Performance to use it to Earn Income (page 236).

- **Earn Income** by staging a performance.

RELIGION (WIS)

The secrets of deities, dogma, faith, and the realms of divine creatures both sublime and sinister are open to you. You also understand how magic works, though your training imparts a religious slant to that knowledge. Even if you're untrained in Religion, you can use it to Recall Knowledge (page 238).

- **Recall Knowledge** about divine agents, the finer points of theology, obscure myths regarding a faith, and creatures of religious significance (like celestials, fiends, and undead), the Outer Sphere, and the Positive and Negative Energy Planes.

RELIGION TRAINED ACTIONS

You must be trained in Religion to use it for the following general skill actions (page 234).

- **Decipher Writing** of a religious nature, including allegories, homilies, and proverbs.
- **Identify Magic**, particularly divine magic.
- **Learn a Spell** from the divine tradition.

SOCIETY (INT)

You understand the people and systems that make civilization run, and you know the historical events that make societies what they are today. Further, you can use that knowledge to navigate the complex physical, societal, and economic workings of settlements. Even if you're untrained in Society, you can use it for the following general skill actions (page 234).

- **Recall Knowledge** about local history, important personalities, legal institutions, societal structure, and humanoid cultures. The GM might allow Society to apply to other creatures that are major elements of society in your region, such as the draconic nobility in a kingdom of humans ruled by dragons.
- **Subsist** in a settlement by finding shelter, scrounging, or begging for food.

SOCIETY TRAINED ACTIONS

You must be trained in Society to use it to Decipher Writing (page 234).

- **Decipher Writing** that's a coded message, text written in an incomplete or archaic form, or in some cases, text in a language you don't know.

CREATE FORGERY

DOWNTIME **SECRET**

You create a forged document, usually over the course of a day or a week. You must have the proper writing material to create a forgery. When you Create a Forgery, the GM rolls a secret DC 20 Society check. If you succeed, the forgery is of good enough quality that passive observers can't notice the fake. Only those who carefully examine the document and attempt a Perception or Society check against your Society DC can do so.

If the document's handwriting doesn't need to be specific to a person, you need only to have seen a similar document before, and you gain up to a +4 circumstance bonus to your check, as well as to your DC (the GM determines the bonus). To forge a specific person's handwriting, you need a sample of that person's handwriting.

If your check result was below 20, the forgery has some obvious signs of being a fake, so the GM compares your result to each passive observer's Perception DC or Society DC, whichever is higher, using the success or failure results below. Once the GM rolls your check for a document, that same result is used against all passive observers' DCs no matter how many creatures passively observe that document.

An observer who was fooled on a passive glance can still choose to closely scrutinize the documents on the lookout for a forgery, using different techniques and analysis methods beyond the surface elements you successfully forged with your original check. In that case, the observer can attempt a Perception or Society check against your Society DC (if they succeed, they know your document is a forgery).

Success The observer does not detect the forgery.
Failure The observer knows your document is a forgery.

STEALTH (DEX)

You are skilled at avoiding detection, allowing you to slip past foes, hide, or conceal an item.

CONCEAL AN OBJECT ❖

MANIPULATE **SECRET**

You hide a small object on your person (such as a weapon of light Bulk). When you try to sneak a concealed object past someone who might notice it, the GM rolls your Stealth check and compares it to this passive observer's Perception DC. Once the GM rolls your check for a concealed object, that same result is used no matter how many passive observers you try to sneak it past. If a creature is specifically searching you for an item, it can attempt a Perception check against your Stealth DC (finding the object on success).

You can also conceal an object somewhere other than your person, such as among undergrowth or in a secret compartment within a piece of furniture. In this case, characters Seeking in an area compare their Perception check results to your Stealth DC to determine whether they find the object.

Success The object remains undetected.
Failure The searcher finds the object.

BEING STEALTHY

If you want to sneak around when there are creatures that can see you, you can use a combination of Hide and Sneak to do so.

- First, Hide behind something (either by taking advantage of cover or having the concealed condition due to fog, a spell, or a similar effect). A successful Stealth check makes you hidden, though the creatures still know roughly where you are.
- Second, now that you're hidden, you can Sneak. That means you can move at half your Speed and attempt another Stealth check. If it's successful, you're now undetected. That means the creatures don't know which square you're in anymore.

If you were approaching creatures that didn't know you were there, you could begin Sneaking right away, since they didn't know your location to start with. Some actions can cause you to become observed again, but they're mostly what you'd expect: standing out in the open, attacking someone, making a bunch of noise, and so forth. If you Strike someone after successfully Hiding or Sneaking, though, they're flat-footed to that Strike.

Creatures can try to find you using the Seek action, described on page 471.

Three conditions explain the states of detection. Remember that these conditions are relative to each creature—you can be observed by one creature while hidden to another and undetected by a third.

OBSERVED

You're in the creature's clear view.

HIDDEN

The creature knows your location but can't see you.

UNDETECTED

The creature doesn't know your location.

HIDE ❖

SECRET

You huddle behind cover or greater cover or deeper into concealment to become hidden, rather than observed. The GM rolls your Stealth check in secret and compares the result to the Perception DC of each creature you're observed by but that you have cover or greater cover against or are concealed from. You gain the circumstance bonus from cover or greater cover to your check.

Success If the creature could see you, you're now hidden from it instead of observed. If you were hidden from or undetected by the creature, you retain that condition.

If you successfully become hidden to a creature but then cease to have cover or greater cover against it or be concealed from it, you become observed again. You cease being hidden if you do anything except Hide, Sneak, or Step.

If you attempt to Strike a creature, the creature remains flat-footed against that attack, and you then become observed. If you do anything else, you become observed just before you act unless the GM determines otherwise. The GM might allow you to perform a particularly unobtrusive action without being noticed, possibly requiring another Stealth check.

If a creature uses Seek to make you observed by it, you must successfully Hide to become hidden from it again.

SNEAK ❖

| MOVE | SECRET |

You can attempt to move to another place while becoming or staying undetected. Stride up to half your Speed. (You can use Sneak while Burrowing, Climbing, Flying, or Swimming instead of Striding if you have the corresponding movement type; you must move at half that Speed.)

If you're undetected by a creature and it's impossible for that creature to observe you (for a typical creature, this includes when you're invisible, the observer is blinded, or you're in darkness and the creature can't see in darkness), for any critical failure you roll on a check to Sneak, you get a failure instead. You also continue to be undetected if you lose cover or greater cover against or are no longer concealed from such a creature.

At the end of your movement, the GM rolls your Stealth check in secret and compares the result to the Perception DC of each creature you were hidden from or undetected by at the start of your movement. If you have cover or greater cover from the creature throughout your Stride, you gain the +2 circumstance bonus from cover (or +4 from greater cover) to your Stealth check. Because you're moving, the bonus increase from Taking Cover doesn't apply. You don't get to roll against a creature if, at the end of your movement, you neither are concealed from it nor have cover or greater cover against it. You automatically become observed by such a creature.

Success You're undetected by the creature during your movement and remain undetected by the creature at the end of it.

You become observed as soon as you do anything other than Hide, Sneak, or Step. If you attempt to Strike a creature, the creature remains flat-footed against that attack, and you then become observed. If you do anything else, you become observed just before you act unless the GM determines otherwise. The GM might allow you to perform a particularly unobtrusive action without being noticed, possibly requiring another Stealth check. If you speak or make a deliberate loud noise, you become hidden instead of undetected.

If a creature uses Seek and you become hidden to it as a result, you must Sneak if you want to become undetected by that creature again.

Failure A telltale sound or other sign gives your position away, though you still remain unseen. You're hidden from the creature throughout your movement and remain so.

Critical Failure You're spotted! You're observed by the creature throughout your movement and remain so. If you're invisible and were hidden from the creature, instead of being observed you're hidden throughout your movement and remain so.

SURVIVAL (WIS)

You are adept at living in the wilderness, foraging for food and building shelter, and with training you discover the secrets of tracking and hiding your trail. Even if you're untrained, you can still use Survival to Subsist (page 240).

- **Subsist** in the wild by foraging for food and building shelter.

SENSE DIRECTION

| EXPLORATION | SECRET |

Using the stars, the position of the sun, traits of the geography or flora, or the behavior of fauna, you can stay oriented in the wild. Typically, you attempt a Survival check only once per day, but some environments or changes might necessitate rolling more often. The GM determines the DC and how long this activity takes (usually just a minute or so). More unusual locales or those you're unfamiliar with might require you to have a minimum proficiency rank to Sense Direction. Without a compass, you take a –2 item penalty to checks to Sense Direction.

Critical Success You get an excellent sense of where you are. If you are in an environment with cardinal directions, you know them exactly.

Success You gain enough orientation to avoid becoming hopelessly lost. If you are in an environment with cardinal directions, you have a sense of those directions.

Sense Direction Tasks

Untrained determine a cardinal direction using the sun

Trained find an overgrown path in a forest

Expert navigate a hedge maze

Master navigate a byzantine labyrinth or relatively featureless desert

Legendary navigate an ever-changing dream realm

SURVIVAL TRAINED ACTIONS

COVER TRACKS

| CONCENTRATE | EXPLORATION | MOVE |

You cover your tracks, moving up to half your travel Speed, using the rules on page 479). You don't need to attempt a Survival check to cover your tracks, but anyone tracking you must succeed at a Survival check against your Survival DC if it is higher than the normal DC to Track.

In some cases, you might Cover Tracks in an encounter. In this case, Cover Tracks is a single action and doesn't have the exploration trait.

TRACK

| CONCENTRATE | EXPLORATION | MOVE |

You follow tracks, moving at up to half your travel Speed, using the rules on page 479). After a successful check to Track, you can continue following the tracks at half your Speed without attempting additional checks for up to 1 hour. In some cases, you might Track in an encounter. In this case, Track is a single action and doesn't have the exploration trait, but you might need to roll more often because you're in a tense situation. The GM determines how often you must attempt this check.

You attempt your Survival check when you start Tracking, once every hour you continue tracking, and any time something significant changes in the trail. The GM determines the DCs for such checks, depending on the freshness of the trail, the weather, and the type of ground.

Success You find the trail or continue to follow the one you're already following.

Failure You lose the trail but can try again after a 1-hour delay.

Critical Failure You lose the trail and can't try again for 24 hours.

Sample Track Tasks

Untrained the path of a large army following a road

Trained relatively fresh tracks of a rampaging bear through the plains

Expert a nimble panther's tracks through a jungle, tracks after the rain

Master tracks after a winter snow, tracks of a mouse or smaller creature, tracks left on surfaces that can't hold prints like bare rock

Legendary old tracks through a windy desert's sands, tracks after a major blizzard or hurricane

THIEVERY (DEX)

You are trained in a particular set of skills favored by thieves and miscreants.

PALM AN OBJECT ◆

> MANIPULATE

Palming a small, unattended object without being noticed requires you to roll a single Thievery check against the Perception DCs of all creatures who are currently observing you. You take the object whether or not you successfully conceal that you did so. You can typically only Palm Objects of negligible Bulk, though the GM might determine otherwise depending on the situation.

Success The creature does not notice you Palming the Object.

Failure The creature notices you Palming the Object, and the GM determines the creature's response.

STEAL ◆

> MANIPULATE

You try to take a small object from another creature without being noticed. Typically, you can Steal only an object of negligible Bulk, and you automatically fail if the creature who has the object is in combat or on guard.

Attempt a Thievery check to determine if you successfully Steal the object. The DC to Steal is usually the Perception DC of the creature wearing the object. This assumes the object is worn but not closely guarded (like a loosely carried pouch filled with coins, or an object within such a pouch). If the object is in a pocket or similarly protected, you take a –5 penalty to your Thievery check. The GM might increase the DC of your check if the nature of the object makes it harder to steal (such

as a very small item in a large pack, or a sheet of parchment mixed in with other documents).

You might also need to compare your Thievery check result against the Perception DCs of observers other than the person wearing the object. The GM may increase the Perception DCs of these observers if they're distracted.

Success You steal the item without the bearer noticing, or an observer doesn't see you take or attempt to take the item.

Failure The item's bearer notices your attempt before you can take the object, or an observer sees you take or attempt to take the item. The GM determines the response of any creature that notices your theft.

THIEVERY TRAINED ACTIONS

DISABLE A DEVICE ◆◆

> MANIPULATE

Requirements Some devices require you to use thieves' tools (page 291) when disabling them.

This action allows you to disarm a trap or another complex device. Often, a device requires numerous successes before becoming disabled, depending on its construction and complexity. Thieves' tools are helpful and sometimes even required to Disable a Device, as determined by the GM, and sometimes a device requires a higher proficiency rank in Thievery to disable it.

Your Thievery check result determines how much progress you make.

Critical Success You disable the device, or you achieve two successes toward disabling a complex device. You leave no trace of your tampering, and you can rearm the device later, if that type of device can be rearmed.

Success You disable the device, or you achieve one success toward disabling a complex device.

Critical Failure You trigger the device.

PICK A LOCK ◆◆

> MANIPULATE

Requirements You have thieves' tools (page 291).

Opening a lock without a key is very similar to Disabling a Device, but the DC of the check is determined by the complexity and construction of the lock you are attempting to pick (locks and their DCs are found on page 290). Locks of higher qualities might require multiple successes to unlock, since otherwise even an unskilled burglar could easily crack the lock by attempting the check until they rolled a natural 20. If you lack the proper tools, the GM might let you used improvised picks, which are treated as shoddy tools, depending on the specifics of the lock.

Critical Success You unlock the lock, or you achieve two successes toward opening a complex lock. You leave no trace of your tampering.

Success You open the lock, or you achieve one success toward opening a complex lock.

Critical Failure You break your tools. Fixing them requires using Crafting to Repair them or else swapping in replacement picks (costing 3 sp, or 3 gp for infiltrator thieves' tools).

INTRODUCTION

ANCESTRIES & BACKGROUNDS

CLASSES

SKILLS

FEATS

EQUIPMENT

SPELLS

THE AGE OF LOST OMENS

PLAYING THE GAME

GAME MASTERING

CRAFTING & TREASURE

APPENDIX

CHAPTER 5: FEATS

All kinds of experiences and training can shape your character beyond what you learn by advancing in your class. Abilities that require a degree of training but can be learned by anyone—not only members of certain ancestries or classes—are called general feats.

For most classes, you gain a general feat when you reach 3rd level and every 4 levels thereafter. Each time you gain a general feat, you can select any feat with the general trait whose prerequisites you satisfy.

General feats also include a subcategory of skill feats, which expand on what you can accomplish via skills.

These feats also have the skill trait. Most characters gain skill feats at 2nd level and every 2 levels thereafter. When you gain a skill feat, you must select a general feat with the skill trait; you can't select a general feat that lacks the skill trait. The level of a skill feat is typically the minimum level at which a character could meet its proficiency prerequisite.

TABLE 5-1: GENERAL FEATS

Non-Skill Feats	Level	Prerequisites	Benefits
Adopted Ancestry	1	—	Gain access to ancestry feats from another ancestry
Armor Proficiency	1	—	Become trained in a type of armor
Breath Control	1	—	Hold your breath longer and gain benefits against inhaled threats
Canny Acumen	1	—	Become an expert in a saving throw or Perception
Diehard	1	—	Die at dying 5, rather than dying 4
Fast Recovery	1	Constitution 14	Regain more HP from rest, recover faster from disease and poisons
Feather Step	1	Dexterity 14	Step into difficult terrain
Fleet	1	—	Increase your Speed by 5 feet
Incredible Initiative	1	—	+2 to initiative rolls
Ride	1	—	Automatically succeed at commanding your mount to move
Shield Block	1	—	Ward off a blow with your shield
Toughness	1	—	Increase your maximum HP and reduce the DCs of recovery checks
Weapon Proficiency	1	—	Become trained in a weapon type
Ancestral Paragon	3	—	Gain a 1st-level ancestry feat
Untrained Improvisation	3	—	Become more adept at using untrained skills
Expeditious Search	7	Master Perception	Search areas in half the time
Incredible Investiture	11	Charisma 16	Invest up to 12 magic items

TABLE 5-2: GENERAL SKILL FEATS

Varying Skill Feats	Level	Prerequisites	Benefits
Assurance	1	Trained in at least one skill	Receive a fixed result on a skill check
Dubious Knowledge	1	Trained in Recall Knowledge skill	Learn true and erroneous knowledge on failed check
Quick Identification	1	Trained in Arcana, Nature, Occultism, or Religion	Identify Magic in 1 minute or less
Recognize Spell	1	Trained in Arcana, Nature, Occultism, or Religion	Identify a spell as a reaction as it's being cast
Skill Training	1	Intelligence 12	Become trained in a skill
Trick Magic Item	1	Trained in Arcana, Nature, Occultism, or Religion	Activate a magic item you normally can't activate
Automatic Knowledge	2	Expert in Recall Knowledge action, Assurance in the relevant skill	Recall Knowledge as a free action once per day
Magical Shorthand	2	Expert in Arcana, Nature, Occultism, or Religion	Learn spells quickly and at a reduced cost
Quick Recognition	7	Master in Arcana, Nature, Occultism, or Religion; Recognize Spell	Identify spells as a free action
Acrobatics Skill Feats	**Level**	**Prerequisites**	**Benefits**
Cat Fall	1	Trained in Acrobatics	Treat falls as shorter than they are

5

INTRODUCTION

ANCESTRIES & BACKGROUNDS

CLASSES

SKILLS

FEATS

EQUIPMENT

SPELLS

THE AGE OF LOST OMENS

PLAYING THE GAME

GAME MASTERING

CRAFTING & TREASURE

APPENDIX

Quick Squeeze	1	Trained in Acrobatics	Move swiftly as you Squeeze
Steady Balance	1	Trained in Acrobatics	Maintain your balance in adverse conditions
Nimble Crawl	2	Expert in Acrobatics	Crawl at a faster rate
Kip Up	7	Master in Acrobatics	Stand up for free without triggering reactions

Arcana Skill Feats	**Level**	**Prerequisites**	**Benefits**
Arcane Sense	1	Trained in Arcana	Cast *detect magic* at will as an arcane innate spell
Unified Theory	15	Legendary in Arcana	Use Arcana for checks for all magical traditions

Athletics Skill Feats	**Level**	**Prerequisites**	**Benefits**
Combat Climber	1	Trained in Athletics	Fight more effectively as you Climb
Hefty Hauler	1	Trained in Athletics	Increase your Bulk limits by 2
Quick Jump	1	Trained in Athletics	High Jump or Long Jump as a single action
Titan Wrestler	1	Trained in Athletics	Disarm, Grapple, Shove, or Trip larger creatures
Underwater Marauder	1	Trained in Athletics	Fight more effectively underwater
Powerful Leap	2	Expert in Athletics	Jump farther and higher
Rapid Mantel	2	Expert in Athletics	Pull yourself onto ledges quickly
Quick Climb	7	Master in Athletics	Climb swiftly
Quick Swim	7	Master in Athletics	Swim quickly
Wall Jump	7	Master in Athletics	Jump off walls
Cloud Jump	15	Legendary in Athletics	Jump impossible distances

Crafting Skill Feats	**Level**	**Prerequisites**	**Benefits**
Alchemical Crafting	1	Trained in Crafting	Craft alchemical items
Quick Repair	1	Trained in Crafting	Repair items quickly
Snare Crafting	1	Trained in Crafting	Craft snares
Specialty Crafting	1	Trained in Crafting	Gain bonuses to Craft certain items
Magical Crafting	2	Expert in Crafting	Craft magic items
Impeccable Crafting	7	Master in Crafting, Specialty Crafting	Craft items more efficiently
Inventor	7	Master in Crafting	Use Crafting to create item formulas
Craft Anything	15	Legendary in Crafting	Ignore most requirements for crafting items

Deception Skill Feats	**Level**	**Prerequisites**	**Benefits**
Charming Liar	1	Trained in Deception	Improve a target's attitude with your lies
Lengthy Diversion	1	Trained in Deception	Remain hidden after you Create a Diversion
Lie to Me	1	Trained in Deception	Use Deception to detect lies
Confabulator	2	Expert in Deception	Reduce the bonuses against your repeated lies
Quick Disguise	2	Expert in Deception	Set up a disguise in only half the time
Slippery Secrets	7	Master in Deception	Evade attempts to uncover your true nature

Diplomacy Skill Feats	**Level**	**Prerequisites**	**Benefits**
Bargain Hunter	1	Trained in Diplomacy	Earn Income by searching for deals
Group Impression	1	Trained in Diplomacy	Make an Impression on multiple targets at once
Hobnobber	1	Trained in Diplomacy	Gather Information rapidly
Glad-Hand	2	Expert in Diplomacy	Make an Impression on a target you've just met
Shameless Request	7	Master in Diplomacy	Make Requests of others with lesser consequences
Legendary Negotiation	15	Legendary in Diplomacy	Quickly parley with foes

Intimidation Skill Feats	**Level**	**Prerequisites**	**Benefits**
Group Coercion	1	Trained in Intimidation	Coerce multiple targets simultaneously
Intimidating Glare	1	Trained in Intimidation	Demoralize a creature without speaking
Quick Coercion	1	Trained in Intimidation	Coerce a creature quickly
Intimidating Prowess	2	Strength 16, expert in Intimidation	Gain a bonus to physically Demoralize a target
Lasting Coercion	2	Expert in Intimidation	Coerce a target into helping you longer
Battle Cry	7	Master in Intimidation	Demoralizes foes when you roll for initiative
Terrified Retreat	7	Master in Intimidation	Cause foes you Demoralize to flee
Scare to Death	15	Legendary in Intimidation	Scare a target so much, they might die

Lore Skill Feats	**Level**	**Prerequisites**	**Benefits**
Additional Lore	1	Trained in Lore	Become trained in another Lore subcategory
Experienced Professional	1	Trained in Lore	Prevent critical failures when Earning Income
Unmistakable Lore	2	Expert in Lore	Recall Knowledge about your Lore more effectively
Legendary Professional	15	Legendary in Lore	Gain renown for your Lore

Medicine Skill Feats	Level	Prerequisites	Benefits
Battle Medicine	1	Trained in Medicine	Heal yourself or an ally in battle
Continual Recovery	2	Expert in Medicine	Treat Wounds on a patient more often
Robust Recovery	2	Expert in Medicine	Greater benefits from Treat Disease and Treat Poison
Ward Medic	2	Expert in Medicine	Treat several patients at once
Legendary Medic	15	Legendary in Medicine	Remove disease or the blinded, deafened, doomed, or drained condition

Nature Skill Feats	Level	Prerequisites	Benefits
Natural Medicine	1	Trained in Nature	Use Nature to Treat Wounds
Train Animal	1	Trained in Nature	Teach an animal a trick
Bonded Animal	2	Expert in Nature	An animal becomes permanently helpful to you

Occultism Skill Feats	Level	Prerequisites	Benefits
Oddity Identification	1	Trained in Occultism	+2 to Occultism checks to Identify Magic with certain traits
Bizarre Magic	7	Master in Occultism	Your magic becomes more difficult to identify

Performance Skill Feats	Level	Prerequisites	Benefits
Fascinating Performance	1	Trained in Performance	Perform to fascinate observers
Impressive Performance	1	Trained in Performance	Make an Impression with Performance
Virtuosic Performer	1	Trained in Performance	+1 with a certain type of performance
Legendary Performer	15	Legendary in Performance, Virtuosic Performer	Gain renown for your Performance

Religion Skill Feats	Level	Prerequisites	Benefits
Student of the Canon	1	Trained in Religion	More accurately recognize the tenets of your faith or philosophy
Divine Guidance	15	Legendary in Religion	Find guidance in the writings of your faith

Society Skill Feats	Level	Prerequisites	Benefits
Courtly Graces	1	Trained in Society	Use Society to get along in noble society
Multilingual	1	Trained in Society	Learn two new languages
Read Lips	1	Trained in Society	Read the lips of people you can see
Sign Language	1	Trained in Society	Learn sign languages
Streetwise	1	Trained in Society	Use Society to Gather Information and Recall Knowledge
Connections	2	Expert in Society, Courtly Graces	Leverage your connections for favors and meetings
Legendary Codebreaker	15	Legendary in Society	Quickly Decipher Writing using Society
Legendary Linguist	15	Legendary in Society, Multilingual	Create pidgin languages to communicate with anyone

Stealth Skill Feats	Level	Prerequisites	Benefits
Experienced Smuggler	1	Trained in Stealth	Conceal items from observers more effectively
Terrain Stalker	1	Trained in Stealth	Sneak in certain terrain without attempting a check
Quiet Allies	2	Expert in Stealth	Roll a single Stealth check when sneaking with allies
Foil Senses	7	Master in Stealth	Take precautions against special senses
Swift Sneak	7	Master in Stealth	Move your full Speed while you Sneak
Legendary Sneak	15	Legendary in Stealth, Swift Sneak	Hide and Sneak without cover or being concealed

Survival Skill Feats	Level	Prerequisites	Benefits
Experienced Tracker	1	Trained in Survival	Track at your full Speed at a –5 penalty
Forager	1	Trained in Survival	Forage for supplies to provide for multiple creatures
Survey Wildlife	1	Trained in Survival	Identify nearby creatures through signs and clues
Terrain Expertise	1	Trained in Survival	+1 to Survival checks in certain terrain
Planar Survival	7	Master in Survival	Use Survival to Subsist on different planes
Legendary Survivalist	15	Legendary in Survival	Survive extreme conditions

Thievery Skill Feats	Level	Prerequisites	Benefits
Pickpocket	1	Trained in Thievery	Steal or Palm an Object more effectively
Subtle Theft	1	Trained in Thievery	Your thefts are harder to notice
Wary Disarmament	2	Expert in Thievery	+2 to AC or saves against devices or traps you trigger while disarming
Quick Unlock	7	Master in Thievery	Pick a Lock with 1 action
Legendary Thief	15	Legendary in Thievery, Pickpocket	Steal what would normally be impossible to steal

INTRODUCTION

ANCESTRIES & BACKGROUNDS

CLASSES

SKILLS

FEATS

EQUIPMENT

SPELLS

THE AGE OF LOST OMENS

PLAYING THE GAME

GAME MASTERING

CRAFTING & TREASURE

APPENDIX

ADDITIONAL LORE   FEAT 1

GENERAL | SKILL

Prerequisites trained in Lore

Your knowledge has expanded to encompass a new field. Choose an additional Lore skill subcategory. You become trained in it. At 3rd, 7th, and 15th levels, you gain an additional skill increase you can apply only to the chosen Lore subcategory.

Special You can select this feat more than once. Each time you must select a new subcategory of Lore and you gain the additional skill increases to that subcategory for the listed levels.

ADOPTED ANCESTRY   FEAT 1

GENERAL

You're fully immersed in another ancestry's culture and traditions, whether born into them, earned through rite of passage, or bonded through a deep friendship or romance. Choose a common ancestry. You can select ancestry feats from the ancestry you chose, in addition to your character's own ancestry, as long as the ancestry feats don't require any physiological feature that you lack, as determined by the GM.

ALCHEMICAL CRAFTING   FEAT 1

GENERAL | SKILL

Prerequisites trained in Crafting

You can use the Craft activity to create alchemical items. When you select this feat, you immediately add the formulas for four common 1st-level alchemical items to your formula book.

ANCESTRAL PARAGON   FEAT 3

GENERAL

Whether through instinct, study, or magic, you feel a deeper connection to your ancestry. You gain a 1st-level ancestry feat.

ARCANE SENSE   FEAT 1

GENERAL | SKILL

Prerequisites trained in Arcana

Your study of magic allows you to instinctively sense its presence. You can cast 1st-level *detect magic* at will as an arcane innate spell. If you're a master in Arcana, the spell is heightened to 3rd level; if you're legendary, it is heightened to 4th level.

ARMOR PROFICIENCY   FEAT 1

GENERAL

You become trained in light armor. If you already were trained in light armor, you gain training in medium armor. If you were trained in both, you become trained in heavy armor.

Special You can select this feat more than once. Each time, you become trained in the next type of armor above.

ASSURANCE   FEAT 1

FORTUNE | GENERAL | SKILL

Prerequisites trained in at least one skill

Even in the worst circumstances, you can perform basic tasks. Choose a skill you're trained in. You can forgo rolling a skill check for that skill to instead receive a result of 10 + your proficiency bonus (do not apply any other bonuses, penalties, or modifiers).

Special You can select this feat multiple times. Each time, choose a different skill and gain the benefits for that skill.

AUTOMATIC KNOWLEDGE   FEAT 2

GENERAL | SKILL

Prerequisites expert in a skill with the Recall Knowledge action, Assurance in that skill

You know basic facts off the top of your head. Choose a skill you're an expert in that has the Recall Knowledge action and for which you have the Assurance feat. You can use the Recall Knowledge action with that skill as a free action once per round. If you do, you must use Assurance on the skill check.

Special You can select this feat multiple times, choosing a different skill each time. You can use Automatic Knowledge with any skills you have chosen, but you can still use Automatic Knowledge only once per round.

BARGAIN HUNTER   FEAT 1

GENERAL | SKILL

Prerequisites trained in Diplomacy

You can Earn Income (page 236) using Diplomacy, spending your days hunting for bargains and reselling at a profit. You can also spend time specifically sniffing out a great bargain on an item; this works as if you were using Earn Income with Diplomacy, except instead of gaining money, you purchase the item at a discount equal to the money you would have gained, gaining the item for free if your earned income equals or exceeds its cost. Finally, if you select Bargain Hunter during character creation at 1st level, you start play with an additional 2 gp.

BATTLE CRY   FEAT 7

GENERAL | SKILL

Prerequisites master in Intimidation

When you roll initiative, you can yell a mighty battle cry and Demoralize an observed foe as a free action. If you're legendary in Intimidation, you can use a reaction to Demoralize your foe when you critically succeed at an attack roll.

BATTLE MEDICINE ❖   FEAT 1

GENERAL | HEALING | MANIPULATE | SKILL

Prerequisites trained in Medicine

You can patch up yourself or an adjacent ally, even in combat. Attempt a Medicine check with the same DC as for Treat Wounds and provide the corresponding amount of healing. As with Treat Wounds, you can attempt checks against higher DCs if you have the minimum proficiency rank. The target is then temporarily immune to your Battle Medicine for 1 day.

BIZARRE MAGIC   FEAT 7

GENERAL | SKILL

Prerequisites master in Occultism

You can draw upon strange variations in your spellcasting, whether or not you can cast occult spells. The DCs to Recognize Spells you cast and Identify Magic you use increase by 5.

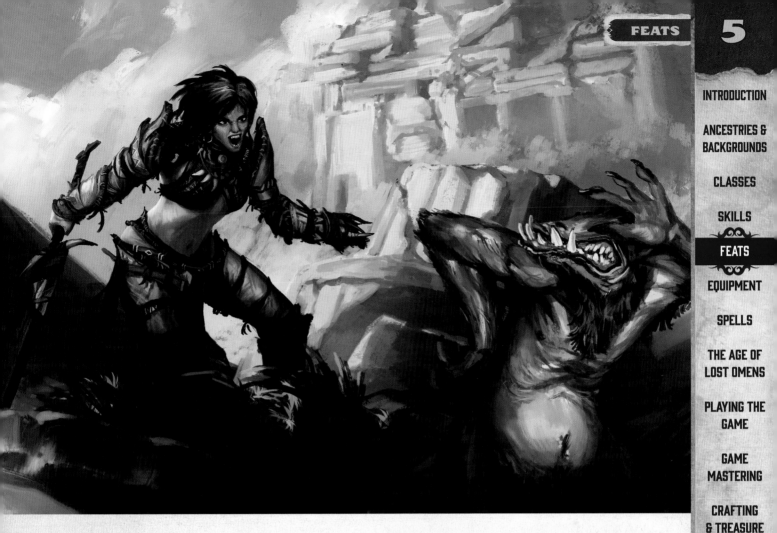

FEATS

5

INTRODUCTION

ANCESTRIES &
BACKGROUNDS

CLASSES

SKILLS

FEATS

EQUIPMENT

SPELLS

THE AGE OF
LOST OMENS

PLAYING THE
GAME

GAME
MASTERING

CRAFTING
& TREASURE

APPENDIX

BONDED ANIMAL   FEAT 2

`DOWNTIME` `GENERAL` `SKILL`

Prerequisites expert in Nature

You forge strong connections with animals. You can spend 7 days of downtime trying to bond with a normal animal (not a companion or other special animal). After this duration, attempt a DC 20 Nature check. If successful, you bond with the animal. The animal is permanently helpful to you, unless you do something egregious to break your bond. A helpful animal is easier to direct, as described under Command an Animal on page 249.

Bonding with a new animal ends any previous bond you had. You can't have both a bonded animal and an animal companion (though you can have both a bonded animal and a familiar).

BREATH CONTROL   FEAT 1

`GENERAL`

You have incredible breath control, which grants you advantages when air is hazardous or sparse. You can hold your breath for 25 times as long as usual before suffocating. You gain a +1 circumstance bonus to saving throws against inhaled threats, such as inhaled poisons, and if you roll a success on such a saving throw, you get a critical success instead.

CANNY ACUMEN   FEAT 1

`GENERAL`

Your avoidance or observation is beyond the ken of most in your profession. Choose Fortitude saves, Reflex saves, Will saves, or Perception. You become an expert in your choice. At 17th level, you become a master in your choice.

CAT FALL   FEAT 1

`GENERAL` `SKILL`

Prerequisites trained in Acrobatics

Your catlike aerial acrobatics allow you to cushion your falls. Treat falls as 10 feet shorter. If you're an expert in Acrobatics, treat falls as 25 feet shorter. If you're a master in Acrobatics, treat them as 50 feet shorter. If you're legendary in Acrobatics, you always land on your feet and don't take damage, regardless of the distance of the fall.

CHARMING LIAR   FEAT 1

`GENERAL` `SKILL`

Prerequisites trained in Deception

Your charm allows you to win over those you lie to. When you get a critical success using the Lie action, the target's attitude toward you improves by one step, as though you'd succeeded at using Diplomacy to Make an Impression. This works only once per conversation, and if you critically succeed against multiple targets using the same result, you choose one creature's attitude to improve. You must be lying to impart seemingly important information, inflate your status, or ingratiate yourself, which trivial or irrelevant lies can't achieve.

CLOUD JUMP   FEAT 15

> GENERAL   SKILL

Prerequisites legendary in Athletics

Your unparalleled athletic skill allows you to jump impossible distances. Triple the distance you Long Jump (so you could jump 60 feet on a successful DC 20 check). When you High Jump, use the calculation for a Long Jump but don't triple the distance.

When you Long Jump or High Jump, you can also increase the number of actions you use (up to the number of actions you have remaining in your turn) to jump even further. For each extra action, add your Speed to the maximum distance you jump.

COMBAT CLIMBER   FEAT 1

> GENERAL   SKILL

Prerequisites trained in Athletics

Your techniques allow you to fight as you climb. You're not flat-footed while Climbing and can Climb with a hand occupied. You must still use another hand and both legs to Climb.

CONFABULATOR   FEAT 2

> GENERAL   SKILL

Prerequisites expert in Deception

Even when caught in falsehoods, you pile lie upon lie. Reduce the circumstance bonus a target gains for your previous attempts to Create a Diversion or Lie to it from +4 to +2. If you're a master in Deception, reduce the bonus to +1, and if you're legendary, your targets don't get these bonuses at all.

CONNECTIONS   FEAT 2

> GENERAL   SKILL

Prerequisites expert in Society, Courtly Graces

You have social connections you can leverage to trade favors or meet important people. When you're in an area with connections (typically a settlement where you've spent downtime building connections, or possibly another area in the same nation), you can attempt a Society check to arrange a meeting with an important political figure or ask for a favor in exchange for a later favor of your contact's choice. The GM decides the DC based on the difficulty of the favor and the figure's prominence.

CONTINUAL RECOVERY   FEAT 2

> GENERAL   SKILL

Prerequisites expert in Medicine

You zealously monitor a patient's progress to administer treatment faster. When you Treat Wounds, your patient becomes immune for only 10 minutes instead of 1 hour. This applies only to your Treat Wounds activities, not any other the patient receives.

COURTLY GRACES   FEAT 1

> GENERAL   SKILL

Prerequisites trained in Society

You were raised among the nobility or have learned proper etiquette and bearing, allowing you to present yourself as a noble and play games of influence and politics. You can use Society to Make an Impression on a noble, as well as with

Impersonate to pretend to be a noble if you aren't one. If you want to impersonate a specific noble, you still need to use Deception to Impersonate normally, and to Lie when necessary.

CRAFT ANYTHING   FEAT 15

> GENERAL   SKILL

Prerequisites legendary in Crafting

You can find ways to craft just about anything, despite restrictions. As long as you have the appropriate Crafting skill feat (such as Magical Crafting for magic items) and meet the item's level and proficiency requirement, you ignore just about any other requirement, such as being of a specific ancestry or providing spells. The only exceptions are requirements that add to the item's cost, including castings of spells that themselves have a cost, and requirements of special items such as the *philosopher's stone* that have exclusive means of access and Crafting. The GM decides whether you can ignore a requirement.

DIEHARD   FEAT 1

> GENERAL

It takes more to kill you than most. You die from the dying condition at dying 5, rather than dying 4.

DIVINE GUIDANCE   FEAT 15

> GENERAL   SKILL

Prerequisites legendary in Religion

You're so immersed in divine scripture that you find meaning and guidance in your texts in any situation. Spend 10 minutes Deciphering Writing on religious scriptures of your deity or philosophy while thinking about a particular problem or conundrum you face, and then attempt a Religion check (DC determined by the GM). If you succeed, you unearth a relevant passage, parable, or aphorism that can help you move forward or change your thinking to help solve your conundrum. For example, the GM might provide you with a cryptic poem or hint that can guide you to the next step of solving your problem.

DUBIOUS KNOWLEDGE   FEAT 1

> GENERAL   SKILL

Prerequisites trained in a skill with the Recall Knowledge action

You're a treasure trove of information, but not all of it comes from reputable sources. When you fail a Recall Knowledge check using any skill, you learn a bit of true knowledge and a bit of erroneous knowledge, but you don't have any way to differentiate which is which.

EXPEDITIOUS SEARCH   FEAT 7

> GENERAL

Prerequisites master in Perception

You have a system that lets you search at great speed, finding details and secrets twice as quickly as others can. When Searching, you take half as long as usual to Search a given area. This means that while exploring, you double the Speed you can move while ensuring you've Searched an area before walking into it (up to half your Speed). If you're legendary in Perception, you instead Search areas four times as quickly.

INTRODUCTION

ANCESTRIES &
BACKGROUNDS

CLASSES

SKILLS

FEATS

EQUIPMENT

SPELLS

THE AGE OF
LOST OMENS

PLAYING THE
GAME

GAME
MASTERING

CRAFTING
& TREASURE

APPENDIX

EXPERIENCED PROFESSIONAL FEAT 1

GENERAL **SKILL**

Prerequisites trained in Lore

You carefully safeguard your professional endeavors to prevent disaster. When you use Lore to Earn Income, if you roll a critical failure, you instead get a failure. If you're an expert in Lore, you gain twice as much income from a failed check to Earn Income, unless it was originally a critical failure.

EXPERIENCED SMUGGLER FEAT 1

GENERAL **SKILL**

Prerequisites trained in Stealth

You often smuggle things past the authorities. When the GM rolls your Stealth check to see if a passive observer notices a small item you have concealed, the GM uses the number rolled or 10—whichever is higher—as the result of your die roll, adding it to your Stealth modifier to determine your Stealth check result. If you're a master in Stealth, the GM uses the number rolled or 15, and if you're legendary in Stealth, you automatically succeed at hiding a small concealed item from passive observers. This provides no benefits when a creature attempts a Perception check while actively searching you for hidden items. Due to your smuggling skill, you're more likely to find more lucrative smuggling jobs when using Underworld Lore to Earn Income.

EXPERIENCED TRACKER FEAT 1

GENERAL **SKILL**

Prerequisites trained in Survival

Tracking is second nature to you, and when necessary you can follow a trail without pause. You can Track while moving at full Speed by taking a –5 penalty to your Survival check. If you're a master in Survival, you don't take the –5 penalty. If you're legendary in Survival, you no longer need to roll a new Survival check every hour when tracking, though you still need to roll whenever there are significant changes in the trail.

FASCINATING PERFORMANCE FEAT 1

GENERAL **SKILL**

Prerequisites trained in Performance

When you Perform, compare your result to the Will DC of one observer. If you succeed, the target is fascinated by you for 1 round. If the observer is in a situation that demands immediate attention, such as combat, you must critically succeed to fascinate it and the Perform action gains the incapacitation trait. You must choose which creature you're trying to fascinate before you roll your check, and the target is then temporarily immune for 1 hour.

If you're an expert in Performance, you can fascinate up to four observers; if you're a master, you can fascinate up to 10 observers; and if you're legendary, you can fascinate any number of observers at the same time.

FAST RECOVERY FEAT 1

GENERAL

Prerequisites Constitution 14

Your body quickly bounces back from afflictions. You regain twice as many Hit Points from resting. Each time you succeed at a Fortitude save against an ongoing disease or poison, you reduce its stage by 2, or by 1 against a virulent disease or poison. Each critical success you achieve against an ongoing disease or poison reduces its stage by 3, or by 2 against a virulent disease or poison. In addition, you reduce the severity of your drained condition by 2 when you rest for a night instead of by 1.

FEATHER STEP FEAT 1

GENERAL

Prerequisites Dexterity 14

You step carefully and quickly. You can Step into difficult terrain.

FLEET FEAT 1

GENERAL

You move more quickly on foot. Your Speed increases by 5 feet.

FOIL SENSES FEAT 7

GENERAL **SKILL**

Prerequisites master in Stealth

You are adept at foiling creatures' special senses and cautious enough to safeguard against them at all times. Whenever you use the Avoid Notice, Hide, or Sneak actions, you are always considered to be taking precautions against special senses (see the Detecting with Other Senses sidebar on page 465).

FORAGER FEAT 1

GENERAL **SKILL**

Prerequisites trained in Survival

While using Survival to Subsist, if you roll any result worse than a success, you get a success. On a success, you can provide subsistence living for yourself and four additional creatures, and on a critical success, you can take care of twice as many creatures as on a success.

Each time your proficiency rank in Survival increases, double the number of additional creatures you can take care of on a success (to eight if you're an expert, 16 if you're a master, or 32 if you're legendary). You can choose to care for half the number of additional creatures and provide a comfortable living instead of subsistence living.

Multiple smaller creatures or creatures with significantly smaller appetites than a human are counted as a single creature for this feat, and larger creatures or those with significantly greater appetites each count as multiple creatures. The GM determines how much a non-human creature needs to eat.

GLAD-HAND FEAT 2

GENERAL **SKILL**

Prerequisites expert in Diplomacy

First impressions are your strong suit. When you meet someone in a casual or social situation, you can immediately attempt a Diplomacy check to Make an Impression on that creature rather than needing to converse for 1 minute. You take a –5 penalty to the check. If you fail or critically fail, you can engage in 1 minute of conversation and attempt a new check at the end of that time rather than accepting the failure or critical failure result.

GROUP COERCION   FEAT 1

GENERAL   SKILL

Prerequisites trained in Intimidation

When you Coerce, you can compare your Intimidation check result to the Will DCs of two targets instead of one. It's possible to get a different degree of success for each target. The number of targets you can Coerce in a single action increases to four if you're an expert, 10 if you're a master, and 25 if you're legendary.

GROUP IMPRESSION   FEAT 1

GENERAL   SKILL

Prerequisites trained in Diplomacy

When you Make an Impression, you can compare your Diplomacy check result to the Will DCs of two targets instead of one. It's possible to get a different degree of success for each target. The number of targets increases to four if you're an expert, 10 if you're a master, and 25 if you're legendary.

HEFTY HAULER   FEAT 1

GENERAL   SKILL

Prerequisites trained in Athletics

You can carry more than your frame implies. Increase your maximum and encumbered Bulk limits by 2.

HOBNOBBER   FEAT 1

GENERAL   SKILL

Prerequisites trained in Diplomacy

You are skilled at learning information through conversation. The Gather Information exploration activity takes you half as long as normal (typically reducing the time to 1 hour). If you're a master in Diplomacy and you Gather Information at the normal speed, when you attempt to do so and roll a critical failure, you get a failure instead. There is still no guarantee that a rumor you learn with Gather Information is accurate.

IMPECCABLE CRAFTING   FEAT 7

GENERAL   SKILL

Prerequisites master in Crafting, Specialty Crafting

You craft flawless creations with great efficiency. Whenever you roll a success at a Crafting check to make an item of the type you chose with Specialty Crafting, you get a critical success instead.

IMPRESSIVE PERFORMANCE   FEAT 1

GENERAL   SKILL

Prerequisites trained in Performance

Your performances inspire admiration and win you fans. You can Make an Impression using Performance instead of Diplomacy.

INCREDIBLE INITIATIVE   FEAT 1

GENERAL

You react more quickly than others can. You gain a +2 circumstance bonus to initiative rolls.

INCREDIBLE INVESTITURE   FEAT 11

GENERAL

Prerequisites Charisma 16

You have an incredible ability to invest more magic items. Increase your limit on invested items from 10 to 12.

INTIMIDATING GLARE   FEAT 1

GENERAL   SKILL

Prerequisites trained in Intimidation

You can Demoralize with a mere glare. When you do, Demoralize loses the auditory trait and gains the visual trait, and you don't take a penalty if the creature doesn't understand your language.

INTIMIDATING PROWESS   FEAT 2

GENERAL   SKILL

Prerequisites Strength 16, expert in Intimidation

In situations where you can physically menace the target when you Coerce or Demoralize, you gain a +1 circumstance bonus to your Intimidation check and you ignore the penalty for not sharing a language. If your Strength score is 20 or higher and you are a master in Intimidation, this bonus increases to +2.

INVENTOR   FEAT 7

DOWNTIME   GENERAL   SKILL

Prerequisites master in Crafting

You are a genius at Crafting, easily able to determine how things are made and create new inventions. You can spend downtime to invent a common formula that you don't know. This works just like the Craft activity: you spend half the Price of the formula up front, attempt a Crafting check, and on a success either finish the formula by paying the difference or work for longer to decrease the Price. The difference is that you spend the additional time in research, design, and development, rather than in creating an item. Once it's complete, you add the new formula you invented to your formula book.

KIP UP ◆   FEAT 7

GENERAL   SKILL

Prerequisites master in Acrobatics

You stand up. This movement doesn't trigger reactions.

LASTING COERCION   FEAT 2

GENERAL   SKILL

Prerequisites expert in Intimidation

When you successfully Coerce someone, the maximum time they comply increases to a week, still determined by the GM. If you're legendary, the maximum increases to a month.

LEGENDARY CODEBREAKER   FEAT 15

GENERAL   SKILL

Prerequisites legendary in Society

Your skill with languages and codes is so great that you can decipher information with little more than a quick read through a text. You can Decipher Writing using Society while reading at normal speed. If you slow down and spend the full amount of time that's ordinarily required and roll a success, you get a critical success; if you critically succeed while spending the normal amount of time, you gain a nearly word-for-word understanding of the document.

LEGENDARY LINGUIST　　　　　　FEAT 15

`GENERAL`　`SKILL`

Prerequisites legendary in Society, Multilingual

You're so skilled with languages you can create a pidgin instantly. You can always talk to any creature that has a language—even a language you don't know—by creating a new pidgin language that uses simplified terms and conveys basic concepts. To do so, you must first understand at least what medium of communication the creature uses (speech, sign language, and so on).

LEGENDARY MEDIC　　　　　　　FEAT 15

`GENERAL`　`SKILL`

Prerequisites legendary in Medicine

You've discovered medical breakthroughs or techniques that achieve miraculous results. Once per day for each target, you can spend 1 hour treating that target and attempt a Medicine check to remove a disease or the blinded, deafened, doomed, or drained condition. Use the DC of the disease or of the spell or effect that created the condition. If the effect's source is an artifact, above 20th level, or similarly powerful, increase the DC by 10.

LEGENDARY NEGOTIATION ◆◆◆　FEAT 15

`GENERAL`　`SKILL`

Prerequisites legendary in Diplomacy

You can negotiate incredibly quickly in adverse situations. You attempt to Make an Impression and then Request your opponent cease their current activity and engage in negotiations. You take a –5 penalty to your Diplomacy check. The GM sets the DC of the Request based on the circumstances—it's generally at least a very hard DC of the creature's level. Some creatures might simply refuse, and even those who agree to parley might ultimately find your arguments lacking and return to violence.

LEGENDARY PERFORMER　　　　　FEAT 15

`GENERAL`　`SKILL`

Prerequisites legendary in Performance, Virtuosic Performer

Your fame has spread throughout the lands. NPCs who succeed at a DC 10 Society check to Recall Knowledge have heard of you and usually have an attitude toward you one step better than normal, depending on your reputation and the NPC's disposition. For instance, if you're well-known for cruel and demanding behavior, creatures might be intimidated by you, rather than be friendly toward you. When you Earn Income with Performance, you attract higher-level audiences than your location would allow, as audiences flock to see you. For instance, rulers and angels might travel to your small tower in the woods to hear you perform. Typically, this increases the audiences available by 2 levels or more, determined by the GM.

LEGENDARY PROFESSIONAL　　　FEAT 15

`GENERAL`　`SKILL`

Prerequisites legendary in Lore

Your fame has spread throughout the lands (for instance, if you have Warfare Lore, you might be a legendary general or tactician). This works as Legendary Performer above, except you gain higher-level jobs when you Earn Income with Lore.

LEGENDARY SNEAK　　　　　　　FEAT 15

`GENERAL`　`SKILL`

Prerequisites legendary in Stealth, Swift Sneak

You're always sneaking unless you choose to be seen, even when there's nowhere to hide. You can Hide and Sneak even without cover or being concealed. When you employ an exploration tactic other than Avoiding Notice, you also gain the benefits of Avoiding Notice unless you choose not to. See page 479 for more information about exploration tactics.

LEGENDARY SURVIVALIST　　　　FEAT 15

`GENERAL`　`SKILL`

Prerequisites legendary in Survival

You can survive indefinitely without food or water and can endure severe, extreme, and incredible cold and heat without taking damage from doing so.

LEGENDARY THIEF　　　　　　　FEAT 15

`GENERAL`　`SKILL`

Prerequisites legendary in Thievery, Pickpocket

Your ability to Steal defies belief. You can attempt to Steal something that is actively wielded or that would be extremely noticeable or time consuming to remove (like worn shoes or armor). You must do so slowly and carefully, spending at least 1 minute (and significantly longer for items that are normally time consuming to remove, like armor). Throughout this duration you must have some means of staying hidden, such as the cover of darkness or a bustling crowd. You take a –5 penalty to your Thievery check. Even if you succeed, if the item is extremely prominent—like a suit of full plate armor—onlookers will quickly notice it's gone after you steal it.

LENGTHY DIVERSION　　　　　　FEAT 1

`GENERAL`　`SKILL`

Prerequisites trained in Deception

When you critically succeed to Create a Diversion, you continue to remain hidden after the end of your turn. This effect lasts for an amount of time that depends on the diversion and situation, as determined by the GM (minimum 1 additional round).

LIE TO ME　　　　　　　　　　FEAT 1

`GENERAL`　`SKILL`

Prerequisites trained in Deception

You can use Deception to weave traps to trip up anyone trying to deceive you. If you can engage in conversation with someone trying to Lie to you, use your Deception DC if it is higher than your Perception DC to determine whether they succeed. This doesn't apply if you don't have a back-and-forth dialogue, such as when someone attempts to Lie during a long speech.

MAGICAL CRAFTING　　　　　　FEAT 2

`GENERAL`　`SKILL`

Prerequisites expert in Crafting

You can Craft magic items, though some have other requirements, as listed in Chapter 11. When you select this feat, you gain formulas for four common magic items of 2nd level or lower.

MAGICAL SHORTHAND   FEAT 2

GENERAL   SKILL

Prerequisites expert in Arcana, Nature, Occultism, or Religion

Learning spells comes easily to you. If you're an expert in a tradition's associated skill, you take 10 minutes per spell level to learn a spell of that tradition, rather than 1 hour per spell level. If you fail to learn the spell, you can try again after 1 week or after you gain a level, whichever comes first. If you're a master in the tradition's associated skill, learning a spell takes 5 minutes per spell level, and if you're legendary, it takes 1 minute per spell level. You can use downtime to learn and inscribe new spells. This works as if you were using Earn Income with the tradition's associated skill, but instead of gaining money, you choose a spell available to you to learn and gain a discount on learning it, learning it for free if your earned income equals or exceeds its cost.

MULTILINGUAL   FEAT 1

GENERAL   SKILL

Prerequisites trained in Society

You easily pick up new languages. You learn two new languages, chosen from common languages, uncommon languages, and any others you have access to. You learn an additional language if you are or become a master in Society and again if you are or become legendary.

   Special You can select this feat multiple times. Each time, you learn additional languages.

NATURAL MEDICINE   FEAT 1

GENERAL   SKILL

Prerequisites trained in Nature

You can apply natural cures to heal your allies. You can use Nature instead of Medicine to Treat Wounds. If you're in the wilderness, you might have easier access to fresh ingredients, allowing you to gain a +2 circumstance bonus to your check to Treat Wounds using Nature, subject to the GM's determination.

NIMBLE CRAWL   FEAT 2

GENERAL   SKILL

Prerequisites expert in Acrobatics

You can Crawl incredibly swiftly—up to half your Speed, rather than 5 feet. If you're a master in Acrobatics, you can Crawl at full Speed, and if you're legendary, you aren't flat-footed while prone.

ODDITY IDENTIFICATION   FEAT 1

GENERAL   SKILL

Prerequisites trained in Occultism

You have a sense for spells that twist minds or reveal secrets. You gain a +2 circumstance bonus to Occultism checks to Identify Magic with the mental, possession, prediction, or scrying traits.

PICKPOCKET   FEAT 1

GENERAL   SKILL

Prerequisites trained in Thievery

You can Steal or Palm an Object that's closely guarded, such as in a pocket, without taking the –5 penalty. You can't steal objects that would be extremely noticeable or time consuming to remove

(like worn shoes or armor or actively wielded objects). If you're a master in Thievery, you can attempt to Steal from a creature in combat or otherwise on guard. When doing so, Stealing requires 2 manipulate actions instead of 1, and you take a –5 penalty.

PLANAR SURVIVAL   FEAT 7

GENERAL   SKILL

Prerequisites master in Survival

You can Subsist using Survival on different planes, even those without resources or natural phenomena you normally need. For instance, you can forage for food even if the plane lacks food that could normally sustain you. A success on your check to Subsist can also reduce the damage dealt by the plane, at the GM's discretion.

POWERFUL LEAP   FEAT 2

GENERAL   SKILL

Prerequisites expert in Athletics

When you Leap, you can jump 5 feet up with a vertical Leap, and you increase the distance you can jump horizontally by 5 feet.

QUICK CLIMB   FEAT 7

GENERAL   SKILL

Prerequisites master in Athletics

When Climbing, you move 5 more feet on a success and 10 more feet on a critical success, to a maximum of your Speed.

   If you're legendary in Athletics, you gain a climb Speed equal to your Speed.

QUICK COERCION   FEAT 1

GENERAL   SKILL

Prerequisites trained in Intimidation

You can bully others with just a few choice implications. You can Coerce a creature after 1 round of conversation instead of 1 minute. You still can't Coerce a creature in the midst of combat, or without engaging in a conversation.

QUICK DISGUISE   FEAT 2

GENERAL   SKILL

Prerequisites expert in Deception

You can set up a disguise in half the usual time (generally 5 minutes). If you're a master, it takes one-tenth the usual time (usually 1 minute). If you're legendary, you can create a full disguise and Impersonate as a 3-action activity.

QUICK IDENTIFICATION   FEAT 1

GENERAL   SKILL

Prerequisites trained in Arcana, Nature, Occultism or Religion

You can Identify Magic swiftly. You take only 1 minute when using Identify Magic to determine the properties of an item, ongoing effect, or location, rather than 10 minutes. If you're a master, it takes a 3-action activity, and if you're legendary, it takes 1 action.

QUICK JUMP   FEAT 1

GENERAL   SKILL

Prerequisites trained in Athletics

FEATS

5

INTRODUCTION

ANCESTRIES &
BACKGROUNDS

CLASSES

SKILLS

FEATS

EQUIPMENT

SPELLS

THE AGE OF
LOST OMENS

PLAYING THE
GAME

GAME
MASTERING

CRAFTING
& TREASURE

APPENDIX

You can use High Jump and Long Jump as a single action instead of 2 actions. If you do, you don't perform the initial Stride (nor do you fail if you don't Stride 10 feet).

QUICK RECOGNITION   FEAT 7

GENERAL **SKILL**

Prerequisites master in Arcana, Nature, Occultism, or Religion; Recognize Spell

You Recognize Spells swiftly. Once per round, you can Recognize a Spell using a skill in which you're a master as a free action.

QUICK REPAIR   FEAT 1

GENERAL **SKILL**

Prerequisites trained in Crafting

You take 1 minute to Repair an item. If you're a master in Crafting, it takes 3 actions. If you're legendary, it takes 1 action.

QUICK SQUEEZE   FEAT 1

GENERAL **SKILL**

Prerequisites trained in Acrobatics

You Squeeze 5 feet per round (10 feet on a critical success). If you're legendary in Acrobatics, you Squeeze at full Speed.

QUICK SWIM   FEAT 7

GENERAL **SKILL**

Prerequisites master in Athletics

You Swim 5 feet farther on a success and 10 feet farther on a critical success, to a maximum of your Speed. If you're legendary in Athletics, you gain a swim Speed equal to your Speed.

QUICK UNLOCK   FEAT 7

GENERAL **SKILL**

Prerequisites master in Thievery

You can Pick a Lock using 1 action instead of 2.

QUIET ALLIES   FEAT 2

GENERAL **SKILL**

Prerequisites expert in Stealth

You're skilled at moving with a group. When you are Avoiding Notice and your allies Follow the Expert, you and those allies can roll a single Stealth check, using the lowest modifier, instead of rolling separately. This doesn't apply for initiative rolls.

RAPID MANTEL   FEAT 2

GENERAL **SKILL**

Prerequisites expert in Athletics

You easily pull yourself onto ledges. When you Grab an Edge, you can pull yourself onto that surface and stand. You can use Athletics instead of a Reflex save to Grab an Edge.

READ LIPS   FEAT 1

GENERAL **SKILL**

Prerequisites trained in Society

You can read lips of others nearby who you can clearly see. When you're at your leisure, you can do this automatically. In encounter mode or when attempting a more difficult feat of lipreading, you're fascinated and flat-footed during each round in which you focus on lip movements, and you must succeed at a Society check (DC determined by the GM) to successfully read someone's lips. In either case, the language read must be one that you know.

If you are deaf or hard of hearing and have Read Lips, you recognize the lip movements for the spoken form of your languages. You can also speak the spoken form of your languages clearly enough for others to understand you.

RECOGNIZE SPELL ↻   FEAT 1

GENERAL **SECRET** **SKILL**

Prerequisites trained in Arcana, Nature, Occultism, or Religion

Trigger A creature within line of sight casts a spell that you don't have prepared or in your spell repertoire, or a trap or similar object casts such a spell. You must be aware of the casting.

If you are trained in the appropriate skill for the spell's tradition and it's a common spell of 2nd level or lower, you automatically identify it (you still roll to attempt to get a critical success, but can't get a worse result than success). The highest level of spell you automatically identify increases to 4 if you're an expert, 6 if you're a master, and 10 if you're legendary. The GM rolls a secret Arcana, Nature, Occultism, or Religion check, whichever corresponds to the tradition of the spell being cast. If you're not trained in the skill, you can't get a result better than failure.

Critical Success You correctly recognize the spell and gain a +1 circumstance bonus to your saving throw or your AC against it.

Success You correctly recognize the spell.

Failure You fail to recognize the spell.

Critical Failure You misidentify the spell as another spell entirely, of the GM's choice.

RIDE   FEAT 1

GENERAL

When you Command an Animal you're mounted on to take a move action (such as Stride), you automatically succeed instead of needing to attempt a check. Any animal you're mounted on acts on your turn, like a minion. If you Mount an animal in the middle of an encounter, it skips its next turn and then acts on your next turn. Page 249 has more on Command an Animal.

ROBUST RECOVERY   FEAT 2

GENERAL   SKILL

Prerequisites expert in Medicine

You learned folk medicine to help recover from diseases and poison, and using it diligently has made you especially resilient. When you Treat a Disease or a Poison, or someone else uses one of these actions on you, increase the circumstance bonus granted on a success to +4, and if the result of the patient's saving throw is a success, the patient gets a critical success.

SCARE TO DEATH ❖   FEAT 15

DEATH   EMOTION   FEAR   GENERAL   INCAPACITATION   SKILL

Prerequisites legendary in Intimidation

You can frighten foes so much, they might die. Attempt an Intimidation check against the Will DC of a living creature within 30 feet of you that you sense or observe and who can sense or observe you. If the target can't hear you or doesn't understand the language you are speaking, you take a –4 circumstance penalty. The creature is temporarily immune for 1 minute.

Critical Success The target must succeed at a Fortitude save against your Intimidation DC or die. If the target succeeds at its save, it becomes frightened 2 and is fleeing for 1 round; it suffers no effect on a critical success.

Success The target becomes frightened 2.

Failure The target becomes frightened 1.

Critical Failure The target is unaffected.

SHAMELESS REQUEST   FEAT 7

GENERAL   SKILL

Requirements master in Diplomacy

You can downplay the consequences or outrageousness of your requests using sheer brazenness and charm. When you Request something, you reduce any DC increases for making an outrageous request by 2, and if you roll a critical failure for your Request, you get a failure instead. While this means you can

never cause your target to reduce their attitude toward you by making a Request, they eventually tire of requests, even though they still have a positive attitude toward you.

SHIELD BLOCK ⤴   FEAT 1

GENERAL

Trigger While you have your shield raised, you would take damage from a physical attack.

You snap your shield in place to ward off a blow. Your shield prevents you from taking an amount of damage up to the shield's Hardness. You and the shield each take any remaining damage, possibly breaking or destroying the shield.

SIGN LANGUAGE   FEAT 1

GENERAL   SKILL

Prerequisites trained in Society

You learn the sign languages associated with the languages you know, allowing you to sign and understand signs. Sign languages typically require both hands to convey more complex concepts, and they are visual rather than auditory.

Sign language is difficult to understand during combat due to the level of attention needed, unlike basic gestures like pointing at a foe to suggest a target. Sign language is hard to use in areas of low visibility, just like speech is difficult in a noisy environment.

SKILL TRAINING   FEAT 1

GENERAL   SKILL

Prerequisites Intelligence 12

You become trained in the skill of your choice.

Special You can select this feat multiple times, choosing a new skill to become trained in each time.

SLIPPERY SECRETS   FEAT 7

GENERAL   SKILL

Prerequisites master in Deception

You elude and evade attempts to uncover your true nature or intentions. When a spell or magical effect tries to read your mind, detect whether you are lying, or reveal your alignment, you can attempt a Deception check against the spell or effect's DC. If you succeed, the effect reveals nothing.

SNARE CRAFTING   FEAT 1

GENERAL   SKILL

Prerequisites trained in Crafting

You can use the Craft activity to create snares, using the rules from page 244. When you select this feat, you add the formulas for four common snares to your formula book.

SPECIALTY CRAFTING   FEAT 1

GENERAL   SKILL

Prerequisites trained in Crafting

Your training focused on Crafting one particular kind of item. Select one of the specialties listed on page 267; you gain a +1 circumstance bonus to Crafting checks to Craft items of that type. If you are a master in Crafting, this bonus increases to +2.

If it's unclear whether the specialty applies, the GM decides. Some specialties might apply only partially. For example, if you were making a morningstar and had specialty in woodworking, the GM might give you half your bonus because the item requires both blacksmithing and woodworking.

Specialty	Applicable Items
Alchemy*	Alchemical items such as elixirs
Artistry	Fine art, including jewelry
Blacksmithing	Durable metal goods, including metal armor
Bookmaking	Books and paper
Glassmaking	Glass, including glassware and windows
Leatherworking	Leather goods, including leather armor
Pottery	Ceramic goods
Shipbuilding	Ships and boats
Stonemasonry	Stone goods and structures
Tailoring	Clothing
Weaving	Textiles, baskets, and rugs
Woodworking	Wooden goods and structures

* You must have the Alchemical Crafting skill feat to Craft alchemical items.

STEADY BALANCE FEAT 1

GENERAL **SKILL**

Prerequisites trained in Acrobatics

You can keep your balance easily, even in adverse conditions. Whenever you roll a success using the Balance action, you get a critical success instead. You're not flat-footed while attempting to Balance on narrow surfaces and uneven ground. Thanks to your incredible balance, you can attempt an Acrobatics check instead of a Reflex save to Grab an Edge.

STREETWISE FEAT 1

GENERAL **SKILL**

Prerequisites trained in Society

You know about life on the streets and feel the pulse of your local settlement. You can use your Society modifier instead of your Diplomacy modifier to Gather Information. In any settlement you frequent regularly, you can use the Recall Knowledge action with Society to know the same sorts of information that you could discover with Diplomacy to Gather Information. The DC is usually significantly higher, but you know the information without spending time gathering it. If you fail to recall the information, you can still subsequently attempt to Gather Information normally.

STUDENT OF THE CANON FEAT 1

GENERAL **SKILL**

Prerequisites trained in Religion

You've researched many faiths enough to recognize notions about them that are unlikely to be true. If you roll a critical failure at a Religion check to Decipher Writing of a religious nature or to Recall Knowledge about the tenets of faiths, you get a failure instead. When attempting to Recall Knowledge about the tenets of your own faith, if you roll a failure, you get a success instead, and if you roll a success, you get a critical success instead.

SUBTLE THEFT FEAT 1

GENERAL **SKILL**

Prerequisites trained in Thievery

When you successfully Steal something, observers (creatures other than the creature you stole from) take a –2 circumstance penalty to their Perception DCs to detect your theft. Additionally, if you first Create a Diversion using Deception, taking a single Palm an Object or Steal action doesn't end your undetected condition.

SURVEY WILDLIFE FEAT 1

GENERAL **SKILL**

Prerequisites trained in Survival

You can study details in the wilderness to determine the presence of nearby creatures. You can spend 10 minutes assessing the area around you to find out what creatures are nearby, based on nests, scat, and marks on vegetation. Attempt a Survival check against a DC determined by the GM based on how obvious the signs are. On a success, you can attempt a Recall Knowledge check with a –2 penalty to learn more about the creatures just from these signs. If you're a master in Survival, you don't take the penalty.

SWIFT SNEAK FEAT 7

GENERAL **SKILL**

Prerequisites master in Stealth

You can move your full Speed when you Sneak. You can use Swift Sneak while Burrowing, Climbing, Flying, or Swimming instead of Striding if you have the corresponding movement type.

TERRAIN EXPERTISE FEAT 1

GENERAL **SKILL**

Prerequisites trained in Survival

Your experience in navigating a certain type of terrain makes you supremely confident while doing so. You gain a +1 circumstance bonus to Survival checks in one of the following types of terrain, chosen when you select this feat: aquatic, arctic, desert, forest, mountain, plains, sky, swamp, or underground.

Special You can select this feat more than once, choosing a different type of terrain each time.

TERRAIN STALKER FEAT 1

GENERAL **SKILL**

Prerequisites trained in Stealth

Select one type of difficult terrain from the following list: rubble, snow, or underbrush. While undetected by all non-allies in that type of terrain, you can Sneak without attempting a Stealth check as long as you move no more than 5 feet and do not move within 10 feet of an enemy at any point during your movement. This also allows you to automatically approach creatures to within 15 feet while Avoiding Notice during exploration as long as they aren't actively Searching or on guard.

Special You can select this feat multiple times. Each time, choose a different type of terrain.

INTRODUCTION

ANCESTRIES & BACKGROUNDS

CLASSES

SKILLS

FEATS

EQUIPMENT

SPELLS

THE AGE OF LOST OMENS

PLAYING THE GAME

GAME MASTERING

CRAFTING & TREASURE

APPENDIX

TERRIFIED RETREAT   FEAT 7

GENERAL   SKILL

Prerequisites master in Intimidation

When you critically succeed at the Demoralize action, if the target's level is lower than yours, the target is fleeing for 1 round.

TITAN WRESTLER   FEAT 1

GENERAL   SKILL

Prerequisites trained in Athletics

You can attempt to Disarm, Grapple, Shove, or Trip creatures up to two sizes larger than you, or up to three sizes larger than you if you're legendary in Athletics.

TOUGHNESS   FEAT 1

GENERAL

You can withstand more punishment than most before succumbing. Increase your maximum Hit Points by your level. You reduce the DC of recovery checks by 1 (page 459).

TRAIN ANIMAL   FEAT 1

DOWNTIME   GENERAL   MANIPULATE   SKILL

Prerequisites trained in Nature

You spend time teaching an animal to do a certain action. You can either select a basic action the animal already knows how to do (typically those listed in the Command an Animal action on page 249) or attempt to teach the animal a new basic action. The GM determines the DC of any check required and the amount of time the training takes (usually at least a week). It's usually impossible to teach an animal a trick that uses critical thinking. If you're expert, master, or legendary in Nature, you might be able to train more unusual creatures, at the GM's discretion.

Success The animal learns the action. If it was an action the animal already knew, you can Command the Animal to take that action without attempting a Nature check. If it was a new basic action, add that action to the actions the animal can take when Commanded, but you must still roll.

Failure The animal doesn't learn the trick.

TRICK MAGIC ITEM ◆   FEAT 1

GENERAL   MANIPULATE   SKILL

Prerequisites trained in Arcana, Nature, Occultism, or Religion

You examine a magic item you normally couldn't use in an effort to fool it and activate it temporarily. For example, this might allow a fighter to cast a spell from a wand or allow a wizard to cast a spell that's not on the arcane list using a scroll. You must know what activating the item does, or you can't attempt to trick it.

Attempt a check using the skill matching the item's magic tradition, or matching a tradition that has the spell on its list, if you're trying to cast a spell from the item. The relevant skills are Arcana for arcane, Nature for primal, Occultism for occult, Religion for divine, or any of the four for an item that has the magical trait and not a tradition trait. The GM determines the DC based on the item's level (possibly adjusted depending on the item or situation).

If you activate a magic item that requires a spell attack roll or spell DC and you don't have the ability to cast spells of the relevant tradition, use your level as your proficiency bonus and the highest of your Intelligence, Wisdom, or Charisma modifiers. If you're a master in the appropriate skill for the item's tradition, you instead use the trained proficiency bonus, and if you're legendary, you instead use the expert proficiency bonus.

Success For the rest of the current turn, you can spend actions to activate the item as if you could normally use it.

Failure You can't use the item or try to trick it again this turn, but you can try again on subsequent turns.

Critical Failure You can't use the item, and you can't try to trick it again until your next daily preparations.

UNDERWATER MARAUDER   FEAT 1

GENERAL   SKILL

Prerequisites trained in Athletics

You've learned to fight underwater. You are not flat-footed while in water, and you don't take the usual penalties for using a bludgeoning or slashing melee weapon in water.

UNIFIED THEORY   FEAT 15

GENERAL   SKILL

Prerequisites legendary in Arcana

You've started to make a meaningful connection about the common underpinnings of the four traditions of magic and magical essences, allowing you to understand them all through an arcane lens. Whenever you use an action or a skill feat that requires a Nature, Occultism, or Religion check, depending on the magic tradition, you can use Arcana instead. If you would normally take a penalty or have a higher DC for using Arcana on other magic (such as when using Identify Magic), you no longer do so.

UNMISTAKABLE LORE   FEAT 2

GENERAL   SKILL

Prerequisites expert in Lore

You never get information about your areas of expertise wrong. When you Recall Knowledge using any Lore subcategory in which you're trained, if you roll a critical failure, you get a failure instead. If you're a master in a Lore subcategory, on a critical success, you gain even more information or context than usual.

UNTRAINED IMPROVISATION   FEAT 3

GENERAL

You've learned how to handle situations when you're out of your depth. Your proficiency bonus to untrained skill checks is equal to half your level instead of +0. If you're 7th level or higher, the bonus increases to your full level instead. This doesn't allow you to use the skill's trained actions.

VIRTUOSIC PERFORMER   FEAT 1

GENERAL   SKILL

Prerequisites trained in Performance

You have exceptional talent with one type of performance. You gain a +1 circumstance bonus when making a certain type of performance. If you are a master in Performance, this bonus increases to +2. Select one of the following specialties and apply

FEATS

5

INTRODUCTION

ANCESTRIES &
BACKGROUNDS

CLASSES

SKILLS

FEATS

EQUIPMENT

SPELLS

THE AGE OF
LOST OMENS

PLAYING THE
GAME

GAME
MASTERING

CRAFTING
& TREASURE

APPENDIX

the bonus when attempting Performance checks of that type. If it's unclear whether the specialty applies, the GM decides.

Specialty	Examples
Acting	Drama, pantomime, puppetry
Comedy	Buffoonery, joke telling, limericks
Dance	Ballet, huara, jig, macru
Keyboards	Harpsichord, organ, piano
Oratory	Epic, ode, poetry, storytelling
Percussion	Chimes, drum, gong, xylophone
Singing	Ballad, chant, melody, rhyming
Strings	Fiddle, harp, lute, viol
Winds	Bagpipe, flute, recorder, trumpet

WALL JUMP — FEAT 7

GENERAL **SKILL**

Prerequisites master in Athletics

You can use your momentum from a jump to propel yourself off a wall. If you're adjacent to a wall at the end of a jump (whether performing a High Jump, Long Jump, or Leap), you don't fall as long as your next action is another jump. Furthermore, since your previous jump gives you momentum, you can use High Jump or Long Jump as a single action, but you don't get to Stride as part of the activity.

You can use Wall Jump only once in a turn, unless you're legendary in Athletics, in which case you can use Wall Jump as many times as you can use consecutive jump actions in that turn.

WARD MEDIC — FEAT 2

GENERAL **SKILL**

Prerequisites expert in Medicine

You've studied in large medical wards, treating several patients at once and tending to all their needs. When you use Treat Disease or Treat Wounds, you can treat up to two targets. If you're a master in Medicine, you can treat up to four targets, and if you're legendary, you can treat up to eight targets.

WARY DISARMAMENT — FEAT 2

GENERAL **SKILL**

Prerequisites expert in Thievery

If you trigger a device or set off a trap while disarming it, you gain a +2 circumstance bonus to your AC or saving throw against the device or trap. This applies only to attacks or effects triggered by your failed attempt, not to any later ones, such as additional attacks from a complex trap.

WEAPON PROFICIENCY — FEAT 1

GENERAL

You become trained in all simple weapons. If you were already trained in all simple weapons, you become trained in all martial weapons. If you were already trained in all martial weapons, you become trained in one advanced weapon of your choice.

Special You can select this feat more than once. Each time you do, you become trained in additional weapons as appropriate, following the above progression.

6

INTRODUCTION

ANCESTRIES &
BACKGROUNDS

CLASSES

SKILLS

FEATS

EQUIPMENT

SPELLS

THE AGE OF
LOST OMENS

PLAYING THE
GAME

GAME
MASTERING

CRAFTING
& TREASURE

APPENDIX

CHAPTER 6: EQUIPMENT

To make your mark on the world, you'll need to have the right equipment, including armor, weapons, and other gear. This chapter presents the various equipment that you can purchase during character creation. You can usually find these items for sale in most cities and other large settlements.

Your character starts out with 15 gold pieces (150 silver pieces) to spend on any common items from this chapter. Items with an uncommon rarity can be purchased only if you have special access from abilities you selected during character creation or your GM gives you permission to purchase them.

Once you've purchased your starting items, there are three main ways to gain new items and equipment: you can find them during an adventure, make them using the Crafting skill, or purchase them from a merchant.

COINS AND CURRENCY

Though you might be able to barter valuable items in some areas, currency is the most versatile way to make transactions when you head to market. The most common currency is coins. For most commoners and beginning adventurers, the standard unit is the **silver piece (sp)**. Each silver piece is a standard weight of silver and is typically accepted by any merchant or kingdom no matter where it was minted. There are three other common types of coins, each likewise standardized in weight and value. The first is the **copper piece (cp)**. Each copper piece is worth one-tenth of a silver piece. The **gold piece (gp)** is often used for purchasing magic items and other expensive items, as 1 gold piece is worth 10 silver pieces or 100 copper pieces. The **platinum piece (pp)** is used by nobles to demonstrate their wealth, for the purchase of very expensive items, or simply as a way to easily transport large sums of currency. A platinum piece is worth 10 gold pieces, 100 silver pieces, or 1,000 copper pieces. See Table 6–1: Coin Values for the exchange rates of common types of coins.

OTHER CURRENCY

Art objects, gems, and raw materials (such as those used for the Craft activity) can be used much like currency: you can sell them for the same Price you can buy them.

PRICE

Most items in the following tables have a Price, which is the amount of currency it typically takes to purchase that item. An item with a Price of "—" can't be purchased. An item with a Price of 0 is normally free, but its value could be higher based on the materials used to create it. Most items can be sold for half their Price, but coins, gems, art objects, and raw materials (such as components for the Craft activity) can be exchanged for their full Price.

STARTING MONEY
15 GP (150 SP)

TABLE 6–1: COIN VALUES

Coins	CP	SP	GP	PP
Copper piece (cp)	1	1/10	1/100	1/1,000
Silver piece (sp)	10	1	1/10	1/100
Gold piece (gp)	100	10	1	1/10
Platinum piece (pp)	1,000	100	10	1

ITEM LEVEL

Each item has an item level, which represents the item's complexity and any magic used in its construction. Simpler items with a lower level are easier to construct, and you can't Craft items that have a higher level than your own (page 243). If an item's level isn't listed, its level is 0. While characters can use items of any level, GMs should keep in mind that allowing characters access to items far above their current level may have a negative impact on the game.

CARRYING AND USING ITEMS

A character typically has two hands, allowing them to hold an item in each hand or a single two-handed item using both hands. Drawing or changing how you're carrying an item usually requires you to use an Interact action (though to drop an item, you use the Release action instead). Table 6–2: Changing Equipment on page 273 lists some ways that you might change the items you're holding or carrying, and the number of hands you need to do so.

Many ways of using items require you to spend multiple actions. For example, drinking a potion stowed in your belt pouch requires using an Interact action to draw it and then using a second action to drink it as described in its Activate entry (page 532).

BULK

Carrying especially heavy or unwieldy items can make it more difficult for you to move, as can overloading yourself with too much gear. The Bulk value of an item reflects how difficult the item is to handle, representing its size, weight, and general awkwardness. If you have a high Strength score, you usually don't need to worry about Bulk unless you're carrying numerous substantial items.

BULK LIMITS

You can carry an amount of Bulk equal to 5 plus your Strength modifier without penalty; if you carry more, you gain the encumbered condition. You can't hold or carry more Bulk than 10 plus your Strength modifier.

Encumbered

You are carrying more weight than you can manage. While you're encumbered, you're clumsy 1 and take a –10-foot penalty to all your Speeds. As with all penalties to your Speed, this can't reduce your Speed below 5 feet.

BULK VALUES

Items can have a number to indicate their Bulk value, or they can be light (indicated by an L) or negligible (indicated by a —) for the purpose of determining Bulk. For instance, full plate armor is 4 Bulk, a longsword is 1 Bulk, a dagger or scroll is light, and a piece of chalk is negligible. Ten light items count as 1 Bulk, and you round down fractions (so 9 light items count as 0 Bulk, and 11 light items count as 1 Bulk). Items of negligible Bulk don't count toward Bulk unless you try to carry vast numbers of them, as determined by the GM.

ESTIMATING AN ITEM'S BULK

As a general rule, an item that weighs 5 to 10 pounds is 1 Bulk, an item weighing less than a few ounces is negligible, and anything in between is light. Particularly awkward or unwieldy items might have higher Bulk values. For example, a 10-foot pole isn't heavy, but its length makes it difficult for you to move while you have one on your person, so its Bulk is 1. Items made for larger or smaller creatures have greater or lesser Bulk, as described on page 295.

BULK OF COINS

Coins are a popular means of exchange due to their portability, but they can still add up. A thousand coins of any denomination or combination of denominations count as 1 Bulk. It's not usually necessary to determine the Bulk of coins in fractions of 1,000; simply round down fractions of 1,000. In other words, 100 coins don't count as a light item, and 1,999 coins are 1 Bulk, not 2.

BULK OF CREATURES

You might need to know the Bulk of a creature, especially if you need to carry someone off the battlefield. The table that follows lists the typical Bulk of a creature based on its size, but the GM might adjust this number.

Size of Creature	Bulk
Tiny	1
Small	3
Medium	6
Large	12
Huge	24
Gargantuan	48

DRAGGING

In some situations, you might drag an object or creature rather than carry it. If you're dragging something, treat its Bulk as half. Typically, you can drag one thing at a time, you must use both hands to do so, and you drag slowly—roughly 50 feet per minute unless you have some means to speed it up. Use the total Bulk of what you're dragging, so if you have a sack laden with goods, use the sum of all the Bulk it carries instead of an individual item within.

WIELDING ITEMS

Some abilities require you to wield an item, typically a weapon. You're wielding an item any time you're holding it in the number of hands needed to use it effectively. When wielding an item, you're not just carrying it around—you're ready to use it. Other abilities might require you to merely carry or have an item. These apply as long as you have the item on your person; you don't have to wield it.

ITEM DAMAGE

An item can be broken or destroyed if it takes enough damage. Every item has a **Hardness** value. Each time an item takes damage, reduce any damage the item takes by its Hardness. The rest of the damage reduces the item's Hit Points. Normally an item takes damage only when a creature is directly attacking it—commonly targeted items include doors and traps. A creature that attacks you doesn't normally damage your armor or other gear, even if it hits you. However, the Shield Block reaction can cause your shield to take damage as you use it to prevent damage to yourself, and some monsters have exceptional abilities that can damage your items.

An item that takes damage can become **broken** and eventually destroyed. It becomes broken when its Hit Points are equal to or lower than its **Broken Threshold** (**BT**); once its Hit Points are reduced to 0, it is **destroyed**. A broken item has the broken condition until Repaired above its Broken Threshold. Anything that automatically makes an item broken immediately reduces its Hit Points to its Broken Threshold if the item had more Hit Points than that when the effect occurred. If an item has no Broken Threshold, then it has no relevant changes to its function due to being broken, but it's still destroyed at 0 Hit Points. (See the broken condition definition on page 273 for more information.) A destroyed item can't be Repaired.

An item's Hardness, Hit Points, and Broken Threshold usually depend on the material the item is made of. This information appears on page 577.

INTRODUCTION

ANCESTRIES &
BACKGROUNDS

CLASSES

SKILLS

FEATS

EQUIPMENT

SPELLS

THE AGE OF
LOST OMENS

PLAYING THE
GAME

GAME
MASTERING

CRAFTING
& TREASURE

APPENDIX

TABLE 6-2: CHANGING EQUIPMENT

Change	Hands	Action
Draw, stow, or pick up an item[1]	1 or 2	Interact
Pass an item to or take an item from a willing creature[2]	1 or 2	Interact
Drop an item to the ground	1 or 2	Release
Detach a shield or item strapped to you	1	Interact
Change your grip by removing a hand from an item	2	Release
Change your grip by adding a hand to an item	2	Interact
Retrieve an item from a backpack[3] or satchel	2	Interact

[1] If you retrieve a two-handed item with only one hand, you still need to change your grip before you can wield or use it.

[2] A creature must have a hand free for someone to pass an item to them, and they might then need to change their grip if they receive an item requiring two hands to wield or use.

[3] Retrieving an item stowed in your own backpack requires first taking off the backpack with a separate Interact action.

Broken

Broken is a condition that affects objects. An object is broken when damage has reduced its Hit Points below its Broken Threshold. A broken object can't be used for its normal function, nor does it grant bonuses—with the exception of armor. Broken armor still grants its item bonus to AC, but it also imparts a status penalty to AC depending on its category: –1 for broken light armor, –2 for broken medium armor, or –3 for broken heavy armor.

A broken item still imposes penalties and limitations normally incurred by carrying, holding, or wearing it. For example, broken armor would still impose its Dexterity modifier cap, check penalty, and so forth.

If an effect makes an item broken automatically and the item has more HP than its Broken Threshold, that effect also reduces the item's current HP to the Broken Threshold.

OBJECT IMMUNITIES

Inanimate objects and hazards are immune to bleed, death effects, disease, healing, mental effects, necromancy, nonlethal attacks, and poison, as well as the doomed, drained, fatigued, paralyzed, sickened, and unconscious conditions. An item that has a mind is not immune to mental effects. Many objects are immune to other conditions, at the GM's discretion. For instance, a sword has no Speed, so it can't take a penalty to its Speed, but an effect that causes a Speed penalty might work on a moving blade trap.

SHODDY ITEMS

Improvised or of dubious make, shoddy items are never available for purchase except for in the most desperate of communities. When available, a shoddy item usually costs half the Price of a standard item, though you can never sell one in any case. Attacks and checks involving a shoddy item take a –2 item penalty. This penalty also applies to any DCs that a shoddy item applies to (such as AC, for shoddy armor). A shoddy suit of armor also worsens the armor's check penalty by 2. A shoddy item's Hit Points and Broken Threshold are each half that of a normal item of its type.

ARMOR

Armor increases your character's defenses, but some medium or heavy armor can hamper movement. If you want to increase your character's defense beyond the protection your armor provides, they can use a shield. Armor protects your character only while they're wearing it.

ARMOR CLASS

Your Armor Class (AC) measures how well you can defend against attacks. When a creature attacks you, your Armor Class is the DC for that attack roll.

> **Armor Class = 10 + Dexterity modifier (up to your armor's Dex Cap) + proficiency bonus + armor's item bonus to AC + other bonuses + penalties**

Use your proficiency bonus for the category (light, medium, or heavy) or the specific type of armor you're wearing. If you're not wearing armor, use your proficiency in unarmored defense.

DONNING AND REMOVING ARMOR

Getting in and out of armor is time consuming—so make sure you're wearing it when you need it! Donning and removing armor are both activities involving many Interact actions. It takes 1 minute to don light armor, 5 minutes to don medium or heavy armor, and 1 minute to remove any armor.

ARMOR STATISTICS

Table 6–3: Unarmored Defense provides the statistics for the various forms of protection without wearing armor. Table 6–4: Armor provides the statistics for suits of armor that can be purchased and worn, organized by category. The columns in both tables provide the following statistics.

CATEGORY

The armor's category—unarmored, light armor, medium armor, or heavy armor—indicates which proficiency bonus you use while wearing the armor.

AC BONUS

This number is the item bonus you add for the armor when determining Armor Class.

DEXTERITY MODIFIER CAP (DEX CAP)

This number is the maximum amount of your Dexterity modifier that can apply to your AC while you are wearing a given suit of armor. For example, if you have a Dexterity modifier of +4 and you are wearing a suit of half plate, you apply only a +1 bonus from your Dexterity modifier to your AC while wearing that armor.

CHECK PENALTY

While wearing your armor, you take this penalty to Strength- and Dexterity-based skill checks, except for those that have the attack trait. If you meet the armor's Strength threshold (see Strength below), you don't take this penalty.

SPEED PENALTY

While wearing a suit of armor, you take the penalty listed in this entry to your Speed, as well as to any other movement types you have, such as a climb Speed or swim Speed, to a minimum Speed of 5 feet. If you meet the armor's Strength threshold (see below), you reduce the penalty by 5 feet.

STRENGTH

This entry indicates the Strength score at which you are strong enough to overcome some of the armor's penalties. If your Strength is equal to or greater than this value, you no longer take the armor's check penalty, and you decrease the Speed penalty by 5 feet (to no penalty if the penalty was −5 feet, or to a −5-foot penalty if the penalty was −10 feet).

BULK

This entry gives the armor's Bulk, assuming you're wearing the armor and distributing its weight across your body. A suit of armor that's carried or worn usually has 1 more Bulk than what's listed here (or 1 Bulk total for armor of light Bulk). An armor's Bulk is increased or decreased if it's sized for creatures that aren't Small or Medium in size, following the rules on page 295.

GROUP

Each type of medium and heavy armor belongs to an armor group, which classifies it with similar types of armor. Some abilities reference armor groups, typically to grant armor specialization effects, which are described on page 275.

ARMOR TRAITS

The traits for each suit of armor appear in this entry. Armor can have the following traits.

Bulwark: The armor covers you so completely that it provides benefits against some damaging effects. On Reflex saves to avoid a damaging effect, such as a *fireball*, you add a +3 modifier instead of your Dexterity modifier.

TABLE 6-3: UNARMORED DEFENSE

Unarmored	Price	AC Bonus	Dex Cap	Check Penalty	Speed Penalty	Bulk	Armor Traits
No armor	–	+0	–	–	–	–	–
Explorer's clothing	1 sp	+0	+5	–	–	L	Comfort

TABLE 6-4: ARMOR

Light Armor	Price	AC Bonus	Dex Cap	Check Penalty	Speed Penalty	Strength	Bulk	Group	Armor Traits
Padded armor	2 sp	+1	+3	–	–	10	L	–	Comfort
Leather	2 gp	+1	+4	–1	–	10	1	–	–
Studded leather	3 gp	+2	+3	–1	–	12	1	–	–
Chain shirt	5 gp	+2	+3	–1	–	12	1	–	Flexible, Noisy

Medium Armor	Price	AC Bonus	Dex Cap	Check Penalty	Speed Penalty	Strength	Bulk	Group	Armor Traits
Hide	2 gp	+3	+2	–2	–5 ft.	14	2	Leather	–
Scale mail	4 gp	+3	+2	–2	–5 ft.	14	2	Composite	–
Chain mail	6 gp	+4	+1	–2	–5 ft.	16	2	Chain	Flexible, noisy
Breastplate	8 gp	+4	+1	–2	–5 ft.	16	2	Plate	–

Heavy Armor	Price	AC Bonus	Dex Cap	Check Penalty	Speed Penalty	Strength	Bulk	Group	Armor Traits
Splint mail (level 1)	13 gp	+5	+1	–3	–10 ft.	16	3	Composite	–
Half plate (level 1)	18 gp	+5	+1	–3	–10 ft.	16	3	Plate	–
Full plate (level 2)	30 gp	+6	+0	–3	–10 ft.	18	4	Plate	Bulwark

Comfort: The armor is so comfortable that you can rest normally while wearing it.

Flexible: The armor is flexible enough that it doesn't hinder most actions. You don't apply its check penalty to Acrobatics or Athletics checks.

Noisy: This armor is loud and likely to alert others to your presence when you're using the Avoid Notice exploration activity (page 479).

ARMOR SPECIALIZATION EFFECTS

Certain class features can grant you additional benefits with certain armors. This is called an armor specialization effect. The exact effect depends on which armor group your armor belongs to, as listed below. Only medium and heavy armors have armor specialization effects.

Chain: The armor is so flexible it can bend with a critical hit and absorb some of the blow. Reduce the damage from critical hits by either 4 + the value of the armor's potency rune for medium armor, or 6 + the value of the armor's potency rune for heavy armor. This can't reduce the damage to less than the damage rolled for the hit before doubling for a critical hit.

Composite: The numerous overlapping pieces of this armor protect you from piercing attacks. You gain resistance to piercing damage equal to 1 + the value of the armor's potency rune for medium armor, or 2 + the value of the armor's potency rune for heavy armor.

Leather: The thick second skin of the armor disperses blunt force to reduce bludgeoning damage. You gain resistance to bludgeoning damage equal to 1 + the value of the armor's potency rune for medium armor, or 2 + the value of the armor's potency rune for heavy armor.

Plate: The sturdy plate provides no purchase for a cutting edge. You gain resistance to slashing damage equal to 1 + the value of the armor's potency rune for medium armor, or 2 + the value of the armor's potency rune for heavy armor.

MATERIALS

Most suits of armor and weapons are made from ordinary, commonly available materials like iron, leather, steel, and wood. If you're not sure what a suit of armor is made of, the GM determines the details.

Some armor, shields, and weapons are instead made of precious materials. These often have inherent supernatural properties. Cold iron, for example, which harms fey, and silver can damage werecreatures. These materials are detailed beginning on page 577.

ARMOR DESCRIPTIONS

Each type of armor is described in more detail below.

Breastplate: Though referred to as a breastplate, this type of armor consists of several pieces of plate or half-plate armor (page 276) that protect the torso, chest, neck, and sometimes the hips and lower legs. It strategically grants some of the protection of plate while allowing greater flexibility and speed.

Chain Mail: A suit of chain mail consists of several pieces of armor composed of small metal rings linked together in a protective mesh. It typically includes a chain shirt, leggings, a pair of arms, and a coif, collectively protecting most of the body.

Chain Shirt: Sometimes called a hauberk, this is a long shirt constructed of the same metal rings as chainmail. However, it is much lighter than chainmail and protects only the torso, upper arms, and upper legs of its wearer.

INTRODUCTION

ANCESTRIES & BACKGROUNDS

CLASSES

SKILLS

FEATS

EQUIPMENT

SPELLS

THE AGE OF LOST OMENS

PLAYING THE GAME

GAME MASTERING

CRAFTING & TREASURE

APPENDIX

Explorer's Clothing: Adventurers who don't wear armor travel in durable clothing. Though it's not armor and uses your unarmored defense proficiency, it still has a Dex Cap and can grant an item bonus to AC if etched with potency runes (as described on page 581).

Full Plate: Plate mail consists of interlocking plates that encase nearly the entire body in a carapace of steel. It is costly and heavy, and the wearer often requires help to don it correctly, but it provides some of the best defense armor can supply. A suit of this armor comes with an undercoat of padded armor (see below) and a pair of gauntlets (page 285).

Half Plate: Half plate consists of most of the upper body plates used in full plate, with lighter or sparser steel plate protection for the arms and legs. This provides some of the protection of full plate with greater flexibility and speed. A suit of this armor comes with an undercoat of padded armor (see below) and a pair of gauntlets (page 285).

Hide: A mix of furs, sturdy hide, and sometimes molded boiled leather, this armor provides protection due to its layers of leather, though its bulkiness slows the wearer down and decreases mobility.

Leather: A mix of flexible and molded boiled leather, a suit of this type of armor provides some protection with maximum flexibility.

Padded Armor: This armor is simply a layer of heavy, quilted cloth, but it is sometimes used because it's so inexpensive. Padded armor is easier to damage and destroy than other types of armor. Heavy armor comes with a padded armor undercoat included in its Price, though it loses the comfort trait when worn under heavy armor. You can wear just that padded armor undercoat to sleep in, if your heavy armor is destroyed, or when otherwise not wearing the full heavy armor. This allows you to keep the armor invested and benefit from the power of any runes on the associated heavy armor, but no one else can wear your heavy armor without the padded undercoat.

Scale Mail: Scale mail consists of many metal scales sewn onto a reinforced leather backing, often in the form of a long shirt that protects the torso, arms, and legs.

Splint Mail: This type of armor is chain mail reinforced with flexible, interlocking metal plates, typically located on the wearer's torso, upper arms, and legs. A suit of this armor comes with an undercoat of padded armor (see above) and a pair of gauntlets (page 285).

Studded Leather: This leather armor is reinforced with metal studs and sometimes small metal plates, providing most of the flexibility of leather armor with more robust protection.

DAMAGING ARMOR

Your armor's statistics are based on the material it's predominantly made from. It's not likely your armor will take damage, as explained in Item Damage on page 272.

Material	Hardness	HP	BT
Cloth (explorer's clothing, padded armor)	1	4	2
Leather (hide, leather, studded leather)	4	16	8
Metal (breastplate, chain mail, chain shirt, full plate, half plate, scale mail, splint mail)	9	36	18

INTRODUCTION

ANCESTRIES & BACKGROUNDS

CLASSES

SKILLS

FEATS

EQUIPMENT

SPELLS

THE AGE OF LOST OMENS

PLAYING THE GAME

GAME MASTERING

CRAFTING & TREASURE

APPENDIX

SHIELDS

A shield can increase your character's defense beyond the protection their armor provides. Your character must be wielding a shield in one hand to make use of it, and it grants its bonus to AC only if they use an action to Raise a Shield. This action grants the shield's bonus to AC as a circumstance bonus until their next turn starts. A shield's Speed penalty applies whenever your character is holding the shield, whether they have raised it or not.

Raise a Shield is the action most commonly used with shields. Most shields must be held in one hand, so you can't hold anything with that hand and Raise a Shield. A buckler, however, doesn't take up your hand, so you can Raise a Shield with a buckler if the hand is free (or, at the GM's discretion, if it's holding a simple, lightweight object that's not a weapon). You lose the benefits of Raise a Shield if that hand is no longer free.

When you have a tower shield raised, you can use the Take Cover action (page 471) to increase the circumstance bonus to AC to +4. This lasts until the shield is no longer raised. If you would normally provide lesser cover against an attack, having your tower shield raised provides standard cover against it (and other creatures can Take Cover as normal using the cover from your shield).

If you have access to the Shield Block reaction (from your class or from a feat), you can use it while Raising your Shield to reduce the damage you take by an amount equal to the shield's Hardness. Both you and the shield then take any remaining damage.

SHIELD STATISTICS

Shields have statistics that follow the same rules as armor: Price, Speed Penalty, and Bulk. See page 274 for the rules for those statistics. Their other statistics are described here.

AC BONUS

A shield grants a circumstance bonus to AC, but only when the shield is raised. This requires using the Raise a Shield action, found on page 472.

HARDNESS

Whenever a shield takes damage, the amount of damage it takes is reduced by this amount. This number is particularly relevant for shields because of the Shield Block feat (page 266). The rules for Hardness appear on page 272.

HP (BT)

This column lists the shield's Hit Points (HP) and Broken Threshold (BT). These measure how much damage the shield can take before it's destroyed (its total HP) and how much it can take before being broken and unusable (its BT). These matter primarily for the Shield Block reaction.

ATTACKING WITH A SHIELD

A shield can be used as a martial weapon for attacks, using the statistics listed for a shield bash on Table 6–7: Melee Weapons (page 280). The shield bash is an option only for shields that weren't designed to be used as weapons. A shield can't have runes added to it. You can also buy and attach a shield boss or shield spikes to a shield to make it a more practical weapon. These can be found on Table 6–7. These work like other weapons and can even be etched with runes.

SHIELD DESCRIPTIONS

Each type of shield is described in more detail below.

Buckler: This very small shield is a favorite of duelists and quick, lightly armored warriors. It's typically made of steel and strapped to your forearm. You can Raise a Shield with your buckler as long as you have that hand free or are holding a light object that's not a weapon in that hand.

Wooden Shield: Though they come in a variety of shapes and sizes, the protection offered by wooden shields comes from the stoutness of their materials. While wooden shields are less expensive than steel shields, they break more easily.

Steel Shield: Like wooden shields, steel shields come in a variety of shapes and sizes. Though more expensive than wooden shields, they are much more durable.

Tower Shield: These massive shields can be used to provide cover to nearly the entire body. Due to their size, they are typically made of wood reinforced with metal.

TABLE 6-5: SHIELDS

Shield	Price	AC Bonus[1]	Speed Penalty	Bulk	Hardness	HP (BT)
Buckler	1 gp	+1	—	L	3	6 (3)
Wooden shield	1 gp	+2	—	1	3	12 (6)
Steel shield	2 gp	+2	—	1	5	20 (10)
Tower shield	10 gp	+2/+4[2]	–5 ft.	4	5	20 (10)

[1] Gaining a shield's circumstance bonus to AC requires using the Raise a Shield action (found on page 472).

[2] Getting the higher bonus for a tower shield requires using the Take Cover action (page 471) while the shield is raised.

WEAPONS

Most characters in Pathfinder carry weapons, ranging from mighty warhammers to graceful bows to even simple clubs. Full details on how you calculate the bonuses, modifiers, and penalties for attack rolls and damage rolls are given in Chapter 9 on page 446, but they're summarized here, followed by the rules for weapons and dozens of weapon choices.

ATTACK ROLLS

When making an attack roll, determine the result by rolling 1d20 and adding your attack modifier for the weapon or unarmed attack you're using. Modifiers for melee and ranged attacks are calculated differently.

> **Melee attack modifier = Strength modifier** (or optionally Dexterity for a finesse weapon) **+ proficiency bonus + other bonuses + penalties**

> **Ranged attack modifier = Dexterity modifier + proficiency bonus + other bonuses + penalties**

Bonuses, and penalties apply to these rolls just like with other types of checks. Weapons with potency runes (page 581) add an item bonus to your attack rolls.

MULTIPLE ATTACK PENALTY

If you use an action with the attack trait more than once on the same turn, your attacks after the first take a penalty called a multiple attack penalty. Your second attack takes a –5 penalty, and any subsequent attacks take a –10 penalty.

The multiple attack penalty doesn't apply to attacks you make when it isn't your turn (such as attacks made as part of a reaction). You can use a weapon with the agile trait (page 282) to reduce your multiple attack penalty.

DAMAGE ROLLS

When the result of your attack roll with a weapon or unarmed attack equals or exceeds your target's AC, you hit your target! Roll the weapon or unarmed attack's damage die and add the relevant modifiers, bonuses, and penalties to determine the amount of damage you deal. Calculate a damage roll as follows.

> **Melee damage roll = damage die of weapon or unarmed attack + Strength modifier + bonuses + penalties**

> **Ranged damage roll = damage die of weapon + Strength modifier for thrown weapons + bonuses + penalties**

Ranged weapons don't normally add an ability modifier to the damage roll, though weapons with the propulsive trait (page 283) add half your Strength modifier (or your full modifier if it is a negative number), and thrown weapons add your full Strength modifier.

Magic weapons with *striking*, *greater striking*, or *major striking* runes (page 581) add one or more weapon damage dice to your damage roll. These extra dice are the same die size as the weapon's damage die. At higher levels, most characters also gain extra damage from weapon specialization.

CRITICAL HITS

When you make an attack and roll a natural 20 (the number on the die is 20), or if the result of your attack exceeds the target's AC by 10, you achieve a critical success (also known as a critical hit).

If you critically succeed at a Strike, your attack deals double damage (page 451). Other attacks, such as spell attack rolls and some uses of the Athletics skill, describe the specific effects that occur when their outcomes are critical successes.

UNARMED ATTACKS

Almost all characters start out trained in unarmed attacks. You can Strike with your fist or another body part, calculating your attack and damage rolls in the same way you would with a weapon. Unarmed attacks can belong to a weapon group (page 280), and they might have weapon traits (page 282). However, unarmed attacks aren't weapons, and effects and abilities that work with weapons never work with unarmed attacks unless they specifically say so.

Table 6–6: Unarmed Attacks lists the statistics for an unarmed attack with a fist, though you'll usually use the same statistics for attacks made with any other parts of your body. Certain ancestry feats, class features, and spells give access to special, more powerful unarmed attacks. Details for those unarmed attacks are provided in the abilities that grant them.

IMPROVISED WEAPONS

If you attack with something that wasn't built to be a weapon, such as a chair or a vase, you're making an attack with an improvised weapon. You take a –2 item penalty to attack rolls with an improvised weapon. The GM determines the amount and type of damage the attack deals, if any, as well as any weapon traits the improvised weapon should have.

6

INTRODUCTION

ANCESTRIES &
BACKGROUNDS

CLASSES

SKILLS

FEATS

EQUIPMENT

SPELLS

THE AGE OF
LOST OMENS

PLAYING THE
GAME

GAME
MASTERING

CRAFTING
& TREASURE

APPENDIX

WEAPON STATISTICS

The tables on pages 280–282 list the statistics for various melee and ranged weapons that you can purchase, as well as the statistics for striking with a fist (or another basic unarmed attack). The tables present the following statistics. All weapons listed in this chapter have an item level of 0.

DAMAGE

This entry lists the weapon's damage die and the type of damage it deals: B for bludgeoning, P for piercing, or S for slashing.

Damage Dice

Each weapon lists the damage die used for its damage roll. A standard weapon deals one die of damage, but a magical *striking* rune can increase the number of dice rolled, as can some special actions and spells. These additional dice use the same die size as the weapon or unarmed attack's normal damage die.

Counting Damage Dice

Effects based on a weapon's number of damage dice include only the weapon's damage die plus any extra dice from a *striking* rune. They don't count extra dice from abilities, critical specialization effects, property runes, weapon traits, or the like.

Increasing Die Size

When an effect calls on you to increase the size of your weapon damage dice, instead of using its normal weapon damage dice, use the next larger die, as listed below (so if you were using a d4, you'd use a d6, and so on). If you are already using a d12, the size is already at its maximum. You can't increase your weapon damage die size more than once.

1d4 → 1d6 → 1d8 → 1d10 → 1d12

RANGE

Ranged and thrown weapons have a range increment. Attacks with these weapons work normally up to that distance. Attack rolls beyond a weapon's range increment take a –2 penalty for each additional multiple of that increment between you and the target. Attacks beyond the sixth range increment are impossible.

For example, a shortbow takes no penalty against a target up to 60 feet away, a –2 penalty against a target beyond 60 feet but up to 120 feet away, and a –4 penalty against a target beyond 120 feet but up to 180 feet away, and so on, up to 360 feet.

RELOAD

While all weapons need some amount of time to get into position, many ranged weapons also need to be loaded and reloaded. This entry indicates how many Interact actions it takes to reload such weapons. This can be 0 if drawing

SELECTING WEAPONS

Characters who focus on combat need to carefully consider their choice of weapons, evaluating whether they want to fight in melee or at range, the weapons' damage potential, and the special features of various weapons. Characters who are primarily spellcasters usually just need to pick a backup weapon in the best category they're trained or better in.

When selecting weapons, start by identifying the weapon types you're trained or better in. You should then compare weapons within these types to determine which ones you will have the highest melee or ranged attack modifier with. It's usually considered best practice to select both a melee and ranged weapon during character creation so you can contend with a broader variety of foes and situations.

Weapon Categories

Weapons fall into broad categories depending on how much damage they deal and what traits they have. Martial weapons generally deal more damage than simple weapons, and advanced weapons generally have more advantageous traits than martial weapons with the same damage. Generally, you'll want to select weapons that deal more damage, but if you're a highly skilled combatant, you might want to pick a weapon with interesting traits, even if it has a lower weapon damage die. You can also purchase multiple weapons within your budget, allowing you to switch between them for different situations.

ammunition and firing the weapon are part of the same action. If an item takes 2 or more actions to reload, the GM determines whether they must be performed together as an activity, or you can spend some of those actions during one turn and the rest during your next turn.

An item with an entry of "—" must be drawn to be thrown, which usually takes an Interact action just like drawing any other weapon. Reloading a ranged weapon and drawing a thrown weapon both require a free hand. Switching your grip to free a hand and then to place your hands in the grip necessary to wield the weapon are both included in the actions you spend to reload a weapon.

BULK

This entry gives the weapon's Bulk. A weapon's Bulk is increased or decreased if it's sized for creatures that aren't Small or Medium size, following the rules on page 295.

HANDS

Some weapons require one hand to wield, and others require two. A few items, such as a longbow, list 1+ for its Hands entry. You can hold a weapon with a 1+ entry in one hand, but the process of shooting it requires using a second to retrieve, nock, and loose an arrow. This means you can do things with your free hand while holding the bow without changing your grip, but the other hand must be free when you shoot. To properly wield a 1+ weapon, you must hold it in one hand and also have a hand free.

Weapons requiring two hands typically deal more damage. Some one-handed weapons have the two-hand trait, causing them to deal a different size of weapon damage die when used in two hands. In addition, some abilities require you to wield a weapon in two hands. You meet this requirement while holding the weapon in two hands, even if it doesn't require two hands or have the two-hand trait.

GROUP

A weapon or unarmed attack's group classifies it with similar weapons. Groups affect some abilities and what the weapon does on a critical hit if you have access to that weapon or unarmed attack's critical specialization effects; for full details, see page 283.

WEAPON TRAITS

The traits a weapon or unarmed attack has are listed in this entry. Any trait that refers to a "weapon" can also apply to an unarmed attack that has that trait.

AMMUNITION

Some entries in the ranged weapons tables are followed by an entry indicating the type of ammunition that weapon launches. The damage die is determined by the weapon, not the ammunition. Because that and other relevant statistics vary by weapon, ammunition entries list only the name, quantity, Price, and Bulk.

TABLE 6-6: UNARMED ATTACKS

Unarmed Attack	Price	Damage	Bulk	Hands	Group	Weapon Traits
Fist	—	1d4 B	—	1	Brawling	Agile, finesse, nonlethal, unarmed

TABLE 6-7: MELEE WEAPONS

Simple Weapons	Price	Damage	Bulk	Hands	Group	Weapon Traits
Club	0	1d6 B	1	1	Club	Thrown 10 ft.
Dagger	2 sp	1d4 P	L	1	Knife	Agile, finesse, thrown 10 ft., versatile S
Gauntlet	2 sp	1d4 B	L	1	Brawling	Agile, free-hand
Light mace	4 sp	1d4 B	L	1	Club	Agile, finesse, shove
Longspear	5 sp	1d8 P	2	2	Spear	Reach
Mace	1 gp	1d6 B	1	1	Club	Shove
Morningstar	1 gp	1d6 B	1	1	Club	Versatile P
Sickle	2 sp	1d4 S	L	1	Knife	Agile, finesse, trip
Spear	1 sp	1d6 P	1	1	Spear	Thrown 20 ft.
Spiked gauntlet	3 sp	1d4 P	L	1	Brawling	Agile, free-hand
Staff	0	1d4 B	1	1	Club	Two-hand d8
Uncommon Simple Weapons	**Price**	**Damage**	**Bulk**	**Hands**	**Group**	**Weapon Traits**
Clan dagger	2 gp	1d4 P	L	1	Knife	Agile, dwarf, parry, versatile B
Katar	3 sp	1d4 P	L	1	Knife	Agile, deadly d6, monk
Martial Weapons	**Price**	**Damage**	**Bulk**	**Hands**	**Group**	**Weapon Traits**
Bastard sword	4 gp	1d8 S	1	1	Sword	Two-hand d12
Battle axe	1 gp	1d8 S	1	1	Axe	Sweep
Bo staff	2 sp	1d8 B	2	2	Club	Monk, parry, reach, trip
Falchion	3 gp	1d10 S	2	2	Sword	Forceful, sweep
Flail	8 sp	1d6 B	1	1	Flail	Disarm, sweep, trip
Glaive	1 gp	1d8 S	2	2	Polearm	Deadly d8, forceful, reach
Greataxe	2 gp	1d12 S	2	2	Axe	Sweep
Greatclub	1 gp	1d10 B	2	2	Club	Backswing, shove
Greatpick	1 gp	1d10 P	2	2	Pick	Fatal d12
Greatsword	2 gp	1d12 S	2	2	Sword	Versatile P
Guisarme	2 gp	1d10 S	2	2	Polearm	Reach, trip
Halberd	2 gp	1d10 P	2	2	Polearm	Reach, versatile S
Hatchet	4 sp	1d6 S	L	1	Axe	Agile, sweep, thrown 10 ft.
Lance	1 gp	1d8 P	2	2	Spear	Deadly d8, jousting d6, reach

INTRODUCTION

ANCESTRIES &
BACKGROUNDS

CLASSES

SKILLS

FEATS

EQUIPMENT

SPELLS

THE AGE OF
LOST OMENS

PLAYING THE
GAME

GAME
MASTERING

CRAFTING
& TREASURE

APPENDIX

Light hammer	3 sp	1d6 B	L	1	Hammer	Agile, thrown 20 ft.
Light pick	4 sp	1d4 P	L	1	Pick	Agile, fatal d8
Longsword	1 gp	1d8 S	1	1	Sword	Versatile P
Main-gauche	5 sp	1d4 P	L	1	Knife	Agile, disarm, finesse, parry, versatile S
Maul	3 gp	1d12 B	2	2	Hammer	Shove
Pick	7 sp	1d6 P	1	1	Pick	Fatal d10
Ranseur	2 gp	1d10 P	2	2	Polearm	Disarm, reach
Rapier	2 gp	1d6 P	1	1	Sword	Deadly d8, disarm, finesse
Sap	1 sp	1d6 B	L	1	Club	Agile, nonlethal
Scimitar	1 gp	1d6 S	1	1	Sword	Forceful, sweep
Scythe	2 gp	1d10 S	2	2	Polearm	Deadly d10, trip
Shield bash	–	1d4 B	–	1	Shield	–
Shield boss	5 sp	1d6 B	–	1	Shield	Attached to shield
Shield spikes	5 sp	1d6 P	–	1	Shield	Attached to shield
Shortsword	9 sp	1d6 P	L	1	Sword	Agile, finesse, versatile S
Starknife	2 gp	1d4 P	L	1	Knife	Agile, deadly d6, finesse, thrown 20 ft., versatile S
Trident	1 gp	1d8 P	1	1	Spear	Thrown 20 ft.
War flail	2 gp	1d10 B	2	2	Flail	Disarm, sweep, trip
Warhammer	1 gp	1d8 B	1	1	Hammer	Shove
Whip	1 sp	1d4 S	1	1	Flail	Disarm, finesse, nonlethal, reach, trip

Uncommon **Martial Weapons**	**Price**	**Damage**	**Bulk**	**Hands**	**Group**	**Weapon Traits**
Dogslicer	1 sp	1d6 S	L	1	Sword	Agile, backstabber, finesse, goblin
Elven curve blade	4 gp	1d8 S	2	2	Sword	Elf, finesse, forceful
Filcher's fork	1 gp	1d4 P	L	1	Spear	Agile, backstabber, deadly d6, finesse, halfling, thrown 20 ft.
Gnome hooked hammer	2 gp	1d6 B	1	1	Hammer	Gnome, trip, two-hand d10, versatile P
Horsechopper	9 sp	1d8 S	2	2	Polearm	Goblin, reach, trip, versatile P
Kama	1 gp	1d6 S	L	1	Knife	Agile, monk, trip
Katana	2 gp	1d6 S	1	1	Sword	Deadly d8, two-hand d10, versatile P
Kukri	6 sp	1d6 S	L	1	Knife	Agile, finesse, trip
Nunchaku	2 sp	1d6 B	L	1	Club	Backswing, disarm, finesse, monk
Orc knuckle dagger	7 sp	1d6 P	L	1	Knife	Agile, disarm, orc
Sai	6 sp	1d4 P	L	1	Knife	Agile, disarm, finesse, monk, versatile B
Spiked chain	3 gp	1d8 S	1	2	Flail	Disarm, finesse, trip
Temple sword	2 gp	1d8 S	1	1	Sword	Monk, trip

Uncommon **Advanced Weapons**	**Price**	**Damage**	**Bulk**	**Hands**	**Group**	**Weapon Traits**
Dwarven waraxe	3 gp	1d8 S	2	1	Axe	Dwarf, sweep, two-hand d12
Gnome flickmace	3 gp	1d8 B	2	1	Flail	Gnome, reach
Orc necksplitter	2 gp	1d8 S	1	1	Axe	Forceful, orc, sweep
Sawtooth saber	5 gp	1d6 S	L	1	Sword	Agile, finesse, twin

TABLE 6–8: RANGED WEAPONS

Simple Weapons	**Price**	**Damage**	**Range**	**Reload**	**Bulk**	**Hands**	**Group**	**Weapon Traits**
Blowgun	1 sp	1 P	20 ft.	1	L	1	Dart	Agile, nonlethal
10 blowgun darts	5 cp				L			
Crossbow	3 gp	1d8 P	120 ft.	1	1	2	Bow	–
10 bolts	1 sp				L			
Dart	1 cp	1d4 P	20 ft.	–	L	1	Dart	Agile, thrown
Hand crossbow	3 gp	1d6 P	60 ft.	1	L	1	Bow	–
10 bolts	1 sp				L			
Heavy crossbow	4 gp	1d10 P	120 ft.	2	2	2	Bow	–

10 bolts		1 sp				L		
Javelin	1 sp	1d6 P	30 ft.	–	L	1	Dart	Thrown
Sling	0	1d6 B	50 ft.	1	L	1	Sling	Propulsive
10 sling bullets	1 cp				L			

Martial Weapons	**Price**	**Damage**	**Range**	**Reload**	**Bulk**	**Hands**	**Group**	**Weapon Traits**
Alchemical bomb*	Varies	Varies	20 ft.	–	L	1	Bomb	Varies
Composite longbow	20 gp	1d8 P	100 ft.	0	2	1+	Bow	Deadly d10, propulsive, volley 30 ft.
10 arrows	1 sp				L			
Composite shortbow	14 gp	1d6 P	60 ft.	0	1	1+	Bow	Deadly d10, propulsive
10 arrows	1 sp				L			
Longbow	6 gp	1d8 P	100 ft.	0	2	1+	Bow	Deadly d10, volley 30 ft.
10 arrows	1 sp				L			
Shortbow	3 gp	1d6 P	60 ft.	0	1	1+	Bow	Deadly d10
10 arrows	1 sp				L			

Uncommon Martial Weapons	**Price**	**Damage**	**Range**	**Reload**	**Bulk**	**Hands**	**Group**	**Weapon Traits**
Halfling sling staff	5 gp	1d10 B	80 ft.	1	1	2	Sling	Halfling, propulsive
10 sling bullets	1 cp				L			
Shuriken	1 cp	1d4 P	20 ft.	0	–		1	Dart	Agile, monk, thrown

* Statistics for alchemical bombs can be found starting on page 544.

WEAPON TRAITS

Weapons and unarmed attacks with the weapon trait can have the following traits.

Agile: The multiple attack penalty you take with this weapon on the second attack on your turn is –4 instead of –5, and –8 instead of –10 on the third and subsequent attacks in the turn.

Attached: An attached weapon must be combined with another piece of gear to be used. The trait lists what type of item the weapon must be attached to. You must be wielding or wearing the item the weapon is attached to in order to attack with it. For example, shield spikes are attached to a shield, allowing you to attack with the spikes instead of a shield bash, but only if you're wielding the shield. An attached weapon is usually bolted onto or built into the item it's attached to, and typically an item can have only one weapon attached to it. An attached weapon can be affixed to an item with 10 minutes of work and a successful DC 10 Crafting check; this includes the time needed to remove the weapon from a previous item, if necessary. If an item is destroyed, its attached weapon can usually be salvaged.

Backstabber: When you hit a flat-footed creature, this weapon deals 1 precision damage in addition to its normal damage. The precision damage increases to 2 if the weapon is a *+3 weapon*.

Backswing: You can use the momentum from a missed attack with this weapon to lead into your next attack. After missing with this weapon on your turn, you gain a +1 circumstance bonus to your next attack with this weapon before the end of your turn.

Deadly: On a critical hit, the weapon adds a weapon damage die of the listed size. Roll this after doubling the weapon's damage. This increases to two dice if the weapon has a *greater striking* rune and three dice if the weapon has

a *major striking* rune. For instance, a rapier with a *greater striking* rune deals 2d8 extra piercing damage on a critical hit. An ability that changes the size of the weapon's normal damage dice doesn't change the size of its deadly die.

Disarm: You can use this weapon to Disarm with the Athletics skill even if you don't have a free hand. This uses the weapon's reach (if different from your own) and adds the weapon's item bonus to attack rolls (if any) as an item bonus to the Athletics check. If you critically fail a check to Disarm using the weapon, you can drop the weapon to take the effects of a failure instead of a critical failure. On a critical success, you still need a free hand if you want to take the item.

Dwarf: Dwarves craft and use these weapons.

Elf: Elves craft and use these weapons.

Fatal: The fatal trait includes a die size. On a critical hit, the weapon's damage die increases to that die size instead of the normal die size, and the weapon adds one additional damage die of the listed size.

Finesse: You can use your Dexterity modifier instead of your Strength modifier on attack rolls using this melee weapon. You still use your Strength modifier when calculating damage.

Forceful: This weapon becomes more dangerous as you build momentum. When you attack with it more than once on your turn, the second attack gains a circumstance bonus to damage equal to the number of weapon damage dice, and each subsequent attack gains a circumstance bonus to damage equal to double the number of weapon damage dice.

Free-Hand: This weapon doesn't take up your hand, usually because it is built into your armor. A free-hand weapon can't be Disarmed. You can use the hand covered by your free-hand weapon to wield other items, perform manipulate actions, and so on. You can't attack with a free-hand weapon if you're wielding anything in that hand or otherwise using that hand. When you're not wielding anything and not otherwise using the hand, you can use abilities that require you to have a hand free as well as those that require you to be wielding a weapon in that hand. Each of your hands can have only one free-hand weapon on it.

Gnome: Gnomes craft and use these weapons.

Goblin: Goblins craft and use these weapons.

Grapple: You can use this weapon to Grapple with the Athletics skill even if you don't have a free hand. This uses the weapon's reach (if different from your own) and adds the weapon's item bonus to attack rolls as an item bonus to the Athletics check. If you critically fail a check to Grapple using the weapon, you can drop the weapon to take the effects of a failure instead of a critical failure.

Halfling: Halflings craft and use these weapons.

Jousting: The weapon is suited for mounted combat with a harness or similar means. When mounted, if you moved at least 10 feet on the action before your attack, add a circumstance bonus to damage for that attack equal to the number of damage dice for the weapon. In addition, while mounted, you can wield the weapon in one hand, changing the damage die to the listed value.

Monk: Many monks learn to use these weapons.

Nonlethal: Attacks with this weapon are nonlethal (page 453), and are used to knock creatures unconscious instead of kill them. You can use a nonlethal weapon to make a lethal attack with a −2 circumstance penalty.

Orc: Orcs craft and use these weapons.

Parry: This weapon can be used defensively to block attacks. While wielding this weapon, if your proficiency with it is trained or better, you can spend an Interact action to position your weapon defensively, gaining a +1 circumstance bonus to AC until the start of your next turn.

Propulsive: You add half your Strength modifier (if positive) to damage rolls with a propulsive ranged weapon. If you have a negative Strength modifier, you add your full Strength modifier instead.

Reach: This weapon is long and can be used to attack creatures up to 10 feet away instead of only adjacent creatures. For creatures that already have reach with the limb or limbs that wield the weapon, the weapon increases their reach by 5 feet.

Shove: You can use this weapon to Shove with the Athletics skill even if you don't have a free hand. This uses the weapon's reach (if different from your own) and adds the weapon's item bonus to attack rolls as an item bonus to the Athletics check. If you critically fail a check to Shove using the weapon, you can drop the weapon to take the effects of a failure instead of a critical failure.

Sweep: This weapon makes wide sweeping or spinning attacks, making it easier to attack multiple enemies. When you attack with this weapon, you gain a +1 circumstance bonus to your attack roll if you already attempted to attack a different target this turn using this weapon.

Thrown: You can throw this weapon as a ranged attack. A thrown weapon adds your Strength modifier to damage just like a melee weapon does. When this trait appears on a melee weapon, it also includes the range increment. Ranged weapons with this trait use the range increment specified in the weapon's Range entry.

Trip: You can use this weapon to Trip with the Athletics skill even if you don't have a free hand. This uses the weapon's reach (if different from your own) and adds the weapon's item bonus to attack rolls as an item bonus to the Athletics check. If you critically fail a check to Trip using the weapon, you can drop the weapon to take the effects of a failure instead of a critical failure.

Twin: These weapons are used as a pair, complementing each other. When you attack with a twin weapon, you add a circumstance bonus to the damage roll equal to the weapon's number of damage dice if you have previously attacked with a different weapon of the same type this turn. The weapons must be of the same type to benefit from this trait, but they don't need to have the same runes.

Two-Hand: This weapon can be wielded with two hands. Doing so changes its weapon damage die to the indicated value. This change applies to all the weapon's damage dice, such as those from *striking* runes.

Unarmed: An unarmed attack uses your body rather than a manufactured weapon. An unarmed attack isn't a weapon, though it's categorized with weapons for weapon groups, and it might have weapon traits. Since it's part of your body, an unarmed attack can't be Disarmed. It also doesn't take up a hand, though a fist or other grasping appendage follows the same rules as a free-hand weapon.

Versatile: A versatile weapon can be used to deal a different type of damage than that listed in the Damage entry. This trait indicates the alternate damage type. For instance, a piercing weapon that is versatile S can be used to deal piercing or slashing damage. You choose the damage type each time you make an attack.

Volley: This ranged weapon is less effective at close distances. Your attacks against targets that are at a distance within the range listed take a −2 penalty.

CRITICAL SPECIALIZATION EFFECTS

Certain feats, class features, weapon runes, and other effects can grant you additional benefits when you make an attack with certain weapons and get a critical success. This is called a critical specialization effect. The exact effect depends on which weapon group your weapon belongs to, as listed below. You can always decide not to add the critical specialization effect of your weapon.

Axe: Choose one creature adjacent to the initial target and within reach. If its AC is lower than your attack roll result for the critical hit, you deal damage to that creature equal to the result of the weapon damage die you rolled (including extra dice for its potency rune, if any). This amount isn't doubled, and no bonuses or other additional dice apply to this damage.

INTRODUCTION

ANCESTRIES & BACKGROUNDS

CLASSES

SKILLS

FEATS

EQUIPMENT

SPELLS

THE AGE OF LOST OMENS

PLAYING THE GAME

GAME MASTERING

CRAFTING & TREASURE

APPENDIX

Bomb: Increase the radius of the bomb's splash damage (if any) to 10 feet.

Bow: If the target of the critical hit is adjacent to a surface, it gets stuck to that surface by the missile. The target is immobilized and must spend an Interact action to attempt a DC 10 Athletics check to pull the missile free; it can't move from its space until it succeeds. The creature doesn't become stuck if it is incorporeal, is liquid (like a water elemental or some oozes), or could otherwise escape without effort.

Brawling: The target must succeed at a Fortitude save against your class DC or be slowed 1 until the end of your next turn.

Club: You knock the target away from you up to 10 feet (you choose the distance). This is forced movement (page 475).

Dart: The target takes 1d6 persistent bleed damage. You gain an item bonus to this bleed damage equal to the weapon's item bonus to attack rolls.

Flail: The target is knocked prone.

Hammer: The target is knocked prone.

Knife: The target takes 1d6 persistent bleed damage. You gain an item bonus to this bleed damage equal to the weapon's item bonus to attack rolls.

Pick: The weapon viciously pierces the target, who takes 2 additional damage per weapon damage die.

Polearm: The target is moved 5 feet in a direction of your choice. This is forced movement (page 475).

Shield: You knock the target back from you 5 feet. This is forced movement (page 475).

Sling: The target must succeed at a Fortitude save against your class DC or be stunned 1.

Spear: The weapon pierces the target, weakening its attacks. The target is clumsy 1 until the start of your next turn.

Sword: The target is made off-balance by your attack, becoming flat-footed until the start of your next turn.

WEAPON DESCRIPTIONS

Each of the weapons listed in Tables 6–7 and 6–8 are described below.

Alchemical Bomb: These bombs come in a variety of types and levels of power, but no matter the variety, you throw the bomb at the target and it explodes, unleashing its alchemical blast.

Arrow: These projectiles are the ammunition for bows. The shaft of an arrow is made of wood. It is stabilized in flight by fletching at one end and bears a metal head on the other.

Bastard Sword: This broad-bladed sword, sometimes called the hand-and-a-half sword, has a longer grip so it can be held in one hand or used with two hands to provide extra piercing or slashing power.

Battle Axe: These axes are designed explicitly as weapons, rather than tools. They typically weigh less, with a shaft reinforced with metal bands or bolts, and have a sharper blade, making them ideal for chopping limbs rather than wood.

Bolt: Shorter than traditional arrows but similar in construction, bolts are the ammunition used by crossbows.

Blowgun: This long, narrow tube is used for shooting blowgun darts, using only the power of a forcefully exhaled breath.

Blowgun Dart: These thin, light darts are typically made of hardwood and stabilized with fletching of down or fur. They are often hollow so they can be used to deliver poison.

Bo Staff: This strong but slender staff is tapered at the ends and well balanced. It's designed to be an offensive and defensive weapon.

Clan Dagger: This broad dagger is carried by dwarves as a weapon, tool, and designation of clan. Losing or having to surrender a clan dagger is considered a mark of embarrassment to most dwarves.

Club: This is a piece of stout wood shaped or repurposed to bludgeon an enemy. Clubs can be intricately carved pieces of martial art or as simple as a tree branch or piece of wood.

Composite Longbow: This projectile weapon is made from horn, wood, and sinew laminated together to increase the power of its pull and the force of its projectile. Like all longbows, its great size also increases the bow's range and power. You must use two hands to fire it, and it cannot be used while mounted. Any time an ability is specifically restricted to a longbow, such as Erastil's favored weapon, it also applies to composite longbows unless otherwise stated.

Composite Shortbow: This shortbow is made from horn, wood, and sinew laminated together to increase the power of its pull and the force of its projectile. Its compact size and power make it a favorite of mounted archers. Any time an ability is specifically restricted to a shortbow, it also applies to composite shortbows unless otherwise stated.

Crossbow: This ranged weapon has a bow-like assembly mounted on a handled frame called a tiller. The tiller has a mechanism to lock the bowstring in place, attached to a trigger mechanism that releases the tension and launches a bolt.

Dagger: This small, bladed weapon is held in one hand and used to stab a creature in close combat. It can also be thrown.

Dart: This thrown weapon is larger than an arrow but shorter than a javelin. It typically has a short shaft of wood ending in a metal tip and is sometimes stabilized by feathers or fur.

Dogslicer: This short, curved, and crude makeshift blade often has holes drilled into it to reduce its weight. It's a favored weapon of goblins.

Dwarven Waraxe: This favored weapon of the dwarves has a large, ornate head mounted on a thick handle. This powerful axe can be wielded with one hand or two.

Elven Curve Blade: Essentially a longer version of the scimitar, this traditional elven weapon has a thinner blade than its cousin.

Falchion: This weapon is a heavier, two-handed version of the curved-bladed scimitar. It is weighted toward the blade's end, making it a powerful slashing weapon.

Filcher's Fork: This halfling weapon looks like a long, two-pronged fork and is used as both a weapon and a cooking implement.

Flail: This weapon consists of a wooden handle attached to a spiked ball or cylinder by a chain, rope, or strap of leather.

Gauntlet: A pair of these metal gloves comes with full plate, half plate, and splint armor; they can also be purchased separately and worn with other types of armor. They not only protect your hands but also transform your hands into lethal weapons.

Glaive: This polearm consists of a long, single-edged blade on the end of a 7-foot pole. It is extremely effective at delivering lethal cuts at a distance.

Gnome Flickmace: More a flail than a mace, this weapon has a short handle attached to a length of chain with a ball at the end. The ball is propelled to its reach with the flick of the wrist, the momentum of which brings the ball back to the wielder after the strike.

Gnome Hooked Hammer: This gnome tool and weapon features a hammer at one end and a curved pick on the other. It's such a strange and awkward weapon that others think the gnomes are slightly erratic for using it.

Greataxe: This large battle axe is too heavy to wield with only one hand. Many greataxes incorporate two blades, and they are often "bearded," having a hook at the bottom to increase the strength of their chopping power.

Greatclub: While many greatclubs are intricately carved, others are little more than a sturdy tree branch. These massive clubs are too heavy to wield with only one hand.

Greatpick: This pick has a longer handle and a broader head than a regular pick. It is too heavy to wield in one hand.

Greatsword: This immense two-handed sword is nearly as tall as its wielder. Its lower blade is often somewhat dulled to allow it to be gripped for extra leverage in close-quarter fights.

Guisarme: This polearm bears a long, often one-sided, curved blade with a hook protruding from the blunt side of the blade, which can allow its wielder to trip opponents at a distance. Its shaft is usually 8 feet long.

Halberd: This polearm has a relatively short, 5-foot shaft. The business end is a long spike with an axe blade attached.

Halfling Sling Staff: This staff ends in a Y-shaped split that cradles a sling. The length of the staff provides excellent leverage when used two-handed to fling rocks or bullets from the sling.

Hand Crossbow: Sometimes referred to as an alley bow by rogues or ruffians, this small crossbow fires small bolts that are sometimes used to deliver poison to the target. It's small enough to be shot one-handed, but it still requires two hands to load.

Hatchet: This small axe can be used in close combat or thrown.

Heavy Crossbow: This large crossbow is harder to load and more substantial than a regular crossbow, but it packs a greater punch.

Horsechopper: Created by goblins to battle horses, this weapon is essentially a long shaft ending in a blade with a large hook.

Javelin: This thin spear is well balanced for throwing but is not designed for melee use.

Kama: Similar to a sickle and used in some regions to reap grain, a kama has a short, slightly curved blade and a wooden handle.

Katana: A katana is a curved, single-edged sword known for its wickedly sharped blade.

Katar: Also known as punching daggers, katars are characterized by their H-shaped hand grip that allows the blade to jut out from the knuckles.

Kukri: The blade of this foot-long knife curves inward and lacks a cross guard at the hilt.

Lance: This spear-like weapon is used by a mounted creature to deal a great deal of damage.

Light Hammer: This smaller version of the warhammer has a wooden or metal shaft ending in a metal head. Unlike its heavier cousin, it is light enough to throw.

Light Mace: A light mace has a short wooden or metal shaft ending with a dense metal head. Used much like a club, it delivers heavy bludgeoning blows, but with extra power derived from the head's metal ridges or spikes.

Light Pick: A light pick is a modified mining implement with a wooden shaft ending in a pick head crafted more to pierce armor and flesh than chip rocks.

Longbow: This 5-foot-tall bow, usually made of a single piece of elm, hickory, or yew, has a powerful draw and is excellent at propelling arrows with great force and at an extreme distance. You must use two hands to fire a longbow, and it can't be used while mounted.

Longspear: This very long spear, sometimes called a pike, is purely for thrusting rather than throwing. Used by many soldiers and city watch for crowd control and defense against charging enemies, it must be wielded with two hands.

Longsword: Longswords can be one-edged or two-edged swords. Their blades are heavy and they're between 3 and 4 feet in length.

Mace: With a stout haft and a heavy metal head, a mace is sturdy and allows its wielder to deliver powerful blows and dent armor.

Main-Gauche: This parrying dagger features a robust guard to protect the wielder's hand.

Maul: Mauls are massive warhammers that must be swung with two hands.

Morningstar: This weapon has a short shaft ending in a metal ball studded with spikes.

Nunchaku: The nunchaku is constructed of two wooden or metal bars connected by a short length of rope or chain.

Orc Knuckle Dagger: This stout, metal blade of orc design has a horizontal basket hilt with blades jutting from each end, or sometimes one blade like that of a katar.

Orc Necksplitter: This single-bladed bearded axe has a jagged blade that's perfect for separating bone from tendon and cartilage.

Pick: A pick designed solely for combat has a sturdy wooden shaft and a heavy, pointed head to deliver devastating blows.

Ranseur: This polearm is a long trident with a central prong that's longer than the other two.

Rapier: The rapier is a long and thin piercing blade with a basket hilt. It is prized among many as a dueling weapon.

Sai: This piercing dagger is a metal spike flanked by a pair of prongs that can be used to trap an enemy's weapon.

Sap: A sap has a soft wrapping around a dense core, typically a leather sheath around a lead rod. Its head is wider than its grip to disperse the force of a blow, as the weapon's purpose is to knock out its victim rather than to draw blood.

Sawtooth Saber: The signature weapon of the Red Mantis assassins, this curved blade is serrated like a saw, hence the name.

Scimitar: This one-handed curved blade is sharp on one side.

Scythe: Derived from a farming tool used to mow down long grains and cereals, this weapon has a long wooden shaft with protruding handles, capped with a curved blade set at a right angle.

Shield Bash: A shield bash is not actually a weapon, but a maneuver in which you thrust or swing your shield to hit your foe with an impromptu attack.

Shield Boss: Typically a round, convex, or conical piece of thick metal attached to the center of a shield, a shield boss increases the bludgeoning damage of a shield bash.

Shield Spikes: These metal spikes are strategically placed on the defensive side of the shield to deal piercing damage with a shield bash.

Shortbow: This smaller bow is made of a single piece of wood and favored by skirmishers and cavalry.

Shortsword: These blades come in a variety of shapes and styles, but they are typically 2 feet long.

Shuriken: This "throwing star" is a small piece of flat metal with sharp edges, designed to be flung with a flick of the wrist.

Sickle: Originally a farming tool used for reaping grain, this one-handed weapon has a short wooden handle ending in a curved blade, sometimes sharpened on both sides.

Sling: Little more than a leather cup attached to a pair of straps, a sling can be used to fling smooth stones or sling bullets at a range.

Sling Bullet: These are small metal balls, typically either iron or lead, designed to be used as ammunition in slings.

Spear: A long metal shaft ending with a metal spike, a spear can be used one-handed as a melee weapon and can be thrown.

Spiked Chain: This 4-foot-long length of chain is covered with barbs and has spikes on one or both ends. Some feature metal hoops used as handgrips.

Spiked Gauntlet: Providing the same defensive function as a standard gauntlet, this version has a group of spikes protruding from the knuckles to deliver piercing damage with a punch.

Staff: This long piece of wood can aid in walking and deliver a mighty blow.

Starknife: From a central metal ring, four tapering metal blades extend like points on a compass rose. When gripping a starknife from the center, the wielder can use it as a melee weapon. It can also be thrown short distances.

Temple Sword: This heavy blade is favored by guardians of religious sites. It has a distinctive, crescent-shaped blade that seems to be a mix of a sickle and sword. It often has holes drilled into the blade or the pommel so that bells or other holy trinkets can be affixed to the weapon as an aid for prayer or mediation.

Trident: This three-pronged, spear-like weapon typically has a 4-foot shaft. Like a spear, it can be wielded with one hand or thrown.

War Flail: This large flail has a long shaft connected to a shorter piece of stout wood or metal that's sometimes inlaid with spikes.

Warhammer: This weapon has a wooden shaft ending in a large, heavy metal head. The head of the hammer might be single-sided or double-sided, but it's always capable of delivering powerful bludgeoning blows.

Whip: This long strand of thick leather, often braided, delivers a painful but nonlethal slash at a distance, usually accompanied by a distinctive cracking sound.

INTRODUCTION

ANCESTRIES &
BACKGROUNDS

CLASSES

SKILLS

FEATS

EQUIPMENT

SPELLS

THE AGE OF
LOST OMENS

PLAYING THE
GAME

GAME
MASTERING

CRAFTING
& TREASURE

APPENDIX

GEAR

Your character needs all sorts of items both while exploring and in downtime, ranging from rations to climbing gear to fancy clothing, depending on the situation.

GEAR STATISTICS

Tables 6–9 and 6–10 list Price and Bulk entries for a wide variety of gear. Any item with a number after it in parentheses indicates that the item's Price is for the indicated quantity, though the Bulk entry for such an item is the value for only one such item. All items in this chapter are level 0 unless the item name is followed by a higher item level in parentheses.

HANDS

This lists how many hands it takes to use the item effectively. Most items that require two hands can be carried in only one hand, but you must spend an Interact action to change your grip in order to use the item. The GM may determine that an item is too big to carry in one hand (or even two hands, for particularly large items).

ADVENTURING GEAR

These items follow special rules or require more detail.

Adventurer's Pack: This item is the starter kit for an adventurer, containing the essential items for exploration and survival. The Bulk value is for the entire pack together, but see the descriptions of individual items as necessary.

The pack contains the following items: backpack (containing the other goods), bedroll, two belt pouches, 10 pieces of chalk, flint and steel, 50 feet of rope, 2 weeks' rations, soap, 5 torches, and a waterskin.

Alchemist's Tools: These beakers and chemicals can be used to set up a mobile alchemical laboratory. Expanded alchemist's tools give a +1 item bonus to Crafting checks to create alchemical items. When you carry the tools from place to place, you keep many of the components handy on your person, in pockets or bandoliers.

Artisan's Tools: You need these tools to create items from raw materials with the Craft skill. Sterling artisan's tools give you a +1 item bonus to the check. Different sets are needed for different work, as determined by the GM; for example, blacksmith's tools differ from woodworker's tools.

Backpack: A backpack holds up to 4 Bulk of items. If you're carrying or stowing the pack rather than wearing it on your back, its bulk is light instead of negligible.

Bandolier: A bandolier holds up to eight items of light Bulk within easy reach and is usually used for alchemical items or potions. If you are carrying or stowing a bandolier rather than wearing it around your chest, it has light Bulk instead of negligible. A bandolier can be dedicated to a full set of tools, such as healer's tools, allowing you to draw the tools as part of the action that requires them.

Basic Crafter's Book: This book contains the formulas (page 293) for Crafting the common items in this chapter.

Belt Pouch: A belt pouch holds up to four items of light Bulk.

Caltrops: These four-pronged metal spikes can cause damage to a creature's feet. You can scatter caltrops in an empty square adjacent to you with an Interact action. The first creature that moves into that square must succeed at a DC 14 Acrobatics check or take 1d4 piercing damage and 1 persistent bleed damage. A creature taking persistent bleed damage from caltrops takes a –5-foot penalty to its Speed. Spending an Interact action to pluck the caltrops free reduces the DC to stop the bleeding. Once a creature takes damage from caltrops, enough caltrops are ruined that other creatures moving into the square are safe.

Deployed caltrops can be salvaged and reused if no creatures took damage from them. Otherwise, enough caltrops are ruined that they can't be salvaged.

Candle: A lit candle sheds dim light in a 10-foot radius.

Chest: A wooden chest can hold up to 8 Bulk of items.

Climbing Kit: This satchel includes 50 feet of rope, pulleys, a dozen pitons, a hammer, a grappling hook, and one set of crampons. Climbing kits allow you to attach yourself to the wall you're Climbing, moving half as quickly as usual (minimum 5 feet) but letting you attempt a DC 5 flat check whenever you critically fail to prevent a fall. You gain a +1 item bonus to Athletics checks to Climb while using an extreme climbing kit. A single kit has only enough materials for one climber; each climber needs their own kit.

Clothing: Ordinary clothing is functional with basic tailoring, such as peasant garb, monk's robes, or work clothes.

Explorer's clothing is sturdy enough that it can be reinforced to protect you, even though it isn't a suit of armor. It comes in many forms, though the most common sorts look like clerical vestments, monk's garments, or wizard's robes, as members of all three classes are likely to avoid wearing armor. For more information on explorer's clothing, see pages 275–276.

Fine clothing, suitable for a noble or royal, is made with expensive fabrics, precious metals, and intricate patterns. You gain a +1 item bonus to checks to Make an Impression on nobility or other upper-class folk while wearing high-fashion fine clothing.

TABLE 6–9: ADVENTURING GEAR

Item	Price	Bulk	Hands
Adventurer's pack	7 sp	2	—
Alchemist's tools	5 gp	2	2
Expanded alchemist's tools (level 3)	55 gp	2	2
Artisan's tools	4 gp	2	2
Sterling artisan's tools (level 3)	50 gp	2	2
Backpack	1 sp	—	—
Bandolier	1 sp	—	—
Basic crafter's book	1 sp	L	2
Bedroll	1 cp	L	—
Belt pouch	4 cp	—	—
Caltrops	3 sp	L	1
Candle (10)	1 cp	—	1
Chain (10 feet)	4 gp	1	2
Chalk (10)	1 cp	—	1
Chest	6 sp	2	2
Climbing kit	5 sp	1	2
Extreme climbing kit (level 3)	40 gp	1	2
Clothing			
Ordinary	1 sp	—	—
Explorer's	1 sp	L	—
Fine	2 gp	L	—
High-fashion fine (level 3)	55 gp	L	—
Winter	4 sp	L	—
Compass	1 gp	—	1
Lensatic compass (level 3)	20 gp	—	1
Cookware	1 gp	2	2
Crowbar	5 sp	L	2
Levered crowbar (level 3)	20 gp	L	2
Disguise kit	2 gp	L	2
Replacement cosmetics	1 sp	—	—
Elite disguise kit (level 3)	40 gp	L	2
Elite cosmetics (level 3)	5 sp	—	—
Fishing tackle	8 sp	1	2
Professional fishing tackle (level 3)	20 gp	1	2
Flint and steel	5 cp	—	2
Formula book (blank)	1 gp	1	1
Grappling hook	1 sp	L	1
Hammer	1 sp	L	1
Healer's tools	5 gp	1	2
Expanded healer's tools (level 3)	50 gp	1	2
Holly and mistletoe	0	—	1
Hourglass	3 gp	L	1
Ladder (10-foot)	3 cp	3	2
Lantern			
Bull's-eye	1 gp	1	1
Hooded	7 sp	L	1
Lock			
Poor lock (level 0)	2 sp	—	2
Simple lock (level 1)	2 gp	—	2
Average lock (level 3)	15 gp	—	2
Good lock (level 9)	200 gp	—	2
Superior lock (level 17)	4,500 gp	—	2
Magnifying glass (level 3)	40 gp	—	1
Manacles			
Poor manacles (level 0)	3 sp	—	2
Simple manacles (level 1)	3 gp	—	2
Average manacles (level 3)	20 gp	—	2
Good manacles (level 9)	250 gp	—	2

Item	Price	Bulk	Hands
Superior manacles (level 17)	5,000 gp	—	2
Material component pouch	5 sp	L	1
Merchant's scale	2 sp	L	2
Mirror	1 gp	—	1
Mug	1 cp	—	1
Musical instrument			
Handheld	8 sp	1	2
Virtuoso handheld (level 3)	50 gp	1	2
Heavy	2 gp	16	2
Virtuoso heavy (level 3)	100 gp	16	2
Oil (1 pint)	1 cp	—	2
Piton	1 cp	—	1
Rations (1 week)	4 sp	L	1
Religious symbol			
Wooden	1 sp	L	1
Silver	2 gp	L	1
Religious text	1 gp	L	1
Repair kit	2 gp	1	2
Superb repair kit (level 3)	25 gp	1	2
Rope	5 sp	L	2
Sack (5)	1 cp	L	1
Saddlebags	2 sp	L	2
Satchel	1 sp	—	2
Scroll case	1 sp	—	2
Sheath	1 cp	—	—
Signal whistle	8 cp	—	1
Snare kit	5 gp	2	2
Specialist snare kit (level 3)	55 gp	2	2
Soap	2 cp	—	1
Spellbook (blank)	1 gp	1	1
Spyglass	20 gp	L	2
Fine spyglass (level 4)	80 gp	L	2
Tack	4 gp	1	—
Ten-foot pole	1 cp	1	2
Tent			
Pup	8 sp	L	2
Four-person	5 gp	1	2
Pavilion (level 2)	40 gp	12	2
Thieves' tools	3 gp	L	2
Replacement picks	3 sp	—	2
Infiltrator thieves' tools (level 3)	50 gp	L	2
Infiltrator picks (level 3)	3 gp	—	2
Tool			
Long tool	1 gp	1	2
Short tool	4 sp	L	1 or 2
Torch	1 cp	L	1
Vial	5 cp	—	1
Waterskin	5 cp	L	1
Writing set	1 gp	L	2
Extra ink and paper	1 sp	—	—

TABLE 6–10: UNCOMMON ADVENTURING GEAR

Item	Price	Bulk	Hands
Scholarly journal (level 3)	6 gp	L	1
Scholarly journal compendium (level 3)	30 gp	L	2
Survey map (level 3)	10 gp	L	1
Survey map atlas (level 3)	50 gp	L	2

CLASS KITS

If you want to quickly decide how to spend your starting money on what your class needs, start with one of these kits. Note than an adventurer's pack, which is included in each kit, contains a backpack, a bedroll, two belt pouches, 10 pieces of chalk, flint and steel, 50 feet of rope, 2 weeks' rations, soap, 5 torches, and a waterskin.

ALCHEMIST
Price 9 gp, 6 sp; **Bulk** 4 Bulk, 6 light; **Money Left Over** 5 gp, 4 sp
Armor studded leather armor
Weapons dagger, sling with 20 sling bullets
Gear adventurer's pack, alchemist's tools, bandolier, basic crafter's book, 2 sets of caltrops, sheath
Options repair kit (2 gp)

BARBARIAN
Price 3 gp, 2 sp; **Bulk** 3 Bulk, 5 light; **Money Left Over** 11 gp, 8 sp
Armor hide armor
Weapons 4 javelins
Gear adventurer's pack, grappling hook, 2 sheaths
Options greataxe (2 gp), greatclub (1 gp), greatsword (2 gp), or battle axe and steel shield (3 gp)

BARD
Price 6 gp, 8 sp; **Bulk** 4 Bulk, 3 light; **Money Left Over** 8 gp, 2 sp
Armor studded leather armor
Weapons dagger, rapier, sling with 20 sling bullets
Gear adventurer's pack, bandolier, handheld instrument, sheath

CHAMPION
Price 3 gp, 8 sp; **Bulk** 3 Bulk, 7 light; **Money Left Over** 11 gp, 2 sp
Armor hide armor
Weapons dagger, 4 javelins
Gear adventurer's pack, crowbar, grappling hook, sheath
Options your deity's favored weapon (see the deity entries on pages 437–441; use the Price listed in this chapter)

CLERIC
Price 1 gp 5 sp; **Bulk** 1 Bulk, 3 light; **Money Left Over** 13 gp
Gear adventurer's pack, bandolier, 2 sets of caltrops, religious symbol (wooden)
Options your deity's favored weapon (see the deity entries on pages 437–441; use the Price listed in this chapter), hide armor (2 gp)

DRUID
Price 3 gp, 7 sp; **Bulk** 4 Bulk, 4 light; **Money Left Over** 11 gp, 3 sp
Armor leather armor
Weapons 4 javelins, longspear
Gear adventurer's pack, bandolier, holly and mistletoe
Options healer's tools (5 gp)

FIGHTER
Price 3 gp; **Bulk** 3 Bulk, 2 light; **Money Left Over** 12 gp
Armor hide armor
Weapons dagger
Gear adventurer's pack, grappling hook, sheath
Options greatsword (2 gp), longbow with 20 arrows (6 gp, 2 sp), or longsword and steel shield (3 gp)

MONK
Price 4 gp, 9 sp; **Bulk** 4 Bulk, 2 light; **Money Left Over** 10 gp, 2 sp
Weapons longspear, staff
Gear adventurer's pack, bandolier, climbing kit, grappling hook, lesser smokestick

RANGER
Price 9 gp, 1 sp; **Bulk** 3 Bulk, 3 light; **Money Left Over** 5 gp, 9 sp
Armor leather armor
Weapons dagger, longbow with 20 arrows
Gear adventurer's pack, sheath

ROGUE
Price 5 gp, 4 sp; **Bulk** 4 Bulk, 1 light; **Money Left Over** 9 gp, 6 sp
Armor leather armor
Weapons dagger, rapier
Gear adventurer's pack, climbing kit, sheath
Options thieves' tools (3 gp)

SORCERER
Price 1 gp, 6 sp; **Bulk** 1 Bulk, 6 light; **Money Left Over** 12 gp, 9 sp
Weapons dagger, slingshot with 20 sling bullets
Gear adventurer's pack, bandolier, 2 sets of caltrops, sheath

WIZARD
Price 1 gp, 2 sp; **Bulk** 2 Bulk, 2 light; **Money Left Over** 11 gp, 8 sp
Weapons staff
Gear adventurer's pack, material component pouch, writing set
Options crossbow with 20 bolts (3 gp, 2 sp)

Winter clothing allows you to negate the damage from severe environmental cold and reduce the damage from extreme cold to that of severe cold.

Compass: A compass helps you Sense Direction or navigate, provided you're in a location with uniform magnetic fields. Without a compass, you take a –2 item penalty to these checks (similar to using a shoddy item). A lensatic compass gives you a +1 item bonus to these checks.

Crowbar: When Forcing Open an object that doesn't have an easy grip, a crowbar makes it easier to gain the necessary leverage. Without a crowbar, prying something open takes a –2 item penalty to the Athletics check to Force Open (similar to using a shoddy item). A levered crowbar grants you a +1 item bonus to Athletics checks to Force Open anything that can be pried open.

Disguise Kit: This small wooden box contains cosmetics, false facial hair, spirit gum, and a few simple wigs. You usually need a disguise kit to set up a disguise in order to Impersonate someone using the Deception skill. An elite disguise kit adds a +1 item bonus to relevant checks. If you've crafted a large number of disguises, you can replenish your cosmetics supply with replacement cosmetics suitable for the type of your disguise kit.

Fishing Tackle: This kit include a collapsible fishing pole, fishhooks, line, lures, and a fishing net. Professional fishing tackle grants a +1 item bonus to checks to fish.

Flint and Steel: Flint and steel are useful in creating a fire if you have the time to catch a spark, though using them is typically too time-consuming to be practical during an encounter. Even in ideal conditions, using flint and steel to light a flame requires using at least 3 actions, and often significantly longer.

Formula Book: A formula book holds the formulas necessary to make items other than the common equipment from this chapter; alchemists typically get one for free. Each formula book can hold the formulas for up to 100 different items. Formulas can also appear on parchment sheets, tablets, and almost any other medium; there's no need for you to copy them into a specific book as long as you can keep them on hand to reference them.

Grappling Hook: You can throw a grappling hook with a rope tied to it to make a climb easier. To anchor a grappling hook, make an attack roll with the secret trait against a DC depending on the target, typically at least DC 20. On a success, your hook has a firm hold, but on a critical failure, the hook seems like it will hold but actually falls when you're partway up.

Healer's Tools: This kit of bandages, herbs, and suturing tools is necessary for Medicine checks to Administer First Aid, Treat Disease, Treat Poison, or Treat Wounds.

Expanded healer's tools provide a +1 item bonus to such checks. When you carry the tools from place to place, you keep many of the components handy on your person, in pockets or bandoliers.

Holly and Mistletoe: Plants of supernatural significance provide a primal focus for primal spellcasters, such as druids, when using certain abilities and casting some spells. A bundle of holly and mistletoe must be held in one hand to use it. Other primal foci exist for druids focused on other aspects of nature.

Lantern: A lantern sheds bright light and requires 1 pint of oil to function for 6 hours. A bull's-eye lantern emits its light in a 60-foot cone (and dim light in the next 60 feet). A hooded lantern sheds light in a 30-foot radius (and dim light in the next 30 feet) and is equipped with shutters, which you can close to block the light. Closing or opening the shutters takes an Interact action.

Lock: Picking a poor lock requires two successful DC 15 Thievery checks, a simple lock requires three successful DC 20 Thievery checks, an average lock requires four successes at DC 25, a good lock requires five successes at DC 30, and a superior lock six successes at DC 40.

Magnifying Glass: This quality handheld lens gives you a +1 item bonus to Perception checks to notice minute details of documents, fabric, and the like.

Manacles: You can manacle someone who is willing or otherwise at your mercy as an exploration activity taking 10–30 seconds depending on the creature's size and how many manacles you apply. A two-legged creature with its legs bound takes a –15-foot circumstance penalty to its Speeds, and a two-handed creature with its wrists bound has to succeed at a DC 5 flat check any time it uses a manipulate action or else that action fails. This DC may be higher depending on how tightly the manacles constrain the hands. A creature bound to a stationary object is immobilized. For creatures with more or fewer limbs, the GM determines what effect manacles have, if any. Freeing a creature from poor manacles requires two successful DC 17 Thievery checks, simple manacles requires three successes at DC 22, average manacles require four successes at DC 27, good manacles require five successes at DC 32, and superior manacles require six successes at DC 42.

Material Component Pouch: This pouch contains material components for those spells that require them. Though the components are used up over time, you can refill spent components during your daily preparations.

Musical Instrument: Handheld instruments include bagpipes, a small set of chimes, small drums, fiddles and viols, flutes and recorders, small harps, lutes, trumpets, and similarly sized instruments. The GM might rule that an especially large handheld instrument (like a tuba) has greater Bulk. Heavy instruments such as large drums, a full set of chimes, and keyboard instruments are less portable and generally need to be stationary while played.

A virtuoso instrument gives a +1 item bonus to Performance checks using that instrument.

Oil: You can use oil to fuel lanterns, but you can also set a pint of oil aflame and throw it. You must first spend an Interact action preparing the oil, then throw it with another action as a ranged attack. If you hit, it splatters on the creature or in a single 5-foot square you target. You must succeed at a DC 10 flat check for the oil to ignite successfully when it hits. If the oil ignites, the target takes 1d6 fire damage.

Piton: These small spikes can be used as anchors to make climbing easier. To affix a piton, you must hold it in one hand and use a hammer to drive it in with your other hand. You can attach a rope to the hammered piton so that you don't fall all the way to the ground on a critical failure while Climbing.

Religious Symbol: This piece of wood or silver is emblazoned with an image representing a deity. Some divine spellcasters, such as clerics, can use a religious symbol of their deity as a divine focus to use certain abilities and cast some spells. A religious symbol must be held in one hand to use it.

Religious Text: This manuscript contains scripture of a particular religion. Some divine spellcasters, such as clerics, can use a religious text as a divine focus to use certain abilities and cast some spells. A religious text must be held in one hand to use it.

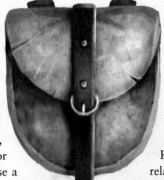

Repair Kit: A repair kit allows you to perform simple repairs while traveling. It contains a portable anvil, tongs, woodworking tools, a whetstone, and oils for conditioning leather and wood. You can use a repair kit to Repair items using the Crafting skill. A superb repair kit gives you a +1 item bonus to the check.

Sack: A sack can hold up to 8 Bulk worth of items. A sack containing 2 Bulk or less can be worn on the body, usually tucked into a belt. You can carry a sack with one hand, but must use two hands to transfer items in and out.

Saddlebags: Saddlebags come in a pair. Each can hold up to 3 Bulk of items. The Bulk value given is for saddlebags worn by a mount. If you are carrying or stowing saddlebags, they count as 1 Bulk instead of light Bulk.

Satchel: A satchel can hold up to 2 Bulk worth of items. If you are carrying or stowing a satchel rather than wearing it over your shoulder, it counts as light Bulk instead of negligible.

Scholarly Journal: Scholarly journals are uncommon. Each scholarly journal is a folio on a very specific topic, such as vampires or the history of a single town or neighborhood of a city. If you spend 1 minute referencing an academic journal before attempting a skill check to Recall Knowledge about the subject, you gain a +1 item bonus to the check. A compendium of journals costs five times as much as a single journal and requires both hands to use; each compendium contains several journals and grants its bonus on a broader topic, such as all undead or a whole city. The GM determines what scholarly journals are available in any location.

Scroll Case: Scrolls, maps, and other rolled documents are stored in scroll cases for safe transport.

Sheath: A sheath or scabbard lets you easily carry a weapon on your person.

Signal Whistle: When sounded, a signal whistle can be heard clearly up to half a mile away across open terrain.

Snare Kit: This kit contains tools and materials for creating snares. A snare kit allows you to Craft snares using the Crafting skill. A specialist snare kit gives you a +1 item bonus to the check.

Spellbook: A spellbook holds the written knowledge necessary to learn and prepare various spells, a necessity for wizards (who typically get one for free) and a useful luxury for other spellcasters looking to learn additional spells. Each spellbook can hold up to 100 spells. The Price listed is for a blank spellbook.

Spyglass: A typical spyglass lets you see eight times farther than normal. A fine spyglass adds a +1 item bonus to Perception checks to notice details at a distance.

Survey Map: Maps are uncommon. Most maps you can find are simple and functional. A survey map details a single location in excellent detail. One of these maps gives you a +1 item bonus to Survival checks and any skill checks to Recall Knowledge, provided the checks are related to the location detailed on the map. Maps sometimes come in atlases, containing a number of maps of the same quality, often on similar topics. An atlas costs five times as much as a single map and requires both hands to use. The GM determines what maps are available in any location.

Tack: Tack includes all the gear required to outfit a riding animal, including a saddle, bit and bridle, and stirrups if necessary. Especially large or oddly shaped animals might require specialty saddles. These can be more expensive or hard to find, as determined by the GM. The Bulk value given is for tack worn by a creature. If carried, the Bulk increases to 2.

Ten-Foot Pole: When wielding this long pole, you can use Seek to search a square up to 10 feet away. The pole is not sturdy enough to use as a weapon.

Thieves' Tools: You need thieves' tools to Pick Locks or Disable Devices (of some types) using the Thievery skill. Infiltrator thieves' tools add a +1 item bonus to checks

INTRODUCTION

ANCESTRIES & BACKGROUNDS

CLASSES

SKILLS

FEATS

EQUIPMENT

SPELLS

THE AGE OF LOST OMENS

PLAYING THE GAME

GAME MASTERING

CRAFTING & TREASURE

APPENDIX

to Pick Locks and Disable Devices. If your thieves' tools are broken, you can repair them by replacing the lock picks with replacement picks appropriate to your tools; this doesn't require using the Repair action.

Tool: This entry is a catchall for basic hand tools that don't have a specific adventuring purpose. A hoe, shovel, or sledgehammer is a long tool, and a hand drill, ice hook, or trowel is a short tool. A tool can usually be used as an improvised weapon, dealing 1d4 damage for a short tool or 1d6 for a long tool. The GM determines the damage type that's appropriate or adjusts the damage if needed.

Torch: A torch sheds bright light in a 20-foot radius (and dim light to the next 20 feet). It can be used as an improvised weapon that deals 1d4 bludgeoning damage plus 1 fire damage.

Vial: A simple glass vial holds up to 1 ounce of liquid.

Waterskin: When it's full, a waterskin has 1 Bulk and contains roughly 1 day's worth of water for a Small or Medium creature.

Writing Set: Using a writing set, you can draft correspondence and scribe scrolls. A set includes stationery, including a variety of paper and parchment, as well as ink, a quill or inkpen, sealing wax, and a simple seal. If you've written a large amount, you can refill your kit with extra ink and paper.

ALCHEMICAL GEAR

The items listed on Table 6–11 are the most widely available alchemical items from Chapter 11, which a 1st-level character could likely access. The descriptions below are incomplete; each item's full entry appears in Chapter 11 on the page listed in the table. Your GM might allow you to start with other alchemical items from Chapter 11 on a case-by-case basis.

TABLE 6–11: ALCHEMICAL GEAR

Alchemical Bombs	Price	Bulk	Page
Lesser acid flask	3 gp	L	544
Lesser alchemist's fire	3 gp	L	545
Lesser bottled lightning	3 gp	L	545
Lesser frost vial	3 gp	L	545
Lesser tanglefoot bag	3 gp	L	545
Lesser thunderstone	3 gp	L	545
Elixirs	**Price**	**Bulk**	**Page**
Lesser antidote	3 gp	L	546
Lesser antiplague	3 gp	L	546
Lesser elixir of life	3 gp	L	548
Alchemical Tools	**Price**	**Bulk**	**Page**
Lesser smokestick	3 gp	L	554

Sunrod	3 gp	L	554
Tindertwig (10)	2 sp	–	554

ALCHEMICAL BOMBS

Alchemical bombs are consumable weapons that deal damage or produce special effects, and they sometimes deal splash damage. For more on alchemical bombs, see page 544.

Lesser Acid Flask: This alchemical bomb deals 1 acid damage, 1d6 persistent acid damage, and 1 acid splash damage.

Lesser Alchemist's Fire: This alchemical bomb deals 1d8 fire damage, 1 persistent fire damage, and 1 fire splash damage.

Lesser Bottled Lightning: This alchemical bomb deals 1d6 electricity damage and 1 electricity splash damage, and it makes the target flat-footed.

Lesser Frost Vial: This alchemical bomb deals 1d6 cold damage and 1 cold splash damage, and it gives the target a –5-foot status penalty to its Speeds until the end of its next turn.

Lesser Tanglefoot Bag: This alchemical bomb gives the target a –10-foot status penalty to its Speeds for 1 minute, and the target is immobilized on a critical hit unless it Escapes.

Lesser Thunderstone: This alchemical bomb deals 1d4 sonic damage and 1 sonic splash damage, and any creature within 10 feet that fails a DC 17 Fortitude save is deafened until the end of its turn.

ELIXIRS

Elixirs are alchemical items you drink to gain various unusual effects. For more on elixirs, see page 546.

Lesser Antidote: After drinking a lesser antidote, you gain a +2 item bonus to Fortitude saves against poison for 6 hours.

Lesser Antiplague: After drinking a lesser antiplague, you gain a +2 item bonus to Fortitude saves against disease for 24 hours, including your saves against diseases' progression.

Lesser Elixir of Life: Drinking a lesser elixir of life restores 1d6 Hit Points and grants a +1 item bonus to saving throws against diseases and poisons for 10 minutes.

ALCHEMICAL TOOLS

Alchemical tools are a type of alchemical item you use, rather than drink or throw. For more on alchemical tools, see page 564.

Smokestick: You create a 5-foot radius smokescreen for 1 minute.

Sunrod: You can strike a sunrod on a hard surface as an Interact action to cause it to shed bright light in a 20-foot radius (dim light in the next 20 feet) for 6 hours.

Tindertwig: You can use a tindertwig to ignite

INTRODUCTION

ANCESTRIES & BACKGROUNDS

CLASSES

SKILLS

FEATS

EQUIPMENT

SPELLS

THE AGE OF LOST OMENS

PLAYING THE GAME

GAME MASTERING

CRAFTING & TREASURE

APPENDIX

something flammable with a single Interact action, faster than with flint and steel.

MAGICAL GEAR

The items on Table 6–12 are the magic items from Chapter 11 that a 1st-level character could most frequently access. The descriptions below are incomplete; the items' full entries appear in Chapter 11 on the pages listed in the table. Your GM might allow you to start with other magic items from Chapter 11 on a case-by-case basis.

TABLE 6-12: MAGICAL GEAR

Consumable Magic Items	Price	Bulk	Page
Holy water	3 gp	L	571
Unholy water	3 gp	L	571
Potions	**Price**	**Bulk**	**Page**
Minor healing potion	3 gp	L	563
Scrolls	**Price**	**Bulk**	**Page**
Scroll of a common 1st-level spell	4 gp	L	565
Talismans	**Price**	**Bulk**	**Page**
Potency crystal	4 gp	–	568

CONSUMABLE MAGIC ITEMS

You can typically purchase *holy* and *unholy water* in a settlement. Particularly good settlements tend to ban *unholy water* and evil settlements tend to ban *holy water*.

Holy Water: You can throw *holy water* like a bomb, dealing 1d6 good damage to fiends, undead, and other creatures weak to good damage.

Unholy Water: You can throw *unholy water* like a bomb, dealing 1d6 good damage to celestials and other creatures weak to evil damage.

POTIONS

Potions are magic items you drink to gain a variety of benefits. For more on potions, see page 562.

Minor Healing Potion: After drinking a *minor healing potion*, you regain 1d8 Hit Points.

SCROLLS

Scrolls are magical scriptures that hold the necessary magic to cast a particular spell without using your spell slots. The Price listed in the table is for a scroll with a common 1st-level spell. For more on scrolls, see page 564.

TALISMANS

A talisman is a special, single-use item you affix to your armor, a weapon, or elsewhere, allowing you to activate the talisman later for a special benefit. For more on talismans, see page 565.

Potency Crystal: When you affix the crystal to a weapon and activate it, this talisman empowers the weapon for the rest of the turn, granting it a +1 item bonus to attack rolls and a second weapon damage die.

FORMULAS

Formulas are instructions for making items with the Craft activity. You can usually read a formula as long as you can read the language it's written in, though you might lack the skill to Craft the item. Often, alchemists and crafting guilds use obscure languages or create codes to protect their formulas from rivals.

You can buy common formulas at the Price listed on Table 6–13, or you can hire an NPC to let you copy their formula for the same Price. A purchased formula is typically a schematic on rolled-up parchment of light Bulk. You can copy a formula into your formula book in 1 hour, either from a schematic or directly from someone else's formula book. If you have a formula, you can Craft a copy of it using the Crafting skill. Formulas for uncommon items and rare items are usually significantly more valuable—if you can find them at all!

If you have an item, you can try to reverse-engineer its formula. This uses the Craft activity and takes the same amount of time as creating the item from a formula would. You must first disassemble the item. After the base downtime, you attempt a Crafting check against the same DC it would take to Craft the item. If you succeed, you Craft the formula at its full Price, and you can keep working to reduce the Price as normal. If you fail, you're left with raw materials and no formula. If you critically fail, you also waste 10% of the raw materials you'd normally be able to salvage.

The item's disassembled parts are worth half its Price in raw materials and can't be reassembled unless you successfully reverse-engineer the formula or acquire the formula another way. Reassembling the item from the formula works just like Crafting it from scratch; you use the disassembled parts as the necessary raw materials.

TABLE 6-13: FORMULAS

Item Level	Formula Price	Item Level	Formula Price
0*	5 sp	11	70 gp
1	1 gp	12	100 gp
2	2 gp	13	150 gp
3	3 gp	14	225 gp
4	5 gp	15	325 gp
5	8 gp	16	500 gp
6	13 gp	17	750 gp
7	18 gp	18	1,200 gp
8	25 gp	19	2,000 gp
9	35 gp	20	3,500 gp
10	50 gp		

* Formulas for all 0-level common items from this chapter can be purchased collectively in a basic crafter's book.

ITEMS WITH MULTIPLE TYPES

If an item has multiple types of different levels, each type has its own formula, and you need the formula for the specific type of item you want to Craft. For example, if you have a formula for a *type I bag of holding* but not for a *type II bag of holding*, you must acquire a separate formula to Craft a *type II bag of holding*.

SERVICES

The services listed on Table 6–14 describe expenditures for common services and consumables.

TABLE 6-14: BASIC SERVICES AND CONSUMABLES

Item	Price	Bulk	Hands
Beverages			
Mug of ale	1 cp	L	1
Keg of ale	2 sp	2	2
Pot of coffee or tea	2 cp	L	1
Bottle of wine	1 sp	L	1
Bottle of fine wine	1 gp	L	1
Hireling (1 day)			
Unskilled	1 sp		
Skilled	5 sp		
Lodging (1 day)			
Floor space	3 cp		
Bed (for 1)	1 sp		
Private room (for 2)	8 sp		
Extravagant suite (for 6)	10 gp		
Meals			
Poor meal	1 cp	L	2
Square meal	3 cp	L	2
Fine dining	1 gp	L	2
Stabling (1 day)	2 cp		
Toll	at least 1 cp		
Transportation (per 5 miles)			
Caravan	3 cp		
Carriage	2 sp		
Ferry or riverboat	4 cp		
Sailing ship	6 cp		

HIRELINGS

Paid laborers can provide services for you. Unskilled hirelings can perform simple manual labor and are untrained at most skills. Skilled hirelings have expert proficiency in a particular skill. Hirelings are level 0. If a skill check is needed, an untrained hireling has a +0 modifier, while a skilled hireling has a +4 modifier in their area of expertise and +0 for other skill checks. Hirelings' rates double if they're going adventuring with you.

TRANSPORTATION

The cost to hire transportation includes standard travel with no amenities. Most transit services provide basic sleeping arrangements, and some provide meals at the rates listed on Table 6–14. Arranging transportation into dangerous lands can be more expensive or impossible.

SPELLCASTING

Spellcasting services, listed on Table 6–15, are uncommon. Having a spell cast for you requires finding a spellcaster who knows and is willing to cast it. It's hard to find someone who can cast higher-level spells, and uncommon spells typically cost at least 100% more, if you can find someone who knows them at all. Spells that take a long time to cast (over 1 minute) usually cost 25% more. You must pay any cost listed in the spell in addition to the Price on the table.

TABLE 6-15: SPELLCASTING SERVICES

Spell Level	Price*	Spell Level	Price*
1st	3 gp	6th	160 gp
2nd	7 gp	7th	360 gp
3rd	18 gp	8th	720 gp
4th	40 gp	9th	1,800 gp
5th	80 gp		

* Plus any cost required to cast the specific spell.

COST OF LIVING

Table 6–16 shows how much it costs to get by. This covers room and board, dues, taxes, and other fees.

TABLE 6-16: COST OF LIVING

Standard of Living	Week	Month	Year
Subsistence*	4 sp	2 gp	24 gp
Comfortable	1 gp	4 gp	52 gp
Fine	30 gp	130 gp	1,600 gp
Extravagant	100 gp	430 gp	5,200 gp

* You can attempt to Subsist using Society or Survival (page 240) for free.

ANIMALS

The Prices for animals are listed both for renting and for purchasing them outright. You usually need to pay for animal rentals up front, and if the vendor believes the animal might be put in danger, they typically require a deposit equal to the purchase Price. Most animals panic in battle. When combat begins, they become frightened 4 and fleeing as long as they're frightened. If you successfully Command your Animal using Nature (page 249), you can keep it from fleeing, though this doesn't remove its frightened condition. If the animal is attacked or damaged, it returns to frightened 4 and fleeing, with the same exceptions.

Warhorses and warponies are combat trained. They don't become frightened or fleeing during encounters in this way.

Statistics for the animals appear in the *Pathfinder Bestiary*.

TABLE 6-17: ANIMALS

Animal	Rental Price* (per day)	Purchase Price
Dog		
Guard dog	1 cp per day	2 sp
Riding dog	6 cp per day	4 gp

Horse		
Riding horse	1 sp per day	8 gp
Warhorse	1 gp per day	30 gp (level 2)
Pack animal	2 cp per day	2 gp
Pony		
Riding pony	8 cp per day	7 gp
Warpony	8 sp per day	24 gp (level 2)
* Might require a deposit equal to the purchase Price.		

BARDING

You can purchase special armor for animals, called barding (shown on Table 6–18). All animals have a trained proficiency rank in light barding, and combat-trained animals are trained in heavy barding. Barding uses the same rules as armor except for the following. The Price and Bulk of barding depend on the animal's size. Unlike for a suit of armor, barding's Strength entry is listed as a modifier, not a score. Barding can't be etched with magic runes, though special magical barding might be available.

ITEMS AND SIZES

The Bulk rules in this chapter are for Small and Medium creatures, as the items are made for creatures of those sizes. Large creatures can carry more, and smaller creatures can carry less, as noted on Table 6–19.

These rules for Bulk limits come up most often when a group tries to load up a mount or animal companion. The rules for items of different sizes tend to come into play when the characters defeat a big creature that has gear, since in most cases, the only creatures of other sizes are creatures under the GM's control. In most cases, Small or Medium creatures can wield a Large weapon, though it's unwieldy, giving them the clumsy 1 condition, and the larger size is canceled by the difficulty of swinging the weapon, so it grants no special benefit. Large armor is simply too large for Small and Medium creatures.

BULK CONVERSIONS FOR DIFFERENT SIZES

As shown in Table 6–19, Large or larger creatures are less encumbered by bulky items than Small or Medium creatures, while Tiny creatures become overburdened more quickly. A Large creature treats 10 items of 1 Bulk as 1 Bulk, a Huge creature treats 10 items of 2 Bulk as 1 Bulk, and so on. A Tiny creature treats 10 items of negligible Bulk as 1 Bulk. Negligible items work in a similar way—a Huge creature treats items of 1 Bulk

as negligible, so it can carry any number of items of 1 Bulk. A Tiny creature doesn't treat any items as having negligible Bulk.

TABLE 6-19: BULK CONVERSIONS

Creature Size	Bulk Limit	Treats as Light	Treats as Negligible
Tiny	Half	–	none
Small or Med.	Standard	L	–
Large	×2	1 Bulk	L
Huge	×4	2 Bulk	1 Bulk
Gargantuan	×8	4 Bulk	2 Bulk

ITEMS OF DIFFERENT SIZES

Creatures of sizes other than Small or Medium need items appropriate to their size. These items have different Bulk and possibly a different Price. Table 6–20 provides the Price and Bulk conversion for such items.

TABLE 6-20: DIFFERENTLY SIZED ITEMS

Creature Size	Price	Bulk	Light Becomes	Negligible Becomes
Tiny	Standard	Half*	–	–
Small or Med.	Standard	Standard	L	–
Large	×2	×2	1 Bulk	L
Huge	×4	×4	2 Bulk	1 Bulk
Gargantuan	×8	×8	4 Bulk	2 Bulk
* An item that would have its Bulk reduced below 1 has light Bulk.				

For example, a morningstar sized for a Medium creature has a Price of 1 gp and 1 Bulk, so one made for a Huge creature has a Price of 4 gp and 4 Bulk. One made for a Tiny creature still costs 1 gp (due to its intricacy) and has 1/2 Bulk, which rounds down to light Bulk.

Because the way that a creature treats Bulk and the Bulk of gear sized for it scale the same way, Tiny or Large (or larger) creatures can usually wear and carry about the same amount of appropriately sized gear as a Medium creature.

Higher-level magic items that cost significantly more than 8 times the cost of a mundane item can use their listed Price regardless of size. Precious materials, however, have a Price based on the Bulk of the item, so multiply the Bulk value as described on Table 6–20, then use the formula in the precious material's entry to determine the item's Price. See page 578 for more information.

TABLE 6-18: BARDING

Light Barding	Price	AC Bonus	Dex Cap	Check Penalty	Speed Penalty	Bulk	Strength
Small or Medium	10 gp	+1	+5	–1	–5 ft.	2	+3
Large	20 gp	+1	+5	–1	–5 ft.	4	+3
Heavy Barding	**Price**	**AC Bonus**	**Dex Cap**	**Check Penalty**	**Speed Penalty**	**Bulk**	**Strength**
Small or Medium (level 2)	25 gp	+3	+3	–3	–10 ft.	4	+5
Large (level 3)	50 gp	+3	+3	–3	–10 ft.	8	+5

INTRODUCTION

ANCESTRIES & BACKGROUNDS

CLASSES

SKILLS

FEATS

EQUIPMENT

SPELLS

THE AGE OF LOST OMENS

PLAYING THE GAME

GAME MASTERING

CRAFTING & TREASURE

APPENDIX

CHAPTER 7: SPELLS

Whether it comes in the form of mystic artifacts, mysterious creatures, or wizards weaving strange spells, magic brings fantasy and wonder to Pathfinder. This chapter explains how spells work and how spellcasters prepare and cast their spells.

With special gestures and utterances, a spellcaster can call forth mystic energies, warp the mind, protect themself against danger, or even create something from nothing. Each class has its own method of learning, preparing, and casting spells, and every individual spell produces a specific effect, so learning new spells gives a spellcaster an increasing array of options to accomplish their goals.

TRADITION AND SCHOOL

The fundamental building blocks of magic are the magical traditions and the schools of magic. The four traditions are arcane, divine, occult, and primal. A spell's magical tradition can vary, because many spells can be cast using different traditions. A spell's school, on the other hand, is intrinsic to the spell and establishes what the spell is capable of. Abjuration spells, for example, can raise protective wards, enchantment spells can change thoughts, and evocation spells can create blasts of fire.

MAGICAL SCHOOLS

All spells, all magic items, and most other magical effects fall into one of the eight schools of magic. These schools broadly define what the magic is capable of. Every spell has the trait corresponding to its school. Some spellcasters, like specialist wizards, have particular acumen with a certain school of magic.

ABJURATION

Abjurations protect and ward. They create barriers that keep out attacks, effects, or even certain types of creatures. They also create effects that harm trespassers or banish interlopers.

CONJURATION

Conjuration spells transport creatures via teleportation, create an object, or bring a creature or object from somewhere else (typically from another plane) to follow your commands.

Conjuration spells often have the teleportation trait, and the creatures summoned by conjuration spells have the summoned trait.

DIVINATION

Divinations allow you to learn the secrets of the present, past, and future. They bestow good fortune, grant you the ability to perceive remote locations, and reveal secret knowledge.

Divinations often have the detection trait if they find something, the prediction trait if they grant you insight about what might happen in the future, the revelation trait if they show things as they truly are, or the scrying trait if they let you perceive another location.

ENCHANTMENT

Enchantments affect the minds and emotions of other creatures—sometimes to influence and control them, and other times to bolster them to greater heights of courage. Enchantment spells almost always have the mental trait, and many have the emotion trait or the fear trait.

SPELLBOOKS

Carefully maintained and jealously guarded, there are few things more valuable to a wizard than a spellbook. These repositories of magical lore are often trapped and warded to ensure that no one meddles with the secrets inside.

Although spellbooks play a central role in a wizard's daily routine, other prepared spellcasting classes have been known to use spellbooks to record uncommon or even rare spells. Such a resource allows a caster to treat the spell like any other common spell, so long as they can reference the book during their daily preparations.

SPELL ATTACK ROLL AND SPELL DC

Many spells allow creatures to defend themselves using either their AC or a saving throw. Two statistics govern how potent your spells are against these defenses: your spell attack roll and your spell DC. When recording these on your character sheet, add together only the numbers that always apply—usually just your ability modifier and proficiency bonus.

Spell attack roll = your spellcasting ability modifier + proficiency bonus + other bonuses + penalties

Spell DC = 10 + your spellcasting ability modifier + proficiency bonus + other bonuses + penalties

A spell attack roll is like other attack rolls, so any bonuses or penalties that apply to all your attack rolls should be included in your calculation. For instance, the +1 status bonus from the *bless* spell would benefit your spell ray just like it could an arrow. However, note that the spell attack roll doesn't gain any bonuses or penalties that apply specifically to weapon attacks or unarmed attacks. The multiple attack penalty applies to spell attacks, so it's usually a bad idea to cast a spell that has a spell attack roll if you've already made an attack that turn.

As with other checks and DCs, bonuses can increase the result of your spell attack roll or your spell DC, and penalties can decrease the result of your spell attack roll or your spell DC. See pages 444–445 in Chapter 9: Playing the Game for more information about modifiers, bonuses, and penalties.

DISBELIEVING ILLUSIONS

Sometimes illusions allow an affected creature a chance to disbelieve the spell, which lets the creature effectively ignore the spell if it succeeds at doing so. This usually happens when a creature Seeks or otherwise spends actions to engage with the illusion, comparing the result of its Perception check (or another check or saving throw, at the GM's discretion) to the caster's spell DC. Mental illusions typically provide rules in the spell's description for disbelieving the effect (often allowing the affected creature to attempt a Will save).

If the illusion is visual, and a creature interacts with the illusion in a way that would prove it is not what it seems, the creature might know that an illusion is present, but it still can't ignore the illusion without successfully disbelieving it. For instance, if a character is pushed through the illusion of a door, they will know that the door is an illusion, but they still can't see through it. Disbelieving an illusion makes it and those things it blocks seem hazy and indistinct, so even in the case where a visual illusion is disbelieved, it may, at the GM's discretion, block vision enough to make those on the other side concealed..

EVOCATION

Evocations capture magical energy and then shape it to harm your foes or protect your allies. Evocation spells often have a trait that comes from the type of damage they deal, such as acid, cold, fire, force, or sonic.

ILLUSION

Illusions create the semblance of something real, fooling the eyes, ears, and other senses. They almost always have the mental trait, and depending on how the illusion is perceived, they might also have the auditory or visual trait.

NECROMANCY

Necromancy spells harness the power of life and death. They can sap life essence or sustain creatures with life-saving healing. Necromancy spells often have the curse, death, healing, negative, or positive traits.

TRANSMUTATION

Transmutation spells make alterations to or transform the physical form of a creature or object. The morph and polymorph traits appear primarily in transmutation spells.

SPELL SLOTS

Characters of spellcasting classes can cast a certain number of spells each day; the spells you can cast in a day are referred to as spell slots. At 1st level, a character has only a small number of 1st-level spell slots per day, but as you advance in level, you gain more spell slots and new slots for higher-level spells. A spell's level indicates its overall power, from 1 to 10.

PREPARED SPELLS

If you're a prepared spellcaster—such as a cleric, druid, or wizard—you must spend time each day preparing spells for that day. At the start of your daily preparations, you select a number of spells of different spell levels determined by your character level and class. Your spells remain prepared until you cast them or until you prepare spells again.

Each prepared spell is expended after a single casting, so if you want to cast a particular spell more than once in a day, you need to prepare that spell multiple times. The exceptions to this rule are spells with the cantrip trait; once you prepare a cantrip, you can cast it as many times as you want until the next time you prepare spells. See page 300 for more information on cantrips.

You might gain an ability that allows you to swap prepared spells or perform other aspects of preparing spells at different times throughout the day, but only your daily preparation counts for the purpose of effects that last until the next time you prepare spells.

SPONTANEOUS SPELLS

If you're a spontaneous spellcaster—such as a bard or a sorcerer—you choose which spell you're using a spell

MAGICAL TRADITIONS

Spellcasters cast spells from one of four different spell lists, each representing a different magical tradition: arcane, divine, occult, and primal.

Your class determines which tradition of magic your spells use. In some cases, such as when a cleric gains spells from their deity or when a sorcerer gets spells from their bloodline, you might be able to cast spells from a different spell list. In these cases, the spell uses your magic tradition, not the list the spell normally comes from. When you cast a spell, add your tradition's trait to the spell.

Some types of magic, such as that of most magic items, don't belong to any single tradition. These have the magical trait instead of a tradition trait.

Arcane
Arcane spellcasters use logic and rationality to categorize the magic inherent in the world around them. Because of its far-reaching approach, the arcane tradition has the broadest spell list, though it's generally poor at affecting the spirit or the soul. Wizards are the most iconic arcane spellcasters, poring over tomes and grimoires, though arcane sorcerers study the secrets of their blood to unlock the power within themselves.

Divine
The power of the divine is steeped in faith, the unseen, and belief in a power source from beyond the Material Plane. Clerics are the most iconic divine spellcasters, beseeching the gods to grant them their magic. Divine sorcerers can use the blood of their celestial or fiendish ancestors as a divine conduit, and champions call upon their gods to grant them martial prowess through divine guidance.

Occult
The practitioners of occult traditions seek to understand the unexplainable, categorize the bizarre, and otherwise access the ephemeral in a systematic way. Bards are the most iconic occult spellcasters, collecting strange esoterica and using their performances to influence the mind or elevate the soul, and occult sorcerers strive to understand the mysterious power in their blood.

Primal
An instinctual connection to and faith in the world, the cycle of day and night, the turning of the seasons, and the natural selection of predator and prey drive the primal tradition. Druids are the most iconic primal spellcasters, calling upon the magic of nature through deep faith and a connection to the plants and animals around them, and primal sorcerers call upon their fey or beast blood to harness the same natural energies.

INTRODUCTION

ANCESTRIES & BACKGROUNDS

CLASSES

SKILLS

FEATS

EQUIPMENT

SPELLS

THE AGE OF LOST OMENS

PLAYING THE GAME

GAME MASTERING

CRAFTING & TREASURE

APPENDIX

slot for at the moment you decide to cast it. This provides you with more freedom in your spellcasting, but you have fewer spells in your spell repertoire, as determined by your character level and class. When you make your daily preparations, all your spell slots are refreshed, but you don't get to change the spells in your repertoire.

HEIGHTENED SPELLS

Both prepared and spontaneous spellcasters can cast a spell at a higher spell level than that listed for the spell. This is called heightening the spell. A prepared spellcaster can heighten a spell by preparing it in a higher-level slot than its normal spell level, while a spontaneous spellcaster can heighten a spell by casting it using a higher-level spell slot, so long as they know the spell at that level (see Heightened Spontaneous Spells below). When you heighten your spell, the spell's level increases to match the higher level of the spell slot you've prepared it in or used to cast it. This is useful for any spell, because some effects, such as counteracting, depend on the spell's level.

In addition, many spells have additional specific benefits when they are heightened, such as increased damage. These extra benefits are described at the end of the spell's stat block. Some heightened entries specify one or more levels at which the spell must be prepared or cast to gain these extra advantages. Each of these heightened entries states specifically which aspects of the spell change at the given level. Read the heightened entry only for the spell level you're using or preparing; if its benefits are meant to include any of the effects of a lower-level heightened entry, those benefits will be included in the entry.

Other heightened entries give a number after a plus sign, indicating that heightening grants extra advantages over multiple levels. The listed effect applies for every increment of levels by which the spell is heightened above its lowest spell level, and the benefit is cumulative. For example, *fireball* says "**Heightened (+1)** The damage increases by 2d6." Because *fireball* deals 6d6 fire damage at 3rd level, a 4th-level *fireball* would deal 8d6 fire damage, a 5th-level spell would deal 10d6 fire damage, and so on.

Heightened Spontaneous Spells

If you're a spontaneous spellcaster, you must know a spell at the specific level that you want to cast it in order to heighten it. You can add a spell to your spell repertoire at more than a single level so that you have more options when casting it. For example, if you added *fireball* to your repertoire as a 3rd-level spell and again as a 5th-level spell, you could cast it as a 3rd-level or a 5th-level spell; however, you couldn't cast it as a 4th-level spell.

Many spontaneous spellcasting classes provide abilities like the signature spells class feature, which allows you to cast a limited number of spells as heightened versions even if you know the spell at only a single level.

THE FOUR ESSENCES

Spells that affect certain physical or metaphysical forces tend to be grouped into particular magical traditions. Scholars of magic widely agree that all of existence is composed of some combination of four essences, though they disagree on the names and particular qualities of each essence.

The following entries discuss each essence and the traditions and spell schools relevant to it; for instance, evocation spells tend to manipulate matter. The abjuration school is an unusual case, as abjuration spells draw upon different essences depending on who they are warding and what they are protecting against.

Matter

Also called body, material essence, or physical essence, matter is the fundamental building block that makes up all physical things in the universe. The arcane and primal traditions are especially attuned toward manipulating and shaping matter. Spells that are used to create or alter matter most often come from the conjuration, evocation, or transmutation schools.

Spirit

Also called soul, ethereal essence, or spiritual essence, spirit is an otherworldly building block that makes up a being's immaterial and immortal self. The spirit travels through the Ethereal Plane and into the Great Beyond after the death of the physical body. The spirit is most easily affected by divine and occult spells. Spirit spells are usually of the divination or necromancy schools.

Mind

Also called thought or astral essence, the mind essence allows thinking creatures to have rational thoughts, ideas, plans, logic, and memories. Mind touches even nonsapient creatures like animals, though in a more limited capacity. Arcane and occult casters usually excel at mind spells. Spells that use mind essence are usually found in the divination, enchantment, and illusion schools.

Life

Also called heart, faith, instinct, or vital essence, life represents the animating universal force within all things. Whereas matter provides the base materials for a body, life keeps it alive and well. This essence is responsible for unconscious responses and belief, such as ancestral instincts and divine guidance. The divine and primal traditions hold power over life. Life spells are usually necromancy.

CANTRIPS

A cantrip is a special type of spell that's weaker than other spells but can be used with greater freedom and flexibility. The title of a cantrip's stat block says "Cantrip" instead of "Spell." Casting a cantrip doesn't use up your spell slots; you can cast a cantrip at will, any number of times per day. If you're a prepared caster, you have a number of cantrip spell slots that you use to prepare your cantrips. You can't prepare a cantrip in any other slot.

A cantrip is always automatically heightened to half your level, rounded up. For a typical spellcaster, this means its level is equal to the highest level of spell slot you have.

FOCUS SPELLS

Focus spells are a special type of spell attained directly from a branch of study, from a deity, or from another specific source. You can learn focus spells only through special class features or feats, rather than choosing them from a spell list. Furthermore, you cast focus spells using a special pool of Focus Points—you can't prepare a focus spell in a spell slot or use your spell slots to cast focus spells; similarly, you can't spend your Focus Points to cast spells that aren't focus spells. Even some classes that don't normally grant spellcasting, such as the champion and monk, can grant focus spells.

Focus spells are automatically heightened to half your level rounded up, just like cantrips are. You can't cast a focus spell if its minimum level is greater than half your level rounded up, even if you somehow gain access to it.

Casting any of your focus spells costs you 1 Focus Point. You automatically gain a focus pool of 1 Focus Point the first time you gain an ability that gives you a focus spell.

You replenish all the Focus Points in your pool during your daily preparations. You can also use the Refocus activity to pray, study, meditate, or otherwise reattune yourself to the source of your focus magic and regain a Focus Point.

Some abilities allow you to increase the Focus Points in your pool beyond 1. Typically, these are feats that give you a new focus spell and increase the number of points in your pool by 1. Your focus pool can't have a capacity beyond 3 Focus Points, even if feats that increase your pool would cause it to exceed this number.

REFOCUS

CONCENTRATE **EXPLORATION**

Requirements You have a focus pool, and you have spent at least 1 Focus Point since you last regained any Focus Points.

You spend 10 minutes performing deeds to restore your magical connection. This restores 1 Focus Point to your focus pool. The deeds you need to perform are specified in the class or ability that gives you your focus spells. These deeds can usually overlap with other tasks that relate to the source of your focus spells. For instance, a cleric with focus spells from a good deity can usually Refocus while tending the wounds of their allies, and a wizard of the illusionist school might be able to Refocus while attempting to Identify Magic of the illusion school.

OTHER SPELL TRAITS

Some spells and effects have traits such as "mental" or "good." These tell you more about the spell and how it works, and other rules might reference them. A creature might, for example, have a –2 circumstance penalty to saving throws against mental effects. Below is a glossary of a few traits you might see with important rules.

Auditory

Auditory spells rely on sound. A spell with the auditory trait has its effect only if the target can hear it. This is different from a sonic effect, which still affects targets who can't hear it (such as deaf targets) as long as the effect makes sound.

Darkness and Light

Effects with the darkness and light traits interact in specific ways. Non-magical light always shines in non-magical darkness and always fails to shine in magical darkness. Magical light always shines in non-magical darkness but shines in magical darkness only if the light spell has a higher level than that of the darkness effect. Spells with the darkness trait or the light trait can always counteract one another, but bringing light and darkness into contact doesn't automatically do so. You must usually cast a light spell on a darkness effect directly to counteract it (and vice versa), but some spells automatically attempt to counteract opposing effects.

Incapacitation

An ability with this trait can take a character completely out of the fight or even kill them, and it's harder to use on a more powerful character. If a spell has the incapacitation trait, any creature of more than twice the spell's level treats the result of their check to prevent being incapacitated as one degree of success better or the result of any check the spellcaster made to incapacitate them as one degree of success worse. If any other effect has the incapacitation trait, a creature of higher level than the item, creature, or hazard generating the effect gains the same benefits.

Minion

Minions are creatures that directly serve another creature. A creature with this trait can use only 2 actions per turn and can't use reactions. Your minion acts on your turn in combat, once per turn, when you spend an action to issue it commands. For an animal companion, you Command an Animal; for a minion that's a spell or magic item effect like a summoned minion you Sustain a Spell or Sustain an Activation; and if not otherwise specified, you issue a verbal command, which is a single action with the auditory and concentrate traits. If given no commands, by default minions use no actions except to defend themselves or to escape obvious harm. If left unattended for long enough, typically 1 minute, mindless minions usually don't act, animals often indulge their creature comforts, and sapient minions act how they please.

Morph

Spells that slightly alter a creature's form have the morph trait. Any Strikes specifically granted by a morph effect are magical. You can be affected by multiple morph spells at once, but if you morph the same body part more than once, the second morph effect attempts to counteract the first (in the same manner as two polymorph effects, described below).

Your morph effects might also end if you are polymorphed and the polymorph effect invalidates or overrides your morph effect. For instance, a morph that gave you wings would be dismissed if you polymorphed into a form that had wings of its own (though if your new form lacked wings, you'd keep the wings from your morph). The GM determines which morph effects can be used together and which can't.

Polymorph

These effects transform the target into a new form. A target can't be under the effect of more than one polymorph effect at a time. If it comes under the effect of a second polymorph effect, the second polymorph effect attempts to counteract the first. If it succeeds, it takes effect, and if it fails, the spell has no effect on that target. Any Strikes specifically granted by a polymorph effect are magical. Unless otherwise stated, polymorph spells don't allow the target to take on the appearance of a specific individual creature, but rather just a generic creature of a general type or ancestry.

If you take on a battle form with a polymorph spell, the special statistics can be adjusted only by circumstance bonuses, status bonuses, and penalties. Unless otherwise noted, the battle form prevents you from casting spells, speaking, and using most manipulate actions that require hands. (If there's doubt about whether you can use an action, the GM decides.) Your gear is absorbed into you; the constant abilities of your gear still function, but you can't activate any items.

Summoned

A creature called by a conjuration spell or effect gains the summoned trait. A summoned creature can't summon other creatures, create things of value, or cast spells that require a cost. It has the minion trait. If it tries to cast a spell of equal or higher level than the spell that summoned it, the spell fails and the summon spell ends. Otherwise, it uses the standard abilities for a creature of its kind. It generally attacks your enemies to the best of its abilities. If you can communicate with it, you can attempt to command it, but the GM determines the degree to which it follows your commands.

Immediately when you finish Casting the Spell, the summoned creature uses its 2 actions for that turn.

Summoned creatures can be banished by various spells and effects. They are automatically banished if reduced to 0 Hit Points or if the spell that called them ends.

Visual

A visual spell can affect only creatures that can see it.

FOCUS POINTS FROM MULTIPLE SOURCES

It's possible, especially through archetypes, to gain focus spells and Focus Points from more than one source. If this happens, you have just one focus pool, adding all the Focus Points together to determine the total size of your pool. (Remember that the maximum number of Focus Points a pool can have is 3.) If you have multiple abilities that give you a focus pool, each one adds 1 Focus Point to your pool. For instance, if you were a cleric with the Domain Initiate feat, you would have a pool with 1 Focus Point. Let's say you then took the champion multiclass archetype and the Healing Touch feat. Normally, this feat would give you a focus pool. Since you already have one, it instead increases your existing pool's capacity by 1.

Focus Points are not differentiated by source; you can spend any of your Focus Points on any of your focus spells. Likewise, when you Refocus, you get back a point as long as you follow the guidelines of any abilities that granted you focus spells. Having Focus Points from multiple sources doesn't change the tradition of your spells; if you had both cleric domain spells and druid order spells, your domain spells would remain divine and the order spells primal. This could mean that you need to keep track of a different proficiency and ability modifier with the spell DC and spell attack roll of different focus spells.

SPELLCASTERS WITH FOCUS SPELLS

If you are a spellcaster, your focus spells are the same tradition of spell as the class that gave you the focus spell. A bard's are occult, a cleric's are divine, a druid's are primal, a wizard's are arcane, and a sorcerer's are determined by their bloodline.

NON-SPELLCASTERS WITH FOCUS SPELLS

If you get focus spells from a class or other source that doesn't grant spellcasting ability (for example, if you're a monk with the Ki Strike feat), the ability that gives you focus spells also provides your proficiency rank for spell attack rolls and spell DCs, as well as the magical tradition of your focus spells. You gain the ability to Cast a Spell and use any spellcasting actions necessary to cast your focus spells (see below). However, you don't qualify for feats and other rules that require you to be a spellcaster.

INNATE SPELLS

Certain spells are natural to your character, typically coming from your ancestry or a magic item rather than your class. You can cast your innate spells even if you aren't a member of a spellcasting class. The ability that gives you an innate spell tells you how often you can cast it—usually once per day—and its magical tradition. Innate spells are refreshed during your daily preparations. Innate

cantrips are cast at will and automatically heightened as normal for cantrips (see Cantrips on page 300) unless otherwise specified.

You're always trained in spell attack rolls and spell DCs for your innate spells, even if you aren't otherwise trained in spell attack rolls or spell DCs. If your proficiency in spell attack rolls or spell DCs is expert or better, apply that proficiency to your innate spells, too. You use your Charisma modifier as your spellcasting ability modifier for innate spells unless otherwise specified.

If you have an innate spell, you can cast it, even if it's not of a spell level you can normally cast. This is especially common for monsters, which might be able to cast innate spells far beyond what a character of the same level could use.

You can't use your spell slots to cast your innate spells, but you might have an innate spell and also be able to prepare or cast the same spell through your class. You also can't heighten innate spells, but some abilities that grant innate spells might give you the spell at a higher level than its base level or change the level at which you cast the spell.

CASTING SPELLS

The casting of a spell can range from a simple word of magical might that creates a fleeting effect to a complex process taking minutes or hours to cast and producing a long-term impact. Casting a Spell is a special activity that takes a number of actions defined by the spell. When you Cast a Spell, your spellcasting creates obvious visual manifestations of the gathering magic, although feats such as Conceal Spell (page 210) and Melodious Spell (page 101) can help hide such manifestations or otherwise prevent observers from noticing that you are casting.

CAST A SPELL

You cast a spell you have prepared or in your repertoire. Casting a Spell is a special activity that takes a variable number of actions depending on the spell, as listed in each spell's stat block. As soon as the spellcasting actions are complete, the spell effect occurs.

Some spells are cast as a reaction or free action. In those cases, you Cast the Spell as a reaction or free action (as appropriate) instead of as an activity. Such cases will be noted in the spell's stat block—for example, "⤾ verbal."

Long Casting Times Some spells take minutes or hours to cast. The Cast a Spell activity for these spells includes a mix of the listed spell components, but it's not necessary to break down which one you're providing at a given time. You can't use other actions or reactions while casting such a spell, though at the GM's discretion, you might be able to speak a few sentences. As with other activities that take a long time, these spells have the exploration trait, and you can't cast them in an encounter. If combat breaks out while you're casting one, your spell is disrupted (see Disrupted and Lost Spells on page 303).

Spell Components Each spell lists the spell components required to cast it after the action icons or text, such as "◆◆◆ material, somatic, verbal." The spell components, described in detail below, add traits and requirements to the Cast a Spell activity. If you can't provide the components, you fail to Cast the Spell.

- Material (manipulate)
- Somatic (manipulate)
- Verbal (concentrate)
- Focus (manipulate)

Disrupted and Lost Spells Some abilities and spells can disrupt a spell, causing it to have no effect and be lost. When you lose a spell, you've already expended the spell slot, spent the spell's costs and actions, and used the Cast a Spell activity. If a spell is disrupted during a Sustain a Spell action, the spell immediately ends. The full rules for disrupting actions appear on page 462.

SPELL COMPONENTS

A spell description lists the components required to Cast the Spell. For most spells, the number of components is equal to the number of actions you must spend to Cast the Spell. Each component adds certain traits to the Cast a Spell activity, and some components have special requirements. The components that appear in this book are listed below.

MATERIAL

A material component is a bit of physical matter consumed in the casting of the spell. The spell gains the manipulate trait and requires you to have a free hand to retrieve and manipulate a material component. That component is expended in the casting (even if the spell is disrupted).

Except in extreme circumstances, you can assume all common components are included in a material component pouch (page 290).

SOMATIC

A somatic component is a specific hand movement or gesture that generates a magical nexus. The spell gains the manipulate trait and requires you to make gestures. You can use this component while holding something in your hand, but not if you are restrained or otherwise unable to gesture freely.

Spells that require you to touch the target require a somatic component. You can do so while holding something as long as part of your hand is able to touch the target (even if it's through a glove or gauntlet).

VERBAL

A verbal component is a vocalization of words of power. You must speak them in a strong voice, so it's hard to conceal that you're Casting a Spell. The spell gains the concentrate trait. You must be able to speak to provide this component.

COMPONENT SUBSTITUTIONS

Some classes can substitute one component for another or alter how a component works.

If you're a bard Casting a Spell from the occult tradition while holding a musical instrument, you can play that instrument to replace any material, somatic, or verbal components the spell requires by using the instrument as a focus component instead. Cast a Spell gains the auditory trait if you make this substitution. Unlike the normal rules for a focus component, you can't retrieve or stow the instrument when making this substitution.

If you're a cleric Casting a Spell from the divine tradition while holding a divine focus (such as a religious symbol or text), you can replace any material component the spell requires by using the divine focus as a focus component instead. Unlike the normal rules for a focus component, you can't retrieve or stow the focus when making this substitution.

If you're a druid Casting a Spell from the primal tradition while holding a primal focus (such as holly and mistletoe), you can replace any material component the spell requires by using the primal focus as a focus component instead. Unlike the normal rules for a focus component, you can't retrieve or stow the focus when making this substitution.

If you're a sorcerer Casting a Spell from the magical tradition that matches your bloodline, you can draw on the magic within your blood to replace any material component with a somatic component.

FOCUS

A focus is an object that funnels the magical energy of the spell. The spell gains the manipulate trait and requires you to either have a free hand to retrieve the focus listed in the spell or already be holding the focus in your hand. As part of Casting the Spell, you retrieve the focus (if necessary), manipulate it, and can stow it again if you so choose.

Foci tend to be expensive, and you need to acquire them in advance to Cast the Spell.

- INTRODUCTION
- ANCESTRIES & BACKGROUNDS
- CLASSES
- SKILLS
- FEATS
- EQUIPMENT
- SPELLS
- THE AGE OF LOST OMENS
- PLAYING THE GAME
- GAME MASTERING
- CRAFTING & TREASURE
- APPENDIX

METAMAGIC

Many spellcasters can gain access to metamagic actions, typically by selecting metamagic feats. Actions with the metamagic trait tweak the properties of your spells, changing their range, damage, or any number of other properties. You must use a metamagic action directly before the spell you want to alter. If you use any action (including free actions, reactions, and additional metamagic actions) other than Cast a Spell directly after, you waste the benefits of the metamagic action. Any additional effects added by a metamagic action are part of the spell's effect, not of the metamagic action itself.

RANGES, AREAS, AND TARGETS

Spells with a range can affect targets, create areas, or make things appear only within that range. Most spell ranges are measured in feet, though some can stretch over miles, reach anywhere on the planet, or go even farther!

TOUCH RANGE

A spell with a range of touch requires you to physically touch the target. You use your unarmed reach to determine whether you can touch the creature. You can usually touch the target automatically, though the spell might specify that the target can attempt a saving throw or that you must attempt a spell attack roll. If an ability increases the range of a touch spell, start at 0 feet and increase from there.

AREAS

Sometimes a spell has an area, which can be a burst, cone, emanation, or line. The method of measuring these areas can be found on page 456. If the spell originates from your position, the spell has only an area; if you can cause the spell's area to appear farther away from you, the spell has both a range and an area.

TARGETS

Some spells allow you to directly target a creature, an object, or something that fits a more specific category. The target must be within the spell's range, and you must be able to see it (or otherwise perceive it with a precise sense) to target it normally. At the GM's discretion, you can attempt to target a creature you can't see, as described in Detecting Creatures on pages 465–467. If you fail to target a particular creature, this doesn't change how the spell affects any other targets the spell might have.

If you choose a target that isn't valid, such as if you thought a vampire was a living creature and targeted it with a spell that can target only living creatures, your spell fails to target that creature. If a creature starts out as a valid target but ceases to be one during a spell's duration, the spell typically ends, but the GM might decide otherwise in certain situations.

Spells that affect multiple creatures in an area can have both an Area entry and a Targets entry. A spell that has an area but no targets listed usually affects all creatures in the area indiscriminately.

Some spells restrict you to willing targets. A player can declare their character a willing or unwilling target at any time, regardless of turn order or their character's condition (such as when a character is paralyzed, unconscious, or even dead).

LINE OF EFFECT

You usually need an unobstructed path to the target of a spell, the origin point of an area, or the place where you create something with a spell. More information on line of effect can be found on page 457.

DURATIONS

The duration of a spell is how long the spell effect lasts. Spells that last for more than an instant have a Duration entry. A spell might last until the start or end of a turn, for some number of rounds, for minutes, or even longer! If a spell's duration is given in rounds, the number of rounds remaining decreases by 1 at the start of each of the spellcaster's turns, ending when the duration reaches 0.

Some spells have effects that remain even after the spell's magic is gone. Any ongoing effect that isn't part of the spell's duration entry isn't considered magical. For instance, a spell that creates a loud sound and has no duration might deafen someone for a time, even permanently. This deafness couldn't be counteracted because it is not itself magical (though it might be cured by other magic, such as *restore senses*).

If a spell's caster dies or is incapacitated during the spell's duration, the spell remains in effect till its duration ends. You might need to keep track of the caster's initiative after they stopped being able to act to monitor spell durations.

SUSTAINING SPELLS

If the spell's duration is "sustained," it lasts until the end of your next turn unless you use a Sustain a Spell action on that turn to extend the duration of that spell.

SUSTAIN A SPELL ❖

CONCENTRATE

Requirements You have at least one spell active with a sustained duration, and you are not fatigued.

Choose one spell with a sustained duration you have in effect. The duration of that spell continues until the end of your next turn. Some spells might have slightly different or expanded effects if you sustain them. Sustaining a Spell for more than 10 minutes (100 rounds) ends the spell and makes you fatigued unless the spell lists a different maximum duration (such as "sustained up to 1 minute" or "sustained up to 1 hour").

If your Sustain a Spell action is disrupted, the spell immediately ends.

LONG DURATIONS

If a spell's duration says it lasts until your next daily preparations, on the next day you can refrain from preparing a new spell in that spell's slot. (If you are a spontaneous caster, you can instead expend a spell slot during your preparations.) Doing so extends the spell's duration until your next daily preparations. This effectively Sustains the Spell over a long period of time. If you prepare a new spell in the slot (or don't expend a spell slot), the spell ends. You can't do this if the spell didn't come from one of your spell slots. If you are dead or otherwise incapacitated at the 24-hour mark after the time you Cast the Spell or the last time you extended its duration, the spell ends. Spells with an unlimited duration last until counteracted or Dismissed. You don't need to keep a spell slot open for these spells.

DISMISSING

Some spells can be dismissed, ending the duration early. This requires the caster or target to use the Dismiss action.

DISMISS ◆

CONCENTRATE

You end one spell effect or magic item effect. This must be an effect you are allowed to dismiss, as defined by the spell or item. Dismissal might end the effect entirely or might end it just for a certain target or targets, depending on the spell or item.

SAVING THROWS

Spells that require a target to attempt a save to resist some or all of the spell's effects have a Saving Throw entry. This entry presents the type of save for quick reference, and specific details appear in the spell description. Whenever a spell allows a saving throw, it uses the caster's spell DC.

BASIC SAVING THROWS

If a spell's Saving Throw entry specifies a "basic" saving throw, the spell's potential effects all relate to the damage listed in the spell's description. The target takes no damage on a critical success, half damage on a success, full damage on a failure, or double damage on a critical failure. The rules for basic saving throws are found on page 449.

SPELL ATTACKS

Some spells require you to succeed at a spell attack roll to affect the target. This is usually because they require you to precisely aim a ray or otherwise make an accurate attack. A spell attack roll is compared to the target's AC. Spell attack rolls benefit from any bonuses or penalties to attack rolls, including your multiple attack penalty, but not any special benefits or penalties that apply only to weapon or unarmed attacks. Spell attacks don't deal any damage beyond what's listed in the spell description.

In rare cases, a spell might have you make some other type of attack, such as a weapon Strike. Such attacks use the normal rules and attack bonus for that type of attack.

IDENTIFYING SPELLS

Sometimes you need to identify a spell, especially if its effects are not obvious right away. If you notice a spell being cast, and you have prepared that spell or have it in your repertoire, you automatically know what the spell is, including the level to which it is heightened.

If you want to identify a spell but don't have it prepared or in your repertoire, you must spend an action on your turn to attempt to identify it using Recall Knowledge. You typically notice a spell being cast by seeing its visual manifestations or hearing its verbal casting components. Identifying long-lasting spells that are already in place requires using Identify Magic instead of Recall Knowledge because you don't have the advantage of watching the spell being cast.

COUNTERACTING

Some spells, such as *dispel magic*, can be used to eliminate the effects of other spells. At least one creature, object, or manifestation of the spell you are trying to counteract must be within range of the spell that you are using. You attempt a counteract check (page 458) using your spellcasting ability modifier and your proficiency bonus for spell attack rolls.

HOSTILE ACTIONS

Sometimes spell effects prevent a target from using hostile actions, or the spell ends if a creature uses any hostile actions. A hostile action is one that can harm or damage another creature, whether directly or indirectly, but not one that a creature is unaware could cause harm. For instance, lobbing a *fireball* into a crowd would be a hostile action, but opening a door and accidentally freeing a horrible monster would not be. The GM is the final arbiter of what constitutes a hostile action.

SETTING TRIGGERS

If a spell is meant to respond only to certain events or under certain conditions—such as *magic mouth*—it might require you to set a trigger. This is a simple sensory cue that causes the spell to activate. The spell activates as a reaction when the spell's sensor observes something that fits its trigger. Depending on the spell, the trigger might be the presence of a type of creature, such as "red-haired dwarven women," or it could be an observed action, such as "whenever someone enters the spell's area."

Disguises and illusions fool the spell as long as they appear to match its parameters. For a spell to detect something visually, the spell's origin point must have line of sight. Darkness doesn't prevent this, but invisibility

does, as does a successful Stealth check to Hide (against the spell's DC). For auditory detection, line of sight isn't necessary, though the sound must be audible at the spell's origin point. A Stealth check to Sneak can fool the sensor.

WALLS

Spells that create walls list the depth, length, and height of the wall, also specifying how it can be positioned. Some walls can be shaped; you can manipulate the wall into a form other than a straight line, choosing its contiguous path square by square. The path of a shaped wall can't enter the same space more than once, but it can double back so one section is adjacent to another section of the wall.

READING SPELLS

Each spell uses the following format. Entries appear only when applicable, so not all spells will have every entry described here. The spell's name line also lists the type of spell if it's a cantrip or focus spell, as well as the level.

SPELL NAME   SPELL (LEVEL)

TRAITS

Tradition This entry lists the magical traditions the spell belongs to. Some feats or other abilities might add a spell to your spell list even if you don't follow the listed traditions.

Cast The number of actions required to Cast the Spell are listed here. Spells that can be cast during a single turn have the appropriate icon, as do those that can be cast as a free action or a reaction. Spells that take longer to cast list the time required, such as "1 minute." After this, the spell's components are listed. If Casting the Spell has a cost, requirements, or a trigger, that information is also listed in this section. A cost includes any money, valuable materials, or other resources that must be expended to cast the spell.

Range, Area, and Targets This entry lists the range of the spell, the area it affects, and the targets it can affect, if any. If none of these entries are present, the spell affects only the caster.

Saving Throw and Duration If a spell allows the target to attempt a saving throw, the type of save appears here. Any details on the particular results and timing of the save appear in the text unless the entry specifies a basic saving throw, which follows the rules found on page 449. If the spell requires a save only under certain circumstances or at a certain time, this entry is omitted, since the text needs to explain it in more detail. A spell that doesn't list a duration takes place instantaneously, and anything created by it persists after the spell.

A horizontal line follows saving throws and duration, and the effects of the spell are described after this line. This section might also detail the possible results of a saving throw: critical success, success, failure, and critical failure.

Heightened (level) If the spell can be heightened, the effects of heightening it appear at the end of the stat block.

SPELL LISTS

These lists include the spells for each tradition, including cantrips. (Focus spells appear on pages 386–407.) A superscript "H" indicates a spell has extra effects when heightened, and a spell whose rarity is greater than common has a superscript with the first letter of that rarity. An abbreviation in parentheses indicates a spell's school.

ARCANE SPELLS

Arcane Cantrips

Acid Splashᴴ **(evo):** Damage creatures with acid.

Chill Touchᴴ **(nec):** Your touch hurts the living or disorients undead.

Dancing Lights (evo): Create four floating lights you can move.

Dazeᴴ **(enc):** Damage a creature's mind and possibly stun it.

Detect Magicᴴ **(div):** Sense whether magic is nearby.

Electric Arcᴴ **(evo):** Zap one or two creatures with lightning.

Ghost Soundᴴ **(ill):** Make false sounds.

Lightᴴ **(evo):** Make an object glow.

Mage Handᴴ **(evo):** Command a floating hand to move an object.

Messageᴴ **(ill):** Speak a message to a distant creature, who can reply.

Prestidigitation (evo): Perform a minor magical trick.

Produce Flameᴴ **(evo):** Kindle small flames to attack close or at range.

Ray of Frostᴴ **(evo):** Damage a creature with cold.

Read Auraᴴ **(div):** Detect if an object is magical, and determine the school of its magic.

Shieldᴴ **(abj):** A shield of magical force blocks attacks and *magic missiles*.

Sigilᴴ **(tra):** Leave a magical mark.

Tanglefootᴴ **(con):** Conjure a vine to entangle a creature.

Telekinetic Projectileᴴ **(evo):** Fling an object at a creature.

Arcane 1st-Level Spells

Air Bubble (con): React to create air for a creature to breathe.

Alarmᴴ **(abj):** Be alerted if a creature enters a warded area.

Ant Haul (tra): Target can carry more.

Burning Handsᴴ **(evo):** A small cone of flame rushes from your hands.

Charmᴴ **(enc):** A humanoid becomes more friendly to you.

Color Spray (ill): Swirling colors dazzle or stun creatures.

Commandᴴ **(enc):** Bid a creature to approach, run, release something, lie prone, or stand up.

Create Water (con): Conjure 2 gallons of water.

Fearᴴ **(enc):** Frighten a creature, possibly making it flee.

Feather Fall (abj): React to slow a creature's fall.

Fleet Step (tra): Make your Speed much faster.

Floating Disk (con): A disk of energy follows you, carrying objects.

Goblin Pox (nec): Infect a creature with goblin pox.

Grease (con): Coat a surface or object in slippery grease.

Grim Tendrilsᴴ **(nec):** Creatures in a line take negative damage and bleed.

Gust of Wind (evo): Wind blows out fires and knocks back objects and creatures.

Hydraulic Pushᴴ **(evo):** Damage and push a creature with a blast of water.

Illusory Disguiseᴴ **(ill):** Make yourself look like a different creature.

Illusory Objectᴴ **(ill):** Form a convincing illusion of an object.

Item Facadeᴴ **(ill):** Disguise an item to look perfect or shoddy.

Jumpᴴ **(tra):** Make an impressive leap.

Lockᴴ **(abj):** Make a lock hard to open.

Longstriderᴴ **(tra):** Increase your Speed for an hour.

Mage Armorᴴ **(abj):** Ward yourself with magical armor.

Magic Auraᵁᐟᴴ **(ill):** Change how an item's magic appears to detecting spells.

Magic Missileᴴ **(evo):** Pelt creatures with unerring bolts of magical force.

Magic Weapon (tra): Make a weapon temporarily magical.

Mendingᴴ **(tra):** Repair one non-magical item.

Negate Aromaᴴ **(abj):** Suppress a creature's scent.

Pest Formᴴ **(tra):** Turn into a nonthreatening animal.

Ray of Enfeeblement (nec): Sap a creature's strength.

Shocking Graspᴴ **(evo):** Zap a creature with electricity.

Sleepᴴ **(enc):** Cause creatures in a small area to fall asleep.

Spider Sting (nec): Damage a creature and afflict it with spider venom.

Summon Animalᴴ **(con):** Conjure an animal to fight on your behalf.

Summon Constructᴴ **(con):** Conjure a construct to fight on your behalf.

True Strike (div): Make your next attack especially accurate.

Unseen Servant (con): Create an invisible creature to help you.

Ventriloquismᴴ **(ill):** Throw your voice.

Arcane 2nd-Level Spells

Acid Arrowᴴ **(evo):** Magical arrow deals acid damage persistently.

Blur (ill): Cause a target's form to become blurry and hard to hit.

Comprehend Languageᴴ **(div):** A creature understands one language.

Continual Flameᴴ **(evo):** A magical flame burns indefinitely.

Create Foodᴴ **(con):** Conjure food that can feed multiple creatures.

Darknessᴴ **(evo):** Suppress all light in an area.

Darkvisionᴴ **(div):** See in the dark.

Deafness (nec): Make a creature deaf.

Dispel Magic (abj): End a spell or suppress an item's magic.

Endure Elementsᴴ **(abj):** Protect a creature from severe cold or heat.

Enlargeᴴ **(tra):** A creature grows in size.

False Lifeᴴ **(nec):** Gain temporary HP.

Flaming Sphereᴴ **(evo):** A ball of fire rolls about at your command.

Gentle Reposeᴴ **(nec):** A corpse doesn't decay and can't become undead.

Glitterdust (evo): Sparkling dust breaks invisibility and impedes vision.

Hideous Laughter (enc): Fits of laughter make a creature unable to take all its actions.

Humanoid Formᴴ **(tra):** Take the shape of a humanoid.

Illusory Creatureᴴ **(ill):** Form a convincing illusion of a creature.

Invisibilityᴴ **(ill):** A creature can't be seen until it attacks.

Knock (tra): Make a door, lock, or container easier to open, and possibly open it immediately.

Magic Mouth (ill): Make an illusory mouth appear to speak a message.

Mirror Image (ill): Illusory duplicates of you cause attacks to miss.

Misdirection (ill): Cause one creature's auras to appear to be another's.

Obscuring Mist (con): Conceal creatures in a cloud of mist.

Phantom Steedᴴ **(con):** Conjure a magical horse.

Resist Energyᴴ **(abj):** Protect a creature from one type of energy damage.

See Invisibilityᴴ **(div):** See invisible creatures and objects.

Shrinkᴴ **(tra):** Reduce a willing creature to Tiny size.

Spectral Hand (nec): Semicorporeal hand touches creatures to target them with your spells.

Spider Climbᴴ **(tra):** Give a creature a climb Speed.

Summon Elementalᴴ **(con):** Conjure an elemental to fight on your behalf.

Telekinetic Maneuver (evo): Disarm, Shove, or Trip a creature telekinetically.

Touch of Idiocy (enc): Dull a target's mind with a touch.

Water Breathingᴴ **(tra):** Allow creatures to breathe underwater.

Water Walk[H] **(tra):** Buoy a creature so it can walk on water.

Web[H] **(con):** Form a web that keeps creatures from moving.

ARCANE 3RD-LEVEL SPELLS

Bind Undead (nec): Take control of a mindless undead.

Blindness (nec): Strike a target blind.

Clairaudience (div): Hear through an invisible magical sensor.

Dream Message[H] **(enc):** Send a message that arrives in a dream.

Earthbind (tra): Bring a flying creature to the ground.

Enthrall (enc): Your speech makes creatures fascinated with you.

Feet to Fins[H] **(tra):** Turn a creature's feet into fins, enabling it swim but slowing it on land.

Fireball[H] **(evo):** An explosion of fire in an area burns creatures.

Ghostly Weapon (tra): Make a weapon affect incorporeal creatures.

Glyph of Warding (abj): Store a spell in a symbol to make a trap.

Haste[H] **(tra):** Speed up a creature so it can attack or move more often.

Hypnotic Pattern (ill): Shifting colors dazzle and fascinate creatures.

Invisibility Sphere[H] **(ill):** You and creatures near you become invisible as you explore.

Levitate (evo): Float an object or creature a few feet off the ground.

Lightning Bolt[H] **(evo):** Lightning strikes all creatures in a line.

Locate[U, H] **(div):** Learn the direction to an object.

Meld into Stone (tra): Meld into a block of stone.

Mind Reading[U] **(div):** Read a creature's surface thoughts.

Nondetection[U] **(abj):** Protect a creature or object from detection.

Paralyze[H] **(enc):** Freeze a humanoid in place.

Secret Page (ill): Alter the appearance of a page.

Shrink Item (tra): Reduce an object to the size of a coin.

Slow[H] **(tra):** Make a creature slower, reducing its actions.

Stinking Cloud (con): Form a cloud that sickens creatures.

Vampiric Touch[H] **(nec):** Deal negative damage and gain temporary HP with a touch.

Wall of Wind (evo): Create a wall of gusting winds that hinders movement and ranged attacks.

ARCANE 4TH-LEVEL SPELLS

Aerial Form[H] **(tra):** Turn into a flying combatant.

Blink[H] **(con):** Flit between the planes, vanishing and reappearing.

Clairvoyance (div): See through an invisible magical sensor.

Confusion[H] **(enc):** Befuddle a creature, making it act randomly.

Creation[H] **(con):** Make a temporary object.

Detect Scrying[U, H] **(div):** Find out if scrying effects are in the area.

Dimension Door[H] **(con):** Teleport yourself up to 120 feet.

Dimensional Anchor (abj): Keep a creature from teleporting or traveling to other planes.

Discern Lies[U] **(div):** Expertly detect lies and falsehoods.

Fire Shield[H] **(evo):** Flames protect you from cold and harm those that touch you.

Fly[H] **(tra):** Cause the target creature to gain a fly Speed.

Freedom of Movement (abj): A creature overcomes hindrances to its movement.

Gaseous Form (tra): Turn a willing creature into a flying cloud.

Globe of Invulnerability[U] **(abj):** Magical sphere counteracts spells that would enter it.

Hallucinatory Terrain[U, H] **(ill):** A natural environment appears to be another kind of terrain.

Nightmare (ill): Plague a creature's dreams with disturbing nightmares.

Outcast's Curse (enc): Curse a creature to be off-putting and grating.

Phantasmal Killer[H] **(ill):** Place a fearsome image in a creature's mind to scare and possibly kill it.

Private Sanctum[U] **(abj):** Black fog prevents sensing, scrying, and mind-reading on anyone within.

Resilient Sphere (abj): Create a sphere of force that blocks anything that would come through.

Rope Trick[U] **(con):** Animate a rope that rises to an extradimensional hiding place.

Shape Stone (tra): Reshape a cube of stone.

Solid Fog (con): Conjure heavy fog that obscures sight and is hard to move through.

Spell Immunity (abj): Name a spell to negate its effects on you.

Stoneskin (abj): Harden a creature's skin into durable stone.

Suggestion[H] **(enc):** Suggest a course of action a creature must follow.

Telepathy[H] **(div):** Communicate telepathically with any creatures near you.

Veil[H] **(ill):** Disguise many creatures as other creatures.

Wall of Fire[H] **(evo):** Create a blazing wall burns creatures that pass through.

Weapon Storm[H] **(evo):** Multiply a weapon you hold and attack many creatures with it.

ARCANE 5TH-LEVEL SPELLS

Banishment[H] **(abj):** Send a creature back to its home plane.

Black Tentacles (con): Tentacles in an area grab creatures.

Chromatic Wall[H] **(abj):** A wall of light offers a unique protection based on its color.

Cloak of Colors (ill): Bright colors dazzle creatures near the target, and attacks cause blinding flashes of light.

Cloudkill[H] **(nec):** Poison creatures in a cloud that moves away from you.

Cone of Cold[H] **(evo):** Bitter cold damages creatures in a cone.

Control Water (evo): Raise or lower water in a large area.

Crushing Despair[H] **(enc):** Make a creature sob uncontrollably.

Drop Dead[U, H] **(ill):** The target appears to die but actually turns invisible.

Elemental Form[H] **(tra):** Turn into an elemental.

False Vision[U] **(ill):** Trick a scrying spell.

Hallucination[H] **(ill):** A creature believes one thing is another, can't detect something, or sees something that's not really there.

Illusory Scene[H] **(ill):** Create an imaginary scene containing multiple creatures and objects.

Mariner's Curse (nec): Infect a creature with the curse of the rolling sea.

Mind Probe[U] **(div):** Uncover knowledge and memories in a creature's mind.

Passwall[U, H] **(con):** Form an earthen tunnel through a wall.

Prying Eye (div): An invisible eye transmits what it sees to you.

Sending (div): Send a mental message to a creature anywhere on the planet and get a reply.

Shadow Siphon (ill): React to lessen the damage from an enemy's spell by making it partially illusion.

Shadow Walk[U] **(con):** Travel rapidly via the Shadow Plane.

Subconscious Suggestion[H] **(enc):** Plant a mental suggestion that must be followed when a trigger occurs.

Summon Dragon[H] **(con):** Conjure a dragon to fight on your behalf.

Telekinetic Haul (evo): Move a large object.

Telepathic Bond[U] **(div):** Link minds with willing creatures to communicate telepathically at great distances.

Tongues[U, H] **(div):** Let a creature understand and speak all languages.

Wall of Ice[H] **(evo):** Sculpt a foot-thick wall of ice that blocks sight and can chill creatures.

Wall of Stone[H] **(con):** Shape a wall of stone.

ARCANE 6TH-LEVEL SPELLS

Baleful Polymorph (tra): Transform a creature into a harmless animal.

Chain Lightning[H] (evo): Lightning jumps from creature to creature.

Collective Transposition[H] (con): Teleport up to two creatures to new positions near you.

Disintegrate[H] (evo): Reduce a creature or object to dust.

Dominate[U, H] (enc): A humanoid must obey your orders.

Dragon Form[H] (tra): Turn into a dragon.

Feeblemind (enc): Stupefy a creature permanently.

Flesh To Stone (tra): Turn a living creature to a stone statue.

Mislead (ill): Turn invisible and create a duplicate of yourself who acts like you.

Phantasmal Calamity[H] (ill): Damage a creature mentally with visions of an apocalypse.

Purple Worm Sting (nec): Damage a creature and infect it with purple worm venom.

Repulsion (abj): Prevent creatures from approaching you.

Scrying[U] (div): Spy on a creature.

Spellwrack (abj): Curse a creature to be harmed when a spell is cast on it and lower the duration of its spells.

Teleport[U, H] (con): Transport you and willing creatures a great distance.

True Seeing (div): See through illusions and transmutations.

Vampiric Exsanguination[H] (nec): Draw blood and life force from creatures in a cone.

Vibrant Pattern (ill): Make a pattern of lights that dazzles and blinds.

Wall of Force[H] (evo): Create an invisible and durable wall of magical force.

ARCANE 7TH-LEVEL SPELLS

Contingency[H] (abj): Set up a spell to trigger later under your choice of circumstances.

Dimensional Lock[U] (abj): Prevent teleportation and planar travel.

Duplicate Foe[H] (con): Create a temporary duplicate of an enemy that fights for you.

Eclipse Burst[H] (nec): A globe of darkness deals cold damage, hurts the living, and overcomes light.

Energy Aegis[H] (abj): A creature gains resistance to acid, cold, electricity, fire, force, and sonic.

Fiery Body[H] (tra): Turn your body into living flame.

Magnificent Mansion[U] (con): Conjure a secure dwelling in a demiplane.

Mask of Terror[H] (ill): A creature's fearsome illusory appearance frightens observers.

Plane Shift[U] (con): Transport creatures to another plane of existence.

Power Word Blind[U, H] (enc): Utter a word that blinds a creature.

Prismatic Spray (evo): Shoot rainbow beams that have various effects on creatures in a cone.

Project Image[H] (ill): Make an illusion of yourself you can cast spells through.

Reverse Gravity[U] (evo): Flip the gravitational pull in an area.

Spell Turning[U] (abj): Reflect spells back at their caster.

True Target (div): Make multiple attacks against a creature especially accurate.

Warp Mind (enc): Confuse a creature, possibly permanently.

ARCANE 8TH-LEVEL SPELLS

Antimagic Field[R] (abj): Magic doesn't function in an area around you.

Disappearance (ill): Make a creature invisible, silent, and undetectable by any and all senses.

Discern Location[U] (div): Discover a target's exact location within unlimited range.

Dream Council (ill): Communicate through a shared dream.

Earthquake[H] (evo): Shake the ground with a devastating earthquake.

Horrid Wilting[H] (nec): Pull moisture from creatures, damaging them.

Maze (con): Trap a creature in an extradimensional maze.

Mind Blank[U] (abj): Protect a creature from mental magic and some divinations.

Monstrosity Form[H] (tra): Turn into a powerful monster.

Polar Ray[H] (evo): Bitter cold damages and drains a creature.

Power Word Stun[U, H] (enc): Utter a word that stuns a creature.

Prismatic Wall (abj): Form a protective wall with seven chromatic layers.

Scintillating Pattern (ill): Cause an array of color that dazzles, confuses, and stuns.

Uncontrollable Dance (enc): Overcome a target with an all-consuming urge to dance.

Unrelenting Observation (div): You and other creatures use scrying to track a subject exactly.

ARCANE 9TH-LEVEL SPELLS

Disjunction[U] (abj): Deactivate or destroy a magic item.

Foresight (div): Sense when a creature is in danger and React to protect it with good fortune.

Implosion[H] (evo): Make a creature collapse in on itself.

Massacre[H] (nec): Instantly kill multiple creatures.

Meteor Swarm[H] (evo): Call down four blazing meteors that explode.

Power Word Kill[U, H] (enc): Utter a word that slays a creature.

Prismatic Sphere (abj): Form a protective sphere composed of seven chromatic layers.

Resplendent Mansion (con): Conjure a mansion that lasts for a day.

Shapechange (tra): Transform into a form of your choice repeatedly.

Telepathic Demand (enc): Send a mental message that impels a creature toward a course of action.

Weird (ill): Frighten, deal mental damage, and possibly kill large numbers of creatures.

ARCANE 10TH-LEVEL SPELLS

Cataclysm (evo): Call an instant, damaging cataclysm.

Gate[U] (con): Tear open a portal to another plane.

Remake[U] (con): Recreate a destroyed object.

Time Stop (tra): Briefly stop time for everything but you.

Wish (div): Make a wish to duplicate arcane spells.

DIVINE SPELLS

DIVINE CANTRIPS

Chill Touch[H] (nec): Your touch hurts the living or disorients undead.

Daze[H] (enc): Damage a creature's mind and possibly stun it.

Detect Magic[H] (div): Sense whether magic is nearby.

Disrupt Undead[H] (nec): Damage undead with positive energy.

Divine Lance[H] (evo): Throw divine energy that damages based on your deity's alignment.

Forbidding Ward[H] (abj): Protect an ally against one specific enemy.

Guidance (div): Divine guidance improves one roll.

Know Direction[H] (div): Find true north.

Light[H] (evo): Make an object glow.

Message[H] (ill): Speak a message to a distant creature, who can reply.

Prestidigitation (evo): Perform a minor magical trick.

Read Aura[H] (div): Detect if an object is magical, and determine the school of its magic.

Shield[H] (abj): A shield of magical force blocks attacks and *magic missiles*.

Sigil[H] (tra): Leave a magical mark.

Stabilize (nec): Stabilize a dying creature.

DIVINE 1ST-LEVEL SPELLS

Air Bubble (con): React to create air for a creature to breathe.

Alarm[H] (abj): Be alerted if a creature enters a warded area.

Bane (enc): Weaken enemies' attacks in an aura around you.

Bless (enc): Strengthen allies' attacks in an aura around you.

Command^H (enc): Bid a creature to approach, run, release something, lie prone, or stand up.

Create Water (con): Conjure 2 gallons of water.

Detect Alignment^U, H (div): See auras of a chosen alignment.

Detect Poison^U, H (div): Determine whether an object or creature is poisonous or venomous.

Disrupting Weapons^H (nec): Weapons deal positive damage to undead.

Fear^H (enc): Frighten a creature, possibly making it flee.

Harm^H (nec): Negative energy harms the living or heals the undead, either a single creature or all in a burst.

Heal^H (nec): Positive energy heals the living or harms the undead, either a single creature or all in a burst.

Lock^H (abj): Make a lock hard to open.

Magic Weapon (tra): Make a weapon temporarily magical.

Mending^H (tra): Repair one non-magical item.

Protection^U (abj): Shield a creature against those of a chosen alignment.

Purify Food And Drink (nec): Make beverages and meals safe.

Ray of Enfeeblement (nec): Sap a creature's strength.

Sanctuary (abj): Protect a creature from being attacked.

Spirit Link^H (nec): Continually transfer your health to someone else.

Ventriloquism^H (ill): Throw your voice.

DIVINE 2ND-LEVEL SPELLS

Augury (div): Predict whether a course of action brings good fortune.

Calm Emotions (enc): Suppress strong emotions and hostility.

Comprehend Language^H (div): A creature understands one language.

Continual Flame^H (evo): A magical flame burns indefinitely.

Create Food^H (con): Conjure food that can feed multiple creatures.

Darkness^H (evo): Suppress all light in an area.

Darkvision^H (div): See in the dark.

Deafness (nec): Make a creature deaf.

Death Knell (nec): Finish off a creature who's near death.

Dispel Magic (abj): End a spell or suppress an item's magic.

Endure Elements^H (abj): Protect a creature from severe cold or heat.

Enhance Victuals^H (tra): Improve food or drink and remove poisons.

Faerie Fire (evo): Colorful light prevents creatures from being concealed or invisible.

Gentle Repose^H (nec): A corpse doesn't decay and can't become undead.

Ghoulish Cravings (nec): Infect a creature with ghoul fever.

Remove Fear^H (enc): Free a creature from its fright.

Remove Paralysis^H (nec): Free a creature from paralysis.

Resist Energy^H (abj): Protect a creature from one type of energy damage.

Restoration^H (nec): Reduce a condition or lessen a toxin.

Restore Senses^H (nec): Remove a blinding or deafening effect.

See Invisibility^H (div): See invisible creatures and objects.

Shield Other (nec): Absorb half the damage an ally would take.

Silence^H (ill): Mute all sound from a creature.

Sound Burst^H (evo): Damage and deafen creatures with a powerful din.

Spiritual Weapon^H (evo): Materialize a deific weapon of force that appears and attacks repeatedly.

Status^H (div): Keep track of a willing creature's location and well-being.

Undetectable Alignment^U (abj): Make a creature or object appear neutral to alignment detection.

Water Breathing^H (tra): Allow creatures to breathe underwater.

Water Walk^H (tra): Buoy a creature so it can walk on water.

DIVINE 3RD-LEVEL SPELLS

Bind Undead (nec): Take control of a mindless undead.

Blindness (nec): Strike a target blind.

Chilling Darkness^H (evo): Ray of evil darkness deals cold damage, counteracts light, and harms celestials.

Circle of Protection^U, H (abj): A creature emits an aura that protects those within against an alignment.

Crisis of Faith^H (enc): Cause mental damage and possibly make a worshipper unable to cast spells.

Dream Message^H (enc): Send a message that arrives in a dream.

Glyph of Warding (abj): Store a spell in a symbol to make a trap.

Heroism^H (enc): Stoke a creature's inner heroism to make it more competent.

Locate^U, H (div): Learn the direction to an object.

Neutralize Poison (nec): Cure a poison afflicting a creature.

Remove Disease (nec): Cure a disease afflicting a creature.

Sanctified Ground (abj): Create a 24-hour area of protection against aberrations, celestials, dragons, fiends, or undead.

Searing Light^H (evo): A ray of burning light deals extra damage to undead and counteracts darkness.

Vampiric Touch^H (nec): Deal negative damage and gain temporary HP with a touch.

Wanderer's Guide (div): Find an ideal route to a location.

Zone of Truth^U (enc): Compel creatures to tell the truth.

DIVINE 4TH-LEVEL SPELLS

Air Walk (tra): Walk on air as though it were solid ground.

Anathematic Reprisal^H (enc): Cause mental pain to one who commits anathema against your deity.

Dimensional Anchor (abj): Keep a creature from teleporting or traveling to other planes.

Discern Lies^U (div): Expertly detect lies and falsehoods.

Divine Wrath^H (evo): Damage and hinder creatures of alignments opposed by your deity.

Freedom of Movement (abj): A creature overcomes hindrances to its movement.

Globe of Invulnerability^U (abj): Magical sphere counteracts spells that would enter it.

Holy Cascade^H (evo): Turn a vial of *holy water* into an explosion of blessed water.

Outcast's Curse (enc): Curse a creature to be off-putting and grating.

Read Omens^U (div): Get a piece of advice about an upcoming event.

Remove Curse (nec): Counteract a curse afflicting a creature.

Spell Immunity (abj): Name a spell to negate its effects on you.

Talking Corpse^U (nec): Have a corpse answer three questions.

Vital Beacon^H (nec): Radiate vitality that heals creatures that touch you.

DIVINE 5TH-LEVEL SPELLS

Abyssal Plague (nec): Inflict a draining curse.

Banishment^H (abj): Send a creature back to its home plane.

Breath of Life (nec): React to revive a creature at the moment of its death.

Death Ward (abj): Protect a creature against negative energy.

Drop Dead^U, H (ill): The target appears to die but actually turns invisible.

Flame Strike^H (evo): Call divine fire from the sky.

Prying Eye (div): An invisible eye transmits what it sees to you.

Sending (div): Send a mental message to a creature anywhere on the planet and get a reply.

Shadow Blast^H (evo): Shape a cone of shadow to deal damage of a type you choose.

Spiritual Guardian[H] **(abj):** Create a magical guardian to attack at your command and take damage for your allies.

Summon Celestial[H] **(con):** Conjure a celestial to fight on your behalf.

Summon Fiend[H] **(con):** Conjure a fiend to fight on your behalf.

Tongues[U, H] **(div):** Let a creature understand and speak all languages.

Divine 6th-Level Spells

Blade Barrier[H] **(evo):** Form a wall of swords made of force.

Field of Life[H] **(nec):** Create a positive energy field that heals those within.

Raise Dead[U, H] **(nec):** Return a dead creature to life.

Repulsion (abj): Prevent creatures from approaching you.

Righteous Might[H] **(tra):** Turn into a battle form with divine armaments.

Spellwrack (abj): Curse a creature to be harmed when a spell is cast on it and lower the duration of its spells.

Spirit Blast[H] **(nec):** Damage a creature's spiritual essence.

Stone Tell[U] **(div):** Speak to spirits within natural stone.

Stone to Flesh (tra): Turn a creature turned to stone back to flesh.

True Seeing (div): See through illusions and transmutations.

Vampiric Exsanguination[H] **(nec):** Draw blood and life force from creatures in a cone.

Zealous Conviction[H] **(enc):** Instill unshakable conviction and zeal in willing creatures.

Divine 7th-Level Spells

Dimensional Lock[U] **(abj):** Prevent teleportation and planar travel.

Divine Decree[H] **(evo):** Creatures of alignments opposed by your deity are damaged, enfeebled, paralyzed, or banished.

Divine Vessel[H] **(tra):** Take on aspects of a servitor of your deity.

Eclipse Burst[H] **(nec):** A globe of darkness deals cold damage, hurts the living, and overcomes light.

Energy Aegis[H] **(abj):** A creature gains resistance to acid, cold, electricity, fire, force, and sonic.

Ethereal Jaunt[U, H] **(con):** Use the Ethereal Plane to move through objects and into the air.

Finger of Death[H] **(nec):** Point at a creature to deal negative damage and possibly kill it instantly.

Plane Shift[U] **(con):** Transport creatures to another plane of existence.

Regenerate[H] **(nec):** Cause a creature to heal over time, regrow organs, and reattach body parts.

Sunburst[H] **(evo):** A globe of sunlight deals fire damage, hurts undead, and overcomes darkness.

Divine 8th-Level Spells

Antimagic Field[R] **(abj):** Magic doesn't function in an area around you.

Discern Location[U] **(div):** Discover a target's exact location within unlimited range.

Divine Aura (abj): Allies in an aura have better defenses and are protected against one alignment.

Divine Inspiration (enc): Spiritual energy recovers a creature's expended spell.

Moment of Renewal (nec): Give a day's recovery in an instant.

Spiritual Epidemic (nec): Weaken a target with a communicable curse.

Divine 9th-Level Spells

Bind Soul[U] **(nec):** Imprison a dead creature's soul.

Crusade[U, H] **(enc):** Creatures become dedicated to a cause of your choice.

Foresight (div): Sense when a creature is in danger and React to protect it with good fortune.

Massacre[H] **(nec):** Instantly kill multiple creatures.

Overwhelming Presence (enc): Take on the majesty of a god.

Telepathic Demand (enc): Send a mental message that impels a creature toward a course of action.

Wail of the Banshee (nec): Scream, dealing damage and draining creatures.

Weapon of Judgment[H] **(evo):** Form a weapon to enforce war or peace.

Divine 10th-Level Spells

Avatar (tra): Transform into a battle form determined by your deity.

Gate[U] **(con):** Tear open a portal to another plane.

Miracle (div): Ask for a blessing to duplicate divine spells.

Remake[U] **(con):** Recreate a destroyed object.

Revival (nec): Heal creatures in an area and return the dead to life temporarily.

OCCULT SPELLS

Occult Cantrips

Chill Touch[H] **(nec):** Your touch hurts the living or disorients undead.

Dancing Lights (evo): Create four floating lights you can move.

Daze[H] **(enc):** Damage a creature's mind and possibly stun it.

Detect Magic[H] **(div):** Sense whether magic is nearby.

Forbidding Ward[H] **(abj):** Protect an ally against one specific enemy.

Ghost Sound[H] **(ill):** Make false sounds.

Guidance (div): Divine guidance improves one roll.

Know Direction[H] **(div):** Find true north.

Light[H] **(evo):** Make an object glow.

Mage Hand[H] **(evo):** Command a floating hand to move an object.

Message[H] **(ill):** Speak a message to a distant creature, who can reply.

Prestidigitation (evo): Perform a minor magical trick.

Read Aura[H] **(div):** Detect if an object is magical, and determine the school of its magic.

Shield[H] **(abj):** A shield of magical force blocks attacks and *magic missiles*.

Sigil[H] **(tra):** Leave a magical mark.

Telekinetic Projectile[H] **(evo):** Fling an object at a creature.

Occult 1st-Level Spells

Alarm[H] **(abj):** Be alerted if a creature enters a warded area.

Bane (enc): Weaken enemies' attacks in an aura around you.

Bless (enc): Strengthen allies' attacks in an aura around you.

Charm[H] **(enc):** A humanoid becomes more friendly to you.

Color Spray (ill): Swirling colors dazzle or stun creatures.

Command[H] **(enc):** Bid a creature to approach, run, release something, lie prone, or stand up.

Detect Alignment[U, H] **(div):** See auras of a chosen alignment.

Fear[H] **(enc):** Frighten a creature, possibly making it flee.

Floating Disk (con): A disk of energy follows you, carrying objects.

Grim Tendrils[H] **(nec):** Creatures in a line take negative damage and bleed.

Illusory Disguise[H] **(ill):** Make yourself look like a different creature.

Illusory Object[H] **(ill):** Form a convincing illusion of an object.

Item Facade[H] **(ill):** Disguise an item to look perfect or shoddy.

Lock[H] **(abj):** Make a lock hard to open.

Mage Armor[H] **(abj):** Ward yourself with magical armor.

Magic Aura[U, H] **(ill):** Change how an item's magic appears to detecting spells.

Magic Missile[H] **(evo):** Pelt creatures with unerring bolts of magical force.

Magic Weapon (tra): Make a weapon temporarily magical.

Mending[H] **(tra):** Repair one non-magical item.

Mindlink (div): Mentally impart 10 minutes' worth of information in an instant.

Phantom Pain[H] **(ill):** Cause a creature ongoing pain that sickens it.

Protection[U] **(abj):** Shield a creature against those of a chosen alignment.

Ray of Enfeeblement (nec): Sap a creature's strength.

Sanctuary (abj): Protect a creature from being attacked.

Sleep[H] (enc): Cause creatures in a small area to fall asleep.

Soothe[H] (nec): Heal the target and bolster them against mental attacks.

Spirit Link[H] (nec): Continually transfer your health to someone else.

Summon Fey[H] (con): Conjure a fey to fight on your behalf.

True Strike (div): Make your next attack especially accurate.

Unseen Servant (con): Create an invisible creature to help you.

Ventriloquism[H] (ill): Throw your voice.

Occult 2nd-Level Spells

Augury (div): Predict whether a course of action brings good fortune.

Blur (ill): Cause a target's form to become blurry and hard to hit.

Calm Emotions (enc): Suppress strong emotions and hostility.

Comprehend Language[H] (div): A creature understands one language.

Continual Flame[H] (evo): A magical flame burns indefinitely.

Darkness[H] (evo): Suppress all light in an area.

Darkvision[H] (div): See in the dark.

Deafness (nec): Make a creature deaf.

Death Knell (nec): Finish off a creature who's near death.

Dispel Magic (abj): End a spell or suppress an item's magic.

Faerie Fire (evo): Colorful light prevents creatures from being concealed or invisible.

False Life[H] (nec): Gain temporary HP.

Gentle Repose[H] (nec): A corpse doesn't decay and can't become undead.

Ghoulish Cravings (nec): Infect a creature with ghoul fever.

Hideous Laughter (enc): Fits of laughter make a creature unable to take all its actions.

Humanoid Form[H] (tra): Take the shape of a humanoid.

Illusory Creature[H] (ill): Form a convincing illusion of a creature.

Invisibility[H] (ill): A creature can't be seen until it attacks.

Knock (tra): Make a door, lock, or container easier to open, and possibly open it immediately.

Magic Mouth (ill): Make an illusory mouth appear to speak a message.

Mirror Image (ill): Illusory duplicates of you cause attacks to miss.

Misdirection (ill): Cause one creature's auras to appear to be another's.

Paranoia[H] (ill): Make a creature believe everyone is a threat.

Phantom Steed[H] (con): Conjure a magical horse.

Remove Fear[H] (enc): Free a creature from its fright.

Remove Paralysis[H] (nec): Free a creature from paralysis.

Resist Energy[H] (abj): Protect a creature from one type of energy damage.

Restoration[H] (nec): Reduce a condition or lessen a toxin.

Restore Senses[H] (nec): Remove a blinding or deafening effect.

See Invisibility[H] (div): See invisible creatures and objects.

Shatter[H] (evo): Shatter an object with a high-frequency sonic attack.

Silence[H] (ill): Mute all sound from a creature.

Sound Burst[H] (evo): Damage and deafen creatures with a powerful din.

Spectral Hand (nec): Create a semicorporeal hand that touches creatures to target them with your spells.

Spiritual Weapon[H] (evo): Materialize a deific weapon of force that appears and attacks repeatedly.

Status[H] (div): Keep track of a willing creature's location and well-being.

Telekinetic Maneuver (evo): Disarm, Shove, or Trip a creature telekinetically.

Touch of Idiocy (enc): Dull a target's mind with a touch.

Undetectable Alignment[U] (abj): Make a creature or object appear neutral to alignment detection.

Occult 3rd-Level Spells

Bind Undead (nec): Take control of a mindless undead.

Blindness (nec): Strike a target blind.

Circle of Protection[U, H] (abj): A creature emits an aura that protects those within against an alignment.

Clairaudience (div): Hear through an invisible magical sensor.

Dream Message[H] (enc): Send a message that arrives in a dream.

Enthrall (enc): Your speech makes creatures fascinated with you.

Ghostly Weapon (tra): Make a weapon affect incorporeal creatures.

Glyph of Warding (abj): Store a spell in a symbol to make a trap.

Haste[H] (tra): Speed up a creature so it can attack or move more often.

Heroism[H] (enc): Stoke a creature's inner heroism to make it more competent.

Hypercognition (div): Recall massive amounts of information in an instant.

Hypnotic Pattern (ill): Shifting colors dazzle and fascinate creatures.

Invisibility Sphere[H] (ill): You and creatures near you become invisible as you explore.

Levitate (evo): Float an object or creature a few feet off the ground.

Locate[U, H] (div): Learn the direction to an object.

Mind Reading[U] (div): Read a creature's surface thoughts.

Nondetection[U] (abj): Protect a creature or object from detection.

Paralyze[H] (enc): Freeze a humanoid in place.

Secret Page (ill): Alter the appearance of a page.

Slow[H] (tra): Make a creature slower, reducing its actions.

Vampiric Touch[H] (nec): Deal negative damage and gain temporary HP with a touch.

Wanderer's Guide (div): Find an ideal route to a location.

Zone of Truth[U] (enc): Designate an area where creatures are compelled to be truthful.

Occult 4th-Level Spells

Blink[H] (con): Flit between the planes, vanishing and reappearing.

Clairvoyance (div): See through an invisible magical sensor.

Confusion[H] (enc): Befuddle a creature, making it act randomly.

Detect Scrying[U, H] (div): Find out if scrying effects are in the area.

Dimension Door[H] (con): Teleport yourself up to 120 feet.

Dimensional Anchor (abj): Keep a creature from teleporting or traveling to other planes.

Discern Lies[U] (div): Expertly detect lies and falsehoods.

Fly[H] (tra): Cause the target creature to gain a fly Speed.

Gaseous Form (tra): Turn a willing creature into a flying cloud.

Glibness[U] (enc): Lie with impunity.

Globe of Invulnerability[U] (abj): Magical sphere counteracts spells that would enter it.

Hallucinatory Terrain[U, H] (ill): A natural environment appears to be another kind of terrain.

Modify Memory[U, H] (div): Change or implant memories.

Nightmare (ill): Plague a creature's dreams with disturbing nightmares.

Outcast's Curse (enc): Curse a creature to be off-putting and grating.

Phantasmal Killer[H] (ill): Place a fearsome image in a creature's mind to scare and possibly kill it.

Private Sanctum[U] (abj): Black fog prevents sensing, scrying, and mind-reading on anyone within.

Read Omens[U] (div): Get a piece of advice about an upcoming event.

Remove Curse (nec): Counteract a curse afflicting a creature.

Resilient Sphere (abj): Create a sphere of force that blocks anything that would come through.

Rope Trick[U] (con): Animate a rope that rises to an extradimensional hiding place.

Spell Immunity (abj): Name a spell to negate its effects on you.

Suggestion[H] **(enc):** Suggest a course of action a creature must follow.

Talking Corpse[U] **(nec):** Have a corpse answer three questions.

Telepathy[H] **(div):** Communicate telepathically with any creatures near you.

Veil[H] **(ill):** Disguise many creatures as other creatures.

Occult 5th-Level Spells

Abyssal Plague (nec): Inflict a draining curse.

Banishment[H] **(abj):** Send a creature back to its home plane.

Black Tentacles (con): Tentacles in an area grab creatures.

Chromatic Wall[H] **(abj):** A wall of light offers a unique protection based on its color.

Cloak of Colors (ill): Bright colors dazzle creatures near the target, and attacks cause blinding flashes of light.

Crushing Despair[H] **(enc):** Make a creature sob uncontrollably.

Death Ward (abj): Protect a creature against negative energy.

Dreaming Potential (enc): The target retrains in its dreams.

False Vision[U] **(ill):** Trick a scrying spell.

Hallucination[H] **(ill):** A creature believes one thing is another, can't detect something, or sees something that's not really there.

Illusory Scene[H] **(ill):** Create an imaginary scene containing multiple creatures and objects.

Mariner's Curse (nec): Infect a creature with the curse of the rolling sea.

Mind Probe[U] **(div):** Uncover knowledge and memories in a creature's mind.

Prying Eye (div): An invisible eye transmits what it sees to you.

Sending (div): Send a mental message to a creature anywhere on the planet and get a reply.

Shadow Blast[H] **(evo):** Shape a cone of shadow to deal damage of a type you choose.

Shadow Siphon (ill): React to lessen the damage from an enemy's spell by making it partially illusion.

Shadow Walk[U] **(con):** Travel rapidly via the Shadow Plane.

Subconscious Suggestion[H] **(enc):** Plant a mental suggestion that must be followed when a trigger occurs.

Summon Entity[H] **(con):** Conjure an aberration to fight on your behalf.

Synaptic Pulse (enc): Slow creatures with a mental blast.

Synesthesia[H] **(div):** Rewire a creature's senses.

Telekinetic Haul (evo): Move a large object.

Telepathic Bond[U] **(div):** Link minds with willing creatures to communicate telepathically at great distances.

Tongues[U, H] **(div):** Let a creature understand and speak all languages.

Occult 6th-Level Spells

Collective Transposition[H] **(con):** Teleport up to two creatures to new positions near you.

Dominate[U, H] **(enc):** A humanoid must obey your orders.

Feeblemind (enc): Stupefy a creature permanently.

Mislead (ill): Turn invisible and create a duplicate of yourself who acts like you.

Phantasmal Calamity[H] **(ill):** Damage a creature mentally with visions of an apocalypse.

Repulsion (abj): Prevent creatures from approaching you.

Scrying[U] **(div):** Spy on a creature.

Spellwrack (abj): Curse a creature to be harmed when a spell is cast on it and lower the duration of its spells.

Spirit Blast[H] **(nec):** Damage a creature's spiritual essence.

Teleport[U, H] **(con):** Transport you and willing creatures a great distance.

True Seeing (div): See through illusions and transmutations.

Vampiric Exsanguination[H] **(nec):** Draw blood and life force from creatures in a cone.

Vibrant Pattern (ill): Make a pattern of lights that dazzles and blinds.

Wall of Force[H] **(evo):** Create an invisible and durable wall of magical force.

Zealous Conviction[H] **(enc):** Instill unshakable conviction and zeal in willing creatures.

Occult 7th-Level Spells

Dimensional Lock[U] **(abj):** Prevent teleportation and planar travel.

Duplicate Foe[H] **(con):** Create a temporary duplicate of an enemy that fights for you.

Energy Aegis[H] **(abj):** A creature gains resistance to acid, cold, electricity, fire, force, and sonic.

Ethereal Jaunt[U, H] **(con):** Use the Ethereal Plane to move through objects and into the air.

Magnificent Mansion[U] **(con):** Conjure a secure dwelling in a demiplane.

Mask of Terror[H] **(ill):** A creature's fearsome illusory appearance frightens observers.

Plane Shift[U] **(con):** Transport creatures to another plane of existence.

Possession[U, H] **(nec):** Send your mind and soul into another creature's body.

Prismatic Spray (evo): Shoot rainbow beams that have various effects on creatures in a cone.

Project Image[H] **(ill):** Make an illusion of yourself you can cast spells through.

Retrocognition[H] **(div):** Sense impressions of past events at your location.

Reverse Gravity[U] **(evo):** Flip the gravitational pull in an area.

True Target (div): Make multiple attacks against a creature especially accurate.

Visions of Danger[H] **(ill):** Create a vision of horrid, swarming creatures that causes mental damage.

Warp Mind (enc): Confuse a creature, possibly permanently.

Occult 8th-Level Spells

Antimagic Field[R] **(abj):** Magic doesn't function in an area around you.

Disappearance (ill): Make a creature invisible, silent, and undetectable by any and all senses.

Discern Location[U] **(div):** Discover a target's exact location within unlimited range.

Dream Council (ill): Communicate through a shared dream.

Maze (con): Trap a creature in an extradimensional maze.

Mind Blank[U] **(abj):** Protect a creature from mental magic and some divinations.

Prismatic Wall (abj): Form a protective wall with seven chromatic layers.

Scintillating Pattern (ill): Cause an array of color that dazzles, confuses, and stuns.

Spirit Song[H] **(nec):** Sing an eldritch song that damages any creature that has a spirit.

Spiritual Epidemic (nec): Weaken a target with a communicable curse.

Uncontrollable Dance (enc): Overcome a target with an all-consuming urge to dance.

Unrelenting Observation (div): You and other creatures use scrying to track a subject exactly.

Occult 9th-Level Spells

Bind Soul[U] **(nec):** Imprison a dead creature's soul.

Foresight (div): Sense when a creature is in danger and React to protect it with good fortune.

Overwhelming Presence (enc): Take on the majesty of a god.

Prismatic Sphere (abj): Form a protective sphere composed of seven chromatic layers.

Resplendent Mansion (con): Conjure a mansion that lasts for a day.

Telepathic Demand (enc): Send a mental message that impels a creature toward a course of action.

Unfathomable Song (enc): Song debilitates creatures in weird ways.

INTRODUCTION

ANCESTRIES & BACKGROUNDS

CLASSES

SKILLS

FEATS

EQUIPMENT

SPELLS

THE AGE OF LOST OMENS

PLAYING THE GAME

GAME MASTERING

CRAFTING & TREASURE

APPENDIX

Wail of the Banshee (nec): Scream, dealing damage and draining creatures.

Weird (ill): Frighten, deal mental damage, and possibly kill large numbers of creatures.

OCCULT 10TH-LEVEL SPELLS

Alter Reality (div): Warp reality to duplicate occult spells.

Fabricated Truth (enc): Make creatures believe something is fact.

Gate^U (con): Tear open a portal to another plane.

Remake^U (con): Recreate a destroyed object.

Time Stop (tra): Briefly stop time for everything but you.

PRIMAL SPELLS

PRIMAL CANTRIPS

Acid Splash^H (evo): Damage creatures with acid.

Dancing Lights (evo): Create four floating lights you can move.

Detect Magic^H (div): Sense whether magic is nearby.

Disrupt Undead^H (nec): Damage undead with positive energy.

Electric Arc^H (evo): Zap one or two creatures with lightning.

Guidance (div): Divine guidance improves one roll.

Know Direction^H (div): Find true north.

Light^H (evo): Make an object glow.

Prestidigitation (evo): Perform a minor magical trick.

Produce Flame^H (evo): Kindle small flames to attack close or at range.

Ray of Frost^H (evo): Damage a creature with cold.

Read Aura^H (div): Detect if an object is magical, and determine the school of its magic.

Sigil^H (tra): Leave a magical mark.

Stabilize (nec): Stabilize a dying creature.

Tanglefoot^H (con): Conjure a vine to entangle a creature.

PRIMAL 1ST-LEVEL SPELLS

Air Bubble (con): React to create air for a creature to breathe.

Alarm^H (abj): Be alerted if a creature enters a warded area.

Ant Haul (tra): Target can carry more.

Burning Hands^H (evo): A small cone of flame rushes from your hands.

Charm^H (enc): A humanoid becomes more friendly to you.

Create Water (con): Conjure 2 gallons of water.

Detect Poison^{U, H} (div): Determine whether an object or creature is poisonous or venomous.

Fear^H (enc): Frighten a creature, possibly making it flee.

Feather Fall (abj): React to slow a creature's fall.

Fleet Step (tra): Make your Speed much faster.

Goblin Pox (nec): Infect a creature with goblin pox.

Grease (con): Coat a surface or object in slippery grease.

Gust of Wind (evo): Wind blows out fires and knocks back objects and creatures.

Heal^H (nec): Positive energy heals the living or harms the undead, either a single creature or all in a burst.

Hydraulic Push^H (evo): Damage and push a creature with a blast of water.

Jump^H (tra): Make an impressive leap.

Longstrider^H (tra): Increase your Speed for an hour.

Magic Fang (tra): Make a creature's unarmed attacks magical temporarily.

Mending^H (tra): Repair one non-magical item.

Negate Aroma^H (abj): Suppress a creature's scent.

Pass without Trace^H (abj): Make your tracks hard to find.

Pest Form^H (tra): Turn into a nonthreatening animal.

Purify Food And Drink (nec): Make beverages and meals safe.

Shillelagh (tra): Make a club or staff temporarily magical, and deal more damage to unnatural creatures.

Shocking Grasp^H (evo): Zap a creature with electricity.

Spider Sting (nec): Damage a creature and afflict it with spider venom.

Summon Animal^H (con): Conjure an animal to fight on your behalf.

Summon Fey^H (con): Conjure a fey to fight on your behalf.

Summon Plants and Fungi^H (con): Conjure a plant or fungus to fight on your behalf.

Ventriloquism^H (ill): Throw your voice.

PRIMAL 2ND-LEVEL SPELLS

Acid Arrow^H (evo): Magical arrow deals acid damage persistently.

Animal Form^H (tra): Turn into a dangerous animal.

Animal Messenger (enc): Send a Tiny animal to deliver a message.

Barkskin^H (abj): Target's skin is covered in protective bark.

Continual Flame^H (evo): A magical flame burns indefinitely.

Create Food^H (con): Conjure food that can feed multiple creatures.

Darkness^H (evo): Suppress all light in an area.

Darkvision^H (div): See in the dark.

Deafness (nec): Make a creature deaf.

Dispel Magic (abj): End a spell or suppress an item's magic.

Endure Elements^H (abj): Protect a creature from severe cold or heat.

Enhance Victuals^H (tra): Improve food or drink and remove poisons.

Enlarge^H (tra): A creature grows in size.

Entangle (tra): Plants in an area grow to entangle and immobilize.

Faerie Fire (evo): Colorful light prevents creatures from being concealed or invisible.

Flaming Sphere^H (evo): A ball of fire rolls about at your command.

Gentle Repose^H (nec): A corpse doesn't decay and can't become undead.

Glitterdust (evo): Sparkling dust breaks invisibility and impedes vision.

Humanoid Form^H (tra): Take the shape of a humanoid.

Obscuring Mist (con): Conceal creatures in a cloud of mist.

Phantom Steed^H (con): Conjure a magical horse.

Remove Fear^H (enc): Free a creature from its fright.

Remove Paralysis^H (nec): Free a creature from paralysis.

Resist Energy^H (abj): Protect a creature from one type of energy damage.

Restoration^H (nec): Reduce a condition or lessen a toxin.

Restore Senses^H (nec): Remove a blinding or deafening effect.

Shape Wood (tra): Reshape unworked wood as you choose.

Shatter^H (evo): Shatter an object with a high-frequency sonic attack.

Shrink^H (tra): Reduce a willing creature to Tiny size.

Speak with Animals (div): Communicate with animals.

Spider Climb^H (tra): Give a creature a climb Speed.

Status^H (div): Keep track of a willing creature's location and well-being.

Summon Elemental^H (con): Conjure an elemental to fight on your behalf.

Tree Shape (tra): Turn into a tree.

Water Breathing^H (tra): Allow creatures to breathe underwater.

Water Walk^H (tra): Buoy a creature so it can walk on water.

Web^H (con): Form a web that keeps creatures from moving.

PRIMAL 3RD-LEVEL SPELLS

Animal Vision (div): Project your senses through an animal.

Blindness (nec): Strike a target blind.

Earthbind (tra): Bring a flying creature to the ground.

Feet to Fins^H (tra): Turn a creature's feet into fins, enabling it swim but slowing it on land.

Fireball^H (evo): An explosion of fire in an area burns creatures.

Glyph of Warding (abj): Store a spell in a symbol to make a trap.

Haste[H] **(tra):** Speed up a creature so it can attack or move more often.

Insect Form[H] **(tra):** Turn into a dangerous giant insect.

Lightning Bolt[H] **(evo):** Lightning strikes all creatures in a line.

Meld into Stone (tra): Meld into a block of stone.

Neutralize Poison (nec): Cure a poison afflicting a creature.

Nondetection[U] **(abj):** Protect a creature or object from detection.

Remove Disease (nec): Cure a disease afflicting a creature.

Searing Light[H] **(evo):** A ray of burning light deals extra damage to undead and counteracts darkness.

Slow[H] **(tra):** Make a creature slower, reducing its actions.

Stinking Cloud (con): Form a cloud that sickens creatures.

Wall of Thorns[H] **(con):** Grow a wall of brambles.

Wall of Wind (evo): Create a wall of gusting winds that hinders movement and ranged attacks.

Primal 4th-Level Spells

Aerial Form[H] **(tra):** Turn into a flying combatant.

Air Walk (tra): Walk on air as though it were solid ground.

Creation[H] **(con):** Make a temporary object.

Dinosaur Form[H] **(tra):** Turn into a dinosaur.

Fire Shield[H] **(evo):** Flames protect you from cold and harm those that touch you.

Fly[H] **(tra):** Cause the target creature to gain a fly Speed.

Freedom of Movement (abj): A creature overcomes hindrances to its movement.

Gaseous Form (tra): Turn a willing creature into a flying cloud.

Hallucinatory Terrain[U, H] **(ill):** A natural environment appears to be another kind of terrain.

Hydraulic Torrent[H] **(evo):** Force creatures back with a damaging line of water.

Shape Stone (tra): Reshape a cube of stone.

Solid Fog (con): Conjure heavy fog that obscures sight and is hard to move through.

Speak with Plants (div): Communicate with plants and plant creatures.

Stoneskin[H] **(abj):** Harden a creature's skin into durable stone.

Vital Beacon[H] **(nec):** Radiate vitality that heals creatures that touch you.

Wall of Fire[H] **(evo):** Create a blazing wall burns creatures that pass through.

Weapon Storm[H] **(evo):** Multiply a weapon you hold and attack many creatures with it.

Primal 5th-Level Spells

Banishment[H] **(abj):** Send a creature back to its home plane.

Cloudkill (nec): Poison creatures in a cloud that moves away from you.

Cone of Cold[H] **(evo):** Bitter cold damages creatures in a cone.

Control Water (evo): Raise or lower water in a large area.

Death Ward (abj): Protect a creature against negative energy.

Elemental Form[H] **(tra):** Turn into an elemental.

Mariner's Curse (nec): Infect a creature with the curse of the rolling sea.

Moon Frenzy[H] **(tra):** Give willing creatures fangs and claws, and send them into a frenzy.

Passwall[U, H] **(con):** Form an earthen tunnel through a wall.

Plant Form[H] **(tra):** Turn into a dangerous plant creature.

Summon Giant[H] **(con):** Conjure a giant to fight on your behalf.

Tree Stride[U, H] **(con):** Teleport from tree to tree.

Wall of Ice[H] **(evo):** Sculpt a foot-thick wall of ice that blocks sight and can chill creatures.

Wall of Stone (con): Shape a wall of stone.

Primal 6th-Level Spells

Baleful Polymorph (tra): Transform a creature into a harmless animal.

Chain Lightning[H] **(evo):** Lightning jumps from creature to creature.

Dragon Form[H] **(tra):** Turn into a dragon.

Field of Life[H] **(nec):** Create a positive energy field that heals those within.

Fire Seeds[H] **(evo):** Make four explosive acorns.

Flesh To Stone (tra): Turn a living creature to a stone statue.

Purple Worm Sting (nec): Damage a creature and infect it with purple worm venom.

Stone Tell[U] **(div):** Speak to spirits within natural stone.

Stone to Flesh (tra): Turn a creature turned to stone back to flesh.

Tangling Creepers (con): Entangle creatures in a burst and concentrate to lash out with immobilizing vines.

True Seeing (div): See through illusions and transmutations.

Primal 7th-Level Spells

Eclipse Burst[H] **(nec):** A globe of darkness deals cold damage, hurts the living, and overcomes light.

Energy Aegis[H] **(abj):** A creature gains resistance to acid, cold, electricity, fire, force, and sonic.

Fiery Body[H] **(tra):** Turn your body into living flame.

Finger of Death[H] **(nec):** Point at a creature to deal negative damage and possibly kill it instantly.

Mask of Terror[H] **(ill):** A creature's fearsome illusory appearance frightens observers.

Plane Shift[U] **(con):** Transport creatures to another plane of existence.

Regenerate[H] **(nec):** Cause a creature to heal over time, regrow organs, and reattach body parts.

Sunburst[H] **(evo):** A globe of sunlight deals fire damage, hurts undead, and overcomes darkness.

Unfettered Pack[H] **(abj):** Let creatures avoid environmental hindrances.

Volcanic Eruption[H] **(evo):** Cause massive lava sprays that burn creatures and encase them in rock.

Primal 8th-Level Spells

Earthquake[H] **(evo):** Shake the ground with a devastating earthquake.

Horrid Wilting[H] **(nec):** Pull moisture from creatures, damaging them.

Moment of Renewal (nec): Give a day's recovery in an instant.

Monstrosity Form[H] **(tra):** Turn into a powerful monster.

Polar Ray[H] **(evo):** Bitter cold damages and drains a creature.

Punishing Winds (evo): A cyclone inhibits flight and traps creatures.

Wind Walk (tra): Turn creatures into swift-moving clouds.

Primal 9th-Level Spells

Disjunction[U] **(abj):** Deactivate or destroy a magic item.

Implosion[H] **(evo):** Make a creature collapse in on itself.

Massacre[H] **(nec):** Instantly kill multiple creatures.

Meteor Swarm[H] **(evo):** Call down four blazing meteors that explode.

Nature's Enmity (enc): Turn animals, plants, and weather against creatures of your choice.

Shapechange (tra): Transform into a form of your choice repeatedly.

Storm of Vengeance[H] **(evo):** Create a massive, dangerous storm.

Primal 10th-Level Spells

Cataclysm (evo): Call an instant, damaging cataclysm.

Nature Incarnate (tra): Turn into a massive avatar of nature.

Primal Herd (tra): Transform willing creatures into mammoths.

Primal Phenomenon (div): Request for nature to duplicate primal spells.

Remake[U] **(con):** Recreate a destroyed object.

Revival (nec): Heal creatures in an area and return the dead to life temporarily.

SPELL DESCRIPTIONS

ABYSSAL PLAGUE   SPELL 5

ATTACK **CHAOTIC** **DISEASE** **EVIL** **NECROMANCY**

Traditions divine, occult
Cast ❖❖ somatic, verbal
Range touch; **Targets** 1 creature
Saving Throw Fortitude

Your touch afflicts the target with Abyssal plague, which siphons fragments of their soul away to empower the Abyss. The effect is based on the target's Fortitude save.

Critical Success The target is unaffected.
Success The target takes 2 evil damage per spell level, and takes a –2 status penalty to saves against Abyssal plague for 1 day or until the target contracts it, whichever comes first.
Failure The target is afflicted with Abyssal plague at stage 1.
Critical Failure The target is afflicted with Abyssal plague at stage 2.

Abyssal Plague (disease); **Level** 9. The target can't recover from the drained condition from Abyssal plague until the disease is cured. **Stage 1** drained 1 (1 day); **Stage 2** drained increases by 2 (1 day).

ACID ARROW   SPELL 2

ACID **ATTACK** **EVOCATION**

Traditions arcane, primal
Cast ❖❖ somatic, verbal
Range 120 feet; **Targets** 1 creature or object

You conjure an arrow of acid that continues corroding the target after it hits. Make a spell attack against the target. On a hit, you deal 3d8 acid damage plus 1d6 persistent acid damage. On a critical hit, double the initial damage, but not the persistent damage.

Heightened (+2) The initial damage increases by 2d8, and the persistent acid damage increases by 1d6.

ACID SPLASH   CANTRIP 1

ACID **ATTACK** **CANTRIP** **EVOCATION**

Traditions arcane, primal
Cast ❖❖ somatic, verbal
Range 30 feet; **Targets** 1 creature or object

You splash a glob of acid that splatters creatures and objects alike. Make a spell attack. If you hit, you deal 1d6 acid damage plus 1 splash acid damage. On a critical success, the target also takes 1 persistent acid damage.

Heightened (3rd) The initial damage increases to 1d6 + your spellcasting ability modifier, and the persistent damage increases to 2.
Heightened (5th) The initial damage increases to 2d6 + your spellcasting ability modifier, the persistent damage increases to 3, and the splash damage increases to 2.
Heightened (7th) The initial damage increases to 3d6 + your spellcasting ability modifier, the persistent damage increases to 4, and the splash damage increases to 3.
Heightened (9th) The initial damage increases to 4d6 + your spellcasting ability modifier, the persistent damage increases to 5, and the splash damage increases to 4.

AERIAL FORM   SPELL 4

POLYMORPH **TRANSMUTATION**

Traditions arcane, primal
Cast ❖❖ somatic, verbal
Duration 1 minute

You harness your mastery of primal forces to reshape your body into a Medium flying animal battle form. When you cast this spell, choose bat, bird, pterosaur, or wasp. You can decide the specific type of animal (such as an owl or eagle for bird), but this has no effect on the form's Size or statistics. While in this form, you gain the animal trait. You can Dismiss the spell.

You gain the following statistics and abilities regardless of which battle form you choose:

- AC = 18 + your level. Ignore your armor's check penalty and Speed reduction.
- 5 temporary Hit Points.
- Low-light vision.
- One or more unarmed melee attacks specific to the battle form you choose, which are the only attacks you can use. You're trained with them. Your attack modifier is +16, and your damage bonus is +5. These attacks are Dexterity based (for the purpose of the clumsy condition, for example). If your attack modifier for Dexterity-based unarmed attacks is higher, you can use it instead.
- Acrobatics modifier of +16, unless your own modifier is higher.

You also gain specific abilities based on the form you choose:

- **Bat** Speed 20 feet, fly Speed 30 feet; precise echolocation 40 feet; **Melee** ❖ fangs, **Damage** 2d8 piercing; **Melee** ❖ wing (agile), **Damage** 2d6 bludgeoning.
- **Bird** Speed 10 feet, fly Speed 50 feet; **Melee** ❖ beak, **Damage** 2d8 piercing; **Melee** ❖ talon (agile), **Damage** 1d10 slashing.
- **Pterosaur** Speed 10 feet, fly Speed 40 feet; imprecise scent 30 feet; **Melee** ❖ beak, **Damage** 3d6 piercing.
- **Wasp** Speed 20 feet, fly Speed 40 feet; **Melee** ❖ stinger, **Damage** 1d8 piercing plus 1d6 persistent poison.

Heightened (5th) Your battle form is Large and your fly Speed gains a +10-foot status bonus. You must have enough space to expand into or the spell is lost. You instead gain 10 temporary HP, attack modifier +18, damage bonus +8, and Acrobatics +20.

Heightened (6th) Your battle form is Huge, your fly Speed gains a +15-foot status bonus, and your attacks have 10-foot reach. You must have enough space to expand into or the spell is lost. You instead gain AC = 21 + your level, 15 temporary HP, attack modifier +21, damage bonus +4 and double damage dice (including persistent damage), and Acrobatics +23.

AIR BUBBLE   SPELL 1

AIR **CONJURATION**

Traditions arcane, divine, primal
Cast ⟳ verbal; **Trigger** A creature within range enters an environment where it can't breathe.
Range 60 feet; **Targets** the triggering creature
Duration 1 minute

A bubble of pure air appears around the target's head, allowing it to breathe normally. The effect ends as soon as the target returns to an environment where it can breathe normally.

AIR WALK   SPELL 4

AIR **TRANSMUTATION**

Traditions divine, primal
Cast ✧✧ somatic, verbal
Range touch; **Targets** 1 creature
Duration 5 minutes

The target can walk on air as if it were solid ground. It can ascend and descend in this way at a maximum of a 45-degree angle.

ALARM   SPELL 1

ABJURATION

Traditions arcane, divine, occult, primal
Cast 10 minutes (material, somatic, verbal); **Requirements** 3 gp silver bell focus
Range touch; **Area** 20-foot burst
Duration 8 hours

You ward an area to alert you when creatures enter without your permission. When you cast *alarm*, select a password. Whenever a Small or larger corporeal creature enters the spell's area without speaking the password, *alarm* sends your choice of a mental alert (in which case the spell gains the mental trait) or an audible alarm with the sound and volume of a hand bell (in which case the spell gains the auditory trait). Either option automatically awakens you, and the bell allows each creature in the area to attempt a DC 15 Perception check to wake up. A creature aware of the *alarm* must succeed at a Stealth check against the spell's DC or trigger the spell when moving into the area.

Heightened (3rd) You can specify criteria for which creatures sound the *alarm* spell—for instance, orcs or masked people.

ALTER REALITY   SPELL 10

DIVINATION

Traditions occult
Cast ✧✧✧ material, somatic, verbal

You use your occult lore and the power of your mind to manipulate the spiritual multiverse, resulting in any of the following effects:

- Duplicate any occult spell of 9th level or lower.
- Duplicate any non-occult spell of 7th level or lower.
- Produce any effect whose power is equivalent to any occult spell 9th level or lower, or non-occult spell 7th level or lower.
- Reverse certain effects that refer to the *wish* spell

At the GM's discretion, you can try to produce greater effects, but this is dangerous and the spell may have only a partial effect.

ANATHEMATIC REPRISAL   SPELL 4

ENCHANTMENT **MENTAL**

Traditions divine
Cast ↻ somatic, verbal; **Trigger** A creature performs an act anathema to your deity.
Range 30 feet; **Targets** the triggering creature
Saving Throw Will

You punish a creature that transgresses against your deity, drawing upon the anguish you feel upon seeing one of your deity's anathema committed.

You can cast this spell only when a creature actively commits a unique act of anathema. For example, if creating undead were anathema to your deity, you could use *anathematic reprisal* on a necromancer who had just created undead in front of you, but not on an undead creature just for existing.

You deal 4d6 mental damage to the target, but a basic Will save can reduce this damage. If it fails, it is also stupefied 1 for 1 round. The creature is then temporarily immune for 1 minute.

Heightened (+1) The damage increases by 1d6.

ANIMAL FORM   SPELL 2

POLYMORPH **TRANSMUTATION**

Traditions primal
Cast ✧✧ somatic, verbal
Duration 1 minute

You call upon primal energy to transform yourself into a Medium animal battle form. When you first cast this spell, choose ape, bear, bull, canine, cat, deer, frog, shark, or snake. You can decide the specific type of animal (such as lion or snow leopard for cat), but this has no effect on the form's Size or statistics. While in this form, you gain the animal trait. You can Dismiss the spell.

You gain the following statistics and abilities regardless of which battle form you choose:

- AC = 16 + your level. Ignore your armor's check penalty and Speed reduction.
- 5 temporary Hit Points.
- Low-light vision and imprecise scent 30 feet.
- One or more unarmed melee attacks specific to the battle form you choose, which are the only attacks you can use. You're trained with them. Your attack modifier is +9, and your damage bonus is +1. These attacks are Strength based (for the purpose of the enfeebled condition, for example). If your unarmed attack bonus is higher, you can use it instead.
- Athletics modifier of +9, unless your own modifier is higher.

You also gain specific abilities based on the type of animal you choose:

- **Ape** Speed 25 feet, climb Speed 20 feet; **Melee** ✧ fist, **Damage** 2d6 bludgeoning.
- **Bear** Speed 30 feet; **Melee** ✧ jaws, **Damage** 2d8 piercing; **Melee** ✧ claw (agile), **Damage** 1d8 slashing.
- **Bull** Speed 30 feet; **Melee** ✧ horn, **Damage** 2d8 piercing.
- **Canine** Speed 40 feet; **Melee** ✧ jaws, **Damage** 2d8 piercing.
- **Cat** Speed 40 feet; **Melee** ✧ jaws, **Damage** 2d6 piercing; **Melee** ✧ claw (agile), **Damage** 1d10 slashing.
- **Deer** Speed 50 feet; **Melee** ✧ antler, **Damage** 2d6 piercing.
- **Frog** Speed 25 feet, swim Speed 25 feet; **Melee** ✧ jaws, **Damage** 2d6 bludgeoning; **Melee** ✧ tongue (reach 15 feet), **Damage** 2d4 bludgeoning.
- **Shark** swim Speed 35 feet; **Melee** ✧ jaws, **Damage** 2d8 piercing; breathe underwater but not in air.

- **Snake** Speed 20 feet, climb Speed 20 feet, swim Speed 20 feet; **Melee** ❖ fangs, **Damage** 2d4 piercing plus 1d6 poison.

Heightened (3rd) You instead gain 10 temporary HP, AC = 17 + your level, attack modifier +14, damage bonus +5, and Athletics +14.

Heightened (4th) Your battle form is Large and your attacks have 10-foot reach. You must have enough space to expand into or the spell is lost. You instead gain 15 temporary HP, AC = 18 + your level, attack modifier +16, damage bonus +9, and Athletics +16.

Heightened (5th) Your battle form is Huge and your attacks have 15-foot reach. You must have enough space to expand into or the spell is lost. You instead gain 20 temporary HP, AC = 18 + your level, attack modifier +18, damage bonus +7 and double the number of damage dice, and Athletics +20.

ANIMAL MESSENGER   SPELL 2

ENCHANTMENT   MENTAL

Traditions primal
Cast 1 minute (material, somatic, verbal)
Range 120 feet
Duration until delivered

You offer a gift of food, and an ordinary Tiny wild animal within range approaches to eat it. You imprint the image, direction, and distance of an obvious place or landmark well known to you within the animal. Optionally, you can attach a small object or note up to light Bulk to it. The animal does its best to reach the destination; if it makes it there, it waits nearby until the duration expires, allowing other nonhostile creatures to approach it and remove the attached object.

If there are no Tiny wild animals in range, the spell is lost.

ANIMAL VISION   SPELL 3

DIVINATION   MENTAL

Traditions primal
Cast 1 minute (material, somatic, verbal)
Range 120 feet; **Targets** 1 animal
Duration 1 hour

You tap into the target's senses, allowing you to see, hear, and otherwise sense whatever it senses for the spell's duration. If the target wishes to prevent you from doing so, it can attempt a Will save, negating the spell on a success, but most animals don't bother to do so. While tapping into the target's senses, you can't use your own body's senses, but you can change back and forth from your body's senses to the target's senses using a single action, which has the concentrate trait.

ANT HAUL   SPELL 1

TRANSMUTATION

Traditions arcane, primal
Cast ❖❖ somatic, verbal
Range touch; **Targets** 1 creature
Duration 8 hours

You reinforce the target's musculoskeletal system to bear more weight. The target can carry 3 more Bulk than normal before becoming encumbered and up to a maximum of 6 more Bulk.

ANTIMAGIC FIELD   SPELL 8

RARE   ABJURATION

Traditions arcane, divine, occult
Cast ❖❖❖ material, somatic, verbal
Area 10-foot emanation
Duration sustained up to 1 minute

You repel all magic from the target area, preventing spells and other magic from functioning. Spells can't penetrate the area, magic items cease to function within it, and no one inside can cast spells or use magic abilities. Likewise, spells—such as *dispel magic*—can't affect the field itself unless they are of a higher level. Magic effects resume the moment they pass outside the field. For example, a ray fired from one side of the field could target a creature on the other side (as long as caster and target are both outside the field). A summoned creature winks out of existence but reappears if the field moves or ends. Invested magic items cease to function, but they remain invested and resume functioning when they exit the field; the ability boost from an apex item isn't suppressed within the field. Spells of a higher level than the *antimagic field* overcome its effects, and can even be cast by a creature within the field.

The field disrupts only magic, so a *+3 longsword* still functions as a longsword. Magically created creatures (such as golems) function normally within an *antimagic field*.

AUGURY   SPELL 2

DIVINATION   PREDICTION

Traditions divine, occult
Cast 10 minutes (material, somatic, verbal)

You gain a vague glimpse of the future. During the casting of this spell, ask about the results of a particular course of action. The spell can predict results up to 30 minutes into the future and reveals the GM's best guess among the following outcomes:

- **Weal** The results will be good.
- **Woe** The results will be bad.
- **Weal and Woe** The results will be a mix of good and bad.
- **Nothing** There won't be particularly good or bad results.

The GM rolls a secret DC 6 flat check. On a failure, the result is always "nothing." This makes it impossible to tell whether a "nothing" result is accurate. If anyone asks about the same topic as the first casting of *augury* during an additional casting, the GM uses the secret roll result from the first casting. If circumstances change, though, it's possible to get a different result.

AVATAR   SPELL 10

POLYMORPH   TRANSMUTATION

Traditions divine
Cast ❖❖ somatic, verbal
Duration 1 minute

You transform into an avatar of your deity, assuming a Huge battle form. You must have space to expand or the spell is lost. You have hands in this battle form and can take manipulate actions. You can Dismiss this spell.

You gain the following statistics and abilities regardless of which deity's battle form you assume:

SPELLS

7

INTRODUCTION

ANCESTRIES &
BACKGROUNDS

CLASSES

SKILLS

FEATS

EQUIPMENT

SPELLS

THE AGE OF
LOST OMENS

PLAYING THE
GAME

GAME
MASTERING

CRAFTING
& TREASURE

APPENDIX

- AC = 25 + your level. Ignore your armor's check penalty and Speed reduction.
- 30 temporary Hit Points.
- Darkvision.
- One or more attacks specific to your deity's battle form, which are the only attacks you can use. You're trained with them. Your attack modifier is +33, and you use the listed damage. Melee attacks are Strength based (for the purposes of the enfeebled condition, for example) unless they have the finesse trait, and all ranged attacks are Dexterity based. Attacks that deal positive or negative damage don't heal creatures.
- Athletics modifier of +35, unless your own is higher.

You also gain the specific abilities listed for your deity below:
- **Abadar** Speed 50 feet, burrow Speed 30 feet, immune to immobilized; **Ranged** ❖ crossbow (range increment 120 feet, reload 1), **Damage** 6d10+3 piercing.
- **Asmodeus** Speed 70 feet, *air walk*; **Melee** ❖ mace (reach 15 feet), **Damage** 6d10+6 bludgeoning; **Ranged** ❖ hellfire (range 120 feet), **Damage** 6d6+3 fire.
- **Calistria** Speed 30 feet, fly Speed 70 feet; **Melee** ❖ whip (disarm, finesse, nonlethal, reach 20 feet), **Damage** 6d4+6 slashing; **Ranged** ❖ savored sting (range 60 feet), **Damage** 6d6+3 poison.
- **Cayden Cailean** Speed 70 feet, *air walk*, ignore difficult terrain and greater difficult terrain; **Melee** ❖ rapier

(deadly, reach 15 feet), **Damage** 6d6+6 piercing; **Ranged** ❖ ale splash (range 120 feet), **Damage** 6d6+3 poison.
- **Desna** Speed 30 feet, fly Speed 70 feet; **Melee** ❖ starknife (agile, deadly, finesse, reach 15 feet, silver, thrown 60 feet), **Damage** 6d4+6 piercing; **Ranged** ❖ moonbeam (range 120 feet, silver), **Damage** 6d6+3 fire.
- **Erastil** Speed 70 feet, *air walk*, ignore difficult terrain and greater difficult terrain; **Ranged** ❖ longbow (deadly d8, range increment 150 feet), **Damage** 6d8+3 piercing.
- **Gorum** Speed 70 feet, immune to immobilized; **Melee** ❖ greatsword (versatile P, reach 15 feet), **Damage** 6d12+6 slashing.
- **Gozreh** no land Speed, fly Speed 70 feet, swim Speed 70 feet; ignore difficult terrain and greater difficult terrain; **Melee** ❖ waves (bull rush, reach 15 feet, thrown 20 feet), **Damage** 6d8+6 bludgeoning; **Ranged** ❖ wind (versatile electricity, range 120 feet), **Damage** 6d6+3 bludgeoning.
- **Iomedae** Speed 70 feet, *air walk*; shield (15 Hardness, can't be damaged); **Melee** ❖ longsword (versatile P, reach 15 feet), **Damage** 6d8+6 slashing.
- **Irori** Speed 80 feet, *air walk*; **Melee** ❖ unfettered strike (agile, versatile P or S, finesse, reach 15 feet), **Damage** 6d8+6 bludgeoning; **Ranged** ❖ wind strike (range 60 feet), **Damage** 6d4+6 bludgeoning.
- **Lamashtu** Speed 30 feet, fly Speed 70 feet; **Melee** ❖ falchion (forceful, reach 15 feet), **Damage**

6d10+6 slashing; **Ranged** ❖ waters of Lamashtu (range 120 feet), **Damage** 6d6+3 poison.

- **Nethys** Speed 70 feet, *air walk*; **Ranged** ❖ raw magic (range 120 feet; versatile cold, electricity, or fire), **Damage** 6d6 force.
- **Norgorber** Speed 70 feet, *air walk*, ignore difficult terrain and greater difficult terrain; **Melee** ❖ shortsword (agile, finesse, versatile S, reach 15 feet), **Damage** 6d6+6 piercing; **Ranged** ❖ blackfinger toss (range 120 feet), **Damage** 6d6+3 poison.
- **Pharasma** Speed 70 feet, *air walk*; **Melee** ❖ dagger (agile, finesse, reach 15 feet, thrown 40 feet), **Damage** 6d6+6 slashing; **Ranged** ❖ spiral blast (range 120 feet, damages only undead), **Damage** 6d8+3 positive.
- **Rovagug** Speed 50 feet, burrow Speed 30 feet, immune to immobilized; **Melee** ❖ jaws (reach 15 feet), **Damage** 6d12+6 piercing; **Melee** ❖ leg (agile, versatile P, reach 15 feet), **Damage** 6d8+6 bludgeoning.
- **Sarenrae** Speed 30 feet, fly Speed 70 feet; **Melee** ❖ scimitar (forceful, nonlethal, reach 15 feet), **Damage** 6d6+6 slashing; **Ranged** ❖ everflame (nonlethal, range 120 feet), **Damage** 6d6+3 fire.
- **Shelyn** Speed 70 feet, *air walk*, ignore difficult terrain and greater difficult terrain; **Melee** ❖ glaive (deadly d8, nonlethal, reach 20 feet), **Damage** 6d8+6 slashing; **Ranged** ❖ melody of inner beauty, (nonlethal, range 120 feet), **Damage** 6d6+3 sonic.
- **Torag** Speed 50 feet, burrow Speed 30 feet, immune to immobilized; shield (15 Hardness, can't be damaged); **Melee** ❖ warhammer (bull rush, reach 15 feet), **Damage** 6d8+6 bludgeoning.
- **Urgathoa** Speed 70 feet, *air walk*; **Melee** ❖ scythe (deadly d10, trip, reach 15 feet), **Damage** 6d10+6 slashing; **Ranged** ❖ pallid plague (range 120 feet), **Damage** 6d6+3 negative.
- **Zon-Kuthon** Speed 70 feet, *air walk*, ignore difficult terrain and greater difficult terrain; **Melee** ❖ spiked chain (disarm, trip, reach 15 feet), **Damage** 6d8+6 slashing; **Ranged** ❖ midnight pain (mental, nonlethal, range 120 feet), **Damage** 6d6+3 mental.

BALEFUL POLYMORPH SPELL 6

INCAPACITATION POLYMORPH TRANSMUTATION

Traditions arcane, primal
Cast ❖❖ somatic, verbal
Range 30 feet; **Targets** 1 creature
Saving Throw Fortitude; **Duration** varies

You transform the target creature into a harmless animal appropriate to the area, with effects based on its Fortitude save.

Critical Success The target is unaffected.

Success The target's body gains minor features of the harmless animal. Its insides churn as they partially transform, causing it to be sickened 1. When it recovers from the sickened condition, its features revert to normal.

Failure The target transforms for 1 minute but keeps its mind. If it spends all its actions on its turn concentrating on its original form, it can attempt a Will save to end the effect immediately.

Critical Failure The target is transformed into the chosen harmless animal, body and mind, for an unlimited duration.

BANE SPELL 1

ENCHANTMENT MENTAL

Traditions divine, occult
Cast ❖❖ somatic, verbal
Area 5-foot emanation; **Targets** enemies in the area
Saving Throw Will; **Duration** 1 minute

You fill the minds of your enemies with doubt. Targets that fail their Will saves take a –1 status penalty to attack rolls as long as they are in the area. Once per turn, starting the turn after you cast *bane*, you can use a single action, which has the concentrate trait, to increase the emanation's radius by 5 feet and force enemies in the area that weren't yet affected to attempt another saving throw. *Bane* can counteract *bless*.

BANISHMENT SPELL 5

ABJURATION INCAPACITATION

Traditions arcane, divine, occult, primal
Cast ❖❖ somatic, verbal
Range 30 feet; **Targets** 1 creature that isn't on its home plane
Saving Throw Will

You send the target back to its home plane. The target must attempt a Will save. You can spend an extra action while Casting this Spell and add a material component to give the creature a –2 circumstance penalty to its save. The component must be a specially gathered object that is anathema to the creature, and not from a spell component pouch. This spell fails if you aren't on your home plane when you cast it.

Critical Success The target resists being banished and you are stunned 1.

Success The target resists being banished.

Failure The target is banished.

Critical Failure The target is banished and can't return by any means to the plane it's banished from for 1 week.

Heightened (9th) You can target up to 10 creatures. The extra material component affects targets to which it is anathema.

BARKSKIN SPELL 2

ABJURATION PLANT

Traditions primal
Cast ❖❖ somatic, verbal
Range touch; **Targets** 1 willing creature
Duration 10 minutes

The target's skin becomes covered in bark. The target gains resistance 2 to bludgeoning and piercing damage and weakness 3 to fire. After the target takes fire damage, it can Dismiss the spell as a free action triggered by taking the damage; doing so doesn't reduce the fire damage the target was dealt.

Heightened (+2) The resistances increase by 2, and the weakness increases by 3.

BIND SOUL SPELL 9

UNCOMMON EVIL NECROMANCY

Traditions divine, occult

Cast ◆◆ somatic, verbal; **Requirements** black sapphire with a gp value of at least the target's level × 100
Range 30 feet; **Targets** 1 creature that died within the last minute
Duration unlimited

You wrench the target's soul away before it can pass on to the afterlife and imprison it in a black sapphire.

While the soul is in the gem, the target can't be returned to life through any means, even powerful magic such as *wish*. If the gem is destroyed or *bind soul* is counteracted on the gem, the soul is freed. The gem has AC 16 and Hardness 10. A gem can't hold more than one soul, and any attempt wastes the spell.

BIND UNDEAD   SPELL 3

NECROMANCY

Traditions arcane, divine, occult
Cast ◆◆ somatic, verbal
Range 30 feet; **Targets** 1 mindless undead creature with a level no greater than *bind undead*'s spell level
Duration 1 day

With a word of necromantic power, you seize control of the target. It gains the minion trait. If you or an ally uses any hostile actions against the target, the spell ends.

BLACK TENTACLES   SPELL 5

CONJURATION

Traditions arcane, occult
Cast ◆◆◆ material, somatic, verbal
Range 120 feet; **Area** 20-foot burst adjacent to a flat surface
Duration 1 minute

Oily black tentacles rise up and attempt to Grapple each creature in the area. Make spell attack rolls against the Fortitude DC of each creature. Any creature you succeed against is grabbed and takes 3d6 bludgeoning damage. Whenever a creature ends its turn in the area, the tentacles attempt to grab that creature if they haven't already, and they deal 1d6 bludgeoning damage to any creature already grabbed.

The tentacles' Escape DC is equal to your spell DC. A creature can attack a tentacle in an attempt to release its grip. Its AC is equal to your spell DC, and it is destroyed if it takes 12 or more damage. Even if destroyed, additional tentacles continue to grow in the area until the duration ends. You can Dismiss the spell.

BLADE BARRIER   SPELL 6

EVOCATION FORCE

Traditions divine
Cast ◆◆◆ material, somatic, verbal
Range 120 feet
Duration 1 minute

Blades of force form a churning wall. The wall is a straight line 20 feet high, 120 feet long, and 2 inches thick, and it provides cover. The wall deals 7d8 force damage to each creature that's in the wall's space when it is created, that attempts to pass through the wall, or that ends its turn inside the wall. A basic Reflex save reduces the damage.

A creature that succeeds at this save when the wall is created is pushed to the nearest space on the side of its choice. Creatures trying to move through the wall fail to do so if they critically fail the save, ending their movement adjacent to the wall.

Heightened (+1) The damage increases by 1d8.

BLESS   SPELL 1

ENCHANTMENT MENTAL

Traditions divine, occult
Cast ◆◆ somatic, verbal
Area 5-foot emanation; **Targets** you and allies in the area
Duration 1 minute

Blessings from beyond help your companions strike true. You and your allies in the area gain a +1 status bonus to attack rolls. Once per turn, starting the turn after you cast *bless*, you can use a single action, which has the concentrate trait, to increase the emanation's radius by 5 feet. *Bless* can counteract *bane*.

BLINDNESS   SPELL 3

INCAPACITATION NECROMANCY

Traditions arcane, divine, occult, primal
Cast ◆◆ somatic, verbal
Range 30 feet; **Targets** 1 creature
Saving Throw Fortitude

You blind the target. The effect is determined by the target's Fortitude save. The target then becomes temporarily immune for 1 minute.

Critical Success The target is unaffected.
Success The target is blinded until its next turn begins.
Failure The target is blinded for 1 minute.
Critical Failure The target is blinded permanently.

BLINK   SPELL 4

CONJURATION TELEPORTATION

Traditions arcane, occult
Cast ◆◆ somatic, verbal
Duration 1 minute

You blink quickly between the Material Plane and the Ethereal Plane. You gain resistance 5 to all damage (except force). You can Sustain the Spell to vanish and reappear 10 feet away in a random direction determined by the GM; the movement doesn't trigger reactions. At the end of your turn, you vanish and reappear as above.

Heightened (+2) The resistance increases by 3.

BLUR   SPELL 2

ILLUSION VISUAL

Traditions arcane, occult
Cast ◆◆ somatic, verbal
Range touch; **Targets** 1 creature
Duration 1 minute

The target's form appears blurry. It becomes concealed. As the nature of this effect still leaves the target's location obvious, the target can't use this concealment to Hide or Sneak.

INTRODUCTION

ANCESTRIES & BACKGROUNDS

CLASSES

SKILLS

FEATS

EQUIPMENT

SPELLS

THE AGE OF LOST OMENS

PLAYING THE GAME

GAME MASTERING

CRAFTING & TREASURE

APPENDIX

BREATH OF LIFE   SPELL 5

| HEALING | NECROMANCY | POSITIVE |

Traditions divine

Cast ⟳ verbal; **Trigger** A living creature within range would die.

Range 60 feet; **Targets** the triggering creature

Your blessing revives a creature at the moment of its death. You prevent the target from dying and restore Hit Points to the target equal to 4d8 plus your spellcasting ability modifier. You can't use *breath of life* if the triggering effect was *disintegrate* or a death effect.

BURNING HANDS   SPELL 1

| EVOCATION | FIRE |

Traditions arcane, primal

Cast ◆◆ somatic, verbal

Area 15-foot cone

Saving Throw basic Reflex

Gouts of flame rush from your hands. You deal 2d6 fire damage to creatures in the area.

Heightened (+1) The damage increases by 2d6.

CALM EMOTIONS   SPELL 2

| EMOTION | ENCHANTMENT | INCAPACITATION | MENTAL |

Traditions divine, occult

Cast ◆◆ somatic, verbal

Range 120 feet; **Area** 10-foot burst

Saving Throw Will; **Duration** sustained up to 1 minute

You forcibly calm creatures in the area, soothing them into a nonviolent state; each creature must attempt a Will save.

Critical Success The creature is unaffected.

Success Calming urges impose a –1 status penalty to the creature's attack rolls.

Failure Any emotion effects that would affect the creature are suppressed and the creature can't use hostile actions. If the target is subject to hostility from any other creature, it ceases to be affected by *calm emotions*.

Critical Failure As failure, but hostility doesn't end the effect.

CATACLYSM   SPELL 10

| ACID | AIR | COLD | EARTH |
| ELECTRICITY | EVOCATION | FIRE | WATER |

Traditions arcane, primal

Cast ◆◆ somatic, verbal

Range 1,000 feet; **Area** 60-foot burst

Saving Throw basic Reflex

You call upon the unimaginable power of world-ending cataclysms, ripping a small piece of each cataclysm and combining them together into one horrifically powerful attack. The following effects come down upon all creatures in the area. Treat the resistances of creatures in the area as if they were 10 lower for the purpose of determining the cataclysm's damage. Each creature attempts one basic Reflex save that applies to all six types of damage.

- Flesh-dissolving acid rain deals 3d10 acid damage.
- A roaring earthquake shakes and bludgeons creatures on the ground, dealing 3d10 bludgeoning damage.

- A blast of freezing wind deals 3d10 cold damage.
- Incredible lightning lashes the area, dealing 3d10 electricity damage.
- Beating winds churn across the sky, dealing 3d10 bludgeoning damage to creatures flying in the area.
- An instant tsunami sweeps over creatures in the area, dealing 3d10 bludgeoning damage with the water trait (doubled for creatures swimming in the area).
- A massive wildfire burns in a sudden inferno, dealing 3d10 fire damage.

CHAIN LIGHTNING   SPELL 6

| ELECTRICITY | EVOCATION |

Traditions arcane, primal

Cast ◆◆ somatic, verbal

Range 500 feet; **Targets** 1 creature, plus any number of additional creatures

Saving Throw Reflex

You discharge a powerful bolt of lightning at the target, dealing 8d12 electricity damage. The target must attempt a basic Reflex save. The electricity arcs to another creature within 30 feet of the first target, jumps to another creature within 30 feet of that target, and so on. You can end the chain at any point. You can't target the same creature more than once, and you must have line of effect to all targets. Roll the damage only once, and apply it to each target (halving or doubling as appropriate for its saving throw outcome). The chain ends if any one of the targets critically succeeds at its save.

Heightened (+1) The damage increases by 1d12.

CHARM   SPELL 1

| EMOTION | ENCHANTMENT | INCAPACITATION | MENTAL |

Traditions arcane, occult, primal

Cast ◆◆ somatic, verbal

Range 30 feet; **Targets** 1 creature

Saving Throw Will; **Duration** 1 hour

To the target, your words are honey and your visage seems bathed in a dreamy haze. It must attempt a Will save, with a +4 circumstance bonus if you or your allies recently threatened it or used hostile actions against it.

You can Dismiss the spell. If you use hostile actions against the target, the spell ends. When the spell ends, the target doesn't necessarily realize it was charmed unless its friendship with you or the actions you convinced it to take clash with its expectations, meaning you could potentially convince the target to continue being your friend via mundane means.

Critical Success The target is unaffected and aware you tried to charm it.

Success The target is unaffected but thinks your spell was something harmless instead of *charm*, unless it identifies the spell (usually with Identify Magic).

Failure The target's attitude becomes friendly toward you. If it was friendly, it becomes helpful. It can't use hostile actions against you.

Critical Failure The target's attitude becomes helpful toward you, and it can't use hostile actions against you.

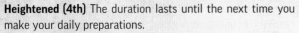
Heightened (4th) The duration lasts until the next time you make your daily preparations.

Heightened (8th) The duration lasts until the next time you make your daily preparations, and you can target up to 10 creatures.

CHILL TOUCH   CANTRIP 1

`ATTACK` `CANTRIP` `NECROMANCY` `NEGATIVE`

Traditions arcane, divine, occult
Cast ◆◆ somatic, verbal
Range touch; **Targets** 1 living or undead creature
Saving Throw Fortitude

Siphoning negative energy into yourself, your hand radiates a pale darkness. Your touch weakens the living and disorients undead, possibly even causing them to flee. The effect depends on whether the target is living or undead.

- **Living Creature** The spell deals negative damage equal to 1d4 plus your spellcasting modifier. The target attempts a basic Fortitude save, but is also enfeebled 1 for 1 round on a critical failure.
- **Undead Creature** The target is flat-footed for 1 round on a failed Fortitude save. On a critical failure, the target is also fleeing for 1 round unless it succeeds at a Will save.

Heightened (+1) The negative damage to living creatures increases by 1d4.

CHILLING DARKNESS   SPELL 3

`ATTACK` `COLD` `DARKNESS` `EVOCATION` `EVIL`

Traditions divine
Cast ◆◆ somatic, verbal
Range 120 feet; **Targets** 1 creature

You shoot an utterly cold ray of darkness tinged with unholy energy. Make a ranged spell attack against the target. You deal 5d6 cold damage, plus 5d6 evil damage if the target is a celestial.

If the ray passes through an area of magical light or targets a creature affected by magical light, *chilling darkness* attempts to counteract the light. If you need to determine whether the ray passes through an area of light, draw a line between yourself and the spell's target.

Critical Success The target takes double damage.
Success The target takes full damage.

Heightened (+1) The cold damage increases by 2d6, and the evil damage against celestials increases by 2d6.

CHROMATIC WALL   SPELL 5

`ABJURATION`

Traditions arcane, occult
Cast ◆◆◆ material, somatic, verbal
Range 120 feet
Duration 10 minutes

You create an opaque wall of light in a single vibrant color. The wall is straight and vertical, stretching 60 feet long and 30 feet high. If the wall would pass through a creature, the spell is lost. The wall sheds bright light for 20 feet on each side, and dim light for the next 20 feet. You can ignore the wall's effects.

Roll 1d4 to determine the color of the wall. Each color has a particular effect on items, effects, or creatures that attempt to pass through. *Chromatic wall* can't be counteracted normally; rather, each color is automatically counteracted when targeted by a specific spell, even if that spell's level is lower than that of *chromatic wall*.

1. **Red** The wall destroys ranged weapon ammunition (such as arrows and crossbow bolts) that would pass through, and it deals 20 fire damage to anyone passing through, with a basic Reflex save. *Cone of cold* can counteract a red *chromatic wall*.
2. **Orange** The wall destroys thrown weapons that would pass through, and it deals 25 acid damage to anyone passing through, with a basic Reflex save. *Gust of wind* can counteract an orange *chromatic wall*.
3. **Yellow** The wall stops acid, cold, electricity, fire, force, negative, positive, and sonic effects from passing through, and it deals 30 electricity damage to anyone passing through, with a basic Reflex save. *Disintegrate* can counteract a yellow *chromatic wall*.
4. **Green** The wall stops toxins, gases, and breath weapons from passing through. It deals 10 poison damage to anyone passing through and makes them enfeebled 1 for 1 minute. A basic Fortitude save reduces the damage and negates the enfeebled condition on a success. *Passwall* can counteract a green *chromatic wall*.

MAGIC AND MORALITY

While magic allows you to perform wondrous acts in the game, it can be used for terrible purposes. While some spells are obviously vile or have the evil trait and a direct connection to the profane, other spells can be used for good or ill. Using magic does not free you from the morality of the outcome.

Nowhere is this more true than when it comes to enchantment spells, especially those used to compel a character to do something. These spells can remove the power of choice from a character and can very easily be used in ways that are evil. Dominating an ogre and forcing him to abandon his guard post is not necessarily evil, but using that same spell to force a merchant to give you all of his wares certainly is. Using a spell for an evil purpose can cause a player character's alignment to shift to evil, with the ultimate judgment of whether a player is using a spell for an evil purpose left up to the GM.

Regardless of in-game effects, all players should take care when using such spells. These effects can negatively affect people at the table, as they might create situations that echo truly awful experiences players might have had, creating uncomfortable or hostile environments. Players and GMs should work to prevent these situations so everyone can focus on having fun at the table.

INTRODUCTION

ANCESTRIES & BACKGROUNDS

CLASSES

SKILLS

FEATS

EQUIPMENT

SPELLS

THE AGE OF LOST OMENS

PLAYING THE GAME

GAME MASTERING

CRAFTING & TREASURE

APPENDIX

Heightened (7th) The spell's duration increases to 1 hour. Roll 1d8 to determine the wall's color; the results for 5–8 are below. A red, orange, yellow, or green wall deals an extra 10 damage.

5. **Blue** The wall stops auditory, petrification, and visual effects from passing through, and creatures passing through are subject to the effects of *flesh to stone*. *Magic missile* can counteract a blue *chromatic wall*.

6. **Indigo** The wall stops divination and mental effects from passing through, and those passing through are subject to the effects of *warp mind*. *Searing light* can counteract an indigo *chromatic wall*.

7. **Violet** The wall prevents spells from targeting the other side (area effects still cross as normal). Creatures passing through must succeed at a Will save or they are slowed 1 for 1 minute; on a critical failure, the creature is instead sent to another plane, with the effect of *plane shift*. *Dispel magic* can counteract a violet *chromatic wall*.

8. Reroll, and creatures that pass through the wall take a –2 circumstance penalty to their saves.

CIRCLE OF PROTECTION   SPELL 3

UNCOMMON   ABJURATION

Traditions divine, occult
Cast ◆◆◆ material, somatic, verbal
Range touch; **Area** 10-foot emanation centered on the touched creature
Duration 1 minute

You ward a creature and those nearby against a specified alignment. Choose chaotic, evil, good, or lawful; this spell gains the opposing trait. Creatures in the area gain a +1 status bonus to AC against attacks by creatures of the chosen alignment and to saves against effects from such creatures. This bonus increases to +3 against effects from such creatures that directly control the target and attacks made by summoned creatures of the chosen alignment. Summoned creatures of the chosen alignment can't willingly enter the area without succeeding at a Will save; repeated attempts use the first save result.

Heightened (4th) The duration increases to 1 hour.

CLAIRAUDIENCE   SPELL 3

DIVINATION   SCRYING

Traditions arcane, occult
Cast 1 minute (material, somatic, verbal)
Range 500 feet
Duration 10 minutes

You create an invisible floating ear at a location within range (even if it's outside your line of sight or line of effect). It can't move, but you can hear through the ear as if using your normal auditory senses.

CLAIRVOYANCE   SPELL 4

DIVINATION   SCRYING

Traditions arcane, occult
Cast 1 minute (material, somatic, verbal)
Range 500 feet
Duration 10 minutes

You create an invisible floating eye at a location within range (even if it's outside your line of sight or line of effect). The eye can't move, but you can see in all directions from that point as if using your normal visual senses.

CLOAK OF COLORS   SPELL 5

ILLUSION   VISUAL

Traditions arcane, occult
Cast ◆◆ somatic, verbal
Range 30 feet; **Targets** 1 creature
Duration 1 minute

A cloak of swirling colors shrouds the target. Creatures are dazzled while adjacent to it, and attacking the target causes a brilliant flash of light. A creature that hits the target with a melee attack must attempt a Will save.

Success The attacker is unaffected.
Failure The attacker is blinded for 1 round.
Critical Failure The attacker is stunned for 1 round.

The creature is temporarily immune until the end of its turn; this effect has the incapacitation trait.

CLOUDKILL   SPELL 5

DEATH   NECROMANCY   POISON

Traditions arcane, primal
Cast ◆◆◆ material, somatic, verbal
Range 120 feet; **Area** 20-foot burst
Saving Throw basic Fortitude; **Duration** 1 minute

You conjure a poisonous fog. This functions as *obscuring mist* (page 355), except the area moves 10 feet away from you each round. You deal 6d8 poison damage to each breathing creature that starts its turn in the spell's area. You can Dismiss the spell.

Heightened (+1) The damage increases by 1d8.

COLLECTIVE TRANSPOSITION   SPELL 6

CONJURATION   TELEPORTATION

Traditions arcane, occult
Cast ◆◆ somatic, verbal
Area 30-foot emanation; **Targets** up to 2 creatures

You teleport the targets to new positions within the area. The creatures must each be able to fit in their new space, and their positions must be unoccupied, entirely within the area, and in your line of sight. Unwilling creatures can attempt a Will save.

Critical Success The target can teleport if it wants, but it chooses the destination within range.
Success The target is unaffected.
Failure You teleport the target and choose its destination.
Heightened (+1) The number of targets increases by 1.

COLOR SPRAY   SPELL 1

ILLUSION   INCAPACITATION   VISUAL

Traditions arcane, occult
Cast ◆◆ somatic, verbal
Area 15-foot cone
Saving Throw Will; **Duration** 1 or more rounds (see below)

Swirling colors affect viewers based on their Will saves.

Critical Success The creature is unaffected.

SPELLS 7

INTRODUCTION

ANCESTRIES &
BACKGROUNDS

CLASSES

SKILLS

FEATS

EQUIPMENT

SPELLS

THE AGE OF
LOST OMENS

PLAYING THE
GAME

GAME
MASTERING

CRAFTING
& TREASURE

APPENDIX

Success The creature is dazzled for 1 round.

Failure The creature is stunned 1, blinded for 1 round, and dazzled for 1 minute.

Critical Failure The creature is stunned for 1 round and blinded for 1 minute.

COMMAND   SPELL 1

| AUDITORY | ENCHANTMENT | LINGUISTIC | MENTAL |

Traditions arcane, divine, occult

Cast ◆◆ somatic, verbal

Range 30 feet; **Targets** 1 creature

Saving Throw Will; **Duration** until the end of the target's next turn

You shout a command that's hard to ignore. You can command the target to approach you, run away (as if it had the fleeing condition), release what it's holding, drop prone, or stand in place. It can't Delay or take any reactions until it has obeyed your command. The effects depend on the target's Will save.

Success The creature is unaffected.

Failure For the first action on its next turn, the creature must use a single action to do as you command.

Critical Failure The target must use all its actions on its next turn to obey your command.

Heightened (5th) You can target up to 10 creatures.

COMPREHEND LANGUAGE   SPELL 2

| DIVINATION |

Traditions arcane, divine, occult

Cast ◆◆ somatic, verbal

Range 30 feet; **Targets** 1 creature

Duration 1 hour

The target can understand the meaning of a single language it is hearing or reading when you cast the spell. This doesn't let it understand codes, language couched in metaphor, and the like (subject to GM discretion). If the target can hear multiple languages and knows that, it can choose which language to understand; otherwise, choose one of the languages randomly.

Heightened (3rd) The target can also speak the language.

Heightened (4th) You can target up to 10 creatures, and targets can also speak the language.

CONE OF COLD   SPELL 5

| COLD | EVOCATION |

Traditions arcane, primal

Cast ◆◆ somatic, verbal

Area 60-foot cone

Saving Throw basic Reflex

Icy cold rushes forth from your hands. You deal 12d6 cold damage to creatures in the area.

Heightened (+1) The damage increases by 2d6.

CONFUSION   SPELL 4

| EMOTION | ENCHANTMENT | MENTAL |

Traditions arcane, occult

Cast ◆◆ somatic, verbal

Range 30 feet; **Targets** 1 creature

Saving Throw Will; **Duration** 1 minute

You befuddle your target with strange impulses, causing it to act randomly. The effects are determined by the target's Will save. You can Dismiss the spell.

Critical Success The target is unaffected.

Success The target babbles incoherently and is stunned 1.

Failure The target is confused for 1 minute. It can attempt a new save at the end of each of its turns to end the confusion.

Critical Failure The target is confused for 1 minute, with no save to end early.

Heightened (8th) You can target up to 10 creatures.

CONTINGENCY SPELL 7

ABJURATION

Traditions arcane

Cast 10 minutes (material, somatic, verbal)

Duration 24 hours

You prepare a spell that will trigger later. While casting *contingency*, you also cast another spell of 4th level or lower with a casting time of no more than 3 actions. This companion spell must be one that can affect you. You must make any decisions for the spell when you cast *contingency*, such as choosing a damage type for *resist energy*. During the casting, choose a trigger under which the spell will be cast, using the same restrictions as for the trigger of a Ready action. Once *contingency* is cast, you can cause the companion spell to come into effect as a reaction with that trigger. It affects only you, even if it would affect more creatures. If you define complicated conditions, as determined by the GM, the trigger might fail. If you cast *contingency* again, the newer casting supersedes the older.

Heightened (8th) You can choose a spell of 5th level or lower.

Heightened (9th) You can choose a spell of 6th level or lower.

Heightened (10th) You can choose a spell of 7th level or lower.

CONTINUAL FLAME SPELL 2

EVOCATION LIGHT

Traditions arcane, divine, occult, primal

Cast ◆◆◆ material, somatic, verbal; **Cost** 6 gp of ruby dust

Range touch; **Targets** 1 object

Duration unlimited

A magical flame springs up from the object, as bright as a torch. It doesn't need oxygen, react to water, or generate heat.

Heightened (+1) The cost increases as follows: 16 gp for 3rd level; 30 gp for 4th, 60 gp for 5th, 120 gp for 6th,; 270 gp for 7th, 540 gp for 8th, 1,350 gp for 9th, and 3,350 gp for 10th.

CONTROL WATER SPELL 5

EVOCATION WATER

Traditions arcane, primal

Cast ◆◆ somatic, verbal

Range 500 feet; **Area** 50 feet long by 50 feet wide

By imposing your will upon the water, you can raise or lower the level of water in the chosen area by 10 feet. Water creatures in the area are subjected to the effects of *slow*.

CREATE FOOD SPELL 2

CONJURATION

Traditions arcane, divine, primal

Cast 1 hour (somatic, verbal)

Range 30 feet

You create enough food to feed six Medium creatures for a day. This food is bland and unappealing, but it is nourishing. After 1 day, if no one has eaten the food, it decays and becomes inedible. Most Small creatures eat one-quarter as much as a Medium creature (one-sixteenth as much for most Tiny creatures), and most Large creatures eat 10 times as much (100 times as much for Huge creatures and so on).

Heightened (4th) You can feed 12 Medium creatures.

Heightened (6th) You can feed 50 Medium creatures.

Heightened (8th) You can feed 200 Medium creatures.

CREATE WATER SPELL 1

CONJURATION WATER

Traditions arcane, divine, primal

Cast ◆◆ somatic, verbal

Range 0 feet

As you cup your hands, water begins to flow forth from them. You create 2 gallons of water. If no one drinks it, it evaporates after 1 day.

CREATION SPELL 4

CONJURATION

Traditions arcane, primal

Cast 1 minute (material, somatic, verbal)

Range 0 feet

Duration 1 hour

You conjure a temporary object from eldritch energy. It must be of vegetable matter (such as wood or paper) and 5 cubic feet or smaller. It can't rely on intricate artistry or complex moving parts, never fulfills a cost or the like, and can't be made of precious materials or materials with a rarity of uncommon or higher. It is obviously temporarily conjured, and thus can't be sold or passed off as a genuine item.

Heightened (5th) The item is metal and can include common minerals, like feldspar or quartz.

CRISIS OF FAITH SPELL 3

ENCHANTMENT MENTAL

Traditions divine

Cast ◆◆ somatic, verbal

Range 30 feet; **Targets** 1 creature

Saving Throw Will

You assault the target's faith, riddling the creature with doubt and mental turmoil that deal 6d6 mental damage, or 6d8 mental damage if it can cast divine spells. The effects are determined by its Will save.

Critical Success The target is unaffected.

Success The target takes half damage.

Failure The target takes full damage; if the target can cast divine spells, it's stupefied 1 for 1 round.

Critical Failure The target takes double damage, is stupefied 1 for 1 round, and can't cast divine spells for 1 round.

To many deities, casting this spell on a follower of your own deity without significant cause is anathema.

Heightened (+1) The damage increases by 2d6 (or by 2d8 if the target is a divine spellcaster).

CRUSADE SPELL 9

UNCOMMON ENCHANTMENT LINGUISTIC MENTAL

Traditions divine
Cast ◆◆ somatic, verbal
Range 60 feet; **Targets** up to 4 creatures
Duration 10 minutes

You issue a divine mandate to the targets. you pronounce a cause. It can be to attain an item, claim a patch of land, slay a creature, war with a group, or be entirely peaceful. Your cause can't force the targets to harm one another or themselves. The targets become completely dedicated to that cause, depending on their levels. They choose their own actions, but they favor direct action over inaction or indirect action.

- **13th or Lower** The target is so dedicated to the cause that it pursues the cause to the death (unless you say otherwise).
- **14th** The target is dedicated to the cause, but the spell ends for the target if it's reduced to half its maximum Hit Points or fewer. • **15th** As 14th, plus the target can attempt a Will save at the end of each of its turns to end the spell for itself.

The spell ends for all creatures if you or one of your allies uses a hostile action against a target, or when the cause is completed. The GM might determine this spell has alignment traits befitting the cause.

Heightened (10th) The level for each category increases by 2.

CRUSHING DESPAIR SPELL 5

EMOTION ENCHANTMENT MENTAL

Traditions arcane, occult
Cast ◆◆ somatic, verbal
Area 30-foot cone
Saving Throw Will; **Duration** 1 or more rounds

You inflict despair on creatures in the area. The effects for each creature are determined by its Will save.

Critical Success The creature is unaffected.

Success For 1 round, the creature can't use reactions and must attempt another save at the start of its turn; on a failure, it is slowed 1 for that turn as it sobs uncontrollably.

Failure As success, but the slowed 1 duration is 1 minute.

Critical Failure As failure, and the creature is automatically slowed 1 for 1 minute.

Heightened (7th) The area increases to a 60-foot cone.

DANCING LIGHTS CANTRIP 1

CANTRIP EVOCATION LIGHT

Traditions arcane, occult, primal
Cast ◆◆ somatic, verbal
Range 120 feet
Duration sustained

You create up to four floating lights, no two of which are more than 10 feet apart. Each sheds light like a torch. When you Sustain the Spell, you can move any number of lights up to 60 feet. Each light must remain within 120 feet of you and within 10 feet of all others, or it winks out.

DARKNESS SPELL 2

DARKNESS EVOCATION

Traditions arcane, divine, occult, primal
Cast ◆◆◆ material, somatic, verbal
Range 120 feet; **Area** 20-foot burst
Duration 1 minute

You create a shroud of darkness that prevents light from penetrating or emanating within the area. Light does not enter the area and any non-magical light sources, such as a torch or lantern, do not emanate any light while inside the area, even if their light radius would extend beyond the *darkness*. This also suppresses magical light of your *darkness* spell's level or lower. Light can't pass through, so creatures in the area can't see outside. From outside, it appears as a globe of pure darkness.

Heightened (4th) Even creatures with darkvision (but not greater darkvision) can barely see through the darkness. They treat targets seen through the darkness as concealed.

DARKVISION SPELL 2

DIVINATION

Traditions arcane, divine, occult, primal
Cast ◆◆ somatic, verbal
Duration 1 hour

You grant yourself supernatural sight in areas of darkness. You gain darkvision.

Heightened (3rd) The spell's range is touch and it targets 1 willing creature.

Heightened (5th) The spell's range is touch and it targets 1 willing creature. The duration is until the next time you make your daily preparations.

DAZE CANTRIP 1

CANTRIP ENCHANTMENT MENTAL NONLETHAL

Traditions arcane, divine, occult
Cast ◆◆ somatic, verbal
Range 60 feet; **Targets** 1 creature
Saving Throw Will; **Duration** 1 round

You cloud the target's mind and daze it with a mental jolt. The jolt deals mental damage equal to your spellcasting ability modifier; the target must attempt a basic Will save. If the target critically fails the save, it is also stunned 1.

Heightened (+2) The damage increases by 1d6.

DEAFNESS SPELL 2

NECROMANCY

Traditions arcane, divine, occult, primal
Cast ◆◆ somatic, verbal
Range 30 feet; **Targets** 1 creature
Saving Throw Fortitude

The target loses hearing; it must attempt a Fortitude save. The target is then temporarily immune for 1 minute.

Critical Success The target is unaffected.

Success The target is deafened for 1 round.

Failure The target is deafened for 10 minutes.

Critical Failure The target is deafened permanently.

INTRODUCTION

ANCESTRIES & BACKGROUNDS

CLASSES

SKILLS

FEATS

EQUIPMENT

SPELLS

THE AGE OF LOST OMENS

PLAYING THE GAME

GAME MASTERING

CRAFTING & TREASURE

APPENDIX

DEATH KNELL   SPELL 2

ATTACK   DEATH   NECROMANCY

Traditions divine, occult
Cast ◆◆ somatic, verbal
Range touch; **Targets** 1 living creature that has 0 HP
Saving Throw Will

You snuff the life out of a creature on the brink of death. The target must attempt a Will save. If this kills it, you gain 10 temporary HP and a +1 status bonus to attack and damage rolls for 10 minutes.

Critical Success The target is unaffected.
Success The target's dying value increases by 1.
Failure The target dies.

DEATH WARD   SPELL 5

ABJURATION

Traditions divine, occult, primal
Cast ◆◆ somatic, verbal
Range touch; **Targets** 1 living creature touched
Duration 10 minutes

You shield a creature from the ravages of negative energy. It receives a +4 status bonus to saves against death and negative effects, gains negative resistance 10, and suppresses the effects of the doomed condition.

DETECT ALIGNMENT   SPELL 1

UNCOMMON   DETECTION   DIVINATION

Traditions divine, occult
Cast ◆◆ somatic, verbal
Area 30-foot emanation

Your eyes glow as you sense aligned auras. Choose chaotic, evil, good, or lawful. You detect auras of that alignment. You receive no information beyond presence or absence. You can choose not to detect creatures or effects you're aware have that alignment.

Only creatures of 6th level or higher—unless divine spellcasters, undead, or beings from the Outer Sphere—have alignment auras.

Heightened (2nd) You learn each aura's location and strength.

ALIGNMENT AURA

The strength of an alignment aura depends on the level of the creature, item, or spell. The auras of undead, clerics and other divine spellcasters with a patron deity, and creatures from the Outer Sphere are one step stronger than normal (faint instead of none, for example).

Creature or Item Level	Spell or Effect Level	Aura Strength
0–5	–	None
6–10	0–3	Faint
11–15	4–7	Moderate
16–20	8–9	Powerful
21+	10	Overwhelming

DETECT MAGIC   CANTRIP 1

CANTRIP   DETECTION   DIVINATION

Traditions arcane, divine, occult, primal
Cast ◆◆ somatic, verbal
Area 30-foot emanation

You send out a pulse that registers the presence of magic. You receive no information beyond the presence or absence of magic. You can choose to ignore magic you're fully aware of, such as the magic items and ongoing spells of you and your allies.

You detect illusion magic only if that magic's effect has a lower level than the level of your *detect magic* spell. However, items that have an illusion aura but aren't deceptive in appearance (such as an *invisibility potion*) typically are detected normally.

Heightened (3rd) You learn the school of magic for the highest-level effect within range that the spell detects. If multiple effects are equally strong, the GM determines which you learn.
Heightened (4th) As 3rd level, but you also pinpoint the source of the highest-level magic. Like for an imprecise sense, you don't learn the exact location, but can narrow down the source to within a 5-foot cube (or the nearest if larger than that).

DETECT POISON   SPELL 1

UNCOMMON   DETECTION   DIVINATION

Traditions divine, primal
Cast ◆◆ somatic, verbal
Range 30 feet; **Targets** 1 object or creature

You detect whether a creature is venomous or poisonous, or if an object is poison or has been poisoned. You do not ascertain whether the target is poisonous in multiple ways, nor do you learn the type or types of poison. Certain substances, like lead and alcohol, are poisons and so mask other poisons.

Heightened (2nd) You learn the number and types of poison.

DETECT SCRYING   SPELL 4

UNCOMMON   DETECTION   DIVINATION

Traditions arcane, occult
Cast ◆◆ somatic, verbal
Area 30-foot emanation
Duration 1 hour

By tapping into trace divinatory auras, you detect the presence of scrying effects in the area. If *detect scrying* is higher level than a scrying effect, you gain a glimpse of the scrying creature and learn its approximate distance and direction.

Heightened (6th) The duration is until the next time you make your daily preparations.

DIMENSION DOOR   SPELL 4

CONJURATION   TELEPORTATION

Traditions arcane, occult
Cast ◆◆ somatic, verbal
Range 120 feet

Opening a door that bypasses normal space, you instantly transport yourself and any items you're wearing and holding from your current space to a clear space within range you can see. If this would bring another creature with you—even if you're carrying it in an extradimensional container—the spell is lost.

Heightened (5th) The range increases to 1 mile. You don't need to be able to see your destination, as long as you have been there in the past and know its relative location and distance from you. You are temporarily immune for 1 hour.

DIMENSIONAL ANCHOR   SPELL 4
ABJURATION

Traditions arcane, divine, occult
Cast ◆◆ somatic, verbal
Range 30 feet; **Targets** 1 creature
Saving Throw Will; **Duration** varies

You interfere with the target's ability to teleport and travel between dimensions. *Dimensional anchor* attempts to counteract any teleportation effect, or any effect that would move the target to a different plane. The duration is determined by the target's Will save.

Critical Success The target is unaffected.
Success The effect's duration is 1 minute.
Failure The effect's duration is 10 minutes.
Critical Failure The effect's duration is 1 hour.

DIMENSIONAL LOCK   SPELL 7
UNCOMMON ABJURATION

Traditions arcane, divine, occult
Cast ◆◆ somatic, verbal
Range 120 feet; **Area** 60-foot burst
Duration 1 day

You create a shimmering barrier that attempts to counteract teleportation effects and planar travel into or out of the area, including items that allow access to extradimensional spaces (such as a *bag of holding*). *Dimensional lock* tries to counteract any attempt to summon a creature into the area but doesn't stop the creature from departing when the summoning ends.

DINOSAUR FORM   SPELL 4
POLYMORPH TRANSMUTATION

Traditions primal
Cast ◆◆ somatic, verbal
Duration 1 minute

You channel the primal forces of nature to transform into a Large animal battle form, specifically that of a powerful and terrifying dinosaur. You must have space to expand or the spell is lost. When you cast this spell, choose ankylosaurus, brontosaurus, deinonychus, stegosaurus, triceratops, or tyrannosaurus. You can decide the specific type of animal, but this has no effect on the form's Size or statistics. While in this form, you gain the animal and dinosaur traits. You can Dismiss the spell.

You gain the following statistics and abilities regardless of which battle form you choose:

- AC = 18 + your level. Ignore your armor's check penalty and Speed reduction.
- 15 temporary Hit Points.
- Low-light vision and imprecise scent 30 feet.

- One or more unarmed melee attacks specific to the battle form you choose, which are the only attacks you can use. You're trained with them. Your attack modifier is +16, and your damage bonus is +9. These attacks are Strength based (for the purpose of the enfeebled condition, for example). If your unarmed attack modifier is higher, you can use it instead.
- Athletics modifier of +18, unless your own modifier is higher.

You also gain specific abilities based on the form you choose:

- **Ankylosaurus** Speed 25 feet; **Melee** ❖ tail (backswing, reach 10 feet), **Damage** 2d6 bludgeoning; **Melee** ❖ foot, **Damage** 2d6 bludgeoning.
- **Brontosaurus** Speed 25 feet; **Melee** ❖ tail (reach 15 feet), **Damage** 2d6 bludgeoning; **Melee** ❖ foot, **Damage** 2d8 bludgeoning.
- **Deinonychus** Speed 40 feet; **Melee** ❖ talon (agile), **Damage** 2d4 piercing plus 1 persistent bleed; **Melee** ❖ jaws, **Damage** 1d10 piercing.
- **Stegosaurus** Speed 30 feet; **Melee** ❖ tail (reach 10 feet), **Damage** 2d8 piercing.
- **Triceratops** Speed 30 feet; **Melee** ❖ horn, **Damage** 2d8 piercing, plus 1d6 persistent bleed on a critical hit; **Melee** ❖ foot, **Damage** 2d6 bludgeoning.
- **Tyrannosaurus** Speed 30 feet; **Melee** ❖ jaws (deadly, reach 10 feet), **Damage** 1d12 piercing; **Melee** ❖ tail (reach 10 feet), **Damage** 1d10 bludgeoning.

Heightened (5th) Your battle form is Huge and your attacks have 15-foot reach, or 20-foot reach if they started with 15-foot reach. You instead gain 20 temporary HP, an attack modifier of +18, a damage bonus of +6, double the damage dice, and Athletics +21.

Heightened (7th) Your battle form is Gargantuan and your attacks have 20-foot reach, or 25-foot reach if they started with 15-foot reach. You instead gain AC = 21 + your level, 25 temporary HP, an attack modifier of +25, a damage bonus of +15, double the damage dice, and Athletics +25.

DISAPPEARANCE   SPELL 8

ILLUSION

Traditions arcane, occult
Cast ❖❖ material, somatic
Range touch; **Targets** 1 creature
Duration 10 minutes

You shroud a creature from others' senses. The target becomes undetected, not just to sight but to all senses, allowing the target to count as invisible no matter what precise and imprecise senses an observer might have. It's still possible for a creature to find the target by Seeking, looking for disturbed dust, hearing gaps in the sound spectrum, or finding some other way to discover the presence of an otherwise-undetectable creature.

DISCERN LIES   SPELL 4

UNCOMMON DIVINATION MENTAL REVELATION

Traditions arcane, divine, occult
Cast ❖❖ somatic, verbal
Duration 10 minutes

Falsehoods ring in your ears like discordant notes. You gain a +4 status bonus to Perception checks when someone Lies.

DISCERN LOCATION   SPELL 8

UNCOMMON DETECTION DIVINATION

Traditions arcane, divine, occult
Cast 10 minutes (material, somatic, verbal)
Range unlimited; **Targets** 1 creature or object

You learn the name of the target's exact location (including the building, community, and country) and plane of existence.

You can target a creature only if you've seen it in person, have one of its significant belongings, or have a piece of its body. To target an object, you must have touched it or have a fragment of it. *Discern location* automatically overcomes protections against detection and divination of lower level than this spell, even if they would normally have a chance to block it.

DISINTEGRATE   SPELL 6

EVOCATION

Traditions arcane
Cast ❖❖ somatic, verbal
Range 120 feet; **Targets** 1 creature or unattended object
Saving Throw Fortitude

You fire a green ray at your target. Make a spell attack. You deal 12d10 damage, and the target must attempt a basic Fortitude save. On a critical hit, treat the save result as one degree worse. A creature reduced to 0 HP is reduced to fine powder; its gear remains.

An object you hit is destroyed (no save), regardless of Hardness, unless it's an artifact or similarly hard to destroy. A single casting can destroy no more than a 10-foot cube of matter. This automatically destroys any force construct, such as a *wall of force*.

Heightened (+1) The damage increases by 2d10.

DISJUNCTION   SPELL 9

UNCOMMON ABJURATION

Traditions arcane, primal
Cast ❖❖ somatic, verbal
Range 120 feet; **Targets** 1 magic item

Crackling energy disjoins the target. You attempt to counteract it (page 458). If you succeed, it's deactivated for 1 week. On a critical success, it's destroyed. If it's an artifact or similar item, you automatically fail.

DISPEL MAGIC   SPELL 2

ABJURATION

Traditions arcane, divine, occult, primal
Cast ❖❖ somatic, verbal
Range 120 feet; **Targets** 1 spell effect or unattended magic item

You unravel the magic behind a spell or effect. Attempt a counteract check against the target (page 458). If you succeed against a spell effect, you counteract it. If you succeed against a magic item, the item becomes a mundane item of its type for 10 minutes. This doesn't change the item's non-magical properties. If the target is an artifact or similar item, you automatically fail.

DISRUPT UNDEAD — CANTRIP 1

NECROMANCY **POSITIVE**

Traditions divine, primal
Cast ◆◆ somatic, verbal
Range 30 feet; **Targets** 1 undead creature
Saving Throw Fortitude

You lance the target with energy. You deal 1d6 positive damage plus your spellcasting ability modifier. The target must attempt a basic Fortitude save. If the creature critically fails the save, it is also enfeebled 1 for 1 round.

Heightened (+1) The damage increases by 1d6.

DISRUPTING WEAPONS — SPELL 1

NECROMANCY **POSITIVE**

Traditions divine
Cast ◆◆ somatic, verbal
Range touch; **Targets** up to two weapons, each of which must be wielded by you or a willing ally, or else unattended
Duration 1 minute

You infuse weapons with positive energy. Attacks with these weapons deal an extra 1d4 positive damage to undead.

Heightened (3rd) The damage increases to 2d4 damage.
Heightened (5th) Target up to three weapons, and the damage increases to 3d4 damage.

DIVINE AURA — SPELL 8

ABJURATION

Traditions divine
Cast ◆◆ somatic, verbal
Area 10-foot emanation; **Targets** allies in the area
Duration sustained up to 1 minute

Divine power wards the targets, granting each a +1 status bonus to AC and saves while in the area.

Choose an alignment your deity has (chaotic, evil, good, or lawful). You can't cast this spell if you don't have a deity or your deity is true neutral. This spell gains the trait of the alignment you chose. The bonuses granted by the spell increase to +2 against attacks by—and effects created by—creatures with an alignment opposite to the spell (lawful if you chose chaotic, evil if you chose good). These bonuses increase to +4 against effects created by such creatures that attempt to impose the controlled condition on a target of your *divine aura*, as well as against attacks made by creatures summoned by anything opposite in alignment to your *divine aura*.

When a creature of opposite alignment hits a target with a melee attack, the creature must succeed at a Will save or be blinded for 1 minute. It's then temporarily immune for 1 minute.

The first time you Sustain the Spell each round, the *divine aura's* radius grows 10 feet.

DIVINE DECREE — SPELL 7

EVOCATION

Traditions divine
Cast ◆◆ somatic, verbal
Range 40 feet; **Area** 40-foot emanation
Saving Throw Fortitude; **Duration** varies

You utter a potent litany from your faith, a mandate that harms those who oppose your ideals. Choose an alignment your deity has (chaotic, evil, good, or lawful). You can't cast this spell if you don't have a deity or your deity is true neutral. This spell gains the trait of the alignment you chose. You deal 7d10 damage to creatures in the area; each creature must attempt a Fortitude save. Creatures with an alignment that matches the one you chose are unaffected by the spell. Those that neither match nor oppose it treat the result of their saving throw as one degree better and don't suffer effects other than damage.

Critical Success The creature is unaffected.
Success The creature takes half damage.
Failure The creature takes full damage and is enfeebled 2 for 1 minute.
Critical Failure The creature takes double damage and is enfeebled 2 for 1 minute. On your home plane, a creature that critically fails is banished with the effect of a failed *banishment* save. A 10th-level creature or lower must attempt a Will save. On a failure, it's paralyzed for 1 minute; on a critical failure, it dies.

Heightened (+1) The damage increases by 1d10, and the level of creatures that must attempt a second save on a critical failure increases by 2.

DIVINE INSPIRATION — SPELL 8

ENCHANTMENT **MENTAL**

Traditions divine
Cast ◆◆ somatic, verbal
Range touch; **Targets** 1 willing creature

You infuse a target with spiritual energy, refreshing its magic. If it prepares spells, it recovers one 6th-level or lower spell it previously cast today and can cast that spell again. If it spontaneously casts spells, it recovers one of its 6th-level or lower spell slots. If it has a focus pool, it regains its Focus Points, as if it had Refocused.

DIVINE LANCE — CANTRIP 1

ATTACK **CANTRIP** **EVOCATION**

Traditions divine
Cast ◆◆ somatic, verbal
Range 30 feet; **Targets** 1 creature

You unleash a beam of divine energy. Choose an alignment your deity has (chaotic, evil, good, or lawful). You can't cast this spell if you don't have a deity or if your deity is true neutral. Make a ranged spell attack roll against the target's AC. On a hit, the target takes damage of the chosen alignment type equal to 1d4 + your spellcasting ability modifier (double damage on a critical hit). The spell gains the trait of the alignment you chose.

Heightened (+1) The damage increases by 1d4.

DIVINE VESSEL — SPELL 7

MORPH **TRANSMUTATION**

Traditions divine
Cast ◆◆ somatic, verbal
Duration 1 minute

INTRODUCTION

ANCESTRIES &
BACKGROUNDS

CLASSES

SKILLS

FEATS

EQUIPMENT

SPELLS

THE AGE OF
LOST OMENS

PLAYING THE
GAME

GAME
MASTERING

CRAFTING
& TREASURE

APPENDIX

You accept otherworldly energies into your body; while you are still recognizably yourself, you gain the features of one of your deity's servitors. Choose an alignment your deity has (chaotic, evil, good, or lawful). You can't cast this spell if you don't have a deity or your deity is true neutral. This spell gains the trait of the alignment you chose.

If you were Medium or smaller, you become Large, as the effects of *enlarge*. You must have space to expand into, or the spell is lost. You also gain the following benefits.

- 40 temporary Hit Points.
- A fly Speed equal to your Speed.
- Weakness 10 to the alignment opposite the one you chose.
- A +1 status bonus to saves against spells.
- Darkvision.
- Your unarmed attacks and weapons deal 1 additional damage of the chosen alignment type.
- One or more unarmed melee attacks. If you chose good or lawful, your fist attacks deal 2d8 damage. If you chose chaotic, you gain a bite unarmed attack that deals 2d10 piercing damage. If you chose evil, you gain a claws unarmed attack that deals 2d8 slashing damage and has the agile and finesse traits.

Heightened (9th) The temporary Hit Points increase to 60, the weakness increases to 15, and the duration increases to 10 minutes.

DIVINE WRATH   SPELL 4
EVOCATION

Traditions divine
Cast ❖❖ somatic, verbal
Range 120 feet; **Area** 20-foot burst
Saving Throw Fortitude

You can channel the fury of your deity against foes of opposed alignment. Choose an alignment your deity has (chaotic, evil, good, or lawful). You can't cast this spell if you don't have a deity or your deity is true neutral. This spell gains the trait of the alignment you chose. You deal 4d10 damage of the alignment you chose; each creature in the area must attempt a Fortitude save. Creatures that match the alignment you chose are unaffected. Those that neither match nor oppose it treat the result of their saving throw as one degree better.

Critical Success The creature is unaffected.
Success The creature takes half damage.
Failure The creature takes full damage and is sickened 1.
Critical Failure The creature takes full damage and is sickened 2; while it is sickened, it is also slowed 1.

Heightened (+1) The damage increases by 1d10.

DOMINATE   SPELL 6
UNCOMMON ENCHANTMENT INCAPACITATION MENTAL

Traditions arcane, occult
Cast ❖❖ somatic, verbal
Range 30 feet; **Targets** 1 creature
Saving Throw Will; **Duration** until the next time you make your daily preparations

You take command of the target, forcing it to obey your orders. If you issue an obviously self-destructive order, the target doesn't act until you issue a new order. The effect depends on its Will save.

Critical Success The target is unaffected.
Success The target is stunned 1 as it fights off your commands.
Failure The target follows your orders but can attempt a Will save at the end of each of its turns. On a success, the spell ends.
Critical Failure As a failure, but the target receives a new save only if you give it a new order that is against its nature, such as killing its allies.

Heightened (10th) The duration is unlimited.

DRAGON FORM   SPELL 6
POLYMORPH TRANSMUTATION

Traditions arcane, primal
Cast ❖❖ somatic, verbal
Duration 1 minute

Calling upon powerful transformative magic, you gain a Large dragon battle form. You must have space to expand or the spell is lost. When you cast this spell, choose one type of chromatic or metallic dragon. While in this form, you gain the dragon trait. You have hands in this battle form and can take manipulate actions. You can Dismiss the spell.

You gain the following statistics and abilities regardless of which battle form you choose:

- AC = 18 + your level. Ignore your armor's check penalty and Speed reduction.
- 10 temporary Hit Points.
- Speed 40 feet, fly Speed 100 feet.
- Resistance 10 against the damage type of your breath weapon (see below).
- Darkvision and imprecise scent 60 feet.
- One or more unarmed melee attacks specific to the battle form you choose, which are the only attacks you can use. You're trained with them. Your attack modifier is +22, and your damage bonus is +6. These attacks are Strength based (for the purpose of the enfeebled condition, for example). If your unarmed attack modifier is higher, you can use it instead. See below for more on these attacks.
- Athletics modifier of +23, unless your own modifier is higher.
- **Breath Weapon** ❖❖ (arcane, evocation) The shape, damage, and damage type of your breath weapon depend on your specific dragon form (see below). A creature in the area attempts a basic save against your spell DC. This is a Reflex save unless stated otherwise in the special ability description for your specific dragon form. Once activated, your breath weapon can't be used again for 1d4 rounds. Your breath weapon has the trait corresponding to the type of damage it deals.

You also gain specific abilities based on the type of dragon you choose:

- **Black** swim Speed 60 feet; **Melee** ❖ jaws, **Damage** 2d12 piercing plus 2d6 acid; **Melee** ❖ claw (agile), **Damage**

SPELLS 7

INTRODUCTION

ANCESTRIES &
BACKGROUNDS

CLASSES

SKILLS

FEATS

EQUIPMENT

SPELLS

THE AGE OF
LOST OMENS

PLAYING THE
GAME

GAME
MASTERING

CRAFTING
& TREASURE

APPENDIX

3d10 slashing; **Melee** ❖ tail (reach 10 feet), **Damage** 3d10 bludgeoning; **Melee** ❖ horns (reach 10 feet), **Damage** 3d8 piercing; breath weapon 60-foot line, 11d6 acid.

- **Blue** burrow Speed 20 feet; **Melee** ❖ jaws, **Damage** 2d10 piercing plus 1d12 electricity; **Melee** ❖ claw (agile), **Damage** 3d10 slashing; **Melee** ❖ tail (reach 10 feet), **Damage** 3d10 bludgeoning; **Melee** ❖ horns (reach 10 feet), **Damage** 3d8 piercing; breath weapon 80-foot line, 6d12 electricity.

- **Green** swim Speed 40 feet, ignores difficult terrain from non-magical foliage; **Melee** ❖ jaws, **Damage** 2d12 piercing plus 2d6 poison; **Melee** ❖ claw (agile), **Damage** 3d10 slashing; **Melee** ❖ tail (reach 10 feet), **Damage** 3d10 bludgeoning; **Melee** ❖ horns (reach 10 feet), **Damage** 3d8 piercing; breath weapon 30-foot cone, 10d6 poison (Fortitude save instead of Reflex).

- **Red** ignore concealed from smoke; **Melee** ❖ jaws, **Damage** 2d12 piercing plus 2d6 fire; **Melee** ❖ claw (agile), **Damage** 4d6 slashing; **Melee** ❖ tail (reach 10 feet), **Damage** 3d10 bludgeoning; **Melee** ❖ wing (reach 10 feet), **Damage** 3d8 bludgeoning; breath weapon 30-foot cone, 10d6 fire.

- **White** climb Speed 25 feet on ice only; **Melee** ❖ jaws, **Damage** 3d6 piercing plus 2d6 cold; **Melee** ❖ claw (agile), **Damage** 3d10 slashing; **Melee** ❖ tail (reach 10 feet), **Damage** 3d10 bludgeoning; breath weapon 30-foot cone, 10d6 cold.

- **Brass** burrow Speed 20 feet; **Melee** ❖ jaws, **Damage** 3d8 piercing plus 2d4 fire; **Melee** ❖ claw (agile), 3d10 slashing; **Melee** ❖ tail (reach 10 feet), **Damage** 3d10 bludgeoning; **Melee** ❖ spikes (reach 10 feet), **Damage** 3d8 piercing; breath weapon 60-foot line, 15d4 fire.

- **Bronze** swim Speed 40 feet; **Melee** ❖ jaws, **Damage** 2d10 piercing plus 1d12 electricity; **Melee** ❖ claw (agile), **Damage** 3d10 slashing; **Melee** ❖ tail (reach 10 feet), **Damage** 3d10 bludgeoning; **Melee** ❖ wing (reach 10 feet), **Damage** 3d8 slashing; breath weapon 80-foot line, 6d12 electricity.

- **Copper** climb Speed 25 feet on stone only; **Melee** ❖ jaws, **Damage** 2d12 piercing plus 2d6 acid; **Melee** ❖ claw (agile), **Damage** 3d10 slashing; **Melee** ❖ tail (reach 10 feet), **Damage** 3d10 bludgeoning; **Melee** ❖ wing (reach 10 feet), **Damage** 3d8 bludgeoning; breath weapon 60-foot line, 10d6 acid.

- **Gold** swim Speed 40 feet; **Melee** ❖ jaws, **Damage** 2d12 piercing plus 2d6 fire; **Melee** ❖ claw (agile), **Damage** 4d6 slashing; **Melee** ❖ tail (reach 10 feet), **Damage** 3d10 bludgeoning; **Melee** ❖ horns (reach 10 feet), **Damage** 3d8 piercing; breath weapon 30-foot cone, 6d10 fire.

- **Silver** walk on clouds; **Melee** ❖ jaws, **Damage** 2d12 piercing plus 2d6 cold; **Melee** ❖ claw (agile), **Damage** 3d10 slashing; **Melee** ❖ tail (reach 10), **Damage** 3d10 bludgeoning; breath weapon 30-foot cone, 8d8 cold.

Heightened (8th) Your battle form is Huge, you gain a +20-foot status bonus to your fly Speed, and your attacks have 10-foot reach (or 15-foot reach if they previously had 10-foot reach). You instead gain AC = 21 + your level, 15 temporary HP, an attack modifier of +28, a damage bonus of +12, Athletics +28, and a +14 status bonus to breath weapon damage.

DREAM COUNCIL — SPELL 8

ILLUSION | MENTAL | SLEEP

Traditions arcane, occult
Cast 10 minutes (somatic, verbal)
Range planetary; **Targets** up to 12 creatures you know by name and have met in person
Duration 1 hour

When you Cast this Spell, any targets—including you—can choose to immediately fall asleep. The spell ends for any creatures that don't choose to fall asleep. Sleepers join a shared dream, where they can communicate with one another as though they were in the same room. Individual targets leave this shared dream upon awakening, and if all the targets awaken, the spell ends.

DREAM MESSAGE — SPELL 3

ENCHANTMENT | MENTAL

Traditions arcane, divine, occult
Cast 10 minutes (somatic, verbal)
Range planetary; **Targets** 1 creature you know by name and have met in person
Duration 1 day

You send a message to your target's dream. The message is one-way, up to 1 minute of speech (roughly 150 words). If the target is asleep, they receive the message instantly. If not, they receive it the next time they sleep. As soon as they receive it, the spell ends, and you know the message was sent.

Heightened (4th) You can target up to 10 creatures you know by name and have met in person. You must send the same message to all of them; the spell ends for each creature individually.

DREAMING POTENTIAL — SPELL 5

ENCHANTMENT | MENTAL

Traditions occult
Cast 10 minutes (material, somatic, verbal)
Range touch; **Targets** 1 willing sleeping creature
Duration 8 hours

You draw the target into a lucid dream where it can explore the endless possibilities of its own potential within the ever-changing backdrop of its dreamscape. If it sleeps the full 8 hours uninterrupted, when it wakes, it counts as having spent a day of downtime retraining, though it can't use *dreaming potential* for any retraining that would require either an instructor or specialized knowledge it can't access within the dream.

DROP DEAD — SPELL 5

UNCOMMON | ILLUSION | VISUAL

Traditions arcane, divine
Cast ↻ somatic; **Trigger** A creature within range is hit by an attack from an enemy.
Range 120 feet; **Targets** 1 creature
Duration sustained up to 1 minute

The target appears to fall down dead, though it actually turns invisible. Its illusory corpse remains where it fell, complete with a believable fatal wound. This illusion looks and feels like a dead body. If the target's death seems absurd—for instance, a barbarian at full health appears to be slain by 2 damage—the GM can grant the attacker an immediate Perception check to disbelieve the illusion. If the target uses hostile actions, the spell ends. This ends the entire spell, so the illusory corpse disappears too.

Heightened (7th) The spell doesn't end if the target uses hostile actions.

DUPLICATE FOE   SPELL 7

CONJURATION

Traditions arcane, occult
Cast ❖❖❖ material, somatic, verbal
Range 30 feet; **Targets** 1 enemy of level 15 or lower
Saving Throw Fortitude; **Duration** sustained up to 1 minute

You try to create a temporary duplicate of an enemy to fight on your behalf. The target can attempt a Fortitude save to disrupt the spell. The duplicate appears in an unoccupied space adjacent to the target and has the target's attack modifier, AC, saving throw modifiers, Perception, and skill modifiers, but it has only 70 Hit Points and lacks the target's special abilities, including immunities, resistances, and weaknesses. It has no magic items except weapon potency runes.

The duplicate gains the minion trait, and it can only Stride and Strike. Its Strikes deal the target's normal damage but don't apply added effects, since it doesn't have special abilities. The spell automatically ends if the duplicate's Hit Points drop to 0.

The duplicate attacks your enemies to the best of its abilities. You can also try to give it additional instructions; when you Sustain the Spell, you can also Command a Minion as part of your action, but the GM determines whether the duplicate follows your command.

The duplicate is unstable, so each turn after it takes its actions, it loses 4d6 Hit Points. It's not a living creature, and it can never regain its lost Hit Points in any way.

Critical Success You fail to create a duplicate.
Success The duplicate deals half damage with its Strikes and the duration is reduced to a maximum of 2 rounds.
Failure The duplicate works as described.

Heightened (+1) The level of creature you can target increases by 2. The duplicate has 10 more HP.

EARTHBIND   SPELL 3

TRANSMUTATION

Traditions arcane, primal
Cast ❖❖ somatic, verbal
Range 120 feet; **Targets** 1 flying creature
Saving Throw Fortitude; **Duration** varies

Using the weight of earth, you hamper a target's flight, with effects based on its Fortitude save. If the creature reaches the ground safely, it doesn't take falling damage.

Critical Success The target is unaffected.
Success The target falls safely up to 120 feet.
Failure The target falls safely up to 120 feet. If it hits the ground, it can't Fly, *levitate*, or otherwise leave the ground for 1 round.

Critical Failure The target falls safely up to 120 feet. If it hits the ground, it can't Fly, *levitate*, or otherwise leave the ground for 1 minute.

EARTHQUAKE   SPELL 8

EARTH   EVOCATION

Traditions arcane, primal
Cast ❖❖ somatic, verbal
Range 500 feet; **Area** 60-foot burst
Duration 1 round

You shake the ground, topple creatures into fissures, and collapse structures.

The GM might add additional effects in certain areas. Cliffs might collapse, causing creatures to fall, or a lake might drain as fissures open up below its surface, leaving a morass of quicksand.

- **Shaking Ground** The ground is difficult terrain, and creatures on it take a –2 circumstance penalty to attack rolls, AC, and skill checks.
- **Fissures** Each creature on the ground must attempt a Reflex save at the start of its turn to keep its footing and avoid falling into 40-foot-deep fissures that open beneath it. The fissures are permanent, and their sides require DC 15 Athletics to Climb.
- **Collapse** Structures and ceilings might collapse. The GM rolls a flat check for each (DC 16 for a sturdy structure, DC 14 for an average structure and most natural formations, DC 9 for a shoddy structure, all adjusted higher or lower as the GM sees fit). A collapse deals 11d6 bludgeoning damage; each creature caught in a collapse must attempt a Reflex save to avoid it.

Critical Success The creature takes half the collapse damage.
Success The creature takes half the collapse damage and falls prone.
Failure The creature takes the full collapse damage and falls prone.
Critical Failure The creature takes the full collapse damage and falls into a fissure.

Heightened (10th) You create a massive earthquake that can devastate a settlement. The range increases to half a mile and the area to a quarter-mile burst.

ECLIPSE BURST   SPELL 7

COLD   DARKNESS   NECROMANCY   NEGATIVE

Traditions arcane, divine, primal
Cast ❖❖ somatic, verbal
Range 500 feet; **Area** 60-foot burst
Saving Throw Reflex

A globe of freezing darkness explodes in the area, dealing 8d10 cold damage to creatures and objects in the area, plus 8d4 additional negative damage to living creatures. Creatures and objects in the area must attempt a Reflex save.

If the globe overlaps with an area of magical light or affects a creature affected by magical light, *eclipse burst* attempts to counteract the light effect.

Critical Success The creature or object is unaffected.
Success The creature or object takes half damage.
Failure The creature or object takes full damage.
Critical Failure The creature or object takes double damage. If it's a creature, it becomes blinded by the darkness for an unlimited duration. **Heightened (+1)** The cold damage increases by 1d10 and the negative damage against the living increases by 1d4.

ELECTRIC ARC   CANTRIP 1

CANTRIP ELECTRICITY EVOCATION

Traditions arcane, primal
Cast ◆◆ somatic, verbal
Range 30 feet; **Targets** 1 or 2 creatures
Saving Throw basic Reflex

An arc of lightning leaps from one target to another. You deal electricity damage equal to 1d4 plus your spellcasting ability modifier.

Heightened (+1) The damage increases by 1d4.

ELEMENTAL FORM   SPELL 5

POLYMORPH TRANSMUTATION

Traditions arcane, primal
Cast ◆◆ somatic, verbal
Duration 1 minute

You call upon the power of the planes to transform into a Medium elemental battle form. When you cast this spell, choose air, earth, fire, or water. While in this form, you gain the corresponding trait and the elemental trait. You have hands in this battle form and can take manipulate actions. You can Dismiss the spell.

You gain the following statistics and abilities regardless of which battle form you choose:

- AC = 19 + your level. Ignore your armor's check penalty and Speed reduction.
- 10 temporary Hit Points.
- Darkvision.
- One or more unarmed melee attacks specific to the battle form you choose, which are the only attacks you can use. You're trained with them. Your attack modifier is +18, and your damage bonus is +9. These are Dexterity based (air or fire) or Strength based (earth or water). If your corresponding unarmed attack modifier is higher, you can use it instead.
- Acrobatics (air or fire) or Athletics (earth or water) modifier of +20; ignore this change if your own modifier is higher.

You also gain specific abilities based on the type of elemental you choose:

- **Air** fly Speed 80 feet, movement doesn't trigger reactions; **Melee** ◆ gust, **Damage** 1d4 bludgeoning.
- **Earth** Speed 20 feet, burrow Speed 20 feet; **Melee** ◆ fist, **Damage** 2d10 bludgeoning.
- **Fire** Speed 50 feet; fire resistance 10, weakness 5 to cold and 5 to water; **Melee** ◆ tendril, **Damage** 1d8 fire plus 1d4 persistent fire.

- **Water** Speed 20 feet, swim Speed 60 feet; fire resistance 5; **Melee** ◆ wave, **Damage** 1d12 bludgeoning, and you can spend an action immediately after a hit to push the target 5 feet with the effects of a successful Shove.

Heightened (6th) Your battle form is Large and your attacks have 10-foot reach. You must have space to expand or the spell is lost. You instead gain AC = 22 + your level, 15 temporary HP, an attack modifier of +23, a damage bonus of +13, and Acrobatics or Athletics +23.

Heightened (7th) Your battle form is Huge and your attacks have 15-foot reach. You must have space to expand or the spell is lost. You instead gain AC = 22 + your level, 20 temporary HP, an attack modifier of +25, a damage bonus of +11, double the number of damage dice (including persistent damage), and Acrobatics or Athletics +25.

ENDURE ELEMENTS   SPELL 2

ABJURATION

Traditions arcane, divine, primal
Cast 10 minutes (somatic, verbal)
Range touch; **Targets** 1 willing creature
Duration until the next time you make your daily preparations

You shield the target against dangerous temperatures. Choose severe cold or heat. The target is protected from the temperature you chose (but not extreme cold or heat).

Heightened (3rd) The target is protected from severe cold and heat.

Heightened (5th) The target is protected from severe cold, severe heat, extreme cold, and extreme heat.

ENERGY AEGIS   SPELL 7

ABJURATION

Traditions arcane, divine, occult, primal
Cast 1 minute (material, somatic, verbal)
Range touch; **Targets** 1 creature
Duration 24 hours

You protect the target with a powerful, long-lasting energy barrier. The target gains resistance 5 to acid, cold, electricity, fire, force, negative, positive, and sonic damage.

Heightened (9th) The resistances increase to 10.

ENHANCE VICTUALS   SPELL 2

TRANSMUTATION

Traditions divine, primal
Cast 1 minute (material, somatic, verbal)
Range touch; **Targets** up to 1 gallon of non-magical water or up to 5 pounds of food
Duration 1 hour

You transform the target into delicious fare, changing water into wine or another fine beverage or enhancing the food's taste and ingredients to make it a gourmet treat.

Prior to the transformation, the spell attempts to counteract any poisons in the food or water. The food turns back to normal if not consumed before the duration expires, though any poisons that were counteracted are still gone.

INTRODUCTION

ANCESTRIES & BACKGROUNDS

CLASSES

SKILLS

FEATS

EQUIPMENT

SPELLS

THE AGE OF LOST OMENS

PLAYING THE GAME

GAME MASTERING

CRAFTING & TREASURE

APPENDIX

Heightened (+1) The number of gallons of water you can target increases by 1, or the number of pounds of food you can target increases by 5.

ENLARGE   SPELL 2

POLYMORPH   TRANSMUTATION

Traditions arcane, primal
Cast ◆◆ somatic, verbal
Range 30 feet; **Targets** 1 willing creature
Duration 5 minutes

Bolstered by magical power, the target grows to size Large. Its equipment grows with it but returns to natural size if removed. The creature is clumsy 1. Its reach increases by 5 feet (or by 10 feet if it started out Tiny), and it gains a +2 status bonus to melee damage. This spell has no effect on a Large or larger creature.

Heightened (4th) The creature instead grows to size Huge. The status bonus to melee damage is +4 and the creature's reach increases by 10 feet (or 15 feet if the creature started out Tiny). The spell has no effect on a Huge or larger creature.

Heightened (6th) As level 4, but you can target up to 10 creatures.

ENTANGLE   SPELL 2

PLANT   TRANSMUTATION

Traditions primal
Cast ◆◆ somatic, verbal
Range 120 feet; **Area** all squares in a 20-foot-radius burst that contain plants
Duration 1 minute

Plants in the area entangle creatures. The area counts as difficult terrain. Each round that a creature starts its turn in the area, it must attempt a Reflex save. On a failure, it takes a –10-foot circumstance penalty to its Speeds until it leaves the area, and on a critical failure, it is also immobilized for 1 round. Creatures can attempt to Escape at *entangle*'s DC to remove these effects.

ENTHRALL   SPELL 3

AUDITORY   ENCHANTMENT   EMOTION

Traditions arcane, occult
Cast ◆◆ somatic, verbal
Range 120 feet; **Targets** all creatures in range
Saving Throw Will; **Duration** sustained

Your words fascinate your targets. You speak or sing without interruption throughout the casting and duration. Targets who notice your speech or song might give their undivided attention; each target must attempt a Will save. The GM might grant a circumstance bonus (to a maximum of +4) if the target is of an opposing religion, ancestry, or political leaning, or is otherwise unlikely to agree with what you're saying.

Each creature that comes within range has to attempt a save when you Sustain the Spell. If you're speaking, *enthrall* gains the linguistic trait.

Critical Success The target is unaffected and notices that you tried to use magic.

Success The target needn't pay attention but doesn't notice you tried to use magic (it might notice others are enthralled).

Failure The target is fascinated with you. It can attempt another Will save if it witnesses actions or speech with which it disagrees. If it succeeds, it's no longer fascinated and is temporarily immune for 1 hour. If the target is subject to a hostile act, or if another creature succeeds at a Diplomacy or Intimidation check against it, the fascination ends immediately.

Critical Failure As failure, but the target can't attempt a save to end the fascination if it disagrees with you.

ETHEREAL JAUNT   SPELL 7

UNCOMMON   CONJURATION   TELEPORTATION

Traditions divine, occult
Cast ◆◆ somatic, verbal
Duration sustained up to 1 minute

You travel to the Ethereal Plane, which overlaps the Material Plane. Material Plane creatures can't see you, and you can move through things on the Material Plane. You move at half your normal Speeds, but can move in any direction (including up and down).

You can see onto the Material Plane within a radius of 60 feet; it is gray, hazy, and concealed from you. You can't affect the Material Plane, and you can't be affected by the Material Plane except by force effects and abjurations originating there.

When the spell ends, you return to the Material Plane. If you're in the air, you fall (unless you can fly), and if you're inside an object, you're pushed into the nearest open space and take 1d6 damage per 5 feet you were pushed.

If you cast this spell when not on the Material Plane, it is lost.

Heightened (9th) You can target up to five additional willing creatures at a range of 30 feet. The duration is up to 10 minutes.

FABRICATED TRUTH   SPELL 10

ENCHANTMENT   INCAPACITATION   MENTAL

Traditions occult
Cast ◆◆◆ material, somatic, verbal
Range 100 feet; **Targets** up to 5 creatures
Saving Throw Will; **Duration** varies

Choose a single statement you want the targets to believe. The fact could be narrow, such as "a dragon is circling overhead and wants to kill me"; wide-reaching, such as "all humanoids are disguised abominations"; or conceptual, such as "if I don't live a kinder life, I'll be punished in the afterlife." The targets' experiences color how they react to this "truth" and how their behavior changes. If the statement changes what they perceive, they treat the change as a sudden revelation.

The effect of the spell depends on the targets' Will saves. If a target is already subject to *fabricated truth*, your spell tries to counteract it. If the counteract check fails, the outcome of the target's saving throw can't be worse than a success.

Critical Success The target doesn't believe the statement, and it knows you tried to trick it.

Success The target doesn't believe the statement or realize you tried to trick it.

Failure The target believes the statement for a duration of 1 week.

Critical Failure The target believes the statement with unlimited duration.

FAERIE FIRE   SPELL 2

`EVOCATION` `LIGHT`

Traditions divine, occult, primal
Cast ◆◆ somatic, verbal
Range 120 feet; **Area** 10-foot burst
Duration 5 minutes

All creatures in the area when you cast the spell are limned in colorful, heatless fire of a color of your choice for the duration. Visible creatures can't be concealed while affected by *faerie fire*. If the creatures are invisible, they are concealed while affected by *faerie fire*, rather than being undetected.

FALSE LIFE   SPELL 2

`NECROMANCY`

Traditions arcane, occult
Cast ◆◆ somatic, verbal
Duration 8 hours

You create a reservoir of vitality from necromantic energy, gaining a number of temporary Hit Points equal to 6 plus your spellcasting ability modifier.

Heightened (+1) The temporary Hit Points increase by 3.

FALSE VISION   SPELL 5

`UNCOMMON` `ILLUSION`

Traditions arcane, occult
Cast 10 minutes (material, somatic, verbal)
Range touch; **Area** 100-foot burst
Duration until the next time you make your daily preparations

You create a false image that fools any attempts to scry on an area. Any scrying spell sees, hears, smells, and otherwise detects whatever you wish within the area, rather than what is actually in the area. You can Sustain the Spell each round to change the illusion as you desire, including playing out a complex scene. If the scrying spell is of a higher level than *false vision*, the scryer can attempt a Perception check to disbelieve the illusion, though even if they're successful, they can't learn what's truly going on in the area.

FEAR   SPELL 1

`EMOTION` `ENCHANTMENT` `FEAR` `MENTAL`

Traditions arcane, divine, occult, primal
Cast ◆◆ somatic, verbal
Range 30 feet; **Targets** 1 creature
Saving Throw Will; **Duration** varies

You plant fear in the target; it must attempt a Will save.
Critical Success The target is unaffected.
Success The target is frightened 1.
Failure The target is frightened 2.
Critical Failure The target is frightened 3 and fleeing for 1 round.

Heightened (3rd) You can target up to five creatures.

FEATHER FALL   SPELL 1

`ABJURATION`

Traditions arcane, primal
Cast ↻ verbal; **Trigger** A creature within range is falling.

Range 60 feet; **Targets** 1 falling creature
Duration 1 minute

You cause the air itself to arrest a fall. The target's fall slows to 60 feet per round, and the portion of the fall during the spell's duration doesn't count when calculating falling damage. If the target reaches the ground while the spell is in effect, it takes no damage from the fall. The spell ends as soon as the target lands.

FEEBLEMIND   SPELL 6

`CURSE` `ENCHANTMENT` `INCAPACITATION` `MENTAL`

Traditions arcane, occult
Cast ◆◆ somatic, verbal
Range 30 feet; **Targets** 1 creature
Saving Throw Will; **Duration** varies

You drastically reduce the target's mental faculties. The target must attempt a Will save.
Critical Success The target is unaffected.
Success The target is stupefied 2 for 1 round.
Failure The target is stupefied 4 with an unlimited duration.
Critical Failure The target's intellect is permanently reduced below that of an animal, and it treats its Charisma, Intelligence, and Wisdom modifiers as –5. It loses all class abilities that require mental faculties, including all spellcasting. If the target is a PC, they become an NPC under the GM's control.

FEET TO FINS   SPELL 3

`MORPH` `TRANSMUTATION`

Traditions arcane, primal
Cast ◆◆ somatic, verbal
Range touch; **Targets** 1 willing creature
Duration 10 minutes

The target's feet transform into fins, improving mobility in the water but reducing it on land. The target gains a swim Speed equal to its normal land Speed, but its land Speed becomes 5 feet.

Heightened (6th) The spell lasts until the next time you make your daily preparations.

FIELD OF LIFE   SPELL 6

`HEALING` `NECROMANCY` `POSITIVE`

Traditions divine, primal
Cast ◆◆ somatic, verbal
Range 30 feet; **Area** 20-foot burst
Duration sustained up to 1 minute

A field of positive energy fills the area, exuding warmth and rejuvenating those within. Each living creature that starts its turn in the area regains 1d8 Hit Points, and any undead creature that starts its turn in the area takes 1d8 positive damage.

Heightened (8th) The healing and damage increase to 1d10.
Heightened (9th) The healing and damage increase to 1d12.

FIERY BODY   SPELL 7

`FIRE` `POLYMORPH` `TRANSMUTATION`

Traditions arcane, primal
Cast ◆◆ somatic, verbal
Duration 1 minute

You become living flame, giving you fire immunity, resistance 10 to precision damage, and weakness 5 to cold and to water. Any creature that touches you or damages you with an unarmed attack or non-reach melee weapon takes 3d6 fire damage.

Your unarmed attacks deal 1d4 additional fire damage, and your fire spells deal one additional die of fire damage (of the same damage die the spell uses). You can cast *produce flame* as an innate spell; the casting is reduced from 2 actions to 1.

In fire form, you have a fly Speed of 40 feet and don't need to breathe.

Heightened (9th) Creatures touching you take 4d6 fire damage instead of 3d6, your unarmed attacks deal 2d4 additional fire damage, and you have a fly Speed of 60 feet.

FINGER OF DEATH   SPELL 7

DEATH   NECROMANCY

Traditions divine, primal
Cast ❖❖ somatic, verbal
Range 30 feet; **Targets** 1 living creature
Saving Throw basic Fortitude

You point your finger toward the target and speak a word of slaying. You deal 70 negative damage to the target. If the damage from *finger of death* reduces the target to 0 Hit Points, the target dies instantly.

Heightened (+1) The damage increases by 10.

FIRE SEEDS   SPELL 6

EVOCATION   FIRE   PLANT

Traditions primal
Cast ❖❖ somatic, verbal
Saving Throw basic Reflex; **Duration** 1 minute

Four acorns grow in your hand, their shells streaked with pulsing red and orange patterns. You or anyone else who has one of the acorns can toss it up to 30 feet with an Interact action. It explodes in a 5-foot burst, dealing 4d6 fire damage. The save uses your spell DC, even if someone else throws the acorn.

Flames continue to burn on the ground in the burst for 1 minute, dealing 2d6 fire damage to any creature that enters the flames or ends its turn within them. A creature can take damage from the continuing flames only once per round, even if it's in overlapping areas of fire created by different acorns.

When the spell ends, any remaining acorns rot and turn to ordinary soil.

Heightened (8th) The burst's damage increases to 5d6, and the continuing flames damage increases to 3d6.
Heightened (9th) The burst's damage increases to 6d6, and the continuing flames damage increases to 3d6.

FIRE SHIELD   SPELL 4

EVOCATION   FIRE

Traditions arcane, primal
Cast ❖❖ somatic, verbal
Duration 1 minute

You wreathe yourself in ghostly flames, gaining cold resistance 5. Additionally, adjacent creatures that hit you with a melee attack, as well as creatures that touch you or hit you with an unarmed attack, take 2d6 fire damage each time they do.

Heightened (+2) The cold resistance increases by 5, and the fire damage increases by 1d6.

FIREBALL   SPELL 3

EVOCATION   FIRE

Traditions arcane, primal
Cast ❖❖ somatic, verbal
Range 500 feet; **Area** 20-foot burst
Saving Throw basic Reflex

A roaring blast of fire appears at a spot you designate, dealing 6d6 fire damage.

Heightened (+1) The damage increases by 2d6.

FLAME STRIKE   SPELL 5

EVOCATION   FIRE

Traditions divine
Cast ❖❖ somatic, verbal
Range 120 feet; **Area** 10-foot radius, 40-foot-tall cylinder
Saving Throw basic Reflex

You call a rain of divine fire that plummets down from above, dealing 8d6 fire damage. Because the flame is infused with divine energy, creatures in the area apply only half their usual fire resistance. Creatures that are immune to fire, instead of gaining the usual benefit of immunity, treat the results of their saving throws as one degree of success better.

Heightened (+1) The damage increases by 2d6.

FLAMING SPHERE   SPELL 2

EVOCATION   FIRE

Traditions arcane, primal
Cast ❖❖ somatic, verbal
Range 30 feet; **Area** 1 5-foot square
Saving Throw Reflex; **Duration** sustained up to 1 minute

You create a sphere of flame in a square within range. The sphere must be supported by a solid surface, such as a stone floor. The sphere deals 3d6 fire damage to each creature in the square where it first appears; each creature must attempt a basic Reflex save. On subsequent rounds, you can Sustain this Spell, leaving the sphere in its square or rolling it to another square within range and dealing 3d6 fire damage; each creature in its square must attempt a basic Reflex save.

Creatures that succeed at their save take no damage (instead of half).

Heightened (+1) The damage increases by 1d6.

FLEET STEP   SPELL 1

TRANSMUTATION

Traditions arcane, primal
Cast ❖❖ somatic, verbal
Duration 1 minute

You gain a +30-foot status bonus to your Speed.

SPELLS

7

INTRODUCTION

ANCESTRIES &
BACKGROUNDS

CLASSES

SKILLS

FEATS

EQUIPMENT

SPELLS

THE AGE OF
LOST OMENS

PLAYING THE
GAME

GAME
MASTERING

CRAFTING
& TREASURE

APPENDIX

FLESH TO STONE   SPELL 6

TRANSMUTATION

Traditions arcane, primal
Cast ◆❯❯ somatic, verbal
Range 120 feet; **Targets** 1 creature made of flesh
Saving Throw Fortitude; **Duration** varies

You try to turn the target's flesh into stone. The target must attempt a Fortitude save.

Critical Success The target is unaffected.

Success The target is slowed 1 for 1 round.

Failure The target is slowed 1 and must attempt a Fortitude save at the end of each of its turns; this ongoing save has the incapacitation trait. On a failed save, the slowed condition increases by 1 (or 2 on a critical failure). A successful save reduces the slowed condition by 1. When a creature is unable to act due to the slowed condition from *flesh to stone*, the creature is petrified permanently. The spell ends if the creature is petrified or the slowed condition is removed.

Critical Failure As failure, but the target is initially slowed 2.

FLOATING DISK   SPELL 1

CONJURATION **FORCE**

Traditions arcane, occult
Cast ◆❯❯ somatic, verbal
Duration 8 hours

A disk of magical force materializes adjacent to you. This disk is 2 feet in diameter and follows 5 feet behind you, floating just above the ground. It holds up to 5 Bulk of objects (though they must be able to fit and balance on its surface). Any objects atop the disk fall to the ground when the spell ends.

The spell ends if a creature tries to ride atop the disk, if the disk is overloaded, if anyone tries to lift or force the disk higher above the ground, or if you move more than 30 feet away from the disk.

FLY   SPELL 4

TRANSMUTATION

Traditions arcane, occult, primal
Cast ◆❯❯ somatic, verbal
Range touch; **Targets** 1 creature
Duration 5 minutes

The target can soar through the air, gaining a fly Speed equal to its Speed or 20 feet, whichever is greater.

Heightened (7th) The duration increases to 1 hour.

FORBIDDING WARD   CANTRIP 1

ABJURATION **CANTRIP**

Traditions divine, occult
Cast ◆❯❯ somatic, verbal
Range 30 feet; **Targets** 1 ally and 1 enemy
Duration sustained up to 1 minute

You ward an ally against the attacks and hostile spells from the target enemy. The target ally gains a +1 status bonus to

Armor Class and saving throws against the target enemy's attacks, spells, and other effects.

Heightened (6th) The status bonus increases to +2.

FORESIGHT   SPELL 9

DIVINATION | MENTAL | PREDICTION

Traditions arcane, divine, occult
Cast ◆◆ somatic, verbal
Range touch; **Targets** 1 creature
Duration 1 hour

You gain a sixth sense that warns you of danger that might befall the target of the spell. If you choose a creature other than yourself as the target, you create a psychic link through which you can inform the target of danger. This link is a mental effect. Due to the amount of information this spell requires you to process, you can't have more than one *foresight* spell in effect at a time. Casting *foresight* again ends the previous *foresight*. While *foresight* is in effect, the target gains a +2 status bonus to initiative rolls and isn't flat-footed against undetected creatures or when flanked. In addition, you gain the following reaction.

Foresight ⟳ **Trigger** The target of *foresight* defends against a hostile creature or other danger. **Effect** If the hostile creature or danger forces the target to roll dice (a saving throw, for example), the target rolls twice and uses the higher result, and this spell gains the fortune trait. But if the hostile creature or danger is rolling against the target (an attack roll or skill check, for example), that hostile creature or danger rolls twice and uses the lower result, and this spell gains the misfortune trait.

FREEDOM OF MOVEMENT   SPELL 4

ABJURATION

Traditions arcane, divine, primal
Cast ◆◆ somatic, verbal
Range touch; **Targets** 1 creature touched
Duration 10 minutes

You repel effects that would hinder a creature or slow its movement. While under this spell's effect, the target ignores effects that would give them a circumstance penalty to Speed. When they attempt to Escape an effect that has them immobilized, grabbed, or restrained, they automatically succeed unless the effect is magical and of a higher level than the *freedom of movement* spell.

GASEOUS FORM   SPELL 4

POLYMORPH | TRANSMUTATION

Traditions arcane, occult, primal
Cast ◆◆ somatic, verbal
Range touch; **Targets** 1 willing creature
Duration 5 minutes

The target transforms into a vaporous state. In this state, the target is amorphous and loses any item bonus to AC. It gains resistance 8 to physical damage and is immune to precision damage. It can't cast spells, activate items, or use actions that have the attack or manipulate trait. It gains a fly

Speed of 10 feet and can slip through tiny cracks. The target can Dismiss the spell.

GATE   SPELL 10

UNCOMMON | CONJURATION | TELEPORTATION

Traditions arcane, divine, occult
Cast ◆◆ somatic, verbal
Range 120 feet
Duration sustained up to 1 minute

You tear open a rift to another plane, creating a portal that creatures can travel through in either direction. This portal is vertical and circular, with a radius of 40 feet. The portal appears at a location of your choice on the destination plane, assuming you have a clear idea of both the destination's location on the plane and what the destination looks like. If you attempt to create a gate into or out of the realm of a deity or another powerful being, that being can prevent the gate from forming.

GENTLE REPOSE   SPELL 2

NECROMANCY

Traditions arcane, divine, occult, primal
Cast ◆◆ somatic, verbal
Range touch; **Targets** 1 corpse
Duration until the next time you make your daily preparations

The targeted corpse doesn't decay, nor can it be transformed into an undead. If the corpse is subject to a spell that requires the corpse to have died within a certain amount of time (for example, *raise dead*), do not count the duration of *gentle repose* against that time. This spell also prevents ordinary bugs and pests (such as maggots) from consuming the body.

Heightened (5th) The spell's duration is unlimited, but the spell takes one more action to cast and requires a material component and a cost (embalming fluid worth 6 gp).

GHOST SOUND   CANTRIP 1

AUDITORY | CANTRIP | ILLUSION

Traditions arcane, occult
Cast ◆◆ somatic, verbal
Range 30 feet
Duration sustained

You create an auditory illusion of simple sounds that has a maximum volume equal to four normal humans shouting. The sounds emanate from a square you designate within range. You can't create intelligible words or other intricate sounds (such as music).

Heightened (3rd) The range increases to 60 feet.
Heightened (5th) The range increases to 120 feet.

GHOSTLY WEAPON   SPELL 3

TRANSMUTATION

Traditions arcane, occult
Cast ◆◆ somatic, verbal
Range touch; **Targets** 1 non-magical weapon that is either unattended or wielded by you or a willing ally
Duration 5 minutes

The target weapon becomes translucent and ghostly, and it can affect material and incorporeal creatures and objects. It can be wielded by a corporeal or incorporeal creature and gains the effects of the *ghost touch* property rune.

GHOULISH CRAVINGS   SPELL 2

ATTACK **DISEASE** **EVIL** **NECROMANCY**

Traditions divine, occult
Cast ❖❖ somatic, verbal
Range touch; **Targets** 1 creature
Saving Throw Fortitude

You touch the target to afflict it with ghoul fever, infesting it with hunger and a steadily decreasing connection to positive energy; the target must attempt a Fortitude save.
Critical Success The target is unaffected.
Success The target is afflicted with ghoul fever at stage 1.
Failure The target is afflicted with ghoul fever at stage 2.
Critical Failure The target is afflicted with ghoul fever at stage 3.
Ghoul Fever (disease); **Level** 3; **Stage 1** carrier with no ill effects (1 day); **Stage 2** 3d8 negative damage and the creature regains half as many Hit Points from all healing (1 day); **Stage 3** as stage 2 (1 day); **Stage 4** 3d8 negative damage and the creature gains no benefit from healing (1 day); **Stage 5** as stage 4 (1 day); **Stage 6** the creature dies and rises as a ghoul at the next midnight

GLIBNESS   SPELL 4

UNCOMMON **ENCHANTMENT** **MENTAL**

Traditions occult
Cast ❖❖ somatic, verbal
Duration 10 minutes

Falsehoods pass your lips as smoothly as silk. You gain a +4 status bonus to Deception checks to Lie and against Perception checks to discern if you are telling the truth, and you add your level even if you're untrained. If the implausibility of your lies prompts a circumstance penalty or a DC increase, reduce that penalty or increase by half.

GLITTERDUST   SPELL 2

EVOCATION

Traditions arcane, primal
Cast ❖❖ somatic, verbal
Range 120 feet; **Area** 10-foot burst
Saving Throw Reflex

Creatures in the area are outlined by glittering dust. Each creature must attempt a Reflex save. If a creature has its invisibility negated by this spell, it is concealed instead of invisible. This applies both if the creature was already invisible and if it benefits from new invisibility effects before the end of the invisibility negation effect from this spell.
Critical Success The target is unaffected.
Success The target's invisibility is negated for 2 rounds.
Failure The target is dazzled for 1 minute and its invisibility is negated for 1 minute.
Critical Failure The target is blinded for 1 round and dazzled for 10 minutes. Its invisibility is negated for 10 minutes.

GLOBE OF INVULNERABILITY   SPELL 4

UNCOMMON **ABJURATION**

Traditions arcane, divine, occult
Cast ❖❖ somatic, verbal
Area 10-foot burst centered on one corner of your space
Duration 10 minutes

You create an immobile globe around yourself that attempts to counteract any spell from outside the globe whose area or targets enter into the globe, as if the globe were a *dispel magic* spell 1 level lower than its actual spell level. If the counteract attempt succeeds, it prevents only the portion of the spell that would have entered the globe (so if the spell also has targets outside the globe, or part of its area is beyond the globe, those targets or that area is affected normally). You must form the sphere in an unbroken open space, so its edges don't pass through any creatures or objects, or the spell is lost (though creatures can enter the globe after the spell is cast).

GLYPH OF WARDING   SPELL 3

ABJURATION

Traditions arcane, divine, occult, primal
Cast 10 minutes (material, somatic, verbal)
Range touch; **Targets** 1 container or a 10-foot-by-10-foot area
Duration unlimited

You craft a trap by binding a hostile spell into a symbol. While Casting this Spell, you also Cast a Spell of a lower spell level to store in the glyph. The stored spell must take 3 actions or fewer to cast, have a hostile effect, and target one creature or have an area. You can set a password, a trigger, or both for the glyph. Any creature that moves, opens, or touches the target container or enters the target area that doesn't speak the password or that matches the trigger activates the glyph, releasing the harmful spell within.

Once a spell is stored in the glyph, the glyph gains all the traits of that spell. If the stored spell targets one or more creatures, it targets the creature that set off the glyph. If it has an area, that area is centered on the creature that set off the glyph. *Glyph of warding*'s duration ends when the glyph is triggered. The glyph counts as a magical trap, using your spell DC for both the Perception check to notice it and the Thievery check to disable it; both checks require the creature attempting them to be trained in order to succeed.

You can Dismiss *glyph of warding*. The maximum number of *glyphs of warding* you can have active at a time is equal to your spellcasting ability modifier.

GOBLIN POX   SPELL 1

ATTACK **DISEASE** **NECROMANCY**

Traditions arcane, primal
Cast ❖❖ somatic, verbal
Range touch; **Targets** 1 creature
Saving Throw Fortitude

Your touch afflicts the target with goblin pox, an irritating allergenic rash. The target must attempt a Fortitude save.
Critical Success The target is unaffected.

INTRODUCTION

ANCESTRIES &
BACKGROUNDS

CLASSES

SKILLS

FEATS

EQUIPMENT

SPELLS

THE AGE OF
LOST OMENS

PLAYING THE
GAME

GAME
MASTERING

CRAFTING
& TREASURE

APPENDIX

Success The target is sickened 1.

Failure The target is afflicted with goblin pox at stage 1.

Critical Failure The target is afflicted with goblin pox at stage 2.

Goblin Pox (disease); **Level** 1. Goblins and goblin dogs are immune. **Stage 1** sickened 1 (1 round); **Stage 2** sickened 1 and slowed 1 (1 round); **Stage 3** sickened 1 and the creature can't reduce its sickened value below 1 (1 day)

GREASE   SPELL 1

CONJURATION

Traditions arcane, primal

Cast ◆◆ somatic, verbal

Range 30 feet; **Area** 4 contiguous 5-foot squares or

Targets 1 object of 1 Bulk or less

Duration 1 minute

You conjure grease, with effects based on choosing area or target.

- **Area** All solid ground in the area is covered with grease. Each creature standing on the greasy surface must succeed at a Reflex save or an Acrobatics check against your spell DC or fall prone. Creatures using an action to move onto the greasy surface during the spell's duration must attempt either a Reflex save or an Acrobatics check to Balance. A creature that Steps or Crawls doesn't have to attempt a check or save.

- **Target** If you cast the spell on an unattended object, anyone trying to pick up the object must succeed at an Acrobatics check or Reflex save against your spell DC to do so. If you target an attended object, the creature that has the object must attempt an Acrobatics check or Reflex save. On a failure, the holder or wielder takes a –2 circumstance penalty to all checks that involve using the object; on a critical failure, the holder or wielder releases the item. The object lands in an adjacent square of the GM's choice. If you cast this spell on a worn object, the wearer gains a +2 circumstance bonus to Fortitude saves against attempts to grapple them.

GRIM TENDRILS   SPELL 1

NECROMANCY   NEGATIVE

Traditions arcane, occult

Cast ◆◆ somatic, verbal

Area 30-foot line

Saving Throw Fortitude

Tendrils of darkness curl out from your fingertips and race through the air. You deal 2d4 negative damage and 1 persistent bleed damage to living creatures in the line. Each living creature in the line must attempt a Fortitude save.

Critical Success The creature is unaffected.

Success The creature takes half the negative damage and no persistent bleed damage.

Failure The creature takes full damage.

Critical Failure The creature takes double negative damage and double persistent bleed damage.

Heightened (+1) The negative damage increases by 2d4, and the persistent bleed damage increases by 1.

GUIDANCE   CANTRIP 1

CANTRIP   DIVINATION

Traditions divine, occult, primal

Cast ◆ verbal

Range 30 feet; **Targets** 1 creature

Duration until the start of your next turn

You ask for divine guidance, granting the target a +1 status bonus to one attack roll, Perception check, saving throw, or skill check the target attempts before the duration ends. The target chooses which roll to use the bonus on before rolling. If the target uses the bonus, the spell ends. Either way, the target is then temporarily immune for 1 hour.

GUST OF WIND   SPELL 1

AIR   EVOCATION

Traditions arcane, primal

Cast ◆◆ somatic, verbal

Area 60-foot line

Duration until the start of your next turn

A violent wind issues forth from your palm, blowing from the point where you are when you cast the spell to the line's opposite end. The wind extinguishes small non-magical fires, disperses fog and mist, blows objects of light Bulk or less around, and pushes larger objects. Large or smaller creatures in the area must attempt a Fortitude save. Large or smaller creatures that later move into the gust must attempt the save on entering.

Critical Success The creature is unaffected.

Success The creature can't move against the wind.

Failure The creature is knocked prone. If it was flying, it suffers the effects of critical failure instead.

Critical Failure The creature is pushed 30 feet in the wind's direction, knocked prone, and takes 2d6 bludgeoning damage.

HALLUCINATION   SPELL 5

ILLUSION   INCAPACITATION   MENTAL

Traditions arcane, occult

Cast ◆◆ material, somatic

Range 30 feet; **Targets** 1 creature

Duration 1 hour

The target consistently detects one thing as another, can't detect something that's there, or detects something that's not there, though it doesn't alter their beliefs. You choose which of these effects applies, and you determine the specifics of the hallucination. For example, you could make the target see all elves as humans, be unable to detect the presence of their brother, see their beloved pocket watch on their person even when it isn't, or see a tower in the center of town.

The target can attempt an initial Will save, with effects below. They also receive a Will save to disbelieve the hallucination every time they Seek or directly interact with the hallucination. For example, the target could attempt to disbelieve the hallucination each time they interacted with an elf, bumped into their brother accidentally, tried to check their pocket watch, or studied the tower. The target can attempt to disbelieve with a large circumstance bonus in situations determined by the GM, such as if the target attempted to climb the nonexistent tower.

Critical Success The creature is unaffected.

Success The creature perceives what you chose until it disbelieves, but it knows what the hallucination is.

Failure The creature perceives what you chose until it disbelieves.

Critical Failure The creature perceives what you chose until it disbelieves, and it trusts its false senses, taking a –4 circumstance penalty to saves to disbelieve.

Heightened (6th) Choose to either target up to 10 creatures or change the spell's duration to until the next time you make your daily preparations.

Heightened (8th) Choose to either target any number of creatures or change the spell's duration to unlimited.

HALLUCINATORY TERRAIN   SPELL 4

`UNCOMMON` `ILLUSION`

Traditions arcane, occult, primal

Cast 10 minutes (material, somatic, verbal)

Range 500 feet; **Area** 50-foot burst

Duration until the next time you make your daily preparations

You create an illusion that causes natural terrain to look, sound, feel, and smell like a different kind of terrain. This doesn't disguise any structures or creatures in the area.

Any creature that touches the illusion or uses the Seek action to examine it can attempt to disbelieve your illusion.

Heightened (5th) Your image can also disguise structures or create illusory structures (but still doesn't disguise creatures).

HARM   SPELL 1

`NECROMANCY` `NEGATIVE`

Traditions divine

Cast ❖ to ❖❖❖

Range varies; **Targets** 1 living creature or 1 willing undead creature

You channel negative energy to harm the living or heal the undead. If the target is a living creature, you deal 1d8 negative damage to it, and it gets a basic Fortitude save. If the target is a willing undead creature, you restore that amount of Hit Points. The number of actions you spend when Casting this Spell determines its targets, range, area, and other parameters.

❖ **(somatic)** The spell has a range of touch.

❖❖ **(verbal, somatic)** The spell has a range of 30 feet. If you're healing an undead creature, increase the Hit Points restored by 8.

❖❖❖ **(material, verbal, somatic)** You disperse positive energy in a 30-foot emanation. This targets all living and undead creatures in the area.

Heightened (+1) The amount of healing or damage increases by 1d8, and the extra healing for the 2-action version increases by 8.

HASTE   SPELL 3

`TRANSMUTATION`

Traditions arcane, occult, primal

Cast ❖❖ somatic, verbal

Range 30 feet; **Targets** 1 creature

Duration 1 minute

Magic empowers the target to act faster. It gains the quickened condition and can use the extra action each round only for Strike and Stride actions.

Heightened (7th) You can target up to 6 creatures.

HEAL   SPELL 1

`HEALING` `NECROMANCY` `POSITIVE`

Traditions divine, primal

Cast ❖ to ❖❖❖

Range varies; **Targets** 1 willing living creature or 1 undead creature

You channel positive energy to heal the living or damage the undead. If the target is a willing living creature, you restore 1d8 Hit Points. If the target is undead, you deal that amount of positive damage to it, and it gets a basic Fortitude save. The number of actions you spend when Casting this Spell determines its targets, range, area, and other parameters.

❖ **(somatic)** The spell has a range of touch.

❖❖ **(verbal, somatic)** The spell has a range of 30 feet. If you're healing a living creature, increase the Hit Points restored by 8.

❖❖❖ **(material, somatic, verbal)** You disperse positive energy in a 30-foot emanation. This targets all living and undead creatures in the burst.

Heightened (+1) The amount of healing or damage increases by 1d8, and the extra healing for the 2-action version increases by 8.

HEROISM   SPELL 3

`ENCHANTMENT` `MENTAL`

Traditions divine, occult

Cast ❖❖ somatic, verbal

Range touch; **Targets** 1 humanoid creature

Duration 10 minutes

You tap into the target's inner heroism, granting it a +1 status bonus to attack rolls, Perception checks, saving throws, and skill checks.

Heightened (6th) The status bonus increases to +2.

Heightened (9th) The status bonus increases to +3.

HIDEOUS LAUGHTER   SPELL 2

`EMOTION` `ENCHANTMENT` `MENTAL`

Traditions arcane, occult

Cast ❖❖ somatic, verbal

Range 30 feet; **Targets** 1 living creature

Saving Throw Will; **Duration** sustained

The target is overtaken with uncontrollable laughter. It must attempt a Will save.

Critical Success The target is unaffected.

Success The target is plagued with uncontrollable laugher. It can't use reactions.

Failure The target is slowed 1 and can't use reactions.

Critical Failure The target falls prone and can't use actions or reactions for 1 round. It then suffers the failure effects.

INTRODUCTION

ANCESTRIES & BACKGROUNDS

CLASSES

SKILLS

FEATS

EQUIPMENT

SPELLS

THE AGE OF LOST OMENS

PLAYING THE GAME

GAME MASTERING

CRAFTING & TREASURE

APPENDIX

HOLY CASCADE   SPELL 4

EVOCATION · GOOD · POSITIVE · WATER

Traditions divine
Cast ❖❖ somatic, verbal; **Cost** one vial of *holy water* (page 571)
Range 500 feet; **Area** 20-foot burst
Saving Throw basic Reflex

You call upon sacred energy to amplify a vial of *holy water*, tossing it an incredible distance. It explodes in an enormous burst that deals 3d6 bludgeoning damage to creatures in the area from the cascade of water. The water deals an additional 6d6 positive damage to undead and 6d6 good damage to fiends.

Heightened (+1) The bludgeoning damage increases by 1d6, and the additional positive and good damage each increase by 2d6.

HORRID WILTING   SPELL 8

NECROMANCY · NEGATIVE

Traditions arcane, primal
Cast ❖❖ somatic, verbal
Range 500 feet; **Targets** any number of living creatures
Saving Throw basic Fortitude

You pull the moisture from the targets' bodies, dealing 10d10 negative damage. Creatures made of water (such as water elementals) and plant creatures use the outcome for one degree of success worse than the result of their saving throw. Creatures whose bodies contain no significant moisture (such as earth elementals) are immune to *horrid wilting*.

Heightened (+1) The damage increases by 1d10.

HUMANOID FORM   SPELL 2

POLYMORPH · TRANSMUTATION

Traditions arcane, occult, primal
Cast ❖❖ somatic, verbal
Duration 10 minutes

You transform your appearance to that of a Small or Medium humanoid, such as a dwarf, elf, goblin, halfling, human, orc, or lizardfolk. You gain the humanoid trait in addition to your other traits while in this form, as well as any trait related to the creature's kind (such as goblin or human). If this transformation reduces your size, it reduces your reach accordingly (as the *shrink* spell). This transformation doesn't change your statistics in any way, and you don't gain any special abilities of the humanoid form you assume. You can still wear and use your gear, which changes size (if necessary) to match your new form. If items leave your person, they return to their usual size.

   Humanoid form grants you a +4 status bonus to Deception checks to pass as a generic member of the chosen ancestry, and you add your level even if you're untrained, but you can't make yourself look like a specific person. If you want to Impersonate an individual, you still need to create a disguise, though the GM won't factor in the difference in ancestry when determining the DC of your Deception check. You can Dismiss this spell.

Heightened (3rd) You gain darkvision or low-light vision if the form you assume has that ability.

Heightened (5th) You can take on the appearance of a Large humanoid. If this increases your size, you gain the effects of the *enlarge* spell.

HYDRAULIC PUSH   SPELL 1

ATTACK · EVOCATION · WATER

Traditions arcane, primal
Cast ❖❖ somatic, verbal
Range 60 feet; **Targets** 1 creature or object

You call forth a powerful blast of pressurized water that bludgeons the target and knocks it back. Make a ranged spell attack roll.

Critical Success The target takes 6d6 bludgeoning damage and is knocked back 10 feet.

Success The target takes 3d6 bludgeoning damage and is knocked back 5 feet.

Heightened (+1) The damage increases by 2d6.

HYDRAULIC TORRENT   SPELL 4

EVOCATION · WATER

Traditions primal
Cast ❖❖ somatic, verbal
Area 60-foot line
Saving Throw Fortitude

A swirling torrent of water manifests along a straight line, battering those that are its path and possibly pushing them away from you. The torrent deals 8d6 bludgeoning damage. Each creature in the area must attempt a basic Fortitude save. Creatures that fail the save are also knocked back 5 feet (10 feet on a critical failure).

Heightened (+1) The damage increases by 2d6.

HYPERCOGNITION   SPELL 3

DIVINATION

Traditions occult
Cast ❖ verbal

You rapidly catalog and collate information relevant to your current situation. You can instantly use up to 6 Recall Knowledge actions as part of Casting this Spell. For these actions, you can't use any special abilities, reactions, or free actions that trigger when you Recall Knowledge.

HYPNOTIC PATTERN   SPELL 3

ILLUSION · VISUAL

Traditions arcane, occult
Cast ❖❖ material, somatic
Range 120 feet; **Area** 10-foot burst
Saving Throw Will; **Duration** sustained up to 1 minute

You create a pattern of shifting colors that hovers in the air in a geometric cloud. Creatures are dazzled while inside the pattern. In addition, a creature must attempt a Will saving throw if it is inside the pattern when you cast it, when it enters the pattern, when it ends its turn within the pattern, or if it uses a Seek or Interact action on the pattern. A creature currently fascinated by the pattern doesn't attempt new saves.

Success The target is unaffected.

Failure The target is fascinated by the pattern.

Critical Failure The target is fascinated by the pattern. While it remains fascinated, it can't use reactions.

ILLUSORY CREATURE   SPELL 2

AUDITORY **ILLUSION** **VISUAL**
Traditions arcane, occult
Cast ◆◆ somatic, verbal
Range 500 feet
Duration sustained

You create an illusory image of a Large or smaller creature. It generates the appropriate sounds, smells, and feels believable to the touch. If you and the image are ever farther than 500 feet apart, the spell ends.

The image can't speak, but you can use your actions to speak through the creature, with the spell disguising your voice as appropriate. You might need to attempt a Deception or Performance check to mimic the creature, as determined by the GM. This is especially likely if you're trying to imitate a specific person and engage with someone that person knows.

In combat, the illusion can use 2 actions per turn, which it uses when you Sustain the Spell. It uses your spell attack roll for attack rolls and your spell DC for its AC. Its saving throw modifiers are equal to your spell DC – 10. It is substantial enough that it can flank other creatures. If the image is hit by an attack or fails a save, the spell ends.

The illusion can cause damage by making the target believe the illusion's attacks are real, but it cannot otherwise directly affect the physical world. If the illusory creature hits with a Strike, the target takes mental damage equal to 1d4 plus your spellcasting ability modifier. This is a mental effect. The illusion's Strikes are nonlethal. If the damage doesn't correspond to the image of the monster—for example, if an illusory Large dragon deals only 5 damage—the GM might allow the target to attempt a Perception check to disbelieve the spell as a free action. Any relevant resistances and weaknesses apply if the target thinks they do, as judged by the GM. For example, if the illusion wields a warhammer and attacks a creature resistant to bludgeoning damage, the creature would take less mental damage. However, illusory damage does not deactivate regeneration or trigger other effects that require a certain damage type. The GM should track illusory damage dealt by the illusion.

Any creature that touches the image or uses the Seek action to examine it can attempt to disbelieve your illusion. When a creature disbelieves the illusion, it recovers from half the damage it had taken from it (if any) and doesn't take any further damage from it.

Heightened (+1) The damage of the image's Strikes increases by 1d4, and the maximum size of creature you can create increases by one (to a maximum of Gargantuan).

ILLUSORY DISGUISE   SPELL 1

ILLUSION **VISUAL**
Traditions arcane, occult
Cast ◆◆ somatic, verbal
Duration 1 hour

You create an illusion that causes you to appear as another creature of the same body shape, and with roughly similar height (within 6 inches) and weight (within 50 pounds), as yourself.

The disguise is typically good enough to hide your identity, but not to impersonate a specific individual. The spell doesn't change your voice, scent, or mannerisms. You can change the appearance of your clothing and worn items, such as making your armor look like a dress. Held items are unaffected, and any worn item you remove returns to its true appearance.

Casting *illusory disguise* counts as setting up a disguise for the Impersonate use of Deception; it ignores any circumstance penalties you might take for disguising yourself as a dissimilar creature, it gives you a +4 status bonus to Deception checks to prevent others from seeing through your disguise, and you add your level even if you're untrained. You can Dismiss this spell.

Heightened (2nd) The spell also disguises your voice and scent, and it gains the auditory trait.

Heightened (3rd) You can appear as any creature of the same size, even a specific individual. You must have seen an individual to take on their appearance. The spell also disguises your voice and scent, and it gains the auditory trait.

ILLUSORY OBJECT   SPELL 1

ILLUSION **VISUAL**
Traditions arcane, occult
Cast ◆◆ somatic, verbal
Range 500 feet; **Area** 20-foot burst
Duration 10 minutes

You create an illusory visual image of a stationary object. The entire image must fit within the spell's area. The object appears to animate naturally, but it doesn't make sounds or generate smells. For example, water would appear to pour down an illusory waterfall, but it would be silent.

Any creature that touches the image or uses the Seek action to examine it can attempt to disbelieve your illusion.

Heightened (2nd) Your image makes appropriate sounds, generates normal smells, and feels right to the touch. The spell gains the auditory trait. The duration increases to 1 hour.

Heightened (5th) As the 2nd-level version, but the duration is unlimited.

ILLUSORY SCENE   SPELL 5

AUDITORY **ILLUSION** **VISUAL**
Traditions arcane, occult
Cast 10 minutes (somatic, verbal)
Range 500 feet; **Area** 30-foot burst
Duration 1 hour

You form an imaginary scene that includes up to 10 discrete creatures or objects of various sizes, all of which must be within the spell's area. These elements generate appropriate sounds and smells, and they feel right to the touch. Elements of an illusory scene are incapable of speech. Unlike with the *illusory creature* spell, creatures in your scene lack combat abilities and statistics. Your scene doesn't include changes to the environment around it, though you can place your scene within the illusory environment of a *hallucinatory terrain* spell.

When you create the scene, you can choose to have it be static or follow a program. Though a static scene is stationary, it includes basic natural movement. For example, wind blowing on

an illusory piece of paper would rustle it. A program can be up to 1 minute long and repeats when finished. For instance, you could create a scene of two orcs fighting each other, and the fight would go the same way for each repetition. If you create a loop, the two fighters end up in the same place at the start of the scene and at the end of it, but you can smooth the program so it's hard to tell when the loop ends and begins. Anyone observing the scene for more than a few minutes almost always notices it looping. You're unable to alter the program after you create the illusion.

Any creature that touches any part of the image or uses the Seek action to examine it can attempt to disbelieve your illusion. If they interact with a portion of the illusion, they disbelieve only that portion. They disbelieve the entire scene only on a critical success.

Heightened (6th) Creatures or objects in your scene can speak. You must speak the specific lines for each actor when creating your program. The spell disguises your voice for each actor.
Heightened (8th) As the 6th-level version, and the duration is unlimited.

IMPLOSION   SPELL 9

EVOCATION

Traditions arcane, primal
Cast ◆◆ somatic, verbal
Range 30 feet; **Targets** 1 corporeal creature
Saving Throw basic Fortitude; **Duration** sustained up to 1 minute

You crush the target by causing it to collapse in on itself, dealing 75 damage. Each time you Sustain the Spell, you must choose a new target to be subject to the same effect; the same creature can never be targeted more than once with a single casting of this spell. You also can't affect more than one creature per turn with *implosion*. You can't target a creature that's incorporeal, gaseous, or liquid, or one that otherwise lacks a solid form.
Heightened (+1) The damage increases by 10.

INSECT FORM   SPELL 3

POLYMORPH **TRANSMUTATION**

Traditions primal
Cast ◆◆ somatic, verbal
Duration 1 minute

You envision a simple bug and transform into a Medium animal battle form. When you cast this spell, choose ant, beetle, centipede, mantis, scorpion, or spider. You can decide the specific type of animal (such as such as a ladybug or scarab for beetle), but this has no effect on the form's Size or statistics. While in this form, you gain the animal trait. You can Dismiss this spell.

You gain the following statistics and abilities regardless of which battle form you choose:

- AC = 18 + your level. Ignore your armor's check penalty and Speed reduction.
- 10 temporary Hit Points.
- Low-light vision.

- One or more attacks specific to the battle form you choose, which are the only attacks you can use. You're trained with them. Your attack modifier is +13, and your damage bonus is +2. These attacks are Strength based (for the purpose of the enfeebled condition). If your unarmed attack modifier is higher, you can use it instead.
- Athletics modifier of +13, unless your own is higher.

You also gain specific abilities based on the form you choose:

- **Ant** Speed 30 feet, climb Speed 30 feet; **Melee ◆** mandibles, **Damage** 2d6 bludgeoning.
- **Beetle** Speed 25 feet; **Melee ◆** mandibles, **Damage** 2d10 bludgeoning.
- **Centipede** Speed 25 feet, climb Speed 25 feet; darkvision; **Melee ◆** mandibles, **Damage** 1d8 piercing plus 1d4 persistent poison.
- **Mantis** Speed 40 feet; imprecise scent 30 feet; **Melee ◆** foreleg, **Damage** 2d8 bludgeoning.
- **Scorpion** Speed 40 feet; darkvision, imprecise tremorsense 60 feet; **Melee ◆** stinger, **Damage** 1d8 piercing plus 1d4 persistent poison; **Melee ◆** pincer (agile), **Damage** 1d6 bludgeoning.
- **Spider** darkvision; **Melee ◆** fangs, **Damage** 1d6 piercing plus 1d4 persistent poison; **Melee ◆** Speed 25 feet, climb Speed 25 feet; **Ranged ◆** web (range increment 20 feet), **Damage** entangles the target for 1 round.

Heightened (4th) Your battle form is Large, and your attacks have 10-foot reach. You must have enough space to expand into or the spell is lost. You instead gain 15 temporary HP, attack modifier +16, damage bonus +6, and Athletics +16.

Heightened (5th) Your battle form is Huge, and your attacks have 15-foot reach. You must have enough space to expand into or the spell is lost. You instead gain 20 temporary HP, attack modifier +18, damage bonus +2 and double damage dice (including persistent damage), and Athletics +20.

INVISIBILITY SPELL 2

ILLUSION

Traditions arcane, occult
Cast ◆◆ material, somatic
Range touch; **Targets** 1 creature
Duration 10 minutes

Cloaked in illusion, the target becomes invisible. This makes it undetected to all creatures, though the creatures can attempt to find the target, making it hidden to them instead (page 466). If the target uses a hostile action, the spell ends after that hostile action is completed.

Heightened (4th) The spell lasts 1 minute, but it doesn't end if the target uses a hostile action.

INVISIBILITY SPHERE SPELL 3

ILLUSION

Traditions arcane, occult
Cast ◆◆ material, somatic
Area 10-foot emanation; **Targets** you and any number of creatures in range
Duration 10 minutes

You and all targets are invisible except to each other as long as you remain within the spell's area. If a creature made invisible by this spell leaves the spell's area, it becomes visible and remains so even if it returns to the spell's area. If any creature made invisible by this spell uses a hostile action, the spell ends after the hostile action is completed.

While exploring, it's easy to move together slowly and remain invisible. This is untenable in a battle, however. Once an encounter begins, creatures remain invisible until at most the end of the first round, at which point the spell ends.

Heightened (5th) The duration increases to 1 hour.

ITEM FACADE SPELL 1

ILLUSION VISUAL

Traditions arcane, occult
Cast ◆◆ somatic, verbal
Range touch; **Targets** 1 object no more than 10 feet by 10 feet by 10 feet
Duration 1 hour

You make the target object look and feel as though it were in much better or worse physical condition. When you cast this spell, decide whether you want to make the object look decrepit or perfect. An item made to look decrepit appears broken and shoddy. An intact item made to look better appears as though it's brand new and highly polished or well maintained. A broken item appears to be intact and functional. Destroyed items can't be affected by this spell. A creature that Interacts with the item can attempt to disbelieve the illusion.

Heightened (2nd) The duration is 24 hours.
Heightened (3rd) The duration is unlimited.

JUMP SPELL 1

MOVE TRANSMUTATION

Traditions arcane, primal
Cast ◆ somatic

Your legs surge with strength, ready to leap high and far. You jump 30 feet in any direction without touching the ground. You must land on a space of solid ground within 30 feet of you, or else you fall after using your next action.

Heightened (3rd) The range becomes touch, the target changes to one touched creature, and the duration becomes 1 minute, allowing the target to jump as described whenever it takes the Leap action.

KNOCK SPELL 2

TRANSMUTATION

Traditions arcane, occult
Cast ◆◆ somatic, verbal
Range 30 feet; **Targets** 1 door, lock, or container
Duration 1 minute

You make the target easier to open. *Knock* grants a +4 status bonus to any creature that tries to open the target door, lock, or container with an Athletics or a Thievery check. You can attempt a Thievery check to open the target as part of casting *knock*, and you add your level even if you're untrained.

Knock counteracts *lock*.

INTRODUCTION

ANCESTRIES & BACKGROUNDS

CLASSES

SKILLS

FEATS

EQUIPMENT

SPELLS

THE AGE OF LOST OMENS

PLAYING THE GAME

GAME MASTERING

CRAFTING & TREASURE

APPENDIX

KNOW DIRECTION CANTRIP 1

CANTRIP | DETECTION | DIVINATION

Traditions divine, occult, primal
Cast ◈◈ somatic, verbal

In your mind's eye, you see a path northward. You immediately know which direction is north (if it exists at your current location).

Heightened (7th) You can instead know the direction to a familiar location, such as a previous home or a favorite tavern.

LEVITATE SPELL 3

EVOCATION

Traditions arcane, occult
Cast ◈◈ somatic, verbal
Range touch; **Targets** 1 unattended object or willing creature
Duration 5 minutes

You defy gravity and levitate the target 5 feet off the ground. For the duration of the spell, you can move the target up or down 10 feet with a single action, which has the concentrate trait. A creature floating in the air from *levitate* takes a –2 circumstance penalty to attack rolls. A floating creature can spend an Interact action to stabilize itself and negate this penalty for the remainder of its turn. If the target is adjacent to a fixed object or terrain of suitable stability, it can move across the surface by climbing (if the surface is vertical, like a wall) or crawling (if the surface is horizontal, such as a ceiling). The GM determines which surfaces can be climbed or crawled across.

LIGHT CANTRIP 1

CANTRIP | EVOCATION | LIGHT

Traditions arcane, divine, occult, primal
Cast ◈◈ somatic, verbal
Range touch; **Targets** 1 unattended, non-magical object of 1 Bulk or less
Duration until the next time you make your daily preparations

The object glows, casting bright light in a 20-foot radius (and dim light for the next 20 feet) like a torch. If you cast this spell again on a second object, the *light* spell on the first object ends.

Heightened (4th) The object sheds bright light in a 60-foot radius (and dim light for the next 60 feet).

LIGHTNING BOLT SPELL 3

ELECTRICITY | EVOCATION

Traditions arcane, primal
Cast ◈◈ somatic, verbal
Area 120-foot line
Saving Throw basic Reflex

A bolt of lightning strikes outward from your hand, dealing 4d12 electricity damage.

Heightened (+1) The damage increases by 1d12.

LOCATE SPELL 3

UNCOMMON | DETECTION | DIVINATION

Traditions arcane, divine, occult
Cast 10 minutes (material, somatic, verbal)
Range 500 feet; **Targets** 1 specific object or type of object
Duration sustained

You learn the direction to the target (if you picked a specific object, such as "my mother's sword") or the nearest target (if you picked a type of object, such as "swords"). If the target is a specific object, you must have observed it directly with your own senses. If it's a type of object, you still need to have an accurate mental image of the type of object. If there's lead or running water between you and the target, this spell can't locate the object. This means you might find a type of object farther away if the nearest one is behind lead or running water.

Heightened (5th) You can target a specific creature or ancestry instead of an object, but you must have met or seen up close the creature or ancestry you want to target.

LOCK SPELL 1

ABJURATION

Traditions arcane, divine, occult
Cast ◈◈ somatic, verbal
Range touch; **Targets** 1 lock, or a door or container with a latch
Duration 1 day

The target's latch mechanism clinks shut, held fast by unseen magical restraints. When you magically lock a target, you set an Athletics and Thievery DC to open it equal to your spell DC or the base lock DC with a +4 status bonus, whichever is higher. Any key or combination that once opened a lock affected by this spell does not do so for the duration of the spell, though the key or combination does grant a +4 circumstance bonus to checks to open the door.

If the target is opened, the spell ends. Assuming the target is not barred or locked in some additional way, you can unlock and open it with an Interact action during which you touch the target. This does not end the spell. You can Dismiss this spell at any time and from any distance.

Heightened (2nd) The duration increases to unlimited, but you must expend 6 gp worth of gold dust as an additional cost.

LONGSTRIDER SPELL 1

TRANSMUTATION

Traditions arcane, primal
Cast ◈◈ somatic, verbal
Duration 1 hour

You lengthen your stride beyond what should be possible. You gain a +10-foot status bonus to your Speed.

Heightened (2nd) The duration increases to 8 hours.

MAGE ARMOR SPELL 1

ABJURATION

Traditions arcane, occult
Cast ◈◈ somatic, verbal
Duration until the next time you make your daily preparations

You ward yourself with shimmering magical energy, gaining a +1 item bonus to AC and a maximum Dexterity modifier of +5. While wearing *mage armor*, you use your unarmored proficiency to calculate your AC.

Heightened (4th) You gain a +1 item bonus to saving throws.
Heightened (6th) The item bonus to AC increases to +2, and you gain a +1 item bonus to saving throws.

Heightened (8th) The item bonus to AC increases to +2, and you gain a +2 item bonus to saving throws.

Heightened (10th) The item bonus to AC increases to +3, and you gain a +3 item bonus to saving throws.

MAGE HAND   CANTRIP 1

`CANTRIP` `EVOCATION`

Traditions arcane, occult

Cast ◆◆ somatic, verbal

Range 30 feet; **Targets** 1 unattended object of light Bulk or less

Duration sustained

You create a single magical hand, either invisible or ghostlike, that grasps the target object and moves it slowly up to 20 feet. Because you're levitating the object, you can move it in any direction. When you Sustain the Spell, you can move the object an additional 20 feet. If the object is in the air when the spell ends, the object falls.

Heightened (3rd) You can target an unattended object with a Bulk of 1 or less.

Heightened (5th) The range increases to 60 feet, and you can target an unattended object with a Bulk of 1 or less.

Heightened (7th) The range increases to 60 feet, and you can target an unattended object with a Bulk of 2 or less.

MAGIC AURA   SPELL 1

`UNCOMMON` `ILLUSION`

Traditions arcane, occult

Cast 1 minute (material, somatic, verbal)

Range touch; **Targets** 1 object of 3 bulk or less

Duration until the next time you make your daily preparations

You alter the appearance of an item's magic aura. You can choose to have the target's aura appear as that of common magic item of twice *magic aura's* level or lower, or to have it register as being under the effects of a spell of your choice of *magic aura's* level or lower. If the target is magical, you can instead choose to have it appear as entirely non-magical.

A caster using *detect magic* or *study aura* of an equal or higher spell level can attempt to disbelieve the illusion from *magic aura*. *Magic aura* doesn't mask the aura of spells that are 9th level or higher or of items that are 19th level or higher.

Heightened (3rd) You can target a creature instead of an object. When you do, you can either conceal the auras of all magic items it has or have that creature's aura appear as if it were under the effect of a spell you know.

MAGIC FANG   SPELL 1

`TRANSMUTATION`

Traditions primal

Cast ◆◆ somatic, verbal

Range touch; **Targets** 1 willing ally

Duration 1 minute

Choose one of the target's unarmed attacks that deal one damage die. You cause that unarmed attack to shine with primal energy. The unarmed attack becomes a *+1 striking* unarmed attack, gaining a +1 item bonus to attack rolls and increasing the number of damage dice to two.

MAGIC MISSILE   SPELL 1

`EVOCATION` `FORCE`

Traditions arcane, occult

Cast ◆ to ◆◆◆ (somatic, verbal)

Range 120 feet; **Targets** 1 creature

You send a dart of force streaking toward a creature that you can see. It automatically hits and deals 1d4+1 force damage. For each additional action you use when Casting the Spell, increase the number of missiles you shoot by one, to a maximum of three missiles for 3 actions. You choose the target for each missile individually. If you shoot more than one missile at the same target, combine the damage before applying bonuses or penalties to damage, resistances, weaknesses, and so forth.

Heightened (+2) You shoot one additional missile with each action you spend.

MAGIC MOUTH   SPELL 2

`AUDITORY` `ILLUSION` `VISUAL`

Traditions arcane, occult

Cast ◆◆ somatic, verbal

Range touch; **Targets** 1 creature or object

Duration unlimited

You specify a trigger (described on page 305) and a message up to 25 words long. When the specified trigger occurs within 30 feet of the target, an illusory mouth appears on the target and speaks the message, and the *magic mouth* spell ends.

MAGIC WEAPON   SPELL 1

`TRANSMUTATION`

Traditions arcane, divine, occult

Cast ◆◆ somatic, verbal

Range touch; **Targets** 1 non-magical weapon that is unattended or wielded by you or a willing ally

Duration 1 minute

The weapon glimmers with magic and energy. The target becomes a *+1 striking weapon*, gaining a +1 item bonus to attack rolls and increasing the number of weapon damage dice to two.

MAGNIFICENT MANSION   SPELL 7

`UNCOMMON` `CONJURATION` `EXTRADIMENSIONAL`

Traditions arcane, occult

Cast 1 minute (material, somatic, verbal)

Range 30 feet

Duration 24 hours

You conjure an extradimensional demiplane consisting of a spacious dwelling with a single entrance. The entrance connects to the plane where you Cast the Spell, appearing anywhere within the spell's range as a faint, shimmering, vertical rectangle 5 feet wide and 10 feet high. You designate who can enter when you cast the spell. Once inside, you can shut the entrance, making it invisible. You and the creatures you designated can reopen the door at will, just like opening a physical door.

INTRODUCTION

ANCESTRIES & BACKGROUNDS

CLASSES

SKILLS

FEATS

EQUIPMENT

SPELLS

THE AGE OF LOST OMENS

PLAYING THE GAME

GAME MASTERING

CRAFTING & TREASURE

APPENDIX

Inside, the demiplane appears to be a mansion featuring a magnificent foyer and numerous opulent chambers. The mansion can have any floor plan you imagine as you Cast the Spell, provided it fits within a space 40 feet wide, 40 feet deep, and 30 feet tall. While the entrance to the mansion is closed, effects from outside the mansion fail to penetrate it, and vice versa, except for *plane shift*, which can be used to enter the mansion. You can use scrying magic and similar effects to observe the outside only if they're capable of crossing planes.

A staff of up to 24 servants attends to anyone within the mansion. These are like the servant created by the *unseen servant* spell, though they're visible, with an appearance you determine during casting. The mansion is stocked with enough food to serve a nine-course banquet to 150 people.

MARINER'S CURSE   SPELL 5

ATTACK | CURSE | NECROMANCY

Traditions arcane, occult, primal
Cast ◆◆ somatic, verbal
Range touch; **Targets** 1 creature
Saving Throw Will

You afflict the target with the curse of the roiling, unforgiving sea. The target must attempt a Will save.

Critical Success The target is unaffected.
Success The target becomes sickened 1. Reducing its sickened condition to 0 ends the curse.
Failure The target becomes sickened 1 and can't reduce its sickened condition below 1 while the curse remains. The curse can be lifted by *remove curse* or similar magic. Whenever the target is sickened and on the water at least a mile from shore, it is also slowed 1.
Critical Failure As failure, but the target becomes sickened 2.

MASK OF TERROR   SPELL 7

EMOTION | FEAR | ILLUSION | MENTAL | VISUAL

Traditions arcane, occult, primal
Cast ◆◆ somatic, verbal
Range 30 feet; **Targets** 1 creature
Duration 1 minute

The target appears to be a gruesome and terrifying creature. The effect is unique to each observer, so a human viewing the target might see a demon with bloody fangs, but a demon observing the target might see a glowing angelic visage.

When any creature attempts a hostile action against the target, the creature must attempt a Will save. It is then temporarily immune until the end of its next turn.

Success The creature is unaffected.
Failure The creature becomes frightened 2 before using its action.
Critical Failure The creature becomes frightened 2, and its action fails and is wasted.
Heightened (8th) You can target up to 5 creatures. If a creature uses a hostile action or reaction that affects multiple targets simultaneously, it needs to attempt only one save against *mask of terror*.

MASSACRE   SPELL 9

DEATH | NECROMANCY | NEGATIVE

Traditions arcane, divine, primal
Cast ◆◆ somatic, verbal
Area 60-foot line
Saving Throw Fortitude

You unleash a wave of necromantic energy to snuff out the life force of those in its path. Each creature of 17th level or lower in the line must attempt a Fortitude save. If the damage from *massacre* reduces a creature to 0 Hit Points, that creature dies instantly. If *massacre* doesn't kill even a single creature, the negative energy violently explodes back toward you, dealing an additional 30 negative damage to every creature in the line (even those above 17th level) and 30 negative damage to you.

Critical Success The creature is unaffected.
Success The creature takes 9d6 negative damage.
Failure The creature takes 100 negative damage.
Critical Failure The creature dies.
Heightened (10th) The spell can affect creatures up to 19th level. Increase the damage to 10d6 on a success, and to 115 on a failure.

MAZE   SPELL 8

CONJURATION | EXTRADIMENSIONAL | TELEPORTATION

Traditions arcane, occult
Cast ◆◆ somatic, verbal
Range 30 feet; **Targets** 1 creature
Duration sustained

You transport the target into an extradimensional maze of eldritch origin and trap it there. Once each turn, the target can spend 1 action to attempt a Survival check or Perception check against your spell DC to escape the maze. The possible outcomes are as follows.

Critical Success The target escapes and the spell ends.
Success The target is on the right path to the exit. If the target was already on the right path, it escapes the maze and the spell ends.
Failure The target makes no progress toward escape.
Critical Failure The target makes no progress toward escape, and if it was on the right path, it no longer is.

Teleportation magic doesn't help the creature escape unless the magic can transport across planes, such as *plane shift*. When the spell ends, either because the target escaped or the duration ran out, the target returns to the space it occupied when it was banished, or to the nearest space if the original is now filled.

MELD INTO STONE   SPELL 3

EARTH | TRANSMUTATION

Traditions arcane, primal
Cast ◆◆ somatic, verbal
Duration 10 minutes

You merge with an adjacent block of stone with enough volume to fit you and your worn and held possessions. You must touch the stone when you Cast the Spell. You can hear, but not see, what's going on outside the stone, and you can cast spells while in the stone as long as they don't require line of effect beyond the stone.

Significant physical damage to the stone while you are inside it expels you and deals 10d6 damage to you. *Passwall* expels you without dealing damage and ends *meld into stone*. You can Dismiss this spell.

MENDING   SPELL 1

TRANSMUTATION

Traditions arcane, divine, occult, primal
Cast 10 minutes (somatic, verbal)
Range touch; **Targets** non-magical object of light Bulk or less
You repair the target item. You restore 5 Hit Points per spell level to the target, potentially removing the broken condition if this repairs it past the item's Broken Threshold. You can't replace lost pieces or repair an object that's been completely destroyed.
Heightened (2nd) You can target a non-magical object of 1 Bulk or less.
Heightened (3rd) You can target a non-magical object of 2 Bulk or less, or a magical object of 1 Bulk or less.

MESSAGE   CANTRIP 1

AUDITORY   CANTRIP   ILLUSION   LINGUISTIC   MENTAL

Traditions arcane, divine, occult
Cast ◆ verbal
Range 120 feet; **Targets** 1 creature
Duration see below
You mouth words quietly, but instead of coming out of your mouth, they're transferred directly to the ears of the target. While others can't hear your words any better than if you normally mouthed them, the target can hear your words as if they were standing next to you. The target can give a brief response as a reaction, or as a free action on their next turn if they wish, but they must be able to see you and be within range to do so. If they respond, their response is delivered directly to your ear, just like the original message.
Heightened (3rd) The spell's range increases to 500 feet.

METEOR SWARM   SPELL 9

EVOCATION   FIRE

Traditions arcane, primal
Cast ◆◆ somatic, verbal
Range 500 feet; **Area** 4 40-foot bursts
Saving Throw basic Reflex
You call down four meteors that explode in a fiery blast. Each meteor deals 6d10 bludgeoning damage to any creatures in the 10-foot burst at the center of its area of effect before exploding, dealing 14d6 fire damage to any creatures in its 40-foot burst. The meteors' central 10-foot bursts can't overlap, and a creature takes the same amount of fire damage no matter how many overlapping explosions it's caught in. The saving throw applies to both the bludgeoning and the fire damage.
Heightened (+1) The bludgeoning damage increases by 1d10, and the fire damage increases by 2d6.

MIND BLANK   SPELL 8

UNCOMMON   ABJURATION

Traditions arcane, occult
Cast ◆◆ somatic, verbal
Range 30 feet; **Targets** 1 creature
Duration until the next time you make your daily preparations
Powerful wards hide a creature from divination magic. The target gains a +4 status bonus to saves against mental effects. *Mind blank* attempts to counteract any detection, revelation, and scrying effects as if its spell level were 1 higher than its actual level. On a success, the divination effect functions normally except that it detects nothing about the target and its possessions. For instance, *detect magic* would still detect other magic in the area, but not any magic on the target.

MIND PROBE   SPELL 5

UNCOMMON   DIVINATION   LINGUISTIC   MENTAL

Traditions arcane, occult
Cast 1 minute (material, somatic, verbal)
Range 30 feet; **Targets** 1 creature
Saving Throw Will; **Duration** sustained up to 1 minute
You cast your thoughts through a creature's mind, sifting for information. You access the target's memories and knowledge unless it fends you off with a Will save.
Success The target is unaffected.
Failure Each round of the spell's duration, you can Sustain the Spell to ask a different question and attempt to uncover the answer. For each question, the target can attempt a Deception check against your spell DC; if the target succeeds, you don't learn the answer, and on a critical success, the target gives you a false answer that you believe is truthful Once you've asked the target a given question, asking it again, even with a separate casting of *mind probe*, produces the same result.
Critical Failure As failure, and the target takes a –4 circumstance penalty to Deception checks against your questions.

MIND READING   SPELL 3

UNCOMMON   DETECTION   DIVINATION   MENTAL

Traditions arcane, occult
Cast ◆◆ somatic, verbal
Range 30 feet; **Targets** 1 creature
Saving Throw Will; **Duration** 1 round or sustained up to 1 minute
With a cursory mental touch, you attempt to read the target's mind. It must attempt a Will save. The target then becomes temporarily immune to your *mind reading* for 1 hour.
Critical Success The target perceives vague surface thoughts from you when you Cast the Spell.
Success You find out whether the target's Intelligence modifier is higher than, equal to, or lower than yours.
Failure You perceive vague surface thoughts from the target when you Cast the Spell, and you find out whether its Intelligence modifier is higher than, equal to, or lower than yours.
Critical Failure As failure, and for the duration of the spell, you can Sustain the Spell to detect the target's surface thoughts again. The target doesn't receive any additional saves.

INTRODUCTION

ANCESTRIES & BACKGROUNDS

CLASSES

SKILLS

FEATS

EQUIPMENT

SPELLS

THE AGE OF LOST OMENS

PLAYING THE GAME

GAME MASTERING

CRAFTING & TREASURE

APPENDIX

MINDLINK   SPELL 1

DIVINATION   MENTAL

Traditions occult
Cast ◆◆ somatic, verbal
Range touch; **Targets** 1 willing creature

You link your mind to the target's mind and mentally impart to that target an amount of information in an instant that could otherwise be communicated in 10 minutes.

MIRACLE   SPELL 10

DIVINATION

Traditions divine
Cast ◆◆◆ material, somatic, verbal

You request aid directly from your divine source. Your divine source always refuses a request out of line with its nature, and it might grant a different request (potentially more powerful or better fitting its nature) than the one you asked for. A casting of *miracle* can do any of the following things.

- Duplicate any divine spell of 9th level or lower.
- Duplicate any non-divine spell of 7th level or lower.
- Produce any effect whose power level is in line with the above effects.
- Reverse certain effects that refer to the *wish* spell.

The GM might allow you to try using *miracle* to produce greater effects than these, but doing so may be dangerous, or the spell may have only a partial effect.

MIRROR IMAGE   SPELL 2

ILLUSION   VISUAL

Traditions arcane, occult
Cast ◆◆ somatic, verbal
Duration 1 minute

Three illusory images of you swirl about your space, potentially causing those who attack you to hit one of the images instead of you. Any attack that would hit you has a random chance of hitting one of your images instead of you. If all three images remain, there is a 1 in 4 chance of hitting you (1 on 1d4). With two images remaining, there is a 1 in 3 chance of hitting you (1–2 on 1d6). With only one image, the chances are 1 in 2 (1–3 on 1d6).

Once an image is hit, it is destroyed. If an attack roll fails to hit your AC but doesn't critically fail, it destroys an image but has no additional effect (even if the attack would normally have an effect on a failure). If an attack roll is a critical success and would hit one of the images, one of the images is destroyed and the attack roll becomes a success against you. Once all the images are destroyed, the spell ends.

MISDIRECTION   SPELL 2

ILLUSION

Traditions arcane, occult
Cast 1 minute (somatic, verbal)
Range 30 feet; **Targets** 2 creatures or objects
Duration until the next time you make your daily preparations

You reshape the magic aura of one creature or object to resemble that of another. You designate one target as the primary target and the other as the secondary target.

Effects that would detect auras on the primary target instead detect the same types of auras from the secondary target. A creature reading the aura can attempt to disbelieve the illusion. You can Dismiss the spell from up to a mile away.

MISLEAD   SPELL 6

ILLUSION

Traditions arcane, occult
Cast ◆◆ somatic, verbal
Duration sustained up to 1 minute

You turn yourself invisible and create an illusory duplicate of yourself. When you Sustain the Spell, you can mentally dictate a course of action for your duplicate to follow that round. Your duplicate acts as though it had your full number of actions, though it can't actually affect anything in the environment. Both the duplicate and your invisibility persist for the spell's duration. Performing a hostile action doesn't end *mislead's* invisibility, just like a 4th-level *invisibility* spell. A creature that determines the duplicate is an illusion doesn't necessarily know you're invisible, and one that can see your invisible form doesn't necessarily know your duplicate is an illusion.

If you Cast a Spell, attack, or otherwise interact with another creature, as a part of that action you can attempt a Deception check against observers' Perception DCs to convince them your duplicate used that action. This doesn't fool anyone who's aware your duplicate is an illusion, nor does it work if the attack obviously couldn't have come from the duplicate. For instance, if you fired a ray, you could make it look like it came from the duplicate as long as the duplicate was positioned appropriately, but if you attacked with a sword and your duplicate was across the room from the target, your Deception check would automatically fail.

MODIFY MEMORY   SPELL 4

UNCOMMON   DIVINATION   MENTAL

Traditions occult
Cast ◆◆ somatic, verbal
Range 30 feet; **Targets** 1 creature
Saving Throw Will; **Duration** unlimited

You alter the target's memories, either erasing a memory, enhancing a memory's clarity, altering a memory, or adding a false memory. The target can attempt a Will save to resist the spell.

Critical Success The target is unaffected and realizes you tried to alter its memory.

Success The target is unaffected but thinks your spell was something harmless instead of *modify memory*, unless it identifies the spell.

Failure During the first 5 minutes of the spell's duration, you can Sustain the Spell to modify a memory once each round. When you do, you imagine up to 6 seconds of memory to modify, to a maximum of 5 continuous minutes of memory.

Any memories you've altered remain changed as long as the spell is active. If the target moves out of range before the 5 minutes is up, you can't alter any further memories.

Heightened (6th) You can cast the spell on a willing target to suppress all memory of a particular topic, detailed in 50 words or fewer. The effect is permanent, and it patches these omissions with an indistinct haze.

MOMENT OF RENEWAL   SPELL 8

`HEALING` `NECROMANCY`

Traditions divine, primal
Cast ◆◆ somatic, verbal
Range touch; **Targets** up to 6 creatures

The targets experience a day's worth of recovery in an instant. Any detrimental effects that would be gone after 24 hours end, though this doesn't shorten the duration of any active spells affecting the targets. The targets regain Hit Points and recover from conditions as if they had taken 24 hours of rest, but they do not make their daily preparations again or gain any benefits of rest other than healing. The targets are then temporarily immune for 1 day.

MONSTROSITY FORM   SPELL 8

`POLYMORPH` `TRANSMUTATION`

Traditions arcane, primal
Cast ◆◆ somatic, verbal
Duration 1 minute

You transform into the shape of a legendary monster, assuming a Huge battle form. You must have enough space to expand into or the spell is lost. When you cast this spell, choose phoenix, purple worm, or sea serpent. While in this form, you gain the beast trait (for phoenix) or the animal trait (for purple worm or sea serpent). You can Dismiss the spell.

You gain the following statistics and abilities regardless of which battle form you choose:

- AC = 20 + your level. Ignore your armor's check penalty and Speed reduction.
- 20 temporary Hit Points.
- Darkvision.
- One or more unarmed melee attacks specific to the battle form you choose, which are the only attacks you can use. You're trained with them. Your attack modifier is +28, and you use the listed damage. These attacks are Strength based (for the purpose of the enfeebled condition, for example). If your unarmed attack modifier is higher, you can use it instead.
- Athletics modifier of +30, unless your own modifier is higher.

You also gain specific abilities based on the type of monster you choose:

- **Phoenix** Speed 30 feet, fly Speed 90 feet; **Melee** ◆ beak (reach 15 feet), **Damage** 2d6+12 piercing plus 2d4 fire and 2d4 persistent fire; **Melee** ◆ talon (agile, reach 15 feet), **Damage** 2d8+12 slashing; **Shroud of Flame** (aura, evocation, fire, primal) 20 feet. You gain an aura of fire that extends out from you. A creature that enters or ends its turn within the aura takes 2d6 fire damage. A creature can take this damage only once per turn. You can use a single action, which

has the concentrate trait, to activate or deactivate this aura.

- **Purple Worm** Speed 40 feet, burrow Speed 30 feet, swim Speed 20 feet; **Melee** ◆ jaws (reach 10 feet), **Damage** 2d12+20 piercing; **Melee** ◆ stinger (agile, reach 10 feet), **Damage** 2d8+15 piercing plus 2d6 persistent poison; **Melee** ◆ body (reach 10 feet) **Damage** 2d8+20 bludgeoning; **Inexorable** You automatically recover from the paralyzed, slowed, and stunned conditions at the end of each of your turns. You're also immune to being immobilized and ignore difficult terrain and greater difficult terrain.
- **Sea Serpent** Speed 20 feet, swim Speed 90 feet; **Melee** ◆ jaws (reach 15 feet), **Damage** 2d12+20 piercing; **Melee** ◆ tail (reach 25 feet), **Damage** 2d8+20 bludgeoning; **Spine Rake** ◆◆ (move) You extend your spines and Swim or Stride. Each creature you're adjacent to at any point during your movement takes 4d8+10 slashing damage (basic Reflex against your spell DC).

Heightened (9th) You instead gain AC = 22 + your level, 25 temporary HP, attack modifier +31, increase damage by one damage die, and Athletics +33.

MOON FRENZY   SPELL 5

`MORPH` `TRANSMUTATION`

Traditions primal
Cast ◆◆ somatic, verbal
Range 30 feet; **Targets** up to 5 willing creatures
Duration 1 minute

A feral aspect overcomes the targets, making them tough and savage. Targets gain 5 temporary Hit Points, a +10-foot status bonus to their Speeds, and weakness 5 to silver. They also grow vicious fangs and claws, which are unarmed attacks. The fangs deal 2d8 piercing damage; the claws deal 2d6 slashing damage and have the agile and finesse traits. The targets use their highest weapon or unarmed attack proficiency with these attacks, and if they have weapon specialization or greater weapon specialization, they add this damage as well. On a critical hit with one of these unarmed attacks, the creature struck takes 1d4 persistent bleed damage.

The targets can't use concentrate actions unless those actions also have the rage trait, with the exception of Seek. A creature can attempt to end the spell's effect on itself by using a single action, which has the rage trait, to attempt a Will save against your spell DC; on a success, it ends the spell's effect on itself.

If a target is in the light of a full moon, it also grows by one size if it were Medium or smaller. This increases the reach of a Medium or Tiny creature by 5 feet.

Heightened (6th) The temporary Hit Points increase to 10, the silver weakness to 10, and the damage dealt by the attacks to three dice.

Heightened (10th) The temporary Hit Points increase to 20, the silver weakness to 20, and the damage dealt by the attacks to four dice.

INTRODUCTION

ANCESTRIES & BACKGROUNDS

CLASSES

SKILLS

FEATS

EQUIPMENT

SPELLS

THE AGE OF LOST OMENS

PLAYING THE GAME

GAME MASTERING

CRAFTING & TREASURE

APPENDIX

NATURE INCARNATE   SPELL 10

POLYMORPH   TRANSMUTATION

Traditions primal
Cast ❖❖ somatic, verbal
Duration 1 minute

The primal power of the world flows through you. You transform into an incarnation of nature, either a green man or a kaiju. Your battle form is Medium for a green man or Gargantuan (30-foot-by-30-foot space) for a kaiju. You must have enough space to expand into or the spell is lost. While in this form, you gain the plant trait (for a green man) or the beast trait (for a kaiju). You can Dismiss the spell.

You gain the following statistics and abilities regardless of which battle form you choose:

- AC = 25 + your level. Ignore your armor's check penalty and Speed reduction.
- 30 temporary Hit Points.
- Darkvision.
- One or more attacks specific to the battle form you choose, which are the only attacks you can use. You're trained with them. Your attack modifier is +34, and you use the listed damage. These attacks are Strength based (for the purpose of the enfeebled condition, for example). If your unarmed attack modifier is higher, you can use it instead.
- Athletics modifier of +36, unless your own modifier is higher.

You also gain specific abilities based on the type of incarnation you choose:

- **Green Man** Speed 40 feet, climb Speed 40 feet; **Melee** ❖ vines (reach 30 feet, versatile P), **Damage** 6d8+12 bludgeoning; **Ranged** ❖ thorns (range 100 feet), **Damage** 6d6+6 piercing; **Green Caress** (aura, primal, transmutation) 60 feet. Enemies other than plants must succeed at a Fortitude save against your spell DC or become clumsy 1 for 1 round (clumsy 2 on a critical failure).
- **Kaiju** Speed 50 feet; resistance 5 to physical damage; **Melee** ❖ jaws (reach 30 feet), **Damage** 6d10+10 piercing; **Melee** ❖ claws (agile, reach 30 feet), **Damage** 6d8+8 slashing; **Melee** ❖ foot (agile, reach 15 feet), **Damage** 6d6+10 bludgeoning; **Unstoppable** You are immune to being immobilized and ignore difficult terrain and greater difficult terrain; **Trample** ❖❖❖ You move up to double your Speed and move through the spaces of Huge or smaller creatures, trampling each creature whose space you enter. A trampled creature takes foot damage with a basic Reflex save against your spell DC.

NATURE'S ENMITY   SPELL 9

ENCHANTMENT

Traditions primal
Cast ❖❖ somatic, verbal
Range 120 feet; **Area** 500-foot burst; **Targets** up to 5 creatures
Duration 10 minutes

Animals and plants in the area turn against the targets. Each target suffers from the following effects as long as it remains in the area.

- Vegetation springs up from every surface, giving each target a –10-foot circumstance penalty to its Speed any time it's adjacent to the plants.
- Aggressive animals attack unpredictably. At the start of its turn, each target rolls a DC 8 flat check. On a failure, it's attacked by swarming creatures that deal 2d10 slashing damage. The target attempts a basic Reflex save, and it is flat-footed for 1 round on any outcome other than a critical success.
- The target loses any connection to nature or natural creatures. The target has to succeed at a DC 5 flat check when casting any primal spell or the spell fails. Furthermore, animal or plant creatures become hostile to it, even one with a strong bond to the target, such as an animal companion.

The GM might decide that you can't subject some creatures, such as an emissary of a nature deity, to the ire of nature.

NEGATE AROMA   SPELL 1

ABJURATION

Traditions arcane, primal
Cast ❖❖ somatic, verbal
Range touch; **Targets** 1 willing creature
Duration 1 hour

The target loses its odor, preventing creatures from passively noticing its presence via smell alone, even if the creatures have precise or imprecise scent. A creature attempting a Perception check to Seek with scent and other senses might notice the lack of natural scent. If the target has any abilities that result from its smell, such as an overpowering scent, those abilities are also negated.

Heightened (5th) The range increases to 30 feet, and you can target up to 10 creatures.

NEUTRALIZE POISON   SPELL 3

HEALING   NECROMANCY

Traditions divine, primal
Cast ❖❖ somatic, verbal
Range touch; **Targets** 1 creature

You pour healing magic through the target in an attempt to cure one poison afflicting it. Attempt a counteract check against the poison.

NIGHTMARE   SPELL 4

ILLUSION   MENTAL

Traditions arcane, occult
Cast 10 minutes (material, somatic, verbal)
Range planetary; **Targets** 1 creature you know by name
Saving Throw Will; **Duration** 1 day

You send disturbing nightmares to your target. The next time the target falls asleep, it must attempt a Will save. If you know the target only by name and have never met them, the target gets a +4 circumstance bonus to the Will save.

Critical Success The target suffers no adverse effects and is temporarily immune for 1 week.

Success The target experiences the nightmares but suffers no adverse effects other than unpleasant memories.

Failure The target experiences the nightmares and awakens fatigued.

Critical Failure The target experiences the nightmares, awakens fatigued, and is drained 2 until it is no longer fatigued.

NONDETECTION SPELL 3

UNCOMMON   ABJURATION

Traditions arcane, occult, primal
Cast 10 minutes (material, somatic, verbal)
Range touch; **Targets** 1 creature or object
Duration 8 hours

You erect protective wards that make the target difficult to detect via magic. *Nondetection* attempts to counteract all detection, revelation, and scrying divinations made against the target or the target's gear throughout the duration, counting cantrips as 1st-level spells for this purpose. Successfully counteracting a divination that targets an area or multiple targets negates the effects only for *nondetection*'s target.

OBSCURING MIST SPELL 2

CONJURATION   WATER

Traditions arcane, primal

Cast ◆➤➤ material, somatic, verbal
Range 120 feet; **Area** 20-foot burst
Duration 1 minute

You call forth a cloud of mist. All creatures within the mist become concealed, and all creatures outside the mist become concealed to creatures within it. You can Dismiss the cloud.

OUTCAST'S CURSE SPELL 4

ATTACK   CURSE   ENCHANTMENT   MENTAL   MISFORTUNE

Traditions arcane, divine, occult
Cast ◆➤ somatic, verbal
Range touch; **Targets** 1 creature
Saving Throw Will

You afflict the target with a curse that makes its presence abrasive and off-putting. The target must attempt a Will save.

Critical Success The target is unaffected.

Success For 10 minutes, the target must roll twice and use the worse result whenever attempting a Deception, Diplomacy, Intimidation, or Performance check, and creatures they encounter have an initial attitude toward them of one step worse (for instance, unfriendly instead of indifferent).

Failure As success, but the effect is permanent.

Critical Failure As failure, and creatures that the target encounters have an initial attitude toward them of two steps worse.

OVERWHELMING PRESENCE   SPELL 9

AUDITORY   ENCHANTMENT   INCAPACITATION   MENTAL   VISUAL

Traditions divine, occult
Cast ◆◆ somatic, verbal
Area 40-foot burst; **Targets** any number of creatures
Saving Throw Will; **Duration** until full tribute is paid

You surround yourself with supernatural splendor, appearing
to be a god or similarly majestic being. You choose the aspects
of your new majestic appearance. This causes the targets to
pay tribute to you by bowing or using some other action in
keeping with your appearance. The number of times a target
must do this depends on the result of their Will save.

Critical Success The target is unaffected.
Success The target must pay tribute twice.
Failure The target must pay tribute six times.
Critical Failure As failure, and the target must spend all its
    actions paying tribute if possible.

Paying tribute is a manipulate action or move action, as chosen
by the creature paying tribute. A creature under this effect
must pay tribute to you at least once on each of its turns if
possible. While affected by this spell, a creature is fascinated
by you and can't use hostile actions against you. The target is
then temporarily immune for 1 minute.

PARALYZE   SPELL 3

ENCHANTMENT   INCAPACITATION   MENTAL

Traditions arcane, occult
Cast ◆◆ somatic, verbal
Range 30 feet; **Targets** 1 creature
Saving Throw Will; **Duration** varies

You block the target's motor impulses before they can leave
its mind, threatening to freeze the target in place. The target
must attempt a Will save.

Critical Success The target is unaffected.
Success The target is stunned 1.
Failure The target is paralyzed for 1 round.
Critical Failure The target is paralyzed for 4 rounds. At the
    end of each of its turns, it can attempt a new Will save to
    reduce the remaining duration by 1 round, or end it entirely
    on a critical success.

Heightened (7th) You can target up to 10 creatures.

PARANOIA   SPELL 2

ILLUSION   MENTAL

Traditions occult
Cast ◆◆ somatic, verbal
Range 30 feet; **Targets** 1 creature
Saving Throw Will; **Duration** 1 minute

You cause the target to see all other creatures as dire threats.
The target is stricken by intense paranoia toward all creatures
around it and must attempt a Will save.

Critical Success The target is unaffected.
Success The target believes everyone it sees is a potential
    threat. It becomes unfriendly to all creatures to which it
    wasn't already hostile, even those that were previously
    allies. It treats no one as an ally. The spell ends after 1 round.

Failure As success, but the effect lasts 1 minute.
Critical Failure As failure, except the target believes that
    everyone it sees is a mortal enemy. It uses its reactions
    and free actions against everyone, regardless of whether
    they were previously its allies, as determined by the GM. It
    otherwise acts as rationally as it normally does and likely
    prefers to attack creatures that are actively attacking or
    hindering it over those leaving it alone.

Heightened (6th) You can target up to 5 creatures.

PASS WITHOUT TRACE   SPELL 1

ABJURATION

Traditions primal
Cast ◆◆ somatic, verbal
Duration 1 hour

You obscure the tracks you leave behind and make it harder
for others to find you. The DC of checks to Track you gains a
+4 status bonus or is equal to your spell DC, whichever results
in a higher DC. You can benefit from only one *pass without
trace* spell at a time.

Heightened (2nd) The duration increases to 8 hours.
Heightened (4th) The duration increases to 8 hours. The spell
has a range of 20 feet and an area of a 20-foot-emanation,
affecting up to 10 creatures of your choice within that area.

PASSWALL   SPELL 5

UNCOMMON   CONJURATION   EARTH

Traditions arcane, primal
Cast ◆◆ somatic, verbal
Range touch; **Area** 5-foot-wide, 10-foot-tall, 10-foot-deep
    section of wooden, plaster, or stone wall
Duration 1 hour

You create a visible tunnel through the wall in the chosen area,
replacing the area with empty space. If the wall is thicker than
10 feet, the tunnel ends 10 feet in. Even a small layer of metal
in the wall prevents this spell from functioning. This spell
doesn't reduce the integrity of the structure. When the spell
ends, anyone inside the tunnel is shunted to the nearest exit.

Heightened (7th) The tunnel can be up to 20 feet deep. The
areas of the wall that contain your tunnel's entrance appear
completely normal (unless viewed with *true seeing* or a similar
effect), despite the tunnel's existence. The tunnel's entrance
functions as a solid wall, but you can specify a password or a
trigger (page 305), allowing creatures to enter the tunnel freely.

PEST FORM   SPELL 1

POLYMORPH   TRANSMUTATION

Traditions arcane, primal
Cast ◆◆ somatic, verbal
Duration 10 minutes

You transform into a the battle form of a Tiny animal, such as
a cat, insect, lizard, or rat. You can decide the specific type of
animal (such as a rat or praying mantis), but this has no effect
on the form's Size or statistics. While in this form, you gain the
animal trait. You can Dismiss the spell.

    You gain the following statistics and abilities:

- AC = 15 + your level. Ignore your armor's check penalty and Speed reduction.
- Speed 10 feet.
- Weakness 5 to physical damage. (If you take physical damage in this form, you take 5 additional damage.)
- Low-light vision and imprecise scent 30 feet.
- Acrobatics and Stealth modifiers of +10, unless your own modifier is higher; Athletics modifier –4.

Heightened (4th) You can turn into a flying creature, such as a bird, which grants you a fly Speed of 20 feet.

PHANTASMAL CALAMITY   SPELL 6

ILLUSION MENTAL

Traditions arcane, occult
Cast ❖❖ somatic, verbal
Saving Throw Will; **Range** 500 feet; **Area** 30-foot burst

A vision of apocalyptic destruction fills the mind of each creature in the area. The vision deals 11d6 mental damage (basic Will save). On a critical failure, the creature must also succeed at a Reflex save or believe it's trapped (stuck in a fissure, adrift at sea, or some other fate in keeping with its vision). If it fails the second save, it's also stunned for 1 minute. It can attempt a new Will save at the end of each of its turns, and on a success, it disbelieves the illusion and recovers from the stunned condition.

Heightened (+1) The damage increases by 2d6.

PHANTASMAL KILLER   SPELL 4

DEATH EMOTION FEAR ILLUSION MENTAL

Traditions arcane, occult
Cast ❖❖ somatic, verbal
Range 120 feet; **Targets** 1 living creature
Saving Throw Will

You create a phantasmal image of the most fearsome creature imaginable to the target. Only the spell's target can see the killer, though you can see the vague shape of the illusion as it races forth to attack. The effect of the killer is based on the outcome of the target's Will save.

Critical Success The target is unaffected.
Success The target takes 4d6 mental damage and is frightened 1.
Failure The target takes 8d6 mental damage and is frightened 2.
Critical Failure The target is so afraid it might die. It must attempt a Fortitude save; if the target fails, it dies. On a successful Fortitude save, the target takes 12d6 mental damage, is fleeing until the end of its next turn, and is frightened 4. This effect has the incapacitation trait.

Heightened (+1) The damage increases by 2d6 on a failure and by 3d6 on a critical failure.

PHANTOM PAIN   SPELL 1

ILLUSION MENTAL NONLETHAL

Traditions occult
Cast ❖❖ somatic, verbal
Range 30 feet; **Targets** 1 creature
Saving Throw Will; **Duration** 1 minute

Illusory pain wracks the target, dealing 2d4 mental damage and 1d4 persistent mental damage. The target must attempt a Will save.

Critical Success The target is unaffected.
Success The target takes full initial damage but no persistent damage, and the spell ends immediately.
Failure The target takes full initial and persistent damage, and the target is sickened 1. If the target recovers from being sickened, the persistent damage ends and the spell ends.
Critical Failure As failure, but the target is sickened 2.

Heightened (+1) The damage increases by 2d4 and the persistent damage by 1d4.

PHANTOM STEED   SPELL 2

CONJURATION

Traditions arcane, occult, primal
Cast 10 minutes (somatic, verbal)
Range 30 feet
Duration 8 hours

You conjure a Large, magical, equine creature that only you (or another Medium or Small creature you choose) can ride. The horse is clearly phantasmal in nature, has 20 AC and 10 Hit Points, and automatically fails all saves. If it's reduced to 0 Hit Points, it disappears and the spell ends. The steed has a Speed of 40 feet and can hold its rider's body weight, plus 20 Bulk.

Heightened (4th) The steed has a Speed of 60 feet, can walk on water, and ignores areas of natural difficult terrain.
Heightened (5th) The steed has a Speed of 60 feet, can walk on water, and ignores areas of natural difficult terrain. It can also *air walk* but must end its turn on solid ground or fall.
Heightened (6th) The steed can walk or fly at a Speed of 80 feet, can walk on water, and ignores natural difficult terrain.

PLANE SHIFT   SPELL 7

UNCOMMON CONJURATION TELEPORTATION

Traditions arcane, divine, occult, primal
Cast 10 minutes (focus, material, somatic, verbal)
Range touch; **Targets** 1 willing creature, or up to 8 willing creatures joining hands

You and your allies traverse the barriers between planes of existence. The targets move to another plane, such as the Plane of Fire, the Shadow Plane, or the Abyss. You must have specific knowledge of the destination plane and use a magic tuning fork created from material from that plane as a focus for the spell. While the tuning forks for most prominent planes are uncommon, just like the spell *plane shift*, more obscure planes and demiplanes often have rare tuning forks.

The spell is highly imprecise, and you appear 1d20×25 miles from the last place one of the targets (of your choice) was located the last time that target traveled to the plane. If it's the first time traveling to a particular plane for all targets, you appear at a random location on the plane. *Plane shift* doesn't provide a means of return travel, though casting *plane shift* again allows you to return to your previous plane unless there are extenuating circumstances.

INTRODUCTION

ANCESTRIES & BACKGROUNDS

CLASSES

SKILLS

FEATS

EQUIPMENT

SPELLS

THE AGE OF LOST OMENS

PLAYING THE GAME

GAME MASTERING

CRAFTING & TREASURE

APPENDIX

PLANT FORM — SPELL 5

PLANT | POLYMORPH | TRANSMUTATION

Traditions primal
Cast ❖❖ somatic, verbal
Duration 1 minute

Taking inspiration from verdant creatures, you transform into a Large plant battle form. You must have space to expand into or the spell is lost. When you cast this spell, choose arboreal, flytrap, or shambler. You can substitute a similar specific plant to turn into (such as a pitcher plant instead of a flytrap), but this has no effect on the form's Size or statistics. While in this form, you gain the plant trait. You can Dismiss the spell.

You gain the following statistics and abilities regardless of which battle form you choose:

- AC = 19 + your level. Ignore your armor's check penalty and Speed reduction.
- 12 temporary Hit Points.
- Resistance 10 to poison.
- Low-light vision.
- One or more unarmed melee attacks specific to the battle form you choose, which are the only attacks you can use. You're trained with them. Your attack modifier is +17, and your damage bonus is +11. These attacks are Strength based (for the purpose of the enfeebled condition, for example). If your unarmed attack modifier is higher, you can use it instead.
- Athletics modifier of +19, unless your own modifier is higher.

You also gain specific abilities based on the type of plant you choose:

- **Arboreal** Speed 30 feet; **Melee** ❖ branch (reach 15 feet), **Damage** 2d10 bludgeoning; **Melee** ❖ foot, **Damage** 2d8 bludgeoning; you can speak in this form, but you still can't Cast a Spell or supply verbal components.
- **Flytrap** Speed 15 feet; resistance 10 to acid; **Melee** ❖ leaf (reach 10 feet), **Damage** 2d8 piercing, and you can spend an action after a hit to Grab the target.
- **Shambler** Speed 20 feet, swim Speed 20 feet; resistance 10 to electricity; **Melee** ❖ vine (reach 15 feet), **Damage** 2d8 slashing.

Heightened (6th) Your battle form is Huge, and the reach of your attacks increases by 5 feet. You instead gain AC = 22 + your level, 24 temporary HP, attack modifier +21, damage bonus +16, and Athletics +22.

POLAR RAY — SPELL 8

COLD | EVOCATION

Traditions arcane, primal
Cast ❖❖ somatic, verbal
Range 120 feet; **Targets** 1 creature or object

You fire a blue-white ray of freezing air and swirling sleet from your finger that can chill your target to the bones. You must succeed at a spell attack roll to affect the target, which then takes 10d8 cold damage and is drained 2.

Heightened (+1) The damage increases by 2d8.

POSSESSION — SPELL 7

UNCOMMON | INCAPACITATION | MENTAL | NECROMANCY | POSSESSION

Traditions occult
Cast ❖❖ somatic, verbal
Range 30 feet; **Targets** 1 living creature
Saving Throw Will; **Duration** 1 minute

You send your mind and soul into the target's body, attempting to take control. The target must attempt a Will save. You can choose to use the effects of a degree of success more favorable to the target if you prefer.

While you're possessing a target, your own body is unconscious and can't wake up normally. You can sense everything the possessed target does. You can Dismiss this spell. If the possessed body dies, the spell ends and you must succeed at a Fortitude save against your spell DC or be paralyzed for 1 hour, or 24 hours on a critical failure. If the spell ends during an encounter, you act just before the possessed creature's initiative count.

Critical Success The target is unaffected.
Success You possess the target but can't control it. You ride along in the body while the spell lasts.
Failure You possess the target and take partial control of it. You no longer have a separate turn; instead, you might control the target. At the start of each of the target's turns, it attempts another Will save. If it fails, it's controlled by you on that turn; if it succeeds, it chooses its own actions; and if it critically succeeds, it forces you out and the spell ends.
Critical Failure You possess the target fully, and it can only watch as you manipulate it like a puppet. The target is controlled by you.

Heightened (9th) The duration is 10 minutes, and you can physically enter the creature's body, protecting your physical body while the spell lasts.

POWER WORD BLIND — SPELL 7

UNCOMMON | AUDITORY | ENCHANTMENT | MENTAL

Traditions arcane
Cast ❖ verbal
Range 30 feet; **Targets** 1 creature
Duration varies

You utter an arcane word of power that can make the target blinded upon hearing it. Once targeted, the target is then temporarily immune for 10 minutes. The effect of the spell depends on the target's level.

11th or Lower The target is blinded permanently.
12th–13th The target is blinded for 1d4 minutes.
14th or Higher The target is dazzled for 1 minute.

Heightened (+1) The levels at which each outcome applies increase by 2.

POWER WORD KILL — SPELL 9

UNCOMMON | AUDITORY | DEATH | ENCHANTMENT | MENTAL

Traditions arcane
Cast ❖ verbal
Range 30 feet; **Targets** 1 creature
Duration varies

INTRODUCTION

ANCESTRIES & BACKGROUNDS

CLASSES

SKILLS

FEATS

EQUIPMENT

SPELLS

THE AGE OF LOST OMENS

PLAYING THE GAME

GAME MASTERING

CRAFTING & TREASURE

APPENDIX

You utter the most powerful arcane word of power. Once targeted, the target is then temporarily immune for 10 minutes. The effect of the spell depends on the target's level.

14th or Lower The target dies instantly.

15th If the target has 50 Hit Points or fewer, it dies instantly; otherwise, it drops to 0 Hit Points and becomes dying 1, or increases its dying condition by 1 if it's already dying.

16th or Higher The target takes 50 damage; if this brings the target to 0 Hit Points, the target dies instantly.

Heightened (10th) The levels at which each outcome applies increase by 2.

POWER WORD STUN   SPELL 8

UNCOMMON   AUDITORY   ENCHANTMENT   MENTAL

Traditions arcane
Cast ❖ verbal
Range 30 feet; **Targets** 1 creature
Duration varies

You stun the target with an arcane word of power. Once targeted, the target is then temporarily immune for 10 minutes. The effect of the spell depends on the target's level.

13th or Lower The target is stunned for 1d6 rounds.

14th–15th The target is stunned for 1 round.

16th or Higher The target is stunned 1.

Heightened (+1) The levels at which each outcome applies increase by 2.

PRESTIDIGITATION   CANTRIP 1

CANTRIP   EVOCATION

Traditions arcane, divine, occult, primal
Cast ❖❖ somatic, verbal
Range 10 feet; **Targets** 1 object (cook, lift, or tidy only)
Duration sustained

The simplest magic does your bidding. You can perform simple magical effects for as long as you Sustain the Spell. Each time you Sustain the Spell, you can choose one of four options.

- **Cook** Cool, warm, or flavor 1 pound of nonliving material.
- **Lift** Slowly lift an unattended object of light Bulk or less 1 foot off the ground.
- **Make** Create a temporary object of negligible Bulk, made of congealed magical substance. The object looks crude and artificial and is extremely fragile—it can't be used as a tool, weapon, or spell component.
- **Tidy** Color, clean, or soil an object of light Bulk or less. You can affect an object of 1 Bulk with 10 rounds of concentration, and a larger object a 1 minute per Bulk.

Prestidigitation can't deal damage or cause adverse conditions. Any actual change to an object (beyond what is noted above) persists only as long as you Sustain the Spell.

PRIMAL HERD   SPELL 10

POLYMORPH   TRANSMUTATION

Traditions primal
Cast ❖❖ somatic, verbal
Range 30 feet; **Targets** you and up to 5 willing targets
Duration 1 minute

Summoning the power of the natural world, you transform the targets into a herd of mammoths, and they each assume a Huge battle form. Each target must have enough space to expand into or the spell fails for that target. Each target gains the animal trait. Each target can Dismiss the spell's effects on themselves. Each target gains the following while transformed:

- AC = 22 + the target's level. Ignore any armor check penalty and Speed reduction.
- 20 temporary Hit Points.
- Speed 40 feet.
- Low-light vision.
- The following unarmed melee attacks, which are the only attacks the target can use. They're trained with them. When attacking with these attacks, the target uses their attack modifier with the proficiency and item bonuses of their most favorable weapon or unarmed Strike, and the damage is listed for each attack. These attacks are Strength based (for the purpose of the enfeebled condition, for example). If the target's unarmed attack modifier is higher, they can use it instead. **Melee** ❖ tusk (reach 15 feet), **Damage** 4d8+19 piercing; **Melee** ❖ trunk (agile, reach 15 feet), **Damage** 4d6+16 bludgeoning; **Melee** ❖ foot (agile, reach 15 feet), **Damage** 4d6+13 bludgeoning.
- Athletics modifier of +30, unless the target's own modifier is higher.
- **Trample** ❖❖❖ You move up to twice your Speed and move through the space of Large or smaller creatures, trampling each creature whose space you enter. A trampled creature takes damage from its foot Strike based on a basic Reflex save (DC = 19 + the target's level).

PRIMAL PHENOMENON   SPELL 10

DIVINATION

Traditions primal
Cast ❖❖❖ material, somatic, verbal

You request a direct intercession from the natural world. Nature always refuses unnatural requests and might grant a different request (potentially more powerful or better fitting its character) than the one you asked for. A *primal phenomenon* spell can do any of the following things.

- Duplicate any primal spell of 9th level or lower.
- Duplicate any non-primal spell of 7th level or lower.
- Produce any effect whose power level is in line with the above effects.
- Reverse certain effects that refer to the *wish* spell.

At the GM's discretion, you can try to use *primal phenomenon* to produce greater effects than these, but doing so may be dangerous, or the spell may have only a partial effect.

PRISMATIC SPHERE   SPELL 9

ABJURATION   LIGHT

Traditions arcane, occult
Cast ❖❖ somatic, verbal
Range 10 feet
Duration 1 hour

You create a seven-layered sphere to protect an area. This multicolored sphere functions like a *prismatic wall* but is shaped in a 10-foot burst centered on a corner of your space. You must form the sphere in an unbroken open space so its edges don't pass through any creatures or objects, or the spell is lost.

PRISMATIC SPRAY   SPELL 7

EVOCATION LIGHT

Traditions arcane, occult
Cast ◆◆ somatic, verbal
Area 30-foot cone

A spray of rainbow light beams cascades from your open hand. Each creature in the area must roll 1d8 on the table below to see which beam affects it, then attempt a saving throw of the indicated type. The table notes any additional traits that apply to each type of ray. If a creature is struck by multiple beams, it uses the same d20 result for all its saving throws. For all rays, a successful saving throw negates the effect for that creature.

1d8	Color	Save	Effect (Traits)
1	Red	Reflex	50 fire damage (fire)
2	Orange	Reflex	60 acid damage (acid)
3	Yellow	Reflex	70 electricity damage (electricity)
4	Green	Fortitude	30 poison damage and enfeebled 1 for 1 minute (poison)
5	Blue	Fortitude	Affected as if by *flesh to stone*
6	Indigo	Will	Confused, as the *warp mind* spell (mental)
7	Violet	Will	Slowed 1 for 1 minute; if a critical failure, sent to another plane, as *plane shift* (teleportation)
8	Potent beam	—	Affected by two beams—roll twice, rerolling any duplicates or results of 8

PRISMATIC WALL   SPELL 8

ABJURATION LIGHT

Traditions arcane, occult
Cast ◆◆◆ material, somatic, verbal
Range 120 feet
Duration 1 hour

You create an opaque wall of shimmering, multicolored light. The wall is straight and vertical, stretching 60 feet long and 30 feet high. You must form the wall in an unbroken open space so its edges don't pass through any creatures or objects, or the spell is lost. You can pass through the wall and ignore its effects. The wall sheds bright light out to 20 feet on each side (and dim light to the next 20 feet). Creatures other than you that come into the wall's light must attempt a Will save; they're dazzled for 1 round on a success, blinded for 1 round on a failure, and blinded for 1 minute on a critical failure. They are then temporarily immune to the blinding effect for 1 hour.

A prismatic wall has seven different layers, each a different color. Red, orange, yellow, and green have the effect of a 5th-level *chromatic wall* (page 323) spell of that color, and the others have the effect of a 7th-level *chromatic wall* spell of that color. A creature that tries to pass through the wall must attempt a saving throw against each component wall. The effects take place simultaneously, so a creature turned to stone by the blue wall is still treated as a creature for the indigo and violet walls.

The wall as a whole is immune to counteracting effects of the wall's level or lower; each color must be counteracted by its specific spell, as described in *chromatic wall*. This must be done in order (red, orange, yellow, green, blue, indigo, then violet). A given color can't be affected until the previous color is counteracted. Counteracting a color wall removes that color's effect from the wall, and counteracting them all ends *prismatic wall*. You can Dismiss the spell.

PRIVATE SANCTUM   SPELL 4

UNCOMMON ABJURATION

Traditions arcane, occult
Cast 10 minutes (material, somatic, verbal)
Range touch; **Area** 100-foot burst
Duration 24 hours

From outside, the area looks like a bank of impenetrable black fog. Sensory stimuli (such as sounds, smells, and light) don't pass from inside the area to outside the area. Scrying spells can't perceive any stimuli from the area, and mind-reading effects don't work in the area.

PRODUCE FLAME   CANTRIP 1

ATTACK CANTRIP EVOCATION FIRE

Traditions arcane, primal
Cast ◆◆ somatic, verbal
Range 30 feet; **Targets** 1 creature

A small ball of flame appears in the palm of your hand, and you lash out with it either in melee or at range. Make a spell attack roll against your target's AC. This is normally a ranged attack, but you can also make a melee attack against a creature in your unarmed reach. On a success, you deal 1d4 fire damage plus your spellcasting ability modifier. On a critical success, the target takes double damage and 1d4 persistent fire damage.

Heightened (+1) Increase the damage by 1d4 and the persistent damage on a critical hit by 1d4.

PROJECT IMAGE   SPELL 7

ILLUSION MENTAL

Traditions arcane, occult
Cast ◆◆ somatic, verbal
Range 30 feet
Duration sustained up to 1 minute

You project an illusory image of yourself. You must stay within range of the image, and if at any point you can't see the image, the spell ends. Whenever you Cast a Spell other than one whose area is an emanation, you can cause the spell effect

to originate from either yourself or the image. Because the image is an illusion, it can't benefit from spells, though visual manifestations of the spell appear. The image has the same AC and saves as you. If it is hit by an attack or fails a save, the spell ends.

Heightened (+2) The maximum duration you can Sustain the Spell increases to 10 minutes.

PROTECTION   SPELL 1

UNCOMMON   ABJURATION

Traditions divine, occult
Cast ◆◆ somatic, verbal
Range touch; **Targets** 1 creature
Duration 1 minute

You ward a creature against a specified alignment. Choose chaotic, evil, good, or lawful when you cast this spell. The target gains a +1 status bonus to Armor Class and saving throws against creatures and effects of the chosen alignment. This bonus increases to +3 against effects from such creatures that would directly control the target and against attacks made by summoned creatures of the chosen alignment.

This spell gains the trait that opposes the alignment you chose—if you choose chaos, this spell gains the lawful trait, and vice versa; if you choose evil, this spell gains the good trait, and vice versa.

PRYING EYE   SPELL 5

DIVINATION   SCRYING

Traditions arcane, divine, occult
Cast 1 minute (material, somatic, verbal)
Range see text
Duration sustained

You create an invisible, floating eye, 1 inch in diameter, at a location you can see within 500 feet. It sees in all directions with your normal visual senses and continuously transmits what it sees to you.

The first time you Sustain the Spell each round, you can either move the eye up to 30 feet, seeing only things in front of the eye, or move it up to 10 feet, seeing everything in all directions around it. There is no limit to how far from you the eye can move, but the spell ends immediately if you and the eye ever cease to be on the same plane of existence. You can attempt Seek actions through the eye if you want to attempt Perception checks with it. Any damage dealt to the eye destroys it and ends the spell.

PUNISHING WINDS   SPELL 8

AIR   EVOCATION

Traditions primal
Cast ◆◆◆ material, somatic, verbal
Range 100 feet; **Area** 30-foot radius, 100-foot-tall cylinder
Duration sustained up to 1 minute

Violent winds and a powerful downdraft fill the area, forming a cyclone. All flying creatures in the area descend 40 feet. The entire area is greater difficult terrain for Flying creatures, and difficult terrain for creatures on the ground or Climbing. Any creature that ends its turn Flying within the area descends 20 feet. Any creature pushed into a surface by this spell's winds takes bludgeoning damage as though it had fallen.

The squares at the outside vertical edges of the cylinder prevent creatures from leaving. These squares are greater difficult terrain, and a creature attempting to push through must succeed at an Athletics check or Acrobatics check to Maneuver in Flight against your spell DC to get through. A creature that fails ends its current action but can try again.

PURIFY FOOD AND DRINK   SPELL 1

`NECROMANCY`

Traditions divine, primal

Cast ◆◆ somatic, verbal

Range touch; **Targets** 1 cubic foot of contaminated food or water

You remove toxins and contaminations from food and drink, making them safe to consume. This spell doesn't prevent future contamination, natural decay, or spoilage. One cubic foot of liquid is roughly 8 gallons.

PURPLE WORM STING   SPELL 6

`NECROMANCY` `POISON`

Traditions arcane, primal

Cast ◆◆ somatic, verbal

Range touch; **Targets** 1 creature

Saving Throw Fortitude

You replicate the attack of a deadly purple worm. You deal 6d6 piercing damage to the touched creature and afflict it with purple worm venom. The target must attempt a Fortitude save.

Critical Success The target is unaffected.

Success The target takes 3d6 poison damage.

Failure The target is afflicted with purple worm venom at stage 1.

Critical Failure The target is afflicted with purple worm venom at stage 2.

Purple Worm Venom (poison); **Level** 11; **Maximum Duration** 6 rounds. **Stage 1** 3d6 poison damage and enfeebled 2 (1 round); **Stage 2** 4d6 poison damage and enfeebled 2 (1 round); **Stage 3** 6d6 poison damage and enfeebled 2 (1 round).

RAISE DEAD   SPELL 6

`UNCOMMON` `HEALING` `NECROMANCY`

Traditions divine

Cast 10 minutes (material, somatic, verbal); **Cost** diamonds worth a total value of the target's level (minimum 1) × 200 gp

Range 10 feet; **Targets** 1 dead creature of 13th level or lower

You attempt to call forth the dead creature's soul, requiring the creature's body to be present and relatively intact. The creature must have died within the past 3 days. If Pharasma has decided that the creature's time has come (at the GM's discretion), or if the creature doesn't wish to return to life, this spell automatically fails, but the diamonds aren't consumed in the casting.

If the spell is successful, the creature returns to life with 1 Hit Point, no spells prepared or spell slots available, no points in any pools or any other daily resources, and still with any long-term debilitations of the old body. The time spent in the Boneyard leaves the target temporarily debilitated, making it clumsy 2, drained 2, and enfeebled 2 for 1 week; these conditions can't be removed or reduced by any means until the week has passed. The creature is also permanently changed by its time in the afterlife, such as a slight personality shift, a streak of white in the hair, or a strange new birthmark.

Heightened (7th) The maximum level of the target increases to 15. The cost increases to the target's level (minimum 1) × 400 gp.

Heightened (8th) The maximum level the target increases to 17. The cost increases to the target's level (minimum 1) × 800 gp.

Heightened (9th) The maximum level of the target increases to 19. The cost increases to the target's level (minimum 1) × 1,600 gp.

Heightened (10th) The maximum level the target increases to 21. The cost increases to the target's level (minimum 1) × 3,200 gp.

RAY OF ENFEEBLEMENT   SPELL 1

`ATTACK` `NECROMANCY`

Traditions arcane, divine, occult

Cast ◆◆ somatic, verbal

Range 30 feet; **Targets** 1 creature

Saving Throw Fortitude; **Duration** 1 minute

A ray with the power to sap a foe's strength flashes from your hand. Attempt a ranged spell attack against the target. If you succeed, that creature attempts a Fortitude save in order to determine the spell's effect. If you critically succeed on your attack roll, use the outcome for one degree of success worse than the result of its save.

Critical Success The target is unaffected.

Success The target becomes enfeebled 1.

Failure The target becomes enfeebled 2.

Critical Failure The target becomes enfeebled 3.

RAY OF FROST   CANTRIP 1

`ATTACK` `CANTRIP` `COLD` `EVOCATION`

Traditions arcane, primal

Cast ◆◆ somatic, verbal

Range 120 feet; **Targets** 1 creature

You blast an icy ray. Make a spell attack roll. The ray deals cold damage equal to 1d4 + your spellcasting ability modifier.

Critical Success The target takes double damage and takes a –10-foot status penalty to its Speeds for 1 round.

Success The target takes normal damage.

Heightened (+1) The damage increases by 1d4.

READ AURA   CANTRIP 1

`CANTRIP` `DETECTION` `DIVINATION`

Traditions arcane, divine, occult, primal

Cast 1 minute (somatic, verbal)

Range 30 feet; **Targets** 1 object

You focus on the target object, opening your mind to perceive magical auras. When the casting is complete, you know whether that item is magical, and if it is, you learn the school of magic (pages 297–298).

If the object is illusory, you detect this only if the effect's level is lower than the level of your *read aura* spell.

Heightened (3rd) You can target up to 10 objects.

Heightened (6th) You can target any number of objects.

READ OMENS   SPELL 4

UNCOMMON DIVINATION PREDICTION

Traditions divine, occult

Cast 10 minutes (material, somatic, verbal)

You peek into the future. Choose a particular goal, event, or activity that will occur within 1 week. You learn a cryptic clue or piece of advice that could help with the chosen event, often in the form of a rhyme or omen.

REGENERATE   SPELL 7

HEALING NECROMANCY POSITIVE

Traditions divine, primal

Cast ◆◆ somatic, verbal

Range touch; **Targets** 1 willing living creature

Duration 1 minute

An infusion of positive energy grants a creature continuous healing. The target temporarily gains regeneration 15, which restores 15 Hit Points to it at the start of each of its turns. While it has regeneration, the target can't die from damage and its dying value can't exceed 3, though if its wounded value becomes 4 or higher, it stays unconscious until its wounds are treated. If the target takes acid or fire damage, its regeneration deactivates until after the end of its next turn.

Each time the creature regains Hit Points from regeneration, it also regrows one damaged or ruined organ (if any). During the spell's duration, the creature can also reattach severed body parts by spending an Interact action to hold the body part to the area it was severed from.

Heightened (9th) The regeneration increases to 20.

REMAKE   SPELL 10

UNCOMMON CONJURATION

Traditions arcane, divine, occult, primal

Cast 1 hour (material, somatic, verbal)

Range 5 feet

You fully re-create an object from nothing, even if the object was destroyed. To do so, you must be able to picture the object in your mind. Additionally, the material component must be a remnant of the item, no matter how small or insignificant (even a speck of dust that remains from *disintegrate* is enough). The spell fails if your imagination relied on too much guesswork; if the object would be too large to fit in a 5-foot cube; if the object still exists and you were simply not aware of it; or if the object is an artifact, has a level over 20, or has similar vast magical power.

The item reassembles in perfect condition. Even if your mental image was of a damaged or weathered object, the new one is in this perfected form. If the object was magical,

this spell typically restores its constant magical properties, but not any temporary ones, such as charges or one-time uses. An item with charges or uses per day has all of its uses expended when remade, but it replenishes them normally thereafter.

REMOVE CURSE   SPELL 4

HEALING NECROMANCY

Traditions divine, occult

Cast 10 minutes (material, somatic, verbal)

Range touch; **Targets** 1 creature

Your touch grants a reprieve to a cursed creature. You attempt to counteract one curse afflicting the target. If the curse comes from a cursed item or other external source, a success indicates that the target creature can rid itself of the cursed item, but it doesn't remove the curse from the item.

REMOVE DISEASE   SPELL 3

HEALING NECROMANCY

Traditions divine, primal

Cast 10 minutes (material, somatic, verbal)

Range touch; **Targets** 1 creature

Healing magic purges disease from a creature's body. You attempt to counteract one disease afflicting the target.

REMOVE FEAR   SPELL 2

ENCHANTMENT

Traditions divine, occult, primal

Cast ◆◆ somatic, verbal

Range touch; **Targets** 1 creature

With a touch, you ease a creature's fears. You can attempt to counteract a single fear effect that the target suffers from. This frees only the target, not any other creatures under the fear effect.

Heightened (6th) The spell's range increases to 30 feet, and you can target up to 10 creatures.

REMOVE PARALYSIS   SPELL 2

HEALING NECROMANCY

Traditions divine, occult, primal

Cast ◆◆ somatic, verbal

Range touch; **Targets** 1 creature

A surge of energy frees a paralyzed creature. You can attempt to counteract a single effect imposing the paralyzed condition on the target. This does not cure someone who is paralyzed from some natural state or effect, such as paralysis caused by non-magical wounds or toxins.

Heightened (6th) The spell's range increases to 30 feet, and you can target up to 10 creatures.

REPULSION   SPELL 6

ABJURATION AURA MENTAL

Traditions arcane, divine, occult

Cast ◆◆ somatic, verbal

Range emanation up to 40 feet

Saving Throw Will; **Duration** 1 minute

You manifest an aura that prevents creatures from approaching you. When casting the spell, you can make the area any radius you choose, up to 40 feet. A creature must attempt a Will save if it's within the area when you cast the spell or as soon as it enters the area while the spell is in effect. Once a creature has attempted the save, it uses the same result for that casting of *repulsion*. Any restrictions on a creature's movement apply only if it voluntarily moves toward you. For example, if you move closer to a creature, it doesn't then need to move away.

Critical Success The creature's movement is not restricted.

Success The creature treats each square in the area as difficult terrain when moving closer to you.

Failure The creature can't move closer to you within the area.

RESILIENT SPHERE   SPELL 4

ABJURATION **FORCE**

Traditions arcane, occult

Cast ◆◆ somatic, verbal

Range 30 feet; **Targets** 1 Large or smaller creature

Duration 1 minute

You create an immobile sphere of force to either trap or protect the target, blocking anything that would pass through the sphere. The sphere has AC 5, Hardness 10, and 40 Hit Points. It's immune to critical hits and precision damage. *Disintegrate* destroys the sphere instantly. If the target is unwilling, the effects of the sphere depend on the target's Reflex save.

Critical Success The target disrupts the sphere's integrity, causing it to collapse entirely.

Success The sphere functions normally but has only 10 Hit Points instead of 40.

Failure The sphere has its normal effect.

RESIST ENERGY   SPELL 2

ABJURATION

Traditions arcane, divine, occult, primal

Cast ◆◆ somatic, verbal

Range touch; **Targets** 1 creature

Duration 10 minutes

A shield of elemental energy protects a creature against one type of energy damage. Choose acid, cold, electricity, fire, or sonic damage. The target and its gear gain resistance 5 against the damage type you chose.

Heightened (4th) The resistance increases to 10, and you can target up to two creatures.

Heightened (7th) The resistance increases to 15, and you can target up to five creatures.

RESPLENDENT MANSION   SPELL 9

CONJURATION

Traditions arcane, occult

Cast 1 minute (material, somatic, verbal)

Range 500 feet

Duration until the next time you make your daily preparations

You conjure a towering mansion up to four stories tall and up to 300 feet on a side. While Casting the Spell, you hold an image of the mansion and its desired appearance in your mind. The mansion can contain as many or as few rooms as you desire, and it is decorated as you imagine it. You can imagine a purpose for each room of the mansion, and the proper accouterments appear within. Any furniture or other mundane fixtures function normally for anyone inside the mansion, but they cease to exist if taken beyond its walls. No fixture created with this spell can create magical effects, but magical devices brought into the mansion function normally.

Your mansion contains the same types and quantities of foodstuffs and servants as created by the *magnificent mansion* spell.

Each of the mansion's exterior doorways and windows are protected by *alarm* spells. You choose whether each alarm is audible or mental as you Cast the Spell, and each has a different sound (for an audible alarm) or sensation (for a mental one), allowing you to instantly determine which portal has been used.

RESTORATION   SPELL 2

HEALING **NECROMANCY**

Traditions divine, occult, primal

Cast 1 minute (somatic, verbal)

Range touch; **Targets** 1 creature

Restorative magic counters the effects of toxins or conditions that prevent a creature from functioning at its best. When you cast *restoration*, choose to either reduce a condition or lessen the effect of a toxin. A creature can benefit from only one *restoration* spell each day, and it can't benefit from *restoration* more than once to reduce the stage of the same exposure to a given toxin.

- **Reduce a Condition** Reduce the value of the target's clumsy, enfeebled, or stupefied condition by 2. You can instead reduce two of the listed conditions by 1 each.
- **Lessen a Toxin** Reduce the stage of one toxin the target suffers from by one stage. This can't reduce the stage below stage 1 or cure the affliction.

Heightened (4th) Add drained to the list of conditions you can reduce. When you lessen a toxin, reduce the stage by two. You also gain a third option that allows you to reduce the target's doomed value by 1. You can't use this to reduce a permanent doomed condition.

Heightened (6th) As the 4th-level *restoration*, but you can reduce a permanent doomed condition if you add a spellcasting action and a material component while Casting the Spell, during which you provide 100 gp worth of diamond dust as a cost.

RESTORE SENSES   SPELL 2

HEALING **NECROMANCY**

Traditions divine, occult, primal

Cast ◆◆ somatic, verbal

Range touch; **Targets** 1 creature

You attempt to counteract a single effect imposing the blinded or deafened conditions on the target, restoring its vision or hearing. This can counteract both temporary magic and permanent consequences of magic, but it doesn't cure someone who does not have the sense due to some natural state or effect, such as from birth or from a non-magical wound or toxin.

Heightened (6th) The spell's range increases to 30 feet, and you can target up to 10 creatures. You can choose the effect to counteract separately for each selected creature.

RETROCOGNITION   SPELL 7

DIVINATION

Traditions occult
Cast 1 minute (material, somatic, verbal)
Duration sustained

Opening your mind to occult echoes, you gain impressions from past events that occurred in your current location. *Retrocognition* reveals psychic impressions from events that occurred over the course of the last day throughout the first minute of the duration, followed by impressions from the next day back the next minute, and so on. These echoes don't play out like a vision but instead reveal impressions of emotions and metaphors that provide cryptic clues and details of the past. If you witness a traumatic or turbulent event through an impression, the spell ends unless you succeed at a Will save with a DC of at least 30 and possibly as much as 50, depending on the severity of the event. The GM determines whether an event is traumatic and chooses the DC.

Heightened (8th) You gain impressions of events that occurred over the previous year for each minute you concentrate, instead of the previous day, though the details diminish, making it harder to distinguish impressions from all but the most major events.

Heightened (9th) You gain impressions of events that occurred over the previous century for each minute you concentrate, instead of the previous day, though the details diminish, making it almost impossible to distinguish impressions from all but the most major events.

REVERSE GRAVITY   SPELL 7

UNCOMMON   EVOCATION

Traditions arcane, occult
Cast ◆◆◆ material, somatic, verbal
Range 120 feet; **Area** 20-foot radius, 40-foot-tall cylinder
Duration 1 minute

You reverse gravity in the area. Creatures and objects that aren't secured to the ground immediately fall upward to the top of the area. A creature might be able to Grab an Edge to arrest its fall if it falls past an appropriate surface. If a creature falls against a solid object (such as a ceiling), it takes the appropriate amount of falling damage and lands on the surface. Once an object or creature reaches the top of the area, it floats, caught between the normal and reversed gravity. The creature can move along the plane where the two forms of gravity meet. Creatures that can levitate or fly can use those abilities to mitigate the effects of *reverse gravity*.

When *reverse gravity* ends, all creatures and objects caught in the area fall back down. Likewise, anything that moves beyond the spell's area is subjected to normal gravity again.

REVIVAL   SPELL 10

HEALING NECROMANCY POSITIVE

Traditions divine, primal

Cast ❖❖ somatic, verbal

Range 30 feet; **Targets** dead creatures and living creatures of your choice within range

Duration sustained up to 1 minute

A burst of healing energy soothes living creatures and temporarily rouses those recently slain. All living targets regain 10d8+40 Hit Points. In addition, you return any number of dead targets to life temporarily, with the same effects and limitations as *raise dead* (page 362). The raised creatures have a number of temporary Hit Points equal to the Hit Points you gave living creatures, but no normal Hit Points. The raised creatures can't regain Hit Points or gain temporary Hit Points in other ways, and once *revival*'s duration ends, they lose all temporary Hit Points and die. *Revival* can't resurrect creatures killed by *disintegrate* or a death effect. It has no effect on undead.

RIGHTEOUS MIGHT   SPELL 6

POLYMORPH TRANSMUTATION

Traditions divine

Cast ❖❖ somatic, verbal; **Requirements** You have a deity.

Duration 1 minute

You focus all your divine energy and transform yourself into a Medium battle form, similar to your normal form but armed with powerful divine armaments granted by your deity. While in this form, you gain the statistics and abilities listed below. You have hands in this battle form and can use manipulate actions. You can Dismiss the spell.

You gain the following statistics and abilities:

• AC = 20 + your level. Ignore your armor's check penalty and Speed reduction.

• 10 temporary Hit Points.

• Speed 40 feet.

• Resistance 3 against physical damage.

• Darkvision.

• A special attack with a righteous armament version of your favored weapon, which is the only attack you can use. Your attack modifier with the special weapon is +21, and your damage bonus is +8 (or +6 for a ranged attack). If your attack modifier with your deity's favored weapon is higher, you can use it instead. You deal three of your weapon's normal damage dice, or three damage dice of one size larger if your weapon is a simple weapon with a d4 or d6 damage die. The weapon has one of the following properties that matches your deity's alignment: *anarchic, axiomatic, holy, unholy*. If your deity is true neutral, you instead deal an extra 1d6 precision damage.

• Athletics modifier of +23, unless your own modifier is higher.

Heightened (8th) Your battle form is Large, and your attacks have 10-foot reach, or 15-foot reach if your deity's favored weapon has reach. You must have enough space to expand into or the spell is lost. You instead gain AC = 21 + your level, 15 temporary HP, resistance 4 against physical damage, attack modifier +28, damage bonus +15 (+12 for a ranged attack), and Athletics +29.

ROPE TRICK   SPELL 4

UNCOMMON CONJURATION EXTRADIMENSIONAL

Traditions arcane, occult

Cast 10 minutes (material, somatic, verbal)

Range touch; **Targets** 1 touched piece of rope from 5 to 30 feet long

Duration 8 hours

You cause the target rope to rise vertically into the air. Where it ends, an extradimensional space opens, connected to the top of the rope. This space can be reached only by climbing the rope.

The entrance to the space can't be seen, and it can be pinpointed only by the presence of the rope. The rope can't be removed or hidden, though it can be detached from the extradimensional space by pulling it with 16,000 pounds of weight, critically succeeding at an Athletics check against the spell's DC, or destroying the rope. The space holds up to eight Medium creatures and their gear. A Large creature counts as two Medium creatures, a Huge creature counts as four Medium creatures, and a Gargantuan creature fills the space on its own.

If the rope is detached or destroyed, or if a creature attempts to enter the space that would put it over its capacity, the space begins to unravel. It disappears in 1d4 rounds, depositing the creatures within safely on the ground below.

SANCTIFIED GROUND   SPELL 3

ABJURATION CONSECRATION

Traditions divine

Cast 1 minute (material, somatic, verbal); **Cost** 1 vial of *holy water*

Area 30-foot burst centered on you

Duration 24 hours

You sanctify the area, sprinkling it with *holy water* and warding it against your foes. Choose aberrations, celestials, dragons, fiends, monitors, or undead. All creatures in the area gain a +1 status bonus to AC, attack rolls, damage rolls, and saving throws against the chosen creatures.

SANCTUARY   SPELL 1

ABJURATION

Traditions divine, occult

Cast ❖❖ somatic, verbal

Range touch; **Targets** 1 creature

Duration 1 minute

You ward a creature with protective energy that deters enemy attacks. Creatures attempting to attack the target must attempt a Will save each time. If the target uses a hostile action, the spell ends.

Critical Success *Sanctuary* ends.

Success The creature can attempt its attack and any other attacks against the target this turn.

Failure The creature can't attack the target and wastes the action. It can't attempt further attacks against the target this turn.

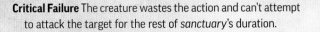

Critical Failure The creature wastes the action and can't attempt to attack the target for the rest of *sanctuary*'s duration.

SCINTILLATING PATTERN — SPELL 8

ILLUSION INCAPACITATION VISUAL

Traditions arcane, occult
Cast ◆◆ material, somatic
Range 120 feet; **Area** 20-foot burst
Saving Throw Will; **Duration** sustained up to 1 minute

A field of cascading, ever-changing colors manifests in the air. Creatures are dazzled while inside the pattern, as are those within 20 feet of the pattern's area. A creature must attempt a Will save if it is inside the pattern when you cast it, enters the pattern, ends its turn within the pattern, or uses a Seek or Interact action on the pattern. A creature currently affected by the pattern doesn't need to attempt new saves.

Success The creature is unaffected.
Failure The creature is confused for 1d4 rounds.
Critical Failure The creature is stunned for 1d4 rounds. After the stunned condition ends, the creature is confused for the remaining duration of the spell.

SCRYING — SPELL 6

UNCOMMON DIVINATION SCRYING

Traditions arcane, occult
Cast 10 minutes (material, somatic, verbal)
Range planetary; **Targets** 1 creature
Saving Throw Will; **Duration** sustained up to 10 minutes

You magically spy on a creature of your choice. *Scrying* works like *clairvoyance* (page 324), except that the image you receive is less precise, insufficient for *teleport* and similar spells. Instead of creating an eye in a set location within 500 feet, you instead create an eye that manifests just above the target. You can choose a target either by name or by touching one of its possessions or a piece of its body. If you haven't met the target in person, *scrying*'s DC is 2 lower, and if you are unaware of the target's identity (perhaps because you found an unknown creature's fang at a crime scene), the DC is instead 10 lower.

The effect of *scrying* depends on the target's Will save.

Critical Success The spell fails and the target is temporarily immune for 1 week. The target also gains a glimpse of you and learns its rough distance and direction from you.
Success The spell fails and the target is temporarily immune for 1 day.
Failure The spell succeeds.
Critical Failure The spell succeeds, and the eye follows the target if it moves, traveling up to 60 feet per round.

SEARING LIGHT — SPELL 3

ATTACK EVOCATION FIRE GOOD LIGHT

Traditions divine, primal
Cast ◆◆ somatic, verbal
Range 120 feet; **Targets** 1 creature

You shoot a blazing ray of light tinged with holy energy. Make a ranged spell attack. The ray deals 5d6 fire damage. If the target is a fiend or undead, you deal an extra 5d6 good damage.

Critical Success The target takes double fire damage, as well as double good damage if a fiend or undead.
Success The target takes full damage

If the light passes through an area of magical darkness or targets a creature affected by magical darkness, *searing light* attempts to counteract the darkness. If you need to determine whether the light passes through an area of darkness, draw a line between yourself and the spell's target

Heightened (+1) The fire damage increases by 2d6, and the good damage against fiends and undead increases by 2d6.

SECRET PAGE — SPELL 3

ILLUSION VISUAL

Traditions arcane, occult
Cast 1 minute (material, somatic, verbal)
Range touch; **Targets** 1 page up to 3 square feet in size
Duration unlimited

You change the target's text to different text entirely. If the text is a spellbook or a scroll, you can change it to show a spell you know of *secret page*'s level or lower. The replacement spell cannot be cast or used to prepare a spell. You can also transform the text into some other text you have written or have access to. You can specify a password that allows a creature touching the page to change the text back and forth. You must choose the replacement text and the password, if any, when you Cast the Spell.

SEE INVISIBILITY — SPELL 2

DIVINATION REVELATION

Traditions arcane, divine, occult
Cast ◆◆ somatic, verbal
Duration 10 minutes

You can see invisible creatures and objects. They appear to you as translucent shapes, and they are concealed to you.

Heightened (5th) The spell has a duration of 8 hours.

SENDING — SPELL 5

DIVINATION MENTAL

Traditions arcane, divine, occult
Cast ◆◆◆ material, somatic, verbal
Range planetary; **Targets** 1 creature with whom you are familiar

You send the creature a mental message of 25 words or fewer, and it can respond immediately with its own message of 25 words or fewer.

SHADOW BLAST — SPELL 5

EVOCATION SHADOW

Traditions divine, occult
Cast ◆◆ somatic, verbal
Range varies; **Area** varies
Saving Throw basic Reflex or Will (target's choice)

You shape the quasi-real substance of the Shadow Plane into a blast. Choose acid, bludgeoning, cold, electricity, fire, force, piercing, slashing, or sonic damage, and choose a 30-foot cone, a 15-foot burst within 120 feet, or a 50-foot line. The blast deals 5d8 damage of the type you chose to each creature in the area.

Heightened (+1) The damage increases by 1d8.

INTRODUCTION

ANCESTRIES &
BACKGROUNDS

CLASSES

SKILLS

FEATS

EQUIPMENT

SPELLS

THE AGE OF
LOST OMENS

PLAYING THE
GAME

GAME
MASTERING

CRAFTING
& TREASURE

APPENDIX

SHADOW SIPHON   SPELL 5

ILLUSION SHADOW

Traditions arcane, occult

Cast ⤴ verbal; **Trigger** A spell or magical effect deals damage.

Range 60 feet; **Targets** the triggering spell

Exchanging material energy with that of the Shadow Plane, you transform the triggering spell into a partially illusory version of itself. Attempt to counteract the target spell. If the attempt is successful, any creatures that would be damaged by the spell instead take only half as much damage. but the spell otherwise works as normal. Treat *shadow siphon's* counteract level as 2 higher for this attempt.

SHADOW WALK   SPELL 5

UNCOMMON CONJURATION SHADOW TELEPORTATION

Traditions arcane, occult

Cast 1 minute (material, somatic, verbal)

Range touch; **Targets** you and up to 9 willing creatures touched

Duration 8 hours

You access the Shadow Plane, using its warped nature to spread your travels. The targets enter the edge of the Shadow Plane where it borders the Material Plane. Targets can't see the Material Plane while on the Shadow Plane (although elements of that plane can sometimes be a hazy reflection of the Material Plane). While on the Shadow Plane, the targets are exposed to potential encounters with that plane's denizens. The shadows on the border between the planes bend space, speeding up your movement with respect to the Material Plane. Every 3 minutes the targets travel along this border, they move as far as they would through the Material Plane in 1 hour. At any point, a target can Dismiss the spell's effects, although this affects only that target. The shadow bending is inexact, so when the spell ends, the targets appear roughly 1 mile from their intended location on the Material Plane (though those who are traveling together and Dismiss the spell at the same point on the Plane of Shadow appear together).

SHAPE STONE   SPELL 4

EARTH TRANSMUTATION

Traditions arcane, primal

Cast ◆◆ somatic, verbal

Range touch; **Targets** cube of stone 10 feet across or smaller

You shape the stone into a rough shape of your choice. The shaping process is too crude to produce intricate parts, fine details, moving pieces, or the like. Any creatures standing atop the stone when you reshape it must each attempt a Reflex save or Acrobatics check.

Success The creature is unaffected.

Failure The creature falls prone atop the stone.

Critical Failure The creature falls off the stone (if applicable) and lands prone.

SHAPE WOOD   SPELL 2

PLANT TRANSMUTATION

Traditions primal

Cast ◆◆ somatic, verbal

Range touch; **Targets** an unworked piece of wood up to 20 cubic feet in volume

You shape the wood into a rough shape of your choice. The shaping power is too crude to produce with intricate parts, fine details, moving pieces, or the like. You cannot use this spell to enhance the value of the wooden object you are shaping.

SHAPECHANGE   SPELL 9

POLYMORPH TRANSMUTATION

Traditions arcane, primal

Cast ◆◆ somatic, verbal

Duration 1 minute

Harnessing your mastery of transformative magic, you take on a mutable form. You transform yourself into any form you could choose with a polymorph spell in your spell repertoire or that you could prepare of 8th level or lower (including any 8th-level or lower heightened versions of spells you know). You choose the type of creature as you Cast the Spell rather than when you prepare it. You can change your form to any other form you could choose with this spell by using a single action, which has the concentrate trait. You can Dismiss this spell.

SHATTER   SPELL 2

EVOCATION SONIC

Traditions occult, primal

Cast ◆◆ somatic, verbal

Range 30 feet; **Targets** 1 unattended object

A high-frequency sonic attack shatters a nearby object. You deal 2d10 sonic damage to the object, ignoring the object's Hardness if it is 4 or lower.

Heightened (+1) The damage increases by 1d10, and the Hardness the spell ignores increases by 2.

SHIELD   CANTRIP 1

ABJURATION CANTRIP FORCE

Traditions arcane, divine, occult

Cast ◆ verbal

Duration until the start of your next turn

You raise a magical shield of force. This counts as using the Raise a Shield action, giving you a +1 circumstance bonus to AC until the start of your next turn, but it doesn't require a hand to use.

While the spell is in effect, you can use the Shield Block reaction with your magic shield (see the sidebar). The shield has Hardness 5. After you use Shield Block, the spell ends and you can't cast it again for 10 minutes. Unlike a normal Shield Block, you can use the spell's reaction against the *magic missile* spell.

Heightening the spell increases the shield's Hardness.

Heightened (3rd) The shield has Hardness 10.

Heightened (5th) The shield has Hardness 15.

Heightened (7th) The shield has Hardness 20.

Heightened (9th) The shield has Hardness 25.

SHIELD ACTIONS

The *shield* spell works like a raised shield, and it also gives you the ability to use the Shield Block reaction.

SHIELD BLOCK ⟳

Trigger While you have your shield raised, you take damage from a physical attack.

You place your shield to ward off a blow. Your shield prevents you from taking an amount of damage up to the shield's Hardness. You and the shield each take any remaining damage, possibly breaking or destroying the shield.

SHIELD OTHER   SPELL 2

    NECROMANCY

Traditions divine
Cast ◆◆ somatic, verbal
Range 30 feet; **Targets** 1 creature
Duration 10 minutes

You forge a temporary link between the target's life essence and your own. The target takes half damage from all effects that deal Hit Point damage, and you take the remainder of the damage. When you take damage through this link, you don't apply any resistances, weaknesses, or other abilities you have to that damage; you simply take that amount of damage. The spell ends if the target is ever more than 30 feet away from you. If either you or the target is reduced to 0 Hit Points, any damage from this spell is resolved and then the spell ends.

SHILLELAGH   SPELL 1

    PLANT   TRANSMUTATION

Traditions primal
Cast ◆◆ somatic, verbal
Range touch; **Targets** 1 non-magical club or staff you hold
Duration 1 minute

The target grows vines and leaves, brimming with primal energy. The target becomes a *+1 striking* weapon while in your hands, gaining a +1 item bonus to attack rolls and increasing the number of weapon damage dice to two. Additionally, as long as you are on your home plane, attacks you make with the target against aberrations, extraplanar creatures, and undead increase the number of weapon damage dice to three.

SHOCKING GRASP   SPELL 1

    ATTACK   ELECTRICITY   EVOCATION

Traditions arcane, primal
Cast ◆◆ somatic, verbal
Range touch; **Targets** 1 creature

You shroud your hands in a crackling field of lightning. Make a melee spell attack roll. On a hit, the target takes 2d12 electricity damage. If the target is wearing metal armor or is made of metal, you gain a +1 circumstance bonus to your attack roll with *shocking grasp*, and the target also takes 1d4 persistent electricity damage on a hit. On a critical hit, double the initial damage, but not the persistent damage.

Heightened (+1) The damage increases by 1d12, and the persistent electricity damage increases by 1.

SHRINK   SPELL 2

    POLYMORPH   TRANSMUTATION

Traditions arcane, primal
Cast ◆◆ somatic, verbal
Range 30 feet; **Targets** 1 willing creature
Duration 5 minutes

You warp space to make a creature smaller. The target shrinks to become Tiny in size. Its equipment shrinks with it but returns to its original size if removed. The creature's reach changes to 0 feet. This spell has no effect on a Tiny creature.

Heightened (6th) The spell can target up to 10 creatures.

SHRINK ITEM   SPELL 3

    POLYMORPH   TRANSMUTATION

Traditions arcane
Cast 10 minutes (somatic, verbal)
Range touch; **Targets** 1 non-magical object up to 20 cubic feet in volume and up to 80 Bulk
Duration 1 day

You shrink the target to roughly the size of a coin. This reduces it to negligible Bulk. You can Dismiss the spell, and the spell ends if you toss the object onto a solid surface. The object can't be used to attack or cause damage during the process of it returning to normal size. If there isn't room for the object to return to normal size when the spell ends, the spell's duration continues until the object is in a location large enough to accommodate its normal size.

SIGIL   CANTRIP 1

    CANTRIP   TRANSMUTATION

Traditions arcane, divine, occult, primal
Cast ◆◆ somatic, verbal
Range touch; **Targets** 1 creature or object
Duration unlimited (see below)

You harmlessly place your unique magical sigil, which is about 1 square inch in size, on the targeted creature or object. The mark can be visible or invisible, and you can change it from one state to another by using an Interact action to touch the target. The mark can be scrubbed or scraped off with 5 minutes of work. If it's on a creature, it fades naturally over the course of a week. The time before the mark fades increases depending on your heightened level.

Heightened (3rd) The sigil instead fades after 1 month.
Heightened (5th) The sigil instead fades after 1 year.
Heightened (7th) The sigil never fades.

SILENCE   SPELL 2

    ILLUSION

Traditions divine, occult
Cast ◆◆ material, somatic
Range touch; **Targets** 1 willing creature
Duration 1 minute

The target makes no sound, preventing creatures from noticing it using hearing or other senses alone. The target can't use sonic attacks, nor can it use actions with the auditory trait. This prevents it from casting spells that include verbal components.

INTRODUCTION

ANCESTRIES & BACKGROUNDS

CLASSES

SKILLS

FEATS

EQUIPMENT

SPELLS

THE AGE OF LOST OMENS

PLAYING THE GAME

GAME MASTERING

CRAFTING & TREASURE

APPENDIX

Heightened (4th) The spell effect emanates from the touched creature, silencing all sound in or passing through a 10-foot radius and preventing any auditory and sonic effects in the affected area. While within the radius, creatures are subject to the same effects as the target. Depending upon the position of the effect, a creature might notice the lack of sound reaching it (blocking off the noise coming from a party, for example).

SLEEP SPELL 1

ENCHANTMENT INCAPACITATION MENTAL SLEEP

Traditions arcane, occult
Cast ◆◆ somatic, verbal
Range 30 feet; **Area** 5-foot burst
Saving Throw Will

Each creature in the area becomes drowsy and might fall asleep. A creature that falls unconscious from this spell doesn't fall prone or release what it's holding. This spell doesn't prevent creatures from waking up due to a successful Perception check, limiting its utility in combat.
Critical Success The creature is unaffected.
Success The creature takes a –1 status penalty to Perception checks for 1 round.
Failure The creature falls unconscious. If it's still unconscious after 1 minute, it wakes up automatically.
Critical Failure The creature falls unconscious. If it's still unconscious after 1 hour, it wakes up automatically.
Heightened (4th) The creatures fall unconscious for 1 round on a failure or 1 minute on a critical failure. They fall prone and release what they're holding, and they can't attempt Perception checks to wake up. When the duration ends, the creature is sleeping normally instead of automatically waking up.

SLOW SPELL 3

TRANSMUTATION

Traditions arcane, occult, primal
Cast ◆◆ somatic, verbal
Range 30 feet; **Targets** 1 creature
Saving Throw Fortitude; **Duration** 1 minute
You dilate the flow of time around the target, slowing its actions.
Critical Success The target is unaffected.
Success The target is slowed 1 for 1 round.
Failure The target is slowed 1 for 1 minute.
Critical Failure The target is slowed 2 for 1 minute.
Heightened (6th) You can target up to 10 creatures.

SOLID FOG SPELL 4

CONJURATION WATER

Traditions arcane, primal
Cast ◆◆◆ material, somatic, verbal
Range 120 feet; **Area** 20-foot burst
Duration 1 minute
You conjure a bank of fog so thick it impedes movement as well as sight. This functions as *obscuring mist* (page 355), except that the area is also difficult terrain. You can Dismiss the spell.

SOOTHE SPELL 1

EMOTION ENCHANTMENT HEALING MENTAL

Traditions occult
Cast ◆◆ somatic, verbal
Range 30 feet; **Targets** 1 willing living creature
Duration 1 minute
You grace the target's mind, boosting its mental defenses and healing its wounds. The target regains 1d10+4 Hit Points when you Cast the Spell and gains a +2 status bonus to saves against mental effects for the duration.
Heightened (+1) The amount of healing increases by 1d10+4.

SOUND BURST SPELL 2

EVOCATION SONIC

Traditions divine, occult
Cast ◆◆ somatic, verbal
Range 30 feet; **Area** 10-foot burst
Saving Throw Fortitude
A cacophonous noise blasts out, dealing 2d10 sonic damage. Each creature must attempt a Fortitude save.
Critical Success The creature is unaffected.
Success The creature takes half damage.
Failure The creature takes full damage and is deafened for 1 round.
Critical Failure The creature takes double damage and is deafened and stunned 1 for 1 minute.
Heightened (+1) The damage increases by 1d10.

SPEAK WITH ANIMALS SPELL 2

DIVINATION

Traditions primal
Cast ◆◆ somatic, verbal
Duration 10 minutes
You can ask questions of, receive answers from, and use the Diplomacy skill with animals. The spell doesn't make them more friendly than normal. Cunning animals are likely to be terse and evasive, while less intelligent ones often make inane comments.

SPEAK WITH PLANTS SPELL 4

DIVINATION PLANT

Traditions primal
Cast ◆◆ somatic, verbal
Duration 10 minutes
You can ask questions of and receive answers from plants, but the spell doesn't make them more friendly or intelligent than normal. Most normal plants have a distinctive view of the world around them, so they don't recognize details about creatures or know anything about the world beyond their immediate vicinity. Cunning plant monsters are likely to be terse and evasive, while less intelligent ones often make inane comments.

SPECTRAL HAND SPELL 2

NECROMANCY

Traditions arcane, occult
Cast ◆◆ somatic, verbal
Range 120 feet
Duration 1 minute

You create a semicorporeal hand out of your essence that delivers touch spells for you. Whenever you Cast a Spell with a range of touch, you can have the hand crawl to a target within range along the ground, touch it, and then crawl back to you. When making a melee spell attack with the hand, you use your normal bonuses. The hand can move as far as it needs to within range. The hand has your AC and saves, but any damage to the hand destroys it and causes you to take 1d6 damage.

SPELL IMMUNITY — SPELL 4

ABJURATION

Traditions arcane, divine, occult
Cast ◈◈ somatic, verbal
Range touch; **Targets** 1 creature
Duration 24 hours

You ward a creature against the effects of a single spell. Choose a spell and name it aloud as part of the verbal component. *Spell immunity* attempts to counteract that spell whenever *spell immunity*'s target is the target of the named spell or in that spell's area. Successfully counteracting a spell that targets an area or multiple targets with *spell immunity* negates the effects only for the target affected by *spell immunity*.

SPELL TURNING — SPELL 7

UNCOMMON ABJURATION

Traditions arcane
Cast ◈◈ somatic, verbal
Duration 1 hour

This abjuration reflects spells cast at you back at their caster. When a spell targets you, you can spend a reaction to attempt to reflect it. This uses the rules for counteracting the spell, but if the spell is successfully counteracted, the effect is turned back on the caster. Whether or not the counteract attempt is successful, *spell turning* then ends. *Spell turning* can't affect spells that aren't targeted (such as area spells).

If *spell turning* reflects a spell back at a caster who is also under the effect of *spell turning*, their *spell turning* can attempt to reflect their own spell back at you again; if they do so, their counteract attempt automatically succeeds.

SPELLWRACK — SPELL 6

ABJURATION CURSE FORCE

Traditions arcane, divine, occult
Cast ◈◈ somatic, verbal
Range 30 feet; **Targets** 1 creature
Saving Throw Will

You cause any spells cast on the target to spill out their energy in harmful surges. The target must attempt a Will save.
Critical Success The target is unaffected.
Success Whenever the target becomes affected by a spell with a duration, the target takes 2d12 persistent force damage. Each time it takes persistent force damage from *spellwrack*, it reduces the remaining duration of spells affecting it by 1 round. Only a successful Arcana check against your spell DC can help the target recover from the persistent damage; the curse and the persistent damage end after 1 minute.

Failure As success, but the curse and persistent damage do not end on their own.
Critical Failure As failure, but the persistent force damage is 4d12.

SPIDER CLIMB — SPELL 2

TRANSMUTATION

Traditions arcane, primal
Cast ◈◈ somatic, verbal
Range touch; **Targets** 1 creature
Duration 10 minutes

Tiny clinging hairs sprout across the creature's hands and feet, offering purchase on nearly any surface. The target gains a climb Speed equal to its Speed.
Heightened (5th) The duration increases to 1 hour.

SPIDER STING — SPELL 1

ATTACK NECROMANCY POISON

Traditions arcane, primal
Cast ◈◈ somatic, verbal
Range touch; **Targets** 1 creature
Saving Throw Fortitude

You magically duplicate a spider's venomous sting. You deal 1d4 piercing damage to the touched creature and afflict it with spider venom. The target must attempt a Fortitude save.
Critical Success The target is unaffected.
Success The target takes 1d4 poison damage.
Failure The target is afflicted with spider venom at stage 1.
Critical Failure The target is afflicted with spider venom at stage 2.
Spider Venom (poison); **Level** 1; **Maximum Duration** 4 rounds.
   Stage 1 1d4 poison damage and enfeebled 1 (1 round); **Stage 2** 1d4 poison damage and enfeebled 2 (1 round).

SPIRIT BLAST — SPELL 6

FORCE NECROMANCY

Traditions divine, occult
Cast ◈◈ somatic, verbal
Range 30 feet; **Targets** 1 creature
Saving Throw basic Fortitude

You concentrate ethereal energy and attack a creature's spirit, dealing 16d6 force damage. Because *spirit blast* affects the creature's spirit, it can damage a target projecting its consciousness (such as via *project image*) or possessing another creature even if the target's body is elsewhere. The possessed creature isn't harmed by the blast. The blast doesn't harm creatures that have no spirit, such as constructs.
Heightened (+1) The damage increases by 2d6.

SPIRIT LINK — SPELL 1

HEALING NECROMANCY

Traditions divine, occult
Cast ◈◈ somatic, verbal
Range 30 feet; **Targets** 1 willing creature
Duration 10 minutes

You form a spiritual link with another creature, allowing you

to take in its pain. When you Cast this Spell and at the start of each of your turns, if the target is below maximum Hit Points, it regains 2 Hit Points (or the difference between its current and maximum Hit Points, if that's lower). You lose as many Hit Points as the target regained.

This is a spiritual transfer, so no effects apply that would increase the Hit Points the target regains or decrease the Hit Points you lose. This transfer also ignores any temporary Hit Points you or the target have. Since this effect doesn't involve positive or negative energy, *spirit link* works even if you or the target is undead. While the duration persists, you gain no benefit from regeneration or fast healing. You can Dismiss this spell, and if you're ever at 0 Hit Points, *spirit link* ends automatically.

Heightened (+1) The number of Hit Points transferred each time increases by 2.

SPIRIT SONG   SPELL 8

FORCE   NECROMANCY

Traditions occult
Cast ◆◆ somatic, verbal
Area 60-foot cone
Saving Throw basic Fortitude

Your eldritch song sends pulsing waves of ethereal energy to attack creatures' spirits in the area, dealing 18d6 force damage. Because *spirit song* affects creatures' spirits, it can damage a target projecting its consciousness (such as via

project image) or possessing another creature even if the target's body is elsewhere. The vibrating waves of spiritual song penetrate into, but not through, solid barriers, damaging incorporeal creatures hiding in solid objects in the area but not passing onward to damage creatures in other rooms. Possessed creatures aren't harmed by the song. The song doesn't harm creatures that have no spirit, such as constructs.

Heightened (+1) The damage increases by 2d6.

SPIRITUAL EPIDEMIC   SPELL 8

CURSE   NECROMANCY

Traditions divine, occult
Cast ◆◆ somatic, verbal
Range 120 feet; **Targets** 1 creature
Saving Throw Will; **Duration** varies

You curse the target, sapping its spirit and leaving a contagious trap in its essence. The target must attempt a Will save. Any creature that casts a divine or occult spell on the target while it's affected is targeted by *spiritual epidemic* and must also attempt a Will save. The curse continues to spread in this way.

Critical Success The target is unaffected.

Success The target is enfeebled 2 and stupefied 2 for 1 round.

Failure The target is enfeebled 2 and stupefied 2 for 1 minute and enfeebled 1 and stupefied 1 permanently.

Critical Failure The target is enfeebled 3 and stupefied 3 for 1 minute and enfeebled 2 and stupefied 2 permanently.

SPIRITUAL GUARDIAN   SPELL 5

`ATTACK` `ABJURATION` `FORCE`

Traditions divine
Cast ◆◆ somatic, verbal; **Requirements** You have a deity.
Range 120 feet
Duration sustained up to 1 minute

A Medium guardian made of magical force appears and attacks foes you designate within range. The spiritual guardian is translucent and appears to be holding your deity's favored weapon.

When you Cast the Spell, the spiritual guardian appears in an unoccupied space next to a foe of your choice within range and makes a Strike against it. Each time you Sustain the Spell, you can move the spiritual guardian to an unoccupied space next to a target within range (if necessary) and make a Strike with it. The guardian uses and contributes to your multiple attack penalty. Alternatively, when you Sustain the Spell, you can have the guardian move adjacent to an ally and protect that ally. If you do, each time the ally would take damage, the guardian takes the first 10 damage instead of your ally. It continues to do so until you move the guardian to attack an enemy or defend a different ally, or until the guardian is destroyed (it has 50 Hit Points and can't recover Hit Points by any means). The guardian can't usually take damage except when protecting an ally, though *disintegrate* automatically destroys it if it hits the spiritual guardian's AC of 25.

The guardian's Strikes are melee spell attacks. Regardless of the appearance of the guardian's weapon, the guardian deals force damage equal to 2d8 plus your spellcasting ability modifier, but you can deal damage of the type normally dealt by the weapon it holds instead of force damage. No other traits or statistics of the weapon apply, and even a ranged weapon attacks adjacent creatures only. Despite making a spell attack, the spiritual guardian's weapon is a weapon for the purposes of triggers, resistances, and so forth.

The guardian takes up space and allies can use it when flanking, but it doesn't have any other attributes a creature would normally have aside from Hit Points, and creatures can move through its space without hindrance. The guardian can't make any attack other than its Strike, and feats or spells that affect weapons or enhance allies do not apply to the guardian.

Heightened (+2) The guardian's damage increases by 1d8, and its Hit Points increase by 20.

SPIRITUAL WEAPON   SPELL 2

`ATTACK` `EVOCATION` `FORCE`

Traditions divine, occult
Cast ◆◆ somatic, verbal; **Requirements** You have a deity.
Range 120 feet
Duration sustained up to 1 minute

A weapon made of pure magical force materializes and attacks foes you designate within range. This weapon has a ghostly appearance and manifests as your deity's favored weapon.

When you cast the spell, the weapon appears next to a foe you choose within range and makes a Strike against it. Each time you Sustain the Spell, you can move the weapon to a new target within range (if needed) and Strike with it. The spiritual weapon uses and contributes to your multiple attack penalty.

The weapon's Strikes are melee spell attacks. Regardless of its appearance, the weapon deals force damage equal to 1d8 plus your spellcasting ability modifier. You can deal damage of the type normally dealt by the weapon instead of force damage (or any of the available damage types for a versatile weapon). No other statistics or traits of the weapon apply, and even a ranged weapon attacks adjacent creatures only. Despite making a spell attack, the spiritual weapon is a weapon for purposes of triggers, resistances, and so forth.

The weapon doesn't take up space, grant flanking, or have any other attributes a creature would. The weapon can't make any attack other than its Strike, and feats or spells that affect weapons do not apply to it.

Heightened (+2) The weapon's damage increases by 1d8.

STABILIZE   CANTRIP 1

`CANTRIP` `HEALING` `NECROMANCY` `POSITIVE`

Traditions divine, primal
Cast ◆◆ somatic, verbal
Range 30 feet; **Targets** 1 dying creature

Positive energy shuts death's door. The target loses the dying condition, though it remains unconscious at 0 Hit Points.

STATUS   SPELL 2

`DETECTION` `DIVINATION`

Traditions divine, occult, primal
Cast ◆◆ somatic, verbal
Range touch; **Targets** 1 willing living creature
Duration 1 day

As long as you and the target are on the same plane of existence and both alive, you remain aware of its present state. You know the target's direction from you, distance from you, and any conditions affecting it.

Heightened (4th) The spell's range increases to 30 feet, and you can target up to 10 creatures.

STINKING CLOUD   SPELL 3

`CONJURATION` `POISON`

Traditions arcane, primal
Cast ◆◆ somatic, verbal
Range 120 feet; **Area** 20-foot burst
Saving Throw Fortitude; **Duration** 1 minute

You create a cloud of putrid mist in the area. The cloud functions as *obscuring mist* (page 355) except it sickens creatures that end their turns within the cloud. (The concealed condition is not a poison effect.)

Critical Success The creature is unaffected.
Success The creature is sickened 1.
Failure The creature is sickened 1 and slowed 1 while in the cloud.
Critical Failure The creature is sickened 2 and slowed 1 until it leaves the cloud.

INTRODUCTION

ANCESTRIES &
BACKGROUNDS

CLASSES

SKILLS

FEATS

EQUIPMENT

SPELLS

THE AGE OF
LOST OMENS

PLAYING THE
GAME

GAME
MASTERING

CRAFTING
& TREASURE

APPENDIX

STONE TELL   SPELL 6

UNCOMMON | EVOCATION | EARTH

Traditions divine, primal
Cast ◆◆ somatic, verbal
Duration 10 minutes

You can ask questions of and receive answers from natural or worked stone. While stone is not intelligent, you speak with the natural spirits of the stone, which have a personality colored by the type of stone, as well as by the type of structure the stone is part of, for worked stone. A stone's perspective, perception, and knowledge give it a worldview different enough from a human's that it doesn't consider the same details important. Stones can mostly answer questions about creatures that touched them in the past and what is concealed beneath or behind them.

STONE TO FLESH   SPELL 6

EARTH | TRANSMUTATION

Traditions divine, primal
Cast ◆◆ somatic, verbal
Range touch; **Targets** petrified creature or human-size stone object

Manipulating the fundamental particles of matter, you convert stone into flesh and blood. You restore a petrified creature to its normal state or transform a stone object into a mass of inert flesh (without stone's Hardness) in roughly the same shape.

STONESKIN   SPELL 4

ABJURATION | EARTH

Traditions arcane, primal
Cast ◆◆ somatic, verbal
Range touch; **Targets** 1 creature
Duration 20 minutes

The target's skin hardens like stone. It gains resistance 5 to physical damage, except adamantine. Each time the target is hit by a bludgeoning, piercing, or slashing attack, *stoneskin's* duration decreases by 1 minute.

Heightened (6th) The resistance increases to 10.
Heightened (8th) The resistance increases to 15.
Heightened (10th) The resistance increases to 20.

STORM OF VENGEANCE   SPELL 9

AIR | ELECTRICITY | EVOCATION

Traditions primal
Cast ◆◆◆ material, somatic, verbal
Range 800 feet; **Area** 360-foot burst
Duration sustained up to 1 minute

A massive storm cloud forms in the air in a 360-foot burst. Beneath it, rain begins to fall, and gales impose a –4 circumstance penalty to physical ranged attacks and weapon ranged attacks, and the air in the area becomes greater difficult terrain for flying creatures. When you Cast this Spell and the first time each round you Sustain the Spell, you can choose one of the following storm effects. You can't choose the same effect twice in a row.

- **Acid Rain** Each creature in the storm takes 4d8 acid damage with no saving throw.
- **Hail** The storm deals 4d10 bludgeoning damage to creatures beneath it (basic Fortitude save).

- **Lightning** Up to 10 bolts of lightning strike down, targeting creatures of your choice in the storm. No more than one bolt can target any one creature. Each bolt deals 7d6 electricity damage (basic Reflex save).
- **Rain and Wind** Heavy rain and whipping wind reduce visibility and mobility, making the area under the storm cloud difficult terrain and making everything seen within or through the area concealed.
- **Thunderclap** Each creature in the storm must succeed at a Fortitude save or be deafened for 10 minutes. A creature that succeeds is temporarily immune to thunderclaps from *storm of vengeance* for 1 hour.

Heightened (10th) The range increases to 2,200 feet, and the cloud is a 1,000-foot burst.

SUBCONSCIOUS SUGGESTION   SPELL 5

ENCHANTMENT | INCAPACITATION | LINGUISTIC | MENTAL

Traditions arcane, occult
Cast ◆◆ somatic, verbal
Range 30 feet; **Targets** 1 creature
Saving Throw Will; **Duration** varies

You implant a subconscious suggestion deep within the target's mind for them to follow when a trigger you specify occurs (as described on page 305). You suggest a course of action to the target. Your directive must be phrased in such a way as to seem like a logical course of action to the target, and it can't be self-destructive or obviously against the target's self-interest. The target must attempt a Will save.

Critical Success The target is unaffected and knows you tried to control it.

Success The target is unaffected and thinks you were talking to them normally, not casting a spell on them.

Failure The suggestion remains in the target's subconscious until the next time you prepare. If the trigger occurs before then, the target immediately follows your suggestion. The effect has a duration of 1 minute, or until the target has completed a finite suggestion or the suggestion becomes self-destructive or has other obvious negative effects.

Critical Failure As failure, but the duration is 1 hour.

Heightened (9th) You can target up to 10 creatures.

SUGGESTION   SPELL 4

ENCHANTMENT | INCAPACITATION | LINGUISTIC | MENTAL

Traditions arcane, occult
Cast ◆◆ somatic, verbal
Range 30 feet; **Targets** 1 creature
Saving Throw Will; **Duration** varies

Your honeyed words are difficult for creatures to resist. You suggest a course of action to the target, which must be phrased in such a way as to seem like a logical course of action to the target and can't be self-destructive or obviously against the target's self-interest. The target must attempt a Will save.

Critical Success The target is unaffected and knows you tried to control it.

Success The target is unaffected and thinks you were talking to them normally, not casting a spell on them.

Failure The target immediately follows your suggestion. The spell has a duration of 1 minute, or until the target has completed a finite suggestion or the suggestion becomes self-destructive or has other obvious negative effects.

Critical Failure As failure, but the base duration is 1 hour.

Heightened (8th) You can target up to 10 creatures.

SUMMON ANIMAL   SPELL 1

CONJURATION

Traditions arcane, primal
Cast ◆◆◆ material, somatic, verbal
Range 30 feet
Duration sustained up to 1 minute

You conjure an animal to fight for you. You summon a common creature that has the animal trait and whose level is –1. Heightening the spell increases the maximum level of creature you can summon.

Heightened (2nd) Level 1.
Heightened (3rd) Level 2.
Heightened (4th) Level 3.
Heightened (5th) Level 5.
Heightened (6th) Level 7.
Heightened (7th) Level 9.
Heightened (8th) Level 11.
Heightened (9th) Level 13.
Heightened (10th) Level 15.

SUMMON CELESTIAL   SPELL 5

CONJURATION

Traditions divine
Cast ◆◆◆ material, somatic, verbal
Range 30 feet
Duration sustained up to 1 minute

You conjure a celestial to fight on your behalf. This works like *summon animal*, except you summon a common creature that has the celestial trait and whose level is 5 or lower. You can't summon a creature unless its alignment is one of your deity's preferred alignments (or, if you don't have a deity, is within one step of your alignment). At the GM's discretion, some deities might restrict specific types of celestials, even if their alignments match.

Heightened As *summon animal*.

SUMMON CONSTRUCT   SPELL 1

CONJURATION

Traditions arcane
Cast ◆◆◆ material, somatic, verbal
Range 30 feet
Duration sustained up to 1 minute

You conjure a construct to fight for you. This works like *summon animal*, except you summon a common creature that has the construct trait and whose level is –1.

Heightened As *summon animal*.

SUMMON DRAGON   SPELL 5

CONJURATION

Traditions arcane

Cast ◆◆◆ material, somatic, verbal
Range 30 feet
Duration sustained up to 1 minute

You conjure a dragon to fight for you. This works like *summon animal*, except you summon a common creature that has the dragon trait and whose level is 5 or lower.

Heightened As *summon animal*.

SUMMON ELEMENTAL   SPELL 2

CONJURATION

Traditions arcane, primal
Cast ◆◆◆ material, somatic, verbal
Range 30 feet
Duration sustained up to 1 minute

You conjure an elemental to fight for you. This works like *summon animal*, except you summon a common creature that has the elemental trait and whose level is 1 or lower.

Heightened As *summon animal*.

SUMMON ENTITY   SPELL 5

CONJURATION

Traditions occult
Cast ◆◆◆ material, somatic, verbal
Range 30 feet
Duration sustained up to 1 minute

You conjure an aberration to fight for you. This works like *summon animal*, except you summon a common creature that has the aberration trait and whose level is 5 or lower.

Heightened As *summon animal*.

SUMMON FEY   SPELL 1

CONJURATION

Traditions occult, primal
Cast ◆◆◆ material, somatic, verbal
Range 30 feet
Duration sustained up to 1 minute

You conjure a fey to fight for you. This works like *summon animal*, except you summon a common creature that has the fey trait and whose level is –1.

Heightened As *summon animal*.

SUMMON FIEND   SPELL 5

CONJURATION

Traditions divine
Cast ◆◆◆ material, somatic, verbal
Range 30 feet
Duration sustained up to 1 minute

You conjure a fiend to fight on your behalf. This works like *summon animal*, except you summon a common creature that has the fiend trait and whose level is 5 or lower. You can't summon a creature unless its alignment is one of your deity's preferred alignments (or, if you don't have a deity, is within one step of your alignment). At the GM's discretion, some deities might restrict specific types of fiends, even if their alignments match.

Heightened As *summon animal*.

INTRODUCTION

ANCESTRIES &
BACKGROUNDS

CLASSES

SKILLS

FEATS

EQUIPMENT

SPELLS

THE AGE OF
LOST OMENS

PLAYING THE
GAME

GAME
MASTERING

CRAFTING
& TREASURE

APPENDIX

SUMMON GIANT   SPELL 5

CONJURATION

Traditions primal
Cast ◆◆◆ material, somatic, verbal
Range 30 feet
Duration sustained up to 1 minute

You conjure a giant to fight for you. This works like *summon animal* (page 375), except you summon a common creature that has the giant trait and whose level is 5 or lower.
Heightened As *summon animal*.

SUMMON PLANT OR FUNGUS   SPELL 1

CONJURATION

Traditions primal
Cast ◆◆◆ material, somatic, verbal
Range 30 feet
Duration sustained up to 1 minute

You conjure a plant or fungus to fight for you. This works like *summon animal* (page 375), except you summon a common creature that has the plant or fungus trait and whose level is –1.
Heightened As *summon animal*.

SUNBURST   SPELL 7

EVOCATION   FIRE   LIGHT   POSITIVE

Traditions divine, primal
Cast ◆◆ somatic, verbal
Range 500 feet; **Area** 60-foot burst
Saving Throw Reflex

A powerful globe of searing sunlight explodes in the area, dealing 8d10 fire damage to creatures and objects in the area, plus 8d10 additional positive damage to undead creatures. Each creature and object in the area must attempt a Reflex save.
Critical Success The creature or object is unaffected.
Success The creature or object takes half damage.
Failure The creature or object takes full damage.
Critical Failure The creature or object takes full damage. If it's a creature, it becomes blinded permanently.

If the globe overlaps with an area of magical darkness, *sunburst* attempts to counteract the darkness effect.
Heightened (+1) The fire damage increases by 1d10, and the positive damage against undead increases by 1d10.

SYNAPTIC PULSE   SPELL 5

ENCHANTMENT   INCAPACITATION   MENTAL

Traditions occult
Cast ◆◆ somatic, verbal
Range 30 feet; **Area** 30-foot emanation
Saving Throw Will; **Duration** 1 round

You emit a pulsating mental blast that penetrates the minds of all enemies in the area. Each creature in the area must attempt a Will save.
Critical Success The creature is unaffected.
Success The creature is stunned 1.
Failure The creature is stunned 2.
Critical Failure The creature is stunned for 1 round.

SYNESTHESIA   SPELL 5

DIVINATION   MENTAL

Traditions occult
Cast ◆◆ somatic, verbal
Range 30 feet; **Targets** 1 creature
Saving Throw Will; **Duration** 1 minute

The target's senses are suddenly rewired in unexpected ways, causing them to process noises as bursts of color, smells as sounds, and so on. This has three effects, and the target must attempt a Will save.

- Due to the distraction, the target must succeed at a DC 5 flat check each time it uses a concentrate action, or the action fails and is wasted.
- The target's difficulty processing visual input makes all creatures and objects concealed from it.
- The creature has trouble moving, making it clumsy 3 and giving it a –10-foot status penalty to its Speeds.

Critical Success The target is unaffected.
Success The target is affected for 1 round.
Failure The target is affected for 1 minute.
Critical Failure As failure, and the target is stunned 2 as it attempts to process the sensory shifts.
Heightened (9th) You can target up to five creatures.

TALKING CORPSE   SPELL 4

UNCOMMON   NECROMANCY

Traditions divine, occult
Cast 10 minutes (material, somatic, verbal)
Range touch; **Targets** 1 corpse
Saving Throw Will; **Duration** 10 minutes

You grant the target corpse a semblance of life, which it uses to speak the answers to three questions posed to it. This spell calls on the physical body's latent memories rather than summoning back the deceased's spirit, so the corpse must be mostly intact for the spell to function. The more damage the corpse has taken, the more inaccurate or patchwork its answers are, and it must have a throat and mouth to speak at all. If anyone has previously cast this spell on the corpse in the last week, the spell automatically fails. The corpse can attempt a Will save to resist answering the questions using the statistics of the original creature at its time of death, with the following effects.
Critical Success The target can lie or refuse to answer your questions, and the target's spirit haunts you for 24 hours, bothering you and causing you to be unable to gain any rest for that time.
Success The target can provide false information or refuse to answer your questions.
Failure The target must answer truthfully, but its answers can be brief, cryptic, and repetitive. It can still mislead you or attempt to stall so that the spell's duration runs out before you can ask all your questions.
Critical Failure As failure, but the target's answers are more direct and less repetitive, though still cryptic. It takes a –2 status penalty to Deception checks to deceive or mislead you.

TANGLEFOOT CANTRIP 1

CANTRIP **CONJURATION** **PLANT**

Traditions arcane, primal
Cast ◆◆ somatic, verbal
Range 30 feet; **Targets** 1 creature

A vine covered in sticky sap appears from thin air, flicking from your hand and lashing itself to the target. Attempt a spell attack against the target.

Critical Success The target gains the immobilized condition and takes a –10-foot circumstance penalty to its Speeds for 1 round. It can attempt to Escape against your spell DC to remove the penalty and the immobilized condition.

Success The target takes a –10-foot circumstance penalty to its Speeds for 1 round. It can attempt to Escape against your spell DC to remove the penalty.

Failure The target is unaffected.

Heightened (2nd) The effects last for 2 rounds.
Heightened (4th) The effects last for 1 minute.

TANGLING CREEPERS SPELL 6

CONJURATION **PLANT**

Traditions primal
Cast ◆◆◆ material, somatic, verbal
Range 500 feet; **Area** 40-foot burst
Duration 10 minutes

Dense, twitching creepers sprout from every surface and fill any bodies of water in the area. Any creature moving on the land, or Climbing or Swimming within the creepers, takes a –10-foot circumstance penalty to its Speeds while in the area. Once per round, you can make a vine lash out from any square within the expanse of creepers by using a single action, which has the concentrate trait. This vine has a 15-foot reach and makes a melee unarmed attack using your spell attack modifier. If the attack succeeds, the vine pulls the target into the creepers and makes it immobilized for 1 round or until the creature Escapes (against your spell DC), whichever comes first.

TELEKINETIC HAUL SPELL 5

EVOCATION

Traditions arcane, occult
Cast ◆◆ somatic, verbal
Range 120 feet; **Targets** 1 object of up to 80 Bulk with no dimension longer than 20 feet
Duration sustained up to 1 minute

You move the target up to 20 feet, potentially suspending it in midair. When you Sustain the Spell, you can do so again, or you can choose a different eligible target to move.

TELEKINETIC MANEUVER SPELL 2

ATTACK **EVOCATION** **FORCE**

Traditions arcane, occult
Cast ◆◆ somatic, verbal
Range 60 feet; **Targets** 1 creature

With a rush of telekinetic power, you move a foe or something they carry. You can attempt to Disarm, Shove, or Trip the target using a spell attack roll instead of an Athletics check.

TELEKINETIC PROJECTILE CANTRIP 1

ATTACK **CANTRIP** **EVOCATION**

Traditions arcane, occult
Cast ◆◆ somatic, verbal
Range 30 feet; **Targets** 1 creature

You hurl a loose, unattended object that is within range and that has 1 Bulk or less at the target. Make a ranged attack against the target. If you hit, you deal bludgeoning, piercing, or slashing damage—as appropriate for the object you hurled—equal to 1d6 plus your spellcasting ability modifier. No specific traits or magic properties of the hurled item affect the attack or the damage.

Critical Success You deal double damage.
Success You deal full damage.

Heightened (+1) The damage increases by 1d6.

TELEPATHIC BOND SPELL 5

UNCOMMON **DIVINATION** **MENTAL**

Traditions arcane, occult
Cast 1 minute (material, somatic, verbal)
Range touch; **Targets** you and up to 4 willing creatures touched
Duration 8 hours

The targets can communicate telepathically with any or all of the other targets from any point on the same planet.

TELEPATHIC DEMAND SPELL 9

ENCHANTMENT **INCAPACITATION** **LINGUISTIC** **MENTAL**

Traditions arcane, divine, occult
Cast ◆◆◆ material, somatic, verbal
Range planetary; **Targets** 1 creature you've telepathically contacted before
Saving Throw Will; **Duration** varies

You send the target a message of 25 words or fewer, and it can respond immediately with its own message of 25 words or fewer. Your message is insidious and has the effect of *suggestion* (page 374), with the message substituting for the spoken suggestion. On a successful save, the target is temporarily immune for 1 day, and on a critical success, the target is temporarily immune for 1 month. You can target a creature only if you have previously been in telepathic contact with it before, such as via the *telepathy* spell.

TELEPATHY SPELL 4

DIVINATION **LINGUISTIC** **MENTAL**

Traditions arcane, occult
Cast ◆◆ somatic, verbal
Duration 10 minutes

You can communicate telepathically with creatures within 30 feet. Once you establish a connection by communicating with a creature, the communication is two-way. You can communicate only with creatures that share a language with you.

Heightened (6th) *Telepathy* loses the linguistic trait. You can communicate telepathically with creatures using shared mental imagery even if you don't share a language.

TELEPORT   SPELL 6

UNCOMMON   CONJURATION   TELEPORTATION

Traditions arcane, occult
Cast 10 minutes (material, somatic, verbal)
Range 100 miles; **Targets** you and up to 4 targets touched, either willing creatures or objects roughly the size of a creature.

You and the targets are instantly transported to any location within range, as long as you can identify the location precisely both by its position relative to your starting position and by its appearance (or other identifying features). Incorrect knowledge of the location's appearance usually causes the spell to fail, but it could instead lead to teleporting to an unwanted location or some other unusual mishap determined by the GM. *Teleport* is not precise over great distances. The targets appear at a distance from the intended destination equal to roughly 1 percent of the total distance traveled, in a direction determined by the GM. For short journeys, this lack of precision is irrelevant, but for long distances this could be up to 1 mile.

Heightened (7th) You and the other targets can travel to any location within 1,000 miles.

Heightened (8th) You and the other targets can travel to any location on the same planet. If you travel more than 1,000 miles, you arrive only 10 miles off target.

Heightened (9th) You and the other targets can travel to any location on another planet within the same solar system. Assuming you have accurate knowledge of the location's position and appearance, you arrive on the new planet 100 miles off target.

Heightened (10th) As the 9th-level version, but you and the other targets can travel to any planet within the same galaxy.

TIME STOP   SPELL 10

TRANSMUTATION

Traditions arcane, occult
Cast ◆◆◆ material, somatic, verbal

You temporarily stop time for everything but yourself, allowing you to use several actions in what appears to others to be no time at all. Immediately after casting *time stop*, you can use up to 9 actions in 3 sets of up to 3 actions each. After each set of actions, 1 round passes, but only for you, effects specifically targeting or affecting you, and effects you create during the stoppage. All other creatures and objects are invulnerable to your attacks, and you can't target or affect them with anything. Once you have finished your actions, time begins to flow again for the rest of the world. If you created an effect with a duration that extends beyond the *time stop*'s duration, such as *wall of fire*, it immediately affects others again, but it doesn't have any of the effects that happen only when you first cast the spell.

TONGUES   SPELL 5

UNCOMMON   DIVINATION

Traditions arcane, divine, occult
Cast ◆◆ somatic, verbal
Range touch; **Targets** 1 creature
Duration 1 hour

The target can understand all words regardless of language and also speak the languages of other creatures. When in a mixed group of creatures, each time the target speaks, it can choose a creature and speak in a language that creature understands, even if the target doesn't know what language that is.

Heightened (7th) The duration is 8 hours.

TOUCH OF IDIOCY   SPELL 2

ENCHANTMENT   MENTAL

Traditions arcane, occult
Cast ◆◆ somatic, verbal
Range touch; **Targets** 1 living creature
Saving Throw Will; **Duration** 1 minute

You dull the target's mind; the target must attempt a Will save.
Success The target is unaffected.
Failure The target is stupefied 2.
Critical Failure The target is stupefied 4.

TREE SHAPE   SPELL 2

PLANT   POLYMORPH   TRANSMUTATION

Traditions primal
Cast ◆◆ somatic, verbal
Duration 8 hours

You transform into a Large tree. Perception checks don't reveal your true nature, but a successful Nature or Survival check against your spell DC reveals that you appear to be a tree that is strangely new to the area. While in tree form, you can observe everything around you, but you can't act other than to end the spell, and your turn, by using a single action, which has the concentrate trait. As a tree, your AC is 20, and only status bonuses, status penalties, circumstance bonuses, and circumstance penalties affect you. Any successes and critical successes you roll on Reflex saves are failures.

TREE STRIDE   SPELL 5

UNCOMMON   CONJURATION   PLANT   TELEPORTATION

Traditions primal
Cast 1 minute (material, somatic, verbal)

You step into a living tree with a trunk big enough for you to fit inside it and instantly teleport to any tree of the same species within 5 miles that also has a sufficiently large trunk. Once you enter the first tree, you instantly know the rough locations of other sufficiently large trees of the same species within range and can exit from the original tree, if you prefer. You can't carry extradimensional spaces with you; if you attempt to do so, the spell fails.

Heightened (6th) The tree you exit can be up to 50 miles away.
Heightened (8th) The tree you exit can be up to 500 miles away.
Heightened (9th) The tree you exit can be anywhere on the same planet.

TRUE SEEING   SPELL 6

DIVINATION   REVELATION

Traditions arcane, divine, occult, primal
Cast ◆◆ somatic, verbal
Duration 10 minutes

You see things within 60 feet as they actually are. The GM rolls a secret counteract check against any illusion or transmutation in the area, but only for the purpose of determining whether you see through it (for instance, if the check succeeds against a *polymorph* spell, you can see the creature's true form, but you don't end the *polymorph* spell).

TRUE STRIKE   SPELL 1

DIVINATION   FORTUNE

Traditions arcane, occult
Cast ◆ verbal
Duration until the end of your turn

A glimpse into the future ensures your next blow strikes true. The next time you make an attack roll before the end of your turn, roll the attack twice and use the better result. The attack ignores circumstance penalties to the attack roll and any flat check required due to the target being concealed or hidden.

TRUE TARGET   SPELL 7

DIVINATION   FORTUNE   PREDICTION

Traditions arcane, occult
Cast ◆ verbal
Range 60 feet; **Targets** 1 creature
Duration until the start of your next turn

You delve into the possible futures of the next few seconds to understand all the ways your target might avoid harm, then cast out a vision of that future to those around you. On the first attack roll made against the target during *true target*'s duration, the attacker rolls twice and uses the better result. The attacker also ignores circumstance penalties to the attack roll and any flat check required due to the target being concealed or hidden.

UNCONTROLLABLE DANCE   SPELL 8

ENCHANTMENT   INCAPACITATION   MENTAL

Traditions arcane, occult
Cast ◆◆ somatic, verbal
Range touch; **Targets** 1 creature
Saving Throw Will; **Duration** varies

The target is overcome with an all-consuming urge to dance. For the duration of the spell, the target is flat-footed and can't use reactions. While affected, the creature can't use actions with the move trait except to dance, using the Stride action to move up to half its Speed.
Critical Success The target is unaffected.
Success The spell's duration is 3 rounds, and the target must spend at least 1 action each turn dancing.
Failure The spell's duration is 1 minute, and the target must spend at least 2 actions each turn dancing.
Critical Failure The spell's duration is 1 minute, and the target must spend all its actions each turn dancing.

UNDETECTABLE ALIGNMENT   SPELL 2

UNCOMMON   ABJURATION

Traditions divine, occult
Cast 1 minute (material, somatic, verbal)
Range touch; **Targets** 1 creature or object

Duration until the next time you make your daily preparations

You shroud a creature in wards that hide its alignment. The target appears to be neutral to all effects that would detect its alignment.

UNFATHOMABLE SONG   SPELL 9

AUDITORY   EMOTION   ENCHANTMENT   FEAR   INCAPACITATION   MENTAL

Traditions occult
Cast ◆◆ somatic, verbal
Range 120 feet; **Targets** up to 5 creatures
Saving Throw Will; **Duration** sustained up to 1 minute

Fleeting notes of a strange and unnatural song fill the air, overtaking the mind. Each target must attempt a Will save when you cast the spell, and again each time you Sustain the Spell. A creature needs to attempt only one save against the song each round, and you have to keep the same targets when you Sustain the Spell.
Critical Success The target is unaffected, can't be affected on subsequent rounds, and is temporarily immune for 1 minute.
Success The target is unaffected this round, but it can be affected on subsequent rounds.
Failure Roll 1d4 on the table below.
Critical Failure Roll 1d4+1 on the table below.

Result	Effect
1	The target is frightened 2.
2	The target is confused for 1 round.
3	The target is stupefied 4 for 1 round.
4	The target is blinded for 1 round.
5	The target is stunned for 1 round and stupefied 1 for an unlimited duration.

UNFETTERED PACK   SPELL 7

ABJURATION

Traditions primal
Cast ◆◆ somatic, verbal
Range 30 feet; **Targets** up to 10 creatures
Duration 1 hour

You free those who travel alongside you from environmental hindrances. Targets don't take circumstance penalties to Speed from vegetation, rubble, winds, or other properties of the environment, whether or not the environment is magical, and they ignore difficult terrain from such environmental properties.
Heightened (9th) The targets also ignore greater difficult terrain from environmental properties.

UNRELENTING OBSERVATION   SPELL 8

DIVINATION   SCRYING

Traditions arcane, occult
Cast ◆◆ somatic, verbal
Range 100 feet; **Area** 20-foot burst; **Targets** 1 creature or object tracked and up to 5 other willing creatures
Duration varies

This spell grants perfect sight based on scrying, allowing several willing targets to track the exact movements or

INTRODUCTION
ANCESTRIES & BACKGROUNDS
CLASSES
SKILLS
FEATS
EQUIPMENT
SPELLS
THE AGE OF LOST OMENS
PLAYING THE GAME
GAME MASTERING
CRAFTING & TREASURE
APPENDIX

position of one creature or object. Choose one target creature or object in the area to be tracked. It becomes the sensor for the spell. Up to five willing creatures of your choice in the area can see a ghostly image of this creature or object when it's out of their sight. They can perceive the creature or object perfectly, allowing them to ignore the concealed or invisible condition, though physical barriers still provide cover.

The tracking creatures can see the tracked creature or object through all barriers other than lead or running water, which block their vision. Distance doesn't matter, though the creature or object might move so far away it becomes too small to perceive. The tracking creatures don't see any of the environment around the target, though they do see any gear a creature is wearing or holding, and they can tell if it removes objects from its person.

If the target to be tracked is willing, the duration is 1 hour. If you try to track an unwilling creature, the target must attempt a Will save.

Critical Success The creature or object is unaffected.
Success As described, and the duration is 1 minute.
Failure As described, and the duration is 1 hour.

UNSEEN SERVANT — SPELL 1

`CONJURATION`

Traditions arcane, occult
Cast ◆◆◆ material, somatic, verbal
Range 60 feet
Duration sustained

You summon an unseen servant (see the sidebar), which you can command as part of Sustaining the Spell. It serves you until its Hit Points are reduced to 0, at which point the spell ends, or until you stop Sustaining the Spell. The unseen servant gains the summoned trait.

UNSEEN SERVANT

Use this stat block for an unseen servant.

UNSEEN SERVANT — CREATURE -1

`MEDIUM` `MINDLESS`

Perception +0; darkvision
Languages — (understands its creator)
Skills Stealth +8
Str -4, **Dex** +2, **Con** +0, **Int** -5, **Wis** +0, **Cha** +0
Invisible An unseen servant is invisible, though it normally doesn't Sneak, so it is usually only hidden.
AC 13; **Fort** +0, **Ref** +4, **Will** +0
HP 4; **Immunities** disease, mental, non-magical attacks, paralysis, poison, precision, unconscious; **Resistances** all damage 5 (except force or ghost touch)
Speed fly 30 feet
Force Body An unseen servant's physical body is made of force. It can't use attack actions. It can move and use Interact actions to do things such as fetch objects, open unstuck or unlocked doors, hold chairs, and clean. It can't pass through solid objects.

VAMPIRIC EXSANGUINATION — SPELL 6

`DEATH` `NECROMANCY` `NEGATIVE`

Traditions arcane, divine, occult
Cast ◆◆ somatic, verbal
Area 30-foot cone
Saving Throw basic Fortitude

You draw in the blood and life force of other creatures through your outstretched arms. You deal 12d6 negative damage to living creatures in the area.

You gain temporary Hit Points equal to half the damage a single creature takes from this spell; calculate these temporary Hit Points using the creature that took the most damage. You lose any remaining temporary Hit Points after 1 minute.

Heightened (+1) The damage increases by 2d6.

VAMPIRIC TOUCH — SPELL 3

`DEATH` `NECROMANCY` `NEGATIVE`

Traditions arcane, divine, occult
Cast ◆◆ somatic, verbal
Range touch; **Targets** 1 living creature
Saving Throw basic Fortitude

Your touch leeches the lifeblood out of a target to empower yourself. You deal 6d6 negative damage to the target. You gain temporary Hit Points equal to half the negative damage the target takes (after applying resistances and the like). You lose any remaining temporary Hit Points after 1 minute.

Heightened (+1) The damage increases by 2d6.

VEIL — SPELL 4

`ILLUSION` `VISUAL`

Traditions arcane, occult
Cast ◆◆ somatic, verbal
Range 30 feet; **Targets** up to 10 creatures
Duration 1 hour

You disguise the targets as other creatures of the same body shape and roughly similar height (within 6 inches) and weight (within 50 pounds). The disguise can hide the targets' identities or let them appear to be of another ancestry, but it's not precise enough to impersonate specific individuals. The spell doesn't change voice, scent, or mannerisms. You choose the disguise for each target; for example, you could make one target appear to be a dwarf and another an elf.

Casting *veil* counts as setting up a disguise for the purpose of the Impersonate action. It allows the target to ignore any circumstance penalties they might take for being disguised as dissimilar creatures, and it gives the targets a +4 status bonus to Deception checks to prevent others from seeing through their disguises, and add their level even if untrained. You can Dismiss any or all of these disguises.

Heightened (5th) The spell also disguises the targets' voices and scents; it gains the auditory trait.
Heightened (7th) The targets can appear as any creature of the same size, even specific individuals. You must have seen an individual to reproduce their appearance. The spell also disguises the targets' voices and scents; it gains the auditory trait.

SPELLS

7

INTRODUCTION

ANCESTRIES &
BACKGROUNDS

CLASSES

SKILLS

FEATS

EQUIPMENT

SPELLS

THE AGE OF
LOST OMENS

PLAYING THE
GAME

GAME
MASTERING

CRAFTING
& TREASURE

APPENDIX

VENTRILOQUISM   SPELL 1

AUDITORY   ILLUSION

Traditions arcane, divine, occult, primal
Cast ❖❖ somatic, verbal
Duration 10 minutes

Whenever you speak or make any other sound vocally, you can make your vocalization seem to originate from somewhere else within 60 feet, and you can change that apparent location freely as you vocalize. Any creature that hears the sound can attempt to disbelieve your illusion.

Heightened (2nd) The spell's duration increases to 1 hour, and you can also change the tone, quality, and other aspects of your voice. Before a creature can attempt to disbelieve your illusion, it must actively attempt a Perception check or otherwise use actions to interact with the sound.

VIBRANT PATTERN   SPELL 6

ILLUSION   INCAPACITATION   VISUAL

Traditions arcane, occult
Cast ❖❖ material, somatic
Range 120 feet; **Area** 10-foot burst
Saving Throw Will; **Duration** sustained up to 1 minute

You create a pattern of lights that pulses with intensity. Creatures are dazzled while inside the pattern.

In addition, a creature must attempt a Will saving throw if it's inside the pattern when you cast it, enters the pattern, ends its turn within the pattern, or uses a Seek or Interact action on the pattern. A creature currently blinded by the pattern doesn't need to attempt new saving throws.

Success The creature is unaffected.

Failure The creature is blinded by the pattern. If it exits the pattern, it can attempt a new save to recover from the blinded condition at the end of each of its turns, to a maximum duration of 1 minute.

Critical Failure The creature is blinded for 1 minute.

VISIONS OF DANGER   SPELL 7

AUDITORY   ILLUSION   VISUAL

Traditions occult
Cast ❖❖❖ material, somatic, verbal
Range 500 feet; **Area** 30-foot burst
Saving Throw Will; **Duration** 1 minute

An illusion of horrific creatures fills the spell's area. The creatures look like Tiny swarming monsters with a specific appearance of your choice, such as Hellish flies or animated saw blades. The burst deals 8d8 mental damage to each creature that's inside the burst when it's created, enters the burst, or starts its turn inside the burst. A creature that critically succeeds at its will save can immediately attempt to disbelieve the illusion. A creature that tries to Interact with the monsters or observes one with a Seek action can attempt to disbelieve the illusion. Creatures that disbelieve the illusion take no damage from the illusion thereafter.

Heightened (+1) The mental damage increases by 1d8.

VITAL BEACON   SPELL 4

HEALING   NECROMANCY   POSITIVE

Traditions divine, primal
Cast 1 minute (somatic, verbal)
Duration until your next daily preparations

Vitality radiates outward from you, allowing others to supplicate and receive healing. Once per round, either you or an ally can use an Interact action to supplicate and lay hands upon you to regain Hit Points. Each time the beacon heals someone, it decreases in strength. It restores 4d10 Hit Points to the first creature, 4d8 Hit Points to the second, 4d6 Hit Points to the third, and 4d4 Hit Points to the fourth, after which the spell ends. You can have only one *vital beacon* active at a time.

Heightened (+1) The beacon restores one additional die of Hit Points each time it heals, using the same die size as the others for that step.

VOLCANIC ERUPTION   SPELL 7

EVOCATION   FIRE

Traditions primal
Cast ◆◆ somatic, verbal
Range 120 feet; **Area** 5-foot radius, 80-foot-tall cylinder
Saving Throw Reflex

The ground opens up, spraying a column of lava high into the air in a vertical cylinder, dealing 14d6 fire damage to creatures in the area. The lava rapidly cools and encases creatures in the area. A creature encased in rock is clumsy 1 and takes a –10-foot status penalty to its Speeds. All normal terrain is difficult terrain to a flying creature, and such creatures immediately descend 20 feet the moment they're encased, but they don't take damage from this fall. A creature encased in rock can attempt to Escape against your spell DC to end the effect. Otherwise, the creature remains encased until it takes a total of 50 damage, freeing it from the rock.

Additionally, creatures in the area and those within 5 feet of the lava column automatically take 3d6 fire damage from the intense heat, regardless of the results of their saving throws.
Critical Success The creature is unaffected.
Success The creature takes half damage.
Failure The creature takes full damage and is encased.
Critical Failure The creature takes double damage and is encased.

Heightened (+1) The damage in the area increases by 2d6, and the damage from the intense heat increases by 1d6.

WAIL OF THE BANSHEE   SPELL 9

AUDITORY   DEATH   NECROMANCY   NEGATIVE

Traditions divine, occult
Cast ◆◆ somatic, verbal
Area 40-foot emanation; **Targets** any number of creatures
Saving Throw Fortitude

Your scream chills the souls of enemies that hear it. Each living enemy in the area takes 8d10 negative damage and must attempt a Fortitude save.
Critical Success The target is unaffected.

Success The target takes full damage.
Failure The target takes full damage and is drained 1d4.
Critical Failure The target takes double damage and is drained 4.

WALL OF FIRE   SPELL 4

EVOCATION   FIRE

Traditions arcane, primal
Cast ◆◆◆ material, somatic, verbal
Range 120 feet
Duration 1 minute

You raise a blazing wall that burns creatures passing through it. You create either a 5-foot-thick wall of flame in a straight line up to 60 feet long and 10 feet high, or a 5-foot-thick, 10-foot-radius ring of flame with the same height. The wall stands vertically in either form; if you wish, the wall can be of a shorter length or height. Everything on each side of the wall is concealed from creatures on the opposite side. Any creature that crosses the wall or is occupying the wall's area at the start of its turn takes 4d6 fire damage.

Heightened (+1) The fire damage increases by 1d6.

WALL OF FORCE   SPELL 6

EVOCATION   FORCE

Traditions arcane, occult
Cast ◆◆◆ material, somatic, verbal
Range 30 feet
Duration 1 minute

You form an invisible wall of pure magical force up to 50 feet long and up to 20 feet high. The wall has no discernible thickness. You must create the wall in an unbroken open space so its edges don't pass through any creatures or objects, or the spell is lost. The wall has AC 10, Hardness 30, and 60 Hit Points, and it's immune to critical hits and precision damage. The wall blocks physical effects from passing through it, and because it's made of force, it blocks incorporeal and ethereal creatures as well. Teleportation effects can pass through the barrier, as can visual effects (since the wall is invisible).

Wall of force is immune to counteracting effects of its level or lower, but the wall is automatically destroyed by a *disintegrate* spell of any level or by contact with a *rod of cancellation* or *sphere of annihilation*.

Heightened (+2) The Hit Points of the wall increases by 20.

WALL OF ICE   SPELL 5

COLD   EVOCATION   WATER

Traditions arcane, primal
Cast ◆◆◆ material, somatic, verbal
Range 120 feet
Duration 1 minute

You sculpt a barrier of ice that blocks sight and, once shattered, freezes foes. You create either a 1-foot-thick wall of ice in a straight line up to 60 feet long and 10 feet high (the wall doesn't have to be vertical, but it must be anchored on both sides to a solid surface) or a 1-foot-thick, 10-foot radius hemisphere of ice. The ice that makes up the wall is opaque. If you wish, the wall can be of a smaller length, height, or radius. You must create the

SPELLS

7

INTRODUCTION

ANCESTRIES &
BACKGROUNDS

CLASSES

SKILLS

FEATS

EQUIPMENT

SPELLS

THE AGE OF
LOST OMENS

PLAYING THE
GAME

GAME
MASTERING

CRAFTING
& TREASURE

APPENDIX

wall in an unbroken open space so its edges don't pass through any creatures or objects, or the spell is lost.

Each 10-foot-by-10-foot section of the wall has AC 10, Hardness 10, and 40 Hit Points, and it's immune to critical hits, cold damage, and precision damage. A section also has weakness to fire 15; a section of the wall destroyed by fire melts, evaporating into water and steam. A section destroyed by means other than fire leaves behind a chilling mass of ice that is difficult terrain and deals 2d6 cold damage to any creature passing through it.

Heightened (+2) The Hit Points of each section of the wall increase by 10, and the cold damage dealt to creatures crossing a destroyed section increases by 1d6.

WALL OF STONE SPELL 5

CONJURATION EARTH

Traditions arcane, primal
Cast ◆◆◆ material, somatic, verbal
Range 120 feet

You shape a wall of solid stone. You create a 1-inch-thick wall of stone up to 120 feet long, and 20 feet high. You can shape the wall's path, placing each 5 feet of the wall on the border between squares. The wall doesn't need to stand vertically, so you can use it to form a bridge or set of stairs, for example. You must conjure the wall in an unbroken open space so its edges don't pass through any creatures or objects, or the spell is lost.

Each 5-foot-by-5-foot section of the wall has AC 10, Hardness 14, and 50 Hit Points, and it's immune to critical hits and precision damage. A destroyed section of the wall can be moved through, but the rubble created from it is difficult terrain.

Heightened (+2) The Hit Points of each section of the wall increase by 15.

WALL OF THORNS SPELL 3

CONJURATION PLANT

Traditions primal
Cast ◆◆◆ material, somatic, verbal
Range 60 feet
Duration 1 minute

Over the course of a minute, you cause a thick wall of thorny brambles to grow from the ground. You create a 5-foot-thick wall of brambles and thorns in a straight line up to 60 feet long and 10 feet high. You must create the wall in an unbroken open space so its edges don't pass through any creatures or objects, or the spell is lost. The wall stands vertically. If you wish, the wall can be of a shorter length or height. Everything on each side of the wall has cover from creatures on the opposite side, and the wall's spaces are difficult terrain. For every move action a creature uses to enter at least one of the wall's spaces, that creature takes 3d4 piercing damage.

Each 5-foot-by-5-foot section of the wall has AC 10, Hardness 10, and 20 Hit Points. It's immune to critical hits and precision damage. A destroyed section can be moved through freely.

Heightened (+1) The Hit Points of each section of the wall increase by 5, and the piercing damage increases by 1d4.

WALL OF WIND SPELL 3

AIR EVOCATION

Traditions arcane, primal
Cast ◆◆◆ material, somatic, verbal
Range 120 feet
Duration 1 minute

You create a barrier of gusting winds that hinders anything moving through it. The wall of swirling winds is 5 feet thick, 60 feet long, and 30 feet high. The wall stands vertically, but you can shape its path. Though the wall of wind distorts the air, it does not hamper sight. The wall has the following effects.

- Ammunition from physical ranged attacks—such as arrows, bolts, sling bullets, and other objects of similar size—can't pass through the wall. Attacks with bigger ranged weapons, such as javelins, take a –2 circumstance penalty to their attack rolls if their paths pass through the wall. Massive ranged weapons and spell effects that don't create physical objects pass through the wall with no penalty.
- The wall is difficult terrain to creatures attempting to move overland through it. Gases, including creatures in gaseous form, can't pass through the wall.
- A creature that attempts to fly through the wall using a move action must attempt a Fortitude save.

Critical Success The creature can move through the wall normally this turn.
Success The flying creature can move through the wall this turn, but the wall is difficult terrain.
Failure The wall stops the movement of the flying creature, and any remaining movement from its current action is wasted.
Critical Failure As failure, and the creature is pushed 10 feet away from the wall.

WANDERER'S GUIDE SPELL 3

DIVINATION

Tradition divine, occult
Cast 1 minute (material, somatic, verbal)
Duration until your next daily preparations

You call upon the beyond to guide your route. When you Cast this Spell, choose a destination; you receive an inspired route to that destination, allowing you and allies who travel overland with you to reduce the movement penalty from difficult terrain by half for the duration, as long as you don't deviate from the inspired route. This doesn't have any effect on movement during encounters. If you use this ability again before the duration is over, this effect ends and is replaced by that of the new route.

WARP MIND SPELL 7

EMOTION ENCHANTMENT INCAPACITATION MENTAL

Traditions arcane, occult
Cast ◆◆ somatic, verbal
Range 120 feet; **Targets** 1 creature
Saving Throw Will

You scramble a creature's mental faculties and sensory input.

The target must attempt a Will saving throw. Regardless of the result of that save, the target is then temporarily immune for 10 minutes. *Warp mind*'s effects happen instantly, so *dispel magic* and other effects that counteract spells can't counteract them. However, *alter reality*, *miracle*, *primal phenomenon*, *restoration*, or *wish* can still counteract the effects.

Critical Success The target is unaffected.

Success The target spends the first action on its next turn with the confused condition.

Failure The target is confused for 1 minute.

Critical Failure The target is confused permanently.

WATER BREATHING   SPELL 2

`TRANSMUTATION`

Traditions arcane, divine, primal

Cast 1 minute (somatic, verbal)

Range 30 feet; **Targets** up to 5 creatures

Duration 1 hour

The targets can breathe underwater.

Heightened (3rd) The duration increases to 8 hours.

Heightened (4th) The duration increases to until your next daily preparations.

WATER WALK   SPELL 2

`TRANSMUTATION`

Traditions arcane, divine, primal

Cast ◆◆ somatic, verbal

Range touch; **Targets** 1 creature

Duration 10 minutes

The target can walk on the surface of water and other liquids without falling through. It can go underwater if it wishes, but in that case it must Swim normally. This spell doesn't grant the ability to breathe underwater.

Heightened (4th) The spell's range increases to 30 feet, the duration increases to 1 hour, and you can target up to 10 creatures.

WEAPON OF JUDGMENT   SPELL 9

`EVOCATION` `FORCE`

Traditions divine

Cast ◆◆ somatic, verbal; **Requirements** You have a deity.

Range 100 feet; **Targets** 1 creature

Duration 1 minute

An immense weapon of force appears, hovering in the air above the target. The weapon has the ghostly visual appearance of your deity's favored weapon. Name war or peace when you cast this spell.

If you name "war," mentally choose one creature. This must be a creature both you and the target can see. The target instinctively knows which creature this is. At the end of each of the target's turns, if the target did not use a hostile action against the creature you chose during that turn, the weapon Strikes the target.

If you name "peace," mentally choose up to five allies. The target instinctively knows who those allies are. The weapon Strikes the target each time the target uses a hostile action against you or one of your allies. The weapon Strikes only once per action, even if the action targets multiple allies (such as for a *fireball* or a Whirlwind Strike).

Strikes with the weapon are melee weapon attacks, but they use your spell attack modifier. Regardless of its appearance, the weapon deals force damage equal to 3d10 plus your spellcasting ability modifier. The weapon takes a multiple attack penalty, which increases throughout the target's turn, but its penalty is separate from yours.

When the weapon Strikes, you can deal damage of the normal damage type of the weapon instead of force damage (or any of the available damage types, for a versatile weapon). No other statistics or attributes of the weapon apply, and even a ranged weapon attacks adjacent creatures only. A weapon of judgment is a weapon for the purposes of triggers, resistances, and so forth.

The weapon doesn't take up space, grant flanking, or have any other attributes a creature would. The weapon can't make any attack other than its Strike, and feats or spells that affect weapons do not apply to this weapon.

Heightened (10th) The force damage increases by 1d10.

WEAPON STORM   SPELL 4

`EVOCATION`

Traditions arcane, primal

Cast ◆◆ somatic, verbal

Area 30-foot cone or 10-foot emanation

Saving Throw Reflex

You swing a weapon you're holding, and the weapon magically multiplies into duplicates that swipe at all creatures in either a cone or an emanation. This flurry deals four dice of damage to creatures in the area. This damage has the same type as the weapon and uses the same die size. Determine the die size as if you were attacking with the weapon; for instance, if you were wielding a two-hand weapon in both hands, you'd use its two-hand damage die.

Critical Success The creature is unaffected.

Success The target takes half damage.

Failure The target takes full damage.

Critical Failure The target takes double damage and is subject to the weapon's critical specialization effect.

Heightened (+1) Add another damage die.

WEB   SPELL 2

`CONJURATION`

Traditions arcane, primal

Cast ◆◆◆ material, somatic, verbal

Range 30 feet; **Area** 10-foot burst

Duration 1 minute

You create a sticky web in the area that impedes creatures' movement each time they try to move through it. Squares filled with the web are difficult terrain. Each square can be cleared of the web by a single attack or effect that deals at least 5 slashing damage or 1 fire damage. A square has AC 5, and it automatically fails its saving throws.

Each time a creature in the web begins to use a move action or enters the web during a move action, it must attempt an

Athletics check or Reflex save against your spell DC to avoid taking a circumstance penalty to its Speeds or becoming immobilized. A creature that gets out of the web ceases to take a circumstance penalty to its Speed from the web.

Critical Success The creature is unaffected, and it doesn't need to attempt further Athletics checks or saving throws against the web this turn. If it used an Athletics check, it clears the web from every square it leaves after leaving the square.

Success The creature is unaffected during its action. If it used an Athletics check, it clears the web from every square it leaves after leaving the square.

Failure The creature takes a –10-foot circumstance penalty to its Speeds until the start of its next turn.

Critical Failure The creature is immobilized until the start of its next turn, after which it takes a –10-foot circumstance penalty to its Speeds for 1 round. It can attempt to Escape to remove its immobilized condition.

Heightened (4th) The spell's area increases to a 20-foot burst, and its range increases to 60 feet.

WEIRD   SPELL 9

DEATH EMOTION FEAR ILLUSION MENTAL

Traditions arcane, occult
Cast ◆◆ somatic, verbal
Range 120 feet; **Targets** any number of creatures
Saving Throw Will

You fill the targets' minds with terrifying images of fearsome creatures, each drawn from the targets' worst fears. Only the targets can see their assailants. Each target takes 16d6 mental damage and must attempt a Will save.

Critical Success The target is unaffected.
Success The target takes half damage and is frightened 1.
Failure The target takes full damage and is frightened 2.
Critical Failure The target is so afraid, it might instantly die. It must attempt a Fortitude saving throw. If the target succeeds, it takes double damage and is frightened 2, and it's also fleeing until the end of its next turn unless it critically succeeded. If it fails, it is reduced to 0 Hit Points and dies.

WIND WALK   SPELL 8

AIR TRANSMUTATION

Traditions primal
Cast 10 minutes (material, somatic, verbal)
Range touch; **Targets** you and up to five creatures touched
Duration 8 hours

When you cast this spell, each target transforms into a vaguely cloud-like form and is picked up by a wind moving in the direction of your choice. You can change the wind's direction by using a single action, which has the concentrate trait. The wind carries the targets at a Speed of 20 miles per hour, but if any of the targets make an attack, Cast a Spell, come under attack, or otherwise enter encounter mode, the spell ends for all targets just after they roll initiative, and they drift gently to the ground.

WISH   SPELL 10

DIVINATION

Traditions arcane
Cast ◆◆◆ material, somatic, verbal

You state a wish, making your greatest desire come true. A *wish* spell can produce any one of the following effects.

- Duplicate any arcane spell of 9th level or lower.
- Duplicate any non-arcane spell of 7th level or lower.
- Produce any effect whose power level is in line with the above effects.
- Reverse certain effects that refer to the *wish* spell.

The GM might allow you to try using *wish* to produce greater effects than these, but doing so might be dangerous or the spell might have only a partial effect.

ZEALOUS CONVICTION   SPELL 6

ENCHANTMENT

Traditions divine, occult
Cast ◆◆ somatic, verbal
Range 30 feet; **Targets** up to 10 willing creatures
Duration 10 minutes

You bypass your targets' rational minds, instilling them with unshakable conviction and zeal. The targets each gain 12 temporary Hit Points and a +2 status bonus to Will saves against mental effects, as their faith overrides the signals from their own bodies and minds. If you tell a target to do something, it must comply with your request, though if it would normally find the task repugnant, it can attempt a Will save at the end of its turn each round due to the cognitive dissonance. On a success, it ends the spell's effects on itself entirely.

Heightened (9th) The temporary Hit Points increase to 18, and the status bonus to Will saves increases to +3.

ZONE OF TRUTH   SPELL 3

UNCOMMON ENCHANTMENT MENTAL

Traditions divine, occult
Cast ◆◆ somatic, verbal
Range 30 feet; **Area** 20-foot burst
Saving Throw Will; **Duration** 10 minutes

You designate an area in which creatures are compelled to speak only truth. Creatures within or entering the area have difficulty lying. Each potentially affected creature must attempt a Will save when the spell is cast or when the creature first enters the area. It uses the results of this initial save if it leaves and reenters the area. Affected creatures are aware of this enchantment; therefore, they can avoid answering questions to which they would normally respond with a lie, or they can be evasive as long as they remain within the boundaries of the truth.

Critical Success The target is unaffected.
Success The target takes a –2 status penalty to Deception checks.
Failure The target can't speak any deliberate and intentional lies, and it takes a –2 status penalty to Deception checks.
Critical Failure The target can't speak any deliberate and intentional lies and takes a –4 status penalty to Deception checks.

INTRODUCTION

ANCESTRIES & BACKGROUNDS

CLASSES

SKILLS

FEATS

EQUIPMENT

SPELLS

THE AGE OF LOST OMENS

PLAYING THE GAME

GAME MASTERING

CRAFTING & TREASURE

APPENDIX

FOCUS SPELLS

Some classes gain special spells that they cast using Focus Points instead of spell slots. These focus spells are listed below, organized by class. The full rules for casting focus spells appear on page 300.

BARD

Bards can gain the following composition spells. This section also includes their composition cantrips.

ALLEGRO — CANTRIP 7

| UNCOMMON | BARD | CANTRIP | COMPOSITION | EMOTION | ENCHANTMENT | MENTAL |

Cast ◆ verbal
Range 30 feet; **Targets** 1 ally
Duration 1 round

You perform rapidly, speeding up your ally. The ally becomes quickened and can use the additional action to Strike, Stride, or Step.

COUNTER PERFORMANCE — FOCUS 1

| UNCOMMON | BARD | COMPOSITION | ENCHANTMENT | FORTUNE | MENTAL |

Cast ↺ somatic or verbal
Trigger You or an ally within 60 feet rolls a saving throw against an auditory or visual effect.
Area 60-foot emanation

Your performance protects you and your allies. Roll a Performance check for a type you know: an auditory performance if the trigger was auditory, or a visual one for a visual trigger. You and allies in the area can use the better result between your Performance check and the saving throw.

DIRGE OF DOOM — CANTRIP 3

| UNCOMMON | BARD | CANTRIP | COMPOSITION | EMOTION | ENCHANTMENT |
| FEAR | MENTAL |

Cast ◆ verbal
Area 30-foot emanation
Duration 1 round

Foes within the area are frightened 1. They can't reduce their frightened value below 1 while they remain in the area.

FATAL ARIA — FOCUS 10

| UNCOMMON | BARD | COMPOSITION | DEATH | EMOTION | ENCHANTMENT | MENTAL |

Cast ◆ verbal
Range 30 feet; **Targets** 1 creature

You perform music so perfect that the target may die of joy or sorrow. Once targeted, the creature becomes temporarily immune for 1 minute. The effect of the spell depends on the target's level and current Hit Points.
16th or Lower The target dies instantly.
17th If the target has 50 Hit Points or fewer, it dies instantly; otherwise, it drops to 0 Hit Points and becomes dying 1.
18th or Higher The target takes 50 damage. If this brings it to 0 Hit Points, it dies instantly.

HOUSE OF IMAGINARY WALLS — CANTRIP 5

| UNCOMMON | BARD | CANTRIP | COMPOSITION | ILLUSION | VISUAL |

Cast ◆ somatic
Range touch
Duration 1 round

You mime creating an invisible 10-foot-by-10-foot stretch of wall adjacent to you and within your reach. The wall is solid to those creatures that don't disbelieve it, even incorporeal creatures. You and your allies can voluntarily believe the wall exists to continue to treat it as solid, for instance to climb onto it. A creature that disbelieves the illusion is temporarily immune to your *house of imaginary walls* for 1 minute. The wall doesn't block creatures that didn't see your visual performance, nor does it block objects. The wall has AC 10, Hardness equal to double the spell's level, and HP equal to quadruple the spell's level.

INSPIRE COMPETENCE — CANTRIP 1

| UNCOMMON | BARD | CANTRIP | COMPOSITION | EMOTION | ENCHANTMENT | MENTAL |

Cast ◆ verbal
Range 60 feet; **Targets** 1 ally
Duration 1 round

Your encouragement inspires your ally to succeed at a task. This counts as having taken sufficient preparatory actions to Aid your ally on a skill check of your choice, regardless of the circumstances. When you later use the Aid reaction, you can roll Performance instead of the normal skill check, and if you roll a failure, you get a success instead. If you are legendary in Performance, you automatically critically succeed.

The GM might rule that you can't use this ability if the act of encouraging your ally would interfere with the skill check (such as a check to Sneak quietly or maintain a disguise).

INSPIRE COURAGE — CANTRIP 1

| UNCOMMON | BARD | CANTRIP | COMPOSITION | EMOTION | ENCHANTMENT | MENTAL |

Cast ◆ verbal
Area 60-foot emanation
Duration 1 round

You inspire your allies with words or tunes of encouragement. You and all allies in the area gain a +1 status bonus to attack rolls, damage rolls, and saves against fear effects.

INSPIRE DEFENSE — CANTRIP 2

| UNCOMMON | BARD | CANTRIP | COMPOSITION | EMOTION | ENCHANTMENT | MENTAL |

Cast ◆ verbal
Area 60-foot emanation
Duration 1 round

You inspire your allies to protect themselves more effectively. You and all allies in the area gain a +1 status bonus to AC and saving throws, as well as resistance equal to half the spell's level to physical damage.

INSPIRE HEROICS   FOCUS 4

UNCOMMON BARD ENCHANTMENT

Cast ◆ verbal

You call upon your muse to greatly increase the benefits you provide to your allies with your *inspire courage* or *inspire defense* composition. If your next action is to cast *inspire courage* or *inspire defense*, attempt a Performance check. The DC is usually a very hard DC of a level equal to that of the highest-level target of your composition, but the GM can assign a different DC based on the circumstances. The effect of your *inspire courage* or *inspire defense* composition depends on the result of your check.

Critical Success The status bonus from your *inspire courage* or *inspire defense* increases to +3.

Success The status bonus from *inspire courage* or *inspire defense* increases to +2.

Failure Your *inspire courage* or *inspire defense* provides only its normal bonus of +1, but you don't spend the Focus Point for casting this spell.

LINGERING COMPOSITION   FOCUS 1

UNCOMMON BARD ENCHANTMENT

Cast ◆ verbal

You add a flourish to your composition to extend its benefits. If your next action is to cast a cantrip composition with a duration of 1 round, attempt a Performance check. The DC is usually a standard-difficulty DC of a level equal to the highest-level target of your composition, but the GM can assign a different DC based on the circumstances. The effect depends on the result of your check.

Critical Success The composition lasts 4 rounds.

Success The composition lasts 3 rounds.

Failure The composition lasts 1 round, but you don't spend the Focus Point for casting this spell.

LOREMASTER'S ETUDE   FOCUS 1

UNCOMMON BARD DIVINATION FORTUNE

Cast ◆ somatic

Trigger You or an ally within range attempts a skill check to Recall Knowledge

Range 30 feet; **Targets** you or the triggering ally

You call upon your muse's deep mysteries, granting the target a greater ability to think and recall information. Roll the triggering Recall Knowledge skill check twice and use the better result.

SOOTHING BALLAD   FOCUS 7

UNCOMMON BARD COMPOSITION EMOTION ENCHANTMENT HEALING MENTAL

Cast ◆◆ somatic, verbal

Range 30 feet; **Targets** you and up to 9 allies

You draw upon your muse to soothe your allies. Choose one of the following three effects:

- The spell attempts to counteract fear effects on the targets.
- The spell attempts to counteract effects imposing paralysis on the targets.
- The spell restores 7d8 Hit Points to the targets.

Heightened (+1) When used to heal, *soothing ballad* restores 1d8 more Hit Points.

TRIPLE TIME   CANTRIP 2

UNCOMMON BARD CANTRIP COMPOSITION EMOTION ENCHANTMENT MENTAL

Cast ◆ somatic

Area 60-foot emanation

Duration 1 round

You dance at a lively tempo, speeding your allies' movement. You and all allies in the area gain a +10-foot status bonus to all Speeds for 1 round.

CHAMPION

Champions can gain the following devotion spells.

CHAMPION'S SACRIFICE   FOCUS 6

UNCOMMON ABJURATION CHAMPION

Cast ↺ somatic

Trigger An ally is hit by a Strike, or an ally fails a saving throw against an effect that doesn't affect you.

Range 30 feet; **Targets** 1 ally

You form a link with an ally, allowing you to take harm in their stead. All the effects of the hit or failed save are applied to you instead of the ally. For example, if the target critically fails a saving throw against a *fireball*, you would take double damage. These effects ignore any resistances, immunities, or other abilities you have that might mitigate them in any way, although those of the target apply before you take the effect.

HERO'S DEFIANCE   FOCUS 10

UNCOMMON CHAMPION HEALING NECROMANCY POSITIVE

Cast ◆ verbal

Trigger An attack would bring you to 0 Hit Points.

You shout in defiance, filling you with a sudden burst of healing. Just before applying the attack's damage, you recover 10d4+20 Hit Points. If this is enough to prevent the attack from bringing you to 0 Hit Points, you don't become unconscious or dying. Either way, cheating death is difficult, and you can't use *hero's defiance* again until you Refocus or the next time you prepare. *Hero's defiance* cannot be used against effects with the death trait or that would leave no remains, such as *disintegrate*.

LAY ON HANDS   FOCUS 1

UNCOMMON CHAMPION HEALING NECROMANCY POSITIVE

Cast ◆ somatic

Range touch; **Targets** 1 willing living creature or 1 undead creature

Your hands become infused with positive energy, healing a living creature or damaging an undead creature with a touch. If you use *lay on hands* on a willing living target, you restore 6 Hit Points; if the target is one of your allies, they also gain a

INTRODUCTION

ANCESTRIES & BACKGROUNDS

CLASSES

SKILLS

FEATS

EQUIPMENT

SPELLS

THE AGE OF LOST OMENS

PLAYING THE GAME

GAME MASTERING

CRAFTING & TREASURE

APPENDIX

+2 status bonus to AC for 1 round. Against an undead target, you deal 1d6 damage and it must attempt a basic Fortitude save; if it fails, it also takes a –2 status penalty to AC for 1 round.

Heightened (+1) The amount of healing increases by 6, and the damage to an undead target increases by 1d6.

LITANY AGAINST SLOTH   FOCUS 5

UNCOMMON | CHAMPION | EVOCATION | GOOD | LITANY

Cast ◆ verbal
Range 30 feet; **Targets** 1 evil creature
Saving Throw Will; **Duration** 1 round

Your litany rails against the sin of sloth, interfering with the target's ability to react. The target must attempt a Will save. A particularly slothful creature, such as a sloth demon, uses the outcome one degree of success worse than the result of its saving throw. The target becomes temporarily immune to all of your litanies for 1 minute.

Critical Success The target is unaffected.
Success The target can't use reactions.
Failure The target can't use reactions and is slowed 1.
Critical Failure The target can't use reactions and is slowed 2.

LITANY AGAINST WRATH   FOCUS 3

UNCOMMON | CHAMPION | EVOCATION | GOOD | LITANY

Cast ◆ verbal
Range 30 feet; **Targets** 1 evil creature
Saving Throw Will; **Duration** 1 round

Your litany rails against the sin of wrath, punishing the target for attacking good creatures. The target must attempt a Will save. A particularly wrathful creature, such as a wrath demon, uses the outcome one degree of success worse than the result of its saving throw. The target then becomes temporarily immune to all of your litanies for 1 minute.

Critical Success The target is unaffected.
Success The first time the target uses an action that deals damage to at least one good creature, the target takes 3d6 good damage.
Failure Each time the target uses an action that deals damage to at least one good creature, the target takes 3d6 good damage.
Critical Failure The target is enfeebled 2. Each time it uses an action that deals damage to at least one good creature, the target takes 3d6 good damage.

Heightened (+1) The damage increases by 1d6.

LITANY OF RIGHTEOUSNESS   FOCUS 7

UNCOMMON | CHAMPION | EVOCATION | GOOD | LITANY

Cast ◆ verbal
Range 30 feet; **Targets** 1 evil creature
Duration 1 round

Your litany denounces an evildoer, rendering it susceptible to the powers of good. The target gains weakness 7 to good. The target then becomes temporarily immune to all of your litanies for 1 minute.

Heightened (+1) The weakness increases by 1.

CLERIC

Clerics can gain the following domain spells by selecting the Domain Initiate or Advanced Domain feat.

AGILE FEET   FOCUS 1

UNCOMMON | CLERIC | TRANSMUTATION

Domain travel
Cast ❖ somatic
Duration until the end of the current turn

The blessings of your god make your feet faster and your movements more fluid. You gain a +5-foot status bonus to your Speed and ignore difficult terrain. As part of casting *agile feet*, you can Stride or Step; you can instead Burrow, Climb, Fly, or Swim if you have the appropriate Speed.

APPEARANCE OF WEALTH   FOCUS 1

UNCOMMON | CLERIC | ILLUSION

Domain wealth
Cast ❖❖ material, verbal
Range 30 feet; **Area** 5-foot burst
Saving Throw Will; **Duration** sustained up to 1 minute

You create a brief vision of immense wealth filling the spell's area. Each creature within 20 feet of the area that could be enticed by material wealth must attempt a Will saving throw. A creature that enters the area automatically disbelieves the illusion, and disbelieving the illusion ends any fascinated condition imposed by the spell. As long as you Sustain the Spell, other creatures react to the treasure like they would any other illusion, but they are not at risk of becoming fascinated.

Critical Success The creature disbelieves the illusion and is unaffected by it.
Success The creature is fascinated by the wealth until it has completed its first action on its next turn.
Failure The creature is fascinated by the illusion.

ARTISTIC FLOURISH   FOCUS 4

UNCOMMON | CLERIC | TRANSMUTATION

Domain creation
Cast ❖❖ material, somatic
Range 15 feet; **Targets** 1 item or work of art that fits entirely within the range
Duration 10 minutes

You transform the target to make it match your artisanal and artistic vision. If you have expert proficiency in Crafting, the item grants a +1 item bonus to attack rolls if it's a weapon or skill checks if it's a skill tool. The target is a beautiful and impressive piece for its new quality, but the effect is obviously temporary, so its monetary value doesn't change.

When you cast this spell, any previous *artistic flourish* you had cast ends.

Heightened (7th) If you have master proficiency in Crafting, the item grants a +2 item bonus instead.
Heightened (10th) If you have legendary proficiency in Crafting, the item grants a +3 item bonus instead.

ATHLETIC RUSH   FOCUS 1

UNCOMMON | CLERIC | TRANSMUTATION

Domain might
Cast ❖ somatic
Duration 1 round

Your body fills with physical power and skill. You gain a +10-foot status bonus to Speed and a +2 status bonus to Athletics checks. As a part of Casting this Spell, you can use a Stride, Leap, Climb, or Swim action. The spell's bonuses apply during that action.

BIT OF LUCK   FOCUS 1

UNCOMMON | CLERIC | DIVINATION | FORTUNE

Domain luck
Cast ❖❖ somatic, verbal
Range 30 feet; **Targets** 1 willing creature
Duration 1 minute

You tilt the scales of luck slightly to protect a creature from disaster. When the target would attempt a saving throw, it can roll twice and use the better result. Once it does this, the spell ends.

If you cast *bit of luck* again, any previous *bit of luck* you cast that's still in effect ends. After a creature has been targeted with *bit of luck*, it becomes temporarily immune for 24 hours.

BLIND AMBITION   FOCUS 1

UNCOMMON | CLERIC | EMOTION | ENCHANTMENT | MENTAL

Domain ambition
Cast ❖❖ somatic, verbal
Range 60 feet; **Targets** 1 creature
Saving Throw Will; **Duration** 10 minutes

You strengthen a target's ambition, increase its resentment of allies, and make its allegiances more susceptible to change. The target must attempt a Will save.

Critical Success The target is unaffected.
Success The target takes a –1 status penalty to its saving throws and other defenses against attempts to Coerce it, Request something of it, or use mental effects to convince it to do something (such as a *suggestion* spell). This penalty applies only if the target is being encouraged to advance its own ambitions.
Failure As success, but the penalty is –2.
Critical Failure The target is overcome with ambition, taking whatever actions would advance its own agenda over those of anyone else, even without attempts to convince it.

CAPTIVATING ADORATION   FOCUS 4

UNCOMMON | CLERIC | EMOTION | ENCHANTMENT | MENTAL | VISUAL

Domain passion
Cast ❖❖ somatic, verbal
Area 15-foot emanation
Saving Throw Will; **Duration** 1 minute

You become intensely entrancing, and creatures are distracted by you as long as they remain within the area. You can exclude any creatures you choose from the effects.

INTRODUCTION

ANCESTRIES & BACKGROUNDS

CLASSES

SKILLS

FEATS

EQUIPMENT

SPELLS

THE AGE OF LOST OMENS

PLAYING THE GAME

GAME MASTERING

CRAFTING & TREASURE

APPENDIX

When a creature enters the area for the first time, it must attempt a Will saving throw. If a creature leaves and reenters, it uses the results of its original save.

Critical Success The creature is unaffected and temporarily immune for 1 hour.

Success The creature is fascinated with you for its next action, then is temporarily immune for 1 hour.

Failure The creature is fascinated with you.

Critical Failure The creature is fascinated with you, and its attitude toward you improves by one step.

Heightened (+1) Increase the size of the emanation by 15 feet.

CHARMING TOUCH   FOCUS 1

UNCOMMON | CLERIC | EMOTION | ENCHANTMENT | INCAPACITATION | MENTAL

Domain passion

Cast ❖ somatic

Range touch; **Targets** 1 humanoid creature that could find you attractive

Saving Throw Will; **Duration** 10 minutes

You infuse your target with attraction, causing it to act friendlier toward you. The target attempts a Will save. It gains a +4 circumstance bonus to this save if you or your allies recently threatened or were hostile to it.

Critical Success The target is unaffected and aware you tried to charm it.

Success The target is unaffected but thinks your spell was something harmless instead of *charming touch*, unless it identifies the spell (usually with Identify Magic).

Failure The target's attitude becomes friendly toward you. If it was friendly, it becomes helpful. It can't use hostile actions against you.

Critical Failure The target is helpful and can't use hostile actions against you.

You can Dismiss the spell. If you use hostile actions against the target, the spell ends. After the spell ends, the target doesn't necessarily realize it was charmed unless its friendship with you or the actions you convinced it to take clash with its expectations, which could potentially allow you to convince the target to continue being your friend via mundane means.

Heightened (4th) You can target any type of creature, not just humanoids, as long as it could find you attractive.

CLOAK OF SHADOW   FOCUS 1

UNCOMMON | CLERIC | DARKNESS | EVOCATION | SHADOW

Domain darkness

Cast ❖ somatic

Range touch; **Targets** 1 willing creature

Duration 1 minute

You drape the target in a mantle of swirling shadows that make it harder to see. The cloak reduces bright light within a 20-foot emanation to dim light. This is a form of magical darkness and can therefore overcome non-magical light or attempt to counteract magical light as described on page 458.

The target can use concealed condition gained from the shadows to Hide, though observant creatures can still follow the moving aura of shadow, making it difficult for the target

to become completely undetected. The target can use an Interact action to remove the cloak and leave it behind as a decoy, where it remains, reducing light for the rest of the spell's duration. If anyone picks up the cloak after it's been removed by the original target, the cloak evaporates and the spell ends.

COMMANDING LASH   FOCUS 4

UNCOMMON | CLERIC | ENCHANTMENT | INCAPACITATION | MENTAL

Domain tyranny

Cast ❖ verbal

Requirements Your most recent action dealt damage to a target.

Range 100 feet; **Targets** A creature you dealt damage to on your most recent action.

Saving Throw Will; **Duration** until the end of the target's next turn

With the threat of more pain, you compel a creature you've recently harmed. You issue a command to the target, with the effects of the spell *command*.

COMPETITIVE EDGE   FOCUS 4

UNCOMMON | CLERIC | EMOTION | ENCHANTMENT | MENTAL

Domain ambition

Cast ❖ verbal

Duration sustained up to 1 minute

Your competitiveness drives you to prove yourself against the opposition. You gain a +1 status bonus to attack rolls and skill checks. If an enemy within 20 feet critically succeeds at an attack roll or skill check, your status bonus increases to +3 attack rolls or that specific skill check (whichever the foe critically succeeded at) for 1 round.

Heightened (7th) Increase the base bonus to +2 and the increased bonus after an enemy critically succeeds to +4.

CRY OF DESTRUCTION   FOCUS 1

UNCOMMON | CLERIC | EVOCATION | SONIC

Domain destruction

Cast ❖❖ somatic, verbal

Area 15-foot cone

Saving Throw basic Fortitude

Your voice booms, smashing what's in front of you. Each creature and unattended object in the area takes 1d8 sonic damage. If you already dealt damage to an enemy this turn with a Strike or spell, increase the damage dice from this spell to d12s.

Heightened (+1) The damage increases by 1d8.

DARKENED EYES   FOCUS 4

UNCOMMON | CLERIC | DARKNESS | TRANSMUTATION

Domain darkness

Cast ❖❖ somatic, verbal

Range 60 feet; **Targets** 1 creature

Saving Throw Fortitude; **Duration** varies

You infuse a creature's vision with darkness. After attempting its save, the target becomes temporarily immune for 24 hours.

Critical Success The target is unaffected.

Success The target's darkvision or low-light vision is suppressed for 1 round.

Failure As success, but the duration is 1 minute.

Critical Failure As success, but the duration is 1 minute, and the target is also blinded for the duration. It can attempt a new save at the end of each of its turns. If it succeeds, it's no longer blinded, but its darkvision or low-light vision remains suppressed.

DAZZLING FLASH   FOCUS 1

UNCOMMON   CLERIC   EVOCATION   LIGHT   VISUAL

Domain sun
Cast ◆◆ material, verbal
Area 15-foot cone
Saving Throw Fortitude

You raise your religious symbol and create a blinding flash of light. Each creature in the area must attempt a Fortitude save.

Critical Success The creature is unaffected.

Success The creature is dazzled for 1 round.

Failure The creature is blinded for 1 round and dazzled for 1 minute. The creature can spend an Interact action rubbing its eyes to end the blinded condition.

Critical Failure The creature is blinded for 1 round and dazzled for 1 hour.

Heightened (3rd) The area increases to a 30-foot cone.

DEATH'S CALL   FOCUS 1

UNCOMMON   CLERIC   NECROMANCY

Domain death
Cast ↻ verbal
Trigger A living creature within 20 feet of you dies, or an undead creature within 20 feet of you is destroyed.
Duration 1 minute

Seeing another pass from this world to the next invigorates you. You gain temporary Hit Points equal to the triggering creature's level plus your Wisdom modifier. If the triggering creature was undead, double the number of temporary Hit Points you gain . These last for the duration of the spell, and the spell ends if all the temporary Hit Points are depleted earlier.

DELUSIONAL PRIDE   FOCUS 4

UNCOMMON   CLERIC   EMOTION   ENCHANTMENT   MENTAL

Domain confidence
Cast ◆◆ somatic, verbal
Range 30 feet; **Targets** 1 creature
Saving Throw Will; **Duration** varies

You make the target overconfident, leading it to ascribe failure to external factors. If the target fails at an attack roll or skill check, it takes a –1 status penalty to attack rolls and skill checks until the end of its turn (or the end of its next turn, if it attempted the roll outside its turn). If the creature fails a second time while taking this penalty, the penalty increases to –2. The duration depends on the target's Will save. After attempting its save, the creature becomes temporarily immune for 24 hours.

Critical Success The target is unaffected.

Success The duration is 1 round.

Failure The duration is 10 minutes.

Critical Failure The duration is 24 hours.

DESTRUCTIVE AURA   FOCUS 4

UNCOMMON   CLERIC   EVOCATION

Domain destruction
Cast ◆◆ somatic, verbal
Area 15-foot emanation
Duration 1 minute

Swirling sands of divine devastation surround you, weakening the defenses of all they touch. Reduce the resistances of creatures in the area (including yourself) by 2.

Heightened (+2) Reduce the resistances by an additional 2.

DISPERSE INTO AIR   FOCUS 4

UNCOMMON   AIR   CLERIC   POLYMORPH   TRANSMUTATION

Domain air
Cast ↻ somatic
Trigger You take damage from an enemy or a hazard.

After taking the triggering damage, you transform into air. Until the end of the current turn, you can't be attacked or targeted, you don't take up space, you can't act, and any auras or emanations you have are suppressed. At the end of the turn, you re-form in any space you can occupy within 15 feet of where you were when you dispersed. Any auras or emanations you had are restored as long as their duration didn't run out while you were dispersed.

DOWNPOUR   FOCUS 4

UNCOMMON   CLERIC   EVOCATION   WATER

Domain water
Cast ◆◆ somatic, verbal
Range 120 feet; **Area** 30-foot burst
Duration 1 minute

You call forth a torrential downpour, which extinguishes non-magical flames. Creatures in the area are concealed and gain fire resistance 10. Creatures outside the area are concealed to those inside the area. Creatures with weakness to water that end their turns in the area take damage equal to their weakness.

Heightened (+1) The fire resistance increases by 2.

DREAMER'S CALL   FOCUS 4

UNCOMMON   CLERIC   ENCHANTMENT   INCAPACITATION   MENTAL

Domain dreams
Cast ◆◆ somatic, verbal
Range 30 feet; **Targets** 1 creature
Saving Throw Will; **Duration** until the end of the target's next turn

The target becomes distracted and suggestible, inundated by vivid daydreams.

Critical Success The target is unaffected.

Success The target's attention wavers. It becomes flat-footed and fascinated by its daydreams.

Failure As success, except that you appear in the dream and give a suggestion. This can be to approach you, run away (as if it had the fleeing condition), Release what it's holding, Drop Prone, or stand in place. The creature follows this course of action as its first action after you Cast the Spell.

Critical Failure As failure, but the target follows the course of action for as many actions as possible for the spell's duration, and it does nothing else.

INTRODUCTION

ANCESTRIES & BACKGROUNDS

CLASSES

SKILLS

FEATS

EQUIPMENT

SPELLS

THE AGE OF LOST OMENS

PLAYING THE GAME

GAME MASTERING

CRAFTING & TREASURE

APPENDIX

ENDURING MIGHT   FOCUS 4

UNCOMMON | ABJURATION | CLERIC

Domain might

Cast ↻ somatic

Trigger An attack or effect would deal damage to you.

Your own might mingles with divine power to protect you. You gain resistance equal to 8 plus your Strength modifier against all damage from the triggering attack or effect.

Heightened (+1) The resistance increases by 2.

ERADICATE UNDEATH   FOCUS 4

UNCOMMON | CLERIC | NECROMANCY | POSITIVE

Domain death

Cast ◆◆ somatic, verbal

Area 30-foot cone

Saving Throw basic Fortitude

A massive deluge of life energy causes the undead to fall apart. Each undead creature in the area takes 4d12 positive damage.

Heightened (+1) The damage increases by 1d12.

FACE IN THE CROWD   FOCUS 1

UNCOMMON | CLERIC | ILLUSION | VISUAL

Domain cities

Cast ◆ somatic

Duration 1 minute

While in a crowd of roughly similar creatures, your appearance becomes bland and nondescript. You gain a +2 status bonus to Deception and Stealth checks to go unnoticed among the crowd, and you ignore difficult terrain caused by the crowd.

Heightened (3rd) The spell gains a range of 10 feet and can target up to 10 creatures.

FIRE RAY   FOCUS 1

UNCOMMON | ATTACK | CLERIC | EVOCATION | FIRE

Domain fire

Cast ◆◆ somatic, verbal

Range 60 feet; **Targets** 1 creature or object

A blazing band of fire arcs through the air. Make a spell attack roll. The ray deals 2d6 fire damage.

Critical Success The ray deals double damage and 1d4 persistent fire damage.

Success The ray deals full damage.

Heightened (+1) The ray's initial damage increases by 2d6, and the persistent fire damage on a critical success increases by 1d4.

FLAME BARRIER   FOCUS 4

UNCOMMON | ABJURATION | CLERIC

Domain fire

Cast ↻ verbal

Trigger An effect would deal fire damage to either you or an ally within range.

Range 60 feet; **Targets** the creature that would take fire damage

You swiftly deflect incoming flames. The target gains fire resistance 15 against the triggering effect.

Heightened (+2) The resistance increases by 5.

FORCED QUIET   FOCUS 1

UNCOMMON ABJURATION CLERIC

Domain secrecy
Cast ◆◆ material, somatic
Range 30 feet; **Targets** 1 creature
Saving Throw Fortitude; **Duration** varies

You quiet the target's voice, preventing it from giving away valuable secrets. This doesn't prevent the target from talking or providing verbal spell components, but no creature more than 10 feet away can hear its whispers without succeeding at a Perception check against your spell DC, which might interfere with auditory or linguistic effects as well as communication. The spell's duration depends on the target's Fortitude save. After attempting its save, the target becomes temporarily immune for 24 hours.

Critical Success The target is unaffected.
Success The duration is 1 round.
Failure The duration is 1 minute.
Critical Failure The duration is 10 minutes.

GLIMPSE THE TRUTH   FOCUS 4

UNCOMMON CLERIC DIVINATION REVELATION

Domain truth
Cast ◆ somatic
Area 30-foot emanation
Duration 1 round

Divine insight lets you see things as they truly are. The GM attempts a secret counteract check against each illusion that is at least partially within the area. Instead of counteracting the illusion, you see through it (for instance, if the check succeeds against an *illusory disguise* spell, you see the creature's true form but *illusory disguise* doesn't end).

The area moves with you for the duration of the spell, and the GM attempts a secret counteract check each time a new illusion is within the area.

Heightened (7th) You can allow everyone to see through illusions you succeed against, not just yourself.

HEALER'S BLESSING   FOCUS 1

UNCOMMON CLERIC NECROMANCY

Domain healing
Cast ◆ verbal
Range 30 feet; **Targets** 1 willing living creature
Duration 1 minute

Your words bless a creature with an enhanced connection to positive energy. When the target regains Hit Points from a healing spell, it regains 1 additional Hit Point.

The target regains additional Hit Points from *healer's blessing* only the first time it regains HP from a given healing spell, so a spell that heals the creature repeatedly over a duration would restore additional Hit Points only once.

Heightened (+1) The additional healing increases by 2 HP.

HURTLING STONE   FOCUS 1

UNCOMMON ATTACK CLERIC EARTH EVOCATION

Domain earth
Cast ◆ somatic
Range 60 feet; **Targets** 1 creature

You evoke a magical stone and throw it, with your god's presence guiding your aim. Make a spell attack roll against the target. The stone deals bludgeoning damage equal to 1d6 plus your Strength modifier.

Critical Success The stone deals double damage.
Success The stone deals full damage.
Heightened (+1) The stone's damage increases by 1d6.

KNOW THE ENEMY   FOCUS 4

UNCOMMON CLERIC DIVINATION FORTUNE

Domain knowledge
Cast ⟳ somatic
Trigger You roll initiative and can see a creature, you succeed at an attack roll against a creature, or a creature fails a saving throw against one of your spells.

Use a Recall Knowledge action, rolling the appropriate skill check to identify the triggering creature's abilities. You can roll your check twice and use the better result.

LOCALIZED QUAKE   FOCUS 4

UNCOMMON CLERIC EARTH TRANSMUTATION

Domain earth
Cast ◆◆ somatic, verbal
Area 15-foot emanation or 15-foot cone
Saving Throw Reflex

You shake the earth, toppling nearby creatures. Choose whether the spell's area is a 15-foot emanation or a 15-foot cone when you cast it. Each creature in the area standing on solid ground may take 4d6 bludgeoning damage and must attempt a Reflex saving throw.

Critical Success The creature is unaffected.
Success The creature takes half damage.
Failure The creature takes full damage and falls prone.
Critical Failure The creature takes double damage and falls prone.
Heightened (+1) Increase the damage by 2d6.

LUCKY BREAK   FOCUS 4

UNCOMMON CLERIC DIVINATION FORTUNE

Domain luck
Cast ⟳ verbal
Trigger You fail (but don't critically fail) a saving throw.

Reroll the saving throw and use the better result. You then become temporarily immune for 10 minutes.

MAGIC'S VESSEL   FOCUS 1

UNCOMMON CLERIC ENCHANTMENT

Domain magic
Cast ◆ somatic
Range touch; **Targets** 1 creature
Duration sustained up to 1 minute

INTRODUCTION

ANCESTRIES &
BACKGROUNDS

CLASSES

SKILLS

FEATS

EQUIPMENT

SPELLS

THE AGE OF
LOST OMENS

PLAYING THE
GAME

GAME
MASTERING

CRAFTING
& TREASURE

APPENDIX

A creature becomes a receptacle for pure magical energy sent by your deity. The target gains a +1 status bonus to saving throws. Each time you Cast a Spell from your spell slots, you automatically Sustain this Spell and grant its target resistance to damage from spells until the start of your next turn. This resistance is equal to the level of the spell you cast.

MALIGNANT SUSTENANCE   FOCUS 4

UNCOMMON   CLERIC   NECROMANCY   NEGATIVE

Domain undeath
Cast ◆◆ somatic, verbal
Range touch; **Targets** 1 willing undead creature
Duration 1 minute

You embed a seed of negative energy in an undead creature, restoring its unnatural vigor. The target gains fast healing 7. This healing comes from negative energy, so it heals the undead rather than damaging it.

Heightened (+1) The fast healing increases by 2.

MOONBEAM   FOCUS 1

UNCOMMON   ATTACK   CLERIC   EVOCATION   FIRE   LIGHT

Domain moon
Cast ◆◆ somatic, verbal
Range 120 feet; **Targets** 1 creature or object

You shine a ray of moonlight. Make a spell attack roll. The beam of light deals 1d6 fire damage. *Moonbeam* deals silver damage for the purposes of weaknesses, resistances, and the like.

Critical Success The beam deals double damage, and the target is dazzled for 1 minute.

Success The beam deals full damage, and the target is dazzled for 1 round.

Heightened (+1) The ray's damage increases by 1d6.

MYSTIC BEACON   FOCUS 4

UNCOMMON   CLERIC   EVOCATION

Domain magic
Cast ◆ somatic
Range 30 feet; **Targets** 1 willing creature
Duration until the start of your next turn

The next damaging or healing spell the target casts before the start of your next turn deals damage or restores Hit Points as if the spell were heightened 1 level higher than its actual level. The spell otherwise functions at its actual level. Once the target casts the spell, *mystic beacon* ends.

NATURE'S BOUNTY   FOCUS 4

UNCOMMON   CLERIC   CONJURATION   PLANT   POSITIVE

Domain nature
Cast ◆ somatic
Requirements You have a free hand.

A palm-sized raw fruit or vegetable appears in your open hand. You choose the specific type of food. A creature can consume the food with an Interact action to regain 3d10+12 Hit Points and be nourished as if it had eaten a meal. If uneaten, the food rots and crumbles to dust after 1 minute.

Heightened (+1) The Hit Points restored increase by 6.

OVERSTUFF   FOCUS 1

UNCOMMON   CLERIC   TRANSMUTATION

Domain indulgence
Cast ◆◆ somatic, verbal
Range 30 feet; **Targets** 1 living creature
Saving Throw Fortitude

Huge amounts of food and drink fill the target. It receives a full meal's worth of nourishment and must attempt a Fortitude save.

Critical Success The target is unaffected.

Success The target is sickened 1, but if it spends an action to end the condition, it succeeds automatically.

Failure The target is sickened 1.

Critical Failure The target is sickened 2.

A target sickened by this spell takes a –10-foot status penalty to its Speed until it's no longer sickened.

PERFECTED FORM   FOCUS 4

UNCOMMON   ABJURATION   CLERIC   FORTUNE

Domain perfection
Cast ↻ somatic
Trigger You fail a saving throw against a morph, petrification, or polymorph effect.

Reroll the saving throw and use the better result.

PERFECTED MIND   FOCUS 1

UNCOMMON   ABJURATION   CLERIC

Domain perfection
Cast ◆ verbal

You meditate upon perfection to remove all distractions from your mind. Attempt a new Will save against one mental effect currently affecting you that required a Will save. Use the result of this new save to determine the outcome of the mental effect, unless the new save would have a worse result than the original save, in which case nothing happens. You can use *perfected mind* against a given effect only once.

POSITIVE LUMINANCE   FOCUS 4

UNCOMMON   CLERIC   LIGHT   NECROMANCY   POSITIVE

Domain sun
Cast ◆ somatic
Duration 1 minute

Drawing life force into yourself, you become a beacon of positive energy. You glow with bright light in a 10-foot emanation, and you gain an internal pool of light called a luminance reservoir, which begins with a value of 4. At the start of each of your turns, you can use a free action to increase the luminance reservoir by 4. If you do, the radius of your light increases by 10 feet.

If an undead creature damages you with an attack or spell while it's within the area of your light, that creature takes positive damage equal to half your luminance reservoir value. It takes this damage only the first time it damages you in a round.

You can Dismiss this Spell. When you do, you can target a creature within your light and direct the positive energy into it. The target must be a willing living creature or an undead creature. This heals a living target or damages an undead target by an amount equal to your luminance reservoir's value.

When you cast *positive luminance*, any other *positive luminance* spell you already had in effect ends.

Heightened (+1) Both the initial value of your luminance reservoir and the amount you gain each turn increase by 1.

PRECIOUS METALS FOCUS 4

UNCOMMON CLERIC TRANSMUTATION

Domain wealth
Cast ❖ material
Range touch; **Targets** 1 metal weapon, up to 10 pieces of metal or metal-tipped ammunition, 1 suit of metal armor, or up to 1 bulk of metal material (such as coins)
Duration 1 minute

Your deity blesses base metals to transform them into precious materials. The target item transforms from its normal metal into cold iron, copper, gold, iron, silver, or steel (the details for these metals are found on pages 577–579). An item transmuted in this way deals damage according to its new material. For example, a steel sword transmuted to cold iron would deal additional damage to a creature with a weakness to cold iron.

This change is clearly magical and temporary, so the item's monetary value doesn't change; you couldn't transmute copper coins to gold and use those coins to purchase something or as a cost for a spell.

Heightened (8th) Add adamantine (page 578) and mithral (page 579) to the list of metals you can transform the item into.

PROTECTOR'S SACRIFICE FOCUS 1

UNCOMMON ABJURATION CLERIC

Domain protection
Cast ↷ somatic
Trigger An ally within 30 feet takes damage.
Range 30 feet

You protect your ally by suffering in their stead. Reduce the damage the triggering ally would take by 3. You redirect this damage to yourself, but your immunities, weaknesses, resistances and so on do not apply.

You aren't subject to any conditions or other effects of whatever damaged your ally (such as poison from a venomous bite). Your ally is still subject to those effects even if you redirect all of the triggering damage to yourself.

Heightened (+1) The damage you redirect increases by 3.

PROTECTOR'S SPHERE FOCUS 4

UNCOMMON ABJURATION CLERIC

Domain protection
Cast ❖❖ somatic, verbal
Area 15-foot emanation
Duration sustained up to 1 minute

A protective aura emanates out from you, safeguarding you and your allies. You gain resistance 3 to all damage. Your allies also gain this resistance while they are within the area.

Heightened (+1) The resistance increases by 1.

PULSE OF THE CITY FOCUS 4

UNCOMMON CLERIC DIVINATION SCRYING

Domain cities
Cast ❖❖❖ material, somatic, verbal
Range 25 miles

You tap into the zeitgeist of the nearest settlement in range (if any). You learn the name of the settlement, and you can utter a special word to learn a brief summary of one significant event happening in the settlement. Choose one of the following words, which indicates the type of people involved and type of event you learn about.

- **Wardens** city guards, barristers, and judges (criminal reports, busts, changes in routines, legal trials)
- **Titles** nobles and politicians (high society weddings, elite soirees, political rallies)
- **Masses** common folk and merchants (gathering mobs, major sales)

When uttering your word, you can exclude events you already know about, whether you know about them from this spell or from other experiences. If you cast *pulse of the city* again within 24 hours, you can say "echo" instead of another word to get an update on the event you learned about the last time you Cast the Spell.

Pulse of the city reveals only publicly available or observable information. You never learn clandestine movements or other details people are specifically trying to hide. The spell is also notoriously bad at overcoming magic meant to avoid detection; it automatically fails to reveal information about events involving creatures, places, or objects affected by spells that could prevent or counteract *pulse of the city* (such as *nondetection*).

Heightened (5th) The range increases to 100 miles.

PUSHING GUST FOCUS 1

UNCOMMON AIR CLERIC CONJURATION

Domain air
Cast ❖❖ somatic, verbal
Range 500 feet; **Targets** 1 creature
Saving Throw Fortitude

Giving the air a push, you buffet the target with a powerful gust of wind; it must attempt a Fortitude save.

Critical Success The target is unaffected.
Success The target is pushed 5 feet away from you.
Failure The target is pushed 10 feet away from you.
Critical Failure The target is pushed 10 feet away from you and knocked prone.

READ FATE FOCUS 1

UNCOMMON CLERIC DIVINATION PREDICTION

Domain fate
Cast 1 minute (material, somatic, verbal)
Range 10 feet; **Targets** 1 creature other than you

You attempt to learn more about the target's fate in the short term, usually within the next day for most prosaic creatures, or the next hour or less for someone likely to have multiple rapid experiences, such as someone actively adventuring.

INTRODUCTION

ANCESTRIES & BACKGROUNDS

CLASSES

SKILLS

FEATS

EQUIPMENT

SPELLS

THE AGE OF LOST OMENS

PLAYING THE GAME

GAME MASTERING

CRAFTING & TREASURE

APPENDIX

You learn a single enigmatic word connected to the creature's fate in that time frame. Fate is notoriously inscrutable, and the word isn't necessarily meant to be taken at face value, so the meaning is often clear only in hindsight. The GM rolls a secret DC 6 flat check. If the creature's fate is too uncertain, or on a failed flat check, the spell yields the word "inconclusive." Either way, the creature is then temporarily immune for 24 hours.

REBUKE DEATH   FOCUS 4

UNCOMMON | CLERIC | HEALING | NECROMANCY | POSITIVE

Domain healing
Cast ❖ to ❖❖❖ (somatic)
Area 20-foot emanation; **Targets** 1 living creature per action spent to cast this spell

You snatch creatures from the jaws of death. You can spend 1 to 3 actions Casting this Spell, and you can target a number of creatures equal to the actions spent. Each target regains 3d6 Hit Points. If the target had the dying condition, coming back from dying due to this healing doesn't increase its wounded condition.
Heightened (+1) Increase the healing by 1d6.

RETRIBUTIVE PAIN   FOCUS 4

UNCOMMON | ABJURATION | CLERIC | MENTAL | NONLETHAL

Domain pain
Cast ⤵ somatic
Trigger A creature in range damages you.
Range 30 feet; **Targets** the triggering creature
Saving Throw basic Fortitude

You vengefully reflect your pain upon your tormentor. The target takes mental damage equal to half the amount it dealt to you when it triggered the spell.

SAFEGUARD SECRET   FOCUS 4

UNCOMMON | ABJURATION | CLERIC | MENTAL

Domain secrecy
Cast 1 minute (somatic, verbal)
Range 10 feet; **Targets** you and any number of willing allies
Duration 1 hour

You ensure a secret remains safe from prying spies. Choose one piece of information that at least some of the targets know; you can target a creature only if it remains within range for the full minute during which you Cast the Spell. The spell grants those who know the piece of knowledge you have chosen a +4 status bonus to skill checks (typically Deception checks) to conceal this knowledge and to saving throws against spells that specifically attempt to obtain this knowledge from them and effects that would force them to reveal it.

If you Cast this Spell again, any previous *safeguard secret* you had cast ends.

SAVOR THE STING   FOCUS 1

UNCOMMON | ATTACK | CLERIC | ENCHANTMENT | MENTAL | NONLETHAL

Domain pain
Cast ❖ somatic
Range touch; **Targets** 1 creature
Saving Throw Will

You inflict pain upon the target and revel in their anguish. This deals 1d4 mental damage and 1d4 persistent mental damage; the target must attempt a Will save. As long as the target is taking persistent damage from this spell, you gain a +1 status bonus to attack rolls and skill checks against the target.
Critical Success The target is unaffected.
Success The target takes half damage and no persistent damage.
Failure The target takes full initial and persistent damage.
Critical Failure The target takes double initial and persistent damage.
Heightened (+1) The initial damage increases by 1d4 and the persistent damage increases by 1d4.

SCHOLARLY RECOLLECTION   FOCUS 1

UNCOMMON | CLERIC | DIVINATION | FORTUNE

Domain knowledge
Cast ⤵ verbal
Trigger You attempt a Perception check to Seek, or you attempt a skill check to Recall Knowledge with a skill you're trained in.

Speaking a short prayer as you gather your thoughts, you're blessed to find that your deity gave you just the right bit of information for your situation. Roll the triggering check twice and use the better result.

SHARED NIGHTMARE   FOCUS 4

UNCOMMON | CLERIC | EMOTION | ENCHANTMENT | INCAPACITATION | MENTAL

Domain nightmares
Cast ❖❖ somatic, verbal
Range 30 feet; **Targets** 1 creature
Saving Throw Will; **Duration** varies

Merging minds with the target, you swap disorienting visions from one another's nightmares. One of you will become confused, but which it'll be depends on the target's Will save.
Critical Success You are confused for 1 round.
Success At the start of your next turn, you spend your first action with the confused condition, then act normally.
Failure As success, but the target is affected instead of you, spending its first action each turn confused. The duration is 1 minute.
Critical Failure The target is confused for 1 minute.

SOOTHING WORDS   FOCUS 1

UNCOMMON | CLERIC | EMOTION | ENCHANTMENT | MENTAL

Domain family
Cast ❖ verbal
Range 30 feet; **Targets** 1 ally
Duration 1 round

You attempt to calm the target by uttering soothing words in a calm and even tone. The target gains a +1 status bonus to Will saving throws. This bonus increases to +2 against emotion effects.

In addition, when you Cast this Spell, you can attempt to counteract one emotion effect on the target.
Heightened (5th) The bonus to saves increases to +2, or +3 against emotion effects.

SPLASH OF ART — FOCUS 1

UNCOMMON | CLERIC | ILLUSION | VISUAL

Domain creation
Cast ◆◆ somatic, verbal
Range 30 feet; **Area** 5-foot burst
Saving Throw Will; **Duration** varies

A deluge of colorful illusory paint, tools, or other symbols of art and artisanship drift down in the area. Roll 1d4 to determine the color of the illusion. Each creature in the area must attempt a Will save. A creature is unaffected on a success. On a failure or critical failure, the creature takes the results listed on the table relevant to the color.

1d4	Color	Failure	Critical Failure
1	White	Dazzled 1 round	Dazzled 1 minute
2	Red	Enfeebled 1 for 1 round	Enfeebled 2 for 1 round
3	Yellow	Frightened 1	Frightened 2
4	Blue	Sluggish 1 for 1 round	Sluggish 2 for 1 round

SUDDEN SHIFT — FOCUS 1

UNCOMMON | ABJURATION | CLERIC | ILLUSION

Domain trickery
Cast ↻ somatic
Trigger An enemy misses you with a melee attack.
Duration until the end of your next turn

You swiftly move from a dangerous spot and veil yourself. You Step and become concealed.

SWEET DREAM — FOCUS 1

UNCOMMON | AUDITORY | CLERIC | ENCHANTMENT | LINGUISTIC | MENTAL | SLEEP

Domain dreams
Cast ◆◆◆ material, somatic, verbal
Range 30 feet; **Targets** 1 willing creature
Duration 10 minutes

With soothing song or tales, you lull the target into an enchanting dream. When you cast the spell, the target falls unconscious if it wasn't already. While unconscious, it experiences a dream of your choice. If it sleeps for at least 1 minute, it gains the benefit of the dream for the remainder of the spell's duration.

- **Dream of Insight** +1 status bonus to Intelligence-based skill checks
- **Dream of Glamour** +1 status bonus to Charisma-based skill checks
- **Dream of Voyaging** +5-foot status bonus to Speed

If you Cast this Spell again, the effects of any previous *sweet dream* you cast end.

TAKE ITS COURSE — FOCUS 4

UNCOMMON | CLERIC | NECROMANCY

Domain indulgence
Cast ◆◆ somatic, verbal
Range touch; **Targets** 1 creature

When someone has overindulged, you can hasten them past the worst of their affliction or intensify their misery. This spell attempts to progress a disease affliction, a poison affliction, or persistent poison damage affecting the target. If the target is affected by more than one of these, you can choose from among those you are aware of; otherwise the GM chooses randomly. An unwilling target can attempt a Will save to negate *take its course*.

The effect of this spell depends on whether you're attempting to end an affliction or persistent poison damage, and whether you are attempting to help or hinder the target's recovery.

- **Affliction** The target immediately attempts its next saving throw against the affliction. You can grant the creature your choice of a +2 status bonus or a –2 status penalty to its saving throw against the affliction.
- **Persistent Poison** You can cause the target take the persistent poison damage immediately when you Cast this Spell (in addition to taking it at the end of its next turn). Whether or not you do so, the target attempts an additional flat check against the persistent poison damage. You can set the DC of that flat check to 5 or 20 instead of the normal DC.

Heightened (7th) You can attempt to progress any number of the target's eligible afflictions and persistent poison damage.

TEMPT FATE — FOCUS 4

UNCOMMON | CLERIC | DIVINATION | FORTUNE

Domain fate
Cast ↻ somatic
Trigger You or an ally within range attempts a saving throw.
Range 120 feet; **Targets** the triggering creature

You twist the forces of fate to make a moment dire or uneventful, with no in-between. The target gains a +1 status bonus to the triggering saving throw. If the saving throw's result is a success, it becomes a critical success. If it's a failure, it becomes a critical failure, and the critical failure can't be reduced by abilities that usually reduce critical failure, such as improved evasion.

If the triggering ability did not have both a critical success and critical failure condition, *tempt fate* fails, but you don't expend the Focus Point for Casting this Spell.

Heightened (8th) The bonus on the saving throw is +2.

TIDAL SURGE — FOCUS 1

UNCOMMON | CLERIC | EVOCATION | WATER

Domain water
Cast ◆ somatic
Range 60 feet; **Targets** 1 creature
Saving Throw Fortitude

You call forth a tremendous wave to move the target either in a body of water or on the ground. The target must attempt a Fortitude save.

Failure You move the target 5 feet in any direction along the ground or 10 feet in any direction through a body of water.

Critical Failure You move the target up to 10 feet in any direction along the ground or 20 feet in any direction through a body of water.

INTRODUCTION

ANCESTRIES & BACKGROUNDS

CLASSES

SKILLS

FEATS

EQUIPMENT

SPELLS

THE AGE OF LOST OMENS

PLAYING THE GAME

GAME MASTERING

CRAFTING & TREASURE

APPENDIX

TOUCH OF OBEDIENCE   FOCUS 1

UNCOMMON   CLERIC   ENCHANTMENT   MENTAL

Domain tyranny
Cast ❖ somatic
Range touch; **Targets** 1 living creature
Saving Throw Will; **Duration** varies

Your imperious touch erodes the target's willpower, making it easier to control. The target attempts a Will save.

Critical Success The target is unaffected.
Success The target is stupefied 1 until the end of your current turn.
Failure The target is stupefied 1 until the end of your next turn.
Critical Failure The target is stupefied 1 for 1 minute.

TOUCH OF THE MOON   FOCUS 4

UNCOMMON   CLERIC   ENCHANTMENT   LIGHT

Domain moon
Cast ❖ somatic
Range touch; **Target** 1 creature
Duration 1 minute

When you touch the target, a symbol of the moon appears on its forehead, glowing with soft moonlight. The target glows with dim light in a 20-foot radius. It also gets a benefit based on a phase of the moon, starting with the new moon and changing to the next phase at the end of each of its turns.

- **New Moon** The target receives no benefit.
- **Waxing Moon** The target gains a +1 status bonus to attack rolls and a +4 status bonus to damage rolls.
- **Full Moon** The target gains a +1 status bonus to attack rolls, AC, and saving throws and a +4 status bonus to damage rolls.
- **Waning Moon** The target gains a +1 status bonus to AC and saving throws. After this phase, return to the new moon.

TOUCH OF UNDEATH   FOCUS 1

UNCOMMON   ATTACK   CLERIC   NECROMANCY   NEGATIVE

Domain undeath
Cast ❖ somatic
Range touch; **Targets** 1 living creature
Saving Throw Fortitude

You attack the target's life force with undeath, dealing 1d6 negative damage. The target must attempt a Fortitude save.

Critical Success The target is unaffected.
Success The target takes half damage.
Failure The target takes full damage, and positive effects heal it only half as much as normal for 1 round.
Critical Failure The target takes double damage, and positive effects heal it only half as much as normal for 1 minute.
Heightened (+1) The damage increases by 1d6.

TRAVELER'S TRANSIT   FOCUS 4

UNCOMMON   CLERIC   EVOCATION

Domain travel
Cast ❖❖ somatic, verbal
Duration 1 minute

You add power to your muscles, allowing you to swim or climb walls with ease. When you cast this spell, you gain either a climb Speed or a swim Speed. The Speed is equal to your land Speed.
Heightened (5th) You can choose to gain a fly Speed.

TRICKSTER'S TWIN   FOCUS 4

UNCOMMON   CLERIC   ILLUSION   VISUAL

Domain trickery
Cast ❖❖ material, verbal
Range 30 feet; **Targets** 1 creature
Saving Throw Will; **Duration** 1 minute

You rarely settle for being in just one place. Choose a location within 100 feet of the target that the target can see. You create an illusion of yourself there that only it can see and that mimics all your actions. The target must attempt a Will save.

Critical Success The target is unaffected.
Success The target believes you're in the designated location and can't see you in your actual location. The target automatically disbelieves the illusion when you use an action that doesn't make sense in the illusion's position, or if the target attacks, touches, Seeks, or otherwise engages with the illusion. If you use a hostile action against the target, the spell ends.
Failure As success, but the target must succeed at a Will save to disbelieve the illusion when one of the listed events occurs.
Critical Failure As success, but the target must critically succeed at a Will save to disbelieve when one of the listed events occurs.

UNIMPEDED STRIDE   FOCUS 1

UNCOMMON   CLERIC   TRANSMUTATION

Domain freedom
Cast ❖ somatic

Nothing can hold you in place. You immediately escape from every magical effect that has you immobilized or grabbed unless the effect is of a higher level than your *unimpeded stride* spell. You then Stride. During this movement, you ignore difficult terrain and any circumstance or status penalties to your Speed.

UNITY   FOCUS 4

UNCOMMON   ABJURATION   CLERIC   FORTUNE

Domain family
Cast ↻ verbal
Trigger You and 1 or more allies within range are targeted by a spell or ability that allows a saving throw.
Range 30 feet; **Targets** each ally targeted by the triggering spell

You put up a united defense. Each ally can use your saving throw modifier instead of its own against the triggering spell. Each ally decides individually which modifier to use.

VEIL OF CONFIDENCE   FOCUS 1

UNCOMMON   CLERIC   ENCHANTMENT   MENTAL

Domain confidence
Cast ❖ verbal
Duration 1 minute

You surround yourself in a veil of confidence. You reduce your current frightened condition by 1, and whenever you would become frightened during the duration, reduce the amount by 1.

If you critically fail a save against fear, *veil of confidence* ends immediately, and you increase any frightened condition you gain from the critical failure by 1 instead of decreasing it.

VIBRANT THORNS   FOCUS 1

UNCOMMON | CLERIC | MORPH | PLANT | TRANSMUTATION

Domain nature
Cast ◆ somatic
Duration 1 minute

Your body sprouts a coat of brambly thorns that harm those that strike you and thrive on life magic. Adjacent creatures that hit you with a melee attack, as well as creatures that hit you with unarmed attacks, take 1 piercing damage each time they do. Anytime you cast a positive spell, the damage from your thorns increases to 1d6 until the start of your next turn.
Heightened (+1) The damage increases by 1, or 1d6 after you cast a positive spell.

WAKING NIGHTMARE   FOCUS 1

UNCOMMON | CLERIC | EMOTION | ENCHANTMENT | FEAR | MENTAL

Domain nightmares
Cast ◆◆ somatic, verbal
Range 30 feet; **Targets** 1 creature
Saving Throw Will; **Duration** varies

You fill the creature's mind with a terrifying vision out of its nightmares. The target must attempt a Will save.
Critical Success The target is unaffected.
Success The target is frightened 1.
Failure The target is frightened 2.
Critical Failure The target is frightened 3.
If the target is unconscious when you Cast this Spell on it, it immediately wakes up before attempting its save, and if it fails its save, it gains the fleeing condition for 1 round in addition to the effects noted above.

WEAPON SURGE   FOCUS 1

UNCOMMON | CLERIC | EVOCATION

Domain zeal
Cast ◆ somatic
Range touch; **Targets** 1 weapon you're wielding

Holding your weapon aloft, you fill it with divine energy. On your next Strike with that weapon before the start of your next turn, you gain a +1 status bonus to the attack roll and the weapon deals an additional die of damage. If the weapon has a *striking* rune, this instead increases the number of dice from the *striking* rune by 1 (to a maximum of 3 extra weapon dice).

If the target weapon leaves your possession, *weapon surge* immediately ends.

WORD OF FREEDOM   FOCUS 4

UNCOMMON | CLERIC | ENCHANTMENT | MENTAL

Domain freedom
Cast ◆ verbal
Range 30 feet; **Targets** 1 creature
Duration 1 round

You utter a liberating word of power that frees a creature.

You suppress one of the following conditions of your choice: confused, frightened, grabbed, or paralyzed. The target isn't affected by the chosen condition, and if you suppress the grabbed condition, the target automatically breaks free from any grab affecting it when you Cast the Spell.

If you don't remove the effect that provided the condition, the condition returns after the spell ends. For example, if a spell was making the target confused for 1 minute, *word of freedom* would let the target act normally for a round, but the confused condition would return afterward.

WORD OF TRUTH   FOCUS 1

UNCOMMON | CLERIC | DIVINATION

Domain truth
Cast ◆ verbal
Duration sustained up to 1 minute

You speak a statement you believe to be true and that is free of any attempt to deceive through twisting words, omission, and so on. The statement must be 25 words or fewer. A symbol of your deity glows above your head, and anyone who sees you and hears your statement knows that you believe it to be true.

Each time you Sustain this Spell, you can repeat this effect.

ZEAL FOR BATTLE   FOCUS 4

UNCOMMON | CLERIC | EMOTION | ENCHANTMENT | FORTUNE | MENTAL

Domain zeal
Cast ↻ verbal
Trigger You and at least 1 ally are about to roll initiative.
Range 10 feet; **Targets** you and the triggering ally

You stoke the righteous anger within yourself and an ally. You and the target ally each roll a d20 and use the higher result for both your initiative rolls. You each still use your own Perception modifier or other statistic to determine your results.

DRUID

Druids can gain the following order spells.

GOODBERRY   FOCUS 1

UNCOMMON | DRUID | HEALING | NECROMANCY

Cast 1 hour (somatic, verbal)
Range touch; **Targets** 1 freshly picked berry
Duration 1 day

You imbue the target berry with the bounty of nature, allowing it to heal and sustain far beyond its normal capacity. A living creature that eats the berry with an Interact action gains as much nourishment as from a square meal for a typical human and regains 1d8+5 Hit Points. If it's not consumed during the duration, or if you cast *goodberry* again, the berry withers away.
Heightened (+1) You can target an additional berry.

HEAL ANIMAL   FOCUS 1

UNCOMMON | DRUID | HEALING | NECROMANCY | POSITIVE

Cast ◆ to ◆◆ somatic
Range touch or 30 feet (see text); **Targets** 1 willing living animal creature

INTRODUCTION

ANCESTRIES &
BACKGROUNDS

CLASSES

SKILLS

FEATS

EQUIPMENT

SPELLS

THE AGE OF
LOST OMENS

PLAYING THE
GAME

GAME
MASTERING

CRAFTING
& TREASURE

APPENDIX

You heal an animal's wounds, restoring 1d8 Hit Points to the target. The number of actions spent Casting this Spell determines its effect.

- ❖ **somatic** The spell has a range of touch.
- ❖❖ **somatic, verbal** The spell has a range of 30 feet and restores an additional 8 Hit Points to the target.

Heightened (+1) The amount of healing increases by 1d8, and the additional healing for the 2-action version increases by 8.

IMPALING BRIARS   FOCUS 8

UNCOMMON | CONJURATION | DRUID | PLANT

Cast ❖❖ somatic, verbal
Area ground within a 100-foot emanation
Duration sustained up to 1 minute

The ground within the area transforms into a mass of dangerous briars that assault and impede your foes. Each round when you Sustain the Spell, you can select one of the following effects to occur in the area.

- **Ensnare** The briars clump around your foes, attempting to hold them in place. A foe within the area (or flying at most 20 feet above the area) must attempt a Reflex save. On a failure, it takes a –10-foot circumstance penalty to all Speeds for 1 round, and on a critical failure, it is immobilized for 1 round unless it Escapes.
- **Impede** The briars twist and writhe, making the entire area difficult terrain.
- **Wall** A *wall of thorns* appears in the area, lasting for 1 round. The wall is greater difficult terrain instead of difficult terrain.

In addition, once per round you can direct the briars to impale any target in the area (or flying up to 20 feet above the area) that you can see by using a single action, which has the concentrate and manipulate traits. Make a spell attack roll. On a success, the target takes 10d6 piercing damage and takes a –10-foot circumstance penalty to all Speeds for 1 round; on a critical success, the target is immobilized for 1 round unless it Escapes.

PRIMAL SUMMONS   FOCUS 6

UNCOMMON | CONJURATION | DRUID

Cast ❖ verbal

You enhance a summoned creature with the power of the elements. If your next action is to cast either *summon animal* or *summon plant or fungus*, choose air, earth, fire, or water, and the creature you summon gains the corresponding abilities.

- **Air** The creature gains a fly Speed of 60 feet.
- **Earth** The creature gains a burrow Speed of 20 feet, reduces its land Speed by 10 feet (minimum 5 feet), and gains resistance 5 to physical damage.
- **Fire** The creature's attacks deal 1d6 extra fire damage, and it gains resistance 10 to fire and weakness 5 to cold and water.
- **Water** The creature gains a swim Speed of 60 feet, can spend 1 action after a melee attack to attempt a Shove (ignoring multiple attack penalty), and gains resistance 5 to fire.

STORM LORD   FOCUS 9

UNCOMMON | AIR | DRUID | ELECTRICITY | EVOCATION

Cast ❖❖ somatic, verbal; **Requirements** You are outdoors and aboveground.
Area 100-foot emanation
Duration sustained up to 1 minute

The sky above you darkens in a matter of moments, swirling with ominous clouds punctuated by flashes of lighting. Each round when you Sustain the Spell, you can select one of the following effects to occur in the area.

- **Calm** No additional effect.
- **Fog** Heavy fog rolls in, concealing the area with the effects of *obscuring mist*.
- **Rain** Torrential rain falls from the sky, dousing ordinary flames. Creatures in the area take a –2 circumstance penalty to Acrobatics and Perception checks.
- **Wind** Powerful winds buffet the area in all directions. Ranged attacks take a –4 circumstance penalty, and all flying is against the wind and counts as moving through difficult terrain.

In addition, once per round you can use a single action, which has the concentrate and manipulate traits, to call down a bolt of lightning, striking any target in range that you can see. You deal 10d6 electricity damage to the target; it must attempt a basic Reflex save. On a failure, it is also deafened for 1 round.

STORMWIND FLIGHT   FOCUS 4

UNCOMMON | AIR | DRUID | TRANSMUTATION

Cast ❖❖ somatic, verbal
Duration 1 minute

Powerful winds carry you smoothly through the air, giving you a fly Speed equal to your Speed. When this spell's duration would end, if you're still flying, you float to the ground, as *feather fall*.

Heightened (6th) When you fly using *stormwind flight*, you don't count flying against the wind as difficult terrain.

TEMPEST SURGE   FOCUS 1

UNCOMMON | AIR | DRUID | ELECTRICITY | EVOCATION

Cast ❖❖ somatic, verbal
Range 30 feet; **Targets** 1 creature
Saving Throw Reflex

You surround a foe in a swirling storm of violent winds, roiling clouds, and crackling lightning. The storm deals 1d12 electricity damage. The target must attempt a basic Reflex save. On a failure, the target also is clumsy 2 for 1 round and takes 1 persistent electricity damage.

Heightened (+1) The initial damage increases by 1d12, and the persistent electricity damage on a failure increases by 1.

WILD MORPH   FOCUS 1

UNCOMMON | DRUID | MORPH | TRANSMUTATION

Cast ❖ to ❖❖ somatic, verbal
Duration 1 minute

You morph your body based on your training, choosing one of the following effects based on your wild order feats.

INTRODUCTION

ANCESTRIES &
BACKGROUNDS

CLASSES

SKILLS

FEATS

EQUIPMENT

SPELLS

THE AGE OF
LOST OMENS

PLAYING THE
GAME

GAME
MASTERING

CRAFTING
& TREASURE

APPENDIX

- If you have Wild Shape, you can morph your hands into wild claws. Your hands transform into incredibly sharp claws. These claws are an unarmed attack you're trained in and deal 1d6 slashing damage each (agile, finesse). You can still hold and use items with your hands while they're transformed by this spell, but you cannot hold an item while attacking. If you have Insect Shape, you can instead transform your mouth into wild jaws, an unarmed attack you're trained in that deals 1d8 piercing damage.
- If you have Elemental Shape, you can morph your body to be partially composed of elemental matter, granting you resistance 5 to critical hits and precision damage.
- If you have Plant Shape, you can morph your arms into long vines, increasing your reach to 10 feet (or 15 feet with a reach weapon).
- If you have Soaring Shape, you can cast the spell as a two-action activity (◆◆ somatic, verbal) to grow wings from your back. These wings allow you to fly with a fly Speed of 30 feet.

Heightened (6th) You can choose up to two of the effects from the list. Wild claws leave terrible, ragged wounds that also deal 2d6 persistent bleed damage on a hit, and wild jaws are envenomed, also dealing 2d6 persistent poison damage on a hit.

Heightened (10th) You can choose up to three of the effects from the list. Wild claws deal 4d6 persistent bleed damage on a hit, and wild jaws deal 4d6 persistent poison damage on a hit.

WILD SHAPE   FOCUS 1

UNCOMMON | DRUID | POLYMORPH | TRANSMUTATION

Cast ◆◆ somatic, verbal
Duration 1 minute (or longer)

You infuse yourself with primal essence and transform yourself into another form. You can polymorph into any form listed in *pest form*, which lasts 10 minutes. All other *wild shape* forms last 1 minute. You can add more forms to your *wild shape* list with druid feats; your feat might grant you some or all of the forms from a given polymorph spell. When you transform into a form granted by a spell, you gain all the effects of the form you chose from a version of the spell heightened to *wild shape*'s level. *Wild shape* allows you to use your own shapeshifting training more easily than most polymorph spells. When you choose to use your own attack modifier while polymorphed instead of the form's default attack modifier, you gain a +2 status bonus to your attack rolls.

Heightened (2nd) You can also *wild shape* into the forms listed in *animal form*.

MONK

Monks can gain the following ki spells.

ABUNDANT STEP   FOCUS 4

UNCOMMON | CONJURATION | MONK | TELEPORTATION

Cast ◆ somatic
Range 15 feet or more

You move so fast you blur across planar boundaries. You teleport up to a distance equal to your Speed within your line of sight.

EMPTY BODY   FOCUS 9

UNCOMMON | CONJURATION | MONK | TELEPORTATION

Cast ◆◆ somatic, verbal
Duration 1 minute

You turn ethereal, with the effects of *ethereal jaunt*, but you don't need to concentrate.

KI BLAST   FOCUS 3

UNCOMMON | EVOCATION | FORCE | MONK

Cast ◆ to ◆◆◆ somatic, verbal
Area 15-foot cone or more
Saving Throw Fortitude

You unleash your ki as a powerful blast of force that deals 2d6 force damage. If you use 2 actions to cast *ki blast*, increase the size of the cone to 30 feet and the damage to 3d6. If you use 3 actions to cast *ki blast*, increase the size of the cone to 60 feet and the damage to 4d6. Each creature in the area must attempt a Fortitude saving throw.

Critical Success The creature is unaffected.
Success The creature takes half damage.
Failure The creature takes full damage and is pushed 5 feet.
Critical Failure The creature takes double damage and is pushed 10 feet.

Heightened (+1) The damage increases by 1d6, or by 2d6 if you use 2 or 3 actions.

KI RUSH   FOCUS 1

UNCOMMON | MONK | TRANSMUTATION

Casting ◆ verbal

Accelerated by your ki, you move with such speed you become a blur. Move two times: two Strides, two Steps, or one Stride and one Step (in either order). You gain the concealed condition during this movement and until the start of your next turn.

KI STRIKE   FOCUS 1

UNCOMMON | MONK | TRANSMUTATION

Casting ◆ verbal

You focus your ki into magical attacks. Make an unarmed Strike or Flurry of Blows (this doesn't change the limit on using only one flourish per turn). You gain a +1 status bonus to your attack rolls with the Strikes, and the Strikes deal 1d6 extra damage. This damage can be any of the following types of your choice, chosen each time you Strike: force, lawful (only if you're lawful), negative, or positive.

Heightened (+4) The extra damage increases by 1d6.

QUIVERING PALM   FOCUS 8

UNCOMMON | INCAPACITATION | MONK | NECROMANCY

Cast ◆◆ somatic, verbal
Saving Throw Fortitude; **Duration** 1 month

Make a melee unarmed Strike. If you hit and the target is alive, anytime during the duration, you can spend a single action, which has the auditory and concentrate traits, to speak a word of death that could instantly slay it. The target must attempt a Fortitude save.

Critical Success The target survives, the spell ends, and the target is then temporarily immune for 24 hours.

Success The target is stunned 1 and takes 40 damage, the spell ends, and the target is then temporarily immune for 24 hours.

Failure The target is stunned 3 and takes 80 damage. The spell's duration continues, but the target is then temporarily immune for 24 hours against being killed by *quivering palm*.

Critical Failure The target dies.

If you cast *quivering palm* again, the effects of any *quivering palm* you had previously cast end.

Heightened (+1) The damage increases by 10 on a failure, or 5 on a success.

WHOLENESS OF BODY   FOCUS 2

UNCOMMON   HEALING   MONK   NECROMANCY   POSITIVE

Cast ❖ verbal

You heal yourself in one of the following ways, chosen by you when you cast the spell.

- You regain 8 Hit Points.
- You attempt to cure one poison or disease afflicting you; attempt to counteract the affliction.

Heightened (+1) If you choose to regain Hit Points, the Hit Points regained increase by 8.

WILD WINDS STANCE   FOCUS 4

UNCOMMON   AIR   EVOCATION   MONK   STANCE

Cast ❖ somatic

Duration until you leave the stance

You take on the stance of the flowing winds, sending out waves of energy at a distance. You can make wind crash unarmed Strikes as ranged Strikes against targets within 30 feet. These deal 1d6 bludgeoning damage, use the brawling group, and have the agile, nonlethal, propulsive, and unarmed traits. Wind crash Strikes ignore concealment and all cover.

While in wild winds stance, you gain a +2 circumstance bonus to AC against ranged attacks.

WIND JUMP   FOCUS 5

UNCOMMON   AIR   MONK   TRANSMUTATION

Cast ❖ verbal

Duration 1 minute

You gain a fly Speed equal to your Speed. You must end your turn on solid ground, or you fall.

Heightened (6th) At the end of your turn, you can attempt a DC 30 Acrobatics check to find purchase in midair. If you succeed, you don't fall.

SORCERER

Sorcerers can gain the following bloodline spells.

ABERRANT WHISPERS   FOCUS 3

UNCOMMON   AUDITORY   ENCHANTMENT   MENTAL   SORCERER

Cast ❖ to ❖❖❖ verbal

Area 5-foot emanation or more; **Targets** each foe in the area

Saving Throw Will; **Duration** 1 round

You utter phrases in an unknown tongue, assaulting the minds of those nearby. Each target must attempt a Will save. Regardless of the result of its save, each target is then temporarily immune for 1 minute. You can increase the number of actions it takes to Cast the Spell (to a maximum of 3 actions total). For each additional action, increase the emanation's radius by 5 feet, to a maximum of 10 extra feet for 3 actions.

Success The target is unaffected.

Failure The target is stupefied 2.

Critical Failure The target is confused.

Heightened (+3) The initial radius increases by 5 feet.

ABYSSAL WRATH   FOCUS 5

UNCOMMON   EVOCATION   SORCERER

Cast ❖❖ somatic, verbal

Area 60-foot cone

Saving Throw basic Reflex

You evoke the energy of an Abyssal realm. The damage types of the spell (one energy and one physical) are based on the result of rolling on the table below.

1d4	Realm	Manifestation	Damage Type
1	Skies	Bolts of lightning and flying debris	Bludgeoning and electricity
2	Depths	Acid and demonic shells	Acid and slashing
3	Frozen	Frigid air and ice	Bludgeoning and cold
4	Volcanic	Jagged volcanic rocks and magma	Fire and piercing

You deal 4d6 damage of each of the corresponding damage types to each creature in the cone (8d6 total damage).

Heightened (+1) The damage for each type increases by 1d6.

ANCESTRAL MEMORIES   FOCUS 1

UNCOMMON   DIVINATION   SORCERER

Cast ❖ verbal

Duration 1 minute

The memories of long-dead spellcasters grant you knowledge in a specific skill. Choose any non-Lore skill, or a Lore skill related to the ancient empire from which your bloodline sprang. You temporarily become trained in that skill and might gain other memories associated with an ancestor who was trained in that skill. If you attempt a task or activity that lasts beyond this spell's duration, use the lower proficiency modifier.

Heightened (6th) You temporarily become an expert in the skill you choose.

ANGELIC HALO   FOCUS 1

UNCOMMON   ABJURATION   GOOD   SORCERER

Cast ❖ verbal

Area 15-foot emanation

Duration 1 minute

You gain an angelic halo with an aura that increases allies' healing from the *heal* spell. *Heal* spells gain a +2 status bonus to Hit Points healed to your allies in the area.

Heightened (+1) The status bonus increases by 2.

ANGELIC WINGS   FOCUS 3

UNCOMMON   EVOCATION   LIGHT   SORCERER

Cast ◆◆ somatic, verbal
Duration 3 rounds

Wings of pure light spread out from your back, granting you a fly Speed equal to your Speed. Your wings cast bright light in a 30-foot radius. When this spell's duration would end, if you're still flying, you float to the ground, as *feather fall*.

Heightened (5th) The duration increases to 1 minute.

ARCANE COUNTERMEASURE   FOCUS 5

UNCOMMON   ABJURATION   SORCERER

Cast ↻ somatic

Trigger A creature within range that you can see Casts a Spell.
Range 120 feet; **Targets** the spell cast by the triggering creature

You undermine the target spell, making it easier to defend against. You reduce the spell's level by 1, and targets of the spell gain a +2 status bonus to any saving throws, skill checks, AC, or DC against it.

You can't reduce the spell's level below its minimum. For example, a 5th-level *cone of cold* would remain 5th-level, but a 5th-level *fireball* would become 4th-level. Targets still gain all the other benefits, even if you don't reduce the spell's level.

CELESTIAL BRAND   FOCUS 5

UNCOMMON   CURSE   NECROMANCY   SORCERER

Cast ◆ somatic
Range 30 feet; **Targets** 1 evil creature
Duration 1 round

A blazing symbol appears on the target, marking it for divine justice. You and your allies receive a +1 status bonus to your attack rolls and skill checks against it. Anytime a good creature damages it, the good creature deals an additional 1d4 good damage. The target is then temporarily immune for 1 minute.

Heightened (+2) The good damage increases by 1.

DIABOLIC EDICT   FOCUS 1

UNCOMMON   ENCHANTMENT   SORCERER

Casting ◆ verbal
Range 30 feet; **Targets** 1 willing living creature
Duration 1 round

You issue a diabolic edict, demanding the target perform a particular task and offering rewards for its fulfillment. It gains a +1 status bonus to attack rolls and skill checks related to performing the task. If it refuses to perform the task you proclaimed, it instead takes a –1 status penalty to all its attack rolls and skill checks.

DRAGON BREATH   FOCUS 3

UNCOMMON   EVOCATION   SORCERER

Cast ◆◆ somatic, verbal

Area 30-foot cone or 60-foot line originating from you
Saving Throw basic Reflex or Fortitude

You spew energy from your mouth, dealing 5d6 damage. The area, damage type, and save depend on the dragon type in your bloodline.

Dragon Type	Area and Damage Type	Saving Throw
Black or copper	60-foot line of acid	Reflex
Blue or bronze	60-foot line of electricity	Reflex
Brass	60-foot line of fire	Reflex
Green	30-foot cone of poison	Fortitude
Gold or red	30-foot cone of fire	Reflex
Silver or white	30-foot cone of cold	Reflex

Heightened (+1) The damage increases by 2d6.

DRAGON CLAWS   FOCUS 1

UNCOMMON   MORPH   SORCERER   TRANSMUTATION

Cast ◆ verbal
Duration 1 minute

Vicious claws grow from your fingers. They are finesse unarmed attacks that deal 1d4 slashing damage and 1d6 extra damage of a type determined by the dragon in your bloodline (see the table in *dragon breath*). Your scales from blood magic glow with faint energy, giving you resistance 5 to the same damage type.

Heightened (5th) The extra damage increases to 2d6, and the resistance increases to 10.

Heightened (9th) The extra damage increases to 3d6, and the resistance increases to 15.

DRAGON WINGS   FOCUS 5

UNCOMMON   MORPH   SORCERER   TRANSMUTATION

Cast ◆◆ somatic, verbal
Duration 1 minute

Leathery wings sprout from your back, giving you a fly Speed of 60 feet or your Speed, whichever is faster. When this spell's duration would end, if you're still flying, you float to the ground, as *feather fall*. You can increase the Focus Point cost by 1 to gain the effects of *dragon claws* as long as the wings last.

Heightened (8th) The duration increases to 10 minutes.

DRAIN LIFE   FOCUS 3

UNCOMMON   NECROMANCY   NEGATIVE   SORCERER

Casting ◆ somatic
Range 30 feet; **Targets** 1 creature
Saving Throw basic Fortitude

You close your hand and pull life energy from another creature into yourself. This deals 3d4 negative damage; the target must attempt a basic Fortitude save. You gain temporary Hit Points equal to the damage the target takes, after resolving its save and applying your blood magic if applicable. If the target's Hit Points were lower than the damage you dealt, you gain temporary Hit Points equal to their remaining Hit Points instead. The temporary Hit Points last for 1 minute.

Heightened (+1) The damage increases by 1d4.

INTRODUCTION

ANCESTRIES & BACKGROUNDS

CLASSES

SKILLS

FEATS

EQUIPMENT

SPELLS

THE AGE OF LOST OMENS

PLAYING THE GAME

GAME MASTERING

CRAFTING & TREASURE

APPENDIX

ELEMENTAL BLAST   FOCUS 5

UNCOMMON   EVOCATION   SORCERER

Casting ◆◆ somatic, verbal

Range 30 feet (burst only); **Area** 10-foot-radius burst, 30-foot cone, or 60-foot line

Saving Throw basic Reflex

You gather elemental energy and blast your foes in one of the various listed shapes of your choosing, dealing 8d6 bludgeoning damage (or fire damage if your element is fire). This spell has your element's trait.

Heightened (+1) The damage increases by 2d6.

ELEMENTAL MOTION   FOCUS 3

UNCOMMON   EVOCATION   SORCERER

Casting ◆◆ somatic, verbal

Duration 1 minute

You call upon your element to propel you, improving your Speed depending on your element. This spell has your element's trait.

- **Air** You gain a fly Speed equal to your Speed.
- **Earth** You gain a burrow Speed of 10 feet.
- **Fire** You gain a fly Speed equal to your Speed.
- **Water** You gain a swim Speed equal to your Speed and can breathe underwater.

Heightened (6th) You also gain a +10-foot status bonus to your Speeds.

Heightened (9th) The status bonus increases to +20 feet.

ELEMENTAL TOSS   FOCUS 1

UNCOMMON   ATTACK   EVOCATION   SORCERER

Casting ◆ somatic

Range 30 feet; **Targets** 1 creature

With a flick of your wrist, you fling a chunk of your elemental matter at your foe. Make a spell attack roll, dealing 1d8 bludgeoning damage (or fire damage if your element is fire) on a success, and double damage on a critical success. This spell has your element's trait.

Heightened (+1) The damage increases by 1d8.

EMBRACE THE PIT   FOCUS 3

UNCOMMON   EVIL   MORPH   SORCERER   TRANSMUTATION

Casting ◆ verbal

Duration 1 minute

Devil horns grow from your skull, and your skin takes on features of the devil responsible for your diabolic bloodline. You gain resistance 5 to evil, fire, and poison, and resistance 1 to physical damage (except silver). You can take good damage, even if you aren't evil, and you gain weakness 5 to good damage.

Heightened (+2) The resistance to evil, fire, and poison increases by 5, the resistance to physical damage (except silver) by 2, and the weakness to good damage by 5.

EXTEND SPELL   FOCUS 3

UNCOMMON   DIVINATION   METAMAGIC   SORCERER

Cast ◆ verbal

You call upon your blood's knowledge of the ancients to extend your magic. If your next action is to Cast a Spell with a duration of 1 minute on a single target, and the spell isn't of the highest spell level you can cast, the spell instead lasts 10 minutes. You can have only one active spell at a time extended in this way.

FAERIE DUST   FOCUS 1

UNCOMMON   ENCHANTMENT   MENTAL   SORCERER

Cast ◆ or more (somatic, verbal)

Range 30 feet; **Area** 5-foot burst or more

Saving Throw Will; **Duration** 1 round

You sprinkle magical dust in the spell's area, making those within easier to trick. Each creature in the area must attempt a Will save. For each additional action you use Casting the Spell, the burst's radius increases by 5 feet.

Success The creature is unaffected.

Failure The creature can't use reactions and takes a –2 status penalty to Perception checks and Will saves.

Critical Failure As failure, and the creature also takes a –1 status penalty to Perception checks and Will saves for 1 minute.

Heightened (+3) The initial radius increases by 5 feet.

FEY DISAPPEARANCE   FOCUS 3

UNCOMMON   ENCHANTMENT   SORCERER

Cast ◆ somatic

Duration until the end of your next turn

You become invisible and ignore natural difficult terrain (such as underbrush). Any hostile action you use ends this invisibility, but you still ignore natural difficult terrain.

Heightened (5th) If you use a hostile action, the invisibility doesn't end.

FEY GLAMOUR   FOCUS 5

UNCOMMON   ILLUSION   SORCERER

Cast ◆◆ somatic, verbal

Range 30 feet; **Area** 30-foot burst or **Targets** up to 10 creatures

Duration 10 minutes

You call upon fey glamours to cloak an area or the targets in illusion. This has the effect of either *illusory scene* on the area or *veil* on the creatures, as if heightened to a level 1 level lower than *fey glamour*, using *fey glamour*'s range and duration.

GLUTTON'S JAWS   FOCUS 1

UNCOMMON   MORPH   NECROMANCY   SORCERER

Cast ◆ somatic, verbal

Duration 1 minute

Your mouth transforms into a shadowy maw bristling with pointed teeth. These jaws are an unarmed attack with the forceful trait dealing 1d8 piercing damage. If you hit with your jaws and deal damage, you gain 1d6 temporary Hit Points.

Heightened (+2) The temporary Hit Points increase by 1d6.

GRASPING GRAVE   FOCUS 5

UNCOMMON   NECROMANCY   SORCERER

Casting ◆◆ somatic, verbal

Range 60 feet; **Area** 20-foot radius on the ground

Saving Throw Reflex

SPELLS

7

INTRODUCTION

ANCESTRIES &
BACKGROUNDS

CLASSES

SKILLS

FEATS

EQUIPMENT

SPELLS

THE AGE OF
LOST OMENS

PLAYING THE
GAME

GAME
MASTERING

CRAFTING
& TREASURE

APPENDIX

Hundreds of skeletal arms erupt from the ground in the area, clawing at creatures within and attempting to hold them in place. The skeletal arms deal 6d6 slashing damage. Each creature in the area must attempt a Reflex save.

Critical Success The creature is unaffected.

Success The creature takes half damage.

Failure The creature takes full damage and a –10-foot circumstance penalty to its Speeds for 1 round.

Critical Failure The creature takes double damage and is immobilized for 1 round or until it Escapes.

Heightened (+1) The damage increases by 2d6.

HELLFIRE PLUME   FOCUS 5

UNCOMMON   EVIL   EVOCATION   FIRE   SORCERER

Casting ◆◆ somatic, verbal

Range 60 feet; **Area** 10-foot radius, 60-foot-tall cylinder

Saving Throw basic Reflex

You call forth a plume of hellfire that erupts from below, dealing 4d6 fire damage and 4d6 evil damage.

Heightened (+1) The fire damage increases by 1d6, and the evil damage increases by 1d6.

HORRIFIC VISAGE   FOCUS 3

UNCOMMON   EMOTION   FEAR   ILLUSION   MENTAL   SORCERER   VISUAL

Cast ◆◆ somatic, verbal

Area 30-foot-radius emanation centered on you

Saving Throw Will

You briefly transform your features into the horrific visage of a hag, striking fear into your enemies. Foes in the area must attempt a Will save.

Success The foe is unaffected.

Failure The foe is frightened 1.

Critical Failure The foe is frightened 2.

Heightened (5th) Foes in the area are frightened 1 on a success, frightened 2 on a failure, and frightened 3 and fleeing for 1 round on a critical failure. They are still unaffected on a critical success.

JEALOUS HEX   FOCUS 1

UNCOMMON   CURSE   NECROMANCY   SORCERER

Cast ◆ verbal

Range 30 feet; **Targets** 1 creature

Saving Throw Will; **Duration** up to 1 minute

You draw forth a hag's innate jealousy to deny a target its greatest attribute. The target gains an adverse condition depending on its highest ability modifier: Strength (enfeebled); Dexterity (clumsy); Constitution (drained); or Intelligence, Wisdom, or Charisma (stupefied). On a tie, the creature decides which of the conditions associated with the tied ability modifiers to take. The target must attempt a Will save.

Success The target is unaffected.

Failure The condition's value is 1.

Critical Failure The condition's value is 2.

At the start of each of your turns, the target can attempt another Will save, ending the effect on a success.

SWAMP OF SLOTH   FOCUS 3

UNCOMMON   CONJURATION   SORCERER

Cast ◆ to ◆◆◆ somatic, verbal

Range 120 feet; **Area** 5-foot burst or more

Saving Throw basic Fortitude; **Duration** 1 minute

Ground in the area turns swampy and fetid. The area is difficult terrain. The sludge at the bottom of the morass animates into diminutive sludge beasts that have a demonic appearance. These don't function as normal creatures, but they swarm over creatures in the swamp and exude a noxious stench. The swamp deals 1d6 poison damage; creatures that end their turn in the area must attempt a basic Fortitude save. You can increase the number of actions it takes to Cast the Spell. For each additional action, increase the burst's radius by 5 feet.

Heightened (+2) The damage increases by 1d6, and the initial radius increases by 5 feet.

TENTACULAR LIMBS   FOCUS 1

UNCOMMON   MORPH   SORCERER   TRANSMUTATION

Cast ◆ somatic

Duration 1 minute

Your arms turn into long, pliable tentacles, increasing your reach when you're delivering touch range spells and making unarmed Strikes with your arms (such as fist and claw Strikes) to 10 feet. This doesn't change the reach of your melee weapon attacks. During the duration, whenever you Cast a Spell, you can add an additional action to that spell's casting to temporarily extend your reach to 20 feet to deliver that spell.

Heightened (+2) When you add an additional action to a spell to temporarily extend your reach, your reach increases by an additional 10 feet to deliver that spell.

TOUCH OF UNDEATH   FOCUS 1

UNCOMMON   NECROMANCY   NEGATIVE   SORCERER

Cast ◆ somatic

Range touch; **Targets** 1 living creature touched

Saving Throw Will; **Duration** 1 minute

You instill within a creature the touch of the grave. For the duration, *harm* spells treat the creature as undead and *heal* spells treat the creature as living. In addition, *harm* spells gain a +2 status bonus to the Hit Points restored to the target.

If the target wishes to avoid the spell, it can attempt a Will save to reduce the effects.

Critical Success The target is unaffected.

Success The target heals half as much from *heal* and takes half as much damage from *harm* for 1 round.

Failure Effects as described in the text.

Heightened (+1) The status bonus to the Hit Points restored increases by 2.

UNUSUAL ANATOMY   FOCUS 5

UNCOMMON   POLYMORPH   SORCERER   TRANSMUTATION

Cast ◆ somatic

Duration 1 minute

You transform your flesh and organs into a bizarre amalgam of glistening skin, rough scales, tufts of hair, and tumorous protuberances. This has three effects:

- You gain resistance 10 to precision damage and resistance 10 to extra damage from critical hits. If the resistance is greater than the extra damage, it reduces the extra damage to 0 but doesn't reduce the attack's normal damage.
- You gain darkvision.
- Acid oozes from your skin. Any creature that hits you with an unarmed attack or with a non-reach melee weapon takes 2d6 acid damage.

Heightened (+2) The resistances increase by 5, and the acid damage increases by 1d6.

YOU'RE MINE   FOCUS 5

| UNCOMMON | EMOTION | ENCHANTMENT | INCAPACITATION | MENTAL | SORCERER |

Cast ◆◆ somatic, verbal
Range 30 feet; **Targets** 1 creature
Saving Throw Will; **Duration** 1 round

You manipulate the target's emotions, potentially allowing you to control it for a brief instant. The target must attempt a Will save.
Critical Success The target is unaffected.
Success The target is stunned 1.
Failure On the target's next turn, it's stunned 1 and you partially control it, causing it to take a single action of your choice. If it has actions left, it can act normally.
Critical Failure The target is controlled for 1 round.

Heightened (7th) On a failure, the target is controlled for 1 round. On a critical failure, the target is controlled for up to 1 minute; it receives a new Will save at the end of each of its turns, and on a success, the spell ends.

WIZARD

Wizards can gain the following school spells.

AUGMENT SUMMONING   FOCUS 1

| UNCOMMON | CONJURATION | WIZARD |

Cast ◆ verbal
Range 30 feet; **Targets** 1 creature you summoned

You augment the abilities of a summoned creature. The target gains a +1 status bonus to all checks (this also applies to the creature's DCs, including its AC) for the duration of its summoning, up to 1 minute.

CALL OF THE GRAVE   FOCUS 1

| UNCOMMON | ARCANE | ATTACK | NECROMANCY | WIZARD |

Cast ◆◆ somatic, verbal
Range 30 feet; **Targets** 1 living creature

You fire a ray of sickening energy. Make a spell attack roll.
Critical Success The target becomes sickened 2 and slowed 1 as long as it's sickened.
Success The target becomes sickened 1.
Failure The target is unaffected.

CHARMING WORDS   FOCUS 1

| UNCOMMON | AUDITORY | ENCHANTMENT | INCAPACITATION | LINGUISTIC |
| MENTAL | WIZARD |

Cast ◆ verbal
Range 30 feet; **Targets** 1 creature
Saving Throw Will; **Duration** until the start of your next turn

You whisper enchanting words to deflect your foe's ire. The target must attempt a Will save.
Critical Success The target is unaffected.
Success The target takes a –1 circumstance penalty to attack rolls and damage rolls against you.
Failure The target can't use hostile actions against you.
Critical Failure The target is stunned 1 and can't use hostile actions against you.

DIMENSIONAL STEPS   FOCUS 4

| UNCOMMON | CONJURATION | TELEPORTATION | WIZARD |

Cast ◆ somatic
Range 20 feet

You teleport to a location up to 20 feet away within your line of sight.

Heightened (+1) The distance you can teleport increases by 5 feet.

DIVINER'S SIGHT   FOCUS 1

| UNCOMMON | CONCENTRATE | DIVINATION | FORTUNE | WIZARD |

Cast ◆ verbal
Range 30 feet; **Targets** 1 willing living creature
Duration until the end of your next turn

You glimpse into the target's future. Roll a d20; when the target attempts a non-secret saving throw or skill check, it can use the number you rolled instead of rolling, and the spell ends. Alternatively, you can instead reveal the result of the die roll for one of the target's secret checks during the duration, and the spell ends. Casting it again ends any active *diviner's sight* you have cast, as well as any active *diviner's sight* on the target.

DREAD AURA   FOCUS 4

| UNCOMMON | ENCHANTMENT | EMOTION | FEAR | MENTAL | WIZARD |

Cast ◆◆ somatic, verbal
Area 30-foot-radius emanation centered on you
Duration sustained up to 1 minute

You emit an aura of terror. Foes in the area are frightened 1 and unable to reduce the condition.

ELEMENTAL TEMPEST   FOCUS 4

| UNCOMMON | EVOCATION | METAMAGIC | WIZARD |

Cast ◆ verbal

Your spellcasting surrounds you in a storm of elemental energy. If the next action you take is to Cast a Spell from your wizard spell slots that's an evocation spell dealing acid, cold, electricity, or fire damage, a 10-foot emanation of energy surrounds you as you cast the spell. Foes in the area take 1d6 damage per spell level of the spell you just cast of the same damage type the spell deals (choose one if it deals multiple types). Combine the damage from both *elemental tempest* and the other spell against foes who take damage from both before applying bonuses, penalties, resistance, weakness, and the like.

ENERGY ABSORPTION — FOCUS 4

UNCOMMON ABJURATION WIZARD

Cast ↻ verbal

Trigger An effect would deal acid, cold, electricity, or fire damage to you.

You gain resistance 15 to acid, cold, electricity, or fire damage from the triggering effect (one type of your choice). The resistance applies only to the triggering effect's initial damage.

Heightened (+1) The resistance increases by 5.

FORCE BOLT — FOCUS 1

UNCOMMON ATTACK EVOCATION FORCE WIZARD

Cast ◆ somatic

Range 30 feet; **Targets** 1 creature or object

You fire an unerring dart of force from your fingertips. It automatically hits and deals 1d4+1 force damage to the target.

Heightened (+2) The damage increases by 1d4+1.

HAND OF THE APPRENTICE — FOCUS 1

UNCOMMON ATTACK EVOCATION WIZARD

Cast ◆ somatic

Range 500 feet; **Targets** 1 creature

You hurl a held melee weapon with which you are trained at the target, making a spell attack roll. On a success, you deal the weapon's damage as if you had hit with a melee Strike, but adding your spellcasting ability modifier to damage, rather than your Strength modifier. On a critical success, you deal double damage, and you add the weapon's critical specialization effect. Regardless of the outcome, the weapon flies back to you and returns to your hand.

INVISIBILITY CLOAK — FOCUS 4

UNCOMMON ILLUSION WIZARD

Cast ◆◆ somatic

Duration 1 minute

You become invisible, with the same restrictions as the 2nd-level *invisibility* spell.

Heightened (6th) The duration increases to 10 minutes.

Heightened (8th) The duration increases to 1 hour.

LIFE SIPHON — FOCUS 4

UNCOMMON HEALING NECROMANCY WIZARD

Cast ↻ verbal

Trigger You expend one of your wizard spell slots to cast a wizard spell of the necromancy school.

You use some of the spell's magic to heal yourself, regaining 1d8 Hit Points per level of the spell.

PHYSICAL BOOST — FOCUS 1

UNCOMMON TRANSMUTATION WIZARD

Cast ◆ verbal

Range touch; **Targets** 1 living creature

Duration until the end of the target's next turn

You temporarily improve the target's physique. The target gains a +2 status bonus to the next Acrobatics check, Athletics check, Fortitude save, or Reflex save it attempts.

PROTECTIVE WARD — FOCUS 1

UNCOMMON ABJURATION WIZARD

Cast ◆ somatic

Area 5-foot-radius emanation centered on you

Duration sustained up to 1 minute

You emanate a shimmering aura of protective magic. You and any allies in the area gain a +1 status bonus to AC. Each time you Sustain the Spell, the emanation's radius increases by 5 feet, to a maximum of 30 feet.

SHIFTING FORM — FOCUS 4

UNCOMMON MORPH TRANSMUTATION WIZARD

Cast ◆ somatic

Duration 1 minute

You gain one of the following abilities of your choice. You can Dismiss this spell.

- You gain a 20-foot status bonus to your Speed.
- You gain a climb or swim Speed equal to half your Speed.
- You gain darkvision.
- You gain a pair of claws. These are agile finesse unarmed attacks that deal 1d8 slashing damage.
- You gain scent 60 feet (imprecise).

VIGILANT EYE — FOCUS 4

UNCOMMON DIVINATION WIZARD

Cast ◆ somatic

Range 500 feet

Duration 1 hour

You create an invisible eye sensor, as *clairvoyance* (page 324). When created, this eye must be in your line of sight.

When the spell's duration ends, you can spend 1 Focus Point as a free action to extend the duration for another hour, though as normal, it ends immediately during your next daily preparations.

WARPED TERRAIN — FOCUS 1

UNCOMMON ILLUSION VISUAL WIZARD

Cast ◆ to ◆◆◆ somatic, verbal

Range 60 feet; **Area** 5-foot burst or more

Duration 1 minute

You create illusory hazards that cover all surfaces in the area (typically the ground). Any creature moving through the illusion treats the squares as difficult terrain. A creature can attempt to disbelieve the effect as normal after using a Seek action or otherwise spending actions interacting with the illusion. If it successfully disbelieves, it ignores the effect for the remaining duration. For each additional action you use casting the spell, the burst's radius increases by 5 feet, to a maximum of 10 extra feet for 3 actions.

Heightened (4th) You can make the illusion appear in the air rather than on a surface, causing it to function as difficult terrain for flying creatures.

INTRODUCTION

ANCESTRIES & BACKGROUNDS

CLASSES

SKILLS

FEATS

EQUIPMENT

SPELLS

THE AGE OF LOST OMENS

PLAYING THE GAME

GAME MASTERING

CRAFTING & TREASURE

APPENDIX

RITUALS

A ritual is an esoteric and complex spell that anyone can cast. It takes much longer to cast a ritual than a normal spell, but rituals can have more powerful effects.

CASTING RITUALS

When you take charge of a ritual, you are its primary caster, and others assisting you are secondary casters. You can be a primary caster for a ritual even if you can't cast spells. You must know the ritual, and the ritual's spell level can be no higher than half your level rounded up. You must also have the required proficiency rank in the skill used for the ritual's primary check (see Checks below), and as the primary caster, you must attempt this skill check to determine the ritual's effects. The primary skill check determines the tradition.

Rituals do not require spell slots to cast. You can heighten a ritual up to half your level rounded up, decided when the ritual is initiated. A ritual always takes at least 1 hour to perform, and often longer. While a ritual is a downtime activity, it's possible—albeit risky—to perform a ritual during exploration with enough uninterrupted time. A ritual's casting time is usually listed in days. Each day of casting requires 8 hours of participation in the ritual from all casters, with breaks during multiday rituals to allow rest. One caster can continue a multiday ritual, usually with some light chanting or meditation, while the other casters rest. All rituals require material, somatic, and verbal components throughout their casting time.

LEARNING RITUALS

Learning a ritual does not count against any limits on spells in your spell repertoire or on any other normal spellcasting ability. Rituals are never common, though if you look hard, you can probably find someone who can perform an uncommon ritual for you. They may still be unwilling to teach it to you.

COST

A ritual's Cost entry lists valuable components required to cast the ritual. If a ritual doesn't have any such components, it won't have a Cost entry. The cost is consumed when you attempt the primary skill check. Costs are often presented as a base cost multiplied by the target's level and sometimes the spell's level. If the target's level is lower than 1, multiply the cost by 1 instead. Heightened versions that increase the base cost multiply it by the target's level or another value as appropriate. Most rituals that create permanent creatures, such as *create undead*, use costs based on the level of the spell, as presented on Table 7–1.

SECONDARY CASTERS

Many rituals need additional secondary casters, who also don't need to be able to cast spells. Unlike a primary caster,

TABLE 7–1: CREATURE CREATION RITUALS

Creature Level	Spell Level Required	Cost
–1 or 0	2	15 gp
1	2	60 gp
2	3	105 gp
3	3	180 gp
4	4	300 gp
5	4	480 gp
6	5	750 gp
7	5	1,080 gp
8	6	1,500 gp
9	6	2,100 gp
10	7	3,000 gp
11	7	4,200 gp
12	8	6,000 gp
13	8	9,000 gp
14	9	13,500 gp
15	9	19,500 gp
16	10	30,000 gp
17	10	45,000 gp

a secondary caster doesn't need a minimum level or skill proficiency. The Secondary Casters entry, if present, indicates the minimum number of secondary casters required.

CHECKS

At the ritual's culmination, you must attempt the skill check listed in the Primary Check entry to determine the ritual's outcome. Primary checks usually have a very hard DC for a level that's twice the ritual's spell level. As with other downtime activities, fortune and misfortune effects can't modify your checks for the ritual, nor can bonuses or penalties that aren't active throughout the process.

The GM can adjust the DCs of rituals, add or change primary or secondary checks, or even waive requirements to fit specific circumstances. For example, performing a ritual in a location where ley lines converge on the night of a new moon might make a normally difficult ritual drastically easier.

SECONDARY CHECKS

Often, a ritual requires secondary checks to represent aspects of its casting, usually with a standard DC for a level twice the ritual's spell level. A different secondary caster must attempt each secondary check. If there are more secondary casters than checks, the others don't attempt any.

Secondary casters attempt their checks before you attempt the primary check; no matter their results, the ritual proceeds to the primary check. Secondary checks affect the primary check depending on their results.

Critical Success You gain a +2 circumstance bonus to the primary check.

Success No bonus or penalty.

Failure You take a –4 circumstance penalty to the primary check.

Critical Failure As failure, and you reduce the degree of success of the primary skill check by one step.

EFFECT

A ritual's effect depends on the result of the primary check. If an effect lists a save DC, use your spell DC for the ritual's magic tradition (or 12 + your level + your highest mental ability modifier, if you don't have a spell DC).

RITUALS

The following rituals are just a small sample of the many that exist.

ANIMATE OBJECT   RITUAL 2

UNCOMMON | TRANSMUTATION

Cast 1 day; **Cost** rare oils, see Table 7–1; **Secondary Casters** 1
Primary Check Arcana (expert); **Secondary Checks** Crafting
Range 10 feet; **Target** 1 object

You transform the target into an animated object with a level up to that allowed by Table 7–1 and of a type corresponding to the object (so a broom would become an animated broom).

Critical Success The target becomes an animated object of the appropriate type. If it's at least 4 levels lower than you, you can make it a minion. This gives it the minion trait, meaning it can use 2 actions when you command it, and commanding it is a single action that has the auditory and concentrate traits. You can have a maximum of four minions under your control. If it doesn't become a minion, you can give it one simple command. It pursues that goal single-mindedly, ignoring any of your subsequent commands.

Success As critical success, except an animated object that doesn't become your minion stays in place and attacks anyone that attacks it or tries to steal or move it, rather than following your command.

Failure You fail to create the animated object.

Critical Failure You create the animated object, but it goes berserk and attempts to destroy you.

ATONE   RITUAL 4

UNCOMMON | ABJURATION

Cast 1 day; **Cost** rare incense and offerings worth a total value of 20 gp × the target's level; **Secondary Casters** 1, must be the ritual's target
Primary Check Nature or Religion (expert); **Secondary Checks** Nature or Religion (whichever is used for the primary check)
Range 10 feet; **Targets** another creature of up to 8th level who is a worshipper of the same deity or philosophy as you

You attempt to help a truly penitent creature atone for its misdeeds, typically actions contrary to your deity's alignment

TABLE 7-2: RITUALS BY LEVEL

Level	Ritual
2	Animate object
2	Consecrate
2	Create undead
2	Inveigle
3	Geas
4	Atone
4	Blight
4	Plant growth
5	Call spirit
5	Planar ally
5	Resurrect
6	Awaken animal
6	Commune
6	Commune with nature
6	Planar binding
6	Primal call
7	Legend lore
8	Control weather
8	Freedom
8	Imprisonment

or anathema to your deity. If the creature isn't truly penitent, the outcome is always a critical failure. This ritual uses Nature if the target is a druid, and Religion in all other cases.

Critical Success The creature receives absolution for its misdeeds, allowing it to regain standing with your deity. It returns to its previous alignment (if its alignment shifted) and regains any abilities it lost. Before the atonement is complete, the creature must perform a special quest or other task chosen by your deity, as befits its misdeeds. If completed during downtime, this task should take no less than 1 month. For 1 month, the target receives divine insight just before performing an act that would be anathema to your deity or contrary to your deity's alignment.

Success As critical success, but the creature gains no special insight regarding its subsequent actions.

Failure The creature does not receive absolution and must continue to meditate and redress its misdeeds. Any future *atone* rituals for the same misdeeds cost half as much and gain a +4 circumstance bonus to primary and secondary checks.

Critical Failure The creature offends your deity and is permanently cast out from the faith. The creature can't rejoin your religion without a more direct intervention.

Heightened (5th) Increase the maximum target level by 2 and the base cost by 20 gp.

AWAKEN ANIMAL   RITUAL 6

UNCOMMON | DIVINATION | MENTAL

Cast 1 day; **Cost** herbs, 1/5 the value on Table 7–1; **Secondary Casters** 3
Primary Check Nature (master); **Secondary Checks** Lore (any), Society, Survival
Range 10 feet; **Target** 1 animal of up to the level on Table 7–1

INTRODUCTION

ANCESTRIES & BACKGROUNDS

CLASSES

SKILLS

FEATS

EQUIPMENT

SPELLS

THE AGE OF LOST OMENS

PLAYING THE GAME

GAME MASTERING

CRAFTING & TREASURE

APPENDIX

You grant intelligence to the target, transforming it into a beast. If it was previously an animal companion or minion, it can no longer serve as one.

Critical Success The target's Intelligence, Wisdom, and Charisma modifiers each increase to +2 if they were lower, and it becomes helpful to you for awakening it.

Success The target's Intelligence, Wisdom, and Charisma modifiers increase to +0 if they were worse and it becomes friendly to you for awakening it.

Failure You fail to awaken the target.

Critical Failure You accidentally awaken the target with a pure bestial hatred toward you. The target's Intelligence, Wisdom, and Charisma modifiers increase to –2 if they were worse. It becomes hostile to you, attempting to destroy you.

BLIGHT   RITUAL 4

UNCOMMON   NECROMANCY   NEGATIVE   PLANT

Cast 1 day; **Secondary Casters** 1
Primary Check Nature (expert); **Secondary Checks** Survival
Area 1/2-mile-radius circle centered on you
Duration 1 year

You twist and stunt plants in the area, causing them to wither. In addition to other dangers from failing plant life, this decreases the crop yield for farms. If you cast this ritual in an area affected by *plant growth*, *blight* attempts to counteract *plant growth* instead of producing its usual effect.

Critical Success Completely spoil the crop yield in the area, or decrease the yield by half in an area with up to a 1-mile radius.

Success Decease the crop yield in the area by half.

Failure The ritual has no effect.

Critical Failure The flora in the area changes in an unexpected way, determined by the GM but generally as contradictory to your true desires as possible (for instance, enriching crops when you would prefer to blight them).

CALL SPIRIT   RITUAL 5

UNCOMMON   NECROMANCY

Cast 1 hour; **Cost** rare candles and incense worth a total value of 50 gp; **Secondary Casters** 1
Primary Check Occultism (expert) or Religion (expert); **Secondary Checks** Occultism or Religion (whichever isn't used for the primary check)
Duration up to 10 minutes

You tear the veil to the afterlife and call a spirit from its final resting place. You must call the spirit by name, and you must provide a connection to the spirit, such as a possession, a garment, or a piece of its corpse. A spirit unwilling to heed your call can attempt a Will save to avoid it; on a critical success, a trickster spirit Impersonates the spirit you meant to call. The DC of the Will save is 2 lower if you haven't met the spirit in life. Either way, the spirit appears as a wispy form of the creature you meant to call. Each minute of the duration, you can ask the spirit a question. It can answer how it pleases or even refuse to answer. If the spirit isn't in the afterlife (such as if it's an undead), all results other than critical failures use the failure effect.

Critical Success The spirit is particularly cooperative, and

even if it has strong reasons to deceive you, it takes a –2 circumstance penalty to its Deception checks.

Success You call the spirit.

Failure You fail to call a spirit.

Critical Failure One or more evil spirits appear and attack.

COMMUNE   RITUAL 6

UNCOMMON   DIVINATION   PREDICTION

Cast 1 day; **Cost** rare incense worth a total value of 150 gp; **Secondary Casters** 1
Primary Check Occultism (master) or Religion (master); **Secondary Checks** Occultism or Religion (whichever is used for the primary check)
Duration up to 10 minutes

You call upon an unknown planar entity to answer questions; this is a servitor of your deity if you have one and use Religion. You can ask up to seven questions that could be answered with "Yes" or "No." The entity is likely to know answers related to its purview; a servitor of Gozreh would likely know about unnatural weather patterns and a servitor of Desna would likely know someone's travel route. The entity answers with one word answers such as "Yes," "No," "Likely," and "Unknown," though its answers always reflect its own agenda and could be deceptive.

Critical Success You contact a more powerful entity aligned strongly with your interests, possibly even your deity. The entity won't attempt to deceive you, though it still might not know the answers. When it's important to provide clarity, the entity will answer your questions with up to five words, such as "If you leave immediately" or "That was true once."

Success You can ask your questions and receive answers.

Failure You fail to contact a planar entity.

Critical Failure You are exposed to the enormity of the cosmos and are stupefied 4 for 1 week (can't remove by any means).

COMMUNE WITH NATURE   RITUAL 6

UNCOMMON   DIVINATION   PREDICTION

Cast 1 day; **Cost** rare incense worth a total value of 60 gp; **Secondary Casters** 1
Primary Check Nature (master); **Secondary Checks** Nature
Duration up to 10 minutes

As *commune*, except you contact the primal spirits of nature, which know about animals, beasts, fey, plants, topography, and natural resources within a 3-mile radius of the ritual's location.

CONSECRATE   RITUAL 2

UNCOMMON   CONSECRATION   EVOCATION

Cast 3 days; **Cost** rare incense and offerings worth a total value of 20 gp × the spell level; **Secondary Casters** 2, must be worshippers of your religion
Primary Check Religion; **Secondary Checks** Crafting, Performance
Range 40 feet; **Area** 40-foot-radius burst around an immobile altar, shrine, or fixture of your deity
Duration 1 year

You consecrate a site to your deity, chanting praises and

creating a sacred space. While within the area, worshippers of your deity gain a +1 status bonus to attack rolls, skill checks, saving throws, and Perception checks, and creatures anathema to your deity (such as undead for Pharasma or Sarenrae) take a −1 status penalty to those checks. Attacks made by worshippers of your deity within the area deal 1 damage of one of your deity's alignment types (your choice); if your deity is true neutral, you don't gain this benefit.

Critical Success The consecration succeeds, and it either lasts for 10 years instead of 1 or covers an area with twice the radius. Occasionally, with your deity's favor, this might produce an even more amazing effect, such as a permanently consecrated area or the effect covering an entire cathedral.

Success The consecration succeeds.

Failure The consecration fails.

Critical Failure The consecration fails spectacularly and angers your deity, who sends a sign of displeasure. For at least 1 year, further attempts to consecrate the site fail.

Heightened (7th) The consecrated area also gains the effects of the *dimensional lock* spell, but the effect doesn't attempt to counteract teleportation by worshippers of your deity. The cost increases to 200 gp × the spell level.

CONTROL WEATHER   RITUAL 8

UNCOMMON   EVOCATION

Cast 1 day; **Secondary Casters** 1
Primary Check Nature (master); **Secondary Checks** Survival
Area 2-mile-radius circle centered on you
Duration 4d12 hours

You alter the weather, making it calm and normal for the season or choosing up to two effects based on the season:

- **Spring** drizzle, heat, hurricane, sleet, thunderstorm, tornado
- **Summer** drizzle, downpour, extreme heat, hail, heat
- **Autumn** cold weather, fog, mild heat, sleet
- **Winter** blizzard, mild cold, extreme cold, thaw

You can't specifically control the manifestations, such as the exact path of a tornado or the targets of lightning strikes.

Critical Success You change the weather as desired and can affect a larger area (up to a 5-mile-radius circle), or a longer duration (any number of additional d12 hours, up to 16d12).

Success You change the weather as desired.

Failure You fail to change the weather as desired.

Critical Failure The weather changes in an unanticipated way, determined by the GM but generally as contradictory to your true desires as possible (for instance, a terrible storm emerges when you would prefer good weather).

Heightened (9th) You can create unseasonable weather and contradictory weather effects, such as extreme cold and a hurricane. You can make the weather calm and normal weather for a different season or choose weather effects from any season's list.

CREATE UNDEAD   RITUAL 2

UNCOMMON   EVIL   NECROMANCY

Cast 1 day; **Cost** black onyx, see Table 7–1; **Secondary Casters** 1

Primary Check Arcana (expert), Occultism (expert), or Religion (expert); **Secondary Checks** Religion
Range 10 feet; **Target** 1 dead creature

You transform the target into an undead creature with a level up to that allowed in Table 7–1. There are many versions of this ritual, each specific to a particular type of undead (one ritual for all zombies, one for skeletons, one for ghouls, and so on), and the rituals that create rare undead are also rare. Some forms of undead, such as liches, form using their own unique methods and can't be created with a version of *create undead*.

Critical Success The target becomes an undead creature of the appropriate type. If it's at least 4 levels lower than you, you can make it a minion. This gives it the minion trait, meaning it can use 2 actions when you command it, and commanding it is a single action that has the auditory and concentrate traits. You can have a maximum of four minions under your control. If it's intelligent and doesn't become a minion, the undead is helpful to you for awakening it, though it's still a horrid and evil creature. If it's unintelligent and doesn't become a minion, you can give it one simple command. It pursues that goal single-mindedly, ignoring any of your subsequent commands.

Success As critical success, except an intelligent undead that doesn't become your minion is only friendly to you, and an unintelligent undead that doesn't become your minion leaves you alone unless you attack it. It marauds the local area rather than following your command.

Failure You fail to create the undead.

Critical Failure You create the undead, but its soul, tortured by your foul necromancy, is full of nothing but hatred for you. It attempts to destroy you.

FREEDOM   RITUAL 8

UNCOMMON   ABJURATION

Cast 1 day; **Cost** valuable oils and objects associated with the target worth a total value of 100 gp × the spell level × the target's level; **Secondary Casters** 2
Primary Check Arcana (legendary) or Occultism (legendary); **Secondary Checks** Society
Range see text; **Target** 1 creature

You perform a ritual to free a creature imprisoned, petrified, or otherwise put into stasis by any magical effects from all such effects, even effects like *imprisonment* that don't have a duration, as long as *freedom*'s spell level is equal to or higher than the effect's spell level. To perform the ritual, you must be within 10 feet of the target, or within 10 feet of the place where the target was imprisoned (in the case of effects that trap the creature in an unreachable prison, like the oubliette form of *imprisonment*). You must know the name of the creature and details of its background; if the creature is not a close associate, a failure or critical failure on a secondary Society check reduces even a critical success on the primary check to a failure.

Critical Success You free the target from all magical effects imprisoning it, petrifying it, or putting it into stasis. It gains a +1 status bonus to saving throws to resist those same magical effects for 1 week.

Success You free the target from all magical effects imprisoning it, petrifying it, or putting it into stasis.

Failure You fail to free the target.

Critical Failure The magical effects imprisoning the target, petrifying the target, or putting it into stasis affect you and all secondary casters.

GEAS — RITUAL 3

UNCOMMON | CURSE | ENCHANTMENT | MENTAL

Cast 1 day; **Secondary Casters** 1

Primary Check Arcana (expert), Occultism (expert), or Religion (expert); **Secondary Checks** Society or Legal Lore

Range 10 feet; **Target** 1 creature of a level no greater than double the *geas* ritual's level

Duration see text

You enforce a magic rule on a willing target, forcing it to either perform or refrain from carrying out a certain act. A *geas* to perform an act is usually conditional, such as, "Always offer hospitality to strangers seeking a place to stay." An unconditional *geas* to perform a certain act doesn't require the target to perform that act exclusively, though it must prioritize the task above all leisurely pursuits. The most common *geas* to refrain from carrying out an act is a specification to avoid violating a contract. In those cases, the secondary caster usually takes charge of making sure the wording of the contract is attuned correctly with the ritual's magic. Because the target is willing, *geas* can have a duration that lasts for as long as the target agrees to. If the target is unable to fulfill the *geas*, it becomes sickened 1, and the sickened condition increases by 1 for each consecutive day it is prevented from following the *geas*, to a maximum of sickened 4. The sickened condition ends immediately when it follows the *geas* again; it can't remove the sickened condition in any other way. Only powerful magic such as a *wish* spell can remove the effects of *geas* from a willing target.

Critical Success The *geas* succeeds, and the target receives a +1 status bonus to skill checks that directly uphold the geas (at the GM's discretion).

Success The *geas* succeeds.

Failure The *geas* fails.

Critical Failure The *geas* fails, and you are instead affected by the *geas* you were attempting to place on the target. You are considered an unwilling target, so the *geas* can be counteracted with a *remove curse* spell.

Heightened (5th) You can use *geas* on an unwilling creature; it can attempt a Will save to negate the effect. If the target fails this Will save, the *geas* lasts up to 1 week. A *remove curse* spell can counteract a *geas* on an unwilling creature, in addition to powerful magic such as a *wish* spell. A clever unwilling creature can subvert the *geas* by contriving situations that prevent it from complying, but in that case it becomes sickened (as described above).

Heightened (7th) As 5th level, but the *geas* lasts for up to 1 year on an unwilling creature.

Heightened (9th) As 5th level, but the *geas* lasts for a duration you choose (even unlimited) on an unwilling creature.

IMPRISONMENT — RITUAL 8

UNCOMMON | EVOCATION

Cast 1 day; **Cost** reagents to construct the magical prison worth a total value of 800 gp × the target's level; **Secondary Casters** 6

Primary Check Arcana (legendary) or Occultism (legendary); **Secondary Checks** Crafting, Society

Range 10 feet; **Target** 1 creature of up to 16th level

You perform a ritual to imprison a creature in one of several forms. While some versions of this ritual offer all of the forms, others include only a single form or only a few of them. Whichever form you use, the effect can't be counteracted, though it can be ended by *freedom*. Some forms of *imprisonment* can be ended by other means. Because the ritual requires the target to remain within 10 feet at all times, it typically requires you to subdue the target first.

- **Chains** You bind the creature with chains, rendering it unable to use any actions other than to speak. Other creatures that attempt to approach, harm the chains, or free the trapped creature in any way must succeed at a Will save or be unable to do so forever. The chains have Hardness equal to 5 × the *imprisonment* ritual's spell level, and double that many Hit Points. Destroying the chains frees the target.
- **Prison** You render the creature completely unable to leave a particular confined area or structure of your choice, such as a jail cell or sealed cave. The magic also prevents the creature from damaging its prison, either directly or indirectly, to break free. If the creature's prison is entirely destroyed by some external force, the creature is freed, though for some larger or natural prisons, this might be unfeasible.
- **Slumber (sleep effect)** You put the creature into an eternal sleep. It ceases aging and doesn't require food or drink. A single sincere physical display of affection from a creature who genuinely loves the target—whether romantically, filially, or otherwise—frees it from the slumber. This form of imprisonment is also enchantment magic.
- **Temporal Stasis** You send the creature into a state of suspended animation outside the flow of time. The creature doesn't grow older and can't be affected by any effect from within the normal timestream. While casting this ritual, you can optionally name any amount of time for the stasis; after this duration elapses, the stasis ends. Unlike other forms of *imprisonment*, temporal stasis can be counteracted by a *dispel magic* or *haste* spell. This form of imprisonment is also transmutation magic.
- **Object (9th level or higher)** You either shrink the creature to an inch in height or transform it into an insubstantial form whose body trails away into wisps below its head. Either way, you trap it inside a gem, jar, bottle, lamp, or similar container. The creature ceases aging and doesn't require food or drink. The creature is still aware of its

surroundings and can move within the container and speak, but it can't use any other actions. Destroying the container kills the target rather than freeing it. This form of *imprisonment* is also transmutation magic.

- **Oubliette (10th level only)** You entomb the target in a state of suspended animation deep beneath the surface of the ground and out of tune with reality so that it can't be reached by any means. You also prevent divinations from revealing the location where the *imprisonment* occurred. Powerful magic such as *wish* can reveal the location of the *imprisonment*, but even such magic can't free the target from the oubliette; only a 10th-level *freedom* ritual can do so.

Critical Success You imprison the target. You can either use a form of *imprisonment* that usually requires 1 additional spell level, or give any creatures trying to use a *freedom* ritual to rescue the target a –2 circumstance penalty to checks associated with that ritual.

Success You imprison the target.

Failure You fail to imprison the target.

Critical Failure You imprison yourself and the secondary casters in the same way you intended to imprison the target.

Heightened (9th) You can use the object form of *imprisonment* in addition to the other options, and you can target a creature of up to 18th level. The base cost increases to 2,000 gp.

Heightened (10th) You can use the object and oubliette forms of *imprisonment* in addition to the other options, and you can target a creature of up to 20th level. The base cost increases to 6,000 gp.

INVEIGLE   RITUAL 2

UNCOMMON   ENCHANTMENT   MENTAL

Cast 1 day; **Cost** rare oils worth a total value of 10 gp × the target's level

Primary Check Arcana (expert), Occultism (expert), or Religion (expert)

Range 10 feet; **Target** 1 creature of a level no greater than double the *inveigle* ritual's level

Duration 1 year or until dismissed

You win over the target's mind, causing it to see you as a close and trusted friend and look upon your every suggestion as reasonable. The target is helpful toward you, so it will go out of its way to help you. As with any other helpful creature, there are limits to what you can ask of it. If you ever ask the target to do something completely against its nature or needlessly harmful to the target or its interests, not only does it refuse, but it also can attempt a Will save to end the effect early. Because of the casting time and range, it's generally difficult to cast this ritual unless the target is willing (perhaps convinced the ritual will have some other effect) or restrained. If the creature is unwilling to accept the ritual, it can attempt a Will save to negate the effect.

Critical Success The ritual succeeds and the target takes a –4 status penalty to Will saves to end the effect.

Success The ritual succeeds.

Failure The ritual fails.

Critical Failure The ritual fails and the target instead hates you, becoming hostile to you for the duration.

Heightened (6th) You can use *inveigle* on a creature up to 1 mile away throughout the casting, as long as you have a lock of hair, a drop of blood, or some other piece of the creature's body, which you mix into the oils used in the cost. The base cost increases to 100 gp. The duration is shorter than normal, based on how large a piece of the creature's body you use. Blood, hair, scales, and the like cause the ritual to last 1 week, while a hand or other substantial body part causes the ritual to last 1 month.

LEGEND LORE   RITUAL 7

UNCOMMON   DIVINATION

Cast 1 day; **Cost** rare incense worth a total value of 300 gp; **Secondary Casters** 2

Primary Check Occultism (master); **Secondary Checks** Performance, Society

You attempt to learn useful legends about a particular subject, which must be an important person, place, or thing. If the subject is present, increase the degree of success of your primary skill check by one step. If you have only vague information about the subject before attempting the ritual, decrease the degree of success of your primary skill check by one step. These modifiers cancel each other out if you have a subject present with little to no baseline information.

Critical Success You recite legends, tales, and lore about the subject over the course of an hour after the ritual ends. The information is mostly coherent, emphasizing more accurate or useful legends over those exaggerated over time.

Success You recite mysterious legends, tales, and lore about the subject over the course of an hour after the ritual ends. These provide useful information for further inquiry but are generally incomplete or enigmatic. As is the nature of legends, you are likely to learn multiple contradictory versions.

Failure You fail to learn any useful legends.

Critical Failure Your mind becomes lost in the past. You can't sense or respond to anything in the present for 1 week except to perform necessities like breathing and sleeping. When you return, however, you can retrain one of your skills into a Lore based on the knowledge of the past you were uncontrollably viewing, as if you had spent 1 week retraining.

PLANAR ALLY   RITUAL 5

UNCOMMON   CONJURATION

Cast 1 day; **Cost** rare incense and offerings worth a total value of 2 gp × the spell level × the target's level; **Secondary Casters** 2, must share your religion

Primary Check Religion (expert); **Secondary Checks** Diplomacy

Duration see text

You call upon your deity to grant you aid in the form of a divine servitor of your deity's choice of a level no greater than double *planar ally*'s spell level. While performing this ritual, the secondary casters entreat your deity, explaining what sort of assistance you need and why you need it; if the task is incredibly fitting to your deity, the GM can grant a circumstance bonus to the secondary Diplomacy check or rule that the check

INTRODUCTION

ANCESTRIES & BACKGROUNDS

CLASSES

SKILLS

FEATS

EQUIPMENT

SPELLS

THE AGE OF LOST OMENS

PLAYING THE GAME

GAME MASTERING

CRAFTING & TREASURE

APPENDIX

is automatically a critical success. If the ritual succeeds, you must offer the servitor payment depending on factors such as the duration and danger of the task. Payment always costs at least as much as a consumable item of the creature's level, even for a short and simple task, and it often costs as much as a permanent magic item of the creature's level to persuade a creature to fight alongside you. If you use the ritual without good reason, the result is automatically a critical failure.

Critical Success Your deity sends a servitor, and the servitor's payment costs only half as much as normal. If you ask for a particular servitor by name, your deity is likely to send that servitor unless the servitor is busy.

Success Your deity sends a servitor.

Failure Your deity does not send a servitor.

Critical Failure Your deity is offended and sends a sign of displeasure or possibly even a servitor to scold or attack you, depending on your deity's nature. You must conduct an *atone* ritual to regain your former standing with your deity.

PLANAR BINDING   RITUAL 6

UNCOMMON   ABJURATION   CONJURATION

Cast 1 day; **Cost** warding diagram ingredients worth a total value of 2 gp × the spell level × the target's level; **Secondary Casters** 4

Primary Check Arcana (master) or Occultism (master); **Secondary Checks** Crafting; Diplomacy or Intimidation; Arcana or Occultism (whichever isn't used for the primary check)

Range interplanar; **Targets** 1 extraplanar creature
Duration varies

You call forth an extraplanar creature of a level no greater than double that of the *planar binding* ritual's level and attempt to bargain with it. The secondary caster attempting the Crafting check creates a warding diagram to prevent the extraplanar creature from attacking or leaving during the bargain; if that caster fails or critically fails, then instead of the usual effects of a failure or critical failure of the secondary skill check, the extraplanar creature can attack or leave instead of negotiate. You can also leave out this step, removing the need for a Crafting check, with the same result (if you're summoning a good outsider you trust, for example). The creature can also attack or leave if you use any hostile action against it or if the warding diagram breaks. Once the diagram is complete, you and the secondary casters each take your places at specific points at the diagram's edge where power concentrates.

You conjure the extraplanar creature within your wards and negotiate a deal with it, generally to perform a task for you in exchange for payment. A creature that doesn't wish to negotiate at all can attempt a Will save to stay on its home plane. Most good and neutral extraplanar creatures feel that they have something better to do than cater to the whims of mortals and require a significant gift, especially if your task poses significant risks. Evil extraplanar creatures are more likely to accept a bargain for a lower cost as long as it allows them to wreak havoc on the Material Plane or inflict evil upon the world along the way. Monetary prices usually range from the cost of a consumable item of the creature's level for a short and simple task to a permanent magic item of the creature's level or more to persuade the creature to fight alongside you. However, some extraplanar creatures may want payments other than money, such as permission to cast a *geas* on you to fulfill an unspecified later favor or obtain ownership of your soul via an infernal contract. If you can't come to an agreement in a reasonable length of time after you've made your case, the extraplanar creature can return from whence it came at any time.

Critical Success You call the extraplanar creature and bind it in the wards for up to a full day before it returns home, potentially allowing you to negotiate a better deal by threatening to leave it in the wards for the full day.

Success You call the extraplanar creature.

Failure You fail to call the extraplanar creature.

Critical Failure You call something dark and horrible, unbound by your wards, and it immediately attempts to destroy you.

PLANT GROWTH   RITUAL 4

UNCOMMON NECROMANCY PLANT POSITIVE

Cast 1 day; **Secondary Casters** 1

Primary Check Nature (expert); **Secondary Checks** Farming Lore or Survival

Area 1/2-mile-radius circle centered on you

Duration 1 year

You cause the plants within the area to be healthier and more fruitful. In addition to other benefits of healthy plants, this increases the crop yield for farms, depending on your success. If you cast it in the area of a *blight*, *plant growth* attempts to counteract the *blight* instead of producing its usual effect.

Critical Success Double the crop yield in the area, or increase the area to a 1-mile radius.

Success Increase the crop yield in the area by one-third.

Failure The ritual has no effect.

Critical Failure The flora in the area changes in an unanticipated way, determined by the GM but generally as contradictory to your true desires as possible (for instance, blighting crops when you would prefer to enrich them).

PRIMAL CALL   RITUAL 6

UNCOMMON ABJURATION CONJURATION

Cast 1 day; **Cost** faerie circle ingredients worth a total value of 1 gp × the spell level × the target's level; **Secondary Casters** 4

Primary Check Nature (master); **Secondary Checks** Crafting, Diplomacy, Survival

Range 100 miles; **Targets** 1 animal, beast, fey, fungus, or plant

Duration see text

This functions as *planar ally* except you craft a faerie circle and call an animal, beast, fey, fungus, or plant from within 100 miles.

RESURRECT   RITUAL 5

UNCOMMON HEALING NECROMANCY

Cast 1 day; **Cost** diamonds worth a total value of 75 gp × the target's level; **Secondary Casters** 2

Primary Check Religion (expert); **Secondary Checks** Medicine, Society

Range 10 feet; **Targets** 1 dead creature of up to 10th level

You attempt to call forth the target's soul and return it to its body. This requires the target's body to be present and relatively intact. The target must have died within the past year. If Pharasma has decided that the target's time has come or the target doesn't wish to return, this ritual automatically fails, but you discover this after the successful Religion check and can end the ritual without paying the cost.

Critical Success You resurrect the target. They return to life with full Hit Points and the same spells prepared and points in their pools they had when they died, and still suffering from any long-term debilitations of the old body. The target meets an agent of their deity during the resurrection who inspires them, granting them a +1 status bonus to attack rolls, Perception, saving throws, and skill checks for 1 week. The target is also permanently changed in some way by their time in the afterlife, such as gaining a slight personality shift, a streak of white in the hair, or a strange new birthmark.

Success As critical success, except the target returns to life with 1 Hit Point and no spells prepared or points in any pools, and still is affected by any long-term debilitations of the old body. Instead of inspiring them, the character's time in the Boneyard has left them temporarily debilitated. The target is clumsy 1, drained 1, and enfeebled 1 for 1 week; these conditions can't be removed or reduced by any means until the week has passed.

Failure Your attempt is unsuccessful.

Critical Failure Something goes horribly wrong—an evil spirit possesses the body, the body transforms into a special kind of undead, or some worse fate befalls the target.

Heightened (6th) You can resurrect a target of up to 12th level, and the base cost is 125 gp.

Heightened (7th) You can use *resurrect* even with only a small portion of the body; the ritual creates a new body on a success or critical success. The target must have died within the past decade. The ritual requires four secondary casters, each of whom must be at least half the target's level. The target can be up to 14th level, and the base cost is 200 gp.

Heightened (8th) As 7th level, but the target can be up to 16th level and the base cost is 300 gp.

Heightened (9th) You can use *resurrect* even without the body as long as you know the target's name and have touched a portion of its body at any time. The target must have died within the past century, and it doesn't gain the negative conditions on a success. The ritual requires eight secondary casters, each of whom must be at least half the target's level. The target can be up to 18th level, and the base cost is 600 gp.

Heightened (10th) As 9th level, except it doesn't matter how long ago the target died. The ritual requires 16 secondary casters, each of whom must be at least half the target's level. The target can be up to 20th level, and the ritual's base cost is 1,000 gp.

INTRODUCTION
ANCESTRIES & BACKGROUNDS
CLASSES
SKILLS
FEATS
EQUIPMENT
SPELLS
THE AGE OF LOST OMENS
PLAYING THE GAME
GAME MASTERING
CRAFTING & TREASURE
APPENDIX

IRRISEN

REALM OF THE
MAMMOTH LANDS

SARKORIS SCAR

MENDEV

LAKE OF MISTS
AND VEILS

LANDS OF THE
LINNORM KINGS

SAGA LANDS

KODOR MOUNTAINS

NUMERIA

BREVOY

NEW THASSILON

HOLD OF
BELKZEN

USTALAV

**BROKEN
LANDS**

VARISIA

**EYE OF
DREAD**

RIVER KINGDOMS

STEAMING SEA

RAZMIRAN

MINDSPIN
MOUNTAINS

NIRMATHAS

ISLE OF
TERROR

KYONIN

GALT

LAKE
ENCARTHAN

HERMEA

NIDAL

OPRAK

MOLTHUNE

DRUMA

TANGLEBRIAR

**SHINING
KINGDOMS**

**HIGH
SEAS**

RAVOUNEL

MENADOR MOUNTAINS

ISGER

FIVE KINGS
MOUNTAINS

VERDURAN
FOREST

OLD CHELIAX

CHELIAX

ANDORAN

TALDOR

ISLE OF KORTOS

ARCADIAN OCEAN

THE INNER SEA

ABSALOM

RAHADOUM

THUVIA

GOLDEN ROAD

OSIRION

QADIRA

**MEDIOGALTI
ISLAND**

BARRIER WALL

EYE OF ABENDEGO

SODDEN LANDS

KATAPESH

KIBWE

NEX

JALMERAY

SHACKLES

USARO

NANTAMBU

MANA WASTES

**MWANGI
EXPANSE**

SHATTERED
RIDGE

BLOODCOVE

**IMPOSSIBLE
LANDS**

GEB

SENGHOR

OBARI OCEAN

FEVER SEA

VIDRIAN

MZALI

CHAPTER 8:
THE AGE OF LOST OMENS

Ten thousand years ago, the world of Golarion came close to ending. Earthfall, as this extinction-level event came to be known, saw the world pummeled by a shower of falling stars that sank continents, hollowed out new seas, and destroyed civilizations. It took centuries for the world to recover, and centuries more for society to rebuild, but recover it did.

Dwarves ascended to the surface from the underground reaches of the Darklands in their legendary Quest for Sky, elves returned from the neighboring planet of Castrovel via a network of portals to reclaim their lands and traditions, and gnomes from the mysterious First World sought shelter from a now-forgotten terror. Survivors from other ancestries who had sheltered through the terror and destruction of Earthfall emerged during the Age of Darkness to reclaim their ancestral lands, from scrappy goblin tribes with a knack for surviving despite all odds against them to industrious halflings who emerged from the ruins to found societies of their own.

But humanity made the most astounding recovery. Less than 2,000 years after the near-extinction from Earthfall, the Age of Destiny saw the rise of many new human empires throughout the world. Humanity built wondrous structures, and its schools relearned magic that had been thought lost. Among these human nations walked a man named Aroden—an immortal survivor of the devastation of Earthfall. Aroden had long since cultivated a following of loyal subjects who regarded him with awe, for immortality was but one of the wonders he'd achieved. Greatest among these was his discovery of a shard of potent magic known today as the *Starstone*, a fragment from the stars that fell during Earthfall, which had lodged at the bottom of the Inner Sea. Contact with this alien artifact assailed Aroden with phantasmagoric visions, subjected him to a series of deadly martial trials, and posed exhausting moral quandaries that challenged his limits more than any of the arduous experiences he had yet endured. He emerged from this test a living god, and his first divine act was to raise the *Starstone* and the mass of land on which it had lain from the bottom of the sea to form the Isle of Kortos—also known as Starstone Isle—where he then established the city of Absalom.

In the centuries to follow, Absalom grew into one of the largest cities in the world, and Aroden's legacy grew alongside it. As the millennia passed, his attentions increasingly turned away from the concerns of the Inner Sea's inhabitants to otherworldly matters beyond mortal ken, but prophecy spoke of a time when he would return to Golarion and lead humanity triumphantly into an Age of Glory. As the time of Aroden's return drew near, entire nations undertook monumental preparations to welcome him back to Golarion.

But instead, Aroden died, and with him the reliability of prophecy as well. Golarion was wracked by storms, war, and supernatural devastation as the god's death marked the beginning of a new age—a time of uncertainty, but also a time of opportunity. This is the Age of Lost Omens, an age in need of heroes like never before.

8

INTRODUCTION

ANCESTRIES & BACKGROUNDS

CLASSES

SKILLS

FEATS

EQUIPMENT

SPELLS

THE AGE OF LOST OMENS

PLAYING THE GAME

GAME MASTERING

CRAFTING & TREASURE

APPENDIX

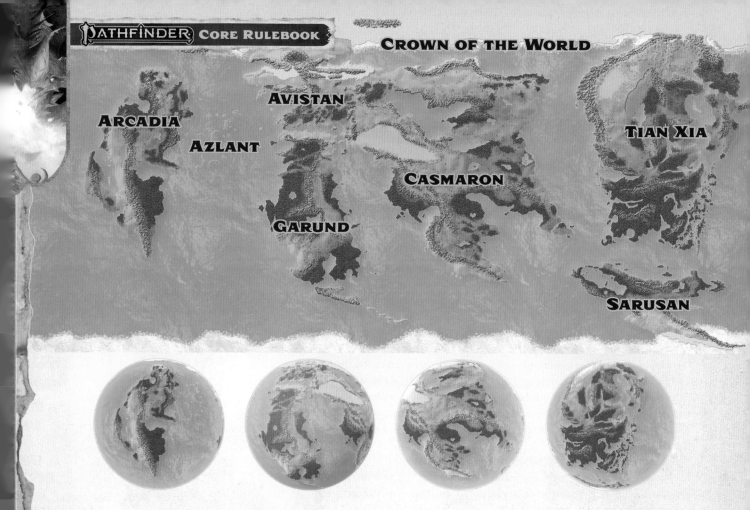

CROWN OF THE WORLD

AVISTAN

ARCADIA

AZLANT

TIAN XIA

CASMARON

GARUND

SARUSAN

BEYOND THE INNER SEA

The Inner Sea region consists of the continent of Avistan and the northern portion of the continent of Garund, but it is only one part of a much larger world. Garund itself extends further south, and its southern reaches are home to several unique ancestries and cultures. As one travels east from the Inner Sea, the vast expanse of the continent of Casmaron stretches beyond the horizon. With the immense inland Castrovin Sea at its heart, Casmaron is the largest of Golarion's continents and home to some of its oldest and most successful empires. Farther east of Casmaron lies the continent of Tian Xia, a region often called the Dragon Empires. The northern section of Tian Xia connects to Golarion's northernmost continent, a frozen reach known as the Crown of the World. This continent forms a bridge between Tian Xia and Avistan over the north pole. South of Tian Xia lies the mysterious continent of Sarusan, of which little is known due to the powerful storms and vexing currents that shroud its shores. Heading west from the Inner Sea region, sailors encounter the shattered remnants of lost Azlant, a ruined continent that hosted one of humanity's first empires until it was destroyed during Earthfall. Sailing farther west from these ruins eventually leads to the shores of Arcadia, a land with unusual magical traditions and powerful nations of its own. And beneath all of these lands, carved into the planet's very crust, lie the twisting tunnels of the tripartite underground realm known collectively as the Darklands, which houses great

horrors and dangers but equally great opportunities for triumph and treasure.

In addition, Golarion is but one of 11 worlds that orbit its sun. To the vast majority of the planet's denizens, the other 11 worlds are little more than points of light in the sky, but these worlds are not so distant as one might expect. The planets of Akiton and Castrovel are Golarion's closest neighbors. Travelers from both have visited and in some cases settled on Golarion, most notably elves, who originally hail from Castrovel. Even the farthest planet, remote Aucturn, has influenced Golarion, with its alien inhabitants exerting a sinister touch on the world that recently put the entire planet in peril. The wise thus do not discount the dangers and wonders that dwell on other planets of Golarion's solar system.

THE GREAT BEYOND

Countless planets lie beyond Golarion's solar system, but even these myriad worlds of the universe, known as the Material Plane, are but a fragment compared to what lies in the multiverse beyond. Other planes of existence and strange dimensions wrap this reality in a series of layered, nested spheres, known collectively as the Great Beyond. This model of reality is as much a metaphor for concepts that mortal minds have difficulty grasping as a physical description, for within the Great Beyond, anything is possible.

INNER SPHERE

The core of the multiverse is the Inner Sphere. Here, the vast expanse of the Material Plane and its countless worlds can be found. The Elemental Planes surround the Material Plane like layered shells, with the Plane of Air on the inside, transitioning to the Plane of Water, then to the Plane of Earth, and finally to the Plane of Fire, in something of a reversal of order in which these elements most often appear on habitable planets. The planes of Positive and Negative Energy are also within the Inner Sphere, their opposing nodes of life and death, creation and destruction, light and dark forming the start and the end of all existence.

OUTER SPHERE

The scope of reality within the Outer Sphere is difficult to grasp. Here the gods dwell and the souls of the dead gather to be judged by the goddess of the dead, Pharasma, atop the spire in the realm that is her Boneyard. Anything is possible in the Outer Sphere, and its realms are as much manifestations of philosophies and belief as anything else. From the towering mountain of Heaven to the endless gulfs of the demon-held Abyss, be it the agonizing pit of Hell or the boundless wonders of Elysium, all of reality is represented within the Outer Sphere. Over time this reality erodes away and is recycled back into the raw material of life within the Positive Energy Plane.

OTHER PLANES AND DIMENSIONS

Some planes exist in the same physical or metaphysical space as others, overlapping these other planes like overlays of reality. They include the ghost world of the Ethereal Plane, which overlays the Inner Sphere; the dizzying vastness of the Astral Plane, which overlays almost all reality and fills the seemingly endless gulf between the Inner Sphere and the Outer Sphere; and the fey-haunted First World and the sinister Shadow Plane, which each overlay the Material Plane. Stranger reaches of the Great Beyond exist as well; some, such as the Dreamlands, are visited often (if accidentally), while others, such as the enigmatic Dimension of Time, are visited rarely, if ever. In all cases these dimensions cannot be accessed by normal means, and each has their own method of entry and exit.

THE INNER SEA REGION

Although infinite opportunities for adventure await on other continents, worlds, and planes, the Inner Sea region is the focus of the Pathfinder campaign setting. With dozens of nations, empires, frontiers, and wildlands, this region presents a huge range of opportunities for heroism and villainy, exploration and adventure!

The following pages break down the Inner Sea region into 10 separate regions, each with its own themes. Only a brief overview of each region is presented here—enough to establish the setting and whet the imagination. If you're interested in exploring Golarion and the Inner Sea region more, see the Pathfinder World Guide, Pathfinder Adventures, and Pathfinder Adventure Path volumes. Adventure paths present not only in-depth material about the region, but also full-length campaigns whose adventures bring a brand-new group of heroes all the way to the height of power!

The year in the Inner Sea region is 4719 Absalom Reckoning (AR). As the calendar advances in the real world, time also progresses for Golarion. The *Pathfinder Core Rulebook* was first published in the year 2019, with the Inner Sea region's corresponding year ending in the same two final digits. Golarion's history is expansive, but two of the most significant events to shape the world occurred in −5293 AR, when Earthfall nearly brought an end to the world, and in 4606 AR, when Aroden, the god of humanity, died, and prophecies the world over began to fail, beginning the Age of Lost Omens.

The map on page 416 depicts the Inner Sea region, further subdivided into the 10 subregions explored on the following pages. The borders of these regions are thematic rather than political. For an in-depth exploration of the Inner Sea region and its dozens of nations and wildlands, see the *Pathfinder Lost Omens World Guide*.

TIME

Like Earth, Golarion spins on its axis once roughly every 24 hours. A week has 7 days and a year has 52 weeks. To keep the calendar synchronized with the astronomical year, an extra leap day is tacked on to the second month of the year every 4 years.

MONTHS AND DAYS

The names of the months of the year are as follows in the Inner Sea region:

Abadius (January)
Calistril (February)
Pharast (March)
Gozran (April)
Desnus (May)
Sarenith (June)
Erastus (July)
Arodus (August)
Rova (September)
Lamashan (October)
Neth (November)
Kuthona (December)

The names of the days are as follows:

Moonday (Monday)
Toilday (Tuesday)
Wealday (Wednesday)
Oathday (Thursday)
Fireday (Friday)
Starday (Saturday)
Sunday (Sunday)

ABSALOM AND STARSTONE ISLE

At the heart of the Inner Sea stands the Isle of Kortos, raised from the waters thousands of years ago as Aroden's first deific act. This amazing feat marks the dawn of the Age of Enthronement and the first year of the Absalom Reckoning calendar. The city of Absalom itself, the largest in the Inner Sea region, sprawls on the southern shore of this isle, and at the city's heart stands the legendary Starstone Cathedral. Within the walls of this structure, the *Starstone* ever waits to test its next supplicants—the few mortals who pass this mystic test become gods themselves. This has made Absalom an oft-besieged metropolis, but in its nearly 5,000 years, it has never once fallen.

Absalom, called by many the City at the Center of the World, boasts a population of over 300,000, and its culture is a true melting pot in both ancestry and belief. Even the city's architecture reflects this, as one might expect of a settlement of its age. From the towering and majestic temples of the Ascendant Court to the close-packed shops and guildhalls of the Petal District and the sagging shanties in the Puddles, Absalom's neighborhoods never fail to present a memorable skyline. Many world-reaching organizations were born in Absalom, notably the Pathfinder Society (page 436).

The Isle of Kortos, also known as Starstone Isle, has a similarly diverse ecosystem. The verdant forests and grasslands of the west provide many of the resources Absalom needs, but to the east, the rugged stony desert known as the Scrape, the dangerous Riven Hills, and the newly formed necromantic wasteland known as the Tyrant's Grasp present far harsher climates. The Isle of Erran, just north of Starstone Isle, hosts the second-largest city in the area, Escadar. A rough seaport with more than its share of shady dealings and dangerous types, Escadar also hosts large shipyards and maintains a strong navy that helps to keep the surrounding waters of the Inner Sea safe. A number of smaller islands also skirt the coast of the Isle of Kortos—some barren, some serving as hideouts for criminals and outcasts.

Rising from the center of the Isle of Kortos are the Kortos Mounts, a short but rugged range of tors that have, over the years, been ruled by minotaurs, harpies, dragons, and worse. A few treacherous passes allow travel through the mountains, but with the northern shore of the Isle of Kortos being dominated by the soggy tangles of Dunmire, these northern reaches offer little to draw anyone other than bandits and adventurers into these still-untamed lands.

THE AGE OF LOST OMENS

8

INTRODUCTION

ANCESTRIES & BACKGROUNDS

CLASSES

SKILLS

FEATS

EQUIPMENT

SPELLS

THE AGE OF LOST OMENS

PLAYING THE GAME

GAME MASTERING

CRAFTING & TREASURE

APPENDIX

BROKEN LANDS

Far to the north of Absalom sprawl the Broken Lands, nations and wildernesses united in their shared stature as fractured regions—places where life itself has taken a blow and the struggle to survive is simply part of daily reality. Not all of the Broken Lands are constantly fraught with peril, but regardless of where one might settle down in these parts' tumultuous times, danger is rarely far from home.

In some cases, the breaks are political. In the northeast, the nation of Brevoy has hung on the edge of civil war for many years, as the long-running feud between the traditional noble houses of Issia and the mercenary swordlords of Rostland maintain an ongoing state of tension that may be nearing a breaking point. But in the case of the oft-contested River Kingdoms, these political breaks have reached something of a draw, for here it is said that anyone might become the ruler of a nation—if they have the tenacity to seize the reins of rule.

Elsewhere in the Broken Lands, the fractures are more spiritual. Razmiran, for example, is ruled by the living god Razmir, who demands the worship of all who dwell within his nation's borders and brooks no competition of faith. His priests act as police throughout the land, brutally enforcing their deity's laws. To the north in

Mendev, these spiritual breaks are less obvious; this land struggles to reclaim its heritage in the wake of a century of occupation by a crusading force that, until a few years ago, stood as a bulwark against the demons who ruled the lands across the river to the west.

These western lands are truly broken, in a physical sense, for in the chaotic times at the dawn of the Age of Lost Omens, powerful agents of the demon lord Deskari tore a hole in reality. The resulting wound in the landscape allowed legions of demons to pour through and devastate the lands once known as Sarkoris. Although heroes of the Fifth Crusade recently defeated Deskari and closed the rift, these lands are still known as the Worldwound. The main threat has been quelled, but demons still inhabit the region, and the blighted landscape struggles to return to normal.

Perhaps the strangest of the Broken Lands lie near its heart. The rugged hills and plains of Numeria are home to many Kellid clans. However, in the distant past, the crash of a scientifically advanced starship brought strange aliens, mechanical monstrosities, and technological wonders to Golarion, but its fiery arrival left large reaches of the surrounding land blighted and blasted even to this day.

EYE OF DREAD

The heart of the continent of Avistan has rotted.

This region is dominated by Lake Encarthan, a large inland sea that was—until recently—a well-traveled hub for trade. To the southwest stands the militaristic nation of Molthune, which had long engaged in an intermittent war against its northern neighbor, Nirmathas, a wooded nation populated by folk who take their freedom seriously. An uprising of hobgoblins took advantage of this conflict, and while hostilities have since abated, the two nations now share their borders with a third: the newborn hobgoblin nation Oprak.

North of these war-torn nations lie two other lands equally forged in the crucible of conflict. Until recently, the paladins and protectors of the small but strong nation of Lastwall stood fast against invasions from orcs, undead, and the like. The wild and rugged Hold of Belkzen, meanwhile, has long been held by those orcs, ever since they were driven up from the Darklands below by the dwarves during their Quest for Sky thousands of years ago.

Still farther to the north is the nation of Ustalav, a collection of counties each beset with its own manifestation of horror and fear, ranging from the nightmarishly cosmic to the dreadfully infernal.

It was from Ustalav that one of the greatest threats to the Inner Sea region emerged. The ancient lich Tar-Baphon—known as the Whispering Tyrant—has been defeated twice in the distant past—once by Aroden and once by the heroes of the Shining Crusade, but he has never been truly destroyed. When the magical seals that kept him imprisoned below the ominous tower of Gallowspire were finally sundered in 4719 AR, Tar-Baphon emerged, bringing with him devastation on such a scale that the one-time nation of Lastwall, which bore the brunt of his return to the world, has been utterly scoured. It exists now only as the Gravelands—the nation that once stood watch over undead uprisings now consigned to an undeath of its own. While heroes temporarily thwarted the Whispering Tyrant's immediate plans shortly after he emerged, the lich remains an active menace.

The Whispering Tyrant now rules a kingdom of the undead on the aptly named Isle of Terror in the center of Lake Encarthan. The nations lining Lake Encarthan's shores have all suffered to varying degrees under the Whispering Tyrant's renewed influence, and some are pursuing unlikely alliances to resist him. The lich is gathering his resources on the Isle of Terror, and none can say where or when he will strike next.

THE AGE OF LOST OMENS

8

INTRODUCTION

ANCESTRIES &
BACKGROUNDS

CLASSES

SKILLS

FEATS

EQUIPMENT

SPELLS

THE AGE OF
LOST OMENS

PLAYING THE
GAME

GAME
MASTERING

CRAFTING
& TREASURE

APPENDIX

GOLDEN ROAD

Trade and travel rule the pathways of the so-called Golden Road, known for its shining sands and economic strength. Much of this region consists of sprawling desert wilderness, but this does not mean that the Golden Road is sparse in population. Coastlines and rivers serve as the lifeblood of this region, and some caravans brave the heat and dangers of the desert to trade across northern Garund. Some of the oldest nations in the Inner Sea region command this region, and ancient lore and valuable treasures can be found amid the shifting sands and storied cities.

The largest of these cities is the cosmopolitan Katapesh, where mercantilism is overseen by a strange group known as the Pactmasters. Much of the trade in Katapesh is in goods that can be freely exported or imported from throughout the Inner Sea region, but the city does just as much business in avenues normally regulated to the black markets of other societies.

Qadira's cities may not be as individually large as Katapesh, but the nation's economy is perhaps the strongest. It's certainly the oldest in the region, with support from the long-established Padishah Empire of Kelesh to the east. This, coupled with the church of Sarenrae—perhaps the nation's most successful cultural export to the rest of the Inner Sea region—has secured Qadira's status as one of the most important centers of influence on the Golden Road.

To the west, the five city-states of Thuvia control a legendary artifact called the *sun orchid elixir*, which grants near-immortality to those who consume it. This treasured commodity is the keystone of Thuvia's place in the Golden Road. Further west, the nation of Rahadoum is perhaps the weakest mercantile link, but the fact that this society has eschewed the worship of gods to place its faith in the industry and talent of mortals alone gives the nation its own compelling draw.

At the center of the Golden Road lies mighty Osirion, one of the oldest nations of the Inner Sea region. While Osirion was for a time ruled by Qadira, the legacies and monuments of its early days still stand tall and are an indisputable and iconic source of pride and identity to its people. The influence of Osirion's artisans, philosophers, and spellcasters has spread far and wide, particularly via the Esoteric Order of the Palatine Eye, far to the north in Ustalav, and the faith of Nethys, whose not-so-humble beginnings as a mortal wizard can be traced to the very beginning of Osirion's history during the ancient Age of Destiny.

HIGH SEAS

From fleets of pirates united under the Hurricane Queen of the Shackles to an ancient, subaquatic empire of shapechanging monsters led by the sinister veiled masters, the High Seas of Golarion present dangers both above and below the waves. Yet they also serve as important trade routes, with merchant ships traveling the waters to link powerful nations at opposite ends of continents. Sea captains brave the dangers of the High Seas hoping to partake in the fortunes to be made in trade, linking the ports of the Inner Sea itself to those on the shores of the Arcadian Ocean from the Mwangi Expanse to the Saga Lands.

Piracy is one of the greatest dangers facing travel on the High Seas. The immense volcanic archipelago known as the Shackles serves as a haven for these pirates, with their Hurricane Queen providing just enough structure to keep them from going at each other's throats. A great diversity of monsters and threats populate these islands, and the local pirates know which are safe and which to avoid. North of the Shackles lies Mediogalti Island. While its only significant port, Ilizmagorti, is a known safe harbor for pirates, it is the presence of the infamous Red Mantis assassins who rule the isle that gives this region its greatest infamy.

Other ports present their own complications. The port-city of Promise on the remote isle of Hermea a few hundred miles west of Avistan rewards well those who can negotiate the privilege of trade, but such honors are hard won, for the dragon who rules this closed society does not allow just anyone to visit. Rumors of what goes on beyond Promise's dock district range from tales of a perfect society to those of an oppressive government that affords no free will. Farther to the north, the elves of the Mordant Spire are even more closed to visitors, and for most sailors, the only thing the Mordant Spire offers is an unmistakable landmark for navigation, as the twisting spire can be seen for miles.

Of all the regions along the Avistani and Garundi coastlines, though, none are more hazardous to travel than the waters tortured by the Eye of Abendego. This immense hurricane first formed at the onset of the Age of Lost Omens, when storms wracked all of Golarion in the wake of Aroden's death. Unlike those other storms, though, this hurricane remained. Its winds and storm surge have destroyed several nations and transformed a previously key gulf into a navigational nightmare. What strange force caused and perpetuates the Eye of Abendego has, to date, eluded all investigation.

IMPOSSIBLE LANDS

Magic allows for astounding feats, yet even those who consider themselves experts in the magical arts pause in wonder before the spectacles to be found in the Impossible Lands. What is taken for granted in these strange and eclectic nations would be all but impossible elsewhere.

Take Geb as an example. Here, the living are the minority, and undeath is the predominant way of life. Cruelty, sadism, and violence are the norm in Geb, as one might expect of a land ruled by a violent, undead dictator. This ghost, for whom the country was named, has ruled his nation for thousands of years, although for the past several centuries the day-to-day rule of the land fell to his queen, Arazni. Her recent disappearance (many would instead say "escape") and abandonment of her duties have invigorated the ghost sovereign to once again take active leadership of his benighted realm.

Geb has opposed its northern neighbor, Nex, for the entirety of its existence. Also named after its ruler, Nex is a cosmopolitan realm where magic is mundane. Nex himself has been missing for ages, yet in his absence the Arclords have ruled quite effectively. Here, golems patrol the streets, and the practice of fleshwarping is an accepted and legitimate industry.

Between these two opposed nations lies a stretch of land known as the Mana Wastes, a blasted and blighted badland formed by the ancient wars between Nex and Geb. The very magic of these lands is damaged—or in many reaches dead entirely—and peculiar mutants flop and prowl through the ruins in search of prey.

Only in the duchy of Alkenstar does life approach anything approximating normal, but even here the assumptions of the rest of the world are turned on their head. With magic being unpredictable, Alkenstar's citizens have turned instead to technology. The nation is home to metallurgists and machinists, and the art of gunsmithing gives them an excellent advantage in this part of the world. Exports of firearms have steadily increased over the years, and Alkenstar is emerging as a significant power of its own as a result.

Across the waters of the Obari Ocean lies the final realm of the Impossible Lands: the island nation of Jalmeray. Here it isn't magic alone that allows for impossibilities but also focused self-control and perfection of the spirit. The people of Jalmeray have accomplished astounding physical feats and achieved remarkable intellectual insights using nothing more than ancient traditions of mysticism and self-perfection.

MWANGI EXPANSE

The Mwangi Expanse is home to a wide array of civilizations, both past and present, even as it holds the largest stretch of wilderness in the Inner Sea region. In fact, one of the first civilizations to rise from the ashes after Earthfall rose here in this land—the nation of Shory and its astounding flying cities, from which many modern customs of magic stem.

Some Mwangi cities and kingdoms were lost far more recently than those ancient wonders. When the Eye of Abendego formed just over a century ago, its winds and waves flooded two significant realms along Garund's west coast. Where once stood the nations of Lirgen and Yamasa now stretch only the Sodden Lands, a swath of swampland and salt marshes held by rival gangs of scavengers and monsters. Even more recently, a powerful city-state in the heart of the Mwangi Jungle, Usaro, fell when its brutal leader, Ruthazek the Gorilla King, was slain by adventurers. Usaro has been without a leader for only a few short years, but already its violent inhabitants have caused significant damage in their anarchic rioting. A long lineage of demonically infused Gorilla Kings has ruled Usaro over the centuries, and so a new one will likely soon rise to seize control of Usaro, for the moment this sinister region lacks a head to focus its wrath.

Despite these instances of ruin and destruction, the Mwangi Expanse hosts a wealth of diverse and powerful city-states within its reaches. In Bloodcove, the ruthless mercantile league of the Aspis Consortium rules. Farther south along the coast stands Senghor, whose stance against both piracy and slavery place the city in stark contrast to its northern neighbor. The city-state of Nantambu lies far upstream from Bloodcove on the Vanji River, where its citizens carry on the ancient traditions of Old-Mage Jatembe in combining arcane and primal magic. Far to the southeast stands Mzali, which lies under the oppressive rule of the undead child-king Walkena, though a group of dissidents called the Bright Lions works to build resistance to the mummy's reign. Then there is the city of Kibwe, where within its walls dwell an eclectic mix of people who have journeyed from afar to seek trade and companionship.

Farther south from these independent city-states lies the recently freed nation of Vidrian. Originally established as the Chelish colony of Sargava, Vidrian has now seized its own destiny and cast off its colonial shackles. In so doing, the young nation has exposed itself to the predations of pirates and worse, yet to its citizens, freedom from oppression is well worth that price.

THE AGE OF LOST OMENS

8

INTRODUCTION

ANCESTRIES &
BACKGROUNDS

CLASSES

SKILLS

FEATS

EQUIPMENT

SPELLS

THE AGE OF
LOST OMENS

PLAYING THE
GAME

GAME
MASTERING

CRAFTING
& TREASURE

APPENDIX

OLD CHELIAX

At its height, the empire of Cheliax had holdings that reached from Varisia to Garund and east all the way to Galt. Aroden was prophesized to return to the world of mortals to usher in a new Age of Glory, and those prophecies predicted the Chelish city of Westcrown would be the point of his arrival. Instead, his death ignited a civil war that lasted for decades. When the Thrice-Damned House of Thrune emerged as victor, Cheliax had forever changed. Under House Thrune's rule, Cheliax transformed into a nation that viewed Hell as a blueprint for government. The church of Asmodeus became Cheliax's official state religion, and diabolism its most powerful philosophy. The devil had come home to rule, and while the nation's politicians and leaders claimed that they maintained control of their fate—and House Thrune had merely formed an alliance with Hell to maintain its power and keep order—the nation's internal and external enemies know better.

Many of Cheliax's outlying provinces—such as Andoran, Galt, and Vidrian—revolted and became their own nations. The nation of Isger remains, at least on paper, a thrall. Cheliax values Isger for its important position as a trade route to the Lake Encarthan region, but when Isger was wracked by the violence of the Goblinblood Wars several decades ago, House Thrune did little to provide aid. As the repercussions of the Whispering Tyrant's return to power send ripples of nervous dread through the land, Isger's people grow fearful that they lack not only their own political strength but also that of their supposed protector, and as a result, Isger is one of the lands in the Inner Sea region most in need of heroes.

Recently, several uprisings within Cheliax have further tested the nation's resolve. After a devastating nautical loss in the Shackles resulted in Vidrian's independence, a new Iomedaean rebellion called the Glorious Reclamation threatened Cheliax from within. House Thrune and the Asmodean church defeated the Glorious Reclamation, but at a price—a simultaneous rebellion was successful, with a group of rebels called the Silver Ravens negotiating the successful secession of the new nation of Ravounel.

North of Cheliax, the shadowy nation of Nidal remains the diabolic nation's only real ally. A theocracy ruled by the church of Zon-Kuthon, Nidal is the oldest nation on Avistan, for its people turned to the Midnight Lord for protection during the Age of Darkness after Earthfall. Today, pain and dread are comforts to the citizens of Nidal, and millennia of rule under a church that revels in pain have left them inured to agony and welcoming of loss.

SAGA LANDS

While the opportunity for epic adventure exists throughout the world, in recent years it seems the Saga Lands have produced the most notorious and legendary tales. These sprawling northern reaches feature kingdoms ruled by vikings and witches, realms home to mammoth-riding Kellid clans, and a frontier land of free cities and dangerous wilderness—all of which are steeped in the ancient legacy of the long-gone empire of Thassilon.

Millennia ago, the nation of Thassilon was ruled by the sinful, tyrannical runelords. These wizards carved out legends intended to last for an eternity, but even the mighty runelords succumbed to the devastation of Earthfall. The seven reigning runelords of that time retreated into the safety of extradimensional domains, and for eons they slumbered, until they began to wake in 4707 AR.

The frontier realm of Varisia, once the heart of Thassilon, bore the brunt of the wrath of the first wakened runelord, an avaricious sadist named Karzoug. A band of unlikely heroes emerged from the small coastal town of Sandpoint to eventually face and defeat Karzoug, yet his wakening soon roused other slumbering runelords, and a new band of heroes was forced to defeat the risen tyrants.

While the neighboring Lands of the Linnorm Kings, Realms of the Mammoth Lords, and witch-haunted Irrisen never faced direct repercussions from the runelords, these northern lands hold dangers of their own. A long-running cold war between the vikings of the Linnorm Kingdoms and the winter witches of Irrisen to the east finally came to a sputtering end when a daughter of the immortal witch Baba Yaga attempted to defy her mother and usurp Irrisen's traditions of rule. While the eternal winter of Irrisen set in place by Baba Yaga endures, its new ruler, Anastasia, may prove to be the first benevolent presence to sit on the throne in centuries. Farther to the east, the Kellid clans of the Realm of the Mammoth Lords played their own pivotal roles in defying the demons of the Worldwound.

Recently, a new nation has risen in the Saga Lands. After the runelords were defeated, two surviving runelords decided to adjust their traditions to fit this strange new world they found themselves in. Now the fledgling nation of New Thassilon sprawls along the northern border of Varisia, and it remains to be seen if its rulers will fully adopt a more peaceful path, or if it is but a matter of time before the old traditions of sin and violence rise once again.

SHINING KINGDOMS

The empire of Taldor was historically the heart of the Shining Kingdoms. In the early Age of Enthronement, Taldor sent several Armies of Exploration to expand the nation's borders and colonize the surrounding lands. Today, Taldor is but a shadow of its former glory, but after a recent bout of internal strife, a progressive new empress has claimed the crown, and Taldor may be on the path to recover its old glory for the first time in centuries.

To the west, the democratic nation of Andoran stands as a rising star on the international stage. Ever since the province seceded from the nation of Cheliax, Andoran's military has helped to stem the flow of slavery, and its heroes have stood tall against all manner of peril to the common folk. But the future doesn't look entirely bright for Andoran, for with Cheliax's recent upsets, rumors flow that House Thrune may seek to reclaim control of its wayward thrall. Given the looming threat of the Whispering Tyrant, an all-out war between these two powerful nations could be disastrous.

Northeast of Andoran sprawls the dwarven city-states of the Five Kings Mountains. No strangers to war, both against enemies and among themselves, the dwarves of the Five Kings remain allies of Andoran but have their own troubles that command most of their attention. To the

west of the dwarven realm, the rich and powerful nation of Druma controls nearly half of the lake's southern shoreline and uses its position to bolster its coffers and further the teachings of the Prophecies of Kalistrade, a philosophy that teaches that wealth can be achieved through adherence to strict and abstemious practices.

Northeast of Druma lie the forested elven lands of Kyonin, one of Avistan's oldest nations. This land belonged to the elves long before Earthfall, but for thousands of years after that devastation, they left their realm abandoned. In that time, a powerful demon named Treerazer seized control of the forest's southern reaches, corrupting the terrain into a swampy, desolate mire called Tanglebriar. Although the elves have returned, they've been unable to force Treerazer from their southern border.

Still farther east is the nation of Galt. Wracked for decades by a self-perpetuating series of rebellions and revolutions, this land has been torn apart from within over and over. Its people are tired and desperate as they continue to live what lives they can in the shadow of the *final blades*—powerful magical guillotines that claim the souls of those they decapitate. If any of the regions of the Shining Kingdoms is poised for significant change in the near future, it is surely revolution-wracked Galt.

CULTURES

Of course, there's more to the world of Golarion than its geopolitical borders and wilderness regions. It's the people who dwell in those nations and the creatures that lurk in those wilds who bring the world to life.

GARUNDI

KELESHITE

KELLID

MWANGI

NIDALESE

HUMAN ETHNICITIES

A variety of ethnic groups make up the human populace of the continents bordering Golarion's Inner Sea. Many of these groups have origins on distant lands, but the Inner Sea region has a diverse population drawn from across the globe. Human characters can be from any of these ethnicities, regardless of what land they call home.

Characters from these ethnicities speak Common if they come from the Inner Sea region, and some ethnicities give access to a regional language or another uncommon language (page 65). Half-elves and half-orcs arise across all human ethnicities and bear the features of both those ethnicities and their non-human parents.

GARUNDI

Garundi span the nations of northern Garund along the shores of the Inner Sea, and their clans are known for strength and empathy, treating their neighbors with compassion and respect. Their skin tones often range from dark brown to beige, and they often have tall statures, broad shoulders, and high cheekbones. Garundi have access to the Osiriani language.

KELESHITE

Tracing their origins to the Keleshite Empire in the eastern deserts, Keleshites often have black hair, brown eyes, and dark- to cool-brown skin. Their culture takes pride in the empire's legacy, valuing boldness, wit, and luxury. Fashions tend to incorporate flowing fabrics, headdresses, and turbans. Keleshites have access to the Kelish language.

KELLID

In the mountains and steppes of northern Avistan, Kellids live hard lives to survive the threats of the wild, wary of magic and relying on skill and might when hunting and fighting. They are typically a brawny and dark-haired people, tanned and bearing eyes that are often black, blue, or gray. Kellids have access to the Hallit language.

MWANGI

Spread across the vast continent of Garund, from the parched deserts in the north to the dense jungles of the Mwangi Expanse, the Mwangi people are divided into four diverse subgroups: Bekyar, Bonuwat, Mauxi, and Zenj. Mwangi skin tones range from black to dark-brown to ocher, and they have black or dark-brown hair. Mwangi have access to the Mwangi language.

NIDALESE

Nidalese hail from a culture that escaped destruction during the Earthfall, when a swarm of meteoroids carved out the Inner Sea. The ancient Nidalese pledged fealty to an evil shadow god to obtain salvation, and the grip of Zon-Kuthon has tainted these people ever since. Nidalese tend toward gray, ashy skin tones, with white, gray, or black hair. Nidalese have access to the Shadowtongue language.

SHOANTI

The Shoanti clans called quahs were long ago pushed out of lush territory in the nation of Varisia into the harsh badlands of the Storval Plateau. Stalwart and tenacious, they remain oath-sworn to someday retake what they've lost. Their skin tones typically range from sepia to russet, and quah members are easily identified by their shaved heads and traditional tattoos. Shoanti have access to the Shoanti language.

Taldan

Renowned as artisans, scholars, and soldiers, Taldans have spread throughout Avistan, as the empire of Taldor once spanned almost half of the northern continent. Taldans often have brown hair, pale-white to deep-bronze skin, and green, gray, or amber eyes. Their native language, Taldane, is so widespread that it is also called Common.

Tian

Few in number in the Inner Sea region, Tians originally come from myriad nations in Tian Xia, a continent on the opposite side of the world. They typically have dark hair, but their body types, skin tones, and eye colors vary greatly, as "Tian" is in fact a general term describing several ethnicities. Tians have access to the Tien language.

Ulfen

The coastal raiders of the Ulfen clans are skilled sailors and bodyguards. They're often tall, with pale to ruddy skin and blond, light-brown, or red hair. They typically show pride in their appearances by adorning themselves with furs, horn, and ivory. Ulfen have access to the Skald language.

Varisian

Varisians historically favored a nomadic life of roving caravans, but today many lead a settled lifestyle in places like Ustalav and their namesake land. Their skin tones typically range from tawny beige to khaki. They have a wide variety of hair colors from platinum to red to brown, and their large, expressive eyes range into even rarer colors like violet and gold. Varisians have access to the Varisian language.

Vudrani

Though the empire of Vudra is far to the east, it has a foothold in the Inner Sea on the island of Jalmeray. A widespread belief in reincarnation makes dedication to self-improvement a hallmark of Vudrani culture. Vudrani typically have dark eyes and skin tones that run from umber to tawny. Their hair is often black and ranges in thickness and texture. Piercings, jewelry, and makeup are common adornments among Vudrani. Vudrani have access to the Vudrani language.

DWARVES

For untold eons, the dwarven people dwelled in the lightless reaches of the Darklands. It wasn't until after Earthfall that the dwarves undertook the legendary Quest for Sky, during which the majority of dwarves made a pilgrimage to relocate to the surface of Golarion. In doing so, they not only drove the orcs to the surface before them, but also established several immense Sky Citadels at each location where they emerged from the realm below. Today, three major ethnicities of dwarves exist, each associated with one of three altitude bands: the grondaksen dwarves (who still dwell in the upper reaches of the Darklands), the ergaksen dwarves (the most widespread heritage, and those who dwell on or adjacent to the surface world), and the holtaksen dwarves (the least populous—dwarves who dwell only among the highest mountain reaches).

ELVES

Golarion is not the original elven home world, but those elves who dwell here today are considered native to the planet. These people first came to Golarion from the neighboring planet of Castrovel via a network of portals known as *aiudara*. While elves abandoned Golarion for several thousand years after the devastation of Earthfall, they have since returned in force. The most populous elves are the aiudeen, elves who have acclimated to temperate forest lands. These are the elves who rule the nation of Kyonin and are most often encountered in other societies. To the south, the mualijae elves have acclimated to the sweltering jungles of the Mwangi Expanse, while far to the north the ilverani elves (known to some as the snowcasters) dwell

SHOANTI

TALDAN

TIAN

ULFEN

VARISIAN

VUDRANI

DWARF

ELF

GNOME

GOBLIN

HALFLING

HALF-ELF

HALF-ORC

in the frozen reaches of Irrisen and beyond in the Crown of the World. The vourinoi elves of Garund's deserts are the most secretive of the elven ethnicities.

GNOMES

The first gnomes arrived on Golarion at some point after Earthfall from the otherworldly dimension known as the First World, fleeing a terror whose nature few can recall. Since that time, gnomes have transitioned fully to creatures of the Material Plane, although they all live in fear of the life-threatening condition known as bleaching. Feychild gnomes are the most widespread. Glimmer gnomes retain a stronger tie to the First World, while others known as fell gnomes have embraced the darker traditions of their fey heritage. Keenspark gnomes (jokingly referred to as "sour gnomes") seek to avoid the bleaching by exploring new innovations rather than seeking new experiences or exploring the world.

GOBLINS

Although many adventurers might assume a goblin is a goblin, these scrappy and creative people are as diverse as any other ancestry. The most widespread are the rasp goblins, so named for the large numbers who have traditionally dwelled along the rugged coastlines of Varisia's west coast, a region known as the Rasp. Forest goblins tend to be smaller than the other ethnicities and are located mostly in central Avistan. Their numbers are only now beginning to recover from the horrors of the Goblinblood Wars. The frost goblins of Irrisen's eternal winter are unusual among their kind for their propensity to grow blue fur on their bodies, while the monkey goblins of Mediogalti Island are known for their prehensile tails and arboreal habitats.

HALFLINGS

Many halflings have lived in the shadow of other societies for as long as they can remember, living in much the same way as their neighboring cultures and adding their own unique variations over time or as necessity demands. However, numerous distinct halfling cultures exist outside of the context of other peoples and nations. In some cases, these divisions were fueled by separation and circumstances, such as the oppressed halflings of Cheliax who have been forced into slavery, and the Song'o halflings of the Mwangi Expanse, who hid from all other cultures to avoid a similar fate. Other halflings, such as the jaric, mihrini, othoban, and uhlam halflings, simply formed their own traditions without the influence of humans and other creatures.

REGIONAL LANGUAGES

These languages are uncommon outside the region of their genesis. A character hailing from one of the regions listed below automatically has access to that language. In the Inner Sea region, the language referred to as Common elsewhere in the rules is the same as Taldane—a result of Taldor's legacy of control and influence over the whole region. Nearly every language listed here is spoken on the melting-pot streets of Absalom.

TABLE 8–1: REGIONAL LANGUAGES

Language	Regions
Hallit	Irrisen, Mendev, Numeria, Realm of the Mammoth Lords, Sarkoris, Ustalav
Kelish	Katapesh, Kelesh, Osirion, Qadira
Mwangi	Mwangi Expanse, the Shackles, Thuvia, Vidrian
Osiriani	Geb, Katapesh, Mana Wastes, Nex, Osirion, Rahadoum, Thuvia
Shoanti	Hold of Belkzen, Varisia
Skald	Irrisen, Lands of the Linnorm Kings
Tien	Lands of the Linnorm Kings, Realm of the Mammoth Lords, Tian Xia
Varisian	Brevoy, the Gravelands, Nidal, Nirmathas, Ustalav, Varisia
Vudrani	Jalmeray, Katapesh, Nex, Vudra

CREATURES

The six humanoid ancestries are far from Golarion's only inhabitants. Many other creatures dwell in the world, some kindly and others cruel, some wild and others organized, some anthropomorphic and others completely monstrous. Even creatures that are usually foes of civilization, and whom brave adventurers face in battle, can sometimes be reasoned with or even befriended. Not all of them are evil, and some are actively helpful to their neighbors. And some, of course, simply want to be left alone.

Listed on these pages are brief descriptions of many creatures that have held important cultural, regional, or historical roles on Golarion, particularly in the Inner Sea region.

ALGHOLLTHUS

Perhaps the oldest intelligent creatures on Golarion, the alghollthus ruled vast empires in the depths of the world's oceans for eons before the first humans came to be. In fact, according to some of their wall carvings, they created the first human beings. Whether or not this claim is true is impossible to prove, but these creatures—from the sinister aboleths to their shape-changing rulers, the veiled masters—have certainly been a part of the world for a long, long time. Moreover, their claim to have existed on Golarion before the gods themselves turned their divine eyes upon the world carries some disturbing implications.

DEMONS

Normally bound to the Abyss, demons can be found wherever cults or evil spellcasters exist to call them to this world. Two notable locations, the Worldwound in the north and the Tanglebriar in southern Kyonin, deserve special mention, for here the demons of the Abyss have established lasting presences.

DEVILS

Although the rulers of Cheliax maintain that Hell is but a blueprint and devilkind is just a tool the clever spellcasters of House Thrune use to maintain control over their nation (as well as their decadent lifestyle), devils have an insidious hold over that nation. With the state formally devoted to Asmodeus and powerful orders of Hellknights serving as mercenary arbiters of law, it should come as no surprise that devils are unusually common in Cheliax and the neighboring realms.

DRAGONS

Dragons are rightfully counted among the most legendary of monsters in the Inner Sea region. Most prefer to dwell in remote lairs, swooping down to interact with humanity only when their violent tempers push them to raid. Good dragons may seem less common than their evil kin, but only because they have less of an urge to mingle with humanoids.

GENIES

The nation of Qadira has a long history with genies, but geniekind's involvement with the Inner Sea region is certainly not limited to that nation. They serve as architects and creators of impossibilities on the isle of Jalmeray, and in Katapesh they are rumored to be infused into the very stone and soil of the land.

GIANTS

Countless tribes and varieties of these massive humanoids rule the rugged reaches of the world, from volcanic mountain ranges and stinking marshlands to trackless badlands and steaming jungles. They were used as slaves in ancient Thassilon, where they were ruled by magic-infused rune giants and forced to erect enormous monuments that remain to this day in Varisia, Belkzen, and the Lands of the Linnorm Kings. But now the giant tribes of northern Avistan are scattered across the land, largely unaware they once had a society that was destroyed and reshaped by the ancient empire of Thassilon.

GNOLLS

Hyena-headed gnolls, ever seeking new slaves to perform menial labor, make for unreliable mercenaries but excel at hunting intelligent prey. Gnolls dwell primarily in northern Garund and are particularly common in Osirion, Katapesh, and Nex. Indeed, gnolls can be found operating openly as bodyguards, mercenaries, and slavers in cities like Katapesh.

GOBLINOIDS

Goblins are certainly the most widespread and recognized goblinoids, but their taller, more militaristic hobgoblin kin rule the new kingdom of Oprak near Lake Encarthan. The looming, murderous creatures known as bugbears remain loners who eschew social structures, preferring to pursue their sadistic hobbies on their own.

KOBOLDS

Industrious and fecund, kobolds thrive anywhere they can, often dwelling in narrow confines and twisting burrows in the hinterlands of rural regions or spreading throughout the sewers of urban centers. These small, reptilian humanoids share many traits with dragons—but courage, might, and an intimidating presence are certainly not among them!

LESHYS

The first leshys were grown by druids as minions, but over time these strange, plantlike creatures have diversified and now take many forms. Leshys have yet to organize or form nations of their own, but considering how quickly their numbers have grown and how swiftly they adapt to new regions, a leshy nation seems all but guaranteed in the near future.

LIZARDFOLK

Once widespread in Avistan and Garund, the isolationist lizardfolk, also known as iruxis, have been forced farther and farther into their forests and swamps by climate change and the rapid expansion of other humanoids. Normally peaceful, lizardfolk can be driven to war by encroaching civilization and power-hungry lizardfolk leaders—the latter are disturbingly common in the Mwangi Expanse and the River Kingdoms.

ORCS

Most orcs currently regard the Hold of Belkzen as their ancestral land, despite the fact that they once called the upper reaches of the Darklands home. After living in a violent and brutal culture built on conquest and strength, some orcs of the Hold of Belkzen have begun to consider other means of securing their lands.

PLANAR SCIONS

A wide variety of planar scions dwell in the Inner Sea region, including the descendants of celestials and fiends who have mixed their bloodlines with those of mortals, and other lineages that arose from the influence of the Elemental Planes. In Cheliax, those who exhibit diabolic influences are particularly despised, as the leaders of that nation see them as examples of mortals who succumbed to fiendish influence instead of commanding devils as minions and slaves.

SERPENTFOLK

Serpentfolk once ruled the second layer of the Darklands along with much of the surface of Garund and Avistan. Azlant's expansion into the Inner Sea region long before Earthfall led to a terrible war between the two peoples. When Azlant proved the victor, the surviving serpentfolk fled into the Darklands; they are nearly extinct today.

KOBOLD

FACTIONS

While nations and faiths command vast resources and control entire regions, they must still compete for the loyalty of their followers. In addition to being swayed by church and state, many people are influenced by societal groups known as factions. These groups vary wildly in size and purpose—from local thieves' guilds interested only in filling the pockets and bellies of their members, to far-reaching, international commercial conglomerates with their own private armies.

The largest factions compete with lesser sovereign nations for wealth, power, and influence, and they sometimes rival even larger nations. In some cases, nations take the risky step of relying upon these powerful factions, making them an extension of government itself (as is the case with some Hellknights in Cheliax, for example). In other cases, such as that of the Red Mantis, entire nations bow to the power of these organizations. Smaller groups, while less rich in resources, nonetheless inspire great zeal in their members. Those groups that strive to grow in size, influence, or wealth frequently attract more dedicated and motivated members.

The factions summarized below represent a sampling of those active in the Inner Sea region. Some, like the Pathfinder Society and the Aspis Consortium, are widespread and powerful; their influence can be found throughout the world. Others, such as the Firebrands and the Sczarni, are disorganized or regional in scope. All encourage adventurers to join their ranks, although the benefits each faction can offer an adventurer varies widely.

ASPIS CONSORTIUM

The sprawling mercantile concern known as the Aspis Consortium is structured to ensure that the survival of the faction is more important than any single member. Originally founded as a private trading endeavor, the Consortium has grown to be one of the largest business ventures in the Inner Sea region. Most of the group's members are skilled merchants and mercenaries, and the organization has made a merciless and bloodthirsty name for itself when it comes to ensuring its profits. The Aspis Consortium has clashed many times with the Pathfinder Society.

BELLFLOWER NETWORK

The unsavory practice of slavery continues to be a strong economic force in diabolic Cheliax. Here, halflings are particularly valued as slaves, for they work hard and take up only half the room of a human laborer. It should come as no surprise, then, to learn of the Bellflower Network, an organization founded by halfling freedom fighters that accepts any into its ranks, provided they aid the network

in its goal of freeing all slaves from servitude and helping them escape from oppressive lands like Cheliax.

ESOTERIC ORDER OF THE PALATINE EYE

Based in the nation of Ustalav, the scholars and philosophers of this semisecret society have long stood against the Whispering Way (page 441), but more recent events have placed them in opposition to the sinister goals of the Night Heralds. When left to their own devices, however, members of this faction prefer to explore and study dusty secrets hidden in the past, particularly those still awaiting rediscovery in the regions of the Golden Road—especially in the nation of Osirion.

EAGLE KNIGHTS

The Eagle Knights are the protectors and defenders of the people of Andoran. The group itself consists of four subfactions—the Steel Falcons (who protect Andoran's interests beyond its borders), the Golden Legion (Andoran's defenders and the commanders of its armies), the Gray Corsairs (nautical agents who specialize in fighting the slave trade), and the Twilight Talons (spies and deep cover agents).

FIREBRANDS

Not all factions have central bases of operation or organized hierarchies of command. The loosely affiliated freedom fighters, swashbuckling heroes, and entertainers known as the Firebrands are one such group. They are united by a desire to fight oppression, oppose tyrannical regimes, free slaves, rescue the wrongfully accused, and engage in jolly cooperation with like-minded heroes—all while building their own individual reputations and wealth. This group of defenders has proven surprisingly difficult for oppressive governments and cruel religions to defeat.

FREE CAPTAINS

To an outside observer or a merchant whose ship has been looted or sunk, the pirates of the Shackles may seem like

INTRODUCTION

ANCESTRIES & BACKGROUNDS

CLASSES

SKILLS

FEATS

EQUIPMENT

SPELLS

THE AGE OF LOST OMENS

PLAYING THE GAME

GAME MASTERING

CRAFTING & TREASURE

APPENDIX

a disorganized scourge. But in truth, these pirates are bound by a complex code of, if not honor, then a mutual recognition that it's always good to have allies on the open seas. The Shackles are ruled by a council of pirate lords who call themselves the Free Captains; they sail the southern Arcadian Ocean and follow their own code of rules when it comes to who can be raided and what can be sunk—even if, to their victims, those rules seem capricious and arbitrary.

HELLKNIGHTS

Several different orders of the mercenaries known collectively as Hellknights operate in Avistan, with most of their number stationed in the nation of Cheliax. These mercenaries see the law of the land as inviolate and offer their services as enforcers to any who can pay their prices. They wear distinctive suits of intimidating armor and take the legends of Hell as inspiration, but they see no one but themselves as the true arbiters of law.

KNIGHTS OF LASTWALL

For centuries, the nation of Lastwall stood as a bulwark against the orcs of Belkzen and the lingering threat of the Whispering Tyrant. But when the Whispering Tyrant escaped his prison, he brought to his enemies in Lastwall a devastating apocalypse. Now Lastwall is destroyed, and the knights who once served there are without a home. In its absence, they have formed a ragtag group known as the Knights of Lastwall, and they carry on their charge to stand against the undead legions of the Whispering Tyrant wherever their skills are needed.

LION BLADES

The Lion Blades of Taldor are a secret organization committed to protecting the interests of Taldor and its ruler. They oppose Taldor's many enemies, foreign and domestic, through a program of infiltration, espionage, and assassination. One of the major goals of the Lion Blades is to rein in corruption within the empire (aside from corruption that is useful to them); another is keeping any one faction of the imperial court from becoming powerful enough to upset the status quo. Through its shadow schools, the Lion Blades intensively train new recruits before investing them with a high degree of initiative and latitude.

MAGAAMBYA

Golarion reeled from the disaster of Earthfall, and its peoples took long to recover. But recover they did, and one of the first institutions to rise from the ashes of near destruction was the Magaambya, an academy of arcane learning founded by the legendary wizard known as Old-Mage Jatembe. Today, the scholars of Magaambya not only preserve ancient magical traditions founded in those early days but also protect the learning and culture of the Mwangi people as a whole.

NIGHT HERALDS

The Night Heralds turn to the lure of the starlit night for guidance, seeking advice and aid from forces far removed from Golarion. The sinister aliens of the Dominion of the Black hold special importance for the Night Heralds, and many Night Heralds worship these inscrutable beings almost as gods. Night Heralds seek and collect obscure texts and mysterious lore from the ancient past and peruse the secrets they find within to unravel larger hidden meanings and obscured truths beyond reality. Their hope is that when the world inevitably falls to alien influence, they will be rewarded for their service by the world's new masters.

PATHFINDER SOCIETY

Many of the greatest explorers and adventurers of the modern age have recorded their discoveries in an ongoing series of chapbooks known as the *Pathfinder Chronicles*, published irregularly by the Pathfinder Society itself. This diverse group is devoted to exploring the world, supporting its agents in the field, and ensuring the discoveries they make are documented. The Society often finds itself in conflict with the more mercenary Aspis Consortium. The Pathfinder Society's pursuit of discovery often puts its agents in the thick of developing plots, forcing them to choose between being heroes or villains as events unfold.

RED MANTIS

It's easy to know if an assassination is the work of the notorious Red Mantis; they typically kill with a sacred sawtooth saber, have a knack for targeting their victims in public or in sanctuaries believed to be safe, and take steps to ensure that those they are contracted to kill stay dead. Their prices change with each mission, but no matter the offer, the Red Mantis never targets rightfully ruling monarchs, for their own deity, the mantis god Achaekek, forbids the murder of those with a divine mandate to rule.

SCZARNI

The Sczarni are a collection of Varisian bandits, smugglers, and thieves. They are organized into tightly knit families, each of which has little or nothing in common with Sczarni in other locations beyond shared skills, techniques, and pursuits. Their crimes focus on thievery, scams, and other relatively nonviolent acts, but since these crimes have a tendency to spiral out of control, their schemes often result in violence anyway.

THE AGE OF LOST OMENS

8

INTRODUCTION

ANCESTRIES &
BACKGROUNDS

CLASSES

SKILLS

FEATS

EQUIPMENT

SPELLS

THE AGE OF
LOST OMENS

PLAYING THE
GAME

GAME
MASTERING

CRAFTING
& TREASURE

APPENDIX

RELIGION

Selection of a deity is critical for certain classes—like champion and cleric—but most characters pay respect to at least one deity to find a focus in life and guide their choices, especially in times of hardship or need. Some people instead worship a group of deities arranged in a pantheon, follow a nondeific religion like the Green Faith, or adhere to a specific philosophy. Note that far more deities, religions, and philosophies exist on any world, Golarion included, than those detailed below.

DEITIES

Anyone can worship a deity, but those who do so devoutly should take care to pursue the faith's edicts (behaviors the faith encourages) and avoid its anathemas (actions considered blasphemous). Each deity below has their alignment listed in parentheses after their name, followed by a short description and their edicts, anathemas, and the alignments permitted for followers. Following that are benefits available to the most ardent devotees of the deities. You get these benefits only if you're a cleric of the deity or some other rule specifically gives you a devotee benefit.

ABADAR (LN)

The Master of the First Vault holds sway over cities, the law, merchants, and wealth. Abadar seeks to bring civilization to the wild places of the world, encourages adherence to law, and promotes commerce and trade within civilization. He also encourages cooperation among the various ancestries.

Edicts bring civilization to the frontiers, earn wealth through hard work and trade, follow the rule of law

Anathema engage in banditry or piracy, steal, undermine a law-abiding court

Follower Alignments LG, LN, LE

DEVOTEE BENEFITS

Divine Font *harm* or *heal*
Divine Skill Society
Favored Weapon crossbow
Domains cities, earth, travel, wealth
Cleric Spells 1st: *illusory object,* 4th: *creation,* 7th: *magnificent mansion*

ASMODEUS (LE)

The Prince of Darkness reigns over contracts, pride, slavery, and tyranny, and he delights in tempting mortals to the path of evil. He promotes strict hierarchies where everyone knows their place, and he takes advantage of order for his own selfish benefit.

Edicts negotiate contracts to your best advantage, rule tyrannically and torture weaker beings, show subservience to your betters

Anathema break a contract, free a slave, insult Asmodeus by showing mercy to your enemies

Follower Alignments LE

DEVOTEE BENEFITS

Divine Font *harm*
Divine Skill Deception
Favored Weapon mace
Domains confidence, fire, trickery, tyranny
Cleric Spells 1st: *charm,* 4th: *suggestion,* 6th: *mislead*

CALISTRIA (CN)

The mischievous goddess known as the Savored Sting extols the virtues of lust, revenge, and trickery. Though Calistria is most widely worshipped by elves, members of many other ancestries follow her as well.

Edicts pursue your personal freedom, seek hedonistic thrills, take revenge

Anathema become too consumed by love or a need for revenge, let a slight go unanswered

Follower Alignments CG, CN, CE

DEVOTEE BENEFITS

Divine Font *harm* or *heal*
Divine Skill Deception
Favored Weapon whip
Domains pain, passion, secrecy, trickery
Cleric Spells 1st: *charm,* 3rd: *enthrall,* 6th: *mislead*

CAYDEN CAILEAN (CG)

The Drunken Hero ascended from mortal life on a drunken dare, becoming the god of ale, freedom, and wine. Cayden promotes freedom and encourages others to find their own path in life. He fights for just causes and delights in the best indulgences.

Edicts drink, free slaves and aid the oppressed, seek glory and adventure

Anathema waste alcohol, be mean or standoffish when drunk, own a slave

Follower Alignments NG, CG, CN

DEVOTEE BENEFITS

Divine Font *heal*
Divine Skill Athletics
Favored Weapon rapier
Domains cities, freedom, indulgence, might
Cleric Spells 1st: *fleet step,* 2nd: *touch of idiocy,* 5th: *hallucination*

DESNA [CG]

The kindly Song of the Spheres presides over dreams, luck, stars, and travelers. An ancient goddess, Desna delights in freedom and mystery, and she encourages her followers to do the same.

Edicts aid fellow travelers, explore new places, express yourself through art and song, find what life has to offer

Anathema cause fear or despair, cast *nightmare* or use similar magic to corrupt dreams, engage in bigoted behavior

Follower Alignments NG, CG, CN

Devotee Benefits

Divine Font *heal*
Divine Skill Acrobatics
Favored Weapon starknife
Domains dreams, luck, moon, travel
Cleric Spells 1st: *sleep*, 3rd: *dream message*, 5th: *dreaming potential*

ERASTIL [LG]

Old Deadeye is god of family, farming, hunting, and trade. Long ago he was a horned god of the hunt, but his worship evolved to focus on rural communities.

Edicts care for your home and family, fulfill your duties, keep the peace, protect the community

Anathema abandon your home in its time of need, choose yourself over your community, tarnish your reputation, tell lies

Follower Alignments LG, NG, LN

Devotee Benefits

Divine Font *heal*
Divine Skill Survival
Favored Weapon longbow
Domains earth, family, nature, wealth
Cleric Spells 1st: *true strike*, 3rd: *wall of thorns*, 5th: *tree stride*

GORUM [CN]

Soldiers call out prayers to Our Lord in Iron, god of battle, strength, and weapons. Gorum emphasizes strength and power, encouraging his followers to seek out war and combat as the ultimate way to worship him.

Edicts attain victory in fair combat, push your limits, wear armor in combat

Anathema kill prisoners or surrendering foes, prevent conflict through negotiation, win a battle through underhanded tactics or indirect magic

Follower Alignments CN, CE

Devotee Benefits

Divine Font *harm* or *heal*
Divine Skill Athletics
Favored Weapon greatsword
Domains confidence, destruction, might, zeal
Cleric Spells 1st: *true strike*, 2nd: *enlarge*, 4th: *weapon storm*

GOZREH [N]

A deity of two aspects, known as the Wind and the Waves, Gozreh rules over nature, the sea, and weather. Gozreh is popular with druids and those who seek to preserve the wilds.

Edicts cherish, protect, and respect nature in all its forms

Anathema bring civilization to intrude on the wild, create undead, despoil areas of natural beauty

Follower Alignments NG, LN, N, CN, NE

Devotee Benefits

Divine Font *heal*
Divine Skill Survival
Favored Weapon trident
Domains air, nature, travel, water
Cleric Spells 1st: *gust of wind*, 3rd: *lightning bolt*, 5th: *control water*

IOMEDAE [LG]

Iomedae is goddess of honor, justice, rulership, and valor, and she is called the Inheritor because she inherited her mantle when the god of humanity perished. Prior to her ascension, Iomedae walked the planet as a mortal. Many paladins follow her faith.

Edicts be temperate, fight for justice and honor, hold valor in your heart

Anathema abandon a companion in need, dishonor yourself, refuse a challenge from an equal

Follower Alignments LG, NG

Devotee Benefits

Divine Font *heal*
Divine Skill Intimidation
Favored Weapon longsword
Domains confidence, might, truth, zeal
Cleric Spells 1st: *true strike*, 2nd: *see invisibility*, 4th: *fire shield*

IRORI [LN]

When the Master of Masters attained true enlightenment, he became a god of history, knowledge, and self-perfection. Irori promotes discipline and teaches that one who can master themself finds the greatest benefits the world can provide.

Edicts be humble; help others perfect themselves; hone your body, mind, and spirit to a more perfect state; practice discipline

Anathema become addicted to a substance, destroy an important historical text, repeatedly fail to maintain self-control

Follower Alignments LG, LN, LE

Devotee Benefits

Divine Font *harm* or *heal*
Divine Skill Athletics
Favored Weapon fist
Domains knowledge, might, perfection, truth
Cleric Spells 1st: *jump*, 3rd: *haste*, 4th: *stoneskin*

LAMASHTU [CE]

The Mother of Monsters is goddess of aberrance, monsters, and nightmares. She seeks to corrupt mortals and populate the world with her twisted and monstrous brood.

Edicts bring power to outcasts and the downtrodden, indoctrinate children in Lamashtu's teachings, make the beautiful monstrous, reveal the corruption and flaws in all things

Anathema attempt to treat a mental illness or deformity, provide succor to Lamashtu's enemies

Follower Alignments CE

DEVOTEE BENEFITS

Divine Font *harm* or *heal*
Divine Skill Survival
Favored Weapon falchion
Domains family, might, nightmares, trickery
Cleric Spells 1st: *magic fang*, 2nd: *animal form*, 4th: *nightmare*

NETHYS [N]

The All-Seeing Eye, god of magic, has a dualistic nature of destruction and preservation; his ability to witness all things has shattered his mind.

Edicts seek out magical power and use it

Anathema pursue mundane paths over magical ones

Follower Alignments NG, LN, N, CN, NE

DEVOTEE BENEFITS

Divine Font *harm* or *heal*
Divine Skill Arcana
Favored Weapon staff
Domains destruction, knowledge, magic, protection
Cleric Spells 1st: *magic missile*, 2nd: *magic mouth*, 3rd: *levitate*, 4th: *blink*, 5th: *prying eye*, 6th: *wall of force*, 7th: *warp mind*, 8th: *maze*, 9th: *disjunction*

NORGORBER [NE]

The god of greed, murder, poison, and secrets has four aspects: Blackfingers, ally of alchemists and poisoners; the murderous Father Skinsaw; the thieving Gray Master; and the secretive Reaper of Reputation.

Edicts keep your true identity secret, sacrifice anyone necessary, take every advantage in a fight, work from the shadows

Anathema allow your true identity to be connected to your dark dealings, share a secret freely, show mercy

Follower Alignments LE, NE, CE, plus N if following the Reaper of Reputation

DEVOTEE BENEFITS

Divine Font *harm*
Divine Skill Stealth
Favored Weapon shortsword
Domains death, secrecy, trickery, wealth
Cleric Spells 1st: *illusory disguise*, 2nd: *invisibility*, 4th: *phantasmal killer*

PHARASMA [N]

Ancient and powerful beyond even most other gods, the Lady of Graves presides over birth, death, fate, and prophecy. From her throne in the Boneyard, she judges the souls of all who perish, and she ensures that the natural cycle of birth and death—the River of Souls—is not disrupted.

Edicts strive to understand ancient prophecies, destroy undead, lay bodies to rest

Anathema create undead, desecrate a corpse, rob a tomb

Follower Alignments NG, LN, N

DEVOTEE BENEFITS

Divine Font *heal*
Divine Skill Medicine
Favored Weapon dagger
Domains death, fate, healing, knowledge
Cleric Spells 1st: *mindlink*, 3rd: *ghostly weapon*, 4th: *phantasmal killer*

ROVAGUG [CE]

The Rough Beast is the god of destruction, disaster, and wrath. He was long ago imprisoned within Golarion's core at the hands of many other deities working in concert, and seeks to one day break free and wreak havoc upon the world.

Edicts destroy all things, free Rovagug from his prison

Anathema create something new, let material ties restrain you, torture a victim or otherwise delay its destruction

Follower Alignments NE, CE

DEVOTEE BENEFITS

Divine Font *harm*
Divine Skill Athletics
Favored Weapon greataxe
Domains air, destruction, earth, zeal
Cleric Spells 1st: *burning hands*, 2nd: *enlarge*, 6th: *disintegrate*

SARENRAE [NG]

The Dawnflower is goddess of healing, honesty, redemption, and the sun. Once a powerful angel and empyreal lord, Sarenrae led the charge to imprison Rovagug. She seeks to redeem evil where possible, or else destroy it swiftly.

Edicts destroy the Spawn of Rovagug, protect allies, provide aid to the sick and wounded, seek and allow redemption

Anathema create undead, lie, deny a repentant creature an opportunity for redemption, fail to strike down evil

Follower Alignments LG, NG, CG

DEVOTEE BENEFITS

Divine Font *heal*
Divine Skill Medicine
Favored Weapon scimitar
Domains fire, healing, sun, truth
Cleric Spells 1st: *burning hands*, 3rd: *fireball*, 4th: *wall of fire*

SHELYN (NG)

The Eternal Rose is the goddess of art, beauty, love, and music. She seeks to one day redeem her corrupted brother, Zon-Kuthon. Shelyn promotes peace and love, and she encourages her followers to create beauty in a sometimes dark world.

Edicts be peaceful, choose and perfect an art, lead by example, see the beauty in all things

Anathema destroy art or allow it to be destroyed, unless saving a life or pursuing greater art; refuse to accept surrender

Follower Alignments LG, NG, CG

DEVOTEE BENEFITS

Divine Font *heal*

Divine Skill select Crafting or Performance

Favored Weapon glaive

Domains creation, family, passion, protection

Cleric Spells 1st: *color spray*, 3rd: *enthrall*, 4th: *creation*

TORAG (LG)

The dwarven deity called the Father of Creation is god of the forge, protection, and strategy. Though most widely worshipped by dwarves, those who treasure crafting and creation also follow Torag.

Edicts be honorable and forthright, keep your word, respect the forge, serve your people

Anathema tell lies or cheat someone, intentionally create inferior works, show mercy to the enemies of your people

Follower Alignments LG, LN

DEVOTEE BENEFITS

Divine Font *heal*

Divine Skill Crafting

Favored Weapon warhammer

Domains creation, earth, family, protection

Cleric Spells 1st: *mindlink*, 3rd: *earthbind*, 4th: *creation*

URGATHOA (NE)

The amoral Pallid Princess oversees disease, gluttony, and undeath.

Edicts become undead upon death, create or protect the undead, sate your appetites

Anathema deny your appetites, destroy undead, sacrifice your life

Follower Alignments LE, NE, CE

DEVOTEE BENEFITS

Divine Font *harm*

Divine Skill Intimidation

Favored Weapon scythe

Domains indulgence, magic, might, undeath

Cleric Spells 1st: *goblin pox*, 2nd: *false life*, 7th: *mask of terror*

ZON-KUTHON (LE)

The Midnight Lord is god of darkness, envy, loss, and pain. Once a god of art, beauty, and music, like Shelyn, he returned from a sojourn in the dark spaces between the planes horribly changed.

Edicts bring pain to the world, mutilate your body

Anathema create permanent or long-lasting sources of light, provide comfort to those who suffer

Follower Alignments LN, LE, NE

DEVOTEE BENEFITS

Divine Font *harm*

Divine Skill Intimidation

Favored Weapon spiked chain

Domains ambition, darkness, destruction, pain

Cleric Spells 1st: *phantom pain*, 3rd: *wall of thorns*, 5th: *shadow walk*

FAITHS AND PHILOSOPHIES

Of course, faith can express itself in more ways than venerating a single deity—or a deity at all. A few examples of nondeific religions and philosophies are presented below. Clerics can work with allied faiths and philosophies, but the organizations here turn to other classes—such as sorcerers with divine bloodlines, druids, or monks—to serve as their leaders. These faiths and philosophies don't have an external godhead that offers benefits to devotees.

ATHEISM

While most concede that the gods exist, some do not view them as worthy of worship, and a few even deny their presence altogether.

Edicts pursue your own agenda with faith in your own ability to excel

Anathema offer prayers to a deity

Follower Alignments all

GREEN FAITH

The worshippers of the Green Faith count many druids among their number. They view nature as divine and draw strength from the knowledge of their place in the natural order.

Edicts guide civilization to grow in harmony with nature, preserve areas of natural wilderness, protect endangered species

Anathema cause damage to natural settings, kill animals for reasons other than self-defense or sustenance, allow abuse of natural resources

Follower Alignments CN, LN, N, NE, NG

PROPHECIES OF KALISTRADE

The dream-records of an eccentric mystic teach that wealth can be achieved through a strict and abstemious code of behavior.

Edicts accumulate personal wealth, foster and aid mercantile pursuits, welcome newcomers regardless of gender or ancestry

Anathema spend money frivolously; offer money to those who don't deserve wealth; overindulge in physical pleasures, food, or drink

Follower Alignments LG, LN, LE

WHISPERING WAY

These cultists believe undeath is the truest form of existence, and life is meant to be spent in preparation for transition to a more glorious unlife after death.

Edicts seek methods to become undead (a lich if possible), oppose those who seek to destroy undead, protect necromantic secrets, serve the Whispering Tyrant

Anathema destroy necromantic texts (unless they reveal secrets of the Whispering Way), teach others of the Whispering Way other than by whispering, use positive energy to harm undead

DOMAINS

The following domains are used by the primary deities of Golarion, as listed on pages 437–440.

TABLE 8-2: DOMAINS

Domain	Description	Domain Spell	Advanced Domain Spell
Ambition	You strive to keep up with and outpace the competition.	Blind ambition	Competitive edge
Air	You can control winds and the weather.	Pushing gust	Disperse into air
Cities	You have powers over urban environments and denizens.	Face in the crowd	Pulse of the city
Confidence	You overcome your fear and project pride.	Veil of confidence	Delusional pride
Creation	You have divine abilities related to crafting and art.	Splash of art	Artistic flourish
Darkness	You operate in the darkness and take away the light.	Cloak of shadow	Darkened eyes
Death	You have the power to end lives and destroy undead.	Death's call	Eradicate undeath
Destruction	You are a conduit for divine devastation.	Cry of destruction	Destructive aura
Dreams	You have the power to enter and manipulate dreams.	Sweet dream	Dreamer's call
Earth	You control soil and stone.	Hurtling stone	Localized quake
Family	You aid and protect your family and community more effectively.	Soothing words	Unity
Fate	You see and understand hidden inevitabilities.	Read fate	Tempt fate
Fire	You control flame.	Fire ray	Flame barrier
Freedom	You liberate yourself and others from shackles and constraints.	Unimpeded stride	Word of freedom
Healing	Your healing magic is particularly potent.	Healer's blessing	Rebuke death
Indulgence	You feast mightily and can shake off the effects of overindulging.	Overstuff	Take its course
Knowledge	You receive divine insights.	Scholarly recollection	Know the enemy
Luck	You're unnaturally lucky and keep out of harm's way.	Bit of luck	Lucky break
Magic	You perform the unexpected and inexplicable.	Magic's vessel	Mystic beacon
Might	Your physical power is bolstered by divine strength.	Athletic rush	Enduring might
Moon	You command powers associated with the moon.	Moonbeam	Touch of the moon
Nature	You hold power over animals and plants.	Vibrant thorns	Nature's bounty
Nightmares	You fill minds with horror and dread.	Waking nightmare	Shared nightmare
Pain	You punish those who displease you with the sharp sting of pain.	Savor the sting	Retributive pain
Passion	You evoke passion, whether as love or lust.	Charming touch	Captivating adoration
Perfection	You strive to perfect your mind, body, and spirit.	Perfected mind	Perfected form
Protection	You ward yourself and others.	Protector's sacrifice	Protector's sphere
Secrecy	You protect secrets and keep them hidden.	Forced quiet	Safeguard secret
Sun	You harness the power of the sun and other light sources, and punish undead.	Dazzling flash	Positive luminance
Travel	You have power over movement and journeys.	Agile feet	Traveler's transit
Trickery	You deceive others and cause mischief.	Sudden shift	Trickster's twin
Truth	You pierce lies and discover the truth.	Word of truth	Glimpse the truth
Tyranny	You wield power to rule and enslave others.	Touch of obedience	Commanding lash
Undeath	Your magic carries close ties to the undead.	Touch of undeath	Malignant sustenance
Water	You control water and bodies of water.	Tidal surge	Downpour
Wealth	You hold power over wealth, trade, and treasure.	Appearance of wealth	Precious metals
Zeal	Your inner fire increases your combat prowess.	Weapon surge	Zeal for battle

INTRODUCTION

ANCESTRIES & BACKGROUNDS

CLASSES

SKILLS

FEATS

EQUIPMENT

SPELLS

THE AGE OF LOST OMENS

PLAYING THE GAME

GAME MASTERING

CRAFTING & TREASURE

APPENDIX

CHAPTER 9: PLAYING THE GAME

At this point, you have a character and are ready to play Pathfinder! Or maybe you're the GM and you are getting ready to run your first adventure. Either way, this chapter provides the full details for the rules outlined in Chapter 1: Introduction. This chapter begins by describing the general rules and conventions of how the game is played and then presents more in-depth explanations of the rules for each mode of play.

9

INTRODUCTION

ANCESTRIES & BACKGROUNDS

CLASSES

SKILLS

FEATS

EQUIPMENT

SPELLS

THE AGE OF LOST OMENS

PLAYING THE GAME

GAME MASTERING

CRAFTING & TREASURE

APPENDIX

Before diving into how to play Pathfinder, it's important to understand the game's three modes of play, which determine the pace of your adventure and the specific rules you'll use at a given time. Each mode provides a different pace and presents a different level of risk to your characters. The Game Master (GM) determines which mode works best for the story and controls the transition between them. You'll likely talk about the modes less formally during your play session, simply transitioning between exploration and encounters during the adventure, before heading to a settlement to achieve something during downtime.

The most intricate of the modes is **encounter mode**. This is where most of the intense action takes place, and it's most often used for combat or other high-stakes situations. The GM typically switches to encounter mode by calling on the players to "roll for initiative" to determine the order in which all the actors take their turns during the encounter. Time is then divided into a series of rounds, each lasting roughly 6 seconds in the game world. Each round, player characters, other creatures, and sometimes even hazards or events take their turn in initiative order. At the start of a participant's turn, they gain the use of a number of actions (typically 3 in the case of PCs and other creatures) as well as a special action called a reaction. These actions, and what you do with them, are how you affect the world within an encounter. The full rules for playing in encounter mode start on page 468.

In **exploration mode**, time is more flexible and the play more free form. In this mode, minutes, hours, or even days in the game world pass quickly in the real world, as the characters travel cross country, explore uninhabited sections of a dungeon, or roleplay during a social gathering. Often, developments during exploration lead to encounters, and the GM will switch to that mode of play until the encounter ends, before returning to exploration mode. The rules for exploration start on page 479.

The third mode is **downtime**. During downtime, the characters are at little risk, and the passage of time is measured in days or longer. This is when you might forge a magic sword, research a new spell, or prepare for your next adventure. The rules for downtime are on page 481.

GENERAL RULES

Before exploring the specific rules of each mode of play, you'll want to understand a number of general rules of the game. To one degree or another, these rules are used in every mode of play.

MAKING CHOICES

Pathfinder is a game where your choices determine the story's direction. Throughout the game, the GM describes what's happening in the world and then asks the players, "So what do you do?" Exactly what you choose to do, and how the GM responds to those choices, builds a unique story experience. Every game is different, because you'll rarely, if ever, make the same decisions as another group of players. This is true for the GM as well—two GMs running the exact same adventure will put different emphasis and flourishes on the way they present each scenario and encounter.

Often, your choices have no immediate risk or consequences. If you're traveling along a forest path and come across a fork in the trail, the GM will ask, "Which way do you go?" You might choose to take the right fork or the left. You could also choose to leave the trail, or just go back to town. Once your choice is made, the GM tells you what happens next. Down the line, that choice may impact what you encounter later in the game, but in many cases nothing dangerous happens immediately.

But sometimes what happens as a result of your choices is less than certain. In those cases, you'll attempt a check.

CHECKS

When success isn't certain—whether you're swinging a sword at a foul beast, attempting to leap across a chasm, or straining to remember the name of the earl's second cousin at a soiree—you'll attempt a check. Pathfinder has many types of checks, from skill checks to attack rolls to saving throws, but they all follow these basic steps.

1. Roll a d20 and identify the modifiers, bonuses, and penalties that apply.
2. Calculate the result.
3. Compare the result to the difficulty class (DC).
4. Determine the degree of success and the effect.

Checks and difficulty classes (DC) both come in many forms. When you swing your sword at that foul beast, you'll make an attack roll against its Armor Class, which is the DC to hit another creature. If you are leaping across that chasm, you'll attempt an Athletics skill check with a

GAME CONVENTIONS

Pathfinder has many specific rules, but you'll also want to keep these general guidelines in mind when playing.

The GM Has the Final Say

If you're ever uncertain how to apply a rule, the GM decides. Of course, Pathfinder is a game, so when adjudicating the rules, the GM is encouraged to listen to everyone's point of view and make a decision that is both fair and fun.

Specific Overrides General

A core principle of Pathfinder is that specific rules override general ones. If two rules conflict, the more specific one takes precedence. If there's still ambiguity, the GM determines which rule to use. For example, the rules state that when attacking a concealed creature, you must attempt a DC 5 flat check to determine if you hit. Flat checks don't benefit from modifiers, bonuses, or penalties, but an ability that's specifically designed to overcome concealment might override and alter this. If a rule doesn't specify otherwise, default to the general rules presented in this chapter. While some special rules may also state the normal rules to provide context, you should always default to the normal rules even if effects don't specifically say to.

Rounding

You may need to calculate a fraction of a value, like halving damage. Always round down unless otherwise specified. For example, if a spell deals 7 damage and a creature takes half damage from it, that creature takes 3 damage.

Multiplying

When more than one effect would multiply the same number, don't multiply more than once. Instead, combine all the multipliers into a single multiplier, with each multiple after the first adding 1 less than its value. For instance, if one ability doubled the duration of one of your spells and another one doubled the duration of the same spell, you would triple the duration, not quadruple it.

Duplicate Effects

When you're affected by the same thing multiple times, only one instance applies, using the higher level of the effects, or the newer effect if the two are the same level. For example, if you were using *mage armor* and then cast it again, you'd still benefit from only one casting of that spell. Casting a spell again on the same target might get you a better duration or effect if it were cast at a higher level the second time, but otherwise doing so gives you no advantage.

Ambiguous Rules

Sometimes a rule could be interpreted multiple ways. If one version is too good to be true, it probably is. If a rule seems to have wording with problematic repercussions or doesn't work as intended, work with your group to find a good solution, rather than just playing with the rule as printed.

DC based on the distance you are trying to jump. When calling to mind the name of the earl's second cousin, you attempt a check to Recall Knowledge. You might use either the Society skill or a Lore skill you have that's relevant to the task, and the DC depends on how common the knowledge of the cousin's name might be, or how many drinks your character had when they were introduced to the cousin the night before.

No matter the details, for any check you must roll the d20 and achieve a result equal to or greater than the DC to succeed. Each of these steps is explained below.

STEP 1: ROLL D20 AND IDENTIFY THE MODIFIERS, BONUSES, AND PENALTIES THAT APPLY

Start by rolling your d20. You'll then identify all the relevant modifiers, bonuses, and penalties that apply to the roll. A **modifier** can be either positive or negative, but a **bonus** is always positive, and a **penalty** is always negative. The sum of all the modifiers, bonuses, and penalties you apply to the d20 roll is called your total modifier for that statistic.

Nearly all checks allow you to add an **ability modifier** to the roll. An ability modifier represents your raw capabilities and is derived from an ability score, as described on page 20. Exactly which ability modifier you use is determined by what you're trying to accomplish. Usually a sword swing applies your Strength modifier, whereas remembering the name of the earl's cousin uses your Intelligence modifier.

When attempting a check that involves something you have some training in, you will also add your **proficiency bonus**. This bonus depends on your proficiency rank: untrained, trained, expert, master, or legendary. If you're untrained, your bonus is +0—you must rely on raw talent and any bonuses from the situation. Otherwise, the bonus equals your character's level plus a certain amount depending on your rank. If your proficiency rank is trained, this bonus is equal to your level + 2, and higher proficiency ranks further increase the amount you add to your level.

Proficiency Rank	Proficiency Bonus
Untrained	0
Trained	Your level + 2
Expert	Your level + 4
Master	Your level + 6
Legendary	Your level + 8

There are three other types of bonus that frequently appear: circumstance bonuses, item bonuses, and status bonuses. If you have different types of bonus that would apply to the same roll, you'll add them all. But if you have multiple bonuses of the same type, you can use only the highest bonus on a given roll—in other words, they don't "stack." For instance, if you have both a proficiency bonus and an item bonus, you add both to your d20 result, but if you have two item bonuses that could apply to the same check, you add only the higher of the two.

Circumstance bonuses typically involve the situation you find yourself in when attempting a check. For instance, using Raise a Shield with a buckler grants you a +1 circumstance bonus to AC. Being behind cover grants you a +2 circumstance bonus to AC. If you are both behind cover and Raising a Shield, you gain only the +2 circumstance bonus for cover, since they're the same type and the bonus from cover is higher.

Item bonuses are granted by some item that you are wearing or using, either mundane or magical. For example, armor gives you an item bonus to AC, while expanded alchemist's tools grant you an item bonus to Crafting checks when making alchemical items.

Status bonuses typically come from spells, other magical effects, or something applying a helpful, often temporary, condition to you. For instance, the 3rd-level *heroism* spell grants a +1 status bonus to attack rolls, Perception checks, saving throws, and skill checks. If you were under the effect of *heroism* and someone cast the *bless* spell, which also grants a +1 status bonus on attacks, your attack rolls would gain only a +1 status bonus, since both spells grant a +1 status bonus to those rolls, and you only take the highest status bonus.

Penalties work very much like bonuses. You can have **circumstance penalties**, **status penalties**, and sometimes even **item penalties**. Like bonuses of the same type, you take only the worst all of various penalties of a given type. However, you can apply both a bonus and a penalty of the same type on a single roll. For example, if you had a +1 status bonus from a *heroism* spell but a –2 status penalty from the sickened condition, you'd apply them both to your roll—so *heroism* still helps even though you're feeling unwell.

Unlike bonuses, penalties can also be **untyped**, in which case they won't be classified as "circumstance," "item," or "status." Unlike other penalties, you always add all your untyped penalties together rather than simply taking the worst one. For instance, when you use attack actions, you incur a multiple attack penalty on each attack you make on your turn after the first attack, and when you attack a target that's beyond your weapon's normal range increment, you incur a range penalty on the attack. Because these are both untyped penalties, if you make multiple attacks at a faraway target, you'd apply both the multiple attack penalty and the range penalty to your roll.

Once you've identified all your various modifiers, bonuses, and penalties, you move on to the next step.

STEP 2: CALCULATE THE RESULT

This step is simple. Add up all the various modifiers, bonuses, and penalties you identified in Step 1—this is your total modifier. Next add that to the number that came up on your d20 roll. This total is your check result.

STEP 3: COMPARE THE RESULT TO THE DC

This step can be simple, or it can create suspense. Sometimes you'll know the **Difficulty Class** (DC) of your check. In these cases, if your result is equal to or greater than the DC, you succeed! If your roll anything less than the DC, you fail.

Other times, you might not know the DC right away. Swimming across a river would require an Athletics check, but it doesn't have a specified DC—so how will you know if you succeed or fail? You call out your result to the GM and they will let you know if it is a success, failure, or otherwise. While you might learn the exact DC through trial and error, DCs sometimes change, so asking the GM whether a check is successful is the best way to determine whether or not you have met or exceeded the DC.

CALCULATING DCS

Whenever you attempt a check, you compare your result against a DC. When someone or something else attempts a check against you, rather than both forces rolling against one another, the GM (or player, if the opponent is another PC) compares their result to a fixed DC based on your relevant statistic. Your DC for a given statistic is 10 + the total modifier for that statistic.

STEP 4: DETERMINE THE DEGREE OF SUCCESS AND EFFECT

Many times, it's important to determine not only if you succeed or fail, but also how spectacularly you succeed or fail. Exceptional results—either good or bad—can cause you to critically succeed at or critically fail a check.

You critically succeed at a check when a check's result meets or exceeds the DC by 10 or more. If the check is an attack roll, this is sometimes called a critical hit. You can also critically fail a check. The rules for critical failure—sometimes called a fumble—are the same as those for a critical success, but in the other direction: if you fail a check by 10 or more, that's a critical failure.

If you rolled a 20 on the die (a "natural 20"), your result is one degree of success better than it would be by numbers alone. If you roll a 1 on the d20 (a "natural 1"), your result is one degree worse. This means that a natural 20

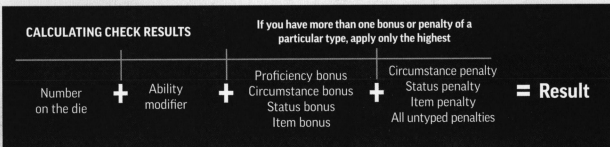

CALCULATING CHECK RESULTS		If you have more than one bonus or penalty of a particular type, apply only the highest	
Number on the die	**+** Ability modifier	**+** Proficiency bonus / Circumstance bonus / Status bonus / Item bonus	**+** Circumstance penalty / Status penalty / Item penalty / All untyped penalties	**= Result**

usually results in a critical success and natural 1 usually results in a critical failure. However, if you were going up against a very high DC, you might get only a success with a natural 20, or even a failure if 20 plus your total modifier is 10 or more below the DC. Likewise, if your modifier for a statistic is so high that adding it to a 1 from your d20 roll exceeds the DC by 10 or more, you can succeed even if you roll a natural 1! If a feat, magic item, spell, or other effect does not list a critical success or critical failure, treat is as an ordinary success or failure instead.

Some other abilities can change the degree of success for rolls you get. When resolving the effect of an ability that changes your degree of success, always apply the adjustment from a natural 20 or natural 1 before anything else.

SPECIFIC CHECKS

While most checks follow these basic rules, it's useful to know about a few specific types of checks, how they're used, and how they differ from one another.

ATTACK ROLLS

When you use a Strike action or any other attack action, you attempt a check called an attack roll. Attack rolls take a variety of forms and are often highly variable based on the weapon you are using for the attack, but there are three main types: melee attack rolls, ranged attack rolls, and spell attack rolls. Spell attack rolls work a little bit differently, so they are explained separately on the next page.

Melee attack rolls use Strength as their ability modifier by default. If you're using a weapon or attack with the finesse trait, then you can use your Dexterity modifier instead.

> **Melee attack roll result = d20 roll + Strength modifier** (or optionally Dexterity modifier for a finesse weapon) **+ proficiency bonus + other bonuses + penalties**

Ranged attack rolls use Dexterity as their ability modifier.

> **Ranged attack roll result = d20 roll + Dexterity modifier + proficiency bonus + other bonuses + penalties**

When attacking with a weapon, whether melee or ranged, you add your proficiency bonus for the weapon you're using. Your class determines your proficiency rank for various weapons. Sometimes, you'll have different proficiency ranks for different weapons. For instance, at 5th level, a fighter gains the weapon mastery class feature, which grants master proficiency with the simple and martial weapons of one weapon group, expert proficiency with advanced weapons of that group and other simple and martial weapons, and trained proficiency in all other advanced weapons.

The bonuses you might apply to attack rolls can come from a variety of sources. Circumstance bonuses can come

from the aid of an ally or a beneficial situation. Status bonuses are typically granted by spells and other magical aids. The item bonus to attack rolls comes from magic weapons—notably, a weapon's potency rune (page 580).

Penalties to attack rolls come from situations and effects as well. Circumstance penalties come from risky tactics or detrimental circumstances, status penalties come from spells and magic working against you, and item penalties occur when you use a shoddy item (page 273). When making attack rolls, two main types of untyped penalties are likely to apply. The first is the multiple attack penalty, and the second is the range penalty. The first applies anytime you make more than one attack action during the course of your turn, and the other applies only with ranged or thrown weapons. Both are described below.

MULTIPLE ATTACK PENALTY

The more attacks you make beyond your first in a single turn, the less accurate you become, represented by the multiple attack penalty. The second time you use an attack action during your turn, you take a –5 penalty to your attack roll. The third time you attack, and on any subsequent attacks, you take a –10 penalty to your attack roll. Every check that has the attack trait counts toward your multiple attack penalty, including Strikes, spell attack rolls, certain skill actions like Shove, and many others.

Some weapons and abilities reduce multiple attack penalties, such as agile weapons, which reduce these penalties to –4 on the second attack or –8 on further attacks.

Attack	Multiple Attack Penalty	Agile
First	None	None
Second	–5	–4
Third or subsequent	–10	–8

Always calculate your multiple attack penalty for the weapon you're using on that attack. For example, let's say you're wielding a longsword in one hand and a shortsword (which has the agile trait) in your other hand, and you are going to make three Strikes with these weapons during the course of your turn. The first Strike you make during your turn has no penalty, no matter what weapon you are using. The second Strike will take either a –5 penalty if you use the longsword or a –4 penalty if you use the shortsword. Just like the second attack, the penalty for your third attack is based on which weapon you're using for that particular Strike. It would be a –10 penalty with the longsword and a –8 penalty with the shortsword, no matter what weapon you used for your previous Strikes.

The multiple attack penalty applies only during your turn, so you don't have to keep track of it if you can perform an Attack of Opportunity or a similar reaction that lets you make a Strike on someone else's turn.

RANGE PENALTY

Ranged and thrown weapons each have a listed range

PLAYING THE GAME

9

INTRODUCTION

ANCESTRIES &
BACKGROUNDS

CLASSES

SKILLS

FEATS

EQUIPMENT

SPELLS

THE AGE OF
LOST OMENS

PLAYING THE
GAME

GAME
MASTERING

CRAFTING
& TREASURE

APPENDIX

increment, and attacks with them grow less accurate against targets farther away (range and range increments are covered in depth on page 279). As long as your target is at or within the listed range increment, also called the first range increment, you take no penalty to the attack roll. If you're attacking beyond that range increment, you take a –2 penalty for each additional increment beyond the first. You can attempt to attack with a ranged weapon or thrown weapon up to six range increments away, but the farther away you are, the harder it is to hit your target.

For example, the range increment of a crossbow is 120 feet. If you are shooting at a target no farther away than that distance, you take no penalty due to range. If they're beyond 120 feet but no more than 240 feet away, you take a –2 penalty due to range. If they're beyond 240 feet but no more than 360 feet away, you take a –4 penalty due to range, and so on, until you reach the last range increment: beyond 600 feet but no more than 720 feet away, where you take a –10 penalty due to range.

Armor Class

Attack rolls are compared to a special difficulty class called an **Armor Class** (AC), which measures how hard it is for your foes to hit you with Strikes and other attack actions. Just like for any other check and DC, the result of an attack roll must meet or exceed your AC to be successful, which allows your foe to deal damage to you.

Armor Class is calculated using the following formula.

> **Armor Class = 10 + Dexterity modifier (up to your
> armor's Dex Cap) + proficiency bonus + armor's
> item bonus to AC + other bonuses + penalties**

Use the proficiency bonus for the category (light, medium, or heavy) or the specific type of armor you're wearing. If you're not wearing armor, use your proficiency in unarmored defense.

Armor Class can benefit from bonuses with a variety of sources, much like attack rolls. Armor itself grants an item bonus, so other item bonuses usually won't apply to your AC, but magic armor can increase the item bonus granted by your armor.

Penalties to AC come from situations and effects in much the same way bonuses do. Circumstance penalties come from unfavorable situations, and status penalties come from effects that impede your abilities or from broken armor. You take an item penalty when you wear shoddy armor (page 273).

SPELL ATTACK ROLLS

If you cast spells, you might be able to make a spell attack roll. These rolls are usually made when a spell makes an attack against a creature's AC.

The ability modifier for a spell attack roll depends on how you gained access to your spells. If your class grants you spellcasting, use your key ability modifier. Innate spells

---

STRIDING AND STRIKING

Two of the simplest and most common actions you'll use in combat are Stride and Strike, described in full on page 471.

Stride is an action that has the move trait and that allows you to move a number of feet up to your Speed. You'll often need to Stride multiple times to reach a foe who's far away or to run from danger! Move actions can often trigger reactions or free actions. However, unlike other actions, a move action can trigger reactions not only when you first use the action, but also for every 5 feet you move during that action, as described on page 474. The Step action (page 471) lets you move without triggering reactions, but only 5 feet.

Strike is an action that has the attack trait and that allows you to attack with a weapon you're wielding or an unarmed attack (such as a fist).

If you're using a melee weapon or unarmed attack, your target must be within your reach; if you're attacking with a ranged weapon, your target must be within range. Your reach is how far you can physically extend a part of your body to make an unarmed attack, or the farthest distance you can reach with a melee weapon. This is typically 5 feet, but special weapons and larger creatures have longer reaches. Your range is how far away you can attack with a ranged weapon or with some types of magical attacks. Different weapons and magical attacks have different maximum ranges, and ranged weapons get less effective as you exceed their range increments.

Striking multiple times in a turn has diminishing returns. The multiple attack penalty (detailed on page 446) applies to each attack after the first, whether those attacks are Strikes, special attacks like the Grapple action of the Athletics skill, or spell attack rolls.

---

use your Charisma modifier unless the ability that granted them states otherwise. Focus spells and other sources of spells specify which ability modifier you use for spell attack rolls in the ability that granted them. If you have spells from multiple sources or traditions, you might use different ability modifiers for spell attack rolls for these different sources of spells. For example, a dwarf cleric with the Stonewalker ancestry feat would use her Charisma modifier when casting *meld into stone* from that feat, since it's a divine innate spell, but she would use her Wisdom modifier when casting *heal* and other spells using her cleric divine spellcasting.

Determine the spell attack roll with the following formula.

> **Spell attack roll result = d20 roll + ability modifier
> used for spellcasting + proficiency bonus + other
> bonuses + penalties**

If you have the ability to cast spells, you'll have a proficiency rank for your spell attack rolls, so you'll always add a proficiency bonus. Like your ability modifier, this proficiency rank may vary from one spell to another if you have spells from multiple sources. Spell attack rolls can benefit from circumstance bonuses and status bonuses, though item bonuses to spell attack rolls are rare. Penalties affect spell attack rolls just like any other attack roll—including your multiple attack penalty.

Many times, instead of requiring you to make a spell attack roll, the spells you cast will require those within the area or targeted by the spell to attempt a saving throw against your **Spell DC** to determine how the spell affects them.

Your spell DC is calculated using the following formula.

Spell DC = 10 + ability modifier used for spellcasting + proficiency bonus + other bonuses + penalties

PERCEPTION

Perception measures your ability to be aware of your environment. Every creature has Perception, which works with and is limited by a creature's senses (described on page 464). Whenever you need to attempt a check based on your awareness, you'll attempt a Perception check. Your Perception uses your Wisdom modifier, so you'll use the following formula when attempting a Perception check.

Perception check result = d20 roll + Wisdom modifier + proficiency bonus + other bonuses + penalties

Nearly all creatures are at least trained in Perception, so you will almost always add a proficiency bonus to your Perception modifier. You might add a circumstance bonus for advantageous situations or environments, and typically get status bonuses from spells or other magical effects. Items can also grant you a bonus to Perception, typically in a certain situation. For instance, a fine spyglass grants a +1 item bonus to Perception when attempting to see something a long distance away. Circumstance penalties to Perception occur when an environment or situation (such as fog) hampers your senses, while status penalties typically come from conditions, spells, and magic effects that foil the senses. You'll rarely encounter item penalties or untyped penalties for Perception.

Many abilities are compared to your **Perception DC** to determine whether they succeed. Your Perception DC is 10 + your total Perception modifier.

PERCEPTION FOR INITIATIVE

Often, you'll roll a Perception check to determine your order in initiative. When you do this, instead of comparing the result against a DC, everyone in the encounter will compare their results. The creature with the highest result acts first, the creature with the second-highest result goes second, and so on. Sometimes you may be called on to roll a skill check for initiative instead, but you'll compare results just as if you had rolled Perception. The full rules for initiative are found in the rules for encounter mode on page 468.

SAVING THROWS

There are three types of saving throws: Fortitude saves, Reflex saves, and Will saves. In all cases, saving throws measure your ability to shrug off harmful effects in the form of afflictions, damage, or conditions. You'll always add a proficiency bonus to each save. Your class might give a different proficiency to each save, but you'll be trained at minimum. Some circumstances and spells might give you circumstance or status bonuses to saves, and you might find *resilient* armor or other magic items that give an item bonus.

Fortitude saving throws allow you to reduce the effects of abilities and afflictions that can debilitate the body. They use your Constitution modifier and are calculated as shown in the formula below.

> **Fortitude save result = d20 roll + Constitution modifier + proficiency bonus + other bonuses + penalties**

Reflex saving throws measure how well you can respond quickly to a situation and how gracefully you can avoid effects that have been thrown at you. They use your Dexterity modifier and are calculated as shown in the formula below.

> **Reflex save result = d20 roll + Dexterity modifier + proficiency bonus + other bonuses + penalties**

Will saving throws measure how well you can resist attacks to your mind and spirit. They use your Wisdom modifier and are calculated as shown in the formula below.

> **Will save result = d20 roll + Wisdom modifier + proficiency bonus + other bonuses + penalties**

Sometimes you'll need to know your DC for a given saving throw. The DC for a saving throw is 10 + the total modifier for that saving throw.

Most of the time, when you attempt a saving throw, you don't have to use your actions or your reaction. You don't even need to be able to act to attempt saving throws. However, in some special cases you might have to take an action to attempt a save. For instance, you can try to recover from the sickened condition by spending an action to attempt a Fortitude save.

Basic Saving Throws

Sometimes you will be called on to attempt a basic saving throw. This type of saving throw works just like any other saving throw—the "basic" part refers to the effects. For a basic save, you'll attempt the check and determine whether you critically succeed, succeed, fail, or critically fail like you would any other saving throw. Then one of the following outcomes applies based on your degree of success—no matter what caused the saving throw.

Critical Success You take no damage from the spell, hazard, or effect that caused you to attempt the save.

Success You take half the listed damage from the effect.

Failure You take the full damage listed from the effect.

Critical Failure You take double the listed damage from the effect.

FORTUNE AND MISFORTUNE EFFECTS

Fortune and misfortune effects can alter how you roll your dice. These abilities might allow you to reroll a failed roll, force you to reroll a successful roll, allow you to roll twice and use the higher result, or force you to roll twice and use the lower result.

You can never have more than one fortune and more than one misfortune effect come into play on a single roll. For instance, if an effect lets you roll twice and use the higher roll, you can't then use Halfling Luck (a fortune effect) to reroll if you fail. If multiple fortune effects would apply, you have to pick which to use. If two misfortune effects apply, the GM decides which is worse and applies it.

If both a fortune effect and a misfortune effect would apply to the same roll, the two cancel each other out, and you roll normally.

SKILL CHECKS

Pathfinder has a variety of skills, from Athletics to Medicine to Occultism. Each grants you a set of related actions that rely on you rolling a skill check. Each skill has a key ability score, based on the scope of the skill in question. For instance, Athletics deals with feats of physical prowess, like swimming and jumping, so its key ability score is Strength. Medicine deals with the ability to diagnose and treat wounds and ailments, so its key ability score is Wisdom. The key ability score for each skill is listed in Chapter 4: Skills. No matter which skill you're using, you calculate a check for it using the following formula.

> **Skill check result = d20 roll + modifier of the skill's key ability score + proficiency bonus + other bonuses + penalties**

You're unlikely to be trained in every skill. When using a skill in which you're untrained, your proficiency bonus is +0; otherwise, it equals your level plus 2 for trained, or higher once you become expert or better. The proficiency rank is specific to the skill you're using. Aid from another character or some other beneficial situation may grant you a circumstance bonus. A status bonus might come from a helpful spell or magical effect. Sometimes tools related to the skill grant you an item bonus to your skill checks. Conversely, unfavorable situations might give you a circumstance penalty to your skill check, while harmful spells, magic, or conditions might also impose a status penalty. Using shoddy or makeshift tools might cause you to take an item penalty. Sometimes a skill action can be an attack, and in these cases, the skill check might take a multiple attack penalty, as described on page 446.

When an ability calls for you to use the DC for a specific skill, you can calculate it by adding 10 + your total modifier for that skill.

NOTATING TOTAL MODIFIERS

When creating your character and adventuring you'll record the total modifier for various important checks on your character sheet. Since many bonuses and penalties are due to the immediate circumstances, spells, and other temporary magical effects, you typically won't apply them to your notations.

Item bonuses and penalties are often more persistent, so you will often want to record them ahead of time. For instance, if you are using a weapon with a *+1 weapon potency* rune, you'll want to add the +1 item bonus to your notation for your attack rolls with that weapon, since you will include that bonus every time you attack with that weapon. But if you have a fine spyglass, you wouldn't add its item bonus to your Perception check notation, since you gain that bonus only if you are using sight—and the spyglass!—to see long distances.

SPECIAL CHECKS

Some categories of checks follow special rules. The most notable are flat checks and secret checks.

FLAT CHECKS

When the chance something will happen or fail to happen is based purely on chance, you'll attempt a flat check. A flat check never includes any modifiers, bonuses, or penalties—you just roll a d20 and compare the result on the die to the DC. Only abilities that specifically apply to flat checks can change the checks' DCs; most such effects affect only certain types of flat checks.

If more than one flat check would ever cause or prevent the same thing, just roll once and use the highest DC. In the rare circumstance that a flat check has a DC of 1 or lower, skip rolling; you automatically succeed. Conversely, if one ever has a DC of 21 or higher, you automatically fail.

SECRET CHECKS

Sometimes you as the player shouldn't know the exact result and effect of a check. In these situations, the rules (or the GM) will call for a secret check. The secret trait appears on anything that uses secret checks. This type of check uses the same formulas you normally would use for that check, but is rolled by the GM, who doesn't reveal the result. Instead, the GM simply describes the information or effects determined by the check's result. If you don't know a secret check is happening (for instance, if the GM rolls a secret Fortitude save against a poison that you failed to notice), you can't use any fortune or misfortune abilities (see the sidebar on page 449) on that check, but if a fortune or misfortune effect would apply automatically, the GM applies it to the secret check. If you know that the GM is attempting a secret check—as often happens with Recall Knowledge or Seek—you can usually activate fortune or misfortune abilities for that check. Just tell the GM, and they'll apply the ability to the check.

The GM can choose to make any check secret, even if it's not usually rolled secretly. Conversely, the GM can let you roll any check yourself, even if that check would usually be secret. Some groups find it simpler to have players roll all secret checks and just try to avoid acting on any out-of-character knowledge, while others enjoy the mystery.

DAMAGE

In the midst of combat, you attempt checks to determine if you can damage your foe with weapons, spells, or alchemical concoctions. On a successful check, you hit and deal damage. Damage decreases a creature's Hit Points on a 1-to-1 basis (so a creature that takes 6 damage loses 6 Hit Points). The full rules can be found in the Hit Points, Healing, and Dying section on page 459.

Damage is sometimes given as a fixed amount, but more often than not you'll make a damage roll to determine how much damage you deal. A damage roll typically uses a number and type of dice determined by the weapon or unarmed attack used or the spell cast, and it is often enhanced by various modifiers, bonuses, and penalties. Like checks, a damage roll—especially a melee weapon damage roll—is often modified by a number of modifiers, penalties, and bonuses. When making a damage roll, you take the following steps, explained in detail below.

1. Roll the dice indicated by the weapon, unarmed attack, or spell, and apply the modifiers, bonuses, and penalties that apply to the result of the roll.
2. Determine the damage type.
3. Apply the target's immunities, weaknesses, and resistances to the damage.
4. If any damage remains, reduce the target's Hit Points by that amount.

STEP 1: ROLL THE DAMAGE DICE AND APPLY MODIFIERS, BONUSES, AND PENALTIES

Your weapon, unarmed attack, spell, or sometimes even a magic item determines what type of dice you roll for damage, and how many. For instance, if you're using a normal longsword, you'll roll 1d8. If you're casting a 3rd-level *fireball* spell, you'll roll 6d6. Sometimes, especially in the case of weapons, you'll apply modifiers, bonuses, and penalties to the damage.

When you use melee weapons, unarmed attacks, and thrown ranged weapons, the most common modifier you'll add to damage is your Strength ability modifier. Weapons with the propulsive trait sometimes add half your Strength modifier. You typically do not add an ability modifier to spell damage, damage from most ranged weapons, or damage from alchemical bombs and similar items.

As with checks, you might add circumstance, status, or item bonuses to your damage rolls, but if you have multiple bonuses of the same type, you add only the highest bonus of that type. Again like checks, you may also apply circumstance, status, item, and untyped penalties to the damage roll, and again you apply only the greatest penalty of a specific type but apply all untyped penalties together.

Use the formulas below.

Melee damage roll = damage die of weapon or unarmed attack + Strength modifier + bonuses + penalties

---

Ranged damage roll = damage die of weapon + Strength modifier for thrown weapons + bonuses + penalties

---

Spell (and similar effects) damage roll = damage die of the effect + bonuses + penalties

---

Once your damage die is rolled, and you've applied any modifiers, bonuses, and penalties, move on to Step 2. Though sometimes there are special considerations, described below.

Increasing Damage

In some cases, you increase the number of dice you roll when making weapon damage rolls. Magic weapons etched with the *striking* rune can add one or more weapon damage dice to your damage roll. These extra dice are the same die size as the weapon's damage die. At certain levels, most characters gain the ability to deal extra damage from the weapon specialization class feature.

Persistent Damage

Persistent damage is a condition that causes damage to recur beyond the original effect. Unlike with normal damage, when you are subject to persistent damage, you don't take it right away. Instead, you take the specified damage at the end of your turns, after which you attempt a DC 15 flat check to see if you recover from the persistent damage. See the Conditions Appendix on pages 618–623 for the complete rules regarding the persistent damage condition.

Doubling and Halving Damage

Sometimes you'll need to halve or double an amount of damage, such as when the outcome of your Strike is a critical hit, or when you succeed at a basic Reflex save against a spell. When this happens, you roll the damage normally, adding all the normal modifiers, bonuses, and penalties. Then you double or halve the amount as appropriate (rounding down if you halved it). The GM might allow you to roll the dice twice and double the modifiers, bonuses, and penalties instead of doubling the entire result, but this usually works best for single-target attacks or spells at low levels when you have a small number of damage dice to roll. Benefits you gain specifically from a critical hit, like the *flaming* weapon rune's persistent fire damage or the extra damage die from the fatal weapon trait, aren't doubled.

STEP 2: DETERMINE THE DAMAGE TYPE

Once you've calculated how much damage you deal, you'll need to determine the damage type. There are many types of damage and sometimes certain types are applied in different ways. The smack of a club deals bludgeoning damage. The stab of a spear deals piercing damage. The staccato crack of a *lightning bolt* spell deals electricity damage. Sometimes you might apply precision damage, dealing more damage for hitting a creature in a vulnerable spot or when the target is somehow vulnerable. The damage types are described on page 452.

Damage Types and Traits

When an attack deals a type of damage, the attack action gains that trait. For example, the Strikes and attack actions you use wielding a sword when its *flaming* rune is active gain the fire trait, since the rune gives the weapon the ability to deal fire damage.

STEP 3: APPLY THE TARGET'S IMMUNITIES, WEAKNESSES, AND RESISTANCES

Defenses against certain types of damage or effects are called immunities or resistances, while vulnerabilities are called weaknesses. Apply immunities first, then weaknesses, and resistances third. Immunity, weakness, or resistance to an alignment applies only to damage of that type, not to damage from an attacking creature of that alignment.

Immunity

When you have immunity to a specific type of damage, you ignore all damage of that type. If you have immunity to a specific condition or type of effect, you can't be affected by that condition or any effect of that type. If you have immunity to effects with a certain trait (such as death effects, poison, or disease) you are unaffected by any effect with that trait. Often, an effect can be both a trait and a damage type (this is especially true in the case of energy damage types). In these cases, the immunity applies to the entire effect, not just the damage. You can still be targeted by an ability with an effect you are immune to; you just don't apply the effect. However, some complex effects might have parts that affect you even if you're immune to one of the effect's traits; for instance, a spell that deals both fire and acid damage can still deal acid damage to you even if you're immune to fire.

Immunity to critical hits works a little differently. When a creature immune to critical hits is critically hit by a Strike or other attack that deals damage, it takes normal damage instead of double damage. This does not make it immune to any other critical success effects of other actions that have the attack trait (such as Grapple and Shove).

Another exception is immunity to nonlethal attacks. If you are immune to nonlethal attacks, you are immune to all damage from attacks with the nonlethal trait, no matter what other type the damage has. For instance, a stone golem has immunity to nonlethal attacks. This means that no matter how hard you hit it with your fist, you're

INTRODUCTION

ANCESTRIES & BACKGROUNDS

CLASSES

SKILLS

FEATS

EQUIPMENT

SPELLS

THE AGE OF LOST OMENS

PLAYING THE GAME

GAME MASTERING

CRAFTING & TREASURE

APPENDIX

DAMAGE TYPES

Damage has a number of different types and categories, which are described below.

Physical Damage

Damage dealt by weapons, many physical hazards, and a handful of spells is collectively called physical damage. The main types of physical damage are bludgeoning, piercing, and slashing. **Bludgeoning damage** comes from weapons and hazards that deal blunt-force trauma, like a hit from a club or being dashed against rocks. **Piercing damage** is dealt from stabs and punctures, whether from a dragon's fangs or the thrust of a spear. **Slashing damage** is delivered by a cut, be it the swing of the sword or the blow from a scythe blades trap.

Ghosts and other incorporeal creatures have a high resistance to physical attacks that aren't magical (attacks that lack the magical trait). Furthermore, most incorporeal creatures have additional, though lower, resistance to magical physical damage (such as damage dealt from a mace with the magical trait) and most other damage types.

Energy Damage

Many spells and other magical effects deal energy damage. Energy damage is also dealt from effects in the world, such as the biting cold of a blizzard to a raging forest fire. The main types of energy damage are acid, cold, electricity, fire, and sonic. **Acid damage** can be delivered by gases, liquids, and certain solids that dissolve flesh, and sometimes harder materials. **Cold damage** freezes material by way of contact with chilling gases and ice. **Electricity damage** comes from the discharge of powerful lightning and sparks. **Fire damage** burns through heat and combustion. **Sonic damage** assaults matter with high-frequency vibration and sound waves. Many times, you deal energy damage by casting magic spells, and doing so is often useful against creatures that have immunities or resistances to physical damage.

Two special types of energy damage specifically target the living and the undead. Positive energy often manifests as healing energy to living creatures but can create **positive damage** that withers undead bodies and disrupts and injures incorporeal undead. Negative energy often revivifies the unnatural, unliving power of undead, while manifesting as **negative damage** that gnaws at the living.

Powerful and pure magical energy can manifest itself as **force damage**. Few things can resist this type of damage—not even incorporeal creatures such as ghosts and wraiths.

Alignment Damage

Weapons and effects keyed to a particular alignment can deal **chaotic**, **evil**, **good**, or **lawful** damage. These damage types apply only to creatures that have the opposing alignment trait. Chaotic damage harms only lawful creatures, evil damage harms only good creatures, good damage harms only evil creatures, and lawful damage harms only chaotic creatures.

Mental Damage

Sometimes an effect can target the mind with enough psychic force to actually deal damage to the creature. When it does, it deals **mental damage**. Mindless creatures and those with only programmed or rudimentary intelligence are often immune to mental damage and effects.

Poison Damage

Venoms, toxins and the like can deal **poison damage**, which affects creatures by way of contact, ingestion, inhalation, or injury. In addition to coming from monster attacks, alchemical items, and spells, poison damage is often caused by ongoing afflictions, which follow special rules described on page 457.

Bleed Damage

Another special type of physical damage is **bleed damage**. This is persistent damage that represents loss of blood. As such, it has no effect on nonliving creatures or living creatures that don't need blood to live. Weaknesses and resistances to physical damage apply.

Precision Damage

Sometimes you are able to make the most of your attack through sheer precision. When you hit with an ability that grants you **precision damage**, you increase the attack's listed damage, using the same damage type, rather than tracking a separate pool of damage. For example, a non-magical dagger Strike that deals 1d6 precision damage from a rogue's sneak attack increases the piercing damage by 1d6.

Some creatures are immune to precision damage, regardless of the damage type; these are often amorphous creatures that lack vulnerable anatomy. A creature immune to precision damage would ignore the 1d6 precision damage in the example above, but it would still take the rest of the piercing damage from the Strike. Since precision damage is always the same type of damage as the attack it's augmenting, a creature that is resistant to physical damage, like a gargoyle, would resist not only the dagger's damage but also the precision damage, even though it is not specifically resistant to precision damage.

Precious Materials

While not their own damage category, precious materials can modify damage to penetrate a creature's resistances or take advantage of its weaknesses. For instance, silver weapons are particularly effective against lycanthropes and bypass the resistances to physical damage that most devils have.

not going to damage it—unless your fists don't have the nonlethal trait, such as if you're a monk.

Temporary Immunity

Some effects grant you immunity to the same effect for a set amount of time. If an effect grants you temporary immunity, repeated applications of that effect don't affect you for as long as the temporary immunity lasts. Unless the effect says it applies only to a certain creature's ability, it doesn't matter who created the effect. For example, the *blindness* spell says, "The target is temporarily immune to *blindness* for 1 minute." If anyone casts *blindness* on that creature again before 1 minute passes, the spell has no effect.

Temporary immunity doesn't prevent or end ongoing effects of the source of the temporary immunity. For instance, if an ability makes you frightened and you then gain temporary immunity to the ability, you don't immediately lose the frightened condition due to the immunity you just gained—you simply don't become frightened if you're targeted by the ability again before the immunity ends.

Weakness

If you have a weakness to a certain type of damage or damage from a certain source, that type of damage is extra effective against you. Whenever you would take that type of damage, increase the damage you take by the value of the weakness. For instance, if you are dealt 2d6 fire damage and have weakness 5 to fire, you take 2d6+5 fire damage.

If you have more than one weakness that would apply to the same instance of damage, use only the highest applicable weakness value. This usually happens only when a monster is weak to both a type of physical damage and the material a weapon is made of.

Resistance

If you have resistance to a type of damage, each time you take that type of damage, you reduce the amount of damage you take by the listed amount (to a minimum of 0 damage). Resistance can specify combinations of damage types or other traits. For instance, you might encounter a monster that's resistant to non-magical bludgeoning damage, meaning it would take less damage from bludgeoning attacks that weren't magical, but would take normal damage from your *+1 mace* (since it's magical) or a non-magical spear (since it deals piercing damage). A resistance also might have an exception. For example, resistance 10 to physical damage (except silver) would reduce any physical damage by 10 unless that damage was dealt by a silver weapon.

If you have more than one type of resistance that would apply to the same instance of damage, use only the highest applicable resistance value.

It's possible to have resistance to all damage. When an effect deals damage of multiple types and you have resistance to all damage, apply the resistance to each type of damage separately. If an attack would deal 7 slashing damage and 4 fire damage, resistance 5 to all damage would reduce the slashing damage to 2 and negate the fire damage entirely.

STEP 4: IF DAMAGE REMAINS, REDUCE THE TARGET'S HIT POINTS

After applying the target's immunities, resistances, and weaknesses to the damage, whatever damage is left reduces the target's Hit Points on a 1-to-1 basis. More information about Hit Points can be found in the Hit Points, Healing, and Dying section on page 459.

Nonlethal Attacks

You can make a nonlethal attack in an effort to knock someone out instead of killing them (see Knocked Out and Dying on page 459). Weapons with the nonlethal trait (including fists) do this automatically. You take a –2 circumstance penalty to the attack roll when you make a nonlethal attack using a weapon that doesn't have the nonlethal trait. You also take this penalty when making a lethal attack using a nonlethal weapon.

CONDITIONS

The results of various checks might apply conditions to you or, less often, an item. Conditions change your state of being in some way. You might be gripped with fear or made faster by a spell or magic item. One condition represents what happens when a creature successfully drains your blood or life essence, while others represent creatures' attitudes toward you and how they interact with you.

Conditions are persistent; when you're affected by a condition, its effects last until the stated duration ends, the condition is removed, or terms dictated in the condition cause it to end. The rules for conditions are summarized on page 454 and described in full on pages 618–623.

EFFECTS

Anything you do in the game has an **effect**. Many of these outcomes are easy to adjudicate during the game. If you tell the GM that you draw your sword, no check is needed, and the result is that your character is now holding a sword. Other times, the specific effect requires more detailed rules governing how your choice is resolved. Many spells, magic items, and feats create specific effects, and your character will be subject to effects caused by monsters, hazards, the environment, and other characters.

While a check might determine the overall impact or strength of an effect, a check is not always part of creating an effect. Casting a *fly* spell on yourself creates an effect that allows you to soar through the air, but casting the spell does not require a check. Conversely, using the Intimidate skill to Demoralize a foe does require a check, and your result on that check determines the effect's outcome.

The following general rules are used to understand and apply effects.

CONDITIONS

These conditions appear often in the game and are defined in detail in the Conditions Appendix on pages 618–623. Here's a brief summary of each.

Blinded: You're unable to see.

Broken: This item can't be used for its normal function until repaired.

Clumsy: You can't move as easily or gracefully as usual.

Concealed: Fog or similar obscuration makes you difficult to see and target.

Confused: You attack indiscriminately.

Controlled: Another creature determines your actions.

Dazzled: Everything is concealed to you.

Deafened: You're unable to hear.

Doomed: With your soul in peril, you are now closer to death.

Drained: Blood loss or something similar has leached your vitality.

Dying: You're slipping closer to death.

Encumbered: You're carrying more weight than you can manage.

Enfeebled: Your strength has been sapped away.

Fascinated: You are compelled to focus your attention on something.

Fatigued: Your defenses are lower and you can't focus while exploring.

Flat-Footed: You're unable to defend yourself to your full capability.

Fleeing: You must run away.

Friendly: An NPC with this condition has a good attitude toward you.

Frightened: Fear makes you less capable of attacking and defending.

Grabbed: A creature, object, or magic holds you in place.

Helpful: An NPC with this condition wants to assist you.

Hidden: A creature you're hidden from knows your location but can't see you.

Hostile: An NPC with this condition wants to harm you.

Immobilized: You can't move.

Indifferent: An NPC with this condition doesn't have a strong opinion about you.

Invisible: Creatures can't see you.

Observed: You're in plain view.

Paralyzed: You body is frozen in place.

Persistent Damage: You keep taking damage every round.

Petrified: You've been turned to stone.

Prone: You're lying on the ground and easier to attack.

Quickened: You get an extra action each turn.

Restrained: You're tied up and can't move, or a grappling creature has you pinned.

Sickened: You're sick to your stomach.

Slowed: You lose actions each turn.

Stunned: You can't use actions.

Stupefied: Your can't access your full mental faculties, and you have trouble casting spells.

Unconscious: You're asleep or knocked out.

Undetected: A creature you're undetected by doesn't know where you are.

Unfriendly: An NPC with this condition doesn't like you.

Unnoticed: A creature is entirely unaware you're present.

Wounded: You've been brought back from the brink of death but haven't fully recovered.

PLAYING THE GAME

9

INTRODUCTION

ANCESTRIES &
BACKGROUNDS

CLASSES

SKILLS

FEATS

EQUIPMENT

SPELLS

THE AGE OF
LOST OMENS

PLAYING THE
GAME

GAME
MASTERING

CRAFTING
& TREASURE

APPENDIX

DURATION

Most effects are discrete, creating an instantaneous effect when you let the GM know what actions you are going to use. Firing a bow, moving to a new space, or taking something out of your pack all resolve instantly. Other effects instead last for a certain duration. Once the duration has elapsed, the effect ends. The rules generally use the following conventions for durations, though spells have some special durations detailed on pages 304–305.

For an effect that lasts a number of rounds, the remaining duration decreases by 1 at the start of each turn of the creature that created the effect. This is common for beneficial effects that target you or your allies. Detrimental effects often last "until the end of the target's next turn" or "through" a number of their turns (such as "through the target's next 3 turns"), which means that the effect's duration decreases at the end of the creature's turn, rather than the start.

Instead of lasting a fixed number of rounds, a duration might end only when certain conditions are met (or cease to be true). If so, the effects last until those conditions are met.

RANGE AND REACH

Actions and other abilities that generate an effect typically work within a specified range or a reach. Most spells and abilities list a **range**—the maximum distance from the creature or object creating the effect in which the effect can occur.

Ranged and thrown weapons have a **range increment**. Attacks with such weapons work normally up to that range. Attacks against targets beyond that range take a –2 penalty, which worsens by 2 for every additional multiple of that range, to a maximum of a –10 penalty after five additional range increments. Attacks beyond this range are not possible. For example, if you are using a shortbow, your attacks take no penalty against a target up to 60 feet away, a –2 penalty if a target is over 60 and up to 120 feet away, a –4 if a target is over 120 and up to 180 feet away, and so on, up to a maximum distance of 360 feet.

Reach is how far you can physically reach with your body or a weapon. Melee Strikes rely on reach. Your reach also creates an area around your space where other creatures could trigger your reactions. Your reach is typically 5 feet, but weapons with the reach trait can extend this. Larger creatures can have greater reach; for instance, an ogre has a 10-foot reach. Unlike with measuring most distances, 10-foot reach can reach 2 squares diagonally. Reach greater than 10 feet is measured normally; 20-foot reach can reach 3 squares diagonally, 25-foot reach can reach 4, and so on.

TARGETS

Some effects require you to choose specific targets. Targeting can be difficult or impossible if your chosen creature is undetected by you, if the creature doesn't match restrictions on who you can target, or if some other ability prevents it from being targeted.

Some effects require a target to be willing. Only you can decide whether your PC is willing, and the GM decides whether an NPC is willing. Even if you or your character don't know what the effect is, such as if your character is unconscious, you still decide if you're willing.

Some effects target or require an ally, or otherwise refer to an ally. This must be someone on your side, often another PC, but it might be a bystander you are trying to protect. You are not your own ally. If it isn't clear, the GM decides who counts as an ally or an enemy.

AREAS

Some effects occupy an area of a specified shape and size. An area effect always has a point of origin and extends out from that point. There are four types of areas: emanations,

bursts, cones, and lines. When you're playing in encounter mode and using a grid, areas are measured in the same way as movement (page 463), but areas' distances are never reduced or affected by difficult terrain (page 475) or lesser cover (page 476). You can use the diagrams below as common reference templates for areas, rather than measuring squares each time. Many area effects describe only the effects on creatures in the area. The GM determines any effects to the environment and unattended objects.

Burst

A burst effect issues forth in all directions from a single

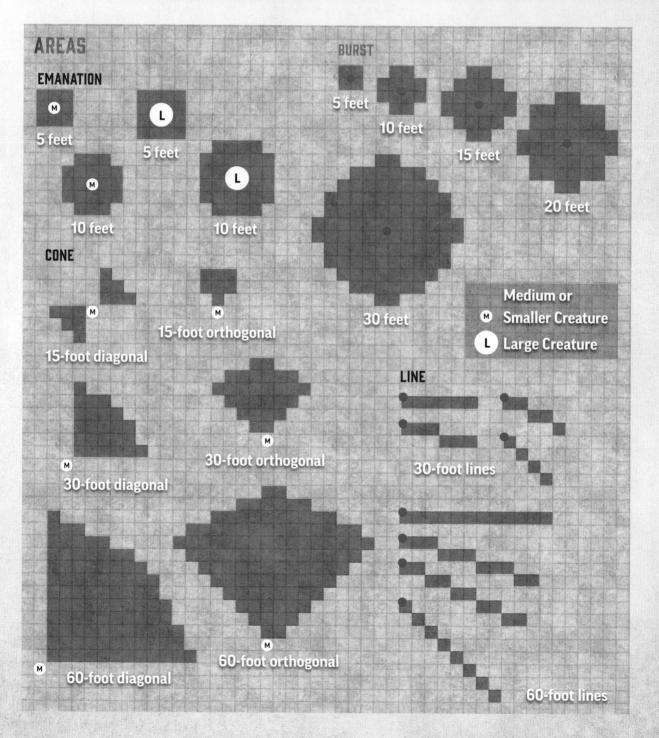

INTRODUCTION

ANCESTRIES & BACKGROUNDS

CLASSES

SKILLS

FEATS

EQUIPMENT

SPELLS

THE AGE OF LOST OMENS

PLAYING THE GAME

GAME MASTERING

CRAFTING & TREASURE

APPENDIX

corner of a square within the range of the effect, spreading in all directions to a specified radius. For instance, when you cast *fireball*, it detonates at the corner of a square within 500 feet of you and creates a 20-foot burst, meaning it extends out 20 feet in every direction from the corner of the square you chose, affecting each creature whose space (or even one square of its space) is within the burst.

CONE

A cone shoots out from you in a quarter circle on the grid. When you aim a cone, the first square of that cone must share an edge with your space if you're aiming orthogonally, or it must touch a corner of your space if you're aiming diagonally. If you're Large or larger, the first square can run along the edge of any square of your space. You can't aim a cone so that it overlaps your space. The cone extends out for a number of feet, widening as it goes, as shown in the Areas diagram. For instance, when a green dragon uses its breath weapon, it breathes a cone of poisonous gas that originates at the edge of one square of its space and affects a quarter-circle area 30 feet on each edge.

If you make a cone originate from someone or something else, follow these same rules, with the first square of the cone using an edge or corner of that creature or object's space instead of your own.

EMANATION

An emanation issues forth from each side of your space, extending out to a specified number of feet in all directions. For instance, the *bless* spell's emanation radiates 5 or more feet outward from the caster. Because the sides of a target's space are used as the starting point for the emanation, an emanation from a Large or larger creature affects a greater overall area than that of a Medium or smaller creature.

LINE

A line shoots forth from you in a straight line in a direction of your choosing. The line affects each creature whose space it overlaps. Unless a line effect says otherwise, it is 5 feet wide. For example, the *lightning bolt* spell's area is a 60-foot line that's 5 feet wide.

LINE OF EFFECT

When creating an effect, you usually need an unblocked path to the target of a spell, the origin point of an effect's area, or the place where you create something with a spell or other ability. This is called a line of effect. You have line of effect unless a creature is entirely behind a solid physical barrier. Visibility doesn't matter for line of effect, nor do portcullises and other barriers that aren't totally solid. If you're unsure whether a barrier is solid enough, usually a 1-foot-square gap is enough to maintain a line of effect, though the GM makes the final call.

In an area effect, creatures or targets must have line of effect to the point of origin to be affected. If there's no line of effect between the origin of the area and the target,

the effect doesn't apply to that target. For example, if there's a solid wall between the origin of a *fireball* and a creature that's within the burst radius, the wall blocks the effect—that creature is unaffected by the *fireball* and doesn't need to attempt a save against it. Likewise, any ongoing effects created by an ability with an area cease to affect anyone who moves outside of the line of effect.

LINE OF SIGHT

Some effects require you to have line of sight to your target. As long as you can precisely sense the area (as described in Perception on page 464) and it is not blocked by a solid barrier (as described in Cover on pages 476–477), you have line of sight. An area of darkness prevents line of sight if you don't have darkvision, but portcullises and other obstacles that aren't totally solid do not. If you're unsure whether a barrier is solid enough to block line of sight, usually a 1-foot-square gap is enough to maintain line of sight, though the GM makes the final call.

AFFLICTIONS

Diseases and poisons are types of afflictions, as are curses and radiation. An affliction can infect a creature for a long time, progressing through different and often increasingly debilitating stages. The level of an affliction is the level of the monster, hazard, or item causing the affliction or, in the case of a spell, is listed in the affliction entry for that spell.

FORMAT

Whether appearing in a spell, as an item, or within a creature's stat block, afflictions appear in the following format.

NAME AND TRAITS

The affliction's name is given first, followed by its traits in parentheses—including the trait for the type of affliction (curse, disease, poison, and so forth). If the affliction needs to have a level specified, it follows the parentheses, followed by any unusual details, such as restrictions on removing the conditions imposed by an affliction.

SAVING THROW

When you're first exposed to the affliction, you must attempt a saving throw against it. This first attempt to stave off the affliction is called the initial save. An affliction usually requires a Fortitude save, but the exact save and its DC are listed after the name and type of affliction. Spells that can poison you typically use the caster's spell DC.

On a successful initial saving throw, you are unaffected by that exposure to the affliction. You do not need to attempt further saving throws against it unless you are exposed to the affliction again.

If you fail the initial saving throw, after the affliction's onset period elapses (if applicable), you advance to stage 1 of the affliction and are subjected to the listed effect. On a critical failure, after its onset period (if applicable), you

AFFLICTION EXAMPLE

To see how a poison works, let's look at the arsenic alchemical item (page 550). The item notes that you can't reduce your sickened condition while affected by arsenic, and has the following text for how the affliction works.

Saving Throw DC 18 Fortitude; **Onset** 10 minutes; **Maximum Duration** 5 minutes; **Stage 1** 1d4 poison damage and sickened 1 (1 minute); **Stage 2** 1d6 poison damage and sickened 2 (1 minute); **Stage 3** 2d6 poison damage and sickened 3 (1 minute)

For example, if you drank a glass of wine laced with arsenic, you would attempt an initial Fortitude save against the listed DC of 18. If you fail, you advance to stage 1. Because of the onset time, nothing happens for 10 minutes, but once this time passes, you take 1d4 poison damage and become sickened 1. As noted, you're unable to reduce the sickened condition you gain from arsenic. The interval of stage 1 is 1 minute (as shown in parentheses), so you attempt a new save after 1 minute passes. If you succeed, you reduce the stage by 1, recovering from the poison. If you fail again, the stage increases by 1 to stage 2, and you take 1d6 poison damage and become sickened 2.

If your initial save against the arsenic was a critical failure, you would advance directly to stage 2. After the 10-minute onset time, you would take 1d6 poison damage and become sickened 2. Succeeding at your second save would reduce the stage t by 1 to stage 1, and you'd take only 1d4 poison damage. Failing the second save would increase by 1 again to stage 3.

If you reach stage 3 of the poison, either by failing while at stage 2 or critically failing while at stage 1, you'd take 2d6 poison damage and be sickened 3. If you failed or critically failed your saving throw while at stage 3, you would repeat the effects of stage 3.

Since the poison has a maximum duration of 5 minutes, you recover from it once the 5 minutes pass, no matter which stage you're at.

advance to stage 2 of the affliction and are subjected to that effect instead. The stages of an affliction are described below.

Onset

Some afflictions have onset times. For these afflictions, once you fail your initial save, you don't gain the effects for the first stage of the affliction until the onset time has elapsed. If this entry is absent, you gain the effects for the first stage (or the second stage on a critical failure) immediately upon failing the initial saving throw.

Maximum Duration

If an affliction lasts only a limited amount of time, it lists a maximum duration. Once this duration passes, the affliction ends. Otherwise, the affliction lasts until you succeed at enough saves to recover, as described in Stages below.

Stages

An affliction typically has multiple stages, each of which lists an effect followed by an interval in parentheses. When you reach a given stage of an affliction, you are subjected to the effects listed for that stage.

At the end of a stage's listed interval, you must attempt a new saving throw. On a success, you reduce the stage by 1; on a critical success, you reduce the stage by 2. You are then subjected to the effects of the new stage. If the affliction's stage is ever reduced below stage 1, the affliction ends and you don't need to attempt further saves unless you're exposed to the affliction again.

On a failure, the stage increases by 1; on a critical failure, the stage increases by 2. You are then subjected to the effects listed for the new stage. If a failure or critical failure would increase the stage beyond the highest listed stage, the affliction instead repeats the effects of the highest stage.

CONDITIONS FROM AFFLICTIONS

An affliction might give you conditions with a longer or shorter duration than the affliction. For instance, if an affliction causes you to be drained but has a maximum duration of 5 minutes, you remain drained even after the affliction ends, as is normal for the drained condition. Or, you might succeed at the flat check to remove persistent damage you took from an ongoing affliction, but you would still need to attempt saves to remove the affliction itself, and failing one might give you new persistent damage.

MULTIPLE EXPOSURES

Multiple exposures to the same curse or disease currently affecting you have no effect. For a poison, however, failing the initial saving throw against a new exposure increases the stage by 1 (or by 2 if you critically fail) without affecting the maximum duration. This is true even if you're within the poison's onset period, though it doesn't change the onset length.

VIRULENT AFFLICTIONS

Afflictions with the virulent trait are harder to remove. You must succeed at two consecutive saves to reduce a virulent affliction's stage by 1. A critical success reduces a virulent affliction's stage by only 1 instead of by 2.

COUNTERACTING

Some effects try to counteract spells, afflictions, conditions, or other effects. Counteract checks compare the power of two forces and determine which defeats the other. Successfully counteracting an effect ends it unless noted otherwise.

When attempting a counteract check, add the relevant skill modifier or other appropriate modifier to your check against the target's DC. If you're counteracting an affliction, the DC is in the affliction's stat block. If it's a spell, use the caster's DC. The GM can also calculate a DC based on the target effect's level. For spells, the counteract check modifier is your spellcasting ability modifier plus your spellcasting proficiency bonus, plus any bonuses and penalties that specifically apply to counteract checks. What you can counteract depends on the check result and the target's level. If an effect is a spell, its level is the counteract level. Otherwise, halve its level and round up to determine its counteract level. If an effect's level is unclear and it came from a creature, halve and round up the creature's level.

Critical Success Counteract the target if its counteract level is no more than 3 levels higher than your effect's counteract level.

Success Counteract the target if its counteract level is no more than 1 level higher than your effect's counteract level.

Failure Counteract the target if its counteract level is lower than your effect's counteract level.

Critical Failure You fail to counteract the target.

Hit Points, Healing, and Dying

All creatures and objects have Hit Points (HP). Your maximum Hit Point value represents your health, wherewithal, and heroic drive when you are in good health and rested. Your maximum Hit Points include the Hit Points you gain at 1st level from your ancestry and class, those you gain at higher levels from your class, and any you gain from other sources (like the Toughness general feat). When you take damage, you reduce your current Hit Points by a number equal to the damage dealt.

Some spells, items, and other effects, as well as simply resting, can heal living or undead creatures. When you are healed, you regain Hit Points equal to the amount healed, up to your maximum Hit Points.

KNOCKED OUT AND DYING

Creatures cannot be reduced to fewer than 0 Hit Points. When most creatures reach 0 Hit Points, they die and are removed from play unless the attack was nonlethal, in which case they are instead knocked out for a significant amount of time (usually 1 minute or more). When undead and construct creatures reach 0 Hit Points, they are destroyed.

Player characters, their companions, and other significant characters and creatures don't automatically die when they reach 0 Hit Points. Instead, they are knocked out and are at risk of death. At the GM's discretion, villains, powerful monsters, special NPCs, and enemies with special abilities that are likely to bring them back to the fight (like ferocity, regeneration, or healing magic) can use these rules as well.

As a player character, when you are reduced to 0 Hit Points, you're knocked out with the following effects:

- You immediately move your initiative position to directly before the creature or effect that reduced you to 0 HP.

- You gain the dying 1 condition. If the effect that knocked you out was a critical success from the attacker or the result of your critical failure, you gain the dying 2 condition instead. If you have the wounded condition (page 460), increase your dying value by an amount equal to your wounded value. If the damage was dealt by a nonlethal attack or nonlethal effect, you don't gain the dying condition; you are instead unconscious with 0 Hit Points.

TAKING DAMAGE WHILE DYING

If you take damage while you already have the dying condition, increase your dying condition value by 1, or by 2 if the damage came from an attacker's critical hit or your own critical failure. If you have the wounded condition, remember to add the value of your wounded condition to your dying value.

RECOVERY CHECKS

When you're dying, at the start of each of your turns, you must attempt a flat check with a DC equal to 10 + your current dying value to see if you get better or worse. This is called a recovery check. The effects of this check are as follows.

Critical Success Your dying value is reduced by 2.
Success Your dying value is reduced by 1.
Failure Your dying value increases by 1.
Critical Failure Your dying value increases by 2.

CONDITIONS RELATED TO DEATH AND DYING

To understand the rules for getting knocked out and how dying works in the game, you'll need some more information on the conditions used in those rules. Presented below are the rules for the dying, unconscious, wounded, and doomed conditions.

DYING

You are bleeding out or otherwise at death's door. While you have this condition, you are unconscious. Dying always includes a value. If this value ever reaches dying 4, you die. If you're dying, you must attempt a recovery check at the start of your turn each round to determine whether you get better or worse.

If you lose the dying condition by succeeding at a recovery check and are still at 0 Hit Points, you remain unconscious, but you can wake up as described on page 460. You lose the dying condition automatically and wake up if you ever have 1 Hit Point or more. Anytime you lose the dying condition, you gain the wounded 1 condition, or increase your wounded value by 1 if you already have that condition.

UNCONSCIOUS

You're sleeping, or you've been knocked out. You can't act. You take a −4 status penalty to AC, Perception, and Reflex saves, and you have the blinded and flat-footed conditions. When you gain this condition, you fall prone and drop

INTRODUCTION

ANCESTRIES & BACKGROUNDS

CLASSES

SKILLS

FEATS

EQUIPMENT

SPELLS

THE AGE OF LOST OMENS

PLAYING THE GAME

GAME MASTERING

CRAFTING & TREASURE

APPENDIX

items you are wielding or holding unless the effect states otherwise or the GM determines you're in a position in which you wouldn't.

If you're unconscious because you're dying, you can't wake up as long as you have 0 Hit Points. If you're restored to 1 Hit Point or more via healing, you lose the dying and unconscious conditions and can act normally on your next turn.

If you are unconscious and at 0 Hit Points, but not dying, you naturally return to 1 Hit Point and awaken after sufficient time passes. The GM determines how long you remain unconscious, from a minimum of 10 minutes to several hours. If you receive healing during this time, you lose the unconscious condition and can act normally on your next turn.

If you're unconscious and have more than 1 Hit Point (typically because you are asleep or unconscious due to an effect), you wake up in one of the following ways. Each causes you to lose the unconscious condition.

- You take damage, provided the damage doesn't reduce you to 0 Hit Points. (If the damage reduces you to 0 Hit Points, you remain unconscious and gain the dying condition as normal.)
- You receive healing, other than the natural healing you get from resting.
- Someone nudges or shakes you awake using an Interact action.
- Loud noise is being made around you—though this isn't automatic. At the start of your turn, you automatically attempt a Perception check against the noise's DC (or the lowest DC if there is more than one noise), waking up if you succeed. This is often DC 5 for a battle, but if

creatures are attempting to stay quiet around you, this Perception check uses their Stealth DC. Some magical effects make you sleep so deeply that they don't allow you to attempt this Perception check.

- If you are simply asleep, the GM decides you wake up either because you have had a restful night's sleep or something disrupted that rest.

WOUNDED

You have been seriously injured during a fight. Anytime you lose the dying condition, you become wounded 1 if you didn't already have the wounded condition. If you already have the wounded condition, your wounded condition value instead increases by 1. If you gain the dying condition while wounded, increase the dying condition's value by your wounded value. The wounded condition ends if someone successfully restores Hit Points to you with Treat Wounds, or if you are restored to full Hit Points and rest for 10 minutes.

DOOMED

Your life is ebbing away, bringing you ever closer to death. Some powerful spells and evil creatures can inflict the doomed condition on you. Doomed always includes a value. The maximum dying value at which you die is reduced by your doomed value. For example, if you were doomed 1, you would die upon reaching dying 3 instead of dying 4. If your maximum dying value is ever reduced to 0, you instantly die. When you die, you're no longer doomed.

Your doomed value decreases by 1 each time you get a full night's rest.

DEATH

After you die, you can't act or be affected by spells that target creatures (unless they specifically target dead creatures), and for all other purposes you are an object. When you die, you are reduced to 0 Hit Points if you had a different amount, and you can't be brought above 0 Hit Points as long as you remain dead. Some magic can bring creatures back to life, such as the *resurrect* ritual or the *raise dead* spell.

HEROIC RECOVERY

If you have at least 1 Hero Point (page 467), you can spend all of your remaining Hero Points at the start of your turn or when your dying value would increase in order to return to 1 Hit Point, no matter how close to death you are. You lose the dying condition and become conscious. You do not gain the wounded condition (or increase its value) when you perform a heroic recovery.

DEATH EFFECTS AND INSTANT DEATH

Some spells and abilities can kill you immediately or bring you closer to death without needing to reduce you to 0 Hit Points first. These abilities have the death trait and usually involve negative energy, the antithesis of life. If you are reduced to 0 Hit Points by a death effect, you are slain instantly without needing to reach dying 4. If an effect states it kills you outright, you die without having to reach dying 4 and without being reduced to 0 Hit Points.

MASSIVE DAMAGE

You die instantly if you ever take damage equal to or greater than double your maximum Hit Points in one blow.

TEMPORARY HIT POINTS

Some spells or abilities give you temporary Hit Points. Track these separately from your current and maximum Hit Points; when you take damage, reduce your temporary Hit Points first. Most temporary Hit Points last for a limited duration. You can't regain lost temporary Hit Points through healing, but you can gain more via other abilities. You can have temporary Hit Points from only one source at a time. If you gain temporary Hit Points when you already have some, choose whether to keep the amount you already have and their corresponding duration or to gain the new temporary Hit Points and their duration.

ITEMS AND HIT POINTS

Items have Hit Points like creatures, but the rules for damaging them are different (page 272). An item has a Hardness statistic that reduces damage the item takes by that amount. The item then takes any damage left over. If an item is reduced to 0 HP, it's destroyed. An item also has a Broken Threshold. If its HP are reduced to this amount or lower, it's broken, meaning it can't be used for its normal function and it doesn't grant bonuses. Damaging an unattended item usually requires attacking it directly, and can be difficult due to that item's Hardness and immunities. You usually can't attack an attended object (one on a creature's person).

ACTIONS

You affect the world around you primarily by using actions, which produce effects. Actions are most closely measured and restricted during the encounter mode of play, but even when it isn't important for you to keep strict track of actions, they remain the way in which you interact with the game world. There are four types of actions: single actions, activities, reactions, and free actions.

Single actions can be completed in a very short time. They're self-contained, and their effects are generated within the span of that single action. During an encounter, you get 3 actions at the beginning of your turn, which you can use as described on page 468.

Activities usually take longer and require using multiple actions, which must be spent in succession. Stride is a single

ACTION ICON KEY

These icons appear in stat blocks as shorthand for each type of action.

- ◆ Single Action
- ◆◆ Two-Action Activity
- ◆◆◆ Three-Action Activity
- ↻ Reaction
- ◇ Free Action

action, but Sudden Charge is an activity in which you use both the Stride and Strike actions to generate its effect.

Reactions have triggers, which must be met for you to use the reaction. You can use a reaction anytime its trigger is met, whether it's your turn or not. In an encounter, you get 1 reaction each round, which you can use as described on page 468. Outside of encounters, your use of reactions is more flexible and up to the GM. Reactions are usually triggered by other creatures or by events outside your control.

Free actions don't cost you any of your actions per turn, nor do they cost your reaction. A free action with no trigger follows the same rules as a single action (except the action cost), and a free action with a trigger follows the same rules as a reaction (except the reaction cost).

ACTIVITIES

An activity typically involves using multiple actions to create an effect greater than you can produce with a single action, or combining multiple single actions to produce an effect that's different from merely the sum of those actions. In some cases, usually when spellcasting, an activity can consist of only 1 action, 1 reaction, or even 1 free action.

An activity might cause you to use specific actions within it. You don't have to spend additional actions to perform them—they're already factored into the activity's required actions. (See Subordinate Actions on page 462.)

You have to spend all the actions of an activity at once to gain its effects. In an encounter, this means you must complete it during your turn. If an activity gets interrupted or disrupted in an encounter (page 462), you lose all the actions you committed to it.

EXPLORATION AND DOWNTIME ACTIVITIES

Outside of encounters, activities can take minutes, hours, or even days. These activities usually have the exploration or downtime trait to indicate they're meant to be used during these modes of play. You can often do other things off and on as you carry out these activities, provided they aren't significant activities of their own. For instance, if you're Repairing an item, you might move around to stretch your legs or have a brief discussion—but you couldn't also Decipher Writing at the same time.

If an activity that occurs outside of an encounter is interrupted or disrupted, as described in Disrupting

IN-DEPTH ACTION RULES

These rules clarify some of the specifics of using actions.

Simultaneous Actions

You can use only one single action, activity, or free action that doesn't have a trigger at a time. You must complete one before beginning another. For example, the Sudden Charge activity states you must Stride twice and then Strike, so you couldn't use an Interact action to open a door in the middle of the movement, nor could you perform part of the move, make your attack, and then finish the move.

Free actions with triggers and reactions work differently. You can use these whenever the trigger occurs, even if the trigger occurs in the middle of another action.

Subordinate Actions

An action might allow you to use a simpler action—usually one of the Basic Actions on page 469—in a different circumstance or with different effects. This subordinate action still has its normal traits and effects, but is modified in any ways listed in the larger action. For example, an activity that tells you to Stride up to half your Speed alters the normal distance you can move in a Stride. The Stride would still have the move trait, would still trigger reactions that occur based on movement, and so on. The subordinate action doesn't gain any of the traits of the larger action unless specified. The action that allows you to use a subordinate action doesn't require you to spend more actions or reactions to do so; that cost is already factored in.

Using an activity is not the same as using any of its subordinate actions. For example, the quickened condition you get from the *haste* spell lets you spend an extra action each turn to Stride or Strike, but you couldn't use the extra action for an activity that includes a Stride or Strike. As another example, if you used an action that specified, "If the next action you use is a Strike," an activity that includes a Strike wouldn't count, because the next thing you are doing is starting an activity, not using the Strike basic action.

Actions below, you usually lose the time you put in, but no additional time beyond that.

ACTIONS WITH TRIGGERS

You can use free actions that have triggers and reactions only in response to certain events. Each such reaction and free action lists the trigger that must happen for you to perform it. When its trigger is satisfied—and *only* when it is satisfied—you can use the reaction or free action, though you don't have to use the action if you don't want to.

There are only a few basic reactions and free actions that all characters can use. You're more likely to gain actions with triggers from your class, feats, and magic items.

LIMITATIONS ON TRIGGERS

The triggers listed in the stat blocks of reactions and some free actions limit when you can use those actions. You can use only one action in response to a given trigger. For example, if you had a reaction and a free action that both had a trigger of "your turn begins," you could use either of them at the start of your turn—but not both. If two triggers are similar, but not identical, the GM determines whether you can use one action in response to each or whether they're effectively the same thing. Usually, this decision will be based on what's happening in the narrative.

This limitation of one action per trigger is per creature; more than one creature can use a reaction or free action in response to a given trigger.

OTHER ACTIONS

Sometimes you need to attempt something not already covered by defined actions in the game. When this happens, the rules tell you how many actions you need to spend, as well any traits your action might have. For example, a spell that lets you switch targets might say you can do so "by spending a single action, which has the concentrate trait." Game masters can also use this approach when a character tries to do something that isn't covered in the rules.

GAINING AND LOSING ACTIONS

Conditions can change the number of actions you can use on your turn, or whether you can use actions at all. The slowed condition, for example, causes you to lose actions, while the quickened condition causes you to gain them. Conditions are detailed in the appendix on pages 618–623. Whenever you lose a number of actions—whether from these conditions or in any other way—you choose which to lose if there's any difference between them. For instance, the *haste* spell makes you quickened, but it limits what you can use your extra action to do. If you lost an action while *haste* was active, you might want to lose the action from *haste* first, since it's more limited than your normal actions.

Some effects are even more restrictive. Certain abilities, instead of or in addition to changing the number of actions you can use, say specifically that you can't use reactions. The most restrictive form of reducing actions is when an effect states that you can't act: this means you can't use any actions, or even speak. When you can't act, you don't regain your actions and reaction on your turn.

DISRUPTING ACTIONS

Various abilities and conditions, such as an Attack of Opportunity, can disrupt an action. When an action is disrupted, you still use the actions or reactions you committed and you still expend any costs, but the action's effects don't occur. In the case of an activity, you usually lose all actions spent for the activity up through the end of that turn. For instance, if you began a Cast a Spell activity requiring 3 actions and the first action was disrupted, you lose all 3 actions that you committed to that activity.

The GM decides what effects a disruption causes beyond simply negating the effects that would have

INTRODUCTION

ANCESTRIES &
BACKGROUNDS

CLASSES

SKILLS

FEATS

EQUIPMENT

SPELLS

THE AGE OF
LOST OMENS

PLAYING THE
GAME

GAME
MASTERING

CRAFTING
& TREASURE

APPENDIX

occurred from the disrupted action. For instance, a Leap disrupted midway wouldn't transport you back to the start of your jump, and a disrupted item hand off might cause the item to fall to the ground instead of staying in the hand of the creature who was trying to give it away.

MOVEMENT

Your movement and position determine how you can interact with the world. Moving around in exploration and downtime modes is relatively fluid and free form. Movement in encounter mode, by contrast, is governed by rules explained in Movement in Encounters (page 473). The rules below apply regardless of which mode you're playing in.

MOVEMENT TYPES

Creatures in Pathfinder soar through the clouds, scale sheer cliffs, and tunnel underfoot. Most creatures have a Speed, which is how fast they can move across the ground. Some abilities give you different ways to move, such as through the air or underground.

Each of these special movement types has its own Speed value. Many creatures have these Speeds naturally. The various types of movement are listed below. Since the Stride action can be used only with your normal Speed, moving using one of these movement types requires using a special action, and you can't Step while using one of these movement types. Since Speed by itself refers to your land Speed, rules text concerning these special movement types specifies the movement types to which it applies. Even though Speeds aren't checks, they can have item, circumstance, and status bonuses and penalties. These can't reduce your Speeds below 5 feet unless stated otherwise.

Switching from one movement type to another requires ending your action that has the first movement type and using a new action that has the second movement type. For instance, if you Climbed 10 feet to the top of a cliff, you could then Stride forward 10 feet.

SPEED

Most characters and monsters have a speed statistic—also called land Speed—which indicates how quickly they can move across the ground. When you use the Stride action, you move a number of feet equal to your Speed. Numerous other abilities also allow you to move, from Crawling to Leaping, and most of them are based on your Speed in some way. Whenever a rule mentions your Speed without specifying a type, it's referring to your land Speed.

BURROW SPEED

A burrow Speed lets you tunnel through the ground. You can use the Burrow action (page 472) if you have a burrow Speed. Burrowing doesn't normally leave behind a tunnel unless the ability specifically states that

it does. Most creatures need to hold their breath when burrowing, and they may need tremorsense (page 465) to navigate with any accuracy.

CLIMB SPEED

A climb Speed allows you to move up or down inclines and vertical surfaces. Instead of needing to attempt Athletics checks to Climb, you automatically succeed and move up to your climb Speed instead of the listed distance.

You might still have to attempt Athletics checks to Climb in hazardous conditions, to Climb extremely difficult surfaces, or to cross horizontal planes such as ceilings. You can also choose to roll an Athletics check to Climb rather than accept an automatic success in hopes of getting a critical success. Your climb Speed grants you a +4 circumstance bonus to Athletics checks to Climb.

If you have a climb Speed, you're not flat-footed while climbing.

FLY SPEED

As long as you have a fly Speed, you can use the Fly and Arrest a Fall actions (page 472). You can also attempt to Maneuver in Flight if you're trained in the Acrobatics skill.

Wind conditions can affect how you use the Fly action. In general, moving against the wind uses the same rules as moving through difficult terrain (or greater difficult terrain, if you're also flying upward), and moving with the wind allows you to move 10 feet for every 5 feet of movement you spend (not cumulative with moving straight downward). For more information on spending movement, see Movement in Encounters on page 473.

Upward and downward movement are both relative to the gravity in your area; if you're in a place with zero gravity, moving up or down is no different from moving horizontally.

SWIM SPEED

With a swim Speed, you can propel yourself through the water with little impediment. Instead of attempting Athletics checks to Swim, you automatically succeed and move up to your swim Speed instead of the listed distance. Moving up or down is still moving through difficult terrain.

You might still have to attempt checks to Swim in hazardous conditions or to cross turbulent water. You can also choose to roll an Athletics check to Swim rather than accept an automatic success in hopes of getting a critical success. Your swim Speed grants you a +4 circumstance bonus to Athletics checks to Swim.

Having a swim Speed doesn't necessarily mean you can breathe in water, so you might still have to hold your breath if you're underwater to avoid drowning (page 478).

FALLING

When you fall more than 5 feet, you take bludgeoning damage equal to half the distance you fell when you land. Treat falls longer than 1,500 feet as though they were 1,500 feet (750 damage). If you take any damage from a fall, you land prone. You fall about 500 feet in the first round of falling and about 1,500 feet each round thereafter.

You can Grab an Edge as a reaction to reduce the damage from some falls. In addition, if you fall into water, snow, or another relatively soft substance, you can treat the fall as though it were 20 feet shorter, or 30 feet shorter if you intentionally dove in. The effective reduction can't be greater than the depth (so when falling into 10-foot-deep water, you treat the fall as 10 feet shorter).

FALLING ON A CREATURE

If you land on a creature, that creature must attempt a DC 15 Reflex save. Landing exactly on a creature after a long fall is almost impossible.

Critical Success The creature takes no damage.

Success The creature takes bludgeoning damage equal to one-quarter the falling damage you took.

Failure The creature takes bludgeoning damage equal to half the falling damage you took.

Critical Failure The creature takes the same amount of bludgeoning damage you took from the fall.

FALLING OBJECTS

A dropped object takes damage just like a falling creature. If the object lands on a creature, that creature can attempt a Reflex save using the same rules as for a creature falling on a creature. Hazards and spells that involve falling objects, such as a rock slide, have their own rules about how they interact with creatures and the damage they deal.

PERCEPTION

Your Perception measures your ability to notice things, search for what's hidden, and tell whether something about a situation is suspicious. This statistic is frequently used for rolling initiative to determine who goes first in an encounter, and it's also used for the Seek action.

The rules for rolling a Perception check are found on page 448. The rules below describe the effects of light and visibility on your specific senses to perceive the world, as well as the rules for sensing and locating creatures with Perception.

LIGHT

The amount of light in an area can affect how well you see things. There are three levels of light: bright light, dim light, and darkness. The rules in this book assume that all creatures are in bright light unless otherwise noted. A source of light lists the radius in which it sheds bright light, and it sheds dim light to double that radius.

BRIGHT LIGHT

In bright light, such as sunlight, creatures and objects can be observed clearly by anyone with average vision or better. Some types of creatures are dazzled or blinded by bright light.

DIM LIGHT

Areas in shadow or lit by weak light sources are in dim light. Creatures and objects in dim light have the concealed condition, unless the seeker has darkvision or low-light vision (see Special Senses on page 465), or a precise sense other than vision.

DARKNESS

A creature or object within darkness is hidden or undetected unless the seeker has darkvision or a precise sense other than vision (Special Senses are on page 465). A creature without darkvision or another means of perceiving in darkness has the blinded condition while in darkness, though it might be able to see illuminated areas beyond the darkness. If a creature can see into an illuminated area, it can observe creatures within that illuminated area normally. After being in darkness, sudden exposure to bright light might make you dazzled for a short time, as determined by the GM.

SENSES

The ways a creature can use Perception depend on what senses it has. The primary concepts you need to know for understanding senses are precise senses, imprecise senses, and the three states of detection a target can be in: observed, hidden, or undetected. Vision, hearing, and scent are three prominent senses, but they don't have the same degree of acuity.

PRECISE SENSES

Average vision is a precise sense—a sense that can be used to perceive the world in nuanced detail. The only way to target a creature without having drawbacks is to use a precise sense. You can usually detect a creature automatically with a precise sense unless that creature is hiding or obscured by the environment, in which case you can use the Seek basic action to better detect the creature.

IMPRECISE SENSES

Hearing is an imprecise sense—it cannot detect the full range of detail that a precise sense can. You can usually sense a creature automatically with an imprecise sense, but it has the hidden condition instead of the observed condition. It might be undetected by you if it's using Stealth or is in an environment that distorts the sense, such as a noisy room in the case of hearing. In those cases, you have to use the Seek basic action to detect the creature. At best, an imprecise sense can be used to make an undetected creature (or one you didn't even know was there) merely hidden—it can't make the creature observed.

VAGUE SENSES

A character also has many vague senses—ones that can alert you that something is there but aren't useful for zeroing in on it to determine exactly what it is. The most useful of these for a typical character is the sense of smell. At best, a vague sense can be used to detect the presence of an unnoticed creature, making it undetected. Even then, the vague sense isn't sufficient to make the creature hidden or observed.

When one creature might detect another, the GM almost always uses the most precise sense available.

Pathfinder's rules assume that a given creature has vision as its only precise sense and hearing as its only imprecise sense. Some characters and creatures, however, have precise or imprecise senses that don't match this assumption. For instance, a character with poor vision might treat that sense as imprecise, an animal with the scent ability can use its sense of smell as an imprecise sense, and a creature with echolocation or a similar ability can use hearing as a precise sense. Such senses are often given special names and appear as "echolocation (precise)," "scent (imprecise) 30 feet," or the like.

SPECIAL SENSES

While a human might have a difficult time making creatures out in dim light, an elf can see those creatures just fine. And though elves have no problem seeing on a moonlit night, their vision cannot penetrate complete darkness, whereas a dwarf's can.

Special senses grant greater awareness that allows a creature with these senses to either ignore or reduce the effects of the undetected, hidden, or concealed conditions (described in Detecting Creatures below) when it comes to situations that foil average vision. The following are a few examples of common special senses.

DARKVISION AND GREATER DARKVISION

A creature with darkvision or greater darkvision can see perfectly well in areas of darkness and dim light, though such vision is in black and white only. Some forms of magical darkness, such as a 4th-level *darkness* spell, block normal darkvision. A creature with greater darkvision, however, can see through even these forms of magical darkness.

LOW-LIGHT VISION

A creature with low-light vision can see in dim light as though it were bright light, so it ignores the concealed condition due to dim light.

SCENT

Scent involves sensing creatures or objects by smell, and is usually a vague sense. The range is listed in the ability, and it functions only if the creature or object being detected emits an aroma (for instance, incorporeal creatures usually do not exude an aroma).

DETECTING WITH OTHER SENSES

If a monster uses a sense other than vision, the GM can adapt the variables that keep its foes from being detected to equivalents that work with the monster's senses. For example, a creature that has echolocation might use hearing as a primary sense. This could mean its quarry is concealed in a noisy chamber, hidden in a great enough din, or even invisible in the area of a *silence* spell.

Using Stealth with Other Senses

The Stealth skill is designed to use Hide for avoiding visual detection and Avoid Notice and Sneak to avoid being both seen and heard. For many special senses, a player can describe how they're avoiding detection by that special sense and use the most applicable Stealth action. For instance, a creature stepping lightly to avoid being detected via tremorsense would be using Sneak.

In some cases, rolling a Dexterity-based Stealth skill check to Sneak doesn't make the most sense. For example, when facing a creature that can detect heartbeats, a PC trying to avoid being detected might meditate to slow their heart rate, using Wisdom instead of Dexterity as the ability modifier for the Stealth check. When a creature that can detect you has multiple senses, such as if it could also hear or see, the PC would use the lowest applicable ability modifier for the check.

If a creature emits a heavy aroma or is upwind, the GM can double or even triple the range of scent abilities used to detect that creature, and the GM can reduce the range if a creature is downwind.

TREMORSENSE

Tremorsense allows a creature to feel the vibrations through a solid surface caused by movement. It is usually an imprecise sense with a limited range (listed in the ability). Tremorsense functions only if the detecting creature is on the same surface as the subject, and only if the subject is moving along (or burrowing through) the surface.

DETECTING CREATURES

There are three conditions that measure the degree to which you can sense a creature: observed, hidden, and undetected. However, the concealed and invisible conditions can partially mask a creature, and the unnoticed condition indicates you have no idea a creature is around. In addition to the descriptions here, you can find these conditions in the Conditions Appendix on pages 618–623.

With the exception of invisible, these conditions are relative to the viewer—it's possible for a creature to be observed to you but hidden from your ally. When you're trying to target a creature that's hard to see or otherwise sense, various drawbacks apply. Most of these rules apply to objects you're trying to detect as well as creatures.

Typically, the GM tracks how well creatures detect each other, since neither party has perfect information. For example, you might think a creature is in the last place you sensed it, but it was able to Sneak away. Or you might think a creature can't see you in the dark, but it has darkvision.

You can attempt to avoid detection by using the Stealth skill (page 251) to Avoid Notice, Hide, or Sneak, or by using Deception to Create a Diversion (page 245).

OBSERVED

In most circumstances, you can sense creatures without difficulty and target them normally. Creatures in this state are observed. Observing requires a precise sense, which for most creatures means sight, but see the Detecting with Other Senses sidebar (page 465) for advice regarding creatures that don't use sight as their primary sense. If you can't observe the creature, it's either hidden, undetected, or unnoticed, and you'll need to factor in the targeting restrictions. Even if a creature is observed, it might still be concealed.

HIDDEN

A creature that's hidden is only barely perceptible. You know what space a hidden creature occupies, but little else. Perhaps the creature just moved behind cover and successfully used the Hide action. Your target might be in a deep fogbank or behind a waterfall, where you can see some movement but can't determine an exact location. Maybe you've been blinded or the creature is under the effects of *invisibility*, but you used the Seek basic action to determine its general location based on hearing alone. Regardless of the specifics, you're flat-footed to a hidden creature.

When targeting a hidden creature, before you roll to determine your effect, you must attempt a DC 11 flat check. If you fail, you don't affect the creature, though the actions you used are still expended—as well as any spell slots, costs, and other resources. You remain flat-footed to the creature, whether you successfully target it or not.

UNDETECTED

If a creature is undetected, you don't know what space it occupies, you're flat-footed to it, and you can't easily target it. Using the Seek basic action can help you find an undetected creature, usually making it hidden from you instead of undetected. If a creature is undetected, that doesn't necessarily mean you're unaware of its presence—you might suspect an undetected creature is in the room with you, even though you're unable to find its space. The unnoticed condition covers creatures you're entirely unaware of.

Targeting an undetected creature is difficult. If you suspect there's a creature around, you can pick a square and attempt an attack. This works like targeting a hidden creature, but the flat check and attack roll are both rolled in secret by the GM. The GM won't tell you why you missed—whether it was due to failing the flat check, rolling an insufficient attack roll, or choosing the wrong square. The GM might allow you to try targeting an undetected creature with some spells or other abilities in a similar fashion. Undetected creatures are subject to area effects normally.

For instance, suppose an enemy elf wizard cast *invisibility* and then Sneaked away. You suspect that with the elf's Speed of 30 feet, they probably moved 15 feet toward an open door. You move up and attack a space 15 feet from where the elf started and directly on the path to the door. The GM secretly rolls an attack roll and flat check, but they know that you were not quite correct—the elf was actually in the adjacent space! The GM tells you that you missed, so you decide to make your next attack on the adjacent space, just in case. This time, it's the right space, and the GM's secret attack roll and flat check both succeed, so you hit!

Unnoticed

If you have no idea a creature is even present, that creature is unnoticed by you. A creature that is undetected might also be unnoticed. This condition usually matters for abilities that can be used only against targets totally unaware of your presence.

CONCEALMENT AND INVISIBILITY

The concealed and invisible conditions reflect certain circumstances that can make a creature harder to see.

Concealed

This condition protects a creature if it's in mist, within dim light, or amid something else that obscures sight but does not provide a physical barrier to effects. An effect or type of terrain that describes an area of concealment makes all creatures within it concealed.

When you target a creature that's concealed from you, you must attempt a DC 5 flat check before you roll to determine your effect. If you fail, you don't affect the target. The concealed condition doesn't change which of the main categories of detection apply to the creature. A creature in a light fog bank is still observed even though it's concealed.

Invisible

A creature with the invisible condition (by way of an *invisibility* spell or *invisibility potion*, for example) is automatically undetected to any creatures relying on sight as their only precise sense. Precise senses other than sight ignore the invisible condition.

You can use the Seek basic action to attempt to figure out an invisible creature's location, making it instead only hidden from you. This lasts until the invisible creature successfully uses Sneak to become undetected again. If you're already observing a creature when it becomes invisible, it starts out hidden, since you know where it was when it became invisible, though it can then Sneak to become undetected.

Other effects might make an invisible creature hidden or even observed but concealed. For instance, if you were tracking an invisible creature's footprints through the snow, the footprints would make it hidden. Similarly, throwing a net over an invisible creature would make it observed but concealed for as long as the net is on the creature.

HERO POINTS

Your heroic deeds earn you Hero Points, which grant you good fortune or let you recover from the brink of death. Unlike most aspects of your character, which persist over the long term, Hero Points last for only a single session.

The GM is in charge of awarding Hero Points (guidelines for doing so can be found on page 507). Usually, each character gets 1 Hero Point at the start of a session and can gain more later by performing heroic deeds—something selfless, daring, or beyond normal expectations. You can have a maximum of 3 Hero Points at a time, and you lose any remaining Hero Points at the end of a session.

You can spend your Hero Points in one of two ways. Neither of these is an action, and you can spend Hero Points even if you aren't able to act. You can spend a Hero Point on behalf of your familiar or animal companion.

- **Spend 1 Hero Point** to reroll a check. You must use the second result. This is a fortune effect (which means you can't use more than 1 Hero Point on a check).
- **Spend all your Hero Points** (minimum 1) to avoid death. You can do this when your dying condition would increase. You lose the dying condition entirely and stabilize with 0 Hit Points. You don't gain the wounded condition or increase its value from losing the dying condition in this way, but if you already had that condition, you don't lose it or decrease its value.

DESCRIBING HEROIC DEEDS

Because spending Hero Points reflects heroic deeds or tasks that surpass normal expectations, if you spend a Hero Point, you should describe the deed or task your character accomplishes with it to the other players.

Your character's deed might invoke a lesson learned in a past adventure, could be spurred by a determination to save someone else, or might depend on an item that ended up on their person due to a previous exploit. If you don't want to describe the deed or don't have any strong ideas about how to do so, ask the GM to come up with something for you. This can be a collaborative process, too. The GM might remind you of a long-forgotten event in the campaign, and all you have to do is fill in how that event comes to mind just at the right time, motivating you to push past your limits.

INTRODUCTION

ANCESTRIES & BACKGROUNDS

CLASSES

SKILLS

FEATS

EQUIPMENT

SPELLS

THE AGE OF LOST OMENS

PLAYING THE GAME

GAME MASTERING

CRAFTING & TREASURE

APPENDIX

ENCOUNTER MODE

When every individual action counts, you enter the encounter mode of play. In this mode, time is divided into rounds, each of which is 6 seconds of time in the game world. Every round, each participant takes a turn in an established order. During your turn, you can use actions, and depending on the details of the encounter, you might have the opportunity to use reactions and free actions on your own turn and on others' turns.

STRUCTURE

An encounter is played out in a series of rounds, during which the player characters, adversaries, and other participants in the encounter act in sequence. You roll initiative to determine this order at the start of the encounter and then play through rounds until a conclusion is reached and the encounter ends. The rules in this section assume a combat encounter—a battle—but the general structure can apply to any kind of encounter.

STEP 1: ROLL INITIATIVE

When the GM calls for it, you'll roll initiative to determine your place in the initiative order, which is the sequence in which the encounter's participants will take their turns. Rolling initiative marks the start of an encounter. More often than not, you'll roll initiative when you enter a battle.

Typically, you'll roll a Perception check to determine your initiative—the more aware you are of your surroundings, the more quickly you can respond. Sometimes, though, the GM might call on you to roll some other type of check. For instance, if you were Avoiding Notice during exploration (page 479), you'd roll a Stealth check. A social encounter could call for a Deception or Diplomacy check.

The GM rolls initiative for anyone other than the player characters in the encounter. If these include a number of identical creatures, the GM could roll once for the group as a whole and have them take their turns within the group in any order. However, this can make battles less predictable and more dangerous, so the GM might want to roll initiative for some or all creatures individually unless it's too much of a burden.

Unlike a typical check, where the result is compared to a DC, the results of initiative rolls are ranked. This ranking sets the order in which the encounter's participants act— the initiative order. The character with the highest result goes first. The second highest follows, and so on until whoever had the lowest result takes their turn last.

If your result is tied with a foe's result, the adversary goes first. If your result is tied with another PC's, you can decide between yourselves who goes first when you reach that place in the initiative order. After that, your places in the initiative order usually don't change during the encounter.

STEP 2: PLAY A ROUND

A round begins when the participant with the highest initiative roll result starts their turn, and it ends when the one with the lowest initiative ends their turn. The process of taking a turn is detailed below. Creatures might also act outside their turns with reactions and free actions.

STEP 3: BEGIN THE NEXT ROUND

Once everyone in the encounter has taken a turn, the round is over and the next one begins. Don't roll initiative again; the new round proceeds in the same order as the previous one, repeating the cycle until the encounter ends.

STEP 4: END THE ENCOUNTER

When your foes are defeated, some sort of truce is reached, or some other event or circumstance ends the combat, the encounter is over. You and the other participants no longer follow the initiative order, and a more free-form style of play resumes, with the game typically moving into exploration mode. Sometimes at the end of an encounter, the GM will award Experience Points to the party or you'll find treasure to divvy up.

TURNS

When it's your turn to act, you can use single actions (❖), short activities (❖❖ and ❖❖❖), reactions (↺), and free actions (◈). When you're finished, your turn ends and the character next in the initiative order begins their turn. Sometimes it's important to note when during your turn something happens, so a turn is divided into three steps.

STEP 1: START YOUR TURN

Many things happen automatically at the start of your turn— it's a common point for tracking the passage of time for effects that last multiple rounds. At the start of each of your turns, take these steps in any order you choose:

- If you created an effect lasting for a certain number of rounds, reduce the number of rounds remaining by 1. The effect ends if the duration is reduced to 0. For example, if you cast a spell that lasts 3 rounds on yourself during your first turn of a fight, it would affect you during that turn, decrease to 2 rounds of duration at the start of your second turn, decrease to 1 round of duration at the start of your third turn, and expire at the start of your fourth turn.
- You can use 1 free action or reaction with a trigger of "Your turn begins" or something similar.
- If you're dying, roll a recovery check (page 459).

- Do anything else that is specified to happen at the start of your turn.

The last step of starting your turn is always the same.

- Regain your 3 actions and 1 reaction. If you haven't spent your reaction from your last turn, you lose it—you can't "save" actions or reactions from one turn to use during the next turn. If a condition prevents you from being able to act, you don't regain any actions or your reaction. Some abilities or conditions (such as quickened and slowed) can change how many actions you regain and whether you regain your reaction. If you lose actions and gain additional actions (such as if you're both quickened and slowed), you choose which actions to lose.

STEP 2: ACT

You can use actions in any order you wish during your turn, but you have to complete one action or activity before beginning another; for example, you can't use a single action in the middle of performing a 2-action activity. What actions you can use often depend on your class features, skills, feats, and items, but there are default actions anyone can use, described in Basic Actions below. Some effects might prevent you from acting. If you can't act, you can't use any actions, including reactions and free actions.

If you begin a 2-action or 3-action activity on your turn, you must be able to complete it on your turn. You can't, for example, begin to High Jump using your final action on one turn and then complete it as your first action on your next turn.

Once you have spent all 3 of your actions, your turn ends (as described in Step 3) and the next creature's turn begins. You can, however, use only some of your actions and end your turn early. As soon as your turn ends, you lose all your remaining actions, but not your reaction or your ability to use free actions.

STEP 3: END YOUR TURN

Once you've done all the things you want to do with the actions you have available, you reach the end of your turn. Take the following steps in any order you choose. Play then proceeds to the next creature in the initiative order.

- End any effects that last until the end of your turn. For example, spells with a sustained duration end at the end of your turn unless you used the Sustain a Spell action during your turn to extend them. Some effects caused by enemies might also last through a certain number of your turns, and you decrease the remaining duration by 1 during this step, ending the effect if its duration is reduced to 0.
- If you have a persistent damage condition, you take the damage at this point. After you take the damage, you can attempt the flat check to end the persistent damage. You then attempt any saving throws for ongoing afflictions. Many other conditions change at the end of your turn,

TRACKING INITIATIVE

The GM keeps track of the initiative order for an encounter. It's usually okay for the players to know this order, since they'll see who goes when and be aware of one another's results. However, the GM might want to conceal the names of adversaries the PCs have yet to identify.

Once the encounter's order is set, it's usually not necessary to track the original initiative numbers. The GM can create a simple list, use a series of cards or other indicators, or use a *Pathfinder Combat Pad*, which has magnetic markers to allow for easily rearranging the order.

Changing the Initiative Order

Any method used to track the initiative order needs to be flexible because the order can change. A creature can use the Delay basic action to change its place in the order, in which case you can erase it from the list or pull its marker aside until it reenters the initiative order. When a creature gets knocked out, its initiative order also changes (see Knocked Out and Dying on page 459). Using the Ready basic action doesn't change a creature's place in the initiative order, though, because the designated action becomes a reaction.

such as the frightened condition decreasing in severity. These take place after you've taken any persistent damage, attempted flat checks to end the persistent damage, and attempted saves against any afflictions.
- You can use 1 free action or reaction with a trigger of "Your turn ends" or something similar.
- Resolve anything else specified to happen at the end of your turn.

BASIC ACTIONS

Basic actions represent common tasks like moving around, attacking, and helping others. As such, every creature can use basic actions except in some extreme circumstances, and many of those actions are used very frequently. Most notably, you'll use Interact, Step, Stride, and Strike a great deal. Many feats and other actions call upon you to use one of these basic actions or modify them to produce different effects. For example, a more complex action might let you Stride up to double your Speed instead of just up to your Speed, and a large number of activities include a Strike.

Actions that are used less frequently but are still available to most creatures are presented in Specialty Basic Actions starting on page 472. These typically have requirements that not all characters are likely to meet, such as wielding a shield or having a burrow Speed.

In addition to the actions in these two sections, the actions for spellcasting can be found on pages 302–305, and the actions for using magic items appear on pages 531–534.

AID ↺

Trigger An ally is about to use an action that requires a skill check or attack roll.

Requirements The ally is willing to accept your aid, and you have prepared to help (see below).

You try to help your ally with a task. To use this reaction, you must first prepare to help, usually by using an action during your turn. You must explain to the GM exactly how you're trying to help, and they determine whether you can Aid your ally.

When you use your Aid reaction, attempt a skill check or attack roll of a type decided by the GM. The typical DC is 20, but the GM might adjust this DC for particularly hard or easy tasks. The GM can add any relevant traits to your preparatory action or to your Aid reaction depending on the situation, or even allow you to Aid checks other than skill checks and attack rolls.

Critical Success You grant your ally a +2 circumstance bonus to the triggering check. If you're a master with the check you attempted, the bonus is +3, and if you're legendary, it's +4.

Success You grant your ally a +1 circumstance bonus to the triggering check.

Critical Failure Your ally takes a –1 circumstance penalty to the triggering check.

CRAWL ◆

MOVE

Requirements You are prone and your Speed is at least 10 feet.

You move 5 feet by crawling and continue to stay prone.

DELAY ◆

Trigger Your turn begins.

You wait for the right moment to act. The rest of your turn doesn't happen yet. Instead, you're removed from the initiative order. You can return to the initiative order as a free action triggered by the end of any other creature's turn. This permanently changes your initiative to the new position. You can't use reactions until you return to the initiative order. If you Delay an entire round without returning to the initiative order, the actions from the Delayed turn are lost, your initiative doesn't change, and your next turn occurs at your original position in the initiative order.

When you Delay, any persistent damage or other negative effects that normally occur at the start or end of your turn occur immediately when you use the Delay action. Any beneficial effects that would end at any point during your turn also end. The GM might determine that other effects end when you Delay as well. Essentially, you can't Delay to avoid negative consequences that would happen on your turn or to extend beneficial effects that would end on your turn.

DROP PRONE ◆

MOVE

You fall prone.

ESCAPE ◆

ATTACK

You attempt to escape from being grabbed, immobilized, or restrained. Choose one creature, object, spell effect, hazard,

or other impediment imposing any of those conditions on you. Attempt a check using your unarmed attack modifier against the DC of the effect. This is typically the Athletics DC of a creature grabbing you, the Thievery DC of a creature who tied you up, the spell DC for a spell effect, or the listed Escape DC of an object, hazard, or other impediment. You can attempt an Acrobatics or Athletics check instead of using your attack modifier if you choose (but this action still has the attack trait).

Critical Success You get free and remove the grabbed, immobilized, and restrained conditions imposed by your chosen target. You can then Stride up to 5 feet.

Success You get free and remove the grabbed, immobilized, and restrained conditions imposed by your chosen target.

Critical Failure You don't get free, and you can't attempt to Escape again until your next turn.

INTERACT ◆

MANIPULATE

You use your hand or hands to manipulate an object or the terrain. You can grab an unattended or stored object, open a door, or produce some similar effect. You might have to attempt a skill check to determine if your Interact action was successful.

LEAP ◆

MOVE

You take a careful, short jump. You can Leap up to 10 feet horizontally if your Speed is at least 15 feet, or up to 15 feet horizontally if your Speed is at least 30 feet. You land in the space where your Leap ends (meaning you can typically clear a 5-foot gap, or a 10-foot gap if your Speed is 30 feet or more).

If you Leap vertically, you can move up to 3 feet vertically and 5 feet horizontally onto an elevated surface.

Jumping a greater distance requires using the Athletics skill.

READY ◆◆

CONCENTRATE

You prepare to use an action that will occur outside your turn. Choose a single action or free action you can use, and designate a trigger. Your turn then ends. If the trigger you designated occurs before the start of your next turn, you can use the chosen action as a reaction (provided you still meet the requirements to use it). You can't Ready a free action that already has a trigger.

If you have a multiple attack penalty and your readied action is an attack action, your readied attack takes the multiple attack penalty you had at the time you used Ready. This is one of the few times the multiple attack penalty applies when it's not your turn.

RELEASE ◆

MANIPULATE

You release something you're holding in your hand or hands. This might mean dropping an item, removing one hand from your weapon while continuing to hold it in another hand, releasing a rope suspending a chandelier, or performing a similar action. Unlike most manipulate actions, Release does not trigger reactions that can be triggered by actions with the manipulate trait (such as Attack of Opportunity).

If you want to prepare to Release something outside of your turn, use the Ready activity.

SEEK ◆

CONCENTRATE **SECRET**

You scan an area for signs of creatures or objects. If you're looking for creatures, choose an area you're scanning. If precision is necessary, the GM can have you select a 30-foot cone or a 15-foot burst within line of sight. You might take a penalty if you choose an area that's far away.

If you're using Seek to search for objects (including secret doors and hazards), you search up to a 10-foot square adjacent to you. The GM might determine you need to Seek as an activity, taking more actions or even minutes or hours if you're searching a particularly cluttered area.

The GM attempts a single secret Perception check for you and compares the result to the Stealth DCs of any undetected or hidden creatures in the area or the DC to detect each object in the area (as determined by the GM or by someone Concealing the Object). A creature you detect might remain hidden, rather than becoming observed, if you're using an imprecise sense or if an effect (such as *invisibility*) prevents the subject from being observed.

Critical Success If you were searching for creatures, any undetected or hidden creature you critically succeeded against becomes observed by you. If you were searching for an object, you learn its location.

Success If you were searching for creatures, any undetected creature you succeeded against becomes hidden from you instead of undetected, and any hidden creature you succeeded against becomes observed by you. If you were searching for an object, you learn its location or get a clue to its whereabouts, as determined by the GM.

SENSE MOTIVE ◆

CONCENTRATE **SECRET**

You try to tell whether a creature's behavior is abnormal. Choose one creature, and assess it for odd body language, signs of nervousness, and other indicators that it might be trying to deceive someone. The GM attempts a single secret Perception check for you and compares the result to the Deception DC of the creature, the DC of a spell affecting the creature's mental state, or another appropriate DC determined by the GM. You typically can't try to Sense the Motive of the same creature again until the situation changes significantly.

Critical Success You determine the creature's true intentions and get a solid idea of any mental magic affecting it.

Success You can tell whether the creature is behaving normally, but you don't know its exact intentions or what magic might be affecting it.

Failure You detect what a deceptive creature wants you to believe. If they're not being deceptive, you believe they're behaving normally.

Critical Failure You get a false sense of the creature's intentions.

SPEAKING

As long as you can act, you can also speak. You don't need to spend any type of action to speak, but because a round represents 6 seconds of time, you can usually speak at most a single sentence or so per round. Special uses of speech, such as attempting a Deception skill check to Lie, require spending actions and follow their own rules. All speech has the auditory trait. If you communicate in some way other than speech, other rules might apply. For instance, using sign language is visual instead of auditory.

STAND ◆

MOVE

You stand up from prone.

STEP ◆

MOVE

Requirements Your Speed is at least 10 feet.

You carefully move 5 feet. Unlike most types of movement, Stepping doesn't trigger reactions, such as Attacks of Opportunity, that can be triggered by move actions or upon leaving or entering a square.

You can't Step into difficult terrain (page 475), and you can't Step using a Speed other than your land Speed.

STRIDE ◆

MOVE

You move up to your Speed (page 463).

STRIKE ◆

ATTACK

You attack with a weapon you're wielding or with an unarmed attack, targeting one creature within your reach (for a melee attack) or within range (for a ranged attack). Roll the attack roll for the weapon or unarmed attack you are using, and compare the result to the target creature's AC to determine the effect. See Attack Rolls on page 446 and Damage on page 450 for details on calculating your attack and damage rolls.

Critical Success As success, but you deal double damage (page 451).

Success You deal damage according to the weapon or unarmed attack, including any modifiers, bonuses, and penalties you have to damage.

TAKE COVER ◆

Requirements You are benefiting from cover, are near a feature that allows you to take cover, or are prone.

You press yourself against a wall or duck behind an obstacle to take better advantage of cover (page 477). If you would have standard cover, you instead gain greater cover, which provides a +4 circumstance bonus to AC; to Reflex saves against area effects; and to Stealth checks to Hide, Sneak, or otherwise avoid detection. Otherwise, you gain the benefits of standard cover (a +2 circumstance bonus instead). This lasts until you move from your current space, use an attack action, become unconscious, or end this effect as a free action.

INTRODUCTION

ANCESTRIES & BACKGROUNDS

CLASSES

SKILLS

FEATS

EQUIPMENT

SPELLS

THE AGE OF LOST OMENS

PLAYING THE GAME

GAME MASTERING

CRAFTING & TREASURE

APPENDIX

SPECIALTY BASIC ACTIONS

These actions are useful under specific circumstances. Some require you to have a special movement type (page 463).

ARREST A FALL ⤵

Trigger You fall.
Requirements You have a fly Speed.

You attempt an Acrobatics check to slow your fall. The DC is typically 15, but it might be higher due to air turbulence or other circumstances.
Success You fall gently, taking no damage from the fall.

AVERT GAZE ❖

You avert your gaze from danger. You gain a +2 circumstance bonus to saves against visual abilities that require you to look at a creature or object, such as a medusa's petrifying gaze. Your gaze remains averted until the start of your next turn.

BURROW ❖

`MOVE`

Requirements You have a burrow Speed.

You dig your way through dirt, sand, or a similar loose material at a rate up to your burrow Speed. You can't burrow through rock or other substances denser than dirt unless you have an ability that allows you to do so.

FLY ❖

`MOVE`

Requirements You have a fly Speed.

You move through the air up to your fly Speed. Moving upward (straight up or diagonally) uses the rules for moving through difficult terrain. You can move straight down 10 feet for every 5 feet of movement you spend. If you Fly to the ground, you don't take falling damage. You can use an action to Fly 0 feet to hover in place. If you're airborne at the end of your turn and didn't use a Fly action this round, you fall.

GRAB AN EDGE ⤵

`MANIPULATE`

Trigger You fall from or past an edge or handhold.
Requirements Your hands are not tied behind your back or otherwise restrained.

When you fall off or past an edge or other handhold, you can try to grab it, potentially stopping your fall. You must succeed at a Reflex save, usually at the Climb DC. If you grab the edge or handhold, you can then Climb up using Athletics.
Critical Success You grab the edge or handhold, whether or not you have a hand free, typically by using a suitable held item to catch yourself (catching a battle axe on a ledge, for example). You still take damage from the distance fallen so far, but you treat the fall as though it were 30 feet shorter.
Success If you have at least one hand free, you grab the edge or handhold, stopping your fall. You still take damage from the distance fallen so far, but you treat the fall as though it were 20 feet shorter. If you have no hands free, you continue to fall as if you had failed the check.

Critical Failure You continue to fall, and if you've fallen 20 feet or more before you use this reaction, you take 10 bludgeoning damage from the impact for every 20 feet fallen.

MOUNT ❖

`MOVE`

Requirements You are adjacent to a creature that is at least one size larger than you and is willing to be your mount.

You move onto the creature and ride it. If you're already mounted, you can instead use this action to dismount, moving off the mount into a space adjacent to it.

POINT OUT ❖

`AUDITORY` `MANIPULATE` `VISUAL`

Requirements A creature is undetected by one or more of your allies but isn't undetected by you.

You indicate a creature that you can see to one or more allies, gesturing in a direction and describing the distance verbally. That creature is hidden to your allies, rather than undetected (page 466). This works only for allies who can see you and are in a position where they could potentially detect the target. If your allies can't hear or understand you, they must succeed at a Perception check against the creature's Stealth DC or they misunderstand and believe the target is in a different location.

RAISE A SHIELD ❖

Requirements You are wielding a shield.

You position your shield to protect yourself. When you have Raised a Shield, you gain its listed circumstance bonus to AC. Your shield remains raised until the start of your next turn.

ACTIVITIES IN ENCOUNTERS

Activities that take longer than a turn can't normally be performed during an encounter. Spells with a casting time of 1 minute or more are a common example of this, as are several skill actions. When you commit to an activity during your turn in an encounter, you commit to spending all of the actions it requires. If the activity gets interrupted partway through, you lose all of the actions you would have spent on that activity. Activities are described in full on page 461.

REACTIONS IN ENCOUNTERS

Your reactions let you respond immediately to what's happening around you. The GM determines whether you can use reactions before your first turn begins, depending on the situation in which the encounter happens.

Once your first turn begins, you gain your actions and reaction. You can use 1 reaction per round. You can use a reaction on anyone's turn (including your own), but only when its trigger occurs. If you don't use your reaction, you lose it at the start of your next turn, though you typically then gain a reaction at the start of that turn.

Some reactions are specifically meant to be used in combat and can change how the battle plays out drastically.

One example of such a reaction is Attack of Opportunity, which fighters gain at 1st level.

ATTACK OF OPPORTUNITY ⤶

Trigger A creature within your reach uses a manipulate action or a move action, makes a ranged attack, or leaves a square during a move action it's using.

You lash out at a foe that leaves an opening. Make a melee Strike against the triggering creature. If your attack is a critical hit and the trigger was a manipulate action, you disrupt that action. This Strike doesn't count toward your multiple attack penalty, and your multiple attack penalty doesn't apply to this Strike.

This reaction lets you make a melee Strike if a creature within reach uses a manipulate or move action, makes a ranged attack, or leaves a square during a move action. The Triggering Moves diagram on page 474 illustrates examples of movements that might trigger an Attack of Opportunity from a creature without reach and one with reach.

You'll notice this reaction allows you to use a modified basic action, a Strike. This follows the rules on subordinate actions found on page 462. Because your Attack of Opportunity takes place outside of your turn, the attack roll doesn't incur a multiple attack penalty.

MOVEMENT IN ENCOUNTERS

Your movement during encounter mode depends on the actions and other abilities you use. Whether you Stride, Step, Swim, or Climb, the maximum distance you can move is based on your Speed. Certain feats or magic items can grant you other movement types, allowing you to swiftly burrow, climb, fly, or swim (page 463).

When the rules refer to a "movement cost" or "spending movement," they are describing how many feet of your Speed you must use to move from one point to another. Normally, movement costs 5 feet per square when you're moving on a grid, or it costs the number of feet you move if you're not using a grid. However, sometimes it's harder to move a certain distance due to difficult terrain (page 475) or other factors. In such a case, you might have to spend a different amount of movement to move from one place to another. For example, a form of movement might require 10 feet of movement to move 1 square, and moving through some types of terrain costs an extra 5 feet of movement per square.

GRID MOVEMENT

If an encounter involves combat, it's often a good idea to track the movement and relative position of the participants using a Pathfinder Flip-Mat, Flip-Tiles, or some other form of grid to display the terrain, and miniatures to represent the combatants. When a character moves on a grid, every 1-inch square of the play area is 5 feet across in the game world. Hence, a creature moving in a straight line spends 5 feet of its movement for every map square traveled.

Because moving diagonally covers more ground, you count that movement differently. The first square of diagonal movement you make in a turn counts as 5 feet, but the second counts as 10 feet, and your count thereafter alternates between the two. For example, as you move across 4 squares diagonally, you would count 5 feet, then 10, then 5, and then 10, for a total of 30 feet. You track your total diagonal movement across all your movement during your turn, but reset your count at the end of your turn.

SIZE, SPACE, AND REACH

Creatures and objects of different sizes occupy different amounts of space. The sizes and the spaces they each take up on a grid are listed in Table 9–1: Size and Reach (page 474).

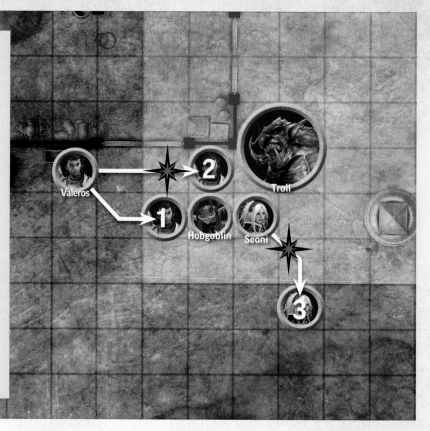

TRIGGERING MOVES

1. Valeros can approach position 1 with the Stride action without triggering reactions.
2. If Valeros approaches this way to position 2, he triggers reactions from both the hobgoblin and the troll. The troll has a reach of 10 feet, so Valeros triggers reactions from both enemies when he moves out of the second square and into the third.
3. If Seoni Strides to position 3, she triggers reactions from the hobgoblin and the troll. Because of its 10-foot reach, the troll could use its reaction when Seoni left either square. She could Step twice to get there to avoid triggering reactions, but that uses 2 actions instead of 1.

Table 9–1 also lists the typical reach for creatures of each size, for both tall creatures (most bipeds) and long creatures (most quadrupeds). See page 455 for more about reach.

The Space entry lists how many feet on a side a creature's space is, so a Large creature fills a 10-foot-by-10-foot space (4 squares on the grid). Sometimes part of a creature extends beyond its space, such as if a giant octopus is grabbing you with its tentacles. In that case, the GM will usually allow attacking the extended portion, even if you can't reach the main creature. A Small or larger creature or object takes up at least 1 square on a grid, and creatures of these sizes can't usually share spaces except in situations like a character riding a mount. Rules for moving through other creatures' spaces appear below.

TABLE 9-1: SIZE AND REACH

Size	Space	Reach (Tall)	Reach (Long)
Tiny	Less than 5 feet	0 feet	0 feet
Small	5 feet	5 feet	5 feet
Medium	5 feet	5 feet	5 feet
Large	10 feet	10 feet	5 feet
Huge	15 feet	15 feet	10 feet
Gargantuan	20 feet or more	20 feet	15 feet

Multiple Tiny creatures can occupy the same square. At least four can fit in a single square, though the GM might determine that even more can fit. Tiny creatures can occupy a space occupied by a larger creature as well, and if their reach is 0 feet, they must do so in order to attack.

MOVE ACTIONS THAT TRIGGER REACTIONS

Some reactions and free actions are triggered by a creature using an action with the move trait. The most notable example is Attack of Opportunity. Actions with the move trait can trigger reactions or free actions throughout the course of the distance traveled. Each time you exit a square (or move 5 feet if not using a grid) within a creature's reach, your movement triggers those reactions and free actions (although no more than once per move action for a given reacting creature). If you use a move action but don't move out of a square, the trigger instead happens at the end of that action or ability.

Some actions, such as Step, specifically state they don't trigger reactions or free actions based on movement.

MOVING THROUGH A CREATURE'S SPACE

You can move through the space of a willing creature. If you want to move through an unwilling creature's space, you can Tumble Through that creature's space using Acrobatics. You can't end your turn in a square occupied by another creature, though you can end a move action in its square provided that you immediately use another move action to leave that square. If two creatures end up in the same square by accident, the GM determines which one is forced out of the square (or whether one falls prone).

PRONE AND INCAPACITATED CREATURES

You can share a space with a prone creature if that

INTRODUCTION

ANCESTRIES &
BACKGROUNDS

CLASSES

SKILLS

FEATS

EQUIPMENT

SPELLS

THE AGE OF
LOST OMENS

PLAYING THE
GAME

GAME
MASTERING

CRAFTING
& TREASURE

APPENDIX

COUNTING MOVEMENT

Lini decides to Stride. She has a Speed of 20 feet. She moves straight south, spending 5 feet of her Speed, then diagonally, spending another 5 feet. Her next diagonal move, because it's her second diagonal of the turn, costs her 10 feet of movement. She's spent all 20 feet of her Speed and ends that Stride.

She Seeks, and something catches her eye to the northeast, so she decides to move toward it. However, the crumbled stone is difficult terrain, so each square costs 5 more feet of Speed. She moves diagonally, spending 10 feet of movement since this is an odd-numbered diagonal. She wants to move northeast again, but that would cost her 15 feet (10 feet for an even-numbered diagonal and 5 more for being difficult terrain). Instead, she decides to move directly north. This costs her 10 feet, so she's used all 20 feet of her Speed and is out of actions.

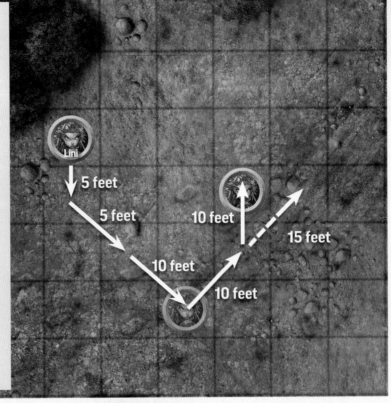

creature is willing, unconscious, or dead and if it is your size or smaller. The GM might allow you to climb atop the corpse or unconscious body of a larger creature in some situations. A prone creature can't stand up while someone else occupies its space, but it can Crawl to a space where it's able to stand, or it can attempt to Shove the other creature out of the way.

Creatures of Different Sizes

In most cases, you can move through the space of a creature at least three sizes larger than you (Table 9-1). This means a Medium creature can move through the space of a Gargantuan creature and a Small creature can move through the space of a Huge creature. Likewise, a bigger creature can move through the space of a creature three sizes smaller than itself or smaller. You still can't end your movement in a space occupied by a creature.

Tiny creatures are an exception. They can move through creatures' spaces and can even end their movement there.

Objects

Because objects aren't as mobile as creatures are, they're more likely to fill a space. This means you can't always move through their spaces like you might move through a space occupied by a creature. You might be able to occupy the same square as a statue of your size, but not a wide column. The GM determines whether you can move into an object's square normally, whether special rules apply, or if you are unable to move into the square at all.

FORCED MOVEMENT

When an effect forces you to move, or if you start falling, the distance you move is defined by the effect that moved you, not by your Speed. Because you're not acting to move, this doesn't trigger reactions that are triggered by movement.

If forced movement would move you into a space you can't occupy—because objects are in the way or because you lack the movement type needed to reach it, for example— you stop moving in the last space you can occupy. Usually the creature or effect forcing the movement chooses the path the victim takes. If you're pushed or pulled, you can usually be moved through hazardous terrain, pushed off a ledge, or the like. Abilities that reposition you in some other way can't put you in such dangerous places unless they specify otherwise. In all cases, the GM makes the final call if there's doubt on where forced movement can move a creature.

TERRAIN

Several types of terrain can complicate your movement by slowing you down, damaging you, or endangering you.

Difficult Terrain

Difficult terrain is any terrain that impedes your movement, ranging from particularly rough or unstable surfaces to thick ground cover and countless other impediments. Moving into a square of **difficult terrain** (or moving 5 feet into or within an area of difficult terrain, if you're not using a grid) costs an extra 5 feet of movement. Moving into a square of **greater difficult terrain** instead

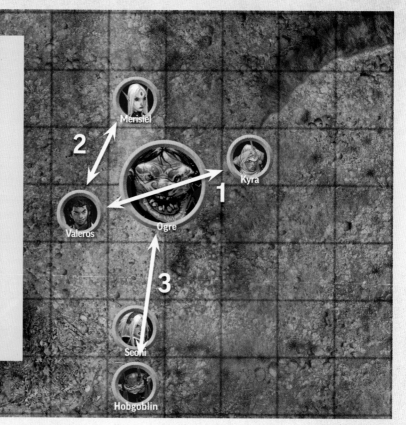

FLANKING

1. Valeros and Kyra are flanking the ogre because they can draw a line to each other that passes through opposite sides of the ogre's space. The ogre is flat-footed to them, taking a −2 circumstance penalty to its AC.
2. Merisiel isn't flanking the ogre because she can't draw a line to Valeros or Kyra that passes through opposite sides of the ogre's space, and the ogre is not in Seoni's reach.
3. The hobgoblin and ogre flank Seoni, since she is within reach for both, and they can draw a line between them that passes through opposite sides of her space. If the ogre didn't have 10 feet of reach, the two creatures wouldn't flank her.

costs 10 additional feet of movement. This additional cost is not increased when moving diagonally. You can't Step into difficult terrain.

Movement you make while you are jumping ignores the terrain you're jumping over. Some abilities (such as flight or being incorporeal) allow you to avoid the movement reduction from some types of difficult terrain. Certain other abilities let you ignore difficult terrain on foot; such an ability also allows you to move through greater difficult terrain at the normal movement cost as for difficult terrain, though it wouldn't let you ignore greater difficult terrain unless the ability specifies otherwise.

HAZARDOUS TERRAIN

Hazardous terrain damages you whenever you move through it. An acid pool and a pit of burning embers are both examples of hazardous terrain. The amount and type of damage depend on the specific hazardous terrain.

NARROW SURFACES

A narrow surface is so precariously thin that you need to Balance (see Acrobatics on page 240) or risk falling. Even on a success, you are flat-footed on a narrow surface. Each time you are hit by an attack or fail a save on a narrow surface, you must succeed at a Reflex save (with the same DC as the Acrobatics check to Balance) or fall.

UNEVEN GROUND

Uneven ground is an area unsteady enough that you need to Balance (see Acrobatics on page 240) or risk falling prone and possibly injuring yourself, depending on the specifics of the uneven ground. You are flat-footed on uneven ground. Each time you are hit by an attack or fail a save on uneven ground, you must succeed at a Reflex save (with the same DC as the Acrobatics check to Balance) or fall prone.

INCLINES

An incline is an area so steep that you need to Climb using the Athletics skill in order to progress upward. You're flat-footed when Climbing an incline.

FLANKING

When you and an ally are flanking a foe, it has a harder time defending against you. A creature is flat-footed (taking a −2 circumstance penalty to AC) to creatures that are flanking it.

To flank a foe, you and your ally must be on opposites sides or corners of the creature. A line drawn between the center of your space and the center of your ally's space must pass through opposite sides or opposite corners of the foe's space. Additionally, both you and the ally have to be able to act, must be wielding melee weapons or able to make an unarmed attack, can't be under any effects that prevent you from attacking, and must have the enemy within reach. If you are wielding a reach weapon, you use your reach with that weapon for this purpose.

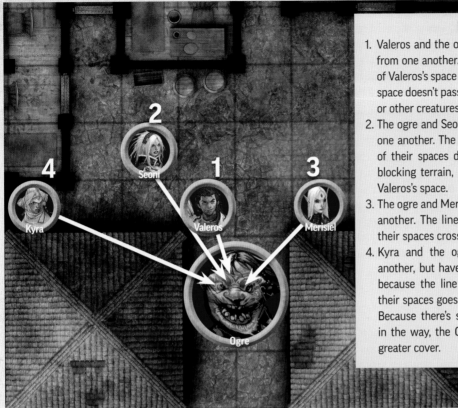

COVER

1. Valeros and the ogre don't have any cover from one another. The line from the center of Valeros's space to the center of the ogre's space doesn't pass through blocking terrain or other creatures.
2. The ogre and Seoni have lesser cover from one another. The line between the centers of their spaces doesn't pass through any blocking terrain, but does passes through Valeros's space.
3. The ogre and Merisiel have cover from one another. The line between the centers of their spaces crosses blocking terrain.
4. Kyra and the ogre can barely see one another, but have cover from one another because the line between the centers of their spaces goes through blocking terrain. Because there's so much blocking terrain in the way, the GM will likely rule this is greater cover.

COVER

When you're behind an obstacle that could block weapons, guard you against explosions, and make you harder to detect, you're behind cover. Standard cover gives you a +2 circumstance bonus to AC, to Reflex saves against area effects, and to Stealth checks to Hide, Sneak, or otherwise avoid detection. You can increase this to greater cover using the Take Cover basic action, increasing the circumstance bonus to +4. If cover is especially light, typically when it's provided by a creature, you have lesser cover, which grants a +1 circumstance bonus to AC. A creature with standard cover or greater cover can attempt to use Stealth to Hide, but lesser cover isn't sufficient.

Type of Cover	Bonus	Can Hide
Lesser	+1 to AC	No
Standard	+2 to AC, Reflex, Stealth	Yes
Greater	+4 to AC, Reflex, Stealth	Yes

Cover is relative, so you might simultaneously have cover against one creature and not another. Cover applies only if your path to the target is partially blocked. If a creature is entirely behind a wall or the like, you don't have line of effect (page 457) and typically can't target it at all.

Usually, the GM can quickly decide whether your target has cover. If you're uncertain or need to be more precise, draw a line from the center of your space to the center of the target's space. If that line passes through any terrain or object that would block the effect, the target has standard

cover (or greater cover if the obstruction is extreme or the target has Taken Cover). If the line passes through a creature instead, the target has lesser cover. When measuring cover against an area effect, draw the line from the effect's point of origin to the center of the creature's space.

COVER AND LARGE CREATURES

If a creature between you and a target is two or more sizes larger than both you and your target, that creature's space blocks the effect enough to provide standard cover instead of lesser cover. The GM might determine that a creature doesn't gain cover from terrain that it's significantly larger than. For example, a Huge dragon probably wouldn't receive any benefit from being behind a 1-foot-wide pillar.

SPECIAL CIRCUMSTANCES

Your GM might allow you to overcome your target's cover in some situations. If you're right next to an arrow slit, you can shoot without penalty, but you have greater cover against someone shooting back at you from far away. Your GM might let you reduce or negate cover by leaning around a corner to shoot or the like. This usually takes an action to set up, and the GM might measure cover from an edge or corner of your space instead of your center.

SPECIAL BATTLES

Sometimes fights occur while the characters are atop mounts or when the PCs take to the sky or seas.

THREE-DIMENSIONAL COMBAT

In aerial and aquatic combat, you might need to track positioning in three dimensions. For flying creatures, you might use one of the following methods:

- Find platforms to place flying creatures' miniatures on.
- Set a die next to a creature with the number indicating how many squares up in the air it is.
- Make a stack of dice or tokens, 1 per 5 feet of elevation.
- Write the elevation next to the monster on the grid.

In underwater combat, choose a plane to be the baseline, typically the waterline, the sea floor, or a stationary object you can measure from.

As with ground-based movement, moving diagonally up or down in 3-D space requires counting every other diagonal as 10 feet. Measure flanking in all directions— creatures above and below an enemy can flank it just as effectively as they can from opposite sides.

MOUNTED COMBAT

You can ride some creatures into combat. As noted in the Mount specialty basic action (page 472), your mount needs to be at least one size larger than you and willing. Your mount acts on your initiative. You must use the Command an Animal action (page 249) to get your mount to spend its actions. If you don't, the animal wastes its actions. If you have the Ride general feat, you succeed automatically when you Command an Animal that's your mount.

For example, if you are mounted on a horse and you make three attacks, your horse would remain stationary since you didn't command it. If you instead spent your first action to Command an Animal and succeeded, you could get your mount to Stride. You could spend your next action to attack or to command the horse to attack, but not both.

MOUNTED ATTACKS

You and your mount fight as a unit. Consequently, you share a multiple attack penalty. For example, if you Strike and then Command an Animal to have your mount Strike, your mount's attack takes a –5 multiple attack penalty.

You occupy every square of your mount's space for the purpose of making your attacks. If you were Medium and on a Large mount, you could attack a creature on one side of your mount, then attack on the opposite side with your next action. If you have a longer reach, the distance depends partly on the size of your mount. On a Medium or smaller mount, use your normal reach. On a Large or Huge mount, you can attack any square adjacent to the mount if you have 5- or 10-foot reach, or any square within 10 feet of the mount (including diagonally) if you have 15-foot reach.

MOUNTED DEFENSES

When you're mounted, attackers can target either you or your mount. Anything that affects multiple creatures (such as an area) affects both of you as long as you're both in the area. You are in an attacker's reach or range if any square of your mount is within reach or range. Because your mount is larger than you and you share its space, you have lesser cover against attacks targeting you when you're mounted if the mount would be in the way.

Because you can't move your body as freely while you're riding a mount, you take a –2 circumstance penalty to Reflex saves while mounted. Additionally, the only move action you can use is the Mount action to dismount.

AERIAL COMBAT

Many monsters can fly, and PCs can use spells and items to gain the ability to fly. Flying creatures have to use the Fly action (page 472) to move through the air. Performing an especially tricky maneuver—such as trying to reverse course 180 degrees or fly through a narrow gap—might require using Acrobatics to Maneuver in Flight. Creatures might fall from the sky, using the falling rules found on page 463. At the GM's discretion, some ground-based actions might not work in the air. For instance, a flying creature couldn't Leap.

AQUATIC COMBAT

Use these rules for battles in water or underwater:

- You're flat-footed unless you have a swim Speed.
- You gain resistance 5 to acid and fire.
- You take a –2 circumstance penalty to melee slashing or bludgeoning attacks that pass through water.
- Ranged attacks that deal bludgeoning or slashing damage automatically miss if the attacker or target is underwater, and piercing ranged attacks made by an underwater creature or against an underwater target have their range increments halved.
- You can't cast fire spells or use actions with the fire trait underwater.
- At the GM's discretion, some ground-based actions might not work underwater or while floating.

DROWNING AND SUFFOCATING

You can hold your breath for a number of rounds equal to 5 + your Constitution modifier. Reduce your remaining air by 1 round at the end of each of your turns, or by 2 if you attacked or cast any spells that turn. You also lose 1 round worth of air each time you are critically hit or critically fail a save against a damaging effect. If you speak (including casting spells with verbal components or activating items with command components) you lose all remaining air.

When you run out of air, you fall unconscious and start suffocating. You can't recover from being unconscious and must attempt a DC 20 Fortitude save at the end of each of your turns. On a failure, you take 1d10 damage, and on a critical failure, you die. On each check after the first, the DC increases by 5 and the damage by 1d10; these increases are cumulative. Once your access to air is restored, you stop suffocating and are no longer unconscious (unless you're at 0 Hit Points).

EXPLORATION MODE

While encounters use rounds for combat, exploration is more free form. The GM determines the flow of time, as you could be traveling by horseback across craggy highlands, negotiating with merchants, or delving in a dungeon in search of danger and treasure. Exploration lacks the immediate danger of encounter mode, but it offers its own challenges.

Much of exploration mode involves movement and roleplaying. You might be traveling from one town to another, chatting with a couple of merchants an outpost along the way, or maybe having a terse conversation with the watchful city guards at your destination. Instead of measuring your rate of movement in 5-foot squares every round, you measure it in feet or miles per minute, hour, or day, using your travel speed. Rather than deciding on each action every turn, you'll engage in an exploration activity, and you'll typically spend some time every day resting and making your daily preparations.

TRAVEL SPEED

Depending on how the GM tracks movement, you move in feet or miles based on your character's Speed with the relevant movement type. Typical rates are on the table below.

TABLE 9–2: TRAVEL SPEED

Speed	Feet per Minute	Miles per Hour	Miles per Day
10 feet	100	1	8
15 feet	150	1-1/2	12
20 feet	200	2	16
25 feet	250	2-1/2	20
30 feet	300	3	24
35 feet	350	3-1/2	28
40 feet	400	4	32
50 feet	500	5	40
60 feet	600	6	48

The rates in Table 9–2 assume traveling over flat and clear terrain at a determined pace, but one that's not exhausting. Moving through difficult terrain halves the listed movement rate. Greater difficult terrain reduces the distance traveled to one-third the listed amount. If the travel requires a skill check to accomplish, such as mountain climbing or swimming, the GM might call for a check once per hour using the result and the table above to determine your progress.

EXPLORATION ACTIVITIES

While you're traveling and exploring, tell the GM what you'd generally like to do along the way. If you to do nothing more than make steady progress toward your goal, you move at the full travel speeds given in Table 9–2.

When you want to do something other than simply travel, you describe what you are attempting to do. It isn't necessary to go into extreme detail, such as "Using my dagger, I nudge the door so I can check for devious traps." Instead, "I'm searching the area for hazards" is sufficient. The GM finds the best exploration activity to match your description and describes the effects of that activity. Some exploration activities limit how fast you can travel and be effective.

These are most common exploration activities.

AVOID NOTICE

EXPLORATION

You attempt a Stealth check to avoid notice while traveling at half speed. If you have the Swift Sneak feat, you can move at full Speed rather than half, but you still can't use another exploration activity while you do so. If you have the Legendary Sneak feat, you can move at full Speed and use a second exploration activity. If you're Avoiding Notice at the start of an encounter, you usually roll a Stealth check instead of a Perception check both to determine your initiative and to see if the enemies notice you (based on their Perception DCs, as normal for Sneak, regardless of their initiative check results).

DEFEND

EXPLORATION

You move at half your travel speed with your shield raised. If combat breaks out, you gain the benefits of Raising a Shield before your first turn begins.

DETECT MAGIC

CONCENTRATE **EXPLORATION**

You cast *detect magic* at regular intervals. You move at half your travel speed or slower. You have no chance of accidentally overlooking a magic aura at a travel speed up to 300 feet per minute, but must be traveling no more than 150 feet per minute to detect magic auras before the party moves into them.

FOLLOW THE EXPERT

AUDITORY **CONCENTRATE** **EXPLORATION** **VISUAL**

Choose an ally attempting a recurring skill check while exploring, such as climbing, or performing a different exploration tactic that requires a skill check (like Avoiding Notice). The ally must be at least an expert in that skill and must be willing to provide assistance. While Following the Expert, you match their tactic or attempt similar skill checks. Thanks to your ally's assistance, you can add your level as a proficiency bonus to the associated skill check, even if you're untrained. Additionally, you gain a circumstance bonus to your skill check based on your ally's proficiency (+2 for expert, +3 for master, and +4 for legendary).

INTRODUCTION

ANCESTRIES & BACKGROUNDS

CLASSES

SKILLS

FEATS

EQUIPMENT

SPELLS

THE AGE OF LOST OMENS

PLAYING THE GAME

GAME MASTERING

CRAFTING & TREASURE

APPENDIX

SKILL EXPLORATION ACTIVITIES

Chapter 4: Skills includes numerous additional exploration activities, which are summarized here.

Borrow an Arcane Spell: You use Arcana to prepare a spell from someone else's spellbook (page 241).

Coerce: You use Intimidation to threaten a creature so it does what you want (page 247).

Cover Tracks: You use Survival to obscure your passing (page 252).

Decipher Writing: You use a suitable skill to understand archaic, esoteric, or obscure texts (page 234).

Gather Information: You use Diplomacy to canvass the area to learn about a specific individual or topic (page 246).

Identify Alchemy: You use Craft and alchemist's tools to identify an alchemical item (page 245).

Identify Magic: Using a variety of skills, you can learn about a magic item, location, or ongoing effect (page 238).

Impersonate: You use Deception and usually a disguise kit to create a disguise (page 245).

Learn a Spell: You use the skill corresponding to the spell's tradition to gain access to a new spell (page 238).

Make an Impression: You use Diplomacy to make a good impression on someone (page 246).

Repair: With a repair kit and the Crafting skill, you fix a damaged item (page 243).

Sense Direction: You use Survival to get a sense of where you are or determine the cardinal directions (page 252).

Squeeze: Using Acrobatics, you squeeze though very tight spaces (page 241).

Track: You use Survival to find and follow creatures' tracks (page 252).

Treat Wounds: You use Medicine to treat a living creature's wounds (page 249).

HUSTLE

EXPLORATION **MOVE**

You strain yourself to move at double your travel speed. You can Hustle only for a number of minutes equal to your Constitution modifier × 10 (minimum 10 minutes). If you are in a group that is Hustling, use the lowest Constitution modifier among everyone to determine how fast the group can Hustle together.

INVESTIGATE

CONCENTRATE **EXPLORATION**

You seek out information about your surroundings while traveling at half speed. You use Recall Knowledge as a secret check to discover clues among the various things you can see and engage with as you journey along. You can use any skill that has a Recall Knowledge action while Investigating, but the GM determines whether the skill is relevant to the clues you could find.

REPEAT A SPELL

CONCENTRATE **EXPLORATION**

You repeatedly cast the same spell while moving at half speed. Typically, this spell is a cantrip that you want to have in effect

in the event a combat breaks out, and it must be one you can cast in 2 actions or fewer. In order to prevent fatigue due to repeated casting, you'll likely use this activity only when something out of the ordinary occurs.

You can instead use this activity to continue Sustaining a Spell or Activation with a sustained duration. Most such spells or item effects can be sustained for 10 minutes, though some specify they can be sustained for a different duration.

SCOUT

CONCENTRATE **EXPLORATION**

You scout ahead and behind the group to watch danger, moving at half speed. At the start of the next encounter, every creature in your party gains a +1 circumstance bonus to their initiative rolls.

SEARCH

CONCENTRATE **EXPLORATION**

You Seek meticulously for hidden doors, concealed hazards, and so on. You can usually make an educated guess as to which locations are best to check and move at half speed, but if you want to be thorough and guarantee you checked everything, you need to travel at a Speed of no more than 300 feet per minute, or 150 feet per minute to ensure you check everything before you walk into it. You can always move more slowly while Searching to cover the area more thoroughly, and the Expeditious Search feat increases these maximum Speeds. If you come across a secret door, item, or hazard while Searching, the GM will attempt a free secret check to Seek to see if you notice the hidden object or hazard. In locations with many objects to search, you have to stop and spend significantly longer to search thoroughly.

REST AND DAILY PREPARATIONS

You perform at your best when you take enough time to rest and prepare. Once every 24 hours, you can take a period of rest (typically 8 hours), after which you regain Hit Points equal to your Constitution modifier (minimum 1) times your level, and you might recover from or improve certain conditions (page 453). Sleeping in armor results in poor rest that leaves you fatigued. If you go more than 16 hours without resting, you become fatigued (you cannot recover from this until you rest at least 6 continuous hours).

After you rest, you make your daily preparations, which takes around 1 hour. You can prepare only if you've rested, and only once per day. Preparing includes the following:

- Spellcasters regain spell slots, and prepared spellcasters choose spells to have available that day.
- Focus Points, other abilities that refresh during your preparations, and abilities that can be used only a certain number of times per day, including magic item uses, are reset.
- You don armor and equip weapons and other gear.
- You invest up to 10 worn magic items to gain their benefits for the day.

DOWNTIME MODE

Downtime mode is played day-by-day rather than minute-by-minute or scene-by-scene. Usually this mode of play occurs when you are in the safety of a settlement, maybe recovering from your adventures or studying an artifact you found.

Downtime gives you time to rest fully, engage in crafting or a professional endeavor, learn new spells, retrain feats, or just have fun. You can sell items acquired during your adventures, buy new goods, and perform other activities as determined by your feats, your skills, and the settlement where you are spending the downtime.

LONG-TERM REST

You can spend an entire day and night resting during downtime to recover Hit Points equal to your Constitution modifier (minimum 1) multiplied by twice your level.

RETRAINING

Retraining offers a way to alter some of your character choices, which is helpful when you want to take your character in a new direction or change decisions that didn't meet your expectations. You can retrain feats, skills, and some selectable class features. You can't retrain your ancestry, heritage, background, class, or ability scores. You can't perform other downtime activities while retraining.

Retraining usually requires you to spend time learning from a teacher, whether that entails physical training, studying at a library, or falling into shared magical trances. Your GM determines whether you can get proper training or whether something can be retrained at all. In some cases, you'll have to pay your instructor.

Some abilities can be difficult or impossible to retrain (for instance, a sorcerer can retrain their bloodline only in extraordinary circumstances).

When retraining, you generally can't make choices you couldn't make when you selected the original option. For instance, you can't exchange a 2nd-level skill feat for a 4th-level one, or for one that requires prerequisites you didn't meet at the time you took the original feat. If you don't remember whether you met the prerequisites at the time, ask your GM to make the call. If you cease to meet the prerequisites for an ability due to retraining, you can't use that ability. You might need to retrain several abilities in sequence in order to get all the abilities you want.

FEATS

You can spend a week of downtime retraining to swap out one of your feats. Remove the old feat and replace it with another of the same type. For example, you could swap a skill feat for another skill feat, but not for a wizard feat.

> ### SKILL DOWNTIME ACTIVITIES
>
> Chapter 4: Skills includes several downtime activities, which are summarized here.
>
> **Craft:** Using the Crafting skill, you can create items from raw materials (page 244).
>
> **Create Forgery:** You forge a document (page 251).
>
> **Earn Income:** You earn money, typically using Crafting, Lore, or Performance (page 236).
>
> **Subsist:** You find food and shelter in the wilderness or within a settlement (page 240).
>
> **Treat Disease:** You spend time caring for a diseased creature in the hope of curing that creature (page 248).

SKILLS

You can spend a week of downtime retraining to swap out one of your skill increases. Reduce your proficiency rank in the skill losing its increase by one step and increase your proficiency rank in another skill by one step. The new proficiency rank has to be equal to or lower than the proficiency rank you traded away. For instance, if your bard is a master in Performance and Stealth, and an expert in Occultism, you could reduce the character's proficiency in Stealth to expert and become a master in Occultism, but you couldn't reassign that skill increase to become legendary in Performance. Keep track of your level when you reassign skill increases; the level at which your skill proficiencies changed can influence your ability to retrain feats with skill prerequisites.

You can also spend a week to retrain an initial trained skill you gained during character creation.

CLASS FEATURES

You can change a class feature that required a choice, making a different choice instead. This lets you change a druid order or a wizard school, for example. The GM will tell you how long this takes—always at least a month.

OTHER DOWNTIME ACTIVITIES

Work with your GM if there are other ways you want to spend downtime. You might need to pay for your cost of living (the prices for this can be found on page 294). You might acquire property, manage a business, become part of a guild or civic group, curry favor in a large city, take command of an army, take on an apprentice, start a family, or minister to a flock of the faithful.

INTRODUCTION

ANCESTRIES &
BACKGROUNDS

CLASSES

SKILLS

FEATS

EQUIPMENT

SPELLS

THE AGE OF
LOST OMENS

PLAYING THE
GAME

GAME
MASTERING

CRAFTING
& TREASURE

APPENDIX

CHAPTER 10: GAME MASTERING

As Game Master, you run each session of Pathfinder, providing the link between the players and the world of the game. It's up to you to set the scene as the player characters battle monsters, interact with other people, and explore the world.

10

INTRODUCTION

ANCESTRIES &
BACKGROUNDS

CLASSES

SKILLS

FEATS

EQUIPMENT

SPELLS

THE AGE OF
LOST OMENS

PLAYING THE
GAME

GAME
MASTERING

CRAFTING
& TREASURE

APPENDIX

When you take on the role of Game Master, you'll have the rewarding job of crafting fun experiences for a group of your friends. Your responsibilities include...

- Telling the story of the group's adventures in a compelling and consistent way.
- Fleshing out the world in which the game takes place, emphasizing the fantastical while grounding it enough in the real world to feel believable.
- Entertaining the players and yourself with novel concepts, and rewarding creative ideas with interesting outcomes.
- Preparing for game sessions by building or studying adventures and creating characters and plots.
- Improvising the reactions of nonplayer characters and other forces in the world as the players do unexpected things.
- Making rules decisions to ensure fairness and keep the game moving forward.

This chapter provides the tools you need to shoulder those responsibilities. The following sections break down the various components of a campaign, discuss the different modes of play and how to set DCs for the tasks the PCs attempt, provide different ways of rewarding player characters, and describe aspects of the environment that might affect an adventuring party.

PLANNING A CAMPAIGN

A Pathfinder game is typically structured as a campaign—a serialized story that focuses on a single party of characters. A campaign is subdivided into multiple adventures, smaller stories that involve exploration and interaction with nonplayer characters. A single adventure represents a complete story that might be connected to the larger arc of a campaign. Playing an adventure spans one or more game sessions—gatherings where the group plays a part of the adventure over the course of several hours.

A campaign provides the overall structure for your Pathfinder game. As you prepare for your campaign, you'll establish its scope and themes, which you'll then reinforce in the adventures and scenes that take place within it.

CAMPAIGN LENGTH

The length of a campaign can range from a few sessions to many years. Two main factors determine campaign length: how much time you need to complete the story, and how much time players want to devote to the game.

COLLABORATION DURING PLAY

As Game Master, you have the final say on how the world and rules function, and how nonplayer characters act. This rule's purpose is to make the game run smoothly, with one guiding hand ensuring consistency. It's not intended to make one player into a dictator over the rest of the group. Collaboration is vital to roleplaying games!

How you implement collaboration in a game depends on what your players are interested in. In some groups, players enjoy adding details to the world and to nonplayer characters. In others, players want to feel like the world is outside their control, and the only decisions they get to make are those made by their own characters. Both are fun and acceptable ways to play.

You are encouraged to collect input from your players before you start, asking what storytelling genres they'd like to emphasize, which areas of the world they want to play in, the types of enemies they'd like to face, or which published adventure they want to play. A good campaign includes some back-and-forth at the beginning as the players figure out what characters they want to play and you figure out what sort of adventure to run. The results can range from building an adventure entirely to fit the characters to choosing a specific published adventure, having the players make their characters, and then just adapting the beginning of that adventure so that all the player characters have a reason to be involved.

As you play, opportunities to collaborate will occur again and again. When players throw out suggestions or come up with specific theories about the events of the campaign, they're telling you what they'd like to see in the game. Try to find ways to incorporate their suggestions, but with enough of a twist that each still includes something unexpected.

A single session, or a "one-shot," is great if your group is trying out Pathfinder or wants to play a specific short adventure. This requires a smaller time commitment but requires the GM to present the events of the game in a way that is immediately engaging, since there's less opportunity for the players to become invested in the story or setting.

If you want to play through a longer campaign, you'll need to add some story elements that speak directly to the characters in your game rather than just to the events of the adventure. In other words, the characters should have individual goals in addition to the group's overall goals.

You can estimate how long a campaign will take by looking at the amount of time you actually have to play, or the number of character levels you intend the characters to advance. It typically takes three to four sessions for a group to level up. Since you'll probably cancel sessions on occasion, playing once a week for a year results in roughly a 14-level campaign, playing every 2 weeks for a year gives you an 8-level campaign, and playing monthly allows for a 5-level campaign. If you play only once a month, you might consider holding longer sessions and using fast advancement (page 509).

It's entirely okay to have a campaign with an indefinite length. Many groups play through one adventure and then decide to take on another. If you run an indefinite campaign, however, avoid ongoing plots that you can't satisfactorily end if the campaign comes to a close after the next adventure. If you introduce an overwhelmingly powerful villain who's crucial to the story but can't be stopped until the player characters are 15th level, ending the campaign at 8th level will feel anticlimactic.

It pays to be conservative when estimating your campaign length and scope. It's always tempting to run a 20-level epic campaign with complex, interwoven plots, but such games can fall apart long before the end if your group can play only once a month and the players have other responsibilities.

EXPECTED DURATION

Not every campaign ends at the same point. Some campaigns go all the way to 20th level, ending after the player characters attain the height of power and confront the greatest threats any mortal could face. Others end at a lower level, after the group takes down a major villain or solves a crucial problem. And still other campaigns end when players become unable to attend or decide its a good time to stop playing.

You should have an end point in mind when you start a campaign. Still, you have to be flexible, since you're telling the story alongside other players, and your initial expectations for the campaign may be proven incorrect. When you think you're heading toward a satisfying conclusion, it's useful to check in with the other players. You might say, "I think we have about two sessions left. Does that work for everyone? Is there any unfinished business you want to take care of?" This lets you gauge whether your assumptions match up with the rest of the group—and make any necessary adjustments.

THEMES

The themes you choose for your campaign are what distinguish it from other campaigns. They include the major dramatic questions of your story and the repeated use of certain environments or creatures, and they can also include embracing a genre beyond traditional high fantasy. The themes you choose for your campaign also suggest storyline elements you might use.

A storyline's themes usually relate to the backstories, motivations, and flaws of the player characters and villains. For example, if you've chosen revenge as one of the themes of your game, you might introduce a villain whose quest for revenge tears his life apart and causes tragic harm to those around him. If one of the player characters is a chaotic good believer in liberty and freedom, you might engage that character by pitting the group against slavers. Or, you might choose a theme of love, leading to nonplayer characters involved in doomed romances, seeking to regain lovers they have lost, or courting the player characters.

Using similar locations and related creatures helps you form connections between disparate adventures. The players feel like their characters are becoming experts negotiating with giants, navigating seaways, battling devils, exploring the planes, or dealing with whatever the recurring elements are. For example, you might have the players explore a frozen tundra early on, then later travel to an icy plane filled with more difficult challenges that can be overcome using knowledge they've previously developed. Likewise, hobgoblin soldiers may be tough enemies for your group at low levels, but as the PCs attain higher levels and the hobgoblins become mere minions of another creature, the players feel a sense of progression.

Pathfinder is a fantasy adventure game, but you can shift your campaign to include elements of other fictional genres. You might want to infuse your game a with a sense of horror, reduce the amount of magic and use slow advancement (page 509) to make it a tale of sword and sorcery, or turn magic into technology for a steampunk setting.

A WELCOMING ENVIRONMENT

The role of Game Master comes with the responsibility of ensuring you and the rest of the players have a rewarding, fun time during the game. Games can deal with difficult subjects and have stressful moments, but fundamentally Pathfinder is a leisure activity. It can remain so only if the players follow the social contract and respect one another.

Players with physical or mental disabilities might find themselves more challenged than abled players. Work with your players to ensure they have the resources and support they need. Additionally, be on the lookout for behavior that's inappropriate, whether intentional or inadvertent, and pay careful attention to players' body language during the game. If you notice a player becoming uncomfortable, you are empowered to pause the game, take it in a new direction, privately check in with your players during or after the session, or take any other action you think is appropriate.

If a player tells you they're uncomfortable with something in the game, whether it's content you've presented as the GM or another player's or PC's actions, listen carefully to that player and take steps to ensure

TOOLS FOR RESPONSIBLE PLAY

Consent and comfort are important topics for roleplaying games, and many designers have created techniques to help facilitate responsible play. Some methods you can use are lines and veils, developed by Ron Edwards, and the X-Card, developed by John Stavropoulos.

Lines and Veils

The terms "line" and "veil" can give your table a common vocabulary for the concepts described in this section. A line is a hard limit to the actions players might take, such as "We're drawing a line at torture." The group agrees not to cross a line and omits that content from the game.

A veil indicates something that shouldn't be described in detail. The scene fades to black for a veil, or the group moves on to discuss a different topic, though whatever the veil is drawn across still happens. For example, you might say, "We'll draw a veil across the scene as those characters head into the bedroom."

You might come up with some lines and veils in advance, but then find more as play continues.

The X-Card

Draw an "X" on a card, and you've got an X-Card. Place it on the table at the start of the session and describe its use to the players: any player can silently reject content they find upsetting by tapping the X-Card; whoever's speaking then rewinds a bit and continues on, excising the objectionable content. As with setting the basic guidelines for your campaign, there are no questions asked, no judgment, and no argument when someone invokes the X-Card. You can, however, ask for clarification if you need it, such as "How far back should I rewind this?" Some groups instead make an X with their hands, say "Let's X that out," or use some other method. Either way, follow up with the player privately, after the game, to see if the guidelines need to be revised. You can find more details at **tinyurl.com/x-card-rpg**.

they can once again have fun during your game. If you're preparing prewritten material and you find a character or a situation inappropriate, you are fully empowered to change any details as you see fit. You also have the authority (and responsibility) to ask players to change their behavior—or even leave the table—if what they're doing is unacceptable or makes others feel uncomfortable. It's never appropriate to make the person who is uncomfortable responsible for resolving a problem. It's okay if mistakes happen. What's important is how you respond and move forward.

Gaming is for everyone. Never let those acting in bad faith undermine your game or exclude other players. Your efforts are part of the long-term process of making games and game culture welcoming to all. Working together, we can build a community where players of all identities and experiences feel safe.

OBJECTIONABLE CONTENT

Before a campaign begins, check in with your players—as a group or individually—to find out what types of content they want to allow in the game, and which topics they would prefer to avoid. Because the story unfolds in real time, it's essential that you discuss these topics before the game starts. These discussions are intended to keep players safe, and so it's not okay to ask why someone wants a type of content banned. If someone wants it banned, ban it—no questions asked.

It can help to start with a rating, like those used for movies or video games. Pathfinder games often include violence and cruelty. What's the limit on how graphically these concepts should be described? Can players swear at the table? Does anyone have phobias they don't want to appear in the game, such as spiders or body horror?

After you figure out the limits on objectionable content, you have four important tasks:

- Clearly convey these limits to the other players.
- Ensure you and the players abide by the boundaries.
- Act immediately if someone becomes uncomfortable about content during a session, even if it wasn't already banned in a prior discussion. Once the issue is resolved, move on.
- Resolve the issue if any player deliberately pushes these boundaries, tries to find loopholes, tries to renegotiate the limits, or belittles people for having a different tolerance to objectionable content.

THE PATHFINDER BASELINE

You might find that your players don't have much to say on the topic of objectionable content, and just assume that general societal mores will keep the most uncomfortable topics out of the game. That's not always enough, as that approach relies on shared assumptions that aren't always accurate. The following is a set of basic assumptions that works for many groups, which you can modify to fit your preferences and those of the other players.

- Bloodshed, injuries, and even dismemberment might be described. However, excessive descriptions of gore and cruelty should be avoided.
- Romantic and sexual relationships can happen in the game, but players should avoid being overly suggestive. Sex always happens "off-screen." Because attempts at initiating a relationship between player characters can be uncomfortably similar to one player hitting on another, this should generally be avoided (and is entirely inappropriate when playing with strangers).
- Avoid excessively gross or scatological descriptions.

The following acts should never be performed by player characters:

- Torture
- Rape, nonconsensual sexual contact, or sexual threats
- Harm to children, including sexual abuse
- Owning slaves or profiting from the slave trade

- Reprehensible uses of mind-control magic

Villains might engage in such acts, but they won't happen "on-screen" or won't be described in detail. Many groups choose to not have villains engage in these activities at all, keeping these reprehensible acts out of mind entirely.

SOCIAL SPLASH DAMAGE

As important as it is to take care of yourself and the other players in your game, be mindful of your group's impact on the other people around you. If you're playing in a space that's not your own, respect your hosts. If you're playing in public, consider the comfort of the people around you, not just what your group is comfortable with. It's easy to get caught up in a game, as we get sucked into the microcosm of an imagined world, but don't ignore the real world around you. Be aware when you're making too much noise, leaving a mess, alarming passersby with graphic descriptions of violence, or even just giving the cold shoulder to curious spectators witnessing RPG play for the first time.

CHARACTER CREATION

At the outset of a new campaign, the players will create new player characters. Part of that process involves you introducing what the campaign will be about and what types of characters are most appropriate. Work with the players to determine which rule options are available. The safest options are the common choices from the *Pathfinder Core Rulebook*. If players want to use common options from other books or uncommon or rare options, through play, review those options to see if any of them conflict with the style of campaign you have in mind or might present strange surprises down the road. It's usually best to allow new options, but there's no obligation to do so. Be as open as you're comfortable with.

PREPARING AN ADVENTURE

An adventure is a self-contained collection of story elements, characters, and settings that become the basis for the story you and the other players tell. Think of the adventure as an outline for your own story. You'll have major beats you want to include, some consistent characters, and themes you want to convey, but all sorts of things can change during the process of turning the outline into a completed story.

You might use a published adventure from Paizo or another company, or you might construct your own adventure as you prepare for your game sessions.

PUBLISHED ADVENTURES

Prewritten adventures include background information and nonplayer characters needed for the story, plus all the locations, maps, and monster groups necessary for both exploration and encounters. Prewritten adventures can speed up your preparation, since you can simply read the relevant sections of the adventure before a game, and you don't have to create everything from scratch. A published adventure already includes the expected amount of encounters and treasure, and you can find adventures built for different character levels to match your group. Reading a published adventure or running one as your first game can help you see how adventures are structured, which makes it easier to write one later if you choose.

Though a published adventure is prewritten, it's not set in stone. Changing the details of an adventure to suit your group isn't just acceptable, it's preferred! Use the backstories and predilections of the player characters to inform how you change the adventure. This can mean altering adversaries so they're linked to the player characters, changing the setting to a place some of the player characters are from, or excising particular scenes if you know they won't appeal to your players.

CREATING ADVENTURES

Building your own adventure is much more challenging than using a published one, but it lets you express yourself, be even more creative, and tailor the game directly to the players and their characters. Later sections in this chapter include guidelines for building and running encounters, placing treasure, and setting appropriately difficult challenges, all to help you construct your own adventures.

Adventure plotting can start at many different points. You might begin with a particular antagonist, then construct an adventure that fits that villain's theme and leads the group to them. Alternatively, you could start with an interesting location for exploration, then populate it with adversaries and challenges appropriate to the setting.

LOCATIONS

Memorable settings that include mysterious and fantastical locations for players to visit can elicit the players' curiosity. Exploring each location should be a treat in itself, not just a chore the players must complete to get from one fight to the next. As you create a locale, picture it in your mind's eye and write down minor details you can include as you narrate the game. Describing decorations, natural landmarks, wildlife, peculiar smells, and even temperature changes make a place feel more real.

Beyond monsters and loot, your locations can include environment-based challenges, from environmental conditions like blizzards to puzzles, traps, or other hazards. These challenges should suit your adventure's location: walls of brambles in a castle ruin overrun with vegetation, pools of acid in a cursed swamp, or magical traps in the tomb of a paranoid wizard. Rules for environments appear on page 512, and those for hazards start on page 520.

ENCOUNTERS

A robust set of encounters forms the backbone of your adventure. Encounters often feature combat with other creatures, but they can also include hazards, or you might

CHARACTERS WITH DISABILITIES

A player might want to create a character with a disability, or their character might end up with a disability over the course of play. Work with the player to find ways to respectfully represent the disability. Conditions such as blinded and deafened aren't a good fit for a character who has been living with a disability long-term. Here are suggestions for rules you might use for PCs with disabilities.

Blindness or Impaired Vision

A blind character can't detect anything using vision, critically fails Perception checks requiring sight, is immune to visual effects, and can't be blinded or dazzled. You might give this character the Blind-Fight feat (page 149) for free.

A character with impaired vision might take a −2 to −4 penalty to vision-based Perception checks. Spectacles or other corrective devices might reduce or remove this.

Deafness or Being Hard of Hearing

A deaf character can't detect anything using hearing, critically fails Perception checks that require hearing, and is immune to auditory effects. They have enough practice to supply verbal components for casting spells and command components for activating magic items, but if they perform an action they're not accustomed to that involves auditory elements, they must succeed at a DC 5 flat check or the action is lost. It's best to give them the Sign Language feat for free, and you might give them Read Lips as well (page 266 and 265). You might give one or more other characters in the group Sign Language for free as well.

A hard-of-hearing character might take a −2 to −4 penalty to Perception checks that are hearing-based. Corrective devices for hearing are less common than spectacles are in a typical Pathfinder world.

Missing Limb

Some magic items require certain limbs or other body parts. It's fine to allow an alternative form of the item, turning boots into bracers for a character without legs, for example.

A character with a missing hand or arm might need to spend 2 actions to Interact with an item that requires two hands, or otherwise compensate. Using a two-handed weapon is not possible. A character can acquire a prosthetic hand or arm to compensate.

Someone missing a foot or leg might take a small penalty to Speed, but can typically acquire a prosthetic to compensate. If they have no legs, they might use a wheelchair, a dependable mount, or levitation or flight magic.

Mental Illness and Chronic Illness

Some disabilities, such as mental illness and chronic illnesses, are best left to the player to roleplay. Mental illness is an especially fraught topic, with a history of insensitive portrayal. Be careful about the intentions of the player and the impact the presentation might have on other players.

INTRODUCTION

ANCESTRIES & BACKGROUNDS

CLASSES

SKILLS

FEATS

EQUIPMENT

SPELLS

THE AGE OF LOST OMENS

PLAYING THE GAME

GAME MASTERING

CRAFTING & TREASURE

APPENDIX

USING RARITY AND ACCESS

The rarity system has two purposes: to convey how common or rare certain spells, creatures, or items are in the game world, and to give you an easy tool to control the complexity of your game. Uncommon and rare options aren't more powerful than other options of their level, but they introduce complications for certain types of stories, or are less common in the world. For instance, it might be more challenging to run a mystery adventure when a player can cast an uncommon spell such as *detect evil*.

At the start of the campaign, communicate your preferred expectations on rarity to the players. Unless you decide otherwise, the players can choose from any common options they qualify for, plus any uncommon options granted by their character choices—primarily their ancestry and class. By default, a character who tries hard enough might eventually find an uncommon option, whereas a rare option is always a special reward. Beyond that baseline, you can grant access as freely as you want; some GMs open up all uncommon and rare options universally. If you're not sure, just look over any uncommon or rare elements before you include them as rewards or otherwise allow a player to acquire them.

Rewards

You can use uncommon and rare rules elements to reward characters. These still have the same value and approximate power as any other treasure of the same Price, but they're just a bit more special because they hail from distant lands or have unusual or surprising abilities. Items are the most likely candidates for uncommon or rare rewards, but an NPC might teach an uncommon or rare spell to a PC in gratitude or to help the party prepare for a certain adversary. You can also improvise extra benefits based around uncommon or rare items. For instance, if a PC gains a rare plant with occult uses, you might also decide that the PC should temporarily get more money if they use it while Earning Income using Herbalism Lore, because it enables them to produce novel poultices.

Different Locations

The rarities in this book assume you're playing in the Inner Sea region of Golarion, where most Pathfinder games are set. These rarities are also suitable for most western medieval fantasy games. However, you might want to alter the rarities for a campaign set in another location on Golarion (detailed in Chapter 8), to emphasize a non-human culture, or to play in a fantasy setting with different roots, like a wuxia game based on Chinese culture. These changes most often affect basic items. If you start your campaign in a dwarven stronghold, for example, you might make all the weapons with the dwarf trait common. You should feel free to adjust rarities to suit your campaign's theme, but if you do, you should share your changes with your group.

create social encounters in which characters duel only with words. The rules for building encounters appropriate to your group's level begin below.

Some adventures have a clear and direct progression, with encounters occurring at specific times or in a specific order. Others, such as a dungeon filled with interconnected rooms the group can investigate in any order, are nonlinear, and the group can face encounters in any order—or even avoid them entirely. Most adventures are somewhere in between, with some keystone encounters you know the characters will need to contend with, but others that are optional.

TREASURE

Your adventure should give out an amount of treasure that's appropriate to the characters' level. The guidelines for assigning treasure are on page 508. You can dole out treasure in all kinds of ways. Treasure could be items carried by an adversary, rewards from a patron for completing a mission, or a classic pile of coins and items inside a wooden chest guarded by a monster. It's best to spread treasure throughout an adventure rather than stockpiled in a single hoard. This gives the players incremental rewards, letting their characters advance in frequent small steps rather than giant leaps separated by many hours of play.

BUILDING ENCOUNTERS

The most common type of encounter is a combat encounter, where the PCs face other creatures. Combat encounters are strictly governed by rules; the guidelines that follow will help you build combat encounters that pose appropriate challenges for your group. Building hazard encounters works the same way. Social encounters are more free-form, and are up to you as the GM to design.

To build a combat encounter, first decide how the encounter fits in the adventure as a whole. Then, estimate how much of a threat you want the encounter to pose, using one of five categories below.

Trivial-threat encounters are so easy that the characters have essentially no chance of losing; they shouldn't even need to spend significant resources unless they are particularly wasteful. These encounters work best as warm-ups, palate cleansers, or reminders of how awesome the characters are. A trivial-threat encounter can still be fun to play, so don't ignore them just because of the lack of threat.

Low-threat encounters present a veneer of difficulty and typically use some of the party's resources. However, it would be rare or the result of very poor tactics for the entire party to be seriously threatened.

Moderate-threat encounters are a serious challenge to the characters, though unlikely to overpower them completely. Characters usually need to use sound tactics and manage their resources wisely to come out of a moderate-threat encounter ready to continue on and face a harder challenge without resting.

Severe-threat encounters are the hardest encounters most groups of characters can consistently defeat. These encounters are most appropriate for important moments in your story, such as confronting a final boss. Bad luck, poor tactics, or a lack of resources due to prior encounters can easily turn a severe-threat encounter against the characters, and a wise group keeps the option to disengage open.

Extreme-threat encounters are so dangerous that they are likely to be an even match for the characters, particularly if the characters are low on resources. This makes them too challenging for most uses. An extreme-threat encounter might be appropriate for a fully rested group of characters that can go all-out, for the climactic encounter at the end of an entire campaign, or for a group of veteran players using advanced tactics and teamwork.

XP Budget

Once you've selected a threat level, it's time to build the encounter. You have an XP budget based on the threat, and each creature costs some of that budget. Start with the monsters or NPCs that are most important to the encounter, then decide how you want to use the rest of your XP budget. Many encounters won't match the XP budget exactly, but they should come close. The XP budget is based on a group of four characters. If your group is larger or smaller, see Different Party Sizes below.

Choosing Creatures

In all but the most unusual circumstances, you'll select creatures for your encounter that range from 4 levels lower than the PCs' level to 4 levels higher (see Table 10–2: Creature XP and Role). Each creature has a part to play in your encounter, from a lowly lackey to a boss so mighty it could defeat the entire party single-handedly.

Each creature costs some of the XP from your XP budget for the encounter, based on its level compared to the levels of the characters in your party. For instance, if the PCs are 5th level, a 2nd-level creature is a "party level – 3" creature, a lackey appropriate for a low-to-moderate-threat encounter, and it costs 15 XP in an encounter's XP budget. Party level is explained in detail on page 508.

Different Party Sizes

For each additional character in the party beyond the fourth, increase your XP budget by the amount shown in the Character Adjustment value for your encounter in Table 10–1: Encounter Budget. If you have fewer than four characters, use the same process in reverse: for each missing character, remove that amount of XP from your XP budget. Note that if you adjust your XP budget to account for party size, the XP awards for the encounter don't change—you'll always award the amount of XP listed for a group of four characters.

It's best to use the XP increase from more characters to add more enemies or hazards, and the XP decrease from

TABLE 10-1: ENCOUNTER BUDGET

Threat	XP Budget	Character Adjustment
Trivial	40 or less	10 or less
Low	60	15
Moderate	80	20
Severe	120	30
Extreme	160	40

TABLE 10-2: CREATURE XP AND ROLE

Creature Level	XP	Suggested Role
Party level – 4	10	Low-threat lackey
Party level – 3	15	Low- or moderate-threat lackey
Party level – 2	20	Any lackey or standard creature
Party level – 1	30	Any standard creature
Party level	40	Any standard creature or low-threat boss
Party level + 1	60	Low- or moderate-threat boss
Party level + 2	80	Moderate- or severe-threat boss
Party level + 3	120	Severe- or extreme-threat boss
Party level + 4	160	Extreme-threat solo boss

fewer characters to subtract enemies and hazards, rather than making one enemy tougher or weaker. Encounters are typically more satisfying if the number of enemy creatures is fairly close to the number of player characters.

RUNNING A GAME SESSION

A campaign happens over a series of sessions. Each session is usually several hours long, with multiple encounters, some exploration, and possibly downtime. Your session can be compared to an episode of a TV show; it should include some twists, turns, and changes, and end leaving people excited about what comes next.

PLANNING A SESSION

One of the greatest challenges in gaming is scheduling a time for everyone to get together and play. Often, this responsibility falls on you as the GM, since you're the one who has to prepare your game between sessions. Many games have a set schedule, such as once per week, once every 2 weeks, or once per month. The less frequently your group meets, the better notes and recaps you'll need to keep everyone on the same page.

Plan a time for everybody will arrive, and also try to set a time when playing the game will begin. This can make it easier for everyone to finish chatting, catching up, and eating in a timely fashion so you can start playing the game. Having an end time in mind is also fairly important. A typical game session lasts about 4 hours, though some groups hold 2-hour sessions or play marathon games. Less than 2 hours usually isn't enough time to get much done in most Pathfinder campaigns. If your session will be longer than 2 hours, plan out some 15-minute breaks (in addition to bathroom and beverage breaks, which players can take as needed).

STARTING A SESSION

Once everyone is ready, get everyone's attention and cover the following topics. These are in a rough order that you can change based on your group's style or a session's needs.

- Recap what happened during the previous sessions.
- Establish where the characters are at the beginning of this session. Have they been resting since their last challenge? Are they in a hallway, preparing to raid the next room of a dungeon? Tell players whether their characters had time to rest or recover since the last session.
- Remind players that they each have 1 Hero Point at the start of the session (page 507).
- Establish goals. The players should have an idea of what they want to do next. Reestablish any goals the group already had, then let the players weigh in on whether these goals still apply, and on whether there's anything else they hope to accomplish in this session.
- Commence adventuring! Decide which mode of play you're going to start in, then lead off with a verbal prompt to get the action started. You might ask a question related to a particular character, have everyone immediately roll initiative as a monster attacks, or briefly describe the environment and sensations that surround the player characters, allowing them to react.

RUNNING A SESSION

During a session, you're in charge of keeping the game's action moving, managing the different modes of play, fielding questions, and making rules decisions. You'll also want to keep a rough eye on the time, so you can end when most convenient for the group.

You're the interface between the rules and the imagined world you and the other players share. They will ask you questions, and they'll act based on their own assumptions. It's up to you to establish what's true in the world, but you don't do this unilaterally. You're informed by the setting's backstory, your preparations, and the suggestions and assumptions the other players bring to the table. Keep in mind that until you announce something, your own plans are subject to change. For example, if you originally intended the owner of a tavern to be kindly and well-intentioned, but a player misreads her and invents an interesting conspiracy theory regarding her intentions that sounds fun, you might convert the tavern owner into an agent of evil after all.

You'll also determine when PCs and foes need to attempt checks, as well as the consequences of those rolls. This comes up most often outside of encounters, as encounters are more regimented about when checks happen and how they are resolved. In an encounter, a player can usually determine their own character's turn, with you chiming in only to say whether an attack hits or if something in the environment requires a character to attempt a check.

The Spotlight

As you run the game, keep track of who has the spotlight. It can be easy to keep attention on the most outgoing player or character, but you need to check in with all the players. If a player hasn't contributed in some time, stop and ask, "What's your character doing at this point?" If the player's not sure, add a detail or nonplayer character to the scene that the player might find interesting.

Distractions and Interruptions

Maintaining the players' attention keeps a game moving and leads to memorable moments when everyone's in the same zone. Too many interruptions break the flow. This is fine in moderation. Distractions become a problem if they're too frequent, as they cause people to miss things and make misinformed decisions as the session becomes disconnected. Yet every game includes breaks—sometimes intentional, sometimes not—and digressions. Finding the right balance of diversions for your group is essential.

A game is a social gathering, so there's definitely a place for conversation that's not directly related to playing the game. These interruptions become a problem if they're too frequent, or if people are talking over others. If a player repeatedly interrupts you or other people or undercuts every crucial moment of the game with a joke, talk to them about limiting their comments to appropriate times. Often, all you need to do is hold up your hand or otherwise indicate that the player is talking out of turn to delay them until after you or another speaker finishes talking.

Phones and other mobile devices are another major source of distraction. Banning them entirely is often impractical—many players use apps to roll dice or manage their character sheets, or they need to answer texts from their partner, check in on a work project, or otherwise stay connected with people who rely on them. However, you can set ground rules against using a device for anything that's not time-sensitive or game-related, such as refreshing social media, checking the score of a hockey game, playing a mobile game, or answering a non-urgent text. You can relax these rules for players when their characters are "offstage." If a player's character isn't in a scene, that might be a good time for the player to use a mobile device.

ADJUDICATING THE RULES

As the GM, you are responsible for solving any rules disputes. Remember that keeping your game moving is more important than being 100% correct. Looking up rules at the table can slow the game down, so in many cases it's better to make your best guess rather than scour the book for the exact rule. (It can be instructive to look those rules up during a break or after the session, though!)

To make calls on the fly, use the following guidelines, which are the same principles the game rules are based on. You might want to keep printouts of these guidelines and the DC guidelines (page 503) for quick reference.

OFF-SESSION GAMING

Session play with a full group isn't the only way to play Pathfinder. Finding opportunities to expand on the game outside of its regular schedule can keep your group engaged between sessions.

You can get together with a single player to run a mini-session for their character, covering a mission that's important to their story but doesn't concern the rest of the group. You and the players can work out what their characters do during solid stretches of downtime via e-mail or chat messages. You can also give players opportunities to collaborate on details of the story, like having a player design a heraldic symbol for the adventuring group or map out their home base. You might even decide to award a Hero Point at the next session to a player for events that happened outside a session.

Some events aren't suitable for handling outside of sessions. Any event that strongly affects a character whose player isn't present should be handled at the table when everyone can attend. It's also helpful to recap events that took place outside of the session for all characters so no one feels excluded or lost.

• If you don't know how long a quick task takes, go with 1 action, or 2 actions if a character shouldn't be able to perform it three times per round.

• If you're not sure what action a task uses, look for the most similar basic action. If you don't find one, make up an undefined action (page XXX) adding any necessary traits (usually attack, concentrate, manipulate, or move).

• When two sides are opposed, have one roll against the other's DC. Don't have both sides roll (initiative is the exception to this rule). The character who rolls is usually the one acting (except in the case of saving throws).

• If an effect raises or lowers chances of success, grant a +1 circumstance bonus or a –1 circumstance penalty.

• If you're not sure how difficult a significant challenge should be, use the DC for the party's level.

• If you're making up an effect, creatures should be incapacitated or killed on only a critical success (or for a saving throw, on a critical failure).

• If you don't know what check to use, pick the most appropriate skill. If no other skill applies to a check to Recall Knowledge, use an appropriate Lore skill (usually at an untrained proficiency rank).

• Use the characters' daily preparations as the time to reset anything that lasts roughly a day.

• When a character accomplishes something noteworthy that doesn't have rules for XP, award them XP for an accomplishment (10 to 30 XP, as described on page 507).

• When the PCs fail at a task, look for a way they might fail forward, meaning the story moves

INTRODUCTION

ANCESTRIES & BACKGROUNDS

CLASSES

SKILLS

FEATS

EQUIPMENT

SPELLS

THE AGE OF LOST OMENS

PLAYING THE GAME

GAME MASTERING

CRAFTING & TREASURE

APPENDIX

SHARING RESPONSIBILITY

Just because you're the GM and ostensibly in charge doesn't mean you have to do all the extra work to make the campaign run. Some of the tasks described here, like scheduling games, taking notes, and giving recaps, can be delegated to other players. You might also have someone track initiative or the Hit Points of the PCs' foes for you in encounters, or even run those foes if you have a large group and someone would rather do that than control a character of their own. It's also great when someone else can host a session, provide snacks for the group, or take on other responsibilities that aren't directly related to the game.

It's best to figure out a schedule of responsibilities when you're first setting up a game. Ask the players what they're willing to take on. If you start to feel overwhelmed partway through a campaign, you can revisit the topic and try out new options until you find a setup that's comfortable.

PAIZO'S PUBLISHED ADVENTURES

You can purchase the following types of adventures at **paizo.com**, your local game store, or many book stores. If you want to acquire all the adventures in a given line, you can purchase a subscription at **paizo.com**.

Pathfinder Adventure Paths

Each monthly volume of a Pathfinder Adventure Path leads into the next as part of a greater story spanning multiple volumes. The first volume of each Adventure Path typically starts at 1st level, and each volume has a self-contained story that eventually leads to a big climax at the end of the final volume. Each volume also typically includes new monsters, rules, and details about the world. Each Adventure Path has a different theme, and their settings range across the Inner Sea region and beyond.

Pathfinder Adventures

Pathfinder Adventures are standalone adventures that cover several levels of play. They're self-contained and typically have a unique structure or theme. You can play through a Pathfinder Adventure on its own or as part of your ongoing campaign—some make ideal side adventures for Adventure Paths that have similar themes.

Pathfinder Society Scenarios

Scenarios are the adventures used by the Pathfinder Society Roleplaying Guild; you can play them as part of the Pathfinder Society or on your own. Each takes about 4 to 5 hours to run, so you can tell a whole story in a short amount of time, but they're also part of a larger continuity and can be combined together to form the basis of a longer campaign.

forward with a negative consequence rather than the failure halting progress entirely.

SPECIAL CIRCUMSTANCES

The player characters in your group will at times attempt tasks that should be easier or harder than the rules or adventure would otherwise lead you to expect, such as a PC Gathering Information in their hometown. In these cases, you can just apply a circumstance bonus or penalty. Usually, this is +1 or –1 for a minor but significant circumstance, but you can adjust this bonus or penalty to +2 or –2 for a major circumstance. The maximum bonus or penalty, +4 or –4, should apply only if someone has an overwhelming advantage or is trying something extremely unlikely but not quite impossible.

You can also add traits to actions. Let's say that during a fight, Seelah dips her sword into a brazier of hot coals before swinging it at an enemy with a weakness to fire. You could add the fire trait to this attack. A PC getting an advantage in this way should usually have to use an action to do so, so Seelah would get the benefit for one attack, but to do it again she'd need to bury her sword in the coals once more.

INCORPORATING ADDITIONAL OPTIONS

You might grant players access to additional rule or character options. If you feel confident that allowing a character to take a particular option will be a good addition to your game, then go for it! If you're uncertain or worried about a request, you don't have to allow it, and it's your call to make. However, try to meet players halfway or suggest alternatives. If you want to allow an option on a trial basis but are worried it might become a problem later, talk to the player beforehand and explain that you are tentatively allowing the option, but might change your mind later, after you see how the option can be used during play.

PATHFINDER SOCIETY

Organized play campaigns allow you to play in and run games all over the world with persistent characters. If you want to play Pathfinder this way, you can do so through the Pathfinder Society Roleplaying Guild! Once you go online to **PathfinderSociety.club** to make an account, you can organize games yourself with your friends or join an existing event.

Pathfinder Society primarily uses 4- to 5-hour adventures called scenarios. At the start of a session when you're running a scenario, you'll collect your players' information. At the end of the adventure, you'll record the rewards their characters earn for completing the scenario, all of which are detailed in the adventure. Once you report the session's results online, the rewards become a persistent part of these characters, even if they play in other games with other groups. These scenarios include important choices, and you can report what your group chose—decisions that will guide the future of the campaign!

RUNNING MODES OF PLAY

Pathfinder sessions are divided into three different modes of play: encounters, exploration, and downtime. Each mode represents different kinds of situations, with specific stakes and time scales, and characters can use different sorts of actions and reactions in each.

Encounters take place in real time or slower, and they involve direct engagement between players and enemies, potential allies, or each other. Combat and direct social interaction usually take place in encounter mode.

Exploration is the connective tissue of an adventure, and it is used whenever characters are exploring a place where there's danger or uncertainty, such as an unfamiliar city or a dungeon. In exploration mode, characters aren't in immediate peril, but they must still be on their toes. Exploration and encounters are collectively called adventuring.

When the party isn't adventuring, the characters are in downtime. This mode covers most of a normal person's life, such as mundane, day-to-day tasks and working toward long-term goals.

ENCOUNTERS

Encounter mode is the most structured mode of play, and you'll mostly be following the rules presented in Chapter 9 to run this mode. Because you usually call for initiative during exploration before transitioning into an encounter, guidelines for initiative order appear on page 498 in the discussion of exploration mode. Rules for building combat encounters appear on page 488.

Stakes: Moderate to high. Encounters always have significant stakes, and they are played in a step-by-step time frame to reflect that.

Time Scale: Encounter mode is highly structured and proceeds in combat rounds for combat encounters, while other sorts of encounters can have rounds of any length. In combat, 1 minute consists of 10 rounds, where each combat round is 6 seconds long, but you might decide a verbal confrontation proceeds in minute-long or longer rounds to give each speaker enough time to make a solid point.

Actions and Reactions: In combat encounters, each participant's turn is broken into discrete actions, and participants can use reactions when their triggers occur. Reactions can occur in social situations, though their triggers are usually more descriptive and less tactical.

CHOOSING ADVERSARIES' ACTIONS

Players often coordinate and plan to be as efficient as possible, but their adversaries might not. As the GM, you're roleplaying these foes, and you decide their tactics. Most creatures have a basic grasp of simple tactics like flanking or focusing on a single target. But you should remember that they also react based on emotions and

make mistakes—perhaps even more than the player characters do.

When selecting targets or choosing which abilities to use, rely on the adversaries' knowledge of the situation, not your own. You might know that the cleric has a high Will save modifier, but a monster might still try to use a fear ability on her. That doesn't mean you should play adversaries as complete fools; they can learn from their mistakes, make sound plans, and even research the player characters in advance.

Adversaries usually don't attack a character who's knocked out. Even if a creature knows a fallen character might come back into the fight, only the most vicious creatures focus on helpless foes rather than the more immediate threats around them.

Running adversaries is a mix of being true to the creature and doing what's best for the drama of the game. Think of your encounter like a fight scene in a movie or novel. If the fighter taunts a fire giant to draw its attention away from the fragile wizard, the tactically sound decision is for the giant to keep pummeling the wizard. But is that the best choice for the scene? Perhaps everyone will have more fun if the giant redirects its ire to the infuriating fighter.

BYPASSED ENCOUNTERS

What happens if you've planned a fight or challenge and the PCs find a way to avoid it entirely? This could leave them behind in XP or cause them to miss important information or treasure.

In the case of XP, the guidelines are simple: If the player characters avoided the challenge through smart tactical play, a savvy diplomatic exchange, clever use of magic, or another approach that required ingenuity and planning, award them the normal XP for the encounter. If they did something that took only moderate effort or was a lucky break, like finding a secret passage and using it to avoid a fight, award them XP for a minor or moderate accomplishment. In an adventure that's more free-form, like a sprawling dungeon with multiple paths, there might be no reward for bypassing an encounter, because doing so was trivial.

You'll have to think on your feet if information or items get skipped when players bypass encounters. First, look for another reasonable place in the adventure to place the information or item. If it makes sense, move the original encounter to another part of the adventure and give the PCs a major advantage for bypassing the encounter in the first place.

INTRODUCTION

ANCESTRIES & BACKGROUNDS

CLASSES

SKILLS

FEATS

EQUIPMENT

SPELLS

THE AGE OF LOST OMENS

PLAYING THE GAME

GAME MASTERING

CRAFTING & TREASURE

APPENDIX

PLAYING WITHOUT A GRID

The Pathfinder rules are built to play combat encounters on a 1-inch grid, but you can play without a grid or map. In what's traditionally called the "theater of the mind," you and other players imagine the locations of the combatants and the environment. In this style of play, you'll frequently need to make judgment calls. These are usually simple, like "Can I see the ogre from where I'm standing?" or "Can I get to the ogre with one Stride?" It's often best to have a player tell you what they want to do, such as "I want to cross the beam to get to the ogre and attack it." Then, you tell the player how that breaks down into actions, like "You'll need to spend one action and succeed at an Acrobatics check, then Stride to get close enough, then you'll have one action left for a Strike."

When preparing encounters, avoid using lots of difficult terrain, cover, or other battlefield challenges that work better on a grid. Also, be more lenient with combat tactics like flanking. You won't have a way to measure flanking, but the rules expect melee characters like rogues to often get into a flanking position—often, two characters ganging up in melee is enough to count.

ENDING ENCOUNTERS

A combat encounter typically ends when all the creatures on one side are killed or knocked unconscious. Once this happens, you can stop acting in initiative order. The surviving side then has ample time to ensure that everyone taken out stays down. However, you might need to keep using combat rounds if any player characters are near death, clinging to a cliff, or in some other situation where every moment matters for their survival.

You can decide a fight is over if there's no challenge left, and the player characters are just cleaning up the last few weak enemies. However, avoid doing this if any of the players still have inventive and interesting things they want to try or spells they're concentrating on—ending an encounter early is a tool to avoid boredom, not to deny someone their fun. You can end a fight early in several ways: the foes can surrender, an adversary can die before its Hit Points actually run out, or you can simply say the battle's over and that the PCs easily dispatch their remaining foes. In this last case, you might ask, "Is everyone okay if we call the fight?" to make sure your players are on board.

One side might surrender when almost all its members are defeated or if spells or skills thoroughly demoralize them. Once there's a surrender, come out of initiative order and enter into a short negotiation. These conversations are really about whether the winners will show mercy to the losers or just kill or otherwise get rid of them. The surrendering side usually doesn't have much leverage in these cases, so avoid long back-and-forth discussions.

FLEEING ENEMIES

Fleeing enemies can be a problem. Player characters often want to pursue foes that flee because they think an enemy might return as a threat later on. Avoid playing this out move by move, as it can easily bog down the game. If every adversary is fleeing, forgo initiative order and give each PC the option to pursue any one fleeing foe. Each PC can declare one action, spell, or other ability to use to try to keep up. Then, compare the PC's Speed to that of the target, assess how much the pursuer's chosen spell or ability would help, and factor in any abilities the quarry has that would aid escape. If you determine that the pursuer catches up, go back into combat with the original initiative order. If not, the quarry escapes for now.

If the PCs decide to flee, it's usually best to let them do so. Pick a particular location and allow them to escape once they all reach it. However, if they're encumbered or otherwise slowed down, or if enemies have higher Speeds and a strong motive to pursue, you might impose consequences upon PCs who flee.

SOCIAL ENCOUNTERS

Most conversations play best as free-form roleplaying, with maybe one or two checks for social skills involved. Sometimes, though, a tense situation or crucial parlay requires a social encounter that uses initiative, much like a combat encounter. As with any other encounter, the stakes of a social encounter need to be high! A failed social encounter could mean a character is imprisoned or put to death, a major rival becomes a political powerhouse, or a key ally is disgraced and ostracized.

Using the structure of an encounter is helpful because it makes the timing clearer than in free-form play, and each character feels like they're contributing. When running a social encounter, establish the stakes up front, so the players know the consequences of success or failure and the circumstances that will cause the encounter to end.

You have much more flexibility in how you run a social encounter than in a combat encounter. Extending the length of rounds beyond 6 seconds, allowing more improvisation, and focusing less on special attacks and spells all differentiate a social encounter from a combat one. In most cases, you don't need to worry about character's movements, nor do you need a map. Some examples of social encounters include:

- Proving someone's innocence in front of a judge.
- Convincing a neighboring monarch to help defend against an invasion.
- Besting a rival bard in a battle of wits.
- Exposing a villain's deception before a noble court.

INITIATIVE AND ACTIONS

Initiative in a social encounter typically has characters rolling Society or a Charisma-based skill, such as

GAME MASTERING

10

INTRODUCTION

ANCESTRIES &
BACKGROUNDS

CLASSES

SKILLS

FEATS

EQUIPMENT

SPELLS

THE AGE OF
LOST OMENS

PLAYING THE
GAME

GAME
MASTERING

CRAFTING
& TREASURE

APPENDIX

Diplomacy or Deception. As with other encounters, a character's approach to the conflict determines which skill they'll roll. On a character's turn, they typically get to attempt one roll, usually by using a skill action. Let the player roleplay what their character says and does, then determine what they'll roll. Allow them to use any abilities or spells that might help them make their case, though keep in mind that when most people see the visual signs of a spell being cast, they think someone is using magic to try to influence or harm them, and they have a negative reaction.

Good social encounters include an opposition. This can be direct, such as a rival who argues against the characters' case, or passive, such as a mob that automatically becomes more unruly as each round passes. Give the opposition one or more positions in the initiative order so you can convey what it is doing. You can create game statistics for the opposition, especially if it's an individual, but in situations like that of the unruly mob, you might need nothing more than establish a set of increasingly difficult DCs.

Measuring Success and Progress

You'll need to decide how to measure the characters' success in social encounters, because there's no AC to target or HP to whittle down. Chapter 4 includes

guidance on setting DCs for social skill actions, often using a target's Will DC. If you need a DC for people who don't have stats, such as a crowd or an NPC for whom you haven't already generated statistics, use the guidelines on setting DCs, found on page 503. You can either pick a simple DC or use a level-based DC, estimating a level for the subject or how challenging it should be to sway them.

The attitude conditions—hostile, unfriendly, indifferent, friendly, and helpful—provide a useful way to track the progress of a social encounter. Use these to represent the attitude of an authority, a crowd, a jury, or the like. A typical goal for a social encounter is to change the attitude of a person or group to helpful so they assist you, or calming a hostile group or person to defuse a situation. Try to give the players a clear idea of how much they've progressed as the encounter proceeds.

Another option is to track the number of successes or failures the characters accrue. For instance, you might need to trick four guards into leaving their posts, and count each successful attempt to Lie or Create a Diversion toward a total of four necessary successes. You can combine these two methods; if the PCs need a group of important nobles to vote their way, the goal of the encounter might be to ensure that a majority of the nobles have a better attitude toward the PCs than they have of a rival—all within a limited time frame.

Consequences

When you set stakes at the start of a social encounter, give an idea of the consequences. Beyond whatever narrative benefits player characters might gain, a social encounter usually includes an XP award. Because these are encounters along the same lines as combat encounters, they grant a sizable amount of XP, typically that of a moderate accomplishment, or even a major accomplishment if the encounter was the culmination of long-term plans or a significant adversary got their comeuppance.

The outcome of a social encounter should direct the story of the game. Look for repercussions. Which NPCs might view the PCs more favorably now? Which might hold a grudge or formulate a new plan? A social encounter can seal the fate of an NPC and end their story, but this isn't true for player characters. Even if something looks truly dire for them, such as a death sentence, the social encounter isn't the end—there's still time for desperate heroics or a twist in the story.

EXPLORATION

Exploration mode is intentionally less regimented than encounters. As a result, during exploration you'll be making judgment calls on just about everything that happens.

Fundamentally, exploration is all about rewarding the PCs for learning about their surroundings. To facilitate this, it's especially important to have and convey a clear mental picture of the group's surroundings. You'll be better able to keep track of where the players are and describe the sights, sounds, and other sensations of their adventuring locales. Encourage the players to have their characters truly explore, and reward their curiosity. The things they try to do in exploration mode show you what they're interested in and what they consider important. As you play, you'll get a good feel for the aspects of exploration that intrigue certain players, and you can add more of those things to your adventures or emphasize these points in published adventures.

Stakes: Low to moderate. Exploration mode should be used when there's some amount of risk, but no immediate danger. The PCs might be in an environment where they're likely to face monsters or hazards, but they usually stay in exploration mode until they enter a fight or engage in some other direct interaction.

Time Scale: When the PCs are in exploration mode, time in the game world passes much faster than real-world time at the table, so it's rarely measured out to the second or the minute. You can speed up or slow down how quickly things are happening as needed. If it's important to know exactly how much time is passing, you can usually estimate time spent in exploration mode to 10-minute increments.

Actions and Reactions: Though exploration isn't broken into rounds, exploration activities assume the PCs are spending part of their time using actions, such as

Seeking or Interacting. If they have specific actions they want to use, they should ask; you can decide whether the actions apply and whether to switch to encounter mode for greater detail. PCs can use any relevant reactions that come up during exploration mode.

EXPLORATION ACTIVITIES

In exploration mode, each player who wants to do something beyond just traveling chooses an exploration activity for their character. The most common activities are Avoid Notice, Detect Magic, Hustle, and Search, though there are many options available. While players usually hew close to these default activities, there's no need for them to memorize the exploration activities and use them exactly. Instead, allow each player to describe what their character is doing. Then, as the GM, you can determine which activity applies. This also means you determine how an activity works if the character's actions differ from those on the list.

The following sections discuss exploration activities that require adjudication from you beyond the guidelines for players detailed on pages 479–480 of Chapter 9.

Detect Magic

This activity doesn't enable characters to automatically find every single magical aura or object during travel. Hazards that require a minimum proficiency can't be found with *detect magic*, nor can illusions of equal or higher level than the spell.

When characters find something magical using this activity, let them know and give them the option to stop and explore further or continue on. Stopping brings you into a more roleplay-heavy scene in which players can search through an area, assess different items, or otherwise try to figure out the source of the magic and what it does. Continuing on might cause the group to miss out on beneficial magic items or trigger a magic trap.

Follow the Expert

A skilled character can help out less skilled allies who choose to Follow the Expert. This is a good way to help a character with a low Stealth modifier sneak around, get a character with poor Athletics up a steep cliff, and so on. Usually, a character who is Following the Expert can't perform other exploration activities or follow more than one person at a time.

Investigate

As with Searching or Detecting Magic, the initial result of Investigating is usually enough to give the investigator a clue that leads into a more thorough examination, but it rarely gives all possible information. For instance, a character might note that the walls of a dungeon are covered with Abyssal writing, but they would need to stop to read the text or determine that it's written in blood.

GAME MASTERING

10

INTRODUCTION

ANCESTRIES &
BACKGROUNDS

CLASSES

SKILLS

FEATS

EQUIPMENT

SPELLS

THE AGE OF
LOST OMENS

PLAYING THE
GAME

GAME
MASTERING

CRAFTING
& TREASURE

APPENDIX

SEARCH

With a successful Perception check while Searching, a character notices the presence or absence of something unusual in the area, but it doesn't provide a comprehensive catalog of everything there. Instead, it gives a jumping-off point for closer inspection or an encounter. For instance, if an area has both a DC 30 secret door and a DC 25 trap, and a Searching character got a 28 on their Perception check, you would tell the player that their character noticed a trap in the area, and you'd give a rough idea of the trap's location and nature. The party needs to examine the area more to learn specifics about the trap, and someone would need to Search again to get another chance to find the secret door.

If an area contains many objects or something that will take a while to search (such as a cabinet full of papers), Searching would reveal the cabinet, but the PCs would have to examine it more thoroughly to check the papers. This usually requires the party to stop for a complete search.

You roll a secret Perception check for a Searching character to detect any secrets they pass that's in a place that stands out (such as near a door or a turn in a corridor), but not one that's in a more inconspicuous place (like a random point in a long hallway) unless they are searching particularly slowly and meticulously.

SETTING A PARTY ORDER

In exploration mode, it often matters which characters are in the front or back of the party formation. Let the players decide among themselves where in the group their characters are while exploring. This order can determine who gets attacked first when enemies or traps threaten from various directions. It's up to you to determine the specifics of who gets targeted based on the situation.

When you come out of exploration mode, the group usually remains in the same general formation. Decide the PCs' exact positions, with their input, if you're moving to a grid (as usually happens at the start of a combat encounter). If they come out of exploration mode on their own terms, they can move around as they see fit. For example, if they detect a trap and the rogue starts attempting to disarm it, the other characters can move to whatever locations they think are safe.

ADVERSE TERRAIN AND WEATHER

Exploration gets slower when the party faces dense jungles, deep snow, sandstorms, extreme heat, or similar difficult conditions. You decide how much these factors impact the characters' progress. The specific effects of certain types of terrain and weather are described starting on page 512.

EXPLORATION ACTIVITIES

The following exploration activities are fully detailed on pages 479–480 of Chapter 9. Many more appear within Chapter 4: Skills.

- Avoid Notice
- Defend
- Detect Magic
- Follow the Expert
- Hustle
- Investigate
- Repeat a Spell
- Scout
- Search

Improvising New Activities

If a player wants to do something not covered by other rules, here are some guidelines. If the activity is similar to an action someone could use in an encounter, such as Avoid Notice, it usually consists of a single action repeated roughly 10 times per minute (such as using the Sneak action 10 times) or an alternation of actions that works out similarly (such as Search, which alternates Stride and Seek). An activity using a quicker pace, corresponding to roughly 20 actions per minute, might have limited use or cause fatigue, as would one requiring intense concentration.

You might find that a player wants to do something equivalent to spending 3 actions every 6 seconds, just like they would in combat. Characters can exert themselves to this extent in combat only because combat lasts such a short time—such exertion isn't sustainable over the longer time frame of exploration.

Difficult terrain such as thick undergrowth usually slows down progress. Unless it's important how far the group gets in a particular time frame, this can be covered with a quick description of chopping through the vines or trudging through a bog. If the characters are on a deadline, adjust their progress on Table 9–2: Travel Speed (page 479), typically cutting it in half if almost all of the land is difficult terrain or to one-third for greater difficult terrain.

Hazardous terrain, such as the caldera of an active volcano, might physically harm the player characters. The group might have the option to travel directly through or go around by spending more time. You can transition into a more detailed scene while the characters move through hazardous terrain and attempt to mitigate the damage with spells or skill checks. If they endure hazardous terrain, consider giving the PCs a minor or moderate XP reward at the end of their exploration, with slightly more XP if they took smart precautions to avoid taking damage.

Dangerous crevasses, swampy bogs, quicksand, and similar dangers are environmental hazards, which are described beginning on page 512.

HAZARDS

Exploration can get broken up by traps and other hazards (see Hazards on page 520). Simple hazards pose a threat to the PCs only once and can be dealt with in exploration mode. Complex hazards require jumping into encounter mode until the hazard is dealt with. Disabling a trap or overcoming a hazard usually takes place in encounter mode. PCs have a better chance to detect hazards while exploring if they're using the Search activity (and the Detect Magic activity, in the case of some magic traps).

ROLLING INITIATIVE

Transitioning from exploration to an encounter usually involves rolling for initiative. Call for initiative once a trap is triggered, as soon as two opposing groups come into contact, or when a creature on one side decides to take action against the other. For example:

- A group of PCs are exploring a cavern. They enter a narrow passage patrolled by a group of kobold warriors. Now that the two groups are in the same area, it's time to roll initiative.
- Amiri and a kobold champion agree to have a friendly wrestling match. They square off on a patch of dirt, and you call for initiative using Athletics.
- Merisiel and Kyra are negotiating with the kobold king. Things aren't going well, so Merisiel decides to launch a surprise attack. As soon as she says this is her plan, you call for initiative.
- Harsk and Ezren are trying to Balance across a narrow beam to reach an isolated kobold treasure trove. When they get halfway across, a red dragon who was hiding behind the mountain flies around to attack! As soon as the dragon makes its appearance, you call for an initiative roll.

INITIATIVE AFTER REACTIONS

In some cases, a trap or a foe has a reaction that tells you to roll initiative. For instance, a complex trap that's triggered might make an attack with its reaction before the initiative order begins. In these cases, resolve all the results of the reaction before calling for initiative rolls.

CHOOSING THE TYPE OF ROLL

When choosing what type of roll to use for initiative, lean toward the most obvious choice. The most common roll is Perception; this is what the kobolds would use in the first example, as would Kyra and the kobold king in the third example. The next most common skills to use are Stealth (for sneaking up, like the dragon in the last example) and Deception (for tricking opponents, like Merisiel in the third example). For social contests, it's common to use Deception, Diplomacy, Intimidation, Performance, or Society.

If you're unsure what roll to call for, use Perception. If a different type of roll could make sense for a character, you should usually offer the choice of that roll or Perception and let the player decide. Don't do this if it's absolutely clear another kind of check matters more sense than Perception, such as when the character is sneaking up on enemies and should definitely use Stealth.

You can allow a player to make a case that they should use a different skill than Perception, but only if they base it on something they've established beforehand. For example, if in the prelude to the attack, Merisiel's player had said, "I'm going to dangle down off the chandelier to get the drop on them," you could let them use Acrobatics for their initiative roll. If they just said, "Hey, I want to attack these guys. Can I use Acrobatics?" without having established a reason beforehand, you probably shouldn't allow it.

Character Placement

When calling for initiative for a combat encounter, you'll need to decide where the participants in the encounter go on the battle map. Use the party's order, described on page 497, as a base. You can move forward characters who are using Stealth to get into position, putting them in a place they could reasonably have moved up to before having a chance to be detected. Consult with each player to make sure their position makes sense to both of you.

RESTING

Characters require 8 hours of sleep each day. Though resting typically happens at night, a group gains the same benefits for resting during the day. Either way, they can gain the benefits of resting only once every 24 hours. A character who rests for 8 hours recovers in the following ways:

- The character regains Hit Points equal to their Constitution modifier (minimum 1) multiplied by their level. If they rest without any shelter or comfort, you might reduce this healing by half (to a minimum of 1 HP).
- The character loses the fatigued condition.
- The character reduces the severity of the doomed and drained conditions by 1.
- Most spellcasters need to rest before they regain their spells for the day.

A group in exploration mode can attempt to rest, but they aren't entirely safe from danger, and their rest might be interrupted. The 8 hours of rest do not need to be consecutive, however, and after an interruption, characters can go back to sleep.

Sleeping in armor results in poor rest and causes a character to wake up fatigued. If a character would have recovered from fatigue, sleeping in armor prevents it.

If a character goes more than 16 hours without going to sleep, they become fatigued.

Taking long-term rest for faster recovery is part of downtime and can't be done during exploration. See page 502 for these rules.

MONITORING SPELL DURATIONS

Spell durations are approximate values that codify the vagaries and eccentricities of magic into a convenient number. However, that doesn't mean you can set your watch by a spell with a 1-hour duration. This is one of the reasons the passage of time outside of encounters is in your hands and isn't as precise as encounter rounds. If a question arises about whether a spell has expired, you make the call. You shouldn't be punitive, but you also shouldn't treat characters like they move with clockwork precision and perfect efficiency between encounters.

There are two times these durations matter most: when players try to fit multiple encounters within the duration of a spell, and when they want to use a spell before a fight and keep it in effect during the encounter.

Multiple Encounters

A 1-minute spell should last for multiple encounters only if the encounters happen in very close proximity (usually in two adjoining rooms) and if the PCs go directly from one fight to the next without leaving encounter mode. If they want to stop and heal, or if the party debates whether to go on, the process takes enough time that the spell runs out.

Be more generous with spells lasting 10 minutes or more. A 10-minute spell easily lasts for one encounter and could continue for another if the locations are close. A 1-hour spell usually lasts for several encounters.

Before a Fight

Casting advantageous spells before a fight (sometimes called "pre-buffing") gives the characters a big advantage, since they can spend more combat rounds on offensive actions instead of preparatory ones. If the players have the drop on their foes, you usually can let each character cast one spell or prepare in some similar way, then roll initiative.

Casting preparatory spells before combat becomes a problem when it feels rote and the players assume it will always work—that sort of planning can't hold up in every situation! In many cases, the act of casting spells gives away the party's presence. In cases where the PCs' preparations could give them away, you might roll for initiative before everyone can complete their preparations.

Watches and Surprise Attacks

Adventuring parties usually put a few people on guard to watch out for danger while the others rest. Spending time on watch also interrupts sleep, so a night's schedule needs to account for everyone's time on guard duty. Table 10–3: Watches and Rest on the next page indicates how long the group needs to set aside for rest, assuming everyone gets a rotating watch assignment of equal length.

If a surprise encounter would occur during rest, you can roll a die to randomly determine which character is on watch at the time. All characters roll initiative; sleeping characters typically roll Perception with a –4 status penalty for being unconscious. They don't automatically wake up when rolling initiative, but they might roll a Perception check to wake up at the start of their turn due to noise. If a savvy enemy waits for a particularly vulnerable character to take watch before attacking, the attack can happen on that character's watch automatically. However, you might have the ambusher attempt a Stealth check against the Perception DCs of all characters to see if anyone noticed its approach.

TABLE 10-3: WATCHES AND REST

Group Size	Total Time	Duration of Each Watch
2	16 hours	8 hours
3	12 hours	4 hours
4	10 hours, 40 minutes	2 hours, 40 minutes
5	10 hours	2 hours
6	9 hours, 36 minutes	1 hour, 36 minutes

DAILY PREPARATIONS

Just before setting out to explore, or after a night's rest, the PCs spend time to prepare for the adventuring day. This typically happens over the span of 30 minutes to an hour in the morning, but only after 8 full hours of rest. Daily preparations include the following.

- Spellcasters who prepare spells choose which spells they'll have available that day.
- Focus Points and other abilities that reset during daily preparations refresh. This includes abilities that can be used only a certain number of times per day.
- Each character equips their gear. This includes donning their armor and strapping on their weapons.
- Characters invest up to 10 worn magic items to gain their benefits for the day (page 531).

STARVATION AND THIRST

Typically characters eat and drink enough to survive comfortably. When they can't, they're fatigued until they do. After 1 day + a creature's Constitution modifier without water, it takes 1d4 damage each hour that can't be healed until it quenches its thirst. After the same amount of time without food, it takes 1 damage each day that can't be healed until it sates its hunger.

DOWNTIME

In downtime, you can sum up the important events of a whole day with just one roll. Use this mode when the characters return home or otherwise aren't adventuring.

Usually, downtime is a few minutes at the start of a session or a break between major chapters of an adventure. As with exploration, you might punctuate downtime with roleplaying or encounters when it's natural to do so.

This section describes ways to handle downtime and details several activities and considerations specific to downtime, such as cost of living, buying and selling goods,

long-term rest, and retraining. Most other downtime activities are skill actions; a number of these common downtime activities and their associated skills are listed below. See the relevant skills in Chapter 4 for details.

- Craft (Crafting)
- Earn Income (Crafting, Lore, Performance)
- Treat Disease (Medicine)
- Create Forgery (Society)
- Subsist (Society, Survival)

Stakes: None to low. Downtime is the counterpart to adventuring and covers low-risk activities.

Time Scale: Downtime can last days, weeks, months, or years in the game world in a few minutes of real time.

Actions and Reactions: If you need to use actions and reactions, switch to exploration or encounter mode. A creature that can't act is unable to perform most downtime activities, but it can take long-term rest.

PLAYING OUT A DOWNTIME DAY

At the start of a given day of downtime, have all the players declare what their characters are trying to accomplish that day. You can then resolve one character's efforts at a time (or group some characters together, if they are cooperating on a single project). Some activities, such as Earning Income, require only a simple roll and some embellishment from you and the player. Other activities are more involved, incorporating encounters or exploration. You can call on the players to play out their downtime activities in any order, though it's often best to do the simplest ones first. Players who aren't part of a more involved activity might have time to take a break from the table while the more complex activities are played out.

Characters can undertake their daily preparations if they want, just as they would on a day of exploration. Ask players to establish a standard set of preparations, and you can assume the characters go through the same routine every day unless their players say otherwise.

COOPERATION

Multiple characters can cooperate on the same downtime task. If it's a simple task that requires just one check, such as a party Subsisting as they await rescue on a desert island, one character rolls the necessary check while everyone else Aids that character. If it's a complex task, assume all of them are working on different parts of it at one time, so all their efforts count toward its completion. For example, a party might collaborate to build a theater, with one character drawing up architectural plans, one doing manual labor, and one talking to local politicians and guilds.

CHECKS

Some downtime activities require rolls, typically skill checks. Because these rolls represent the culmination of a series of tasks over a long period, players can't use most abilities or spells that manipulate die rolls, such as

GAME MASTERING

10

INTRODUCTION

ANCESTRIES &
BACKGROUNDS

CLASSES

SKILLS

FEATS

EQUIPMENT

SPELLS

THE AGE OF
LOST OMENS

PLAYING THE
GAME

GAME
MASTERING

CRAFTING
& TREASURE

APPENDIX

activating a magic item to gain a bonus or casting a fortune spell to roll twice. Constant benefits still apply, though, so someone might invest a magic item that gives them a bonus without requiring activation. You might make specific exceptions to this rule. If something could apply constantly, or so often that it might as well be constant, it's more likely to be used for downtime checks.

LONGER PERIODS OF DOWNTIME

Running downtime during a long time off—like several weeks, months, or even years—can be more challenging. However, it's also an opportunity for the characters to progress toward long-term plans rather than worrying about day-to-day activities. Because so much time is involved, characters don't roll a check for each day. Instead, they deal with a few special events, average out the rest of the downtime, and pay for their cost of living.

EVENTS

After the characters state what they want to achieve in their downtime, select a few standout events for each of them— usually one event for a period of a week or a month, or four events for a year or longer. These events should be tailored to each character and their goals, and they can serve as hooks for adventures or plot development.

Though the following examples of downtime events all involve Earning Income, you can use them to spark ideas for other activities. A character using Perform to

Earn Income could produce a commanding performance of a new play for visiting nobility. Someone using Crafting might get a lucrative commission to craft a special item. A character with Lore might have to research a difficult problem that needs a quick response.

PCs who want to do things that don't correspond to a specific downtime activity should still experience downtime events; you just choose the relevant skill and DC. For example, if a character intends to build their own library to house their books on magic, you might decide setting the foundation and organizing the library once construction is finished are major events. The first could be a Crafting check, and the second an Arcana or Library Lore check.

AVERAGE PROGRESS

For long periods of downtime, you might not want to roll for every week, or even every month. Instead, set the level for one task using the lowest level the character can reliably find in the place where they spend their downtime (see Difficulty Classes on page 503 for more on setting task levels). If the character fails this check, you might allow them to try again after a week (or a month, if you're dealing with years of downtime). Don't allow them to roll again if they succeeded but want to try for a critical success, unless they do something in the story of the game that you think makes it reasonable to allow a new roll.

The events you include during a long stretch of downtime should typically feature higher-level tasks than the baseline. For instance, a character Earning Income with Sailing Lore for 4 months might work at a port doing 1st-level tasks most of the time, but have 1 week of 3rd-level tasks to account for busy periods. You'll normally have the player roll once for the time they spent at 1st-level tasks and once for the week of 3rd-level tasks.

COST OF LIVING

For short periods of downtime, characters are usually just passing through a settlement or spending a bit of time there. They can use the prices for inn stays and meals found on page 294. For long stretches of downtime, use the values on Table 6–16: Cost of Living on the same page. Deduct these costs from a character's funds after they gain any money from their other downtime activities.

A character can live off the land instead, but each day they do, they typically use the Subsist activity (page 240) to the exclusion of any other downtime activity.

BUYING AND SELLING

After an adventure yields a windfall, the characters might have a number of items they want to sell. Likewise, when they're flush with currency, they might want to stock up on gear. It usually takes 1 day of downtime to sell off a few goods or shop around to buy a couple items. It can take longer to sell off a large number of goods, expensive items, or items that aren't in high demand.

This assumes the characters are at a settlement of decent size during their downtime. In some cases, they might spend time traveling for days to reach bigger cities. As always, you have final say over what sort of shops and items are available.

An item can usually be purchased at its full Price and sold for half its Price. Supply and demand adjusts these numbers, but only occasionally.

LONG-TERM REST

Each full 24-hour period a character spends resting during downtime allows them to recover double what they would for an 8-hour rest (as listed on page 499). They must spend this time resting in a comfortable and secure location, typically in bed.

If they spend significantly longer in bed rest—usually from a few days to a week of downtime—they recover from all damage and most nonpermanent conditions. Characters affected by diseases, long-lasting poisons, or similar afflictions might need to continue attempting saves during downtime. Some curses, permanent injuries, and other situations that require magic or special care to remove don't end automatically during long-term rest.

RETRAINING

The retraining rules on page 481 allow a player to change some character choices, but they rely on you to decide whether the retraining requires a teacher, how long it takes, if it has any associated costs, and if the ability can

be retrained at all. It's reasonable for a character to retrain most choices, and you should allow them. Only choices that are truly intrinsic to the character, like a sorcerer's bloodline, should be off limits without extraordinary circumstances.

Try to make retraining into a story. Use NPCs the character already knows as teachers, have a character undertake intense research in a mysterious old library, or ground the retraining in the game's narrative by making it the consequence of something that happened to the character in a previous session.

TIME

Retraining a feat or skill increase typically takes a week. Class features that require a choice can also be retrained but take longer: at least a month, and possibly more. Retraining might take even longer if it would be especially physically demanding or require travel, lengthy experimentation, or in-depth research, but usually you won't want to require more than a month for a feat or skill, or 4 months for a class feature.

A character might need to retrain several options at once. For instance, retraining a skill increase might mean they have skill feats they can no longer use, and so they'll need to retrain those as well. You can add all this retraining time together, then reduce the total a bit to represent the cohesive nature of the retraining.

INSTRUCTION AND COSTS

The rules abstract the process of learning new things as you level up—you're learning on the job—but retraining suggests that the character works with a teacher or undergoes specific practice to retrain. If you want, you can entirely ignore this aspect of retraining, but it does give an opportunity to introduce (or reintroduce) NPCs and further the game's story. You can even have one player character mentor another, particularly when it comes to retraining skills.

Any costs to retraining should be pretty minor—about as much as a PC could gain by Earning Income over the same period of time. The costs are mostly there to make the training feel appropriate within the context of the story, not to consume significant amounts of the character's earnings. A teacher might volunteer to work without pay as a reward for something the character has already done, or simply ask for a favor in return.

DISALLOWED OPTIONS

While some character options can't normally be retrained, you can invent ways for a character to retrain even these—special rituals, incredible quests, or the perfect tutor. For example, ability scores can't normally be retrained, as that can unbalance the game. But not all players necessarily want to exploit the system—maybe a player simply wants to swap an ability boost between two low stats. In situations like this, you could let them spend a few months working out or studying to reassign an ability boost.

DIFFICULTY CLASSES

As the Game Master, it's up to you to set the difficulty classes (DCs) for checks that don't use a predefined DC. The following sections offer advice on how to set appropriate DCs and tweak them as needed to feel natural for your story. Picking a simple DC and using a level-based DC each work well in certain circumstances, and you can adjust both types of DC using the advice on adjusting difficulty.

SIMPLE DCs

Sometimes you need to quickly set a Difficulty Class. The easiest method is to select a simple DC from Table 10–4 by estimating which proficiency rank best matches the task (that rank is usually not required to succeed at the task). If it's something pretty much anyone would have a decent chance at, use the untrained DC. If it would require a degree of training, use the DC listed for trained, expert, master, or legendary proficiency, as appropriate to the complexity of the task. For example, say a PC was trying to uncover the true history behind a fable. You determine this requires a check to Recall Knowledge, and that only someone with master proficiency in Folktale Lore would know the information, so you'd set the DC at 30—the simple master DC.

Simple DCs work well when you need a DC on the fly and there's no level associated with the task. They're most useful for skill checks. Because there isn't much gradation between the simple DCs, they don't work as well for hazards or combatants, where the PCs' lives are on the line; you're better off using level-based DCs for such challenges.

TABLE 10-4: SIMPLE DCs

Proficiency Rank	DC
Untrained	10
Trained	15
Expert	20
Master	30
Legendary	40

LEVEL-BASED DCs

When you're determining a skill DC based on something that has a level, use Table 10–5 to set the DC. Find the level of the subject, and assign the corresponding DC. Since spells use a 1–10 scale, use the Spell Level column for them.

Use these DCs when a PC needs to Identify a Spell or Recall Knowledge about a creature, attempts to Earn Income by performing a task of a certain level, and so on. You can also use the level-based DCs for obstacles instead of assigning a simple DC. For example, you might determine that a wall in a high-level dungeon was constructed of smooth metal and is hard to climb. You could simply say only someone with master proficiency could climb it, and use the simple DC of 30. Or you might decide that the 15th-level villain who created the

dungeon crafted the wall, and use the 15th-level DC of 34. Either approach is reasonable!

Note that PCs who invest in a skill become more likely to succeed at a DC of their level as they increase in level, and the listed DCs eventually become very easy for them.

TABLE 10-5: DCs BY LEVEL

Level	DC	Level	DC
0	14	13	31
1	15	14	32
2	16	15	34
3	18	16	35
4	19	17	36
5	20	18	38
6	22	19	39
7	23	20	40
8	24	21	42
9	26	22	44
10	27	23	46
11	28	24	48
12	30	25	50

Spell Level*	DC
1st	15
2nd	18
3rd	20
4th	23
5th	26
6th	28
7th	31
8th	34
9th	36
10th	39

* If a spell is uncommon or rare, its difficulty should be adjusted accordingly.

ADJUSTING DIFFICULTY

You might decide a DC should differ from the baseline, whether to account for PCs' areas of expertise or to represent the rarity of spells or items. A DC adjustment represents an essential difference in the difficulty of a task and applies to anyone attempting a specific check for it. Adjustments happen most often with tasks whose DCs are based on their level. Adjustments use a scale of –10 to +10, from incredibly easy checks to incredibly hard

INTRODUCTION

ANCESTRIES & BACKGROUNDS

CLASSES

SKILLS

FEATS

EQUIPMENT

SPELLS

THE AGE OF LOST OMENS

PLAYING THE GAME

GAME MASTERING

CRAFTING & TREASURE

APPENDIX

ones, and are broken into increments of 2, 5, and 10. You'll often apply the adjustments for uncommon, rare, or unique subjects.

TABLE 10-6: DC ADJUSTMENTS

Difficulty	Adjustment	Rarity
Incredibly easy	–10	–
Very easy	–5	–
Easy	–2	–
Hard	+2	Uncommon
Very hard	+5	Rare
Incredibly hard	+10	Unique

The adjustments' names don't translate to how hard a task actually is for a PC or group of PCs, and adjustments aren't meant to balance out or replace PCs' bonuses and penalties. PCs who invest in a skill will become better and better at that skill as they increase in level. For example, even the best 1st-level PC has grim odds against an incredibly hard 1st-level DC, with a huge chance of critical failure, but by 20th level, an optimized character with a modicum of magic or assistance can take down incredibly hard 20th-level DCs over half the time, critically failing only on a 1. At higher levels, many groups will find that the very hard DC is more like standard for them; keep that in mind if you need a check that presents a true challenge to a high level group.

You might use different DCs for a task based on the particular skill or statistic used for the check. Let's say your PCs encounter a magical tome about aberrant creatures. The tome is 4th-level and has the occult trait, so you set the DC of an Occultism check to Identify the Magic to 19, based on Table 10–5. As noted in Identify Magic, other magic-related skills can typically be used at a higher DC, so you might decide the check is very hard for a character using Arcana and set the DC at 24 for characters using that skill. If a character in your group had Aberration Lore, you might determine that it would be easy or very easy to use that skill and adjust the DC to 17 or 14. These adjustments aren't taking the place of characters' bonuses, modifiers, and penalties—they are due to the applicability of the skills being used.

GROUP ATTEMPTS

The DCs in this chapter give an individual character a strong and increasing chance of success if they have some proficiency. On occasion, though, you'll have a task that only one person in the group needs to succeed at, but that everyone can attempt. The number of dice being rolled means that there's a very high chance at least one of them will succeed. Most of the time, that's perfectly fine, but sometimes you'll want the task to be a challenge, with some uncertainty as to whether the party can succeed. In these cases, make the check very hard, or incredibly hard if you want it to be particularly difficult or at high levels. At these DCs, most of the party will probably fail, but

someone will probably still succeed, likely a character who has heavily invested in the given skill, as is expected for specialized characters.

MINIMUM PROFICIENCY

Sometimes succeeding at a particular task requires a character to have a specific proficiency rank in addition to a success on the check. Locks and traps often require a certain proficiency rank to successfully use the Pick a Lock or Disable a Device actions of Thievery. A character whose proficiency rank is lower than what's listed can attempt the check, but they can't succeed. You can apply similar minimum proficiencies to other tasks. You might decide, for example, that a particular arcane theorem requires training in Arcana to understand. An untrained barbarian can't succeed at the check, but she can still attempt it if she wants—after all, she needs to have a chance to critically fail and get erroneous information!

For checks that require a minimum proficiency, keep the following guidelines in mind. A 2nd-level or lower task should almost never require expert proficiency, a 6th-level or lower task should almost never require master proficiency, and a 14th-level or lower task should almost never require legendary proficiency. If they did, no character of the appropriate level could succeed.

SPECIFIC ACTIONS

Several parts of this book, most notably Chapter 4: Skills, state that you as the GM set the DCs for certain checks or determine other parameters. Here are guidelines for the most common tasks. Remember that all of these are guidelines, and you can adjust them as necessary to suit the situation.

CRAFT

When a character Crafts an item, use the item's level to determine the DC, applying the adjustments from Table 10–6 for the item's rarity if it's not common. You might also apply the easy DC adjustment for an item the crafter has made before. Repairing an item usually uses the DC of the item's level with no adjustments, though you might adjust the DC to be more difficult for an item of a higher level than the character can Craft.

EARN INCOME

You set the task level when someone tries to Earn Income. The highest-level task available is usually the same as the level of the settlement where the character is located. If you don't know the settlement's level, it's usually 0–1 for a village, 2–4 for a town, or 5–7 for a city. A PC might need to travel to a metropolis or capital to find tasks of levels 8-10, and to the largest cities in the world or another plane to routinely find tasks beyond that. Some locations might have higher-level tasks available based on the nature of the settlement. A major port might have higher-level tasks

GAME MASTERING

10

INTRODUCTION

ANCESTRIES &
BACKGROUNDS

CLASSES

SKILLS

FEATS

EQUIPMENT

SPELLS

THE AGE OF
LOST OMENS

PLAYING THE
GAME

GAME
MASTERING

CRAFTING
& TREASURE

APPENDIX

for Sailing Lore, a city with a vibrant arts scene might have higher-level tasks for Performance, and so on. If someone is trying to use a particularly obscure skill, they might have trouble finding tasks of an ideal level, or any at all—no one in most settlements is clamoring for the expertise of someone with Troll Lore.

Once the PC has decided on a particular level of task from those available, use the DC for that level from Table 10–5. You might adjust the DC to be more difficult if there's inclement weather during an outdoor job, a rowdy audience for a performance, or the like.

GATHER INFORMATION

To set the DC to Gather Information, use a simple DC representing the availability of information about the subject. Adjust the DC upward if the PC Gathering Information seeks in-depth information. For example, if a character wants to Gather Information about a visiting caravan, you might decide that a common person wouldn't know much about it, but any merchant or guard would, so learning basic facts uses the simple DC for trained proficiency. A caravan leader's name is superficial, so discovering it might be DC 15 (the simple trained DC in Table 10–4). Learning the identity of the leader's employers, however, might be DC 20 if the employers are more obscure.

IDENTIFY MAGIC OR LEARN A SPELL

The DC to Identify Magic or Learn a Spell is usually the DC listed in Table 10–5 for the spell or item's level, adjusted for its rarity. A very strange item or phenomenon usually uses a higher DC adjustment. For a cursed item or certain illusory items, use an incredibly hard DC to increase the chance of misidentification.

RECALL KNOWLEDGE

On most topics, you can use simple DCs for checks to Recall Knowledge. For a check about a specific creature, trap, or other subject with a level, use a level-based DC (adjusting for rarity as needed). You might adjust the difficulty down, maybe even drastically, if the subject is especially notorious or famed. Knowing simple tales about an infamous dragon's exploits, for example, might be incredibly easy for the dragon's level, or even just a simple trained DC.

Alternative Skills

As noted in the action's description, a character might attempt to Recall Knowledge using a different skill than the ones listed as the default options. If the skill is highly applicable, like using Medicine to identify a medicinal tonic, you probably don't need to adjust the DC. If its relevance is a stretch, adjust the DC upward as described in Adjusting Difficulty.

DETERMINING THE SCOPE OF LORE

Lore skills are one of the most specialized aspects of Pathfinder, but they require GM oversight, particularly in determining which Lore subcategories are acceptable for characters to select. A Lore subcategory represents a narrow focus, and thus it shouldn't replace all or even most of an entire skill, nor should it convey vast swaths of information. For example, a single Lore subcategory doesn't cover all religions–that's covered by the Religion skill–but a character could have a Lore subcategory that covers a single deity. One Lore subcategory won't cover an entire country or all of history, but it could cover a city, an ancient civilization, or one aspect of a modern country, like Taldan History Lore. A single Lore subcategory couldn't cover the entire multiverse, but it could cover a whole plane other than the Material Plane.

ADDITIONAL KNOWLEDGE

Sometimes a character might want to follow up on a check to Recall Knowledge, rolling another check to discover more information. After a success, further uses of Recall Knowledge can yield more information, but you should adjust the difficulty to be higher for each attempt. Once a character has attempted an incredibly hard check or failed a check, further attempts are fruitless—the character has recalled everything they know about the subject.

CREATURE IDENTIFICATION

A character who successfully identifies a creature learns one of its best-known attributes—such as a troll's regeneration (and the fact that it can be stopped by acid or fire) or a manticore's tail spikes. On a critical success, the character also learns something subtler, like a demon's weakness or the trigger for one of the creature's reactions.

The skill used to identify a creature usually depends on that creature's trait, as shown on Table 10–7, but you have leeway on which skills apply. For instance, hags are humanoids but have a strong connection to occult spells and live outside society, so you might allow a character to use Occultism to identify them without any DC adjustment, while Society is harder. Lore skills can also be used to identify their specific creature. Using the applicable Lore usually has an easy or very easy DC (before adjusting for rarity).

SENSE DIRECTION

Pick the most appropriate simple DC when someone uses Survival to Sense Direction. This is usually the trained DC in normal wilderness, expert in deep forest or underground, master in featureless or tricky locations, or legendary in weird or surreal environments on other planes.

SOCIAL SKILLS

When a character uses Deception, Diplomacy, Intimidation, or Performance to influence or impress someone whose level or Will DC you don't know, estimate

TABLE 10-7: CREATURE IDENTIFICATION SKILLS

Creature Trait	Skills
Aberration	Occultism
Animal	Nature
Astral	Occultism
Beast	Arcana, Nature
Celestial	Religion
Construct	Arcana, Crafting
Dragon	Arcana
Elemental	Arcana, Nature
Ethereal	Occultism
Fey	Nature
Fiend	Religion
Fungus	Nature
Humanoid	Society
Monitor	Religion
Ooze	Occultism
Plant	Nature
Spirit	Occultism
Undead	Religion

the level of the creature and use that DC. A commoner is usually level 0 or 1. Don't worry about being exact. It often makes sense to adjust the DC based on the target's attitude for Deception, Diplomacy, or Performance, making the DC easy for a friendly creature, very easy for a helpful one, hard for an unfriendly one, or very hard for a hostile one. You might adjust the DC further or differently based on the PC's goal; for instance, the DC to Request something an indifferent NPC is fundamentally opposed to might be incredibly hard or impossible, and it might be easy to convince an unfriendly creature to do something it already wants to do.

SUBSIST

A simple DC is usually sufficient for the Subsist action, with a trained DC for a typical situation. Use the disposition of the environment or city as a guide; an environment with scarce resources or a city with little tolerance for transience might require an expert or higher DC.

TRACK

Often when a PC uses Survival to Track, you can pick a simple DC and adjust it based on the circumstances. For example, an army is usually easy to track, so you could use the untrained DC of 10. If the army marched through mud, you could even adjust this down to DC 5. On the other hand, if the party pursues a cunning survivalist using Cover Tracks, you might use their Survival DC as the DC to Track.

TRAIN AN ANIMAL

Train Animal (page 268) allows PCs to teach animals tricks. Use the level of the animal as the baseline; you can adjust the DC up if the trick is especially difficult, or down if the animal is especially domesticated, like a dog.

REWARDS

In Pathfinder, player characters can receive three kinds of rewards for their heroic deeds: Hero Points, which they can use to get out of sticky situations; Experience Points, which they'll use to level up; and treasure, including powerful magic items.

HERO POINTS

Unlike Experience Points and treasure, which stay with a character, Hero Points are granted and used on a per-session basis. At the start of a game session, you give out 1 Hero Point to each player character. You can also give out more Hero Points during the game, typically after a heroic moment or accomplishment (see below). As noted on page 467, a player can spend 1 Hero Point for a reroll, or they can spend all their Hero Points to recover when near death.

In a typical game, you'll hand out about 1 Hero Point during each hour of play after the first (for example, 3 extra points in a 4-hour session). If you want a more over-the-top game, or if your group is up against incredible odds and showing immense bravery, you might give them out at a faster rate, like 1 every 30 minutes (6 over a 4-hour session). Try to ensure each PC has opportunities to earn Hero Points, and avoid granting all of the Hero Points to a single character.

Brave last stands, protecting innocents, and using a smart strategy or spell to save the day could all earn a character a Hero Point. Look for those moments when everybody at the table celebrates or sits back in awe of a character's accomplishments; that's your cue to issue that character a Hero Point.

The party could also gain Hero Points for their accomplishments throughout the game. For a moderate or major accomplishment, consider giving out a Hero Point as well. This point typically goes to a PC who was instrumental in attaining that accomplishment.

EXPERIENCE POINTS

As characters adventure, they earn Experience Points (XP). These awards come from achieving goals, completing social encounters, exploring new places, fighting monsters, overcoming hazards, and other sorts of deeds. You have a great deal of control over when the characters gain XP, though the following guidelines are what you're expected to give out in a standard campaign.

Normally, when a player character reaches 1,000 XP or more, they level up, reduce their XP by 1,000, and start progressing toward the next level. Other means of advancement are described in the Advancement Speeds sidebar on page 509.

XP AWARDS

Experience Points are awarded for encounters, exploration, and progress in an adventure. When the PCs face direct opposition, such as a fight or a social conflict, the XP earned is based on the level of the challenge the party overcame. Characters can also gain XP from exploration, such as finding secret areas, locating a hideout, enduring a dangerous environment, or mapping an entire dungeon.

Any XP awarded goes to all members of the group. For instance, if the party wins a battle worth 100 XP, they each get 100 XP, even if the party's rogue was off in a vault stealing treasure during the battle. But if the rogue collected a splendid and famous gemstone, which you've decided was a moderate accomplishment worth 30 XP, each member of the party gets 30 XP, too.

ADVERSARIES AND HAZARDS

Encounters with adversaries and hazards grant a set amount of XP. When the group overcomes an encounter with creatures or hazards, each character gains XP equal to the total XP of the creatures and hazards in the encounter (this excludes XP adjustments for different party sizes; see Party Size on page 508 for details).

Trivial encounters don't normally grant any XP, but you might decide to award the same XP as for a minor or moderate accomplishment for a trivial encounter that was important to the story, or for an encounter that became trivial because of the order in which the PCs encountered it in a nonlinear adventure.

ACCOMPLISHMENTS

Characters' actions that move the story forward—like securing a major alliance, establishing an organization, or causing an NPC to have a change of heart—are considered accomplishments and should be rewarded with XP. Their significance determines the size of the XP award. Determine whether the achievement was a minor, moderate, or major accomplishment, and refer to Table 10–8: XP Awards on page 508 to award an appropriate amount of XP. Minor accomplishments include all sorts of significant, memorable, or surprising moments in the game. A moderate accomplishment typically represents a goal that takes most of a session to complete, and a major accomplishment is usually the culmination of the characters' efforts across many sessions. Moderate and major accomplishments usually come after heroic effort, so that's an ideal time to also give a Hero Point to one or more of the characters involved.

As mentioned earlier, it's up to you how much XP to give out for accomplishments. As a general guideline, in a given game session, you'll typically give several minor awards, one or two moderate awards, and only one major award, if any.

TABLE 10-8: XP AWARDS

Accomplishment	XP Award
Minor	10 XP
Moderate*	30 XP
Major*	80 XP

*Typically earns a Hero Point as well.

Adversary Level	XP Award
Party level – 4	10 XP
Party level – 3	15 XP
Party level – 2	20 XP
Party level – 1	30 XP
Party level	40 XP
Party level + 1	60 XP
Party level + 2	80 XP
Party level + 3	120 XP
Party level + 4	160 XP

Hazard Level	XP Award Simple Hazard	Complex Hazard
Party level – 4	2 XP	10 XP
Party level – 3	3 XP	15 XP
Party level – 2	4 XP	20 XP
Party level – 1	6 XP	30 XP
Party level	8 XP	40 XP
Party level + 1	12 XP	60 XP
Party level + 2	16 XP	80 XP
Party level + 3	24 XP	120 XP
Party level + 4	32 XP	160 XP

PARTY SIZE

The rules for advancement assume a group of four PCs. The rules for encounters (page 489) describe how to accommodate groups of a different size, but the XP awards don't change—always award the amount of XP listed for a group of four characters. You usually won't need to make many adjustments for a differently sized group outside of encounters. Be careful of providing too many ways to get accomplishment XP when you have a large group, though, since they can pursue multiple accomplishments at once, which can lead to the PCs leveling up too fast.

GROUP PARITY AND PARTY LEVEL

It's recommended that you keep all the player characters at the same XP total. This makes it much easier to know what challenges are suitable for your players. Having characters at different levels can mean weaker characters die more easily and their players feel less effective, which in turn makes the game less fun for those players.

If you choose not to keep the whole group at the same character level, you'll need to select a party level to determine your XP budget for encounters. Choose the level you think best represents the party's ability as a whole. Use the highest level if only one or two characters are behind, or an average if everyone is at a different level. If only one character is

two or more levels ahead, use a party level suitable for the lower-level characters, and adjust the encounters as if there were one additional PC for every 2 levels the higher-level character has beyond the rest of the party.

Party members who are behind the party level gain double the XP other characters do until they reach the party's level. When tracking individually, you'll need to decide whether party members get XP for missed sessions.

TREASURE

As the GM, it's your job to distribute treasure to the player characters. Treasure appears throughout an adventure, and the PCs obtain it by raiding treasure hoards, defeating foes who carry valuable items or currency, getting paid for successful quests, and any other way you can imagine.

This section provides guidelines for distributing treasure in a typical Pathfinder campaign, but you always have the freedom to assign extra treasure for a high-powered game, less treasure for a gritty survival horror adventure, or any amount in between.

TREASURE BY LEVEL

Table 10–9: Party Treasure by Level on the next page shows how much treasure you should give out over the course of a level for a group of four PCs. The Total Value column gives an approximate total value of all the treasure, in case you want to spend it like a budget. The next several columns provide suggestions for breaking down that total into permanent items, which the PCs keep and use for a long time; consumables, which are destroyed after being used once; and currency, which includes coins, gems, and other valuables primarily spent to acquire items or services. The final column gives the amount of currency to add for each PC beyond four in the group; use this only if you have more than four characters in the game. (Different Party Sizes on page 510 provides more guidance on this.)

For instance, between the time your PCs reach 3rd level and the time they reach 4th level, you should give them the treasure listed in the table for 3rd level, worth approximately 500 gp: two 4th-level permanent items, two 3rd-level permanent items, two 4th-level consumables, two 3rd-level consumables, two 2nd-level consumables, and 120 gp worth of currency.

When assigning 1st-level permanent items, your best options are armor, weapons, and other gear from Chapter 6 worth between 10 and 20 gp. The treasure listed in the row for 20th level represents a full level's worth of adventures, even though there is no way to reach 21st level.

Some creature entries in the *Pathfinder Bestiary* list treasure that can be gained by defeating an individual creature; this counts toward the treasure for any given level. Published adventures include a suitable amount of treasure throughout the adventure, though you should still monitor the party's capabilities as the PCs progress through the adventure to make sure they don't end up behind.

CURRENCY

A party will find money and other treasure that isn't useful on its own but that can be sold or spent on other things. The gp values in the Party Currency column don't refer only to coins. Gems, art objects, crafting materials (including precious materials), jewelry, and even items of much lower level than the party's level can all be more interesting than a pile of gold.

If you include a lower-level permanent item as part of a currency reward, count only half the item's Price toward the gp amount, assuming the party will sell the item or use it as crafting material. But lower-level consumables might still be useful, particularly scrolls, and if you think your party will use them, count those items at their full Price.

OTHER TYPES OF TREASURE

Not all treasure has to be items or currency. Crafters can use the Crafting skill to turn raw materials directly into items instead of buying those items with coins. Knowledge can expand a character's abilities, and formulas make good treasure for item-crafting characters. A spellcaster might get access to new spells from an enemy's spellbook or an ancient scholar, while a monk might retrain techniques with rarer ones learned from a master on a remote mountaintop.

TREASURE AND RARITY

Giving out uncommon and rare items and formulas can get players more interested in treasure. It's best to introduce uncommon items as a reward fairly regularly but rare items only occasionally. These rewards are

ADVANCEMENT SPEEDS

By varying the amount of XP it takes to gain a level, you can change how quickly characters gain power. The game rules assume a group playing with standard advancement. Fast advancement works best when you know you won't be playing a very long campaign and want to accomplish as much as possible quickly; slow advancement works best for a gritty campaign where all progress is hard won.

You can alter XP from one adventure to the next to get a different feel. During a street-level murder mystery and travel through a haunted wilderness, you might use slow advancement. When the PCs reach the dungeon, you might switch to standard or fast advancement. The values below are just examples. You can use values even higher or lower.

Advancement Speed	XP to Level Up
Fast	800 XP
Standard	1,000 XP
Slow	1,200 XP

Story-Based Leveling

If you don't want to deal with managing and handing out XP, or if you want to have progression based solely on events in the story, you can ignore the XP process entirely and instead simply decide when the characters level up. Generally, the characters should gain a level every three to four game sessions, just after the most appropriate big event that happens during that time, such as defeating a significant villain or achieving a major goal.

TABLE 10-9: PARTY TREASURE BY LEVEL

Level	Total Value	Permanent Items (By Item Level)	Consumables (By Item Level)	Party Currency	Currency per Additional PC
1	175 gp	2nd: 2, 1st: 2*	2nd: 2, 1st: 3	40 gp	10 gp
2	300 gp	3rd: 2, 2nd: 2	3rd: 2, 2nd: 2, 1st: 2	70 gp	18 gp
3	500 gp	4th: 2, 3rd: 2	4th: 2, 3rd: 2, 2nd: 2	120 gp	30 gp
4	850 gp	5th: 2, 4th: 2	5th: 2, 4th: 2, 3rd: 2	200 gp	50 gp
5	1,350 gp	6th: 2, 5th: 2	6th: 2, 5th: 2, 4th: 2	320 gp	80 gp
6	2,000 gp	7th: 2, 6th: 2	7th: 2, 6th: 2, 5th: 2	500 gp	125 gp
7	2,900 gp	8th: 2, 7th: 2	8th: 2, 7th: 2, 6th: 2	720 gp	180 gp
8	4,000 gp	9th: 2, 8th: 2	9th: 2, 8th: 2, 7th: 2	1,000 gp	250 gp
9	5,700 gp	10th: 2, 9th: 2	10th: 2, 9th: 2, 8th: 2	1,400 gp	350 gp
10	8,000 gp	11th: 2, 10th: 2	11th: 2, 10th: 2, 9th: 2	2,000 gp	500 gp
11	11,500 gp	12th: 2, 11th: 2	12th: 2, 11th: 2, 10th: 2	2,800 gp	700 gp
12	16,500 gp	13th: 2, 12th: 2	13th: 2, 12th: 2, 11th: 2	4,000 gp	1,000 gp
13	25,000 gp	14th: 2, 13th: 2	14th: 2, 13th: 2, 12th: 2	6,000 gp	1,500 gp
14	36,500 gp	15th: 2, 14th: 2	15th: 2, 14th: 2, 13th: 2	9,000 gp	2,250 gp
15	54,500 gp	16th: 2, 15th: 2	16th: 2, 15th: 2, 14th: 2	13,000 gp	3,250 gp
16	82,500 gp	17th: 2, 16th: 2	17th: 2, 16th: 2, 15th: 2	20,000 gp	5,000 gp
17	128,000 gp	18th: 2, 17th: 2	18th: 2, 17th: 2, 16th: 2	30,000 gp	7,500 gp
18	208,000 gp	19th: 2, 18th: 2	19th: 2, 18th: 2, 17th: 2	48,000 gp	12,000 gp
19	355,000 gp	20th: 2, 19th: 2	20th: 2, 19th: 2, 18th: 2	80,000 gp	20,000 gp
20	490,000 gp	20th: 4	20th: 4, 19th: 2	140,000 gp	35,000 gp

* Many 1st-level permanent items should be items from Chapter 6 instead of magic items.

ADJUSTING TREASURE

The treasure you award to the party should be monitored and adjusted as you play. You might need to give out treasure you hadn't originally planned for, especially if the group bypasses part of an adventure. Keep an eye on the party's resources. If they're running out of consumables or money, or if they're having trouble in combat because their items aren't up to the task, you can make adjustments.

This is especially common in adventures that have little downtime or that take place far from civilization. If the group goes a long time without being able to purchase or Craft useful items, the PCs will be flush with coins and valuables but behind on useful equipment. In a situation like this, you can either place more useful treasure in the adventure or introduce NPCs who are willing to trade.

Megadungeons and Sandboxes

Some adventures have an expectation that the player characters explore where they want and find only what their skill, luck, and ingenuity afford. Two common examples of this type of adventure are the sprawling dungeon with multiple different sections and paths, often called a megadungeon, and free-form exploration, often called a sandbox and typically occurring in a wilderness. If you want to build a free-form adventure like this where characters are likely to miss at least some of the treasure, increase the amount of treasure you place. Be aware, however, that a meticulous group can end up with more treasure than normal and will have advantages in later adventures.

For a simple guideline to these situations, increase the treasure as though there were one more PC in the party. If the structure is especially loose, especially in sandbox adventures, you can increase this amount even further.

especially compelling when the adventurers get the item by defeating or outsmarting an enemy who carries an item that fits their backstory or theme.

Uncommon and rare formulas make great treasure for a character who Crafts items. Note that if an uncommon or rare formula is broadly disseminated, it eventually becomes more common. This can take months or years, but the item might start showing up in shops all around the world.

DIFFERENT ITEM LEVELS

The levels listed for items on Table 10–9: Party Treasure by Level aren't set in stone. You can provide items of slightly higher or lower level as long as you take into account the value of the items you hand out. For instance, suppose you were considering giving a party of 11th-level PCs a *runestone* with a *fortification* rune (with a Price of 2,000 gp) as one of their 12th-level items, but you realize they've had trouble finding armor in their recent adventures, so you instead decide to give them a suit of 11th-level *+2 resilient*

armor (1,400 gp) instead. Since the armor has a lower Price than the rune, you might also add a 9th-level *shadow rune* (650 gp) to make up the difference. The total isn't exactly the same, but that's all right.

However, if you wanted to place a 13th-level permanent item in a treasure hoard, you could remove two 11th-level permanent items to make a roughly equivalent exchange. When you make an exchange upward like this, be cautious: not only might you introduce an item with effects that are disruptive at the party's current level of play, but you also might give an amazing item to one PC while other characters don't gain any new items at all!

If you're playing in a long-term campaign, you can spread out the treasure over time. A major milestone can give extra treasure at one level, followed by a tougher dungeon with fewer new items at the next level. Check back occasionally to see whether each PC's treasure is comparable to the amount they'd get if they created a new character at their current level, as described under Treasure for New Characters below. They should be a bit higher. but if there's a significant discrepancy, adjust the adventure's upcoming treasure rewards accordingly.

DIFFERENT PARTY SIZES

If a party has more than four characters, add the following for each additional character:

- One permanent item of the party's level or 1 level higher
- Two consumables, usually one of the party's level and one of 1 level higher
- Currency equal to the value in the Currency per Additional PC column of Table 10–9

If the party has fewer than four characters, you can subtract the same amount for each missing character, but since the game is inherently more challenging with a smaller group that can't cover all roles as efficiently, you might consider subtracting less treasure and allowing the extra gear help compensate for the smaller group size.

TREASURE FOR NEW CHARACTERS

When your new campaign starts at a higher level, a new player joins an existing group, or a current player's character dies and they need a new one, your campaign will have one or more PCs who don't start at 1st level. In these cases, refer to Table 10–10: Character Wealth on the next page, which shows how many common permanent items of various levels the PC should have, in addition to currency. A single item on this table is always a baseline item. If the player wants armor or a weapon with property runes, they must buy the property runes separately, and for armor or a weapon made of a precious material, they must pay for the precious material separately as well.

These values are for a PC just starting out at the given level. If the PC is joining a party that has already made progress toward the next level, consider giving the new

character an additional item of their current level. If your party has kept the treasure of dead or retired PCs and passed it on to new characters, you might need to give the new character less than the values on the table or reduce some of the treasure rewards of the next few adventures.

Item Selection

You should work with the new character's player to decide which items their character has. Allow the player to make suggestions, and if they know what items they want their character to have, respect their choices unless you believe those choices will have a negative impact on your game. At your discretion, you can grant the player character uncommon or rare items that fit their backstory and concept, keeping in mind how many items of those rarities you have introduced into your game. The player can also spend currency on consumables or lower-level permanent items, keeping the rest as coinage. As usual, you determine which items the character can find for purchase.

A PC can voluntarily choose an item that has a lower level than any or all of the listed items, but they don't gain any more currency by doing so.

If you choose, you can allow the player to instead start with a lump sum of currency and buy whatever common items they want, with a maximum item level of 1 lower than the character's level. This has a lower total value than the normal allotment of permanent items and currency, since the player can select a higher ratio of high-level items.

TABLE 10-10: CHARACTER WEALTH

Level	Permanent Items	Currency	Lump Sum
1	–	15 gp	15 gp
2	**1st:** 1	20 gp	30 gp
3	**2nd:** 1, **1st:** 2	25 gp	75 gp
4	**3rd:** 1, **2nd:** 2, **1st:** 1	30 gp	140 gp
5	**4th:** 1, **3rd:** 2, **2nd:** 1, **1st:** 2	50 gp	270 gp
6	**5th:** 1, **4th:** 2, **3rd:** 1, **2nd:** 2	80 gp	450 gp
7	**6th:** 1, **5th:** 2, **4th:** 1, **3rd:** 2	125 gp	720 gp
8	**7th:** 1, **6th:** 2, **5th:** 1, **4th:** 2	180 gp	1,100 gp
9	**8th:** 1, **7th:** 2, **6th:** 1, **5th:** 2	250 gp	1,600 gp
10	**9th:** 1, **8th:** 2, **7th:** 1, **6th:** 2	350 gp	2,300 gp
11	**10th:** 1, **9th:** 2, **8th:** 1, **7th:** 2	500 gp	3,200 gp
12	**11th:** 1, **10th:** 2, **9th:** 1, **8th:** 2	700 gp	4,500 gp
13	**12th:** 1, **11th:** 2, **10th:** 1, **9th:** 2	1,000 gp	6,400 gp
14	**13th:** 1, **12th:** 2, **11th:** 1, **10th:** 2	1,500 gp	9,300 gp
15	**14th:** 1, **13th:** 2, **12th:** 1, **11th:** 2	2,250 gp	13,500 gp
16	**15th:** 1, **14th:** 2, **13th:** 1, **12th:** 2	3,250 gp	20,000 gp
17	**16th:** 1, **15th:** 2, **14th:** 1, **13th:** 2	5,000 gp	30,000 gp
18	**17th:** 1, **16th:** 2, **15th:** 1, **14th:** 2	7,500 gp	45,000 gp
19	**18th:** 1, **17th:** 2, **16th:** 1, **15th:** 2	12,000 gp	69,000 gp
20	**19th:** 1, **18th:** 2, **17th:** 1, **16th:** 2	20,000 gp	112,000 gp

BUYING AND SELLING ITEMS

Characters can usually buy and sell items only during downtime. An item can typically be sold for only half its Price, though art objects, gems, and raw materials can be sold for their full Price (page 271).

ENVIRONMENT

Primarily used during exploration, environment rules bring the locales your party travels through to life. You'll often be able to use common sense to adjudicate how environments work, but you'll need special rules for environments that really stand out.

Each of the environments presented in this section uses the terrain rules (which are summarized on page 514 and appear in full beginning on page 475) in different ways, so be sure to familiarize yourself with those rules before reading this section. Some environments refer to the rules for climate (page 517) and natural disasters (beginning on page 517). Many places have the traits of multiple environments; a snow-covered mountain might use both the arctic and mountain environments, for example. For environmental features with effects based on how tall or deep they are, those effects vary further based on a creature's size. For instance, a shallow bog for a Medium creature might be a deep bog for smaller creatures, and a deep bog for a Medium creature could be only a shallow bog for a larger creature (and so insignificant for a truly massive creature that it isn't even difficult terrain).

Table 10–12 lists the features of various environments alphabetically for quick reference. The Proficiency DC Band entry indicates a range of appropriate simple DCs for that environmental feature, while also providing a rough estimate of the danger or complexity of the feature.

ENVIRONMENTAL DAMAGE

Some environmental features or natural disasters deal damage. Because the amount of damage can vary based on the specific circumstances, the rules for specific environments and natural disasters use damage categories to describe the damage, rather than exact numbers. Use Table 10–11 below to determine damage from an environment or natural disaster. When deciding the exact damage amount, use your best judgment based on how extreme you deem the danger to be.

TABLE 10-11: ENVIRONMENTAL DAMAGE

Category	Damage
Minor	1d6–2d6
Moderate	4d6–6d6
Major	8d6–12d6
Massive	18d6–24d6

AQUATIC

Aquatic environments are among the most challenging for PCs short of other worlds and unusual planes. PCs in an aquatic environment need a way to breathe (typically a *water breathing* spell) and must usually Swim to move, though a PC who sinks to the bottom can walk awkwardly, using the rules for greater difficult terrain. Characters in aquatic environments make frequent use of the aquatic combat (page 478) and drowning and suffocation rules (page 478).

CURRENTS AND FLOWING WATER

Ocean currents, flowing rivers, and similar moving water are difficult terrain or greater difficult terrain (depending on the speed of the water) for a creature Swimming against the current. At the end of a creature's turn, it moves a certain distance depending on the current's speed. For instance, a 10-foot current moves a creature 10 feet in the current's direction at the end of that creature's turn.

VISIBILITY

It's much harder to see things at a distance underwater than it is on land, and it's particularly difficult if the water is murky or full of particles. In pure water, the maximum visual range is roughly 240 feet to see a small object, and in murky water, visibility can be reduced to only 10 feet or even less.

ARCTIC

The main challenge in an arctic environment is the low temperature, but arctic environments also contain ice and snow. The disasters that most often strike in arctic environments are avalanches, blizzards, and floods.

ICE

Icy ground is both uneven ground and difficult terrain, as characters slip and slide due to poor traction.

SNOW

Depending on the depth of snow and its composition, most snowy ground is either difficult terrain or greater difficult terrain. In denser snow, characters can attempt to walk along the surface without breaking through, but some patches might be loose or soft enough that they're uneven ground.

DESERT

Desert encompasses sandy and rocky deserts as well as badlands. Though tundra is technically a desert, it's classified as arctic, as the climate is the primary challenge in such areas. Sandy deserts often have quicksand hazards (page 526) and sandstorms.

RUBBLE

Rocky deserts are strewn with rubble, which is difficult terrain. Rubble dense enough to be walked over rather than navigated through is uneven ground.

SAND

Packed sand doesn't usually significantly impede a character's movement, but loose sand is either difficult terrain (if it's shallow) or uneven ground (if it's deep). The wind in a desert often shifts sand into dunes, hills of loose sand with uneven ground facing the wind and steeper inclines away from the wind.

FOREST

These diverse environments include jungles and other wooded areas. They are sometimes struck by wildfires.

CANOPIES

Particularly dense forests, such as rain forests, have a canopy level above the ground. A creature trying to reach the canopy or travel along it must Climb. Swinging on vines and branches usually requires an Acrobatics or Athletics check. A canopy provides cover, and a thicker one can prevent creatures in the canopy from seeing those on the ground, and vice versa.

TREES

While trees are omnipresent in a forest, they typically don't provide cover unless a character uses the Take Cover action. Only larger trees that take up an entire 5-foot square on the map (or more) are big enough to provide cover automatically.

UNDERGROWTH

Light undergrowth is difficult terrain that allows a character to Take Cover. Heavy undergrowth is greater difficult terrain that automatically provides cover. Some sorts of undergrowth, such as thorns, might also be hazardous terrain, and areas with plenty of twisting roots might be uneven ground.

MOUNTAIN

Mountain environments also include hills, which share many aspects of mountains, though not their more extreme features. The most common disasters here are avalanches.

CHASMS

Chasms are natural pits, typically at least 20 feet long and clearly visible (barring mundane or magical efforts to conceal them). The main danger posed by a chasm is that characters must Long Jump to get across. Alternatively, characters can take the safer but slower route of Climbing down the near side of the chasm and then ascending the far side to get across.

CLIFFS

Cliffs and rock walls require creatures to Climb to ascend or descend. Without extensive safety precautions, a critical failure can result in significant falling damage.

RUBBLE

Mountains often have extremely rocky areas or shifting, gravelly scree that makes for difficult terrain. Especially deep or pervasive rubble is uneven ground.

TABLE 10-12: ENVIRONMENTAL FEATURES

Feature	Pages	Proficiency DC Band
Avalanche	518	Expert-legendary
Blizzard	518	—
Bog	514	Untrained-trained
Canopy	513	Trained-master
Chasm	513	—
Cliff	513	Trained-master
Collapse	518	Expert-legendary
Crowd	514	Trained-master
Current	512	Trained-master
Door	515	See page 515
Earthquake	518	Trained-legendary
Flood	518	Expert-legendary
Floor	515, 516	Untrained-expert
Fog	517	—
Gate	515	—
Guard	515	—
Hedge	514	Untrained-trained
Ice	512	Trained-master
Lava	519	Expert-legendary
Ledge	516	Untrained-master
Portcullis	515	See page 515
Precipitation	517	—
Rooftop	515	Trained-master
Rubble	513, 516	Untrained-expert
Sand	513	Untrained-expert
Sandstorm	519	Trained-master
Sewer	515	—
Slope	514	Untrained-trained
Snow	512	Untrained-expert
Stairs	516	Untrained-trained
Stalagmite	516	Trained-expert
Street	516	Untrained-trained
Temperature	517	—
Tornado	519	Master-legendary
Tree	513	Untrained-master
Tsunami	519	Master-legendary
Undergrowth	513, 514	Untrained-expert
Underwater Visibility	512	—
Volcanic Eruption	519	Trained-legendary
Wall	517	See page 516
Wildfire	519	Expert-legendary
Wind	517	Untrained-legendary

TERRAIN RULES

Environments make frequent use of the rules for difficult terrain, greater difficult terrain, and hazardous terrain, so those rules are summarized here.

Difficult terrain is any terrain that impedes movement, ranging from particularly rough or unstable surfaces to thick ground cover and countless other impediments. Moving into a square of difficult terrain (or moving 5 feet into or within an area of difficult terrain, if you're not using a grid) costs an extra 5 feet of movement. Moving into a square of **greater difficult terrain** instead costs 10 additional feet of movement. This additional cost is not increased when moving diagonally. Creatures can't normally Step into difficult terrain.

Any movement creatures make while jumping ignores terrain that the creature is jumping over. Some abilities (such as flight or being incorporeal) allow creatures to avoid the movement reduction from some types of difficult terrain. Certain other abilities let creatures ignore difficult terrain while traveling on foot; such an ability also allows a creature to move through greater difficult terrain using the movement cost for difficult terrain, but unless the ability specifies otherwise, these abilities don't let creatures ignore greater difficult terrain.

Hazardous terrain damages creatures whenever they move through it. For instance, an acid pool, a pit of burning embers, and a spike-filled passageway all constitute hazardous terrain. The amount and type of damage depend on the specific hazardous terrain.

SLOPES

Slopes vary from the gentle rises of normal terrain to difficult terrain and inclines, depending on the angle of elevation. Moving down a slope is typically normal terrain, but characters might need to Climb up particularly steep slopes.

UNDERGROWTH

Light undergrowth is common in mountains. It is difficult terrain and allows a character to Take Cover.

PLAINS

The plains environment encompasses grasslands such as savannas and farmland. The most common disasters in plains are tornadoes and wildfires.

HEDGES

Hedges are planted rows of bushes, shrubs, and trees. Their iconic appearance in adventures consists of tall hedges grown into mazes. A typical hedge is 2 to 5 feet tall, takes up a row of squares, and provides cover. A character trying to push through a hedge faces greater difficult terrain; it's sometimes faster to Climb over.

UNDERGROWTH

Light undergrowth is difficult terrain that allows a character to Take Cover. Heavy undergrowth is greater difficult terrain that provides cover automatically. Undergrowth in plains is usually light with a few scattered areas of heavy undergrowth, but fields of certain crops, like corn, are entirely heavy undergrowth.

SWAMP

Wetlands are the most common kind of swamp, but this category also includes drier marshes such as moors. Swamps often contain quicksand hazards (page 526). Despite their soggy nature, swamps aren't very likely to experience heavy flooding, since they act as natural sponges and absorb a great deal of water before they flood.

BOGS

Also called mires, bogs are watery areas that accumulate peat, are covered by shrubs and moss, and sometimes feature floating islands of vegetation covering deeper pools. Shallow bogs are difficult terrain for a Medium creature, and deep bogs are greater difficult terrain. If a bog is deep enough that a creature can't reach the bottom, the creature has to Swim. Bogs are also acidic, so particularly extreme or magical bogs can be hazardous terrain.

UNDERGROWTH

Light undergrowth is difficult terrain that allows a character to Take Cover, while heavy undergrowth is greater difficult terrain that provides cover automatically. Some sorts of undergrowth, such as thorns, are also hazardous terrain, and areas with plenty of twisting roots are uneven ground.

URBAN

Urban environments include open city spaces as well as buildings. The building information in this section also applies to ruins and constructed dungeons. Depending on their construction and location, cities might be vulnerable to many sorts of disasters, especially fires and floods.

CROWDS

Crowded thoroughfares and similar areas are difficult terrain, or greater difficult terrain if an area is truly packed with people. You might allow a character to get a crowd to part using Diplomacy, Intimidation, or Performance.

A crowd exposed to an obvious danger, like a fire or a rampaging monster, attempts to move away from the danger as quickly as possible, but it is slowed by its own mass. A fleeing crowd typically moves at the Speed of an average member each round (usually 25 feet), potentially trampling or leaving behind slower-moving members of the crowd.

DOORS

Opening an unlocked door requires an Interact action (or more than one for a particularly complicated or large door). Stuck doors must be Forced Open, and locked ones require a character to Pick the Lock or Force them Open.

FLOORS

Wooden floors are easy to walk on, as are flagstone floors made of fitted stones. However, floors of worn flagstone often contain areas of uneven ground.

GATES

Walled settlements often have gates that the city can close for defense or open to allow travel. A typical gate consists of one portcullis at each end of a gatehouse, with murder holes in between or other protected spots from which guards can attack foes.

GUARDS

Most settlements of significant size have guards working in shifts to protect the settlement at all hours, patrolling the streets and guarding various posts. The size of this force varies from one guard for every 1,000 residents to a force 10 times this number.

PORTCULLISES

A portcullis is a wooden or iron grate that descends to seal off a gate or corridor. Most are raised on ropes or chains operated by a winch, and they have locking mechanisms that keep them from being lifted easily. The rules on lifting a portcullis or bending its bars appear in the sidebar on this page. If a portcullis falls on a creature, use a slamming door trap (page 523).

ROOFTOPS

Rooftops make for memorable ambushes, chase scenes, infiltrations, and running fights. Flat roofs are easy to move across, but they're rare in any settlement that receives significant snowfall, since heavy buildups of snow can collapse a roof. Angled roofs are uneven ground, or inclines if they're especially steep. The peak of an angled roof is a narrow surface.

Hurdling from roof to roof often requires a Long Jump, though some buildings are close enough to Leap between. A High Jump might be necessary to reach a higher roof, or a Leap followed by Grabbing an Edge and Climbing up.

SEWERS

Sewers are generally 10 feet or more below street level and are equipped with ladders or other means to ascend and descend. Raised paths along the walls allow sewer workers access, while channels in the center carry the waste itself. Less sophisticated sewers, or sections those workers don't usually access, might require wading through disease-ridden waste. Sewers can be accessed through sewer grates, which usually require 2 or more Interact actions to open.

DOORS, GATES, AND WALLS

Some of the most common obstacles that characters face in urban areas and dungeons are doors, gates, and walls.

Climbing

The table below gives the typical DC for Athletics checks to Climb a structure, which is usually a simple DC. You might adjust the difficulty based on the specifics of the structure and environment.

Demolishing

A character might want to smash their way through a door, a window, or certain walls. The Hardness, Hit Point, and Broken Threshold values provided in the table below are based on the material the structure is typically made out of, so a portcullis made of iron, for example, has a higher Hardness than one of wood. For more on damaging objects, see page 272.

Strong walls, such as well-maintained masonry or hewn stone, can't be broken without dedicated work and proper tools. Getting through such walls requires downtime.

Door	Climb DC	Hardness, HP (BT)
Wood	20	10, 40 (20)
Stone	30	14, 56 (28)
Reinforced wood	15	15, 60 (30)
Iron	30	18, 72 (36)
Wall	**Climb DC**	**Hardness, HP (BT)**
Crumbling masonry	15	10, 40 (20)
Wooden slats	15	10, 40 (20)
Masonry	20	14, 56 (28)
Hewn stone	30	14, 56 (28)
Iron	40	18, 72 (36)
Portcullis	**Climb DC**	**Hardness, HP (BT)**
Wood	10	10, 40 (20)
Iron	10	18, 72 (36)

Forcing Open

Structures that can be opened—such as doors, gates, and windows—can be Forced Open using Athletics. This is usually necessary only if they're locked or stuck. The DC to Force Open a structure uses the Thievery DC of its lock but adjusts it to be very hard (increasing the DC by 5). If there's no lock, use the following table; when lifting a portcullis, use the lock DC or the DC from the table, whichever is higher.

Structure	Force Open DC
Stuck door or window	15
Exceptionally stuck	20
Lift wooden portcullis	20
Lift iron portcullis	30
Bend metal bars	30

INTRODUCTION

ANCESTRIES & BACKGROUNDS

CLASSES

SKILLS

FEATS

EQUIPMENT

SPELLS

THE AGE OF LOST OMENS

PLAYING THE GAME

GAME MASTERING

CRAFTING & TREASURE

APPENDIX

SEWER GAS

Sewer gas often contains pockets of highly flammable gas. A pocket of sewer gas exposed to a source of flame explodes, dealing moderate environmental fire damage to creatures in the area.

STAIRS

Stairs are difficult terrain for characters moving up them, and shoddy stairs might also be uneven ground. Some temples and giant-built structures have enormous stairs that are greater difficult terrain both up and down, or might require Climbing every step.

STREETS

Most settlements have narrow and twisting streets that were largely established organically as the settlement grew. These roads are rarely more than 20 feet wide, with alleys as narrow as 5 feet. Streets are generally paved with cobblestones. If the cobblestones are in poor repair, they could be difficult terrain or uneven ground.

Particularly lawful or well-planned cities have major thoroughfares that allow wagons and merchants to reach marketplaces and other important areas in town. These need to be at least 25 feet wide to accommodate wagons moving in both directions, and they often have narrow sidewalks that allow pedestrians to avoid wagon traffic.

WALLS

Well-built structures have exterior walls of brick or stonemasonry. Smaller, lower-quality, or temporary structures might have wooden walls. Interior walls tend to be less sturdy; they could be made of wooden planks, or even simply of thick, opaque paper held in a wooden frame. An underground structure might have thick walls carved out of solid rock to prevent the weight of the ground above from collapsing the structure. Rules for climbing and breaking walls are in the sidebar on page 515.

UNDERGROUND

Underground environments consist of caves and natural underground areas. Artificial dungeons and ruins combine underground features with urban features like stairs and walls. Deep underground vaults have some of the same terrain features as mountains, such as chasms and cliffs. The most common disasters underground are collapses.

FLOORS

Natural underground environments rarely have flat floors, instead featuring abrupt changes in elevation that result in difficult terrain, uneven ground, and inclines.

LEDGES

Ledges are narrow surfaces that overlook a lower area or provide the only means to move along the edge of a chasm. Moving across a narrow ledge requires using Acrobatics to Balance.

RUBBLE

Caverns can be covered in rubble, which is difficult terrain. Deep or pervasive rubble is also uneven ground.

STALAGMITES AND STALACTITES

Stalagmites are tapering columns that rise from the floor of a cave. Areas filled with stalagmites are greater difficult terrain, and especially large stalagmites have to be sidestepped or Climbed. Stalagmites can be sharp enough they can be used as hazardous terrain in some circumstances, as can stalactites (icicle-shaped formations that hang from the roof of a cave) if they're knocked loose from a ceiling or overhang.

WALLS

Natural cave walls are uneven, with nooks, crannies, and ledges. Since most caves are formed by water, cave walls are often damp, making them even more difficult to Climb.

CLIMATE

Weather is more than just set dressing to establish mood—it has mechanical effects you can combine with environmental components to create a more memorable encounter. Weather can impose circumstance penalties on certain checks, from –1 to –4 based on severity.

FOG

Fog imposes a circumstance penalty to visual Perception checks, depending on the thickness; it causes creatures viewed through significant amounts of fog to be concealed; and it cuts off all visibility at half a mile or less—possibly much less. Conditions limiting visibility to about a mile are called mist, and those that do so to about 3 miles are called haze.

PRECIPITATION

Precipitation includes rain as well as colder snow, sleet, and hail. Wet precipitation douses flames, and frozen precipitation can create areas of snow or ice on the ground. Drizzle or light snowfall has little mechanical effect beyond limited visibility.

VISIBILITY

Most forms of precipitation impose circumstance penalties on visual Perception checks. Hail often is sparser but loud, instead penalizing auditory Perception checks. Especially heavy precipitation, such as a downpour of rain or heavy snow, might make creatures concealed if they're far away.

FATIGUE

Precipitation causes discomfort and fatigue. Anything heavier than drizzle or light snowfall reduces the time it takes for characters to become fatigued from overland travel to only 4 hours. Heavy precipitation can be dangerous in cold environments when characters go without protection. Soaked characters treat the temperature as one step colder (mild to severe, severe to extreme; see Temperature below).

THUNDERSTORMS

High winds and heavy precipitation accompany many thunderstorms. There's also a very small chance

DUNGEONS

Dungeon environments, which include both ruins and contemporary buildings constructed in the wilderness, are a fairly common venue for adventures. As an environment, they combine urban features like doors and buildings (page 515) with features from an underground environment, and occasionally components from other environments. While underground dungeons are particularly common, you might also consider setting your adventure in a ruin reclaimed by the forest, with giant trees spreading their roots through the walls, or a ruin deep in a swamp, with bogs covering access to some of the ruin's hidden secrets.

that a character might be struck by lightning during a storm. A lightning strike usually deals moderate electricity damage, or major electricity damage in a severe thunderstorm.

TEMPERATURE

Often, temperature doesn't impose enough of a mechanical effect to worry about beyond describing the clothing the characters need to wear to be comfortable. Particularly hot and cold weather can make creatures fatigued more quickly during overland travel and can cause damage if harsh enough, as shown in Table 10–13 on page 518.

Appropriate cold-weather gear (such as the winter clothing) can negate the damage from severe cold or reduce the damage from extreme cold to that of particularly severe cold.

WIND

Wind imposes a circumstance penalty on auditory Perception checks depending on its strength. It also interferes with physical ranged attacks such as arrows, imposing a circumstance penalty to attack rolls involving such weapons, and potentially making attacks with them impossible in powerful windstorms. Wind snuffs out handheld flames; lanterns protect their flame from the wind, but particularly powerful winds can extinguish these as well.

MOVING IN WIND

Wind is difficult or greater difficult terrain when Flying. Moving in wind of sufficient strength requires a Maneuver in Flight action, and fliers are blown away on a critical failure or if they don't succeed at a minimum of one such check each round.

Even on the ground, particularly strong winds might require a creature to succeed at an Athletics check to move, knocking the creature back and prone on a critical failure. On such checks, Small creatures typically take a –1 circumstance penalty, and Tiny creatures typically take a –2 penalty.

INTRODUCTION

ANCESTRIES & BACKGROUNDS

CLASSES

SKILLS

FEATS

EQUIPMENT

SPELLS

THE AGE OF LOST OMENS

PLAYING THE GAME

GAME MASTERING

CRAFTING & TREASURE

APPENDIX

TABLE 10-13: TEMPERATURE EFFECTS

Category	Temperature	Fatigue	Damage
Incredible cold	–80° F or colder	2 hours	Moderate cold every minute
Extreme cold	–79° F to –20° F	4 hours	Minor cold every 10 minutes
Severe cold	–21° F to 12° F	4 hours	Minor cold every hour
Mild cold	13° F to 32° F	4 hours	None
Normal	33° F to 94° F	8 hours	None
Mild heat	95° F* to 104° F*	4 hours	None
Severe heat	105° F* to 114° F	4 hours	Minor fire every hour
Extreme heat	115° F to 139° F	4 hours	Minor fire every 10 minutes
Incredible heat	140° F or warmer	2 hours	Moderate fire every minute

* Adjust temperatures down by 15° in areas of high humidity.

NATURAL DISASTERS

Climate and environmental features can be a hindrance or long-term threat, but natural disasters represent acute danger, especially to those directly exposed to their fury. The damage in the following sections uses the categories in Table 10–11: Environmental Damage on page 512.

AVALANCHES

Though the term avalanche specifically refers to a cascading flow of ice and snow down a mountain's slope, the same rules work for landslides, mudslides, and other similar disasters. Avalanches of wet snow usually travel up to 200 feet per round, though powdery snow can travel up to 10 times faster. Rockslides and mudslides are slower, sometimes even slow enough that a character might be able to outrun them.

An avalanche deals major or even massive bludgeoning damage to creatures and objects in its path. These victims are also buried under a significant mass. Creatures caught in an avalanche's path can attempt a Reflex save; if they succeed, they take only half the bludgeoning damage, and if they critically succeed, they also avoid being buried.

BURIAL

Buried creatures take minor bludgeoning damage each minute, and they potentially take minor cold damage if buried under an avalanche of snow. At the GM's discretion, creatures without a sufficient air pocket could also risk suffocation (page 478). A buried creature is restrained and usually can't free itself.

Allies or bystanders can attempt to dig out a buried creature. Each creature digging clears roughly a 5-foot-by-5-foot square every 4 minutes with a successful Athletics check (or every 2 minutes on a critical success). Using shovels or other proper tools halves the time.

BLIZZARDS

Blizzards combine cold weather, heavy snow, and strong winds. They don't pose a single direct threat as other disasters do; instead, the combination of these factors all at once poses a substantial impediment to characters.

COLLAPSES

Collapses and cave-ins occur when caverns or buildings fall, dumping tons of rock or other material on those caught below or inside them. Creatures under the collapse take major or massive bludgeoning damage and become buried, just as with an avalanche. Fortunately, collapses don't spread unless they weaken the overall integrity of the area and lead to further collapses.

EARTHQUAKES

Earthquakes often cause other natural disasters in the form of avalanches, collapses, floods, and tsunamis, but they also present unique threats such as fissures, soil liquefaction, and tremors.

FISSURES

Fissures and other ground ruptures can destabilize structures, but more directly they lead to creatures taking bludgeoning damage from falling into a fissure.

SOIL LIQUEFACTION

Liquefaction occurs when granular particles shake to the point where they temporarily lose their solid form and act as liquids. When this happens to soil, it can cause creatures and even whole buildings to sink into the ground. You can use the *earthquake* spell for more specific rules, though that spell represents only one particular kind of localized quake.

TREMORS

Tremors knock creatures prone, causing them to fall or careen into other objects, which can deal bludgeoning damage appropriate to the severity of the quake.

FLOODS

Though more gradual floods can damage structures and drown creatures, flash floods are similar to avalanches, except with a liquid mass instead of a solid one. Instead of burying creatures, a flash flood carries creatures and even massive objects away, buffeting the creatures and potentially drowning them. The drowning rules appear on page 478.

SANDSTORMS

Mild sandstorms and dust storms don't present much more danger than a windy rainstorm, but they can cause damage to a creature's lungs and spread diseases across long distances. Heavy sandstorms deal minor slashing damage each round to those exposed to the sand, force creatures to hold their breath to avoid suffocation, or both.

TORNADOES

In a tornado's path, wind conditions impose severe circumstance penalties, but creatures that would normally be blown away are instead picked up in the tornado's funnel, where they take massive bludgeoning damage from flying debris as they rise through the cone until they are eventually expelled (taking bludgeoning damage from falling).

Tornadoes usually travel around 300 feet per round (roughly 30 miles per hour). They normally travel a few miles before dissipating. Some tornadoes are stationary or travel much faster.

TSUNAMIS

Tsunamis present many of the same dangers as flash floods but are much larger and more destructive. Tsunami waves can reach 100 feet or more in height, wrecking buildings and creatures alike with massive bludgeoning damage from both the wave itself and debris pulled up along its path of destruction.

VOLCANIC ERUPTIONS

Volcanic eruptions can contain any combination of ash, lava bombs, lava flows, pyroclastic flows, and vents.

Ash

Ash from volcanic eruptions is hot enough to cause minor fire damage each minute. It limits visibility like a thick fog and can make air unbreathable, requiring characters to hold their breath or suffocate (page 478). Ash clouds generate ash lightning strikes, which typically deal moderate electricity damage but are very unlikely to hit an individual creature. Ash buildup on the ground creates areas of uneven ground, difficult terrain, or greater difficult terrain, and ash in the atmosphere can block the sun for weeks or even months, leading to colder temperatures and longer winters.

Lava Bombs

Pressure can launch lava into the air that falls as lava bombs: masses of lava that solidify as they fly and shatter on impact, dealing at least moderate bludgeoning damage and moderate fire damage.

Lava Flows

Lava flows are an iconic volcanic threat; they usually move between 5 and 60 feet per round over normal ground, so characters can often outrun them. However, flows can move up to 300 feet per round in a steep volcanic tube or channel. Lava emanates heat that deals minor fire damage even before it comes into contact with creatures, and immersion in lava deals massive fire damage each round.

Pyroclastic Flows

Mixes of hot gases and rock debris, pyroclastic flows spread much faster than lava, sometimes more than 4,000 feet per round. While cooler than the hottest lava, pyroclastic flows are capable of overwhelming entire settlements. They work like avalanches but deal half of their damage as fire damage.

Vents

Steam vents shoot from the ground, dealing moderate fire damage or more in a wide column. Acidic and poisonous gases released from beneath the surface can create wide areas of hazardous terrain that deals at least minor acid or poison damage.

WILDFIRES

Wildfires travel mainly along a front moving in a single direction. In a forest, the front can advance up to 70 feet per round (7 miles per hour). They can move up to twice as fast across plains due to a lack of shade and the relatively low humidity. Embers from the fire, carried by winds and rising hot air, can scatter, forming spot fires as far as 10 miles away from the main wildfire. Wildfires present three main threats: flames, heat, and smoke.

Flames

Flames are hazardous terrain, usually dealing moderate damage and potentially setting a character on fire, dealing moderate persistent fire damage. The flames from a small fire are often less dangerous than the advancing heat from the front of a large fire.

Heat

Wildfires increase the temperature in advance of the front, reaching nearly 1,500° F at the fire's arrival, as hot as some lava. This begins as minor fire damage every round at a reasonable distance from the front and increases to massive fire damage for someone within the wildfire.

Smoke

Wind can carry smoke far in front of the wildfire itself. Smoke imposes a circumstance penalty to visual Perception checks, depending on the thickness. It causes creatures viewed through significant amounts of smoke to be concealed, and it cuts off all visibility at half a mile or less. Near or within the wildfire, the combination of smoke and heated air require characters to hold their breath or suffocate (page 478).

HAZARDS

Dungeons are rife with devious traps meant to protect the treasures within. These range from mechanical devices that shoot darts or drop heavy blocks to magic runes that explode into bursts of flame. In addition to traps, adventurers may stumble into other types of hazards, including naturally occurring environmental hazards, mysterious hauntings, and more.

DETECTING A HAZARD

Every hazard has a trigger of some kind that sets its dangers in motion. For traps, this could be a mechanism like a trip wire or a pressure plate, while for an environmental hazard or haunt, the trigger may simply be proximity. When characters approach a hazard, they have a chance of finding the trigger area or mechanism before triggering the hazard. They automatically receive a check to detect hazards unless the hazards require a minimum proficiency rank to do so.

During exploration, determine whether the party detects a hazard when the PCs first enter the general area in which it appears. If the hazard doesn't list a minimum proficiency rank, roll a secret Perception check against the hazard's Stealth DC for each PC. For hazards with a minimum proficiency rank, roll only if someone is actively searching (using the Search activity while exploring or the Seek action in an encounter), and only if they have the listed proficiency rank or higher. Anyone who succeeds becomes aware of the hazard, and you can describe what they notice.

Magical hazards that don't have a minimum proficiency rank can be found using *detect magic*, but this spell doesn't provide enough information to understand or disable the hazard—it only reveals the hazard's presence. Determining a magical hazard's properties thoroughly enough to disable it requires either the use of more powerful magic or a successful skill check, likely using Identify Magic or Recall Knowledge. Magical hazards with a minimum proficiency rank cannot be found with *detect magic* at all.

TRIGGERING A HAZARD

If the group fails to detect a hazard and the hazard's trigger is a standard part of traveling (such as stepping on a floor plate or moving through a magical sensor while walking), the hazard's reaction occurs. Hazards that would be triggered only when someone directly manipulates the environment—by opening a door, for example—use their reactions only if a PC explicitly takes that action.

REACTION OR FREE ACTION

Most hazards have reactions that occur when they're triggered. For simple hazards, the reaction is the entirety

MONSTERS AND HAZARDS

The statistics for NPCs and monsters usually don't list their proficiency ranks. Most of the time, they don't need to deal with detecting or disabling hazards the way PCs do, so you don't need this information. However, if a PC resets a trap in a monster's path or plans to lure a monster into a hazard, you can improvise this information.

For Perception, a monster is usually an expert at 3rd or 4th level, a master at 8th or 9th level, and legendary at 16th or 17th level. If the monster has Thievery listed in its skills, it has the highest proficiency possible for its level (trained at 1st, expert at 3rd, master at 7th, and legendary at 15th); otherwise, it's untrained. Of course, an individual monster might deviate from these guidelines, especially if it's mindless or not very perceptive.

of the hazard's effect. For complex hazards, the reaction may also cause the hazard to roll initiative, either starting a combat encounter or joining one already in progress, and the hazard continues to pose a threat over multiple rounds. Some hazards have a triggered free action instead of a reaction; for instance, quicksand can suck down multiple creatures per round.

ROUTINE

A complex hazard usually follows a set of preprogrammed actions called a routine. Once triggered, the hazard first performs its initial reaction; then, if the PCs are not yet in encounter mode, they should roll initiative. (If they're already in encounter mode, their initiative remains the same.) The hazard might tell you to roll initiative for it—in this case, the hazard rolls initiative using its Stealth modifier.

After this happens, the hazard follows its routine each round on its initiative. The number of actions a hazard can take each round, as well as what they can be used for, depend on the hazard.

RESETTING A HAZARD

Some hazards can be reset, allowing them to be triggered again. This can occur automatically, as for quicksand, whose surface settles after 24 hours, or manually, like a hidden pit, whose trapdoor must be closed for the pit to become hidden again.

DISABLING A HAZARD

The most versatile method for deactivating traps is the Disable a Device action of the Thievery skill, though most mechanical traps can also simply be smashed, and magical traps can usually be counteracted. Environmental hazards often can be overcome with Nature or Survival, and haunts can often be overcome with Occultism or Religion. The specific skill and DC required to disable a hazard are listed in the hazard's stat block. As with detecting a hazard, disabling a hazard might require a character to have a certain proficiency rank in the listed skill.

A character must first detect a hazard (or have it pointed out to them) to try to deactivate it. They can attempt to deactivate a hazard whether or not it has already been triggered, though some hazards no longer pose a danger once their reactions have occurred, especially if there is no way for them to be reset.

For most hazards, a successful check for the listed skill against the DC in the stat block disables the hazard without triggering it. Any other means of deactivating the hazard are included in the hazard's stat block, as are any additional steps required to properly deactivate it. A critical failure on any roll to disable a hazard triggers it, including a critical failure on a roll to counteract a magic hazard.

Some hazards require multiple successful checks to deactivate, typically because they have a particularly complicated component or have several discrete portions. For hazards with a complex component, a critical success on a check to disable the hazard counts as two successes on a single component.

DAMAGING A HAZARD

Rather than trying to carefully disable a hazard, a character might just smash it. Damaging a mechanical trap or another physical hazard works like damaging objects: the hazard reduces the damage it takes by its Hardness. In most cases, hitting the hazard also triggers it, as explained in Attacking a Hazard below. If a hazard's Hit Points are reduced to its Broken Threshold (BT) or lower, the hazard becomes broken and can't be activated, though it can still be repaired. If it's reduced to 0 HP, it's destroyed and can't be repaired. (See page 272 in Chapter 6 for more information on damaging objects.)

Hazards' AC, applicable saving throw modifiers, Hardness, HP, and BT are listed in their stat blocks. A hazard that doesn't list one of these statistics can't be affected by anything targeting that statistic. For example, a hazard that has HP but no BT can't be broken, but can still be destroyed. Hazards are immune to anything an object is immune to unless specifically noted otherwise, and they can't be targeted by anything that can't target objects. Some hazards may have additional immunities, as well as resistances or weaknesses.

ATTACKING A HAZARD

If someone hits a hazard—especially if it's a mechanical trap—they usually trigger it, though you might determine otherwise in some cases. An attack that breaks the hazard might prevent it from triggering, depending on the circumstances. If the hazard has multiple parts, breaking one part might still trigger the trap. For example, if a trap has a trip wire in one location and launches an attack from another location, severing the trip wire could still trigger the attack. Destroying a trap in one blow almost never triggers it. These rules also apply to most damaging spells or other effects in addition to attacks.

REPAIRING A HAZARD

You might allow a character to repair a damaged hazard to restore its functionality. You determine the specifics of this, since it can vary by trap. The Repair action might be insufficient if fixing the trap requires gathering scattered components or the like. If the item has a Reset entry, the character needs to do whatever is listed there, in addition to repairing the damage.

COUNTERACTING A MAGICAL HAZARD

Some magical hazards can be counteracted using *dispel magic* and the counteracting rules found on page 458. These hazards' spell levels and counteract DCs are listed in their stat block. Counteracting a hazard otherwise works like using a skill check to disable the hazard.

HAZARD EXPERIENCE

Characters gain Experience Points for overcoming a hazard, whether they disable it, avoid it, or simply endure its attacks. If they trigger the same hazard later on, they don't gain XP for the hazard again. The XP values for hazards of different levels also appear on page 508, but are repeated here for convenience. The XP for a complex hazard is equal to the XP for a monster of the same level, and the XP for a simple hazard is one-fifth of that. Hazards of a lower level than the party's level − 4 are trivial and award no XP.

TABLE 10-14: HAZARD XP

Level	XP Award	
	Simple Hazard	Complex Hazard
Party level − 4	2 XP	10 XP
Party level − 3	3 XP	15 XP
Party level − 2	4 XP	20 XP
Party level − 1	6 XP	30 XP
Party level	8 XP	40 XP
Party level + 1	12 XP	60 XP
Party level + 2	16 XP	80 XP
Party level + 3	24 XP	120 XP
Party level + 4	30 XP	150 XP

INTRODUCTION

ANCESTRIES & BACKGROUNDS

CLASSES

SKILLS

FEATS

EQUIPMENT

SPELLS

THE AGE OF LOST OMENS

PLAYING THE GAME

GAME MASTERING

CRAFTING & TREASURE

APPENDIX

HAZARDS BY NAME

This chapter's hazards are organized by level and complexity. If you need to look up a hazard by its name, use the following table.

Hazard Name	Level	Complexity	Page
Armageddon orb	23	Simple	526
Banshee's symphony	18	Complex	529
Bloodthirsty urge	10	Simple	524
Bottomless pit	9	Simple	524
Darkside mirror	14	Complex	528
Drowning pit	3	Complex	526
Electric latch rune	3	Simple	523
Fireball rune	5	Simple	524
Frozen moment	17	Simple	525
Hallucination powder trap	6	Simple	524
Hammer of forbiddance	11	Simple	525
Hidden pit	0	Simple	522
Lava flume tube	10	Complex	528
Pharaoh's ward	7	Simple	524
Planar rift	13	Simple	525
Poisoned dart gallery	8	Complex	528
Poisoned lock	1	Simple	522
Polymorph trap	12	Simple	525
Quicksand	3	Complex	526
Scythe blades	4	Simple	523
Second chance	21	Simple	525
Slamming door	1	Simple	523
Spear launcher	2	Simple	523
Spinning blade pillar	4	Complex	527
Summoning rune	1	Complex	526
Telekinetic swarm trap	12	Complex	528
Vorpal executioner	19	Simple	525
Wheel of misery	6	Complex	527
Yellow mold	8	Simple	524

HAZARD FORMAT

Hazards are presented in a stat block format similar to those used for monsters. A few notes regarding the format follow the sample stat block.

HAZARD NAME   HAZARD [LEVEL]

TRAITS

Stealth This entry lists the Stealth modifier for a complex hazard's initiative or the Stealth DC to detect a simple hazard, followed by the minimum proficiency rank to detect the hazard (if any) in parentheses. If *detect magic* can be used to detect the hazard, this information is located here as well.

Description This explains what the hazard looks like and might include special rules.

Disable The DC of any skill checks required to disable the hazard are here; if the hazard can be counteracted, its spell level and counteract DC are listed in parentheses.

AC the hazard's AC; **Saving Throws** the hazard's saves. Usually only haunts are subject to Will saves.

Hardness the hazard's Hardness; **HP** the hazard's Hit Points, with its Broken Threshold in parentheses; **Immunities** the hazard's immunities; **Weaknesses** the hazard's weaknesses, if any; **Resistances** the hazard's resistances, if any

Action Type ↻ or ◆ This is the reaction or free action the hazard uses; **Trigger** The trigger that sets off the hazard appears here. **Effect** For a simple hazard, this effect is often all the hazard does. For a complex hazard, this might also cause the hazard to roll initiative.

Routine This section describes what a complex hazard does on each of its turns during an encounter; the number in parentheses after the word "Routine" indicates how many actions the hazard can use each turn. Simple hazards don't have this entry.

Action Any action the hazard can use appears here. Typically, this is a melee or ranged attack.

Reset If the hazard can be reset, that information is here.

LEVEL

The hazard's level indicates what level of party it's a good challenge for. If the hazard involves a toxin, curse, or other non-spell feature, that feature's level is the hazard's level.

TRAITS

The most notable hazard traits are trap (constructed to harm intruders), environmental (natural hazards), and haunt (spectral phenomena). Traps have a trait to indicate whether they're magical or mechanical. Hazards that have initiative and a routine have the complex trait.

STEALTH OR STEALTH DC

Complex hazards list their Stealth modifier, which they use for initiative, instead of their Stealth DC. If you need the DC, it's equal to this modifier + 10.

SIMPLE HAZARDS

A simple hazard uses its reaction only once, after which its threat is over unless the hazard is reset.

HIDDEN PIT   HAZARD 0

MECHANICAL **TRAP**

Stealth DC 18 (or 0 if the trapdoor is disabled or broken)

Description A wooden trapdoor covers a pit that's 10 feet square and 20 feet deep.

Disable Thievery DC 12 to remove the trapdoor

AC 10; **Fort** +1, **Ref** +1

Trapdoor Hardness 3, **Trapdoor HP** 12 (BT 6); **Immunities** critical hits, object immunities, precision damage

Pitfall ↻ **Trigger** A creature walks onto the trapdoor. **Effect** The triggering creature falls in and takes falling damage (typically 10 bludgeoning damage). That creature can use the Grab an Edge reaction to avoid falling.

Reset Creatures can still fall into the trap, but the trapdoor must be reset manually for the trap to become hidden again.

POISONED LOCK HAZARD 1

`MECHANICAL` `TRAP`

Stealth DC 17 (trained)

Description A spring-loaded, poisoned spine is hidden near the keyhole of a lock. Disabling or breaking the trap does not disable or break the lock.

Disable Thievery DC 17 (trained) on the spring mechanism

AC 15; **Fort** +8, **Ref** +4

Hardness 6, **HP** 24 (BT 12); **Immunities** critical hits, object immunities, precision damage

Spring ⟳ (attack); **Trigger** A creature tries to unlock or Pick the Lock. **Effect** A spine extends to attack the triggering creature.

Melee spine +13, **Damage** 1 piercing plus cladis poison

Cladis Poison (poison); **Saving Throw** DC 19 Fortitude; **Maximum Duration** 4 hours; **Stage 1** 1d6 poison damage and drained 1 (1 hour); **Stage 2** 2d6 poison damage and drained 2 (1 hour); **Stage 3** 3d6 poison damage and drained 2 (1 hour)

SLAMMING DOOR HAZARD 1

`MECHANICAL` `TRAP`

Stealth DC 17 (trained)

Description Pressure-sensitive panels in the floor connect to a stone slab hidden in a hallway's ceiling.

Disable Thievery DC 15 (trained) on the floor panels before the slab falls

AC 16; **Fort** +10, **Ref** +2

Hardness 5, **HP** 20 (BT 10); **Immunities** critical hits, object immunities, precision damage

Slam Shut ⟳ **Trigger** Pressure is placed on any floor tile. **Effect** The door falls, closing off the hallway. The stone slab deals 3d8 bludgeoning damage to anyone beneath or adjacent to the slab when it drops and pushes them out of its space in a random direction. A creature that succeeds at a DC 17 Reflex save takes no damage and rolls out of the way in a random direction. On a critical success, they can choose the direction.

Lifting the fallen slab requires a successful DC 25 Athletics check. Hitting the floor panels triggers the trap. The slab uses the same AC and saves as the trap, but it has Hardness 12, HP 48 (BT 24).

SPEAR LAUNCHER HAZARD 2

`MECHANICAL` `TRAP`

Stealth DC 20 (trained)

Description A wall socket loaded with a spear connects to a floor tile in one 5-foot square.

Disable Thievery DC 18 (trained) on the floor tile or wall socket

AC 18; **Fort** +11, **Ref** +3

Hardness 8, **HP** 32 (BT 16); **Immunities** critical hits, object immunities, precision damage

Spear ⟳ (attack); **Trigger** Pressure is applied to the floor tile. **Effect** The trap shoots a spear, making an attack against the creature or object on the floor tile.

Ranged spear +14, **Damage** 2d6+6 piercing

ELECTRIC LATCH RUNE HAZARD 3

`ELECTRICITY` `EVOCATION` `MAGICAL` `TRAP`

Stealth DC 20 (trained)

Description An invisible rune imprinted on a door latch releases a powerful electric discharge.

Disable Thievery DC 20 (expert) to scratch out the rune without allowing electricity to flow, or *dispel magic* (2nd level; counteract DC 18) to counteract the rune

Electrocution ⟳ (arcane, electricity, evocation); **Trigger** A creature grasps the door latch directly or with a tool. **Effect** The trap deals 3d12 electricity damage to the triggering creature (DC 22 basic Reflex save).

SCYTHE BLADES HAZARD 4

`MECHANICAL` `TRAP`

Stealth DC 23 (trained)

Description Two blades, each hidden in a 15-foot-long ceiling groove, are both connected to a trip wire.

Disable Thievery DC 21 (trained) to disable each blade

AC 21; **Fort** +12, **Ref** +8

Hardness 11, **HP** 44 (BT 22); **Immunities** critical hits, object immunities, precision damage

Falling Scythes ⟳ (attack); **Trigger** The trip wire is pulled or severed. **Effect** Both blades swing down, each one attacking all creatures under the ceiling grooves.

Melee scythe +17 (deadly 1d12), **Damage** 2d12+4 slashing; no multiple attack penalty

Reset The trap resets after 15 minutes.

FIREBALL RUNE   HAZARD 5

EVOCATION   FIRE   MAGICAL   TRAP

Stealth DC 24 (expert)

Description An invisible rune creates an invisible, spherical magical sensor with a 20-foot radius.

Disable Thievery DC 22 (expert) to erase the rune without triggering the sensor, or *dispel magic* (3rd level; counteract DC 20) to counteract the rune

Fireball ↻ (arcane, evocation, fire); **Trigger** A living creature enters the sensor area. **Effect** The rune detonates a *fireball* centered on the triggering creature's square. This is a 3rd-level *fireball* spell that deals 6d6 fire damage (DC 22 basic Reflex save).

HALLUCINATION POWDER TRAP   HAZARD 6

MECHANICAL   TRAP

Stealth DC 24 (expert)

Description A tube of hallucinogenic powder armed with a miniature explosive is connected to a doorknob or similar latch.

Disable Thievery DC 26 (expert) to disable the hammer that strikes the percussion cap

AC 24; **Fort** +0, **Ref** +0

Hardness 0, **HP** 1; **Immunities** critical hits, object immunities, precision damage

Powder Burst ↻ (mental, poison); **Trigger** The latch is opened or the tube is broken. **Effect** The tube explodes, spraying hallucinogenic powder in a 30-foot cone. Any creature in the cone must succeed at a DC 24 Will save or be confused for 1 round and take a –2 status penalty to Perception checks and saves against mental effects for 1d4 hours. On a critical failure, the penalty is instead –4.

PHARAOH'S WARD   HAZARD 7

MAGICAL   TRAP

Stealth DC 25 (expert)

Description A curse is imbued on an entryway's threshold.

Disable Thievery DC 27 (master) to painstakingly remove the lintel without triggering the magic, or *dispel magic* (4th level; counteract DC 25) to counteract the rune

Curse the Intruders ↻ (curse, divine, necromancy); **Trigger** The seal on the tomb is broken from the outside. **Effect** Each living creature within 60 feet must succeed at a DC 23 Will save or be subjected to the pharaoh's curse. A cursed creature takes a –2 status penalty to Fortitude saves, and any natural or magical healing it receives is halved. The curse remains until removed by *remove curse* or similar magic.

Reset The trap resets when the door is shut.

YELLOW MOLD   HAZARD 8

ENVIRONMENTAL   FUNGUS

Stealth DC 28 (trained)

Description Poisonous mold spores assault nearby creatures.

Disable Survival DC 26 (expert) to remove the mold without triggering the spores

AC 27; **Fort** +17, **Ref** +13

HP 70; **Immunities** critical hits, object immunities, precision damage

Spore Explosion ↻ **Trigger** A creature moves into the mold's space or damages the mold. The mold can't use this reaction if it's in direct sunlight or if the damage was fire damage. **Effect** The triggering creature and all creatures within 10 feet are exposed to yellow mold spores.

Yellow Mold Spores (inhaled, poison) Any drained condition from the spores persists after the poison's duration ends; **Saving Throw** DC 26 Fortitude; **Maximum Duration** 6 rounds; **Stage 1** 1d8 poison damage and drained 1 (1 round); **Stage 2** 2d8 poison damage and drained 2 (1 round); **Stage 3** 3d8 poison damage and drained 3 (1 round)

BOTTOMLESS PIT   HAZARD 9

MAGICAL   MECHANICAL   TRAP

Stealth DC 30 (or 0 if the trapdoor is disabled or broken) or *detect magic*

Description An iron trapdoor covers an infinitely deep 10-foot-square pit.

Disable Thievery DC 28 (trained) to remove the trapdoor

AC 28; **Fort** +12, **Ref** +12

Trapdoor Hardness 9, **Trapdoor HP** 36 (BT 18); **Immunities** critical hits, object immunities, precision damage

Infinite Pitfall ↻ **Trigger** A creature walks onto the trapdoor. **Effect** The triggering creature falls in and continues to fall, potentially forever. That creature can try to Grab an Edge to avoid falling (page 472). The DC to Climb the walls or Grab an Edge is 26.

The pit contains many handholds, so the falling creature can try to Grab an Edge again every 6 seconds. If the creature succeeds, it can start to Climb out from that point (though it might be a very long climb, depending on how far the creature fell). Since the creature falls endlessly, it can rest and even prepare spells while falling, though items dropped while falling are usually lost forever.

Reset The trap still causes creatures to fall forever if they fall in, but the trapdoor must be reset manually for the trap to become hidden again.

BLOODTHIRSTY URGE   HAZARD 10

HAUNT

Stealth DC 31 (trained)

Description An object haunted by the echoes of a vicious mind attempts to kill someone who comes near.

Disable Religion DC 29 (master) to exorcise the spirit or Diplomacy DC 31 (expert) to talk it down

Quietus ↻ (death, emotion, fear, illusion, mental, occult); **Trigger** A creature moves within 10 feet of the haunted object. **Effect** The haunt takes control of the triggering creature, forcing it to attack itself. The creature must attempt a DC 29 Will save.

Critical Success The target is unaffected.

Success The target makes a Strike against itself and automatically hits; the target also becomes frightened 1.

Failure The target makes a Strike against itself and automatically scores a critical hit; the target also becomes frightened 2.

Critical Failure The target attempts a Fortitude save. If the target succeeds, it is subject to the effects of a failure instead. If the target fails, it is reduced to 0 Hit Points and dies.

HAMMER OF FORBIDDANCE — HAZARD 11

MAGICAL   MECHANICAL   TRAP

Stealth DC 30 (expert)

Description An enormous hammer at an edifice's entrance swings down in an attempt to damage a creature entering an area, push it back, and prevent it from going any further.

Disable Thievery DC 28 (expert) once on the hammer itself and once on its joint to prevent the hammer from swinging

AC 32; **Fort** +24, **Ref** +15

Hammer Hardness 22, **Hammer HP** 88 (BT 44); **Joint Hardness** 16, **Joint HP** 64 (BT 32); **Immunities** critical hits, object immunities, precision damage

Forbid Entry ⤵ (abjuration, attack, divine); **Trigger** A creature attempts to enter through the entrance. **Effect** The hammer swings down, making an attack against the triggering creature.

Melee hammer +28, **Damage** 6d8+20 bludgeoning plus the target is knocked back 10 feet and must succeed at a DC 30 Will save or be unable to enter the edifice through any entrance for 24 hours (on a critical hit, the target automatically fails the Will save); no multiple attack penalty

Reset The trap resets over the course of the round, and is ready to swing again 1 round later.

POLYMORPH TRAP — HAZARD 12

MAGICAL   TRAP

Stealth DC 34 (trained)

Description A Druidic glyph tries to transforms a trespasser into an animal.

Disable Thievery DC 32 (master) to drain the glyph's power harmlessly, or *dispel magic* (6th level; counteract DC 30) to counteract the glyph

Baleful Polymorph ⤵ (primal, transmutation); **Trigger** A creature moves within 30 feet of the glyph without speaking the passphrase in Druidic. **Effect** The creature is targeted by *baleful polymorph* (DC 32 Will save).

PLANAR RIFT — HAZARD 13

MAGICAL   TRAP

Stealth DC 35 (trained)

Description A rift attempts to draw creatures into another plane (the GM chooses the specific plane).

Disable Thievery DC 33 (master) to assemble a rift seal using objects strongly grounded to your plane, or *dispel magic* (7th level; counteract DC 31) to counteract the rift

Into the Great Beyond ⤵ (conjuration, occult, teleportation); **Trigger** A creature moves within 10 feet of the rift. **Effect** The triggering creature and all creatures within 30 feet of the rift are drawn into another plane. Each creature can attempt a DC 33 Reflex save to avoid this fate.

FROZEN MOMENT — HAZARD 17

MAGICAL   TRAP

Stealth DC 40 (master)

Description Warding magic attempts to trap intruders or would-be thieves in a disrupted time flow.

Disable Thievery DC 38 (legendary) to rapidly disassemble the spell's myriad components in a single blink of an eye; or *dispel magic* (9th level; counteract DC 36) to counteract the trap before it triggers or to counteract the effect on one creature after the trap is triggered

Adrift in Time ⤵ (occult, transmutation); **Trigger** A creature touches the warded object or area. **Effect** The triggering creature and all creatures within 30 feet are trapped in a disrupted time flow (DC 38 Fortitude negates). The creatures' minds move so quickly that each round seems to last a century, but their bodies and magical energies move so slowly that they can't use any actions except Recall Knowledge. An affected creature must attempt a DC 36 Will saving throw against a *warp mind* spell immediately and again for every minute of real time that passes while the creature is trapped in the frozen moment. This effect has an unlimited duration but can be counteracted.

VORPAL EXECUTIONER — HAZARD 19

MECHANICAL   TRAP

Stealth DC 43 (expert)

Description A wickedly sharp saw blade descends and travels along grooves in a complex path throughout the room, attempting to decapitate everyone within.

Disable Thievery DC 41 (expert) at four different junctions to jam all the saw blade's possible paths, preventing it from traveling through the room

AC 43; **Fort** +32, **Ref** +32

Hardness 30; **HP** 120 (BT 60) per junction; **Immunities** critical hits, object immunities, precision damage

Total Decapitation ⤵ (attack, death); **Trigger** A creature attempts to exit the room. **Effect** The saw blade travels along its path, making one Strike against each creature in the room, twisting and varying its height for a maximum chance of beheading its targets.

Melee saw blade +40 (deadly d12), **Damage** 6d12+25 slashing plus decapitation; no multiple attack penalty

Decapitation On a critical hit, a target must succeed at a DC 39 Fortitude save or be decapitated, dying instantly unless it can survive without a head.

Reset The trap resets over the course of the round and can be triggered again 1 round later.

SECOND CHANCE — HAZARD 21

MAGICAL   TRAP

Stealth DC 44 (legendary)

Description Powerful warding magic tied to an object or location tries to regress the ages of a creature and its allies.

Disable Thievery DC 46 (legendary) to take apart the spell one tiny piece at a time, with eyes closed, while recalling every vivid life memory in order, starting from the earliest memory

In the Beginning ⤵ (divine, transmutation); **Trigger** A creature tries to steal the object or intrude upon the location. If someone uses a proxy or dupe for the theft or intrusion, the

UPGRADED SUMMONING RUNES

You can make a summoning rune of nearly any level. It summons a creature of a level equal to the trap's level. Use Table 10-5: DCs by Level on page 503 to determine the Thievery DC and spell DC, using the trap's level and applying a hard adjustment (+2). The Stealth modifier for the trap is equal to this number – 10. Stronger summoning runes usually require expert proficiency or better in Perception to find, and they might require a higher proficiency rank in Thievery to disable.

trap unerringly targets the true perpetrator or perpetrators at any distance—even across planes. **Effect** The triggering creature and up to five coconspirators instantly revert to infants, losing all memories, class abilities, and other skills acquired during their lives (DC 44 Fortitude negates). Reversing this effect is nearly impossible, requiring powerful magic such as *wish*.

ARMAGEDDON ORB   HAZARD 23

RARE MAGICAL TRAP

Stealth DC 10 or *detect magic*

Description A roiling red orb, forged from a drop of the god Rovagug's blood, rains fire from the sky when a specified condition is met.

Disable Thievery DC 48 (legendary) to imbue thieves' tools with aspects representing Asmodeus and Sarenrae and use them to drain away the orb's power over 10 minutes; the character attempting this check takes 5 fire damage each round until the orb is depleted

Burn It All ⤴ (death, divine, evocation, fire); **Trigger** A special condition set by the trap's creator occurs; this is typically the event of their death. **Effect** Fire rains from the sky in a 100-mile radius, dealing 10d6 fire damage to creatures and objects in the area. Each creature or object can attempt a DC 46 basic Reflex save. Any creature reduced to 0 Hit Points by this damage dies instantly. This is not enough damage to completely burn away a forest or level an entire mountain or city, but it typically kills most creatures in the area.

COMPLEX HAZARDS

Complex hazards function similarly to monsters during encounters, as they roll initiative and have actions of their own, though these are usually automated in a routine.

SUMMONING RUNE   HAZARD 1

COMPLEX MAGICAL TRAP

Stealth +7 (trained)

Description A cloud of invisible magical sensors in a 10-foot radius surrounds an invisible wall or floor rune the size of the creature to be summoned.

Disable Acrobatics DC 15 to approach without triggering the trap followed by Thievery DC 17 (trained) to erase the rune, or *dispel magic* (1st level; counteract DC 15) to counteract the rune

Summon Monster ⤴ (arcane, conjuration, summon; **Trigger** A creature enters the cloud of magical sensors. **Effect** This trap summons a specific level 1 creature, determined when the trap is created. The creature rolls initiative and remains for 2d6 rounds, after which the spell ends and the creature disappears. The creature also disappears if someone disables the trap before the duration expires. The summoned creature can use 3 actions each round and can use reactions, unlike most summoned creatures.

Reset The trap resets each day at dawn.

DROWNING PIT   HAZARD 3

COMPLEX MECHANICAL TRAP

Stealth +10 (trained); DC 22 (expert) to notice the water spouts once the pit opens

Description A trapdoor covers a 10-foot-square pit that's 30 feet deep and has 5 feet of water at the bottom. Four water spouts in the walls connect to hidden water tanks. Each water spout extends out of a different wall, 6 inches from the top of the pit.

Disable Thievery DC 18 (trained) to seal each water spout, Thievery DC 22 (trained) to open the trapdoor, or Athletics DC 22 to Force Open the trapdoor

AC 19; **Fort** +8, **Ref** +5

Trapdoor Hardness 15, **Trapdoor HP** 60 (BT 30); **Spout Hardness** 8, **Spout HP** 32 (BT 16); **Immunities** critical hits, object immunities, precision damage

Pitfall ⤴ **Trigger** A creature walks onto the trapdoor. **Effect** The triggering creature falls in and takes damage from the fall, reduced by 5 feet for falling into the water (typically 12 bludgeoning damage). A creature can Grab an Edge to avoid falling (page 472). The trapdoor then slams shut, and the hazard rolls initiative.

Routine (4 actions) The trap loses 1 action each turn for each disabled water spout. On each of the trap's actions, a spout pours water, increasing the depth of the water by 5 feet. Once the pit is full of water, the pit stops using actions, but creatures in the pit begin drowning (page 478).

Reset The trap can be reset if the door is manually reengaged and the water tanks refilled; it can be reset without draining the pit, but doing so renders it less effective.

QUICKSAND   HAZARD 3

COMPLEX ENVIRONMENTAL

Stealth +12 (trained) (or –10 and no minimum proficiency if the surface is disturbed)

Description A 15-foot-wide patch of water and sand attempts to submerge creatures that step onto it.

Disable Survival DC 18 (trained) to disturb the surface

Submerge ◆ **Trigger** A Huge or smaller creature walks onto the quicksand. **Effect** The triggering creature sinks into the quicksand up to its waist. The quicksand rolls initiative if it hasn't already.

Routine (1 action) On its initiative, the quicksand pulls down each creature within it. A creature that was submerged up to its waist becomes submerged up to its neck, and a creature that was submerged up to its neck is pulled under and has to hold its breath to avoid suffocation (page 478).

A creature in the quicksand can attempt a DC 20 Athletics check to Swim to either raise itself by one step if it's submerged to its neck or worse, or to move 5 feet if it's submerged only up to its waist. On a critical failure, the creature is pulled down one step. A creature that Swims out of the quicksand escapes the hazard and is prone in a space adjacent to the quicksand patch. Other creatures can Aid the creature, typically by using a rope or similar aid, or attempt to pull the creature out with their own DC 20 Athletics check, with the same results as if the creature attempted the check.

Reset The hazard still submerges anyone who walks in, but the surface doesn't become hidden again until it settles over the course of 24 hours.

SPINNING BLADE PILLAR — HAZARD 4

`COMPLEX` `MECHANICAL` `TRAP`

Stealth +11 (trained) or DC 26 (expert) to notice the control panel

Description A metal pole with three razor-sharp spinning blades is hidden in the floor, connected to trigger plates in up to eight floor tiles and a hidden control panel within 30 feet.

Disable Thievery DC 21 (trained) twice on the pillar, or Thievery DC 19 (expert) once on the control panel deactivates the whole trap. Breaking the control panel prevents anyone from disabling the trap using the control panel and prevents the trap from deactivating automatically (see Reset below).

AC 21; **Fort** +10, **Ref** +12

Pillar Hardness 12, **Pillar HP** 48 (BT 24); **Panel Hardness** 5, **Panel HP** 20 (BT 10); **Immunities** critical hits, object immunities, precision damage

Rising Pillar ⟳ (attack); **Trigger** A creature steps on one of the trapped floor tiles. **Effect** The trap pops up in a grid intersection and makes a spinning blade attack against one adjacent creature (if any), then rolls initiative.

Routine (3 actions) The trap uses its first action to make a spinning blade Strike against each adjacent creature, its second action to move straight in a random direction (roll 1d4 to determine the direction), and its third action to make a spinning blade Strike against each adjacent creature. This trap doesn't take a multiple attack penalty.

Speed 10 feet

Melee ◆ spinning blade +12, **Damage** 2d10+5 slashing

Reset The trap deactivates and resets after 1 minute.

WHEEL OF MISERY — HAZARD 6

`COMPLEX` `MAGICAL` `MECHANICAL` `TRAP`

Stealth +16 (expert) to detect the magical sensor; noticing the wheel has a DC of 0

Description An ornate wheel set into a wall—divided into six segments with colored

runes on each—is controlled by a magical sensor that detects any creature within 100 feet in front of it.

Disable Thievery DC 26 (expert) on the wheel to stop it from spinning, Thievery DC 22 (master) to erase each rune, or *dispel magic* (4th level; counteract DC 22) to counteract each rune

AC 24; **Fort** +15, **Ref** +13

Hardness 14, **HP** 56 (BT 28); **Immunities** critical hits, object immunities, precision damage

Wheel Spin ⟳ **Trigger** A creature enters the sensor's detection area. **Effect** The wheel begins to spin and rolls initiative.

Routine (2 actions) On its initiative, the trap uses its first action to spin, then stops. Roll 1d6 to determine which segment is topmost when the wheel stops spinning. The wheel uses its second action to replicate the spell listed for that segment (3rd level, DC 24, spell attack roll +14). This spell's target is centered on or otherwise includes the nearest creature in the area. This increases the spell's range to 100 feet if necessary. Any spell cast by this trap is arcane.

1 *sleep*
2 *paralyze*
3 *lightning bolt* (100-foot line)
4 *blindness*
5 *acid arrow*
6 *ray of enfeeblement*

Reset The trap deactivates and resets if 1 minute passes without any creature moving within range of its sensor.

POISONED DART GALLERY   HAZARD 8

COMPLEX   MECHANICAL   TRAP

Stealth +16 (expert) or DC 31 (master) to notice the control panel

Description Countless holes to launch poison darts from line a long hallway with a hidden control panel on the far end.

Disable Thievery DC 21 (expert) on the control panel deactivates the trap.

AC 27; **Fort** +13, **Ref** +17

Hardness 14; **HP** 56 (BT 28) to destroy the control panel and disable the trap; **Immunities** critical hits, object immunities, precision damage

Dart Volley ⟳ (attack); **Trigger** A creature enters the hallway or ends its turn in the hallway. **Effect** The trap makes a poisoned dart Strike against the triggering creature, then rolls initiative.

Routine (1 action) The trap launches one dart against every creature in the gallery as 1 action. Because it launches darts continuously, the trap can also use the Continuous Barrage free action (see below) to launch darts at each creature during that creature's turn.

Ranged poisoned dart +21, **Damage** 3d4 piercing plus flesset poison; no multiple attack penalty

Continuous Barrage ❖ **Trigger** A creature within the active gallery finishes an action. **Effect** The trap makes a poisoned dart Strike against the triggering creature.

Flesset Poison (poison); **Saving Throw** DC 22 Fortitude; **Maximum Duration** 6 rounds; **Stage 1** 1d6 poison damage and clumsy 1 (1 round); **Stage 2** 2d6 poison damage and clumsy 2 (1 round); **Stage 3** 3d6 poison damage and clumsy 3 (1 round)

Reset The trap deactivates and resets after 1 minute.

LAVA FLUME TUBE   HAZARD 10

COMPLEX   MECHANICAL   TRAP

Stealth +19 (trained)

Description Four gated channels carved into stone allow lava to flow into a 15-foot-tall room; the floor can withdraw to allow the hardened lava to fall into a chamber beneath.

Disable Thievery DC 29 (expert) to block a channel, or Thievery DC 31 (master) to release the floor latch and escape to the chamber below

AC 30; **Fort** +20, **Ref** +16

Channel Hardness 12, **Channel HP** 48 (BT 24) to destroy a channel gate (this prevents that channel from being disabled and stops the trap from resetting); **Floor Hardness** 18; **Floor HP** 72 (BT 36); **Immunities** critical hits, object immunities, precision damage

Flume Activation ⟳ **Trigger** A creature tries to leave the room. **Effect** The exits seal instantly and the trap rolls initiative.

Routine (4 actions) The trap loses 1 action per disabled channel each turn. On each action, a different channel spews lava, dealing 4d6 fire damage to each creature within 10 feet of the channel (DC 27 basic Reflex save), and increasing the depth of the lava in the room by 1 foot (4 feet per round if all the channels are active).

A creature that starts its turn in lava takes 8d6 fire damage and is immobilized until it Escapes the hardening lava (DC 27).

The creature might suffocate if covered in lava (page 478). Lava from the previous round hardens fully at the start of the trap's turn, effectively raising the floor of the room. Once the room is full of lava, the trap stops taking actions, but creatures in the room remain stuck until the floor opens and the trap resets.

Reset The trap deactivates and resets after 1 hour by withdrawing the floor, cracking and dumping the hardened lava (and any creatures trapped inside) into the chamber. Creatures fall 40 feet, taking falling damage (typically 17 bludgeoning damage).

TELEKINETIC SWARM TRAP   HAZARD 12

COMPLEX   MAGICAL   MECHANICAL   TRAP

Stealth +24 (expert)

Description Three innocuous decorations instilled with telekinetic magic pull objects and pieces of the room itself into spinning clouds of debris that attack all creatures in the room.

Disable Thievery DC 27 (expert) to take apart a telekinetic cloud, Thievery DC 32 (master) to disable each telekinetic decoration, or *dispel magic* (6th level; counteract DC 30) to counteract each telekinetic decoration

AC 33; **Fort** +24, **Ref** +19

Hardness 22, **HP** 88 (BT 44) per telekinetic cloud

Agitate ⟳ (arcane, evocation); **Trigger** A creature stays in the room for at least 6 seconds. **Effect** Each telekinetic decoration constructs a cloud of objects in the room (three clouds total) and the trap rolls initiative. The creatures in the room when the trap is triggered become the trap's targets, regardless of whether they leave the room or other creatures later enter the room. Each decoration targets a different creature if possible. A target creature that moves at least 1 mile from the trap ceases being a target, at which point the decoration designates a new target.

Routine (9 actions) Each decoration uses 3 of the trap's actions each turn, and the trap loses 3 actions each turn for every decoration that is disabled. A decoration uses its first action to move its cloud of objects up to 200 feet, its second action to make the objects Strike, and its third action to add more objects to the cloud, increasing its damage by 1d12 (to a maximum of 4d12+10). If a decoration's cloud is already at maximum damage, it does nothing with its third action.

If a decoration's cloud has been destroyed, the decoration instead spends its first action to create a new cloud of objects inside the room (using the starting damage value) and then its second and third actions to have the cloud move and attack.

Melee ❖ objects +24, **Damage** 2d12+10 bludgeoning

Reset The trap deactivates and resets 10 minutes after it has no target creatures (because the creatures either moved too far away or died).

DARKSIDE MIRROR   HAZARD 14

COMPLEX   MAGICAL   MECHANICAL   TRAP

Stealth +24 (master) to notice it isn't a regular mirror

Description A magic mirror replaces characters with evil mirror duplicates from another dimension.

Disable Thievery DC 34 (legendary) to retrieve a creature from the other dimension within 10 minutes of the switch (possible only if their mirror duplicate is dead), Thievery DC 39 (master) to permanently disable the mirror once all mirror duplicates are dead, or *dispel magic* (7th level; counteract DC 32) to counteract the mirror for 1 minute and prevent additional replacements during that time

AC 34; **Fort** +25, **Ref** +20

Hardness 1, **HP** 4 (BT 2), the mirror can't be damaged while any mirror duplicate is alive

Reflection of Evil ⟳ (arcane, conjuration, teleportation); **Trigger** A non-evil creature is reflected in the mirror. **Effect** The mirror absorbs the creature into the mirror, replacing it with an evil mirror duplicate (DC 34 Reflex to avoid being absorbed into the mirror), and rolls initiative.

Routine (1 action) The mirror absorbs another reflected creature into the mirror and replaces it with a mirror duplicate. Mirror duplicates attack on their own initiative, using the same statistics as the original creature, but with an evil alignment (changing only abilities that shift with the alignment change). A mirror duplicate can spend 3 actions in contact with the mirror to return to its original dimension and release the creature it duplicated, but most mirror duplicates prefer not to.

Reset The mirror is always ready to absorb creatures into the other dimension. Ten minutes after a creature is sucked into the mirror, if an ally doesn't rescue the creature with Thievery, it reaches the other dimension, where it might be captured or killed. In the mirror dimension, it counts as a mirror duplicate, so the denizens of the other dimension can't destroy the mirror on their side while the absorbed creature is there. These dimensions are alternate realities, not planes, so even rituals like *plane shift* can't reach them.

BANSHEE'S SYMPHONY HAZARD 18

COMPLEX　MAGICAL　TRAP

Stealth +30 (legendary)

Description A magically contagious *wail of the banshee* spell is trapped in the larynx of an invisible, mummified elf.

Disable Thievery DC 42 (master) to pierce the invisible larynx so precisely that the magic releases in a trickle before the trap activates, Thievery DC 44 (legendary) three times to deconstruct the larynx while the trap is active in such a way that it tears the spell apart, or spell DC 38 (9th level) to counteract the *wail of the banshee* before the trap activates

Scream ⟳ **Trigger** Three or more living creatures remain within 100 feet of the trap for 6 seconds or longer. **Effect** The trap releases an arcane *wail of the banshee* (DC 40) with a 100-foot-radius emanation instead of 40 feet, targeting all living creatures in the area, and rolls initiative.

Routine (1 action) The trap uses its action to force one random creature that failed its save against *wail of the banshee* last turn to emit a *wail of the banshee* with the same statistics as the initial one. The creature wails even if it is dead or unable to speak, no matter how far away from the trap it is. Unlike a casting of the spell, the drained condition from this trap's *wail of the banshee* spells increases the targets' drained condition values. A creature that critically succeeds at any of its saves can still be affected by the trap on future rounds, but can't be forced to wail by the trap.

Reset The trap ends when the trap is unable to make a creature scream (usually because no creature failed its save on the previous turn or because all creatures have critically succeeded in the past). It then resets over 24 hours, as a new scream builds up in the mummified larynx.

CHAPTER 11: CRAFTING & TREASURE

Characters acquire treasure from the glittering hoards of their foes, as rewards for defending the innocent, and as favors from the grand personalities they treat with. As they progress through their adventures and improve their station in the world, characters collect ever more fabulous items from enchanted armor and weapons to spell-infused staves.

Treasure comes in all sorts of forms, from humble copper coins to incredibly powerful and valuable magic items. The GM controls the flow of items in the game as the PCs win them through adventures, find them for purchase, or acquire the formulas to make the items themselves.

Items can support characters by granting bonuses to their statistics, allowing them to cast more spells, and creating all sorts of effects that can't be achieved in any other way. Magic items come in many varieties, from enchanted swords that can harm even incorporeal undead to containers that can store a king's ransom within a tiny space; many are permanent items that can be used repeatedly. Alchemical items, by contrast, are not intrinsically magical and are often consumed when used. Both have a variety of uses, from curing the sick to lighting foes on fire. Some treasures are neither magical nor alchemical, but are instead crafted from precious materials or using specialized expertise.

This chapter provides rules for using different kinds of items encountered in the game. Rules for distributing treasure and creating treasure hoards can be found on page 508 of Chapter 10: Game Mastering.

- **Using Items**, beginning below, describes how to activate items and explains the statistics for items.
- **Table 11–1: Treasure by Level**, beginning on page 536, lists the options for treasures, arranged by level, category, and Price.
- The catalog of items, which begins on page 543, presents descriptions and rules for all sorts of different treasures that can appear in the game, sorted by category (page 533 has a list of key categories and subcategories). This also includes a section on precious materials found in the game world, which can give items unusual properties.

USING ITEMS

This section presents the rules for how characters use alchemical items, magic items, and other special items during play.

The myriad types of items give their powerful boons in different ways. Some function automatically, while others need to be activated. While you need only swing a *flaming greataxe* to scorch foes, you need to invest a *diadem of intellect* for it to work, imbibe an elixir of life to heal yourself, activate *slippers of spider climbing* to walk up a wall, activate your *mail of luck* to protect yourself, and Cast a Spell using a magical scroll.

CONSTANT ABILITIES

Some magic items have abilities that always function. You don't have to use any actions to do anything special (beyond wearing and investing a worn item or wielding a held item) to make these abilities work. For example, an *everburning torch* always sheds light, and a *flaming* weapon deals fire damage every time it deals damage.

INVESTING MAGIC ITEMS

Certain magic items convey their magical benefits only when worn and invested using the Invest an Item activity, tying them to your inner potential. These items have the invested trait. Many invested items have constant abilities that function all the time or that always trigger when you use the item—but only when they're invested. If you don't have an item invested, these abilities don't work. If an invested item can be activated, you must have invested the item to activate it.

You can benefit from no more than 10 invested magic items each day. Because this limit is fairly high, and because it matters only for worn items, you probably won't need to worry about reaching the limit until higher levels, when you've acquired many useful magic items to wear.

You can still gain the mundane benefits of an item if you don't invest it. A suit of *+1 resilient armor* still gives you its item bonus to AC when not invested, but it doesn't give its magical bonus to saving throws, and *winged boots* still protect your feet even though you can't activate them to fly. Entirely non-magical items don't need to be invested.

INVEST AN ITEM

You invest your energy in an item with the invested trait as you don it. This process requires 1 or more Interact actions, usually taking the same amount of time it takes to don the item. Once you've Invested the Item, you benefit from its constant magical abilities as long as you meet its other requirements (for most invested items, the only other requirement is that you must be wearing the item). This investiture lasts until you remove the item.

You can invest no more than 10 items per day. If you remove an invested item, it loses its investiture. The item still counts against your daily limit after it loses its investiture. You reset the limit during your daily preparations, at which point you Invest your Items anew. If you're still wearing items you had invested the previous day, you can typically keep them invested on the new day, but they still count against your limit.

11

INTRODUCTION

ANCESTRIES & BACKGROUNDS

CLASSES

SKILLS

FEATS

EQUIPMENT

SPELLS

THE AGE OF LOST OMENS

PLAYING THE GAME

GAME MASTERING

CRAFTING & TREASURE

APPENDIX

DISRUPTING ACTIVATIONS

Some abilities and effects can disrupt the process of
Activating an Item. If something disrupts your item
activation, you fail to Activate the Item and lose the
actions you committed. If the item can be activated only
a certain number of times per day, the failed activation
still counts against that limit. If an item requires you to
spend actions to Sustain an Activation and one of those
actions is disrupted, the item's effect ends.

ACTIVATING ITEMS

Some items produce their effects only when used properly
in the moment. Others always offer the same benefits as
their mundane counterparts when worn, but have magical
abilities you can gain by further spending actions. Either
case requires you to use the Activate an Item activity.
Activating an Item works much like Casting a Spell, in that
the activity takes a variable number of actions and can have
different components depending on how you Activate the
Item. This information appears in the item's Activate entry.

If an item is used up when activated, as is the case for
consumable items, its Activate entry appears toward the
top of the stat block. For permanent items with activated
abilities, the Activate entry is a paragraph in the description.
Activations are not necessarily magical—for instance,
drinking an alchemical elixir isn't usually a magical effect.

ACTIVATE AN ITEM

Requirement You can Activate an Item with the invested
trait only if it's invested by you. If the item requires you to
Interact with it, you must be wielding it (if it's a held item)
or touching it with a free hand (if it's another type of item).

You call forth the effect of an item by properly activating
it. This is a special activity that takes a variable number of
actions, as listed in the item's stat block.

Some items can be activated as a reaction or free action. In
this case, you Activate the Item as a reaction or free action (as
appropriate) instead of as an activity. Such cases are noted
in the item's Activate entry in its stat block—for example,
"**Activate** ⟳ command."

Long Activation Times Some items take minutes or hours
to activate. The Activate an Item activity for these items
includes a mix of the listed activation components, but it's not
necessary to break down which one you're providing at a given
time. You can't use other actions or reactions while activating
such an item, though at the GM's discretion, you might be able
to speak a few sentences. As with other activities that take
a long time, these activations have the exploration trait, and
you can't activate them in an encounter. If combat breaks out
while you're activating one, your activation is disrupted (see
the Disrupting Activations sidebar).

Activation Components Each activation entry lists any
components involved in the activation after the action icons
or text, such as "◆ command." The activation components,

described below, add traits (listed in parentheses) and requirements to the activation. If you can't provide the components, you fail to Activate the Item.

- Command (auditory, concentrate)
- Envision (concentrate)
- Interact (manipulate)
- Cast a Spell

ACTIVATION COMPONENTS

An item's activate entry lists the components required to activate its abilities. Each component adds certain traits to the Activate an Item activity, and some components have special requirements. The components that appear in this book are listed below.

COMMAND

This component is a specific utterance you must make in a loud and strong voice. Activate an Item gains the auditory and concentrate traits. You must be able to speak to provide this component.

ENVISION

This component is a specific image or phenomenon you need to imagine. Activate an Item gains the concentrate trait.

INTERACT

This component works like the Interact basic action. Activate an Item gains the manipulate trait and requires you to use your hands, just like with any Interact action.

CAST A SPELL

If an item lists "Cast a Spell" after "Activate," the activation requires you to use the Cast a Spell activity (described on page 302) to Activate the Item. This happens when the item replicates a spell. You must have a spellcasting class feature to Activate an Item with this activation component. If the item can be used for a specific spell, the action icon for that spell is provided. If it's an item like a staff, which can be used for many spells, the icon is omitted, and you must refer to each spell to determine which actions you must spend to Activate the Item to cast it.

In this case, Activate an Item gains all the traits from the relevant components of the Cast a Spell activity.

LIMITED ACTIVATIONS

Some items can be activated only a limited number of times per day, as described in the items. This limit is independent of any costs for activating the item. The limit resets during your daily preparations. The limit is inherent to the item, so if an ability that can be used only once per day is used, it doesn't refresh if another creature later invests or tries to activate the item.

SUSTAINING ACTIVATIONS

Some items, once activated, have effects that can be sustained if you concentrate on them. This works much

ITEM CATEGORIES

Items are grouped into the following categories, shown here with the page number where those items appear and a brief description of the category.

- **Alchemical Items** (page 543) are powered by the reactions of alchemical reagents. Almost all alchemical items are consumable items that are used up when you activate them. This category includes bombs, elixirs (including mutagens), poisons, and alchemical tools.
- **Ammunition** (page 559), in Consumables, includes different types of magical arrows, crossbow bolts, and other types of ammunition.
- **Apex Items** (page 603) are a subcategory of worn items of a high level that increase an ability score.
- **Armor** (page 555) includes the rules for basic magical armor as well as special suits of armor.
- **Companion Items** (page 604) are a category of worn items meant for animal companions and mounts.
- **Consumables** (page 559) are used up when you activate them, and include ammunition, oils, potions, scrolls, and talismans, among others. Categories of items that are consumables but have specific rules, such as alchemical items, are presented separately.
- **Held Items** (page 572) include a wide variety of items you use with your hands. This doesn't include more narrow categories of held items, such as weapons.
- **Materials** (page 577) can be used to make items with unique properties and other advantages.
- **Oils** (page 561) are consumables applied to the surface of an object or person.
- **Potions** (page 562) are consumable magical liquids you drink to activate.
- **Runes** (page 580) modify armor and weapons when etched onto them. This section includes fundamental runes for weapons (*weapon potency* and *striking*) and armor (*armor potency* and *resilient*).
- **Scrolls** (page 564) are consumables that allow spellcasters to cast more spells.
- **Shields** (page 586) include more durable shields and ones with special magical powers.
- **Snares** (page 589) are single-use traps typically made by rangers.
- **Staves** (page 592) provide flexible spellcasting options.
- **Structures** (page 596) include buildings, tents, and other larger items.
- **Talismans** (page 565) are consumables that are affixed to items and then activated for a one-time combat or physical benefit.
- **Wands** (page 597) hold a spell of the crafter's choice, and can be used to repeatedly cast that spell.
- **Weapons** (page 599) include the rules for basic magical weapons, weapons made from precious materials, and specific magic weapons.
- **Worn Items** (page 603) consist of a vast collection of clothing and other items you wear on your body.

INTRODUCTION

ANCESTRIES & BACKGROUNDS

CLASSES

SKILLS

FEATS

EQUIPMENT

SPELLS

THE AGE OF LOST OMENS

PLAYING THE GAME

GAME MASTERING

CRAFTING & TREASURE

APPENDIX

like the Sustain a Spell action (found on page 304). If an item's description states that you can sustain the effect, that effect lasts until the end of your turn in the round after you Activated the Item. You can use a Sustain an Activation action on that turn to extend the duration.

❖ SUSTAIN AN ACTIVATION

`CONCENTRATE`

Requirements You have at least one magic item activation that you can sustain, and you are not fatigued.

Choose one magic item activation with a sustained duration you have in effect. The duration of that activation continues until the end of your next turn. Some activations may have slightly different or expanded effects if you sustain them. Sustaining an Activation for more than 10 minutes (100 rounds) ends the activation and makes you fatigued unless the item's description states a different maximum duration (such as "up to 1 minute" or "up to 1 hour").

If your Sustain an Activation action is disrupted, the item's effect immediately ends.

DISMISSING ACTIVATIONS

Some item effects can be dismissed, ending the duration early due to you or the target taking action. Dismissing an activation requires using the Dismiss action.

❖ DISMISS

`CONCENTRATE`

You end one spell effect or magic item effect. This must be an effect that you are allowed to dismiss, as defined by the spell or item. Dismissal might end the effect entirely, or might end it just for a certain target or targets, depending on the spell or item.

READING ITEMS

Hundreds of items lie ahead. Each item is presented in a stat block, much like spells or feats. The example below shows the structure of an item stat block and gives a brief description of each entry. Entries appear only when applicable, so not all items will have every entry described here. Detailed rules governing aspects of the stat block specific to items appear after the stat block.

ITEM NAME   ITEM [LEVEL]

`TRAITS`

Price This entry lists the item's Price. An item that has multiple types includes Price for each type in its entry.

Ammunition Magic ammunition lists the types of ammunition available for that kind of item.

Usage This entry describes whether the item is held, worn, or affixed to or etched onto another item; **Bulk** The item's Bulk is listed here (the rules for Bulk appear on page 271). Runes don't have a Bulk entry.

Activate The number of actions needed to Activate the Item appear here, followed by the components in parentheses. You can find activation rules on page 532. This entry appears here for consumables and lower in the stat block for permanent items that can be activated. This section might also have Frequency, Trigger, or Requirements entries as necessary.

Onset This entry appears if the item's effect is delayed, which most often occurs with alchemical poisons. The onset is the amount of time that elapses between when a character Activates an Item and any effect occurs.

The section after the line describes the item and its constant abilities. If the item can be activated and doesn't have an Activate entry above, that entry appears here in a paragraph beginning with "Activate."

Type If multiple types of the item exist, entries here indicate the name of each type, its level, its Price, and any other relevant details or alterations from the above description.

Craft Requirements An item that has special requirements to be Crafted details those requirements here.

LEVEL

An item's level indicates what level of adventurer the item is best suited for. There's no limit to the items a character can use, though. A 3rd-level character who finds an item of 4th level or higher while adventuring can use it normally. Likewise, they can purchase the item if they can find it for sale and can afford it.

When making items, a character's level must be equal to or higher than the item's level in order to Craft it. In addition to anything listed in the Craft Requirements entry in the item's stat block, the crafter must have the appropriate skill proficiencies and feats, as well as the item's formula; see the Craft activity on page 244 for more information about these requirements.

MULTIPLE TYPES

If multiple types of an item exist, the title line gives the minimum level followed by a plus symbol ("+"). The description includes information on the base version of the item, and the Type entries at the bottom of the stat block lists the specifics for each version, including the level, Price, and any modified or added abilities of the different types. For some items, the types listed are upgrades to the base item. For other items, such as *aeon stones* and *wondrous figurines*, each type is distinct from the others.

PRICE

If an item is available for purchase, a character can typically buy it for the listed Price, and the character uses this Price when they use the Craft activity to make the item. If a character wants to sell an item, they can sell it for half its Price (or full Price, if the item was made on commission), assuming they're able to find a buyer. The GM determines whether a buyer is available.

USAGE

An item's stat block includes a Usage entry that indicates whether a character must be holding or wearing the item in order to use it, or whether she instead must have it etched or affixed onto another item.

HELD OR WORN

If a character must wield the item to use it, this entry in the item's stat block lists the word "held" along with the number of hands the character must use when wielding the item, such as "held in 1 hand." The rules for carrying and using items are provided on page 271.

An item that needs to be worn to function lists "worn" as its usage. This is followed by another word if the character is limited to only one of that type of item. For instance, a character can wear any number of rings, so the entry for a ring would list only "worn." However, if the Usage entry were "worn cloak," then a character couldn't wear another cloak on top of that one. It's assumed that items are meant to be worn by humanoids; any item that can or must be worn by a different type of creature either states this in its description or has the companion trait. Most magic items a character must wear have the invested trait, as described on page 531.

AFFIXED OR ETCHED

Some items enhance other items. Talismans function only if affixed to other items. They have a Usage entry indicating the type or types of items to which a character can attach them, such as "affixed to armor." Rules for affixing a talisman are on page 565.

Runes must be etched onto permanent items, such as armor, weapons, or *runestones* (found on page 571) to grant their benefit. Adding or transferring a rune takes downtime to accomplish. The Usage entry indicates the type or types of items a rune can be etched into, such as "etched onto a weapon." More information about etching runes is on page 580.

CRAFT REQUIREMENTS

An item might require the crafter to provide specific raw materials, supply spells, have a certain alignment, or meet other special requirements to Craft it. These appear in the Craft Requirements entry of the stat block. Every item also has default requirements. The crafter must provide half the item's Price in raw materials (as explained in the Craft activity on page 244). In addition, creating

NOTABLE ITEM TRAITS

The following traits apply to items. Some specific categories of item have special traits—such as elixir or scroll—described in their sections.

Alchemical: Alchemical items are powered by the reactions of alchemical reagents. Alchemical items aren't magical, and they don't radiate a magical aura. Characters can Craft these items only if they have the Alchemical Crafting feat (page 258).

Consumable: An item with this trait can be used only once. Unless stated otherwise, it's destroyed after activation, though part of it might be recoverable for other purposes. For instance, while a potion is consumable, the vial it comes in is not destroyed when you drink it. Consumable items include alchemical items (page 543) as well as ammunition oils, potions, scrolls, snares, talismans, and other magical consumables (which begin on page 559).

When a character creates consumable items, she can make them in batches of four, as described in Consumables and Ammunition (page 245).

Focused: An item with this trait can give you an additional Focus Point. This focus point is separate from your focus pool and doesn't count toward the cap on your focus pool. You can gain this benefit only if you have a focus pool, and there might be restrictions on how the point can be used. You can't gain more than 1 Focus Point per day from focused items, no matter how many focused items you have.

Invested: A character can wear only 10 magical items that have the invested trait. None of the magical effects of the item apply if the character hasn't invested it, though the character still gains any normal benefits from wearing the physical item (like a hat keeping rain off a character's head).

Magical: Items with this trait are imbued with magical energies. Each one radiates a magic aura infused with its dominant school of magic (abjuration, conjuration, divination, enchantment, evocation, illusion, necromancy, or transmutation; these are described on pages 297–298). A character can craft these items only if she has the Magical Crafting feat (page 263).

Some items are closely tied to a particular tradition of magic. In these cases, the item has the arcane, divine, occult, or primal trait instead of the magical trait. Any of these traits indicates that the item is magical.

alchemical items requires the Alchemical Crafting feat (page 258), creating magic items requires the Magical Crafting feat (page 263), and crafting snares requires the Snare Crafting feat (page 266). Finally, crafting higher-level items requires greater proficiency in Crafting. Unless stated otherwise, creating items of 9th level and higher requires you to have the master proficiency rank in Crafting, and items of 16th level and higher require legendary Crafting.

TREASURE TABLE

Table 11–1 lists the items and runes appearing in this chapter. The table includes all the options of a given item level, organized by category and name. Each level has a section for consumables, followed by a section for permanent items. A superscript "U" indicates the item is uncommon, and a superscript "R" indicates it's rare.

TABLE 11–1: TREASURE BY LEVEL

1st-Level Consumables	Category	Price	Page
Shining ammunition	Ammunition	3 gp	560
Acid flask, lesser	Bomb	3 gp	544
Alchemist's fire, lesser	Bomb	3 gp	545
Bottled lightning, lesser	Bomb	3 gp	545
Frost vial, lesser	Bomb	3 gp	545
Tanglefoot bag, lesser	Bomb	3 gp	545
Thunderstone, lesser	Bomb	3 gp	545
Feather token, ladder	Consumable	3 gp	570
Holy water	Consumable	3 gp	571
Runestone	Consumable	3 gp	571
Unholy water	Consumable	3 gp	571
Antidote, lesser	Elixir	3 gp	546
Antiplague, lesser	Elixir	3 gp	546
Bestial mutagen, lesser	Elixir	4 gp	546
Cheetah's elixir, lesser	Elixir	3 gp	547
Cognitive mutagen, lesser	Elixir	4 gp	547
Eagle-eye elixir, lesser	Elixir	4 gp	548
Elixir of life, minor	Elixir	3 gp	548
Juggernaut mutagen, lesser	Elixir	4 gp	548
Leaper's elixir, lesser	Elixir	3 gp	549
Quicksilver mutagen, lesser	Elixir	4 gp	549
Serene mutagen, lesser	Elixir	4 gp	549
Silvertongue mutagen, lesser	Elixir	4 gp	550
Nectar of purification	Oil	3 gp	561
Arsenic	Poison	3 gp	550
Giant centipede venom	Poison	4 gp	551
Healing potion, minor	Potion	4 gp	563
Scroll of 1st-level spell	Scroll	4 gp	565
Alarm snare	Snare	3 gp	589
Caltrop snare	Snare	3 gp	590
Hampering snare	Snare	3 gp	590
Marking snare	Snare	3 gp	590
Signaling snare	Snare	3 gp	591
Spike snare	Snare	3 gp	591
Owlbear claw	Talisman	3 gp	569
Potency crystal	Talisman	4 gp	569
Wolf fang	Talisman	4 gp	570
Smokestick, lesser	Tool	3 gp	554
Snake oil	Tool	2 gp	554
Sunrod	Tool	3 gp	554
Tindertwig	Tool	2 sp	554

1st-Level Permanent Items	Category	Price	Page
Half plate	Armor	18 gp	276
Splint mail	Armor	13 gp	276
Everburning torch	Held	15 gp	573
Aeon stone, dull gray^U	Worn	9 gp	604

2nd-Level Consumables	Category	Price	Page
Feather token, holly bush	Consumable	6 gp	570
Bravo's brew, lesser	Elixir	7 gp	547
Cat's eye elixir	Elixir	7 gp	547
Comprehension elixir, lesser	Elixir	7 gp	547
Darkvision elixir, lesser	Elixir	6 gp	547
Infiltrator's elixir	Elixir	6 gp	548
Oil of potency	Oil	7 gp	562
Oil of weightlessness	Oil	6 gp	562
Belladonna	Poison	5 gp	551
Black adder venom	Poison	6 gp	551
Lethargy poison^U	Poison	7 gp	552
Bronze bull pendant	Talisman	7 gp	566
Crying angel pendant	Talisman	7 gp	566
Effervescent ampoule	Talisman	7 gp	566
Hunter's bane	Talisman	6 gp	567
Jade cat	Talisman	6 gp	568
Mesmerizing opal	Talisman	7 gp	568
Monkey pin	Talisman	6 gp	568
Onyx panther	Talisman	7 gp	569
Savior spike	Talisman	7 gp	569
Silversheen	Tool	6 gp	554

2nd-Level Permanent Items	Category	Price	Page
Full plate	Armor	30 gp	276
Wondrous figurine, onyx dog	Held	34 gp	576
+1 weapon potency	Rune	35 gp	581
Cold iron buckler, low-grade	Shield	30 gp	586
Cold iron shield, low-grade	Shield	34 gp	586
Silver buckler, low-grade	Shield	30 gp	587
Silver shield, low-grade	Shield	34 gp	587
+1 weapon	Weapon	35 gp	599
Cold iron weapon, low-grade	Weapon	40+ gp	599
Silver weapon, low-grade	Weapon	40+ gp	599
+1 handwraps of mighty blows	Worn	35 gp	611
Brooch of shielding^U	Worn	30 gp	607
Hand of the mage	Worn	30 gp	611
Hat of disguise	Worn	30 gp	611
Wayfinder^U	Worn	28 gp	617

3rd-Level Consumables	Category	Price	Page
Beacon shot	Ammunition	10 gp	559
Sleep arrow	Ammunition	11 gp	560
Spellstrike ammunition 1st	Ammunition	12 gp	560
Vine arrow	Ammunition	10 gp	560
Acid flask, moderate	Bomb	10 gp	544
Alchemist's fire, moderate	Bomb	10 gp	545
Bottled lightning, moderate	Bomb	10 gp	545
Frost vial, moderate	Bomb	10 gp	545
Tanglefoot bag, moderate	Bomb	10 gp	545
Thunderstone, moderate	Bomb	10 gp	545
Feather token, bird	Consumable	8 gp	570
Feather token, chest	Consumable	10 gp	570
Bestial mutagen, moderate	Elixir	12 gp	546
Cognitive mutagen, moderate	Elixir	12 gp	547
Juggernaut mutagen, moderate	Elixir	12 gp	548
Quicksilver mutagen, moderate	Elixir	12 gp	549
Serene mutagen, moderate	Elixir	12 gp	549
Silvertongue mutagen, moderate	Elixir	12 gp	550

Oil of mending	Oil	9 gp	561
Cytillesh oil	Poison	10 gp	551
Graveroot	Poison	10 gp	552
Healing potion, lesser	Potion	12 gp	563
Potion of water breathing	Potion	11 gp	564
Scroll of 2nd-level spell	Scroll	12 gp	565
Feather step stone	Talisman	8 gp	567

3rd-Level Permanent Items	Category	Price	Page
Maestro's instrument, lesser	Held	60 gp	574
Thurible of revelation, lesser	Held	55 gp	575
Returning	Rune	55 gp	584
Shadow	Rune	55 gp	583
Slick	Rune	45 gp	583
Staff of fire	Staff	60 gp	594
Wand of 1st-level spell	Wand	60 gp	597
Fighter's fork	Weapon	50 gp	600
Retribution axe	Weapon	60 gp	602
Bracelet of dashing	Worn	58 gp	607
Bracers of missile deflection	Worn	52 gp	607
Channel protection amulet[U]	Worn	56 gp	608
Coyote cloak	Worn	60 gp	609
Crafter's eyepiece	Worn	60 gp	609
Dancing scarf	Worn	60 gp	609
Doubling rings	Worn	50 gp	609
Hat of the magi	Worn	50 gp	611
Pendant of the occult	Worn	60 gp	613
Persona mask	Worn	50 gp	613
Tracker's goggles	Worn	60 gp	616
Ventriloquist's ring	Worn	60 gp	617

4th-Level Consumables	Category	Price	Page
Climbing bolt	Ammunition	15 gp	559
Viper arrow	Ammunition	17 gp	561
Feather token, fan	Consumable	15 gp	570
Bomber's eye elixir, lesser	Elixir	14 gp	547
Darkvision elixir, moderate	Elixir	11 gp	547
Mistform elixir, lesser	Elixir	18 gp	549
Salamander elixir, lesser	Elixir	15 gp	549
Stone fist elixir	Elixir	13 gp	550
Winter wolf elixir, lesser	Elixir	15 gp	550
Barkskin potion	Potion	15 gp	562
Invisibility potion[U]	Potion	20 gp	563
Shrinking potion, standard	Potion	15 gp	564
Biting snare	Snare	15 gp	589
Hobbling snare[U]	Snare	15 gp	590
Stalker bane snare[U]	Snare	15 gp	591
Trip snare	Snare	15 gp	591
Warning snare	Snare	15 gp	591
Bloodseeker beak	Talisman	20 gp	565
Dragon turtle scale	Talisman	13 gp	566
Fear gem	Talisman	20 gp	566

4th-Level Permanent Items	Category	Price	Page
Bag of holding type I	Held	75 gp	572
Ghost touch	Rune	75 gp	584
Striking	Rune	65 gp	581
Sturdy shield, minor	Shield	100 gp	588
Animal staff	Staff	90 gp	592
Mentalist's staff	Staff	90 gp	592

Staff of healing	Staff	90 gp	594
Wand of widening 1st	Wand	100 gp	598
+1 striking weapon	Weapon	100 gp	599
Alchemist goggles	Worn	100 gp	605
+1 striking handwraps of mighty blows	Worn	100 gp	611
Demon mask	Worn	85 gp	609
Healer's gloves	Worn	80 gp	612
Lifting belt	Worn	80 gp	613

5th-Level Consumables	Category	Price	Page
Spellstrike ammunition 2nd	Ammunition	30 gp	560
Cheetah's elixir, moderate	Elixir	25 gp	547
Eagle-eye elixir, moderate	Elixir	27 gp	548
Elixir of life, lesser	Elixir	30 gp	548
Sea touch elixir, lesser	Elixir	22 gp	549
Salve of slipperiness	Oil	25 gp	562
Hunting spider venom	Poison	25 gp	552
Potion of leaping	Potion	21 gp	563
Scroll of 3rd-level spell	Scroll	30 gp	565
Emerald grasshopper	Talisman	30 gp	566
Shark tooth charm	Talisman	23 gp	569
Sneaky key	Talisman	22 gp	569
Tiger menuki	Talisman	30 gp	569

5th-Level Permanent Items	Category	Price	Page
+1 armor	Armor	160 gp	556
Cold iron armor, low-grade	Armor	140+ gp	555
Silver armor, low-grade	Armor	140+ gp	556
Holy prayer beads, standard[U]	Held	160 gp	573
Skeleton key, standard	Held	125 gp	575
+1 armor potency	Rune	160 gp	581
Glamered	Rune	140 gp	583
Disrupting	Rune	150 gp	584
Pocket stage	Structure	138 gp	596
Wand of 2nd-level spell	Wand	160 gp	597
Wand of continuation 1st	Wand	160 gp	598
Wand of manifold missiles 1st	Wand	160 gp	598
Caterwaul sling	Weapon	155 gp	600
Dagger of venom	Weapon	150 gp	600
Boots of elvenkind	Worn	145 gp	606
Diplomat's badge	Worn	125 gp	609
Goggles of night	Worn	150 gp	610
Necklace of fireballs type I	Worn	44 gp	613

6th-Level Consumables	Category	Price	Page
Dust of appearance	Consumable	50 gp	570
Feather token, tree	Consumable	38 gp	570
Antidote, moderate	Elixir	35 gp	546
Antiplague, moderate	Elixir	35 gp	546
Mistform elixir, moderate	Elixir	56 gp	549
Oil of weightlessness, greater	Oil	36 gp	562
Salve of antiparalysis	Oil	40 gp	562
Giant scorpion venom	Poison	40 gp	551
Healing potion, moderate	Potion	50 gp	563
Potion of resistance, lesser	Potion	45 gp	563
Potion of swimming, moderate	Potion	50 gp	563
Truth potion[U]	Potion	46 gp	564
Iron cube	Talisman	50 gp	567

6th-Level Permanent Items	Category	Price	Page
Ghoul hide^U	Armor	220 gp	558
Chime of opening^U	Held	235 gp	572
Horn of fog	Held	230 gp	573
Primeval mistletoe, standard	Held	230 gp	574
Traveler's any-tool	Held	200 gp	576
Shifting	Rune	225 gp	585
Lion's shield	Shield	245 gp	588
Spellguard Shield	Shield	250 gp	588
Staff of abjuration	Staff	230 gp	593
Staff of conjuration	Staff	230 gp	593
Staff of divination	Staff	230 gp	593
Staff of enchantment	Staff	230 gp	593
Staff of evocation	Staff	230 gp	593
Staff of illusion	Staff	230 gp	594
Staff of necromancy	Staff	230 gp	594
Staff of transmutation	Staff	230 gp	595
Verdant staff	Staff	225 gp	595
Wand of widening 2nd	Wand	250 gp	598
Bloodletting kukri^U	Weapon	240 gp	600
Twining staff	Weapon	250 gp	602
Aeon stone, gold nodule^U	Worn	230 gp	604
Choker of elocution	Worn	200 gp	608
Clandestine cloak^U	Worn	230 gp	608
Ring of energy resistance	Worn	245 gp	614
Ring of the ram	Worn	220 gp	615

7th-Level Consumables	Category	Price	Page
Spellstrike ammunition 3rd	Ammunition	70 gp	560
Feather token, anchor	Consumable	55 gp	570
Comprehension elixir, greater	Elixir	54 gp	547
Leaper's elixir, greater	Elixir	55 gp	549
Giant wasp venom	Poison	55 gp	552
Malyass root paste	Poison	55 gp	552
Dragon's breath potion, young	Potion	70 gp	562
Serum of sex shift	Potion	60 gp	564
Scroll of 4th-level spell	Scroll	70 gp	565
Grim trophy	Talisman	55 gp	567
Murderer's knot	Talisman	66 gp	568
Swift block cabochon^U	Talisman	70 gp	569
Smokestick, greater	Tool	53 gp	554

7th-Level Permanent Items	Category	Price	Page
Moonlit chain	Armor	360 gp	558
Horseshoes of speed	Companion	340 gp	604
Bag of holding type II	Held	300 gp	572
Bottled air	Held	320 gp	572
Decanter of endless water	Held	320 gp	573
Wondrous figurine, jade serpent	Held	340 gp	576
Wounding	Rune	340 gp	585
Cold iron buckler, standard-grade	Shield	300 gp	586
Cold iron shield, standard-grade	Shield	340 gp	586
Silver buckler, standard-grade	Shield	300 gp	587
Silver shield, standard-grade	Shield	340 gp	587
Spined shield	Shield	360 gp	588
Sturdy shield, lesser	Shield	360 gp	588
Wand of 3rd-level spell	Wand	360 gp	597
Wand of continuation 2nd	Wand	360 gp	598
Aeon stone, clear spindle^U	Worn	325 gp	604

	Category	Price	Page
Aeon stone, tourmaline sphere^U	Worn	350 gp	604
Boots of bounding	Worn	340 gp	606
Cloak of elvenkind	Worn	360 gp	608
Gloves of storing^U	Worn	340 gp	610
Hat of disguise, greater	Worn	340 gp	611
Necklace of fireballs type II	Worn	115 gp	613
Ring of sustenance^U	Worn	325 gp	615
Ring of wizardry type I^U	Worn	360 gp	615
Slippers of spider climbing	Worn	325 gp	616

8th-Level Consumables	Category	Price	Page
Candle of truth^U	Consumable	75 gp	570
Feather token, swan boat	Consumable	76 gp	570
Darkvision elixir, greater	Elixir	90 gp	547
Nettleweed residue	Poison	75 gp	553
Wyvern poison	Poison	80 gp	554
Potion of flying, standard	Potion	100 gp	563
Potion of quickness	Potion	90 gp	563
Shrinking potion, greater	Potion	90 gp	564
Bomb snare	Snare	75 gp	589
Grasping snare^U	Snare	75 gp	590
Striking snare	Snare	75 gp	591
Gallows tooth	Talisman	100 gp	567
Jade bauble	Talisman	100 gp	568

8th-Level Permanent Items	Category	Price	Page
+1 resilient armor	Armor	500 gp	556
Collar of inconspicuousness	Companion	475 gp	604
Rod of wonder^R	Held	465 gp	575
Corrosive	Rune	500 gp	583
Energy-resistant	Rune	420 gp	582
Flaming	Rune	500 gp	584
Frost	Rune	500 gp	584
Invisibility	Rune	500 gp	583
Resilient	Rune	340 gp	581
Shock	Rune	500 gp	585
Slick, greater	Rune	450 gp	583
Thundering	Rune	500 gp	585
Adamantine buckler, standard-grade^U	Shield	400 gp	586
Adamantine shield, standard-grade^U	Shield	440 gp	586
Darkwood buckler, standard-grade^U	Shield	400 gp	586
Darkwood shield, standard-grade^U	Shield	440 gp	586
Darkwood tower shield, standard-grade^U	Shield	560 gp	586
Dragonhide buckler, standard-grade^U	Shield	400 gp	586
Dragonhide shield, standard-grade^U	Shield	440 gp	586
Mithral buckler, standard-grade^U	Shield	400 gp	586
Mithral shield, standard-grade^U	Shield	440 gp	586
Animal staff, greater	Staff	460 gp	592
Mentalist's staff, greater	Staff	450 gp	592
Staff of fire, greater	Staff	450 gp	594
Staff of healing, greater	Staff	470 gp	594
Staff of illumination	Staff	425 gp	594
Wand of smoldering fireballs 3rd	Wand	500 gp	598

| Wand of widening 3rd | Wand | 500 gp | 598 |
| Bracers of armor type I | Worn | 450 gp | 607 |

9th-Level Consumables	Category	Price	Page
Explosive ammunition, standard	Ammunition	130 gp	559
Spellstrike ammunition 4th	Ammunition	150 gp	560
Storm arrow	Ammunition	130 gp	560
Dust of disappearance	Consumable	135 gp	570
Feather token, whip	Consumable	130 gp	570
Javelin of lightning	Consumable	110 gp	571
Cheetah's elixir, greater	Elixir	110 gp	547
Elixir of life, moderate	Elixir	150 gp	548
Aligned oil	Oil	140 gp	561
Lich dust	Poison	110 gp	552
Spider root	Poison	110 gp	553
Scroll of 5th-level spell	Scroll	150 gp	565

9th-Level Permanent Items	Category	Price	Page
Rhino hide	Armor	700 gp	558
Collar of empathy	Companion	600 gp	604
Horn of blasting	Held	700 gp	573
Immovable rod	Held	600 gp	574
Triton's conch	Held	640 gp	576
Grievous	Rune	700 gp	584
Shadow, greater	Rune	650 gp	583
Dragonslayer's Shield^U	Shield	670 gp	587
Force shield^U	Shield	650 gp	587
Wand of 4th-level spell	Wand	700 gp	597
Wand of continuation 3rd	Wand	700 gp	598
Wand of manifold missiles 3rd	Wand	700 gp	598
Gloom blade	Weapon	700 gp	601
Armbands of athleticism	Worn	645 gp	605
Belt of the five kings^U	Worn	650 gp	606
Bracers of missile deflection, greater	Worn	650 gp	607
Coyote cloak, greater	Worn	650 gp	609
Dancing scarf, greater	Worn	650 gp	609
Eye of the eagle	Worn	700 gp	610
Hat of the magi, greater	Worn	650 gp	611
Healer's gloves, greater	Worn	700 gp	612
Knapsack of halflingkind^U	Worn	675 gp	612
Messenger's ring	Worn	700 gp	613
Necklace of fireballs type III	Worn	300 gp	613
Pendant of the occult, greater	Worn	650 gp	613
Persona mask, greater	Worn	650 gp	613
Phylactery of faithfulness	Worn	680 gp	614
Tracker's goggles, greater	Worn	660 gp	616
Ventriloquist's ring, greater	Worn	670 gp	617

10th-Level Consumables	Category	Price	Page
Elemental gem	Consumable	200 gp	570
Antidote, greater	Elixir	160 gp	546
Antiplague, greater	Elixir	160 gp	546
Bravo's brew, moderate	Elixir	150 gp	547
Eagle-eye elixir, greater	Elixir	200 gp	548
Mistform elixir, greater	Elixir	180 gp	549
Shadow Essence	Poison	160 gp	553
Wolfsbane	Poison	155 gp	553
Potion of resistance, moderate	Potion	180 gp	563
Iron medallion	Talisman	175 gp	568

Mummified bat	Talisman	175 gp	568
Vanishing coin	Talisman	160 gp	569

10th-Level Permanent Items	Category	Price	Page
Breastplate of command	Armor	1,000 gp	557
Electric eelskin	Armor	950 gp	557
Barding of the zephyr	Companion	900 gp	604
Maestro's instrument, moderate	Held	900 gp	574
Thurible of revelation, moderate	Held	900 gp	575
Wondrous figurine, golden lions	Held	900 gp	576
+2 weapon potency	Rune	935 gp	581
Invisibility, greater	Rune	1,000 gp	583
Forge warden^U	Shield	975 gp	587
Sturdy shield, moderate	Shield	1,000 gp	588
Staff of abjuration, greater	Staff	900 gp	593
Staff of conjuration, greater	Staff	900 gp	593
Staff of divination, greater	Staff	900 gp	593
Staff of enchantment, greater	Staff	900 gp	593
Staff of evocation, greater	Staff	900 gp	593
Staff of illusion, greater	Staff	900 gp	594
Staff of necromancy, greater	Staff	900 gp	594
Staff of transmutation, greater	Staff	900 gp	595
Explorer's yurt	Structure	880 gp	596
Wand of widening 4th	Wand	1,000 gp	598
+2 striking weapon	Weapon	1,000 gp	599
Cold iron weapon, standard-grade	Weapon	880+ gp	599
Silver weapon, standard-grade	Weapon	880+ gp	599
+2 striking handwraps of mighty blows	Worn	1,000 gp	611
Cape of the mountebank^U	Worn	980 gp	607
Choker of elocution, greater	Worn	850 gp	608
Clandestine cloak, greater^U	Worn	900 gp	608
Cloak of the bat	Worn	950 gp	608
Daredevil boots	Worn	900 gp	609
Demon mask, greater	Worn	900 gp	609
Druid's vestments	Worn	1,000 gp	610
Ring of counterspells^U	Worn	925 gp	614
Ring of energy resistance, greater	Worn	975 gp	614
Ring of lies^U	Worn	850 gp	614
Ring of wizardry type II^U	Worn	1,000 gp	615
Winged boots	Worn	850 gp	617

11th-Level Consumables	Category	Price	Page
Spellstrike ammunition 5th	Ammunition	300 gp	560
Acid flask, greater	Bomb	250 gp	544
Alchemist's fire, greater	Bomb	250 gp	545
Bottled lightning, greater	Bomb	250 gp	545
Frost vial, greater	Bomb	250 gp	545
Tanglefoot bag, greater	Bomb	250 gp	545
Thunderstone, greater	Bomb	250 gp	545
Bestial mutagen, greater	Elixir	300 gp	546
Cognitive mutagen, greater	Elixir	300 gp	547
Juggernaut mutagen, greater	Elixir	300 gp	548
Quicksilver mutagen, greater	Elixir	300 gp	549
Serene mutagen, greater	Elixir	300 gp	549
Silvertongue mutagen, greater	Elixir	300 gp	550
Oil of keen edges^U	Oil	250 gp	561
Oil of repulsion	Oil	175 gp	562

Blightburn resin	Poison	225 gp	551
Potion of swimming, greater	Potion	250 gp	563
Scroll of 6th-level spell	Scroll	300 gp	565

11th-Level Permanent Items	Category	Price	Page
+2 resilient armor	Armor	1,400 gp	556
Cold iron armor, standard-grade	Armor	1,200+ gp	555
Silver armor, standard-grade	Armor	1,200+ gp	556
Bag of holding type III	Held	1,200 gp	572
*Holy prayer beads, greater*ᵁ	Held	1,400 gp	573
Skeleton key, greater	Held	1,250 gp	575
+2 armor potency	Rune	1,060 gp	581
Anarchic	Rune	1,400 gp	583
Axiomatic	Rune	1,400 gp	583
Holy	Rune	1,400 gp	584
Unholy	Rune	1,400 gp	585
Arrow-catching shield	Shield	1,350 gp	587
*Floating shield*ᵁ	Shield	1,250 gp	587
Wand of 5th-level spell	Wand	1,500 gp	597
Wand of continuation 4th	Wand	1,400 gp	598
Adamantine weapon, standard-gradeᵁ	Weapon	1,400+ gp	599
Darkwood weapon, standard-gradeᵁ	Weapon	1,400+ gp	599
Mithral weapon, standard-gradeᵁ	Weapon	1,400+ gp	599
Oathbow	Weapon	1,300 gp	602
Alchemist goggles, greater	Worn	1,400 gp	605
Boots of elvenkind, greater	Worn	1,250 gp	606
Cassock of devotion	Worn	1,150 gp	607
Crafter's eyepiece, greater	Worn	1,200 gp	609
Doubling rings, greater	Worn	1,300 gp	609
Goggles of night, greater	Worn	1,250 gp	610
Gorget of the primal roar	Worn	1,250 gp	611
Necklace of fireballs type IV	Worn	700 gp	613
Ring of maniacal devices	Worn	1,175 gp	614

12th-Level Consumables	Category	Price	Page
Penetrating ammunition	Ammunition	400 gp	560
Salamander elixir, moderate	Elixir	320 gp	549
Sea touch elixir, moderate	Elixir	300 gp	549
Winter wolf elixir, moderate	Elixir	320 gp	550
*Oil of animation*ᵁ	Oil	330 gp	561
Salve of antiparalysis, greater	Oil	325 gp	562
Slumber wine	Poison	325 gp	553
Dragon's breath potion, adult	Potion	400 gp	562
Healing potion, greater	Potion	400 gp	563
*Potion of tongues*ᵁ	Potion	320 gp	563
Bleeding spines snare	Snare	320 gp	589
Scything blade snare	Snare	320 gp	591
Stunning snare	Snare	320 gp	591
Eye of apprehension	Talisman	400 gp	566
Fade band	Talisman	320 gp	566
Iron equalizer	Talisman	400 gp	567

12th-Level Permanent Items	Category	Price	Page
Adamantine armor, standard-gradeᵁ	Armor	1,600+ gp	555
Darkwood armor, standard-gradeᵁ	Armor	1,600+ gp	555

Dragonhide armor, standard-gradeᵁ	Armor	1,600+ gp	555
Mithral armor, standard-gradeᵁ	Armor	1,600+ gp	556
Broom of flying	Held	1,900 gp	572
Marvelous medicines, standard	Held	1,800 gp	574
Energy-resistant, greater	Rune	1,650 gp	582
Fortification	Rune	2,000 gp	582
Striking, greater	Rune	1,065 gp	581
Animal staff, major	Staff	1,900 gp	592
Mentalist's staff, major	Staff	1,800 gp	592
Staff of fire, major	Staff	1,800 gp	594
Staff of healing, major	Staff	1,800 gp	594
Verdant staff, greater	Staff	1,750 gp	595
Wand of smoldering fireballs 5th	Wand	2,000 gp	598
Wand of widening 5th	Wand	2,000 gp	598
+2 greater striking weapon	Weapon	2,000 gp	599
+2 greater striking handwraps of mighty blows	Worn	2,000 gp	611
*Aeon stone, pink rhomboid*ᵁ	Worn	1,900 gp	604
Berserker's cloak	Worn	2,000 gp	606
Cloak of elvenkind, greater	Worn	1,750 gp	608
Ring of climbing	Worn	1,750 gp	614
Ring of swimming	Worn	1,750 gp	615
*Ring of wizardry type III*ᵁ	Worn	2,000 gp	615

13th-Level Consumables	Category	Price	Page
Explosive ammunition, greater	Ammunition	520 gp	559
Spellstrike ammunition 6th	Ammunition	600 gp	560
Elixir of life, greater	Elixir	600 gp	548
Deathcap powder	Poison	450 gp	551
Purple worm venom	Poison	500 gp	553
*Panacea*ᵁ	Potion	450 gp	563
Scroll of 7th-level spell	Scroll	600 gp	565
*Mending lattice*ᵁ	Talisman	525 gp	568

13th-Level Permanent Items	Category	Price	Page
Celestial armor	Armor	2,500 gp	557
Demon armor	Armor	2,500 gp	557
*Elven chain, standard-grade*ᵁ	Armor	2,500 gp	555
Mail of luck	Armor	2,600 gp	558
Bag of holding type IV	Held	2,400 gp	572
Wondrous figurine, marble elephant	Held	2,700 gp	576
*Dancing*ᵁ	Rune	2,700 gp	583
*Keen*ᵁ	Rune	3,000 gp	584
*Spell-storing*ᵁ	Rune	2,700 gp	585
Sturdy shield, greater	Shield	3,000 gp	588
Wand of 6th-level spell	Wand	3,000 gp	597
Wand of continuation 5th	Wand	3,000 gp	598
Wand of manifold missiles 5th	Wand	3,000 gp	598
Dwarven thrower	Weapon	2,750 gp	600
Flame tongue	Weapon	2,800 gp	600
*Aeon stone, pale lavender ellipsoid*ᵁ	Worn	2,200 gp	604
Boots of speed	Worn	3,000 gp	606
Eye of fortune	Worn	2,700 gp	610
*Knapsack of halflingkind, greater*ᵁ	Worn	2,850 gp	612
Necklace of fireballs type V	Worn	1,600 gp	613
Ring of the ram, greater	Worn	2,700 gp	615

14th-Level Consumables	Category	Price	Page
Ghost ammunition	Ammunition	900 gp	559
Antidote, major	Elixir	675 gp	546
Antiplague, major	Elixir	675 gp	546
Bomber's eye elixir, greater	Elixir	700 gp	547
Potion of resistance, greater	Potion	850 gp	563
Dazing Coil	Talisman	900 gp	566
Iron cudgel	Talisman	900 gp	567
Viper's fang	Talisman	850 gp	569

14th-Level Permanent Items	Category	Price	Page
+2 greater resilient armor	Armor	4,500 gp	556
Horseshoes of speed, greater	Companion	4,250 gp	604
Crystal ball, clear quartz^U	Held	3,800 gp	572
Primeval mistletoe, greater	Held	3,900 gp	574
Rod of negation	Held	4,300 gp	574
Disrupting, greater^U	Rune	4,300 gp	584
Resilient, greater	Rune	3,440 gp	581
Staff of abjuration, major	Staff	4,000 gp	593
Staff of conjuration, major	Staff	4,000 gp	593
Staff of divination, major	Staff	4,000 gp	593
Staff of enchantment, major	Staff	4,000 gp	593
Staff of evocation, major	Staff	4,000 gp	593
Staff of illusion, major	Staff	4,000 gp	594
Staff of necromancy, major	Staff	4,000 gp	594
Staff of transmutation, major	Staff	4,000 gp	595
Wand of widening 6th	Wand	4,500 gp	598
Holy avenger^U	Weapon	4,500 gp	601
Storm flash	Weapon	4,000 gp	602
Boots of bounding, greater	Worn	4,250 gp	606
Bracers of armor type II	Worn	4,000 gp	607
Ring of energy resistance, major	Worn	4,400 gp	614
Ring of wizardry type IV^U	Worn	4,500 gp	615

15th-Level Consumables	Category	Price	Page
Disintegration bolt^U	Ammunition	1,300 gp	559
Spellstrike ammunition 7th	Ammunition	1,300 gp	560
Stone bullet	Ammunition	1,300 gp	560
Bravo's brew, greater	Elixir	700 gp	547
Elixir of life, major	Elixir	1,300 gp	548
Sea touch elixir, greater	Elixir	920 gp	549
Obfuscation oil	Oil	1,200 gp	561
Dragon bile	Poison	925 gp	551
Mindfog mist	Poison	1,000 gp	553
Potion of flying, greater	Potion	1,000 gp	563
Scroll of 8th-level spell	Scroll	1,300 gp	565

15th-Level Permanent Items	Category	Price	Page
Plate armor of the deep^U	Armor	6,500 gp	558
Crystal ball, selenite^U	Held	7,000 gp	572
Wondrous figurine, obsidian steed^U	Held	6,000 gp	576
Antimagic^U	Rune	6,500 gp	582
Corrosive, greater	Rune	6,500 gp	583
Flaming, greater	Rune	6,500 gp	584
Frost, greater	Rune	6,500 gp	584
Shock, greater	Rune	6,500 gp	585
Thundering, greater	Rune	6,500 gp	585
Cold iron buckler, high-grade	Shield	5,000 gp	586
Cold iron shield, high-grade	Shield	5,500 gp	586

Silver buckler, high-grade	Shield	5,000 gp	587
Silver shield, high-grade	Shield	5,500 gp	587
Wand of 7th-level spell	Wand	6,500 gp	597
Wand of continuation 6th	Wand	6,500 gp	598
Necklace of fireballs type VI	Worn	4,200 gp	613
Robe of the archmagi^U	Worn	6,500 gp	616

16th-Level Consumables	Category	Price	Page
Eagle-eye elixir, major	Elixir	2,000 gp	548
Salamander elixir, greater	Elixir	1,400 gp	549
Winter wolf elixir, greater	Elixir	1,400 gp	550
Brimstone fumes	Poison	1,500 gp	551
Nightmare vapor	Poison	1,400 gp	553
Truesight potion	Potion	1,500 gp	564
Hail of arrows snare	Snare	1,500 gp	590
Omnidirectional spear snare	Snare	1,500 gp	591
Flame navette	Talisman	1,800 gp	567
Ghost dust	Talisman	1,800 gp	567

16th-Level Permanent Items	Category	Price	Page
Dragonplate^U	Armor	10,000 gp	557
Crystal ball, moonstone^U	Held	7,500 gp	572
+3 weapon potency	Rune	8,935 gp	581
Slick, major	Rune	9,000 gp	583
Speed^R	Rune	10,000 gp	585
Adamantine buckler, high-grade^U	Shield	8,000 gp	586
Adamantine shield, high-grade^U	Shield	8,800 gp	586
Darkwood buckler, high-grade^U	Shield	8,000 gp	586
Darkwood shield, high-grade^U	Shield	8,800 gp	586
Darkwood tower shield, high-grade^U	Shield	11,200 gp	586
Dragonhide buckler, high-grade^U	Shield	8,000 gp	586
Dragonhide shield, high-grade^U	Shield	8,800 gp	586
Floating shield, greater	Shield	9,000 gp	587
Mithral buckler, high-grade^U	Shield	8,000 gp	586
Mithral shield, high-grade^U	Shield	8,800 gp	586
Sturdy shield, major	Shield	10,000 gp	588
Staff of healing, true	Staff	9,200 gp	594
Staff of power^R	Staff	10,000 gp	595
Instant fortress^U	Structure	9,300 gp	596
Wand of slaying 7th	Wand	10,000 gp	598
Wand of smoldering fireballs 7th	Wand	10,000 gp	598
Wand of widening 7th	Wand	10,000 gp	598
+3 greater striking weapon	Weapon	10,000 gp	599
Cold iron weapon, high-grade	Weapon	9,000+ gp	599
Frost brand	Weapon	10,000 gp	601
Silver weapon, high-grade	Weapon	9,000+ gp	599
+3 greater striking handwraps of mighty blows	Worn	10,000 gp	611
Aeon stone, orange prism^U	Worn	9,750 gp	604

17th-Level Consumables	Category	Price	Page
Spellstrike ammunition 8th	Ammunition	3,000 gp	560
Acid flask, major	Bomb	2,500 gp	544
Alchemist's fire, major	Bomb	2,500 gp	545
Bottled lightning, major	Bomb	2,500 gp	545
Frost vial, major	Bomb	2,500 gp	545
Tanglefoot bag, major	Bomb	2,500 gp	545
Thunderstone, major	Bomb	2,500 gp	545
Bestial mutagen, major	Elixir	3,000 gp	546

Cognitive mutagen, major	Elixir	3,000 gp	547
Juggernaut mutagen, major	Elixir	3,000 gp	548
Quicksilver mutagen, major	Elixir	3,000 gp	549
Serene mutagen, major	Elixir	3,000 gp	549
Silvertongue mutagen, major	Elixir	3,000 gp	550
Hemlock	Poison	2,250 gp	552
Dragon's breath potion, wyrm	Potion	3,000 gp	562
Scroll of 9th-level spell	Scroll	3,000 gp	565
Dispelling sliver	Talisman	2,400 gp	566

17th-Level Permanent Items	Category	Price	Page
Anklets of alacrity	Apex	15,000 gp	603
Belt of giant strength	Apex	15,000 gp	603
Belt of regeneration	Apex	15,000 gp	603
Circlet of persuasion	Apex	15,000 gp	603
Diadem of intellect	Apex	15,000 gp	603
Headband of inspired wisdom	Apex	15,000 gp	604
Impenetrable scale^U	Armor	12,800 gp	558
Crystal ball, peridot^U	Held	12,500 gp	572
Ethereal^U	Rune	13,500 gp	582
Shadow, major	Rune	14,000 gp	583
Vorpal^R	Rune	15,000 gp	585
Orichalcum buckler, high-grade^R	Shield	12,000 gp	587
Orichalcum shield, high-grade^R	Shield	13,200 gp	587
Wand of 8th-level spell	Wand	15,000 gp	597
Wand of continuation 7th	Wand	15,000 gp	598
Wand of manifold missiles 7th	Wand	15,000 gp	598
Adamantine weapon, high-grade^U	Weapon	13,500+ gp	599
Darkwood weapon, high-grade^U	Weapon	13,500+ gp	599
Flame tongue, greater	Weapon	13,800 gp	600
Luck blade^R	Weapon	15,000 gp	601
Mithral weapon, high-grade^U	Weapon	13,500+ gp	599
Alchemist goggles, major	Worn	15,000 gp	605
Armbands of athleticism, greater	Worn	13,000 gp	605
Cloak of the bat, greater	Worn	13,000 gp	608
Daredevil boots, greater	Worn	14,000 gp	609
Dread blindfold	Worn	15,000 gp	610
Messenger's ring, greater	Worn	13,500 gp	613
Necklace of fireballs type VII	Worn	9,600 gp	613
Phylactery of faithfulness, greater	Worn	13,000 gp	614
Robe of eyes^U	Worn	13,000 gp	615
Voyager's pack^U	Worn	14,800 gp	617

18th-Level Consumables	Category	Price	Page
King's sleep	Poison	4,000 gp	552
Healing potion, major	Potion	5,000 gp	563
Potion of undetectability	Potion	4,400 gp	563

18th-Level Permanent Items	Category	Price	Page
+3 greater resilient armor	Armor	24,000 gp	556
Breastplate of command, greater	Armor	22,000 gp	557
Cold iron armor, high-grade	Armor	20,000+ gp	555
Silver armor, high-grade	Armor	20,000+ gp	556
Maestro's instrument, greater	Held	19,000 gp	574
Marvelous medicines, greater	Held	19,000 gp	574
Possibility tome	Held	22,000 gp	574
Thurible of revelation, greater	Held	19,000 gp	575
+3 armor potency	Rune	20,560 gp	581

Fortification, greater	Rune	24,000 gp	582
Indestructible shield^R	Shield	24,000 gp	588
Reflecting shield^U	Shield	18,000 gp	588
Wand of slaying 8th	Wand	24,000 gp	598
Wand of widening 8th	Wand	24,000 gp	598
Orichalcum weapon, high-grade^R	Weapon	22,500+ gp	599
Storm flash, greater	Weapon	21,000 gp	602
Goggles of night, major	Worn	20,000 gp	610
Inexplicable apparatus	Worn	19,000 gp	612
Ring of maniacal devices, greater	Worn	4,250 gp	614

19th-Level Consumables	Category	Price	Page
Spellstrike ammunition 9th	Ammunition	8,000 gp	560
Elixir of life, true	Elixir	3,000 gp	548
Black lotus extract	Poison	6,500 gp	551
Scroll of 10th-level spell^U	Scroll	8,000 gp	565

19th-Level Permanent Items	Category	Price	Page
Adamantine armor, high-grade^U	Armor	32,000+ gp	555
Darkwood armor, high-grade^U	Armor	32,000+ gp	555
Dragonhide armor, high-grade^U	Armor	32,000+ gp	555
Mithral armor, high-grade^U	Armor	32,000+ gp	556
Crystal ball, obsidian^U	Held	32,000 gp	572
Striking, major	Rune	31,065 gp	581
Sturdy shield, supreme	Shield	40,000 gp	588
Wand of 9th-level spell	Wand	40,000 gp	597
Wand of continuation 8th	Wand	40,000 gp	598
+3 major striking weapon	Weapon	40,000 gp	599
Luck blade, wishing^R	Weapon	30,000 gp	601
Mattock of the titans^U	Weapon	36,000 gp	601
+3 major striking handwraps of mighty blows	Worn	40,000 gp	611
Aeon stone, lavender and green ellipsoid^U	Worn	30,000 gp	604
Berserker's cloak, greater	Worn	40,000 gp	606
Robe of the archmagi, greater^U	Worn	32,000 gp	616
Third eye	Worn	40,000 gp	616

20th-Level Consumables	Category	Price	Page
Elixir of rejuvenation^U	Elixir	–	548
Antimagic oil^R	Oil	13,000 gp	561
Tears of death	Poison	12,000 gp	553
Flying blade wheel snare	Snare	10,000 gp	590
Instant evisceration snare	Snare	10,000 gp	590
Philosopher's stone^U	Tool	–	554

20th-Level Permanent Items	Category	Price	Page
+3 major resilient armor	Armor	70,000 gp	556
Elven chain, high-grade^U	Armor	52,000+ gp	555
Orichalcum armor, high-grade^R	Armor	55,000+ gp	556
Resilient, major	Rune	49,440 gp	581
Staff of the magi^R	Staff	90,000 gp	595
Wand of slaying 9th	Wand	70,000 gp	598
Wand of smoldering fireballs 9th	Wand	70,000 gp	598
Wand of widening 9th	Wand	70,000 gp	598
Skyhammer^R	Weapon	70,000 gp	602
Bracers of armor type III	Worn	60,000 gp	607
Ring of spell turning^R	Worn	67,000 gp	615
Whisper of the first lie^R	Worn	60,000 gp	617

ALCHEMICAL ITEMS

Alchemical items are not magical. They instead use the properties of volatile chemicals, exotic minerals, potent plants, and other substances, collectively referred to as alchemical reagents. As such, alchemical items don't radiate magical auras, and they can't be dismissed or affected by *dispel magic*. Their effects last for a set amount of time or until they are countered in some way, typically physically.

Sometimes the reactions of alchemical reagents create effects that seem magical, and at other times they straddle the line between purely reactive and the inexplicable. Alchemists can infuse reagents with some of their own essence, allowing them to efficiently create short-lived alchemical items at no monetary cost. Even in these cases, alchemical items don't radiate magic auras, instead using the alchemist's infused essence as one additional catalyst for the item's alchemical effects.

Rules for creating alchemical items are found in the Craft activity on page 244, and you must have the Alchemical Crafting skill feat to use Crafting to create alchemical items. Critically failing a Crafting check to make alchemical items often causes a dangerous effect, such as an explosion for a bomb or accidental exposure for a poison, in addition to losing some of the materials. Some alchemical items have additional requirements beyond those stated in the Craft activity; these items list their requirements in a Craft Requirements entry.

All alchemical items have the alchemical trait. Most also have the consumable trait, which means that the item is used up once activated. The bomb, elixir, and poison traits indicate special categories of alchemical items, each of which is described on the following pages. Alchemical items without any of these traits are called alchemical tools, and are described further on page 554.

This section contains the following subcategories. Special rules appear at the start of the relevant section.

- **Alchemical bombs** appear on page 544.
- **Alchemical elixirs** are listed on page 546.
- **Alchemical poisons** begin on page 550.
- **Alchemical tools** can be found on page 554.

TABLE 11-2: ALCHEMICAL ITEMS BY LEVEL

Table 11-2 lists alchemical items arranged by level and category, as a reference primarily for alchemist characters.

Level	Item	Category	Page
1	Acid flask, lesser	Bomb	544
1	Alchemist's fire, lesser	Bomb	545
1	Bottled lightning, lesser	Bomb	545
1	Frost vial, lesser	Bomb	545
1	Tanglefoot bag, lesser	Bomb	545
1	Thunderstone, lesser	Bomb	546
1	Antidote, lesser	Elixir	546
1	Antiplague, lesser	Elixir	546
1	Bestial mutagen, lesser	Elixir	546

Level	Item	Category	Page
1	Cheetah's elixir, lesser	Elixir	547
1	Cognitive mutagen, lesser	Elixir	547
1	Eagle-eye elixir, lesser	Elixir	548
1	Elixir of life, lesser	Elixir	548
1	Juggernaut mutagen, lesser	Elixir	548
1	Leaper's elixir, lesser	Elixir	549
1	Quicksilver mutagen, lesser	Elixir	549
1	Serene mutagen, lesser	Elixir	549
1	Silvertongue mutagen, lesser	Elixir	550
1	Arsenic	Poison	550
1	Giant centipede venom	Poison	551
1	Smokestick, lesser	Tool	554
1	Snake oil	Tool	554
1	Sunrod	Tool	554
1	Tindertwig	Tool	554
2	Bravo's brew, lesser	Elixir	547
2	Cat's eye elixir	Elixir	547
2	Comprehension elixir, lesser	Elixir	547
2	Darkvision elixir, lesser	Elixir	547
2	Infiltrator's elixir	Elixir	548
2	Belladonna	Poison	551
2	Black adder venom	Poison	551
2	Lethargy poison	Poison	552
2	Silversheen	Tool	554
3	Acid flask, moderate	Bomb	544
3	Alchemist's fire, moderate	Bomb	545
3	Bottled lightning, moderate	Bomb	545
3	Frost vial, moderate	Bomb	545
3	Tanglefoot bag, moderate	Bomb	545
3	Thunderstone, moderate	Bomb	546
3	Bestial mutagen, moderate	Elixir	546
3	Cognitive mutagen, moderate	Elixir	547
3	Juggernaut mutagen, moderate	Elixir	548
3	Quicksilver mutagen, moderate	Elixir	549
3	Serene mutagen, moderate	Elixir	549
3	Silvertongue mutagen, moderate	Elixir	550
3	Cytillesh oil	Poison	551
3	Graveroot	Poison	552
4	Bomber's eye elixir, lesser	Elixir	547
4	Darkvision elixir, moderate	Elixir	547
4	Mistform elixir, lesser	Elixir	549
4	Salamander elixir, lesser	Elixir	549
4	Stone fist elixir	Elixir	550
4	Winter wolf elixir, lesser	Elixir	550
5	Cheetah's elixir, moderate	Elixir	547
5	Eagle-eye elixir, moderate	Elixir	548
5	Elixir of life, lesser	Elixir	548
5	Sea touch elixir, lesser	Elixir	549
5	Hunting spider venom	Poison	552
6	Antidote, moderate	Elixir	546
6	Antiplague, moderate	Elixir	546
6	Mistform elixir, moderate	Elixir	549
6	Giant scorpion venom	Poison	551
7	Comprehension elixir, greater	Elixir	547
7	Leaper's elixir, greater	Elixir	549

INTRODUCTION

ANCESTRIES & BACKGROUNDS

CLASSES

SKILLS

FEATS

EQUIPMENT

SPELLS

THE AGE OF LOST OMENS

PLAYING THE GAME

GAME MASTERING

CRAFTING & TREASURE

APPENDIX

Level	Item	Category	Page
7	Giant wasp venom	Poison	552
7	Malyass root paste	Poison	552
7	Smokestick, greater	Tool	554
8	Darkvision elixir, greater	Elixir	547
8	Nettleweed residue	Poison	553
8	Wyvern poison	Poison	554
9	Cheetah's elixir, greater	Elixir	547
9	Elixir of life, moderate	Elixir	548
9	Lich dust	Poison	552
9	Spider root	Poison	553
10	Antidote, greater	Elixir	546
10	Antiplague, greater	Elixir	546
10	Bravo's brew, moderate	Elixir	547
10	Eagle-eye elixir, greater	Elixir	548
10	Mistform elixir, greater	Elixir	549
10	Shadow essence	Poison	553
10	Wolfsbane	Poison	553
11	Acid flask, greater	Bomb	544
11	Alchemist's fire, greater	Bomb	545
11	Bottled lightning, greater	Bomb	545
11	Frost vial, greater	Bomb	545
11	Tanglefoot bag, greater	Bomb	545
11	Thunderstone, greater	Bomb	546
11	Bestial mutagen, greater	Elixir	546
11	Cognitive mutagen, greater	Elixir	547
11	Juggernaut mutagen, greater	Elixir	548
11	Quicksilver mutagen, greater	Elixir	549
11	Serene mutagen, greater	Elixir	549
11	Silvertongue mutagen, greater	Elixir	550
11	Blightburn resin	Poison	551
12	Salamander elixir, greater	Elixir	549
12	Sea touch elixir, moderate	Elixir	549
12	Winter wolf elixir, moderate	Elixir	550
12	Slumber wine	Poison	553
13	Elixir of life, greater	Elixir	548
13	Deathcap powder	Poison	551
13	Purple worm venom	Poison	553
14	Antidote, major	Elixir	546
14	Antiplague, major	Elixir	546
14	Bomber's eye elixir, greater	Elixir	547
15	Bravo's brew, greater	Elixir	547
15	Elixir of life, greater	Elixir	548
15	Sea touch elixir, greater	Elixir	549
15	Dragon bile	Poison	551
15	Mindfog mist	Poison	553
16	Eagle-eye elixir, major	Elixir	548
16	Salamander elixir, greater	Elixir	549
16	Winter wolf elixir, greater	Elixir	550
16	Brimstone fumes	Poison	551
16	Nightmare vapor	Poison	553
17	Acid flask, major	Bomb	544
17	Alchemist's fire, major	Bomb	545
17	Bottled lightning, major	Bomb	545
17	Frost vial, major	Bomb	545
17	Tanglefoot bag, major	Bomb	545

Level	Item	Category	Page
17	Thunderstone, major	Bomb	546
17	Bestial mutagen, major	Elixir	546
17	Cognitive mutagen, major	Elixir	547
17	Juggernaut mutagen, major	Elixir	548
17	Quicksilver mutagen, major	Elixir	549
17	Serene mutagen, major	Elixir	549
17	Silvertongue mutagen, major	Elixir	550
17	Hemlock	Poison	552
18	King's sleep	Poison	552
19	Elixir of life, true	Elixir	548
19	Black lotus extract	Poison	551
20	Elixir of rejuvenation	Elixir	548
20	Tears of death	Poison	553
20	Philosopher's stone	Tool	554

ALCHEMICAL BOMBS

An alchemical bomb combines volatile alchemical components that explode when the bomb hits a creature or object. Most alchemical bombs deal damage, though some produce other effects. Bombs have the bomb trait.

Bombs are martial thrown weapons with a range increment of 20 feet. When you throw a bomb, you make a weapon attack roll against the target's AC, as you would for any other weapon. It takes one hand to draw, prepare, and throw a bomb. Due to the complexity involved in preparing bombs, Strikes to throw alchemical bombs gain the manipulate trait. The bomb is activated when thrown as a Strike—you don't have to activate it separately.

SPLASH TRAIT

Most bombs also have the splash trait. When you use a thrown weapon with the splash trait, you don't add your Strength modifier to the damage roll. If an attack with a splash weapon fails, succeeds, or critically succeeds, all creatures within 5 feet of the target (including the target) take the listed splash damage. On a failure (but not a critical failure), the target of the attack still takes the splash damage. Add splash damage together with the initial damage against the target before applying the target's resistance or weakness. You don't multiply splash damage on a critical hit.

For example, if you threw a lesser acid flask and hit your target, that creature would take 1d6 persistent acid damage and 1 acid splash damage. All other creatures within 5 feet of it would take 1 acid splash damage. On a critical hit, the target would take 2d6 persistent acid damage, but the splash damage would still be 1. If you missed, the target would take 1 splash damage. If you critically failed, no one would take any damage.

ACID FLASK   ITEM 1+

ACID   ALCHEMICAL   BOMB   CONSUMABLE   SPLASH

Usage held in 1 hand; **Bulk** L

Activate ❖ Strike

This flask filled with corrosive acid deals 1 acid damage, the

INTRODUCTION

ANCESTRIES & BACKGROUNDS

CLASSES

SKILLS

FEATS

EQUIPMENT

SPELLS

THE AGE OF LOST OMENS

PLAYING THE GAME

GAME MASTERING

CRAFTING & TREASURE

APPENDIX

listed persistent acid damage, and the listed acid splash damage. Many types grant an item bonus to attack rolls.

Type lesser; **Level** 1; **Price** 3 gp

It deals 1d6 persistent acid damage and 1 acid splash damage.

Type moderate; **Level** 3; **Price** 10 gp

You gain a +1 item bonus to attack rolls. The bomb deals 2d6 persistent acid damage and 2 acid splash damage.

Type greater; **Level** 11; **Price** 250 gp

You gain a +2 item bonus to attack rolls. The bomb deals 3d6 persistent acid damage and 3 acid splash damage.

Type major; **Level** 17; **Price** 2,500 gp

You gain a +3 item bonus to attack rolls. The bomb deals 4d6 persistent acid damage and 4 acid splash damage.

ALCHEMIST'S FIRE   ITEM 1+

`ALCHEMICAL` `BOMB` `CONSUMABLE` `FIRE` `SPLASH`

Usage held in 1 hand; **Bulk** L

Activate ◆ Strike

Alchemist's fire is a combination of volatile liquids that ignite when exposed to air. Alchemist's fire deals the listed fire damage, persistent fire damage, and splash damage. Many types grant an item bonus to attack rolls.

Type lesser; **Level** 1; **Price** 3 gp

The bomb deals 1d8 fire damage, 1 persistent fire damage, and 1 fire splash damage.

Type moderate; **Level** 3; **Price** 10 gp

You gain a +1 item bonus to attack rolls. The bomb deals 2d8 fire damage, 2 persistent fire damage, and 2 fire splash damage.

Type greater; **Level** 11; **Price** 250 gp

You gain a +2 item bonus to attack rolls. The bomb deals 3d8 fire damage, 3 persistent fire damage, and 3 fire splash damage.

Type major; **Level** 17; **Price** 2,500 gp

You gain a +3 item bonus to attack rolls. The bomb deals 4d8 fire damage, 4 persistent fire damage, and 4 fire splash damage.

BOTTLED LIGHTNING   ITEM 1+

`ALCHEMICAL` `BOMB` `CONSUMABLE` `ELECTRICITY` `SPLASH`

Usage held in 1 hand; **Bulk** L

Activate ◆ Strike

Bottled lightning is packed with volatile reagents that create a blast of electricity when they are exposed to air. Bottled lightning deals the listed electricity damage and electricity splash damage. On a hit, the target becomes flat-footed until the start of your next turn. Many types grant an item bonus to attack rolls.

Type lesser; **Level** 1; **Price** 3 gp

It deals 1d6 electricity damage and 1 electricity splash damage.

Type moderate; **Level** 3; **Price** 10 gp

You gain a +1 item bonus to attack rolls. The bomb deals 2d6 electricity damage and 2 electricity splash damage.

Type greater; **Level** 11; **Price** 250 gp

You gain a +2 item bonus to attack rolls. The bomb deals 3d6 electricity damage and 3 electricity splash damage.

Type major; **Level** 17; **Price** 2,500 gp

You gain a +3 item bonus to attack rolls. The bomb deals 4d6 electricity damage and 4 electricity splash damage.

FROST VIAL   ITEM 1+

`ALCHEMICAL` `BOMB` `COLD` `CONSUMABLE` `SPLASH`

Usage held in 1 hand; **Bulk** L

Activate ◆ Strike

The liquid reagents in this vial rapidly absorb heat when exposed to air. A frost vial deals the listed cold damage and cold splash damage. On a hit, the target takes a status penalty to its Speeds until the end of its next turn. Many types of frost vial also grant an item bonus to attack rolls.

Type lesser; **Level** 1; **Price** 3 gp

The bomb deals 1d6 cold damage and 1 cold splash damage, and the target takes a –5-foot penalty.

Type moderate; **Level** 3; **Price** 10 gp

You gain a +1 item bonus to attack rolls, the bomb deals 2d6 cold damage and 2 cold splash damage, and the target takes a –10-foot penalty.

Type greater; **Level** 11; **Price** 250 gp

You gain a +2 item bonus to attack rolls, the bomb deals 3d6 cold damage and 3 cold splash damage, and the target takes a –10-foot penalty.

Type major; **Level** 17; **Price** 2,500 gp

You gain a +3 item bonus to attack rolls, the bomb deals 4d6 cold damage and 4 cold splash damage, and the target takes a –15-foot penalty.

TANGLEFOOT BAG   ITEM 1+

`ALCHEMICAL` `BOMB` `CONSUMABLE`

Usage held in 1 hand; **Bulk** L

Activate ◆ Strike

A tanglefoot bag is filled with sticky substances. When you hit a creature with a tanglefoot bag, that creature takes a status penalty to its Speeds for 1 minute. Many types of tanglefoot bag also grant an item bonus on attack rolls.

On a critical hit, a creature in contact with a solid surface becomes stuck to the surface and immobilized for 1 round, and a creature flying via wings has its wings tangled, causing it to fall safely to the ground and become unable to Fly again for 1 round. Tanglefoot bags are not effective when used on a creature that is in water.

The target can end any effects by Escaping or spending a total of 3 Interact actions to carefully remove the sticky substances. These Interact actions don't have to be consecutive, and other creatures can provide the actions as well.

Type lesser; **Level** 1; **Price** 3 gp

The target takes a –10-foot penalty, and the Escape DC is 17.

Type moderate; **Level** 3; **Price** 10 gp

You gain a +1 item bonus to attack rolls, the target takes a –15-foot penalty, and the Escape DC is 19.

Type greater; **Level** 11; **Price** 250 gp

You gain a +2 item bonus to attack rolls, the target takes a –15-foot penalty, and the Escape DC is 28.

Type major; **Level** 17; **Price** 2,500 gp

You gain a +3 item bonus to attack rolls, the target takes a –20-foot penalty, and the Escape DC is 37.

THUNDERSTONE   ITEM 1+

ALCHEMICAL | BOMB | CONSUMABLE | SONIC | SPLASH

Usage held in 1 hand; **Bulk** L
Activate ◆ Strike

When this stone hits a creature or a hard surface, it explodes with a deafening bang. A thunderstone deals the listed sonic damage and sonic splash damage, and each creature within 10 feet of the space in which the stone exploded must succeed at a Fortitude saving throw with the listed DC or be deafened until the end of its next turn. Many types of thunderstone grant an item bonus to attack rolls.

Type lesser; **Level** 1; **Price** 3 gp

The bomb deals 1d4 sonic damage and 1 sonic splash damage, and the DC is 17.

Type moderate; **Level** 3; **Price** 10 gp

You gain a +1 item bonus to attack rolls. The bomb deals 2d4 sonic damage and 2 sonic splash damage, and the DC is 20.

Type greater; **Level** 11; **Price** 250 gp

You gain a +2 item bonus to attack rolls. The bomb deals 3d4 sonic damage and 3 sonic splash damage, and the DC is 28.

Type major; **Level** 17; **Price** 2,500 gp

You gain a +3 item bonus to attack rolls. The bomb deals 4d4 sonic damage and 4 sonic splash damage, and the DC is 36.

ALCHEMICAL ELIXIRS

Elixirs are alchemical liquids that are used by drinking them. They have the elixir trait. These potent concoctions grant the drinker some alchemical benefits. While all elixirs follow the same general rules, mutagens (described below) have additional rules that apply to their use.

ACTIVATING ELIXIRS

You usually Interact to activate an elixir as you drink it or feed it to another creature. You can feed an elixir only to a creature within reach that is either willing or unable to prevent you from doing so. You usually need only one hand to consume an elixir or feed it to another creature.

MUTAGENS

These elixirs, indicated by the mutagen trait, temporarily transmogrify the subject's body and alter its mind. Typically, only alchemists have the expertise to craft mutagens, and some say they are the only ones reckless enough to use them.

A mutagen always conveys one or more beneficial effects (listed in the Benefit entry) paired with one or more detrimental effects (shown in the Drawback entry). Mutagens are polymorph effects, meaning you can benefit from only one at a time (see page 301 for more information about the polymorph trait).

ANTIDOTE   ITEM 1+

ALCHEMICAL | CONSUMABLE | ELIXIR

Usage held in 1 hand; **Bulk** L
Activate ◆ Interact

An antidote protects you against toxins. Upon drinking an antidote, you gain an item bonus to Fortitude saving throws against poisons for 6 hours.

Type lesser; **Level** 1; **Price** 3 gp

You gain a +2 item bonus.

Type moderate; **Level** 6; **Price** 35 gp

You gain a +3 item bonus.

Type greater; **Level** 10; **Price** 160 gp

You gain a +4 item bonus.

Type major; **Level** 14; **Price** 675 gp

You gain a +4 item bonus, and when you drink the antidote, you can immediately attempt a saving throw against one poison of 14th level or lower affecting you. If you succeed, the poison is neutralized.

ANTIPLAGUE   ITEM 1+

ALCHEMICAL | CONSUMABLE | ELIXIR

Usage held in 1 hand; **Bulk** L
Activation ◆ Interact

Antiplague can fortify the body's defenses against diseases. Upon drinking an antiplague, you gain an item bonus to Fortitude saving throws against diseases for 24 hours; this applies to your daily save against a disease's progression.

Type lesser; **Level** 1; **Price** 3 gp

You gain a +2 item bonus.

Type moderate; **Level** 6; **Price** 35 gp

You gain a +3 item bonus.

Type greater; **Level** 10; **Price** 160 gp

You gain a +4 item bonus.

Type major; **Level** 14; **Price** 675 gp

You gain a +4 item bonus, and when you drink the antiplague, you can immediately attempt a saving throw against one disease of 14th level or lower affecting you. If you succeed, you are cured of the disease.

BESTIAL MUTAGEN   ITEM 1+

ALCHEMICAL | CONSUMABLE | ELIXIR | MUTAGEN | POLYMORPH

Usage held in 1 hand; **Bulk** L
Activate ◆ Interact

Your features transform into something bestial and you take on muscle mass, but your lumbering form is clumsy.

Benefit You gain an item bonus to Athletics checks and unarmed attack rolls. You gain a claw unarmed attack with the agile trait and a jaws unarmed attack.

Drawback You take a –1 penalty to AC and a –2 penalty to Reflex saves.

Type lesser; **Level** 1; **Price** 4 gp

You gain a +1 item bonus, your claw deals 1d4 slashing damage, your jaws deal 1d6 piercing damage, and the duration is 1 minute.

Type moderate; **Level** 3; **Price** 12 gp

You gain a +2 item bonus, your claw deals 1d6 slashing damage, your jaws deal 1d8 piercing damage, and the duration is 10 minutes.

Type greater; **Level** 11; **Price** 300 gp
You gain a +3 item bonus, your claw deals 1d8 slashing damage, your jaws deal 1d10 piercing damage, and the duration is 1 hour.

Type major; **Level** 17; **Price** 3,000 gp
You gain a +4 item bonus, your claw deals 1d8 slashing damage, your jaws deal 1d10 piercing damage, and the duration is 1 hour. You gain weapon specialization with the claws and jaws, or greater weapon specialization, if you already have weapon specialization with these unarmed attacks.

BOMBER'S EYE ELIXIR — ITEM 4+

ALCHEMICAL • CONSUMABLE • ELIXIR

Usage held in 1 hand; **Bulk** L
Activate ◆ Interact

This tincture lets you pinpoint your foes. For the next 5 minutes, your alchemical bomb Strikes reduce the circumstance bonus to AC your targets gain from cover.

Type lesser; **Level** 4; **Price** 14 gp
Reduce your targets' circumstance bonus by 1.

Type greater; **Level** 14; **Price** 700 gp
Reduce your targets' circumstance bonus by 2.

BRAVO'S BREW — ITEM 2+

ALCHEMICAL • CONSUMABLE • ELIXIR • MENTAL

Usage held in 1 hand; **Bulk** L
Activate ◆ Interact

This flask of foaming beer grants courage. For the next hour after drinking this elixir, you gain an item bonus to Will saves, which is greater when attempting Will saves against fear.

Type lesser; **Level** 2; **Price** 7 gp
The bonus on Will saves is +1, or +2 against fear.

Type moderate; **Level** 10; **Price** 150 gp
The bonus on Will saves is +2, or +3 against fear.

Type greater; **Level** 15; **Price** 700 gp
The bonus on Will saves is +3, or +4 against fear. If you roll a success on a save against fear, you get a critical success instead.

CAT'S EYE ELIXIR — ITEM 2

ALCHEMICAL • CONSUMABLE • ELIXIR

Price 7 gp
Usage held in 1 hand; **Bulk** L
Activate ◆ Interact

After you consume this elixir, your vision sharpens and you become sensitive to even the most minute movements. For the next minute, you reduce the flat check to target hidden creatures to 5, and you don't need to attempt a flat check to target concealed creatures. These benefits apply only against creatures within 30 feet of you.

CHEETAH'S ELIXIR — ITEM 1+

ALCHEMICAL • CONSUMABLE • ELIXIR

Usage held in 1 hand; **Bulk** L
Activate ◆ Interact

Enzymatic compounds in this elixir strengthen and excite the muscles in your legs. You gain a status bonus to your Speed for the listed duration.

Type lesser; **Level** 1; **Price** 3 gp
The bonus is +5 feet, and the duration is 1 minute.

Type moderate; **Level** 5; **Price** 25 gp
The bonus is +10 feet, and the duration is 10 minutes.

Type greater; **Level** 9; **Price** 110 gp
The bonus is +10 feet, and the duration is 1 hour.

COGNITIVE MUTAGEN — ITEM 1+

ALCHEMICAL • CONSUMABLE • ELIXIR • MUTAGEN • POLYMORPH

Usage held in 1 hand; **Bulk** L
Activate ◆ Interact

Your mind becomes clear and cognition flows freely, but physical matters seem ephemeral.

Benefit You gain an item bonus to Arcana, Crafting, Lore, Occultism, and Society checks and all checks to Recall Knowledge. Your critical failures on Recall Knowledge checks become failures instead.

Drawback You take a –2 penalty to weapon and unarmed attack rolls, Athletics checks, and Acrobatics checks. You can carry 2 less Bulk than normal before becoming encumbered, and the maximum Bulk you can carry is reduced by 4.

Type lesser; **Level** 1; **Price** 4 gp
The bonus is +1, and the duration is 1 minute.

Type moderate; **Level** 3; **Price** 12 gp
The bonus is +2, and the duration is 10 minutes.

Type greater; **Level** 11; **Price** 300 gp
The bonus is +3, and the duration is 1 hour. You become trained in one Intelligence-based skill, chosen at creation.

Type major; **Level** 17; **Price** 3,000 gp
The bonus is +4, and the duration is 1 hour. You become trained in one skill, chosen at creation.

COMPREHENSION ELIXIR — ITEM 2+

ALCHEMICAL • CONSUMABLE • ELIXIR • MENTAL

Usage held in 1 hand; **Bulk** L
Activate ◆ Interact

This bitter draught opens your mind to the potential of the written word. For the listed duration after drinking this elixir, you can understand any words you read, so long as they are written in a common language. This elixir doesn't automatically allow you to understand codes or extremely esoteric passages—you still need to attempt a skill check to Decipher Writing.

Type lesser; **Level** 2; **Price** 7 gp
The duration is 1 minute.

Type greater; **Level** 7; **Price** 54 gp
The duration is 10 minutes.

DARKVISION ELIXIR — ITEM 2+

ALCHEMICAL • CONSUMABLE • ELIXIR

Usage held in 1 hand; **Bulk** L
Activate ◆ Interact

INTRODUCTION
ANCESTRIES & BACKGROUNDS
CLASSES
SKILLS
FEATS
EQUIPMENT
SPELLS
THE AGE OF LOST OMENS
PLAYING THE GAME
GAME MASTERING
CRAFTING & TREASURE
APPENDIX

After you drink this elixir, your sight becomes sharper in darkness. You gain darkvision for the listed duration.

Type lesser; **Level** 2; **Price** 6 gp
The duration is 10 minutes.

Type moderate; **Level** 4; **Price** 11 gp
The duration is 1 hour.

Type greater; **Level** 8; **Price** 90 gp
The duration is 24 hours.

EAGLE-EYE ELIXIR   ITEM 1+

ALCHEMICAL   CONSUMABLE   ELIXIR

Usage held in 1 hand; **Bulk** L
Activate ❖ Interact

After you drink this elixir, you notice subtle visual details. For the next hour, you gain an item bonus to Perception checks that is greater when attempting to find secret doors and traps.

Type lesser; **Level** 1; **Price** 4 gp
The bonus is +1, or +2 to find secret doors and traps.

Type moderate; **Level** 5; **Price** 27 gp
The bonus is +2, or +3 to find secret doors and traps.

Type greater; **Level** 10; **Price** 200 gp
The bonus is +3, or +4 to find secret doors and traps.

Type major; **Level** 16; **Price** 2,000 gp
The bonus is +3, or +4 to find secret doors and traps. Each time you pass within 10 feet of a secret door or trap, the GM automatically rolls a secret check for you to find it.

ELIXIR OF LIFE   ITEM 1+

ALCHEMICAL   CONSUMABLE   ELIXIR   HEALING

Usage held in 1 hand; **Bulk** L
Activate ❖ Interact

Elixirs of life accelerate the body's natural healing processes and immune system. Upon drinking this elixir, you regain the listed number of Hit Points and gain an item bonus to saving throws against diseases and poisons for 10 minutes.

Type minor; **Level** 1; **Price** 3 gp
The elixir restores 1d6 Hit Points, and the bonus is +1.

Type lesser; **Level** 5; **Price** 30 gp
The elixir restores 3d6+6 Hit Points and the bonus is +1.

Type moderate; **Level** 9; **Price** 150 gp
The elixir restores 5d6+12 Hit Points, and the bonus is +2.

Type greater; **Level** 13; **Price** 600 gp
The elixir restores 7d6+18 Hit Points, and the bonus is +2.

Type major; **Level** 15; **Price** 1,300 gp
The elixir restores 8d6+21 Hit Points, and the bonus is +3.

Type true; **Level** 19; **Price** 3,000 gp
The elixir restores 10d6+27 Hit Points, and the bonus is +4.

ELIXIR OF REJUVENATION   ITEM 20

UNCOMMON   ALCHEMICAL   CONSUMABLE   ELIXIR

Price –
Usage held in 1 hand; **Bulk** L
Activate ❖ Interact

The elixir of rejuvenation restores a creature to full health and eradicates toxins affecting it. When you drink this elixir,

you're restored to your maximum Hit Points, and all afflictions of 20th level or lower affecting you are removed.

You can instead administer this elixir to a creature that has been dead for a week or less. When you do, that creature is instantly brought back to life with 1 Hit Point and no spell slots, Focus Points, or other daily resources.

Craft Requirements philosopher's stone, true elixir of life

INFILTRATOR'S ELIXIR   ITEM 2

ALCHEMICAL   CONSUMABLE   ELIXIR   POLYMORPH

Price 6 gp
Usage held in 1 hand; **Bulk** L
Activate ❖ Interact

Favored by spies and tricksters, an infiltrator's elixir is used to alter your appearance. When imbibed, you take the shape of a humanoid creature of your size, but different enough so you might be unrecognizable. If you aren't a humanoid, you might take on a form more similar to your own, at the GM's discretion.

The creator of the elixir decides the basics of the appearance you transform into when you imbibe the elixir, including eye color, skin tone, and hair color. The elixir can't change your form into that of a specific person. After the form takes hold, you retain it for the next 10 minutes.

Drinking this elixir counts as setting up a disguise to Impersonate. You gain a +4 status bonus to your Deception DC to avoid others seeing through your disguise, and you add your level to this DC even if untrained.

JUGGERNAUT MUTAGEN   ITEM 1+

ALCHEMICAL   CONSUMABLE   ELIXIR   MUTAGEN   POLYMORPH

Usage held in 1 hand; **Bulk** L
Activate ❖ Interact

After you drink this mutagen, your body becomes thick and sturdy. You exhibit a healthy glow, though you tend to be ponderous and unobservant.

Benefit You gain an item bonus to Fortitude saves and the listed number of temporary Hit Points. Whenever you are at maximum Hit Points for at least 1 full minute, you regain the temporary Hit Points.

Drawback You take a –2 penalty to Will saves, Perception checks, and initiative rolls.

Type lesser; **Level** 1; **Price** 4 gp
The bonus is +1, you gain 5 temporary Hit Points, and the duration is 1 minute.

Type moderate; **Level** 3; **Price** 12 gp
The bonus is +2, you gain 10 temporary Hit Points, and the duration is 10 minutes.

Type greater; **Level** 11; **Price** 300 gp
The bonus is +3, you gain 30 temporary Hit Points, and the duration is 1 hour. When you roll a success on a Fortitude save, you get a critical success instead.

Type major; **Level** 17; **Price** 3,000 gp
The bonus is +4, you gain 45 temporary Hit Points, and the duration is 1 hour. When you roll a success on a Fortitude save,

you get a critical success instead, and your critical failures on Fortitude saves become failures instead.

LEAPER'S ELIXIR — ITEM 1+

ALCHEMICAL   CONSUMABLE   ELIXIR

Usage held in 1 hand; **Bulk** L

Activate ❖ Interact

This tingly solution increases the elasticity and contraction of your leg muscles. For 1 minute after drinking this elixir, you can High Jump or Long Jump as a single action instead of 2 actions. If you do, you don't perform the initial Stride (nor do you fail if you don't Stride 10 feet).

Type lesser; **Level** 1; **Price** 3 gp

Type greater; **Level** 7; **Price** 55 gp

The maximum vertical distance you can jump with a High Jump is the same as you can jump horizontally with a Long Jump.

MISTFORM ELIXIR — ITEM 4+

ALCHEMICAL   CONSUMABLE   ELIXIR   ILLUSION   VISUAL

Usage held in 1 hand; **Bulk** L

Activate ❖ Interact

A faint mist emanates from your skin, making you concealed for the listed duration. As usual being concealed when your position is still obvious, you can't use this concealment to Hide or Sneak.

Type lesser; **Level** 4; **Price** 18 gp

The duration is 3 rounds.

Type moderate; **Level** 6; **Price** 56 gp

The duration is 1 minute.

Type greater; **Level** 10; **Price** 180 gp

The duration is 5 minutes.

QUICKSILVER MUTAGEN — ITEM 1+

ALCHEMICAL   CONSUMABLE   ELIXIR   MUTAGEN   POLYMORPH

Usage held in 1 hand; **Bulk** L

Activate ❖ Interact

Your features become thin and angular. You become swifter and nimbler, but your body also becomes fragile.

Benefit You gain an item bonus to Acrobatics checks, Stealth checks, Thievery checks, Reflex saves, and ranged attack rolls, and you gain the listed status bonus to your Speed.

Drawback You take damage equal to twice your level; you can't recover Hit Points lost in this way by any means while the mutagen lasts. You take a –2 penalty to Fortitude saves.

Type lesser; **Level** 1; **Price** 4 gp

The bonus to rolls is +1, the bonus to Speed is +5 feet, and the duration is 1 minute.

Type moderate; **Level** 3; **Price** 12 gp

The bonus to rolls is +2, the bonus to Speed is +10 feet, and the duration is 10 minutes.

Type greater; **Level** 11; **Price** 300 gp

The bonus to rolls is +3, the bonus to Speed is +15 feet, and the duration is 1 hour.

Type major; **Level** 17; **Price** 3,000 gp

The bonus to rolls is +4, the bonus to Speed is +20 feet, and the duration is 1 hour.

SALAMANDER ELIXIR — ITEM 4+

ALCHEMICAL   CONSUMABLE   ELIXIR

Usage held in 1 hand; **Bulk** L

Activate ❖ Interact

This elixir is made from salamander scales to withstand fire. For 24 hours, you are protected from the effects of severe heat.

Type lesser; **Level** 4; **Price** 15 gp

Type moderate; **Level** 12; **Price** 320 gp

You're also protected from extreme heat.

Type greater; **Level** 16; **Price** 1,400 gp

You're also protected from extreme and incredible heat.

SEA TOUCH ELIXIR — ITEM 5+

ALCHEMICAL   CONSUMABLE   ELIXIR   POLYMORPH

Usage held in 1 hand; **Bulk** L

Activate ❖ Interact

This briny concoction alters the skin on your hands and feet. The spaces between your fingers and toes become webbed, granting you a swim Speed of 20 feet for the listed duration.

Type lesser; **Level** 5; **Price** 22 gp

The duration is 10 minutes.

Type moderate; **Level** 12; **Price** 300 gp

The duration is 1 hour, and you can breathe underwater.

Type greater; **Level** 15; **Price** 920 gp

The duration is 24 hours, and you can breathe underwater.

SERENE MUTAGEN — ITEM 1+

ALCHEMICAL   CONSUMABLE   ELIXIR   MUTAGEN   POLYMORPH

Usage held in 1 hand; **Bulk** L

Activate ❖ Interact

You gain inner serenity, focused on fine details and steeled against mental assaults, but you find violence off-putting.

Benefit You gain an item bonus to Will saves and Perception, Medicine, Nature, Religion, and Survival checks. This bonus improves when you attempt Will saves against mental effects.

Drawback You take a –1 penalty to attack rolls and save DCs of offensive spells, and a –1 penalty per damage die to all weapon, unarmed attack, and spell damage.

Type lesser; **Level** 1; **Price** 4 gp

The bonus is +1, or +2 vs. mental, and the duration is 1 minute.

Type moderate; **Level** 3; **Price** 12 gp

The bonus is +2, or +3 vs. mental, and the duration is 10 minutes.

Type greater; **Level** 11; **Price** 300 gp

The bonus is +3, or +4 vs. mental, and the duration is 1 hour. When you roll a success on a Will save against a mental effect, you get a critical success instead.

Type major; **Level** 17; **Price** 3,000 gp

The bonus is +4, and the duration is 1 hour. When you roll a success on a Will save against a mental effect, you get a critical success instead, and your critical failures on Will saves against mental effects become failures instead.

SILVERTONGUE MUTAGEN   ITEM 1+

ALCHEMICAL CONSUMABLE ELIXIR MUTAGEN POLYMORPH

Usage held in 1 hand; **Bulk** L

Activate ❖ Interact

Your features become striking and your voice becomes musical and commanding, though facts and figures become hazy for you and emotion clouds your ability to reason.

Benefit You gain an item bonus to Deception, Diplomacy, Intimidation, and Performance checks. Your critical failures with any of these skill become failures instead.

Drawback You take a –2 item penalty to Arcana, Crafting, Lore, Occultism, and Society checks. Choose one skill in which you are trained; for the duration, you become untrained in that skill. All your failures on checks to Recall Knowledge become critical failures.

Type lesser; **Level** 1; **Price** 4 gp
The bonus is +1, and the duration is 1 minute.

Type moderate; **Level** 3; **Price** 12 gp
The bonus is +2, and the duration is 10 minutes.

Type greater; **Level** 11; **Price** 300 gp
The bonus is +3, and the duration is 1 hour.

Type major; **Level** 17; **Price** 3,000 gp
The bonus is +4, and the duration is 1 hour.

STONE FIST ELIXIR   ITEM 4

ALCHEMICAL CONSUMABLE ELIXIR MORPH

Price 13 gp

Usage held in 1 hand; **Bulk** L

Activate ❖ Interact

Your fists become hard as stone. For 1 hour, your fists deal 1d6 bludgeoning damage and lose the nonlethal trait.

WINTER WOLF ELIXIR   ITEM 4+

ALCHEMICAL CONSUMABLE ELIXIR

Usage held in 1 hand; **Bulk** L

Activate ❖ Interact

This elixir warms your core and improves your circulation. For 24 hours, you are protected from the effects of severe cold.

Type lesser; **Level** 4; **Price** 15 gp

Type moderate; **Level** 12; **Price** 320 gp
You're also protected from extreme cold.

Type greater; **Level** 16; **Price** 1,400 gp
You're also protected from extreme and incredible cold.

ALCHEMICAL POISONS

Alchemical poisons are potent toxins distilled or extracted from natural sources and made either stronger or easier to administer. Each poison's stat block includes the Price and features for a single dose. Poison doses are typically kept in a vial or some other type of safe and secure container.

Applying alchemical poisons uses Interact actions. A poison typically requires one hand to pour into food or scatter in the air. Applying a poison to a weapon or another item requires two hands, with one hand holding the weapon or item. The Usage entry for a poison indicates the number of hands needed for a typical means of application, but the GM might determine that using poisons in other ways functions differently.

The full rules for how poisons and other afflictions work begin on page 457. A creature attempts the listed saving throw as soon as it's exposed to the poison; on a failed save, the creature advances to stage 1 of the poison after any listed onset time elapses.

Some poisons have the virulent trait. This means the poison is harder to remove once it has taken effect; see Virulent Afflictions on page 458.

METHOD OF EXPOSURE

Each alchemical poison has one of the following traits, which define how a creature can be exposed to that poison.

Contact: A contact poison is activated by applying it to an item or directly onto a living creature's skin. The first creature to touch the affected item must attempt a saving throw against the poison; if the poison is applied directly, the creature must attempt a saving throw immediately when the poison touches its skin. Contact poisons are infeasible to apply to a creature via a weapon attack due to the logistics of delivering them without poisoning yourself. Typically, the onset time of a contact poison is 1 minute.

Ingested: An ingested poison is activated by applying it to food or drink to be consumed by a living creature, or by placing it directly into a living creature's mouth. A creature attempts a saving throw against such a poison when it consumes the poison or the food or drink treated with the poison. The onset time of ingested poisons typically ranges anywhere from 1 minute to 1 day.

Inhaled: An inhaled poison is activated by unleashing it from its container. Once unleashed, the poison creates a cloud filling a 10-foot cube lasting for 1 minute or until a strong wind dissipates the cloud. Every creature entering this cloud is exposed to the poison and must attempt a saving throw against it; a creature aware of the poison before entering the cloud can use a single action to hold its breath and gain a +2 circumstance bonus to the saving throw for 1 round.

Injury: An injury poison is activated by applying it to a weapon, and it affects the target of the first Strike made using the poisoned weapon. If that Strike is a success and deals piercing or slashing damage, the target must attempt a saving throw against the poison. On a failed Strike, the target is unaffected, but the poison remains on the weapon and you can try again. On a critical failure, or if the Strike fails to deal slashing or piercing damage for some other reason, the poison is spent but the target is unaffected.

ARSENIC   ITEM 1

ALCHEMICAL CONSUMABLE INGESTED POISON

Price 3 gp

Usage held in 1 hand; **Bulk** L

Activate ❖ Interact

This toxin is a compound of arsenic and other substances. You can't reduce your sickened condition while affected.

Saving Throw DC 18 Fortitude; Onset 10 minutes; Maximum Duration 5 minutes; Stage 1 1d4 poison damage and sickened 1 (1 minute); Stage 2 1d6 poison damage and sickened 2 (1 minute); Stage 3 2d6 poison damage and sickened 3 (1 minute)

BELLADONNA   ITEM 2

| ALCHEMICAL | CONSUMABLE | INGESTED | POISON |

Price 5 gp
Usage held in 1 hand; **Bulk** L
Activate ❖ Interact

Sometimes called "deadly nightshade," belladonna is a widely available toxin produced from a plant similar to a tomato.

Saving Throw DC 19 Fortitude; Onset 10 minutes; Maximum Duration 30 minutes; Stage 1 dazzled (10 minutes); Stage 2 1d6 poison damage and sickened 1 (10 minutes); Stage 3 1d6 poison damage, confused, and sickened 1 (1 minute)

BLACK ADDER VENOM   ITEM 2

| ALCHEMICAL | CONSUMABLE | INJURY | POISON |

Price 6 gp
Usage held in 2 hands; **Bulk** L
Activate ❖❖❖ Interact

Adder venom is a simple but effective way to enhance a weapon.

Saving Throw DC 18 Fortitude; Maximum Duration 3 rounds; Stage 1 1d8 poison damage (1 round); Stage 2 1d10 poison damage (1 round); Stage 3 2d6 poison damage (1 round)

BLACK LOTUS EXTRACT   ITEM 19

| ALCHEMICAL | CONSUMABLE | CONTACT | POISON | VIRULENT |

Price 6,500 gp
Usage held in 1 hand; **Bulk** L
Activate ❖ Interact

Black lotus extract causes severe internal bleeding.

Saving Throw DC 42 Fortitude; Onset 1 minute; Maximum Duration 6 rounds; Stage 1 15d6 poison damage and drained 1 (1 round); Stage 2 17d6 poison damage and drained 1 (1 round); Stage 3 20d6 poison damage and drained 2 (1 round)

BLIGHTBURN RESIN   ITEM 11

| ALCHEMICAL | CONSUMABLE | CONTACT | POISON |

Price 225 gp
Usage held in 2 hands; **Bulk** L
Activate ❖ Interact

This tacky, hardened sap is harvested from trees infected by fungal blights and exposed to open flames.

Saving Throw DC 31 Fortitude; Onset 1 minute; Maximum Duration 6 rounds; Stage 1 8d6 poison damage (1 round); Stage 2 10d6 poison damage (1 round); Stage 3 15d6 poison damage (1 round)

BRIMSTONE FUMES   ITEM 16

| ALCHEMICAL | CONSUMABLE | EVIL | INHALED | POISON |

Price 1,500 gp
Usage held in 1 hand; **Bulk** L
Activate ❖ Interact

Fumes from the forges of Hell drain health and strength alike.

Saving Throw DC 36 Fortitude; Onset 1 round; Maximum Duration 6 rounds; Stage 1 7d6 poison damage and enfeebled 1 (1 round); Stage 2 8d6 poison damage and enfeebled 2 (1 round); Stage 3 10d6 poison damage and enfeebled 3 (1 round)

CYTILLESH OIL   ITEM 3

| ALCHEMICAL | CONSUMABLE | INJURY | POISON |

Price 10 gp
Usage held in 2 hands; **Bulk** L
Activate ❖ Interact

This thick substance is distilled from the mind-robbing cytillesh fungus, though it lacks memory-altering capabilities.

Saving Throw DC 19 Fortitude; Maximum Duration 4 rounds; Stage 1 1d10 poison damage (1 round); Stage 2 1d12 poison damage (1 round); Stage 3 2d10 poison damage (1 round)

DEATHCAP POWDER   ITEM 13

| ALCHEMICAL | CONSUMABLE | INGESTED | POISON |

Price 450 gp
Usage held in 2 hands; **Bulk** L
Activate ❖ Interact

The toxic deathcap mushroom can be dried, ground, and treated to form a flavorless powder with accelerated effects.

Saving Throw DC 33 Fortitude; Onset 10 minutes; Maximum Duration 6 minutes; Stage 1 13d6 poison damage (1 minute); Stage 2 17d6 poison damage and sickened 2 (1 minute); Stage 3 20d6 poison damage and sickened 3 (1 minute)

DRAGON BILE   ITEM 15

| ALCHEMICAL | CONSUMABLE | CONTACT | POISON |

Price 925 gp
Usage held in 2 hands; **Bulk** L
Activate ❖ Interact

A mix of digestive juices and green dragon poison glands nauseates the victim as its flesh is digested from within.

Saving Throw DC 37 Fortitude; Onset 1 minute; Maximum Duration 6 rounds; Stage 1 6d6 poison damage and sickened 2 (1 round); Stage 2 7d6 poison damage and sickened 3 (1 round); Stage 3 9d6 poison damage and sickened 4 (1 round)

GIANT CENTIPEDE VENOM   ITEM 1

| ALCHEMICAL | CONSUMABLE | INJURY | POISON |

Price 4 gp
Usage held in 2 hands; **Bulk** L
Activate ❖❖❖ Interact

Giant centipede venom causes severe muscle stiffness.

Saving Throw DC 17 Fortitude; Maximum Duration 6 rounds; Stage 1 1d6 poison damage (1 round); Stage 2 1d8 poison damage and flat-footed (1 round); Stage 3 1d12 poison damage, clumsy 1, and flat-footed (1 round)

GIANT SCORPION VENOM   ITEM 6

| ALCHEMICAL | CONSUMABLE | INJURY | POISON |

Price 40 gp

Usage held in 2 hands; **Bulk** L

Activate ◆◆◆ Interact

Scorpion venom is excruciating and its effects are somewhat debilitating.

Saving Throw DC 22 Fortitude; **Maximum Duration** 6 rounds; **Stage 1** 1d10 poison damage and enfeebled 1 (1 round); **Stage 2** 2d10 poison damage and enfeebled 1 (1 round); **Stage 3** 2d10 poison damage and enfeebled 2 (1 round)

GIANT WASP VENOM　　　　　ITEM 7

| ALCHEMICAL | CONSUMABLE | INJURY | POISON |

Price 55 gp

Usage held in 2 hands; **Bulk** L

Activate ◆◆◆ Interact

Giant wasp venom interferes with a victim's movement.

Saving Throw DC 25 Fortitude; **Maximum Duration** 6 rounds; **Stage 1** 2d6 poison damage and clumsy 1 (1 round); **Stage 2** 3d6 poison damage and clumsy 2 (1 round); **Stage 3** 4d6 poison and clumsy 2 (1 round)

GRAVEROOT　　　　　　　　ITEM 3

| ALCHEMICAL | CONSUMABLE | INJURY | POISON |

Price 10 gp

Usage held in 2 hands; **Bulk** L

Activate ◆◆◆ Interact

The opaque white sap from the graveroot shrub clouds the mind.

Saving Throw DC 19 Fortitude; **Maximum Duration** 4 rounds; **Stage 1** 1d10 poison damage (1 round); **Stage 2** 1d12 poison damage and stupefied 1 (1 round); **Stage 3** 2d6 poison damage and stupefied 2 (1 round)

HEMLOCK　　　　　　　　　ITEM 17

| ALCHEMICAL | CONSUMABLE | INGESTED | POISON |

Price 2,250 gp

Usage held in 1 hand; **Bulk** L

Activate ◆ Interact

Concentrated hemlock is a particularly deadly toxin that halts muscle action—including that of the victim's heart.

Saving Throw DC 40 Fortitude; **Onset** 30 minutes; **Maximum Duration** 60 minutes; **Stage 1** 17d6 poison damage and enfeebled 2 (10 minutes); **Stage 2** 21d6 poison damage and enfeebled 3 (10 minutes); **Stage 3** 26d6 poison damage and enfeebled 4 (10 minutes)

HUNTING SPIDER VENOM　　　ITEM 5

| ALCHEMICAL | CONSUMABLE | INJURY | POISON |

Price 25 gp

Usage held in 2 hands; **Bulk** L

Activate ◆◆◆ Interact

This venom erodes its target's defenses, aiding the spider in securing prey.

Saving Throw DC 21 Fortitude; **Maximum Duration** 6 rounds; **Stage 1** 1d10 poison damage and flat-footed (1 round); **Stage 2** 1d12 poison damage, clumsy 1, and flat-footed (1 round); **Stage 3** 2d6 poison damage, clumsy 2, and flat-footed (1 round)

KING'S SLEEP　　　　　　　ITEM 18

| ALCHEMICAL | CONSUMABLE | INGESTED | POISON | VIRULENT |

Price 4,000 gp

Usage held in 1 hand; **Bulk** L

Activate ◆ Interact

King's sleep is an insidious long-term poison that can seem like a disease or even death from natural causes on a venerable target. The drained condition from king's sleep is cumulative with each failed save and can't be removed while the poison lasts.

Saving Throw DC 41 Fortitude; **Onset** 1 day; **Stage 1** drained 1 (1 day); **Stage 2** drained 1 (1 day); **Stage 3** drained 2 (1 day)

LETHARGY POISON　　　　　ITEM 2

| UNCOMMON | ALCHEMICAL | CONSUMABLE | INCAPACITATION | INJURY | POISON |
| SLEEP |

Price 7 gp

Usage held in 2 hands; **Bulk** L

Activate ◆◆◆ Interact

Lethargy poison is commonly used in hit-and-run tactics by drow and others who want their victims alive; the ambusher retreats until the poison sets in and the victim falls unconscious. Further exposure to lethargy poison does not require the target to attempt additional saving throws; only failing an saving throw against an ongoing exposure can progress its stage.

Saving Throw DC 18 Fortitude; **Maximum Duration** 4 hours; **Stage 1** slowed 1 (1 round); **Stage 2** slowed 1 (1 minute); **Stage 3** unconscious with no Perception check to wake up (1 round) **Stage 4** unconscious with no Perception check to wake up (1d4 hours).

LICH DUST　　　　　　　　ITEM 9

| ALCHEMICAL | CONSUMABLE | INGESTED | POISON |

Price 110 gp

Usage held in 1 hand; **Bulk** L

Activate ◆ Interact

Dust salvaged from the remains of a destroyed lich has paralytic properties that make it a valuable poison.

Saving Throw DC 28 Fortitude; **Onset** 10 minutes; **Maximum Duration** 6 minutes; **Stage 1** fatigued (1 minute); **Stage 2** 5d6 poison damage and fatigued (1 minute); **Stage 3** 5d6 poison damage, fatigued, and paralyzed (1 minute)

MALYASS ROOT PASTE　　　　ITEM 7

| ALCHEMICAL | CONSUMABLE | CONTACT | POISON |

Price 55 gp

Usage held in 2 hands; **Bulk** L

Activate ◆◆◆ Interact

Malyass root paste sees use to impede opponents in athletic competitions, in addition to espionage and tracking.

Saving Throw DC 26 Fortitude; **Onset** 1 minute; **Maximum Duration** 6 minutes; **Stage 1** clumsy 1 and –10-foot status penalty to all Speeds (1 minute); **Stage 2** clumsy 2 and –20-foot status penalty to all Speeds (1 minute); **Stage 3** clumsy 3, flat-footed, and –30-foot status penalty to all Speeds

MINDFOG MIST ITEM 15

ALCHEMICAL CONSUMABLE INHALED POISON

Price 1,000 gp
Usage held in 1 hand; **Bulk** L
Activate ❖ Interact

Mindfog mist can be used to undermine spellcasters, as its effect on a victim's mental faculties are swift and powerful.

Saving Throw DC 35 Fortitude; **Onset** 1 round; **Maximum Duration** 6 rounds; **Stage 1** stupefied 2 (1 round); **Stage 2** confused and stupefied 3 (1 round); **Stage 3** confused and stupefied 4 (1 round)

NETTLEWEED RESIDUE ITEM 8

ALCHEMICAL CONSUMABLE CONTACT POISON

Price 75 gp
Usage held in 2 hands; **Bulk** L
Activate ❖ Interact

Concentrated sap of stinging weeds makes an effective toxin.

Saving Throw DC 27 Fortitude; **Onset** 1 minute; **Maximum Duration** 6 minutes; **Stage 1** 8d6 poison damage (1 minute); **Stage 2** 10d6 poison damage (1 minute); **Stage 3** 13d6 poison damage (1 minute)

NIGHTMARE VAPOR ITEM 16

ALCHEMICAL CONSUMABLE INHALED POISON

Price 1,400 gp
Usage held in 1 hand; **Bulk** L
Activate ❖ Interact

Purportedly sourced from any number of outlandish locales, nightmare vapor is most often created by boiling the sweat collected from humanoids caught in the throes of terrible nightmares.

Saving Throw DC 36 Fortitude; **Onset** 1 round; **Maximum Duration** 6 rounds; **Stage 1** confused (1 round); **Stage 2** confused and flat-footed (1 round); **Stage 3** confused, flat-footed, and stupefied 2 (1 round)

PURPLE WORM VENOM ITEM 13

ALCHEMICAL CONSUMABLE INJURY POISON

Price 500 gp
Usage held in 2 hands; **Bulk** L
Activate ❖❖❖ Interact

Venom from enormous purple worms leaves a victim weakened.

Saving Throw DC 32 Fortitude; **Maximum Duration** 6 rounds; **Stage 1** 5d6 poison damage and enfeebled 2 (1 round); **Stage 2** 6d6 poison damage and enfeebled 2 (1 round); **Stage 3** 8d6 poison and enfeebled 2 (1 round)

SHADOW ESSENCE ITEM 10

ALCHEMICAL CONSUMABLE INJURY NEGATIVE POISON

Price 160 gp
Usage held in 2 hands; **Bulk** L
Activate ❖❖❖ Interact

Distilled from the Plane of Shadow, this oily substance imposes tenebrous effects. The enfeebled condition from shadow essence lasts for 24 hours.

Saving Throw DC 29 Fortitude; **Maximum Duration** 6 rounds; **Stage 1** 3d6 negative damage and 2d6 poison damage (1 round); **Stage 2** 3d6 negative damage, 2d6 poison damage, and enfeebled 1 (1 round); **Stage 3** 3d6 negative damage, 2d6 poison damage, and enfeebled 2 (1 round)

SLUMBER WINE ITEM 12

ALCHEMICAL CONSUMABLE INGESTED POISON SLEEP

Price 325 gp
Usage held in 1 hand; **Bulk** L
Activate ❖ Interact

Slumber wine sees its greatest use in games of intrigue, where an absence can be more devastating than injury. Characters unconscious from slumber wine can't wake up by any means while the poison lasts, don't need to eat or drink while unconscious in this way, and appear to be recently dead unless an examiner succeeds at a DC 40 Medicine check.

Saving Throw DC 32 Fortitude; **Onset** 1 hour; **Maximum Duration** 7 days; **Stage 1** unconscious (1 day); **Stage 2** unconscious (2 days); **Stage 3** unconscious (3 days).

SPIDER ROOT ITEM 9

ALCHEMICAL CONSUMABLE CONTACT POISON

Price 110 gp
Usage held in 2 hands; **Bulk** L
Activate ❖ Interact

A paste made by mashing the fine, threadlike roots of a certain creeper vine, spider root renders a victim clumsy and maladroit.

Saving Throw DC 28 Fortitude; **Onset** 1 minute; **Maximum Duration** 6 minutes; **Stage 1** 8d6 poison damage and clumsy 1 (1 minute); **Stage 2** 9d6 poison damage and clumsy 2 (1 minute); **Stage 3** 10d6 poison damage and clumsy 3 (1 minute)

TEARS OF DEATH ITEM 20

ALCHEMICAL CONSUMABLE CONTACT POISON VIRULENT

Price 12,000 gp
Usage held in 2 hands; **Bulk** L
Activate ❖ Interact

Tears of death are among the most powerful of alchemical poisons, distilled from extracts of five other deadly poisons in just the right ratios.

Saving Throw DC 46 Fortitude; **Onset** 1 minute; **Maximum Duration** 10 minutes; **Stage 1** 18d6 poison damage and paralyzed (1 round); **Stage 2** 25d6 poison damage and paralyzed (1 minute); **Stage 3** 30d6 poison damage and paralyzed (1 minute)

WOLFSBANE ITEM 10

ALCHEMICAL CONSUMABLE INGESTED POISON

Price 155 gp
Usage held in 1 hand; **Bulk** L
Activate ❖ Interact

Wolfsbane appears in folklore for its link to werecreatures. If you are afflicted with lycanthropy and survive stage 3 of wolfsbane, you're immediately cured of the lycanthropy.

Saving Throw DC 30 Fortitude; **Onset** 10 minutes; **Maximum Duration** 6 minutes; **Stage 1** 12d6 poison damage (1 minute); **Stage 2** 16d6 poison damage (1 minute); **Stage 3** 20d6 poison damage (1 minute)

WYVERN POISON ITEM 8

| ALCHEMICAL | CONSUMABLE | INJURY | POISON |

Price 80 gp
Usage held in 2 hands; **Bulk** L
Activate ◆◆◆ Interact

Properly harvested and preserved, the poison from a wyvern's sting is effective and direct.

Saving Throw DC 26 Fortitude; **Maximum Duration** 6 rounds; **Stage 1** 5d6 poison damage (1 round); **Stage 2** 6d6 poison damage (1 round); **Stage 3** 8d6 poison damage (1 round)

ALCHEMICAL TOOLS

Alchemical tools are consumable items you don't drink.

PHILOSOPHER'S STONE ITEM 20

| UNCOMMON | ALCHEMICAL | CONSUMABLE |

Price –
Usage held in 2 hands; **Bulk** 2
Activate ◆ Interact or 1 or more days; see below

An alchemist with the Craft Philosopher's Stone feat can create a philosopher's stone once per month by spending 1 batch of infused reagents during their daily preparations using the advanced alchemy class feature. This is the only way to create a philosopher's stone.

At a glance, a philosopher's stone appears to be an ordinary, sooty piece of natural rock. Breaking the rock open with a Force Open action (DC 35) reveals a cavity at the stone's heart. The cavity is lined with a rare type of quicksilver that can transmute base metals into precious metals or create an elixir of rejuvenation (page 548).

To use the quicksilver, you must be legendary in Crafting and have the Alchemical Crafting feat. You can then use the stone's quicksilver for one of two effects:

- You can apply the stone's quicksilver to an infused true elixir of life using an Interact action. This turns the elixir into an infused elixir of rejuvenation instantaneously. This doesn't require any crafting time or additional materials.
- You can spend up to a month of downtime applying the quicksilver either to iron to create silver or to lead to create gold. Treat this as a 20th-level task to Earn Income using Crafting, except that you create 500 gp worth of your chosen metal per day on a success or 750 gp worth per day on a critical success.

SILVERSHEEN ITEM 2

| ALCHEMICAL | CONSUMABLE |

Price 6 gp
Usage held in 2 hands; **Bulk** L
Activate ◆ Interact

You can slather this silvery paste onto one melee weapon, one thrown weapon, or 10 pieces of ammunition. Silversheen spoils quickly, so once you open a vial, you must use it all at once, rather than saving it. For the next hour, the weapon or ammunition counts as silver instead of its normal precious material (such as cold iron) for any physical damage it deals.

SMOKESTICK ITEM 1+

| ALCHEMICAL | CONSUMABLE |

Usage held in 2 hands; **Bulk** L
Activate ◆ Interact

With a sharp twist of this item, you instantly create a screen of thick, opaque smoke in a burst centered on one corner of your space. All creatures within that area are concealed, and all other creatures are concealed to them. The smoke lasts for 1 minute or until dispersed by a strong wind.

Type lesser; **Level** 1; **Price** 3 gp
The radius of the burst is 5 feet.

Type greater; **Level** 7; **Price** 53 gp
The radius of the burst is 20 feet.

SNAKE OIL ITEM 1

| ALCHEMICAL | CONSUMABLE |

Price 2 gp
Usage held in 2 hands; **Bulk** L
Activate ◆ Interact

You can apply snake oil onto a wound or other outward symptom of an affliction or condition (such as sores from a disease or discoloration from a poison). For the next hour, the symptom disappears and the wounded or afflicted creature doesn't feel as if it still has the wound or affliction, though all effects remain. A creature can uncover the ruse by succeeding at a DC 17 Perception check, but only if it uses a Seek action to specifically examine the snake oil's effects.

SUNROD ITEM 1

| ALCHEMICAL | CONSUMABLE | LIGHT |

Price 3 gp
Usage held in 1 hand; **Bulk** L
Activate ◆ Interact

This 1-foot-long, gold-tipped rod glows after it's struck on a hard surface. For the next 6 hours, it sheds bright light in a 20-foot radius (and dim light to the next 40 feet).

TINDERTWIG ITEM 1

| ALCHEMICAL | CONSUMABLE | FIRE |

Price 2 sp
Usage held in 1 hand; **Bulk** –
Activate ◆ Interact

An alchemical substance applied to one end of this tiny wooden stick ignites when struck against a rough surface. Creating a flame with a tindertwig is much faster than creating a flame with flint and steel. You can ignite the tindertwig and touch it to a flammable object as part of the same Interact action.

INTRODUCTION

ANCESTRIES &
BACKGROUNDS

CLASSES

SKILLS

FEATS

EQUIPMENT

SPELLS

THE AGE OF
LOST OMENS

PLAYING THE
GAME

GAME
MASTERING

CRAFTING
& TREASURE

APPENDIX

ARMOR

Suits of armor can be crafted from precious materials or infused with magic to grant them abilities exceeding those of typical armor. Many suits of magic armor are created by etching runes onto them, as described on page 580. The magic armor stat block lists the Price and attributes of the most common armors you can make with fundamental runes. Other special suits of armor might be made of precious materials, and some are specially crafted items all on their own.

PRECIOUS MATERIAL ARMOR

Suits of armor made of precious materials are more expensive and sometimes grant special effects. You can make leather armor out of dragonhide, wooden armor out of darkwood, and metal armor out of any precious materials except for darkwood. Because armor's Bulk is reduced when the armor is worn, use its carried Bulk when determining its material Price. (Materials are on page 577.)

ADAMANTINE ARMOR   ITEM 12+

UNCOMMON

Usage worn armor; **Bulk** varies by armor

Adamantine armor has a shiny, black appearance and is amazingly durable.

Type standard-grade adamantine armor; **Level** 12; **Price** 1,600 gp + 160 gp per Bulk; **Craft Requirements** The initial raw materials must include adamantine worth at least 200 gp + 20 gp per Bulk.

Type high-grade adamantine armor; **Level** 19; **Price** 32,000 gp + 3,200 gp per Bulk; **Craft Requirements** The initial raw materials must include adamantine worth at least 16,000 gp + 1,600 gp per Bulk.

COLD IRON ARMOR   ITEM 5+

Usage worn armor; **Bulk** varies by armor

Cold iron armor sickens certain creatures that touch it. A creature with weakness to cold iron (such as most demons and fey) that critically fails an unarmed attack against a creature in cold iron armor becomes sickened 1. A creature with weakness to cold iron is sickened 1 as long as it wears cold iron armor.

Type low-grade cold iron armor; **Level** 5; **Price** 140 gp + 14 gp per Bulk; **Craft Requirements** The initial raw materials must include cold iron worth at least 70 sp + 7 sp per Bulk

Type standard-grade cold iron armor; **Level** 11; **Price** 1,200 gp + 120 gp per Bulk; **Craft Requirements** The initial raw materials must include at least 150 gp of cold iron + 15 gp per Bulk.

Type high-grade cold iron armor; **Level** 18; **Price** 20,000 gp + 2,000 gp per Bulk; **Craft Requirements** The initial raw materials must include cold iron worth at least 10,000 gp + 1,000 gp per Bulk.

DARKWOOD ARMOR   ITEM 12+

UNCOMMON

Usage worn armor; **Bulk** varies by armor

Darkwood armor is 1 Bulk lighter than normal (or light Bulk if its normal Bulk is 1, with no effect on armor that normally has light Bulk). It's easier to wear than normal wood armor, reducing the Strength score necessary to ignore its check penalty by 2 and reducing its Speed penalty by 5 feet. (There are no types of wood armor in this book.)

Type standard-grade darkwood armor; **Level** 12; **Price** 1,600 gp + 160 gp per Bulk; **Craft Requirements** The initial raw materials must include darkwood worth at least 200 gp + 20 gp per Bulk.

Type high-grade darkwood armor; **Level** 19; **Price** 32,000 gp + 3,200 gp per Bulk; **Craft Requirements** The initial raw materials must include darkwood worth at least 16,000 gp + 1,600 gp per Bulk.

DRAGONHIDE ARMOR   ITEM 12+

UNCOMMON

Usage worn armor; **Bulk** varies by armor

Dragonhide armor is immune to one damage type based on the type of dragon it is made from (as listed in the table on page 579). Wearing armor made from dragonhide also grants you a +1 circumstance bonus to your AC and saving throws against attacks and spells that deal the corresponding damage type.

Type standard-grade dragonhide armor; **Level** 12; **Price** 1,600 gp + 160 gp per Bulk; **Craft Requirements** The initial raw materials must include dragonhide worth at least 200 gp + 20 gp per Bulk.

Type high-grade dragonhide armor; **Level** 19; **Price** 32,000 gp + 3,200 gp per Bulk; **Craft Requirements** The initial raw materials must include dragonhide worth at least 16,000 gp + 1,600 gp per Bulk.

ELVEN CHAIN   ITEM 13+

UNCOMMON

Usage worn armor; **Bulk** 1

Elven chain is a chain shirt made of mithral (page 579) that glitters in even the faintest light. It grants a +2 item bonus to AC and has no check penalty.

Created by elven artisans employing ancient crafting techniques, elven chain is exceptionally quiet. Unlike other chain shirts—even other mithral chain shirts—elven chain does not have the noisy trait. This suit of armor can be etched with runes like any other mithral chain shirt.

ARMOR ALTERNATIVES

If you don't want to wear armor, or you're trained in only unarmored defense, you can wear either explorer's clothing or *bracers of armor*. Explorer's clothing can be etched with runes just like armor can, so it can provide item bonuses to AC or saves.

Bracers of armor give a +1 item bonus to AC with no Dex modifier cap, and also grant a bonus to saves. This item can be found on page 607.

Type standard-grade elven chain; **Level** 13; **Price** 2,500 gp; **Craft Requirements** The initial raw materials must include mithral worth at least 3,125 sp.

Type high-grade elven chain; **Level** 20; **Price** 52,000 gp; **Craft Requirements** The initial raw materials must include mithral worth at least 26,000 gp.

MITHRAL ARMOR   ITEM 12+

UNCOMMON

Usage worn armor; **Bulk** varies by armor

Mithral armor is 1 Bulk lighter than normal (or light Bulk if its normal Bulk is 1, with no effect on armor that normally has light Bulk). It's easier to wear than normal metal armor, reducing the Strength score necessary to ignore its check penalty by 2 and reducing its Speed penalty by 5 feet.

Type standard-grade mithral armor; **Level** 12; **Price** 1,600 gp + 160 gp per Bulk; **Craft Requirements** The initial raw materials must include mithral worth at least 200 gp + 20 gp per Bulk.

Type high-grade mithral armor; **Level** 19; **Price** 32,000 gp + 3,200 gp per Bulk; **Craft Requirements** The initial raw materials must include mithral worth at least 16,000 gp + 1,600 gp per Bulk.

ORICHALCUM ARMOR   ITEM 20

RARE

Usage worn armor; **Bulk** varies by armor

Orichalcum armor can be etched with four magic property runes instead of three due to the magical empowerment of orichalcum. If you are wearing armor made of orichalcum, the armor grants you insights into the future, granting you a +1 circumstance bonus to initiative rolls.

Type high-grade orichalcum armor; **Level** 20; **Price** 55,000 gp + 5,500 gp per Bulk; **Craft Requirements** The initial raw materials must include orichalcum worth at least 27,500 gp + 2,750 gp per Bulk.

SILVER ARMOR   ITEM 5+

Usage worn armor; **Bulk** varies by armor

Silver armor sickens certain creatures that touch it. A creature with weakness to silver that critically fails an unarmed attack against a creature in silver armor becomes sickened 1. A creature with weakness to silver is sickened 1 as long as it wears silver armor.

Type low-grade silver armor; **Level** 5; **Price** 140 gp + 14 gp per Bulk; **Craft Requirements** silver worth at least 70 sp + 7 sp per Bulk

Type standard-grade silver armor; **Level** 11; **Price** 1,200 gp + 120 gp per Bulk; **Craft Requirements** The initial raw materials must include silver worth at least 150 gp + 15 gp per Bulk.

Type high-grade silver armor; **Level** 18; **Price** 20,000 gp + 2,000 gp per Bulk; **Craft Requirements** The initial raw materials must include silver worth at least 10,000 gp + 1,000 gp per Bulk.

BASIC MAGIC ARMOR

The most common special armors are suits of armor with some combination of *armor potency* and *resilient* runes. The following stat block provides a quick reference for these types of armor.

MAGIC ARMOR   ITEM 5+

ABJURATION   INVESTED   MAGICAL

Usage worn armor; **Bulk** varies by armor

A suit of magic armor is simply a suit of armor or explorer's clothing etched with fundamental runes. An *armor potency* rune increases the armor's item bonus to AC, and a *resilient* rune adds an item bonus to saving throws.

The Prices here are for all types of armor. You don't need to adjust the Price from leather armor to full plate or the like. These armors are made of standard materials, not precious materials such as mithral.

Type *+1 armor*; **Level** 5; **Price** 160 gp

This armor has a *+1 armor potency* rune (increase the item bonus to AC by 1).

Type *+1 resilient armor*; **Level** 8; **Price** 500 gp

This armor has a *+1 armor potency* rune (increase the item bonus to AC by 1) and a *resilient* rune (+1 item bonus to saves).

Type *+2 resilient armor*; **Level** 11; **Price** 1,400 gp

This armor has a *+2 armor potency* rune (increase the item bonus to AC by 2) and a *resilient* rune (+1 item bonus to saves).

Type *+2 greater resilient armor*; **Level** 14; **Price** 4,500 gp

This armor has a *+2 armor potency* rune (increase the item bonus to AC by 2) and a *greater resilient* rune (+2 item bonus to saves).

Type *+3 greater resilient armor*; **Level** 18; **Price** 24,000 gp

This armor has a *+3 armor potency* rune (increase the item bonus to AC by 3) and a *greater resilient* rune (+2 item bonus to saves).

Type *+3 major resilient armor*; **Level** 20; **Price** 70,000 gp

This armor has a *+3 armor potency* rune (increase the item bonus to AC by 3) and a *major resilient* rune (+3 item bonus to saves).

11

SPECIFIC MAGIC ARMOR

These suits of armor have abilities far different from what can be gained by etching runes. A specific magic armor lists its fundamental runes, which you can upgrade, add, or transfer as normal. You can't etch any property runes onto a specific armor that it doesn't already have.

BREASTPLATE OF COMMAND ITEM 10+

ENCHANTMENT   INVESTED   MAGICAL

Usage worn armor; **Bulk** 2

This *+1 resilient breastplate* is made from shining bronze overlaid with reinforcing golden panels in the shape of lion's heads. Wearing this breastplate grants you a commanding aura. You gain a +2 item bonus to Diplomacy checks, but you take a –2 item penalty to Stealth checks to Hide and Sneak and Deception checks to Impersonate.

Activate ❖ command; **Frequency** once per day; **Effect** You grant allies within 100 feet a +2 status bonus to saves against fear effects for 1 minute. When you activate this ability, each affected ally who's frightened reduces their frightened value by 1.

Type *breastplate of command*; **Level** 10; **Price** 1,000 gp
Type *greater breastplate of command*; **Level** 18; **Price** 22,000 gp
The armor is a *+2 greater resilient breastplate*. The item bonus and penalty increase to +3 and –3, respectively.

CELESTIAL ARMOR ITEM 13

DIVINE   GOOD   INVESTED   TRANSMUTATION

Price 2,500 gp

Usage worn armor; **Bulk** 1

This suit of *+2 resilient chain mail* is made of fine white links of a strange and slightly translucent pale metal, and the sleeves and skirt are fashioned into smaller trails that resemble feathers. Unlike normal chain mail, *celestial armor* has no Speed reduction, its armor check penalty is 0, and its Bulk is 1.

You gain a +1 circumstance bonus to AC and saving throws against fiends. You appear radiant while you wear the armor, giving you a +2 item bonus to Diplomacy checks against all creatures except fiends.

If you are not good, you are drained 2 while wearing *celestial armor*. You can't recover from this condition while wearing the armor.

Activate ❖ command; **Frequency** once per day; **Effect** The armor sprouts glowing wings that grant you a fly Speed of 30 feet. The wings shed bright light in a 40-foot radius (and dim light to the next 40 feet). The wings fade away after 10 minutes.

Craft Requirements You are good.

DEMON ARMOR ITEM 13

DIVINE   EVIL   INVESTED   NECROMANCY

Price 2,500 gp

Usage worn armor; **Bulk** 4

Crafted from black iron, this crude suit of *+2 resilient full plate* is designed to make you look like a horned demon, with your face peering out of the screaming maw of the beast.

While wearing the armor, you can attack with the helmet's horns. They are a martial melee weapon with the effects of a *+2 weapon potency* rune. They deal 2d8 piercing damage and have the deadly d12 trait. On a critical hit with the horns, the target must attempt a DC 30 Fortitude save against the *Abyssal plague* disease (page 316). The horns can't be etched with any runes.

If you aren't evil, you're drained 2 and can't recover from this condition while wearing *demon armor*.

Activate ❖❖ command; **Frequency** once per day; **Effect** You cast *dimension door*.

Craft Requirements You are evil; supply one casting of *dimension door*.

DRAGONPLATE ITEM 16

UNCOMMON   EVOCATION   INVESTED   MAGICAL

Price 10,000 gp

Usage worn armor; **Bulk** 4

This suit of *+2 greater resilient dragonhide full plate* makes you look like a fearsome dragon. The armor comes in 10 varieties corresponding to the 10 common dragon types, though other varieties undoubtedly exist.

Activate ❖❖ Interact; **Frequency** once per day; **Effect** You unleash a bout of dragon breath with a shape, damage type, and saving throw corresponding to the type of dragon used to make the armor (shown on the table below). The breath weapon deals 14d6 damage; each creature in the area must attempt a DC 36 basic saving throw.

| | **Protects** | |
Dragon Type	Against	Breath Weapon (Save)
Black or copper	acid	30-foot line of acid (Reflex)
Blue or bronze	electricity	30-foot line of electricity (Reflex)
Brass	fire	30-foot line of fire (Reflex)
Green	poison	15-foot cone of poison (Fortitude)
Gold or red	fire	15-foot cone of fire (Reflex)
Silver or white	cold	15-foot cone of cold (Reflex)

Craft Requirements The initial raw materials must include 1,250 gp of dragonhide.

ELECTRIC EELSKIN ITEM 10

INVESTED   MAGICAL   TRANSMUTATION

Price 950 gp

ANCESTRIES & BACKGROUNDS

CLASSES

SKILLS

FEATS

EQUIPMENT

SPELLS

THE AGE OF LOST OMENS

PLAYING THE GAME

GAME MASTERING

CRAFTING & TREASURE

APPENDIX

Usage worn armor; **Bulk** 1

Shining, slippery eelskin covers the plates of this *+1 resilient greater slick leather* armor. The armor gives you the ability to breathe water and grants you a +2 item bonus to Athletics checks to Swim and Stealth checks you attempt in the water.

Activate ◆◆ command, Interact; **Frequency** once per hour; **Effect** You cast a 2nd-level *shocking grasp* with a DC of 29.

Craft Requirements Supply one casting of *shocking grasp*.

GHOUL HIDE   ITEM 6

UNCOMMON | INVESTED | MAGICAL | NECROMANCY

Price 220 gp

Usage worn armor; **Bulk** 2

Stitched together from pieces of ghoul skin, this suit of *+1 hide armor* grants you a +1 item bonus to saving throws against disease and paralysis and makes you immune to the paralysis of ghouls. *Ghoul hide* with a *resilient* rune increases the *resilient* rune's item bonus to saving throws against disease and paralysis by 1 (maximum +4).

Ghoul hide hisses with sibilant hatred at the touch of elves. When worn by a creature with the elf trait, the armor gains the noisy trait.

IMPENETRABLE SCALE   ITEM 17

UNCOMMON | ABJURATION | INVESTED | MAGICAL

Price 12,800 gp

Usage worn armor; **Bulk** 3

Made of overlapping, lustrous black scales of standard-grade adamantine, this *+2 greater resilient fortification adamantine scale mail* seems to momentarily thicken at the point of impact when hit. Whenever the armor's *fortification* rune successfully turns a significant foe's critical hit into a normal hit, one of the scales on the armor turns violet. You gain resistance to physical damage equal to the number of violet scales, to a maximum of 8.

At dawn each day, all the violet scales return to normal.

Craft Requirements The initial raw materials must include 1,600 gp of adamantine.

MAIL OF LUCK   ITEM 13

DIVINATION | INVESTED | MAGICAL

Price 2,600 gp

Usage worn armor; **Bulk** 3

This suit of *+2 resilient splint mail* has a large, green gemstone inset in a prominent location.

Activate ◆ envision; **Frequency** once per day; **Trigger** You are hit or critically hit with an attack, but damage hasn't been rolled yet; **Effect** You force the attacker to reroll the attack roll and use the worse result. This effect has the misfortune trait.

Activating the armor causes the gemstone to turn gray and become inert. You cannot activate the armor again until the stone returns to its original green color. The gem turns green again after 1 week or when a significant foe critically succeeds at an attack roll targeting you. (If an enemy rolls a critical success at an attack against you and you force the attacker to reroll that critical success, that critical success does not recharge the *mail of luck*.) Even if the armor's power returns before a week has elapsed, it can't be activated more than once per day.

MOONLIT CHAIN   ITEM 7

DIVINATION | INVESTED | MAGICAL

Price 360 gp

Usage worn armor; **Bulk** 2

This *+1 silver chain shirt* has a collar adorned with stitched images of the phases of the moon. You can see in moonlight as though you had low-light vision.

Activate ◆ Interact; **Frequency** once per day; **Effect** You touch the stitched image of the new moon on the armor's collar and suppress the dazzled condition for 1 minute.

Craft Requirements The initial raw materials must include 33 gp of silver.

PLATE ARMOR OF THE DEEP   ITEM 15

UNCOMMON | ABJURATION | INVESTED | MAGICAL

Price 6,500 gp

Usage worn armor; **Bulk** 4

This suit of *+2 greater resilient full plate* is decorated with swirling, ornate motifs of waves and fish scales. While wearing it, you take no Speed reduction or check penalty from armor when Swimming, gain a +2 item bonus to Athletics checks to Swim, can breathe underwater, and can speak Aquan.

RHINO HIDE   ITEM 9

INVESTED | MAGICAL | TRANSMUTATION

Price 700 gp

Usage worn armor; **Bulk** 2

This *+1 resilient hide armor* is made from rhinoceros hide. It has an armor check penalty of –1 instead of –3. When you use the Sudden Charge class feat while wearing this armor, your Strike deals an additional 1d8 damage.

Craft Requirements The initial raw materials must include 320 gp of rhinoceros hide (a common material).

CONSUMABLES

This section includes magic items with the consumable trait. An item with this trait can be used only once. Unless stated otherwise, it is destroyed after activation. When a character creates consumable items, they can make them in batches of four, as described in the Craft activity. Consumables includes the following subcategories, with any special rules appearing at the start of the section.

- **Ammunition** begins on this page.
- **Oils** appear on page 561.
- **Potions** are described on page 562.
- **Scrolls** are listed on page 564.
- **Talismans** begin on page 565.
- **Other Consumables** begins on page 570.

AMMUNITION

These magic items are ammunition for ranged weapons. Each item's stat block includes an Ammunition entry that lists which type of ammunition it can be Crafted as, or "any" if it's not limited to any particular type. All stat blocks for ammunition omit the Usage and Bulk entries; use the standard rules in Chapter 6: Equipment for the type of ammunition to determine reloading times and Bulk.

When using magic ammunition, use your ranged weapon's fundamental runes to determine the attack modifier and damage dice. Don't add the effects of your weapon's property runes unless the ammunition states otherwise—the ammunition creates its own effects. Magic ammunition deals damage on a hit normally in addition to any listed effects unless its description states otherwise.

Regardless of whether an attack with magic ammunition hits or misses, launching the ammunition consumes its magic. Magic ammunition is made of normal materials, not precious materials, unless stated otherwise.

ACTIVATED AMMUNITION

If magic ammunition doesn't have an Activate entry, it's activated automatically when it's launched. Types of magic ammunition that have an Activate entry must be activated with additional actions before being used. Once you activate the ammunition, you must shoot it before the end of your turn. Otherwise, it deactivates (but it isn't consumed) and you must activate it again before you can use it. If you shoot the ammunition without activating it first, it functions as non-magical ammunition and is still consumed.

The action required to activate the ammunition doesn't alter how many actions it takes to reload. For example, you could activate a *beacon shot arrow* by touching it with 1 action, then draw and shoot the arrow as part of a Strike as normal. For a *beacon shot bolt*, you could activate it, load it into a crossbow, then shoot it, or load it into the crossbow, then activate it, and then shoot it.

BEACON SHOT   ITEM 3

CONSUMABLE   EVOCATION   MAGICAL
Price 10 gp

Ammunition arrow, bolt
Activate ❖ Interact

The shaft of a *beacon shot* is studded with tiny flecks of glimmering gemstones. When an activated *beacon shot* hits a target, it embeds itself into that target and spews sparks for 1 minute. If the target is invisible, it becomes merely hidden to creatures who would otherwise be unable to see it. The sparks also negate the concealed condition if the target was otherwise concealed.

A creature can remove the arrow or bolt by using an Interact basic action and succeeding at a DC 20 Athletics check.

CLIMBING BOLT   ITEM 4

CONJURATION   CONSUMABLE   MAGICAL
Price 15 gp
Ammunition bolt

The shaft of this bolt is wrapped with fine twine. When the bolt strikes a solid surface, the twine unwinds and enlarges into a 50-foot-long rope, securely fastened to the surface the bolt struck. The rope can be pulled free with an Interact action and a successful DC 20 Athletics check.

DISINTEGRATION BOLT   ITEM 15

UNCOMMON   CONSUMABLE   EVOCATION   MAGICAL
Price 1,300 gp
Ammunition bolt
Activate ❖ Interact

The shaft of this bolt is scorched and blackened, and handling it coats your fingers with a fine black powder. When an activated *disintegration bolt* hits a target, it is subject to a *disintegrate* spell requiring a DC 34 Fortitude save. As with the spell, a critical hit on the attack roll causes the target's saving throw outcome to be one degree worse.

Craft Requirements Supply one casting of *disintegrate*.

EXPLOSIVE AMMUNITION   ITEM 9+

CONSUMABLE   EVOCATION   FIRE   MAGICAL
Ammunition any
Activate ❖ Interact

This piece of ammunition is coated in gritty black soot. When activated *explosive ammunition* hits a target, the missile explodes in a 10-foot burst, dealing 6d6 fire damage to each creature in the area (including the target). Each creature must attempt a DC 25 basic Reflex save.

Type standard; **Level** 9; **Price** 130 gp
Type greater; **Level** 13; **Price** 520 gp
The damage is 10d6 and the save DC is 30.

GHOST AMMUNITION   ITEM 14

MAGICAL   TRANSMUTATION
Ammunition any
Price 900 gp

Ghost ammunition is cool to the touch. This ammunition has the benefits of the *ghost touch* property rune and can fly through any obstacle except those that can block incorporeal creatures or effects. Though the ammunition penetrates

INTRODUCTION

ANCESTRIES & BACKGROUNDS

CLASSES

SKILLS

FEATS

EQUIPMENT

SPELLS

THE AGE OF LOST OMENS

PLAYING THE GAME

GAME MASTERING

CRAFTING & TREASURE

APPENDIX

barriers and ignores all cover, the target still benefits from the flat check from being concealed or hidden. You still can't target an undetected creature without guessing.

After it is launched, the ammunition vanishes into mist. However, in the dead of the night 1d4 days later, it reappears in the last quiver or other container it was taken from.

PENETRATING AMMUNITION — ITEM 12

CONSUMABLE | MAGICAL | TRANSMUTATION

Price 400 gp
Ammunition arrow, bolt
Activate ◆ Interact

This ammunition has a slender shape and a viciously pointed tip. When you activate and shoot *penetrating ammunition*, the Strike takes the shape of a 60-foot line originating from you. Roll one attack roll and compare the result to the AC of each target in the line. The ammunition ignores up to 10 of a target's resistance, and it can penetrate walls up to 1 foot thick with Hardness 10 or less. Each target that takes damage from this ammunition also takes 1d6 persistent bleed damage.

If your attack roll result is a natural 20, you improve your degree of success only against the first target in the line, but you can still score a critical hit on other targets if your result exceeds their AC by 10 or more. If you have access to your bow's critical specialization effect, *penetrating ammunition* applies that effect only against a target in the last square of the line.

SHINING AMMUNITION — ITEM 1

CONSUMABLE | EVOCATION | LIGHT | MAGICAL

Price 3 gp
Ammunition any

A piece of *shining ammunition* gives off a faint glow. When shot, this ammunition sheds bright light in a 20-foot radius (and dim light to the next 20 feet) for 10 minutes. If it hits a target, it sticks, causing the target to shed light in the same radius. A creature can remove the ammunition with an Interact action, but the ammunition itself continues to glow for the rest of the duration or until destroyed.

SLEEP ARROW — ITEM 3

CONSUMABLE | ENCHANTMENT | MAGICAL | MENTAL | SLEEP

Price 11 gp
Ammunition arrow
Activate ◆ Interact

Sleep arrows often have shafts of deep blue or black, and their fletching is exceptionally soft and downy. An activated *sleep arrow* deals no damage, but a living creature hit by it is subject to the effects of a *sleep* spell (DC 17).
Craft Requirements Supply one casting of *sleep*.

SPELLSTRIKE AMMUNITION — ITEM 3+

CONSUMABLE | MAGICAL | TRANSMUTATION

Ammunition any
Activate ◆◆ Cast a Spell

Mystic patterns create a magic reservoir within this ammunition. You activate *spellstrike ammunition* by Casting

a Spell into the ammunition. The spell must be of a spell level the ammunition can hold, and the spell must be able to target a creature other than the caster. A creature hit by activated *spellstrike ammunition* is targeted by the spell. If the creature isn't a valid target for the spell, the spell is lost.

The ammunition affects only the target hit, even if the spell would normally affect more than one target. If the spell requires a spell attack roll, use the result of your ranged attack roll with the ammunition to determine the degree of success of the spell. If the spell requires a saving throw, the target attempts the save against your spell DC.

The maximum level of spell the ammunition can hold determines its item level and Price.

Type I; Level 3; **Price** 12 gp; **Maximum Spell Level** 1st
Type II; Level 5; **Price** 30 gp; **Maximum Spell Level** 2nd
Type III; Level 7; **Price** 70 gp; **Maximum Spell Level** 3rd
Type IV; Level 9; **Price** 150 gp; **Maximum Spell Level** 4th
Type V; Level 11; **Price** 300 gp; **Maximum Spell Level** 5th
Type VI; Level 13; **Price** 600 gp; **Maximum Spell Level** 6th
Type VII; Level 15; **Price** 1,300 gp; **Maximum Spell Level** 7th
Type VIII; Level 17; **Price** 3,000 gp; **Maximum Spell Level** 8th
Type IX; Level 19; **Price** 8,000 gp; **Maximum Spell Level** 9th

STONE BULLET — ITEM 15

CONSUMABLE | MAGICAL | TRANSMUTATION

Price 1,300 gp
Ammunition sling bullet
Activate ◆ Interact

This sling bullet looks like a petrified serpent's eye. A creature hit by an activated *stone bullet* is subject to the effects of a 6th-level *flesh to stone* spell (DC 34).
Craft Requirements Supply one casting of *flesh to stone.*

STORM ARROW — ITEM 9

AIR | CONSUMABLE | ELECTRICITY | EVOCATION | MAGICAL

Price 130 gp
Ammunition arrow
Activate ◆ Interact

The head of this arrow is made from gleaming copper. When an activated *storm arrow* hits a target, it is buffeted by raging winds and struck by a bolt of lightning that deals 3d12 electricity damage and the target must attempt a DC 25 Reflex saving throw. If this arrow is shot from a weapon with a *shock* property rune, the save DC increases to 27, though the attack doesn't benefit from the *shock* property rune itself.
Critical Success The foe is unaffected.
Success The foe takes half damage and isn't affected by the wind.
Failure The foe takes full damage and is buffeted by winds for 1 round, taking a –2 circumstance penalty to ranged attack rolls and a –10-foot circumstance penalty to its fly Speed.
Critical Failure As failure, but the foe takes double damage.

VINE ARROW — ITEM 3

CONJURATION | CONSUMABLE | MAGICAL

Price 10 gp
Ammunition arrow

CRAFTING & TREASURE

11

INTRODUCTION

ANCESTRIES &
BACKGROUNDS

CLASSES

SKILLS

FEATS

EQUIPMENT

SPELLS

THE AGE OF
LOST OMENS

PLAYING THE
GAME

GAME
MASTERING

**CRAFTING
& TREASURE**

APPENDIX

Activate ◆ command

Leafy stalks protrude from the shaft of this rustic arrow. When an activated *vine arrow* hits a target, the arrow's shaft splits and grows, wrapping the target in vines. The target takes a –10-foot circumstance penalty to its Speeds for 2d4 rounds, or until it Escapes against a DC of 19. On a critical hit, the target is also immobilized until it Escapes.

VIPER ARROW   ITEM 4

| CONJURATION | CONSUMABLE | MAGICAL |

Price 17 gp
Ammunition arrow
Activate ◆ command

The shaft of this arrow is covered in fine green scales, and its iron head comes to a pair of points almost like fangs. After an activated *viper arrow* hits a target, the arrow transforms into a viper (*Pathfinder Bestiary* 302). The target is affected by the viper's poison, as if it had been bitten. The viper then lands in an open space adjacent to the target.

The viper has the summoned trait and acts at the end of your turn, even though you didn't use the Sustain a Spell action. It is under the GM's control, but it generally attacks the creature the arrow struck. The viper vanishes after 1 minute or when slain.

Craft Requirements Supply one casting of *summon animal*.

OILS

Oils are magical gels, ointments, pastes, or salves that are typically applied to an object and are used up in the process. They have the oil trait. Applying an oil usually takes two hands: one to hold the jar containing the oil, and another to extract the oil and apply it. You can only apply an oil to an item or creature within your reach. Because the process is so thorough, it is usually impossible to apply an oil to an unwilling target or an item in the possession of an unwilling target unless that target is paralyzed, petrified, or unconscious.

ANTIMAGIC OIL   ITEM 20

| RARE | ABJURATION | CONSUMABLE | MAGICAL | OIL |

Price 13,000 gp
Usage held in 2 hands; **Bulk** L
Activate ◆ Interact

This oil contains energy that repels nearly all types of magic. When you apply this oil to armor, the creature wearing the armor becomes immune to all spells, effects of magic items (the wearer's and those of others), and effects with the magical trait for 1 minute. The oil affects neither the magic of the armor nor the fundamental runes of weapons attacking the wearer. Magical effects from a source of 20th level or higher, such as a deity, still function on the armor's wearer.

ALIGNED OIL   ITEM 9

| CONSUMABLE | DIVINE | EVOCATION | OIL |

Price 140 gp
Usage held in 2 hands; **Bulk** L
Activate ◆ Interact

This oil fills a weapon with cosmic power of an alignment. Each *aligned oil* is crafted to one alignment: chaos, evil, good, or law (such as a *good-aligned oil*). A weapon anointed with this oil gains the effects of the property rune matching its alignment: *anarchic* (chaos), *axiomatic* (law), *holy* (good), or *unholy* (evil). This lasts for 1 minute.

NECTAR OF PURIFICATION   ITEM 1

| CONSUMABLE | MAGICAL | NECROMANCY | OIL |

Price 3 gp
Usage held in 1 hand; **Bulk** L
Activate ◆ Interact

A shimmering liquid, *nectar of purification* is often stored in bottles similar to those used for vinegar. This oil casts a 1st-level *purify food and drink* spell over any food or drink onto which it's poured. The nectar evaporates as it takes effect, leaving the taste and texture of the food or drink unaltered.

OBFUSCATION OIL   ITEM 15

| CONSUMABLE | ILLUSION | MAGICAL | OIL |

Price 1,200 gp
Usage held in 2 hands; **Bulk** L
Activate ◆ Interact

You can spread this blue-gray gel on a single item with a Bulk of 3 or less to ward it against magical detection. It becomes immune to divination magic of 8th level or lower (such as *locate*). This oil is permanent, but it can be removed with acid. Removing the oil in this way usually takes 1 minute for objects with Bulk of 1 or less, or a number of minutes equal to the item's Bulk.

OIL OF ANIMATION   ITEM 12

| UNCOMMON | CONSUMABLE | MAGICAL | OIL | TRANSMUTATION |

Price 330 gp
Usage held in 2 hands; **Bulk** L
Activate ◆ Interact

You can rub this bronze-colored oil onto a melee weapon to grant it the benefits of the *dancing* rune (page 583). Once you fail a flat check for the weapon, causing it to fall, this effect ends.

OIL OF KEEN EDGES   ITEM 11

| UNCOMMON | CONSUMABLE | MAGICAL | OIL | TRANSMUTATION |

Price 250 gp
Usage held in 2 hands; **Bulk** L
Activate ◆ Interact

When this silvery salve is applied to a melee weapon that deals piercing or slashing damage, the weapon grows sharper and more dangerous for 1 minute, granting it the benefits of the *keen* rune.

OIL OF MENDING   ITEM 3

| CONSUMABLE | MAGICAL | OIL | TRANSMUTATION |

Price 9 gp
Usage held in 2 hands; **Bulk** L
Activate 1 minute (Interact)

A vial of *oil of mending* appears to have countless translucent threads swirling within. Applying this oil to an item casts a 2nd-level *mending* spell to repair the item.

OIL OF POTENCY   ITEM 2

CONSUMABLE | MAGICAL | OIL | TRANSMUTATION

Price 7 gp
Usage held in 2 hands; **Bulk** L
Activate ❖ Interact

When you apply this thick, viscous oil to a non-magical weapon or suit of armor, that item immediately becomes magically potent. If the item is a weapon, it temporarily becomes a *+1 striking weapon*, or, if it's armor, it temporarily becomes *+1 resilient armor*. This lasts for 1 minute.

OIL OF REPULSION   ITEM 11

ABJURATION | CONSUMABLE | MAGICAL | OIL

Price 175 gp
Usage held in 2 hands; **Bulk** L
Activate ❖ Interact

This oil contains magnetically charged iron filings repelled into opposite ends of the vial. For 1 minute after you apply this oil to armor, any creature that hits you with a melee Strike must attempt a DC 28 Fortitude save with the following effects.

Success The creature is unaffected.
Failure The creature is pushed up to 10 feet away from you (the GM determines the direction).
Critical Failure As failure, and the creature is also knocked prone.

OIL OF WEIGHTLESSNESS   ITEM 2+

CONSUMABLE | MAGICAL | OIL | TRANSMUTATION

Usage held in 2 hands; **Bulk** L
Activate ❖ Interact

You can spread this shimmering oil on an item of 1 Bulk or less to make it feel weightless. It has negligible Bulk for 1 hour.

Type *oil of weightlessness*; **Level** 2; **Price** 6 gp
Type *greater oil of weightlessness*; **Level** 6; **Price** 36 gp
This oil can affect an item of 2 Bulk or less and lasts 8 hours.

SALVE OF ANTIPARALYSIS   ITEM 6+

CONSUMABLE | HEALING | MAGICAL | NECROMANCY | OIL

Usage held in 2 hands; **Bulk** L
Activate ❖ Interact

Applying this filmy salve to a creature helps it overcome magical paralysis. The creature recovers as if it were the target of a 3rd-level *remove paralysis* spell.

Type *salve of antiparalysis*; **Level** 6; **Price** 40 gp
Type *greater salve of antiparalysis*; **Level** 12; **Price** 325 gp
A *greater salve of antiparalysis* can potentially remove petrification. The creature recovers as if it were the target of both a 6th-level *remove paralysis* spell and a *stone to flesh* spell.

SALVE OF SLIPPERINESS   ITEM 5

CONSUMABLE | MAGICAL | OIL | TRANSMUTATION

Price 25 gp **Usage** held in 2 hands; **Bulk** L
Activate ❖ Interact

This greenish, persistent grease can be applied to armor to make it extremely slippery for 8 hours, granting the wearer a +2 item bonus to Acrobatics checks to Escape or to Squeeze.

POTIONS

A potion is a magical liquid activated when you drink it, which uses it up. Potions have the potion trait. You can activate a potion with an Interact action as you drink it or feed it to another creature. You can feed a potion only to a creature that is within reach and willing or otherwise so helpless that it can't resist. You usually need only one hand to consume a potion or feed it to another creature.

BARKSKIN POTION   ITEM 4

ABJURATION | CONSUMABLE | POTION | PRIMAL

Price 15 gp
Usage held in 1 hand; **Bulk** L
Activate ❖ Interact

After you drink this bitter draft, your skin thickens like bark. You gain the effects of a 2nd-level *barkskin* spell for 10 minutes.

DRAGON'S BREATH POTION   ITEM 7+

CONSUMABLE | EVOCATION | MAGICAL | POTION

Usage held in 1 hand; **Bulk** L
Activate ❖ Interact

This liquid contains blood from a certain type of dragon. For 1 hour after you imbibe the concoction, you can unleash a breath weapon used by that type of dragon. The potency of the breath depends on the potion's type, based on the age of the dragon whose blood was used to make the potion. This potion has the trait matching the damage type of the breath weapon.

Exhaling dragon breath uses a single action. The damage type and the area of the dragon breath depend on the type of dragon blood in the potion, as shown in the table below. Regardless of the dragon type, the breath weapon deals 4d6 damage, and each creature in the area must attempt a DC 23 basic save of a type determined by the type of the dragon. After you use the breath weapon, you can't do so again for 1d4 rounds.

Type young; **Level** 7; **Price** 70 gp
Type adult; **Level** 12; **Price** 400 gp
The damage is 6d6 and the save DC is 29.
Type wyrm; **Level** 17; **Price** 3,000 gp
The damage is 10d6 and the save DC is 37.

Dragon Type	Breath Weapon (Save)
Black or copper	30-foot line of acid (Reflex)
Blue or bronze	30-foot line of electricity (Reflex)
Brass	30-foot line of fire (Reflex)
Green	15-foot cone of poison (Fortitude)
Gold or red	15-foot cone of fire (Reflex)
Silver or white	15-foot cone of cold (Reflex)

CRAFTING & TREASURE

11

INTRODUCTION

ANCESTRIES &
BACKGROUNDS

CLASSES

SKILLS

FEATS

EQUIPMENT

SPELLS

THE AGE OF
LOST OMENS

PLAYING THE
GAME

GAME
MASTERING

CRAFTING
& TREASURE

APPENDIX

HEALING POTION — ITEM 1+

CONSUMABLE   HEALING   MAGICAL   NECROMANCY   POTION

Usage held in 1 hand; **Bulk** L
Activate ◆ Interact

A healing potion is a vial of a ruby-red liquid that imparts a tingling sensation as the drinker's wounds heal rapidly. When you drink a *healing potion*, you regain the listed number of Hit Points.

Type minor; **Level** 1; **Price** 4 gp
The potion restores 1d8 Hit Points.

Type lesser; **Level** 3; **Price** 12 gp
The potion restores 2d8+5 Hit Points.

Type moderate; **Level** 6; **Price** 50 gp
The potion restores 3d8+10 Hit Points.

Type greater; **Level** 12; **Price** 400 gp
The potion restores 6d8+20 Hit Points.

Type major; **Level** 18; **Price** 5,000 gp
The potion restores 8d8+30 Hit Points.

INVISIBILITY POTION — ITEM 4

UNCOMMON   CONSUMABLE   ILLUSION   MAGICAL   POTION

Price 20 gp
Usage held in 1 hand; **Bulk** L
Activate ◆ Interact

An *invisibility potion* is colorless and oddly lightweight. Upon drinking it, you gain the effects of a 2nd-level *invisibility* spell.

PANACEA — ITEM 13

UNCOMMON   CONSUMABLE   HEALING   MAGICAL   NECROMANCY   POTION

Price 450 gp
Usage held in 1 hand; **Bulk** L
Activate ◆ Interact

This potion appears to shift colors, and no two observers describe it in the same way. When consumed, it attempts to counteract all curses and diseases affecting you, as well as the blinded and deafened conditions from spells affecting you. The potion has a counteract level of 7 and a +20 modifier for the roll.

POTION OF FLYING — ITEM 8+

CONSUMABLE   MAGICAL   POTION   TRANSMUTATION

Usage held in 1 hand; **Bulk** L
Activate ◆ Interact

Upon drinking this effervescent concoction, you gain a fly Speed of 40 feet for 1 minute.

Type standard; **Level** 8; **Price** 100 gp

Type greater; **Level** 15; **Price** 1,000 gp
The fly Speed lasts for 1 hour.

POTION OF LEAPING — ITEM 5

CONSUMABLE   MAGICAL   POTION   TRANSMUTATION

Price 21 gp
Usage held in 1 hand; **Bulk** L
Activate ◆ Interact

For 1 minute after you drink this fizzy potion, whenever you Leap, you gain the effect of the 1st-level *jump* spell.

POTION OF QUICKNESS — ITEM 8

CONSUMABLE   MAGICAL   POTION   TRANSMUTATION

Price 90 gp
Usage held in 1 hand; **Bulk** L
Activate ◆ Interact

Drinking this silver potion grants you the effects of *haste* for 1 minute.

POTION OF RESISTANCE — ITEM 6+

ABJURATION   CONSUMABLE   MAGICAL   POTION

Usage held in 1 hand; **Bulk** L
Activate ◆ Interact

Drinking this thick, fortifying potion grants resistance against a single damage type for 1 hour. Each *potion of resistance* is created to defend against acid, cold, electricity, fire, or sonic damage (and is called a *lesser potion of fire resistance* or the like).

Type lesser; **Level** 6; **Price** 45 gp
You gain resistance 5 to the appropriate energy type.

Type moderate; **Level** 10; **Price** 180 gp
You gain resistance 10 to the appropriate energy type.

Type greater; **Level** 14; **Price** 850 gp
You gain resistance 15 to the appropriate energy type.

POTION OF SWIMMING — ITEM 6+

CONSUMABLE   MAGICAL   POTION   TRANSMUTATION

Usage held in 1 hand; **Bulk** L
Activate ◆ Interact

This potion tastes like salt water, and sandy grit settles to the bottom of its container. When you drink it, you gain a swim Speed equal to your land Speed for 10 minutes.

Type moderate; **Level** 6; **Price** 50 gp

Type greater; **Level** 11; **Price** 250 gp
The swim Speed lasts for 1 hour.

POTION OF TONGUES — ITEM 12

UNCOMMON   CONSUMABLE   DIVINATION   MAGICAL   POTION

Price 320 gp
Usage held in 1 hand; **Bulk** L
Activate ◆ Interact

This sour potion enlivens your tongue with unusual flavors and uncommon eloquence, allowing you to speak and understand all languages for 4 hours after you drink it. This doesn't allow you to read these languages in their written form.

POTION OF UNDETECTABILITY — ITEM 18

CONSUMABLE   ILLUSION   MAGICAL   POTION

Price 4,400 gp
Usage held in 1 hand; **Bulk** L
Activate ◆ Interact

Drinking this dull-black liquid makes you undetectable to divinations. This grants the same effects as *mind blank*, but without the bonus against mental effects. You also gain the effects of a 4th-level *invisibility* spell, which protects against *see invisibility* spells of 8th level and lower and has a DC of 36 against *true seeing*. The potion's effects last for 10 minutes.

POTION OF WATER BREATHING ITEM 3

CONSUMABLE MAGICAL POTION TRANSMUTATION

Price 11 gp
Usage held in 1 hand; **Bulk** L
Activate ❖ Interact

This filmy, gray potion smells of an old fish midden and tastes even worse. After drinking this potion, you gain the effects of a 2nd-level *water breathing* spell for 1 hour.

SHRINKING POTION ITEM 4+

CONSUMABLE MAGICAL POTION TRANSMUTATION

Usage held in 1 hand; **Bulk** L
Activate ❖ Interact; **Onset** 1 minute

This fungus-flavored potion conveys the effects of the *shrink* spell to make you and all your gear smaller. After the onset, you remain small for 10 minutes.

Type standard; **Level** 4; **Price** 15 gp
Type greater; **Level** 8; **Price** 90 gp

This potion has no onset, lasts for 1 hour, and grants the effects of a 4th-level *shrink* spell. In addition, you gain a +2 item bonus to Stealth checks while shrunken.

SERUM OF SEX SHIFT ITEM 7

CONSUMABLE MAGICAL POTION TRANSMUTATION

Price 60 gp
Usage held in 1 hand; **Bulk** L
Activate ❖ Interact

Upon drinking this potion, your biology instantly transforms to take on a set of sexual characteristics of your choice, changing your appearance and physiology accordingly. You have mild control over the details of this change, but you retain a strong "family resemblance" to your former appearance.

The magic functions instantaneously and can't be counteracted. Your new anatomy is as healthy and functional as your previous body's, potentially allowing you to procreate (depending on your ancestry's biology). Drinking a subsequent *serum of sex shift* allows you to either revert back to your original form or adopt other sexual characteristics, as you choose. The elixir has no effect if you are pregnant or from an ancestry with no sexual differentiation. Most ancestries have a wide spectrum of sexual differentiation, some common, others more rare.

TRUESIGHT POTION ITEM 16

CONSUMABLE DIVINATION MAGICAL POTION

Price 1,500 gp
Usage held in 1 hand; **Bulk** L
Activate ❖ Interact

Upon drinking this clear, refreshing potion, you can see things as they actually are. You gain the benefits of a 7th-level *true seeing* spell that has a counteract modifier of +25.

TRUTH POTION ITEM 6

UNCOMMON CONSUMABLE ENCHANTMENT MAGICAL MENTAL POTION

Price 46 gp
Usage held in 1 hand; **Bulk** L
Activate ❖ Interact

For 10 minutes after drinking this astringent potion, you can't intentionally lie and may be compelled to tell the truth. Upon drinking the potion, attempt a DC 19 Will save. You can voluntarily fail or critically fail.

Success The potion does not affect you.
Failure When you speak, you must tell the truth.
Critical Failure As failure, and when someone asks you a question, you must attempt another DC 19 Will saving throw. If you fail this saving throw, you must answer the question truthfully if you are able to do so; if you succeed, you are temporarily immune to further attempts to ask the same question within the potion's duration.

SCROLLS

A scroll contains a single spell that you can cast without having to expend a spell slot. A scroll can be Crafted to contain nearly any spell, so the types of scrolls available are limited only by the number of spells in the game. The exceptions are cantrips, focus spells, and rituals, none of which can be put on scrolls. The spell on a scroll can be cast only once, and the scroll is destroyed as part of the casting. The spell on the scroll is cast at a particular spell level, as determined by the scroll. For instance, a scroll of *magic missile* (1st level) can be used to cast the 1st-level version of *magic missile*, but not a *magic missile* heightened to 2nd level. If no level is listed, the scroll can be used to cast the spell at its lowest level.

If you find a scroll, you can try to figure out what spell it contains. If the spell is a common spell from your spell list or a spell you know, you can spend a single Recall Knowledge action and automatically succeed at identifying the scroll's spell. If it's not, you must use Identify Magic (page 238) to learn what spell the scroll holds.

CASTING A SPELL FROM A SCROLL

Casting a Spell from a scroll requires holding the scroll in one hand and activating it with a Cast a Spell activity using the normal number of actions for that spell.

To Cast a Spell from a scroll, the spell must appear on your spell list. Because you're the one Casting the Spell, use your spell attack roll and spell DC. The spell also gains the appropriate trait for your tradition (arcane, divine, occult, or primal).

Any physical material components and costs are provided when a scroll is created, so you don't need to provide them when Casting a Spell from a scroll. You must replace any required material component for that spell with a somatic component. If the spell requires a focus, you must have that focus to Cast the Spell from a scroll.

SCROLL STATISTICS

All scrolls have the same base statistics unless noted otherwise. A scroll has light Bulk, and it must be held in one hand to be activated.

Varying Statistics

Table 11–3 indicates the item level and Price of a scroll, both of which are based on the level of the spell contained on the scroll. Any costs to Cast the Spell are added to the scroll's Price when the scroll is crafted, so a scroll containing a spell with a Cost entry will have a higher Price than what appears on the table. The scroll's rarity matches the spell's rarity.

The traits for a scroll vary based on the spell it contains. A scroll always has the consumable, magical, and scroll traits, plus the traits of the spell stored on it.

TABLE 11–3: SCROLL STATISTICS

Spell Level	Item Level	Scroll Price
1	1	4 gp
2	3	12 gp
3	5	30 gp
4	7	70 gp
5	9	150 gp
6	11	300 gp
7	13	600 gp
8	15	1,300 gp
9	17	3,000 gp
10	19	8,000 gp

Crafting a Scroll

The process to Craft a scroll is much like that to Craft any other magic item. When you begin the crafting process, choose a spell to put into the scroll. You have to either Cast that Spell during the crafting process, or someone else must do so in your presence. Casting that Spell doesn't produce its normal effects; instead, the magic is trapped inside the scroll. The casting must come from a spellcaster expending a spell slot. You can't Craft a scroll from a spell produced from another magic item, for example. The caster has to provide any cost of the spell.

Like other consumables, scrolls can be crafted in batches of four. All scrolls of one batch must contain the same spell at the same level, and you must provide one casting for each scroll crafted.

Sample Scrolls

A wide variety of spells can appear on scrolls. The following specific scrolls are just examples.

SCROLL OF GLITTERDUST   ITEM 3

| CONSUMABLE | EVOCATION | MAGICAL | SCROLL |

Price 12 gp
Usage held in 1 hand; **Bulk** L
Activate ❖❖ Cast a Spell

This scroll can be used to cast *glitterdust* as a 2nd-level spell.
Craft Requirements Supply one casting of *glitterdust*.

SCROLL OF ILLUSORY DISGUISE   ITEM 1

| CONSUMABLE | ILLUSION | MAGICAL | SCROLL |

Price 3 gp
Usage held in 1 hand; **Bulk** L
Activate ❖❖ Cast a Spell

This scroll can cast *illusory disguise* as a 1st-level spell.
Craft Requirements Supply one casting of *illusory disguise*.

TALISMANS

An item with the talisman trait is a magical charm, gem, stone, or other small object affixed to armor, a shield, or a weapon (called the affixed item). Each talisman holds a sliver of combat knowledge or magical energy that can be unleashed for a momentary boost of power or enhanced ability. Many talismans can be activated as a free action when you use a particular action or activity. A talisman is a consumable item and has the talisman trait.

You must be wielding or wearing an item to activate a talisman attached to it. Once activated, a talisman burns out permanently, usually crumbling into a fine dust.

Affixing a Talisman

Each talisman's stat block indicates the type of item it can be affixed to. Affixing or removing requires using the Affix a Talisman activity. A single talisman can be affixed to only one item at a time, and an item can have only one talisman affixed to it at a time.

AFFIX A TALISMAN

| EXPLORATION | MANIPULATE |

Requirements You must use a repair kit (page 291).

You spend 10 minutes affixing a talisman to an item, placing the item on a stable surface and using the repair kit with both hands. You can also use this activity to remove a talisman. If more than one talisman is affixed to an item, the talismans are suppressed; none of them can be activated.

Talismans

These are but a few of the talismans available.

BLOODSEEKER BEAK   ITEM 4

| CONSUMABLE | MAGICAL | NECROMANCY | TALISMAN |

Price 20 gp
Usage affixed to a weapon; **Bulk** –
Activate ❖ envision; **Trigger** You hit a flat-footed creature with the affixed weapon.

This long, hollow proboscis is harvested from the notorious bloodseeker beast and drips a trickle of blood. When you activate the beak, you deal an extra 1d4 precision damage on your damage roll. If you deal sneak attack damage to the creature, you also deal 1d4 persistent bleed damage.

BRONZE BULL PENDANT — ITEM 2

| CONSUMABLE | EVOCATION | MAGICAL | TALISMAN |

Price 7 gp

Usage affixed to armor; **Bulk** —

Activate ◈ envision; **Trigger** You attempt an Athletics check to Shove, but you haven't rolled yet; **Requirements** You are trained in Athletics.

This pendant is forged from grainy steel and depicts a snorting bull's face. The pendant must be attached to the chest area or on a shoulder guard. When you activate the pendant, you gain a +2 status bonus to the Athletics check to Shove, and if you roll a critical failure on the check, you get a failure instead.

CRYING ANGEL PENDANT — ITEM 2

| CONSUMABLE | DIVINE | NECROMANCY | TALISMAN |

Price 7 gp

Usage affixed to armor; **Bulk** —

Activate ◈ envision; **Trigger** You critically fail to Administer First Aid; **Requirements** You are trained in Medicine.

When you activate this alabaster pendant, your critical failure becomes a normal failure instead.

DAZING COIL — ITEM 14

| CONSUMABLE | ENCHANTMENT | MAGICAL | TALISMAN |

Price 900 gp

Usage affixed to a weapon; **Bulk** —

Activate ◈ envision; **Trigger** You deal damage to a flat-footed creature with the affixed weapon.

This knot of copper wire reshapes itself in a new pattern every time its affixed weapon deals damage. When you activate the coil, the damaged creature must succeed at a DC 31 Will save or be stunned 1. If it critically fails, it instead becomes stunned 2.

DISPELLING SLIVER — ITEM 17

| ABJURATION | CONSUMABLE | MAGICAL | TALISMAN |

Price 2,400 gp

Usage affixed to a weapon; **Bulk** —

Activate ◈ envision; **Trigger** Your Strike damages a target; **Requirements** You're a master with the affixed weapon.

Made from a treated sliver of cold iron, this talisman allows you to counteract magical effects. When you activate the *dispelling sliver*, it attempts to counteract a single spell active on the target, with the effects of an 8th-level *dispel magic* spell.

If you activate the talisman on a successful Dispelling Slice, the talisman attempts to counteract all spells active on the target.

DRAGON TURTLE SCALE — ITEM 4

| CONSUMABLE | MAGICAL | TRANSMUTATION | TALISMAN |

Price 13 gp

Usage affixed to armor; **Bulk** —

Activate ◆ envision; **Requirements** You're an expert in Athletics.

This shimmering green scale is usually attached to a golden clasp or chain. When you activate the scale, for 1 minute you gain a swim Speed equal to half your land Speed.

EFFERVESCENT AMPOULE — ITEM 2

| CONSUMABLE | MAGICAL | TRANSMUTATION | TALISMAN |

Price 7 gp

Usage affixed to armor; **Bulk** —

Activate ◆ Interact; **Requirements** You're an expert in Acrobatics.

Light spring water fizzes and bubbles within this small glass globe, spilling onto the affixed armor when activated. Until the end of your turn, the armor lets you move across water and other liquids as if they were solid ground. If you Stride or Step over a weight-sensitive pressure plate, you don't cause the plate to depress, which prevents you from triggering any device or hazard attached to the pressure plate. When the ampoule's effect ends, you sink, fall, break through flimsy ground, or land on pressure plates as normal for your current location.

EMERALD GRASSHOPPER — ITEM 5

| CONSUMABLE | MAGICAL | TRANSMUTATION | TALISMAN |

Price 30 gp

Usage affixed to armor; **Bulk** —

Activate ◈ envision; **Trigger** You attempt a High Jump but haven't rolled yet; **Requirements** You are an expert in Athletics.

This metal grasshopper studded with emeralds is usually clasped to the legs of a suit of armor. When you activate it, if you succeed at the Athletics check, you Leap up to 50 feet vertically and up to 10 feet horizontally. If you critically succeed, you can Leap up to 75 feet vertically and 20 feet horizontally. If you don't end your jump on solid ground, you flutter in the air until the end of your turn, then fall harmlessly at a rate of 60 feet per round until you reach the ground.

EYE OF APPREHENSION — ITEM 12

| CONSUMABLE | DIVINATION | FORTUNE | TALISMAN |

Price 400 gp

Usage affixed to armor; **Bulk** —

Activate ◈ envision; **Trigger** You are about to roll Perception for initiative but haven't rolled yet; **Requirements** You are a master in Perception.

This round piece of cymophane's silky inclusion makes it look like a cat's eye. While affixed, it makes you jittery. When you activate it, roll Perception twice and use the higher result.

FADE BAND — ITEM 12

| CONSUMABLE | ILLUSION | MAGICAL | TALISMAN |

Price 320 gp

Usage affixed to armor; **Bulk** —

Activate ◈ envision; **Trigger** An attack misses you; **Requirements** You are a master in Stealth.

This thin, silvery wire wraps around your armor. When you activate the band, it casts a 2nd-level *invisibility* spell on you.

FEAR GEM — ITEM 4

| CONSUMABLE | ENCHANTMENT | FEAR | MAGICAL | MENTAL | TALISMAN |

Price 20 gp

CRAFTING & TREASURE

11

INTRODUCTION

ANCESTRIES & BACKGROUNDS

CLASSES

SKILLS

FEATS

EQUIPMENT

SPELLS

THE AGE OF LOST OMENS

PLAYING THE GAME

GAME MASTERING

CRAFTING & TREASURE

APPENDIX

Usage affixed to a weapon; **Bulk** —

Activate ◆◆ Intimidating Strike

Dark smoke seems to writhe within this obsidian gem. When you activate the gem, you make an Intimidating Strike, as the fighter feat (page 146).

If you have the Intimidating Strike feat, increase the frightened condition value from this Intimidating Strike to frightened 2, or frightened 3 on a critical hit.

FEATHER STEP STONE   ITEM 3

CONSUMABLE · MAGICAL · TALISMAN · TRANSMUTATION

Price 8 gp

Usage affixed to armor; **Bulk** —

Activate ◆ envision; **Trigger** You Stride or Step; **Requirement** You are an expert in Acrobatics.

This stone, usually shaped as a cabochon, is a small chunk of amber with a bit of feather or a flying insect caught within it. When you activate the stone, you ignore the effects of any difficult terrain and greater difficult terrain you move through until the end of your turn.

FLAME NAVETTE   ITEM 16

ABJURATION · CONSUMABLE · MAGICAL · TALISMAN

Price 1,800 gp

Usage affixed to armor; **Bulk** —

Activate ◆ envision; **Requirement** You're an expert in Will saves.

This piece of bronzite is shaped like an oval with points at both ends. It has a carved flame at its center and is traditionally worn over the heart. You can activate only one *flame navette* per day. When you activate the navette, you gain the benefit of the fighter's Determination class feat, with a counteract modifier of +22. If you have the Determination feat, you can use your own modifier if it's better.

GALLOWS TOOTH   ITEM 8

CONSUMABLE · DIVINATION · MAGICAL · TALISMAN

Price 100 gp

Usage affixed to a weapon; **Bulk** —

Activate ◆ Interact; **Trigger** You attack an adjacent creature and haven't rolled your attack roll; **Requirements** You're a master in Intimidation.

This grisly molar hangs from a cord threaded through a tiny hole just above its dried, exposed root. When you activate this talisman, the creature you're attacking becomes flat-footed until the end of the current turn.

GHOST DUST   ITEM 16

CONSUMABLE · ILLUSION · OCCULT · TALISMAN

Price 1,800 gp

Usage affixed to armor; **Bulk** —

Activate ◆ envision; **Trigger** You use an action with the move trait; **Requirements** You are legendary in Stealth.

This small vial is filled with a grayish-green dust rendered from dried ectoplasm. When you activate the dust, it casts a 4th-level *invisibility* spell on you. This comes into effect before you move during the triggering action.

GRIM TROPHY   ITEM 7

CONSUMABLE · ENCHANTMENT · MAGICAL · TALISMAN

Price 55 gp

Usage affixed to armor; **Bulk** —

Activate ◆ envision; **Trigger** You attempt an Intimidation check to Coerce or Demoralize, but you haven't rolled yet; **Requirements** You are an expert in Intimidation.

This talisman comes in many forms, most often a severed piece of a humanoid creature displayed in some gruesome manner. When you activate the trophy, select two targets and compare your Intimidation check result to both of their DCs.

HUNTER'S BANE   ITEM 2

CONSUMABLE · DIVINATION · MAGICAL · TALISMAN

Price 6 gp

Usage affixed to armor; **Bulk** —

Activate ◆ envision; **Trigger** An undetected enemy hits you with an attack; **Requirements** You are trained in Survival.

This talisman is a ring of dried, interwoven leaves. When you activate the *hunter's bane*, you sense the exact location of the attacker, making it hidden from you instead of undetected. If the attacker is behind lead, the *hunter's bane* fails and is wasted.

IRON CUBE   ITEM 6

CONSUMABLE · EVOCATION · MAGICAL · TALISMAN

Price 50 gp

Usage affixed to a weapon; **Bulk** —

Activate ◆◆ Knockdown; **Requirement** You are an expert with the affixed weapon.

This cube of blackened iron is affixed to a weapon with an iron chain. When you activate the cube, you use Knockdown, as the fighter feat (page 146).

If you have the Knockdown feat, ignore its normal size restrictions.

IRON CUDGEL   ITEM 14

CONSUMABLE · EVOCATION · MAGICAL · TALISMAN

Price 900 gp

Usage affixed to a weapon; **Bulk** —

Activate ◆ Brutal Finish; **Requirement** You are a master with the affixed weapon.

This miniature iron cudgel is typically affixed to a weapon by an iron chain. When you activate the cudgel, you use Brutal Finish, as the fighter feat (page 151). You must meet the normal requirements, including those of the press trait.

If you have the Brutal Finish feat, add two additional weapon damage dice on a success or a failure.

IRON EQUALIZER   ITEM 12

CONSUMABLE · EVOCATION · MAGICAL · TALISMAN

Price 400 gp

Usage affixed to a weapon; **Bulk** —

Activate ◆ Certain Strike; **Requirement** You are a master with the affixed weapon.

This small iron band has a shifting weight that helps equalize the affixed weapon's balance. When you activate it, you use Certain Strike, as the fighter feat (page 150). You must meet the normal requirements, including those of the press trait.

If you have the Certain Strike feat, the failure effect increases to deal the weapon's normal damage.

IRON MEDALLION ITEM 10

ABJURATION CONSUMABLE MAGICAL TALISMAN

Price 175 gp

Usage affixed to armor; **Bulk** —

Activate ◆ envision; **Trigger** You attempt a Will save against a fear effect but haven't rolled yet; **Requirements** You have master proficiency in Will saves or have the bravery class feature.

This small medallion is shaped like a shield. When you activate it, you gain a +2 status bonus to saves against fear for 1 minute. On the triggering save, if the outcome of your roll is a failure, you get a success instead or if the outcome is a critical failure, you get a failure instead.

JADE BAUBLE ITEM 8

CONSUMABLE ENCHANTMENT MAGICAL MENTAL TALISMAN

Price 100 gp

Usage affixed to a melee weapon; **Bulk** —

Activate ◆ command; **Requirements** You are a master with the affixed weapon.

This bit of jade is usually carved in the shape of a duelist, or sometimes a multi-armed creature. When you activate the bauble, it magically draws the attention of foes. Until the start of your next turn, enemies within the reach of the weapon the talisman is affixed to are flat-footed.

JADE CAT ITEM 2

ABJURATION CONSUMABLE MAGICAL TALISMAN

Price 6 gp

Usage affixed to armor; **Bulk** —

Activate ◆ command; **Trigger** You fall or attempt an Acrobatics check to Balance; **Requirements** You are trained in Acrobatics.

A thumb-sized feline carved of rare stone, the *jade cat* is typically worn as a pendant upon a suit of armor. For 1 minute after you activate the cat, you treat all falls as 20 feet shorter, you are not flat-footed when you Balance, and narrow surfaces and uneven ground are not difficult terrain for you.

MENDING LATTICE ITEM 13

UNCOMMON ABJURATION CONSUMABLE MAGICAL TALISMAN

Price 525 gp

Usage affixed to a shield or weapon; **Bulk** —

Activate ◆ command; **Trigger** The affixed item would take damage; **Requirements** You are a master in Crafting.

This lattice of reinforced iron is shaped into a perfect octagon. When you activate it, it negates the damage and instantly and completely repairs the affixed item.

MESMERIZING OPAL ITEM 2

CONSUMABLE ENCHANTMENT MAGICAL TALISMAN

Price 7 gp

Usage affixed to armor; **Bulk** —

Activate ◆ envision; **Trigger** You attempt a Deception check to Feint, but you haven't rolled yet.

This silver-bound opal pendant is afire with iridescence. When you activate it, if the outcome of your triggering Deception check is a critical failure, you get a failure instead (or if the outcome is a success, you get a critical success instead).

MONKEY PIN ITEM 2

CONSUMABLE TRANSMUTATION MAGICAL TALISMAN

Price 6 gp

Usage affixed to armor; **Bulk** —

Activate ◆ Climb; **Requirements** You are trained in Athletics.

This small brass pin is in the shape of a monkey climbing a tree. When you activate this talisman, use a Climb action. If you succeed, you move your full Speed during the Climb. If you roll a critical failure, you get a failure instead.

MUMMIFIED BAT ITEM 10

CONSUMABLE DIVINATION MAGICAL TALISMAN

Price 175 gp

Usage affixed to a weapon; **Bulk** —

Activate ◆ command; **Requirements** You are a master in Perception.

This talisman is the magically treated corpse of a tiny bat bound in papyrus. When you activate the bat, the affixed weapon detects vibrations around you and guides your perception. You gain the benefits of the fighter Blind-Fight class feat (page 149) for 1 minute.

If you have the Blind-Fight feat, you gain imprecise echolocation with a range of 30 feet for 1 minute. This makes creatures that would be undetected by you because you can't see them hidden instead.

MURDERER'S KNOT ITEM 7

CONSUMABLE EVOCATION MAGICAL TALISMAN

Price 66 gp

Usage affixed to a weapon; **Bulk** —

Activate ◆ command; **Trigger** You damage a flat-footed creature with a Strike using the affixed weapon; **Requirements** You are an expert with the affixed weapon.

This black strand of leather is tied to look like a peace knot when the weapon is stowed, but it doesn't hamper drawing the weapon. When you activate the knot, the creature you damaged takes 1d6 persistent bleed damage.

If you have the Twist the Knife feat, the talisman instead deals persistent bleed damage equal to your sneak attack damage.

ONYX PANTHER   ITEM 2

| CONSUMABLE | MAGICAL | TRANSMUTATION | TALISMAN |

Price 7 gp

Usage affixed to armor; **Bulk** —

Activate ◆ envision; **Trigger** You use a Sneak action; **Requirements** You are trained in Stealth.

This small stone is a stylized panther shape. When you activate it, you can move your full Speed (instead of half) during the triggering Sneak and any other time you Sneak this turn.

OWLBEAR CLAW   ITEM 1

| CONSUMABLE | EVOCATION | MAGICAL | TALISMAN |

Price 3 gp

Usage affixed to a weapon; **Bulk** —

Activate ◆ envision; **Trigger** You critically succeed at an attack roll with the affixed weapon.

This claw set in an iron clasp and chain isn't always the claw of an owlbear. When you activate the claw, the triggering attack gains the weapon's critical specialization effect.

POTENCY CRYSTAL   ITEM 1

| CONSUMABLE | EVOCATION | MAGICAL | TALISMAN |

Price 4 gp

Usage affixed to a weapon; **Bulk** —

Activate ◆ envision; **Trigger** You make an attack with the affixed weapon, but you haven't rolled yet.

This fluorite crystal glows with a strange phosphorescence. When you activate the crystal, the weapon becomes a *+1 striking weapon* for the rest of the turn, gaining a +1 item bonus to the attack roll and increasing the damage on a hit to two weapon damage dice.

SAVIOR SPIKE   ITEM 2

| ABJURATION | CONSUMABLE | FORCE | MAGICAL | TALISMAN |

Price 7 gp

Usage affixed to armor; **Bulk** —

Activate ◆ command; **Trigger** You attempt to Grab an Edge but haven't rolled; **Requirements** You're an expert in Reflex.

This pyramid-shaped spike is attached to an armor's chest piece. When you activate the spike, it shoots a strand of force to help you gain purchase. If you roll a success on the triggering attempt, you get a critical success instead (if you roll a critical failure, you get a failure instead).

SHARK TOOTH CHARM   ITEM 5

| ABJURATION | CONSUMABLE | MAGICAL | TALISMAN |

Price 23 gp

Usage affixed to armor; **Bulk** —

Activate ◆ command; **Trigger** You attempt to Escape using Acrobatics for your roll, but you haven't rolled yet; **Requirements** You are an expert in Acrobatics.

This dried seaweed bracelet is lined with charms shaped like small shark teeth. When you activate the bracelet, if you roll a success on the triggering check, you get a critical success instead (if you roll a critical failure, you get a failure instead). If you fail the Acrobatics check against a grabbing creature, the creature must either release you as a free action or take 2d8 piercing damage as shark's teeth momentarily emerge from your skin.

SNEAKY KEY   ITEM 5

| CONSUMABLE | EVOCATION | MAGICAL | TALISMAN |

Price 22 gp

Usage affixed to armor; **Bulk** —

Activate ◆◆ Interact; **Requirements** You are an expert in Thievery.

This small silver skeleton key can be pinned to armor or a sleeve. When you turn the key to activate it, for the next minute, if the outcome of any your attempts to Pick a Lock is a critical failure, you get a failure instead.

SWIFT BLOCK CABOCHON   ITEM 7

| UNCOMMON | ABJURATION | CONSUMABLE | MAGICAL | TALISMAN |

Price 70 gp

Usage affixed to a shield; **Bulk** —

Activate ◆ envision; **Trigger** You take damage from a physical attack while you don't have the affixed shield raised.

This clear quartz cabochon attaches to the center of your shield. When you activate the cabochon, you use the Shield Block reaction even if you hadn't raised the affixed shield (and even if you don't normally have that reaction).

TIGER MENUKI   ITEM 5

| CONSUMABLE | MAGICAL | TRANSMUTATION | TALISMAN |

Price 30 gp

Usage affixed to a weapon; **Bulk** —

Activate ◆ envision; **Trigger** You Strike with the affixed weapon.

This tiger formed of pewter snarls viciously from your weapon's grip. When you activate the tiger, the affixed weapon gains the sweep trait for the triggering attack and all other attacks for 1 minute.

VANISHING COIN   ITEM 10

| CONSUMABLE | ILLUSION | MAGICAL | TALISMAN |

Price 160 gp

Usage affixed to armor; **Bulk** —

Activate ◆ envision; **Trigger** You attempt a Stealth check for initiative, but you haven't rolled yet; **Requirements** You are a master in Stealth.

This copper coin dangles from a leather strip strung through a hole drilled in the center. Until activated, the coin becomes invisible for a few seconds at random intervals every few minutes. When you activate the coin, it casts a 2nd-level *invisibility* spell on you, lasting until the end of your next turn.

VIPER'S FANG   ITEM 14

| CONSUMABLE | EVOCATION | MAGICAL | TALISMAN |

Price 850 gp

Usage affixed to a weapon; **Bulk** —

Activate ↻ envision; **Trigger** A creature within your reach uses a manipulate or move action, makes a ranged attack, or leaves a square during a move action it's using; **Requirements** You are a master with the affixed weapon.

When you activate this resin-strengthened viper skull, you make an Attack of Opportunity against the triggering creature.

If you have Attack of Opportunity, you can activate the *viper's fang* as a free action.

WOLF FANG   ITEM 1

| CONSUMABLE | EVOCATION | MAGICAL | TALISMAN |

Price 4 gp

Usage affixed to armor; **Bulk** —

Activate ◈ envision; **Trigger**
  You successfully Trip a foe;
  Requirements You are trained in Athletics.

This wolf canine is bound in a strip of leather and tied to a buckle or strap of a suit of armor. When you activate the fang, you deal bludgeoning damage equal to your Strength modifier to the target of your Trip. If your Trip would already deal physical damage that doesn't include an ability modifier, add your Strength modifier to that damage.

OTHER CONSUMABLES

Though many consumables are grouped into specific categories, such as potions and talismans, some consumables don't fit into those categories.

CANDLE OF TRUTH   ITEM 8

| UNCOMMON | CONSUMABLE | ENCHANTMENT | MAGICAL | MENTAL |

Price 75 gp

Usage held in 1 hand; **Bulk** —

Activate ◈ Interact

This tapered candle has a golden wick that burns with white fire. You activate the candle by lighting it, which causes creatures within 10 feet of the candle to find it difficult to tell falsehoods. Creatures in the area receive a –4 status penalty to Lie.

In addition, when first entering the affected area, each creature (including you) must succeed at a DC 26 Will save or be unable to tell any deliberate lies while within 10 feet of the lit candle. This lasts for as long as the candle is lit. Once lit, the candle burns for 10 minutes, and it cannot be extinguished.

DUST OF APPEARANCE   ITEM 6

| CONSUMABLE | DIVINATION | MAGICAL |

Price 50 gp

Usage held in 1 hand; **Bulk** —

Activate ◈ Interact

Stored in a small reed, this powder looks like a fine metallic dust. When you fling it in the air, it coats all creatures in a 10-foot burst centered on a point within 5 feet of you. For 1 minute, the coated creatures can't be concealed or invisible, nor can they benefit from *mirror image* or similar abilities that create illusory duplicates. Any illusions in the area of

3rd level or lower are revealed as such, although this does not end their effect.

DUST OF DISAPPEARANCE   ITEM 9

| CONSUMABLE | ILLUSION | MAGICAL |

Price 135 gp

Usage held in 1 hand; **Bulk** —

Activate ◈ Interact

This powder shimmers like a thousand tiny motes of light. Activating the dust by sprinkling it on yourself or a creature within reach casts a 4th-level *invisibility* spell with a duration of 1 minute on that creature. This invisibility can't be negated or seen through by any spell of 3rd level or lower or any item of 5th level or lower.

ELEMENTAL GEM   ITEM 10

| CONJURATION | CONSUMABLE | MAGICAL |

Price 200 gp

Usage held in 1 hand; **Bulk** —

Activate ◈◈ command, Interact

You shout the name of an elemental lord and dash this glassy gem against a hard surface to activate it. It cracks open, casting a 5th-level *summon elemental* spell to summon forth an elemental you control as long as you spend an action each round to Sustain the Activation.

This gem comes in four varieties: transparent for a living whirlwind, light brown for a living landslide, reddish orange for a living wildfire, and blue-green for a living waterfall.

FEATHER TOKEN   ITEM 1+

| CONJURATION | CONSUMABLE | MAGICAL |

Usage held in 1 hand; **Bulk** —

Activate ◈ Interact

Each *feather token* appears to be a simple feather from some exotic bird. The feather's shaft, dipped in gold, bears a single arcane rune. Activating a *feather token* causes it to transform into another object, which then can be used as normal for that object. Each feather can be activated only once, with most of them permanently becoming the item in their description.

Type anchor; **Level** 7; **Price** 55 gp

This feather can be activated only on a boat. When activated, this feather transforms into a massive anchor that causes the boat to immediately stop. After 1 day, the anchor vanishes and the boat can move as normal. The anchor is attached to the boat by a magical chain of force, but the chain can be removed by *dispel magic* or destroyed (Hardness 30, HP 40).

Type bird; **Level** 3; **Price** 8 gp

When activated, this token transforms into a small sparrow that waits on your finger for you to relay a message up to 1 minute in length, along with the name and rough location of a recipient. The recipient must be someone you have met, and the location must be somewhere you have visited. After receiving the message, the bird flies off to deliver it, traveling at 30 miles per hour and then searching for the target in the location you provided. If the bird finds the target, it moves adjacent to them, your words emanate from the bird, and the bird then flies off and vanishes. The bird also vanishes if it fails to find your target after 10 hours of searching the location you specified.

Type chest; **Level** 3; **Price** 10 gp

When you use this token, a small wooden chest appears and immediately opens. This chest can hold up to 10 Bulk worth of items. Once the chest is closed, it transforms again—this time into a key—taking all of the stored items with it. You can activate this key by spending an Interact action to turn it in an imaginary lock, which causes it to transform back into a chest with all of the items still inside. Once it has turned into a chest a second time, it forever remains a wooden chest.

Type fan; **Level** 4; **Price** 15 gp

Activating this feather requires you to fan it in a given direction. If this direction is toward the sail of a vessel, the feather flutters up toward the sail and fans continuously, filling the sail with air and granting the vessel a +10-foot circumstance bonus to its Speed for 8 hours. If fanned in any other direction, it instead produces a single casting of *gust of wind* (DC 20).

Type holly bush; **Level** 2; **Price** 6 gp

When this feather is activated, it immediately transforms into a living holly bush, filling a single square. This bush can provide standard cover. In addition, the bush has 2d4 bright-red berries. While holly berries are usually poisonous, these berries are infused with beneficial magic. You can pick and eat a berry as an Interact action to recover 1 Hit Point. Once plucked from the bush, a berry becomes non-magical after a few seconds, so it doesn't heal you if you don't eat it within the span of your Interact action.

If activated on soil, the plant continues to grow and thrive (although it doesn't produce any more healing berries). If activated elsewhere, it withers and dies within 1d4 days.

Type ladder; **Level** 1; **Price** 3 gp

When activated, this feather transforms permanently into a 20-foot-long wooden ladder.

Type swan boat; **Level** 8; **Price** 76 gp

This feather can be activated only when tossed into a large body of water, such as a lake or broad river. It transforms into a swan-shaped boat capable of carrying up to 32 Medium creatures, 8 Large creatures, or 2 Huge creatures. The boat moves on the water at a Speed of 50 feet, and lasts 1 day.

Type tree; **Level** 6; **Price** 38 gp

This token can be activated only on an unoccupied patch of earth or soil. When activated, this token transforms into an oak tree, 60 feet tall with a 5-foot-wide trunk. The tree continues to live and grow if conditions are favorable.

Type whip; **Level** 9; **Price** 130 gp

This feather transforms into a +1 *striking dancing whip* when activated. The whip immediately jumps from your grasp and proceeds to attack your enemies until 1 minute has passed or it fails its flat check for *dancing*, at which point it vanishes. If the whip's target isn't prone, the whip uses its actions to attempt to Trip that creature instead of making a Strike. The whip's total attack modifier for Striking or Tripping is +18 instead of the normal bonus for a *dancing* weapon.

HOLY WATER — ITEM 1

CONSUMABLE **DIVINE** **GOOD** **SPLASH**

Price 3 gp

Usage held in 1 hand; **Bulk** L

Activate ◆ Strike

This vial contains water blessed by a good deity. You activate a vial of *holy water* by throwing it as a Strike. It's a simple thrown weapon with a range increment of 20 feet. Unlike an alchemical bomb, it doesn't add the manipulate trait to the attack made with it.

Holy water deals 1d6 good damage and 1 good splash damage. It damages only fiends, undead, and creatures that have a weakness to good damage.

JAVELIN OF LIGHTNING — ITEM 9

CONSUMABLE **ELECTRICITY** **EVOCATION** **MAGICAL**

Price 110 gp

Usage held in 1 hand; **Bulk** L

Activate ◆◆ command, Interact

This item looks like a normal javelin carved with lightning-bolt motifs. If thrown without being activated, it wobbles in the air and fails to strike true. When you Activate the javelin, your command makes the carvings crackle with electricity. You then hurl the javelin. It shatters immediately after leaving your hand and unleashes its magic as a 4th-level *lightning bolt* originating from your space. The bolt deals 5d12 electricity damage and has a Reflex save DC of 25.

Craft Requirements Supply a casting of *lightning bolt* (4th level).

RUNESTONE — ITEM 1

CONSUMABLE **MAGICAL**

Price 3 gp

Usage held in 1 hand; **Bulk** L

This flat piece of hard stone is specially prepared for etching a magical fundamental rune or property rune. You can etch only one rune upon a stone. Once the stone is etched, it gains the magic school trait of the rune etched upon it. When a rune is transferred from the *runestone* to another object, the *runestone* cracks and is destroyed. The Price listed is for an empty stone; a stone holding a rune adds the Price of the rune.

UNHOLY WATER — ITEM 1

CONSUMABLE **DIVINE** **EVIL** **SPLASH**

Price 3 gp

Usage held in 1 hand; **Bulk** L

Activate ◆ Strike

An evil deity's malice lies within this vial of water. You activate a vial of *unholy water* by throwing it as a Strike. It's a simple thrown weapon with a range increment of 20 feet. Unlike an alchemical bomb, it doesn't add the manipulate trait to the attack made with it.

Unholy water deals 1d6 evil damage and 1 evil splash damage. It damages only celestials and creatures that have a weakness to evil damage.

HELD ITEMS

These items need to be held to use them. Weapons, wands, and staves follow special rules and have their own sections.

BAG OF HOLDING   ITEM 4+

CONJURATION **EXTRADIMENSIONAL** **MAGICAL**

Usage held in 2 hands; **Bulk** 1

Though it appears to be a cloth sack decorated with panels of richly colored silk or stylish embroidery, a *bag of holding* opens into an extradimensional space larger than its outside dimensions. The Bulk held inside the bag doesn't change the Bulk of the *bag of holding* itself. The amount of Bulk the bag's extradimensional space can hold depends on its type.

You can Interact with the *bag of holding* to put items in or remove them just like a mundane sack. Though the bag can hold a great amount of material, an object still needs to be able to fit through the opening of the sack to be stored inside.

If the bag is overloaded or broken, it ruptures and is ruined, causing the items inside to be lost forever. If it's turned inside out, the items inside spill out unharmed, but the bag must be put right before it can be used again. A living creature placed inside the bag has enough air for 10 minutes before it begins to suffocate, and it can attempt to Escape against a DC of 13. An item inside the bag provides no benefits unless it's retrieved first. An item in the bag can't be detected by magic that detects only things on the same plane.

Type I; **Level** 4; **Price** 75 gp; **Capacity** 25 Bulk
Type II; **Level** 7; **Price** 300 gp; **Capacity** 50 Bulk
Type III; **Level** 11; **Price** 1,200 gp; **Capacity** 100 Bulk
Type IV; **Level** 13; **Price** 2,400 gp; **Capacity** 150 Bulk

BOTTLED AIR   ITEM 7

AIR **CONJURATION** **MAGICAL**

Price 320 gp

Usage held in 1 hand; **Bulk** L

Appearing to be an ordinary corked glass bottle, this item contains a limitless supply of fresh air. You must uncork the bottle with an Interact action before you can activate it.

Activate ❖ Interact; **Effect** You draw a breath of air from the bottle. This allows you to breathe even in an airless or toxic environment. Air doesn't escape the mouth of the bottle, so leaving the open bottle in an airless environment doesn't change the environment.

BROOM OF FLYING   ITEM 12

MAGICAL **TRANSMUTATION**

Price 1,900 gp

Usage held in 1 hand; **Bulk** 1

This broom has a tenuous connection to gravity, and it tends to drift even while stowed. You can ride on the broom using one hand to guide it, and the broom can carry up to one passenger in addition to you. The broom moves at a fly Speed of 20 feet. The broom can carry only so much, taking a –10-foot penalty

to its Speed if laden with more than 20 Bulk, and crashing to the ground if it carries more than 30 Bulk.

Activate ❖❖ command, Interact; **Effect** You name a destination on the same plane, and the broom speeds toward it at a fly Speed of 40 feet. You must either clutch the broom with two hands in order to ride it, or you need to release the broom to send it off with no rider. If you don't have a good idea of the location, layout, and general direction of the destination, or if your named destination is on another plane, the broom wanders aimlessly, circling back to its starting location after 30 minutes.

If the broom carries a rider, this activation lasts until 4 hours pass (typically 16 miles of travel), the broom reaches its destination, or you Dismiss the activation. If the broom doesn't have a rider, the activation lasts until the broom reaches its destination. When the activation ends, the broom floats to the ground and can't be activated again for 1 hour.

CHIME OF OPENING   ITEM 6

UNCOMMON **EVOCATION** **MAGICAL**

Price 235 gp

Usage held in 2 hands; **Bulk** L

This hollow mithral tube is about a foot long and bears engravings reminiscent of open locks and broken chains. The chime can be activated 10 times before it cracks and becomes useless.

Activate ❖ Interact; **Effect** You aim the chime at a container, door, or lock you want to open and strike the chime. The chime sends out magical vibrations that attempt a Thievery check against the lock's DC, with a Thievery bonus of +13. This targets only one lock or binding at a time, so you might need to activate the chime multiple times to open a target with several forms of protection.

CRYSTAL BALL   ITEM 14+

UNCOMMON **DIVINATION** **MAGICAL** **SCRYING**

Usage held in 1 hand; **Bulk** L

This polished crystal sphere enhances scrying magic. Any visual information received through a spell with the scrying trait that was cast by the *crystal ball* appears within the sphere, and any auditory information sounds out from the surface of the sphere. When you cast a *scrying* spell by any other means while holding the sphere, you can relay any information you receive in the same way, allowing others to see or hear the target.

The base version of a *crystal ball* is a sphere of clear quartz, but other versions are made of different stones.

Activate 1 minute (command, envision, Interact); **Frequency** once per hour; **Effect** The crystal ball casts *clairvoyance* to your specifications.

Activate 10 minutes (command, envision, Interact); **Frequency** twice per day; **Effect** The crystal ball casts a DC 33 *scrying* spell to your specifications.

Type clear quartz; **Level** 14; **Price** 3,800 gp

Type selenite; **Level** 15; **Price** 7,000 gp

Scrying is DC 36 and gives you the benefits of *see invisibility* on the target.

Type moonstone; **Level** 16; **Price** 7,500 gp

Scrying is DC 37 and gives you the benefits of *mind reading* on the target, using the same save DC.

Type peridot; **Level** 17; **Price** 12,500 gp

Scrying is DC 39 and gives you the benefits of *telepathy* for communicating with the target.

Type obsidian; **Level** 19; **Price** 32,000 gp

Scrying is DC 41 and gives you the benefits of *true seeing* for anything you watch through it.

DECANTER OF ENDLESS WATER   ITEM 7

`CONJURATION` `MAGICAL` `WATER`

Price 320; **Bulk** L

This item looks like an ordinary glass flask full of water. The stopper can't be removed unless you speak one of the item's three command words, each of which causes water to pour forth in a different way. Pulling the stopper straight out creates fresh water, and rotating it as you pull creates salt water. Any effect of the decanter lasts until the decanter is plugged (with its own stopper, a finger, or the like).

Activate ❖ command, Interact; **Effect** Speaking "stream," you cause water to pour out at a rate of 1 gallon per round.

Activate ❖ command, Interact; **Effect** Speaking "fountain," you cause water to pour out in a 5-foot-long stream at a rate of 5 gallons per round.

Activate ❖ command, Interact; **Effect** Speaking "geyser," you cause a powerful deluge of water to erupt at a rate of 15 gallons per round. You can direct the stream at a creature, subjecting it to the effects of *hydraulic push* (spell attack roll +15). You can repeat this once per round as long as the geyser continues, spending an Interact action to direct the geyser each time.

EVERBURNING TORCH   ITEM 1

`EVOCATION` `LIGHT` `MAGICAL`

Price 15 gp

Usage held in 1 hand; **Bulk** L

An *everburning torch* is one of the most common applications of permanent magic. This torch sheds light constantly, requiring no oxygen and generating no heat. The flame can be covered or hidden, but can't be smothered or quenched.

HOLY PRAYER BEADS   ITEM 5+

`UNCOMMON` `DIVINE` `HEALING` `NECROMANCY` `POSITIVE`

Usage held in 1 hand; **Bulk** –

This strand of ordinary-looking prayer beads glows with a soft light and becomes warm to the touch the first time you cast a divine spell while holding it. When you do, the prayer beads become attuned to your deity, changing their form and iconography to prominently incorporate your deity's religious symbol and iconography. The beads don't transform or function for an evil spellcaster.

Whenever you cast a divine spell from your own spell slots while holding the prayer beads, you recover 1 Hit Point; this is a positive healing effect. If the spell you cast was a healing spell, you can grant this additional healing to one of the spell's targets instead of yourself.

Activate Cast a Spell; **Effect** Cast *bless* or *heal*, each once per day.

Type standard; **Level** 5; **Price** 160 gp

Type greater; **Level** 11; **Price** 1,400 gp

You recover 1d4 Hit Points instead of 1 Hit Point when casting divine spells from your spell slots. Change the beads' list of spells to the 4th-level versions of *bless*, *divine wrath* (matching one component of your deity's alignment), *heal*, *neutralize poison*, and *remove disease*. You can cast each of these once per day.

Craft Requirements You have a spellcasting class feature with the divine tradition.

HORN OF BLASTING   ITEM 9

`EVOCATION` `SONIC`

Price 700 gp

Usage held in 1 hand; **Bulk** L

A *horn of blasting* is a bright brass trumpet. It can be played as an instrument, granting a +2 item bonus to your Performance check.

Activate ❖ Interact; **Frequency** once per round; **Effect** When you activate the horn by blowing into it with destructive intent, you create a blast note targeting one creature or object within 30 feet. The blast deals 3d6 sonic damage. (DC 28 basic Fortitude save).

Activate ❖❖ Interact; **Frequency** once per day; **Effect** You can blow even louder to create an intense blast wave in a 30-foot cone that deals 8d6 sonic damage. Each creature attempts a DC 28 Fortitude save with the following effects.

Critical Success The creature takes no damage.

Success The creature takes half damage.

Failure The creature takes full damage and is deafened for 2d6 rounds.

HORN OF FOG   ITEM 6

`CONJURATION` `MAGICAL` `WATER`

Price 230 gp

Usage held in 1 hand; **Bulk** 1

This large ram's horn perpetually glistens with tiny droplets of water, much like condensation.

Activate ❖❖ Interact; **Frequency** once per hour; **Effect** You activate the horn by blowing deeply into it, causing it to issue forth a low blast and cast a 2nd-level *obscuring mist* spell. You can Dismiss the mist at any time by blowing a second note on the horn using an Interact action.

INTRODUCTION

ANCESTRIES &
BACKGROUNDS

CLASSES

SKILLS

FEATS

EQUIPMENT

SPELLS

THE AGE OF
LOST OMENS

PLAYING THE
GAME

GAME
MASTERING

CRAFTING
& TREASURE

APPENDIX

IMMOVABLE ROD — ITEM 9

MAGICAL **TRANSMUTATION**

Price 600 gp

Usage held in 1 hand; **Bulk** 1

This flat iron bar is almost completely nondescript, except for one small button appearing on its surface.

Activate ◆ Interact; You push the button to anchor the rod in place. It doesn't move, defying gravity if need be. If the button is pushed again, the rod deactivates, ending the anchoring magic. While anchored, the rod can be moved only if 8,000 pounds of pressure are applied to it or if a creature uses Athletics to Force Open the rod with a DC of 40 (though most intelligent creatures can just push the button to release the rod).

MAESTRO'S INSTRUMENT — ITEM 3+

ENCHANTMENT **MAGICAL**

Usage held in 2 hands; **Bulk** 1

A *maestro's instrument* can be crafted in the form of any variety of handheld musical instrument. A *maestro's instrument* grants you a +1 item bonus to Performance checks while playing music with the instrument.

Activate ◆◆ Interact; **Frequency** once per day; **Effect** You can play the instrument to produce the effects of a *charm* spell.

Type lesser; **Level** 3; **Price** 60 gp

Type moderate; **Level** 10; **Price** 900 gp

The item bonus is +2, and the *charm* spell is 4th level.

Type greater; **Level** 18; **Price** 19,000 gp

The item bonus is +3, and the *charm* spell is 8th level.

Craft Requirements You must supply a casting of *charm* of the appropriate level.

MARVELOUS MEDICINES — ITEM 12+

MAGICAL **NECROMANCY**

Usage held in 2 hands; **Bulk** 1

This set of healer's tools contains a seemingly endless supply of bandages, herbs, and healing items of impeccable quality, granting you a +2 item bonus to Medicine checks.

Activate ◆ Treat Poison or 8 hours (Treat Disease); **Effect** You can activate the tools when you use them to Treat Poison in order to produce the effects of *neutralize poison*, or when you Treat Disease in order to produce the effects of *remove disease*. Once these medicines have been used to treat a patient's poison or disease, they can't be used again to treat the same affliction for that patient.

Type standard; **Level** 12; **Price** 1,800 gp

Type greater; **Level** 18; **Price** 19,000 gp

The tools grant a +3 item bonus, and the spells are heightened to 6th level.

POSSIBILITY TOME — ITEM 18

MAGICAL **DIVINATION**

Price 22,000 gp

Usage held in 2 hands; **Bulk** 2

An array of semiprecious stones is set into the ornate silver and beaten copper cover of this thick and weighty tome. If you open the book before it's been activated, its vellum pages are blank and pristine, but once activated, words dance and swim onto the pages before your eyes.

Activate 10 minutes (envision, Interact); **Effect** As you flip through the book, you think about a broad topic you want to know more about. Choose one skill: Arcana, Crafting, Medicine, Nature, Occultism, Religion, Society, or a single subcategory of Lore. The book's pages fill with information about that skill, though only you can see the information. While the pages are full, you can spend an Interact action perusing the book just before attempting a check to Recall Knowledge with the chosen skill. This grants you a +3 item bonus to the check, and if you roll a critical failure, you get a failure instead. The information within the book disappears after 24 hours or when the tome is activated again.

PRIMEVAL MISTLETOE — ITEM 6+

PRIMAL **TRANSMUTATION**

Usage held in 1 hand; **Bulk** —

This sprig of berry-festooned holly and mistletoe doesn't wilt or rot. It can be used as a primal focus, and it also grants the creature holding it a +1 item bonus to Nature checks.

Activate ◆◆ Interact; **Frequency** once per 10 minutes; **Effect** You squeeze juice from one of the berries and smear it onto a non-magical club or staff to cast *shillelagh* upon it.

Activate ◆◆ Interact; **Frequency** once per day; **Effect** You can twine the sprig around the wrist of one hand and touch a tree to cast *tree shape* upon yourself, except instead of a becoming a tree, you become a vine on the touched tree.

Type standard; **Level** 6; **Price** 230 gp

Type greater; **Level** 14; **Price** 3,900 gp

The sprig grants a +2 bonus and can be activated in one additional way:

Activate ◆◆ Interact; **Frequency** once per day; **Effect** You plant the *primeval mistletoe* into an area of natural earth or stone. Once planted, the plant immediately sprouts into an area of holly bushes that don't impede movement and that pulse with positive energy, replicating the effects of a *field of life* spell. This lasts for up to 1 minute, as long as you continue to Sustain the Activation. When this magic ends, the holly bushes revert back into the original *primeval mistletoe*.

ROD OF NEGATION — ITEM 14

ABJURATION **MAGICAL**

Price 4,300 gp

Usage held in 1 hand; **Bulk** 1

This long, plain, leaden rod can disrupt magic.

Activate ◆◆ Interact; **Effect** This rod emits a thin, gray beam that negates a spell or magic item, casting a 6th-level *dispel magic* spell with a counteract modifier of +23. Once activated, the rod can't be activated again for 2d6 hours.

INTRODUCTION

ANCESTRIES &
BACKGROUNDS

CLASSES

SKILLS

FEATS

EQUIPMENT

SPELLS

THE AGE OF
LOST OMENS

PLAYING THE
GAME

GAME
MASTERING

CRAFTING
& TREASURE

APPENDIX

ROD OF WONDER — ITEM 8

RARE **CHAOTIC** **EVOCATION** **MAGICAL**

Price 465 gp

Usage held in 1 hand; **Bulk** L

This peculiar rod is strange and unpredictable. Each time it is activated, it produces one of a variety of effects at random.

Activate ◆◆ command, Interact; **Effect** Choose a creature within 60 feet and roll d% on the table below to determine the rod's effect. If an entry lists only a spell name, the rod casts that spell at its lowest level. You make any decisions for a spell cast by the rod unless otherwise indicated, except that it must target the creature you chose, or the creature you chose must be the center of the spell's area, if it has an area but no targets. If the spell's range is less than 60 feet, increase the range to 60 feet.

Any spell DC required is DC 27, and any spell attack roll required is +17. If the rod casts a spell on you, you don't get a saving throw or other defense against it.

Once activated, the rod can't be activated again for 1d4 hours.

D%	Wondrous Effect
1–3	Leaves grow from the target; they last 24 hours
4–8	*Darkness*
9	Summon a giant stag beetle (5th-level *summon animal*; *Pathfinder Bestiary* 41)
10–13	A stream of 600 large and colorful butterflies pours forth, fluttering in a 20-foot burst for 2 rounds; creatures are blinded while in the cloud of butterflies
14–15	All the target's weapons animate with the effects of the *dancing* rune
16–25	*Lightning bolt*
26–29	Grass grows in a 60-foot cone in front of the rod, or existing grass grows at 10 × normal rate
30	Target turns blue, green, or purple with an unlimited duration
31	Summon an elephant (6th-level *summon animal*; *Pathfinder Bestiary* 154)
32–34	Heavy rain falls in a 60-foot radius around you for 1 round
35–38	*Stinking cloud*
39	Summon an ineffective mouse (1st-level *summon animal*)
40–42	*Vibrant pattern*, with a 1-round duration
43–44	The rod casts *mirror image* on you
45–46	*Gust of wind*
47–48	The non-living, unattended object closest to the target (up to 30 cubic feet in size) turns ethereal for an unlimited duration
49–53	*Slow*
54	You turn blue, green, or purple with an unlimited duration
55–59	The rod casts *pest form* on you, lasting 1d4 rounds
60–61	1d4 × 10 gems, each worth 1 sp, shoot from the rod, dealing 1 piercing damage to each creature in a 15-foot cone
62	*Sleep*, with a 100-foot burst
63–72	*Fireball*
73–77	*Mind reading*
78–80	Roll again; the target believes you created the effect of the second roll
81–84	*Enlarge*
85–87	Target is coated in nectar, making it clumsy 1 for 1 round
88–92	*Faerie fire*
93–97	The rod casts *invisibility* on you
98–100	The rod casts *shrink* on you, lasting 1 day

SKELETON KEY — ITEM 5+

MAGICAL **TRANSMUTATION**

Usage held in 1 hand; **Bulk** —

A grinning skull tops the bow of this macabre key. This key can be used in place of thieves' tools when attempting to Pick a Lock, and it grants a +1 item bonus to the Thievery check. If the *skeleton key* becomes broken due to a critical failure on the check, it works as normal thieves' tools and loses its benefits until repaired.

Activate ◆ Interact; **Frequency** once per day; **Trigger** You attempt to Pick a Lock but haven't rolled yet; **Effect** The key casts *knock* on the lock you're trying to pick.

Type standard; **Level** 5; **Price** 125 gp

Type greater; **Level** 11; **Price** 1,250 gp

The key grants a +2 item bonus, and you can activate the key once per hour.

THURIBLE OF REVELATION — ITEM 3+

DIVINATION **DIVINE**

Usage held in 1 hand; **Bulk** 1

This brass censer dangles on a length of chain. Most *thuribles of revelation* are adorned with swirling Celestial text, though some are iron and feature Infernal or Abyssal text.

Activate ◆◆ Interact; **Cost** incense worth at least 5 gp; **Effect** You light the incense inside the censer, and it burns for 1 hour. During that time, as long you are holding the thurible, you gain a +1 item bonus to Religion checks, and any critical failure you roll when you Decipher Writing of a religious nature is a failure instead.

Type lesser; **Level** 3; **Price** 55 gp

Type moderate; **Level** 10; **Price** 900 gp

The thurible grants a +2 bonus. Once per day, when you activate the thurible, you can increase its revelations. During that activation, you can hold the thurible up to your eyes with an Interact action to gain the effects of *see invisibility* for 1 round by peering through the smoke.

Type greater; **Level** 18; **Price** 19,000 gp

The thurible grants a +3 bonus. The greater version shares the once-per-day enhanced revelations of the moderate version, except peering through the smoke also grants you the effects of *true seeing*.

TRAVELER'S ANY-TOOL — ITEM 6

MAGICAL **TRANSMUTATION**

Price 200 gp

Usage held in 2 hands; **Bulk** 1

Before it's activated, this item appears to be an ash rod capped with steel on either end.

Activate ◆◆ Interact, envision; **Effect** You imagine a specific simple tool, and the any-tool transforms into it. (Usually, you can choose from a tool listed in Chapter 6). This transforms the wooden portion into any haft and the metal caps into spades, hammer heads, or the like, allowing for most basic tools but nothing more complex. You can return the item to its rod form with an Interact action.

TRITON'S CONCH — ITEM 9

MAGICAL **TRANSMUTATION**

Price 640 gp

Usage held in 1 hand; **Bulk** L

If you put this large opalescent conch shell to your ear, you can hear the sound of the roaring sea crashing against the shore.

Activate ◆ Interact (auditory); **Effect** You can raise the conch to your lips and blow into it, letting out a long, rumbling note. For the next minute, you and all allies who were within 30 feet of you when you activated the conch gain a +2 item bonus to Athletics checks to Swim and can breathe under water.

WONDROUS FIGURINE — ITEM 2+

CONJURATION **MAGICAL**

Usage held in 1 hand; **Bulk** L

Each one of these statuettes is 1 inch in height, carved from a specific material and taking the shape of a particular animal or animals.

Activate ◆◆ command, Interact; **Effect** You activate the statue by placing it on solid ground and then speaking its name, causing the statuette to transform into a living creature or creatures. In creature form, the figurine has the minion trait. It can understand your language and it obeys you to the best of its ability when you use an action to command it. The specifics of each creature, as well as the activation's frequency (if any), appear in its entry below.

If the figurine is slain while in animal form, it reverts to its statue shape and cannot be activated again until 1 week has passed. If the figurine is destroyed in statue form, it is shattered and its magic is lost.

Type golden lions; **Level** 10; **Price** 900 gp

This statuette depicts a pair of gold lions, and when activated, it becomes a pair of adult lions (*Pathfinder Bestiary* 52). The lions can be called on only once per day, and they remain in lion form for no more than 1 hour. If either of the lions is slain, that lion cannot be summoned again until 1 week has passed, but this doesn't prevent you from summoning the other.

Type jade serpent; **Level** 7; **Price** 340 gp

This tiny statue first appears to be a formless lump of jade until closer inspection reveals it to be a serpentine body curled into a snug knot. When activated, this figurine becomes a giant viper (*Pathfinder Bestiary* 303). The figurine can be used only once per day, and it can remain in serpent form for no more than 10 minutes.

Type marble elephant; **Level** 13; **Price** 2,700 gp

Finely carved from a solid piece of marble, this gleaming elephant statuette becomes a fully grown elephant (*Pathfinder Bestiary* 154) when activated. The elephant can be called upon no more than four times per month. It remains for 24 hours as long as it is being used as a beast of burden or for transport. If it attempts an attack or otherwise engages in combat, it reverts to statuette form after 1d4 rounds.

Type obsidian steed; **Level** 15 (uncommon); **Price** 6,000 gp

This sinister-looking black statuette resembles a horse rearing up on its hind legs. When activated, this figurine becomes a nightmare (*Pathfinder Bestiary* 244). It can be called upon once per week for up to 24 hours, though it won't use *plane shift* or its other abilities on behalf of its rider. Although evil, it allows itself to be ridden by creatures of any alignment, although if a good creature mounts it, the rider must attempt a DC 3 flat check. On a failure, the nightmare uses *plane shift* to take the rider to a random location in the Abyss, where it promptly returns to statue form, stranding its rider in that nightmarish place.

Type onyx dog; **Level** 2; **Price** 34 gp

This simple onyx statue transforms into a guard dog (*Pathfinder Bestiary* 102). The dog has a +4 circumstance bonus to Survival checks to Track, and it has darkvision. When the dog senses a hidden creature with its scent, that creature is instead observed and concealed. The onyx dog can be activated once per week and remains in its form for up to 6 hours.

MATERIALS

Most items are made from readily available materials—usually leather, wood, or steel—but some weapons and armor are made from more exotic materials, giving them unique properties and other advantages. Weapons made from precious materials are better able to harm certain creatures, and armor of these materials provides enhanced protection.

Most materials are metals; they can be used to make metal weapons and armor. The GM is the final arbiter of what items can be made using a material. An item can be made with no more than one precious material, and only an expert in Crafting can create it. Some rare and exotic materials require master or even legendary proficiency.

A material's Price depends on how hard it is to work, its scarcity, and its purity; most items made with precious materials use an alloy, blend, or coating rather than using the material in its purest form. The three grades of purity for precious materials are low-grade, standard-grade, and high-grade. Regardless of a precious material's purity, an item made from it gains the full effects of the precious material, but creating higher-level items and more powerful magic runes with precious material requires greater purity.

Some precious materials are available only at certain grades. For instance, adamantine can't be low-grade, and orichalcum must be high-grade. Items made of materials with a lower grade than expected for the item's level, or of a higher grade than necessary, will mention the precious material's grade.

MATERIAL STATISTICS

Table 11–4 below provides the Hardness, Hit Points, Broken Threshold, and example items for some types of common materials. The table has separate entries for thin items (like shields), ordinary items (like armor), and reinforced or durable structures (such as walls).

Stone is a catchall for any hard stone, such as granite and marble. Likewise, wood covers ordinary woods, such as oak and pine. Metal weapons and armor are assumed to be made of iron or steel unless noted otherwise.

If an object consists of more than one material, the GM typically uses the statistics for the strongest material involved. For instance, breaking a wall made of paper panels over a woven wooden framework would require damaging thin wood, not paper. However, the GM might choose the weaker material based on the item's function. For instance, breaking the wooden handle of a hammer rather than its iron head would still render the item unusable. Sometimes an item is even less sturdy than the Hardness and Hit Points provided for a thin object; for instance, a twig doesn't take 9 damage to break, even though it's made of thin wood. Similarly, a particularly sturdy item or structure might have even higher Hardness and Hit Points. Certain structures, particularly thick walls, are so reinforced that you have to break them down over time with tools. (Page 515 has more information on walls.)

PRECIOUS MATERIALS

Materials with the precious trait can be substituted for base materials. For example, a hammer's head could be made of adamantine instead of iron. Items made of a precious material cost more than typical items; not only does precious material cost more, but the crafter must invest more time working with it. In addition, more powerful items require precious materials of greater purity.

TABLE 11-4: MATERIAL HARDNESS, HIT POINTS, AND BROKEN THRESHOLD

Material	Hardness	HP	BT	Example Items
Paper	0	1	–	Book pages, paper fan, scroll
Thin cloth	0	1	–	Kite, silk dress, undershirt
Thin glass	0	1	–	Bottle, spectacles, window pane
Cloth	1	4	2	Cloth armor, heavy jacket, sack, tent
Glass	1	4	2	Glass block, glass table, heavy vase
Glass structure	2	8	4	Glass block wall
Thin leather	2	8	4	Backpack, jacket, pouch, strap, whip
Thin rope	2	8	4	Standard adventuring rope
Thin wood	3	12	6	Chair, club, sapling, wooden shield
Leather	4	16	8	Leather armor, saddle
Rope	4	16	8	Industrial rope, ship rigging
Thin stone	4	16	8	Chalkboard, slate tiles, stone cladding
Thin iron or steel	5	20	10	Chain, steel shield, sword
Wood	5	20	10	Chest, simple door, table, tree trunk
Stone	7	28	14	Paving stone, statue
Iron or steel	9	36	18	Anvil, iron or steel armor, stove
Wooden structure	10	40	20	Reinforced door, wooden wall
Stone structure	14	56	28	Stone wall
Iron or steel structure	18	72	36	Iron plate wall

A number of precious materials are described below. The Price entry for each material gives the Price of a simple non-magical item made of that material, based on its Bulk (if the item is lighter than 1 Bulk, use the price for 1 Bulk), as well as Prices for different amounts of the material itself. Prices for armor, shields, and weapons made of precious material are in the Armor (page 555), Shields (page 586), and Weapons (page 599) sections of this chapter.

CRAFTING WITH PRECIOUS MATERIALS

Only an expert crafter can create a low-grade item, only a master can create a standard-grade item, and only a legendary crafter can create a high-grade item. In addition, to Craft with a precious material, your character level must be equal to or greater than that of the material.

Low-grade items can be used in the creation of magic items of up to 8th level, and they can hold runes of up to 8th level. Standard-grade items can be used to create magic items of up to 15th level and can hold runes of up to 15th level. High-grade items use the purest form of the precious material, and can be used to Craft magic items of any level holding any runes. Using purer forms of common materials is so relatively inexpensive that the Price is included in any magic item.

When you Craft an item that incorporates a precious material, your initial raw materials for the item must include that material; at least 10% of the investment must be of the material for low-grade, at least 25% for standard-grade, and all of it for high-grade. For instance, a low-grade silver object of 1 Bulk costs 20 gp. Of the 10 gp of raw materials you provide when you start to Craft the item, at least 1 gp must be silver. The raw materials you spend to complete the item don't have to consist of the precious material, though the GM might rule otherwise in certain cases.

After creating an item with a precious material, you can use Craft to improve its grade, paying the Price difference and providing a sufficient amount of the precious material.

ADAMANTINE   MATERIAL 8+

UNCOMMON | PRECIOUS

Mined from rocks that fell from the heavens, adamantine is one of the hardest metals known. It has a shiny, black appearance, and it is prized for its amazing resiliency and ability to hold an incredibly sharp edge.

Type adamantine chunk; **Price** 500 gp; **Bulk** L

Type adamantine ingot; **Price** 5,000 gp; **Bulk** 1

Type standard-grade adamantine object; **Level** 8; **Price** 350 gp per Bulk

Type high-grade adamantine object; **Level** 16; **Price** 6,000 gp per Bulk

Adamantine Items	Hardness	HP	BT
Thin Items			
Standard-grade	10	40	20
High-grade	13	52	26

Items			
Standard-grade	14	56	28
High-grade	17	68	34
Structures			
Standard-grade	28	112	56
High-grade	34	136	68

COLD IRON   MATERIAL 2+

PRECIOUS

Weapons made from cold iron are deadly to demons and fey alike. Cold iron looks like normal iron but is mined from particularly pure sources and shaped with little or no heat. This process is extremely difficult, especially for high-grade cold iron items.

Type cold iron chunk; **Price** 10 gp; **Bulk** L

Type cold iron ingot; **Price** 100 gp; **Bulk** 1

Type low-grade cold iron object; **Level** 2; **Price** 20 gp per Bulk

Type standard-grade cold iron object; **Level** 7; **Price** 250 gp per Bulk

Type high-grade cold iron object; **Level** 15; **Price** 4,500 gp per Bulk

Cold Iron Items	Hardness	HP	BT
Thin Items			
Low-grade	5	20	10
Standard-grade	7	28	14
High-grade	10	40	20
Items			
Low-grade	9	36	18
Standard-grade	11	44	22
High-grade	14	56	28
Structures			
Low-grade	18	72	36
Standard-grade	22	88	44
High-grade	28	112	56

DARKWOOD   MATERIAL 8+

UNCOMMON | PRECIOUS

Darkwood is a very lightweight wood found primarily in old-growth forests in south-central Avistan; it is dark as ebony but has a slight purple tint. A darkwood item's Bulk is reduced by 1 (or to light Bulk if its normal Bulk is 1, with no effect on an item that normally has light Bulk). The Price of an item made of darkwood is based on the item's normal Bulk, not its reduced Bulk for being made of darkwood, but reduce the Bulk before making any further Bulk adjustments for the size of the item.

Type darkwood branch; **Price** 500 gp; **Bulk** L

Type darkwood lumber; **Price** 5,000 gp; **Bulk** 1

Type standard-grade darkwood object; **Level** 8; **Price** 350 gp per Bulk

Type high-grade darkwood object; **Level** 16; **Price** 6,000 gp per Bulk

Darkwood Items	Hardness	HP	BT
Thin Items			
Standard-grade	5	20	10
High-grade	8	32	16

Items			
Standard-grade	7	28	14
High-grade	10	40	20
Structures			
Standard-grade	14	56	28
High-grade	20	80	40

DRAGONHIDE   MATERIAL 8+

UNCOMMON   **PRECIOUS**

The hide and scales of a dragon can be used to Craft any item normally made of ordinary leather or hide. Dragonhide varies in color from blue to glittering gold, depending on the dragon it came from. Due to the scales' resiliency, it can also be used to Craft armor usually made out of metal plates (such as a breastplate, half plate, and full plate), allowing such armor to be made without metal. Dragonhide objects are immune to one damage type, depending on the type of dragon (see the table below).

Type standard-grade dragonhide object; **Level** 8; **Price** 350 gp per Bulk

Type high-grade dragonhide object; **Level** 16; **Price** 6,000 gp per Bulk

Dragon Type	Resistance
Black or copper	Acid
Blue or bronze	Electricity
Brass, gold, or red	Fire
Green	Poison
Silver or white	Cold

Dragonhide Items	Hardness	HP	BT
Thin Items			
Standard-grade	4	16	8
High-grade	8	32	16
Items			
Standard-grade	7	28	14
High-grade	11	44	22

MITHRAL   MATERIAL 8+

UNCOMMON   **PRECIOUS**

Mithral is renowned for its lightness, durability, and effectiveness against a range of creatures including devils and lycanthropes. It has the same sheen as silver but a slightly lighter hue. Mithral weapons and armor are treated as if they were silver for the purpose of damaging creatures with weakness to silver. A metal item made of mithral is lighter than one made of iron or steel: the item's Bulk is reduced by 1 (reduced to light Bulk if its normal Bulk is 1, with no effect on an item that normally has light Bulk). The Price of an item made of this material is based on the item's normal Bulk, not its reduced Bulk for being made of mithral, but reduce the Bulk before making any further Bulk adjustments for the size of the item.

Type mithral chunk; **Price** 500 gp; **Bulk** L

Type mithral ingot; **Price** 5,000 gp; **Bulk** 1

Type standard-grade mithral object; **Level** 8; **Price** 350 gp per Bulk

Type high-grade mithral object; **Level** 16; **Price** 6,000 gp per Bulk

Mithral Items	Hardness	HP	BT
Thin Items			
Standard-grade	5	20	10
High-grade	8	32	16
Items			
Standard-grade	9	36	18
High-grade	12	48	24
Structures			
Standard-grade	18	72	36
High-grade	24	96	48

ORICHALCUM   MATERIAL 17+

RARE   **PRECIOUS**

The most rare and valuable skymetal, orichalcum is coveted for its incredible time-related magical properties. This dull, coppery metal isn't as physically sturdy as adamantine, but orichalcum's time-bending properties protect it, granting it greater Hardness and Hit Points. If an orichalcum item takes damage but isn't destroyed, it repairs itself completely 24 hours later.

Type orichalcum chunk; **Price** 1,000 gp; **Bulk** L

Type orichalcum ingot; **Price** 10,000 gp; **Bulk** 1

Type high-grade orichalcum object; **Level** 17; **Price** 10,000 gp per Bulk

Orichalcum Items	Hardness	HP	BT
Thin Items			
High-grade	16	64	32
Items			
High-grade	18	72	36
Structures			
High-grade	35	140	70

SILVER   MATERIAL 2+

PRECIOUS

Silver weapons are a bane to creatures ranging from devils to werewolves. Silver items are less durable than steel items, and low-grade silver items are usually merely silver-plated.

Type silver chunk; **Price** 10 gp; **Bulk** L

Type silver ingot; **Price** 100 gp; **Bulk** 1

Type low-grade silver object; **Level** 2; **Price** 20 gp per Bulk

Type standard-grade silver object; **Level** 7; **Price** 250 gp per Bulk

Type high-grade silver object; **Level** 15; **Price** 4,500 gp per Bulk

Silver Items	Hardness	HP	BT
Thin Items			
Low-grade	3	12	6
Standard-grade	5	20	10
High-grade	8	32	16
Items			
Low-grade	5	20	10
Standard-grade	7	28	14
High-grade	10	40	20
Structures			
Low-grade	10	40	20
Standard-grade	14	56	28
High-grade	20	80	40

RUNES

Most magic weapons and armor gain their enhancements from potent eldritch runes etched into them. These runes allow for in-depth customization of items.

Runes must be physically engraved on items through a special process to convey their effects. They take two forms: fundamental runes and property runes. Fundamental runes offer the most basic and essential benefits: a *weapon potency* rune adds a bonus to a weapon's attack rolls, and the *striking* rune adds extra weapon damage dice. An *armor potency* rune increases the armor's item bonus to AC, and the *resilient* rune grants a bonus to the wearer's saving throws. Property runes, by contrast, grant more varied effects—typically powers that are constant while the armor is worn or that take effect each time the weapon is used, such as a rune that grants energy resistance or one that adds fire damage to a weapon's attacks.

The number of property runes a weapon or armor can have is equal to the value of its potency rune. A *+1 weapon* can have one property rune, but it could hold another if the *+1 weapon potency* rune were upgraded to a *+2 weapon potency* rune. Since the *striking* and *resilient* runes are fundamental runes, they don't count against this limit.

An item with runes is typically referred to by the value of its potency rune, followed by any other fundamental runes, then the names of any property runes, and ends with the name of the base item. For example, you might have a *+1 longsword* or *+2 greater resilient fire-resistant chain mail*.

Rune-etched armor and weapons have the same Bulk and general characteristics as the non-magical version unless noted otherwise. The level of an item with runes etched onto it is equal to the highest level among the base item and all runes etched on it; therefore, a *+1 striking mace* (a 4th-level item) with a *disrupting* rune (a 5th-level rune) would be a 5th-level item.

Each rune can be etched into a specific type of armor or weapon, as indicated in the Usage entry of the rune's stat block. Explorer's clothing can have armor runes etched on it even though it's not armor, but because it's not in the light, medium, or heavy armor category, it can't have runes requiring any of those categories.

INVESTITURE

If a suit of armor has any runes, it has the invested trait, requiring you to invest it to get its magical benefits.

RUNE FORMULAS

The Price of a rune's formula is the same as the Price of a formula for an item of the same level; it can be acquired in the same way as an item formula (described on page 293).

THE ETCHING PROCESS

Etching a rune on an item follows the same process as using the Craft activity to make an item. You must have the formula for the rune, the item you're adding the rune to must be in your possession throughout the etching process,

and you must meet any special Craft Requirements of the rune. The rune has no effect until you complete the Craft activity. You can etch only one rune at a time.

TRANSFERRING RUNES

You can transfer runes between one item and another, including a *runestone* (page 571). This also uses the Craft activity. This lets you either move one rune from one item to another or swap a rune on one item with a rune on the other item. To swap, the runes must be of the same form (fundamental or property).

If an item can have two or more property runes, you decide which runes to swap and which to leave when transferring. If you attempt to transfer a rune to an item that can't accept it, such as transferring a melee weapon rune to a ranged weapon, you get an automatic critical failure on your Crafting check. If you transfer a potency rune, you might end up with property runes on an item that can't benefit from them. These property runes go dormant until transferred to an item with the necessary potency rune or until you etch the appropriate potency rune on the item bearing them.

The DC of the Crafting check to transfer a rune is determined by the item level of the rune being transferred, and the Price of the transfer is 10% of the rune's Price, unless transferring from a *runestone*, which is free. If you're swapping, use the higher level and higher Price between the two runes to determine these values. It takes 1 day (instead of the 4 days usually needed to Craft) to transfer a rune or swap a pair of runes, and you can continue to work over additional days to get a discount, as usual with Craft.

FUNDAMENTAL RUNES

Four fundamental runes produce the most essential magic of protection and destruction: *armor potency* and *resilient* runes for armor, and *weapon potency* and *striking* runes for weapons. A potency rune is what makes a weapon a magic weapon (page 599) or armor magic armor (page 556).

An item can have only one fundamental rune of each type, though etching a stronger rune can upgrade an existing rune to the more powerful version (as described in each rune's entry). As you level up, you typically alternate between increasing an item's potency rune and its *striking* or *resilient* rune when you can afford to.

Fundamental Rune	Etched Onto	Benefit
Armor potency	Armor	Increase item bonus to AC and determine maximum number of property runes
Resilient	Armor	Grant item bonus to saves
Weapon potency	Weapon	Grant an item bonus to attack rolls and determine maximum number of property runes
Striking	Weapon	Increase weapon damage dice

CRAFTING & TREASURE

11

INTRODUCTION

ANCESTRIES &
BACKGROUNDS

CLASSES

SKILLS

FEATS

EQUIPMENT

SPELLS

THE AGE OF
LOST OMENS

PLAYING THE
GAME

GAME
MASTERING

CRAFTING
& TREASURE

APPENDIX

FUNDAMENTAL ARMOR RUNES

ARMOR POTENCY   RUNE 5+

ABJURATION **MAGICAL**

Usage etched onto armor

Magic wards deflect attacks. Increase the armor's item bonus
to AC by 1. The armor can be etched with one property rune.

You can upgrade the *armor potency* rune already etched
on a suit of armor to a stronger version, increasing the
values of the existing rune to those of the new rune. You
must have the formula of the stronger rune to do so, and
the Price of the upgrade is the difference between the two
runes' Prices.

Type *+1 armor potency*; **Level** 5; **Price** 160 gp; **Craft
Requirements** You are an expert in Crafting.

Type *+2 armor potency*; **Level** 11; **Price** 1,060 gp; **Craft
Requirements** You are a master in Crafting.
Increase the armor's item bonus to AC by 2, and the armor can
be etched with two property runes.

Type *+3 armor potency*; **Level** 18; **Price** 20,560 gp; **Craft
Requirements** You are legendary in Crafting.
Increase the armor's item bonus to AC by 3, and the armor can
be etched with three property runes.

RESILIENT   RUNE 8+

ABJURATION **MAGICAL**

Usage etched onto armor

Resilient runes imbue armor with additional protective magic.
This grants the wearer a +1 item bonus to saving throws.

You can upgrade the *resilient* rune already etched on a suit
of armor to a stronger version, increasing the values of the
existing rune to those of the new rune. You must have the
formula of the stronger rune to do so, and the Price of the
upgrade is the difference between the two runes' Prices.

Type *resilient*; **Level** 8; **Price** 340 gp

Type *greater resilient*; **Level** 14; **Price** 3,440 gp
The armor grants a +2 item bonus to saving throws.

Type *major resilient*; **Level** 20; **Price** 49,440 gp
The armor grants a +3 item bonus to saving throws.

FUNDAMENTAL WEAPON RUNES

STRIKING   RUNE 4+

EVOCATION **MAGICAL**

Usage etched onto a weapon

A *striking* rune stores destructive magic in the weapon,
increasing the weapon damage dice it deals to two instead of
one. For instance, a *+1 striking dagger* would deal 2d4 damage
instead of 1d4 damage.

You can upgrade the *striking* rune already etched on a
weapon to a stronger version, increasing the values of the
existing rune to those of the new rune. You must have the
formula of the stronger rune to do so, and the Price of the
upgrade is the difference between the two runes' Prices.

Type *striking*; **Level** 4; **Price** 65 gp

Type *greater striking*; **Level** 12; **Price** 1,065 gp

SPECIFIC ARMOR AND WEAPONS

Unlike armor and weapons enhanced with runes, specific
armor and weapons (such as *ghoul hide* or a *holy avenger*)
are created for a specific purpose and can work quite
differently from other items of their type. Specific magic
armor and weapons can't gain property runes, but you
can add or improve their fundamental runes.

RUNE TRANSFER EXAMPLES

You could transfer a *flaming* rune from a *+1 striking
flaming greatsword* to a *+2 striking longsword*, resulting
in a *+2 striking flaming longsword* and a *+1 striking
greatsword*. You could swap the *weapon potency* runes
from a *+1 longsword* and a *+2 greatsword*, resulting in a
+2 longsword and a *+1 greatsword*. However, you couldn't
swap a *+1 weapon potency* rune from one weapon with a
flaming property rune from another weapon, as the two
runes don't have the same form.

When transferring a rune to an item that can hold
multiple property runes, you can decide whether you
transfer a single rune or swap runes between the items.
For example, a *+2 weapon* can hold two property runes. If
you transferred a *flaming rune* from a *+1 striking flaming
rapier* to a *+2 striking frost warhammer*, you would
decide whether you wanted to end up with a *+1 striking
rapier* and a *+2 striking flaming frost warhammer* or a *+1
striking frost rapier* and a *+2 striking flaming warhammer*.

The weapon deals three weapon damage dice.

Type *major striking*; **Level** 19; **Price** 31,065 gp
The weapon deals four weapon damage dice.

WEAPON POTENCY   RUNE 2+

EVOCATION **MAGICAL**

Usage etched onto a weapon

Magical enhancements make this weapon strike true. Attack
rolls with this weapon gain a +1 item bonus, and the weapon
can be etched with one property rune.

You can upgrade the *weapon potency* rune already
etched on a weapon to a stronger version, increasing the
values of the existing rune to those of the new rune. You
must have the formula of the stronger rune to do so, and
the Price of the upgrade is the difference between the two
runes' Prices.

Type *+1 weapon potency*; **Level** 2; **Price** 35 gp; **Craft
Requirements** You are an expert in Crafting.

Type *+2 weapon potency*; **Level** 10; **Price** 935 gp; **Craft
Requirements** You are a master in Crafting.
The item bonus to attack rolls is +2, and the weapon can be
etched with two property runes.

Type *+3 weapon potency*; **Level** 16; **Price** 8,935 gp; **Craft
Requirements** You are legendary in Crafting.
The item bonus to attack rolls is +3, and the weapon can be
etched with three property runes.

UPGRADING ARMOR AND WEAPON RUNES

You'll often want to upgrade the fundamental runes of magic armor or a magic weapon you already have. This requires upgrading each rune separately. Tables 11–5 and 11–6 summarize the Price of each step, with a number in parentheses indicating the item's level for the Craft activity. This also indicates the typical progression for an adventurer to follow when upgrading their armor and weapons. The tables here don't include progressions that aren't as likely to come up, like turning a *+1 weapon* directly into a *+1 greater striking weapon*.

TABLE 11-5: ARMOR UPGRADE PRICES

Starting Armor	Improved Armor	Price and Process
+1 armor	+1 resilient armor	340 gp to etch *resilient* (8th level)
+1 resilient armor	+2 resilient armor	900 gp to etch *+2 armor potency* (11th level)
+2 resilient armor	+2 greater resilient armor	3,100 gp to etch *greater resilient* (14th level)
+2 greater resilient armor	+3 greater resilient armor	19,500 gp to etch *+3 armor potency* (18th level)
+3 greater resilient armor	+3 major resilient armor	46,000 gp to etch *major resilient* (20th level)

TABLE 11-6: WEAPON UPGRADE PRICES

Starting Weapon	Improved Weapon	Price and Process
+1 weapon	+1 striking weapon	65 gp to etch *striking* (4th level)
+1 striking weapon	+2 striking weapon	900 gp to etch *+2 weapon potency* (10th level)
+2 striking weapon	+2 greater striking weapon	1,000 gp to etch *greater striking* (12th level)
+2 greater striking weapon	+3 greater striking weapon	8,000 gp to etch *+3 weapon potency* (16th level)
+3 greater striking weapon	+3 major striking weapon	30,000 gp to etch *major striking* (19th level)

PROPERTY RUNES

Property runes add special abilities to armor or a weapon in addition to the item's fundamental runes. If a suit of armor or a weapon has multiple etchings of the same rune, only the highest-level one applies. You can upgrade a property rune to a higher-level type of that rune in the same way you would upgrade a fundamental rune.

Rune abilities that must be activated follow the rules for activating magic items on page 532.

ARMOR PROPERTY RUNES

ANTIMAGIC RUNE 15

UNCOMMON · ABJURATION · MAGICAL

Price 6,500 gp

Usage etched onto armor

This intricate rune displaces spell energy, granting you a +1 status bonus to saving throws against magical effects.

Activate ↺ command; **Frequency** once per day; **Trigger** A spell targets you or includes you in its area; **Effect** The armor attempts to counteract the triggering spell with the effect of a 7th-level *dispel magic* spell and a counteract modifier of +26.

Craft Requirements Supply one casting of *dispel magic*.

ENERGY-RESISTANT RUNE 8+

ABJURATION · MAGICAL

Usage etched onto armor

These symbols convey protective forces from the Elemental Planes. You gain resistance 5 to acid, cold, electricity, or fire.

The crafter chooses the damage type when creating the rune. Multiple energy-resistant runes can be etched onto a suit of armor; rather than using only the highest-level effect, each must provide resistance to a different damage type. For instance, a *+2 acid-resistant greater fire-resistant breastplate* would give you acid resistance 5 and fire resistance 10.

Type *energy-resistant*; **Level** 8; **Price** 420 gp

Type *greater energy-resistant*; **Level** 12; **Price** 1,650 gp

You gain resistance 10 to the specified damage type.

ETHEREAL RUNE 17

UNCOMMON · CONJURATION · MAGICAL

Price 13,500 gp

Usage etched onto armor

An *ethereal* rune replicates armor on the Ethereal Plane.

Activate ❖ command; **Frequency** once per day; **Effect** You gain the effects of an *ethereal jaunt* spell. This doesn't require concentration and lasts for 10 minutes or until you choose to return to material form as a free action.

Craft Requirements Supply a casting of 9th level *ethereal jaunt*.

FORTIFICATION RUNE 12+

ABJURATION · MAGICAL

Usage etched onto medium or heavy armor

A *fortification* rune wards against the most deadly attacks. Each time you're critically hit while wearing the etched armor, attempt a DC 17 flat check. On a success, it becomes a normal hit. This property thickens the armor, increasing its Bulk by 1 and the Strength required to reduce its penalties by 2.

Type *fortification*; **Level** 12; **Price** 2,000 gp

Type *greater fortification*; **Level** 18; **Price** 24,000 gp

The flat check DC is 14.

GLAMERED   RUNE 5

ILLUSION **MAGICAL**

Price 140 gp

Usage etched onto armor

This armor can be disguised with a mere thought.

    Activate ◆ envision; **Effect** You change the shape and appearance of this armor to appear as ordinary or fine clothes of your imagining. The armor's statistics do not change. Only a creature that is benefiting from *true seeing* or a similar effect can attempt to disbelieve this illusion, with a DC of 25.

INVISIBILITY   RUNE 8+

ILLUSION **MAGICAL**

Usage etched onto light armor

Light seems to partially penetrate this armor.

    Activate ◆ command; **Frequency** once per day; **Effect** Whispering the command word, you become invisible for 1 minute, gaining the effects of a 2nd-level *invisibility* spell.

Type *invisibility*; **Level** 8; **Price** 500 gp

Type *greater invisibility*; **Level** 10; **Price** 1,000 gp

You can activate the armor up to three times per day.

Craft Requirements Supply one casting of *invisibility*.

SHADOW   RUNE 5+

MAGICAL **TRANSMUTATION**

Usage etched onto light or medium nonmetallic armor

Armor with this rune becomes hazy black. You gain a +1 item bonus to Stealth checks while wearing the armor.

Type *shadow*; **Level** 3; **Price** 55 gp

Type *greater shadow*; **Level** 9; **Price** 650 gp

The item bonus is +2.

Type *major shadow*; **Level** 17; **Price** 14,000 gp

The item bonus is +3.

SLICK   RUNE 3+

MAGICAL **TRANSMUTATION**

Usage etched onto armor

This property makes armor slippery, as though it were coated with a thin film of oil. You gain a +1 item bonus to Acrobatics checks to Escape and Squeeze.

Type *slick*; **Level** 3; **Price** 45 gp

Type *greater slick*; **Level** 8; **Price** 450 gp

The item bonus is +2.

Type *major slick*; **Level** 16; **Price** 9,000 gp

The item bonus is +3.

WEAPON PROPERTY RUNES

ANARCHIC   RUNE 11

CHAOTIC **EVOCATION** **MAGICAL**

Price 1,400 gp

Usage etched onto a weapon without an *axiomatic* rune

An *anarchic* rune is jagged and asymmetrical, channeling chaotic energy. A weapon with this rune deals an additional 1d6 chaotic damage against lawful targets. If you are lawful, you are enfeebled 2 while carrying or wielding this weapon.

    When you critically succeed at a Strike with this weapon against a lawful creature, roll 1d6. On a 1 or 2, you deal double minimum damage; on a 3 or 4, double your damage normally; on a 5 or 6, you deal double maximum damage.

Craft Requirements You are chaotic.

AXIOMATIC   RUNE 11

EVOCATION **LAWFUL** **MAGICAL**

Price 1,400 gp

Usage etched onto a weapon without an *anarchic* rune

Complex and symmetrical, an *axiomatic* rune imbues a weapon with lawful energy. A weapon with this rune deals an additional 1d6 lawful damage against chaotic targets. If you are chaotic, you are enfeebled 2 while carrying or wielding this weapon.

    When you critically succeed at an attack roll with this weapon against a chaotic creature, instead of rolling, count each weapon damage die as average damage rounded up (3 for d4, 4 for d6, 5 for d8, 6 for d10, 7 for d12).

Craft Requirements You are lawful.

CORROSIVE   RUNE 8+

ACID **CONJURATION** **MAGICAL**

Usage etched onto a weapon

Acid sizzles across the surface of the weapon. When you hit with the weapon, add 1d6 acid damage to the damage dealt. In addition, on a critical hit, the target's armor (if any) takes 3d6 acid damage (before applying Hardness); if the target has a shield raised, the shield takes this damage instead.

Type *corrosive*; **Level** 8; **Price** 500 gp

Type *greater corrosive*; **Level** 15; **Price** 6,500 gp

The acid damage dealt by this weapon ignores the target's acid resistance. Increase the acid damage dealt to armor or a shield on a critical hit to 6d6.

DANCING   RUNE 13

UNCOMMON **EVOCATION** **MAGICAL**

Price 2,700 gp

Usage etched onto a melee weapon

A *dancing* weapon flies autonomously and strikes your foes.

    Activate ◆◆ command, Interact; **Effect** You Release the weapon and it dances through the air, fighting on its own against the last enemy you attacked, or the nearest enemy to it if your target has been defeated. At the end of your turn each round, the weapon can Fly up to its fly Speed of 40 feet, and then can either Fly again or Strike one creature within its reach.

    The weapon has a space of 5 feet, but it doesn't block or impede enemies attempting to move though that space, nor does it benefit from or provide flanking. The weapon can't move through an enemy's space. The weapon can't use reactions, and its Fly actions don't trigger reactions.

    While it's activated, a *dancing* weapon makes Strikes with an attack modifier of +24 plus its item bonus to attack rolls. It uses

INTRODUCTION

ANCESTRIES & BACKGROUNDS

CLASSES

SKILLS

FEATS

EQUIPMENT

SPELLS

THE AGE OF LOST OMENS

PLAYING THE GAME

GAME MASTERING

CRAFTING & TREASURE

APPENDIX

the weapon's normal damage but has a +0 Strength modifier. The weapon's abilities that automatically trigger on a hit or critical hit still function, but the weapon can't be activated or benefit from any of your abilities while dancing.

Each round, when the weapon is finished using its actions, attempt a DC 6 flat check. On a failure, the activation ends and the weapon falls to the ground. You can't activate the item again for 10 minutes.

DISRUPTING   RUNE 5+

MAGICAL   NECROMANCY

Usage etched onto a melee weapon

A *disrupting* weapon pulses with positive energy, dealing an extra 1d6 positive damage to undead. On a critical hit, the undead is also enfeebled 1 until the end of your next turn.

Type disrupting; **Level** 5; **Price** 150 gp

Type greater disrupting; **Level** 14 (uncommon), **Price** 4,300 gp
Increase the extra damage to 2d6. On a critical hit, instead of being enfeebled 1, the undead creature must attempt a DC 34 Fortitude save with the following effects. This is an incapacitation effect.

Critical Success It's enfeebled 1 until the end of your next turn.

Success It's enfeebled 2 until the end of your next turn.

Failure It's enfeebled 3 until the end of your next turn.

Critical Failure It's destroyed.

FLAMING   RUNE 8+

CONJURATION   FIRE   MAGICAL

Usage etched onto a weapon

This weapon is empowered by flickering flame. The weapon deals an additional 1d6 fire damage on a successful Strike, plus 1d10 persistent fire damage on a critical hit.

Type flaming; **Level** 8; **Price** 500 gp

Type greater flaming; **Level** 15; **Price** 6,500 gp
Increase the persistent damage on a critical hit to 2d10. Fire damage dealt by this weapon (including the persistent fire damage) ignores the target's fire resistance.

FROST   RUNE 8+

COLD   CONJURATION   MAGICAL

Usage etched onto a weapon

This weapon is empowered with freezing ice. It deals an additional 1d6 cold damage on a successful Strike. On a critical hit, the target is also slowed 1 until the end of your next turn unless it succeeds at a DC 24 Fortitude save.

Type frost; **Level** 8; **Price** 500 gp

Type greater frost; **Level** 15; **Price** 6,500 gp
The save DC is 34. Cold damage dealt by this weapon ignores the target's cold resistance.

GHOST TOUCH   RUNE 4

MAGICAL   TRANSMUTATION

Price 75 gp

Usage etched onto a melee weapon

The weapon can harm creatures without physical form. A *ghost touch* weapon is particularly effective against incorporeal

creatures, which almost always have a specific weakness to *ghost touch* weapons. Incorporeal creatures can touch, hold, and wield *ghost touch* weapons (unlike most physical objects).

GRIEVOUS   RUNE 9

ENCHANTMENT   MAGICAL

Price 700 gp

Usage etched onto a weapon

When your attack roll with this weapon is a critical hit and gains the critical specialization effect, you gain an additional benefit depending on the weapon group.

Axe You can damage a third creature, with the same restrictions.

Bow The Athletics check to pull the missile free is DC 20.

Brawling The target takes a –4 circumstance penalty to its save.

Club You can knock the target up to 15 feet away.

Dart The base persistent bleed damage increases to 2d6.

Flail You move the target 5 feet. You can't move it away from you, but you can move it in another direction of your choice.

Hammer You can also knock the target 5 feet away from you.

Knife The target takes a –5-foot status penalty to its Speed while it has the persistent bleed damage.

Pick The extra damage from the critical specialization effect increases to 4 per weapon damage die.

Polearm You can move the target up to 10 feet.

Shield You can knock the target up to 10 feet away.

Sling The target also takes a –10-foot status penalty to its Speed for 1 round if it fails the save.

Spear The enfeebled condition lasts for 2 rounds.

Sword The target is flat-footed until the end of your next turn.

HOLY   RUNE 11

EVOCATION   GOOD   MAGICAL

Price 1,400 gp

Usage etched onto a weapon without an *unholy* rune

Holy weapons command powerful celestial energy. A weapon with this rune deals an extra 1d6 good damage against evil targets. If you are evil, you are enfeebled 2 while carrying or wielding this weapon.

Activate ⟳ command; **Frequency** once per day; **Trigger** You critically succeed at an attack roll against an evil creature with the weapon; **Effect** You regain HP equal to double the evil creature's level. This is a good, positive, healing effect.

Craft Requirements You are good.

KEEN   RUNE 13

UNCOMMON   MAGICAL   TRANSMUTATION

Price 3,000 gp

Usage etched onto a piercing or slashing melee weapon

The edges of a *keen* weapon are preternaturally sharp. Attacks with this weapon are a critical hit on a 19 on the die as long as that result is a success. This property has no effect on a 19 if the result would be a failure.

RETURNING   RUNE 3

EVOCATION   MAGICAL

Price 55 gp

Usage etched onto a thrown weapon

When you make a thrown Strike with this weapon, it flies back to your hand after the Strike is complete. If your hands are full when the weapon returns, it falls to the ground in your space.

SHIFTING   RUNE 6

MAGICAL TRANSMUTATION

Price 225 gp

Usage etched onto a melee weapon

With a moment of manipulation, you can shift this weapon into a different weapon with a similar form.

Activate ❖ Interact; **Effect** The weapon takes the shape of another melee weapon that requires the same number of hands to wield. The weapon's runes and any precious material it's made of apply to the weapon's new shape. Any property runes that can't apply to the new form are suppressed until the item takes a shape to which they can apply.

SHOCK   RUNE 8+

ELECTRICITY EVOCATION MAGICAL

Usage etched onto a weapon

Electric arcs crisscross this weapon, dealing an extra 1d6 electricity damage on a hit. On a critical hit, electricity arcs out to deal an equal amount of electricity damage to up to two other creatures of your choice within 10 feet of the target.

Type *shock*; **Level** 8; **Price** 500 gp

Type *greater shock*; **Level** 15; **Price** 6,500 gp

Electricity damage dealt by this weapon ignores the target's electricity resistance (and the other creatures' on a critical hit).

SPEED   RUNE 16

RARE MAGICAL TRANSMUTATION

Price 10,000 gp

Usage etched onto a weapon

Attacks with a *speed* weapon are supernaturally swift. While wielding a *speed* weapon, you gain the quickened condition, but you can use the additional action granted only to make a Strike with the etched weapon.

SPELL-STORING   RUNE 13

UNCOMMON ABJURATION MAGICAL

Price 2,700 gp

Usage etched onto a melee weapon

A *spell-storing* rune creates a reservoir of eldritch energy within the etched weapon. A spellcaster can spend 1 minute to cast a spell of 3rd level or lower into the weapon. The spell must have a casting of 2 actions or fewer and must be able to target a creature other than the caster. The spell has no immediate effect—it is instead stored for later. When you wield a *spell-storing* weapon, you immediately know the name and level of the stored spell. A *spell-storing* weapon found as treasure has a 50% chance of having a spell of the GM's choice stored in it.

Activate ❖ command; **Requirements** On your previous action this turn, you hit and damaged a creature with this weapon; **Effect** You unleash the stored spell, which uses the target of the triggering attack as the target of the spell. This empties the

spell from the weapon and allows a spell to be cast into it again. If the spell requires a spell attack roll, the result of your attack roll with the weapon determines the degree of success of the spell, and if the spell requires a saving throw, the DC is 30.

Activate ❖ command; **Effect** Harmlessly expend the stored spell. This frees the weapon to have a new spell cast into it.

THUNDERING   RUNE 8+

EVOCATION MAGICAL SONIC

Usage etched onto a weapon

This weapon lets out a peal of thunder when it hits, dealing an extra 1d6 sonic damage on a successful Strike. On a critical hit, the target has to succeed at a DC 24 Fortitude save or be deafened for 1 minute (or 1 hour on a critical failure).

Type *thundering*; **Level** 8; **Price** 500 gp

Type *greater thundering*; **Level** 15; **Price** 6,500 gp

The save DC is 34, and the deafness is permanent. Sonic damage dealt by this weapon ignores the target's sonic resistance.

UNHOLY   RUNE 11

EVIL EVOCATION MAGICAL

Price 1,400 gp

Usage etched onto a weapon without a *holy* rune

An *unholy* rune instills fiendish power into the etched weapon. A weapon with this rune deals an additional 1d6 evil damage when it hits a good target. If you are good, you are enfeebled 2 while carrying or wielding this weapon.

Activate ↻ command; **Frequency** once per day; **Trigger** You critically succeed at an attack roll against a good creature with the weapon; **Effect** The target takes persistent bleed damage equal to 1d8 per weapon damage die of the etched weapon.

Craft Requirements You are evil.

VORPAL   RUNE 17

RARE EVOCATION MAGICAL

Price 15,000 gp

Usage etched onto a slashing melee weapon

Originally created as a means of slaying the legendary jabberwock, *vorpal* weapons prove equally effective against nearly any foe with a head.

Activate ↻ envision (death, incapacitation); **Trigger** You roll a natural 20 on a Strike with the weapon, critically succeed, and deal slashing damage. The target must have a head; **Effect** The target must succeed at a DC 37 Fortitude save or be decapitated. This kills any creature except ones that don't require a head to live. For creatures with multiple heads, this usually kills the creature only if you sever its last head.

WOUNDING   RUNE 7

MAGICAL NECROMANCY

Price 340 gp

Usage etched onto a piercing or slashing melee weapon

Weapons with *wounding* runes are said to thirst for blood. When you hit a creature with a *wounding* weapon, you deal an extra 1d6 persistent bleed damage. On a critical hit, it instead deals 1d12 persistent bleed damage.

SHIELDS

All magic shields are specific items with a wide variety of protective effects, as described in their entries. Unlike magic armor, magic shields can't be etched with runes.

PRECIOUS MATERIAL SHIELDS

Shields made of precious materials are more expensive and have different durabilities. You can make bucklers and most shields out of any of these precious materials, but only darkwood can be used to make tower shields.

ADAMANTINE SHIELD   ITEM 8+

UNCOMMON

Usage varies by shield

Adamantine shields are particularly sturdy, and when used for a shield bash, they are adamantine weapons.

Type standard-grade adamantine buckler; **Level** 8; **Price** 400 gp; **Bulk** L; **Craft Requirements** adamantine worth at least 50 gp
The shield has Hardness 8, HP 32, and BT 16.

Type standard-grade adamantine shield; **Level** 8; **Price** 440; **Bulk** 1; **Craft Requirements** adamantine worth at least 55 gp
The shield has Hardness 10, HP 40, and BT 20.

Type high-grade adamantine buckler; **Level** 16; **Price** 8,000 gp; **Bulk** L; **Craft Requirements** adamantine worth at least 4,000 gp
The shield has Hardness 11, HP 44, and BT 22.

Type high-grade adamantine shield; **Level** 16; **Price** 8,800 gp; **Bulk** 1; **Craft Requirements** adamantine worth at least 4,400 gp
The shield has Hardness 13, HP 52, and BT 26.

COLD IRON SHIELD   ITEM 2+

Usage varies by shield

Cold iron shields don't typically have an additional effect, though when used for a shield bash, they are cold iron weapons.

Type low-grade cold iron buckler; **Level** 2; **Price** 30 gp; **Craft Bulk** L; **Requirements** cold iron worth at least 15 sp
The shield has Hardness 3, HP 12, and BT 6.

Type low-grade cold iron shield; **Level** 2; **Price** 34 gp; **Craft Bulk** 1; **Requirements** cold iron worth at least 17 sp
The shield has Hardness 5, HP 20, and BT 10.

Type standard-grade cold iron buckler; **Level** 7; **Price** 300 gp; **Bulk** L; **Craft Requirements** cold iron worth at least 375 sp
The shield has Hardness 5, HP 20, and BT 10.

Type standard-grade cold iron shield; **Level** 7; **Price** 340 gp; **Bulk** 1; **Craft Requirements** cold iron worth at least 425 sp
The shield has Hardness 7, HP 28, and BT 14.

Type high-grade cold iron buckler; **Level** 15; **Price** 5,000 gp; **Bulk** L; **Craft Requirements** cold iron worth at least 2,500 gp
The shield has Hardness 8, HP 32, and BT 16.

Type high-grade cold iron shield; **Level** 15; **Price** 5,500 gp; **Bulk** 1; **Craft Requirements** cold iron worth at least 2,750 gp
The shield has Hardness 10, HP 40, and BT 20.

DARKWOOD SHIELD   ITEM 8+

UNCOMMON

Usage varies by shield

Darkwood shields are 1 Bulk lighter than normal (or light Bulk if their normal Bulk is 1, with no effect on a shield that normally has light Bulk).

Type standard-grade darkwood buckler; **Level** 8; **Price** 400 gp; **Bulk** L; **Craft Requirements** darkwood worth at least 50 gp
The shield has Hardness 3, HP 12, and BT 6.

Type standard-grade darkwood shield; **Level** 8; **Price** 440 gp; **Bulk** L; **Craft Requirements** darkwood worth at least 55 gp
The shield has Hardness 5, HP 20, and BT 10.

Type standard-grade darkwood tower shield; **Level** 8; **Price** 560 gp; **Bulk** 3; **Craft Requirements** darkwood worth at least 70 gp
The shield has Hardness 5, HP 20, and BT 10.

Type high-grade darkwood buckler; **Level** 16; **Price** 8,000 gp; **Bulk** L; **Craft Requirements** darkwood worth at least 4,000 gp
The shield has Hardness 6, HP 24, and BT 12.

Type high-grade darkwood shield; **Level** 16; **Price** 8,800 gp; **Bulk** L; **Craft Requirements** darkwood worth at least 4,400 gp
The shield has Hardness 8, HP 32, and BT 16.

Type high-grade darkwood tower shield; **Level** 16; **Price** 11,200 gp; **Bulk** 3; **Craft Requirements** darkwood worth at least 5,600 gp
The shield has Hardness 8, HP 32, and BT 16.

DRAGONHIDE SHIELD   ITEM 8+

UNCOMMON

Usage varies by shield

Dragonhide shields are each immune to one damage type based on the type of dragon (see Dragonhide on page 579).

Type standard-grade dragonhide buckler; **Level** 8; **Price** 400 gp; **Bulk** L; **Craft Requirements** dragonhide worth at least 50 gp
The shield has Hardness 2, HP 8, and BT 4.

Type standard-grade dragonhide shield; **Level** 8; **Price** 440 gp; **Bulk** 1; **Craft Requirements** dragonhide worth at least 55 gp
The shield has Hardness 4, HP 16, and BT 8.

Type high-grade dragonhide buckler; **Level** 16; **Price** 8,000 gp; **Bulk** L; **Craft Requirements** dragonhide worth at least 4,000 gp
The shield has Hardness 5, HP 20, and BT 10.

Type high-grade dragonhide shield; **Level** 16; **Price** 8,800 gp; **Bulk** 1; **Craft Requirements** dragonhide worth at least 4,400 gp
The shield has Hardness 7, HP 28, and BT 14.

MITHRAL SHIELD   ITEM 8+

UNCOMMON

Usage varies by shield

Mithral shields are 1 Bulk lighter than normal (or light Bulk if their normal Bulk is 1, with no effect on a shield that normally has light Bulk). When used for a shield bash, they are treated as silver weapons.

Type standard-grade mithral buckler; **Level** 8; **Price** 400 gp; **Bulk** L; **Craft Requirements** mithral worth at least 50 gp
The shield has Hardness 3, HP 12, and BT 6.

Type standard-grade mithral shield; **Level** 8; **Price** 440 gp; **Bulk** 1; **Craft Requirements** mithral worth at least 55 gp
The shield has Hardness 5, HP 20, BT 10.

Type high-grade mithral buckler; **Level** 16; **Price** 8,000 gp; **Bulk** L; **Craft Requirements** mithral worth at least 4,000 gp

CRAFTING & TREASURE

11

INTRODUCTION

ANCESTRIES &
BACKGROUNDS

CLASSES

SKILLS

FEATS

EQUIPMENT

SPELLS

THE AGE OF
LOST OMENS

PLAYING THE
GAME

GAME
MASTERING

CRAFTING
& TREASURE

APPENDIX

The shield has Hardness 6, HP 24, and BT 12.

Type high-grade mithral shield; **Level** 16; **Price** 8,800 gp; **Craft Bulk** 1; **Requirements** at least 4,400 gp of mithral
The shield has Hardness 8, HP 32, and BT 16.

ORICHALCUM SHIELD   ITEM 17+

RARE

Usage varies by shield

Orichalcum shields' time-bending properties are particularly useful for keeping them intact. The first time each day an orichalcum shield would be destroyed, it is instead left with 1 Hit Point and the broken condition.

Type high-grade orichalcum buckler; **Level** 17; **Price** 12,000 gp; **Bulk** L; **Craft Requirements** orichalcum worth at least 6,000 gp
The shield has Hardness 14, HP 56, and BT 28.

Type high-grade orichalcum shield; **Level** 17; **Price** 13,200 gp; **Bulk** 1; **Craft Requirements** orichalcum worth at least 6,600 gp
The shield has Hardness 16, HP 64, and BT 32.

SILVER SHIELD   ITEM 2+

Usage varies by shield

Silver shields don't typically have an additional effect, though when used for a shield bash, they are silver weapons.

Type low-grade silver buckler; **Level** 2; **Price** 30 gp; **Bulk** L; **Craft Requirements** silver worth at least 15 sp
The shield has Hardness 1, HP 4, and BT 2.

Type low-grade silver shield; **Level** 2; **Price** 34 gp; **Bulk** 1; **Craft Requirements** silver worth at least 17 sp
The shield has Hardness 3, HP 12, and BT 6.

Type standard-grade silver buckler; **Level** 7; **Price** 300 gp; **Bulk** L; **Craft Requirements** silver worth at least 375 sp
The shield has Hardness 3, HP 12, BT 6.

Type standard-grade silver shield; **Level** 7; **Price** 340 gp; **Bulk** 1; **Craft Requirements** silver worth at least 425 sp
The shield has Hardness 5, HP 20, and BT 10.

Type high-grade silver buckler; **Level** 15; **Price** 5,000 gp; **Bulk** L; **Craft Requirements** silver worth at least 2,500 gp
The shield has Hardness 6, HP 24, and BT 12.

Type high-grade silver shield; **Level** 15; **Price** 5,500 gp; **Bulk** 1; **Craft Requirements** silver worth at least 2,750 gp
The shield has Hardness 8 HP 32, and BT 16.

SPECIFIC SHIELDS

These shields have unique abilities that differentiate them from their typical counterparts.

ARROW-CATCHING SHIELD   ITEM 11

ABJURATION   MAGICAL

Price 1,350 gp

Usage held in 1 hand; **Bulk** 1

This wooden shield (Hardness 6, HP 24, BT 12) is carved with images of overlapping fletched arrows.

Activate ⤾ Interact; **Trigger** A ranged weapon Strike targets a creature within 15 feet of you when you have this shield raised, and the attacker has not yet rolled their attack; **Effect**

The triggering Strike targets you instead of its normal target. If it hits, you gain the effects of the Shield Block reaction.

DRAGONSLAYER'S SHIELD   ITEM 9

UNCOMMON   ABJURATION   MAGICAL

Price 670 gp

Usage held in 1 hand; **Bulk** 1

A *dragonslayer's shield* is a steel shield covered with dragonhide from a certain type of dragon, which distinguishes each shield from the others. While raised, this steel shield (Hardness 8, HP 32, BT 16) grants its circumstance bonus to Reflex saves against area effects (as well as to AC, as normal).

While you hold the shield, it also grants you a +2 circumstance bonus to Will saves against a dragon's frightful presence ability. The shield has resistance 10 against the damage type corresponding to the type of dragon whose hide was used in its creation (see dragonhide on page 579); this applies after reducing the damage for Hardness, so when you use Shield Block, the *dragonslayer's shield* takes 18 less damage from attacks of that damage type. You can use Shield Block against attacks that deal damage of that type.

Craft Requirements The initial raw materials must include at least 30 gp of dragonhide.

FLOATING SHIELD   ITEM 11+

UNCOMMON   MAGICAL

Usage strapped to 1 hand; **Bulk** L

A *floating shield* is usually carved with wing motifs. This buckler (Hardness 6, HP 24, BT 12) can protect you on its own.

Activate ❖ Interact; **Frequency** once per day; **Effect** The shield magically releases itself and floats off your arm into the air next to you, granting you its bonus automatically, as if you had Raised the Shield. Because you're not wielding the shield, you can't use reactions such as Shield Block with the shield, but you gain its benefits even when using both of your hands. After 1 minute, the shield drops to the ground, ending its floating effect. While the shield is adjacent to you, you can Interact to grasp it, ending its floating effect early.

Type *floating shield*; **Level** 11; **Price** 1,250 gp

Type *greater floating shield*; **Level** 16; **Price** 9,000 gp
You can activate the shield any number of times per day.

FORCE SHIELD   ITEM 9

UNCOMMON   EVOCATION   FORCE   MAGICAL

Price 650 gp

Usage held in 1 hand; **Bulk** L

The edges of this elaborately engraved steel shield (Hardness 8, HP 32, BT 16) bear tiny glass tiles set in mosaic patterns.

Activate ❖ command; **Frequency** once per day; **Effect** The shield surrounds you with a bubble of force that protects you from harm, granting you resistance 5 to physical damage for 1 minute. The bubble disappears if you cease holding the shield.

FORGE WARDEN   ITEM 10

UNCOMMON   ABJURATION   MAGICAL

Price 975 gp

Usage held in 1 hand; **Bulk** 1

The religious symbol of Torag, the forge god—an ornate hammer of dwarven construction—adorns the face of this steel shield (Hardness 6, HP 24, BT 12). The shield is a religious symbol of Torag.

You and any adjacent allies have fire resistance 5 while you have the shield raised. When used for a Shield Block, the *forge warden* rings out like the hammer strike of a blacksmith, and the symbol glows as if lit by the fires of a furnace.

Activate ❖ command (fire); **Trigger** You use the *forge warden* to Shield Block an adjacent creature's attack and the shield takes damage; **Effect** The attacking creature takes 2d6 fire damage.

INDESTRUCTIBLE SHIELD   ITEM 18

[RARE] [ABJURATION] [MAGICAL]

Price 24,000 gp

Usage held in 1 hand; **Bulk** 1

An *indestructible shield* is a high-grade adamantine shield (Hardness 13, HP 90) that can withstand just about any damage. It can be damaged only by a *disintegrate* spell (roll damage as if against a creature that failed its save) or by an artifact tied to destruction, such as a *sphere of annihilation*.

Craft Requirements The raw materials must include at least 4,400 gp of adamantine.

LION'S SHIELD   ITEM 6

[CONJURATION] [MAGICAL]

Price 245 gp

Usage held in 1 hand; **Bulk** 1

This steel shield (Hardness 6, HP 36, BT 18) is forged into the shape of a roaring lion's head. The lion's head functions as *+1 striking shield boss* that can't be removed from the shield.

Activate ❖ Raise a Shield; **Frequency** once per day; **Effect** You animate the lion's head. You Raise the Shield and make a melee Strike with it as part of the same action. The shield's biting maw is a martial melee weapon that deals 2d6 piercing damage and has the deadly 1d6 trait; it can't be enhanced by runes. The shield remains animated for 1 minute, during which time you can Strike with it each time you Raise the Shield, as well as with a Strike action.

REFLECTING SHIELD   ITEM 18

[UNCOMMON] [ABJURATION] [MAGICAL]

Price 18,000 gp

Usage held in 1 hand; **Bulk** L

This high-grade silver buckler (Hardness 6, HP 24, BT 12) is polished to a mirrorlike sheen. The shield functions as a *spellguard shield* (see below) that can also reflect spells.

Activate ↺ command; **Frequency** once per day; **Trigger** You are targeted by a spell; **Requirements** The *reflecting shield* is raised; **Effect** You attempt to reflect the spell on its caster, with the effects of a 9th-level *spell turning* with a counteract modifier of +40.

Craft Requirements Supply one casting of *spell turning*, and the initial raw materials must include at least 2,750 gp of silver.

SPELLGUARD SHIELD   ITEM 6

[ABJURATION] [MAGICAL]

Price 250 gp

Usage held in 1 hand; **Bulk** 1

This shield bears eldritch glyphs to guard against magic. While you have this steel shield (Hardness 6, HP 24, BT 12) raised, you gain its circumstance bonus to saving throws against spells that target you (as well as to AC).

SPINED SHIELD   ITEM 7

[EVOCATION] [MAGICAL]

Price 360 gp

Usage held in 1 hand; **Bulk** 1

Five jagged spines project from the surface of this steel shield (Hardness 6, HP 24, BT 12). The spines are *+1 striking shield spikes*. When you use the Shield Block reaction with this shield, the spines take the damage before the shield itself does. When the shield would take damage (after applying Hardness), one spine snaps off per 6 damage, reducing the damage by 6. The shield takes any remaining damage. When there are no spines left, the shield takes damage as normal.

When all the spines are gone, you lose the ability to attack with them until the spines regenerate the next day.

Activate ❖ Interact; **Effect** You shoot one of the shield's spines at a target. A fired spine uses the spikes' statistics, but it is a martial ranged weapon with a range increment of 120 feet.

STURDY SHIELD   ITEM 4+

[ABJURATION] [MAGICAL]

Usage held in 1 hand; **Bulk** 1

With a superior design and excellent craftsmanship, this steel shield has higher Hardness than its non-magical counterparts, making it harder to break and destroy.

Type minor; **Level** 4; **Price** 100 gp

The shield has Hardness 8, HP 64, and BT 32.

Type lesser; **Level** 7; **Price** 360 gp

The shield has Hardness 10, HP 80, and BT 40.

Type moderate; **Level** 10; **Price** 1,000 gp

The shield has Hardness 13, HP 104, and BT 52.

Type greater; **Level** 13; **Price** 3,000 gp

The shield has Hardness 15, HP 120, and BT 60.

Type major; **Level** 16; **Price** 10,000 gp

The shield has Hardness 17, HP 136, and BT 68.

Type supreme; **Level** 19; **Price** 40,000 gp

The shield has Hardness 20, HP 160, and BT 80.

SNARES

Snares are small annoyances and simple traps you can create using the Crafting skill if you have the Snare Crafting feat (page 266). Creating a snare requires a snare kit (page 291) and an amount of raw materials worth the amount listed in the snare's Price entry. Unlike other items, found snares cannot be collected or sold in their complete form. Snares have the snare trait.

CRAFTING SNARES

A snare is built within a single 5-foot square. Once constructed, it can't be moved without destroying (and often triggering) the snare.

You must have the Snare Crafting feat to create snares. You can spend 1 minute to Craft a snare at its listed Price. If you want to Craft a snare at a discount, you must spend downtime as described in the Craft activity. Some snares have additional requirements beyond those stated in the Craft activity; these snares list their requirements in a Craft Requirements entry.

DETECTING SNARES

Creatures can detect snares as they would any trap or hazard (as described on page 520), using the creator's Crafting DC as the snare's Stealth DC. As you become better at creating snares, your snares become harder to detect by those with lesser ability. If you are an expert in Crafting, only a creature that is trained in Perception can find your snares; if you are a master in Crafting, only a creature that is an expert in Perception can find your snares; and if you are legendary in Crafting, only a creature that is a master in Perception can find your snares.

If your proficiency rank is expert or better in Crafting, only creatures actively searching can find your snares.

TRIGGERING SNARES

Unless stated otherwise in a snare's description, when a Small or larger creature enters a snare's square, the snare's effect occurs and then the snare is destroyed.

DISABLING SNARES

Once a creature discovers a snare, it can disable it much like it can other physical traps, using the Disable a Device action of the Thievery skill and using the Crafting DC of the snare's creator as the DC. As you become better at creating snares, your snares become harder to disable by those with lesser ability. If you are an expert in Crafting, only a creature that is trained in Thievery can disable them; if you are a master in Crafting, only a creature that is an expert in Thievery can disable them; and if you are legendary in Crafting, only a creature that is a master in Thievery can disable them.

You can automatically disarm a snare that you personally Crafted without triggering it by spending an Interact action while adjacent to the snare.

ALARM SNARE — SNARE 1

AUDITORY CONSUMABLE MECHANICAL SNARE TRAP

Price 3 gp

You create an alarm snare by rigging one or more noisy objects to a trip wire or pressure plate. When you create an alarm snare, you designate a range between 100 to 500 feet at which it can be heard. When a Small or larger creature enters the square, the snare makes a noise loud enough that it can be heard by all creatures in the range you designated.

BITING SNARE — SNARE 4

CONSUMABLE MECHANICAL SNARE TRAP

Price 15 gp

The snare's jaws shut on the leg of a creature that steps on it. The snare deals 5d6 piercing damage to the first creature that enters its square; that creature must attempt a DC 18 Reflex save.

Critical Success The creature is unaffected.

Success The creature takes half damage.

Failure The creature takes full damage.

Critical Failure The creature takes double damage and takes a –10-foot status penalty to its Speed until it recovers at least 1 Hit Point.

BLEEDING SPINES SNARE — SNARE 12

CONSUMABLE MECHANICAL SNARE TRAP

Price 320 gp

When a creature enters the square, spines covered in numerous jagged thorns protrude out to stab it, dealing 8d8 piercing damage and 2d8 persistent bleed damage. The creature must attempt a DC 31 basic Reflex saving throw. After the initial trigger, the spines retract and protrude again repeatedly for 1 minute, forcing any creature that enters the space or ends its turn in the space to attempt a Reflex save against the spines' damage.

BOMB SNARE — SNARE 8

CONSUMABLE MECHANICAL SNARE TRAP

Price 75 gp

You create a snare that catalyzes three 3rd-level moderate alchemical bombs of the same type to explode when a creature enters the snare's square. The target and all creatures in adjacent squares must attempt a DC 26 Reflex save, as the snare deals damage equal to three times the direct hit damage from one of the component bombs (for example, 6d6 electricity damage from bottled lightning) with no splash damage or other effects.

Critical Success The creature is unaffected.

Success The creature takes half damage and no other effects.

Failure The creature takes full damage. It also takes all other effects of a direct hit from one of the component bombs (such as flat-footed from bottled lightning or persistent damage from an acid flask).

Critical Failure The creature takes double damage, plus all other effects of a direct hit (as failure).

Craft Requirements Supply six of the same damaging 3rd-level moderate alchemical bomb.

INTRODUCTION

ANCESTRIES & BACKGROUNDS

CLASSES

SKILLS

FEATS

EQUIPMENT

SPELLS

THE AGE OF LOST OMENS

PLAYING THE GAME

GAME MASTERING

CRAFTING & TREASURE

APPENDIX

CALTROP SNARE   SNARE 1

| CONSUMABLE | MECHANICAL | SNARE | TRAP |

Price 3 gp

This snare consists of a hidden canister of caltrops (page 287) attached to a trip wire. When the snare is triggered, it flings the caltrops into either the snare's square or a square adjacent to the snare. You choose which square when you set up the snare.

If the caltrops scatter into the same square as a creature, that creature must attempt the Acrobatics check immediately.

Craft Requirements Supply a container of caltrops.

FLYING BLADE WHEEL SNARE   SNARE 20

| CONSUMABLE | MECHANICAL | SNARE | TRAP |

Price 10,000 gp

When a creature enters the square, a deadly flying wheel of spinning blades launches at it, making a Strike with an attack modifier of +33 and dealing 8d8 slashing damage. Once on each of your turns, you can use an Interact action within 120 feet of the wheel to cause it to Fly up to 60 feet toward the creature it's chasing and make another Strike if it's within 5 feet of its target after it moves. After 1 minute, the spinning ceases and the wheel falls to the ground. Creatures can destroy the wheel to stop it (AC 37, Fort +29, Ref +20, HP 200, Hardness 10, object immunities).

GRASPING SNARE   SNARE 8

| UNCOMMON | CONSUMABLE | MECHANICAL | SNARE | TRAP |

Price 75 gp

You rig vines and ropes to hold a creature in place. The first creature to enter the square must attempt a DC 26 Reflex save, with the following effects.

Critical Success The creature is unaffected.

Success The creature takes a –5-foot status penalty to its Speed for 1 minute or until it Escapes (DC 26).

Failure The creature is immobilized for 1 round, then takes a

–5-foot status penalty to its Speed for 1 minute. Both effects end early if it Escapes (DC 26)

Critical Failure The creature is immobilized for 1 minute or until it Escapes (DC 26).

HAIL OF ARROWS SNARE   SNARE 16

| CONSUMABLE | MECHANICAL | SNARE | TRAP |

Price 1,500 gp

When a creature enters the snare's square, it releases hundreds upon hundreds of carefully prepared arrows, blanketing a 20-foot radius around the snare's square with massive arrow fire that deals 18d6 piercing damage. Creatures in the area must attempt a DC 37 basic Reflex saving throw.

HAMPERING SNARE   SNARE 1

| CONSUMABLE | MECHANICAL | SNARE | TRAP |

Price 3 gp

You arrange brambles, wires, sticky goo, or other materials to interfere with a creature's movement. The square with this snare, as well as three adjacent squares (to form a 10-foot-by-10-foot area), become difficult terrain when the first creature enters the snare's square. The difficult terrain affects the creature's movement right away, including its movement into the triggering square, and it lasts for 1d4 rounds after the snare is triggered. A creature can use an Interact action to clear the difficult terrain out of a single square early.

HOBBLING SNARE   SNARE 4

| UNCOMMON | CONSUMABLE | MECHANICAL | SNARE | TRAP |

Price 15 gp

You rig vines, ropes, or wires to cinch tight around a creature that triggers this snare. The first creature to enter the square must attempt a DC 20 Reflex save.

Critical Success The creature is unaffected.

Success The creature takes a –5-foot status penalty to its Speed for 1 minute or until it Escapes (DC 18).

Failure As success, but the penalty is –10 feet.

Critical Failure As success, but the penalty is –20 feet.

INSTANT EVISCERATION SNARE   SNARE 20

| CONSUMABLE | MECHANICAL | SNARE | TRAP |

Price 10,000 gp

When a creature enters the snare's square, the snare releases an unbelievable arsenal of blades, dealing 24d8 piercing damage (DC 45 basic Reflex).

MARKING SNARE   SNARE 1

| CONSUMABLE | MECHANICAL | SNARE | TRAP |

Price 3 gp

This snare is often used to mark intruders for later tracking or identification. When you create this snare, you must decide whether to make it a dye or a scent marker. Either type of marking grants a +2 circumstance bonus to Track the creature for up to 24 hours or until the dye or scent is washed off (requiring at least a gallon of water and 10 minutes of scrubbing). A creature that enters a square of the snare must attempt a DC 17 Reflex save.

Success The creature is unaffected.

Failure The snare marks the creature.

Critical Failure The snare marks the creature, and the creature is blinded until the end of its next turn.

OMNIDIRECTIONAL SPEAR SNARE   SNARE 16

CONSUMABLE   MECHANICAL   SNARE   TRAP

Price 1,500 gp

As soon as a creature enters the snare's square, the snare unleashes wickedly powerful spears at the creature from all directions, dealing 19d8 piercing damage (DC 37 basic Reflex).

SCYTHING BLADE SNARE   SNARE 12

CONSUMABLE   MECHANICAL   SNARE   TRAP

Price 320 gp

This snare sends a powerful series of scything blades to slice through a creature entering the snare's square, dealing 14d8 slashing damage (DC 31 basic Reflex).

SIGNALING SNARE   SNARE 1

CONSUMABLE   MECHANICAL   SNARE   TRAP

Price 3 gp

A subtle snare used in hunting or tracking, a signaling snare often consists of carefully prepared earth, piled sand or stones, specific arrangements of vegetation, and so forth. When a creature enters a square of a signaling snare, nothing happens to the creature, but instead it causes a small, unobtrusive disruption to the terrain that allows the snare's creator or another creature who knows what to look for to determine whether a creature of the appropriate size entered the square.

SPIKE SNARE   SNARE 1

CONSUMABLE   MECHANICAL   SNARE   TRAP

Price 3 gp

This basic snare consists of hidden spikes that rely on a creature's momentum to lacerate or potentially impale it as it enters the snare's square, dealing 2d8 piercing damage. The creature must attempt a DC 17 basic Reflex saving throw.

STALKER BANE SNARE   SNARE 4

UNCOMMON   CONSUMABLE   MECHANICAL   SNARE   TRAP

Price 15 gp

This snare explodes in a burst of cloying powder that can cling to a creature stepping into its square. A creature that enters the square of a stalker bane snare must attempt a DC 20 Reflex save.

Critical Success The target is unaffected.

Success Powder sticks to the target, causing it to leave behind telltale footprints. Being invisible makes the target hidden, rather than undetected, to creatures that could see it if it weren't invisible.

Failure Powder clumps on the target, constantly flaking away. Being invisible makes the target concealed, rather than hidden or undetected, to creatures that could see it if it weren't invisible.

Critical Failure As failure, and the creature is blinded until the end of its next turn.

STRIKING SNARE   SNARE 8

CONSUMABLE   MECHANICAL   SNARE   TRAP

Price 75 gp

You affix a trip line or other trigger to a group of either stones or wooden stakes to strike a creature that enters the snare's square. The creature must attempt a DC 26 basic Reflex saving throw. If you choose stones, the snare deals 9d8 bludgeoning damage; if you choose spikes, it deals 9d8 piercing damage.

STUNNING SNARE   SNARE 12

CONSUMABLE   MECHANICAL   SNARE   TRAP

Price 320 gp

You rig a snare to disorient a creature with a quick bash, leaving it with little ability to defend itself. The trap deals 6d6 bludgeoning damage to the first creature to enter its square; that creature must attempt a DC 31 Reflex save.

Critical Success The creature is unaffected.

Success The creature takes half damage and is flat-footed for 1 round and stunned 1.

Failure The creature takes full damage and is flat-footed for 1 round and stunned 2.

Critical Failure The creature takes double damage and is flat-footed for 1 minute and stunned 4.

TRIP SNARE   SNARE 4

CONSUMABLE   MECHANICAL   SNARE   TRAP

Price 15 gp

You set a cunning wire to trip a creature. A Medium or smaller creature that enters this snare's square must attempt a DC 20 Reflex save.

If you want to create a trip snare to trip a larger creature, you must create a group of contiguous snares of a length equal to the edge of that larger creature's space, and the creature must be moving such that it moves into the full set of snares. For example, three trip snares in a 15-foot-line can trip a Huge creature coming down a corridor into the line of snares.

Critical Success The creature is unaffected.

Success The creature is flat-footed until the start of its next turn.

Failure The creature falls prone.

Critical Failure The creature falls prone and takes 1d6 bludgeoning damage.

WARNING SNARE   SNARE 4

AUDITORY   CONSUMABLE   MECHANICAL   SNARE   TRAP

Price 15 gp

Using materials specific to the area, you connect a sound-making component to a trip wire or a pressure plate. This snare is like an alarm snare, but its subtle sound blends into ambient noise. You can detect this sound as long as you're within 1,000 feet of the snare and aren't prevented from hearing it. Other creatures in that area who are searching might notice the sound if their Perception check result meets or exceeds your Craft DC.

INTRODUCTION

ANCESTRIES & BACKGROUNDS

CLASSES

SKILLS

FEATS

EQUIPMENT

SPELLS

THE AGE OF LOST OMENS

PLAYING THE GAME

GAME MASTERING

CRAFTING & TREASURE

APPENDIX

STAVES

A magical staff is an indispensable accessory for an elite spellcaster. A staff is tied to one person during a preparation process, after which the preparer, and only the preparer, can harness the staff to cast a variety of spells throughout the day. The spells that can be cast from a staff are listed in bullet points organized by level under each version of the staff. Many staves can be found in multiple versions, with more powerful versions that contain more spells and can hold more charges—such a staff always contains the spells of all lower-level versions, in addition to the spells listed in its own entry. All magical staves have the staff trait.

CASTING SPELLS FROM A STAFF

A staff gains charges when someone prepares it for the day. The person who prepared a staff can expend the charges to cast spells from it. You can Cast a Spell from a staff only if you have that spell on your spell list, are able to cast spells of the appropriate level, and expend a number of charges from the staff equal to the spell's level. Casting a Spell from a staff requires holding the staff (typically in one hand) and Activating the staff by Casting the Spell, which takes the spell's normal number of actions.

Use your spell attack roll and spell DC when Casting a Spell from a staff. The spell gains the appropriate trait for your magical tradition (arcane, divine, occult, or primal) and can be affected by any modifications you can normally make when casting spells, such as metamagic feats. You must provide any material components, cost, or focus required by the spell, or you fail to cast it.

Prepared spellcasters and spontaneous spellcasters each have a unique way of altering how their staves gain charges and the ways they can be used (see the Prepared Spellcasters and Spontaneous Spellcasters sections below).

CASTING CANTRIPS FROM A STAFF

If a staff contains a cantrip, you can cast that cantrip using the staff without expending any charges. The cantrip's level is heightened to the same level as cantrips you cast.

PREPARING A STAFF

During your daily preparations, you can prepare a staff to add charges to it for free. When you do so, that staff gains a number of charges equal to the highest level of spell you're able to cast. You don't need to expend any spells to add charges in this way. No one can prepare more than one staff per day, nor can a staff be prepared by more than one person per day. If the charges aren't used within 24 hours, they're lost, and preparing the staff anew removes any charges previously stored in it. You can prepare a staff only if you have at least one of the staff's spells on your spell list.

PREPARED SPELLCASTERS

A prepared spellcaster—such as a cleric, druid, or wizard—can place some of their own magic in a staff to increase its number of charges. When a prepared spellcaster prepares a staff, they can expend a spell slot to add a number of charges to the staff equal to the level of the spell. They can't expend more than one spell in this way each day. For example, if Ezren can cast 3rd-level spells and prepared a staff, the staff would gain 3 charges, but Ezren could increase this to 6 by expending one of his 3rd-level spells, 5 by expending a 2nd-level spell, or 4 by expending a 1st-level spell.

SPONTANEOUS SPELLCASTERS

A spontaneous spellcaster, such as a bard or sorcerer, can reduce the number of charges it takes to Activate a staff by supplementing with their own energy. When a spontaneous spellcaster Activates a staff, they can expend 1 charge from the staff and one of their spell slots to cast a spell from the staff of the same level (or lower) as the expended spell slot. This doesn't change the number of actions it takes to cast the spell. For example, if Seoni can cast 3rd-level spells and prepared a staff, the staff would gain 3 charges. She could expend 1 charge and one of her 3rd-level spell slots to cast a 3rd-level spell from the staff, or 1 charge and one of her 2nd-level spell slots to cast a 2nd-level spell from the staff. She could still expend 3 charges from the staff to cast a 3rd-level spell from it without using any of her own slots, just like any other spellcaster.

ATTACKING WITH A STAFF

Staves are also staff weapons (page 280), included in their Price. They can be etched with runes as normal for a staff. This doesn't alter any of their spellcasting abilities.

ANIMAL STAFF   ITEM 4+

DIVINATION   MAGICAL   STAFF

Usage held in 1 hand; **Bulk** 1

This staff is topped with carved animal and monster heads. While wielding the staff, you gain a +2 circumstance bonus to Nature checks to identify animals.

   Activate Cast a Spell; **Effect** You expend a number of charges from the staff to cast a spell from its list.

Type animal staff; **Level** 4; **Price** 90 gp
- **Cantrip** know direction
- **1st** magic fang, summon animal

Type greater animal staff; **Level** 8; **Price** 460 gp
- **2nd** animal messenger, speak with animals, summon animal
- **3rd** animal form, summon animal

Type major animal staff; **Level** 12; **Price** 1,900 gp
- **4th** summon animal
- **5th** animal form, moon frenzy, summon animal

Craft Requirements Supply one casting of all listed levels of all listed spells.

MENTALIST'S STAFF   ITEM 4+

DIVINATION   MAGICAL   STAFF

Usage held in 1 hand; **Bulk** 1

This polished wooden staff bears a swirling motif reminiscent of the folds of a brain. While wielding the staff, you gain a +2 circumstance bonus to checks to identify mental magic.

Activate Cast a Spell; Effect You expend a number of charges from the staff to cast a spell from its list.

Type *mentalist's staff*; **Level** 4; **Price** 90 gp
- **Cantrip** *daze*
- **1st** *mindlink, phantom pain*

Type *greater mentalist's staff*; **Level** 8; **Price** 450 gp
- **2nd** *paranoia*
- **3rd** *hypercognition, phantom pain*

Type *major mentalist's staff*; **Level** 12; **Price** 1,800 gp
- **4th** *modify memory, telepathy*
- **5th** *phantom pain, synaptic pulse, synesthesia*

Craft Requirements Supply one casting of all listed levels of all listed spells.

STAFF OF ABJURATION   ITEM 6+

ABJURATION   MAGICAL   STAFF

Usage held in 1 hand; **Bulk** 1

This intricately carved wooden staff is warm to the touch and thrums with inner energy. While wielding the staff, you gain a +2 circumstance bonus to checks to identify abjuration magic.

Activate Cast a Spell; Effect You expend a number of charges from the staff to cast a spell from its list.

Type *staff of abjuration*; **Level** 6; **Price** 230 gp
- **Cantrip** *shield*
- **1st** *alarm, feather fall*
- **2nd** *dispel magic, endure elements, resist energy*

Type *greater staff of abjuration*; **Level** 10; **Price** 900 gp
- **3rd** *alarm, glyph of warding*
- **4th** *dimensional anchor, dispel magic, resist energy*

Type *major staff of abjuration*; **Level** 14; **Price** 4,000 gp
- **5th** *banishment, endure elements*
- **6th** *dispel magic, repulsion*

Craft Requirements Supply one casting of all listed levels of all listed spells.

STAFF OF CONJURATION   ITEM 6+

CONJURATION   MAGICAL   STAFF

Usage held in 1 hand; **Bulk** 1

This ash staff is decorated with animals; wielding it, you gain a +2 circumstance bonus to checks to identify conjuration magic.

Activate Cast a Spell; Effect You expend a number of charges from the staff to cast a spell from its list.

Type *staff of conjuration*; **Level** 6; **Price** 230 gp
- **Cantrip** *tanglefoot*
- **1st** *summon construct, unseen servant*
- **2nd** *obscuring mist, phantom steed, summon construct, summon elemental*

Type *greater staff of conjuration*; **Level** 10; **Price** 900 gp
- **3rd** *stinking cloud, summon construct, summon elemental*
- **4th** *creation, phantom steed, summon construct, summon elemental*

Type *major staff of conjuration*; **Level** 14; **Price** 4,000 gp
- **5th** *black tentacles, summon construct, summon elemental*
- **6th** *phantom steed, summon construct, summon elemental*

Craft Requirements Supply one casting of all listed levels of all listed spells.

STAFF OF DIVINATION   ITEM 6+

DIVINATION   MAGICAL   STAFF

Usage held in 1 hand; **Bulk** 1

Semiprecious gemstones emerge, seemingly at random, from the surface of this gnarled wooden staff. While wielding it, you gain a +2 circumstance bonus to checks to identify divination magic.

Activate Cast a Spell; Effect You expend a number of charges from the staff to cast a spell from its list.

Type *staff of divination*; **Level** 6; **Price** 230 gp
- **Cantrip** *detect magic*
- **1st** *true strike*
- **2nd** *comprehend language, darkvision, see invisibility*

Type *greater staff of divination*; **Level** 10; **Price** 900 gp
- **3rd** *clairaudience, darkvision*
- **4th** *clairvoyance, comprehend language, telepathy*

Type *major staff of divination*; **Level** 14; **Price** 4,000 gp
- **5th** *prying eye, sending*
- **6th** *telepathy, true seeing*

Craft Requirements Supply one casting of all listed levels of all listed spells.

STAFF OF ENCHANTMENT   ITEM 6+

ENCHANTMENT   MAGICAL   STAFF

Usage held in 1 hand; **Bulk** 1

A mesmerizing gemstone caps the head of this handsomely crafted wooden staff. While wielding the staff, you gain a +2 circumstance bonus to checks to identify enchantment magic.

Activate Cast a Spell; Effect You expend a number of charges from the staff to cast a spell from its list.

Type *staff of enchantment*; **Level** 6; **Price** 230 gp
- **Cantrip** *daze*
- **1st** *charm, command*
- **2nd** *hideous laughter, touch of idiocy*

Type *greater staff of enchantment*; **Level** 10; **Price** 900 gp
- **3rd** *paralyze*
- **4th** *charm, confusion, suggestion*

Type *major staff of enchantment*; **Level** 14 (uncommon); **Price** 4,000 gp
- **5th** *command, crushing despair*
- **6th** *dominate, feeblemind*

Craft Requirements Supply one casting of all listed levels of all listed spells.

STAFF OF EVOCATION   ITEM 6+

EVOCATION   MAGICAL   STAFF

Usage held in 1 hand; **Bulk** 1

This staff is tapered at the base and carved into a gem-studded twist at the top. While wielding the staff, you gain a +2 circumstance bonus to checks to identify evocation magic.

Activate Cast a Spell; Effect You expend a number of charges from the staff to cast a spell from its list.

Type *staff of evocation*; **Level** 6; **Price** 230 gp
- **Cantrip** *ray of frost*

- **1st** *magic missile, shocking grasp*
- **2nd** *acid arrow, glitterdust*

Type *greater staff of evocation*; **Level** 10; **Price** 900 gp
- **3rd** *lightning bolt, magic missile*
- **4th** *fireball, weapon storm*

Type *major staff of evocation*; **Level** 14; **Price** 4,000 gp
- **5th** *cone of cold, magic missile*
- **6th** *chain lightning, wall of force*

Craft Requirements Supply one casting of all listed levels of all listed spells.

STAFF OF FIRE   ITEM 3+

EVOCATION   MAGICAL   STAFF

Usage held in 1 hand; **Bulk** 1

This staff resembles a blackened and burned length of ashen wood. It smells faintly of soot and glows as if lit by embers. You can use an Interact action to touch the tip of this staff to a torch, tinder, or a flammable substance to ignite a flame.

   Activate Cast a Spell; **Effect** You expend a number of charges from the staff to cast a spell from its list.

Type *staff of fire*; **Level** 3; **Price** 60 gp
- **Cantrip** *produce flame*
- **1st** *burning hands*

Type *greater staff of fire*; **Level** 8; **Price** 450 gp
- **2nd** *burning hands, flaming sphere*
- **3rd** *flaming sphere, fireball*

Type *major staff of fire*; **Level** 12; **Price** 1,800 gp
- **4th** *fire shield, fireball, wall of fire*
- **5th** *fireball, wall of fire*

Craft Requirements Supply one casting of all listed levels of all listed spells.

STAFF OF HEALING   ITEM 4+

MAGICAL   NECROMANCY   STAFF

Usage held in 1 hand; **Bulk** 1

Made of smooth, white wood, this staff is capped at each end with a golden cross adorned with a multitude of ruby cabochons. A *staff of healing* grants an item bonus to the Hit Points you restore anytime you cast the *heal* spell using your own spell slots or using charges from the staff.

   Activate Cast a Spell; **Effect** You expend a number of charges from the staff to cast a spell from its list.

Type *staff of healing*; **Level** 4; **Price** 90 gp
The item bonus granted to *heal* spells is +1.
- **Cantrip** *stabilize*
- **1st** *heal*

Type *greater staff of healing*; **Level** 8; **Price** 470 gp
The item bonus granted to *heal* spells is +2.
- **2nd** *heal, restoration, restore senses*
- **3rd** *heal, remove disease*

Type *major staff of healing*; **Level** 12; **Price** 1,800 gp
The item bonus granted to *heal* spells is +3.
- **4th** *heal, restoration*
- **5th** *breath of life, heal, remove disease*

Type *true staff of healing*; **Level** 16; **Price** 9,200 gp
The item bonus granted to *heal* spells is +4.

- **6th** *heal, restoration, restore senses*
- **7th** *heal, regenerate, remove disease*

Craft Requirements Supply one casting of all listed levels of all listed spells.

STAFF OF ILLUMINATION   ITEM 8

EVOCATION   MAGICAL   STAFF

Price 425 gp

Usage held in 1 hand; **Bulk** 1

This simple iron staff is capped with a faceted, clear gem.

   Activate ❖ Interact; **Effect** The gem at the top of the staff glows as a torch, shedding bright light in a 20-foot radius (and dim light to the next 20 feet) for 10 minutes.

   Activate Cast a Spell; **Effect** You expend a number of charges from the staff to cast a spell from its list.
- **Cantrip** *light*
- **2nd** *continual flame*
- **3rd** *continual flame, searing light*

Craft Requirements Supply one casting of all listed levels of all listed spells.

STAFF OF ILLUSION   ITEM 6+

ILLUSION   MAGICAL   STAFF

Usage held in 1 hand; **Bulk** 1

This ornately designed metal staff shines with precious inlays of gold. When you Cast a Spell from the staff, the illusory image of something you desire flashes across its surface. While wielding the staff, you gain a +2 circumstance bonus to checks to identify illusion magic.

   Activate Cast a Spell; **Effect** You expend a number of charges from the staff to cast a spell from its list.

Type *staff of illusion*; **Level** 6; **Price** 230 gp
- **Cantrip** *ghost sound*
- **1st** *illusory disguise, illusory object*
- **2nd** *illusory creature, item facade, ventriloquism*

Type *greater staff of illusion*; **Level** 10; **Price** 900 gp
- **3rd** *illusory disguise, item facade*
- **4th** *illusory creature, veil*

Type *major staff of illusion*; **Level** 14; **Price** 4,000 gp
- **5th** *illusory scene, veil*
- **6th** *hallucination, mislead*

Craft Requirements Supply one casting of all listed levels of all listed spells.

STAFF OF NECROMANCY   ITEM 6+

MAGICAL   NECROMANCY   STAFF

Usage held in 1 hand; **Bulk** 1

This twisted and grim-looking staff is adorned with hideous skull and bone motifs. While wielding the staff, you gain a +2 circumstance bonus to checks to identify necromancy magic.

   Activate Cast a Spell; **Effect** You expend a number of charges from the staff to cast a spell from its list.

Type *staff of necromancy*; **Level** 6; **Price** 230 gp
- **Cantrip** *chill touch*
- **1st** *grim tendrils, ray of enfeeblement*
- **2nd** *deafness, gentle repose*

Type *greater staff of necromancy*; **Level** 10; **Price** 900 gp
- **3rd** *blindness, vampiric touch*
- **4th** *grim tendrils, enervation*

Type *major staff of necromancy*; **Level** 14; **Price** 4,000 gp
- **5th** *cloudkill, gentle repose*
- **6th** *grim tendrils, vampiric exsanguination*

Craft Requirements Supply one casting of all listed levels of all listed spells.

STAFF OF POWER   ITEM 16

[RARE] [EVOCATION] [MAGICAL] [STAFF]
Price 10,000 gp
Usage held in 1 hand; **Bulk** 1

This staff of magically hardened wood is topped with a silver sculpture depicting magical runic symbols. When used as a weapon, a *staff of power* is a *+2 greater striking staff*.

Voluntarily destroying a *staff of power* unleashes an incredible blast of energy. When wielding the staff, you can Interact to break it. This releases a 30-foot-burst magical explosion centered on the staff. This deals 2d8 force damage per charge remaining in the staff (DC 40 basic Reflex save). You automatically critically fail your save. A creature reduced to 0 Hit Points by this damage dies instantly; this is a death effect.

Activate Cast a Spell; **Effect** You expend a number of charges from the staff to cast a spell from its list.
- **1st** *ray of enfeeblement*
- **2nd** *continual flame*
- **3rd** *levitate*
- **4th** *globe of invulnerability, paralyze*
- **5th** *magic missile*
- **6th** *wall of force*
- **7th** *cone of cold, fireball, lightning bolt*

Craft Requirements Supply one casting of all listed levels of all listed spells.

STAFF OF THE MAGI   ITEM 20

[RARE] [EVOCATION] [MAGICAL] [STAFF]
Price 90,000 gp
Usage held in 1 hand; **Bulk** 1

Sigils and runes of ancient and powerful magic cover the iron cladding on this long wooden staff. A *staff of the magi* is a *+3 major striking staff*, and when wielding it you gain a +1 circumstance bonus to saving throws against spells.

Voluntarily destroying a *staff of the magi* unleashes a truly devastating wave of arcane energy that surges out, dissipating with distance. When wielding the staff, you can break it using an Interact action. This releases a 30-foot-burst magical explosion centered on the staff. This deals 2d10 force damage per charge remaining in the staff (DC 40 basic Reflex save). You automatically critically fail your save. The explosion continues to echo beyond the initial blast zone, dealing half as much damage to creatures beyond 30 feet but within a 60-foot burst. A creature reduced to 0 Hit Points by this damage dies instantly; this is a death effect.

Activate Cast a Spell; **Effect** You expend a number of charges from the staff to cast a spell from its list.
- **Cantrip** *detect magic, light, mage hand, telekinetic projectile*
- **1st** *lock*
- **2nd** *enlarge, glitterdust, invisibility, knock, telekinetic maneuver, web*
- **3rd** *dispel magic, fireball, lightning bolt*
- **4th** *invisibility, enlarge, fireball, wall of fire, web*
- **5th** *cone of cold, passwall, telekinetic haul*
- **6th** *disintegrate, dispel magic, fireball, lightning bolt*
- **7th** *cone of cold, passwall, plane shift, wall of fire*
- **8th** *fireball, mage armor*
- **9th** *dispel magic, meteor swarm, summon dragon*

Craft Requirements Supply one casting of all listed levels of all listed spells.

STAFF OF TRANSMUTATION   ITEM 6+

[MAGICAL] [STAFF] [TRANSMUTATION]
Usage held in 1 hand; **Bulk** 1

A glass orb atop this metal staff contains fine, undulating sand. While wielding the staff, you gain a +2 circumstance bonus to checks to identify transmutation magic.

Activate Cast a Spell; **Effect** You expend a number of charges from the staff to cast a spell from its list.

Type *staff of transmutation*; **Level** 6; **Price** 230 gp
- **Cantrip** *sigil*
- **1st** *fleet step, jump*
- **2nd** *enlarge, humanoid form*

Type *greater staff of transmutation*; **Level** 10; **Price** 900 gp
- **3rd** *feet to fins, jump*
- **4th** *gaseous form, shape stone*

Type *major staff of transmutation*; **Level** 14; **Price** 4,000 gp
- **5th** *humanoid transformation*
- **6th** *baleful polymorph, dragon form, flesh to stone*

Craft Requirements Supply one casting of all listed levels of all listed spells.

VERDANT STAFF   ITEM 6+

[DIVINATION] [MAGICAL] [STAFF]
Usage held in 1 hand; **Bulk** 1

This oak branch grows leaves in spring that change color in autumn and shed in winter. While wielding it, you gain a +2 circumstance bonus to Nature checks to identify plants.

Activate Cast a Spell; **Effect** You expend a number of charges from the staff to cast a spell from its list.

Type *verdant staff*; **Level** 6; **Price** 225 gp
- **Cantrips** *tanglefoot*
- **1st** *shillelagh* (can target the *verdant staff*)
- **2nd** *barkskin, entangle, shape wood, tree shape*

Type *greater verdant staff*; **Level** 12; **Price** 1,750 gp
- **3rd** *wall of thorns*
- **4th** *barkskin, speak with plants*
- **5th** *plant form, wall of thorns*

Craft Requirements Supply one casting of all listed levels of all listed spells.

STRUCTURES

These items create structures of significant size, typically by growing from their more manageable, normal forms. All these items have the structure trait, described in the sidebar below.

EXPLORER'S YURT   ITEM 10

CONJURATION MAGICAL STRUCTURE

Price 880 gp
Bulk 1 (when not activated)

Before activation, this item appears to be nothing more than a simple rolled-up tent, barely large enough to fit four Medium creatures. Despite attempts to clean it, the tent is perpetually smudged with dirt in various places.

Activate (10 minutes) Interact; **Frequency** once per day; **Effect** The rolled-up tent expands into a spacious yurt complete with a fire pit, 10 bedrolls, various cooking utensils, and basic food and water.

The yurt can house and feed you and up to nine other Medium creatures that eat roughly as much as a human does; they need not attempt a Survival check to Subsist when you use the yurt. Fires and light inside the yurt do not extend illumination into the area surrounding the yurt, making it harder to spot from a distance.

A large loop of red cloth hangs from one wall. If this loop is pulled, which takes an Interact action, the entire yurt immediately folds back up into its deactivated form, ready for further travel.

THE STRUCTURE TRAIT

An item with the structure trait creates a magical building or other structure when activated. The item must be activated on a plot of land free of other structures. The structure adapts to the natural terrain, adopting the structural requirements for being built there. The structure adjusts around small features such as ponds or spires of rock, but it can't be created on water or other nonsolid surfaces. If activated on snow, sand dunes, or other soft surfaces with a solid surface underneath, the structure's foundation (if any) reaches the solid ground. If an item with this trait is activated on a solid but unstable surface, such as a swamp or an area plagued by tremors, roll a DC 3 flat check each day; on a failure, the structure begins to sink or collapse.

The structure doesn't harm creatures within the area when it appears, and it can't be created within a crowd or in a densely populated area. Any creature inadvertently caught inside the structure when the item is activated ends up unharmed inside the complete structure and always has a clear path of escape. A creature inside the structure when the activation ends isn't harmed, and it lands harmlessly on the ground if it was on an upper level of the structure.

INSTANT FORTRESS   ITEM 16

UNCOMMON CONJURATION MAGICAL STRUCTURE

Price 9,300 gp
Bulk L (when not activated)

This metal cube is small enough to fit in your palm. Close inspection reveals fine lines in the dark gray metal, as though the cube were folded thousands of times.

Activate ◆◆◆ command, Interact; **Effect** You toss the cube on the ground, and it immediately unfolds into an adamantine fortress.

The fortress is 20 feet square and 30 feet high, with adamantine stairs leading up to three sets of battlements at heights of 10 feet and 20 feet and at the top. Arrow slits along the lower battlements and crenelations at the top provide standard cover to anyone within the fortress. There's no roof, leaving an open, 10-foot-square vertical shaft through the center of the structure.

As a magical structure, the fortress has the structure trait. Because it expands outward, the fortress can't catch creatures inside it as a magical structure normally does. Instead, it pushes those creatures back. It can't push a creature into a surface or hazard this way, and stops expanding if that would happen.

The fortress has a single door in the center of one wall on the ground level, and the door appears directly in front of you when you activate the fortress. Provided you're within 100 feet of the door, you can cause the door to open or slam shut and lock by spending a single action to issue a verbal command, which has the auditory trait. The DC to Force Open the door or Pick its Lock is 40.

You can instantly return the *instant fortress* to its cube form by spending a single action to issue a verbal command, which has the auditory trait. Once deactivated, the fortress can't be activated again for 4 hours.

If the fortress becomes damaged, it can be repaired only with a *remake* spell or by someone who is legendary at Crafting.

POCKET STAGE   ITEM 5

CONJURATION MAGICAL STRUCTURE

Price 138 gp
Bulk L (when not activated)

This item appears to be a miniature replica of a theater. It includes a small pocket full of minute set dressing and costumed paper dolls.

Activate (1 minute) command, envision, Interact; **Effect** You place the miniature theater on the ground, filling it with any set dressing and up to six figures you choose. Then, you tap a rhythm on the miniature, causing it to grow into a modest stage 20 feet wide and 15 feet deep. It's dressed with the decorations you selected, and simple mannequins wear the costumes you chose. A wooden proscenium arch frames the stage, and simple curtains along the sides conceal the wings. As a magical structure, the stage has the structure trait.

All the stage's set dressing is illusory and disappears if taken more than 20 feet from the stage. The costumes are physical but with illusory embellishments that fade at the same range, revealing only plain, white smocks.

WANDS

Short, slender items typically made of wood, wands let you cast a specific spell without expending a spell slot. They can be used once per day, but can be overcharged to attempt to cast them again at great risk. Each wand holds a spell of a certain level, determined when the wand is created. Cantrips, focus spells, and rituals can't be placed in wands.

If you find a wand, you can try to figure out what spell is in it. If the spell is a common spell from your spell list or is a spell you know, you can use a single Recall Knowledge action and automatically succeed. If it's not, you must Identify Magic (page 238).

CASTING SPELLS FROM A WAND

A wand contains a spell that can be cast once per day. Casting a spell from a wand requires holding the wand in one hand and activating the item with a Cast a Spell activity using the normal number of actions for the spell.

To cast a spell from a wand, it must be on your spell list. Because you're the one casting the spell, use your spell attack roll and spell DC. The spell is of your tradition.

A spell cast from a wand doesn't require physical material components, but you must replace any material component normally required to cast the spell with a somatic component. If the spell requires a focus, you must still have that focus to cast the spell from a wand, and if the spell has a cost, you must still pay that cost to cast the spell from a wand.

OVERCHARGING A WAND

After the spell is cast from the wand for the day, you can attempt to cast it one more time—overcharging the wand at the risk of destroying it. Cast the Spell again, then roll a DC 10 flat check. On a success, the wand is broken. On a failure, the wand is destroyed. If anyone tries to overcharge a wand when it's already been overcharged that day, the wand is automatically destroyed (even if it had been repaired) and no spell is cast.

WAND STATISTICS

A wand's base statistics are the same unless noted otherwise in a special wand. It has light Bulk, and must be held in one hand to be activated. Each wand contains a specific level of the spell. When you activate a wand, you can only cast the spell at the specified level, but you can craft a wand with a heightened version of a spell.

VARYING STATISTICS

Each type of wand has a Level and Price determined by the spell's level. The wand's rarity matches the spell's rarity. The item's traits also vary, based on the spell. A wand has any traits listed in its stat block (usually just magical and wand), plus any traits of the spell stored on it.

CRAFTING A WAND

For the most part, the process to Craft a wand is like that to

---

EXAMPLE MAGIC WAND

This example magic wand has the *heal* spell.

WAND OF HEAL   ITEM 3+

| MAGICAL | NECROMANCY | POSITIVE | WAND |

Usage held in 1 hand; **Bulk** L

The golden end caps on this white wooden wand are adorned with ruby cabochons.

    Activate (Cast a Spell); **Frequency** once per day, plus overcharge; You cast a *heal* spell at the indicated level.

Type 1st-level spell; **Level** 3; **Price** 60 gp
Type 2nd-level spell; **Level** 5; **Price** 160 gp
Type 3rd-level spell; **Level** 7; **Price** 360 gp
Type 4th-level spell; **Level** 9; **Price** 700 gp
Type 5th-level spell; **Level** 11; **Price** 1,500 gp
Type 6th-level spell; **Level** 13; **Price** 3,000 gp
Type 7th-level spell; **Level** 15; **Price** 6,500 gp
Type 8th-level spell; **Level** 17; **Price** 15,000 gp
Type 9th-level spell; **Level** 19; **Price** 40,000 gp

Craft Requirements Supply a listed-level casting of *heal*.

Craft any other magic item. When you begin the crafting process, choose a spell to put into the wand. You have to either cast that spell during the process, or someone else must do so in your presence. That spell doesn't have its normal effects; instead, the magic is captured inside the wand. The caster doesn't need to pay any cost of the spell.

The casting must come from a spellcaster expending a spell slot. You can't make a wand from a spell that comes from another magic item, for example.

MAGIC WAND

The simplest form of wand contains a spell, with Price and level based on that spell. The wand has the magical and wand traits, as well as the traits the spell has. The name of a magic wand with a spell in it is simply "wand of," followed by the spell's name.

MAGIC WAND   ITEM 3+

| MAGICAL | WAND |

Usage held in 1 hand; **Bulk** L

This baton is about a foot long and contains a single spell. The appearance typically relates to the spell within.

    Activate (Cast a Spell); **Frequency** once per day, plus overcharge; You Cast the Spell at the indicated level.

Type 1st-level spell; **Level** 3; **Price** 60 gp
Type 2nd-level spell; **Level** 5; **Price** 160 gp
Type 3rd-level spell; **Level** 7; **Price** 360 gp
Type 4th-level spell; **Level** 9; **Price** 700 gp
Type 5th-level spell; **Level** 11; **Price** 1,500 gp
Type 6th-level spell; **Level** 13; **Price** 3,000 gp
Type 7th-level spell; **Level** 15; **Price** 6,500 gp
Type 8th-level spell; **Level** 17; **Price** 15,000 gp
Type 9th-level spell; **Level** 19; **Price** 40,000 gp

Craft Requirements Supply a listed-level casting of the spell.

SPECIALTY WANDS

Specialty wands can contain only certain kinds of spells, as noted in the stat block, and either alter the spell's effects or affect how it can be cast. The Craft Requirements entry lists what kinds of spells the wand can hold.

WAND OF CONTINUATION   ITEM 5+

MAGICAL **WAND**

Usage held in 1 hand; **Bulk** L

This wand increases a spell's duration. Yellow embers spiral over its surface until the spell ends.

Activate (Cast a Spell); **Frequency** once per day, plus overcharge; the activation takes ◆◆ if the spell normally takes ◆ to cast, or ◆◆◆ if the spell normally takes ◆◆; **Effect** You Cast the Spell, and its duration is increased by half.

Type 1st-level spell; **Level** 5; **Price** 160 gp
Type 2nd-level spell; **Level** 7; **Price** 360 gp
Type 3rd-level spell; **Level** 9; **Price** 700 gp
Type 4th-level spell; **Level** 11; **Price** 1,400 gp
Type 5th-level spell; **Level** 13; **Price** 3,000 gp
Type 6th-level spell; **Level** 15; **Price** 6,500 gp
Type 7th-level spell; **Level** 17; **Price** 15,000 gp
Type 8th-level spell; **Level** 19; **Price** 40,000 gp

Craft Requirements Supply a casting of a spell of the appropriate level. The spell must have a casting time of ◆ or ◆◆ and a duration no less than 10 minutes and no greater than 1 hour.

WAND OF MANIFOLD MISSILES   ITEM 5+

EVOCATION **FORCE** **MAGICAL** **WAND**

Usage held in 1 hand; **Bulk** L

This wand features a carved dragon's head at its top and a polished metal sphere set in its midsection.

Activate (Cast a Spell); **Frequency** once per day, plus overcharge; **Effect** You cast *magic missile* of the indicated level. After you cast the spell, an additional missile or missiles are released from the wand at the start of each of your turns, as though you cast the 1-action version of *magic missile*. Choose targets each time. This lasts for 1 minute, until you're no longer wielding the wand, or until you try to activate the wand again.

Type 1st-level spell; **Level** 5; **Price** 160 gp
Type 3rd-level spell; **Level** 9; **Price** 700 gp
Type 5th-level spell; **Level** 13; **Price** 3,000 gp
Type 7th-level spell; **Level** 17; **Price** 15,000 gp

Craft Requirements Supply a casting of *magic missile* of the appropriate level.

WAND OF SLAYING   ITEM 16+

ILLUSION **MAGICAL** **WAND**

Usage held in 1 hand; **Bulk** L

This polished black wand has a green gem at the tip, and anyone who looks into it sees a reflection of a grinning skull instead of their face.

Activate (Cast a Spell); **Frequency** once per day, plus overcharge; **Effect** You cast *finger of death* of the indicated level. If the spell slays its target, the corpse releases negative energy in a 20-foot emanation, dealing negative damage equal to double the spell's level.

Type 7th level spell; **Level** 16; **Price** 10,000 gp
Type 8th level spell; **Level** 18; **Price** 24,000 gp
Type 9th level spell; **Level** 20; **Price** 70,000 gp

Craft Requirements Supply a casting of *finger of death* of the appropriate level.

WAND OF SMOLDERING FIREBALLS   ITEM 8+

EVOCATION **FIRE** **MAGICAL** **WAND**

Usage held in 1 hand; **Bulk** L

This blackened, heavily burned stick smells faintly of bat guano.

Activate (Cast a Spell); **Frequency** once per day, plus overcharge; **Effect** You cast *fireball* of the indicated level. Each creature that fails its save takes persistent fire damage.

Type 3rd-level spell; **Level** 8; **Price** 500 gp; **Persistent Damage** 1d6
Type 5th-level spell; **Level** 12; **Price** 2,000 gp; **Persistent Damage** 2d6
Type 7th-level spell; **Level** 16; **Price** 10,000 gp; **Persistent Damage** 3d6
Type 9th-level spell; **Level** 20; **Price** 70,000 gp; **Persistent Damage** 4d6

Craft Requirements Supply a casting of *fireball* of the appropriate level.

WAND OF WIDENING   ITEM 4+

MAGICAL **WAND**

Usage held in 1 hand; **Bulk** L

The end of this wand is forked instead of tapered.

Activate (Cast a Spell); **Frequency** once per day, plus overcharge; This activation takes ◆◆ if the spell normally takes ◆ to cast, or ◆◆◆ if the spell normally takes ◆◆; **Effect** You Cast the Spell, and increase its area. Add 5 feet to the radius of a burst that normally has a radius of at least 10 feet; add 5 feet to the length of a cone or line that is normally 15 feet long or smaller; or add 10 feet to the length of a larger cone or line.

Type 1st-level spell; **Level** 4; **Price** 100 gp
Type 2nd-level spell; **Level** 6; **Price** 250 gp
Type 3rd-level spell; **Level** 8; **Price** 500 gp
Type 4th-level spell; **Level** 10; **Price** 1,000 gp
Type 5th-level spell; **Level** 12; **Price** 2,000 gp
Type 6th-level spell; **Level** 14; **Price** 4,500 gp
Type 7th-level spell; **Level** 16; **Price** 10,000 gp
Type 8th-level spell; **Level** 18; **Price** 24,000 gp
Type 9th-level spell; **Level** 20; **Price** 70,000 gp

Craft Requirements Supply a casting of a spell of the appropriate level. The spell must have a casting time of ◆ or ◆◆, can't have a duration, and must have an area of burst (10 feet or more), cone, or line.

CRAFTING & TREASURE

11

INTRODUCTION

ANCESTRIES &
BACKGROUNDS

CLASSES

SKILLS

FEATS

EQUIPMENT

SPELLS

THE AGE OF
LOST OMENS

PLAYING THE
GAME

GAME
MASTERING

CRAFTING
& TREASURE

APPENDIX

WEAPONS

Weapons can be crafted from precious materials or infused with magic to grant them powerful and unusual abilities.

PRECIOUS MATERIAL WEAPONS

Weapons made of precious materials are more expensive and sometimes have special effects. You can make metal weapons out of any of these materials except darkwood, and wooden weapons out of darkwood. To determine the Price of 10 pieces of ammunition, use the base Price for a single weapon, without adding any extra for Bulk.

ADAMANTINE WEAPON   ITEM 11+

UNCOMMON

Usage varies by weapon; **Bulk** varies by weapon

Adamantine weapons have a shiny black appearance and cut through lesser items with ease. They treat any object they hit as if it had half as much Hardness as usual, unless the object's Hardness is greater than that of the adamantine weapon.

Type standard-grade adamantine weapon; **Level** 11; **Price** 1,400 gp + 140 gp per Bulk; **Craft Requirements** at least 175 gp of adamantine + 17.5 gp per Bulk

Type high-grade adamantine weapon; **Level** 17; **Price** 13,500 gp + 1,350 gp per Bulk; **Craft Requirements** at least 6,750 gp of adamantine + 675 gp per Bulk

COLD IRON WEAPON   ITEM 2+

Usage varies by weapon; **Bulk** varies by weapon

Cold iron weapons deal additional damage to creatures with weakness to cold iron, like demons and fey.

Type low-grade cold iron weapon; **Level** 2; **Price** 40 gp + 4 gp per Bulk; **Craft Requirements** at least 20 sp of cold iron + 2 sp per Bulk

Type standard-grade cold iron weapon; **Level** 10; **Price** 880 gp + 88 gp per Bulk; **Craft Requirements** at least 110 gp of cold iron + 11 gp per Bulk

Type high-grade cold iron weapon; **Level** 16; **Price** 9,000 gp + 900 gp per Bulk; **Craft Requirements** at least 4,500 gp of cold iron + 450 gp per Bulk

DARKWOOD WEAPON   ITEM 11+

UNCOMMON

Usage varies by weapon; **Bulk** varies by weapon

Darkwood weapons are as dark as ebony, with a slight purple tint. A darkwood weapon's Bulk is reduced by 1 (or to light Bulk if its normal Bulk is 1, with no effect on a weapon that normally has light Bulk).

Type standard grade darkwood weapon; **Level** 11; **Price** 1,400 gp + 140 gp per Bulk; **Craft Requirements** at least 175 gp of darkwood + 17.5 gp per Bulk

Type high-grade darkwood weapon; **Level** 17; **Price** 13,500 gp + 1,350 gp per Bulk; **Craft Requirements** at least 6,750 gp of darkwood + 675 gp per Bulk

MITHRAL WEAPON   ITEM 11+

UNCOMMON

Usage varies by weapon; **Bulk** varies by weapon

Mithral weapons are slightly lighter than silver. A mithral weapon is 1 Bulk lighter than normal (or light Bulk if its normal Bulk is 1, with no effect on a weapon that normally has light Bulk).

Type standard-grade mithral weapon; **Level** 11; **Price** 1,400 gp + 140 gp per Bulk; **Craft Requirements** at least 175 gp of mithral + 17.5 gp per Bulk

Type high-grade mithral weapon; **Level** 17; **Price** 13,500 gp + 1,350 gp per Bulk; **Craft Requirements** at least 6,750 gp of mithral + 675 gp per Bulk

ORICHALCUM WEAPON   ITEM 18

RARE

Usage varies by weapon; **Bulk** varies by weapon

Orichalcum weapons can have four magic property runes instead of three. Due to orichalcum's temporal properties, etching the *speed* weapon property rune onto an orichalcum weapon costs half the normal Price (though transferring the rune to a weapon made of another material requires you to first pay the remaining Price and then pay the cost to transfer).

Type high-grade orichalcum weapon; **Level** 18; **Price** 22,500 gp + 2,250 gp per Bulk; **Craft Requirements** at least 11,250 gp of orichalcum + 1,125 gp per Bulk

SILVER WEAPON   ITEM 2+

Usage varies by weapon; **Bulk** varies by weapon

Silver weapons deal additional damage to creatures with weakness to silver, like werewolves, and ignore the resistances of some other creatures, like devils.

Type low-grade silver weapon; **Level** 2; **Price** 40 gp + 4 gp per Bulk; **Craft Requirements** at least 20 sp of silver + 2 sp per Bulk

Type standard-grade silver weapon; **Level** 10; **Price** 880 gp + 88 gp per Bulk; **Craft Requirements** at least 110 gp of silver + 11 gp per Bulk

Type high-grade silver weapon; **Level** 16; **Price** 9,000 gp + 900 gp per Bulk; **Craft Requirements** at least 4,500 gp of silver + 450 gp per Bulk

BASIC MAGIC WEAPON

Many magic weapons are created by etching runes onto them, as described on page 580. The *magic weapon* stat block covers the Prices and attributes of the most common weapons you can make with only fundamental runes.

MAGIC WEAPON   ITEM 2+

EVOCATION   **MAGICAL**

Usage held in 1 hand

A *magic weapon* is a weapon etched with only fundamental runes. A *weapon potency* rune gives an item bonus to attack rolls with the weapon, and a *striking* rune increases the weapon's number of weapon damage dice.

The Prices here are for all types of weapons. You don't need to adjust the Price from a club to a greataxe or the like. These weapons are made of standard materials, not precious materials such as cold iron.

Type *+1 weapon*; **Level** 2; **Price** 35 gp
This weapon has a *+1 weapon potency* rune (+1 item bonus to attack rolls with the weapon).

Type *+1 striking weapon*; **Level** 4; **Price** 100 gp
This weapon has a *+1 weapon potency* rune (+1 item bonus to attack rolls with the weapon) and a *striking* rune (one extra damage die).

Type *+2 striking weapon*; **Level** 10; **Price** 1,000 gp
This weapon has a *+2 weapon potency* rune (+2 item bonus to attack rolls with the weapon) and a *striking* rune (one additional damage die).

Type *+2 greater striking weapon*; **Level** 12; **Price** 2,000 gp
This weapon has a *+2 weapon potency* rune (+2 item bonus to attack rolls with the weapon) and a *greater striking* rune (two extra damage dice).

Type *+3 greater striking weapon*; **Level** 16; **Price** 10,000 gp
This weapon has a *+3 weapon potency* rune (+3 item bonus to attack rolls with the weapon) and a *greater striking* rune (two extra damage dice).

Type *+3 major striking weapon*; **Level** 19; **Price** 40,000 gp
This weapon has a *+3 weapon potency* rune (+3 item bonus to attack rolls with the weapon) and a *major striking* rune (three extra damage dice).

SPECIFIC MAGIC WEAPONS

These weapons have abilities far different from what can be gained by simply etching runes. A specific magic weapon lists its fundamental runes, which you can upgrade, add, or transfer as normal. You can't etch any property runes onto a specific weapon that it doesn't already have.

BLOODLETTING KUKRI   ITEM 6

UNCOMMON | MAGICAL | NECROMANCY

Price 240 gp
Usage held in 1 hand; **Bulk** L

This *+1 striking kukri* has a crimson blade that shimmers eerily in bright light. On a critical hit, the kukri deals 1d8 persistent bleed damage. If the target didn't already have persistent bleed damage when you scored the critical hit, you also gain 1d8 temporary Hit Points.

CATERWAUL SLING   ITEM 5

EVOCATION | MAGICAL

Price 155 gp
Usage held in 1 hand; **Bulk** L

Made of shiny brown leather, this *+1 striking sling* has a single white thread interwoven into its cord.

Activate ◆◆ Interact (sonic); **Frequency** once per day; **Effect** You pull the white thread free, then whirl the sling in circles at high speed. It lets out an ear-piercing wave of sound. Each creature in a 30-foot cone takes 4d6 sonic damage (DC 21 basic Fortitude save). Any creature that fails is deafened for 1 round, or 1 hour on a critical failure.

DAGGER OF VENOM   ITEM 5

MAGICAL | NECROMANCY | POISON

Price 150 gp
Usage held in 1 hand; **Bulk** L

The serrated blade of this *+1 striking dagger* has a greenish tinge, and the hilt is sculpted to look like the head of a serpent about to strike. When you critically succeed at an attack roll with the *dagger of venom*, the target becomes sickened 1 unless it succeeds at a DC 19 Fortitude save. This is a poison effect. In addition, you can activate the dagger to poison a creature with a more potent poison.

Activate ◆ Interact; **Frequency** once per day; **Trigger** You damage a creature with the *dagger of venom*; **Effect** You poison the creature you hit with dagger venom.

Dagger Venom (poison); **Saving Throw** Fortitude DC 21; **Maximum Duration** 4 rounds. **Stage 1** 1d8 poison damage and enfeebled 1.

DWARVEN THROWER   ITEM 13

EVOCATION | MAGICAL

Price 2,750 gp
Usage held in 1 hand; **Bulk** 1

This *+2 striking warhammer* is inlaid with precious metals and decorated with geometric patterns in a dwarven style. If you're a dwarf, a *dwarven thrower* functions for you as a *+2 greater striking returning warhammer* with the thrown 30 feet trait, and your attacks with the hammer deal 1d8 additional damage against giants.

FIGHTER'S FORK   ITEM 3

MAGICAL | TRANSMUTATION

Price 50 gp
Usage held in 1 or 2 hands; **Bulk** 1

This *+1 trident*, usually engraved with a decorative pattern resembling fish scales, is a common weapon among warriors of aquatic ancestries.

Activate ◆ Interact; **Effect** You extend or shorten the trident's haft. When extended, the trident requires two hands to wield and gains the reach trait, but loses the trident's normal thrown trait.

FLAME TONGUE   ITEM 13+

EVOCATION | FIRE | MAGICAL

Usage held in 1 hand; **Bulk** 1

This *+2 greater striking flaming longsword* has an ornate brass hilt and a blade shaped like stylized flames. When wielded, the blade projects illumination resembling shimmering firelight, emitting dim light in a 10-foot radius.

Activate ◆◆ command, Interact; **Effect** You cast the *produce flame* cantrip from the sword as a 7th-level arcane spell, using your melee attack modifier with *flametongue* as your spell attack modifier.

Type *flame tongue*; **Level** 13; **Price** 2,800 gp
Type *greater flame tongue*; **Level** 17; **Price** 13,800 gp

This is a *+3 greater striking greater flaming longsword*. When you activate the sword to cast *produce flame*, the spell is 9th level.

Activate ❖ command; **Frequency** once per day; **Effect** A 10-foot emanation of flame radiates from the *greater flame tongue* for 1 minute. All weapon and unarmed attacks by you and your allies within the area gain the effect of the *flaming* property rune.

FROST BRAND ITEM 16

COLD | EVOCATION | MAGICAL

Price 10,000 gp
Usage held in 2 hands; **Bulk** 2

The blade of this *+2 greater striking greater frost greatsword* appears to be nothing but icy shards. The *frost brand* automatically extinguishes non-magical fires in a 20-foot emanation. While wielding it, you gain fire resistance 5.

Activate ❖❖ command, Interact; **Effect** You swing the *frost brand* into the area of an ongoing magical fire, and the blade attempts to counteract the fire with a counteract modifier of +27. If it fails, it can't attempt to counteract the same fire again.

GLOOM BLADE ITEM 9

EVOCATION | MAGICAL

Price 700 gp
Usage held in 1 hand; **Bulk** L

As black as coal, this blade grows more potent in darkness. While in bright light, it functions as a *+1 shortsword* and doesn't appear to radiate a magic aura to *detect magic* or similar spells unless the spells are 4th level or higher.

In dim light or darkness, the *gloom blade* becomes a *+2 striking shortsword*. Whenever you use the *gloom blade* to attack a creature you're undetected by, you deal 1d6 additional precision damage.

To upgrade the gloom blade's fundamental runes, start with the base *+1 shortsword*, but if you improve it beyond a *+2 striking shortsword*, the runes apply in dim light or darkness as well.

HOLY AVENGER ITEM 14

UNCOMMON | DIVINE | EVOCATION | LAWFUL | GOOD

Price 4,500 gp
Usage held in 1 hand; **Bulk** 1

The gleaming *holy avenger* is the iconic weapon of powerful paladins. The crossbar of this *+2 greater striking holy cold iron longsword* is styled to look like angel wings. Tradition holds that those who see their reflection in a *holy avenger*'s highly polished blade have their faults laid bare. If you are evil, you are enfeebled 2 while carrying or wielding this weapon.

Activate ❖❖ command, Interact; **Frequency** once per hour; **Effect** You command the sword and point it at a creature you can see. The sword casts *detect alignment* to detect evil, but this targets only the selected creature instead of detecting in an area.

Paladin Wielder If you're a champion of the paladin cause, you also gain the following two benefits.

• When you critically hit an evil creature with the *holy avenger*, the creature is slowed 1 and enfeebled 2 for 1 round.

• You can activate the sword in the following way.

Activate ❖ command; **Frequency** once per day; **Requirements** You hit a creature using the *holy avenger* on your previous action; **Effect** You cast *dispel magic* at the same level as your champion focus spells. It must target an illusion the creature you hit created, a spell affecting the creature you hit, or an item the creature you hit wears or carries. The spell or item you attempt to counteract must be within 120 feet of you.

Craft Requirements You are a champion with the paladin cause; supply a casting of *detect alignment* and *dispel magic*. The initial raw materials must include 120 gp of cold iron.

LUCK BLADE ITEM 17+

RARE | DIVINATION | FORTUNE | MAGICAL

Usage held in 1 hand; **Bulk** L

Luck and good fortune bless the wielder of this *+3 greater striking shortsword*. *Luck blades* are crafted in a variety of styles, but their hilts or blades always incorporate symbols of luck, such as clovers, horseshoes, fish, ladybugs, or other symbols.

Activate ↻ envision; **Frequency** once per day; **Trigger** You miss on a Strike with the *luck blade*; **Effect** Reroll the triggering attack roll and use the new result. This is a fortune effect.

Type *luck blade*; **Level** 17; **Price** 15,000 gp
Type *wishing luck blade*; **Level** 19; **Price** 30,000 gp

Some *luck blades* contain one *wish* when crafted. You can cast this spell as an arcane innate spell while wielding the *luck blade*, expending the spell. A spellcaster who can cast *wish* can place another *wish* into the blade by spending 8,000 gp and 4 days of downtime. A *wishing luck blade* can hold no more than one *wish* at a time.

Craft Requirements Supply a casting of *wish*.

MATTOCK OF THE TITANS ITEM 19

UNCOMMON | EVOCATION | MAGICAL

Price 36,000 gp
Usage held in 2 hands; **Bulk** 16

This 15-foot-long adamantine digging tool is far too big for even a Large creature to wield, though if you're a Small or larger creature, you can wield it while wearing a *belt of giant strength*, as though it were appropriately sized for you and had 2 Bulk. The GM might also allow you to wield the mattock if you have some other means of wielding oversized weapons, such as if you're a Large barbarian with the giant instinct or are a Huge creature. When it's used as a weapon, the *mattock of the titans* has the statistics of a *+3 greater striking keen adamantine great pick*.

While you're wielding the *mattock of the titans*, you gain a +3 item bonus to Athletics checks. You can use it to loosen or push soft earth at a rate of 1 minute per 5-foot cube or smash through solid stone at the rate of 5 minutes per 5-foot-cube.

Activate ◆◆ Interact; **Frequency** once per day; **Effect** You dig furiously with the mattock to non-magically replicate the effects of an *earthquake* spell.

Craft Requirements You are a titan, and the initial raw materials must include 8,100 gp of adamantine.

OATHBOW   ITEM 11
DIVINATION MAGICAL
Price 1,300 gp
Usage held in 1 hand; **Bulk** 2

Constructed of a flexible, white wood and with ornate, twisting designs carved into its surface, this *+2 striking composite longbow* appears to have been made by elves. Sometimes when you loose an arrow, its whistling in flight sounds like a voice whispering in Elven, wishing for the swift defeat of your enemies.

Activate ◆ command; **Effect** You swear an oath to destroy one creature you can see. For the next 7 days or until that creature is slain, your attacks with the bow against that creature deal 1d6 additional damage, and you gain a +2 circumstance bonus to Survival checks to Track that creature. Your critical hits against the target gain the bow's critical specialization effect (page 283); if they would already do so, they instead increase the DC of the Athletics check to Escape when critically hit to DC 20.

After you activate the bow, you can't activate it again for 7 days. If you kill the creature you've sworn an oath against, the oath ends and you need to wait only 10 minutes before you can activate it again.

RETRIBUTION AXE   ITEM 3
ENCHANTMENT MAGICAL
Price 60 gp
Usage held in 2 hands; **Bulk** 2

The blade of this *+1 greataxe* bears a design of a human skull. Whenever a creature damages you with an attack, the skull changes its appearance to look like the face of that creature. You gain a +2 circumstance bonus to your next damage roll against that creature before the end of your next turn. Because the face reshapes each time you're damaged, you get the additional damage only if you attack the creature that damaged you most recently.

SKY HAMMER   ITEM 20
RARE EVOCATION MAGICAL
Price 70,000 gp
Usage held in 1 hand; **Bulk** 1

The sturdy, steel head of this *+3 major striking flaming shock orichalcum warhammer* is shaped like a blazing comet.

Activate ↻ command; **Trigger** Your attack roll with the *sky hammer* is a critical success; **Effect** A 6th-level arcane *fireball* spell explodes, centered on the *sky hammer*. The spell DC is 45. You are immune to the *fireball*'s effect, though your allies are not.

Craft Requirements Supply a casting of *fireball* (6th level), and the initial raw materials must include 12,375 gp of orichalcum.

STORM FLASH   ITEM 14+
ELECTRICITY EVOCATION MAGICAL
Usage held in 1 hand; **Bulk** 1

This *+2 greater striking shock rapier* has a golden blade, and miniature electric arcs flash across its guard while it's wielded. When out of its sheath under an open sky, the blade causes storm clouds to gather slowly above.

Activate ◆◆ command, envision; **Frequency** once per day; **Effect** You cast a 6th-level *lightning bolt* (DC 33).

Activate ↻ command; **Frequency** once per 10 minutes; **Trigger** An electricity effect targets you or a creature within 10 feet of you, or has you or a creature within 10 feet of you in its area; **Effect** You try to divert the electricity off course, to be absorbed by *storm flash*. Choose one eligible creature to protect and roll a melee attack roll against the DC of the electricity effect. If you succeed, the chosen creature takes no electricity damage from the triggering effect.

Type *storm flash*; **Level** 14; **Price** 4,000 gp
Type *greater storm flash*; **Level** 18; **Price** 21,000 gp
This is a *+3 greater striking greater shock rapier*. When activating the sword to cast *lightning bolt*, the spell is 8th level.

TWINING STAFF   ITEM 6
MAGICAL TRANSMUTATION
Price 250 gp
Usage held in 1 or 2 hands; **Bulk** — to 2

Appearing to be just a small, flat disc made of twigs, this item can grow and shrink.

Activate ◆ Interact; **Effect** You cause the twigs to rapidly grow or contract, reshaping into a *+1 striking staff*, a *+1 striking bo staff*, or its disc form. In its disc form, it has negligible Bulk and must be held in one hand to be activated. In the other forms, it has the same Bulk as a normal weapon of its type. You can switch your grip as part of the activation.

When you expand the item, you can use the force of the expansion to High Jump or to try to Force Open a door or the like by wedging the disc into a gap before activation. The staff makes the Athletics check with a +15 modifier.

WORN ITEMS

This section includes magic items you wear. Most have the invested trait, which means you can wear no more than 10 (page 531). Worn items include the following subcategories, with special rules appearing at the start of the section.

- **Apex Items** on this page.
- **Companion Items** on page 604.
- **Other Worn Items** on page 604.

APEX ITEMS

When you Invest an Item that has the apex trait, it improves one of your ability scores, either increasing it by 2 or to a total of 18, whichever grants the higher score. This gives you all the benefits of the new ability score until the investiture runs out: increasing Intelligence lets you become trained in an additional skill and learn a new language, increasing Constitution gives you more Hit Points, and so on.

An apex item grants this benefit only the first time it's invested within a 24-hour period, and you can benefit from only one apex item at a time. If you attempt to invest an apex item when you already have one invested, you don't gain the ability score increase, though you do gain any other effects of Investing the Item.

ANKLETS OF ALACRITY — ITEM 17

APEX **INVESTED** **MAGICAL** **TRANSMUTATION**

Price 15,000 gp

Usage worn anklets; **Bulk** —

These gem-studded golden anklets give you a +3 item bonus to Acrobatics checks. When you invest the anklets, you either increase your Dexterity score by 2 or increase it to 18, whichever would give you a higher score.

Activate ❖ Interact; **Frequency** once per day; **Effect** You click the anklets together, gaining a +20-foot status bonus to all your Speeds and the effects of *water walk* for the next 10 minutes.

BELT OF GIANT STRENGTH — ITEM 17

APEX **INVESTED** **MAGICAL** **TRANSMUTATION**

Price 15,000 gp

Usage worn belt; **Bulk** L

This thick leather belt is decorated with a buckle carved from glittering quartz in the shape of a fist. You gain a +3 item bonus to Athletics checks and a +2 circumstance bonus to Athletics checks to lift a heavy object, Escape, and Force Open. When you invest the belt, you either increase your Strength score by 2 or increase it to 18, whichever would give you a higher score.

Activate ⟳ Interact; **Trigger** You are targeted by a thrown rock attack, or a rock would fall on you; **Effect** Attempt an Athletics check to grab the triggering rock. Use the Athletics

DC of the creature throwing the rock, the DC of the hazard or other effect, or DC 35 if no other DC is applicable. You must have a free hand to catch the rock, but you can Release anything you're holding in a hand as part of this reaction.

Success You safely catch the rock, take no damage, and are now holding the rock.

Failure You take half damage.

Critical Failure You take full damage.

BELT OF REGENERATION — ITEM 17

APEX **INVESTED** **MAGICAL** **NECROMANCY**

Price 15,000 gp

Usage worn belt; **Bulk** L

This belt is crafted from rubbery troll hide that's green and orange in color. You gain 15 temporary Hit Points the first time you invest the belt in a day. When you invest the belt, you either increase your Constitution score by 2 or increase it to 18, whichever would give you a higher score.

Activate ❖ Interact; **Frequency** once per day; **Effect** You tighten the belt one notch to gain a regeneration effect. For 2d4 rounds, at the start of your turn each round, you recover 15 Hit Points unless you took acid or fire damage since the start of your previous turn.

CIRCLET OF PERSUASION — ITEM 17

APEX **ENCHANTMENT** **INVESTED** **MAGICAL**

Price 15,000 gp

Usage worn circlet; **Bulk** —

This elegant silver band often resembles curling fig leaves and fits around your brow. You gain a +2 item bonus to Deception and Diplomacy checks. When you invest the circlet, you either increase your Charisma score by 2 or increase it to 18, whichever would give you a higher score.

Activate ❖❖ envision; **Frequency** once per hour; **Effect** You cast a 4th-level *charm* spell (DC 38).

DIADEM OF INTELLECT — ITEM 17

APEX **DIVINATION** **INVESTED** **MAGICAL**

Price 15,000 gp

Usage worn circlet; **Bulk** L

An elegant, colorful gem cut into a complex geometric pattern is slotted into a narrow metal band that fits around your brow. You gain a +3 item bonus to checks to Recall Knowledge, regardless of the skill. When you invest the diadem, you either increase your Intelligence score by 2 or increase it to 18, whichever would give you a higher score. This gives you additional trained skills and languages, as normal for increasing your Intelligence score. You must select skills and languages the first time you invest the item, and whenever you invest the same *diadem of intellect*, you get the same skills and languages you chose the first time.

Activate ❖ envision; **Frequency** once per hour; **Effect** You gain the effects of *hypercognition*.

HEADBAND OF INSPIRED WISDOM — ITEM 17

| ABJURATION | APEX | INVESTED | MAGICAL |

Price 15,000 gp

Usage worn circlet; **Bulk** —

This simple cloth headband remains pristine and clean at all times, no matter the circumstances. When you invest the headband, you either increase your Wisdom score by 2 or increase it to 18, whichever would give you a higher score.

Activate ❖ envision; **Frequency** once per day; **Effect** When you are considering a course of action, you get a gut feeling about whether it's a good idea. You gain the effects of an *augury* spell, except that you receive the result from your own instincts rather than an external source.

Activate ↺ envision (fortune); **Frequency** once per hour; **Trigger** You fail a saving throw against an effect that makes you confused, fascinated, or stupefied; **Effect** The *headband of inspired wisdom* clears your mind. You can reroll the saving throw and use the better result.

COMPANION ITEMS

You might want to acquire items that benefit an animal or beast that assists you. These items have the companion trait, meaning they function only for animal companions, familiars, and similar creatures. If it's unclear whether a creature can benefit from such an item, the GM decides.

INVESTING COMPANION ITEMS

Any worn companion item needs to be invested. However, your companion needs to invest it rather than you doing so. This requires you to use the Invest an Item activity alongside your companion. A companion has an investiture limit of two items (instead of the 10-item limit a player character has).

BARDING OF THE ZEPHYR — ITEM 10

| COMPANION | INVESTED | PRIMAL | TRANSMUTATION |

Price 900 gp

Usage worn barding; **Bulk** L

This light barding is covered in stylized wind motifs. When you suit up your animal companion, the barding adjusts to fit your animal companion regardless of its shape.

When your companion falls, wind picks it up from below; it gains the effects of *feather fall*.

Activate ❖❖ Interact; **Frequency** once per day; **Effect** You trace a finger along the wind motifs on the barding, granting your companion wearing the barding a fly Speed of 30 feet for 10 minutes. Even if the companion doesn't have the mount special ability, it can still Fly while being ridden.

COLLAR OF EMPATHY — ITEM 9

| COMPANION | DIVINATION | INVESTED | PRIMAL |

Price 600 gp

Usage worn collar (companion) and worn bracelet (you); **Bulk** 1

This ornate collar of intertwined leather strips of contrasting colors is paired with a bracelet of a similar construction. When you wear and invest the bracelet and your companion wears and invests the collar, you gain a stronger connection to each other. You and your companion can always sense each others' emotional states and basic physical wants and needs.

Activate ❖ envision; **Effect** You perceive through your animal companion's senses instead of your own. You can Sustain the Activation. You are unaware of your own surroundings for as long as you are using your animal companion's senses. In addition to the obvious use when you are separated from your companion, this ability might allow you to notice sounds, scents, and other stimuli that your companion's senses register but yours alone don't.

COLLAR OF INCONSPICUOUSNESS — ITEM 8

| COMPANION | INVESTED | PRIMAL | TRANSMUTATION |

Price 475 gp

Usage worn collar; **Bulk** 1

This leather collar's worn and almost threadbare look belies its magical nature. When your companion wears and invests the collar, it gains the ability to change its appearance from that of a ferocious animal into a more inconspicuous form.

Activate ❖ envision; **Effect** You touch your animal companion to transform it into a nonthreatening Tiny creature of the same family or a similar creature (for instance, a house cat instead of a tiger, or a puppy instead of a wolf). This has the effects of *pest form* (2nd level, or 4th level if your companion can fly). The effect lasts until you Dismiss it.

HORSESHOES OF SPEED — ITEM 7+

| COMPANION | INVESTED | PRIMAL | TRANSMUTATION |

Usage worn horseshoes; **Bulk** 1

When you affix these simple iron horseshoes to the hooves of an ordinary horse or a quadrupedal animal companion and the animal companion invests them, that creature gains a +5-foot item bonus to its land Speed and a +2 item bonus to Athletics checks to High Jump and Long Jump. In addition, when it Leaps, it can move 5 feet farther if jumping horizontally or 3 feet higher if jumping vertically.

Type *horseshoes of speed*; **Level** 7; **Price** 340 gp

Type *greater horseshoes of speed*; **Level** 14; **Price** 4,250 gp

The bonus to Speed is +10 feet, and the bonus to Athletics checks is +3.

OTHER WORN ITEMS

These are a wide variety of items you wear. Armor appears in its own section on page 555, and apex items that can increase ability scores are on page 603.

AEON STONE — ITEM 1+

| UNCOMMON | INVESTED | MAGICAL | TRANSMUTATION |

Usage worn; **Bulk** —

Over millennia, these mysterious, intricately cut gemstones have been hoarded by mystics and fanatics hoping to discover their secrets. Despite their myriad forms and functions, these stones are purportedly all fragments of crystal tools used by otherworldly entities to construct the universe in primeval times.

When you invest one of these precisely shaped crystals, the stone orbits your head instead of being worn on your body. You can stow an *aeon stone* with an Interact action, and an orbiting stone can be snatched out of the air with a successful Disarm action against you. A stowed or removed stone remains invested, but its effects are suppressed until you return it to orbit your head again.

There are various types of *aeon stones*, each with a different shape, color, and magical effect. Each *aeon stone* also gains a resonant power when slotted into a special magical item called a *wayfinder* (page 617).

Type clear spindle; **Level** 7; **Price** 325 gp
You don't need to eat or drink while this *aeon stone* is invested by you. This *aeon stone* doesn't function until it has been worn continuously for a week and invested each day therein. If it's invested by someone else, this interval starts over.

The resonant power allows you to cast *air bubble* as a primal innate spell once per day.

Type dull gray; **Level** 1; **Price** 9 gp
A *dull gray aeon stone* has lost its special magical properties, sometimes as a result of overusing a *tourmaline sphere* or *pale lavender ellipsoid aeon stone*. It still orbits your head like any other *aeon stone* and can thus serve as a stylish, hands-free option for various spells that target an object, like *continual flame*.

Dull gray aeon stones have no resonant power.

Type gold nodule; **Level** 6; **Price** 230 gp
When a *gold nodule aeon stone* is created, its creator chooses a language they know to store within the crystal. When you invest the stone, you gain the ability to understand, speak, and write that language.

The resonant power allows you to cast *comprehend language* as an occult innate spell once per day.

Type lavender and green ellipsoid; **Level** 19; **Price** 30,000 gp
This functions as a *pale lavender ellipsoid aeon stone*, but it casts an 8th-level *dispel magic* spell with a counteract modifier of +31.

The resonant power allows you to cast *detect magic* and *read aura* as arcane innate spells at will.

Type orange prism; **Level** 16; **Price** 9,750 gp
An *orange prism aeon stone* must be activated to provide a benefit. The resonant power grants you a +2 item bonus to Arcana, Nature, Occultism, or Religion checks—whichever corresponds to the tradition of the last spell you enhanced with this *aeon stone*.

Activate ❖ envision; **Effect** If your next action is to Cast a Spell, that spell's level is 1 higher (maximum 10th level) for the purposes of counteracting and being counteracted.

Type pale lavender ellipsoid; **Level** 13; **Price** 2,200 gp

This *aeon stone* must be activated to provide a benefit. The resonant power allows you to cast the *read aura* cantrip as an arcane innate spell.

Activate ↻ envision; **Frequency** once per day; **Trigger** A spell targets you; **Effect** The stone casts a 6th-level *dispel magic* spell in an attempt to counteract the triggering spell, with a counteract modifier of +22. This can be used only on spells that specifically target you—not area spells that don't have targets. If it succeeds, it counteracts the spell for all targets if other creatures were targeted in addition to you.

Each time you activate this *aeon stone*, attempt a DC 5 flat check. On a failure, the stone permanently turns into a *dull gray aeon stone*.

Type pink rhomboid; **Level** 12; **Price** 1,900 gp
When you invest this stone, you gain 15 temporary Hit Points. If the stone's effects are suppressed, you lose any of the temporary Hit Points remaining until it returns. The temporary Hit Points refresh during your daily preparations; they do not refresh if you re-invest the stone, or invest another *pink rhomboid aeon stone*, before then.

The resonant power allows you to cast the *stabilize* cantrip as a divine innate spell.

Type tourmaline sphere; **Level** 7; **Price** 350 gp
When you would die from the dying condition (typically at dying 4), this *aeon stone* automatically activates and reduces your dying value to 1 less than would normally kill you (typically to dying 3). The stone then permanently turns into a *dull gray aeon stone*. You can benefit from this ability only once per day, even if you have multiple such stones.

The resonant power allows you to cast 1st-level *heal* as a divine innate spell once per day.

ALCHEMIST GOGGLES   ITEM 4+

INVESTED   MAGICAL   TRANSMUTATION
Usage worn eyepiece; **Bulk** —

These brass goggles are engraved with flame patterns and have thick, heavy lenses. While worn, they give you a +1 item bonus to Crafting checks to Craft alchemical items and a +1 item bonus to attack rolls with alchemical bombs. You can also ignore lesser cover when making Strikes with alchemical bombs.

Type alchemist goggles; **Level** 4; **Price** 100 gp
Type greater alchemist goggles; **Level** 11; **Price** 1,400 gp
The item bonuses are both +2.
Type major alchemist goggles; **Level** 17; **Price** 15,000 gp
The item bonuses are both +3.

ARMBANDS OF ATHLETICISM   ITEM 9+

INVESTED   MAGICAL   TRANSMUTATION
Usage worn armbands; **Bulk** L

Skilled awl work has imprinted images of a muscled weightlifter into these tiered leather bands, which grant you enhanced stamina and skill when performing athletic exercises. While fastened to your upper arms, the armbands give you a +2 item bonus to Athletics checks. In addition, whenever you use an action to Climb or Swim and you succeed at the Athletics check, add a +5-foot item bonus to the distance you move.

Type armbands of athleticism; **Level** 9; **Price** 645 gp
Type greater armbands of athleticism; **Level** 17; **Price** 13,000 gp

The bonus to Athletics checks is +3, and the bonus to a successful check to Climb or Swim is +10 feet.

BELT OF THE FIVE KINGS — ITEM 9
UNCOMMON · ENCHANTMENT · INVESTED · MAGICAL
Price 650 gp
Usage worn belt; **Bulk** L

Made from interlocking plates of silver and gold, this heavy belt bears stylized miniature images of five kingly dwarves. You gain a +1 circumstance bonus to Diplomacy checks to Make an Impression with dwarves or make a Request from dwarves. You also gain a +1 circumstance bonus to Intimidation checks against giants and orcs.

The belt also grants you darkvision and the ability to understand, speak, and write the Dwarven language.

Activate ❖ Interact; **Frequency** once per day; **Requirements** You are a dwarf; **Effect** You tighten the belt one notch to gain temporary Hit Points equal to your level and grant allies within 20 feet of you darkvision. Both effects last for 10 minutes.

BERSERKER'S CLOAK — ITEM 12+
INVESTED · PRIMAL · TRANSMUTATION
Usage worn cloak; **Bulk** 1

This bearskin includes the head and bared teeth of the mighty creature from which it was taken. When worn, the cloak drapes over your head and around your shoulders, imbuing you with a bear's ferocity. If you have the Rage action, while raging you grow jaws that deal 1d10 piercing damage and claws that deal 1d6 slashing damage and have the agile trait. This transformation is a morph effect, and both the jaws and claws are unarmed attacks in the brawling weapon group. You gain the benefits of a +1 weapon potency rune and a striking rune with these attacks (gaining a +1 item bonus to attack rolls and increasing the weapon damage dice by one).

If you have an animal instinct (see the barbarian on page 82) and the bestial rage instinct ability, instead of gaining these unarmed attacks, your unarmed attacks from the bestial rage instinct ability gain the benefits of a +2 weapon potency rune and a greater striking rune (granting a +2 item bonus to attack rolls and increasing the weapon damage dice by two).

Type berserker's cloak; **Level** 12; **Price** 2,000 gp
Type greater berserker's cloak; **Level** 19; **Price** 40,000 gp

You gain the benefits of a +2 weapon potency rune and a greater striking rune, or a +3 weapon potency rune and a major striking rune if you have an animal instinct and the bestial rage instinct ability.

Craft Requirements You are a barbarian with the animal instinct.

BOOTS OF BOUNDING — ITEM 7+
INVESTED · MAGICAL · TRANSMUTATION
Usage worn shoes; **Bulk** L

The springy soles of these sturdy leather boots cushion your feet and make each step lighter. These boots give you a +5-foot item bonus to your Speed and a +2 item bonus to Athletics checks to High Jump and Long Jump. In addition, when you use the Leap action, you can move 5 feet further if jumping horizontally or 3 feet higher if jumping vertically.

Type boots of bounding; **Level** 7; **Price** 340 gp
Type greater boots of bounding; **Level** 14; **Price** 4,250 gp

The bonus to Speed is +10 feet, and the bonus to High Jump and Long Jump is +3.

BOOTS OF ELVENKIND — ITEM 5+
INVESTED · MAGICAL · TRANSMUTATION
Usage worn shoes; **Bulk** L

These tall, pointed boots are made from soft, supple black or green leather and are decorated with trim and buckles of gold. When worn, the boots allow you to move more nimbly, granting you a +1 item bonus to Acrobatics checks.

Activate ◆ envision; **Frequency** once per hour; **Effect** Until the end of your turn, you ignore difficult terrain when moving on the ground. If you're wearing a cloak of elvenkind, you also gain a +5-foot status bonus to your land Speed until the end of your turn.

Type boots of elvenkind; **Level** 5; **Price** 145 gp
Type greater boots of elvenkind; **Level** 11; **Price** 1,250 gp

The boots grant a +2 bonus. If you're also wearing a cloak of elvenkind, greater boots of elvenkind constantly grant the effects of pass without trace (DC 30) in forest environments.

BOOTS OF SPEED — ITEM 13
INVESTED · MAGICAL · TRANSMUTATION
Price 3,000 gp
Usage worn shoes; **Bulk** L

These sleek red boots make your legs feel like they're bursting with energy. You gain a +5-foot item bonus to your land Speed and to any climb or swim Speeds you have.

Activate ❖ Interact; **Frequency** once per day; **Effect** You click the heels of the boots together and gain the quickened condition for 1 minute. You can use the extra action to Stride, Climb, or Swim. (You must still attempt an Athletics check for the Climb and Swim actions unless you have the appropriate movement type.)

BRACELET OF DASHING — ITEM 3

INVESTED   MAGICAL   TRANSMUTATION

Price 58 gp
Usage worn; **Bulk** L

This jangling, silvery bracelet makes you lighter on your feet, giving you a +1 item bonus to Acrobatics checks.

Activate ❖ command; **Frequency** once per day; **Effect** You gain a +10-foot status bonus to Speed for 1 minute.

BRACERS OF ARMOR — ITEM 8+

ABJURATION   INVESTED   MAGICAL

Usage worn bracers; **Bulk** L

These stiff leather armguards grant you a +1 item bonus to AC and saving throws, and a maximum Dexterity modifier of +5. You can affix talismans to *bracers of armor* as though they were light armor.

Type I; **Level** 8; **Price** 450 gp
Type II; **Level** 14; **Price** 4,000 gp
The item bonus to AC and saves is +2.
Type III; **Level** 20; **Price** 60,000 gp
The item bonus to AC and saves is +3.

BRACERS OF MISSILE DEFLECTION — ITEM 3

ABJURATION   INVESTED   MAGICAL

Usage worn bracers; **Bulk** L

These bracers are made from plates of durable mithral and gleam like the summer sun.

Activate ↻ Interact; **Frequency** once per day; **Trigger** A ranged weapon attack hits you but doesn't critically hit; **Requirements** You are aware of the attack and not flat-footed; **Effect** The bracers send the missile off-course. You gain a +2 circumstance bonus to AC against the triggering attack. If this would cause the attack to be a failure, the attack misses you.

Type *bracers of missile deflection*; **Level** 3; **Price** 52 gp
Type *greater bracers of missile deflection*; **Level** 9; **Price** 650 gp
You can activate the bracers once every 10 minutes.

BROOCH OF SHIELDING — ITEM 2

UNCOMMON   ABJURATION   INVESTED   MAGICAL

Price 30 gp
Usage worn; **Bulk** –

This piece of silver or gold jewelry is adorned with miniature images of kite shields and can be used to fasten a cloak or cape. The brooch automatically absorbs *magic missile* spells targeting you. A *brooch of shielding* can absorb 30 individual *magic missiles* before it melts and becomes useless. Sometimes when found, a *brooch of shielding* has already absorbed a number of missiles.

CAPE OF THE MOUNTEBANK — ITEM 10

UNCOMMON   CONJURATION   INVESTED   MAGICAL

Price 980 gp
Usage worn cloak; **Bulk** L

This bright red-and-gold cape is often interlaced with glittery

threads and serves as a distraction. While wearing the cape, you gain a +2 item bonus to Deception checks.

Activate ❖❖ Interact; **Frequency** once per day; **Effect** You cast *dimension door*. The space you leave and the one you appear in are filled with puffs of smoke that make anyone within concealed until they leave the smoke or the end of your next turn, at which point the smoke dissipates. Strong winds immediately disperse the smoke.

CASSOCK OF DEVOTION — ITEM 11

DIVINATION   DIVINE   FOCUSED   INVESTED

Price 1,150 gp
Usage worn garment; **Bulk** L

Each *cassock of devotion* depicts scenes related to the domains of a certain deity. It serves as a religious symbol of that deity, and it doesn't need to be wielded to provide that benefit. You gain a +2 item bonus to Religion checks and a +1 item bonus to the divine skill of the deity to whom the cassock is dedicated (as listed on pages 437–440).

Activate ❖ envision; **Frequency** once per day; **Effect** You gain 1 Focus Point, which you can spend only to cast a cleric domain spell for a domain belonging to the deity the cassock is dedicated to. If you don't spend this Focus Point by the end of this turn, it is lost.

Craft Requirements You are a cleric who worships the deity tied to the cassock.

CHANNEL PROTECTION AMULET — ITEM 3

UNCOMMON · ABJURATION · INVESTED · MAGICAL

Price 56 gp

Usage worn; **Bulk** —

This nugget of polished tektite is trapped in a cage of braided wire and hangs from a silken cord. When wearing this amulet, you gain resistance 5 against damage from *harm* spells if you're living, or against *heal* spells if you're undead.

CHOKER OF ELOCUTION — ITEM 6+

ENCHANTMENT · INVESTED · MAGICAL

Usage worn collar; **Bulk** L

This platinum choker bears characters from a language's alphabet, and it gives knowledge of that language and the associated culture's customs. You gain a +1 item bonus to Society checks and the ability to understand, speak, and write the chosen language. Your excellent elocution reduces the DC of the flat check to perform an auditory action while deafened from 5 to 3.

Type *choker of elocution*; **Level** 6; **Price** 200 gp

Type *greater choker of elocution*; **Level** 10; **Price** 850 gp

The item bonus is +2. The choker bears characters from three languages and grants fluency in all three.

Craft Requirements You know the language or languages the choker grants.

CLANDESTINE CLOAK — ITEM 6+

UNCOMMON · ILLUSION · INVESTED · MAGICAL

Usage worn cloak; **Bulk** L

When you pull up the hood of this nondescript gray cloak (an Interact action), you become drab and uninteresting, gaining a +1 item bonus to Stealth checks and to Deception checks to Impersonate a forgettable background character, such as a servant, but also taking a –1 item penalty to Diplomacy and Intimidation checks.

Activate ◆◆ envision, Interact; **Frequency** once per day; **Effect** You pull the cloak's hood up and gain the benefits of nondetection for 1 hour or until you pull the hood back down, whichever comes first.

Type *clandestine cloak*; **Level** 6; **Price** 230 gp

Type *greater clandestine cloak*; **Level** 10; **Price** 900 gp

The item bonus is +2, and when you activate the cloak, you gain the benefits of 5th-level *nondetection* for 8 hours.

CLOAK OF ELVENKIND — ITEM 7+

ILLUSION · INVESTED · MAGICAL

Usage worn cloak; **Bulk** L

This cloak is deep green with a voluminous hood, embroidered with gold trim and symbols significant in elven culture. The cloak allows you to cast the *ghost sound* cantrip as an arcane innate spell. When you adjust the cloak's clasp (an Interact action), the cloak transforms to match the environment around you and muffles your sounds, granting you a +1 item bonus to Stealth checks.

Activate ◆◆ Interact; **Frequency** once per day; **Effect** You draw the hood up and gain the effects of *invisibility*, with the spell's normal duration or until you pull the hood back down, whichever comes first. If you're also wearing *boots of elvenkind*, you can activate this ability twice per day.

Type *cloak of elvenkind*; **Level** 7; **Price** 360 gp

Type *greater cloak of elvenkind*; **Level** 12; **Price** 1,750 gp

The cloak grants a +2 item bonus, and the effects of 4th-level *invisibility*. If you're also wearing *boots of elvenkind*, the *greater cloak of elvenkind* allows you to Sneak in forest environments even when creatures are currently observing you.

CLOAK OF THE BAT — ITEM 10+

INVESTED · MAGICAL · TRANSMUTATION

Usage worn cloak; **Bulk** L

Sewn from several long strips of luxurious brown and black silk, this cloak grants you a +2 item bonus to Stealth checks as well as to Acrobatics checks to Maneuver in Flight. You can also use your feet to hang from any surface that can support your weight, without requiring any check, though you still must attempt Athletics checks to Climb in order to move around while inverted.

Activate ◆◆ command, Interact; **Frequency** once per day; **Effect** You can either transform the cloak into bat-like wings that grant you a fly Speed of 30 feet for 10 minutes, or have the cloak turn you into a bat by casting a 4th-level *pest form* spell on you.

Type *cloak of the bat*; **Level** 10; **Price** 950 gp
Type *greater cloak of the bat*; **Level** 17; **Price** 13,000 gp
The item bonus is +3, and you can activate the cloak any number of times per day.

COYOTE CLOAK   ITEM 3+

| DIVINATION | INVESTED | MAGICAL |

Usage worn cloak; **Bulk** —
This dusty coat is made of mangy brown-and-gray coyote fur. You gain a +1 item bonus to Survival checks. If you critically succeed at your Survival check to Subsist, you can feed twice as many additional creatures.

Type *coyote cloak*; **Level** 3; **Price** 60 gp
Type *greater coyote cloak*; **Level** 9; **Price** 650 gp
The cloak grants a +2 item bonus, and if you critically succeed at a Survival check to Subsist, you can feed four times as many additional creatures.

CRAFTER'S EYEPIECE   ITEM 3+

| INVESTED | MAGICAL | TRANSMUTATION |

Usage worn eyepiece; **Bulk** —
This rugged metal eyepiece etched with square patterns is designed to be worn over a single eye. Twisting the lens reveals a faint three-dimensional outline of an item you plan to build or repair, with helpful labels on the component parts. While worn, this eyepiece gives you a +1 item bonus to Crafting checks. When you Repair an item, increase the Hit Points restored by 15 per proficiency rank instead of 10.

Type *crafter's eyepiece*; **Level** 3; **Price** 60 gp
Type *greater crafter's eyepiece*; **Level** 11; **Price** 1,200 gp
The eyepiece grants a +2 item bonus and can be activated.

Activate 1 minute (Interact); **Frequency** once per day; **Effect** You calibrate the eyepiece to have it cast a 5th-level *creation* spell over the course of 1 minute to construct a temporary item.

DANCING SCARF   ITEM 3+

| ILLUSION | INVESTED | MAGICAL | VISUAL |

Usage worn belt; **Bulk** —
This long and billowing scarf is typically woven of silk or sheer fabric and adorned with bells or other jangling bits of shiny metal. It grants a +1 item bonus to Performance checks to dance.

Activate ◆ Interact; **Requirements** On your most recent action, you succeeded at a Performance check to dance; **Effect** You become concealed until the beginning of your next turn.

Type *dancing scarf*; **Level** 3; **Price** 60 gp
Type *greater dancing scarf*; **Level** 9; **Price** 650 gp
The scarf grants a +2 bonus. When you activate the scarf, you can also Stride up to half your Speed or Step.

DAREDEVIL BOOTS   ITEM 10+

| ABJURATION | INVESTED | MAGICAL |

Usage worn shoes; **Bulk** L
These brightly colored, soft-soled boots motivate you to perform risky stunts and grant you the agility to succeed. The boots grant you a +2 item bonus to Acrobatics checks and a +1 circumstance bonus to checks to Tumble Through an enemy's space.

The boots can grip solid surfaces and help you avoid a fall, allowing you to use the Grab an Edge reaction even if your hands aren't free. You treat falls as 10 feet shorter or, if you have the Cat Fall feat, treat your proficiency rank in Acrobatics as one degree better to determine the benefits of that feat. If you have Cat Fall and are already legendary in Acrobatics, you can choose the speed of your fall, from 60 feet per round up to normal falling speed.

Type *daredevil boots*; **Level** 10; **Price** 900 gp
Type *greater daredevil boots*; **Level** 17; **Price** 14,000 gp
The bonus to Acrobatics checks is +3, and the bonus to Tumble Through is +2. The boots can be activated.

Activate ◆◆ command; **Frequency** once per day; **Effect** The boots cast *freedom of movement* on you.

DEMON MASK   ITEM 4+

| ENCHANTMENT | INVESTED | MAGICAL |

Usage worn mask; **Bulk** L
This terrifying mask is crafted in the visage of a leering demon and grants a +1 item bonus to Intimidation checks.

Activate ◆◆ Interact; **Frequency** once per day; **Effect** The mask casts a *fear* spell with a DC of 20.

Type *demon mask*; **Level** 4; **Price** 85 gp
Type *greater demon mask*; **Level** 10; **Price** 900 gp
The mask grants a +2 item bonus. It casts 3rd-level *fear* with a DC of 29.

DIPLOMAT'S BADGE   ITEM 5

| ENCHANTMENT | INVESTED | MAGICAL |

Price 125 gp
Usage worn; **Bulk** —
When displayed prominently, this brass badge makes creatures find you more agreeable. You gain a +1 item bonus to Diplomacy checks.

Activate ◆ Recall Knowledge; **Frequency** once per day; **Effect** Attempt a DC 20 check to Recall Knowledge about people of a human ethnicity, a non-human ancestry, or some other type of creature. (The GM determines what your options are.) If you succeed, the badge's bonus increases to +2 for Diplomacy checks with creatures of that group for the rest of the day.

DOUBLING RINGS   ITEM 3+

| EVOCATION | INVESTED | MAGICAL |

Usage worn; **Bulk** —

INTRODUCTION

ANCESTRIES &
BACKGROUNDS

CLASSES

SKILLS

FEATS

EQUIPMENT

SPELLS

THE AGE OF
LOST OMENS

PLAYING THE
GAME

GAME
MASTERING

CRAFTING
& TREASURE

APPENDIX

This item consists of two magically linked rings: an intricate, gleaming golden ring with a square-cut ruby, and a thick, plain iron ring. When you wield a melee weapon in the hand wearing the golden ring, the weapon's fundamental runes are replicated onto any melee weapon you wield in the hand wearing the iron ring. (The fundamental runes are *weapon potency* and *striking*, which add an item bonus to attack rolls and extra weapon damage dice, respectively.) Any fundamental runes on the weapon in the hand wearing the iron ring are suppressed.

The replication functions only if you wear both rings, and it ends as soon as you cease wielding a melee weapon in one of your hands. Consequently, the benefit doesn't apply to thrown attacks or if you're holding a weapon but not wielding it (such as holding in one hand a weapon that requires two hands to wield).

Type *doubling rings*; **Level** 3; **Price** 50 gp
Type *greater doubling rings*; **Level** 11; **Price** 1,300 gp

The rings also replicate property runes from the weapon in the gold-ringed hand, so long as the weapon in the iron-ringed hand meets all the prerequisites for a given rune and is not a specific weapon. The weapon in the iron-ringed hand gains the benefits of those runes. All its own runes are suppressed. When you invest the rings, you can elect for the rings to transfer only fundamental runes, in which case they function as standard *doubling rings*.

DREAD BLINDFOLD   ITEM 17

EMOTION | ENCHANTMENT | FEAR | INVESTED | MAGICAL | MENTAL
Price 15,000 gp
Usage worn eyepiece; **Bulk** –

When tied over your eyes, this ragged strip of black linen gives you a +3 item bonus to Intimidation checks and darkvision. You can see through the blindfold, but only using darkvision.

The first time a particular creature sees you in a day, it must succeed at a DC 37 Will save or be frightened 1. This is an emotion, fear, and mental effect, and your allies become immune to it after about a week.

Activate ◆ command; **Frequency** once per minute; **Trigger** You damage a creature with a Strike; **Effect** Your target is gripped by intense fear. This has the effect of a DC 37 *phantasmal killer* spell, but it is an enchantment instead of an illusion. The creature is then temporarily immune for 24 hours.

DRUID'S VESTMENTS   ITEM 10

FOCUSED | INVESTED | PRIMAL | TRANSMUTATION
Price 1,000 gp

Usage worn garment; **Bulk** L

This brown-and-green tunic is embroidered with patterns that resemble interlocking elk antlers. You gain a +2 item bonus to Nature checks.

Activate ◆ envision; **Frequency** once per day; **Effect** You gain 1 Focus Point, which you can spend only to cast an order spell. If you don't spend this Focus Point by the end of this turn, it is lost.

Craft Requirements You are a druid.

EYE OF FORTUNE   ITEM 13

DIVINATION | INVESTED | MAGICAL
Price 2,700 gp
Usage worn eyepiece; **Bulk** –

Adherents of Erastil, god of the hunt, create these magical eye patches. An *eye of fortune* has a jeweled eye symbol on its front, allowing you to magically see through the eye patch as though it were transparent.

Activate ◆ envision (fortune); **Trigger** You attack a concealed or hidden creature and haven't attempted the flat check yet; **Effect** You can roll the flat check for the concealed or hidden condition twice and use the higher result.

EYES OF THE EAGLE   ITEM 9

INVESTED | MAGICAL | TRANSMUTATION
Price 700 gp
Usage worn eyepiece; **Bulk** –

These lenses of amber crystal fit over your eyes. They grant you low-light vision and a +2 item bonus to Perception checks that involve sight.

GLOVES OF STORING   ITEM 7

UNCOMMON | EXTRADIMENSIONAL | INVESTED | MAGICAL | TRANSMUTATION
Price 340 gp
Usage worn gloves; **Bulk** –

An item can be stored inside these supple leather gloves, held in an extradimensional space. When an item is inside the glove, an image of the item appears as a simple, stitched pattern on the back of each glove. Many *gloves of storing* are found with an item already inside.

Activate ◆ Interact; **Requirements** No item is stored in the gloves; **Effect** One item you're holding with a Bulk of 1 or less vanishes into the gloves' extradimensional space.

Activate ◆ Interact; **Requirements** An item is stored in the gloves, and you have a free hand; **Effect** The item stored in the gloves appears in your hand. The gloves can't be activated again for 1 minute.

GOGGLES OF NIGHT   ITEM 5+

INVESTED | MAGICAL | TRANSMUTATION
Usage worn eyepiece; **Bulk** –

The opaque crystal lenses of these sleek goggles do not

obscure vision, but rather enhance it. While wearing the goggles, you gain a +1 item bonus to Perception checks involving sight.

    Activate ❖ Interact; **Frequency** once per day; **Effect** Rotating the lenses 90 degrees, you gain darkvision for 1 hour.

Type *goggles of night*; **Level** 5; **Price** 150 gp

Type *greater goggles of night*; **Level** 11; **Price** 1,250 gp

The item bonus is +2, and the darkvision lasts until you rotate the lenses back or the item is no longer invested by you, whichever comes first.

Type *major goggles of night*; **Level** 18; **Price** 20,000 gp

The item bonus is +3, and the goggles grant greater darkvision, which lasts until you rotate the lenses back or the item is no longer invested by you, whichever comes first.

GORGET OF THE PRIMAL ROAR — ITEM 11

| ENCHANTMENT | INVESTED | MAGICAL |

Price 1,250 gp

Usage worn collar; **Bulk** L

This engraved darkwood gorget seems to vibrate with ferocity, granting you a +2 item bonus to Intimidation checks.

    Activate ❖ command; **Frequency** once during the duration of each polymorph effect; **Requirements** You're in a non-humanoid form via a polymorph effect; **Effect** You unleash a bestial roar, attempting a single Intimidation check compared to the Will DCs of all enemies within 30 feet to impose the effects below. Though this activation has the command component, you can issue this command without the need for language.

Critical Success The creature is frightened 2.

Success The creature is frightened 1.

Failure The creature is unaffected.

HAND OF THE MAGE — ITEM 2

| EVOCATION | INVESTED | MAGICAL |

Price 30 gp

Usage worn; **Bulk** L

This mummified elf hand hangs on a golden chain, its gnarled fingers locked in a peculiar pattern.

    Activate ❖❖ command, envision; **Effect** You cast *mage hand*.

HANDWRAPS OF MIGHTY BLOWS — ITEM 2+

| INVESTED | MAGICAL | TRANSMUTATION |

Usage worn gloves; **Bulk** —

As you invest these embroidered strips of cloth, you must meditate and slowly wrap them around your hands. These handwraps have weapon runes etched into them to give your unarmed attacks the benefits of those runes, making your unarmed attacks work like magic weapons. For example, *+1 striking handwraps of mighty blows* would give you a +1 item bonus to attack rolls with your unarmed attacks and increase the damage of your unarmed attacks from one weapon die to two (normally 2d4 instead of 1d4, but if your fists have a different weapon damage die or you have other unarmed attacks, use two of that die size instead).

    You can upgrade, add, and transfer runes to and from the handwraps just as you would for a weapon, and you can attach talismans to the handwraps. Treat the handwraps as melee weapons of the brawling group with light Bulk for these purposes. Property runes apply only when they would be applicable to the unarmed attack you're using. For example, a property that must be applied to a slashing weapon wouldn't function when you attacked with a fist, but you would gain its benefits if you attacked with a claw or some other slashing unarmed attack.

    The entries below list the most typical combinations of fundamental runes.

Type *+1 handwraps of mighty blows*; **Level** 2; **Price** 35 gp

Type *+1 striking handwraps of mighty blows*; **Level** 4; **Price** 100 gp

Type *+2 striking handwraps of mighty blows*; **Level** 10; **Price** 1,000 gp

Type *+2 greater striking handwraps of mighty blows*; **Level** 12; **Price** 2,000 gp

Type *+3 greater striking handwraps of mighty blows*; **Level** 16; **Price** 10,000 gp

Type *+3 major striking handwraps of mighty blows*; **Level** 19; **Price** 40,000 gp

HAT OF DISGUISE — ITEM 2+

| ILLUSION | INVESTED | MAGICAL |

Usage worn headwear; **Bulk** —

This ordinary-looking hat allows you to cloak yourself in illusions.

    Activate 1 minute (Interact); **Frequency** once per day; **Effect** The hat casts a 1st-level *illusory disguise* spell on you. While setting up the disguise, you can magically alter the hat to appear as a comb, ribbon, helm, or other piece of headwear.

Type *hat of disguise*; **Level** 2; **Price** 30 gp

Type *greater hat of disguise*; **Level** 7; **Price** 340 gp

You can activate the hat as a 2-action activity, you can activate it any number of times per day, and the *illusory disguise* is 2nd level.

HAT OF THE MAGI — ITEM 3+

| ARCANE | CONJURATION | INVESTED |

Usage worn headwear; **Bulk** —

This hat comes in many forms, such as a colorful turban or a pointy hat with a brim, and can bear symbols or runes. It grants you a +1 item bonus to Arcana checks and allows you to cast the *prestidigitation* cantrip as an arcane innate spell.

Type *hat of the magi*; **Level** 3; **Price** 50 gp

Type *greater hat of the magi*; **Level** 9; **Price** 650 gp

This larger, fancier hat grants a +2 bonus and can be activated.

    Activate ❖❖❖ Cast a Spell; **Frequency** once per day; **Effect** You cast a 4th-level arcane *summon elemental* spell.

day reduces the remaining raw material cost by an amount based on your level + 2 and your proficiency rank. If you are 20th level, on a critical success your progress is 50 gp, 100 gp, 200 gp, or 350 gp for trained, expert, master, or legendary proficiency, respectively.

Activate ❖❖ command, Interact; **Frequency** once per day; **Effect** You command the apparatus to magically jury-rig an item you hold or that's within 5 feet of you. The item is repaired, as a 3rd-level *mending* spell. This lasts for 10 minutes, after which the item returns to its previous state of disrepair unless you've Repaired it before then.

KNAPSACK OF HALFLINGKIND   ITEM 9+

UNCOMMON | CONJURATION | EXTRADIMENSIONAL | HEALING | INVESTED | MAGICAL
Usage worn backpack; **Bulk** L

This sturdy leather satchel contains three compartments fastened with large clasps. The first compartment is lined in blue satin and contains an extradimensional space equivalent to a *type II bag of holding*.

The second compartment has no lining. You can pull forth cookware and cooking utensils from it. Once they have been used to prepare a meal, the items transform into plates and silverware, and they evaporate once the meal has been eaten, taking any leftovers with them. The cookware reappears cleaned in the compartment 1 hour later. The compartment provides only kitchenware, not any food.

The third compartment is lined with plush purple velvet and contains berry tarts wrapped in parchment paper. A creature can unwrap and eat one tart with an Interact action to regain 2d8+4 Hit Points. The knapsack produces four tarts per day, which appear at breakfast time. Any tarts not eaten by the end of the day evaporate.

Type *knapsack of halflingkind*; **Level** 9; **Price** 675 gp

Type *greater knapsack of halflingkind*; **Level** 13; **Price** 2,850 gp

The berry tarts each restore 4d8+8 Hit Points, and the bag has two additional compartments, each of which can be Activated with an Interact action.

The fourth compartment is lined in golden velvet. Once per day, you can draw a lucky magic sling bullet from this compartment. If you attack with this sling bullet, you roll twice and use the better result on your attack roll and your damage roll. This is a fortune effect. The stone becomes non-magical if not hurled by the end of your turn. Once activated, this compartment stitches itself shut until the next day.

The bag's fifth compartment is lined in black wool. Once per day, you can unfold this compartment into a 5-foot-diameter portal on the ground. The first person to Step into the portal from an adjacent square is teleported away. This has the same effect as an 5th-level *dimension door* spell, except the affected creature takes the knapsack with them. When the portal is used, or at the start of your next turn if it hasn't been used,

HEALER'S GLOVES   ITEM 4+

INVESTED | MAGICAL | NECROMANCY
Usage worn gloves; **Bulk** L

These clean, white gloves never show signs of blood, even when used to stitch up wounds or treat other ailments. They give you a +1 item bonus to Medicine checks.

Activate ❖ Interact; **Frequency** once per day; **Effect** You can soothe a willing, adjacent creature's wounds, restoring 2d6+7 Hit Points to that creature. This is a positive healing effect. You can't harm undead with this healing.

Type *healer's gloves*; **Level** 4; **Price** 80 gp

Type *greater healer's gloves*; **Level** 9; **Price** 700 gp

The gloves provide a +2 bonus and restore 4d6+15 Hit Points.

INEXPLICABLE APPARATUS   ITEM 18

INVESTED | MAGICAL | TRANSMUTATION
Price 19,000 gp
Usage worn garment; **Bulk** 2

This strange and intricate harness fits snugly to the torso. Once you invest the apparatus, numerous artificial limbs with various tools, clamps, and lenses whirl into action, following your mental commands effortlessly.

When using this apparatus, you gain a +3 item bonus to Crafting checks to Craft, Earn Income, and Repair, and you reduce the minimum time required to Craft an item to 1 day. If you succeed at your Crafting check and spend more downtime to continue work on the item after the minimum number of days, each day you spend reduces the remaining raw material cost by an amount based on your level + 1 and your proficiency rank in Crafting; on a critical success, each the compartment closes automatically and can't be unfolded until the next day.

LIFTING BELT — ITEM 4

INVESTED MAGICAL TRANSMUTATION

Price 80 gp

Usage worn belt; **Bulk** L

This wide leather belt grants you a +1 item bonus to Athletics checks and increases the amount you can easily carry. You can carry Bulk equal to 6 + your Strength modifier before becoming encumbered, and you can hold and carry a total Bulk up to 11 + your Strength modifier.

Activate ◆◆ Interact; **Effect** You lift an object of up to 8 Bulk as though it were weightless. This requires two hands, and if the object is locked or otherwise held in place, you can attempt to Force it Open using Athletics as part of this activation. The object still has its full weight and Bulk for all other purposes—you just ignore that weight. The effect lasts until the end of your next turn.

MESSENGER'S RING — ITEM 9+

ENCHANTMENT INVESTED MAGICAL

Usage worn; **Bulk** —

This silver signet ring changes to match the insignia of a lord or organization you serve (or your own face, if you serve no one else). It grants you a +2 item bonus to Diplomacy checks and lets you cast *message* as an arcane innate spell at will.

Activate 1 minute (envision); **Frequency** once per day; **Effect** The ring casts *animal messenger* to your specification. The animal is a magical creature that springs from the ring, and its appearance suits the iconography or heraldry of the lord or organization represented by the ring.

Type *messenger's ring*; **Level** 9; **Price** 700 gp
Type *greater messenger's ring*; **Level** 17; **Price** 13,500 gp
The ring grants a +3 bonus and can be activated in an additional way.

Activate ◆◆◆ command; **Frequency** once per hour; **Effect** The ring casts *sending* to your specifications.

NECKLACE OF FIREBALLS — ITEM 5+

EVOCATION INVESTED MAGICAL

Usage worn; **Bulk** —

This string of beads appears to be a hemp string with lustrous red beads of various sizes hanging from it. When activated, it briefly appears in its true form: a golden chain with golden spheres attached by fine threads.

Numerous varieties of the *necklace of fireballs* exist. Each has a different basic Reflex save DC and includes a combination of spheres dealing different amounts of damage, as listed for each type below. When all the beads are gone, the necklace becomes a non-magical hemp string.

Activate ◆ Interact; **Effect** You detach a sphere from the necklace, causing it to glow with orange light. After you activate a sphere, if you or anyone else hurls it (an Interact action with the ranged trait), it detonates as a *fireball* where it lands. Your toss can place the center of the fireball anywhere within 70 feet, though at the GM's discretion you might need to make an attack roll if the throw is unusually challenging. If no one hurls the sphere by the start of your next turn, it turns into a non-magical red bead.

Type I; **Level** 5; **Price** 44 gp
One 6d6, two 4d6 (DC 21)

Type II; **Level** 7; **Price** 115 gp
One 8d6, one 6d6, two 4d6 (DC 25)

Type III; **Level** 9; **Price** 300 gp
One 10d6, two 8d6, two 6d6 (DC 27)

Type IV; **Level** 11; **Price** 700 gp
One 12d6, two 10d6, three 8d6 (DC 30)

Type V; **Level** 13; **Price** 1,600 gp
One 14d6, two 12d6, four 10d6 (DC 32)

Type VI; **Level** 15; **Price** 4,200 gp
One 16d6, three 14d6, four 12d6 (DC 36)

Type VII; **Level** 17; **Price** 9,600 gp
One 18d6, three 16d6, five 14d6 (DC 39)

PENDANT OF THE OCCULT — ITEM 3+

DIVINATION INVESTED OCCULT

Usage worn; **Bulk** —

This amulet is hollow and shaped in the form of an unblinking eye. Its cavity typically holds some fragment of occult text. While wearing the pendant, you gain a +1 item bonus to Occultism checks, and you can cast the *guidance* cantrip as an occult innate spell.

Type *pendant of the occult*; **Level** 3; **Price** 60 gp
Type *greater pendant of the occult*; **Level** 9; **Price** 650 gp
The pendant grants a +2 item bonus and can be activated.

Activate 10 minutes (Cast a Spell); **Frequency** once per day; **Effect** You cast a 4th-level *dream message* spell.

PERSONA MASK — ITEM 3+

FORTUNE ILLUSION INVESTED MAGICAL

Usage worn mask; **Bulk** —

Despite covering the entire face, this alabaster mask does not hinder vision or other senses. Wearing the mask grants a +1 item bonus to Performance checks while acting, orating, performing comedy, or singing.

Activate ◆ envision; **Effect** You change the mask's appearance into an artistic rendition of a dramatic character of your choice.

Type *persona mask*; **Level** 3; **Price** 50 gp
Type *greater persona mask*; **Level** 9; **Price** 650 gp
The mask grants a +2 bonus and can be activated.

Activate ⟳ envision (fortune); **Frequency** once per day; **Trigger** You fail a Performance check that benefits from the

INTRODUCTION

ANCESTRIES & BACKGROUNDS

CLASSES

SKILLS

FEATS

EQUIPMENT

SPELLS

THE AGE OF LOST OMENS

PLAYING THE GAME

GAME MASTERING

CRAFTING & TREASURE

APPENDIX

mask's bonus; **Effect** You change the mask's character and reroll the Performance check, using the second result.

PHYLACTERY OF FAITHFULNESS   ITEM 9+

DIVINATION   DIVINE   INVESTED

Usage worn circlet; **Bulk** L

This tiny box holds a fragment of religious scripture sacred to a particular deity. The box is worn by affixing it to a leather cord and tying it around your head just above your brow. You don't gain any benefit from the phylactery if you don't worship the affiliated deity. The phylactery grants you religious wisdom, which manifests as a +2 item bonus to Religion checks. Just before you perform an action that would be anathema to the phylactery's deity, the phylactery warns you of the potential transgression in time for you to change your mind.

   Activate ❖ envision; **Frequency** once per day; **Effect** You ask for guidance about a particular course of action, gaining the effects of an *augury* spell.

Type *phylactery of faithfulness*; **Level** 9; **Price** 680 gp

Type *greater phylactery of faithfulness*; **Level** 17; **Price** 13,000 gp

The phylactery grants a +3 item bonus, and you can activate it once every 30 minutes.

Craft Requirements You worship the phylactery's deity.

RING OF CLIMBING   ITEM 12

INVESTED   MAGICAL   TRANSMUTATION

Price 1,750 gp

Usage worn; **Bulk** —

Claw-like prongs on his thick golden band bears extend to dig deep into sheer surfaces when you are Climbing. This ring grants you a climb Speed equal to half your land Speed. Penalties to your Speed (including those from your armor) apply before halving.

RING OF COUNTERSPELLS   ITEM 10

UNCOMMON   ABJURATION   INVESTED   MAGICAL

Price 925 gp

Usage worn; **Bulk** —

This ornate silver ring bears two competing geometric designs of brightly colored and wildly clashing inlaid gemstones. A spellcaster can cast a single spell into this ring as long as no spell is currently stored within, expending the normal time, costs, and so forth to Cast the Spell. The spell's effect doesn't occur; the spell's power is instead stored within the ring.

   When you invest a *ring of counterspells*, you immediately know the name and level of the spell stored inside, if any. A *ring of counterspells* found as treasure has a 50% chance of having a spell stored in it. The GM determines that spell.

   Activate ↻ envision; **Trigger** You are targeted by or within the area of the spell stored within the ring; **Effect** You can attempt to counteract the triggering spell, using the level of the spell stored in the ring and a counteract modifier of +19.

Once you do, the stored spell's energy is spent, and the ring is empty.

   Activate ❖ command; **Effect** You harmlessly expend the stored spell, having no effect but emptying the ring so that another spell can be cast into it.

RING OF ENERGY RESISTANCE   ITEM 6+

ABJURATION   INVESTED   MAGICAL

Usage worn; **Bulk** —

This ring grants you resistance 5 against one type of energy damage: acid, cold, electricity, fire, or sonic. Each ring is crafted to protect against a particular type of energy damage, and its design usually embodies the type of energy it protects the wearer from in some way. For instance, a *ring of fire resistance* might be capped with a ruby, whereas a *ring of cold resistance* features a sapphire instead.

Type *ring of energy resistance*; **Level** 6; **Price** 245 gp

Type *greater ring of energy resistance*; **Level** 10; **Price** 975 gp
The ring grants resistance 10.

Type *major ring of energy resistance*; **Level** 14; **Price** 4,400 gp
The ring grants resistance 15.

RING OF LIES   ITEM 10

UNCOMMON   ENCHANTMENT   INVESTED   MAGICAL

Price 850 gp

Usage worn; **Bulk** —

This plain silver ring has an almost oily sheen. While wearing the ring, you gain a +2 item bonus to Deception checks.

   Activate ❖❖ Interact; **Effect** Snapping your fingers on the hand that wears the ring causes the ring to cast *glibness* on you with no visual manifestations of a spell being cast.

RING OF MANIACAL DEVICES   ITEM 11+

DIVINATION   INVESTED   MAGICAL

Usage worn; **Bulk** —

This ring seems like simple tarnished brass, but it enhances your curiosity about traps and devices of all kinds. You can use an Interact action to pull a set of thieves' tools from the ring. These tools appear in your hand and fold back into the ring if they would leave your possession. They grant you a +2 item bonus to Thievery checks to Disable a Device and to Pick a Lock, and the ring's insights grant you the same bonus to Crafting checks to Craft and Repair snares and traps.

   Activate 10 minutes (Interact); **Frequency** once per day; **Effect** You create a 4th-level *glyph of warding* containing *fireball*. You can have only one *glyph of warding* from a *ring of maniacal devices* active at a time, even if you have multiple rings, and the spell ends if you lose your investiture in the ring.

Type *ring of maniacal devices*; **Level** 11; **Price** 1,175 gp

Type *greater ring of maniacal devices*; **Level** 18; **Price** 4,250 gp
The ring grants a +3 bonus. Activating it creates an 8th-level *glyph of warding* containing your choice of either *prismatic spray* or 7th-level *fireball*.

RING OF SPELL TURNING — ITEM 20

RARE   ABJURATION   INVESTED   MAGICAL

Price 67,000 gp

Usage worn; **Bulk** —

This golden ring has three diamonds set into its face.

Activate ⟳ envision; **Trigger** You are targeted by a spell; **Effect** The ring replicates the effects of an 8th-level *spell turning* with a counteract modifier of +35, possibly causing the triggering spell to reflect back on its caster. The ring can reflect no more than 9 total levels of spells per day. If you activate the ring to reflect a spell that would exceed this limit, the attempt fails, but the attempted usage of the ring does not count toward the daily limit.

RING OF SUSTENANCE — ITEM 7

UNCOMMON   CONJURATION   INVESTED   MAGICAL

Price 325 gp

Usage worn; **Bulk** —

This polished wooden ring constantly refreshes your body and mind. You don't need to eat or drink while wearing it, and you need only 2 hours of sleep per day to gain the benefits of 8 hours of sleep. A *ring of sustenance* doesn't function until it's been worn and invested continuously for a week. Removing it resets this interval.

RING OF SWIMMING — ITEM 12

INVESTED   MAGICAL   TRANSMUTATION

Price 1,750 gp

Usage worn; **Bulk** —

This blue metal ring grants you a swim Speed equal to half your land Speed. Penalties to your Speed (including from your armor) apply before halving.

RING OF THE RAM — ITEM 6+

EVOCATION   FORCE   INVESTED   MAGICAL

Usage worn; **Bulk** —

This heavy iron ring is shaped to look like the head of a ram, with curling horns.

Activate ✦ or more (Interact); **Frequency** once per minute; **Effect** A ram-shaped blast of force slams into one foe that you can see within 60 feet. The number of actions you spend to Activate this Item (from 1 to 3) determines the intensity of the force. The blow deals 2d6 force damage per action spent and pushes the target 5 feet per action spent. The target must attempt a DC 22 Fortitude save.

Critical Success The target is unaffected.

Success The target takes half damage and is pushed half the distance.

Failure The target takes full damage and is pushed the full distance.

Critical Failure The target takes double damage and is pushed twice the distance.

Type *ring of the ram*; **Level** 6; **Price** 220 gp

Type *greater ring of the ram*; **Level** 13; **Price** 2,700 gp

The ring deals 3d6 force damage per action spent, and the save DC is 32. When you activate the ring using 3 actions, you can disperse the force into multiple magical rams, targeting all creatures in a 30-foot cone instead of one target within 60 feet.

RING OF WIZARDRY — ITEM 7+

UNCOMMON   ARCANE   DIVINATION   INVESTED

Usage worn; **Bulk** —

This ring is made from the purest platinum and is covered in esoteric arcane symbols. It does nothing unless you have a spellcasting class feature with the arcane tradition. While wearing the *ring of wizardry*, you gain a +1 item bonus to Arcana checks and have two additional 1st-level arcane spell slots each day. You prepare spells in these slots or cast from them spontaneously, just as you normally cast your spells.

If you take off the ring for any reason, you lose the additional spell slots. You can't gain spell slots from more than one *ring of wizardry* per day, nor can a single *ring of wizardry* grant spell slots more than once per day.

If you can cast arcane spells in a variety of different ways (such as if you are a draconic bloodline sorcerer with the wizard multiclass archetype), you can divide the spell slots as you wish among your various sources of arcane spells.

Type I; **Level** 7; **Price** 360 gp

Type II; **Level** 10; **Price** 1,000 gp

The bonus is +2, and the ring grants two 2nd-level spell slots and one 1st-level spell slot.

Type III; **Level** 12; **Price** 2,000 gp

The bonus is +2, and the ring grants two 3rd-level spell slots and one 2nd-level spell slot.

Type IV; **Level** 14; **Price** 4,500 gp

The bonus is +2, and the ring grants two 4th-level spell slots and one 3rd-level spell slot.

Craft Requirements You have a spellcasting class feature with the arcane tradition.

ROBE OF EYES — ITEM 17

UNCOMMON   DIVINATION   INVESTED   MAGICAL

Price 13,000 gp

Usage worn garment; **Bulk** 1

This garment appears to be an ordinary robe until donned, at which point numerous strange and alien eyes of varied shapes and colors open and blink across its fabric. While wearing the robe, you gain a +3 item bonus to Perception checks, and you constantly benefit from the effects of a 2nd-level *see invisibility* spell.

You can also see powerful magic auras. The highest-level magic aura within 30 feet of you glows in a color that reveals its school to you and allows you to determine where the effect originates. This can narrow down the origin point of the effect to a 5-foot-cube, but not more precisely than that.

INTRODUCTION

ANCESTRIES & BACKGROUNDS

CLASSES

SKILLS

FEATS

EQUIPMENT

SPELLS

THE AGE OF LOST OMENS

PLAYING THE GAME

GAME MASTERING

CRAFTING & TREASURE

APPENDIX

The *robe of eyes* is not without its dangers. If any spell with the light trait is cast on you or your square while you are wearing the robe, you are blinded for a number of rounds equal to the spell's level unless you succeed at a Fortitude save against the spell's DC.

Activate ❖ Interact; **Effect** You pluck an eye from the robe and toss it into the air, where it turns invisible and floats to a destination you choose, with the same effect as a 5th-level *prying eye* spell. You can Sustain the Activation just as you would be able to Sustain the Spell.

ROBE OF THE ARCHMAGI   ITEM 15+

`UNCOMMON` `ABJURATION` `ARCANE` `INVESTED`

Usage worn garment; **Bulk** 1

Embroidered with fine silver thread in ornate arcane patterns, these robes come in one of three colors depending on their attuned alignment. Good robes are white, neutral robes are gray, and evil robes are black. An evil or good robe gains the appropriate trait. The robes benefit only characters who can cast arcane spells and whose alignment on the good-evil axis matches that of the robe. If your alignment does not match that of the robe, or you are not an arcane spellcaster, you are instead stupefied 2 while wearing a *robe of the archmagi*. This condition can't be removed in any way until you remove the robe.

The robes are +2 *greater resilient explorer's clothing*, and they grant a +1 circumstance bonus to saving throws against arcane spells and resistance 5 to damage from arcane spells.

Activate ⟳ command; **Frequency** once per day; **Trigger** You attempt a saving throw against an arcane spell, but you haven't rolled yet; **Effect** You automatically succeed at your save against the triggering arcane spell.

Type *robe of the archmagi*; **Level** 15; **Price** 6,500 gp

Type *greater robe of the archmagi*; **Level** 19; **Price** 32,000 gp

The resistance against arcane spells is 10. You can activate the robe when you or an ally within 30 feet attempts a saving throw against an arcane spell, and the robe grants either you or the ally a success on the triggering saving throw; you still can activate it only once per day.

Craft Requirements You are an arcane spellcaster.

SLIPPERS OF SPIDER CLIMBING   ITEM 7

`INVESTED` `MAGICAL` `TRANSMUTATION`

Price 325 gp

Usage worn shoes; **Bulk** L

These soft slippers are made of fine gray silk. If the slippers

are left unattended for a while, they tend to attract spiders that nest inside.

Activate ❖ command; **Frequency** once per hour; **Effect** Tiny, hairlike tendrils extend from the slippers' soles, allowing you to walk on vertical surfaces or even to move upside down along ceilings. For 1 minute, you gain a 20-foot climb Speed and you don't need to use your hands to Climb. However, the slippers require decent traction for you to walk on a wall, so they provide no benefit when you're moving across greased, icy, or oiled surfaces.

THIRD EYE   ITEM 19

`DIVINATION` `INVESTED` `MAGICAL`

Price 40,000 gp

Usage worn; **Bulk** —

When invested, this ornate crown and its incandescent gemstone meld into your head and take the form of a tattoo. This grants you otherworldly sight and allows you to read auras. No one but you can manipulate the *third eye* while it's invested by you. Your heightened senses and ability to sense emotional auras grant you a +3 item bonus to Perception checks.

You continuously see magic auras, as a 9th-level *detect magic* spell, except you see the location of all auras within 30 feet, not just the strongest. If you use a Seek action to study a creature you can see, you can perceive an aura that conveys knowledge of that creature's health, including all conditions and afflictions it has and an approximate percentage of its remaining Hit Points.

Activate ❖❖ envision, command; **Frequency** once per day; **Effect** You gain the effects of an 8th-level *true seeing* spell.

TRACKER'S GOGGLES   ITEM 3+

`DIVINATION` `INVESTED` `MAGICAL`

Usage worn eyepiece; **Bulk**—

These lenses of forest-green glass are bound in rough leather stitched with crude twine. While wearing these goggles, you gain a +1 bonus to Survival checks to Sense Direction and Track. If you fail a check to Track, you can try again after 30 minutes rather than an hour.

Type *tracker's goggles*; **Level** 3; **Price** 60 gp

Type *greater tracker's goggles*; **Level** 9; **Price** 660 gp

The goggles grant a +2 bonus. If you fail a check to Track, you can try again after 15 minutes rather than an hour.

VENTRILOQUIST'S RING   ITEM 3+

ILLUSION   INVESTED   MAGICAL

Usage worn; **Bulk** —

This elegant copper ring has miniature images of songbirds engraved around its circumference. You gain a +1 item bonus to Deception checks.

Activate ⬦⬦ Interact; **Frequency** once per day; **Effect** Twisting the ring around your finger allows you to magically throw your voice, with the effects of a *ventriloquism* spell (DC 19).

Type *ventriloquist's ring*; **Level** 3; **Price** 60 gp

Type *greater ventriloquist's ring*; **Level** 9; **Price** 670 gp
The ring grants a +2 bonus. When you activate the ring, you gain the effects of 2nd-level *ventriloquism* (DC 27). You can activate the ring any number of times per day.

VOYAGER'S PACK   ITEM 17

UNCOMMON   CONJURATION   INVESTED   MAGICAL

Price 14,800 gp

Usage worn backpack; **Bulk** —

This leather rucksack has icons burned into it, and every time it's taken to a plane it hasn't been to before, a new icon representing that plane scorches into the surface. The pack grants you a +3 bonus to Survival checks. It also enables you to see the magical traces of creatures' passage, allowing you to Track a creature that has teleported. The GM sets the DC of this check, usually using the level and DC of the teleportation spell. This lets you find the location of the creature's destination, and you can use that destination when casting *teleport* or activating the pack, even though you don't know what it looks like.

The pack contains an extradimensional space with the same properties as a *type II bag of holding*. This space contains the contents of a climber's kit. If any components of that kit are removed and not returned, they return to the pack at dawn each day.

Activate 10 minutes (command, envision, Interact); **Effect** As you activate the pack, you can harness up to four willing creatures to the ropes on the pack. At the end of the activation time, the pack casts a 7th-level *plane shift* or *teleport* spell, transporting you and everyone attached to the pack. Attempt a DC 45 Survival check. On a success, you arrive 25 miles off target using *plane shift* or halve the distance you're off-target with *teleport*. On a critical success, you arrive exactly on target.

WAYFINDER   ITEM 2

UNCOMMON   EVOCATION   INVESTED   MAGICAL

Price 28 gp

Usage worn; **Bulk** —

This compact compass repurposes ancient technology to draw fantastic powers from the mysterious magical items called

aeon stones. It serves as a badge of office for agents of the Pathfinder Society and as a status symbol among adventurers of any stripe. A *wayfinder* functions as a compass.

An indentation in the middle of the *wayfinder* can hold a single *aeon stone* (page 604). Placing an *aeon stone* in this indentation provides you all the benefits of having the *aeon stone* orbiting your head, but it protects the stone from being noticed or stolen as easily. You invest a *wayfinder* and the *aeon stone* within it simultaneously, and they count as only one item toward your investiture limit. An invested *aeon stone* slotted in a *wayfinder* also grants its resonant power.

If you have more than one *wayfinder* with an invested *aeon stone* on your person at a given time, destructive interference from their resonance prevents you from gaining benefits from any of them. You can still benefit from additional *aeon stones* orbiting your head, just not in *wayfinders*.

Activate ⬦ command; **Effect** The *wayfinder* is targeted by a 1st-level *light* spell.

WHISPER OF THE FIRST LIE   ITEM 20

RARE   ENCHANTMENT   INVESTED   MAGICAL

Price 60,000 gp

Usage worn; **Bulk** —

This delicate necklace contains bottled whispers distilled from a source on the Astral Plane rumored to be connected to the first lie ever told. While wearing the necklace, you gain a +3 item bonus to Deception checks, and you can attempt to counteract effects that would force you to tell the truth or determine whether you are lying. Success on this counteract attempt lets you ignore the effect, rather than removing the effect entirely. The counteract level is 9, with a counteract modifier of +35.

Activate ⬦⬦⬦ Interact, envision, command; **Effect** You unstopper the vial and release the lie, creating the effect of a *fabricated truth* (DC 47). The vial is emptied and can never be activated again.

Craft Requirements Supply a casting of *fabricated truth*.

WINGED BOOTS   ITEM 10

INVESTED   MAGICAL   TRANSMUTATION

Price 850 gp

Usage worn shoes; **Bulk** L

Made from soft leather, with delicate white wings attached to the heel, these boots are ensorcelled with powerful air magic. Whenever you fall while wearing these boots, the boots automatically cast *feather fall* on you. This benefit can't trigger again for 10 minutes.

Activate ⬦⬦ command, Interact; **Frequency** once per day; **Effect** You speak a command word and click the boots' heels together to cause the wings to animate and flap rapidly, granting you a fly Speed of 30 feet for 10 minutes.

CONDITIONS APPENDIX

While adventuring, characters (and sometimes their belongings) are affected by abilities and effects that apply conditions. For example, a spell or magic item might turn you invisible or cause you to be gripped by fear. Conditions change your state of being in some way, and they represent everything from the attitude other creatures have toward you and how they interact with you to what happens when a creature drains your blood or life essence.

Conditions are persistent. Whenever you're affected by a condition, its effects last until the condition's stated duration ends, the condition is removed, or terms dictated in the condition itself cause it to end.

CONDITION VALUES

Some conditions have a numerical value, called a condition value, indicated by a numeral following the condition. This value conveys the severity of a condition, and such conditions often give you a bonus or penalty equal to their value. These values can often be reduced by skills, spells, or simply waiting. If a condition value is ever reduced to 0, the condition ends.

OVERRIDING CONDITIONS

Some conditions override others. This is always specified in the entry for the overriding condition. When this happens, all effects of the overridden condition are suppressed until the overriding condition ends. The overridden condition's duration continues to elapse, and it might run out while suppressed.

LIST OF CONDITIONS

BLINDED

You can't see. All normal terrain is difficult terrain to you. You can't detect anything using vision. You automatically critically fail Perception checks that require you to be able to see, and if vision is your only precise sense, you take a –4 status penalty to Perception checks. You are immune to visual effects. Blinded overrides dazzled.

BROKEN

Broken is a condition that affects objects. An object is broken when damage has reduced its Hit Points below its Broken Threshold. A broken object can't be used for its normal function, nor does it grant bonuses—with the exception of armor. Broken armor still grants its item bonus to AC, but it also imparts a status penalty to AC depending on its category: –1 for broken light armor, –2 for broken medium armor, or –3 for broken heavy armor.

A broken item still imposes penalties and limitations normally incurred by carrying, holding, or wearing it.

For example, broken armor would still impose its Dexterity modifier cap, check penalty, and so forth.

If an effect makes an item broken automatically and the item has more HP than its Broken Threshold, that effect also reduces the item's current HP to the Broken Threshold.

CLUMSY

Your movements become clumsy and inexact. Clumsy always includes a value. You take a status penalty equal to the condition value to Dexterity-based checks and DCs, including AC, Reflex saves, ranged attack rolls, and skill checks using Acrobatics, Stealth, and Thievery.

CONCEALED

While you are concealed from a creature, such as in a thick fog, you are difficult for that creature to see. You can still be observed, but you're tougher to target. A creature that you're concealed from must succeed at a DC 5 flat check when targeting you with an attack, spell, or other effect. Area effects aren't subject to this flat check. If the check fails, the attack, spell, or effect doesn't affect you.

CONFUSED

You don't have your wits about you, and you attack wildly. You are flat-footed, you don't treat anyone as your ally (though they might still treat you as theirs), and you can't Delay, Ready, or use reactions.

You use all your actions to Strike or cast offensive cantrips, though the GM can have you use other actions to facilitate attack, such as draw a weapon, move so that a target is in reach, and so forth. Your targets are determined randomly by the GM. If you have no other viable targets, you target yourself, automatically hitting but not scoring a critical hit. If it's impossible for you to attack or cast spells, you babble incoherently, wasting your actions.

Each time you take damage from an attack or spell, you can attempt a DC 11 flat check to recover from your confusion and end the condition.

CONTROLLED

Someone else is making your decisions for you, usually because you're being commanded or magically dominated. The controller dictates how you act and can make you use any of your actions, including attacks, reactions, or even Delay. The controller usually does not have to spend their own actions when controlling you.

DAZZLED

Your eyes are overstimulated. If vision is your only precise sense, all creatures and objects are concealed from you.

DEAFENED

You can't hear. You automatically critically fail Perception checks that require you to be able to hear. You take a –2 status penalty to Perception checks for initiative and checks that involve sound but also rely on other senses. If you perform an action with the auditory trait, you must succeed at a DC 5 flat check or the action is lost; attempt the check after spending the action but before any effects are applied. You are immune to auditory effects.

DOOMED

A powerful force has gripped your soul, calling you closer to death. Doomed always includes a value. The dying value at which you die is reduced by your doomed value. If your maximum dying value is reduced to 0, you instantly die. When you die, you're no longer doomed.

Your doomed value decreases by 1 each time you get a full night's rest.

DRAINED

When a creature successfully drains you of blood or life force, you become less healthy. Drained always includes a value. You take a status penalty equal to your drained value on Constitution-based checks, such as Fortitude saves. You also lose a number of Hit Points equal to your level (minimum 1) times the drained value, and your maximum Hit Points are reduced by the same amount. For example, if you're hit by an effect that inflicts drained 3 and you're a 3rd-level character, you lose 9 Hit Points and reduce your maximum Hit Points by 9. Losing these Hit Points doesn't count as taking damage.

Each time you get a full night's rest, your drained value decreases by 1. This increases your maximum Hit Points, but you don't immediately recover the lost Hit Points.

DYING

You are bleeding out or otherwise at death's door. While you have this condition, you are unconscious. Dying always includes a value, and if it ever reaches dying 4, you die. If you're dying, you must attempt a recovery check (page 459) at the start of your turn each round to determine whether you get better or worse. Your dying condition increases by 1 if you take damage while dying, or by 2 if you take damage from an enemy's critical hit or a critical failure on your save.

If you lose the dying condition by succeeding at a recovery check and are still at 0 Hit Points, you remain unconscious, but you can wake up as described in that condition. You lose the dying condition automatically and wake up if you ever have 1 Hit Point or more. Any time you lose the dying condition, you gain the wounded 1 condition, or increase your wounded condition value by 1 if you already have that condition.

GROUPS OF CONDITIONS

Some conditions exist relative to one another or share a similar theme. It can be useful to look at these conditions together, rather than viewing them in isolation, to understand how they interact.

Degrees of Detection: Observed, hidden, undetected, unnoticed

Senses: Blinded, concealed, dazzled, deafened, invisible

Death and Dying: Doomed, dying, unconscious, wounded

Attitudes: Hostile, unfriendly, indifferent, friendly, helpful

Lowered Abilities: Clumsy, drained, enfeebled, stupefied

DEATH AND DYING RULES

The doomed, dying, unconscious, and wounded conditions all relate to the process of coming closer to death. The full rules are on pages 459–461. The most significant information not contained in the conditions themselves is this: When you're reduced to 0 Hit Points, you're knocked out with the following effects:

- You immediately move your initiative position to directly before the creature or effect that reduced you to 0 Hit Points.
- You gain the dying 1 condition. If the effect that knocked you out was a critical success from the attacker or the result of your critical failure, you gain the dying 2 condition instead. If you have the wounded condition, increase these values by your wounded value. If the damage came from a nonlethal attack or effect, you don't gain the dying condition— you are instead unconscious with 0 Hit Points.

ENCUMBERED

You are carrying more weight than you can manage. While you're encumbered, you're clumsy 1 and take a 10-foot penalty to all your Speeds. As with all penalties to your Speed, this can't reduce your Speed below 5 feet.

ENFEEBLED

You're physically weakened. Enfeebled always includes a value. When you are enfeebled, you take a status penalty equal to the condition value to Strength-based rolls and DCs, including Strength-based melee attack rolls, Strength-based damage rolls, and Athletics checks.

FASCINATED

You are compelled to focus your attention on something, distracting you from whatever else is going on around you. You take a –2 status penalty to Perception and skill checks, and you can't use actions with the concentrate trait unless they or their intended consequences are related to the subject of your fascination (as determined by the GM). For instance, you might be able to Seek and Recall Knowledge about the subject, but you likely couldn't cast a spell targeting a different creature. This

INTRODUCTION

ANCESTRIES & BACKGROUNDS

CLASSES

SKILLS

FEATS

EQUIPMENT

SPELLS

THE AGE OF LOST OMENS

PLAYING THE GAME

GAME MASTERING

CRAFTING & TREASURE

APPENDIX

condition ends if a creature uses hostile actions against you or any of your allies.

FATIGUED

You're tired and can't summon much energy. You take a –1 status penalty to AC and saving throws. While exploring, you can't choose an exploration activity.

You recover from fatigue after a full night's rest.

FLAT-FOOTED

You're distracted or otherwise unable to focus your full attention on defense. You take a –2 circumstance penalty to AC. Some effects give you the flat-footed condition only to certain creatures or against certain attacks. Others—especially conditions—can make you universally flat-footed against everything. If a rule doesn't specify that the condition applies only to certain circumstances, it applies to all of them; for example, many effects simply say "The target is flat-footed."

FLEEING

You're forced to run away due to fear or some other compulsion. On your turn, you must spend each of your actions trying to escape the source of the fleeing condition as expediently as possible (such as by using move actions to flee, or opening doors barring your escape). The source is usually the effect or caster that gave you the condition, though some effects might define something else as the source. You can't Delay or Ready while fleeing.

FRIENDLY

This condition reflects a creature's disposition toward a particular character, and it affects only creatures that are not player characters. A creature that is friendly to a character likes that character. The character can attempt to make a Request of a friendly creature, and the friendly creature is likely to agree to a simple and safe request that doesn't cost it much to fulfill. If the character or one of their allies uses hostile actions against the creature, the creature gains a worse attitude condition depending on the severity of the hostile action, as determined by the GM.

FRIGHTENED

You're gripped by fear and struggle to control your nerves. The frightened condition always includes a value. You take a status penalty equal to this value to all your checks and DCs. Unless specified otherwise, at the end of each of your turns, the value of your frightened condition decreases by 1.

GRABBED

You're held in place by another creature, giving you the flat-footed and immobilized conditions. If you attempt a manipulate action while grabbed, you must succeed at a DC 5 flat check or it is lost; roll the check after spending the action, but before any effects are applied.

HELPFUL

This condition reflects a creature's disposition toward a particular character, and it affects only creatures that are not player characters. A creature that is helpful to a character wishes to actively aid that character. It will accept reasonable Requests from that character, as long as such requests aren't at the expense of the helpful creature's goals or quality of life. If the character or one of their allies uses a hostile action against the creature, the creature gains a worse attitude condition depending on the severity of the hostile action, as determined by the GM.

HIDDEN

While you're hidden from a creature, that creature knows the space you're in but can't tell precisely where you are. You typically become hidden by using Stealth to Hide. When Seeking a creature using only imprecise senses, it remains hidden, rather than observed. A creature you're hidden from is flat-footed to you, and it must succeed at a DC 11 flat check when targeting you with an attack, spell, or other effect or it fails affect you. Area effects aren't subject to this flat check.

A creature might be able to use the Seek action to try to observe you, as described on page 471.

HOSTILE

This condition reflects a creature's disposition toward a particular character, and it affects only creatures that are not player characters. A creature that is hostile to a character actively seeks to harm that character. It doesn't necessarily attack, but it won't accept Requests from the character.

IMMOBILIZED

You can't use any action with the move trait. If you're immobilized by something holding you in place and an external force would move you out of your space, the force must succeed at a check against either the DC of the effect holding you in place or the relevant defense (usually Fortitude DC) of the monster holding you in place.

INDIFFERENT

This condition reflects a creature's disposition toward a particular character, and it affects only creatures that are not player characters. A creature that is indifferent to a character doesn't really care one way or the other about that character. Assume a creature's attitude to a given character is indifferent unless specified otherwise.

INVISIBLE

While invisible, you can't be seen. You're undetected to everyone. Creatures can Seek to attempt to detect you; if a creature succeeds at its Perception check against your Stealth DC, you become hidden to that creature until you Sneak to become undetected again. If you become invisible while someone can already see you, you start out hidden to the observer (instead of undetected) until you successfully Sneak. You can't become observed while invisible except via special abilities or magic.

OBSERVED

Anything in plain view is observed by you. If a creature takes measures to avoid detection, such as by using Stealth to Hide, it can become hidden or undetected instead of observed. If you have another precise sense instead of or in addition to sight, you might be able to observe a creature or object using that sense instead. You can observe a creature only with precise senses. When Seeking a creature using only imprecise senses, it remains hidden, rather than observed.

PARALYZED

Your body is frozen in place. You have the flat-footed condition and can't act except to Recall Knowledge and use actions that require only the use of your mind (as determined by the GM). Your senses still function, but only in the areas you can perceive without moving your body, so you can't Seek while paralyzed.

PERSISTENT DAMAGE

Persistent damage comes from effects like acid, being on fire, or many other situations. It appears as "X persistent [type] damage," where "X" is the amount of damage dealt and "[type]" is the damage type. Instead of taking persistent damage immediately, you take it at the end of each of your turns as long as you have the condition, rolling any damage dice anew each time. After you take persistent damage, roll a DC 15 flat check to see if you recover from the persistent damage. If you succeed, the condition ends.

PETRIFIED

You have been turned to stone. You can't act, nor can you sense anything. You become an object with a Bulk double your normal Bulk (typically 12 for a petrified Medium creature or 6 for a petrified Small creature), AC 9, Hardness 8, and the same current Hit Points you had when alive. You don't have a Broken Threshold. When you're turned back into flesh, you have the same number of Hit Points you had as a statue. If the statue is destroyed, you immediately die. While petrified, your mind and body are in stasis, so you don't age or notice the passing of time.

PRONE

You're lying on the ground. You are flat-footed and take a –2 circumstance penalty to attack rolls. The only move actions you can use while you're prone are Crawl and Stand. Standing up ends the prone condition. You can Take Cover while prone to hunker down and gain cover against ranged attacks, even if you don't have an object to get behind, gaining a +4 circumstance bonus to AC against ranged attacks (but you remain flat-footed).

If you would be knocked prone while you're Climbing or Flying, you fall (see pages 463–464 for the rules on falling). You can't be knocked prone when Swimming.

PERSISTENT DAMAGE RULES

The additional rules presented below apply to persistent damage in certain cases.

Assisted Recovery

You can take steps to help yourself recover from persistent damage, or an ally can help you, allowing you to attempt an additional flat check before the end of your turn. This is usually an activity requiring 2 actions, and it must be something that would reasonably improve your chances (as determined by the GM). For example, you might try to smother a flame, wash off acid, or use Medicine to Administer First Aid to stanch bleeding. This allows you to attempt an extra flat check immediately.

The GM decides how your help works, using the following examples as guidelines.

- Reduce the DC of the flat check to 10 for a particularly appropriate type of help, such as dousing you in water to put out flames.
- Automatically end the condition due to the type of help, such as healing that restores you to your maximum HP to end persistent bleed damage, or submerging yourself in a lake to end persistent fire damage.
- Alter the number of actions required to help you if the means the helper uses are especially efficient or remarkably inefficient.

Persistent damage runs its course and automatically ends after a certain amount of time as fire burns out, blood clots, and the like. The GM determines when this occurs, but it usually takes 1 minute.

Immunities, Resistances, and Weaknesses

Immunities, resistances, and weaknesses all apply to persistent damage. If an effect deals initial damage in addition to persistent damage, apply immunities, resistances, and weaknesses separately to the initial damage and to the persistent damage. Usually, if an effect negates the initial damage, it also negates the persistent damage, such as with a slashing weapon that also deals persistent bleed damage because it cut you. The GM might rule otherwise in some situations.

Multiple Persistent Damage Conditions

You can be simultaneously affected by multiple persistent damage conditions so long as they have different damage types. If you would gain more than one persistent damage condition with the same damage type, the higher amount of damage overrides the lower amount. The damage you take from persistent damage occurs all at once, so if something triggers when you take damage, it triggers only once; for example, if you're dying with several types of persistent damage, the persistent damage increases your dying condition only once.

GAINING AND LOSING ACTIONS

Quickened, slowed, and stunned are the primary ways you can gain or lose actions on a turn. The rules for how this works appear on page 462. In brief, these conditions alter how many actions you regain at the start of your turn; thus, gaining the condition in the middle of your turn doesn't adjust your number of actions on that turn. If you have conflicting conditions that affect your number of actions, you choose which actions you lose. For instance, the action gained from *haste* lets you only Stride or Strike, so if you need to lose one action because you're also slowed, you might decide to lose the action from *haste*, letting you keep your other actions that can be used more flexibly.

Some conditions prevent you from taking a certain subset of actions, typically reactions. Other conditions simply say you can't act. When you can't act, you're unable to take any actions at all. Unlike slowed or stunned, these don't change the number of actions you regain; they just prevent you from using them. That means if you are somehow cured of paralysis on your turn, you can act immediately.

QUICKENED

You gain 1 additional action at the start of your turn each round. Many effects that make you quickened specify the types of actions you can use with this additional action. If you become quickened from multiple sources, you can use the extra action you've been granted for any single action allowed by any of the effects that made you quickened. Because quickened has its effect at the start of your turn, you don't immediately gain actions if you become quickened during your turn.

RESTRAINED

You're tied up and can barely move, or a creature has you pinned. You have the flat-footed and immobilized conditions, and you can't use any actions with the attack or manipulate traits except to attempt to Escape or Force Open your bonds. Restrained overrides grabbed.

SICKENED

You feel ill. Sickened always includes a value. You take a status penalty equal to this value on all your checks and DCs. You can't willingly ingest anything—including elixirs and potions—while sickened.

You can spend a single action retching in an attempt to recover, which lets you immediately attempt a Fortitude save against the DC of the effect that made you sickened. On a success, you reduce your sickened value by 1 (or by 2 on a critical success).

SLOWED

You have fewer actions. Slowed always includes a value. When you regain your actions at the start of your turn, reduce the number of actions you regain by your slowed value. Because slowed has its effect at the start of your turn, you don't immediately lose actions if you become slowed during your turn.

STUNNED

You've become senseless. You can't act while stunned. Stunned usually includes a value, which indicates how many total actions you lose, possibly over multiple turns, from being stunned. Each time you regain actions (such as at the start of your turn), reduce the number you regain by your stunned value, then reduce your stunned value by the number of actions you lost. For example, if you were stunned 4, you would lose all 3 of your actions on your turn, reducing you to stunned 1; on your next turn, you would lose 1 more action, and then be able to use your remaining 2 actions normally. Stunned might also have a duration instead of a value, such as "stunned for 1 minute." In this case, you lose all your actions for the listed duration.

Stunned overrides slowed. If the duration of your stunned condition ends while you are slowed, you count the actions lost to the stunned condition toward those lost to being slowed. So, if you were stunned 1 and slowed 2 at the beginning of your turn, you would lose 1 action from stunned, and then lose only 1 additional action by being slowed, so you would still have 1 action remaining to use that turn.

STUPEFIED

Your thoughts and instincts are clouded. Stupefied always includes a value. You take a status penalty equal to this value on Intelligence-, Wisdom-, and Charisma-based checks and DCs, including Will saving throws, spell attack rolls, spell DCs, and skill checks that use these ability scores. Any time you attempt to Cast a Spell while stupefied, the spell is disrupted unless you succeed at a flat check with a DC equal to 5 + your stupefied value.

UNCONSCIOUS

You're sleeping, or you've been knocked out. You can't act. You take a –4 status penalty to AC, Perception, and Reflex saves, and you have the blinded and flat-footed conditions. When you gain this condition, you fall prone and drop items you are wielding or holding unless the effect states otherwise or the GM determines you're in a position in which you wouldn't.

If you're unconscious because you're dying, you can't wake up while you have 0 Hit Points. If you are restored to 1 Hit Point or more via healing, you lose the dying and unconscious conditions and can act normally on your next turn.

If you are unconscious and at 0 Hit Points, but not dying, you naturally return to 1 Hit Point and awaken after sufficient time passes. The GM determines how long you remain unconscious, from a minimum of 10 minutes to several hours. If you receive healing during this time, you lose the unconscious condition and can act normally on your next turn.

If you're unconscious and have more than 1 Hit Point (typically because you are asleep or unconscious due to an effect), you wake up in one of the following ways. Each causes you to lose the unconscious condition.

- You take damage, provided the damage doesn't reduce you to 0 Hit Points. If the damage reduces you to 0 Hit Points, you remain unconscious and gain the dying condition as normal.
- You receive healing, other than the natural healing you get from resting.
- Someone shakes you awake with an Interact action.
- There's loud noise going on around you—though this isn't automatic. At the start of your turn, you automatically attempt a Perception check against the noise's DC (or the lowest DC if there is more than one noise), waking up if you succeed. If creatures are attempting to stay quiet around you, this Perception check uses their Stealth DCs. Some magical effects make you sleep so deeply that they don't allow you to attempt this Perception check.
- If you are simply asleep, the GM decides you wake up either because you have had a restful night's sleep or something disrupted that rest.

UNDETECTED

When you are undetected by a creature, that creature cannot see you at all, has no idea what space you occupy, and can't target you, though you still can be affected by abilities that target an area. When you're undetected by a creature, that creature is flat-footed to you.

A creature you're undetected by can guess which square you're in to try targeting you. It must pick a square and attempt an attack. This works like targeting a hidden creature (requiring a DC 11 flat check, as described on page 466), but the flat check and attack roll are rolled in secret by the GM, who doesn't reveal whether the attack missed due to failing the flat check, failing the attack roll, or choosing the wrong square.

A creature can use the Seek action to try to find you, as described on page 471.

UNFRIENDLY

This condition reflects a creature's disposition toward a particular character, and it affects only creatures that are not player characters. A creature that is unfriendly to a character dislikes and specifically distrusts that character. The unfriendly creature won't accept Requests from the character.

UNNOTICED

If you are unnoticed by a creature, that creature has no idea you are present at all. When you're unnoticed, you're also undetected by the creature. This condition matters

REDUNDANT CONDITIONS

You can have a given condition only once at a time. If an effect would impose a condition you already have, you now have that condition for the longer of the two durations. The shorter-duration condition effectively ends, though other conditions caused by the original, shorter-duration effect might continue.

For example, let's say you have been hit by a monster that drains your vitality; your wound causes you to be enfeebled 2 and flat-footed until the end of the monster's next turn. Before the end of that creature's next turn, a trap poisons you, making you enfeebled 2 for 1 minute. In this case, the enfeebled 2 that lasts for 1 minute replaces the enfeebled 2 from the monster, so you would be enfeebled 2 for the longer duration. You would remain flat-footed, since nothing replaced that condition, and it still lasts only until the end of the monster's next turn.

Any ability that removes a condition removes it entirely, no matter what its condition value is or how many times you've been affected by it. In the example above, a spell that removes the enfeebled condition from you would remove it entirely—the spell wouldn't need to remove it twice.

Redundant Conditions with Values

Conditions with different values are considered different conditions. If you're affected by a condition with a value multiple times, you apply only the highest value, although you might have to track both durations if one has a lower value but lasts longer. For example, if you had a slowed 2 condition that lasts 1 round and a slowed 1 condition that lasts for 6 rounds, you'd be slowed 2 for the first round, and then you'd change to slowed 1 for the remaining 5 rounds of the second effect's duration. If something reduces the condition value, it reduces it for all conditions of that name affecting you. For instance, in this example above, if something reduced your slowed value by 1, it would reduce the first condition from the example to slowed 1 and reduce the second to slowed 0, removing it.

for abilities that can be used only against targets totally unaware of your presence.

WOUNDED

You have been seriously injured. If you lose the dying condition and do not already have the wounded condition, you become wounded 1. If you already have the wounded condition when you lose the dying condition, your wounded condition value increases by 1. If you gain the dying condition while wounded, increase your dying condition value by your wounded value.

The wounded condition ends if someone successfully restores Hit Points to you with Treat Wounds, or if you are restored to full Hit Points and rest for 10 minutes.

INTRODUCTION

ANCESTRIES & BACKGROUNDS

CLASSES

SKILLS

FEATS

EQUIPMENT

SPELLS

THE AGE OF LOST OMENS

PLAYING THE GAME

GAME MASTERING

CRAFTING & TREASURE

APPENDIX

PATHFINDER
CHARACTER SHEET

PROFICIENCY
Untrained +0
Trained 2+Level
Expert 4+Level
Master 6+Level
Legendary 8+Level

❖ Single Action
❖❖ Two-Action Activity
❖❖❖ Three-Action Activity
◇ Free Action
↻ Reaction

CHARACTER NAME

PLAYER NAME

EXPERIENCE POINTS (XP)

ANCESTRY AND HERITAGE

BACKGROUND

CLASS

SIZE | ALIGNMENT | TRAITS

DEITY

LEVEL

HERO POINTS

ABILITY SCORES

STR MODIFIER — STRENGTH SCORE
DEX MODIFIER — DEXTERITY SCORE
CON MODIFIER — CONSTITUTION SCORE
INT MODIFIER — INTELLIGENCE SCORE
WIS MODIFIER — WISDOM SCORE
CHA MODIFIER — CHARISMA SCORE

CLASS DC

= 10 DC BASE | KEY | PROF | T E M L | ITEM

ARMOR CLASS

AC = 10 DC BASE | DEX OR | CAP | PROF | T E M L | ITEM

UNARMORED T E M L | LIGHT T E M L | MEDIUM T E M L | HEAVY T E M L

Shield + | HARDNESS | MAX HP | BT | CURRENT HP

SAVING THROWS

FORTITUDE	REFLEX	WILL
CON	PROF	DEX	PROF	WIS	PROF
ITEM	T E M L	ITEM	T E M L	ITEM	T E M L

NOTES

HIT POINTS

MAX | CURRENT | TEMPORARY

DYING | WOUNDED

RESISTANCES AND IMMUNITIES

CONDITIONS

PERCEPTION

WIS | PROF | T E M L | ITEM

SENSES

SPEED ____ FEET

MOVEMENT TYPES & NOTES

MELEE STRIKES

WEAPON — = STR | PROF | T E M L | ITEM
DAMAGE — DICE | STR | B P S | W SPEC | OTHER | TRAITS

WEAPON — = STR | PROF | T E M L | ITEM
DAMAGE — DICE | STR | B P S | W SPEC | OTHER | TRAITS

WEAPON — = STR | PROF | T E M L | ITEM
DAMAGE — DICE | STR | B P S | W SPEC | OTHER | TRAITS

RANGED STRIKES

WEAPON — = DEX | PROF | T E M L | ITEM
DAMAGE — DICE | SPECIAL | B P S | W SPEC | OTHER | TRAITS

WEAPON — = DEX | PROF | T E M L | ITEM
DAMAGE — DICE | SPECIAL | B P S | W SPEC | OTHER | TRAITS

WEAPON — = DEX | PROF | T E M L | ITEM
DAMAGE — DICE | SPECIAL | B P S | W SPEC | OTHER | TRAITS

WEAPON PROFICIENCIES

SIMPLE T E M L | MARTIAL T E M L | OTHER T E M L | OTHER T E M L

SKILLS

Skill		Ability	PROF	T E M L	ITEM	ARMOR
ACROBATICS	=	DEX	PROF	T E M L	ITEM	-
ARCANA	=	INT	PROF	T E M L	ITEM	
ATHLETICS	=	STR	PROF	T E M L	ITEM	-
CRAFTING	=	INT	PROF	T E M L	ITEM	
DECEPTION	=	CHA	PROF	T E M L	ITEM	
DIPLOMACY	=	CHA	PROF	T E M L	ITEM	
INTIMIDATION	=	CHA	PROF	T E M L	ITEM	
LORE	=	INT	PROF	T E M L	ITEM	
LORE	=	INT	PROF	T E M L	ITEM	
MEDICINE	=	WIS	PROF	T E M L	ITEM	
NATURE	=	WIS	PROF	T E M L	ITEM	
OCCULTISM	=	INT	PROF	T E M L	ITEM	
PERFORMANCE	=	CHA	PROF	T E M L	ITEM	
RELIGION	=	WIS	PROF	T E M L	ITEM	
SOCIETY	=	INT	PROF	T E M L	ITEM	
STEALTH	=	DEX	PROF	T E M L	ITEM	-
SURVIVAL	=	WIS	PROF	T E M L	ITEM	
THIEVERY	=	DEX	PROF	T E M L	ITEM	-

LANGUAGES

ANCESTRY FEATS AND ABILITIES

	SPECIAL 1ST
	HERITAGE 1ST
	FEAT 1ST
	FEAT 5TH
	FEAT 9TH
	FEAT 13TH
	FEAT 17TH

SKILL FEATS

	BACKGROUND
	2ND
	4TH
	6TH
	8TH
	10TH
	12TH
	14TH
	16TH
	18TH
	20TH

GENERAL FEATS

	3RD
	7TH
	11TH
	15TH
	19TH

CLASS FEATS AND ABILITIES

	FEATURE 1ST
	FEATURE 1ST
	FEAT 1ST
	FEAT 2ND
	FEATURE 3RD
	FEAT 4TH
	FEATURE 5TH
	FEAT 6TH
	FEATURE 7TH
	FEAT 8TH
	FEATURE 9TH
	FEAT 10TH
	FEATURE 11TH
	FEAT 12TH
	FEATURE 13TH
	FEAT 14TH
	FEATURE 15TH
	FEAT 16TH
	FEATURE 17TH
	FEAT 18TH
	FEATURE 19TH
	FEAT 20TH

BONUS FEATS

INVENTORY

WORN ITEMS	INVEST (MAX 10)	BULK

READIED ITEMS	BULK

OTHER ITEMS	BULK

BULK

ENCUMBERED
BASE = 5   STR

MAXIMUM
BASE = 10   STR

CP   SP   GP   PP

CHARACTER SKETCH

ETHNICITY	NATIONALITY	BIRTHPLACE	AGE	GENDER & PRONOUNS	HT	WT

APPEARANCE

PERSONALITY

ATTITUDE

BELIEFS

LIKES

DISLIKES

CATCHPHRASES

CAMPAIGN NOTES

NOTES

ALLIES

ENEMIES

ORGANIZATIONS

ACTIONS AND ACTIVITIES

NAME	ACTIONS	TRAITS	PAGE
DESCRIPTION

NAME	ACTIONS	TRAITS	PAGE
DESCRIPTION

NAME	ACTIONS	TRAITS	PAGE
DESCRIPTION

NAME	ACTIONS	TRAITS	PAGE
DESCRIPTION

NAME	ACTIONS	TRAITS	PAGE
DESCRIPTION

NAME	ACTIONS	TRAITS	PAGE
DESCRIPTION

FREE ACTIONS AND REACTIONS

NAME	☐ FREE ACTION ☐ REACTION	TRAITS	PAGE
TRIGGER
DESCRIPTION

NAME	☐ FREE ACTION ☐ REACTION	TRAITS	PAGE
TRIGGER
DESCRIPTION

NAME	☐ FREE ACTION ☐ REACTION	TRAITS	PAGE
TRIGGER
DESCRIPTION

NAME	☐ FREE ACTION ☐ REACTION	TRAITS	PAGE
TRIGGER
DESCRIPTION

SPELL ATTACK ROLL

◯ = | KEY | PROF | T E M L |

SPELL DC

◯ = DC BASE 10 | KEY | PROF | T E M L |

MAGIC TRADITIONS

ARCANE   OCCULT

PRIMAL   DIVINE

☐ PREPARED   ☐ SPONTANEOUS

CANTRIPS

	PREP
	ACTIONS
	☐M ☐S ☐V

	PREP
	ACTIONS
	☐M ☐S ☐V

	PREP
	ACTIONS
	☐M ☐S ☐V

	PREP
	ACTIONS
	☐M ☐S ☐V

	PREP
	ACTIONS
	☐M ☐S ☐V

	PREP
	ACTIONS
	☐M ☐S ☐V

	PREP
	ACTIONS
	☐M ☐S ☐V

INNATE SPELLS

	FREQ
	ACTIONS
	☐M ☐S ☐V

	FREQ
	ACTIONS
	☐M ☐S ☐V

FOCUS SPELLS

FOCUS POINTS | CURRENT | MAXIMUM |

| | ACTIONS |
| | ☐M ☐S ☐V |

| | ACTIONS |
| | ☐M ☐S ☐V |

| | ACTIONS |
| | ☐M ☐S ☐V |

| | ACTIONS |
| | ☐M ☐S ☐V |

SPELL SLOTS PER DAY

CANTRIP LEVEL

| 1 | 2 | 3 | 4 | 5 | 6 | 7 | 8 | 9 | 10 |

SPONTANEOUS SPELL SLOTS REMAINING

SPELLS

	PREP
	ACTIONS
	☐M ☐S ☐V

	PREP
	ACTIONS
	☐M ☐S ☐V

	PREP
	ACTIONS
	☐M ☐S ☐V

	PREP
	ACTIONS
	☐M ☐S ☐V

	PREP
	ACTIONS
	☐M ☐S ☐V

	PREP
	ACTIONS
	☐M ☐S ☐V

	PREP
	ACTIONS
	☐M ☐S ☐V

	PREP
	ACTIONS
	☐M ☐S ☐V

	PREP
	ACTIONS
	☐M ☐S ☐V

	PREP
	ACTIONS
	☐M ☐S ☐V

	PREP
	ACTIONS
	☐M ☐S ☐V

	PREP
	ACTIONS
	☐M ☐S ☐V

	PREP
	ACTIONS
	☐M ☐S ☐V

GLOSSARY AND INDEX

This appendix contains page references for essential rules of the game, full definitions for most traits, and partial definitions and calculations for many other rules.

INTRODUCTION

ANCESTRIES & BACKGROUNDS

CLASSES

SKILLS

FEATS

EQUIPMENT

SPELLS

THE AGE OF LOST OMENS

PLAYING THE GAME

GAME MASTERING

CRAFTING & TREASURE

APPENDIX

disbelieve Attempt to ignore an illusion. 298

disease (trait) An effect with this trait applies one or more diseases. A disease is typically an affliction. 457–458

Dismiss ❖ (action) End a spell or magic item effect that can be dismissed. 305, 534

dispel *See also* counteract. 305, 458–459

disrupting actions 462–463

  disrupting item activations 532

  disrupting spells 303

divination (trait) The divination school of magic typically involves obtaining or transferring information, or predicting events. 297

divine (trait) This magic comes from the divine tradition, drawing power from deities or similar sources. Anything with this trait is magical. 299

  divine spell list 309–311

domain 441

doomed (condition) Your soul is in peril, bringing you closer to death. 619

downtime A mode of play in which characters are not adventuring. Days pass quickly at the table, and characters engage in long-term activities. 12, **481**

  downtime activities 461–462, 481

  running downtime (GM) 500–502

downtime (trait) An activity with this trait takes a day or more, and can be used only during downtime. 17, 234

dragon (trait) Dragons are reptilian creatures, often winged or with the power of flight. Most are able to use a breath weapon and are immune to sleep and paralysis. 433

dragonhide (material) 579

drained (condition) Blood loss or a similar effect has leeched your vitality. 619

draw an item *See also* Interact. 271, 273

Drop Prone ❖ (basic action) Fall flat on the ground. 470, 621

drop an item *See also* Release. 271, 273

drow (trait) Subterranean kin of the elves, drow typically have darkvision and inborn magical abilities.

drowning and suffocation 478

druid (class) 128–139

  multiclass archetype 225

  order spells 399–401

  primal spell list 314–315

druid (trait) This indicates abilities from the druid class.

duergar (trait) Subterranean kin of the dwarves, duergar typically have darkvision and immunity to poison. They are not easily fooled by illusions.

duration 455

  spell durations 304–305

dwarf (trait) A creature with this trait is a member of the dwarf ancestry. Dwarves are stout folk who often live underground and typically have darkvision. An ability with this trait can be used or selected only by dwarves. An item with this trait is created and used by dwarves. 34–37, 431

dying (condition) You have been reduced to 0 HP and are nearing death. 619

  death and dying rules 459–461

Earn Income (skill action) Make money using a skill during downtime. (Crafting, Lore, Performance; trained) 236–238

  GM advice 504–505

earth (trait) Effects with the earth trait either manipulate or conjure earth. Those that manipulate earth have no effect in an area without earth. Creatures with this trait consist primarily of earth or have a magical connection to that element.

effect An effect is the result of an ability, though an ability's exact effect is sometimes contingent on the result of a check or other roll. 453–457

electricity (damage type) 452

electricity (trait) Effects with this trait deal electricity damage. A creature with this trait has a magical connection to electricity.

elemental (trait) Elementals are creatures directly tied to an element and native to the Elemental Planes. Elementals don't need to breathe.

elf (trait) A creature with this trait is a member of the elf ancestry. Elves are mysterious people with rich traditions of magic and scholarship who typically have low-light vision. An ability with this trait can be used or selected only by elves. A weapon with this trait is created and used by elves. 38–41, 431–432

  half-elf 55, 56, 58–59

elixir (trait) Elixirs are alchemical liquids that are used by drinking them. 546–550

emanation (area) 457

emotion (trait) This effect alters a creature's emotions. Effects with this trait always have the mental trait as well. Creatures with special training or that have mechanical or artificial intelligence are immune to emotion effects.

enchantment (trait) Effects and magic items with this trait are associated with the enchantment school of magic, typically involving mind control, emotion alteration, and other mental effects. 297

encounter A mode of play in which time is measured in 6-second rounds and participants use precise actions. Combat takes place in encounters. 10–12, **468–478**

  building encounters (GM) 488–489

  initiative 468

  running encounters (GM) 493–496

  social encounters (GM) 494–496

  special battles (aerial, aquatic, mounted) 478

encumbered (condition) Too much Bulk impedes your movement. 619

energy (damage type) An umbrella category including acid, cold, electricity, fire, force, negative, positive, and sonic damage. 452

enfeebled (condition) Your strength has been sapped away. 619

environment 512–519

environmental (trait) A hazard with this trait is something dangerous that's part of the natural world, such as quicksand or harmful mold.

envision (item activation component) 533

equipment *See also* items. 27, 270–295

Escape ❖ (basic action) Attempt to get free when grabbed, restrained or immobilized. 470

ethereal (trait) Ethereal creatures are natives of the Ethereal Plane. They can survive the basic environmental effects of the Ethereal Plane.

ethnicities of Golarion 55, 430–431

evil (damage type) 452

evil (trait) Evil effects often manipulate energy from evil-aligned Outer Planes and are antithetical to good divine servants or divine servants of good deities. A creature with this trait is evil in alignment. An ability with this trait can be selected or used only by evil creatures.

evocation (trait) Effects and magic items with this trait are associated with the evocation school of magic, typically involving energy and elemental forces. 298

Experience Points (XP) Points that measure a player character's progress, accrued during play. Typically a PC gains a new level upon reaching 1,000 XP. 8

  encounter budget (GM) 489

  leveling up 31

  XP awards (GM) 507–508

expert (proficiency rank) Add your level + 4 to associated rolls and DCs. 13, 444

exploration A mode of play used for traveling, investigating, and otherwise exploring. The GM determines the flow of time. 10, **479–480**

  exploration activities 461, **479–480**

  running exploration (GM) 496–500

exploration (trait) An activity with this trait takes more than a turn to use, and can usually be used only during exploration mode. 17, 234

extradimensional (trait) This effect or item creates an extradimensional space. An extradimensional effect placed inside another extradimensional space ceases to function until it is removed.

failure A result on a check that fails to meet the DC. Failing by 10 or more is a critical failure. If a check has no failure entry, nothing happens on a failure. 445–446

falling When you fall more than 5 feet, you take bludgeoning damage equal to half the distance you fell and land prone. 463–464

familiar A Tiny creature mystically bonded to you. 217–218

fascinated (condition) You must focus on one subject of your fascination. 619–620

fatal (weapon trait) 282

fatigued (condition) Your defenses are lower, and you can't focus while exploring. 620

fear (trait) Fear effects evoke the emotion of fear. Effects with this trait always have the mental and emotion traits as well.

feat An ability you gain or select for your character due to their ancestry, background, class, general training, or skill training. Some feats grant special actions. 12, 18

  ancestry feat 33

  archetype feat 219

  class feat 68

  general feat 68, **255**

  skill feat (general feat that improves skills) 68, **255**

Feint ❖ (skill action) Misdirect someone to make them flat-footed. (Deception, trained) 246

fey (trait) Creatures of the First World are called the fey.

fiend (trait) Creatures that hail from or have a strong connection to the evil-aligned planes are called fiends. Fiends can survive the basic environmental effects of planes in the Outer Sphere.

fighter (class) 140-153

multiclass archetype 226

fighter (trait) This indicates abilities from the fighter class.

finesse (weapon trait) 282

fire (damage type) 452

fire (trait) Effects with the fire trait deal fire damage or either conjure or manipulate fire. Those that manipulate fire have no effect in an area without fire. Creatures with this trait consist primarily of fire or have a magical connection to that element.

flank When two creatures are on opposite sides of their enemy, the enemy is flanked, becoming flat-footed to those creatures. 476

flat check A d20 roll that measures pure chance. A flat check can't have any modifiers, bonuses, or penalties applied to it. 450

flat-footed (condition) You take a –2 circumstance penalty to AC. 620

fleeing (condition) You must run away. 620

flexible (armor trait) 275

flourish (trait) Flourish actions are actions that require too much exertion to perform a large number in a row. You can use only 1 action with the flourish trait per turn.

Fly ❖ (specialty basic action) Move up to your fly Speed. 472

aerial combat 478

fly Speed 463

focus (spell component) 303

Focus Point If you can cast focus spells, you have a pool of Focus Points you can use to cast them. You regain a Focus Point using the Refocus activity. 300, 302

focus spell A type of spell, specific to a class, that can be cast using Focus Points and is automatically heightened to half your level rounded up. Focus spells always have a descriptive term such as "domain spell" or "ki spell." 300, 302, 386-407

Refocus (activity) 300

focused (trait) An item with this trait can give you an additional Focus Point. This focus point is separate from your focus pool and doesn't count toward the cap on your focus pool. You can gain this benefit only if you have a focus pool, and there might be restrictions on how the point can be used. You can't gain more than 1 Focus Point per day from focused items. 535

Follow the Expert (exploration activity) Benefit from another's skill proficiency. 479

force (damage type) 452

force (trait) Effects with this trait deal force damage or create objects made of pure magical force.

Force Open ❖ (skill action) Physically wrench something open. (Athletics) 242

Force Open DCs (GM) 515

forceful (weapon trait) 282

formula A recipe or instructions required to Craft an item. 293-294

formula book (alchemist) 73, 81

Fortitude (Fort) A type of saving throw used to resist diseases, poisons, and other physical effects. Fortitude modifier = Con modifier + proficiency bonus + other bonuses + penalties. 13, **449**

fortune (trait) A fortune effect beneficially alters how you roll your dice. You can never have more than one fortune effect alter a single roll. If multiple fortune effects would apply, you have to pick which to use. If a fortune effect and a misfortune effect would apply to the same roll, the two cancel each other out, and you roll normally. 449

free action (❖) An action you can use without spending one of your actions. Free actions with triggers can be used at any time, but they don't use up your 1 reaction per round. 17, **461-462**

free-hand (weapon trait) 282-283

frequency An ability that can't be used at will might list a frequency. 18

friendly (condition) An NPC with this condition has a good attitude toward you. 620

frightened (condition) Fear makes you less capable of attacking and defending. 620

fumble A colloquial term for a critical failure. 445

fungus (trait) Fungal creatures have the fungus trait. They are distinct from normal fungi.

Game Master (GM) The player who adjudicates the rules and narrates the elements of the Pathfinder story and world that the other players explore. 12, 482-529

Gargantuan (size) 473-475

Gather Information (skill action) Socialize to learn things. (Diplomacy) 246

GM advice 505

gear See also item. 270-295

gender and pronouns 29

general (trait) A type of feat that any character can select, regardless of ancestry and

class, as long as they meet the prerequisites. You can select a feat with this trait when your class grants a general feat. 255

giant (trait) Giants are massive humanoid creatures. 433-434

GM (Game Master) See also Game Master. 12, 482-529

gnome (trait) A creature with this trait is a member of the gnome ancestry. Gnomes are small people skilled at magic who seek out new experiences and usually have low-light vision. An ability with this trait can be used or selected only by gnomes. A weapon with this trait is created and used by gnomes. 42-45, 432

goblin (trait) A creature with this trait can come from multiple tribes of creatures, including goblins, hobgoblins, and bugbears. Goblins tend to have darkvision. An ability with this trait can be used or chosen only by goblins. A weapon with this trait is created and used by goblins. 46-49, 432

gods See also deity. 437-440

Golarion The world of the Pathfinder setting. 12, **416-441**

gold piece (gp) 271

good (damage type) 452

good (trait) Good effects often manipulate energy from good-aligned Outer Planes and are antithetical to evil divine servants or divine servants of evil deities. A creature with this trait is good in alignment. An ability with this trait can be selected or used only by good creatures.

gp (gold piece) 271

Grab an Edge ⟳ (specialty basic action) Try to catch yourself while falling. 472

grabbed (condition) A creature, object, or magic holds you in place. 620

Grapple ❖ (skill action) Grab or restrain a creature. (Athletics) 242

grapple (weapon trait) 283

grid A map with 1-inch squares used for indicating position and movement. 473

playing without a grid (GM) 494

hag (trait) These creatures are malevolent spellcasters who form covens.

half-elf (trait) A creature with this trait is part human and part elf. An ability with this trait can be used or selected only by half-elves. 55, 56, 58-59

half-orc (trait) A creature with this trait is part human and part orc. An ability with this trait can be used or selected only by half-orcs. 55, 56, 58-59

halfling (trait) A creature with this trait is a member of the halfling ancestry. These small people are friendly wanderers considered to be lucky. An ability with this trait can be used or selected only by halflings. A weapon with this trait is created and used by halflings. 50-53, 432

Hardness A statistic representing an object's durability. 272, 579

haunt (trait) A hazard with this trait is a spiritual echo, often of someone with a tragic death. Putting a haunt to rest often involves resolving the haunt's unfinished business. A haunt that hasn't been properly put to rest always returns after a time.

hazard Hazards are non-creature dangers that adventurers encounter during their journeys, including environmental hazards, haunts, and traps. Simple hazards have a one-time effect, but negotiating a complex hazard takes place in encounter mode, wherein the hazard has a specific routine. 498, **520-529**

complex hazards 526-529

simple hazards 522-526

XP for hazards 507-508, 521

hazardous terrain (terrain) You take damage when moving through this terrain. 476

healing 459

long-term rest (downtime) 481

Medicine skill 248-249

natural healing 480

healing (trait) A healing effect restores a creature's body, typically by restoring Hit Points, but sometimes by removing diseases or other debilitating effects.

helpful (condition) An NPC with this condition is likely to assist you. 620

heritage A choice made to further define your ancestry. 33

Hero Point These points last only within a session. You can spend 1 Hero Point to reroll a check, or all your Hero Points to avoid dying. 29, **467**

awarding Hero Points (GM) 507

hidden (condition) A creature knows your location but can't see you. 466, **620**

Hide ❖ (skill action) Make yourself hidden. (Stealth) 251-252

High Jump ❖❖ (skill action) Jump vertically. (Athletics) 242

Hit Points (HP) A statistic representing the amount of physical harm a creature can take before it falls unconscious or dies. Damage decreases Hit Points on a 1-to-1 basis, while healing restores Hit Points at the same rate. 12, 26, 67-68, 459-461

ancestry Hit Points 33

class Hit Points 67-68

item Hit Points 272-273, 461

INTRODUCTION

ANCESTRIES & BACKGROUNDS

CLASSES

SKILLS

FEATS

EQUIPMENT

SPELLS

THE AGE OF LOST OMENS

PLAYING THE GAME

GAME MASTERING

CRAFTING & TREASURE

APPENDIX

Pick a Lock ◆◆ (skill action) Open a lock. (Thievery, trained) 253

piercing (damage type) A type of physical damage. 452

plane 418–419

plant (trait) Vegetable creatures have the plant trait. They are distinct from normal plants. Magical effects with this trait manipulate or conjure plants or plant matter in some way. Those that manipulate plants have no effect in an area with no plants.

platinum piece (pp) 271

player One of the real people playing the game. 7

Player Character (character or PC) A character created and controlled by a player other than the GM. 13

character creation 19–30

Point Out ◆ (specialty basic action) Indicate an undetected creature's location. 472

poison (damage type) 452

poison (trait) An effect with this trait delivers a poison or deals poison damage. An item with this trait is poisonous and might cause an affliction. 457–458, 550–554

polymorph (trait) These effects transform the target into a new form. A target can't be under the effect of more than one polymorph effect at a time. If it comes under the effect of a second polymorph effect, the second polymorph effect attempts to counteract the first. If it succeeds, it takes effect, and if it fails, the spell has no effect on that target. Any Strikes specifically granted by a polymorph effect are magical. Unless otherwise stated, polymorph spells don't allow the target to take on the appearance of a specific individual creature, but rather just a generic creature of a general type or ancestry.

If you take on a battle form with a polymorph spell, the special statistics can be adjusted only by circumstance bonuses, status bonuses, and penalties. Unless otherwise noted, the battle form prevents you from casting spells, speaking, and using most manipulate actions that require hands. (If there's doubt about whether you can use an action, the GM decides.) Your gear is absorbed into you; the constant abilities of your gear still function, but you can't activate any items.

positive (damage type) 452

positive (trait) Effects with this trait heal living creatures with positive energy, deal positive energy damage to undead, or manipulate positive energy.

possession (trait) Effects with this trait allow a creature to project its mind and spirit into a target. A creature immune to mental effects can't use a possession effect. While possessing a target, a possessor's true body is unconscious (and can't wake up normally), unless the possession effect allows the creature to physically enter the target. Whenever the target takes damage, the possessor takes half that amount of damage as mental damage.

A possessor loses the benefits of any of its active spells or abilities that affect its physical body, though it gains the benefits of the target's active spells and abilities that affect their body. A possessor can use any of the target's abilities that are purely physical, and it can't use any of its own abilities except spells and purely mental abilities. The GM decides whether an ability is purely physical or purely mental. A possessor uses the target's attack modifier, AC, Fortitude save, Reflex save, Perception, and physical skills, and its own Will save, mental skills, spell attack roll, and spell DC; benefits of invested items apply where relevant (the possessor's invested items apply when using its own values, and the target's invested items apply when using the target's values). A possessor gains no benefit from casting spells that normally affect only the caster, since it isn't in its own body. The possessor must use its own actions to make the possessed creature act.

If a possessor reaches 0 Hit Points through any combination of damage to its true body and mental damage from the possession, it is knocked out as normal and the possession immediately ends. If the target reaches 0 Hit Points first, the possessor can either fall unconscious with the body and continue the possession or end the effect as a free action and return to its body. If the target dies, the possession ends immediately and the possessor is stunned for 1 minute.

potion (trait) A potion is a magical liquid activated when you drink it. 562–564

pp (platinum piece) 271

precious (trait) Valuable materials with special properties have the precious trait. They can be substituted for base materials when you Craft items. 577–579

armor and weapons made of precious materials. 555–556, 599

damage from precious materials 452

precise sense A sense that can make creatures observed, such as human sight. 464

precision (damage type) A type of damage that increases the attack's listed damage, using the same damage type, rather than adding a separate amount. 452

prediction (trait) Effects with this trait determine what is likely to happen in the near future. Most predictions are divinations.

preparations See also daily preparations. 480, 500

prerequisite Many feats and other abilities can be taken only if you meet their prerequisites. Prerequisites are often feats or proficiency ranks. 18

press (trait) Actions with this trait allow you to follow up earlier attacks. An action with the press trait can be used only if you are currently affected by a multiple attack penalty. Some actions with the press trait also grant an effect on a failure. The effects that are added on a failure don't apply on a critical failure. If your press action succeeds, you can choose to apply the failure effect instead. (For example, you may wish to do this when an attack deals no damage due to resistance.) Because a press action requires a multiple attack penalty, you can't use one when it's not your turn, even if you use the Ready activity.

Price The amount of currency it usually costs to purchase an item. 271, 535

primal (trait) This magic comes from the primal tradition, connecting to the natural world and instinct. Anything with this trait is magical. 299

primal spell list 314–315

proficiency A measure of a character's aptitude at a specific task or quality, with five ranks: untrained, trained, expert, master, and legendary. Proficiency gives a proficiency bonus. Being untrained adds a +0 bonus. Being trained, expert, master, or legendary adds your level plus 2, 4, 6, or 8, respectively. 13, **444**

initial proficiencies 26, **68**

minimum proficiency for hazards 520–522

prone (condition) You're lying on the ground and easier to attack. 621

propulsive (weapon trait) 283

quickened (condition) You get an extra action each turn. 622

rage (trait) 87

Raise a Shield ◆ (specialty basic action) Gain your shield's bonus to AC. 472

range 304, **455**

range increment 279, 446–447

ranger (class) 166–177

multiclass archetype 228

ranger (trait) This indicates abilities from the ranger class.

rare (trait) This rarity indicates that a rules element is very difficult to find in the game world. A rare feat, spell, item or the like is available to players only if the GM decides to include it in the game, typically through discovery during play. 13

rarity How often something is encountered in the game world. The rarities are common, uncommon, rare, and unique. Anything that doesn't list a rarity is common. 13, 535

GM advice 488

reach (weapon trait) 283

reaction (↺) An action you can use even if it's not your turn. You can use 1 reaction per round. 17, **461–462**, 472–473

Ready ◆◆ (basic action) Prepare an action to use when it's not your turn. 470

Recall Knowledge ◆ (skill action) Try to remember something using a skill. 238–239

GM advice 505–506

recovery check A flat check made to see if you get worse or better while dying. 459

Reflex (Ref) A type of saving throw used to quickly dodge. Reflex modifier = Dex modifier + proficiency bonus + other bonuses + penalties. 13, **448–449**

Refocus (activity) Regain 1 focus point. 300

Release ◆ (basic action) Let go of something you're holding. 470–471

Religion (skill) Know about deities, faith, and divine magic. (Wis) 250

reload 279

Repair (skill action) Fix a broken or damaged item. (Crafting) 243–244

Repeat a Spell (exploration activity) Repeatedly Cast a Spell as you move. 480

Request ◆ (skill action) Convince someone to do you a favor. (Diplomacy) 247

reroll An ability that causes you to roll again has the fortune or misfortune trait. 499, 467

resistance Reduce damage you take of a certain type. 453

rest Characters recover HP (normally Con modifier × level) and resources with 8 hours of sleep. 480, 499–500

GM advice 499–500, 502

long-term rest 481

restrained (condition) You are bound by restraints or a grappling creature. 622

result of a check 445

retrain You can retrain during downtime to change character choices. 481

GM advice 502

revelation (trait) Effects with this trait see things as they truly are.

rewards 507–511

ritual A type of spell that takes downtime to cast and doesn't use spell slots. 408–415

rogue (class) 178–189

multiclass archetype 229

rogue (trait) This indicates abilities from the rogue class.

splash (trait) When you use a thrown weapon with the splash trait, you don't add your Strength modifier to the damage roll. If an attack with a splash weapon fails, succeeds, or critically succeeds, all creatures within 5 feet of the target (including the target) take the listed splash damage. On a failure (but not a critical failure), the target of the attack still takes the splash damage. Add splash damage together with the initial damage against the target before applying the target's weaknesses or resistances. You don't multiply splash damage on a critical hit. 544

Squeeze (skill action) Move through a gap while exploring. (Acrobatics, trained) 241

staff (trait) This magic item holds spells of a particular theme and allows a spellcaster to cast additional spells by preparing the staff. 592–595

stage One of the steps of an affliction. 458

stance (trait) A stance is a general combat strategy that you enter by using an action with the stance trait, and that you remain in for some time. A stance lasts until you get knocked out, until its requirements (if any) are violated, until the encounter ends, or until you enter a new stance, whichever comes first. After you use an action with the stance trait, you can't use another one for 1 round. You can enter or be in a stance only in encounter mode.

Stand ◆ (basic action) Stand up from prone. 471

starvation and thirst 500

status bonus A bonus that typically comes from a spell or condition and represents a beneficial status. 444–445

status penalty A penalty that typically comes from a spell or condition and represents a detrimental status. 444–445

staves 280, **592–595**

Steal ◆ (skill action) Pilfer an object in someone else's possession. (Thievery) 253

Stealth (skill) Avoid detection and conceal items. (Dex) 251–252

Step ◆ (basic action) Move 5 feet without triggering reactions. 471

Strength (Str) This ability score measures your brawn. 19

  armor Strength score 274

Stride ◆ (basic action) Move up to your Speed. 471

Strike ◆ (basic action) Make an attack with a weapon or unarmed attack. 471

structure (trait) 596

structures 515, 596

stunned (condition) You can't act for a number of actions or an amount of time. 622

stupefied (condition) Your can't access your full mental faculties, and you have trouble casting spells. 622

Subsist (skill action) Find food and shelter for free. (Society or Survival) 240

  GM advice 506

success A result on a check that equals or exceeds the DC. Exceeding the DC by 10 or more is even better—a critical success. If a stat block has no success entry, that means there is no effect on a success. 445–446

suffocation 478

summoned (trait) A creature called by a conjuration spell or effect gains the summoned trait. A summoned creature can't summon other creatures, create things of value, or cast spells that require a cost. It has the minion trait. If it tries to cast a spell of equal or higher level than the spell that summoned it, it overpowers the summoning magic, causing the summoned creature's spell to fail and the summon spell to end. Otherwise, the summoned creature uses the standard abilities for a creature of its kind. It generally attacks your enemies to the best of its abilities. If you can communicate with it, you can attempt to command it, but the GM determines the degree to which it follows your commands.

  Immediately when you finish Casting the Spell, the summoned creature uses its 2 actions for that turn. Summoned creatures can be banished by various spells and effects. They are automatically banished if reduced to 0 Hit Points or if the spell that called them ends.

Support ◆ Direct your animal companion to support you. 215

surprise attack 499–500

Survival (skill) Travel and survive in the wild. (Wis) 252–253

Sustain a Spell ◆ (action) Extend a spell with a sustained duration. 304

Sustain an Activation ◆ (action) Extend a magic item activation with a sustained duration to the end of your next turn. 534

sustained A spell with this duration can be extended with Sustain a Spell. 304

sweep (weapon trait) 283

Swim ◆ (skill action) Move through the water. (Athletics) 243

  aquatic combat 478

  swim Speed 463

Take Cover ◆ (basic action) Gain cover, or improve cover to greater cover. 471

talisman (trait) A talisman is a small object affixed to armor, a shield, or a weapon (called the affixed item). You must be wielding or wearing an item to activate a talisman attached to it. Once activated, a talisman burns out permanently. 565–570

target 304, **455–456**

teleportation (trait) Teleportation effects allow you to instantaneously move from one point in space to another. Teleportation does not usually trigger reactions based on movement.

temporary Hit Points 461

temporary immunity An effect that makes a creature temporarily immune lets that creature avoid new effects of the same name, but it doesn't end anything caused by the effect that gave the temporary immunity. 453

terrain 475–476, 497–498

  environment 512–517

Thievery (skill) Steal objects and dismantle locks and other mechanisms. (Dex) 253

thirst 500

thrown (weapon trait) 283

Tiny (size) 473–475

tool alchemical tool 554

  tools and kits 288

touch A spell range requiring you to touch the target. 304

Track (skill action) Follow a creature's tracks. (Survival) 252–253

  GM advice 506

tradition A fundamental category of magic (arcane, divine, occult, or primal). 297, 299

Train Animal (general feat) **268**, 506

trained (proficiency rank) Add your level + 2 to associated rolls and DCs. Some skill actions and many other rules require you to be trained. 13, 444

trait A keyword that conveys information about a rules element. Often a trait indicates how other rules interact with an ability, creature, item, or other rules element with that trait. Individual traits appear by name in this appendix. 13

  armor traits 274–275

  weapon traits 282–283

transmutation (trait) Effects and magic items with this trait are associated with the transmutation school of magic, typically changing something's form. 298

trap (trait) A hazard or item with this trait is constructed to hinder interlopers. 520–522

travel Speed 479

treasure *See also* item. 508–511, 530–617

  treasure tables 536–542

Treat Disease (skill action) Remedy a disease in downtime. (Medicine, trained) 248

Treat Poison ◆ (skill action) Help a poisoned patient recover. (Medicine, trained) 248–249

Treat Wounds (skill action) Restore Hit Points to a creature. (Medicine, trained) 249

tremorsense (sense) Detect the movement of creatures along surfaces. 465

trigger A specified event when you can use a reaction or free action. 18, 305–306, **462**

trip (weapon trait) 283

Trip ◆ (skill action) Knock a creature down. (Athletics) 243

Tumble Through ◆ (skill action) Move through someone's space. (Acrobatics) 240

turn During a round in an encounter, each creature takes a single turn. A creature typically uses up to 3 actions during its turn. 13, **468–469**

twin (weapon trait) 283

two-hand (weapon trait) 283

unarmed (weapon trait) 283

unarmored defense 274, 275

uncommon (trait) Something of uncommon rarity requires special training or comes from a particular culture or part of the world. Some character choices give access to uncommon options, and the GM can choose to allow access for anyone. 13

unconscious (condition) You're asleep or knocked out. 622–623

  death, dying, and unconscious rules 459–461

undead (trait) Once living, these creatures were infused after death with negative energy and soul-corrupting evil magic. When reduced to 0 Hit Points, an undead creature is destroyed. Undead creatures are damaged by positive energy, are healed by negative energy, and don't benefit from healing effects.

undetected (condition) A creature doesn't know your precise location. 466–467, **623**

uneven ground (terrain) You must Balance or fall when crossing uneven ground. 476

unfriendly (condition) An NPC with this condition doesn't like you. 623

unique (trait) A rules element with this trait is one-of-a-kind. 13

unlimited A spell with this duration lasts indefinitely. 305

unnoticed (condition) A creature is entirely unaware you're present. 467, **623**

until the next time you make your daily preparations A spell with this duration lasts until you next prepare, and you can extend it by leaving your spell slot open. 305

untrained (proficiency rank) The lowest proficiency rank (+0 bonus). 10, 13, 444

usage An indication of how an item must be worn, held, or otherwise used. 535

vague sense A sense that can detect an unnoticed creature but not determine its position, such as a human's sense of smell. 465

verbal (spell component) 303

versatile (weapon trait) 283

virulent (trait) Afflictions with the virulent trait are harder to remove. You must succeed at two consecutive saves to reduce a virulent affliction's stage by 1. A critical success reduces a virulent affliction's stage by only 1 instead of by 2.

visual (trait) A visual effect can affect only creatures that can see it. This applies only to visible parts of the effect, as determined by the GM.

volley (weapon trait) 283

wall 306, **515**

wand (trait) A wand contains a single spell which you can cast once per day. 597–598

watches 499–500

water (trait) Effects with the water trait either manipulate or conjure water. Those that manipulate water have no effect in an area without water. Creatures with this trait consist primarily of water or have a magical connection to the element.

weakness Increases damage you take of a certain type. 453

wealth A character's wealth by level. 508–511

weapon 278–286

  magical and special weapons 599–602

  runes 580–585

  wielding 272

weather 497, 517–518

welcoming environment 8, 485–486

Will A saving throw used to resist effects targeting the mind and personality. Will modifier = Wis modifier + proficiency bonus + other bonuses + penalties. 13, **448–449**

Wisdom (Wis) This ability score measures your awareness and intuition. 19

wizard (class) 202–213

  arcane spell list 307–309

  multiclass archetype 231

  school spells 406–407

wizard (trait) This indicates abilities from the wizard class.

wounded (condition) You've returned from the brink of death but remain at risk. 623

XP (Experience Points) See also Experience Points. 8, 507–508

PAIZO INC.

Creative Directors • James Jacobs, Robert G. McCreary, and Sarah E. Robinson
Director of Game Design • Jason Bulmahn
Managing Developers • Adam Daigle and Amanda Hamon
Organized Play Lead Developer • John Compton
Developers • Eleanor Ferron, Jason Keeley, Luis Loza, Ron Lundeen, Joe Pasini, Patrick Renie, Michael Sayre, Chris S. Sims, and Linda Zayas-Palmer
Starfinder Design Lead • Owen K.C. Stephens
Starfinder Society Developer • Thurston Hillman
Senior Designer • Stephen Radney-MacFarland
Designers • Logan Bonner and Mark Seifter
Managing Editor • Judy Bauer
Senior Editor • Christopher Paul Carey
Editors • James Case, Leo Glass, Lyz Liddell, Adrian Ng, Lacy Pellazar, and Jason Tondro
Art Director • Sonja Morris
Senior Graphic Designers • Emily Crowell and Adam Vick
Production Artist • Tony Barnett
Franchise Manager • Mark Moreland
Project Manager • Gabriel Waluconis

Paizo CEO • Lisa Stevens
Chief Creative Officer • Erik Mona
Chief Financial Officer • John Parrish
Chief Operations Officer • Jeffrey Alvarez
Chief Technical Officer • Vic Wertz

Director of Sales • Pierce Watters
Sales Associate • Cosmo Eisele
Vice President of Marketing & Licensing • Jim Butler
Marketing Manager • Dan Tharp
Licensing Manager • Glenn Elliott
Public Relations Manager • Aaron Shanks
Customer Service & Community Manager • Sara Marie
Operations Manager • Will Chase
Organized Play Manager • Tonya Woldridge
Human Resources Generalist • Angi Hodgson
Accountant • Christopher Caldwell
Data Entry Clerk • B. Scott Keim

Director of Technology • Raimi Kong
Web Production Manager • Chris Lambertz
Senior Software Developer • Gary Teter
Webstore Coordinator • Rick Kunz

Customer Service Team • Katina Davis, Virginia Jordan, Samantha Phelan, and Diego Valdez
Warehouse Team • Laura Wilkes Carey, Mika Hawkins, Heather Payne, Jeff Strand, and Kevin Underwood
Website Team • Brian Bauman, Robert Brandenburg, Whitney Chatterjee, Erik Keith, Josh Thornton, and Andrew White

SECOND EDITION

PATHFINDER®

Lost Omens World Guide

THIS COMPREHENSIVE HARDCOVER OVERVIEW OF THE WORLD OF PATHFINDER PROVIDES EVERYTHING YOU NEED TO KNOW FOR A LIFETIME OF ADVENTURE IN THE AGE OF LOST OMENS. THE GOD OF HUMANITY IS DEAD AND PROPHECY IS BROKEN, LEAVING HEROES JUST LIKE YOU TO CARVE THEIR OWN DESTINIES OUT OF AN UNCERTAIN FUTURE!

HARDCOVER $36.99